KU-074-743

Financial Statement Analysis and Security Valuation

Second Edition

Stephen H. Penman
Columbia University

Boston   Burr Ridge, IL   Dubuque, IA   Madison, WI   New York   San Francisco   St. Louis
Bangkok   Bogotá   Caracas   Kuala Lumpur   Lisbon   London   Madrid   Mexico City
Milan   Montreal   New Delhi   Santiago   Seoul   Singapore   Sydney   Taipei   Toronto

LIVERPOOL JOHN MOORES UNIVERSITY
Aldham Roberts L.R.C.

The McGraw-Hill Companies

FINANCIAL STATEMENT ANALYSIS AND SECURITY VALUATION
International Edition 2003

Exclusive rights by McGraw-Hill Education (Asia), for manufacture and export. This book cannot be re-exported from the country to which it is sold by McGraw-Hill. The International Edition is not available in North America.

Published by McGraw-Hill/Irwin, a business unit of The McGraw-Hill Companies, Inc., 1221 Avenue of the Americas, New York, NY 10020. Copyright © 2004, 2001 by The McGraw-Hill Companies, Inc. All rights reserved. No part of this publication may be reproduced or distributed in any form or by any means, or stored in a database or retrieval system, without the prior written consent of The McGraw-Hill Companies, Inc., including, but not limited to, in any network or other electronic storage or transmission, or broadcast for distance learning.
Some ancillaries, including electronic and print components, may not be available to customers outside the United States.

10   09   08   07   06   05   04   03
20   09   08   07   06   05
CTF   BJE

Cover illustration: © *Tom White*

Library of Congress Cataloging-in-Publication Data
Penman, Stephen H.
   Financial statement analysis and security valuation / Stephen H. Penman.—2nd ed.
        p.   cm.
    Includes index.
    ISBN 007-253317-X
      1. Financial statements. I. Title
   HF5681.B2P4134   2004
   332.63'2042—dc21   2003051348

When ordering this title, use ISBN 007-123263-X

Printed in Singapore

www.mhhe.com

Finent

A

Setion

Books are to be returned on or before
the last date below.

**7 – DAY
LOAN**

LIVERPOOL JOHN MOORES UNIVERSITY
Aldham Roberts L.R.C.
TEL 0151 231 3701/3634

WITHDRAWN

LIVERPOOL JMU LIBRARY

3 1111 01156 2673

WITHDRAWN

About the Author

Stephen H. Penman is the George O. May Professor and the Morgan Stanley Research Scholar in the Graduate School of Business, Columbia University. Prior to his appointment at Columbia in 1999, he was the L.H. Penney Professor in the Walter A. Haas School of Business at the University of California at Berkeley. From 1990–95 he served as Chairman of the Professional Accounting Program and Chairman of the Accounting Faculty at Berkeley. He also initiated and chaired Berkeley's Annual Conference on Financial Reporting. He has served as a Visiting Professor at Columbia University and the London Business School, and as the Jan Wallander Visiting Professor at the Stockholm School of Economics.

Professor Penman received a first-class honors degree in Commerce from the University of Queensland, Australia, and M.B.A. and Ph.D. degrees from the University of Chicago. His research is concerned with the valuation of equity and the role of accounting information in security analysis. He has published widely in finance and accounting journals and has conducted seminars on fundamental analysis and equity evaluation for academic and professional audiences. In 1991 he was awarded the Notable Contribution to Accounting Literature Award by the American Accounting Association and the American Institute of Certified Public Accountants, and in 2002 he was awarded the American Accounting Association and Deloitte & Touche Wildman Medal for his book, *Financial Statement Analysis and Security Valuation*, published by McGraw-Hill/Irwin. He is managing editor of the *Review of Accounting Studies* and is on the editorial board of the *Schmalenbach Business Review*.

Preface

Financial statements are the lens on a business. Financial statement analysis calibrates the lens to bring the business into focus. Imperfections in the financial statements can dirty the lens and distort the picture. Financial statement analysis deals with the imperfections in financial statements to improve the focus.

Financial statements have many uses, but the predominant one is to provide information for investing in businesses. Every day millions of shares and corporate bonds are traded in the world's capital markets, and prices are set to value these securities. Investors want to know what firms are worth so they can ascertain at what price to trade. They turn to financial statement analysis to get an indication of the underlying value of firms. This book focuses on these investors.

Underlying value is sometimes referred to as fundamental value, and the analysis of information about fundamental value is referred to as fundamental analysis. This book is about fundamental analysis. Financial statement analysis is central to fundamental analysis. Indeed, in this book, fundamental analysis is developed as a matter of appropriate financial statement analysis. As the lens on a business, financial statements, focused with the techniques of financial statement analysis, provide a way of interpreting the business that enables readers to understand the value it generates for shareholders.

The experience in stock markets in the late 1990s and early 2000s suggests that such understanding is sorely needed. During those years, share prices rose considerably above the value that was indicated by earnings, book values, sales, and other fundamental information, only to collapse as the bubble burst. Spurred on by suspect analysis from those representing themselves as analysts, suspect financial reporting from some companies, the hyping of shares by corporate managements, and the speculative discussions of "talking heads" in the media, investors ignored sound analysis in a wave "irrational exuberance." The time has come to return to fundamentals. This book lays out the techniques of sound fundamental analysis.

THE APPROACH

Conceptual Framework

Good analysis comes from good understanding. And good understanding is provided by a conceptual framework that helps you—the student analyst—organize your thinking. In this information age, there are large amounts of information about firms to be processed. A conceptual framework guides you in using this information intelligently and economically—to turn the information into knowledge.

This book works from a conceptual framework that helps you understand how businesses work, how they generate value, and how the value they generate is captured (or not captured) in financial statements. The framework helps you translate your knowledge of a business into a valuation. The framework helps you interpret what you see in financial statements. It gives you answers to the many important questions facing analysts. What "fundamentals" should the analyst focus on—dividends, cash flows or earnings? How is an analyst's earnings forecast converted into a valuation? How can an investor rely on earnings when earnings are sometimes measured with doubtful accounting methods? What role does the balance sheet play? What is a growth company and how is growth valued? What does a firm's price-earnings (P/E) ratio tell you? What does its price-to-book ratio tell you? How are equity analysis and credit analysis integrated?

Most importantly, the framework gives you the security that your analysis is a sound one. The framework is built block by block from "first principles" so that you see clearly where the analysis comes from and, by the end of the book, have a firm understanding of the principles of fundamental analysis. You will also be able to distinguish good analysis from poor analysis.

Practical Tools

This book is about understanding, but it is primarily about doing. Concepts and frameworks are only important if they lead to analysis tools. Each chapter of the book ends with a list of **Key Concepts**, but also with the **Analyst's Toolkit** that summarizes the key analysis tools in the chapter. By the end of the book, you will have a complete set of tools for practical analysis. The Toolkit is efficiently organized so that the analyst proceeds in a disciplined way with the assurance that his or her analysis is coherent and does not overlook any aspect of the value generation in a firm. The book identifies too-simple methods of analysis and shuns ad hoc methods. However, it also strives to develop simple schemes, with a sense of trade-off between the benefit of more complicated analysis over the cost. At all points in the book, methods are illustrated with applications to recognizable firms such as Dell Computer, Wal-Mart, Nike, Reebok, and many more.

Valuation and Strategy

The tools in the book are those that a security analyst outside the firm uses to advise clients about investing in the firm. These analysts present their recommendations in an equity research report. After studying this text, you will have the ability to write a persuasive, state-of-the-art equity research report. But the tools are also those that a manager within a firm uses to evaluate investments. The analyst outside the firm values the firm on the basis of what he understands the firm's strategy to be, while the manager within the firm uses the same tools to evaluate investments and choose the strategy. The techniques that are used to assess the value of a firm's strategy are also the techniques used to choose among strategies, so this book integrates valuation analysis and strategy analysis.

Accounting-Based Approach to Valuation

Valuation texts typically use discounted cash flow analysis to value businesses. However, analysts typically forecast earnings to indicate business value, and equity research reports primarily discuss firms' earnings, not their cash flows, to get a sense of whether the firm is making money for investors. "Buy earnings" is indeed the mantra of investing. The stock market focuses on earnings; analysts' and managements' earnings forecasts drive share prices, and when a firm announces earnings that are different from analysts' earnings estimates, the stock price responds accordingly. Revelations of overstated earnings result in large drops in stock prices—as with the Xerox, Enron, Qwest, WorldCom, and other accounting scandals that broke as the stock market bubble burst. Investment houses are increasingly moving from cash flow valuation models to earnings-based valuation models.

This book focuses on earnings forecasting and the methods for converting earnings forecasts to a valuation. The reason will become clear as you proceed through the book: earnings, appropriately measured, give a better indication of the value generation in a business, so the analysis of earnings prospects leads to a firmer understanding of fundamental value. Graham and Dodd and the fundamental analysts of earlier generations emphasized "earnings power." This book maintains that focus, but in a way that is consistent with the principles of modern finance.

Earnings differ from cash flows because of the "accruals" of accounting, so the book lays out how accrual accounting helps in understanding a business and its value. Accruals such as depreciation, pension liabilities, and deferred taxes are shown to have a purpose. A cash flow perspective sees accruals, rather, as arbitrary. The book shows how to work with the accounting rather than dismissing it. As accruals affect both the income statement and the balance sheet, earnings forecasts (in the income statement) cannot be interpreted without the balance sheet that lists assets that generate the earnings. Therefore, the accrual-accounting framework is one of income statements and balance sheets working together.

Financial statements are sometimes dismissed as uninformative, but you will see that, with the appropriate analysis, they can be quite revealing. With the appropriate analysis, the financial statements come to life.

The Quality of the Accounting

With an understanding of how accounting should work, you will develop an appreciation in this book of what is good accounting and what is poor accounting. By the end of the book you will recognize the defects in financial statements that are issued by firms and will have developed a critique of the "generally accepted accounting principles" and disclosure rules that determine what is in the statements. You will also understand how the accounting in reports can be distorted, as well as discover tools that detect the distortion and give you an indication of the quality of the accounting that a firm uses.

Integrating Finance and Accounting

Financial statements are prepared according to the dictates of accounting principles, and you take accounting courses to learn these accounting principles. Your appreciation of financial statements from these courses is often in terms of the accounting used to prepare them, not in terms of what the financial statements say about investing in businesses. Principles of finance guide investment analysis and you typically take finance courses to learn these principles. However, the investment analysis in these courses often does not employ financial statements or accounting concepts in any systematic way. Often you see finance and accounting as distinct or, if you see them as related, the relationship is vague in your mind. Finance courses are sometimes dismissive of accounting, while accounting courses sometimes propose analysis that violates the principles of finance. This book integrates your learning from finance and accounting courses. By integrating financial statement analysis and fundamental analysis, the book combines accounting concepts with finance concepts. Accounting is viewed as a matter of accounting for value and the accounting for value is appropriated for investment analysis. The organized structure of the financial statements helps organize fundamental analysis. Accounting principles for measuring balance sheets and income statements are incorporated as principles for measuring value. All analysis is performed in a way that is consistent with the principles of modern finance and with an appreciation of what is good accounting and what is poor accounting.

Activist Approach

Investment texts often take the view that capital markets are "efficient," such that market prices always reflect the underlying value of the securities traded. These texts are primarily concerned with measuring risk, not with valuation. The investor is viewed as relatively passive, accepting prices as fair value, concerned primarily with managing risk through portfolio management. This text takes an activist's perspective. Active investors do not "assume that the market is efficient." Rather, active investors challenge the market price with sound analysis, checking whether that price is a fair price. Indeed, they exploit what is perceived to be mispricing in the market to earn superior returns. Active investors adopt the creed of fundamental analysts: price is what you pay, value is what you get. They believe that an important risk in equity investing is the risk of paying too much for a share, so active investors seek to gain an appreciation of value independently of price. Whether or not the market is efficient, you will find this perspective engaging.

The Overview

Chapter 1 introduces you to financial statement analysis and fundamental analysis, and sets the stage for the rest of the book. Chapter 2 introduces you to the financial statements. The remainder of the book is in five parts:

- **Part I** (Chapters 3–6) develops the thinking that is necessary to perform fundamental analysis. It integrates finance concepts with accounting concepts and shows you how the structure of accounting can be exploited for valuation analysis. Good thinking about valuation is captured in a valuation model, so this part of the book ends with accrual-accounting valuation models that provide the framework for the practical analysis that follows in the rest of the book. These models show you how to calculate intrinsic price-earnings ratios and price-to-book ratios. Alternative models are discussed as competing technologies, so you develop an appreciation of the strength and weaknesses of alternative approaches.

- **Part II** (Chapters 7–12) lays out the financial statement analysis that identifies value generation in a business and provides information for forecasting. In this part of the book you will see the lens being focused on the business.

- **Part III** (Chapters 13–15) deals with forecasting. The value of a firm and its shares is based on the payoffs it is expected to yield investors; thus, using the information from the financial statement analysis, this part of the book shows you how to forecast payoffs. The forecasting is developed within a financial statement framework so that forecasting is an exercise in pro forma financial statement analysis. The analysis then shows how to convert forecasts into valuations of firms and their strategies.

- **Part IV** (Chapters 16 and 17) deals with accounting issues that arise with the use of accounting-based valuation. It shows how to accommodate different accounting methods for measuring earnings and how to analyze the quality of the accounting used in financial statements.

- **Part V** (Chapters 18 and 19) lays out the fundamental analysis of risk, both equity risk and credit risk, and provides a pro forma analysis that integrates equity analysis and credit analysis.

PUTTING IT ALL TOGETHER: A TOOLKIT FOR ANALYSTS AND MANAGERS

The best way to tackle this book is to see yourself as putting together a Toolkit for analyzing financial statements and valuing businesses and business strategies. As a professional analyst or a strategic thinker, you want to be using the best technologies available, so approach the book in the spirit of sorting out what are good methods and what are poor ones. You want methods that are practical as well as conceptually sound.

As you read the text, you will learn the following:

- How fundamental value (or "intrinsic" value) is ascertained

- How to analyze business strategies to understand the value that they add

- How to perform financial statement analysis

- How financial statements are used to value firms

- What a good equity research report looks like

- How to prepare business forecasts

- How "fundamentals" such as dividends, cash flows, earnings, and book values are used in valuation

- What determines a firm's price/earnings ratio

- What determines a firm's price-to-book ratio

- How to analyze the quality of the accounting in financial reports

- How to analyze equity risk from financial statements

- How to analyze credit risk

USING THE BOOK

Background Requirements

To comprehend the text material, you should have a basic course in financial accounting and a basic course in finance. A second course in financial accounting and a course in investments or corporate finance will be helpful but not necessary. Indeed, you may find yourself motivated to take those courses after reading this book.

Chapter Features

The text is written with features designed to enhance your efforts in learning the material. Each chapter of the book begins with a **flow chart** that lays out the material covered in the chapter and connects that material to the preceding and upcoming chapters. This chart will help you see clearly where you've been and where you are going, and how it all ties together. Each chapter also opens with **The Analyst's Checklist**, which has two lists: one covering the conceptual points in the chapter and the other a set of tasks that you should be able to perform after working the chapter. This outlines the goals of the chapter, setting you up for mastery of the material at hand. Each chapter concludes with **The Analyst's Toolkit**, a convenient resource complete with page references, that summarizes the analysis tools in the chapter—ideal for studying and review.

End-of-Chapter Material

Each chapter ends with a set of concept questions, exercises and minicases. Working through this material will enhance your understanding considerably. These problems are designed, not so much to test you, but to further your learning with practical analysis.

Each problem makes a point. **Concept questions** reinforce the thinking in the chapter. **Exercises**, most involving actual companies, highlight specific issues covered in the chapter. **Minicases**, designed for classroom discussion, are more contextual and involve a broader set of issues, some involving ambiguity. They are written more concisely than full cases so that you do not have to handle a large amount of detail, and classroom time is used more efficiently to make the point. However, the minicases involve considerable analysis and insight, providing stimulus for group discussion.

As with the chapter material, the Exercises and Minicases often use the same real-world companies to make different points in different parts of the book. To help you refer back to earlier material on the same company, the Exercises and Minicases are marked with an easy-to-identify **Real World Connection** tagline.

Website Reinforcement

The material in the text is supplemented with further analysis on the book's website at www.mhhe.com/penman2e. The **Student Center** on the website contains the following:

- **Chapter supplements** for each chapter in the book. The flow chart at the beginning of each chapter of the text refers you to the website, and **The Web Connection** at the end of each chapter summarizes what you will find in the supplements.

- **Chapter notes** for each chapter of the book. Use these notes as a summary of the chapter material.

- **Additional exercises** for each chapter, along with solutions. Work these exercises and correct yourself with the solutions to reinforce your learning.

- **Accounting Clinics I–VII** review accounting issues that are particularly relevant to equity and credit analysis. Among the topics covered are revenue recognition, fair value and historical cost accounting, accounting for debt and equity investments, accounting for stock compensation, pension accounting, and the accounting for taxes.

- **Build Your Own Analysis Product (BYOAP)** on the website shows you how to build your own financial statement analysis and valuation spreadsheet product using the principles and methods in the book. It is not a final product that you can immediately appropriate; rather it is a guidebook for constructing your own. As such, it is a learning device; rather than mechanically applying a black-box product, you learn by doing. With the completed product you can analyze financial statements; forecast earnings, residual earnings, abnormal earnings growth, cash flows and dividends; and then value firms and strategies with a variety of techniques. Add your own bells and whistles. In short, the product is the basis for preparing an equity research report and for carrying out due diligence as a professional. You will find the building process will give you a feeling of accomplishment, and the final product—of your own construction—will be a valuable tool to carry into your professional life or to use for your own investing. Off-the-shelf products are also available. **eVal 2000**, authored by Russell Lundholm and Richard Sloan, both at the University of Michigan, is available through McGraw-Hill/Irwin.

- **Links** to firms' financial statements and to many other sources of financial information. You will also find engines to screen and analyze stocks and to help you build your own analysis tools.

- **Market Insight** (Educational Version) from Standard & Poor's contains financial information on 370 companies. Access codes are available from your instructor.

Resources for Instructors

The book is accompanied by ancillaries that support the teaching and learning. The **Instructor Center** on the book's website contains the following:

- **Solutions Manual** with detailed solutions to the end-of-chapter material.

- **Teaching Notes** with advice for teaching from the book, alternative course outlines, a number of teaching tools, and graphs and figures from the book.

- **PowerPoint** slides for each chapter.

- **Large-scale Cases** for use in class discussion. In contrast to the Minicases in the text, which focus on specific issues, these cases are more comprehensive in the issues they cover. Accordingly, they are longer and require more preparation and more class discussion time. Cases are added to the site as they are prepared.

Acknowledgments

This book capsulates what I have learned as a student of the subject. I am indebted to many writers and professors for that learning. The book has the investment philosophy of Graham, Dodd and Cottle's *Security Analysis*, the book assigned for my first finance course as an undergraduate. It also incorporates the accounting concepts from my study of accounting theory at the University of Queensland and from reading the classics of Paton and Littleton, Sprouse and Moonitz, and Edwards and Bell, to name a few. It reflects my training in the principles of "modern finance," first as a graduate student at the University of Chicago and subsequently from colleagues at Berkeley.

I have learned much from carrying out research on accounting and valuation. In seminars, workshops, and informal discussions, I have been stimulated by the insights of many colleagues at universities around the world. I have a particular debt to Jim Ohlson, whose theoretical work on accounting valuation models has inspired me, as have our many conversations on research and teaching. I have learned much from him. I am also indebted to my students at Berkeley, the London Business School, and Columbia University, who have worked with draft versions of this book and given me valuable feedback. Peter Easton and his students at The Ohio State University, the University of Melbourne, and the University of Chicago also used drafts of the first edition and were generous with their comments.

My appreciation also goes to Lorraine Seiji at Berkeley, whose dedication to preparing the manuscript for the first edition was outstanding. Luis Palencia, Doron Nissim, and Nir Yehuda helped in preparing the graphical material, and Guohua Jiang, Siyi Li, and Nir Yehuda provided valuable accuracy checking and help with supporting materials. Jeffrey Jullich, Marylin Batista and David Comstock also worked on parts of the book. To them all I am grateful. Nancy Banks, as always, gave strong support. The administrations at Berkeley, the London Business School and the Columbia Business School, and my colleagues at these schools, lent support at various stages of the book's preparation. George Werthman, Erin Cibula, Gina Huck, Tim Matray, Kari Geltemeyer, and the entire team at McGraw-Hill/Irwin have been outstanding. Stewart Mattson has overseen the development of both the first and second editions with an expert hand. Instructors, too many to mention, gave feedback on their experience with the first edition.

Anonymous reviewers went out of their way to help improve the manuscript. I am very thankful to them. Now identified, they are listed below. Bruce Johnson requires special mention. He went through the manuscript for the first edition word by word, challenged it, and persuaded me to make numerous improvements.

First and Second Edition Reviewers:

Agnes Cheng
University of Houston

Michael Clement
University of Texas at Austin

Peter Easton
The Ohio State University

Patricia Fairfield
Georgetown University

Richard Gore
Boise State University

Bruce Johnson
University of Iowa

Charles Lee
Cornell University

Gerald Lobo
Syracuse University

Ronald King
Washington University

Arijit Mukherji
University of Minnesota

Jane Ou
Santa Clara University

Richard Sloan
University of Michigan

Lenny Soffer
Northwestern University

Theodore Sougiannis
University of Illinois

K. R. Subramanyan
University of Southern California

Mark Trombley
University of Arizona

James Wahlen
Indiana University

Scott Whisenant
University of Houston

Stephen H. Penman
Columbia University

Brief Contents

Contents

List of Cases

Financial Statement Analysis and Security Valuation

Introduction to Investing and Valuation

LINKS

This chapter
This chapter introduces investing and the role of fundamental analysis in investing.

Link to next chapter
Chapter 2 introduces the financial statements that are used in fundamental analysis.

Link to web page
Go to the book's website for this chapter at **http://www. mhhe.com/ penman2e**. It explains how to find your way around the site and gives you more of the flavor of using financial statement analysis in investing.

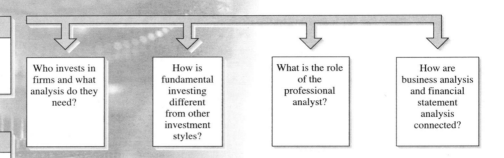

Who invests in firms and what analysis do they need?	How is fundamental investing different from other investment styles?	What is the role of the professional analyst?	How are business analysis and financial statement analysis connected?

Financial statements are the primary information that firms publish about themselves, and investors are the primary users of financial statements. Firms seek capital from investors and prepare financial statements to help investors decide whether to invest. Investors expect the firm to add value to their investment—to return more than was invested—and read financial statements to evaluate the firm's ability to do so. Financial statements are also used for other purposes. Governments use them in social and economic policy-making. Regulators such as the antitrust authorities use them to control business activity. Employees use them in wage negotiations. Senior managers use them to evaluate subordinate managers. Courts, and the expert witnesses who testify in court, use financial statements to assess damages in litigation.

Each type of user needs to understand financial statements. Each needs to know the statements' deficiencies, what they reveal, and what they don't reveal. And each needs to know how to find the pertinent information. **Financial statement analysis** is the method by which users extract information to answer their questions about the firm.

This book presents the principles of financial statement analysis, with a focus on the investor. Many types of investment are entertained. Buying a firm's equity—its common stock—is one, and the book has a particular focus on the shareholder and prospective shareholder. Buying a firm's debt—its bonds—is another. The shareholder is concerned with profitability, the bondholder with default, and financial statement analysis aids in evaluating both. Banks making loans to firms are investors, and they are concerned with default. Firms themselves are also investors when they consider strategies to acquire other firms, go into a new line of business, spin off a division or restructure, or indeed acquire or disinvest in an asset of any form. In all cases financial statements must be analyzed to make a sound decision.

Financial statement analysis inescapably focuses on investors. In market economies, most firms are organized to make money (or "create value") for their owners. So financial statements are prepared primarily with shareholders' investment in mind: The statements are formally presented to shareholders at annual meetings and the main numbers they report are earnings (for the owners) in the income statement and the book value of owners' equity in the balance sheet. But much of the financial statement analysis for investors is relevant to other parties. The shareholder is concerned with profitability. But governmental regulators, suppliers, the firms' competitors, and employees are concerned with profitability also. Shareholders and bondholders are concerned with the riskiness of the business, but so are suppliers and employees. And securities litigation, which involves expert witnesses, usually deals with compensation for loss of profits—or loss of value—to investors. Thus much of the financial statement analysis in this book is relevant to these users also.

Investors typically invest in a firm by buying equity shares or the firm's debt. Their primary concern is the amount to pay—the value of the shares or the debt. The analysis of information that focuses on valuation is called **valuation analysis, fundamental analysis**, or, when securities like stocks and bonds are involved, **security analysis**. This book develops the principles of fundamental analysis. And it shows how financial statement analysis is used in fundamental analysis.

In this chapter we set the stage.

INVESTMENT STYLES AND FUNDAMENTAL ANALYSIS

Millions of shares of business firms are traded every day on the world's stock markets. The investors who buy and sell these shares ask themselves: Am I trading at the right price? What are the shares really worth? They attempt to answer these questions while a discordant background chorus—the printed press, "talking heads" on television financial networks, and Internet chatrooms—voices opinions about what the price should be. They turn to investment advisers who provide an almost endless stream of information and recommendations to sort out. They hear claims that some shares are overpriced, some underpriced, and they hear theories that stock markets can be caught up in the fads and fashions—even mania—that are said to drive share prices away from their appropriate values.

In the absence of any clear indication of what stocks are worth, investors cope in different ways. Some—**intuitive investors**—rely on their own instincts. They go on hunches. Some—called **passive investors**—throw up their hands and trust in "market efficiency." They assume that the market price is a fair price for the risk taken, that market forces have driven the price to the appropriate point.

These investment styles are simple and don't require much effort. But both types of investor run risks beyond those inherent in the firms they buy: paying too much or selling for too little damages investment returns. The intuitive investor has the problem of the intuitive bridge builder: one may be pleased with one's intuition but, before building gets under way, it might pay to check that intuition against the calculations prescribed by modern engineering. Not doing so might lead to disaster. The passive investor is in danger if stocks are mispriced. It is tempting to trust, as a matter of faith, that the market is efficient, and much economic theory says it should be. But it is good practice to check. Both types of investors run the risk of trading with someone who has "done his homework," someone who has analyzed the information thoroughly.

Consider the following:

> Dell Computer Corporation, a leading manufacturer of personal computers, reported earnings for its fiscal year ending February 1, 1998, of $944 million on sales of $12.4 billion. A couple of months later in July 1998, the total market value of Dell's shares surpassed that of General Motors Corporation, which had reported $6.6 billion in earnings for its most recent year on sales of $166.4 billion. Dell traded at 76 times earnings while GM traded at just over 8 times earnings.

General Motors has had its problems. Dell has been a very successful operation with innovative production, "direct marketing," and a made-to-order inventory system. The intuitive investor might identify Dell as a good company and feel confident about buying it. But at 76 times earnings? The P/E ratio for the Standard & Poor's Index (S&P 500) stocks at the time was 28 (very high by historical standards) and microcomputer stocks as a whole traded at 38 times earnings. To pay 76 times earnings seems expensive. The intuitive investor might feel that Dell is a good, well-managed company. But the intuitive investor should recognize that good companies might be overpriced, good companies but bad buys. He might be advised to check the price with some analysis. The passive investor believes that both companies are appropriately priced and ignores the P/E ratios. But with such an extraordinary P/E, she might be advised to check her beliefs. She is at risk of paying too much.

This risk of paying too much for a stock or selling for too little might be reduced by averaging out gains and losses in repeated investments. A passive investor might say: I concede that the market is inefficient at times so sometimes I will pay too much, sometimes too little; but I can still invest passively because, in the end, gains and losses from buying and selling at the wrong price will wash out.

The risk also can be reduced by thoroughly examining information about firms and reaching conclusions about the underlying value that the information implies. This is fundamental analysis and the investor who relies on fundamental analysis is a **fundamental investor**. Fundamental investors ask: Is a P/E of 76 for Dell too expensive? To answer, they make a calculation of what P/E is reasonable given the available information about Dell. They ask: What multiple of earnings is Dell really worth? Fundamental investors distinguish price from value. The creed they follow is "price is what you pay, but value is what you get." They "inspect the goods" as a buyer does with any purchase. Of course, in one sense price is value, for it is the value that other traders put on the shares. You could be cynical about financial analysis and accept price as value. But the fundamental analyst sees price as the cost of the investment, not its value. Oscar Wilde's observation is to the point: "Cynics know the cost of everything, and the value of nothing."

"What you get" from the investment is future payoffs, so the fundamental investor forecasts payoffs to ascertain whether the asking price is a reasonable one. The **defensive investor** does this as a matter of prudence, to avoid trading at the wrong price. The **active investor** uses fundamental analysis to discover mispriced stocks that might earn exceptional rates of return. Box 1.1 further contrasts passive and active investors.

This book shows how to develop forecasts of payoffs and how to use financial statement analysis for forecasting. Fundamental investors speak of discovering intrinsic values, warranted values, or fundamental values. **Intrinsic value** is the worth of an investment that is justified by the information about its payoffs. But this term should not be taken to imply precision. Unlike bridge engineering, fundamental analysis does not take away all uncertainty. It offers principles which, followed faithfully, reduce uncertainty. The analysis in this book develops these principles in a deliberate, systematic way so investors have the security that their investment decisions are sound, intelligent ones. The

Investors buy gambles. They buy a chance to earn a high return against the chance of losing their investment. Passive and active investors differ in their approaches to handling this risk.

Passive investors see risk in business operations delivering less value than expected. They understand that there is a chance that firms' sales will be less than anticipated, that profits from sales will not materialize. But passive investors trust that this **fundamental risk** is efficiently priced in the market. The passive investor realizes, however, that risk can be reduced by diversification and that the market will not reward risk that can be eliminated through diversification. So she holds a diversified portfolio of investments to deal with risk. But, once diversified, the passive investor believes that she is price-protected, with higher risk investments efficiently priced to yield higher expected returns. All she desires from an analyst is information about the level of risk she is taking on, sometimes referred to as *beta risk*. She buys **betas**, and quantitative analysts supply these risk measures using models like the capital asset pricing model (CAPM) and variants— so-called *beta technologies*. No doubt you have been exposed to these models in finance courses.

Active fundamental investors see another source of risk, the risk of paying too much (or selling for too little). That is, they are concerned that securities are not efficiently priced. They see **price risk** in addition to the inherent fundamental risk in business operations. So they carry out an analysis to challenge the market price. Like those who supply betas, they design technologies to do this, sometimes referred to as *alpha technologies* to differentiate them from beta technologies. It is these technologies with which this book is concerned. Active fundamental investors see a reward in this endeavor, for they see the possibility of identifying stocks that can earn abnormal returns—higher expected returns than those implied by beta risk. Indeed, the trade term for these abnormal returns is **alphas** (in contrast to betas), and alpha technologies are brought to bear to predict alphas.

Index investing is an extreme form of passive investing. The index investor buys the market portfolio of stocks or a portfolio like the S&P 500 Index, which closely resembles the market. The market portfolio provides the ultimate diversification, so the investor does not even have to know the beta. The investor does not have to think about anything, and

transaction costs are low. Consider the returns (including dividends) for the S&P 500 for the five years 1998–2002, along with P/E ratios for the index at December 31 of each year:

	1998	1999	2000	2001	2002
S&P 500 returns	28.0%	20.7%	−9.1%	−11.9%	−22.1%
S&P 500 P/E ratio	32.3	33.3	24.7	40.3	28.9

The index investor did very well in the bull market of the 1990s, with the returns for 1998 and 1999 following a string of high returns relative to the historical average for stocks of 13 percent. Her subsequent experience was a little painful, for the S&P 500 returned only −0.6 percent over the five years, compared to 6.8 percent for intermediate term U.S. government bonds. However, the index investor rides out the market, in the belief that stocks are "for the long run"; the historical average return to stocks has been 13 percent, compared with 6 percent for corporate bonds, and 3.5 percent for Treasury bills.

The fundamental investor recognizes these statistical averages but appreciates that these returns are not guaranteed. He also notes another statistic: The historical average P/E ratio for the S&P 500 is 14. P/E ratios over 30 suggest that stocks are too expensive. However, the fundamental investor then begins an investigation as to whether times have changed, whether higher P/E ratios are now justified. Further, rather than holding all of the stocks in the index, he differentiates between those stocks he feels are undervalued in the market, those he thinks are efficiently priced, and those he thinks are overvalued. The indexer's action is HOLD; the active investor expands his action alternatives to BUY, HOLD, or SELL.

It is easy, with hindsight, to say that selling stocks at the end of 1999 would have been a good idea. The appropriate question is whether an analysis in 1999 would have indicated so in advance. The passive investor is skeptical. She points to the fact that active investment funds typically do not perform much better than the S&P 500 Index, net of costs of running the funds. The fundamentalist replies: If no one does fundamental research, how can the market become efficient?

analysis highlights errors that can be made from following simplistic approaches, and how value can be lost by ignoring basic principles.

Traders in securities are not alone in their interest in the value of investments. Within firms, managers daily make investment decisions. They too must ask whether the value of the investment is greater than its cost. And they too, as we will see, must forecast payoffs to ascertain this value.

BUBBLE, BUBBLE

Much is at stake in valuing securities correctly. Trillions of dollars were invested in stock markets around the world in the 1990s. By the end of the decade, nearly 50 percent of adults in the United States held equity shares, either directly or through retirement accounts. In the United Kingdom, this figure was 25 percent, in Germany, 15 percent, and in France, 13 percent. These numbers were up considerably from 10 years earlier. Stock markets in Asia and the Pacific also became very active. Firms in Europe and Asia that once went to banks for capital began raising funds through public stock markets. An equity culture was emerging where firms traded more and more with individual equity investors or their intermediaries. Unfortunately, the growing equity culture was not matched with a growing understanding of how to value stocks. Trillions of dollars were lost as a stock market bubble burst and investors found their savings shrunk significantly.

The experience repeated that of a decade earlier in Japan. On December 29, 1989, The Nikkei 225 Index of Japanese stocks soared to a high of 38,957, a 238 percent gain over a five-year period. Twelve years later in 2001, the Nikkei 225 fell below 10,000 for a loss of over 75 percent from the 1989 high. The stock prices of the 1980s were a bubble, and the bubble burst. The repercussions in Japan were long-term. Some claim that equity investing is rewarded in the long run, but the long run was a long time running. On March 10, 2000, the NASDAQ Composite Index in the United States peaked at 5,060, up 574 percent from the beginning of 1995. By mid-2002, the index was below 1,400, down 75 percent from the high. The S&P 500 Index was down 45 percent and the London FTSE 100 and the Eurotop 300 had lost more than 40 percent. Again, a bubble had burst, leaving investors to wonder how long the long run would be. We are reminded that the Dow Index did not recover its 1929 euphoric level until 1954. During the 1970s, after the bull market of the late 1960s, the Dow stocks returned only 4.8 percent over 10 years and ended the decade down 13.5 percent from their 1960's high.

In January 2000, prior to the bursting of the bubble, Alan Greenspan, chairman of the U.S. Federal Reserve Bank, expressed concern. He asked whether the boom would be remembered as "one of the many euphoric speculative bubbles that have dotted human history." In 1999 he said, "History tells us that sharp reversals in confidence happen abruptly, most often with little advance notice. . . What is so intriguing is that this type of behavior has characterized human interaction with little appreciable difference over the generations. Whether Dutch tulip bulbs or Russian equities, the market price patterns remain much the same."

Indeed, while the usual reference to bubbles is to Dutch tulip bulbs in the seventeenth century or to the South Seas Bubble in the nineteenth century, there has been more recent experience. In 1972, the pricing of the technology stocks of the day—Burroughs, Digital Equipment, Polaroid, IBM, Xerox, Eastman Kodak—looked like a bubble waiting to burst. These stocks were part of the "Nifty Fifty" stocks, deemed a "must buy," that included Coca Cola, Johnson & Johnson, and McDonald's Corporation. The average P/E ratio for the Nifty Fifty was 37 in 1972, nothing like the P/E of over 300 for the NASDAQ 100 stocks in 2000, but considerably above the historical average of 13. The bubble did burst. The S&P 500 P/E ratio declined from 19.0 in 1972 to 7.5 by 1974. The FT 30-share index in London (prior to the days of the FTSE 100) dropped from 543 in May 1972 to 146 in January 1975.

Stock market bubbles damage economies. People form unreasonable expectations of likely returns and so make misguided consumption and investment decisions. Mispriced stocks attract capital to the wrong businesses. Entrepreneurs with poor business models raise cash too easily, deflecting it from firms that can add value for society. Investors borrow to buy paper rather than real productive assets. Debt burdens become intolerable. Banks that feed the borrowing run into trouble. Retirement savings are lost and a pension crisis develops. And, while we have learned something of macroeconomic management since then, the euphoria of the late 1920s and the subsequent depression of the 1930s teach us that systematic failure is possible. Bubble, bubble, toil and trouble.

How Bubbles Work

Bubbles work like a chain letter. You may have joined a chain letter as a teenager for fun (and not much consequence), or as an adult trying to get enough signatures to lobby for a good cause (hopefully with consequence). One letter writer writes to a number of people, instructing each to send the letter on to a number of other people with the same instruction. Letters proliferate, but ultimately the scheme collapses. If the letter involves money—each person in the chain is paid by those joining the chain—the scheme is sometimes referred to as a *Ponzi scheme* or a *pyramid scheme*. A few that are early in the chain make considerable money, but most participants are left with nothing.

In a bubble, investors behave as if they are joining a chain letter. They adopt speculative beliefs that are then fed on to other people, facilitated in recent years by talking heads in the media, Internet chat rooms, and indeed by analysts and poor financial reporting. Each person believes that he will benefit from more people joining the chain, by their buying the stock and pushing the price up. A bubble forms, only to burst as the speculative beliefs are not fulfilled.

The popular investing style called *momentum investing* has features of a chain letter. Advocates of momentum investing advise buying stocks that have gone up, the idea being that those stocks have momentum to continue going up more. What goes up must keep on going up. Indeed, this happens when speculation feeds on itself as the chain letter is passed along.

Analysts During the Bubble

As the renowned fundamental investor Warren Buffett observed, the boom in technology and Internet stocks of the late 1990s was a chain letter, and investment bankers were the "eager postmen." He might well have added sell-side analysts (who recommend stocks to retail investors), some of whom worked with their investment banking colleagues to push stocks at high prices to investors. During the bubble, analysts were recommending buy, buy, buy. In the year 2000, only 2 percent of sell-side analysts' stock recommendations in the U.S. were sells. Only after the NASDAQ index dropped 50 percent did analysts begin to issue sell recommendations. This is not very helpful. One would think that, with such a drop in price, recommendations would tend to change from sell to buy rather than the other way around.

To be fair to analysts, it is difficult to go against the tide of speculation. An analyst might understand that a stock is overvalued, but overvalued stocks can go higher, fed along by the speculation of the moment. The nature of a bubble is for prices to keep rising. So, making a sell call may be foolish in the short run. Analysts are afraid to buck the trend. If they turn out to be wrong when the herd is right, they look bad. If they and the herd are wrong together, they are not penalized as much. But there are big benefits for the star analyst who makes the correct call when the herd is wrong.

The issue calls into question what analysts do. Do they write equity research reports that develop a valuation for a company, or do they speculate on where the stock price will go based on crowd behavior? They might do either or both. However, they should always justify their position with good thinking. Unfortunately, during the 1990s bubble, many analysts promoted poor thinking. They fed the speculation. See Box 1.2.

When speculative fever is high, analysts are tempted to abandon good thinking and promote speculative thinking. They may be compromised because their investment firms make money from brokerage commissions, so they want their analysts to promote stock buying. If their firm has an investment banking arm (where considerable money is made), it may reward analysts for recommending stocks during public offerings, mergers, and acquisitions. Analysts may be reluctant to make sell recommendations on the firms they cover, in fear of being cut off from further information from those firms. Or they may simply get caught up in the speculative fever of the moment.

There was no shortage of speculative analysis during the 1990s bubble, particularly in the coverage of technology, Internet, and telecommunication stocks. Here are some examples. Understand the fallacy in each point.

- Profits were dismissed as unimportant. Most Internet stocks reported losses, but analysts insisted at the time that this did not matter. What was important, they said, was the business model. Well, both are important. A firm has to make profits and, even though it may have losses currently, there must be reasonable scenarios for earning profits. See Box 1.3. As it turned out, the losses reported for dot.com firms during the bubble were a good indicator of outcomes. Many of these firms did not survive.

- Commentators insisted that traditional financial analysis was no longer relevant. The "new economy" demands new ways of thinking, they said. They offered no persuasive new thinking, but discarded the old.

- Analysts appealed to vague terms like "new technology," "web real estate," customer "share of mind," "network effects," and indeed, "new economy" to recommend stocks. Pseudoscientific labels; sound science produces good analysis, not just labels.

- Analysts claimed that the firms' value was in "intangible assets" (and so claimed that the firm must be worth a lot!), but they didn't indicate how one tests for the value of the intangible assets. One even saw analysts calculating the value of intangible assets as the difference between bubble prices and tangible assets of the balance sheet. Beware of analysts recommending firms because they have "knowledge capital." Knowledge is value in this information age, but knowledge must produce goods and services, the goods and services must produce sales, and the sales must produce profits. And knowledge assets must be paid for. Inventors and engineers must be paid. Will there be good profits after paying for knowledge?

- Analysts relied heavily on nonfinancial metrics like page views, usage metrics, customer reach, and capacity utilization. These metrics may give some indication of profitability but they don't guarantee it. The onus is on the analysts to show how these indicators translate into future profits.

- Analysts justified values on the basis of macro variables rather than expected future corporate profits. So they claimed that the high prices for Internet and other technology stocks were justified by the large increase in productivity from technological advances. But productivity increases do not necessarily flow to producers. Employees share in productivity gains. Competition pushes the benefits through to consumers, leaving firms with a normal rate of return, if not immediately, not too far in the future. Indeed, it seems that consumers have been the primary beneficiaries of the Internet revolution, not the e-commerce start-ups.

- Analysts relied on financial measures above the "bottom line" earnings. Revenue growth is one, but while revenue growth is desirable, revenues must result in profits. Some firms published "pro forma" or adjusted earnings that excluded some aspects of earnings. Lynn Turner, chief accountant at the Securities and Exchange Commission (SEC) in 2000, called these numbers EBS, "Everything but the Bad Stuff," in contrast to EPS, earnings per share.

- Analysts moved from focusing on P/E ratios and earnings growth to focusing on price-to-sales (P/S) ratios and sales growth. Sales growth is important, but sales ultimately must produce profits. With analysts' focus on price-to-sales ratios, firms began to manufacture sales through accounting practices like grossing up commissions and barter transactions in advertising.

- Analysts' forecasts of growth rates were high compared to past history. Analysts consistently maintained that companies could maintain exceptional revenue and earnings growth rates for a long time. Analysts' "long-term growth rates" (for 3–5 years in the future) are typically too optimistic in boom times. History says that growth rates usually decline toward average rates quite quickly.

- Rough indicators of mispricing were ignored without justification. A P/E of 33 for the S&P 500 at the height of the bubble is a waving red flag. A P/E of 76 for Dell Computer flashes a warning. One should have good reasons for buying at these multiples.

- Historical perspective was ignored. Cisco Systems, with a market value of half a trillion dollars, traded at a P/E of 135 in 1999. There has never been a company with a large market value that has traded with a P/E over 100.

- Comparisons between firms did not make sense. See the earlier comparison of Dell Computer and General Motors.

- Simple calculations didn't add up. At one point in 1999, an online discount airline ticket seller traded at a market value greater than the total for all U.S. airlines. Internet companies traded at a market value, in total, of over $1 trillion, but had total revenues of only $30 billion, giv-ing them an average price-to-sales ratio of 33. This looks high against the historical average P/S ratio of just 1. All the more so when one recognizes that these firms were reporting losses totaling $9 billion. For $1 trillion, an investor could have purchased quite a number of established firms with significant profits.

- Analysts did not examine the quality of earnings that firms were reporting. The emphasis was on firms reporting earnings that bettered analysts' forecasts, not on the quality of the accounting that went into those earnings.

Fundamental Analysis Anchors Investors

Fundamental analysis cuts through the poor thinking (like that in Box 1.2) that promotes the chain letter. Fundamental analysis challenges speculative beliefs and the prices they ferment, anchoring the investor against the tide of fad and fashion. Speculation promotes momentum in stock prices, but fundamental analysts see gravity at work. Prices, they insist, must gravitate to fundamentals, and the investor anchored to fundamentals has the best prospect for the long run. See Box 1.3.

THE SETTING: INVESTORS, FIRMS, SECURITIES, AND CAPITAL MARKETS

To value business investments we need to have a good understanding of how a business works, how it adds value, and how it returns value to investors. We begin here to build a picture of the firm and its investors—sketchy at first—to be filled out as the book proceeds.

When individuals or institutions invest in firms, they give up cash in hope of a higher return of cash in the future. The investment gives them a **claim** on the firm for a return. This claim if formalized in a *contract*, which may not be tradable (like most partnership interests and bank loan agreements), or in a *security*, which can be traded in security markets (like stocks and bonds).

Corporate claims vary from simple "plain vanilla" types such as equity and debt to more complicated contingent claims. *Contingent claims* such as convertible bonds, options, and warrants are derivative claims whose payoffs are based on the value of firms' stocks or bonds, usually stocks. Despite their contractual complexity, contingent claims are relatively easy to value: once the value of the stocks or bonds is determined, standard option-pricing techniques can be used to get the derivative price. The techniques follow the principles of financial engineering (which will not concern us in this book). Equity and debt claims are more basic: their value is "fundamental" to valuing the contingent claims. Their pricing is guided by principles of fundamental analysis (on which we very much focus in this book).

The *equity* is the most important corporate claim. It is the primary claim, so much so that common stock is sometimes referred to as the fundamental security. The equity is the

During 1998 and 1999 the prices of Internet stocks soared to such a degree that commentators referred to the phenomenon as speculative mania. The stock price of Amazon.com, the leading Internet book retailer, rose from $20 in June 1998 to $200 by January 1999 (adjusted for stock splits), at the same time it was reporting losses. Yahoo's stock rose from $25 to $225 over the same period, giving it a P/E ratio of 1,406 and a price-sales ratio of 199. Shares in America Online (AOL), another Internet portal, rose from $20 in June 1998 to $150 by April 1999 (before its acquisition of Time Warner), giving it a P/E ratio of 649, a price-sales ratio of 46, and a market capitalization of 2½ times that of General Motors.

To investigate whether these prices represent value or speculative mania, the fundamental investor asks what are reasonable expectations for these firms. AOL was reporting annual sales revenue of $3.1 billion at the time, 80 percent from the subscriptions of 18 million members, and the remainder from online advertising and Internet commerce. The fundamental investor might ask: What anticipated sales growth over the next 10 years is required to justify a price of 46 times sales? Well, if AOL were to maintain its 1998 profit margin of 8½ percent of sales, he might calculate that AOL

needs $291 billion in sales in 10 years, or a 9,387 percent increase over current sales, about 57 percent per year. (You will see how to make these calculations later.)

Perspective might tell him this forecast is a high number. Among the largest U.S. firms in stock market value, General Motors had 1998 sales of $154 billion, General Electric's 1998 sales were $100 billion, and Microsoft's were $16 billion. Wal-Mart, the largest U.S. retailer, had 1998 sales of $138 billion and experienced sales growth of 17 percent per year in the 1990s. He might then take a defensive position and not hold AOL stock. Or he might take an active position and sell it short. Or he might come to the conclusion that AOL's future prospects justify the current price of its shares.

The thorough fundamental investor would not be satisfied by assuming that AOL would maintain its profit margin at the 1998 level. He would forecast future profit margins as well. He might anticipate benefits from AOL's recent acquisition of Netscape. But, whatever the scenario, he would anticipate the payoffs from the scenario. And he would ask whether a reasonable scenario could be developed that would justify the current market price.

owners' claim on the business, often referred to as *owners' equity* or *shareholders' equity*. This claim is the residual claim on the value of the firm after other claimants have been satisfied. It is, by far, the most difficult claim to value and it is the valuation of this claim, *equity valuation*, with which we will be preoccupied. But we also will be concerned with debt claims. Debt claims are relatively simple claims for return of interest and principal. So they are relatively simple to value.

Figure 1.1 depicts the *debtholders* and *shareholders* and the cash flows between them and the firm. We ignore the holders of contingent claims here to keep it simple. Debtholders (bondholders, banks, and other creditors) make loans to the firm in exchange for a claim for a **payoff** in the form of interest payments and loan repayments, as shown. Shareholders contribute cash in exchange for equity shares that entitle them to a payoff in the form of dividends or cash from share repurchases. The amount of the payoff, less the amount paid for the claim, is called the **return**.

When a firm sells debt or equity claims it trades in the *capital market*. The capital market can be a formal, organized stock exchange where public, "listed" firms trade, an informal market involving intermediaries such as venture capitalists, banks, and investment brokers, or raising capital from family and friends.

Holders of claims also may sell claims in the capital market if they wish to liquidate their investment. They sell to secondary investors and receive cash, as indicated by the arrows in the diagram, in exchange for surrendering their claims to the new investors. So you see from the diagram that the payoffs to claimants (indicated by the arrows flowing to them) come both from the firm and from sales of their claims in the capital market. For shareholders the payoffs are in the form of dividends from the firm and proceeds from the sale of shares, either to the firm in a share repurchase (where the firm buys back shares) or to other investors in the stock market. Debtholders receive interest and a settlement

FIGURE 1.1   The Firm, Its Claimants, and the Capital Market

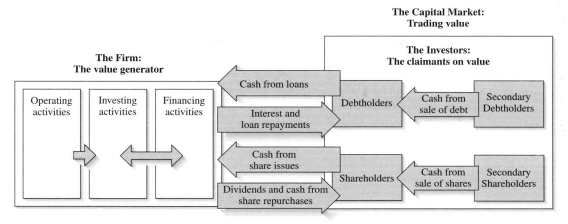

payment, either by the firm redeeming the debt before or at maturity or by selling the debt in the bond market.

The value of a claim traded in the capital market is based on the anticipated payoffs that the firm will ultimately pay on the claim. So the diagram describes the firm as the *value generator*. Debtholders want enough value generated to recover interest and principal. Shareholders get the residual value after the return to the bondholders. To the extent their goals are financial ones, shareholders want to maximize the value generated by the firm. Indeed, as owners they have the authority, in most cases, to hire and fire management to ensure that management strives to increase firm value and the value of their residual claim.

It is always the case that the value of the claims on a firm must add up to the **value of the firm**:

$$\text{Value of the firm} = \text{Value of debt} + \text{Value of equity} \qquad \textbf{(1.1)}$$

This just says that the total value that a firm generates must be divided among the various claims to that value (just the two basic claims are given here). So, in valuation, we can think of valuing the firm and dividing the firm's value among claimants, or we can think of valuing the claims, the sum of which is the value of the firm. The value of the firm is sometimes referred to as the *value of the enterprise* or *enterprise value*.

We will have much more to say about value generation in a business. To start, the diagram shows the firm involved in three activities: financing activities, investing activities, and operating activities. Specifics vary, but these three activities are generic to all businesses.

- **Financing activities** are the transactions with claimants that we have just talked about: raising cash for the business in exchange for equity and debt claims and returning cash to claimants. These activities are investing activities for the claimants but financing activities for the firm.

- **Investing activities** use the cash raised from financing activities and generated in operations to acquire assets to be employed in operations. These assets may be physical assets, like inventories, plant, and equipment, or knowledge and intellectual assets, like technology and know-how.

- **Operating activities** utilize the assets in which the firm has invested to produce and sell products. Operating activities combine assets with labor and materials to produce products and services, sell them to customers, and collect cash from customers. If successful, the operations generate enough cash to reinvest in assets or return to claimants.

Understanding these activities is fundamental to understanding the value generation in a business. The picture is very much incomplete here, so these activities are drawn as opaque windows in the diagram. As the book proceeds, we will open these windows to learn more about how the firm generates value for its investors.

THE BUSINESS OF ANALYSIS: THE PROFESSIONAL ANALYST

Many investors find that choosing and managing investments is not their forte, so they turn to professional **financial analysts**. In any field, the professional is someone who has the specialized technology to get a task done. Indeed professionals present themselves as arbiters of good technology, and a profession is judged by its ability to successfully solve the problem at hand. The professional continually asks: What are good techniques, what are poor ones? The professional, like any other producer, sells products to his customers, the investors. As a competitor with others, the professional asks: How can I enhance the technology to get an edge over my competition? What does a good valuation product look like? What's the best way to go about analyzing information on firms? How can I do financial statement analysis most efficiently? What methods add value for my client? Understanding what a good fundamental analysis technology looks like is at the heart of this book.

As types of investments vary, so do the types of professionals who serve investors. Each needs to tailor analysis to the client's need.

Investing in Firms: The Outside Analyst

Many professionals are outside the business, looking in, and we refer to them as outside analysts. Security analysts, investment consultants, and stockbrokers advise clients on buying and selling corporate securities. Investment bankers and business brokers advise clients on acquiring and selling businesses. Accountants and assessors value firms for tax and estate purposes. And any one of these might serve as an expert witness in litigation involving valuation issues.

Just as there are two main types of business claims, there are two main types of outside analysts. *Credit analysts*, such as those at bond rating agencies (Standard & Poor's Corporation and Moody's Investors Service, for example) or bank loan officers, evaluate the riskiness—and thus the value—of business debt. But prime among business analysts is the *equity analyst*. The equity analyst typically prepares an equity research report. The analyst's main concern: How do I produce an equity research report which is credible and persuasive and gives my client confidence in investing? Many research reports fail this test. They typically close with a prominent buy, hold, or sell recommendation. They present graphs, numbers, and verbiage about the business but it is not always clear how the recommendation follows from the analysis, or indeed whether it is justified.

Investing within Firms: The Inside Analyst

Inside the firm, business managers invest moneys contributed to the firm in business assets. Business investment begins with an idea, a "strategy." These strategies may involve developing new products, exploring new markets, adopting a new production technology, or beginning an entirely new line of business. Strategy may call for acquiring another firm, merging with other firms, or entering into alliances. To evaluate their ideas, business managers, like outside investors, need to analyze the value that their ideas might generate. Such an evaluation is called **strategy analysis**.

Business managers may have good intuition and may feel confident that their ideas are good ones. But they can be overconfident, too persuaded by their own ideas. They, like the outside intuitive investor, need to submit their intuition to analysis. And their fiduciary relationship to claimants requires that they focus on shareholder value. They must value their ideas: Is the strategy likely to add value? The insider's view on analysis should be no different from that of the outsider. The outside investor must be persuaded to buy shares at the market price and, to decide, looks to analysis. The inside investor must be persuaded to buy an idea or a strategy at what it will cost to implement and, to decide, looks to analysis. What value is likely to be added over the cost?

Business strategists develop appealing ideas and each year new strategy paradigms are offered in business schools and in the financial press. Recent examples are the "centerless corporation" and the "knowledge corporation," both of which require investment in reorganization and intellectual capital. The ideas must be tested. Downsizing was a popular idea of the 1990s, but downsizing may reduce revenues as well as costs. Like all strategies, this idea must be subjected to analysis.

Valuation analysis not only helps with the go/no-go decision on whether to commit to an investment, but it also helps in the planning and execution of the investment. Strategic ideas sometimes can be vague; submitting the ideas to formal analysis forces the planner to think concretely about ideas and to develop the specifics; it turns ideas into concrete, dollar numbers. And it forces the planner to examine alternative ways of doing things. Strategies are revised in response to the numbers until a final, best plan emerges. A good strategy is the result of both good ideas and good analysis. Investing and managing with valuation analysis is called **value-based management**.

The chief financial officer (CFO) typically coordinates analysis for management and it is her responsibility to institutionalize the best analysis. She and her corporate analysts evaluate broad strategies and specific proposals to acquire firms, spin off businesses, restructure operations, launch new products, and the like. Managers sometimes complain about "bean counters" being too narrowly focused on the numbers, stifling innovation. Yet "manage by the numbers" they must. The onus is on the CFO to adopt an analysis that not only avoids the criticism but actively promotes innovation and the testing of innovative ideas, with the assurance that good ideas that add value will be recognized.

Inside and outside analysts differ in one respect: Inside analysts have far more information to work with. Outside analysts receive the published financial statements along with much supplementary information, but they are typically not privy to "inside information." Because you, as students, are not privy to inside information either, the financial statement analysis in this book is more oriented to the outside analyst. Most of the applications are to U.S. financial statements, but the focus is not on U.S. accounting practices. Rather it is on how accounting information—be it accounting practices of the United States or any other country—can best be handled in valuation analysis. Statements of other countries as well as the United States will be reformulated and modified according to universal principles to make them more amenable to analysis. And impediments to good analysis due to accounting principles or disclosure deficiencies will be identified. So we develop a critique of financial statements as they are currently prepared.

THE ANALYSIS OF BUSINESS

The techniques to be developed in this book are for both inside and outside investors. Both invest in business operations. The outside investor talks of buying a stock, but buying a stock is not buying a piece of paper; it is buying a piece of a business. An old adage says, "One does not buy a stock, one buys a business." And it goes on: "If you are going to buy a business, know the business."

An accomplished analyst must know the business she is covering. An analyst seeking to value a telecommunications firm must understand that industry and the firm's position in it. She must know the firm's strategy to build networks, to adapt to technological change, and to meet the challenges of its competitors. She must know the products. She must anticipate consumer demand. She must know whether there is excess capacity in the industry. She must understand the evolving technology path, how voice, data, and multimedia might be delivered in the future. The business context gives meaning to information. The significance of high labor costs of, say, 70 percent of sales is much greater for a firm with low labor input and high capital input than for a consulting firm with a large labor input. To understand whether a P/E ratio of 76 for Dell Computer is too high, the analyst must understand the computer business, the prospects for sales growth, and the profit margins on different computer products. Some types of firms work on low profit margins on different computer products. Some types of firms work on low profit margins (profits relative to sales), while others work on high profit margins, depending on how products are produced, and it might be ridiculous to expect a low-margin firm to improve its profit margin substantially. Normal inventory levels differ between retailers and wholesalers, and between manufacturers and retailers. Depreciation charges should be high if a firm is in an industry with rapidly changing technology or excess capacity.

Analysts specialize by industry sector simply because knowing the nature of the business is a necessary condition for analyzing a business. For example, equity research reports are usually prefaced by a discussion of the industry and financial statement analysis usually compares measures like profit margins and inventory ratios to normal benchmarks for the industry.

Understanding business is of course the subject of a whole business school curriculum, to be filled out by years of experience. The more thorough that knowledge, the more confident one is in business valuation. To put it differently, one treads cautiously when investing in firms about which one knows little. Do too many investors (and indeed money managers) buy stocks instead of businesses?

Strategy and Valuation

There are many details of a business with which the analyst must be familiar. To focus his thinking he first identifies the **business model**—sometimes also referred to as the *business concept* or the *business strategy*. What is the firm aiming to do? How does it see itself to be generating value? And what are the consequences of the strategy? These questions are often answered in terms of how the firm represents itself to its customers. Home Depot, the warehouse retailer of home-improvement products, follows the concept of providing high-quality materials for do-it-yourselfers at discount prices, but with training and advice. As a consequence, the combination of discount prices with added customer servicing costs implies that the firm must be very efficient in its purchasing, warehousing, and inventory control. The Gap, Inc., aims to present dress-down clothing as fashion items at reasonable prices in attractive stores, a different concept from warehouse retailing. As a consequence, it must manage image through advertising and be creative in fash-

Managers of firms use valuation analysis to evaluate whether their strategies create value for shareholders. But shareholders and other potential investors also must familiarize themselves with firms' strategies. And they should ask what alternative strategies firms might pursue, for the value of firms is different under different strategies.

Consider America Online. In early 1999 AOL was an Internet portal whose revenues came from subscriptions, advertising, and e-commerce. After its acquisition of Netscape, it added Internet technology services to its product line. Then, in early 2000, it announced its merger with Time Warner, the large media company that owned CNN, Turner Broadcasting Systems, publications like *Time* magazine, Warner Brothers film and recording studios, cable systems, and many other assets with valuable brand names. This acquisition was the first big merger of a new Internet company with an old-style media company, bringing distribution and content together.

Clearly AOL was a company in (rapid) evolution, changing from a portal firm to a content firm in a short space of time. AOL's management would need to understand the value of Netscape and Time Warner to ensure that they were not overpaying for these firms' shares. They would need to understand the value of AOL's own shares to ensure that, in offering shares to make acquisitions, they were not issuing shares that were undervalued in the market. And they would need to understand any value-added synergies that would come from combining the firms.

But outside analysts also benefit from understanding how AOL is likely to evolve. An analyst valuing AOL as a stand-alone portal firm in early 1999 would have arrived at a different valuation from one who had anticipated AOL's acquisition strategy. And an analyst surprised by the Time Warner acquisition would revise his valuation after recognizing the implications of the strategy it revealed.

Strategies are adaptive to changing conditions, so valuations must be revised as strategies change. In mid-2002, AOL Time Warner's stock price was down 65 percent from its level at the time of the merger, and $54 billion of goodwill from the acquisition had to be written off the balance sheet (the largest write-off ever). Commentators insisted that the expected benefits from the merger had not been realized. The CEO position at AOL Time Warner passed from Gerald Levin, who engineered the AOL merger, to Richard Parsons, with the challenge to modify the strategy. Would AOL be spun off from Time Warner? Anticipating that strategy was the first step in valuing AOL Time Warner at that point in time.

ion design while at the same time keeping production costs low. With considerable retail space, both firms require high asset turnover.

For the inside investor, the business strategy is the outcome of valuation analysis: A strategy is chosen after determining whether it will add value. For the outside investor, the business strategy is the starting point for analysis, for firms can be valued only under a specified strategy. But the outside investor also should be aware of alternative strategies that have the potential for enhancing value. Some takeovers occur because outside investors believe that more value can be created with new ideas and with new management. Strategies are ever evolving, so the analyst must be attuned to the way firms adapt to change and adapt also. Indeed, a smart analyst anticipates changes in strategy and the value they might create or destroy. See Box 1.4.

Mastering the Details

Once the business is clearly in mind, the analyst turns to master the details. There are many details of the business to discover, but you can think of them under five categories.

1. Know the firm's product.
    a. Type of product.
    b. Consumer demand for the product.
    c. Price elasticity of demand for the product.
    d. Substitutes for the product. Is it differentiated? On price? On quality?
    e. Brand name association of the product.
    f. Patent protection for the product.

2. Know the technology required to bring the product to market.
   a. Production process.
   b. Marketing process.
   c. Distribution channels.
   d. Supplier network.
   e. Cost structure.
   f. Economies of scale.

3. Know the firm's knowledge base.
   a. Direction and pace of technological change and the firm's grasp of it.
   b. Research and development program.
   c. Tie-in to information networks.
   d. Managerial talent.
   e. Ability to innovate in product development.
   f. Ability to innovate in production technology.
   g. Economies from learning.

4. Know the competitiveness of the industry.
   a. Concentration in the industry, the number of firms, and their sizes.
   b. Barriers to entry in the industry and the likelihood of new entrants and substitute products.
   c. The firm's position in the industry. Is it a first mover or a follower in the industry? Does it have a cost advantage?
   d. Competitiveness of suppliers. Do suppliers have market power? Do labor unions have power?
   e. Capacity in the industry. Is there excess capacity or undercapacity?
   f. Relationships and alliances with other firms.

5. Know the political, legal, regulatory, and ethical environment.
   a. The firm's political influence.
   b. Legal constraints on the firm, including antitrust law, consumer law, labor law, and environmental law.
   c. Regulatory constraints on the firm, including product and price regulations.
   d. Taxation of the business.
   e. The ethical charter under which the firm operates, and the propensity of managers to violate it.

These features are sometimes referred to as the *economic factors* that drive the business. You have studied many of these factors, and more, in courses on business economics, strategy, marketing, and production.

The Key Question: Durability of Competitive Advantage

Armed with an understanding of a firm's strategy and a mastery of the details, the analyst focuses on the key question: *How durable is the firm's competitive advantage?*

Microeconomics tells us that competition drives away abnormal returns, so that a firm ultimately earns a return equal to the required return for the risk assumed. With very few exceptions, the **forces of competition** are at play, and the critical question is how long those forces take to play out. The key to adding value is to design a business where abnormal returns endure for as long as possible. Firms attempt to counter the forces of competition to gain **competitive advantage**. The more enduring the competitive advantage, the more the firms generate value.

The business strategy and all of the economic factors listed ultimately bear upon competitive advantage. Innovative strategies are adopted to "get ahead of the competition." Products are designed to allure customers from the competition. Brands are built to maintain enduring customer loyalty. Patent protection is sought. Innovative production technologies are adopted for cost advantage. And, yes, politicians are lobbied to protect firms from competition. The inside analyst designs strategies to maintain competitive advantage. The outside analyst understands those strategies and strives to answer the question as to the durability of the firm's competitive advantage.

Financial Statements: The Lens on the Business

Understanding economic factors is a prerequisite to forecasting. But we need a way of translating these factors into measures that lead to a valuation. We must recognize the firm's product, the competition in the industry, the firm's ability to develop product innovations, and so on, but we also must interpret this knowledge in a way that leads to a valuation. Economic factors often are expressed in qualitative terms that are suggestive but do not immediately translate into concrete dollar numbers. We might recognize that a firm has "market power," but what numbers would support this attribution? We might recognize that a firm is "under the threat of competition," but how would this show up in the numbers?

Financial statements report the numbers. Financial statements translate economic factors into accounting numbers like assets, sales, margins, cash flows, and earnings, and therefore we analyze the business by analyzing financial statements. We understand the effects of market power from accounting numbers. We evaluate the durability of competitive advantage from sequences of accounting numbers. Financial statement analysis organizes the financial statements in a way that highlights these features of a business.

Financial statements are the lens on the business. However, financial statements often produce a blurred picture. Financial statement analysis focuses the lens to produce a clearer picture. Where accounting measurement is defective, analysis corrects. And where the picture in financial statements is incomplete, the analyst supplements the financial statements with other information. To do so, the analyst must know what the financial statements say and what they do not say. He must have a sense of good accounting and bad accounting. This book develops that facility, beginning in the next chapter, where financial statements are introduced. With this facility and a good knowledge of the business, the analyst proceeds to value the business through the lens of the financial statements.

CHOOSING A VALUATION TECHNOLOGY

The analyst must have a good understanding of the business. He must understand the firm's competitive advantage. He must understand how the financial statements measure the success of the business. But, with all this understanding, he must then have a way of converting that understanding into a valuation of the firm. A valuation technology allows the analyst to make that conversion. However, the analyst must choose an appropriate technology.

Box 1.5 lists valuation technologies that are commonly used in practice. Some have the advantage of being simple, and simplicity is a virtue. But techniques can be too simple, ignoring important elements. Some techniques are dangerous, containing pitfalls for the unwary. The analyst chooses a technology with costs and benefits in mind, weighing simplicity against the costs of ignoring complexities.

The following valuation methods are covered in this book. All involve financial statement numbers in some way. Each method must be evaluated on its costs and benefits.

METHODS THAT DO NOT INVOLVE FORECASTING

The Method of Comparables (Chapter 3)
This method values stocks on the basis of price multiples (stock price divided by earnings, book value, sales, and other financial statement numbers) that are observed for similar firms.

Multiple Screening (Chapter 3)
This method identifies underpriced and overpriced stocks on the basis of their relative multiples. A stock screener buys firms with relative low price-earnings (P/E) ratios, for example, and sells stocks with high P/E ratios. Or he may screen stocks into buys and sells by screening on price-to-book, price-to-sales, and other multiples.

Asset-Based Valuation (Chapter 3)
Asset-based valuation values equities by adding up the value of the assets of a firm and subtracting the value of the liabilities.

METHODS THAT INVOLVE FORECASTING

Dividend Discounting: Forecasting Dividends (Chapter 3)
Value is calculated as the present value of expected dividends.

Discounted Cash Flow Analysis: Forecasting Free Cash Flows (Chapter 4)
Value is calculated as the present value of expected free cash flows.

Residual Earnings Analysis: Forecasting Earnings and Book Values (Chapter 5)
Value is calculated as book value plus the present value of expected residual earnings.

Earnings Growth Analysis: Forecasting Earnings and Earnings Growth (Chapter 6)
Value is calculated as capitalized earnings plus the present value of expected abnormal earnings growth.

This book covers the techniques in Box 1.5, highlighting their advantages and disadvantages. However, by far the most attention will be given to those techniques that attempt to calculate fundamental value from forecasts, for value is based on the expected payoffs to investing. For these methods, the analyst must identify what is to be forecasted. Does the analyst forecast dividends (and thus use dividend discount methods)? Does the analyst forecast cash flows (and thus use discounted cash flow methods)? Earnings? Book value and earnings? To make the choice the analyst must understand the advantages and disadvantages of each and then adopt a technology that provides the most security to the investor.

Classifying and Ordering Information

An important part of a valuation technology is how it handles information. All of the valuation methods in Box 1.5 involve financial statement information, but in different ways. Too-simple techniques ignore information, and the investor ignores information at her peril because she puts herself in danger of trading with someone who knows more than she. Multiple screening methods, for example, use only one or two bits of information, so they can get you into trouble. Forecasting uses the full range of information available, but it requires the appropriate organization of information into a form that facilitates forecasting. Financial statement analysis is a matter of efficient organization of financial statement information.

In organizing the information, fundamental analysts follow the maxim: *Don't mix what you know with speculation.* If the fundamental analyst is to cut across speculation, he must distinguish information that is concrete from information that is more speculative. The fundamental analyst takes care not to contaminate relatively hard information with soft information that leads to speculation. He sees current sales as relatively hard information, for customers have been won, but he sees information indicating that the firm might win more customers in the future as more speculative. He does not ignore the more speculative information, but he treats it differently. Current sales are weighed differently than forecasts of long-run growth rates in sales. He treats information that is used to forecast one or two years ahead in a different light than information that is used to forecast the distant future. And he is considerably more uncomfortable with stock valuations that are dependent on forecasting the long run; he sees such a stock as a more speculative stock.

Anchoring Value in the Financial Statements

Financial statements contain information of varying quality and the accounting is sometimes suspect, but the information they contain is relatively hard information. Financial statements are based on accounting principles that largely exclude speculative information. They are audited. So, while the analyst always tests the quality of the information in the financial statements and organizes that information based on its perceived quality, financial statements are a good place to start when valuating firms.

Financial statements report two summary numbers, book value of equity and earnings. The book value of equity is the "bottom line" number in the balance sheet; earnings is the "bottom line" number in the income statement. The last two methods in Box 1.5 anchor value on these summary numbers. The form of the valuation is as follows:

$$\text{Value} = \text{Anchor} + \text{Extra value}$$

That is, the analyst takes a particular measure in the financial statements as a concrete starting point and then goes about calculating "extra value" not captured by this measure. The anchor might be the book value of shareholders' equity, so that

$$\text{Value} = \text{Book value} + \text{Extra value}$$

Here book value is the starting point, but the analyst realizes that book value is an incomplete measure of value, so he calculates extra value. In doing so, he calculates the intrinsic price-to-book ratio, the multiple of book value that the equity is worth. Valuation then comes down to the method of calculating value that is not in book value.

Alternatively, the anchor might be earnings, so that

$$\text{Value} = \text{Earnings} + \text{Extra value}$$

In this case, earnings is the starting point and the extra value yields the price-earnings ratio, the multiple of earnings that the equity is worth. In both cases, the analyst starts with a hard number (in the financial statements) and adds an analysis of more speculative information.

HOW TO USE THIS BOOK

The best way to tackle this book is to see it as an exercise in building a valuation technology. Think of yourself as an investor who wants to have the best methods to protect and enhance your investments. Or think of yourself as one of the professionals we have talked about, an investment analyst or CFO. This will give you focus. If you think in terms of an outside analyst, ask yourself: How would I build the best valuation product for my clients? How would I prepare a credible equity research report? If you think in terms of an inside analyst, ask yourself: How would I write a strategy document or an investment appraisal? You want an analysis that will be practical, but you want one that is also conceptually sound. And you want an analysis that is understandable and easy to use.

This focus will make you demand a lot of the book, and of yourself. It will help you develop your critique of investment products that are being offered by vendors. It will help you develop your critique of the accounting in published financial statements. And, yes, it will also help you critique the book!

There are three ingredients to a good technology: good thinking, good application, and good balance between cost and benefit. Use the book to develop good thinking about businesses and their valuation: The book takes pains to lay out the concepts clearly. Use the book to translate concepts into methods that work in practice: The book builds a practical technique, block-by-block, from the concepts. Much of the analysis can be built into a spreadsheet program, and you might build this spreadsheet as you go, a product to carry over to your professional life. Use the book to get a sense of cost-benefit tradeoffs. When is more detail worth it? What do I lose by cutting corners? What "bells and whistles" are worth adding?

The text is self-contained. But you will also find the book's web page to be a worthwhile companion. It goes into more "real-life" situations, gives you more data to work with, and opens up the broader literature. It also has numerous links to information, the basic raw materials of analysis. Indeed, you might use this web page as your home base for investment analysis, and carry it with you into your professional life.

Learning comes from reinforcing concepts by application. Exercises are given at the end of each chapter along with larger cases at the end of each section. They are written with learning in mind, to make a point, not solely as tests. More applications are on the web page. Work through as many of these as you can. You will see how the analysis comes to life as you go "hands on."

An Outline of the Book

This chapter has introduced you to fundamental investing and has provided a flavor of the fundamental analysis that supports the investing. Financial statements feature prominently in analysis, so the introduction is completed in Chapter 2, where the financial statements are introduced. There you will understand why an analyst might anchor a valuation in the financial statements. The remainder of the book is then presented in five parts.

Good practice is built on good thinking. Part One (Chapters 3–6) lays out that thinking. Part One evaluates each of the methods presented in Box 1.5 and lays out how financial statement information is incorporated in each. By the end of Part One you will have a good sense of what good analysis is and what poor analysis is, and you will have selected a valuation technology with some confidence. The remainder of the book involves the application of the technology to good practice.

Part Two (Chapters 7–12) deals with the analysis of information. It shows how to understand the business through the lens of the financial statements. It also shows how to carry out financial statement analysis with a view to forecasting payoffs.

Part Three (Chapters 13–15) involves forecasting. It lays out the practical steps for developing forecasts from the information analyzed in Part Two. And it shows how to convert those forecasts into a valuation.

Part Four (Chapters 16–17) deals with accounting issues. A discussion of accounting is intertwined with the development of fundamental analysis throughout the book, beginning in Chapter 2. Part Four pulls the accounting analysis together so that you have a sound understanding of how accounting works in valuation. And, to the financial statement analysis of the earlier parts, it adds an accounting quality analysis.

Part Five (Chapters 18 and 19) discusses how to bring fundamental analysis to the evaluation of risk, both the risk of equities and the risk of corporate debt.

The Web Connection

Find the following on the web page for this chapter:

- A guide to the book's website.
- More on investment styles and the styles that equity funds commit to in their marketing.
- More on the history of investing and the returns to different investments.
- More on stock market bubbles.
- Formal definitions of market efficiency.
- A discussion of arbitrage in equity markets.
- A guide to further reading.

Key Concepts

active investors buy or sell investments after an examination of whether they are mispriced, in order to earn exceptional rates of return. Compare with **passive investors** and **defensive investors**. *4*

alpha is an abnormal return over the expected return for the investment risk taken. *5*

beta is a measure of risk as prescribed by the capital asset pricing model (CAPM). *5*

business model is the concept or strategy under which a firm operates to add value from selling products or services to customers. *14*

claim is an enforceable contract for returns from an investment. *9*

competitive advantage is the ability to earn abnormal returns by resisting the **forces of competition**. *16*

defensive investors buy or sell investments after an examination of whether they are mispriced, in order to avoid trading at the wrong price. *4*

financial analyst is a professional who evaluates aspects of investing; particular types are equity analysts, credit analysts, strategy analysts, risk analysts, and bank loan officers. *12*

financial statement analysis is a set of methods for extracting information from financial statements. *2*

financing activities of a firm are the transactions between a firm and its claimants that involve cash investments in the firm by claimants and cash returns to claimants by the firm. *11*

forces of competition are the challenges of others, in the pursuit of profit, to erode a firm's **competitive advantage**. The forces of competition tend to drive away abnormal returns. *16*

fundamental analysis (or **valuation analysis**) is a set of methods for determining the value of an investment. *3*

fundamental investors buy investments only after thoroughly examining information about firms and reaching conclusions about the underlying value that the information implies. *4*

fundamental risk is the chance of losing value because of the outcome of business activities. Compare with **price risk**. *5*

index investing involves buying and (passively) holding a market index of stocks. *5*

intrinsic value is what an investment is worth based on forecasted payoffs from the investment. Payoffs are forecasted with information so intrinsic value is sometimes said to be the value justified by the information. *4*

intuitive investors trade stocks based on their intuition, without submitting that intuition to analysis. *3*

investing activities of a firm involve the acquisition and disposal of assets used in operations. *11*

operating activities of the firm involve using assets (acquired in **investing activities**) to produce and sell products in markets.   *12*

passive investors buy investments without an examination of whether they are mispriced: Compare with **active investors**.   *3*

payoff is value received from an investment.   *10*

price risk is the chance of losing value from buying or selling investments at prices that differ from intrinsic value.   *5*

return to an investment is the **payoff** to the investment less the amount paid for the investment.   *10*

security analysis is a set of methods for determining the value of an investment when securities like stocks and bonds are involved.   *3*

strategy analysis involves articulating business ideas and discovering the value that might be generated by the ideas.   *13*

value-based management is making business plans by maximizing the likely value to be generated by the business, and monitoring and rewarding business performance with measures of value added.   *13*

value of the equity is the value of the payoffs a firm is expected to yield for its shareholders (its owners).   *11*

value of the firm (or **enterprise value**) is the value of the payoffs a firm is expected to yield for all its claimants.   *13*

Concept Questions

C1.1. Some commentators argue that stock prices "follow a random walk." By this they mean that changes in stock prices in the future are not predictable. Would stock prices follow a random walk if all investors were fundamental investors who use all available information to price stocks?

C1.2. Consider the case where all investors are passive investors: They buy index funds. What is your prediction about how stock prices will behave overtime? Will they follow a random walk?

C1.3. What is the difference between fundamental risk and price risk?

C1.4. What is the difference between an alpha technology and a beta technology?

C1.5. Critique the following statement: Hold stocks for the long run, for in the long run, the return to stocks is always higher than bond returns.

C1.6. What is the difference between a passive investor and an active investor?

C1.7. In the late 1990s, P/E ratios were high by historical standards. The P/E ratio for the S&P 500 stocks was as high as 33 in 1999. In the 1970s it was 8. What do you think would be a "normal" P/E ratio—that is, where multiples higher than normal could be called "high" and multiples less than normal could be called "low"? *Hint:* The P/E ratio is the inverse of the E/P ratio, sometimes called the earnings yield.

C1.8. Should a shareholder be indifferent between selling her shares on the open market and selling them to the firm in a stock repurchase?

C1.9. Figure 1.2 below plots a price-to-value ratio (P/V) for the Dow Jones Industrial Average (DJIA) from 1979 to 1999. A P/V ratio is a metric that compares the market price (P) to an estimate of intrinsic value (V). The intrinsic value in the figure is based on techniques that will be discussed in this book. But how it is calculated is not important for the following questions:

   a. Up to 1996, the P/V ratio fluctuated around 1.0. What do you make of this pattern?

FIGURE 1.2
Price-to-value ratio
(P/V) for the DJIA at
monthly intervals. V
is an estimate of the
intrinsic value of the
Dow.

Source: From the web page of the Parker Center, Cornell University. The graph is an update of one reported in C. Lee, J. Myers, and B. Swaminathan, "What Is the Intrinsic Value of the Dow?" *Journal of Finance,* October 1999, pp. 1693–1741. The Parker Center website is at http://parkercenter.johnson.cornell.edu.

b. If you had purchased the Dow 30 stocks each time the P/V ratio fell below 0.8 and had sold them each time the P/V ratio rose above 1.2, how well would your investment strategy have performed?

c. What interpretation do you put on the continuing upward movement of the P/V ratio after 1995?

Exercises

Exercises in all chapters are rated by their degree of difficulty—easy, medium, or hard.

E1.1. Finding Information on the Internet: Dell Computer and General Motors (Easy)

This chapter compared the market values of Dell Computer Corp. and General Motors Corp. Go to the Internet and find sources that will help research these firms. Two sites to start with are.

   Yahoo! Finance: http://quote.yahoo.com
   Wall Street Research Net: http://www.wsrn.com
Also find the firms' web pages. Look at the book's web page for further sources.

E1.2. Enterprise Market Value: General Mills and Hewlett-Packard (Medium)

a. General Mills, Inc., the large manufacturer of packaged foods, reported the following in its annual report for the year ending May 30, 1999 (in millions):

Short-term borrowing	$ 614.9
Long-term debt	1,702.4
Stockholders' equity	164.2

The firm's 150.0 million shares traded at $80 per share when the annual report was released. From these numbers, calculate General Mills's enterprise market value (the market value of the firm).

b. Hewlett-Packard, the computer equipment manufacturer and systems consultant, had 1,013 million shares outstanding in July 1999, trading at $100 per share. Its most recent quarterly report listed the following (in millions):

Long-term investments in debt securities	$ 5,800
Short-term borrowings	1,380
Long-term debt	1,730
Stockholders' equity	18,198

Calculate the enterprise market value of Hewlett-Packard.

E1.3. **Identifying Operating, Investing, and Financing Transactions: Microsoft (Easy)**

Microsoft Corp. reported the following in its third quarter 10-Q report to the Securities and Exchange Commission for fiscal 1999. Classify each item as involving an operating, investing, or financing activity. Amounts are in millions.

a.	Cash paid to purchase Web TV	$ 190
b.	General and administrative expenses	104
c.	Sales and marketing expenses	829
d.	Common stock issues	650
e.	Common stock repurchases	1,605
f.	Sales revenue	3,774
g.	Research and development expenditures	597
h.	Income taxes	720
i.	Additions to property and equipment	415
j.	Accounts receivable	1,460

E1.4. **Applying Present Value Calculations to Value a Building (Medium)**

In the year 2000, a real estate analyst forecasts that a rental apartment building will generate $5.3 million each year in rents over the five years 2001–2005. Cash expenses are expected to be $4.2 million a year. At the end of five years, the building is expected to sell for $12 million. Real estate investors expect a 12 percent return on their investments. Apply present value discounting techniques to value the building.

E1.5. **Calculating Stock Returns: Nike, Inc. (Easy)**

The shares of Nike, Inc., traded at $58 per share at the beginning of 2002 and closed at $47 per share at the end of the year. Nike paid a dividend of 48 cents per share during the year. What was the return to holding Nike's shares during 2002?

E1.6. **Returns and Dividends: Ford Motor Company (Medium)**

Ford's shares began trading in January 1998 at $48 per share and closed trading at the end of December of that year at $59. Investors earned a 26.5 percent return from holding the stock during 1998. What was the dividend that Ford paid in 1998?

Minicase

M1.1

Critique of an Equity Analysis: America Online Inc.

The so-called Internet Bubble gripped stock markets in 1998, 1999, and 2000, as discussed in the chapter. Internet stocks traded at multiples of earnings and sales rarely seen in stock markets. Start-ups, some with not much more than an idea, launched initial public offerings (IPOs) that sold for very high prices (and made their founders and employees with stock options very rich). Established firms, like Disney, considered launching spinoffs with "dot.com" in their names, just to receive the higher multiple that the market was giving to similar firms.

Commentators argued over whether the high valuations were justified. Many concluded the phenomenon was just speculative mania. They maintained that the potential profits that others were forecasting would be competed away by the low barriers to entry. But others maintained that the ability to establish and protect recognized brand names—like AOL, Netscape, Amazon, Yahoo!, and eBay—would support high profits. And, they argued, consumers would migrate to these sites from more conventional forms of commerce.

America Online (AOL) was a particular focus in the discussion. One of the most well-established Internet portals, AOL was actually reporting profits, in contrast to many Internet firms that were reporting losses. AOL operated two worldwide Internet services, America Online and CompuServe. It sold advertising and e-commerce services on the Web and, with its acquisition of Netscape, had enhanced its Internet technology services.

For the fiscal year ending June 30, 1999, America Online reported total revenue of $4.78 billion, of which $3.32 billion was from the subscriptions of 19.6 million AOL and CompuServe subscribers, $1.00 billion from advertising and e-commerce, and the remainder from network services through its Netscape Enterprises Group. It also reported net income of $762 million, or $0.73 per share.

AOL traded at $105 per share on this report and, with 1.10 billion shares outstanding, a market capitalization of its equity of $115.50 billion. The multiple of revenues of 24.2 was similar to the multiple of earnings for more seasoned firms at the time, so relatively, it was very high. AOL's P/E ratio was 144.

In an article on the op-ed page of *The Wall Street Journal* on April 26, 1999, David D. Alger of Fred Alger Management, a New York–based investment firm, argued that AOL's stock price was justified. He made the following revenue forecasts for 2004, five years later (in billions):

Subscriptions from 39 million subscribers	$12.500
Advertising and other revenues	3.500
Total revenue	16.000
Profits margin on sales, after tax	26%

To answer parts (*A*) and (*B*), forecast earnings for 2004.

A. If AOL's forecasted price-earnings (P/E) ratio for 2004 was at the current level of that for a seasoned firm, 24, what would AOL's shares be worth in 1999? AOL is not expected to pay dividends. Hint: The current price should be the present value of the price expected in the future.

B. Alger made his case by insisting that AOL could maintain a high P/E ratio of about 50 in 2004. What P/E ratio would be necessary in 2004 to justify a per-share price of $105 in 1999? If the P/E were to be 50 in 2004, would AOL be a good buy?

C. What is missing from these evaluations? Do you see a problem with Alger's analysis?

Introduction to the Financial Statements

LINKS

Links to previous chapter

The first chapter introduced active investing based on fundamental analysis and explained how financial statements provide a lens on the business to help carry out the analysis.

This chapter

This chapter gives you a basic understanding of the financial statements with a view to using them as an analysis tool.

Link to Part I

The four chapters in Part One of the book show how financial statements are utilized in valuing business firms.

Link to web page

The web page shows you how to find financial statements and goes into more detail about the statements.

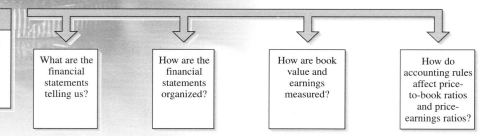

What are the financial statements telling us?

How are the financial statements organized?

How are book value and earnings measured?

How do accounting rules affect price-to-book ratios and price-earnings ratios?

Financial statements contain information that helps the analyst infer fundamental value. The analyst must appreciate what these statements are saying and what they are not saying. She must know where to go in the financial statements to find relevant information. She must understand the deficiencies of the statements, where they fail to provide the necessary information for valuation. This chapter introduces the financial statements.

You probably have some familiarity with financial statements, perhaps at the technical level of how they are prepared. This knowledge will help you here. However, our focus is not on the detailed accounting rules, but on the broad principles behind the statements that determine how they are used in analysis. The coverage is skeletal, to be filled out as the book proceeds (and we will come back to a more detailed accounting analysis in Part Four).

Financial statements are the lens on a business. They draw a picture of the business that is brought into focus with financial statement analysis. The analyst must understand how the picture is drawn and how she might then refine it with analysis. Two features of

The Analyst's Checklist

After reading this chapter you should understand:

- The broad picture of the firm that is painted by the financial statements.

- The component parts of each financial statement.

- How components of the financial statements fit together (or "articulate").

- The accounting relations that govern the financial statements.

- The stocks and flows equation that dictates how shareholders' equity is updated.

- The concept of comprehensive income.

- The concept of dirty-surplus accounting.

- The accounting principles that dictate how the balance sheet is measured.

- How price-to-book ratios are affected by accounting principles.

- The accounting principles that dictate how earnings are measured.

- How price-earnings ratios are affected by accounting principles.

- The difference between market value added and earnings.

- Why fundamental analysts want accountants to enforce the reliability criterion.

- How financial statements anchor investors.

After reading this chapter you should be able to:

- Explain shareholders' equity in terms of assets and liabilities.

- Explain the change in shareholders' equity using the equity statement.

- Explain the change in shareholders' equity using the income statement.

- Explain the change in cash using the cash flow statement.

- Calculate comprehensive income.

- Calculate net payout.

- Generate the financial statements for a savings account.

- Describe, for a particular firm, the picture that is painted by the financial statements.

- Calculate a premium over book value.

- Identify items in the balance sheet that are measured at fair value.

- Calculate market value added (the stock return).

- Recount the history of price-to-book ratios and price-earnings ratios over the past 40 years.

the statements that need to be appreciated are form and content. *Form* describes how the financial statements are organized. Financial statement analysis is an organized way of extracting information from financial statements. To organize financial statement analysis, one must understand how the financial statements themselves are organized. The form of the financial statements sketches the picture in the financial statements, so to understand the form of the financial statements is to understand broadly what the financial statements are depicting. *Content* colors the sketch. Content describes how line items such as earnings, assets, and liabilities, dictated by form, are measured, thus quantifying the message. This chapter lays out the form of the financial statements and then explains the accounting principles that dictate the measurement.

Financial statements are published in firms' annual reports to shareholders. All firms listed for public trading in the United States must also file an annual 10-K report and a quarterly 10-Q report with the Securities and Exchange Commission (SEC). These reports are available online through the SEC's EDGAR database at www.sec.gov. You should familiarize yourself with this source. The book's web page links you to online services that allow you to retrieve the information on EDGAR in spreadsheet form, ready for analysis. Use the resources on the web page.

THE FORM OF THE FINANCIAL STATEMENTS

The form of the financial statements is the way in which the statements, and their component parts, relate to each other. Form is given by a set of **accounting relations** that express the various components of financial statements in terms of other components. Understanding these relations is important because, as you will see in later chapters, they structure the way in which we do fundamental analysis. Indeed, many of these relations specify how you develop a spreadsheet program to value firms and their equity.

Firms are required to publish three primary financial statements in the United States, the *balance sheet*, the *income statement*, and the *cash flow statement*. In addition they must report a statement reconciling beginning and ending shareholders' equity for the reporting period. This is usually done in a fourth statement, the *statement of shareholders' equity*, but the information is sometimes given in footnotes. Other countries have similar requirements. The International Accounting Standards Board (IASB), which is developing financial reporting standards with broad, international application, requires the three primary statements plus an explanation of changes in shareholders' equity. The web page gives examples of financial statements for a number of countries.

Exhibit 2.1 presents the four financial statements for the fiscal year ending February 1, 2002, for Dell Computer Corp., the personal computer manufacturer whose P/E ratio we questioned in Chapter 1. These statements are reproduced from the firm's 10-K annual report filing. We will examine these statements here and use them in discussion, exercises, and cases later.

The Balance Sheet

The balance sheet—Dell's Consolidated Statement of Financial Position in the exhibit—lists assets, liabilities, and stockholders' (shareholders') equity. **Assets** are investments that are expected to generate payoffs. **Liabilities** are claims to the payoffs by claimants other than owners. **Stockholders' equity** is the claim by the owners. So the balance sheet is a statement of the firm's investments (from its investing activities) and the claims to the payoffs from those investments. Both assets and liabilities are divided into current and long-term categories, where "current" means that the assets will generate cash within a year, or that cash will be used to settle liability claims within a year.

The three parts of the balance sheet are tied together in the following accounting relation:

$$\text{Shareholders' equity} = \text{Assets} - \text{Liabilities} \qquad \textbf{(2.1)}$$

This equation (sometimes referred to as the *accounting equation* or *balance sheet equation*) says that shareholders' equity is always equal to the difference between the assets and liabilities (referred to as *net assets*). That is, shareholders' equity is the residual claim on the assets after subtracting liability claims. From an equity valuation point of view, the shareholders' equity is the main summary number on the balance sheet. It's the accountants' attempt to measure the equity claim. In Dell's case, the net assets of $4,694 million in 2002 are given by 12 line items, eight assets and four liabilities. This total of $4,694 million is also explained in the shareholders' equity by common stock issued, net

EXHIBIT 2.1
The financial statements for Dell Computer Corp. for fiscal year ending February 1, 2002. Four statements are published: the balance sheet, the income statement, the cash flow statement, and the statement of stockholders' equity.

DELL COMPUTER CORPORATION
Consolidated Statement of Financial Position (in millions)

	February 1, 2002	February 2, 2001
ASSETS		
Current assets:		
Cash and cash equivalents	$ 3,641	$ 4,910
Short-term investments	273	525
Accounts receivable, net	2,269	2,424
Inventories	278	400
Other	1,416	1,467
Total current assets	7,877	9,726
Property, plant and equipment, net	826	996
Investments	4,373	2,418
Other noncurrent assets	459	530
Total assets	$13,535	$13,670
LIABILITIES AND STOCKHOLDERS' EQUITY		
Current liabilities:		
Accounts payable	$ 5,075	$ 4,286
Accrued and other	2,444	2,492
Total current liabilities	7,519	6,778
Long-term debt	520	509
Other	802	761
Commitments and contingent liabilities	—	—
Total liabilities	8,841	8,048
Stockholders' equity:		
Preferred stock and capital in excess of $.01 par value; shares issued and outstanding: none	—	—
Common stock and capital in excess of $.01 par value; shares authorized: 7,000; shares issued: 2,654 and 2,601, respectively	5,605	4,795
Treasury stock, at cost; 52 shares and no shares, respectively	(2,249)	—
Retained earnings	1,364	839
Other comprehensive income	38	62
Other	(64)	(74)
Total stockholders' equity	4,694	5,622
Total liabilities and stockholders' equity	$13,535	$13,670

of stock repurchases (in treasury stock), of $3,356 million, retained earnings of $1,364 million, and "other" items of $(26) million.

The balance sheet equation (2.1) views the balance sheet from the perspective of shareholders as owners. The web page gives a balance sheet layout that emphasizes this view.

The Income Statement

The income statement—Dell's Consolidated Statement of Income in the exhibit—reports how shareholders' equity increased or decreased as a result of business activities. The

EXHIBIT 2.1 Financial Statements for Dell Computer (continued)

Consolidated Statement of Income (in millions)

	Fiscal Year Ended		
	February 1, 2002	February 2, 2001	January 28, 2000
Net revenue	$31,168	$31,888	$25,265
Cost of revenue	25,661	25,445	20,047
Gross margin	5,507	6,443	5,218
Operating expenses:			
Selling, general and administrative	2,784	3,193	2,387
Research, development and engineering	452	482	374
Special charges	482	105	194
Total operating expenses	3,718	3,780	2,955
Operating income	1,789	2,663	2,263
Investment and other income (loss), net	(58)	531	188
Income before income taxes and cumulative effect of change in accounting principle	1,731	3,194	2,451
Provision for income taxes	485	958	785
Income before cumulative effect of change in accounting principle	1,246	2,236	1,666
Cumulative effect of change in accounting principle, net	—	59	—
Net income	$ 1,246	$ 2,177	$ 1,666
Earnings per common share:			
Before cumulative effect of change in accounting principle:			
Basic	$ 0.48	$ 0.87	$ 0.66
Diluted	$ 0.46	$ 0.81	$ 0.61
After cumulative effect of change in accounting principle:			
Basic	$ 0.48	$ 0.84	$ 0.66
Diluted	$ 0.46	$ 0.79	$ 0.61
Weighted average shares outstanding:			
Basic	2,602	2,582	2,536
Diluted	2,726	2,746	2,728

"bottom line" measure of value added to shareholders' equity is *net income,* also referred to as *earnings* or *net profit.* The income statement displays the sources of net income, broadly classified as **revenue** (value coming in from selling products) and **expenses** (value going out in earning revenue). The accounting relation that determines net income is

$$\text{Net income} = \text{Revenues} - \text{Expenses} \qquad \textbf{(2.2)}$$

Dell's revenue for 2000 was in net revenue from sales of computer products of $31,168 million. Net revenue is sales after deducting estimates for sales returns. From this net revenue, Dell subtracts operating expenses incurred in earning the revenue to yield *operating income,* the income earned from selling its products. Dell holds substantial short-term and long-term interest-bearing securities, listed as "investments" on the balance sheet, and the "investment income" from these investments, net of interest expense on long-term debt and income from "other" activities, is listed below operating income, but before income taxes. Finally, taxes are subtracted to yield net income.

EXHIBIT 2.1   **Financial Statements for Dell Computer (continued)**

Consolidated Statement of Cash Flows (in millions)

	Fiscal Year Ended		
	February 1, 2002	February 2, 2001	January 28, 2000
Cash flows from operating activities:			
Net income	$ 1,246	$ 2,177	$ 1,666
Adjustments to reconcile net income to net cash			(
provided by operating activities:			
Depreciation and amortization	239	240	156
Tax benefits of employee stock plans	487	929	1,040
Special charges	742	105	194
Gains/losses on investments	17	(307)	(80)
Other	178	135	56
Changes in:			
Operating working capital	826	642	812
Noncurrent assets and liabilities	62	274	82
Net cash provided by operating activities	3,797	4,195	3,926
Cash flows from investing activities:			
Investments in securities:			
Purchases	(5,382)	(2,606)	(3,101)
Maturities and sales	3,425	2,331	2,319
Capital expenditures	(303)	(482)	(401)
Net cash used in investing activities	(2,260)	(757)	(1,183)
Cash flows from financing activities:			
Purchase of common stock	(3,000)	(2,700)	(1,061)
Issuance of common stock under employee plans	295	404	289
Other	3	(9)	77
Net cash used in financing activities	(2,702)	(2,305)	(695)
Effect of exchange rate changes on cash	(104)	(32)	35
Net decrease/increase in cash	$(1,269)	$1,101	$2,083

The income statement groups like expenses in categories to report a number of components of net income. Typical groupings in U.S. statements yield the following sequential components:

Net revenue – Cost of goods sold = Gross margin   **(2.2a)**

Gross margin – Operating expenses = Operating income before tax (ebit)

Operating income before tax – Interest expense + Interest income = Income before taxes

Income before taxes – Income taxes = Income after taxes (and before extraordinary items)

Income before extraordinary items + Extraordinary items = Net income

Net income – Preferred dividends = Net income available to common

Most of these subtotals appear on Dell's income statement. (Dell had a cumulative effect of a change in accounting principle as an extraordinary item in 2001.) Names of line items can and do differ among companies. Gross margin is referred to as gross profit and operating income before tax is sometimes referred to as earnings before interest and taxes

EXHIBIT 2.1   **Financial Statements for Dell Computer (concluded)**

	Consolidated Statement of Stockholders' Equity (in millions)							
	Common Stock and Capital in Excess of Par Value		Treasury Stock		Retained Earnings	Other Comprehensive Income	Other	Total
	Shares	Amount	Shares	Amount				
Balances at February 2, 2001	2,601	4,795	—	—	839	62	(74)	5,622
Net income	—	—	—	—	1,246	—	—	1,246
Change in unrealized gain on investments, net of taxes	—	—	—	—	—	(65)	—	(65)
Foreign currency translation adjustments	—	—	—	—	—	2	—	2
Net unrealized gain on derivative instruments, net of taxes	—	—	—	—	—	39	—	39
Total comprehensive income for fiscal 2002								1,222
Stock issuances under employee plans, including tax benefits	69	843	—	—	—	—	10	853
Purchases and retirements	(16)	(30)	52	(2,249)	(721)	—	—	(3,000)
Other	—	(3)	—	—	—	—	—	(3)
Balances at February 1, 2002	2,654	$5,605	52	$(2,249)	$ 1,364	$38	$(64)	$4,694

Notes to financial statements:
1. Description of business and summary of significant accounting policies.
2. Special charges.
3. Financial instruments.
4. Income taxes.
5. Capitalization.
6. Benefit plans.
7. Commitments, contingencies, and certain concentrations.
8. Related party transactions.
9. Supplemental consolidated financial information.
10. Segment information.
11. Unaudited quarterly results.

(ebit), for example. Items included in certain categories can also differ. Interest income is sometimes given as a separate category from interest expense. Preferred dividends are often in the statement of shareholders' equity. But this set of relations gives the basic outline of the income statement in the United States.

Net income is given on a dollar basis and on a per-share basis. *Earnings per share (eps)* is always earnings (after preferred dividends) for the common shareholder (called ordinary shareholders in the United Kingdom and other countries), so the numerator is net income available to common. *Basic earnings per share* is net income available to common shareholders divided by the weighted-average of common shares outstanding during the year; a weighted average is used to accommodate changes in shares outstanding from share issues and repurchases. *Diluted earnings per share* is based on total common shares that would be outstanding if holders of contingent claims on shares (like convertible bonds and stock options) were to exercise their options and hold common shares.

The Cash Flow Statement

The cash flow statement—Dell's Consolidated Statement of Cash Flows in the exhibit—describes how the firm generated and used cash during the period. Cash flows are divided into three types in the statement: cash flows from operating activities, cash flows from investing activities, and cash flows from financing activities. Recall that this is cash generated from the three activities of the firm depicted in Figure 1.1 in Chapter 1. Cash from operations is cash generated from selling products, net of cash used up in doing so. Investing cash flows are cash spent on purchasing assets less cash received from selling assets. Financing cash flows are the cash transactions with claimants that are also depicted in Figure 1.1. The sum of the cash flows from the three activities explains the increase or decrease in the firm's cash (at the bottom of the statement):

$$\text{Cash from operations} + \text{Cash from investment} \qquad \textbf{(2.3)}$$
$$+ \text{Cash from financing} = \text{Change in cash}$$

Dell generated $3,797 million in cash from operations in fiscal 2002, spent a net $2,260 million on investments, and disbursed a net $2,702 million to claimants. The line items in Dell's statement give the specific sources of cash in each category. Some, of course, involve cash outflows rather than cash inflows, and outflows are in parentheses. Dell trades around the world and so holds cash in different currencies. Thus the change in cash in U.S. dollar equivalents is also explained by a change in exchange rates over the year: The U.S. dollar equivalent of cash in other currencies declined by $104 million over the year. The overall decrease in cash was $1,269 million.

The Statement of Stockholders' Equity

The statement of shareholders' equity—Dell's Consolidated Statement of Stockholders' Equity in the exhibit—starts with beginning-of-period equity and ends with end-of-period equity, thus explaining how the equity changed over the period. For purposes of analysis, the change in equity is best explained as follows:

$$\text{Ending equity} = \text{Beginning equity} + \text{Total (comprehensive) income} \qquad \textbf{(2.4)}$$
$$- \text{Net payout to shareholders}$$

This is referred to as the *stocks and flows equation* for equity because it explains how stocks of equity changed with flows of equity. Owners' equity increases from value added in business activities (income) and decreases if there is a net payout to owners. **Net payout** is amounts paid to shareholders less amounts received from share issues. As cash can be paid out in dividends or share repurchases, net payout is stock repurchases plus dividends minus proceeds from share issues.

Unfortunately, the statement is not presented as clearly as this reconciliation of beginning and ending equity prescribes. But the two components, total income and net payout, can (usually) be identified. In Dell's 2002 statement, net payout involves a share issue to employees for $853 million and stock repurchases for $3,003 million. So Dell's shareholders received a net payout, or had a net disinvestment, of $2,150 million in 2002. If the firm had paid dividends, these would have reduced stockholders' equity also. The other component of the statement is the increase in shareholders' equity from business activities. This component is given by the net income for the year of $1,246 million plus three other items of income—an unrealized loss on investments of $65 million, a foreign currency translation gain of $2 million (due to changes in the dollar equivalent of net assets held in other currencies), and an unrealized gain on derivative instruments of $39 million—to report total income of $1,222 million. With these numbers identified, we can proof the relation (equation 2.4) for reconciling beginning and ending equity (in millions): $4,694 = $5,622 + $1,222 − $2,150.

The three additional income items are income recorded in the equity statement rather than in the income statement. This practice is known as **dirty surplus accounting**, for it does not give a clean income number in the income statement. The total dirty surplus income items (a loss of $24 million for Dell) are called *other comprehensive income* and the total of net income (in the income statement) and other comprehensive income (in the equity statement) is **comprehensive income**:

$$\text{Comprehensive income} = \text{Net income} + \text{Other comprehensive income} \qquad \textbf{(2.5)}$$

Dell's comprehensive income is identified on its statement of shareholders' equity: $1,246 − $65 + $2 + $39 = $1,222 million. A few firms report other comprehensive income below net income in the income statement and some report it in a separate "Other Comprehensive Income Statement."

The Footnotes and Supplementary Information to Financial Statements

Dell is a reasonably simple operation in one line of business—it manufactures and sells desktop and notebook computers, workstations, and network servers, along with software and support programs—and its financial statements are also quite simple. However, much more information embellishes these statements in the footnotes. The notes are an integral part of the statements and the statements can be interpreted only with a thorough reading of the notes.

The heading for each of Dell's footnotes in the 10-K is given at the end of Exhibit 2.1. If you go to the 10-K on the SEC's website (through the book's web page) you will see that these footnotes are supplemented with a background discussion of the firm—its strategy, area of operations, product portfolio, product development, marketing, manufacturing, and order backlog. There is a discussion of regulations applying to the firm and a review of factors affecting the company's business and its prospects. Details of executive compensation also are given. This material, along with the more formal "Management's Discussion and Analysis" required in the 10-K, is an aid to knowing the business but is by no means complete. The industry analyst should know considerably more about the personal computer industry before attempting to research Dell.

The Articulation of the Financial Statements: How the Statements Tell a Story

The balance sheet is sometimes referred to as a "stock" statement because the balances it reports are **stocks** of value at a point in time. (The word "stock" here should not be confused with stocks as in "stocks and shares" or "stocks" used in the United Kingdom and elsewhere to mean inventory.) The income statement and the cash flow statement are "flow" statements because they measure **flows**—or changes—in stocks between two points in time. The income statement reports part of the change in owners' equity and the cash flow statement reports the change in cash.

The so-called **articulation** of the income statement, cash flow statement, and balance sheet—or the articulation of stocks and flows—is depicted in Figure 2.1. Articulation is

FIGURE 2.1

The articulation of the financial statements. The stock of cash in the balance sheet increases from cash flows that are detailed in the cash flow statement. The stock of equity value in the balance sheet increases from net income that is detailed in the income statement and other comprehensive income and from net investments by owners that are detailed in the statement of shareholders' equity.

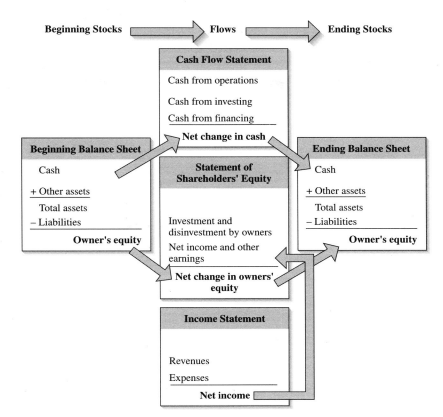

the way in which the statements fit together, their relationship to each other. The articulation of the income statement and balance sheet is through the statement of shareholders' equity and is described by the stocks and flows relation (equation 2.4). Balance sheets give the stock of owners' equity at a point in time. The statement of shareholders' equity explains the changes in owners' equity (the flows) between two balance sheet dates, and the income statement, corrected for other comprehensive income in the equity statement, explains the change in owners' equity that comes from adding value in operations. The balance sheet also gives the stock of cash at a point in time, and the cash flow statement explains how that stock changed over a period. Indeed the cash flow relation (equation 2.3) is a stocks and flows equation for cash.

Much detail buried in the financial statements will be revealed by the financial statement analysis later in the book. But by recognizing the articulation of the financial statements, the reader of the statements understands the overall story that they tell. That story is in terms of stocks and flows: The statements track changes in stocks of cash and owners' equity (net assets). Dell began its 2002 fiscal year with $4,190 million in cash and ended the year with $3,641 million in cash. The cash flow statement reveals that the $1,269 million decrease came from a cash inflow of $3,797 million in operations, less cash spent in investing of $2,260 million, net cash paid out to claimants of $2,702 million, and a drop in the U.S. dollar equivalent of cash held abroad of $104 million. But the main focus of the statements is on the change in the owners' equity during the year. Dell's owners' equity decreased from $5,622 million to $4,694 million over the year by earning $1,222 million in its business activities and paying out a net $2,150 million to its

The Balance Sheet
  Assets
  − Liabilities
  = Shareholders' equity

The Income Statement
  Net revenue
  − Cost of goods sold
  = Gross margin
  − Operating expenses
  = Operating income before taxes (ebit)
  − Interest expense
  = Income before taxes
  − Income taxes
  = Income after tax and before extraordinary items
  + Extraordinary items
  = Net income
  − Preferred dividends
  = Net income available to common

Cash Flow Statement (and the Articulation of the Balance Sheet and Cash Flow Statement)
  Cash flow from operations
  + Cash flow from investing
  + Cash flow from financing
  = Change in cash

Statement of Shareholders' Equity (and the Articulation of the Balance Sheet and Income Statement)

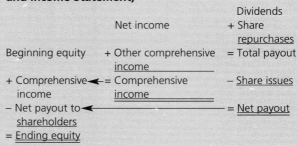

owners. The income statement indicates that the net income portion of the increase in equity from business activities ($1,246 million) came from revenue from selling products and financing revenue of $31,168 million, less expenses incurred in generating the revenue of $29,379 million, net investment and other losses of $58 million, and taxes of $485 million.

And so Dell began its fiscal 2003 year with the stocks in place in the 2002 balance sheet to accumulate more cash and wealth for shareholders. Fundamental analysis involves forecasting that accumulation. As we proceed with the analysis in subsequent chapters we will see how the accounting relations we have laid out are important in developing forecasting tools. See Box 2.1 for a summary. Be sure you have Figure 2.1 firmly in mind. Understand how the statements fit together. Understand how financial reporting tracks the evolution of shareholders' equity, updating stocks of equity value in the balance sheet with value added in earnings from business activities. And understand the accounting equations that govern each statement. Now go to Box 2.2 for a simple example that reinforces these points.

MEASUREMENT IN THE FINANCIAL STATEMENTS

To recap, the balance sheet reports the stock of shareholder value in the firm and the income statement reports the flow, or change, in shareholder value over a period. Using the language of valuation, the balance sheet gives the shareholders' net worth and the income statement gives the value added to their net worth from running the business. However, we must be careful with words for, while financial reporting conveys these ideas conceptually, the reality can be quite different. Value and value added have to be measured, and measurement in the balance sheet and income statement is less than perfect.

A savings account is the simplest of investments. The first investment that many of us made, as children, was in a savings account. We learned some of the basic principles of investing with a savings account, like the concepts of simple interest, dividends (withdrawals), and compound interest (which comes from not withdrawing from the account, but rather reinvesting in the account). Indeed, we first understood the notion of earnings—interest earned in the account—and book value—the balance posted in our passbooks—when we went to the bank to get the book value updated. Perhaps only on reflection can we appreciate the stocks and flows equation (equation 2.4) that tracks how our equity in a savings account changes over time: Book value of the savings account at the end of a quarter = Book value at the beginning of the quarter + Earnings for the quarter – Withdrawals + New deposits. This elementary knowledge will be of considerable help as you move to value more complicated investments, like shares in business firms, and use measures like earnings and book value of equity in the financial statements. Indeed, we will continually refer to the savings account to reinforce principles as we proceed through the book.

To get going, let's construct a set of financial statements for a savings account. Suppose $100 is invested in an account earning an interest rate of 5 percent for one year, Year 1. The earnings of $5 are withdrawn at the end of the year, leaving $100 in the account. The four statements for Year 1 tell the story of this investment:

Balance Sheet

Assets	$100	Owners' equity	$100

Income Statement

Revenue	$5
Expenses	0
Earnings	$5

Statement of Cash Flows

Cash from operations	$5
Cash investment	0
Cash in financing activities:	
Dividends	(5)
Change in cash	$0

Statement of Owners' Equity

Balance, end of Year 0	$100
Earnings, Year 1	5
Dividends (withdrawals), Year 1	(5)
Balance, end of Year 1	$100

You can see that the story is in terms of book values, earnings, cash flows, and dividends. The stocks and flows equation, expressed in the statement of owners' equity, ties the story together for the owner: Equity in an investment at the beginning of the year earned $5 and this $5 was distributed as a dividend to the owner, leaving an equity of $100 in the investment at the end of the year. The statement of cash flows tells the story about the change in cash in the account: Cash generated by the account was not reinvested in the account but instead was paid out in dividends, leaving the investment in cash unchanged. You also can see how the financial statements articulate as in Figure 2.1 to tell these stories.

The Price-to-Book Ratio

The balance sheet equation (2.1) corresponds to the value equation (1.1) that we introduced in the last chapter. The value equation can be written as

$$\text{Value of equity} = \text{Value of the firm} - \text{Value of debt} \qquad \textbf{(2.6)}$$

The value of the firm is the value of the firm's assets and its investments, and the value of the debt is the value of the liability claims. So you see that the value equation and the balance sheet equation are of the same form but differ in how the assets, liabilities, and equity are measured. The measure of stockholders' equity on the balance sheet, the *book value of equity*, typically does not give the intrinsic value of what the equity is worth. Correspondingly, the net assets are not measured at their values. If they were, there would be no analysis to do! It is because the accountant does not, or cannot, calculate the intrinsic value that fundamental analysis is required.

The difference between the intrinsic value of equity and its book value is called the *intrinsic premium:*

$$\text{Intrinsic premium} = \text{Intrinsic value of equity} - \text{Book value of equity}$$

and the difference between the market price of equity and its book value is called the *market premium:*

Market premium = Market price of equity − Book value of equity

If these premiums are negative, they are called *discounts* (from book value). Premiums sometimes are referred to as *unrecorded goodwill* because someone purchasing the firm at a price greater than book value could record the premium paid as an asset, purchased goodwill, on the balance sheet; without a purchase of the firm, the premium is un-recorded.

Premiums are calculated for the total equity or on a per-share basis. When Dell pub-lished its fiscal 2002 report, the market value for its 2,602 million outstanding shares was $67,652 million, or $26 per share.[1] With a book value of $4,694 million, the market pre-mium was $62,958 million: The market saw $62,958 million of shareholder value that was not on the balance sheet. And it saw $62,958 million of net assets that were not on the balance sheet. With 2,602 million shares outstanding, the *book value per share (bps)* was $1.80 and the premium was $24.20 per share.

The ratio of market price to book value is the *price-to-book ratio* or the *market-to-book ratio*, and the ratio of intrinsic value to book value is the *intrinsic price-to-book ratio*. Dell's price-to-book ratio (P/B) in 2002 was 14.4. Investors talk of buying a firm for a number-of-times book value, referring to the P/B ratio. The market P/B ratio is the multiple of book value at the current market price. The intrinsic P/B ratio is the multiple of book value that the equity is worth. We will spend considerable time estimating intrin-sic price-to-book ratios in this book, and we will be asking if those intrinsic ratios indi-cate that the market P/B is mispriced.

In asking such questions, it is important to have a sense of history so that any calcula-tion can be judged against what was normal in the past. The history provides a bench-mark for our analysis. It was said, for example, that P/B ratios in the 1990s were high rel-ative to historical averages, indicating that the stock market was overvalued. Figure 2.2 tracks selected percentiles of the price-to-book ratio for all U.S. listed firms from 1963 to 2001. Median P/B ratios (the 50th percentile) for these firms were indeed high in the 1990s—over 2.0—relative to the 1970s.[2] But they were around 2.0 in the 1960s. The 1970s experienced exceptionally low P/B ratios, with medians below 1.0 in some years.

What causes this variation in ratios? Is it due to mispricing in the stock market or is it due to the way accountants calculate book values? The low P/B ratios in the 1970s cer-tainly preceded a long bull market. Could this bull market have been forecast in 1974 by an analysis of intrinsic P/B ratios? Were market P/B ratios in 1974 too low? Would an analysis of intrinsic P/B ratios in the 1990s find that they were too high? Dell's P/B of 14.4 in 2002 looks high relative to historical averages. Was it too high? The fundamental analyst sees herself as providing answers to these questions. She estimates the intrinsic value of equity that is not recorded on the balance sheet.

---

[1] Shares outstanding are shares issued (2,654 million on Dell's balance sheet) less shares repurchased into treasury shares (52 million).
[2] The median P/B for all firms during the 1990s was considerably lower than that for the Dow Jones Industrial Average stocks (consisting of 30 industrial firms) and the S&P 500 stocks. The P/B for both indexes increased from about 2.5 in 1990 to over 5.0 by 2000. Their P/B ratios were just under 1.0 in the 1970s. The stocks in these indexes tend to be larger than the median stocks but, because they contain a significant portion of the total value of the market, they are representative of the broad market.

FIGURE 2.2

Percentiles of price-to-book ratios for all U.S. listed firms, 1963-2001. P/B ratios were relatively low in the 1970s and high in the 1960s and 1990s. The average is above 1.0.

Source:
Company: Standard & Poor's
Data: Compustat® data.

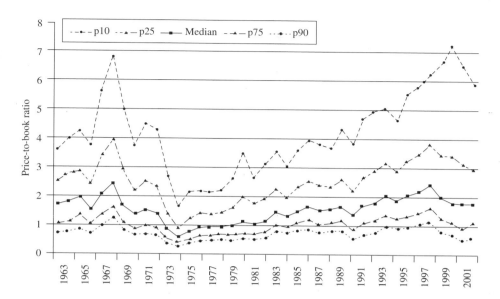

You can view P/B ratios for other firms through the links on the web page. You also can find firms with particular levels of P/B ratios using a stock screener from links on the website.

Measurement in the Balance Sheet

To assess the price-to-book ratio, the analyst must understand how book values are measured, for that measurement determines the price-to-book ratio.

The value of some assets and liabilities are easy to measure, and the accountant does so. He applies **mark-to-market accounting**, thus recording these items on the balance sheets, at **fair value** (in accounting terms). These items do not contribute to the premium over book value. But, for many items, the accountant does not, or cannot, mark to market. He applies **historical cost accounting**. Box 2.3 gives the U.S. GAAP measurement rules for items commonly found on balance sheets, with those carried at fair value and historical cost indicated. International accounting standards broadly follow similar rules.

After reviewing Box 2.3, consider Dell's balance sheet. It lists investments of $3,641 million in cash and cash equivalents measured at their fair value. Dell's short-term investments ($273 million) and long-term investments ($4,373 million) are mainly in interest-bearing debt securities. A market value is usually available for these securities, so they can be *marked to market*, as indeed they are on Dell's balance sheet. Dell's accounts payable ($5,075 million) is close to market value and, while the long-term debt ($520 million) is not marked to market, its book value approximates market value unless interest rates change significantly. So, these items do not contribute to the price premium over book value. Net accounts receivable ($2,269 million), accrued expenses ($2,444 million), and the "other liabilities" ($802 million) involve estimates, but if these are made in an unbiased way, these items, too, are at fair value.

Thus Dell's large premium of $62,958 million over the book value of its equity arises largely from tangible assets, recorded at (depreciated) historical cost, and unrecorded assets. The latter are likely to be quite significant. Dell's value, it is claimed, comes not so

Generally Accepted Accounting Principles in the U.S. prescribe the following rules for measuring assets and liabilities in the balance sheet. Items whose carrying values are typically close to fair value are indicated, but note any exceptions mentioned.

ASSETS

Cash and Cash Equivalents (*Fair Value*)

Cash and cash equivalents (deposits of less than 90-day maturity) are recorded as the amount of cash held which equals their fair value.

Short-Term Investments and Marketable Securities (*Fair Value*)

Short-term investments—in interest-bearing deposits, short-term paper, and shares held for trading in the short-term—are carried at "fair" market value. An exception is a long-term security held to maturity that is reclassified to short-term because it is due to mature. See long-term securities below.

Receivables (*Quasi Fair Value*)

Receivables are recorded at the expected amount of cash to be collected (that is, the nominal claim less a discount for amounts not expected to be received because of bad debts or sales returns). If the estimate of this discount is unbiased, receivables are carried at their fair value. If biased, the carrying amount may not be fair value.

Inventories (*Lower of Cost or Market Value*)

Inventories are recorded at the historical cost of acquiring them. However, the carrying value of inventories is written down to market value if market value is less than historical cost, under the "lower of cost or market" rule. Historical cost is determined under an assumption about the flow of inventory. Under first-in-first-out (FIFO), the cost of more recent inventory goes to the inventory number in the balance sheet, and the cost of older inventory goes to cost of goods sold in the income statement. Under last-in-first-out (LIFO), the balance sheet includes the older costs and cost of goods sold includes the more recent costs. Accordingly, in times of rising inventory prices, the carrying value of inventory in the balance sheet is lower under LIFO than FIFO, but cost of goods sold is higher (and income lower). All else being equal, price-to-book ratios are thus higher for LIFO firms than for FIFO firms.

Long-term Tangible Assets (*Historical Cost*)

Tangible assets—inventory, property, and plant and equipment—are recorded at historical cost (the amount that the firm paid for the assets), less accumulated depreciation. If fair market value is less than amortized historical cost, these assets are impaired (written down to market value),

with the impairment loss as a charge to earnings. In the U.S., assets are never revalued upward to market value, although this practice is followed in the United Kingdom and a number of other jurisdictions.

Recorded Intangible Assets (*Historical Cost*)

Intangible assets that are recorded on the balance sheet—purchased copyrights, patents, and other legal rights—are recorded at historical cost and then either amortized over the life of the right or impaired if market value falls below carrying value.

Goodwill (*Historical Cost*)

Goodwill is the difference between the purchase price of an acquired firm and the fair value of net assets acquired. Since FASB Statement No. 142 in 2001, goodwill is carried at cost and not amortized but is impaired by a write-off if its value is deemed to have declined.

Other Intangible Assets (*Not Recorded*)

Assets such as brand assets, knowledge assets developed from research and development, and assets arising from marketing and supplier relationships are not recorded at all. Brand assets are recorded in the U.K., but not in the U.S.

Long-Term Debt Securities (*Some at Fair Value*)

Some investments in bonds and other debt instruments are marked to market, as prescribed by FASB Statement No. 115. For marking to market, these investments are classified into three types:

1. *Investments held for active trading*. These investments are recorded at fair market value and the unrealized gains and losses from marking them to market are recorded in the income statement, along with interest.

2. *Investments available for sale* (investments not held for active trading but which may be sold before maturity). These investments are also recorded at fair market value, but the unrealized gains and losses are reported outside the income statement as part of other comprehensive income (usually in the equity statement), while interest is reported in the income statement.

3. *Investments held to maturity* (investments where the intent is to hold them until maturity). These investments are recorded at historical cost, with no unrealized gains or losses recognized, but with interest reported in the income statement. Fair market values for these investments are given in the footnotes.

Equity Investments (*Some at Fair Value*)

Equity investments are classified into three types:

1. Investments involving less than 20 percent ownership of another corporation. These equity investments are classified as either "held for active trading," "available for sale," or "held to maturity," with the same mark-to-market accounting for debt investments in these categories.

2. Investments involving *20 percent to 50 percent ownership* of another corporation. The equities are recorded using the "equity method." Under the equity method, the investment is recorded at cost, but the balance sheet carrying value is subsequently increased by the share of earnings reported by the subsidiary corporation and reduced by dividends paid by the subsidiary and write-offs of goodwill acquired on purchase. The share of subsidiaries' earnings (less any write-off of goodwill) is reported in the income statement.

3. Investments involving *greater than 50 percent ownership* of another corporation. The financial statements of the parent and subsidiary corporation are consolidated, after elimination of intercompany transactions, with a deduction for minority interests in the net assets (in the balance sheet) and net income (in the income statement).

LIABILITIES

Short-Term Payables (*Fair Value*)

Payables—such as accounts payable, interest payable, and taxes payable—are measured at the contractual amount of cash to satisfy the obligations. Because these obligations are short-term, the contractual amount is close to its discounted present value, so the amount of these liabilities on the balance sheet approximates market value.

Short-Term and Long-Term Borrowings (*Fair Value*)

Obligations arising from borrowing—short-term debt, long-term bonds, lease obligations, and bank loans—are recorded at the present value of the contractual amount, so they are at market value when initially recorded. The value of these liabilities changes as interest rates change, but the liabilities are not marked to market. However, in periods when interest rates change little, the carrying value of liabilities is typically close to market value. FASB Statement No. 107 requires that the fair market value of liabilities be reported in footnotes, and the debt footnote typically compares market values with carrying values.

Accrued and Estimated Liabilities (*Quasi Fair Value*)

Some liabilities arising in operations—including pension liabilities, accrued liabilities, warranty liabilities, unearned (deferred) revenue, and estimated restructuring liabilities—have to be estimated. If the estimates are unbiased present values of expected cash to be paid out on the obligation, these liabilities reflect their value. If biased, these liabilities contribute to a premium over book value. They are sometimes called *quasi-marked-to-market* liabilities, emphasizing that estimation is involved.

Commitments and Contingencies (*Many Not Recorded*)

If a liability is contingent upon some event, it is recorded on the balance sheet only if two criteria (from FASB Statement No. 5) are satisfied: (1) the contingent event is "probable," and (2) the amount of likely loss can be "reasonably" estimated. Examples include potential losses from lawsuits, product warranties, debt guarantees, and recourse on assignment of receivables or debt. When a liability does not satisfy the two criteria, it must be disclosed in footnotes if it is "reasonably possible." Firms (like Dell) often indicate such a possibility by an entry in the balance sheet with a zero amount and then cover the matter in the footnotes. Understatement of contingent liabilities in the balance sheet reduces the premium over book value.

much from tangible assets, but from its innovative "direct-to-customer" process, its supply chain, its managerial ability, and its brand name. None of these assets are on its balance sheet. Nor might we want them to be. Identifying them and measuring their value is a very difficult task, and we would probably end up with very doubtful, speculative numbers.

Measurement in the Income Statement

Shareholder value added is the change in shareholders' wealth during a period. This comes from two sources: (1) the increase in the value of their equity and (2) any dividends they receive:

$$\text{Value added} = \text{Ending value} - \text{Beginning value} + \text{Dividend} \quad \textbf{(2.7)}$$

LIVERPOOL JOHN MOORES UNIVERSITY
Aldham Roberts L.R.C.
TEL 0151 231 3701/3634

The accounting measure of value added, earnings, is determined by rules for measuring revenues and expenses.

REVENUES: THE REVENUE RECOGNITION PRINCIPLE

Value is added by businesses from a process—a value creation chain—that begins with strategy and product ideas, and then continues with the research and development of those ideas, the building of factories and distribution channels to deliver the product, the persuading of customers to buy the finished product, and finally the collection of cash from customers. Potentially, value could be recognized gradually, as the process proceeds. However, accounting typically recognizes value added at one point in the process. The two broad principles for *revenue recognition* are:

1. The earnings process is substantially accomplished.

2. Receipt of cash is reasonably certain.

In most cases, these two criteria are deemed to be satisfied when the product or service has been delivered to the customer and a receivable has been established as a legal claim against the customer. The revenue recognized at that point is the amount of the sale, discounted to *net revenue* based on an assessment of the probability of not receiving cash (the receivable is also discounted to a net receivable).

In a few cases, revenue is recognized during production, but before final sale—in long-term construction projects, for example—and sometimes revenue is not recognized until cash is collected—as in some retail installment sales where there is considerable doubt that the customer will pay. Gains from securities are sometimes recognized prior to sale—in the form of "unrealized" gains and losses—if the securities are trading securities or are available for sale. (See Box 2.3.)

EXPENSES: THE MATCHING PRINCIPLE

Expenses are recognized in the income statement by their association with the revenues for which they have been incurred. This matching of revenues and expenses yields an earnings number that is net value added from revenues.

Matching is done by direct association of expenses with revenues or by association with periods in which revenue is

In terms of market prices,

$$\text{Market value added} = \text{Ending price} - \text{Beginning price} + \text{Dividend} \qquad \textbf{(2.8)}$$

If the market is pricing the intrinsic value correctly, **market value added** is, of course, (intrinsic) value added. The change in value in the market is the **stock return**. The stock return for a period, t, is

$$\text{Stock return}_t = P_t - P_{t-1} + d_t \qquad \textbf{(2.8a)}$$

where $P_t - P_{t-1}$ is the change in price (the **capital gain** portion of the return) and d_t is the dividend part of the return.

The accounting measure of value added—earnings—does not usually equal value added in the stock market. The reason, again, involves the rules for recognizing value added. Those rules are summarized in Box 2.4. The two driving principles are the **revenue recognition principle** and the **matching principle**. Accounting recognizes that firms add value by selling products and services to customers. Unless a firm wins customers, it does not "make money." So accounting value is added only when a firm makes a sale to a customer: Revenue is booked. The accountant then turns to the task of calculating the net value added, matching the expenses incurred in gaining revenue against the revenue. Accordingly, the difference between revenue and matched expenses is the measure of value added from trading with customers.

The matching principle, however, is violated in practice, introducing accounting quality problems and, as we will see, difficulties for valuation. Firms and analysts can mislead investors by referring to pro forma earnings numbers that fail to match expenses with revenues. See Box 2.4.

recognized. Cost of goods sold, for example, is recognized by directly matching the cost of items sold with the revenue from the sale of those items, to yield gross margin. Interest expenses, in contrast, are matched to the period in which the debt provides the financing of the operations that produce revenue.

Revenue recognition and expense matching are violated in practice, reducing the quality of earnings as a measure of value added from customers. Firms themselves may violate the revenue recognition and matching principles, but violations also are admitted (indeed, required) under GAAP. In these cases, the difference between value added and accounting value added is explained, not only in cases where the revenue recognition and matching principles have been followed, but further by the violation of these principles. Here are come examples of good and poor matching.

Examples of Sound Matching Prescribed by GAAP

- Recording cost of goods sold as the cost of producing goods for which sales have been made and, correspondingly, placing the cost of goods produced, but not sold, in inventory in the balance sheet, to be matched against future revenues when they are sold.

- Recording expenditure on plant as an asset and then allocating the cost of the asset to the income statement (as depreciation expense) over the life of the asset. In this way, income is not affected when the investment is made, but only as revenues from the plant are recognized. Accordingly, income is revenue matched with the plant costs incurred to earn the revenue.

- Recording the cost of employee pensions as expenses in the period in which the employees provide service to produce revenues, rather than in the future when pensions are paid (and employees are not producing, but retired).

Examples of Poor Matching Prescribed by GAAP

- Expensing research and development (R&D) expenditures in the income statement when incurred, rather than recording them as an asset (an investment) in the balance sheet. If the expenditures were recorded as an asset, their cost would be matched (through amortization) against the future revenues that the R&D generates.

- Expensing film production costs as incurred, rather than matching them against revenues earned after the film is released.

- Compensation from stock options is not recognized, so revenues are not charged with the cost of earning them.

Examples of Poor Matching by Firms

- Underestimating bad debts from sales so that net revenue is overstated.

- Estimating long useful lives for plant so that depreciation is understated.

- Overestimating a restructuring charge. The overestimate has the consequence of recording current period's income as less than it would be with an unbiased estimate, while recording future income as higher than it would be because expenses (like depreciation) have already been written off.

THE WORLDCOM CON

In June 2002, WorldCom, the second largest U.S. long-distance telephone carrier through its MCI unit, confessed to overstating income by $3.8 billion over 2001–2002, one of the largest accounting frauds ever. The overstatement was due to a mismatch of revenues with access fees paid to local telephone companies. These fees are necessary to connect long-distance calls through local networks to customers; thus they are a cost of earning current revenue. The WorldCom CFO, however, capitalized these costs as assets in the balance sheet, with the idea of amortizing them against future revenue. This treatment served to inflate income by $3.8 billion and allowed WorldCom to avoid reporting losses. WorldCom shares had traded at a high of $64 per share during the telecom bubble, but they fell below $1 in June 2002, and the firm subsequently filed for bankruptcy.

PRO FORMA EARNINGS OFTEN INVOLVE MISMATCHING

During the stock market bubble, corporations often encouraged investors to evaluate them on "pro forma" earnings numbers that differed from GAAP earnings. Analysts and investment bankers also promoted these numbers. Most pro forma numbers involve mismatching, usually omitting expenses. Indeed they are sometimes referred to as "ebs" (in contrast to eps): Everything but the Bad Stuff. Amazon.com, for example, referred to earnings before amortization and interest (yes, interest!) in press releases; its GAAP numbers (after amortization and interest) were actually losses.

The most prevalent pro forma number is ebitda, *earnings before interest, taxes, depreciation, and amortization*. This number omits taxes and interest. Analysts argue that it is a better number because depreciation and amortization are not cash costs, so ebitda is emphasized in telecom and media companies whose large capital investments result in large depreciation charges. However, while the analyst might be wary of mismeasurement of depreciation, depreciation is a real cost, just like wages expense. Plants rust. Telecom networks become obsolescent. Telecoms can overinvest in networks, producing overcapacity. Depreciation expense recognizes these costs.

Reliance on ebidta encourages firms to substitute capital for labor and, indeed, to invest in overcapacity because the cost of overcapacity does not affect ebitda. Ebitda can be used to deceive. The WorldCom con was a scam to inflate ebitda. Expensing access charges as operating costs reduces ebitda. However, by capitalizing the charges, WorldCom not only increased current ebitda, but also be increased future ebitda as the amortization of capitalized operating costs are classified as depreciation or amortization; thus the charges are not be reflected in ebitda in any period. Growing ebitda would impress the unwary investor and perpetuate the telecom bubble.

In contrast, value added in the stock market, while presumably recognizing value added from selling products during the period, is speculative value. The market prices not only the earnings from current operations, but it also anticipates sales and earnings to be made in future operations. A firm may announce a new product line. In response, investors revalue the firm in the market based on speculation about future sales and earnings from the product. A firm may announce new strategies, new investment plans, and management changes, and the market prices the anticipated profits from these changes. But none of them affects current earnings. The accountant says: Let's wait and see if these actions win customers; let's not book revenues until we have a sale. Investors say: Let's price the anticipated value that will be booked in future revenues.

Thus accounting recognition of value typically lags intrinsic value. Accordingly, fundamental analysis involves anticipation, that is, forecasting value added that has not been recognized in the financial statements but will be recognized in future financial statements as sales are made. In so doing, fundamental analysis estimates value added that is missing from the financial statements. This leads us to the price-earnings ratio.

The Price-Earnings Ratio

The *price-earnings ratio* (P/E) compares current price with earnings. Interpret the P/E ratio as follows. Price, the numerator, is the market's anticipation of value to be added from sales in the future, that is, future earnings. The denominator is current earnings, value added from current sales. So the P/E ratio compares forecasted future earnings to current earnings. If one expects considerably more future earnings than current earnings, the P/E ratio should be high, and if one expects lower future earnings than current earnings, the P/E ratio should be low. To be more concise, the P/E ratio reflects anticipated earnings growth. Accordingly, fundamental analysis evaluates expected earnings growth to estimate *intrinsic P/E ratios*. Intrinsic P/E ratios are then compared with *market P/E ratios* to test the market's anticipations.

With Dell trading at $26 per share in 2002, its P/E ratio on 2002 earnings per share of 48 cents was 54. The analyst's task is to assess whether forecasts of future earnings justify this multiple. As with the P/B ratio, he has the history of P/E ratios in mind and uses these as benchmarks. Figure 2.3 tracks selected percentiles of P/E ratios for U.S. firms. Like P/B ratios, P/E ratios were low in the 1970s, with medians less than 10. But the 1990s saw considerably higher P/E ratios, with medians of 20 and above.[3] A P/E of 54 for Dell certainly looks high against the history of P/E ratios. Can it be justified with fundamental analysis?

---

[3] P/E ratios for the S&P 500 and the Dow index were on the order of 7 to 10 in the mid-1970s and well over 20 in the 1990s. By 2000, the P/E for the S&P 500 reached 33.

FIGURE 2.3
Percentiles of price-earnings ratios for all U.S. listed firms, 1963–2001. P/E ratios were relatively low in the 1970s and high in the 1960s and 1990s. The average is above 10.0. (The figure covers firms with positive earnings only.)

Source:
Company: Standard & Poor's
Data: Compustat® data.

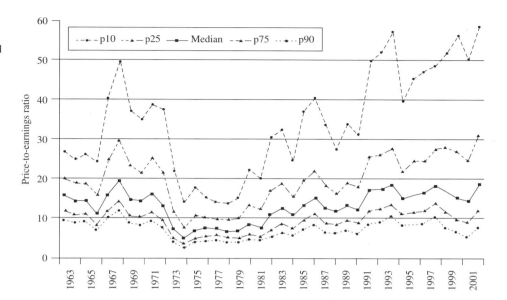

The Reliability Criterion: Don't Mix What You Know with Speculation

We have seen that the balance sheet omits value and the income statement does not recognize all the value that is added in the stock market. Is there justification for these seeming deficiencies? Accountants justify their rules by what is called the **reliability criterion**.

The reliability criterion demands that assets and liabilities be recognized only if they can be measured with reasonable precision and supported by objective evidence, free of opinion and bias. So the reliability criterion rules out recognizing Dell's direct-to-customer marketing asset, its brand name, and its supply chain on its balance sheet. Estimates of these assets are deemed too subjective, too open to manipulation. Indeed, most intangible assets are omitted from the balance sheet. Knowledge assets developed from research and development (R&D) usually are omitted. Only assets that the firm has purchased—such as inventories, plant, R&D acquired by purchasing a patent, and acquired goodwill—are recorded, for then there is an objective market transaction to justify the measurement. Contingent liabilities for which the outcome is not probable or which cannot be reasonably estimated also are not recorded.

The reliability criterion also governs the income statement. Indeed, the revenue recognition principle (see Box 2.4) invokes the reliability criterion: Revenues are recorded only when there is reliable evidence of a customer buying the product. So accountants do not book revenue based on speculation that the firm may get customers in the future—only when they actually do.

The reliability criterion suits the fundamental analyst well. Stock prices are based on speculation about firms' ability to make sales in the future and to generate earnings from those sales. The role of fundamental analysis is to challenge that speculation in order to test whether stocks are appropriately priced. So fundamental analysts have a maxim: *Don't mix what you know with what you don't know*. Don't mix speculation with knowledge. Sales made in the current period, and the earnings derived from them after matching expenses, are something that we know with some reliability (unless the accounting is

During the stock market bubble of 1998–2000, financial reporting came into question. Commentators claimed that the traditional financial reporting model, developed during the Industrial Age, was no longer relevant for the Information Age. Claims were made that "earnings no longer matter." Balance sheets were said to be useless because, in the "new economy," value comes from knowledge assets and other intangibles that are omitted from balance sheets. To justify lofty price-earnings ratios, technology analysts referred to metrics such as clicks and page views rather than earnings. "Value reporting" that relies on soft information outside the financial statements became the vogue. Was this bubble froth or are these claims justified?

Speculative beliefs feed price bubbles. Speculation overlooks hard information and overemphasizes soft information. The role of financial statements is to anchor the investor on the rising tide of speculation with hard information. As we proceed through the book we will learn how to anchor analysis in the financial statements. Consider the following:

- Losses reported by new economy firms during the bubble turned out to be a good predictor: Most of these firms failed. Earnings did matter.

- For firms that did survive, the earnings they reported during the bubble were a much better predictor of subsequent earnings than the speculative forecasts of analysts pushing the stocks.

- Most of the intangible assets imagined by speculative analysts vaporized.

- The much-criticized balance sheets also provided good forecasts. The ratio of debt assumed in pursuit of intangible assets (by telecoms, for example) was large relative to tangible assets on the balance sheet, and that ratio predicted demise.

Financial reporting was rightly criticized after the bubble burst, exposing the poor financial reporting practices of Enron and Arthur Andersen, Xerox (in its earnings restatements), and WorldCom, to mention a few. But the critique was one of accounting that allowed speculation to enter the financial statements (and of the deviance of compromised management, directors, and auditors who wished to inflate profits). The statements did not anchor investors.

Good accounting serves as a check on speculation. Good accounting challenges the pyramid scheme that bubbles perpetuate. Bad accounting perpetuates pyramid schemes. Bad accounting creates false earnings momentum that feeds price momentum. GAAP, unfortunately, does have features that can be used to perpetuate bubbles. The fundamental analyst is aware of these features and brings her quality-of-earnings analysis to bear on the problem. See the web page for further discussion.

suspect). Don't contaminate that knowledge by mixing it with speculation in the income statement, for the analyst wants to use that knowledge to test speculation. Further, don't mix hard assets in the balance sheet with speculative estimates about the value of unobserved intangible assets. See Box 2.5.

The practice of omitting or understating assets on the balance sheet is called **conservative accounting**. Conservative accounting says: Let's be conservative in valuing assets; let's not speculate about the value of assets. So, if there is uncertainty about the value of an asset, don't book the asset at all. In practicing conservative accounting, accountants write down assets, but they will not (in the U.S) write up assets. You understand, then, why price-to-book ratios are typically greater than 1.

Tension in Accounting

To measure value added from sales to customers, accountants match expenses with revenues. The reliability criterion demands that revenues not be recognized until a customer is won. But the reliability criterion also comes into play in matching expenses, and this creates tension.

According to the reliability criterion, investment in assets with uncertain value cannot be booked on the balance sheet. So GAAP requires that investments in R&D assets and brand assets (developed through advertising) be expensed immediately in the income statement rather then booked to the balance sheet. The result is a mismatch: Current rev-

Accounting Clinic I

BASIC ACCOUNTING PRINCIPLES

This chapter has provided an overview of the principles of accounting. Much detail lurks behind the broad principles. Not all will be required of a competent analyst but, as we proceed with the fundamental analysis that is anchored in the financial statements, accounting issues will arise. Those issues will be addressed in the text but, in many cases, the detail is too much to cover. So, on issues important to the equity analyst, you will be introduced to

an **Accounting Clinic** on the book's website. The purpose of these clinics is to help remedy your scant knowledge of accounting or to provide a review of material you have covered in accounting courses. You might also want to refer to the texts you have used in previous accounting courses, to refresh your memory.

Accounting Clinic I expands on the basic principles of accounting measurement that are laid out in this chapter.

enues are charged with the investments to produce future revenues, and future revenues are not charged with the (amortized) cost of earning those revenues. There is a tension between the matching principle and the reliability criterion and, in the case of R&D and advertising, GAAP comes down on the side of mismatching.

The reliability criterion is not absolute, however. Matching requires estimates, and the reliability criterion allows estimates when they can be "reasonably" made. To calculate net sales revenue, accountants match the estimated cost of not receiving cash from the sales, that is, the cost of bad debts. The estimate of this cost is subjective and can be biased, but the estimate is allowed. To match depreciation of plant with the revenues that the plant produces, the accountant must estimate the useful life over which depreciation is calculated, and that estimate is subjective. Estimates can be abused, so the tension in accounting becomes one of making the appropriate matching but possibly admitting biased estimates. Auditors and corporate directors are, of course, a check on abuses if they pursue their job in an unbiased way as fiduciaries for shareholders.

The analyst is aware of these tensions. He adapts to the mismatching that the reliability criterion and conservative accounting introduce. And he develops diagnostics to assess poor quality earnings that are biased by estimates. The quality of earnings is an important issue in equity analysis and is an issue we will visit again and again as the book proceeds.

Summary

Financial statements articulate in a way that tells a story. From the shareholder's point of view, the book value of equity in the balance sheet is the "bottom line" to the financial statements. The accounting system tracks shareholders' equity over time. Each period, equity is updated by recognizing value added from business activities—comprehensive income—and value paid out in net dividends. The statement of shareholders' equity summarizes the tracking. The income statement (along with "other comprehensive income" in the equity statement) gives the details of valued added to the business by matching revenues (value received from customers) with expenses (value given up in servicing customers). As well as tracking owners' equity, the financial statements also track changes in a firm's cash position through the cash flow statement, where the change in cash is explained by cash generated in operations, cash spent on investments, and cash paid out in financing activities.

The Web Connection

Find the following on the web page for this chapter:

- Directions on how to find financial statements on the SEC's EDGAR database.

- Summary of the filings that firms must make with the SEC.

- Directions to online services for recovering financial statement information.

- Financial statement layouts in countries other than the U.S.

- Elaboration on accounting principles.

- A discussion of financial reporting during the 1990s stock market bubble.

These features of the financial statements are expressed in a set of accounting relations that define the structure of the statements. Commit these to memory, for they will come into play as we organize the financial statements into spreadsheets for analysis. Indeed, they will become rules that have to be obeyed as we develop forecasted financial statements for valuation.

Accountants calculate the (book) value of equity, but the analyst is interested in the (intrinsic) value of the equity. This chapter outlined the rules that determine the book value of equity in the balance sheet. The chapter also outlined the rules that determine value added—earnings—in the income statement. These rules lead to differences in prices and book values, so understanding them gives you an understanding of price-to-book ratios. The rules also explain why value added in the stock price is not recognized immediately in earnings, so you also have an understanding of the P/E ratio. That understanding will be enhanced as we establish the technology for determining intrinsic P/B and P/E ratios.

Key Concepts

accounting relation is an equation that expresses components of financial statements in terms of other components. *30*

articulation of the financial statements is the way they relate to each other. *36*

asset is an investment that is expected to produce future payoffs. *30*

capital gain is the amount by which the price of an investment changes. *44*

comprehensive income is total income reported (in the income statement and elsewhere in the financial statements). *36*

conservative accounting is the practice of recording relatively low values for net assets on the balance sheets, or omitting assets altogether. *48*

dirty surplus accounting books income in the equity statement rather than the income statement. *36*

expense is value given up in earning revenue that is recognized in the financial statements. *32*

fair value is the term that accountants use for the amount to which an asset or liability is **marked to market**. It is market value, or an estimate of market value when a liquid market does not exist. *41*

flows in financial statements are changes in stocks between two points in time. Compare with **stocks**. *36*

historical cost accounting records assets and liabilities at their historical cost, then (in most cases) amortizes the cost over periods to the income statement. *41*

intangible asset is an asset without physical form. *42*

liability is a claim on payoffs other than by the owners. *30*

mark-to-market accounting records assets and liabilities at their market value. *41*

market value added is the amount by which shareholder wealth increases in the market, plus any net dividend received. It is equal to the **stock return**. *44*

matching principle is the accounting principle by which *expenses* are matched with the *revenues* for which they are incurred. *44*

net payout is cash distributed to shareholders. *35*

reliability criterion is the accounting principle that requires assets, liabilities, revenues, and expenses to be booked only if they can be measured with reasonable precision based on objective evidence. *47*

revenue is value received from customers that is recognized in the financial statements. *32*

revenue recognition principle is the accounting principle by which revenues are recognized in the income statement. *44*

shareholder value added is the (intrinsic) value added to shareholders' wealth during a period. *43*

stocks in the financial statements are balances at a point in time. Compare with **flows**. *36*

stock return is the return to holding a share, and it is equal to the **capital gain** plus dividend. *44*

stockholders' equity is the claim on the net assets by the owners (the stockholders) of the firm. *30*

The Analyst's Toolkit

Analysis Tools	Page	Key Measures	Page	Acronymns to Remember
Financial statements		Assets	30	bps book value per share
Balance sheet	30	Basic earnings per share (eps)	34	dps dividends per share
Income statement	31	Book value of equity	39	ebit earnings before interest and
Cash flow statement	35	Book value per share (bps)	40	taxes
Statement of shareholders'		Capital gain	44	ebitda earnings before interest,
equity	35	Cash flow		taxes, depreciation and
Financial statement		From operations	35	amortization
footnotes	36	From investing activities	35	eps earnings per share
Management's discussion		From financing activities	35	FASB Financial Accounting
and analysis	36	Comprehensive income	36	Standards Board
Accounting relations		Diluted earnings per share (eps)	35	GAAP Generally Accepted
Balance sheet equation (2.1)	30	Earnings before interest and		Accounting Principles
Income statement		taxes (ebit)	33	IASB International Accounting
equation (2.2)	32	Earnings before interest, taxes,		Standards Board
Income statement component		depreciation, and		NYSE New York Stock Exchange
equations (2.2a)	33	amortization	45	P/B price-to-book ratio
Cash flow statement		Expense	32	P/E price-earnings ratio
equation (2.3)	35	Fair values	41	R&D research and development
Stocks and flows		Gross margin	33	SEC Securities and Exchange
equation (2.4)	35	Liabilities	30	Commission
Comprehensive income		Market value added	44	
calculation (2.5)	36	Net assets	30	
Value equation (2.6)	39	Net income (or net profit)	31	
Value added for shareholders		Net payout	35	
equation (2.7)	43	Net revenue	32	
		Operating income	33	

The Analyst's Toolkit (concluded)

Analysis Tools	Page	Key Measures	Page
Market value added equation (2.8)	44	Premium (or discount) over book value	39
Stock return for a period equation (2.8a)	44	Price/earnings ratio (P/E)	46
		Price-to-book ratio (P/B)	40
		Revenue	32
		Shareholder value added	43
		Stock return	44

Concept Questions

C2.1. Changes in shareholders' equity are determined by earnings minus net payout to shareholders, but they are not equal to net income (in the income statement) minus net payout to shareholders. Why?

C2.2. Dividends are the only way to pay cash out to shareholders. True or False?

C2.3. As the change in shareholders' equity is equal to total earnings minus net payout, and shareholders' equity is also equal to assets minus liabilities, it must be that total earnings minus net payout is equal to the change in assets minus the change in liabilities over a period. True or false?

C2.4. Explain the difference between net income and net income available to common. Which definition of income is used in earnings-per-share calculations?

C2.5. Why might a firm trade at a price-to-book ratio (P/B) greater than 1.0?

C2.6. Explain why firms have different price-earnings (P/E) ratios.

C2.7. Explain the difference between accounting value added (earnings) and shareholder value added.

C2.8. Give some examples in which there is poor matching of revenues and expenses.

C2.9. Price-to-book ratios are determined by how accountants measure book values. Can you think of accounting reasons for why price-to-book ratios were high in the 1990s? What other factors might explain the high P/B ratios?

C2.10. Why are dividends not an expense in the income statement?

C2.11. Why is depreciation of plant and equipment an expense in the income statement?

C2.12. Is amortization of goodwill or a patent right an appropriate expense in measuring value added in operations?

C2.13. Why is the matching principle important?

Exercises

E2.1. Finding Financial Statement Information on the Internet (Easy)

The Securities and Exchange Commission (SEC) maintains the EDGAR database of company filings with the commission. Explore the SEC'S EDGAR site:

http://www.sec.gov/edgarhp.htm

Look at the "Form Descriptions" page to familiarize yourself with the types of filings that firms make. Then click on "Search for Company Filings" for the filings of firms you are interested in. Forms 10-K (annual reports) and 10-Q (quarterly reports) will be of primary interest.

Accessing the database directly on the SEC site gives you the full text of each filing. A number of services deliver the material in small, digestible pieces so you don't have to scroll through the entire filing in search of a particular item. These services also format the filing in a form that can be downloaded into a spreadsheet program. Try, for example,

FreeEDGAR at http://www.freeedgar.com

EdgarScan at http://edgarscan.pwcglobal.com

You also can access these sites through links on the book's web page.

E2.2. Accounting for a Savings Account (Easy)

Review the accounting for the savings account in Box 2.2. Suppose that, instead of withdrawing $5 from the account at the end of Year 1, the owner left the $5 in the account. Construct the financial statements for this "zero payout" case.

Suppose now that the owner has authorized the bank to invest the $5 of cash from earnings for Year 1 in an equity mutual fund, and that there has been no withdrawal from the account. Construct the financial statements that report the owner's investment at the bank.

E2.3. Preparing an Income Statement and Statement of Shareholders' Equity (Easy)

From the following information for the year 2003, prepare an income statement and a statement of shareholders' equity, under GAAP rules, for a company with shareholders' equity at the beginning of 2003 of $3,270 million. Amounts are in millions.

Sales	$4,458
Common dividends paid	140
Selling expenses	1,230
Research and development costs	450
Cost of goods sold	3,348
Share issues	680
Unrealized gain on securities available for sale	76
Income taxes	(200)

Also calculate comprehensive income and net payout. Income taxes are negative. How can this be?

E2.4. Using Accounting Relations: J.C. Penney Co. (Medium)

The following numbers appeared in the annual report of J.C. Penney, the retailer, for fiscal year ending January 27, 1996 (in millions of dollars):

	Fiscal 1996	Fiscal 1995
Total assets	17,102	16,202
Total stockholders' equity	5,884	5,615
Total revenues	21,419	21,082
Net income	838	1,057
Common share issues	383	462
Common dividends	434	392
Preferred dividends	40	40
Common stock repurchases	301	435
Retirement of preferred stock	27	18

For fiscal 1996, calculate

a. Total liabilities.

b. Total expenses.

c. Comprehensive income.

Real World Connection

See Exercises E3.12 and E8.5 for the material on J.C. Penney.

E2.5. Using Accounting Relations: Genentech Inc. (Medium)

Consider the following excerpts from Genentech's 1998 income statement and cash flow statement. (Amounts are in thousands of dollars.) From the 1998 income statement:

Revenues	?
Costs and expenses	
Cost of sales	$138,623
Research and development	396,186
Marketing, general, and administrative	358,931
Interest	4,552
Total costs and expenses	898,292
Income tax provision	70,742
Net income	$181,909

From the 1998 cash flow statement:

Cash flows from operating activities	
Net income	$181,909
Adjustments to reconcile net income to net cash provided by operating activities	
Depreciation and amortization	78,101
Deferred income taxes	29,792
Gain on sales of securities available for sale	(9,542)
Loss on sales of securities available for sale	1,809
Write-down of nonmarketable securities	16,689
Write-down of securities available for sale	20,249
Loss on fixed-asset dispositions	1,015
Changes in assets and liabilities	
Net cash flow from trading securities	12,725
Receivables and other current assets	33,767
Inventories	(32,600)
Accounts payable, other current liabilities, and other long-term liabilities	15,937
Net cash provided by operating activities	$349,851

For 1998 calculate

a. Revenues.

b. ebit (Earnings before interest and taxes).

c. ebitda (Earnings before interest, taxes, depreciation, and amortization).

The following were reported in Genentech's 1998 balance sheet (in millions):

Current assets	$1,242
Total assets	2,855
Long-term liabilities	220
Stockholders' equity	2,344

d. Calculate the long-term assets and short-term liabilities that were reported.

The following were also reported in the 1998 statements (in thousands):

	1998	1997
Cash used in investing activities (in the cash flow statement)	$421,096	$168,378
Cash and cash equivalents (in the balance sheet)	281,162	244,469

e. Calculate cash flows from financing activities reported for 1998.

E2.6. Classifying Accounting Items (Easy)

Indicate where in the financial statements the following appear under GAAP:

 a. Investment in a certificate of deposit maturing in 120 days.
 b. Expenses for bad debts.
 c. Allowances for bad debts.
 d. Research and development expenditures.
 e. A restructuring charge.
 f. A lease of an asset for its entire productive life.
 g. Unrealized gain on shares held for trading purposes.
 h. Unrealized gain on shares available for sale.
 i. Unearned revenue.
 j. Preferred stock issued.
 k. Preferred dividends paid.
 l. Stock option compensation expense.

E2.7. Violations of the Matching Principle (Easy)

Generally accepted accounting principles (GAAP) notionally follow the matching principle. However, there are exceptions. Explain why the following accounting rules, required under GAAP, violate the matching principle.

 a. Expenditures on research and development into new drugs are expensed in the income statement as they are incurred.
 b. Advertising and promotion costs for a new product are expensed as incurred.
 c. Film production costs are expensed prior to the release of films to theaters.

E2.8. Using Accounting Relations to Check Errors (Medium)

A chief executive reported the following numbers for fiscal year 2003 to an annual meeting of shareholders (in millions):

Revenues	$ 2,300
Total expenses, including taxes	1,750
Other comprehensive income	(90)
Total assets, end of year	4,340
Total liabilities, end of year	1,380
Dividends to shareholders	400
Share issues	900
Share repurchases	150
Shareholders' equity, beginning of year	19,140

Show that at least one of these numbers must be wrong because it does not obey accounting relations.

E2.9. Mismatching at WorldCom (Hard)

During the four fiscal quarters of 2001 and the first quarter of 2002, WorldCom incorrectly capitalized access charges to local networks as assets (as explained in Box 2.4). The amount of costs capitalized were as follows:

First quarter, 2001	$780 million
Second quarter, 2001	$605 million
Third quarter, 2001	$760 million
Fourth quarter, 2001	$920 million
First quarter, 2002	$790 million

Suppose WorldCom amortized these capitalized costs straight-line over five years (20 quarters). Calculate the amount of the overstatement of income before tax for each of the five quarters.

Minicase	**M2.1**

Reviewing the Financial Statements of Nike, Inc.

Nike, Inc. is a leading manufacturer and marketer of sport and fashion footwear. Incorporated in 1968 and headquartered in Beaverton, Oregon, its brand name has become almost universal, delivering sales of over $10 billion by 2002 and making it the largest seller of athletic footwear and apparel in the world, with operations in 140 countries. Nike's top-selling product categories are running, basketball, and cross-training shoes, but it also markets shoes designed for tennis, golf, soccer, baseball, football, bicycling, volleyball, wrestling, cheerleading, aquatic activities, hiking, and outdoor activity. Many of its products are purchased as leisurewear.

In the 1990s Nike was a hot stock, trading at a P/E ratio of 35 and a P/B ratio of 5.1 in mid-1999. By early 2003, its P/E ratio had fallen to 18 and its P/B ratio to 3.2.

We will spend considerable time in the book analyzing and valuing Nike and comparing it with a vigorous competitor, Reebok International Ltd. The **Build Your Own Analysis Product (BYOAP)** on the website tracks Nike from 1996 to 2002. The 2002 financial statements that follow introduce you to the firm. You also can find these financial statements in Nike's 10-K report for 2002 on the SEC's EDGAR website, which is accessible through the portals listed in Exercise 2.1, or through links on the book's website. Browse the entire 10-K as an example of what a typical 10-K looks like. Look at the footnotes referred to in the statements below. Read the management's discussion of the business and get a sense of the business model. Look also at the firm's website at www.nike.com.

Examine the financial statements below and use them to test your basic knowledge of accounting. The questions that follow will help you focus on the pertinent features.

A. Using the numbers in the financial statements, show that the following accounting relations hold in Nike's 2002 statements:

Shareholders' equity = Assets – Liabilities

Net income = Revenue – Expenses

Cash from operations + Cash from investment + Cash from financing – Effect of exchange rate = Change in cash and cash equivalents

B. What are the components of other comprehensive income for 2002? Show that the following accounting relation holds:

Comprehensive income = Net income + Other comprehensive income

C. Calculate the net payout to shareholders in 2002 from the Statement of Shareholders' Equity.

D. Calculate the following for 2002: gross margin, effective tax rate, ebit, ebitda, and the sales growth rate for 2002.

E. Explain the difference between basic earnings per share and diluted earnings per share.

F. Explain why some inventory costs are in cost of goods sold and some are in inventory on the balance sheet.

G. Nike carries out research and development. Where is this cost included in the financial statements? Does this treatment satisfy the matching principle?

H. Accounts receivable of $1,807.1 million is the net of $77.4 million. What is this component of the calculation?

I. Why are deferred income taxes both an asset and a liability?

J. What is "goodwill" and how is it accounted for?

K. Why are commitments and contingencies listed on the balance sheet, yet the amount is zero?

L. What is the paid-in value of the common stock at the end of 2002?

M. Explain why there is a difference between net income and cash provided by operations.

N. Why is "income tax benefit from exercise of stock options" included in cash provided by operations (in the Consolidated Statements of Cash Flows)? Why is this tax benefit not a part of net income?

O. Why is there a difference between interest paid ($54.2 million, at the bottom of the cash flow statement) and interest expense ($47.6 million, in the income statement)?

P. The following accounting relation does not work for Nike's statement of equity: Ending equity = Beginning equity + Comprehensive income − Net payout to shareholders Why? Hint: What is unearned stock compensation?

Q. What items in Nike's balance sheet would you say were close to fair market value?

R. Nike's shares traded at $50. Calculate the P/E ratio and the P/B ratio at this price. How do these ratios compare with historical P/E and P/B ratios in Figures 2.2 and 2.3?

NIKE, INC.
Consolidated Statements of Income
Year Ended May 31

	2002	2001	2000
	(in millions, except per share data)		
Revenues	$9,893.0	$9,488.8	$8,995.1
Costs and expenses:			
Cost of sales	6,004.7	5,784.9	5,403.8
Selling and administrative	2,820.4	2,689.7	2,606.4
Interest expense (Notes 4 and 5)	47.6	58.7	45.0
Other income/expense, net (Notes 1, 10 and 11)	3.0	34.1	20.7
Total costs and expenses	8,875.7	8,567.4	8,075.9
Income before income taxes and cumulative effect accounting change	1,017.3	921.4	919.2
Income taxes (Note 6)	349.0	331.7	340.1
Income before cumulative effect of accounting change	668.3	589.7	579.1
Cumulative effect of accounting change, net of income taxes of $3.0 (Note 1)	5.0	—	—
Net income	$ 663.3	$ 589.7	$ 579.1
Basic earnings per common share—before accounting change (Notes 1 and 9)	$ 2.50	$ 2.18	$ 2.10
Cumulative effect of accounting change	0.02	—	—
	$ 2.48	$ 2.18	$ 2.10
Diluted earnings per common share—before accounting change (Notes 1 and 9)	$ 2.46	$ 2.16	$ 2.07
Cumulative effect of accounting change	0.02	—	—
	$ 2.44	$ 2.16	$ 2.07

Consolidated Balance Sheets
May 31

	2002	2001
	\(in millions\)	
ASSETS		
Current Assets		
Cash and equivalents	$ 575.5	$ 304.0
Accounts receivable, less allowance for doubtful accounts of $77.4 and $72.1	1,807.1	1,621.4
Inventories (Note 2)	1,373.8	1,424.1
Deferred income taxes (Notes 1 and 6)	140.8	113.3
Prepaid expenses and other current assets (Note 1)	260.5	162.5
Total current assets	4,157.7	3,625.3
Property, plant and equipment, net (Note 3)	1,614.5	1,618.8
Identifiable intangible assets and goodwill, net (Note 1)	437.8	397.3
Deferred income taxes and other assets (Notes 1 and 6)	233.0	178.2
Total assets	$6,443.0	$5,819.6
LIABILITIES AND SHAREHOLDERS' EQUITY		
Current Liabilities		
Current portion of long-term debt (Note 5)	$ 55.3	$ 5.4
Notes payable (Note 4)	425.2	855.3
Accounts payable (Note 4)	504.4	432.0
Accrued liabilities (Note 15)	768.3	472.1
Income taxes payable	83.0	21.9
Total current liabilities	1,836.2	1,786.7
Long-term debt (Notes 5 and 14)	625.9	435.9
Deferred income taxes and other liabilities (Notes 1 and 6)	141.6	102.2
Commitments and contingencies (Notes 13 and 15)	—	—
Redeemable preferred stock (Note 7)	0.3	0.3
Shareholders' Equity		
Common stock at stated value (Note 8):		
Class A convertible—98.1 and 99.1 shares outstanding	0.2	0.2
Class B—168.0 and 169.5 shares outstanding	2.6	2.6
Capital in excess of stated value	538.7	459.4
Unearned stock compensation	(5.1)	(9.9)
Accumulated other comprehensive loss	(192.4)	(152.1)
Retained earnings	3,495.0	3,194.3
Total shareholders' equity	3,839.0	3,494.5
Total liabilities and shareholders' equity	$6,443.0	$5,819.6

Consolidated Statements of Cash Flows
Year Ended May 31

	2002	2001	2000
		(in millions)	
Cash provided (used) by operations:			
Net income	$ 663.3	$589.7	$579.1
Income charges not affecting cash:			
Depreciation	223.5	197.4	188.0
Deferred income taxes	15.2	79.8	36.8
Amortization and other	53.1	16.7	35.6
Income tax benefit from exercise of stock options	13.9	32.4	14.9
Changes in certain working capital components:			
Increase in accounts receivable	(135.2)	(141.4)	(82.6)
Decrease (increase) in inventories	55.4	(16.7)	(311.8)
Decrease in other current assets and income taxes receivable	16.9	78.0	61.2
Increase (decrease) in accounts payable, accrued liabilities, and income taxes payable	175.4	(179.4)	178.4
Cash provided by operations	1,081.5	656.5	699.6
Cash provided (used) by investing activities:			
Additions to property, plant, and equipment and other	(282.8)	(317.6)	(419.9)
Disposals of property, plant, and equipment	15.6	12.7	25.3
Increase in other assets	(39.1)	(42.5)	(51.3)
Increase in other liabilities	3.5	5.1	5.9
Cash used by investing activities	(302.8)	(342.3)	(440.0)
Cash provided (used) by financing activities:			
Proceeds from long-term debt issuance	329.9	—	—
Reductions in long-term debt including current portion	(80.3)	(50.3)	(1.7)
(Decrease) increase in notes payable	(431.5)	(68.9)	505.1
Proceeds from exercise of stock options and other stock issuances	59.5	56.0	23.9
Repurchase of stock	(226.9)	(157.0)	(646.3)
Dividends—common and preferred	(128.9)	(129.7)	(133.1)
Cash used by financing activities	(478.2)	(349.9)	(252.1)
Effect of exchange rate changes	(29.0)	85.4	48.7
Net increase in cash and equivalents	271.5	49.7	56.2
Cash and equivalents, beginning of year	304.0	254.3	198.1
Cash and equivalents, end of year	$ 575.5	$304.0	$254.3
Supplemental disclosure of cash flow information:			
Cash paid during the year for:			
Interest	$ 54.2	$ 68.5	$ 45.0
Income taxes	262.0	173.1	221.1
Noncash investing and financing activity:			
Assumption of long-term debt to acquire property, plant, and equipment	—	—	$ 108.9

Consolidated Statements of Shareholders' Equity
(in millions, except per share data)

	Common Stock				Capital in Excess of Stated Value	Unearned Stock Compensation	Accumulated Other Comprehensive Loss	Retained Earnings	Total
	Class A		Class B						
	Shares	Amount	Shares	Amount					
Balance at May 31, 2001	99.1	$ 0.2	169.5	$ 2.6	$459.4	$ (9.9)	$ (152.1)	$3,194.3	3,494.5
Stock options exercised			1.7		72.9				72.9
Conversion to Class B common stock	(1.0)		1.0						
Repurchase of Class B common stock			(4.3)		(5.2)			(232.5)	(237.7)
Dividends on common stock ($.48 per share)								(128.6)	(128.6)
Issuance of shares to employees and others			0.2		13.2	(1.9)			11.3
Amortization of unearned compensation						6.5			6.5
Forfeiture of shares from employees			(0.1)		(1.6)	0.2		(1.5)	(2.9)
Comprehensive income (Note 12):									
Net income								663.3	663.3
Other comprehensive income (net of tax benefit of $17.4):									
Foreign currency translation							(1.5)		(1.5)
Cumulative effect of change in accounting principle (Note 1)	—	—	—	—	—		56.8		56.8
Adjustment for fair value of hedge derivatives							(95.6)		(95.6)
Comprehensive income							(40.3)	663.3	623.0
Balance at May 31, 2002	98.1	$ 0.2	168.0	$ 2.6	$538.7	$(5.1)	$(192.4)	$3,495.0	$3,839.0

The notes in these financial statements refer to footnotes in the 10-K report.

Financial Statements and Valuation

Chapter 3

Lays out the alternative ways in which financial statements are used in equity analysis, and discusses how valuation models direct the way to account for value.

Chapter 4

Introduces cash accounting and accrual accounting for valuation, and lays out discounted cash flow valuation methods that employ cash accounting.

Chapter 5

Introduces valuation methods that anchor equity values on book values and lead to an evaluation of the intrinsic price-to-book ratio.

Chapter 6

Introduces valuation methods that anchor equity values on earnings and lead to an evaluation of the intrinsic price-earnings ratio.

With the foundations established in Part One, proceed to **The Analysis of Financial Statements (Part Two) Forecasting, Valuation, and Strategy (Part Three)**

The first step for any analyst is to choose a technology with which to work. This part of the book lays out alternative techniques that can be employed in equity analysis. The diligent analyst wants the best technology, so the material goes to lengths to contrast the advantages and disadvantages of each technique. By the end of Part Two, you will have chosen a technology with which you feel comfortable, one that gives you the security that is necessary for equity investing.

In order to make the appropriate choice, you must have an understanding of the basic principles of fundamental analysis and investing. This part of the book develops that understanding. Crucial to this understanding is an appreciation of the role of a valuation model, for a valuation model directs how analysis is to be done and how valuations are to be carried out. You will understand that valuation models—though often expressed in seemingly cryptic formulas—are really a way of thinking about the analysis and valuation task. You also will understand that a valuation model is actually a statement about how to account for value, thereby tying valuation to the financial statements. You will then see how we accomplish our objective (in Chapter 1) of anchoring value on the financial statements.

Chapter 3 introduces valuation models based on the financial statements, but not before laying out alternative ways of carrying out equity analysis. The chapter describes the method of comparables, multiple screening analysis, and asset-based valuation. These simple schemes are shown to be lacking, and their use comes with the warning that ignoring the principles of sound fundamental analysis is done at one's peril. With the introduction to valuation models in this chapter you will develop an appreciation for how financial statements are utilized in fundamental analysis. You also will gain an appreciation for what a good (and poor) valuation model looks like with an introduction to the dividend discount model for equity analysis.

Chapter 4 introduces discounted cash flow analysis and shows that this valuation technique embraces cash accounting for value. This provides an opportunity to reveal the deficiencies of cash accounting (and discounted cash flow analysis) as a method of accounting for value, and leads to an appreciation of accrual accounting as way of correcting the deficiencies of cash accounting. The discussion of accrual accounting in this chapter builds on the discussion of accounting in Chapter 2, further enhancing your understanding of how accounting works for valuation.

The two "bottom-line" numbers in accrual accounting financial statements are the book value of equity—the bottom line number in the balance sheet—and earnings (income)—the bottom line number in the income statement. It is on these two numbers that accrual accounting valuation is anchored. Chapter 5 shows how to value a firm by anchoring value on book value. Chapter 2 showed that book values are typically an imperfect measure of value, but they provide a starting point for valuation. Using book value as a starting point, Chapter 5 goes on to show how the analyst adds value to complete the valuation, determining the intrinsic price-to-book (P/B) ratio. In a complementary way, Chapter 6 shows how to anchor a valuation on earnings, thus determining the intrinsic price-earnings (P/E) ratio.

The purpose of this part of the book is to give you perspective on the issues and to emphasize some important concepts. Above all, it gets you thinking about design issues in developing valuation tools. Some of the concepts will be familiar to you from finance courses. Some will be familiar from accounting courses. The accounting and finance concepts come together here. In finance people talk of valuation. In accounting people talk of measurement. But valuation is a matter of measurement (of value generated in the firm). So, in discussing valuation principles, we also introduce the principles of accounting measurement. The point is to show you how accounting works—or maybe doesn't work—to reveal the value in a firm. And we will see how accounting is integrated into valuation analysis so that fundamental analysis and financial statement analysis are much the same thing.

Part Two and subsequent parts of the book are about technique. They are about doing financial statement analysis and fundamental analysis. Part One of the book is less about doing and more about thinking about doing. "Look before you leap" applies to investing but it also applies to the analysis of investing. Sometimes the word "sage" is applied to certain investors, and with good cause. Good techniques must be applied with good judgment, with wisdom. And wisdom helps in the selection of techniques. If you read *The Intelligent Investor* by Benjamin Graham, the acclaimed father of fundamental analysis, you will see that the book is more about attitude and approach to investing than it is about technique.[1] Use this part of the book to understand the basics and use it to cultivate wisdom in investing. We purposefully develop the material slowly, so you can read it in a considered way.

---

[1] B. Graham, *The Intelligent Investor,* 4th rev. ed. (New York: Harper & Row, 1973).

Chapter **Three**

How Financial Statements Are Used in Valuation

LINKS

Link to previous chapters

Chapter 1 introduced fundamental analysis and Chapter 2 introduced the financial statements.

This chapter

This chapter shows how fundamental analysis and valuation are carried out and how the financial statements are utilized in the process. It lays out a five-step approach to fundamental analysis that involves the analysis and forecasting of financial statements. Simpler schemes involving financial statements are also presented.

Link to next chapter

Chapter 4 will begin the implementation of the analysis outlined in this chapter with valuation based on forecasting cash flow statements.

Link to web page

The web page offers further treatment of comparables analysis and screening analysis, as well as an extended discussion of valuation techniques and asset pricing. It also links you to fundamental research engines.

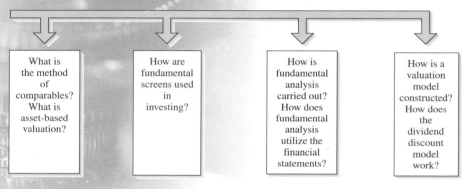

What is the method of comparables? What is asset-based valuation?	How are fundamental screens used in investing?	How is fundamental analysis carried out? How does fundamental analysis utilize the financial statements?	How is a valuation model constructed? How does the dividend discount model work?

This chapter explains how financial statements are used in valuing firms. It is an important chapter, for it sets the stage for developing practical valuation analysis in Chapters 4, 5, and 6. Indeed, the material in the second half of the chapter provides a road map for much of what follows in the rest of the book. As you proceed through the book, you will find yourself looking back to this material to maintain your bearings.

In introducing valuation in Chapter 1, we said that the analyst's first order of business is to choose a technology to work with. You will not be able to commit to a technology until the end of Chapter 6, but this chapter raises the issues involved in making that choice. It lays out the architecture of a competent valuation technology. Here you will develop an appreciation of what a good technology looks like, and you will begin to understand the pitfalls that await those using misguided methods. You also will understand what features of firms are relevant to their valuation, how these features are identified by a competent valuation method, and how they are recognized in financial statements.

In valuation, as with most technologies, there is always a tradeoff between simple approaches that ignore some pertinent features and more elaborate techniques that accommodate complexities. In this book we will always be pushing for the simple approaches, but simple approaches that do not substantially sacrifice the quality of the product. Simple approaches are cheap—they avoid some analysis work—but they can be too cheap, leading to errors. In adopting a simple approach, we want to be sure we know what we are missing relative to a full-fledged analysis. So this chapter begins with simple schemes that use financial statements and progresses to more formal valuation methods. At all points, the tradeoffs are indicated.

The Analyst's Checklist

After reading this chapter you should understand:

- What a valuation technology looks like.
- What a valuation model is and how it differs from an asset pricing model.
- How a valuation model provides the architecture for fundamental analysis.
- The practical steps involved in fundamental analysis.
- How the financial statements are involved in fundamental analysis.
- How one converts a forecast to a valuation.
- The difference between valuing terminal investments and going concern investments (like business firms).
- What business activities generate value.
- The dividend irrelevance concept.
- Why financing transactions do not generate value, except in particular circumstances.
- Why the focus of value creation is on the investing and operating activities of a firm.
- How the dividend discount model works (or does not work).
- How the method of comparables works (or does not work).
- How asset-based valuation works (or does not work).
- How multiple screening strategies work (or do not work).
- What is involved in contrarian investing.
- How fundamental analysis differs from screening.

After reading this chapter you should be able to:

- Carry out a multiple comparison analysis.
- Develop a simple or multiple screen using a stock screener.
- Calculate an array of price multiples for a firm.
- Calculate unlevered price multiples.
- Calculate trailing and forward P/E ratios.
- Calculate a dividend-adjusted P/E ratio.
- Apply asset-based valuation techniques.
- Calculate the breakup value of a firm.
- Value a bond.
- Value a project.
- Calculate the value added from project selection.
- Show that a bond purchased at a price to yield its required return generates no value.
- Calculate the loss to existing shareholders from issuing shares at less than market value.
- Generate "homemade dividends."
- Apply the dividend discount model (or, at least, try to).
- Calculate the value of a perpetuity.
- Calculate the value of a perpetuity with growth.

Simple valuations use a limited amount of information. The chapter begins with multiple analysis that uses just a few numbers in the financial statements—sales, earnings, or book values, for example—and applies pricing multiples to these numbers. Asset-based valuation techniques are then introduced. These techniques attempt to value equities by summing the market value of the firms' assets, net of liabilities. We will see that asset-based valuation, though seemingly simple, is a doubtful exercise for most firms.

Simple methods run the risk of ignoring relevant information. A full-fledged fundamental analysis identifies all the information that is important and extracts the implications of that information for valuing the firm. The chapter concludes with a broad outline of fundamental analysis technologies that accomplish this. It leads you through the five steps involved and shows how financial statements are incorporated in the process. It stresses the importance of adopting a valuation model that captures value created in the firm and shows how that valuation model provides the architecture for fundamental analysis. The chapter distinguishes valuation models for terminal investments from those for going-concern investments (like business firms), and it shows how valuing going concerns raises particular problems. The chapter closes by describing the dividend discounting technique as an example of a method that typically does not work, thereby setting the stage for techniques that deal with the deficiencies, which we discuss in the later chapters.

This chapter is introductory. While The Analyst's Checklist for Chapter 3 indicates that there is much you will be able to do after reading this chapter, the primary goal of the chapter is to provoke your thinking as to what a good valuation technology looks like. With that thinking, you will be prepared to adopt such a technology in the next few chapters.

MULTIPLE ANALYSIS

An acceptable valuation technique must have benefits that outweigh the cost of using it, and its cost-benefit tradeoff must compare favorably with alternative techniques. A full-fledged fundamental analysis comes at some cost because it requires the analyst to consider a large amount of information, which involves considerable effort. We will develop ways of doing this as efficiently as possible but, before proceeding, we should consider shortcuts that avoid those costs. What is lost by taking an easier route? What is gained by taking the more difficult path? Multiple analysis is cheap because it uses minimal information.

A multiple is simply the ratio of the stock price to a particular number in the financial statements. The most common ratios multiply the important summary numbers in the statements—earnings, book values, sales, and cash flows—hence the price-earnings ratio (P/E), the price-to-book ratio (P/B), the price-to-sales ratio (P/S), and the ratio of price-to-cash flow from operations (P/CFO). By using one piece of information in the statements, these multiples are surely parsimonious in using financial statement information. One does not have to know much accounting to calculate these ratios.

Two techniques employ these multiples and variants on them; they are the method of comparables and multiple screening.

The Method of Comparables

The *method of comparables* or *multiple comparison analysis* works as follows:

1. Identify comparable firms that have operations similar to those of the target firm whose value is in question.

2. Identify measures for the comparable firms in their financial statements—earnings, book value, sales, cash flow—and calculate multiples of those measures at which the firms trade.

3. Apply these multiples to the corresponding measures for the target firm to get that firm's value.

We will attempt to value Dell Computer in April 2002 using the method of comparables. Table 3.1 lists the most recent annual sales, earnings, and the book value of equity

TABLE 3.1
Pricing Multiples for Comparable Firms to Dell Computer

	Sales	Earnings before Extraordinary Items	Book Value	Market Value	P/S	P/E	P/B
Hewlett-Packard Co.	$45,226	$ 624	$13,953	$32,963	0.73	52.8	2.4
Gateway Inc.	6,080	(1,290)	1,565	1,944	0.32	—	1.2
Dell Computer Corp.	31,168	1,246	4,694	?	?	?	?

Dollar figures in millions.

TABLE 3.2
Applying Comparable Firms' Multiples to Dell Computer

	Average Multiple for Comparables		Dell's Number		Dell's Valuation
Sales	0.53	×	31,168	=	$16,519
Earnings	52.8*	×	1,246	=	65,789
Book value	1.8	×	4,694	=	8,449
Average of valuations					30,252

Dollar figures in millions.
*HP only, because earnings for Gateway are negative (losses).

for Dell (from the 2002 financial statements in Chapter 2) and two firms that produce similar personal computer products, Hewlett-Packard Company (HP) and Gateway Inc. The price-to-sales (P/S), price-to-earnings (P/E), and price-to-book (P/B) ratios for HP and Gateway are based on their market values in April 2002. Dell is valued by applying the average of multiples for the comparison firms to Dell sales, earnings, and book values, as seen in Table 3.2. The three multiples give three different valuations for Dell, a bit awkward. So the valuations are averaged to give a market value of $30,252 million on 2,602 million shares, or $11.63 per share. The earnings multiple gives the highest valuation of $25.28 per share. Dell was trading at $27 per share in April 2002, more than the average value calculated here. Our analysis says sell.

These calculations are certainly minimal. But the valuation has probably left you a little uneasy. This is not a valuation that makes one feel secure.

Multiple comparison analysis is easy, but it's cheap in more than one sense of the word. Indeed, there's a real fallacy here. If we have the prices of the comps, we can calculate a value for Dell. But if we want to get a value for Gateway (say), would we use the calculated value of $11.63 per share for Dell? This would be circular because Dell's price is based on Gateway's price. The analysis is not anchored in something fundamental that tells us about value independently of prices. It assumes that the market is efficient in setting prices for the comparables. But if this is the case, why doubt that the $27 market price for Dell is also efficient and go through the exercise? If the comps are mispriced, then the exercise is doubtful.

This method is used extensively and there are situations in which it is justified. If the target firm is a private or thinly traded firm with no reliable traded price, we might get a quick feel for the value of its equity from the comparables, but only if their stocks are efficiently priced. We might also be interested in the price at which a stock should trade, whether that price is efficient or not. Investment bankers floating initial public

Does the Method of Comparables Promote Pyramid Schemes?

3.1

Periodically, initial public offerings for particular types of firms become "hot." The 1990s bull market saw hot issues for theme restaurants, technology and computer stocks, brand fashion houses, and Internet stocks. In a hot IPO market, firms sell for high multiples, encouraging comparable firms to go public also. Investment bankers justify the price of an offering on the basis of multiples received in an earlier offering. If they raise the multiples a little, to get the IPO business, a pyramid scheme can develop, with offering prices based on increasing comparable prices without reference to fundamental value.

In 1995 and 1996, teleservicing firms—firms supplying telemarketing and customer service—were offered to the market. In anticipation of other firms outsourcing these functions to the new firms, investors paid high prices in the IPOs. The pyramiding occurred. Lehman Brothers co-managed one

of the initial offers but lost out to other investment banks in handling later IPOs. Quoted in *The Wall Street Journal* on September 15, 1998, Jeffrey Kessler of Lehman Brothers said, "Every time we came out with what we thought was a reasonable valuation for a new IPO in this area, the winning bidder had valuations that were way higher. We were outbid [by other investment banks] by, in some cases, over five multiple points, and we scratched our heads and said this was crazy."

Indeed, the stock prices of teleservicing firms dropped dramatically after the IPO boom. A pyramiding IPO market is another stock price bubble. Pricing IPOs on the basis of the speculative price multiples of comparable firms perpetuates the bubble. Beware of prices estimated from comparables, for you may join a chain letter (a pyramid scheme) that leads you to pay too much for a stock.

offerings (IPOs) use the method of comparables to estimate the price at which the market might value the issue. If the market is mispricing the comps, they estimate it will misprice the IPO also. In litigation for loss of value (in shareholder class action or minority interest suits, for example), the question often asked is what price the stock would have traded at if certain events had or had not occurred, not what it's really worth. But deferring to market prices without a sense of fundamental value can be dangerous. See Box 3.1.

Conceptual problems aside, the method of comparables also has problems in implementation:

- Identifying comps with the same operating characteristics is difficult. Firms are typically matched on industry, product, size, and some measure of risk, but no two firms are exactly alike. For example, one might argue that Hewlett-Packard, with its printer business, is not the same type of firm as Dell. Comps are usually competitors in the same industry that might dominate (or be dominated by) the target firm and thus not be comparable. Increasing the number of comps might average out errors, but the more comps there are, the less homogeneous they are likely to be.

- Different multiples give different valuations. Applying a comp's P/B ratio to the target's book value yields a different price from applying the comp's P/E ratio to the target's earnings, as we just saw with Dell. Which price should we use? In the example we simply took an arithmetic average, but it is not clear that this is correct.

- Negative denominators can occur. When the comp has a loss, the P/E has little meaning, as with Gateway in Table 3.1.

Other multiples are used in comparison analysis. Some adjust for differences in leverage between firms and some adjust for differences in accounting principle. See Box 3.2.

In carrying out multiple analysis the analyst should have a feel for what typical multiples look like, as a benchmark. Table 3.3 lists percentiles for a number of ratios for all

LEVERAGE ADJUSTMENTS

Some multiples are affected by leverage—the amount of debt financing a firm has relative to equity financing. So, to control for differences in leverage between the target firm and comparison firms, these multiples are "unlevered." Typical **unlevered measures** are

$$\text{Unlevered price/sales ratio} = \frac{\text{Market value of equity} + \text{Net debt}}{\text{Sales}}$$

$$\text{Unlevered price/ebit} = \frac{\text{Market value of equity} + \text{Net debt}}{\text{ebit}}$$

where ebit = earnings before interest and taxes (earnings plus interest and tax expenses). Net debt is total debt obligations less any interest-bearing securities that the firm may hold as assets. Typically the book value of net debt is taken as an approximation of its market value. The numerator in these ratios is the market value of the firm, sometimes referred to as the *unlevered value* or *enterprise value*. Unlevered ratios are sometimes referred to as *enterprise multiples*. Price-to-sales and price-to-ebit ratios should be calculated as unleveled ratios because leverage does not produce sales or earnings before interest and taxes.

ACCOUNTING ADJUSTMENTS

As their denominators are accounting numbers, multiples are often adjusted for aspects of the accounting that may differ between firms. Depreciation and amortization methods can differ and some analysts feel that depreciation and amortization are not well measured in income statements. A ratio that adjusts for both leverage and the accounting for these expenses is

$$\text{Unlevered price/ebitda} = \frac{\text{Market value of equity} + \text{Net debt}}{\text{ebitda}}$$

where ebitda = earnings before interest, taxes, depreciation, and amortization (ebit plus depreciation and amortization ex-

pense). Sometimes, ebitda is referred to as "cash flow" (from operations) but, as we will see in Chapter 4, it is only an approximation of cash flow.

Earnings can be affected by one-time events that are particular to one firm. So multiples are adjusted to remove the effects of these events on earnings:

$$\text{Price/earnings before unusual items} = \frac{\text{Market value of equity}}{\text{Earnings before unusual items}}$$

VARIATIONS OF THE P/E RATIO

The trailing P/E ratio compares the stock price to the most recently reported annual earnings. Alternatives are

$$\text{Rolling P/E} = \frac{\text{Price per share}}{\text{Sum of eps for most recent four quarters}}$$

$$\text{Forward or leading P/E} = \frac{\text{Price per share}}{\text{Forecast of next year's eps}}$$

The forward P/E, usually calculated with analysts' forecasts, modifies the trailing P/E for anticipated earnings growth in the coming year.

Price in the numerator of the trailing P/E is affected by dividends: Dividends reduce share prices because value is taken out of the firm. But earnings in the denominator are not affected by dividends. So P/E ratios can differ because of differing dividend payouts. To correct for this difference, trailing P/E ratios are calculated as

$$\text{Dividend-adjusted P/E} = \frac{\text{Price per share} + \text{Annual dps}}{\text{eps}}$$

where dps is dividends per share. The numerator is the **cum-dividend price,** the price before the dividend is paid; the price after the dividend is paid is the **ex-dividend price**.

The web page gives some examples of multiple calculations.

U.S. listed firms for the years 1963–2000. You can see from the table that the median P/B (at the 50th percentile) is 1.5, the median P/E is 17.5, and the median price-to-sales (P/S) ratio is 0.6. Further back in time (to the 1970s), multiples were lower. On the other hand, multiples in the 1990s were considerably higher than historical ratios. You will find more detail on historical multiples on the book's web page.

TABLE 3.3 Percentiles of Common Price Multiples, 1963–2000, for U.S. Listed Firms

				Multiple				
Percentile	P/B	Standard P/E	Forward P/E	P/S	Unlevered P/S	P/CFO	Unlevered P/ebitda	Unlevered P/ebit
95	7.4	Negative earnings	41.7	4.1	4.8	Negative cash flow	120.4	Negative ebit
75	2.5	29.4	19.2	1.3	1.7	21.9	10.0	15.8
50	1.5	17.5	14.3	0.6	0.8	10.0	6.8	9.9
25	0.9	12.3	10.9	0.3	0.4	5.8	4.7	6.6
5	0.5	7.6	7.3	0.1	0.2	2.5	2.6	3.3

Notes: CFO is cash flow from operations. Firms with negative denominators are treated as high multiple firms. Thus firms in the upper percentiles of P/E, P/CFO, and P/ebit are those with negative earnings (losses), cash flows, or ebit, as indicated.

Source: Calculated from Standard & Poor's COMPUSTAT data. Leading P/E ratios are based on consensus analysts' one-year-ahead earnings forecasts, as reported in J. Liu, D. Nissim, and J. Thomas, "Equity Valuation Using Multiples," *Journal of Accounting Research,* March 2002, p. 146, for the years 1982–1999. P/CFO ratios cover the period 1987–2000 only.

Screening on Multiples

The method of comparables takes the view that similar firms should have similar multiples. One would expect this to be the case if market prices were efficient. Investors who doubt that the market prices fundamentals correctly, however, construe multiples a little differently: If firms trade at different multiples, they may be mispriced. This idea leads to screening stocks for buying and selling on the basis of their relative multiples.

Here is how *screening* works in its simplest form:

1. Identify a multiple on which to screen stocks.

2. Rank stocks on that multiple, from highest to lowest.

3. Buy stocks with the lowest multiples and (short) sell stocks with the highest multiples.

Screening on multiples is referred to as *fundamental screening* because multiples price fundamental features of the firm. Box 3.3 contrasts fundamental screening with *technical screening.*

Screening on multiples presumes that stocks whose prices are high relative to a particular fundamental are overpriced and stocks whose prices are low relative to a fundamental are underpriced. Stocks with high multiples are sometimes referred to as **glamour stocks** for, it is claimed, investors view them as glamorous or fashionable and, too enthusiastically, drive up their prices relative to fundamentals. In contrast, stocks with low multiples are sometimes called **contrarian stocks** for they are stocks that have been ignored by the fashion herd. Contrarian investors run against the herd, so they buy unglamorous low multiple stocks and sell glamour stocks. Low multiple stocks are also called **value stocks** because their value is deemed to be high relative to their price.

Fundamental screening is a cheap fundamental analysis. You accept the denominator of the screen as an indicator of intrinsic value and accept the spread between price and this number as an indicator of mispricing. It uses little information, which is an advantage. It's quick-stop shopping for bargains. It may be cost effective if a full-blown fundamental analysis is too expensive, but it can lead you astray if that one number is not a

TECHNICAL SCREENS

Technical screens identify positions on the basis of indicators that relate to trading. Some common ones are:

Price screens: Buy stocks whose prices have dropped a lot relative to the market (sometimes called "losers") and sell stocks whose prices have increased a lot (sometimes called "winners"). The rationale: Large price movements can be deviations from fundamentals that will reverse.

Small-stocks screens: Buy stocks with a low market value (price per share times shares outstanding). The rationale: History has shown that small stocks typically earn higher returns.

Neglected-stock screens: Buy stocks that are not followed by many analysts. The rationale: These stocks are underpriced because the investor "herd" which follows fashions has deemed them uninteresting.

Seasonal screens: Buy stocks at a certain time of year, for example, in early January. The rationale: History shows that stock returns tend to be higher at these times.

Momentum screens: Buy stocks that have had increases in stock prices. The rationale: The momentum will continue.

Insider-trading screens: Mimic the trading of insiders (who must file details of their trades with the Securities and Exchange Commission). The rationale: Insiders have inside information that they use in trading.

FUNDAMENTAL SCREENS

Fundamental screens compare price to a particular number in firms' financial statements. Typical fundamental screens are:

Price-to-earnings (P/E) screens: Buy firms with low P/E ratios and sell firms with high P/E ratios.

Price-to-book value (P/B) screens: Buy firms with low P/B and sell firms with high P/B.

Price-to-cash flow (P/CFO) screens: Buy low price relative to cash flow from operations, sell high P/CFO.

Price-to-dividend (P/d) screens: Buy low P/d, sell high P/d.

The web page for this chapter discusses these screens in more detail and directs you to screening engines.

good indicator of intrinsic value. For this reason, some screeners combine strategies to exploit more information: Buy firms with low P/E and low P/B (two-stop shopping), or buy small firms with low P/B and prior price declines (three-stop shopping), for example.

Figure 3.1 depicts five-year returns from investing in nine portfolios of stocks selected on the basis on high, low, and middle ranges of past sales growth and cash flow-to-price ratios. The investment strategy conjectures that the market overprices firms with high sales growth (glamour stocks) and underprices firms with high cash flow relative to price (low P/CFO firms). Clearly, the two-stop shopping would have paid off. In particular, investing in stocks with high cash flow-to-price but low growth in sales (unglamorous stocks with good cash flow) was especially profitable. Similar patterns are found for glamour stocks matched against stocks with low price-to-earnings or book value: Investors who buy unglamorous stocks with low prices to fundamentals do better than those who jump on the bandwagon.

But danger lurks! By buying high cash flow-to-price firms with low growth in sales, you could be taking on risk. The returns in Figure 3.1 could derive from high cash flow-to-price firms being very risky and firms with high growth in sales having low risk. So the strategy just rewards you for taking on risk. Figure 3.2 displays returns from investing in high cash flow-to-price stocks and shorting high growth-in-sales stocks each year from 1968 to 1989. Returns were negative in 3 of the 22 years, so there is some risk in the strategy. These years were not recession years (R in the figure) or years when the overall stock market declined (D). Therefore, the returns are not related to the economy. But they could be related to some other risk factor.

FIGURE 3.1
Returns to two fundamental screens, 1968–1989.
Compounded five-year returns for portfolios formed on the basis of cash flow-to-price ratio and growth in sales. Stocks are independently sorted in ascending order into three groups: (1) bottom 30 percent, (2) middle 40 percent, and (3) top 30 percent, based on cash flow-to-price and growth in sales.

Source: Lakonishok, Shleifer, and Vishny, "Contrarian Investment, Extrapolation, and Risk," *Journal of Finance,* December 1994, p. 1554.

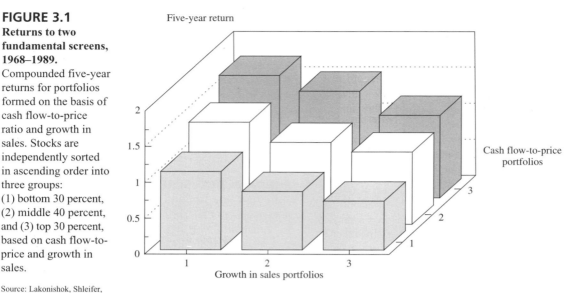

FIGURE 3.2
Year-by-year returns to the cash flow-to-price and growth-in-sales strategy, 1968–1989.
R indicates recession years, identified by the National Bureau of Economic Research, and *D* indicates years in which the stock market declined.

Source: Lakonishok, Shleifer, and Vishny, "Contrarian Investment, Extrapolation, and Risk," *Journal of Finance,* December 1994, p. 1566.

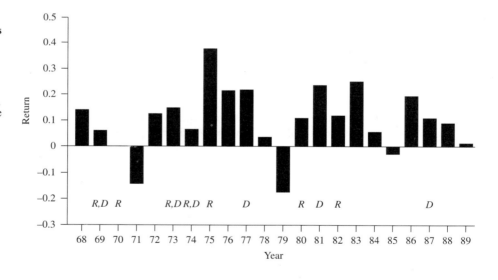

There is a further caveat in running these investment strategies: They use very little information—only two pieces of financial statement information in the two-stop shopping case—and ignoring information has costs. By relying on little information, the trader is in danger of trading with someone who knows more than he, someone who's done her homework on the payoffs a stock is likely to yield. A low P/E stock could be overpriced and a high P/E stock could be underpriced. In such cases, the trader might get caught in the wrong position. The solution to the information problem is to build in a model of anticipations that incorporates all the information about payoffs. This is the subject of formal fundamental analysis, which produces the intrinsic value. And it is the subject that we begin to develop in this chapter.

ASSET-BASED VALUATION

Asset-based valuation estimates a firm's value by identifying and summing the value of its assets. The value of the equity is then calculated by deducting the value of debt: Value of the equity = Value of the firm − Value of the debt. It looks alluringly simple: Identify the assets, get a valuation for each, add them up, and deduct the value of debt.

A firm's balance sheet adds up assets and liabilities, and stockholders' equity equals total assets minus total liabilities, as we saw in Chapter 2. That chapter explained that some assets and liabilities are marked to market. Debt and equity investments are carried at "fair" market value (if part of a trading portfolio or if they are "available for sale"). Liabilities are typically carried close to market value on balance sheets and, in any case, market values of many liabilities can be discovered in financial statement footnotes. Cash and receivables are close to their value (though net receivables involve estimates that may be suspect). However, the bulk of assets that generate value are recorded at amortized historical cost, which usually does not reflect the value of the payoffs expected from them. (Refer back to Box 2.3.)

Further, there may be so-called intangible assets—such as brand assets, knowledge assets, and managerial assets—missing from the balance sheet because accountants find their values too hard to measure under the GAAP "reliability" criterion. Accountants give these assets a value of zero. In Dell's case this is probably the major source of the difference between market value and book value. The firm has a brand name that may be worth more than its tangible assets combined. It has what is hailed as a unique built-to-order production technology. It has marketing networks and distribution channels that generate value. But none of these assets are on the balance sheet.

Asset-based valuation attempts to redo the balance sheet by (1) getting current market values for assets and liabilities listed on the balance sheet and (2) identifying omitted assets and assigning a market value to them. Is this a cheap way out of the valuation problem? The accounting profession has essentially given up on this idea and placed it in the "too difficult" basket. Accountants point out that asset valuation presents some very difficult problems:

- Assets listed on the balance sheet may not be traded often, so market values may not be readily available.

- Market values, if available, might not be efficient measures of intrinsic value if markets for the assets are imperfect.

- Market values, if available, may not represent the value in the particular use to which the asset is put in the firm. One might establish either the current replacement price for an asset or its current selling price (its liquidation value), but neither of these may be indicative of its value in a particular going concern. A building used in computer manufacturing may not have the same value when used for warehousing groceries.

- The omitted assets must be identified for their market value to be determined. What is the brand-name asset? The knowledge asset? What are the omitted assets on Dell's balance sheet? The very term "intangible asset" indicates a difficulty in measuring value.

Asset-based valuation is used to determine the **breakup value** of a firm. While understanding the value of the firm as a going concern, the investor must always ask whether the assets are worth more as a going concern or broken up. If their breakup value is greater, the firm should be liquidated. Some of the large takeover and restructuring activity of the late 1980s came about when takeover specialists saw that a takeover target's assets were worth more broken up than as a whole. This assessment requires a discovery of the liquidation value (selling prices) of assets.

Fundamental analysis estimates value from utilizing assets in a going-concern business. A comparison of this value with breakup value recognizes the maxim that "Value depends on the business strategy." Proceeding as a going concern is just one strategy for using assets, selling them is another, and the value of the two strategies must be compared.

Those who estimate the value of brand assets and knowledge assets have a difficult task. Accountants list intangible assets on the balance sheet only when they have been purchased in the market, because only then is an objective market valuation available.

- Even if individual assets can be valued, the sum of the market values of all identified assets may not (and probably will not) be equal to the value of the assets in total. Assets are used jointly. Indeed, entrepreneurs create firms to combine assets in a unique way to generate value. The value of the "synergy" asset is elusive. Determining the intrinsic value of the firm—the value of the assets combined—is the valuation issue.

Asset-based valuations are feasible in a few instances. For example, we might value an investment fund that invests only in traded stocks by adding up the market values of those stocks. But even in this case, the firm may be worth more than this balance sheet value if one of its assets is the fund's ability to earn superior investment returns. And the market values of the fund's stocks may not be efficient ones—which will be the case if the fund managers can pick mispriced stocks. Asset-based analysis is sometimes applied when a firm's main asset is a natural resource—an oil field, a mineral deposit, or timberlands, for example. Indeed these firms are sometimes called *asset-based companies.* Proven reserves (of oil or minerals) or board feet (of timber) are estimated and priced out at the current market price for the resource, with a discount for estimated extraction costs. See Box 3.4 for an application of asset-based valuation.

Asset-based valuation is not a cheap way to value firms. In fact, it's typically so difficult that it becomes very expensive. This is why accountants dodge it. The difficulty highlights the need for fundamental analysis. The problem of valuing firms is really a problem of the imperfect balance sheet. Fundamental analysis involves forecasting payoffs to get an intrinsic value that corrects for the missing value in the balance sheet. Coca-Cola has a large brand asset that is not on the balance sheet. Therefore, it trades at a high premium over book value. But we will see in this book that the premium can be estimated with fundamental analysis.

FUNDAMENTAL ANALYSIS

The value of a share in a firm is based on the future payoffs that it is expected to deliver, so one cannot avoid forecasting payoffs if one is to do a thorough job in valuing shares. Payoffs are forecasted from information, so one cannot avoid analyzing information. **Fundamental analysis** is the method of analyzing information, forecasting payoffs from that

FIGURE 3.3

The Process of Fundamental Analysis

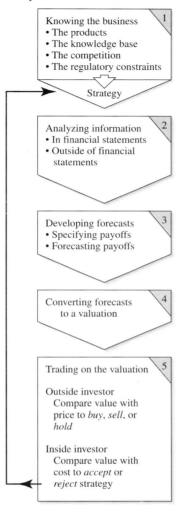

information, and arriving at a valuation based on those forecasts. The method of comparables and screening analysis use little information and avoid forecasting. That makes these methods simple, but their simplicity comes at the cost of ignoring information.

The Process of Fundamental Analysis

Figure 3.3 outlines the process of fundamental analysis. Fundamental analysis produces an estimate of the value of an investment. In the last step in the diagram, Step 5, this value is compared with the price of investing. This step is the *investment decision.* For the investor outside of the firm, the price of investing is the market price of the stock to be traded. If the valuation is greater than the market price, the analysis says *buy;* if less, *sell.* If the warranted value equals the market price, the analyst concludes that the market in the particular investment is efficient. In the analysts' jargon this is a *hold.* For the investor inside the firm, the price of investing is the cost of the investment. If the calculated value of a strategy or investment proposal is greater than the cost, value is added. The analyst says (in the parlance of project evaluation) *accept* the strategy or the proposal if it is greater than the cost, if less, *reject.*

Steps 1–4 in the diagram show how to get the valuation for this investment decision. The value of an investment is based on the payoffs it is likely to yield, so forecasting payoffs (in Step 3) is at the heart of fundamental analysis. Forecasts cannot be made without identifying and analyzing the information that indicates those payoffs, so information analysis (in Step 2) precedes forecasting. And information cannot be interpreted unless one knows the business and the strategy the firm has adopted to produce payoffs (Step 1).

1. *Knowing the business.* Chapter 1 stressed that understanding the business is a prerequisite to valuing the business. An important element is the firm's strategy to add value. The analyst outside the firm values a given strategy, following the steps in the diagram, and adjusts the valuation as the firm modifies its strategy. The analyst inside the firm is, of course, involved in the formulation of strategy, so she proceeds through the steps to test for the value that alternative strategies might add. So you see a feedback loop in Figure 3.3: Once a strategy has been selected, that strategy becomes the one under which the business is valued as a going concern.

2. *Analyzing information.* With a background knowledge of the business, the valuation of a particular strategy begins with an analysis of information about the business. The in-

formation comes in many forms and from many sources. There is typically a vast amount of information to be dealt with, from "hard" dollar numbers in the financial statements like sales, cash flows, and earnings, to "soft" qualitative information on consumer tastes, technological change, and the quality of management. Efficiency is needed in organizing this information for forecasting. Relevant information needs to be distinguished from the irrelevant, and financial statements need to be dissected to extract information for forecasting.

3. *Developing forecasts.* For a shareholder, payoffs come in the form of future dividends and the amount received when the share is sold. But these payoffs are determined by the future success of operations, by selling products for more than it costs to produce them. So the analyst forecasts payoffs from operations.

   Payoffs from operations have to be measured. Are they cash inflows minus cash outflows (net cash flow)? Are they revenues minus expenses (net income)? If so, how is revenue measured and how is expense measured? Specifying and measuring the payoffs is critical to valuation analysis. It is an accounting issue.

   Developing forecasts thus has two steps, as indicated in Step 3 in Figure 3.3. First, specify how payoffs are measured. Then, forecast the specified payoffs. The first step is a nontrivial one, as the validity of a valuation will always depend on how payoffs from operations are measured.

4. *Converting the forecast to a valuation.* Operations pay off over many years, so typically forecasts are made for a stream of future payoffs. To complete the analysis, the stream of expected payoffs has to be reduced to one number, the valuation. Since payoffs are in the future and investors prefer value now rather than in the future, expected payoffs must be discounted for the time value of money. Payoffs are uncertain; there is a chance they will prove considerably worse or better than expected. So, as investors typically prefer less risky expected payoffs to more risky ones, expected payoffs also must be discounted for risk. Therefore, the final step involves combining a stream of expected payoffs into one number in a way that adjusts them for the time value of money and for risk. See Box 3.5.

5. *The investment decision: Trading on the valuation.* The outside investor decides to trade securities by comparing their estimated value to their price. The inside investor compares the estimated value of an investment to its cost. In both cases, the comparison yields the **value added** by the investment. So, rather than comparing price to one piece of information, as in a simple multiple, price is compared to a value number that incorporates all the information used in forecasting. That is, the fundamental analyst screens stocks on their P/V ratios—price-to-value ratios—rather than on a P/E or P/B ratio.

An analyst can specialize in any one of these steps or a combination of them. The analyst needs to get a sense of where in the process his comparative advantage lies, where he can get an edge on his competition. When buying advice from an analyst, the investor needs to know just what the analyst's particular skill is. Is it in knowing a great deal about the business (Step 1)? Is it in discovering and analyzing information (Step 2)? Is it in developing good forecasts from the information (Step 3)? Is it in inferring value from the forecasts (Step 4)? Or is it the function of developing trading strategies from the analysis while minimizing trading costs (Step 5)? An analyst might be a very good earnings forecaster, for example, but might not be good at indicating the intrinsic value implied by the forecast.

Having forecasted payoffs, the investor asks: How much should I pay for the expected payoffs? In answering this question, he understands that he must cover his costs. He has two costs in making the investment. First, he loses interest on the money invested (he loses the "time value of money") and, second, he takes on risk (the cost of possibly losing some or all of his investment). These two costs determine his **required return**, sometimes referred to as his **cost of capital**, sometimes as the **normal return**:

Required return = Risk-free interest return + Premium for risk

So, if one can earn 5 percent on a risk-free investment (like a U.S. government obligation or a government-guaranteed savings account) but requires 10 percent to invest in a firm, one is requiring a 5 percent premium as compensation for risk. The value received from making an investment must compensate the investor for both risk and the time value of money. Therefore, in converting forecasted payoffs to a valuation, the payoffs must be adjusted for the required return. There are two ways of doing this in a valuation model.

1. DISCOUNTING PAYOFFS

Value can be determined by *discounting* expected payoffs at 1 plus the required return. So, the value of an expected cash payoff one period in the future is:

$$\text{Value} = \text{Present value of expected cash flow}$$

$$= \frac{\text{Expected cash flow one year ahead}}{1 + \text{Required return}}$$

So, for an investment of $100 in a savings account that earns 5 percent per year and is to be held for one year, the expected payoff one year ahead is $105, and the value at the beginning of the year is

$$\text{Value} = \frac{\$105}{1.05}$$

$$= \$100$$

which, of course, is what the savings account is worth. The expected cash flow of $105 is discounted by 1.0 + 0.05 = 1.05. The amount 1.05 is the cost of each dollar of investment because it is the (opportunity) cost of not investing a dollar in a similar account (with the same risk) at 5 percent. You will recognize the mechanics here as the standard *present value formula* for one period. Because the formula involves discounting to present value, the required return is

sometimes referred to as the **discount rate.** Note that, the higher the discount rate, the lower the discounted value of the payoff. That is, the higher the cost is in terms of lost interest and risk, the lower is the amount the investor should pay for a dollar of payoff.

2. CAPITALIZING PAYOFFS

Some payoffs are *capitalized* rather than discounted. Capitalization divides the forecast by the required return, rather than 1 plus the required return:

$$\text{Value} = \frac{\text{Expected payoff}}{\text{Required return}}$$

For a savings account, we can specify the payoffs as the earnings on the account rather than the total cash payoff at the end of the holding period. For a $100 savings account, expected earnings for one year (at 5 percent) are $5, and the required return is 5 percent. So,

$$\text{Value} = \frac{\$5}{0.05}$$

$$= \$100$$

The earnings are capitalized at 0.05 rather than 1.05, for 5 cents is the (opportunity) cost of a dollar of earnings lost from not investing in a similar account. In this context, the required return is referred to as the **capitalization rate.** Note that, as with discounting, the higher the required return, the lower the capitalized value of the payoff.

We will see when payoffs are to be discounted and when they are to be capitalized, but note for the moment that total cash payoffs are discounted while earnings are capitalized. The savings account examples here are for payoffs over one period, but discounting and capitalization apply to a stream of payoffs over a number of periods in much the same way, as we will see.

THE REQUIRED RETURN

Clearly, one needs a measure of the required return to complete a valuation. While the required return for a savings account is straightforward, calculating the required return for equities is nontrivial. Discounting or capitalizing expected payoffs is a mechanical exercise that can be left to a spreadsheet program once the required return is known. The substantive aspect of Step 4 is the measurement of the required return. The appendix to this chapter deals with the estimation of the required return.

Financial Statement Analysis, Pro Forma Analysis, and Fundamental Analysis

Financial statements are usually thought of as a place to find information about firms, and indeed we have seen them as such in the "analyzing information" step above. But financial statements play another important role in fundamental analysis.

We have recognized that forecasting payoffs to investments is at the heart of fundamental analysis. Future earnings are the payoffs that analysts forecast, and future earnings will be reported in future income statements. Cash flows might also be forecast, and cash flows will be reported in future cash flow statements. So financial statements are not only information to help in forecasting; they are also what is to be forecast. Figure 3.4 gives a picture of how financial statements are used in valuation.

Along with earnings and cash flows, the financial statements report many line items that explain how firms produce earnings and cash flows. The income statement gives sales, the costs of production, and other expenses necessary to make the sales. The cash flow statement gives the sources of the cash flows. The balance sheet lists the assets employed to generate earnings and cash. Financial statements, in the jargon of valuation analysis, give the "drivers" of earnings and cash flows. So they provide a way of thinking about how to build up a forecast, a framework for forecasting. If we think of the line items in the financial statements—sales, expenses, assets employed—we will understand the value generation. And if we forecast the complete, detailed statements, we will forecast the factors that drive earnings and cash flows, and so construct forecasts.

Forecasting future financial statements is called **pro forma analysis** because it involves preparing pro forma financial statements for the future. A pro forma statement is one that will be reported if expectations are met. Forecasting is at the heart of fundamental analysis and pro forma analysis is at the heart of forecasting. Accordingly, fundamental analysis is a matter of developing pro forma (future) financial statements and converting these pro formas into a valuation. This perspective also directs the analysis of current financial statements. Current financial statements are information for forecasting, so they are analyzed with the purpose of forecasting future financial statements.

FIGURE 3.4

How financial statements are used in valuation. The analyst forecasts future financial statements and converts forecasts in the future financial statements to a valuation. Current financial statements are used to extract information for forecasting.

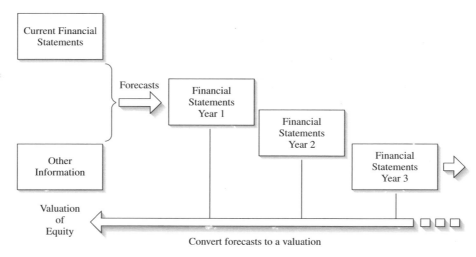

THE ARCHITECTURE OF FUNDAMENTAL ANALYSIS: THE VALUATION MODEL

As Figure 3.3 illustrates, fundamental analysis is a process that transforms your knowledge of the business (Step 1) into a valuation and trading strategy (Step 5). Steps 2, 3, and 4 accomplish the transformation. These three steps are guided by the **valuation model** that the analyst adopts. Forecasting is at the heart of analysis, and the analyst cannot begin the analysis without specifying what's to be forecast. The valuation model specifies the payoffs and, accordingly, directs Step 3—the forecasting step—of fundamental analysis. But it also directs Step 2—information analysis—because the relevant information for forecasting can be identified only after defining what is to be forecast. And, it tells the analyst how to do Step 4—converting forecasts to a valuation. So the valuation model provides the architecture for valuation, and a good or poor valuation technology rides on the particular valuation model adopted.

Box 3.5 contains two valuation models. The first involves forecasting cash flows (Step 3) and discounting those cash flows (Step 4), and the implied information analysis (Step 2) is that which forecasts cash flows. The second involves forecasting earnings (Step 3) and capitalizing those earnings (Step 4), and the implied information analysis (Step 2) is that which forecasts earnings. Both work for a savings account. In the next chapter we question whether both work for equities.

Good practice comes from good thinking. Valuation models embed the concepts regarding how firms generate value. Firms are complex organizations and inferring the value they generate from their many activities requires some orderly thinking. Valuation models supply that thinking. A valuation model is a tool for understanding the business and its strategy. With that understanding, the model is used to translate knowledge of the business into a valuation of the business.

Investment bankers and equity research groups typically have a common discipline, an in-house approach to valuation, that articulates their valuation model. An investment consultant's valuation model is often at the center of its marketing. There are many models being promoted. At one time discounted cash flow (DCF) models were the rage. But now many models focus on "economic profit" and refer to particular economic factors—"value drivers," "fade rates," "franchise factors," and "competitive advantage periods," for example. Are these gimmicks? To what extent, and how, do these factors actually create value? How does one choose between the different models? These are questions that a potential client must ask. And the vendor of the valuation model must have a satisfying answer. The valuation model is at the heart of equity research, and the analyst must have a valuation model that survives scrutiny.

Valuation models calculate the value effects of business activities, and so they also are at the heart of the analysis of strategy within the firm. Firms sometimes hire consultants to aid in strategic analysis and many consultants come with their proprietary models, all with a focus on generating shareholder value. Product names are promoted in their advertising, usually capitalized with symbols indicating they are trade names. There is Value-Based Management from Marakon Associates, Economic Value Added from Stern Stewart & Company, CFROI (Cash Flow Return on Investment) from Holt Value Associates, Economic Profit Model from McKinsey & Co., Value Builder from Pricewaterhouse-Coopers, and Economic Value Management from KPMG, to name a few. These models also are used to measure performance and to reward management on value added after a strategy has been implemented. A CFO deferring to a consultant must recognize the features of a good technology and examine the consultant's model, and the consultant selling

EXHIBIT 3.1

Extract from an equity research report on Electrolux.

Analysts forecast a variety of attributes. Which forecast should be used for valuation?

Source: Reprinted with permission by Carnegie Holding AB, Stockholm.

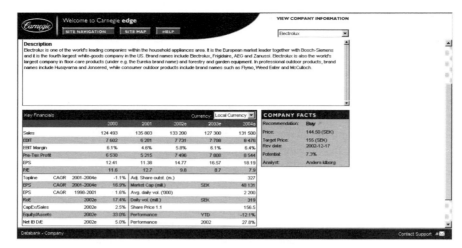

the technology must ensure that it passes scrutiny. Does it capture value added? Does it gain an edge on competitors?

Value management products supposedly forecast "economic profit" or "economic value added." But economic profit is a concept, not a measure. These models really forecast an accounting measure of payoffs—or value added—from operations. Most of these products are similar in form but differ in how value added is accounted for. And, in common, the proponent of each model claims that its measure of value added is superior to the GAAP accounting measure of value added, the GAAP earnings that analysts forecast.

The disciplined equity analyst prepares an equity research report with a valuation model in mind. The standard analyst's report nearly always includes forecasts. For example, Exhibit 3.1 is an extract taken from an equity research report on Electrolux, a Swedish household appliance manufacturer, prepared in 2002 by Carnegie Group, an investment banking, brokerage, and asset management firm based in Stockholm, Sweden. The buy recommendation (from Step 5 in Figure 3.3) is clearly displayed and is supported by forecasts of sales, ebit, ebit margin, eps, return on equity (ROE), and a number of ratios. These forecasts are the analyst's product from Step 3. Supporting text and analysis pertinent to Step 2 came with the report but, as with most reports, it is not clear how the analyst got from the forecasts to the recommendation and what forecasts (Step 3) were relied upon. Was it future sales, ebit, earnings, or return on equity? How was the chosen forecast converted to a valuation in Step 4? What valuation model did the analyst have in mind?

Answering the question of what is to be forecast is the central question in building a valuation model, for forecasting is at the heart of fundamental analysis. To start you thinking about an appropriate valuation model, refer to Figure 3.5. Suppose you make an investment now with the intention of selling it at some time in the future. Your payoff from the investment will come from the total cash it yields, and this arises from two sources: the cash that the investment pays while you are holding it and the cash you get from selling it. These payoffs are depicted for two types of investments on the time line in Figure 3.5. This line starts at the time the investment is made (time zero) and covers T periods, where T is referred to as the **investment horizon**. Investors typically think in terms of annual returns, so think of the periods in the figure as years.

The first investment in the figure is an investment for a fixed term, a **terminal investment**. A bond is an example. It pays a cash flow (CF) in the form of coupon interest each year and a terminal cash flow at maturity. Investment in a single asset—a rental building,

FIGURE 3.5
Periodic payoffs to investing. The first investment is for a terminal investment; the second is for a going-concern investment in a stock. The investments are made at time zero and held for T periods when they terminate or are liquidated.

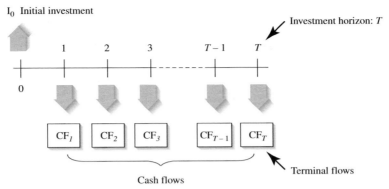

For a terminal investment:

I_0 Initial investment

Investment horizon: T

Cash flows

Terminal flows

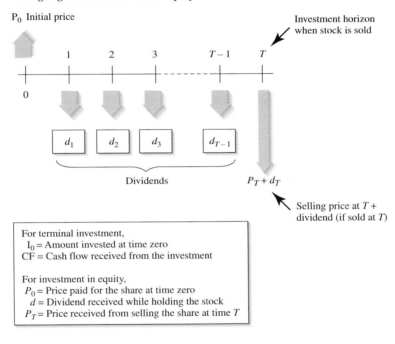

For a going-concern investment in equity:

P_0 Initial price

Investment horizon when stock is sold

Dividends

$P_T + d_T$

Selling price at T + dividend (if sold at T)

For terminal investment,
  I_0 = Amount invested at time zero
  CF = Cash flow received from the investment

For investment in equity,
  P_0 = Price paid for the share at time zero
  d = Dividend received while holding the stock
  P_T = Price received from selling the share at time T

for example—is another. It pays off periodic cash flows (in rents) and a final cash flow when the asset is scrapped. The second investment in the figure differs from a bond or a single asset in that it doesn't terminate. This is a feature of investment in an equity share of a firm. Firms are usually considered to be **going concerns**, that is, to go on indefinitely. There is no terminal date and no liquidating payoff that can be forecast. However, an investor may terminate her investment at some time T in the future by selling the share. This leaves her with the problem of forecasting her terminal payoff. For an investment in equity, P_0 is the price paid for the share and $d_1, d_2, d_3, \ldots, d_T$ are the dividends paid each year by the firm. The dividends are the periodic cash flow payoffs like the coupon on a bond. P_T is the terminal payoff, the price from selling the share. We consider

FIGURE 3.6

Cash flows for a $1,000, five-year, 10 percent p.a. coupon bond and a five-year investment project.
In both cases a cash investment is made at time 0 and cash flows are received over five subsequent years. The investments terminate at the end of Year 5.

For a bond:

Periodic cash coupon	$100	$100	$100	$100	$100
Cash at redemption					$1,000
Purchase price ($1,080)					
Time, *t* 0	1	2	3	4	5

For a project:

Periodic cash flow	$430	$460	$460	$380	$250
Salvage value					$120
Initial investment ($1,200)					
Time, *t* 0	1	2	3	4	5

both terminal investments and going-concern investments in this book, but we focus on going-concern equity investments.

Following the mechanics for the savings account in Box 3.5, we know that the payoffs for the two types of investments must be converted to a valuation with the required return. In this book, we will represent 1 + the required return (used in discounting) by the symbol, ρ. So, if the required return is 5 percent (as for the savings account), $\rho = 1 + 0.05 = 1.05$. When we talk of the required return, we will denote it as $\rho - 1$, so the required return for the savings account is $1.05 - 1.0 = 0.05$. You may be used to using a symbol (r, say) for the required return and using $1 + r$ as a discount rate. So ρ is equivalent to $1 + r$ and $\rho - 1$ to r. You will see that our convention makes for simpler formulas.[2]

Valuation Models for Terminal Investments

The standard *bond valuation formula* is an example of a valuation model. The top of Figure 3.6 depicts the cash payoffs for a five-year, $1,000 bond with an annual coupon rate of 10 percent. The layout follows the time line in Figure 3.5. The bond valuation formula expresses the intrinsic value of the bond at investment date zero, as

$$\text{Value of a bond} = \text{Present value of expected cash flows} \qquad \textbf{(3.1)}$$

$$V_0^D = \frac{CF_1}{\rho_D} + \frac{CF_2}{\rho_D^2} + \frac{CF_3}{\rho_D^3} + \frac{CF_4}{\rho_D^4} + \frac{CF_5}{\rho_D^5}$$

The ρ_D here is the required return on the bond plus 1. The D indicates the valuation is for debt (as a bond is commonly identified). This model states that future cash flows (CF) from the bond are to be forecast and discounted at the required payoff rate on the debt,

---

[2] It is common to talk of a percentage rate as the *required return.* Strictly speaking, we really mean the *required rate of return.*

ρ_D. Specifying what's to be forecast in Step 3 is not difficult here—just refer to the cash flow payoffs as specified in the bond agreement. The formula dictates how these are combined with the required return (Step 4): Cash flows for each period t are weighted by the inverse of the discount rate, $1/\rho_D^t$, to discount them to a "present value."

The only real issue in getting a bond value is calculating the discount rate. This is the rate of return that the lender requires, sometimes called the *cost of capital for debt*. This rate is the yield on a bond with identical features that the lender could buy. Fixed-income analysts who value debt usually specify different rates for different future periods, that is, they give the discount rate a term structure. We will use a constant rate here to keep it simple. Say this is 8 percent per annum. Then

$$V_0^D = \frac{\$100}{1.08} + \frac{\$100}{(1.08)^2} + \frac{\$100}{(1.08)^3} + \frac{\$100}{(1.08)^4} + \frac{\$1,100}{(1.08)^5} = \$1,079.85$$

This is the amount you would pay for the bond if it were correctly priced, as indicated by the cash outflow at time 0 in the figure.

This of course is the standard *present value formula*. It is often applied for project evaluation inside the firm, that is, for making decisions about whether to invest in projects such as new factories or new equipment. Figure 3.6 also depicts expected cash flow payoffs for a project that requires an outlay of $1,200 at time 0 and runs for five years. The present value formula can again be applied:

$$\text{Value of a project} = \text{Present value of expected cash flows} \qquad \textbf{(3.2)}$$

$$V_0^P = \frac{CF_1}{\rho_P} + \frac{CF_2}{\rho_P^2} + \frac{CF_3}{\rho_P^3} + \frac{CF_4}{\rho_P^4} + \frac{CF_5}{\rho_P^5}$$

where P indicates this is for a project and ρ_P is the required payoff per dollar invested in the project, which reflects its risk. The required rate of return for a project is sometimes called a *hurdle rate*. If this is 12 percent ($\rho_P = 1.12$), the value of the investment is $1,530. (Make sure you can calculate this.) This formula is a *project valuation model*. It directs that we should forecast cash flows from the project in Step 3 and combine the forecasts with the required payoff according to the present value formula in Step 4. As with bonds, determining the cost of capital for the project is an issue. But a project's future cash flows are not as transparent as those for bonds, so we must analyze information to forecast them also. So Step 2, information analysis, comes into play. The valuation model directs what to do in the information analysis: Discover information that forecasts future cash flows.

A firm aims to create value for shareholders. The forecasted payoffs in Figure 3.6 are illustrations of two investments that a firm could make with shareholders' money. Consider the bond. If the market is pricing the bond correctly, it will set the price of this bond to yield 8 percent. Thus, if the firm buys the bond, it will pay $1,079.85. What is the anticipated value created by that investment? It's the present value of the payoff minus the cost. This is the *net present value of the investment,* the *NPV,* discovered in Step 5. For the bond priced at $1,079.85, this is zero, so the investment is referred to as a *zero-NPV investment.* Equivalently, it is said that the bond investment does not *create value,* or there is no *value added.* You get what you pay for because it generates payoffs that have the same (present) value as the cost. Of course, if the manager thinks that the market is mispricing the bond—because it has calculated the discount rate incorrectly—then he may buy or sell the bond and create value. This is what bond traders do: They exploit arbitrage opportunities from what they perceive as mispricing of bonds.

Most businesses invest in assets and projects like the one at the bottom of Figure 3.6. This is an example of a *positive-NPV investment,* one that adds value because the value exceeds the cost. In appraising the investment, the manager would conclude that the anticipated net present value was $1,530 − $1,200 = $330, so adopting the project creates value.

Valuation Models for Going-Concern Investments

The valuation of terminal investments like a bond or a project is a relatively easy task. But firms are going concerns, and so are the strategies their managers embark upon. Firms invest in projects but they perpetually roll projects over into new projects. Equity valuation and strategy analysis that involve ongoing operations present two additional complications. First, as going concerns continue (forever?), payoffs have to be forecast for a very long (infinite?) horizon. This raises practical issues. Second, the attribute to be forecasted to capture value added is not as apparent as that for a single terminal investment. Identifying it requires a good understanding of where in the business value is generated. We deal with these two issues in turn.

Criteria for a Practical Valuation Model

We want a valuation model to capture value generated within the firm, to be sure. But we also want it to be practical. We don't want a fancy valuation model that is cumbersome to apply in practice. The following are some considerations.

1. *Finite forecast horizons.* Going concerns are expected to go on forever but the idea that we have to forecast "to infinity" for going concerns is not a practical one. The further into the future we have to forecast, the more uncertain we will be about our forecast. Indeed, in practice analysts issue forecasts for just a few years ahead, or they summarize the long term with long-term growth rates. We prefer a valuation method for which a **finite-horizon forecast** (for a set number of years, for 1, 5, or 10 years, say) does the job. This dictates the specification of the forecast target in Step 3; it must be such that forecasting the payoff over relatively short horizons is equivalent to forecasting perpetual payoffs for going concerns. And the shorter the horizon, the better.

2. *Validation.* Whatever we forecast must be observable after the fact. That is, when the feature that's been forecasted actually occurs, we can see it. We don't want to forecast vague notions such as "economic profit," "technological advantage," "competitive advantage," or "growth opportunities." These may be important to building a forecast but, as a practical matter, we want to forecast something that can be audited and reported in firms' future financial statements. The ability to validate a forecast requires us to be concrete. So, if "growth opportunities" create value, we want to identify them in terms of a feature that will show up in financial statements. The insistence on validation makes the method credible: An analyst's forecast can be validated in financial reports after the fact to confirm that the forecast was a good (or poor) one. From the investor's point of view, the ability to ascertain product quality is important. He's wary of stock tips that use vague criteria. He demands concreteness.

3. *Parsimony.* We want to forecast something for which the information-gathering and analysis task in Step 2 is relatively straightforward. The fewer pieces of information required, the more parsimonious is the valuation. If we could identify one or two pieces of information as being particularly important—because they summarize a lot of information about the payoff—that would be ideal. And if that information is in the financial statements that are ready at hand, all the better.

What Generates Value?

Firms are engaged in the three activities we outlined in Chapter 1: financing activities, investing activities, and operating activities. (Look at Figure 1.1 in Chapter 1 again.) Which of these activities adds value?

The standard answer says that it is the investing and operating activities that add value. Financing activities, the transactions that raise moneys from investors and return cash to them, are of course necessary to run a business. But the standard position among financial economists is that financing activities do not generate value. However, there are some exceptions. We consider transactions with shareholders and bondholders in turn.

Equity Financing Activities

Share Issues in Efficient Markets. A firm with 120 million shares outstanding issues 10 million additional shares at the market price of $42 per share. What happens to the price per share? Well, nothing. The firm's market value prior to the offering was 120 million × $42 = $5,040 million. The offering increases its market value by 10 million × $42 = $420 million, that is, to $5,460 million. With now 130 million shares outstanding, the price per share is still $42. The value of a shareholder's claim is unchanged. The total investment in the firm increases but no value is added to investment. This observation tells us that we should always consider shareholder value on a per-share basis. Value creation is a matter of increasing the per-share value of the equity, not the total value. And managers should not aim at increasing the size of the firm if it does not add to per-share value.

Suppose the same firm were to issue 10 million shares but at $32 a share rather than the market price of $42. This issue increases the market value of the firm by 10 million × $32 = $320 million, that is, to $5,360 million. But the per-share price on the 130 million shares after the issue is $41.23. Has this transaction affected shareholder value? Well, yes. Shareholders have lost 77 cents per share. Their equity has been diluted: The per-share value has declined.

These two scenarios illustrate a standard principle: Issuing shares at market value does not affect shareholders' wealth but issuing them at less than market value erodes their wealth. In valuation we might ignore share issues at market value but we cannot ignore issues at less than market value. The latter occurs, for example, when shares are issued to executives and employees under stock compensation plans. If we ignore these transactions we will miss some value that is lost.

The effect of issuing shares at market value is different from the effect of announcing that a share issue will be made. Sometimes the announcement, in advance of the issue, carries information about the value of the firm, about its investment prospects, for example—and so the market price changes. But this effect—sometimes referred to as a *signaling effect*—is generated by new information, not by the issue itself.

Share Issues in Inefficient Markets. The standard view of the effects of financing assumes that the market price of shares reflects their value, that is, the share market is efficient. If so, value received is value surrendered, on both sides of the transaction. But if shares are mispriced, one party can lose at the expense of the other. If management knows that the shares of their firm are overvalued in the market, they might choose to issue shares. The new shareholder pays the market price but receives less in value. The existing shareholders receive more value than the value surrendered, so they gain. For this reason announcements of share offerings are sometimes greeted as bad news information, and the share price drops. This wealth transfer can only happen in an inefficient market or a market where the manager knows more about the firm's prospects than the market. Buyer beware! Understand the value of the shares before participating in a share issue. See Box 3.6.

In takeovers, acquiring firms often offer shares of their firm in exchange for shares of the firm they are buying. Questions always arise as to whether particular mergers or acquisitions are value-adding transactions: If the shares in the transactions are efficiently priced, the acquirer pays fair value and expects to earn just a normal rate of return on the acquisition.

An acquirer adds value in an acquisition in three ways:

1. Identifying acquirees whose shares are undervalued in the market relative to their fundamental value.

2. Identifying acquirees whose operations, combined with those of the acquirer, will add value.

3. Identifying that the acquirer's own shares are overvalued in the market.

Under the first strategy, the acquirer behaves like any active investor and looks for undervalued assets.

The second strategy looks for so-called synergies from the two companies combined. Cost savings—economies of scale—were said to be the motivation for many bank mergers in the 1990s. Economies from marketing a broad range of financial services under one roof was said to be one of the motivations for the merger of banks, brokerages, and insurance firms, like the merger of Travelers Life, Salomon Smith Barney, and Citibank into Citigroup in 1999. And the announcement of the merger of America Online and Time Warner combined the content of a media company with an Internet portal to that content.

Under the third strategy, the acquirer recognizes that he has "currency" in the form of overvalued stock and so can buy assets cheaply. In the AOL and Time Warner merger, AOL's shares were trading at 190 times earnings and 35 times sales, very high multiples by historical standards. Was AOL using overvalued currency to acquire Time Warner? Indeed, in the agreement to acquire Time Warner, AOL offered its shares at an (unusual) discount of 25 percent of market value, in admission that its shares might have been overvalued.

The second strategy involves adding value in operations. The third involves adding value (to the acquirer's shareholders) by issuing shares. Before going into a transaction, both the acquirer and the acquiree need to understand the value of both the acquirer's shares and the acquiree's shares and how they compare to market values. They then understand value given up and value received.

Share Repurchases. Share repurchases are share issues in reverse. So share repurchases at market price do not affect per-share value and share repurchases at more than market value (should they occur) do. But, like share issues, management can make share repurchases when they see that the share price is below intrinsic value. In this case, shareholders who offer their shares lose; those that don't, gain. For this reason announcements of share repurchases are sometimes seen as signals that the stock is underpriced, increasing share price. In this case, seller beware.

Dividends. Dividends are part of the return to equity investment so it is tempting to think that they are value for shareholders. Indeed fundamental analysts once believed that higher payout meant higher value. But modern finance theory sees it differently. Dividends are one of those things that are not what they appear to be.

If a firm pays a dollar of dividends, the shareholders get a dollar. But there is a dollar less in the firm, so the value of the firm drops by a dollar. Shareholders receive the dollar of dividends, but they can sell the share for a dollar less. The dividend payment makes them no better off; it does not create value. In other words, the investor's cum-dividend payoff is not affected. The return to the shareholder is made up of a dividend and a capital gain. A dividend adds to the return but the capital gain is reduced by the amount of the dividend, leaving the return unaffected.

You might have heard these arguments referred to as the **dividend irrelevance concept,** or as the M&M dividend proposition after the two professors who advanced the arguments, Merton Miller and Franco Modigliani. Some investors might prefer dividends to capital gains because they need the cash. But they can sell some of their shares to convert capital gains into dividends. This ability to make what are called **homemade dividends** means they do not care if their return comes from dividends or capital gains. And if its shareholders want dividends, the firm also can create dividends without affecting the firm's investments, by borrowing against the security in the investments and using the proceeds to pay dividends. Of course, if a firm forgoes value-creating projects to pay dividends it will destroy value. But, given a ready availability of financing, sensible management will borrow or issue shares to pay the dividends rather than affecting good investments.

Homemade dividends and borrowing do involve some transaction costs, but these are usually considered small enough to ignore, given the imprecision we typically have in calculating value. If making homemade dividends is difficult because of illiquidity in the market for the shares (of a nontraded firm, for example), lack of dividends might reduce the value of an investment to a shareholder who desires dividends. The value effect is referred to as the **liquidity discount** (to the value of an equivalent liquid investment). That same shareholder will not demand a liquidity discount, however, if he can generate cash by borrowing against the security of his shares. Just as a firm can borrow to pay dividends (and not affect the value of investments), so shareholders can borrow to generate dividends (and not affect the value of shares).

Like share issues and share repurchases, dividend announcements might convey information that affects stock prices. Dividend increases are often greeted as good news, an indicator that the firm will earn more in the future, and cuts in dividends are often greeted as bad news. These information effects—called *dividend signaling* effects—occur when dividends are announced. The dividend irrelevance notion says that the dividends themselves will not affect (cum-dividend) shareholder value (when the stock goes ex-dividend).

Some argue that dividends might lose value for shareholders if they are taxed at a higher rate than capital gains. This is of no consequence to tax-exempt investors, but the taxable investor might incur more taxes with dividends, and so would prefer to get returns in the form of capital gains. Accordingly, the taxable investor would pay less for a share that pays dividends to yield the same return for a similar share that returns only capital gains. Others argue, however, that investors can shield dividends from taxes with careful tax planning. And some also argue that market prices cannot be lower for dividend-paying stocks because tax-exempt investors (such as the large retirement funds and not-for-profit endowments) dominate the market. A lower price that yields the same after-tax return to a taxable investor as the return without dividends would provide an arbitrage opportunity to the tax-exempt investor, and exploitation of this opportunity would drive the price to yield the same return as a stock with no dividends. Thus dividends have no effect on prices or values. Go to a corporate finance text for the subtleties of this reasoning. Empirical research on the issue has produced conflicting findings.

In this book we accept the presumption that "dividends don't matter" and calculate values accordingly. The investor who expects to pay more taxes on dividends must reduce the before-tax values that we calculate in this book by the present value of any forecasts of taxes on dividends. (She also might consider buying a stock with similar features that does not pay dividends.) The adjusted valuation involves tax planning because this investor must consider how taxes on dividends can be avoided or deferred by holding high dividend yield stocks in retirement funds and employee savings plans (for example). Similarly, the valuations here might be adjusted for liquidity discounts.

Debt Financing Activities

The bond in Figure 3.6 that yields 8 percent per annum has a market value of $1,079.85. We saw that at this price the bond is a zero-NPV investment; it doesn't add value. Most firms accept debt markets as being efficient and issue and buy bonds and other debt instruments at their market value, so do not add value (over the required return for their risk). The exception is financial firms like banks, which can buy debt (lend) at a higher rate than they can sell it (borrow). They add value as financial intermediaries in the capital market. And, as we saw, firms in the business of bond arbitrage might add value if they detect mispricing of bonds.

In debt financing activities, firms sell debt to raise money. They are not in the business of bond arbitrage, so they accept the market price as fair value and sell at that price. The transaction thus does not add value. The firm gets what it pays for. If it issues bonds, it gets cash that is exactly the present value of what it expects to pay back. If it borrows from a bank, it gets the amount of cash equal to the present value, at the interest rate, of the principal plus interest it has to pay back in the future. In the jargon of modern finance, **debt financing is irrelevant** to the value of the firm. It is simply a transaction at fair value to bring moneys into the firm for operations.[3]

Investing and Operating Activities

Value generation in a business is ascribed to many factors—know-how, proprietary technology, good management, brand recognition, brilliant marketing strategy, and so on. At the root of these factors is good ideas. Good entrepreneurs build good businesses and a good entrepreneur is someone with good ideas. But ideas are vague, as are the factors just mentioned, and it is difficult to see the value of ideas without being more concrete. The value of ideas is ascertained from what firms do, and what firms do is engage in investing and operating activities.

Investing activities use the moneys contributed to the firm in financing transactions to invest in the assets necessary to conduct the business envisioned by ideas. The project in Figure 3.6 is a simple example. It adds value. Value is anticipatory; it is based on expected future payoffs from investing. But there has to be follow-through, and operating activities are the follow-through. Operating activities utilize the investments to produce goods or services for sale, and it is these sales that realize the value anticipated in investing. Simply, a firm cannot generate value without finding customers for its products, and the amount of value received is the amount of value those customers are willing to surrender. Net value added in operations is the value received from customers less the value surrendered by the firm in getting products to customers. So investments generate value, but the anticipated value is determined by forecasting the success of the investment in generating value in operations.

Valuation models are developed with the understanding that it is the operations, and the investment in those operations, that generate value. So valuation models value operations, ignoring value that might be created from share issues and share repurchases. Accordingly, the valuation indicates whether the stock market is mispricing the equity, so that the investor understands whether share issues and share repurchases are made at fair value—or whether the firm has the opportunity to create value for shareholders by issuing shares (in an acquisition, for example).

---

[3] Some argue that because interest on debt is deductible against income in assessing corporate taxes, issuing debt gains a tax advantage that shareholders cannot get in paying personal taxes. Thus it generates value for the shareholder. This is controversial and you should go to corporate finance texts for a discussion. If one believes this tax argument, one can add the value of the tax benefit in valuing the firm.

Valuation Models and Asset Pricing Models

You have been introduced to asset pricing models in finance courses and are probably familiar with the most common model, the *capital asset pricing model (CAPM)*. Be sure not to confuse a valuation model with an asset pricing model.

The name "asset pricing model" suggests that the model will give you the price or value of an asset. But it is a misnomer. Asset pricing models yield the required return (the cost of capital), not the value of an asset. The capital asset pricing model, for example, specifies the required return for holding a share of a firm as the risk-free return plus a risk premium, determined by the equity beta for the firm. Valuation models, on the other hand, do yield the value of an asset. Asset pricing models are pertinent to valuing an asset, of course, for we have seen that converting a forecast to a valuation using a valuation model (in Step 4) requires specification of the required return. Valuation models show how, giving a required return from an asset pricing model, the asset pricing is completed.

In this book, we do not spend much time on the technology involved in measuring the required return. You should be familiar with the techniques—students sometimes refer to them as "beta bashing"—from your corporate finance courses. The appendix to this chapter gives a brief overview of asset pricing models and provides some caveats to using these models for the measurement of the required return.

THE DIVIDEND DISCOUNT MODEL

Most investment texts focus on the dividend discount model in their fundamental analysis chapter. At first sight, the model is very appealing. Dividends are the cash flows that shareholders get from the firm, the distributions to shareholders that are reported in the statement of shareholders' equity. In valuing bonds we forecast the cash flows from the bond, so, in valuing stocks, why not forecast the cash flows from stocks?

The dividend discount model values the equity by forecasting future dividends:

$$\text{Value of equity} = \text{Present value of expected dividends} \qquad \textbf{(3.3)}$$

$$V_0^E = \frac{d_1}{\rho_E} + \frac{d_2}{\rho_E^2} + \frac{d_3}{\rho_E^3} + \frac{d_4}{\rho_E^4} + \cdots$$

(The ellipsis in the formula indicates that dividends must be forecast indefinitely into the future, for years 5, 6, and so on.) The dividend discount model instructs us to forecast dividends in Step 3 and to convert the forecasts to a value in Step 4 by discounting them at the equity cost of capital, ρ_E. One might forecast varying discount rates for future periods but for the moment we will treat the discount rate as a constant. The dividend discount model is a straight application of the bond valuation model to equity. That model works for a terminal investment. Will it work for a going-concern investment under the practical criteria we have embraced?

Well, going concerns are expected to pay out dividends for many (infinite?) periods in the future. Clearly, forecasting for infinite periods is a problem. How would we proceed by forecasting for a finite period, say 10 years? Look again at the payoffs for an equity investment in Figure 3.5. For a finite horizon forecast of T years, we might be able to predict the dividends to Year T but we are left with a problem: The payoff for T years includes the terminal price, P_T, as well as the dividends, so we also need to forecast P_T, the price at which we might sell at the forecast horizon. Forecasting just the dividends would be like forecasting the coupon payments on a bond and forgetting the bond repayment. This last component, the terminal payoff, is also called the *terminal value*. So we have the problem of calculating a terminal value such that

Value of equity = Present value of expected dividends to time T **(3.4)**
+ Present value of expected terminal value at T

$$V_0^E = \frac{d_1}{\rho_E} + \frac{d_2}{\rho_E^2} + \frac{d_3}{\rho_E^3} + \cdots + \frac{d_T}{\rho_E^T} + \frac{P_T}{\rho_E^T}$$

You can see that this model is technically correct, for it is simply the present value of all the payoffs from the investment that are laid out in Figure 3.5. The problem is that one of those payoffs is the price that the share will be worth T years ahead, P_T. This is awkward, to say the least: The value of the share at time zero is determined by its expected value in the future, but it is the value we are trying to assess. To break the circularity, we must investigate fundamentals that determine value.

A method often suggested is to assume that the dividend at the forecast horizon will be the same forever afterward. Thus

$$V_0^E = \frac{d_1}{\rho_E} + \frac{d_2}{\rho_E^2} + \frac{d_3}{\rho_E^3} + \cdots + \frac{d_T}{\rho_E^T} + \left(\frac{d_{T+1}}{\rho_E - 1} \right) / \rho_E^T \qquad \textbf{(3.5)}$$

The terminal value here (in the bracketed term) is the **value of a perpetuity**, calculated by capitalizing the forecasted dividend at $T + 1$ at the cost of capital. This terminal value is then discounted to present value.

This perpetuity assumption is a bold one. We are guessing. How do we know the firm will maintain a constant payout? If there is less than full payout of earnings, one would expect dividends to grow as the retained funds earn more in the firm. This idea can be accommodated in a terminal value calculation that incorporates growth:

$$V_0^E = \frac{d_1}{\rho_E} + \frac{d_2}{\rho_E^2} + \frac{d_3}{\rho_E^3} + \cdots + \frac{d_T}{\rho_E^T} + \left(\frac{d_{T+1}}{\rho_E - g} \right) / \rho_E^T \qquad \textbf{(3.6)}$$

where g is 1 plus a forecasted growth rate.[4] The terminal value here is the *value of a perpetuity with growth*. The model is referred to as the *dividend growth model*. If the constant growth starts in the first period, the entire series collapses to $V_0^E = d_1/(\rho_E - g)$, which is sometimes referred to as the *Gordon growth model*.

What would we do, however, for a firm that might be expected to have zero payout for a very long time in the future? For a firm that has exceptionally high payout that can't be maintained? What if payout comes in stock repurchases (that typically don't affect shareholder value) rather than dividends?

The truth of the matter is that dividend payout over the foreseeable future doesn't matter much. Some firms pay a lot of dividends, others none. A firm that is very profitable and worth a lot can have zero payout and a firm that is marginally profitable can have high payout, at least in the short run. Dividends usually are not tied to value creation. Indeed, firms can borrow to pay dividends, and this has nothing to do with their investing and operating activities where value is created. Dividends are distributions of value, not the creation of value.

These observations just restate what we observed in the last section: Dividends are not relevant to value. To be practical we have to forecast over finite horizons. To do so, the

---

[4] The capitalization rate in the denominator of the terminal value can be expressed as $(\rho_E - 1) - (g - 1)$, which is the same as $\rho_E - g$.

ADVANTAGES

Easy concept: Dividends are what shareholders get, so forecast them.

Predictability: Dividends are usually fairly stable in the short run so dividends are easy to forecast (in the short run).

DISADVANTAGES

Relevance: Dividend payout is not related to value, at least in the short run; dividend forecasts ignore the capital gain component of payoffs.

Forecast horizons: Typical requirement is for forecasts for long periods; terminal values for shorter periods are hard to calculate with any reliability.

WHEN IT WORKS BEST

When payout is permanently tied to the value generation in the firm. For example, when a firm has a fixed payout ratio (dividends/earnings).

dividend discount model (equation 3.4) requires us to forecast dividends up to a forecast horizon plus the terminal price. But payoffs are insensitive to the dividend component: if you expect a stock to pay you more dividends, it will pay off a lower terminal price; if the firm pays out cash, the price will drop by this amount to reflect that value has left the firm. Any change in dividends will be exactly offset by a price change such that, in present value terms, the net effect is zero. In other words, paying dividends is a zero-NPV activity. It doesn't create value. If dividends are irrelevant, we are left with the task of forecasting the terminal price, but it is price that we are after. Box 3.7 summarizes the advantages and disadvantages of the dividend discount model.

This leaves us with the so-called **dividend conundrum**: Equity value is based on future dividends, but forecasting dividends over a finite horizon does not give an indication of value. The dividend discount model fails the first criterion for a practical analysis. We have to forecast something else that is tied to the value creation. The model fails the second criterion—validation—also. Dividends can be observed after the fact, so a dividend forecast can be validated for its accuracy. But a change in a dividend from a forecast may not be related to value at all, just a change in payout policy, so ex-post dividends cannot be validation of a valuation.

Summary

This chapter has given you a roadmap for carrying out fundamental analysis. Indeed, the chapter has laid out a roadmap for the rest of the book, and we will be referring to Figure 3.3 quite often as we proceed. It lays out the five steps of fundamental analysis, steps that convert your knowledge of a business and its strategy to a valuation of that business. At the core of the process is the analysis of information (Step 2), making forecasts from that information (Step 3), and converting those forecasts to a valuation (Step 4).

A valuation model provides the architecture for fundamental analysis. A valuation model is a tool for thinking about value creation in a business and translating that thinking into a value. The chapter introduced you to valuation models for bonds and projects and showed that valuation of going concerns is inherently more difficult than valuation of these terminal investments. As an example of a valuation model for going-concern equities, we introduced dividend discounting. This technology simply appropriates the discounted cash flow valuation (which works for bonds) for the valuation of equities. But we saw that dividend discounting does not work, for the reason that dividends are not necessarily related to the value generation in a firm. Dividends are financing activities; they have to do with the distribution of value, not the creation of value. We concluded

The Web Connection

Find the following on the web page for this chapter:

- More on the method of comparables.
- Further detail on typical price multiples.
- Additional screening analysis.

- Links to screening engines.
- A history of returns to equity investing.
- Links to research on issues in this chapter and to further reading.

that a valuation model must focus on the aspects of the firm that generate value, the investing and operating activities, so setting the stage for the development of appropriate valuation models in the following chapters.

Having gained an understanding of fundamental analysis—at least in outline—you can appreciate the limitations of "cheap" methods that use limited information. The chapter outlined three such methods: the method of comparables, screening analysis, and asset-based valuation. You should understand the mechanics of these methods but also be aware of the pitfalls in applying them.

How are financial statements used in valuation? You don't have a complete answer to this question yet, for that is the subject of the whole book. But you do have an outline. Minimal financial statement information is used in the method of comparables and in screening strategies. Balance sheet information is used in asset-based valuation; indeed, asset-based valuation is a matter of marking to market the assets and liabilities of a firm. But financial statements really come into play in full fundamental analysis. Not only are current and past financial statements analyzed as part of the information for forecasting (in Step 2), but also forecasting (in Step 3) is a matter of preparing pro forma financial statements for the future. That is, financial statements are information, but they also must be forecasted. (Figure 3.4 gives the picture.) So you see that financial statements are very much involved in fundamental analysis; indeed preparing pro forma financial statements for the future, and analyzing current financial statements to forecast those statements, is very much what fundamental analysis is all about.

Key Concepts

breakup value is the amount a firm is worth if its assets (net of liabilities) are sold off. *74*

contrarian stock is a stock that is out-of-favor and trades at low multiples (viewed by **contrarian investors** as undervalued). *70*

cost of capital is the opportunity cost of having money tied up in an investment. Also referred to as the **normal return**, the **required return**, or, when calculating values, as the **discount rate** or **capitalization rate.** *77*

cum-dividend price is the price inclusive of the dividend received while holding the investment. Compare with **ex-dividend**

price, which is price without the dividend. *69*

debt financing irrelevance means that the value of a firm is not affected by financing activities, that is, by issuing debt. *88*

dividend conundrum refers to the following puzzle: The value of a share is based on expected dividends but forecasting dividends (over finite horizons) does not yield the value of the share. *91*

dividend irrelevance means that paying dividends does not generate value for shareholders. *86*

finite-horizon forecasting refers to forecasting for a fixed (finite) number of years. *84*

forecast horizon is a point in the future up to which forecasts are made. *84*

fundamental analysis is the method of analyzing information, forecasting payoffs from that information, and arriving at a valuation based on those forecasts. *74*

glamour stock is a stock that is fashionable and trades at high multiples (viewed by **contrarian investors** as overvalued). *70*

going-concern investment is one which is expected to continue indefinitely. Compare with terminal investment. *81*

homemade dividends are dividends a shareholder creates for himself by selling some of his shares, thus substituting dividends for capital gains *87*

investment horizon is the period for which an investment is likely to be held. *80*

liquidity discount is a reduction in the value of an investment due to difficulty in converting value in the investment into cash. *87*

parsimony (in valuation) is the ability to value a firm from a reduced amount of information. *84*

payoff is value received (usually in cash) from an investment. *81*

perpetuity is a flow that continues forever. *90*

pro forma analysis is the preparation of forecasted financial statements for future years. *78*

risk premium is the expected return on an investment over the risk-free return. *77*

terminal investment is an investment that terminates at a point of time in the future. Compare with **going-concern investment**. *80*

unlevered measures are measures that are not affected by how a firm is financed. *69*

value added (or **value created** or **value generated**) is the value from anticipated payoffs to an investment (**fundamental value**) in excess of value given up in making the investment (the cost of the investment). *76*

value stock is a stock that trades at low multiples (viewed by **value investors** as undervalued). *70*

valuation model is the architecture for fundamental analysis that directs what is to be forecast as a payoff, what information is relevant for forecasting, and how forecasts are converted to a valuation. *79*

The Analyst's Toolkit

Analysis Tools	Page	Key Measures	Page	Acronymns to Remember
Method of comparables	66	Adjusted multiples	69	CAPM capital asset pricing model
Screening analysis:	70	Capitalization rate	77	CF cash flow
Technical screening	71	Cost of capital	77	CFO cash flow from operations
Fundamental screening	71	Cum-dividend price	69	dps dividends per share
Glamour screening	70	Dividend-adjusted P/E	69	ebit earnings before interest and
Contrarian screening	70	Discounted dividend value	89	taxes
Value screening	70	Discount rate	77	ebitda earnings before interest,
Momentum screening	71	ebit	69	taxes, depreciation, and
Asset-based valuation	73	ebitda	69	amortization
Breakup valuation	74	Ex-dividend price	69	eps earnings per share
Converting a forecast to a		Hurdle rate	83	GAAP generally accepted
valuation:	76	P/E	69	accounting principles
Discounting payoffs	77	Trailing P/E	69	IPO initial public offering
Capitalizing payoffs	77	Rolling P/E	69	NPV net present value
Five-step fundamental analysis	75	Leading (forward) P/E	69	P/B price-to-book ratio

The Analyst's Toolkit (concluded)

Analysis Tools	Page	Key Measures	Page	Acronymns to Remember
Valuation models:		Price-to-book (P/B)	66	P/B price-to-book ratio
Bond valuation model		Price-to-cash flow (P/CFO)	66	P/CFO price-to-cash flow ratiio
equation (3.1)	82	Price-to-dividend (P/d)	71	P/E price-to-earnings ratio
Project valuation model		Price-to-sales (P/S)	66	P/d price-to-dividends ratio
equation (3.2)	83	Required return	77	P/S price-to-sales ratio
Dividend discount model		Risk-free return	77	P/V price-to-value ratio
equations (3.3, 3.4, 3.5)	89	Risk premium	77	
Dividend growth model		Terminal payoff	81	
equation (3.6)	90	Terminal value	90	
		Unlevered multiples	69	
		Price-to-sales (P/S)	69	
		Price-to-ebit	69	
		Value of a perpetuity	90	
		Value of a perpetuity with		
		growth	90	

Concept Questions

C3.1. What explains differences between firms' price-to-sales ratios?

C3.2. It is common to compare firms on their price-to-ebit ratios. What are the merits of using this measure? What are the problems with it?

C3.3. It is also common to compare firms on their price-to-ebitda ratios. What are the merits of using this measure? What are the dangers?

C3.4. Why do P/E ratios vary with dividend payout?

C3.5. If a firm has a P/E ratio of 12 and a profit margin on sales of 6 percent, what is its price-to-sales (P/S) ratio likely to be?

C3.6. If an Internet firm is expected to have a profit margin of 8 percent but trades at a price-to-sales ratio of 25, what inferences would you make?

C3.7. What do traders mean when they refer to stocks as "growth stocks" and "value stocks?" What is a "glamour stock?"

C3.8. Why would you expect asset-based valuation to be more difficult to apply to a technology firm, like Dell Computer, than to a forest products company, like Weyerhaeuser?

C3.9. The yield on a bond is independent of the coupon rate. Is this true?

C3.10. It is sometimes said that firms prefer to make stock repurchases rather than pay dividends because stock repurchases yield a higher eps. Do they?

C3.11. Your answer to concept question C3.10 should have been: Yes. If share repurchases increase eps more than dividends, do share repurchases also create more value than dividends?

C3.12. Should a firm that pays higher dividends have a higher share value?

C3.13. Reebok International Ltd., the footwear and apparel manufacturer, included the following note in its 1996 annual report.

Dutch Auction Self-Tender Stock Repurchase
On July 28, 1996, the Board of Directors authorized the purchase by the Company of up to 24.0 million shares of the Company's common stock pursuant to a Dutch Auction self-tender offer. The tender offer price range was from $30.00 to $36.00 net per share in

> cash. The self-tender offer commenced on July 30, 1996, and expired on August 27, 1996. As a result of the self-tender offer, the Company repurchased approximately 17.0 million common shares at a price of $36.00 per share. Prior to the tender offer, the Company had 72.5 million common shares outstanding. As a result of the tender offer share repurchase, the Company had 55.8 million common shares outstanding at December 31, 1996. In conjunction with this repurchase and as described in Notes 6 and 8, the Company entered into a new credit agreement underwritten by a syndicate of major banks.

Reebok borrowed $640 million under the credit agreement to finance the stock repurchase. It also announced that it was dropping its quarterly dividend.

What do you think was the effect of these activities on Reebok's share price during August 1996?

Exercises

E3.1. Identifying Firms with Similar Multiples (Easy)

Find a screening engine on the Web, enter a multiple you are interested in, and get a list of firms that have that multiple of a particular size. Choose a particular industry and see how the various multiples—P/E, price-to-book, price-to-sales—differ among firms in the industry.

Screening engines can be found at the following site (among others):

http://www.wsrn.com/apps/companysearch/

E3.2. A Stab at Valuation Using Multiples: Biotech Firms (Easy)

The following table gives accounting data from the 1994 annual reports of six biotechnology firms. The market value of the equity of five of the firms is also given. All numbers are in millions of dollars. From these numbers, estimate a value for Genentech, Inc. Genentech had a book value of $1,349 million in 1994.

Company	Market Value of Equity	Price/Book	Revenue	R&D	Net Income
Amgen	$8,096.71	5.6	$1,571.0	$307.0	$406.0
Biogen	1,379.00	3.6	152.0	101.0	15.0
Chiron	2,233.60	4.6	413.0	158.0	28.0
Genetics Institute	925.00	2.5	138.0	109.0	–7.0
Immunex	588.53	4.5	151.0	81.0	–34.0
Genentech	?	?	795.4	314.3	124.4

E3.3. A Stab at Equity Valuation Using Multiples: Automobiles (Medium)

Earnings, book values, dividends, and year-end prices for firms in automobile manufacturing for 1992 and 1993 are listed in the following table. Data are per share.

	1992				1993			
Company	**eps**	**bps**	**dps**	**Price**	**eps**	**bps**	**dps**	**Price**
Chrysler Corp.	2.21	25.468	0.60	32¼	–7.62	19.320	0.65	53¼
Daimler-Benz AG	Not traded in U.S.				0.74	21.694	8.01	48⅝
Federal Signal Corp.	1.00	5.231	0.42	21¼	1.15	5.807	0.48	28
Ford Motor of Canada Ltd.	–34.50	64.184	0.00	85½	–22.45	39.872	0.00	95½
Ford Motor Co.	–15.61	30.138	1.60	42⅞	4.55	31.210	1.60	64½
General Motors Corp.	–38.28	8.470	1.40	32¼	2.13	7.767	0.80	54⅞
Honda Motor Ltd.	0.67	18.310	0.24	25½	0.47	19.262	0.27	32⅜
Navistar Intl.	–0.95	0.366	0.00	1⅞	–15.19	7.095	0.00	27¼
Paccar Inc.	1.93	30.702	1.30	57¼	4.21	32.777	0.00	61¼

a. Calculate estimated prices in 1992 and 1993 for Chrysler Corp. based on average multiples of earnings, book values, and dividends of the other firms in the industry. Which valuation comes closest to the actual prices?

b. List the reservations you developed in doing this exercise.

c. All else equal, would you expect the price of a firm with a high payout (of dividends) to be higher or lower than that of comparison firms? How would you expect the P/E ratio of a high-payout firm to be affected by the payout?

d. Would you expect the price-to-book ratio to be related to dividends?

E3.4. Pricing Multiples: IBM (Medium)

At the end of its June 30, 1999, quarter, International Business Machines (IBM) had 1.83 billion shares outstanding trading at $125 per share. Its price-to-book ratio was 12.1 and its long-term debt-to-equity ratio was 76 percent. How much long-term debt did IBM have outstanding?

E3.5. Pricing Multiples: Procter & Gamble (Medium)

Procter & Gamble, the consumer products company, traded at 3.5 times sales in 1999. It was reporting a net profit margin on its sales of 9.9 percent. What was its P/E ratio?

E3.6. Measuring Value Added (Medium)

a. *Buying a stock.* A firm is expected to pay an annual dividend of $2 per share forever. Investors require a return of 12 percent per year to compensate for the risk of not receiving the expected dividends. The firm's shares trade for $19 each. What is the value added by buying a share at $19?

b. *An investment within a firm.* The general manager of a soccer club is considering paying $2.5 million per year for five years for a "star" player, along with a $2 million up-front signing bonus. He expects the player to enhance gate receipts and television advertising revenues by $3.5 million per year with no added costs. The club requires a 9 percent return on its investments. What would be the value added from the acquisition of the player?

E3.7. Converting a Price to a Forecast: Charles Schwab (Hard)

Charles Schwab, the discount broker, has the largest Internet stock trading business in the world. In 1999, Schwab had a 25 percent share of the online brokerage business, in competition with the likes of E*Trade, Ameritrade, and TD Waterhouse. Its shares benefited from the run-up in Internet share prices in 1999. The price of its shares rose from $25 in September 1998 to $140 in April 1999, giving it an equity market value of $56 billion. Suppose a normal price-to-sales ratio for a brokerage business is 1.5 and suppose that Schwab earns an average of 1/4 percent commission on stock trades it makes on behalf of customers. What dollar volume of trading must Schwab do for customers to justify the market price of $140 per share?

Real World Connection

See Minicase 16.2 in Chapter 16 on online trading firms.

E3.8. Price-to-Earnings Forecasts and Value: Microsoft Corporation (Hard)

Microsoft traded at $80 per share just after it released its 1999 annual report for the year ending June 30. Analysts were forecasting eps for the June 30, 2000, year of $1.56 and a P/E ratio at June 30, 2000, of 72. Microsoft pays no dividends.

Microsoft's CAPM equity cost of capital at the time was 13 percent, using a 6.0 percent market risk premium.

Do analysts who forecast the P/E ratio of 72 see the stock as mispriced?

Real World Connection

See Minicase 8.1 in Chapter 8 on Microsoft.

E3.9.   Forecasting Prices in an Efficient Market: Weyerhaeuser Company (Easy)

Weyerhaeuser, the forest products producer, traded at $42 at the beginning of 1996. Beta services typically place its beta at 1.0, and the risk-free rate at the end of 1995 was 5.5 percent. The firm was expected to pay dividends of $1.60 per share in 1996 and 1997.

a. At what prices do you expect Weyerhaeuser to sell at the end of 1997?

b. At what price do you expect Weyerhaeuser to sell at the end of 1997 if you forecast it will pay no dividends?

E3.10.   Valuation of Bonds and the Accounting for Bonds, Borrowing Costs, and Bond Revaluations (Medium)

On January 1, 1995, Debtor Corporation issued 10,000 five-year bonds with a face value of $1,000 and an annual coupon of 4 percent. Bonds of similar risk were yielding 8 percent p.a. in the market at the time.

a. What did the firm receive for each bond issued?

b. At the end of 1995 the market was still yielding 8 percent on the bonds.

1. What was the firm's borrowing cost before tax for 1995?
2. How much interest expense was reported in the income statement for 1995?

c. At the end of 1996, the yield on the bonds had dropped to 6 percent.

1. What was the firm's borrowing cost before tax for 1996?
2. How much interest expense was reported in the income statement for 1996?

d. Creditor Corporation purchased 2,000 of the bonds in the issue. FASB Statement No. 115 requires firms to mark these financial investments to market.

1. What were the bonds carried at on the balance sheet at the end of 1996?
2. What was interest income in the income statement for 1996?

E3.11.   Share Issues and Market Prices: Is Value Generated or Lost by Share Issues? (Medium)

a. XYZ Corporation had 158 million shares outstanding on January 1, 2000. On February 2, 2000, it issued an additional 30 million shares to the market at the market price of $55 per share. What was the effect of this share issue on the price per share of the firm?

b. On February 28, 2000, directors of the same XYZ Corporation exercised stock options to acquire 12 million shares at an exercise price of $30 per share. Prior to this transaction the stock traded at $62 per share. What was the effect of the share issue to the directors on the per-share value of the firm?

E3.12.   Stock Repurchases and Value: J.C. Penney Company (Easy)

During fiscal year 1995, J.C. Penney repurchased 7.5 million shares on the market for $335 million. There were 227.4 million shares outstanding prior to the repurchase. What was the effect of the repurchases on the per-share price of Penney's stock?

E3.13.   Dividends, Stock Returns, and Expected Payoffs: Weyerhaeuser Company (Easy)

Weyerhaeuser, the forest products producer, traded at $42 at the beginning of 1996. Its cost of equity capital, calculated with the CAPM, is 13.5 percent. It is expected to pay dividends of $1.60 per share in 1996 and 1997. Straightforward calculations (as in Exercise E3.9) give it an expected price at the end of 1997 of $50.69 per share.

Suppose the company had announced that, instead of paying a cash dividend, it would make share repurchases in 1996 and 1997 equal to the amount of the total annual dividend. It had 198 million shares outstanding at the end of 1995. What now would you expect the per-share price to be at the end of 1997?

Real World Connection

See Exercise E3.9 and Minicase 3.4 for related material on Weyerhaeuser Company.

E3.14. Dividend Payoffs and Value (Medium)

The numbers plotted on the time line below are the average dividends investors received during the first year, second year, third year (etc.) subsequent to buying NYSE, AMEX, and NASDAQ stocks between 1973 and 1991:

Year after investing	1	2	3	4	5	6	7	8	9
Dividend payoff ($)	0.088	0.104	0.120	0.139	0.158	0.180	0.204	0.235	0.252

The dividends include cash dividends, stock repurchases, and liquidating distributions. They are in units of price at the time of the investment, so they are average yearly cash yields on the purchase. Suppose you had an opportunity cost of capital of 10 percent. Is the cash payoff over the nine years sufficient to justify the price paid?

E3.15. Betas, the Market Risk Premium, and the Equity Cost of Capital: Sun Microsystems (Medium)

A risk analyst gives Sun Microsystems, the networking computer firm, a CAPM equity beta of 1.38. The risk-free rate is 5.5 percent.

a. Prepare a table with the cost of capital that you would calculate for the equity with the following estimates of the market risk premium:

4.5%
6.0%
7.5%
9.0%

b. Other analysts disagree on the beta, with estimates ranging from 1.25 to 1.55. Prepare a table that gives the cost of capital for each estimate of the market risk premium and beta estimates of 1.25 and 1.55.

c. In early July 1999, analysts were forecasting earnings of $2.10 per share for the fiscal year ending June 30, 2000. They were also forecasting a P/E ratio for the firm of 67 in June 2000. The company pays no dividends. Calculate the current value of the stock in July 1999 for this P/E forecast using the lowest and highest cost of capital estimates from part b.

E3.16. Implying the Market Risk Premium: Procter & Gamble (Easy)

Analysts give Procter & Gamble, the consumer products firm, an equity beta of 0.78. The risk-free rate is 5.5 percent. An analyst calculates an equity cost of capital for the firm of 11.9 percent using the capital asset pricing model (CAPM). What market risk premium is she assuming?

Real World Connection

See Exercise 3.5 and Minicase 15.4 in Chapter 15 for more material on Procter & Gamble.

Minicases

M3.1

An Arbitrage Opportunity? Cordant Technologies and Howmet International

Cordant Technologies, based in Salt Lake City, manufactures rocket motors, "fasteners" (bolts), and turbine engine components for the aerospace industry. For the first half of 1999, its sales were $1.28 billion, up 7 percent on the same period for the previous year. Net income was $85.7 million, or $2.34 per share, up 16 percent. Cordant's gas turbine business was growing, but production cuts and inventory buildup at Boeing forecast a slowdown in the firm's revenues from other aerospace products. Other data on the firm are as follows:

Rolling 12-month eps to June 30, 1999	$4.11
Book value per share, June 30, 1999	$7.76
Rolling 12-month sales per share to June 30, 1999	$67.20
Profit margin	7.4%
Price per share, September 30, 1999	$32
Market capitalization of equity	$1.17 billion

Analysts were forecasting earnings of $4.00 per share for the full 1999 year and $4.28 for 2000.

Cordant's financial statements consolidate an 85 percent interest in Howmet International, another manufacturer of turbine engine components. Howmet reported net income of $65.3 million for the first half of 1999, up 33 percent, on sales of $742.4 million. Other data on Howmet are:

Rolling 12-month eps to June 30, 1999	$1.21
Book value per share, June 30, 1999	$4.25
Rolling 12-month sales per share to June 30, 1999	$14.28
Profit margin	8.7%
Price per share, September 30, 1999	$14
Market capitalization of equity	$1.40 billion

Analysts were forecasting earnings of $1.24 for 1999 and $1.36 for 2000.

Both firms were categorized by some analysts at the time as "neglected" or "ignored" stocks. Their claim was that the market was irrational not only in overpricing the new technology stocks, but also in underpricing the old, "blue-collar" industrial stocks. For reference, firms like Micosoft, Dell, Yahoo!, and AOL traded at multiples of over 50 times earnings at the time, whereas aerospace firms traded at 11 times earnings.

Calculate price multiples for Cordant and Howmet. Do you see an arbitrage opportunity? What trading strategy do you recommend to exploit the opportunity? Would you call it a riskless arbitrage opportunity?

M3.2

Nifty Stocks? Returns to Stock Screening

In the early 1970s a widely publicized list of the "Nifty Fifty" stocks was drawn up. This list, which included Avon Products, Polaroid, Coca-Cola, McDonald's, Walt Disney, American Express, and Xerox, was touted as a set of "good buys." Most of the firms traded at high multiples. Their P/E ratios were as high as 70 to 90, with an average of 42, while the S&P 500 traded at a multiple of 19 times earnings. Burton Crane, a *New York Times* reporter, wrote the famous words at the time: "Xerox's multiple not only discounts the future but the hereafter as well."

Unfortunately, many of those Nifty Fifty stocks lost considerable value in the subsequent 1970s bear market. Avon's stock fell 80 percent, as did Polaroid's. Coca-Cola, IBM, and Xerox fell dramatically.

The multiples of the Nifty Fifty in 1972 bear a strong resemblance to those of the "nifty" technology stocks of the late 1990s, and indeed to those of mature "quality" firms such as Coca-Cola, General Electric, Pfizer, Merck, and Walt Disney (all of which were in the original Nifty Fifty of 1972). Morgan Stanley published a new set of Nifty Fifty stocks in 1995 that included these stocks. Here are some of the firms with high earnings multiples in September 1999, with their per-share prices at that date:

	P/E	Price per Share ($)
Microsoft (MSFT)	64	90
Dell Computer (DELL)	70	44
Lucent Technologies (LU)	75	64
America Online (AOL)	168	104
Analog Devices (ADI)	65	56
Mattel (MAT)	72	21
CBS Corp. (CBS)	72	46
Cisco Systems (CSCO)	110	68
Home Depot (HD)	51	69
Motorola (MOT)	95	87
Charles Schwab (SCH)	56	34
Time Warner (TWX)	185	61

Track the return to these stocks from October 1999. You might use a price chart that tracks stock splits (for example, Big Charts at http://www.bigcharts.com).

How have these nifty stocks fared?

Here are some less nifty stocks at the time, all of which were in the S&P 500. They have low P/E ratios.

	P/E	Price per Share ($)
Centex (CTX)	7	28
ITT Industries (ITT)	2	32
Seagate Technology (SEG)	7	30
U.S. Airways (U)	3	26
Conseco (CNC)	6	20
Hilton Hotels (HTL)	8	10

How have these stocks fared?

(Note: This case was written in October 1999, without any idea of the outcome.)

M3.3

What Is the Value of the Big Board?

In 1999 the New York Stock Exchange proposed to convert from a membership organization to a traded company. How much might the Big Board be worth if its own shares were traded on the Big Board?

There is little comparative pricing of stock exchanges. But in October 1998, the Australian Stock Exchange (ASX) "demutualized," with its shares listed on its own market. The purpose was to broaden the ASX's ownership and to separate ownership from rights to market access. By mid-1999 the shares were held by more than 8,000 shareholders, with the largest shareholder holding a 1.86 percent share.

Shares of ASX traded at $1.2 billion (Australian) or $780 million (U.S.) in June 1999. The market value of securities traded on the ASX was about $1 trillion (Australian) annually or $650 billion (U.S.). In contrast, the market value of securities traded on the NYSE was $12.7 trillion (U.S.) annually. The following table compares the revenues and net income of the two exchanges in millions of U.S. dollars.

	Revenues	Net Income
NYSE (1998)	728.7	101.3
ASX (estimated for June 1999 year)	145.0	24.4

With the comparison to the Australian Stock Exchange, make a stab at valuing the New York Stock Exchange.

What factors might give the NYSE different multiples than the ASX? What other measures might be useful in making the comparison? You might look at the web pages of the two exchanges:

> http://www.asx.com.au
> http://www.nyse.com

M3.4

Attempting Asset-Based Valuations: Weyerhaeuser Company

Weyerhaeuser Company grows, harvests, and processes timber and develops residential real estate. Incorporated in Washington State, the company has four business segments: timberlands; wood products; pulp, paper, and packaging; and real estate.

The company manages 5.3 million acres of commercial forestland, 5.1 million of them company-owned, with 3.3 million acres in the southern United States and 2 million acres in the Pacific Northwest. The standing timber inventory on these lands was approximately 9.4 million cunits as of early 1999 (a cunit is 100 cubic feet of solid wood).

The wood products division of Weyerhaeuser is the world's largest producer of commercial-grade softwood timber and also produces coated groundwood and coated freesheet. Weyerhaeuser's pulp, paper, and packaging division is the world's largest producer of pulp and a leading producer of corrugated containers. The real estate operations involve home building.

Segments contributed to total revenues and total operating income in 1998 as follows:

	Percent of Revenue	Percent of Operating Income
Timberlands and wood products	47.5%	74.1%
Pulp, paper, and packaging	40.1	18.2
Real estate	11.1	10.9
Corporate operations	1.3	(3.2)

Exhibit 3.2 presents Weyerhaeuser's 1998 income statement and balance sheet. The notes refer to footnotes to the financial statements that can be found on the SEC's EDGAR website.

A. List the assets and liabilities on the balance sheet that you think are probably close to market value.

B. Consider assigning a market value to the assets and liabilities you have not put on the list. Use the following information.

Analysts estimate that the timberlands in the South are worth $1,000 per acre and those in the Pacific Northwest $2,000 per acre. Valuers estimate the replacement cost of plants used in producing pulp, paper, and packaging to be $12,500 million and those producing wood products to be $2,100 million.

Market values are not available for the homes being built or for the land held for building homes, but firms with similar operations sell at seven times pretax earnings.

C. Prepare a balance sheet that purports to give the value of the equity. What do you estimate to be the intrinsic premium?

D. What reservations do you have about the process? What other approaches do you recommend?

For reference, Weyerhaeuser's shares traded at $54 in March 1999, when its annual report was released.

EXHIBIT 3.2

Weyerhaeuser Co.
Consolidated Income Statement
(dollar amounts in millions except per-share figures)

	1998	1997
Net sales and revenues:		
Weyerhaeuser	$ 9,574	$10,117
Real estate and related assets	1,192	1,093
Total net sales and revenues	10,766	11,210
Costs and expenses:		
Weyerhaeuser:		
Costs of products sold	7,468	7,866
Depreciation, amortization, and fee stumpage	611	616
Selling, general, and administrative expenses	649	646
Research and development expenses	57	56
Taxes other than payroll and income taxes	130	142
Charge for closure or disposition of facilities (Note 15)	71	89
Charge for year 2000 remediation	42	1
	9,028	9,416
Real estate and related assets:		
Costs and operating expenses	1,016	909
Depreciation and amortization	5	12
Selling, general, and administrative expenses	53	96
Taxes other than payroll and income taxes	8	8
	1,082	1,025
Total costs and expenses	10,110	10,441
Operating income	656	769
Interest expense and other:		
Weyerhaeuser:		
Interest expense incurred	264	271
Less interest capitalized	7	15
Equity in income (loss) of affiliates (Note 3)	28	(7)
Other income (expense), net (Note 4)	15	(10)
Real estate and related assets:		
Interest expense incurred	77	110
Less interest capitalized	61	69
Equity in income of joint ventures and limited partnerships (Note 3)	14	14
Other income, net (Note 4)	23	70
Earnings before income taxes	463	539
Income taxes (Note 5)	169	197
Net earnings	$ 294	$ 342
Per common share (Note 2)		
Basic net earnings	$ 1.48	$ 1.72
Diluted net earnings	$ 1.47	$ 1.72
Dividends paid	$ 1.60	$ 1.60

EXHIBIT 3.2   *(continued)*

Consolidiated Balance Sheet
(dollar amounts in millions)

	December 27, 1998	December 28, 1997
Assets		
Weyerhaeuser		
Current assets:		
Cash and short-term investments (Note 1)	$ 28	$ 100
Receivables, less allowances $5 and $6	886	913
Inventories (Note 7)	962	983
Prepaid expense	294	298
Total current assets	2,170	2,294
Property and equipment (Note 8)	6,692	6,991
Construction in progress	315	354
Timber and timberlands at cost, less fee stumpage charged to disposals	1,013	996
Investments in and advances to equity affiliates (Note 3)	482	249
Other assets and deferred charges	262	187
	10,934	11,071
Real estate and related assets:		
Cash and short-term investments, including restricted deposits of $16 in 1997	7	22
Receivables, less discounts and allowances of $6 and $6	81	62
Mortgage-related financial instruments, less discounts and allowances of $9 and $27 (Notes 1 and 13)	119	173
Real estate in process of development and for sale (Note 9)	584	593
Land being processed for development	854	845
Investments in and advances to joint ventures and limited partnerships, less reserves of $4 and $6 (Note 3)	120	116
Other assets	135	193
	1,900	2,004
Total assets	$12,834	$13,075
Liabilities and Shareholders' Interest		
Weyerhaeuser		
Current liabilities:		
Notes payable	$ 5	$ 25
Current maturities of long-term debt	88	17
Accounts payable (Note 1)	699	694
Accrued liabilities (Note 10)	707	648
Total current liabilities	1,499	1,384
Long-term debt (Notes 12 and 13)	3,397	3,483
Deferred income taxes (Note 5)	1,404	1,418
Deferred pension, other postretirement benefits, and other liabilities (Note 6)	488	498
Minority interest in subsidiaries	—	121
Commitments and contingencies (Note 14)		
	6,788	6,904

EXHIBIT 3.2 *(concluded)*

	December 27, 1998	December 28, 1997
Real estate and related assets:		
Notes payable and commercial paper (Note 11)	564	228
Long-term debt (Notes 12 and 13)	701	1,032
Other liabilities	255	262
Commitments and contingencies (Note 14)		
	1,520	1,522
Total liabilities	8,308	8,426
Shareholders' interest (Note 16):		
Common shares; authorized 400,000,000 shares, issued		
206,072,890 shares, $1.25 par value	258	258
Other capital	416	407
Retained earnings	4,372	4,397
Cumulative other comprehensive expense	(208)	(123)
Treasury common shares, at cost: 7,063,917 and 6,586,939	(312)	(290)
Total shareholders' interest	4,526	4,649
Total liabilities and shareholders' interest	$12,834	$13,075

Appendix

The Required Return and Asset Pricing Models

The chapter has introduced the *required return* for an investment, otherwise known as the *normal return* or the *cost of capital* and, in the context of project selection, the *hurdle rate*. The required return is the amount that an investor requires to compensate her for the time value of money tied up in the investment and for taking on risk in the investment. These are her costs of taking on the investment, thus the name, cost of capital. In effect, the cost of capital is the opportunity cost of forgoing an alternative investment with the same risk. To add value, an investment must earn more than the cost of capital, so the required return features in valuation: In converting forecasted payoffs to a valuation, the payoffs must be discounted for the cost of capital. (See Box 3.5 again.)

Considerable time is spent in corporate finance courses estimating the cost of capital. The techniques are called *beta technologies*. This appendix gives an overview. Chapter 18 comes back to the topic with a discussion of how fundamental analysis helps in the assessment of the required return.

MEASURING THE REQUIRED RETURN: BETA TECHNOLOGIES

When you invest, you buy a gamble. Different investments will yield different expected payoffs, but the expected payoff is only one feature of the gamble. You are buying a range of possible outcomes with different probabilities of occurring, and you must be concerned about the chance of getting payoffs different from those expected. Most people are risk averse (that is, particularly concerned about the downside), so they want to be rewarded with a higher return for taking on risk. They want to earn at least the risk-free return that one would get on a U.S. government bond, say, but they also want a premium for any risk that they take on.

An *asset-pricing model* supplies the technology to calculate required returns. These models have one insight in common: The market will not price an investment to compensate for risk that can be diversified away in a portfolio. They also have a common form. They characterize required returns as determined by the *risk-free return* plus a *risk premium*:

$$\text{Required return} = \text{Risk-free return} + \text{Risk premium}$$

The risk premium is given by (1) expected returns over the risk-free return on risk factors to which the investor must be exposed because they can't be diversified away, and (2) sensitivities of the returns on a particular investment to these factors, known as *betas*. Multiplying components (1) and (2) together gives the effect of an exposure to a particular risk factor on the risk premium, and the total risk premium is the sum of the effects of all risk factors.

The well-known *capital asset pricing model (CAPM)* identifies the market return (the return on all investment assets) as the (only) risk factor. Box 3.8 outlines the CAPM. This model determines the normal return for an equity investment as the risk-free rate plus a risk premium, which is the expected return on the whole market over the risk-free rate multiplied by the sensitivity of the investment's return to the market return, its *beta*. The risk-free rate is readily measured by the yield on a U.S. government bond that covers the duration of the investment, so the CAPM leaves the analyst with the task of measuring the market risk premium and a stock's beta.

Alternatively, *multifactor pricing models* insist that additional factors are involved in determining the risk premium. The box reviews these models. These models expand the task to identifying the relevant risk factors and estimating betas for each factor. The *arbitrage pricing theory (APT)* is behind these multifactor models. It characterizes investment returns as being sensitive to a number of economywide influences that cannot be diversified away, but is silent as to what these might be and indeed as to the numbers of factors. One might be the CAPM market factor, and the enhancement in practice comes from identifying the other factors. Some that have been suggested are shocks resulting from changes in industrial activity, the inflation rate, the spread between short and long-term interest rates, and the spread between low and high-risk corporate bonds.[1] Firm size and book-to-market ratio are among other factors that have been nominated as risk factors.[2] But these are conjectures.

Playing with Mirrors?

Clearly, this is a tricky business. Not only must the elusive risk factors be identified, but the unobservable risk premiums associated with them also must be measured, along with the beta sensitivities. With these problems it's tempting to play with mirrors, but coming

---

[1] See, for example, N-F. Chen, R. Roll, and S. A. Ross, "Economic Forces and the Stock Market," *Journal of Business,* July 1986, pp. 383–403.
[2] See E. F. Fama and K. R. French, "The Cross-Section of Expected Stock Returns," *Journal of Finance,* June 1992, pp. 427–465.

THE CAPITAL ASSET PRICING MODEL

The CAPM states that the required return for an investment *i* for a period is determined by

Required return (*i*) = Risk-free return
+ [Beta (*i*) × Market risk premium]

The market risk premium is the expected return from holding all risky assets over that from a risk-free asset. The portfolio of all risky assets (stocks, bonds, real estate, human capital, and many more) is sometimes called "the market portfolio" or "the market." So

Market risk premium = Expected return on the market
− Risk-free return

The beta for an investment measures the expected sensitivity of its return to the return on the market. That is, it measures how the price of the investment will move as the price of the market moves. It is defined as

$$\text{Beta}(i) = \frac{\text{Covariance (return on } i, \text{ return on the market)}}{\text{Variance (return on the market)}}$$

The covariance measures the sensitivity but, as it is standardized by the variance of the market, it is scaled so that the market as a whole has a beta of 1.0. A beta greater than 1 means the price of the investment is expected to move up more than the market when the market goes up and drop more when the market declines.

The risk premium for the investment is its beta multiplied by the market risk premium. In 2002, the risk-free rate (on U.S. Treasury bills) was about 3.5 percent. Commercial services that publish beta estimates were giving Cisco Systems a beta of about 2.1. So, if the market risk premium was 6 percent, then the required return for Cisco given by the CAPM was 16.1 percent:

16.1% = 3.5% + (2.1 × 6.0%)

The risk premium for buying Cisco was 12.6 percent, made up of 6.0 percent for the risk in the market as a whole plus an extra 6.6 percent for risk higher than that for the market.

The CAPM is based on the idea that one can diversify away a considerable amount of risk by holding the market portfolio of all investment assets. So the only risk that an investor needs to take on—and the only risk that will be rewarded in the market—is the risk that one cannot avoid, the risk in the market as a whole. The normal return for an investment is thus determined by the risk premium for the market and the investment's sensitivity to market risk.

The required return given by the CAPM is based on two expectations, expected sensitivities to the market and the expected market risk premium. Expectations are difficult to estimate. This is the challenge for a beta technology.

MULTIFACTOR PRICING MODELS

The market is said to be a risk factor. A risk factor is something that affects the returns on all investments in common, so it produces risk that cannot be diversified away. The market is the only risk factor in the CAPM because the model says that risk produced by other factors can be diversified away. Beta analysts suggest, however, that there are other risks, in addition to market risk, that cannot be negated. So they build multifactor models to capture the risk from additional factors:

Required return (*i*) = Risk-free return + [Beta1 (*i*) × Risk
premium for factor 1] + [Beta2 (*i*)
× Risk premium for factor 2]
+ · · · · + [Beta*k*(*i*) × Risk premium for
factor *k*]

The risk premium for each of the *k* factors is the expected return identified with the factor over the risk-free return. The market is usually considered to be risk factor 1, so the beta analyst needs to deal with the measurement problems in the CAPM. But the analyst must also identify the additional factors, calculate their expected risk premiums, and calculate the factor betas that measure the sensitivities of a given investment to the factors.

up with a solid product that gives an edge over the competition is a challenge. Even the one-factor CAPM is demanding. Betas have to be estimated and there are many commercial services that sell betas, each claiming its betas are better than those of the competition. No one knows the true beta and inevitably betas are measured with error. But even if we get a good measure of beta, there is the more difficult problem of determining the market risk premium. We used 6 percent for the market risk premium in calculating Cisco System's equity cost of capital in Box 3.8. But estimates range from 3 percent to

9.2 percent in texts and research papers. With this degree of uncertainty, estimates of required returns are likely to be unreliable. An 8 percent market risk premium would yield a required return for Cisco of 20.3 percent. A 4 percent market risk premium would yield a required return of 11.9 percent. We might well be cynical about the ability to get precise measures of required returns with these methods.

Indeed, there is a case to be made that using these beta technologies is just playing with mirrors. If Cisco's cost of capital can range from 11.9 percent to 20.3 percent depending on the choice of a number for the market risk premium, we cannot be very secure in our estimate. Disappointingly, despite a huge effort to build an empirically valid asset pricing model, research in finance has not delivered a reliable technology. In short, we really don't know what the cost of capital for most firms is.

If you have confidence in the beta technologies you have acquired in finance courses, you may wish to apply them in valuation. In this book, we will be sensitive to the imprecision that is introduced because of uncertainty about the cost of capital. Analysis is about reducing uncertainty. Forecasting payoffs is the first order of business in reducing our uncertainty about the worth of an investment, so our energies, in this book, are devoted to that aspect of fundamental analysis rather than the measurement of the cost of capital. We will, however, find ways to deal with our uncertainty about the cost of capital. Indeed, Chapter 18 brings fundamental analysis to the task of estimating the cost of capital and outlines strategies for finessing the imprecision in measuring the cost of capital in equity investing. You may wish to jump to that chapter, to get a flavor of the approach and how it relates to standard beta technologies.

Also look at the web page for this chapter. It reports historical returns and risk premiums from equity investing and compares them to returns for other types of assets.

LIVERPOOL JOHN MOORES UNIVERSITY
LEARNING & INFORMATION SERVICES

Cash Accounting, Accrual Accounting, and Discounted Cash Flow Valuation

LINKS

Link to previous chapter

Chapter 3 outlined the process of fundamental analysis and depicted valuation as a matter of forecasting future financial statements.

This chapter

This chapter introduces discounted cash flow valuation, a method that involves forecasting future cash flow statements. The chapter also shows how cash flows reported in the cash flow statement differ from accrual earnings in the income statement and how ignoring accruals in discounted cash flow valuation can cause problems.

Link to next chapter

Chapters 5 and 6 lay out valuation methods that forecast accrual accounting income statements and balance sheets.

Link to web page

The web page provides further explanation and additional examples of discounted cash flow analysis, cash accounting, and accrual accounting.

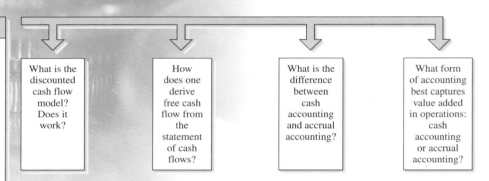

| What is the discounted cash flow model? Does it work? | How does one derive free cash flow from the statement of cash flows? | What is the difference between cash accounting and accrual accounting? | What form of accounting best captures value added in operations: cash accounting or accrual accounting? |

The previous chapter described fundamental analysis as a matter of forecasting future financial statements, with a focus on those features in the statements that have to do with investing and operating activities. We saw that forecasting the dividends that are to be reported as distributions in future statements of shareholders' equity does not work very well—primarily because dividends involve financing activities rather than value generation from investing and operating activities. But there are three other financial statements—the balance sheet, the income statement, and the cash flow statement. Which of these statements should be forecasted for valuation and what features of these statements involve the investing and operating activities?

This chapter examines valuation technologies based on forecasting the cash flow statement. The particular features of the cash flow statement that deal with operating and investment activities are cash flow from operations and cash investment. Forecasting cash flow from operations and cash investment and discounting them to a present value is called *discounted cash flow analysis.* This chapter describes discounted cash flow valuation techniques.

As a student in an introductory financial accounting course, you were no doubt introduced to the difference between cash accounting and accrual accounting. The cash flow statement tracks operating and investment activities with cash accounting. Accordingly,

The Analyst's Checklist

After reading this chapter you should understand:

- What is meant by cash flow from operations.
- What is meant by cash used in investing activities.
- What is meant by free cash flow.
- How discounted cash flow valuation works.
- Problems that arise in applying cash flow valuation.
- Why free cash flow may not measure value added in operations.
- Why free cash flow is a liquidation concept.
- How discounted cash flow valuation involves cash accounting for operating activities.
- Why "cash flow from operations" reported in U.S. financial statements does not measure operating cash flows correctly.
- Why "cash flow in investing activities" reported in U.S. financial statements does not measure cash investment in operations correctly.
- How accrual accounting for operations differs from cash accounting for operations.
- The difference between earnings and cash flow from operations.
- The difference between earnings and free cash flow.
- How accruals and the accounting for investment affect the balance sheet as well as the income statement.
- Why analysts forecast earnings rather than cash flows.
- How a valuation model is a model of accounting for the future.

After reading this chapter you should be able to:

- Apply the discounted cash flow model.
- Make a simple valuation from the current free cash flow.
- Calculate cash flow from operations from a cash flow statement.
- Calculate cash used in investing from a cash flow statement.
- Calculate free cash flow.
- Calculate after-tax net interest payments.
- Calculate levered and unlevered cash flow from operations.
- Calculate total accruals from a cash flow statement.
- Calculate revenue from cash receipts and revenue accruals.
- Calculate expenses for cash payments and expense accruals.
- Explain the difference between earnings and cash from operations.
- Explain the difference between earnings and free cash flow.

discounted cash flow analysis is a cash accounting approach to valuation. Income statements and balance sheets are prepared according to the principles of accrual accounting. In laying out discounted cash flow valuation, this chapter also explores the use of accrual accounting for valuation, and so sets the stage for techniques in the next two chapters that involve forecasting accrual accounting income statements and balance sheets rather than the cash flow statement. After giving an explanation of how accrual accounting works and how it differs from cash accounting, the chapter asks how those differences are relevant in valuation. In the spirit of choosing the best technology, we ask two questions. What problems arise when we forecast cash flows? Can accrual accounting help in remedying those problems?

As we saw in Chapter 1, the value of the firm is equal to the value of the debt plus the value of the equity: $V_0^F = V_0^D + V_0^E$. The *value of the firm* is the value of its investing and operating activities, and this value is divided among the claimants—the debtholders and shareholders. So, one can calculate the value of the equity directly by forecasting value flowing to equity holders, as with the dividend discount model, or one can value the equity by forecasting the value flowing from the firm's investing and operating activities (the value of the firm), and then deduct the value of the net debt. Discounted cash flow analysis, by forecasting operating and investing cash flows, values the firm's operating and investing activities. The value of the equity is then calculated by subtracting the value of the net debt. *Net debt* is the debt the firm holds as liabilities less any debt investments that the firm holds as assets. As we saw in Chapter 2, debt is typically reported on the balance sheet at close to market value so one can subtract the book value of the net debt. In any case, the market value of the debt is reported, in most cases, in the footnotes to the financial statements. When valuing the common equity, both the debt and the preferred equity are subtracted from the value of the firm; from the common shareholder's point of view, preferred equity is really debt.

It is common to refer to investing and operating activities simply as *operating activities,* with investing in operations implicit. Accordingly, the *value of the operations* as used in this text can be taken to mean the value of the investing and operating activities of the firm.

THE DISCOUNTED CASH FLOW MODEL

We saw in Chapter 3 that we can value a project by forecasting its cash flows. We can also anticipate its value added with a calculation of the net present value of expected cash flows. This is a standard approach in project evaluation. The firm is just a lot of projects combined; to discover the value of the firm, we can calculate the present value of expected cash flows from all the projects in the firm's operations.

The total cash flow from all projects is referred to as the *cash flow from operations.* Going concerns invest in new projects as old ones terminate. Investments require cash outlays, called *capital expenditures* or *cash investment* (in operations). Figure 4.1 depicts the cash flow from operations, C_t, and the cash outflows for investments, I_t, for five years for a going concern. After a cash investment is made in a particular year (Year 2, say), cash flow from operations in subsequent years (Year 3 and beyond) will include the cash inflow from that project until it terminates. In any particular year, operations yield a net cash flow, the difference between the cash flow from operations and cash investment, $C_t - I_t$. This is called *free cash flow* because it is the part of the cash from operations that is "free" after the firm reinvests in new assets.[1]

If we forecast free cash flows, we can value the firm's operations by applying the present value formula:

$$\text{Value of the firm} = \text{Present value of expected free cash flows} \qquad \textbf{(4.1)}$$

$$V_0^F = \frac{C_1 - I_1}{\rho_F} + \frac{C_2 - I_2}{\rho_F^2} + \frac{C_3 - I_3}{\rho_F^3} + \frac{C_4 - I_4}{\rho_F^4} + \frac{C_5 - I_5}{\rho_F^5} + \cdots$$

---

[1] Be warned that you will encounter a multitude of "cash flow" definitions in practice: operating cash flow, free cash flow, financing cash flow, and even ebitda (used to approximate "cash flow"). You need to differentiate what is meant with each use of the words.

FIGURE 4.1

Cash Flows from All Projects for a Going Concern. Free cash flow is cash flow from operations that results from investments minus cash used to make investments.

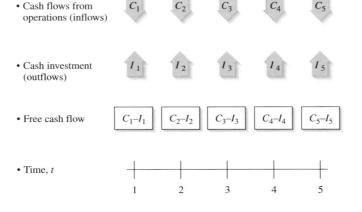

This is a valuation model for the firm, referred to as the *discounted cash flow (DCF) model.* The discount rate here is one that is appropriate for the riskiness of the cash flows from all projects. It is called the *cost of capital for the firm* or the *cost of capital for operations.*[2] The equity claimants have to share the payoffs from the firm's operations with the debt claimants, so the value for the common equity is the value of the firm minus the value of the net debt (including preferred stock): $V_0^E = V_0^F - V_0^D$.

You should have noticed something: This model, like the dividend discount model, requires forecasting over an infinite horizon. If we are to forecast for a finite horizon, we will have to add value at the horizon for the value of free cash flows after the horizon. This value is called the **continuing value**. For a forecast of cash flows for T periods, the value of equity will be

$$V_0^E = \frac{C_1 - I_1}{\rho_F} + \frac{C_2 - I_2}{\rho_F^2} + \frac{C_3 - I_3}{\rho_F^3} + \cdots + \frac{C_T - I_T}{\rho_F^T} + \frac{\text{CV}_T}{\rho_F^T} - V_0^D \qquad \textbf{(4.2)}$$

The continuing value is not to be confused with the terminal value. As explained in the last chapter, the terminal value is the value we expect the firm to be worth at T, the terminal payoff, P_T, to selling the firm at T. The continuing value is the value omitted by the calculation when we forecast only up to T rather than "to infinity." The continuing value is the device by which we reduce an infinite-horizon forecasting problem to a finite-horizon one, so our first criterion for practical analysis is really a question of whether a continuing value can be calculated within a reasonable forecast period. How do we calculate the continuing value so that it captures all the cash flows expected after T? Well, we can proceed in the same way as with the dividend discount model if we forecast that the free cash flows after T will be a constant perpetuity. In this case we capitalize the perpetuity:

$$\text{CV}_T = \frac{C_{T+1} - I_{T+1}}{\rho_F - 1} \qquad \textbf{(4.2a)}$$

---

[2] Chapter 13 discusses the cost of capital for operations and how it relates to the cost of capital for equity.

EXHIBIT 4.1 Discounted Cash Flow Analysis

NEW YORK STATE ELECTRIC AND GAS CORP.
(amounts in millions of dollars except per share data)

	1987	1988	1989	1990	1991	1992	1993	1994	1995	1996
Cash from operations		602	460	381	403	379	499	533	531	534
Cash investments		207	191	211	301	243	302	216	160	212
Free cash flow		395	269	170	102	136	197	317	371	322
Discount factor $(1.09)^t$		1.090	1.188	1.295	1.412	1.539	1.677	1.828	1.993	
PV of cash flows		362	226	131	72	88	117	173	186	
Total PV of cash flows	1,355									
Continuing value*									3,578	
PV of CV	1,795									
Value of the firm (V^F_{1987})	3,150									
Book value of debt and preferred stock	2,290									
Value of equity (V^E_{1987})	860									
Value per share (55.733 million shares)	15.43									
Dividends per share	2.64	2.00	2.02	2.06	2.10	2.14	2.18	2.00	1.40	1.40
Price per share	20.88	22.75	28.88	26.00	29.00	32.50	30.75	19.00	25.88	21.63

*Continuing value = $322/0.09 = $3,578 million.

Or, if we forecast free cash flow growing at a constant rate after the horizon, then

$$CV_T = \frac{C_{T+1} - I_{T+1}}{\rho_F - g} \tag{4.2b}$$

where g is now 1 plus the forecasted rate of growth in free cash flow.

Exhibit 4.1 reproduces actual free cash flows generated by New York State Electric and Gas Corp. (now trading as a parent, Energy East Corp.) from 1988 to 1996. Suppose that these actual cash flows were those you had forecast (with perfect foresight) at the end of 1987 when the stock traded at $20.88. As free cash flows from 1994 to 1996 are at a reasonably constant level, you might have forecast their continuing as a perpetuity after 1996 at the level in 1996. So you might have valued the firm using the DCF model (equation 4.2) with the continuing value (equation 4.2a). Exhibit 4.1 gives the calculation using a cost of capital of 9 percent. The calculation takes the book value of debt and preferred stock as their market value. The approximation is reasonable unless interest rates have moved substantially since the debt was issued.

Actual cash flows differ from forecasted cash flows, so this valuation (based on actual cash flows) cannot be expected to equal the market valuation of $20.88 per share (based on forecasted cash flows) at the end of 1987. The purpose of the exhibit is merely to apply the model and to indicate that using the DCF model is appropriate for firms whose forecasted free cash flows level off like those for this firm from 1994 to 1996. Box 4.1 gives a valuation for New York State Electric and Gas at the end of 1996.

New York State Electric and Gas generates fairly regular and predictable cash flows. Look now at Exhibit 4.2. Wal-Mart has been one of the most successful retailers in the United States since the 1960s. The firm's annual sales are now over $250 billion. From January 1987 to January 1996 its stock rose from $6 per share to $20.38, adjusted for stock splits. Wal-Mart would have been a good buy at the beginning of 1987. If you were

With practical, low-cost solutions in mind, we always want to investigate simple methods of analysis. Simple methods avoid some forecasting (and the associated information analysis), but they lose precision as a consequence. The tradeoff has to be considered, so simple valuations are made as benchmarks to be improved upon with more detailed analysis.

Simple valuations can be made from information in current financial statements. Keep forecasting in mind, but take a number in the current statements as indicative of the future. This avoids the analysis of other information. In valuing New York State Gas and Electric at the end of 1996, conjecture that the 1996 free cash flow will continue at the same level perpetually in the future. Thus the value of the firm is calculated (in millions of dollars) as

$$V^F_{1996} = \frac{\$322}{0.09} = \$3,578$$

The book value of the firm's debt and preferred stock at the end of 1996 was $1,875 million. The book value of debt and preferred stock is usually close to market value so the book value is typically used as an approximation to market value (another simple valuation!). Thus the value of the common equity is calculated (in millions) as

$$V^E_{1996} = \$3,578 - \$1,875 = \$1,703$$

or, with 69.67 million shares outstanding, $24.44 per share. The shares traded at 21.63 at the end of 1996.

Simple valuations may be imprecise but they serve to prompt questions for further analysis. If you value this utility at $24.44 while it trades at 21.63, you ask: What does the market see that I don't see? Well, your cost of capital might be wrong and you'd want to test sensitivity of your valuation to other reasonable rates for the cost of capital. But you might also ask: Does the market see future free cash flows that are different from current free cash flow? This is your leading question for analysis. If you cannot justify the forecast of future cash flows that is implicit in the market price, you conclude that the market is incorrect. You see an arbitrage opportunity.

You may improve a simple valuation by applying an estimated growth rate to a current number in the financial statements. Using current free cash flow (in 1996), calculate

$$V^E_{1996} = \frac{\$322 \times g}{1.09 - g} - \$1,875$$

where g is (1 plus) the forecasted perpetual growth rate in future free cash flows. This simple valuation applies the continuing value in equation (4.2b) at the present point in time rather than at a future horizon, whereas the first simple valuation applies the continuing value in equation (4.2a) to the present. The simple model with growth requires only that a growth rate be forecasted, but clearly this involves additional analysis over the simple valuation without growth.

Using one number in the current financial statements as the basis for a valuation is an example of the parsimony sought under the third criterion for practical analysis discussed in Chapter 3. If one number is sufficient to forecast the future stream, then we certainly have a parsimonious valuation method. The "if" here is a "big if." But we strive for methods that, for a large set of firms, give us reasonable, simple valuation approximations with one (or perhaps two or three) piece of information. Does free cash flow do so? Well, look at the Wal-Mart example in Exhibit 4.2.

EXHIBIT 4.2   A Case with Negative Free Cash Flows

WAL-MART STORES INC.
(fiscal years ending January 31; amounts in millions of dollars except per-share data)

	1988	1989	1990	1991	1992	1993	1994	1995	1996
Cash from operations	536	828	968	1,422	1,553	1,540	2,573	3,410	2,993
Cash investments	627	541	894	1,526	2,150	3,506	4,486	3,792	3,332
Free cash flow	(91)	287	74	(104)	(597)	(1,966)	(1,913)	(382)	(339)
Dividends per share	0.03	0.04	0.06	0.07	0.09	0.11	0.13	0.17	0.20
Price per share	6.88	8.50	10.63	16.50	27.00	32.50	26.50	22.88	20.38

Numbers in parentheses are negative.

to calculate the rate of return over these nine years from the dividends and price payoffs in the exhibit, you would find it is 260.5 percent (using a 12 percent rate for reinvestment of dividends), or 15.2 percent on an annual basis.

Suppose you were thinking of buying Wal-Mart in 1987. Suppose also that, again with perfect foresight, you knew then what Wal-Mart's cash flows were going to be and had sought to apply a DCF valuation. Well, the free cash flows are negative in all except two years and their present value is negative! The last cash flow in 1996 is also negative, so it can't be capitalized to yield a continuing value. You could not have valued Wal-Mart with a nine-year forecast horizon (and a nine-year horizon is considered quite long). A simple valuation like the one in Box 4.1 would be hopeless. And if, in 1996, you had looked back on the free cash flows Wal-Mart had produced, you surely would not conclude that they indicate the value generated in the stock price.

Free Cash Flow and Value Added

Why does DCF valuation not work in some cases? The short answer is that free cash flow does not measure value added from operations over a period. Cash flow from operations is value flowing into the firm from selling products but it is reduced by cash investment. If a firm invests more cash in operations than it takes in from operations, its free cash flow is negative. And even if investment is zero NPV or adds value, free cash flow is reduced, and so is its present value. Of course, the return to these investments will come later in cash flow from operations, but the more investing the firm does for a longer period in the future, the longer the forecasting horizon has to be to capture these cash inflows. Wal-Mart has continually found new investment opportunities—expansion into new stores—so its investment has been greater than its cash inflow. Eventually free cash flow should turn positive as the cash from those investments comes in (but probably only as the rate of investment slows down).

Free cash flow is not really a concept about adding value in operations. It confuses investments (and the value they create) with the payoffs from investments, so it is partly an investment or a liquidation concept. A firm decreases its free cash flow by investing and increases it by liquidating or reducing its investments. But a firm is worth more if it invests profitably, not less. If an analyst forecasts low or negative free cash flow for the next few years, would we take this as a lack of success in operations? Wal-Mart's positive free cash flow in 1989 might have been seen as bad news because it resulted partly from a decrease in investment. Free cash flow would be a measure of value from operations if cash receipts were matched in the same period with the cash investments that generated them. Then we would have value received less value surrendered to gain it. But in DCF analysis, cash receipts from investments are recognized in periods after the investment is made, and this can force us to forecast over long horizons to capture value. DCF analysis violates the matching principle (see Box 2.4 in Chapter 2).

A solution to the Wal-Mart problem is to have a very long forecast horizon. But this offends the first criterion of practical analysis that we established in Chapter 3. Discounted cash flow analysts deal with the problem by making adjustments to cash flows that effectively involve accrual accounting. The question is how to do accrual accounting well. On the second criterion of validating forecasts, DCF analysis also presents problems. Free cash flows subsequent to a forecast are reported in later statements of cash flows, of course, so they can be observed. But those free cash flows include cash inflows from new investments made subsequent to the forecasts, which may not have been anticipated at the time of the forecasts. Disentangling cash flows that are realizations of those forecasted from those deriving from the new investments is very difficult (particularly to an outsider to the firm); thus the ability to validate forecasts after the fact is questionable.

ADVANTAGES

Easy concept: Cash flows are "real" and easy to think about; they are not affected by accounting rules.

Familiarity: Cash flow valuation is a straight-forward application of familiar present value techniques.

DISADVANTAGES

Suspect concept: Free cash flow does not measure value added in the short run; value gained is not matched with value given up.

Free cash flow fails to recognize value generated that does not involve cash flows.

Investment is treated as a loss of value.

Free cash flow is partly a liquidation concept; firms increase free cash flow by cutting back on investments.

Forecast horizons: Typically, long forecast horizons are required to recognize cash inflows from investments, particularly when investments are growing.

Validation: It is hard to validate free cash flow forecasts.

Not aligned with what people forecast: Analysts forecast earnings, not free cash flow; adjusting earnings forecasts to free cash flow forecasts requires further forecasting of accruals.

WHEN IT WORKS BEST

When the investment pattern produces positive constant free cash flow or free cash flow growing at a constant rate.

Another practical problem is that free cash flows are not what professionals forecast. Analysts usually forecast earnings, not free cash flow, probably because earnings, not free cash flow, are a measure of success in operations. To convert an analyst's forecast to a valuation using DCF analysis, we have to convert the earnings forecast to a free cash forecast. This can be done but not without further analysis. Box 4.2 summarizes the advantages and disadvantages of DCF analysis.

THE STATEMENT OF CASH FLOWS

Cash flows are reported in the statement of cash flows, so forecasting cash flows amounts to preparing pro forma cash flow statements for the future. But the cash flows in a U.S. statement (that is, one prepared following GAAP) are not quite what we want for DCF analysis. Exhibit 4.3 gives "cash flows from operating activities" and "cash flows from investing activities" from Dell Computer's statement of cash flows for fiscal year 2002. The extract is from Dell's full cash flow statement, provided in Exhibit 2.1 in Chapter 2. Dell reported 2002 cash flow from operations of $3,797 million and cash used in investing of $2,260 million, so its free cash flow appears to be the difference, $1,537 million.

Cash flow from operations is calculated in the statement as net income less items in income that do not involve cash flows. (These noncash items are the accruals, to be discussed later in the chapter.) But net income includes interest payments, which are not part of operations. Interest payments are cash flows to debtholders out of the cash that operations generate. They are financing flows. Firms are required to report the amount of interest paid as supplementary information to the cash flow statement; Dell reported

EXHIBIT 4.3

Portion of Dell
Computer's 2002
Cash Flow Statement

DELL COMPUTER CORPORATION
Partial Consolidated Statement of Cash Flows
(in millions of dollars)

	Fiscal Year Ended		
	February 1, 2002	February 2, 2001	January 28, 2000
Cash flows from operating activities:			
Net income	$1,246	$2,177	$1,666
Adjustments to reconcile net income to net cash provided by operating activities:			
Depreciation and amortization	239	240	156
Tax benefits of employee stock plans	487	929	1,040
Special charges	742	105	194
Gains/losses on investments	17	(307)	(80)
Other	178	135	56
Changes in operating working capital:			
Accounts receivable, net	222	(531)	(394)
Inventories	111	(11)	(123)
Accounts payable	826	780	988
Accrued and other liabilities	(210)	404	416
Other, net	(123)	—	(75)
Changes in Noncurrent assets and liabilities	62	274	82
Net cash provided by operating activities	3,797	4,195	3,926
Cash flows from investing activities:			
Investments in securities:			
Purchases	(5,382)	(2,606)	(3,101)
Maturities and sales	3,425	2,331	2,319
Capital expenditures	(303)	(482)	(401)
Net cash used in investing activities	(2,260)	(757)	(1,183)
Supplemental statement of cash flows information:			
Interest paid	31	49	34
Investment income, primarily interest	314	305	158

Source: Dell Computer Corporation, 10-K filing, 2002.

$31 million (see Exhibit 4.3.) Net income also includes income (usually interest) earned on excess cash that is temporarily invested in interest-bearing deposits and marketable securities like bonds. These investments are not investments in operations. Rather they are investments to store excess cash until it can be invested in operations later, or to pay off debt or pay dividends later. Dell had over $5 billion of interest-bearing securities on its 2002 balance sheet (in Chapter 2). The supplementary information in Exhibit 4.3 reports $314 million of investment income on these securities. This interest income from the investments was not cash generated by operations.

The difference between interest payments and interest receipts is called *net interest payments*. In the U.K. cash flow statements, net interest payments are not included in cash flow from operations.[3] But in the United States they are, so they must be added back

---

[3] International accounting standards permit firms to classify net interest payments either as part of operations or as a financing cash flow.

DELL COMPUTER CORPORATION, 2002
(in millions of dollars)

Reported cash flow from operations		3,797
Interest payments	31	
Interest income*	(314)	
Net interest payments	(283)	
Taxes (35%)†	99	
Net interest payments after tax (65%)		(184)
Cash flow from operations		3,613
Reported cash used in investing activities	2,260	
Purchases of interest-bearing securities	5,382	
Sales of interest-bearing securities	(3,425)	1,957
Cash investment in operations		303
Free cash flow		3,310

*Interest payments are given as supplemental data to the statement of cash flows, but interest receipts usually are not. Interest income (from the income statement) is used instead; this includes accruals but is usually close to the cash interest received.
†Dell's statutory tax rate (for federal and state taxes) is 35 percent, as indicated in the financial statement footnotes.

to the reported free cash flows from operations to get the actual cash that operations generate. However, interest receipts are taxable and interest payments are deductions for assessing taxable income, so net interest payments must be adjusted for the tax payments they attract or save. The net effect of interest and taxes is *after-tax net interest payments,* calculated as net interest payments $\times$ (1 – tax rate). Cash flow from operations is

$$\text{Cash flow from operations} = \text{Reported cash flow from operations} \quad \textbf{(4.3)}$$
$$+ \text{After-tax net interest payments}$$

The first part of Box 4.3 calculates Dell's cash flow from operations from its reported number. For many firms, interest payments are greater than interest receipts (unlike here), so cash flow from operations is usually larger than the reported number.

The U.S. statement of cash flows has a section headed "cash flow from investing activities." But the investments there include the investments of excess cash in interest-bearing securities. These are not investments in operations, so

$$\text{Cash investment in operations} = \text{Reported cash flow from investing} \quad \textbf{(4.4)}$$
$$- \text{Net investment in interest-bearing}$$
$$\text{securities}$$

Net investment is investments minus liquidations (purchases minus sales) of investments. Dell's revised cash investment in operations is given in Box 4.3, along with its free cash flow.

Cash flow from operations is sometimes referred to as the *unlevered cash flow from operations* but the "unlevered" is redundant. The reported cash flow from operations is sometimes called the *levered cash flow from operations* because it includes the interest from leverage through debt financing. With common shareholders in mind, levered cash flow from operations is the reported cash flow minus preferred dividend payments. But levered cash flow is not a useful measure. Dividends are the cash flows to shareholders and these are calculated after servicing not just interest but the repayment of principal to debtholders also.

DELL COMPUTER CORPORATION, 2002
(in millions of dollars)

Forecast		2000F		2001F		2002F
Earnings		1,666		2,177		1,246
Accrual adjustment		2,260		2,018		2,551
Levered cash flows from operations		3,926		4,195		3,797
Interest payments	34		49		31	
Interest receipts	(158)		(305)		(314)	
Net interest payments	(124)		(256)		(283)	
Tax at 35%	43	(81)	90	(166)	99	(184)
Cash flow from operations		3,845		4,029		3,613
Cash investment in operations		(401)		(482)		(303)
Free cash flow		3,444		3,547		3,310

Forecasting Free Cash Flows

It is difficult to forecast free cash flows without first forecasting earnings. After forecasting earnings (as analysts do), make adjustments to convert earnings to cash flows from operations. Follow these steps:

1. Forecast earnings.

2. Forecast the accrual adjustments to earnings in the cash flow statement.

3. Calculate levered cash flow from operations (Step 1 + Step 2).

4. Forecast after-tax net interest payments.

5. Calculate (unlevered) cash flow from operations (Step 3 + Step 4).

6. Forecast cash investments in operations, excluding net investment in interest-bearing securities.

7. Calculate free cash flow, $C - I$ (Step 5 – Step 6).

Box 4.4 shows how we might have forecasted Dell's free cash flows for 2000–2002 at the end of 1999. The forecasted numbers in the box are actual numbers that Dell reported for 2000–2002 to make a point: The forecasting of free cash flows (Steps 1–7) follows the structure of the cash flow statement.

Forecasting earnings, accruals, and investments is a considerable challenge. It requires an analysis of what's going on inside the firm. Some analysts forecast ebitda for Step 5, to keep it simple, but this is very much an approximation. Indeed ebitda can be quite misleading as a measure of cash flow, because it ignores all accruals other than depreciation and amortization and, further, ignores the taxes incurred in operations. Part Two of the book supplies an analysis in which free cash flows are efficiently forecast, indeed with just one calculation rather than the seven steps here, once income statements and balance sheets are forecast.

However, we also must ask whether the exercise of converting earnings forecasts to cash flows is a useful one. Can we value a firm from earnings forecasts rather than cash flow forecasts and save ourselves the work in making the conversion? The answer is yes. Indeed we will now show that adjusting earnings for accruals can actually introduce more complications to the valuation task.

CASH FLOW, EARNINGS, AND ACCRUAL ACCOUNTING

Analysts forecast earnings rather than cash flows. And the stock market appears to value firms on the basis of expected earnings: A firm's failure to meet analysts' earnings forecasts typically results in a drop in share price, while beating earnings expectations usually results in an increased share price.

There are good reasons to forecast earnings rather than free cash flows if we have valuation in mind. The difference between earnings and cash flow from operations is the accruals. We now show how accruals in principle capture value added in operations that cash flows do not. And we also show how accrual accounting treats investment differently from cash accounting to remedy the problems we have just seen in forecasting free cash flows.

We recognized in the last chapter that value creation is based on expectations of value to be generated in selling goods and services in markets. The net value added in markets is value received from sales to customers less value given up in acquiring inputs to make sales. Earnings is the accrual accounting measure of this value added. We saw in this chapter that the cash flow statement matches cash investment to cash flow from operations to yield free cash flow. But we found that this matching does not capture value added in markets because the cash investment that is subtracted from cash from operations does not usually reduce value and, indeed, is the source of the value creation. Does use of accounting earnings remedy these problems?

Earnings and Cash Flows

Exhibit 4.4 gives the statement of income for Dell Computer for fiscal 2002 along with prior years' comparative statements. The income statement recognizes value inflows from selling products in revenues and reduces revenues by the value outflows in expenses to yield a net number, net income, as we saw in Chapter 2. Adding other comprehensive income and subtracting preferred dividends yields comprehensive income available to common, the measure of value added for the common shareholders.

There are three things you should notice about income statements:

1. Dividends do not appear in the statement. Dividends are a distribution of value, not a part of the value generation. So they do not determine the measure of value added, earnings. Dividends do reduce shareholders' value in the firm, however; appropriately, they reduce the book value of equity in the balance sheet. Accountants get this right.

2. Investment is not subtracted in the income statement, so the value-added earnings number is not affected by investment, unlike free cash flow. (An exception is investment in research and development, so the value-added measure may be distorted in this respect.)

3. There is a matching of value inflows (revenues) to value outflows (expenses). Accountants follow the **matching principle**, which says that expenses should be recorded in the same period that the revenues they generate are recognized, as we saw in Chapter 2. Value surrendered is matched with value gained to get net value added from selling goods or services. Thus, for example, only those inventory costs that apply to goods sold during a period are recognized as value given up in cost of sales (and the

EXHIBIT 4.4
Income Statements
for Dell Computer
Corporation

DELL COMPUTER CORPORATION
Consolidated Statements of Income
(amounts in millions)

	Fiscal Year Ended		
	February 1, 2002	February 2, 2001	January 28, 2000
Net revenue	$31,168	$31,888	$25,265
Cost of revenue	25,661	25,445	20,047
Gross margin	5,507	6,443	5,218
Operating expenses:			
Selling, general and administrative	2,784	3,193	2,387
Research, development and engineering	452	482	374
Special charges	482	105	194
Total operating expenses	3,718	3,780	2,955
Operating income	1,789	2,663	2,263
Investment and other income (loss), net	(58)	531	188
Income before income taxes and cumulative effect of change in accounting principle	1,731	3,194	2,451
Provision for income taxes	485	958	785
Income before cumulative effect of change in accounting principle	1,246	2,236	1,666
Cumulative effect of change in accounting principle, net	—	59	—
Net income	$ 1,246	$ 2,177	$ 1,666

Source: Dell Computer Corporation, 10-K filing, 2002.

remaining costs—value not yet given up—are recorded as inventories in the balance sheet); and a cost to pay pensions to employees arising from their service during the current period is reported as an expense in generating revenue for the period even though the cash flow (during the employees' retirement) may be many years later (and a corresponding pension liability is recorded in the balance sheet). Dell reported 2002 revenues of $31,168 million from the sale of computers and related products. Against this, it matched $25,661 million for the cost of the products sold and another $3,718 million in operating expenses, to report $1,789 million as operating income before taxes—value received less value given up in operations. (Dell also reported a loss of $58 million on investments and "other income.")

Cash flow from operations adds value and is incorporated in the revenue and expenses. But to effect the matching of revenues and expenses, the accountant modifies cash flows from operations with the **accruals**. Accruals are measures of noncash value flows.

Accruals

These are of two types, *revenue accruals* and *expense accruals.*

Revenues are recorded when value is received from sales of products. To measure this value inflow, revenue accruals recognize value increases that are not cash flows and subtract cash inflows that are not value increases. The most common revenue accruals are receivables: A sale on credit is considered an increase in value even though cash has not been received. Correspondingly, cash received in advance of a sale is not included in revenue because value is not deemed to have been added: The recognition of value is deferred until such time as the goods are shipped and the sale is completed. Revenue for a period is calculated as:

Revenue = Cash receipts from sales + New sales on credit − Cash received for previous
periods' sales − Estimates of credit sales not collectible − Estimated sales
returns − Deferred revenue for cash received in advance of sale + Revenue
previously deferred to the current period

You will notice in this calculation that credit sales deemed uncollectible and estimated returns of goods are accruals. That is, they are amounts in sales that are judged not to add value. The net effect of these adjustments is sometimes called *net revenue.*

Expense accruals recognize value given up in generating revenue that is not a cash flow and adjust cash outflows that are not value given up. Cash payments are modified by accruals as follows:

Expense = Cash paid for expenses + Amounts incurred in generating revenues but not
yet paid − Cash paid for generating revenues in future periods + Amounts
paid in the past for generating revenues in the current period

Pension expense is an example of an expense incurred in generating revenue that will not be paid until later. Wages payable is another example. A prepaid wage for work in the future is an example of cash paid for expenses in advance. Depreciation arises from cash flows in the past for investments in plant. Plants wear out. Depreciation is that part of the cost of the investment that is deemed to be used up in producing the revenue of the current period. Dell's expenses have cash and accrual components. Income tax expense, for example, includes taxes due for the period but not paid and cost of goods sold excludes cash paid for production of computers that have not yet been sold.

Total accruals for a period are reported as the difference between net income and cash flow from operations in the statement of cash flows. Reported cash flows from operations are after interest, so

$$\text{Earnings} = \text{Levered cash flow from operations} + \text{Accruals} \qquad \textbf{(4.5)}$$
$$\text{Earnings} = (C - i) + \text{Accruals}$$

This is another accounting relation to be added to those discussed in Chapter 2. See Box 4.5. We use C to indicate (unlevered) cash flow from operations, as before, and i to indicate after-tax net interest payments, so $C - i$ is levered cash flow from operations. We see in Exhibit 4.3 that Dell had $2,551 million in accruals in 2002. That is, $2,551 million less value was deemed to have been added in earnings of $1,246 million than in levered cash flows from operations of $3,797 million.

Accruals change the timing for recognizing value in the financial statements from when cash flows occur. Recognizing a receivable as revenue or recognizing an increase in a pension obligation as expense recognizes value ahead of the future cash flow; recognizing deferred revenue or depreciation recognizes value later than cash flow. In all cases, the concept is to match value inflows and outflows to get a measure of value added in selling products in the market. Timing is important to our first criterion for practical valuation analysis, a reasonably short forecast horizon. You readily see how recognizing a pension expense 30 years before the cash flow at retirement is going to shorten the forecast horizon. We will now see how deferring recognition until after a cash flow also will shorten the forecast horizon.

Cash flow from operations
− Net interest payments (after tax)
+ Accruals
= Earnings

Free cash flow
− Net interest payments (after tax)
+ Accruals
+ Investments
= Earnings

Add these accounting relations to those in Chapter 2 (Box 2.1). They are tools for analysis.

Investments

The performance measure in DCF analysis is free cash flow, not cash flow from operations. Free cash flow is cash generated from operations after cash investments, $C − I$, and we saw that investments are troublesome in the DCF calculation because they are treated as decreases in value. But investments are made to generate value; they lose value only later as the assets are used up in operations. The value lost in operations occurs after the cash flow. The earnings calculation recognizes this:

$$\text{Earnings} = \text{Free cash flow} − \text{Net cash interest} + \text{Investments} + \text{Accruals} \qquad \textbf{(4.6)}$$
$$\text{Earnings} = (C − I) − i + I + \text{Accruals}$$

Accrual accounting adds back investment to free cash flow. Because it places investment in the balance sheet as assets, it does not affect income. Then it recognizes decreases in those assets in subsequent periods in the form of depreciation accruals (and other amortizations) as assets lose value in generating revenue. Look at Box 4.5 again.

We saw in Exhibit 4.2 that forecasting Wal-Mart's free cash flows would not have been a productive valuation exercise in 1987. Exhibit 4.5 adds earnings and eps numbers to the display of cash flow numbers in Exhibit 4.2. The difference between cash from operations and net income is the additional value measured by the accruals. In fiscal 1988, for example, the net income of $628 million recognized $92 million in value added over the $536 million in cash flows from operations. Compare, now, the free cash flows to the net income. The difference, $719 million in 1988, reflects the amount of investment, $627 million, as well as the accruals. The free cash flows are typically negative, as we have observed, but earnings are positive and growing over time, consistent with the increase in share prices. Some of this growth is explained by increased assets from share issues, so focus on per-share earnings that standardizes for share issues.

To appreciate the full details of how accrual accounting is done, you must grasp a good deal of detail. Here we have seen only a broad outline of how the accounting works to measure value flows. This will be embellished later—particularly in Part Four of the book—but now would be a good time to review a financial accounting text.

The outline of earnings measurement here describes nominally how the accounting works and our expression for earnings above looks like a good way to measure value added. But there is no guarantee that a particular set of accounting rules—U.S. GAAP, for example—achieves the ideal. Yes, depreciation nominally matches value lost to value gained, but whether this is achieved depends on how the depreciation is actually measured. And this is true for all accruals. Cash flows are objective, but the accruals depend on accounting rules, and these rules may not be good ones. Indeed, in the case of depreciation,

EXHIBIT 4.5   A Case with Negative Free Cash Flows and Positive Earnings

WAL-MART STORES INC.
(fiscal years ending January 31; amounts in millions of dollars except per-share data)

	1988	1989	1990	1991	1992	1993	1994	1995	1996
Cash from operations	536	828	968	1,422	1,553	1,540	2,573	3,410	2,993
Cash investments	627	541	894	1,526	2,150	3,506	4,486	3,792	3,332
Free cash flow	(91)	287	74	(104)	(597)	(1,966)	(1,913)	(382)	(339)
Net income	628	837	1,076	1,291	1,608	1,995	2,333	2,681	2,740
eps	0.28	0.37	0.48	0.57	0.70	0.87	1.02	1.17	1.19

Accounting Clinic II

HOW ACCRUAL ACCOUNTING WORKS

Accounting Clinic II, on the book's website, lays out in more detail how accrual accounting works and contrasts accrual accounting with cash accounting. After going through this clinic you will understand how and when revenues are recorded and why cash received from customers is not the same as revenues recorded under accrual accounting. You also will understand how accrual accounting records expenses. You will see how the matching principle—to measure value added—that was introduced in Chapter 2 is applied through the rules of accrual accounting. You also will recognize those cases where GAAP violates the principle of good matching. And you will appreciate how accrual accounting affects not only the income statement but also the balance sheet.

firms can choose from different methods. Many accruals involve estimates, which offer a potential for error. Accruals can be manipulated to some degree. And you see in Dell's income statement that R&D expenditures are expensed in the income statement even though they are investments. These observations suggest that the value-added measure, net income, may be mismeasured, so a valuation technique based on forecasting earnings must accommodate this mismeasurement. Indeed, one rationale for DCF analysis is that the accounting is so suspect that one must subtract or "back out" the accruals from income statements to get to the "real cash flows," with the problems this induces. We will come back to the quality of accrual accounting in Part Four of the book.

Accruals, Investments, and the Balance Sheet

Exhibit 4.6 is Dell's 2002 comparative balance sheet. The investments (which are not placed in the income statement) are there—land, buildings, equipment, leasehold improvements, construction in progress, short-term investments, and long-term marketable securities. But the statement also has accruals. Shareholders' equity is assets minus liabilities, so one cannot affect the shareholders' equity through earnings without affecting assets and liabilities also. The cash flow component of earnings affects cash on the balance sheet and the accrual component affects other balance sheet items. That is why some accrual adjustments in the statement of cash flows are expressed as changes in balance sheet items. Credit sales, recognized as a revenue accrual on Dell's income statement, produce receivables on Dell's balance sheet and estimates of bad debts and sales returns reduce net receivables. Inventories are costs incurred ahead of matching against revenue

EXHIBIT 4.6
Balance Sheets for
Dell Computer
Corporation

CONSOLIDATED STATEMENT OF FINANCIAL POSITION
(in millions of dollars)

	Fiscal Year Ended	
	February 1, 2002	February 2, 2001
ASSETS		
Current assets:		
Cash and cash equivalents	$ 3,641	$ 4,910
Short-term investments	273	525
Accounts receivable, net	2,269	2,424
Inventories	278	400
Other	1,416	1,467
Total current assets	7,877	9,726
Property, plant and equipment, net	826	996
Investments	4,373	2,418
Other noncurrent assets	459	530
Total assets	$13,535	$13,670
LIABILITIES AND STOCKHOLDERS' EQUITY		
Current liabilities:		
Accounts payable	$ 5,075	$ 4,286
Accrued and other	2,444	2,492
Total current liabilities	7,519	6,778
Long-term debt	520	509
Other	802	761
Commitments and contingent liabilities	—	—
Total liabilities	8,841	8,048
Stockholders' equity:		
Preferred stock and capital in excess of $.01 par value; shares issued and outstanding: none	—	—
Common stock and capital in excess of $.01 par value; shares authorized: 7,000; shares issued: 2,654 and 2,601, respectively	5,605	4,795
Treasury stock, at cost; 52 shares and no shares, respectively	(2,249)	—
Retained earnings	1,364	839
Other comprehensive income	38	62
Other	(64)	(74)
Total stockholders' equity	4,694	5,622
Total liabilities and stockholders' equity	$13,535	$13,670

Source: Dell Computer Corporation, 10-K filing, 2002.

in the future. Dell's property, plant and equipment are investments whose costs will later be matched against revenues as the assets are used up in producing those revenues. On the liability side, Dell's accrued liabilities and payables are accruals. Accrued marketing and promotion costs, for example, are costs incurred in generating revenue but not yet paid for.

Indeed all balance sheet items, apart from cash, investments that absorb excess cash, and debt and equity financing items, result from either investment or accruals. To modify free cash flow according to the accounting relation (equation 4.6), investments and accruals are put in the balance sheet. And in some cases, balance sheet items involve both

FIGURE 4.2
The Articulation of the Financial Statements through the Recording of Cash Flows and Accruals between Time 0 and Time 1

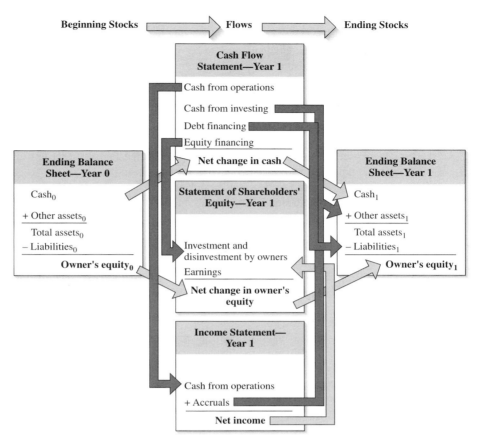

(1) Net cash flows from all activities increases cash in the balance sheet.
(2) Cash from operations increases net income and shareholders equity.
(3) Cash investments increase other assets.
(4) Cash from debt financing increases liabilities.
(5) Cash from equity financing increases shareholders' equity.
(6) Accruals increase net income, shareholders' equity, assets, and liabilities.

investment and accruals. Net property, plant, and equipment in Dell's balance sheet is investment reduced by accumulated accruals for depreciation, for example.

Figure 4.2 depicts how cash flows and accruals affect the income statement and balance sheet. This figure is an embellishment of Figure 2.1 in Chapter 2. Net cash flow from all activities updates cash in the balance sheet, as in Figure 2.1. Its component cash flows from operating, investing, and financing activities update other aspects of the balance sheet: equity financing cash flows update shareholders' equity (through the statement of shareholders' equity), debt financing cash flows update liabilities, and cash investments update assets other than cash in the balance sheet. And cash flow from operations update shareholders' equity as a component of earnings. But just as cash flow from operations updates both shareholders' equity and cash, so accruals update both shareholders' equity (as a component of earnings) and assets and liabilities other than cash.

The accruals in the balance sheet take on a meaning of their own, either as assets or liabilities. An asset is something that will generate future cash. Accounts receivable are assets because they are cash to be received from customers in the future. Inventories are assets because they can generate sales and ultimately cash in the future. A liability is an obligation to pay cash in the future. Accrued compensation, for example, is a liability to pay wages; a pension liability, an obligation to pay pension benefits. And accruals that reduce investments are reductions of assets. Property, plant, and equipment are assets from investment but subtracting accumulated depreciation recognizes that some of the ability to generate future cash has been given up in earning revenues to date. So net assets (assets minus liabilities) are anticipated value that comes from investment but also anticipated value that is recognized by accruals.

The net assets give the book value of shareholders' equity, $4,694 million for Dell in 2002. We observed in Chapter 2 that these net assets in published balance sheets are typically not measured at the (intrinsic) value of the equity. We now see why. The cash, debt investments, and debt liabilities are often close to their appropriate values. But the assets and liabilities that are a result of accrual accounting are measured at the amount of cash investment in the assets (referred to as *historical cost*) plus the accruals made to effect matching in the income statement. **Historical cost accounting** refers to the practice of recording investments at their cash cost and then adding accruals. Historical cost is not the value of an investment; it's the cost incurred to generate value. Accruals are value added (or lost) over cash from operations from selling products. But they are accounting measures of value added that may not be perfect. And, more important, they are only value that has been added to operations to date. The value of investments is based on value to be added in operations in the future. Thus we expect the value of equity to be different from its book value. We expect shares to be worth a premium or discount over book value. GAAP historical cost accounting, through impairment rules, requires assets to be written down if their value is judged to be below their book value but does not permit writing up historical costs. We therefore expect premiums typically to be positive, which, of course, there are.[4]

Summary

A valuation model is a tool for thinking about the value creation in a business and translating that thinking into a valuation. This chapter introduced the discounted cash flow model. This model, like the dividend discount model in the last chapter, forecasts cash flows, but rather than forecasting the cash flow distributions to shareholders that are not related to value, the discounted cash flow model focuses appropriately on the investing and operating activities of the firm, where value is generated.

The chapter demonstrated, however, that cash flows from investing and operating activities, summarized in free cash flow, are doubtful measures of value added. Indeed, as a value-added measure, free cash flow is perverse. Firms reduce free cash flows by investing, whereas investment is made to generate value. Thus very profitable firms, like Wal-Mart, generate negative free cash flow. Firms increase free cash flow by liquidating investments. So we preferred to call free cash flow a (partial) liquidation concept rather than a value-added concept and in doing so called into question the idea of forecasting free cash flows to value firms. We recognized, of course, that forecasting free cash flows

---

[4] In the United Kingdom, Australia, and some other jurisdictions, tangible asset values can be written up to their current market value, and in the United Kingdom, brand assets can be recognized on the balance sheet.

The Web Connection

Find the following on the web page for this chapter:

- Further examples of discounted cash flow valuation.

- Further demonstration of the difference between cash and accrual accounting.

- A discussion of the question: Is cash king?

- A discussion of the statement: Cash valuation models and accrual valuation models must yield the same valuation.

captures value in the long run. But that goes against our criterion of working with relatively short forecast horizons. Forecasting where Wal-Mart will be in 2050 is not an easy task; in the long run, we are all dead, as Keynes said. But the problem is primarily a conceptual one as well as a practical one: Free cash flow is not a measure of value added.

How might we deal with the problems of cash flow valuation? The chapter has outlined the principles of accrual accounting that determine earnings (in the income statement) and book values (in the balance sheet). It has shown that accrual accounting measures earnings in a way that, in principle at least, corrects for deficiencies in free cash flow as a measure of value added. Under accrual accounting, investments are not deducted from revenues (as with free cash flow), but rather they are put in the balance sheet as an asset, to be matched as expenses against revenues at the appropriate time. Additionally, accrual accounting recognizes accruals — noncash value — as part of value added. Accordingly, accrual accounting produces a number, earnings, that measures the value received from customers less the value given up in winning the revenues, that is, value added in operations.

Analysts forecast earnings rather than cash flows, and—as we now see—for very good reasons. But forecasting is only part of the task of valuation, the Step 3 part. Forecasts have to be converted to a valuation in Step 4. The next two chapters develop valuation models based on forecasts of earnings and book values. That is, they are based on forecasted income statements and balance sheets rather than forecasted cash flow statements.

There is one further subtle point to be gleaned from this chapter. A valuation model provides the architecture for valuation. A valuation model specifies what aspect of the firm's activities is to be forecasted, and we have concluded that it is the investing and operating activities. But a valuation model also specifies how those activities are to be measured. This chapter investigated cash accounting for investing and operating activities, but it also raised the possibility of using accrual accounting (which we will do in the next two chapters). Here is the subtle point: A valuation model not only tells you how to think about the value generation in the future, but it also tells you how to *account* for the value generation. *A valuation model is really a model of pro forma accounting for the future*. Should you account for the future in terms of dividends? Should you account for the future in terms of cash flows? Or should you use accrual accounting for the future? You see, then, that accounting and valuation are very much alike. Valuation is a matter of accounting for value.

Accordingly one can think of good accounting and bad accounting for valuation. This chapter has suggested that accrual accounting might be better than cash accounting. But is accrual accounting as specified by U.S. GAAP (or U.K. GAAP, German accounting, Japanese accounting, or international accounting standards) good accounting for valuation? We must proceed with a critical eye toward GAAP accounting.

Key Concepts

accrual is a noncash value flow recorded in the financial statements. See also **income statement accrual** and **balance sheet accrual**. *122*

balance sheet accrual is a change in an asset or liability that does not involve a cash flow. *125*

continuing value is the value calculated at a forecast horizon that captures value added after the horizon. *113*

historical cost accounting measures investments at their cash cost and adjusts the cost with accruals. *128*

income statement accrual is noncash value added that is recognized in the income statement. There are two types, a revenue accrual and an expense accrual. *123*

matching principle is the accounting principle that recognizes expenses when the revenue for which they are incurred is recognized. *121*

revenue recognition is the accounting principle for recording revenue (value from customers). Revenue is usually recorded when sales are made. *122*

The Analyst's Toolkit

Analysis Tools	Page	Key Measures	Page	Acronymns to Remember
Discounted cash flow model		Accruals	122	C cash flow from operations
(equations 4.1, 4.2)	112	After-tax net interest payments	119	CV continuing value
Simple cash valuation model	115	Cash flow from operations	112	DCF discounted cash flow
Cash flow from operations		Cash flow in investing activities	112	ebitda earnings before interest,
equation (4.3)	119	Continuing value	113	taxes, depreciation, and
Cash investment in operations		Discounted cash flow	112	amortization
equation (4.4)	119	Free cash flow	112	I cash flow from investments
Seven-step cash flow forecast	120	Free cash flow growth rate	114	NPV net present value
Accounting relations equations		Levered cash flow from		
Earnings =		operations	119	
$(C - i)$ + Accruals (4.5)	123	Net debt	112	
Earnings = $(C - I) - i$		(Unlevered) cash flow from		
$+ I +$ Accruals (4.6)	124	operations	119	

Concept Questions

C4.1. The following is the lead to an article published in *The Economist* on February 18, 1995, p. 80, under the headline "Where Cash Flow Is King"*

In the 1980s American banks and stockbrokers revolutionized their approach to valuing equities by junking traditional financial measures and concentrating instead on firms' cash flows, analyzing them rather as a corporate financier would. In Europe, many analysts still cling to tired old techniques that present a misleading picture of a stock's underlying worth. But a few more adventurous souls, grappling with the difficulties of valuing equities across European borders, are now embracing the American approach—and trying to improve it.

Corporate financiers consider that a company's worth is determined by the flow of cash it generates for its investors. Bearing this in mind, equity analysts can comb a firm's financial statements and help fund managers and other clients to assess its cash-pumping potential. Traditional investment analysis, however, relies heavily on performance measures that often have little, if anything, to do with cash flow. (© 1995 The Economist Newspaper Group, Inc. Reprinted with permission. Further reproduction prohibited.)

Should cash be enthroned as king?

*Source: © 1995 The Economist Newspaper Ltd. All rights reserved. Reprinted with permission. Further reproduction prohibited. www.economist.com.

C4.2. Should a firm that has higher free cash flows have a higher value?

C4.3. After years of negative free cash flow up to 1996, Wal-Mart Stores reported a positive free cash flow of $4,415 million in 1997, with cash from operations of $6,483 million and cash investment of $2,068 million. Look back at the pattern of Wal-Mart's cash flows displayed in this chapter. Would you interpret the 1997 free cash flow as good news?

C4.4. Which of the following two measures gives a better indication of the value added from selling inventory: (a) cash received from customers minus cash paid for inventory, or (b) accrual revenue minus cost of goods sold. Why?

C4.5. What explains the difference between cash flow from operations and earnings?

C4.6. What explains the difference between free cash flow and earnings?

C4.7. Why is an investment in a T-bill not an investment in operations?

C4.8. Explain the difference between levered cash flow and unlevered cash flow.

C4.9. Why must the interest component of cash flow or earnings be calculated on an after-tax basis?

Exercises   **E4.1.** **Approximate Discounted Cash Flow Valuation of Dell Computer Corporation (Medium)**

Using the free cash flow forecasts for the years 2000, 2001, and 2002 for Dell Computer in Box 4.4, developed at the end of fiscal year 1999, value a Dell share using a cost of capital for the firm of 12 percent. The following information from Dell's balance sheet at the end of fiscal year 1999 will be needed:

Investments in interest-bearing deposits and bonds	$2,661 million
Long-term debt	$ 512 million
Common shares outstanding	2,543 million

Your valuation will be approximate because you have only three years of cash flow forecasts. Value the firm under the following expectations:

a. Free cash flow will continue as a perpetuity after 2002.
b. Free cash flow will grow at a 3 percent rate after 2002.

Dell traded at $40 per share at the end of its 1999 fiscal year. Given the forecasts of free cash flow for 2000–2002, what growth rate in free cash flow after 2002 is the market implicitly forecasting with a $40 price?

E4.2. **Debt Financing and Dividend Discount Techniques (Medium)**

Consider the following cash flow forecasts (in millions of dollars) for a pure equity firm (no debt) with a cost of capital of 8 percent:

Year ahead	1	2	3	4	5
Cash from operations	112	103	179	183	185
Cash investment (including cash)	59	98	130	142	110

a. Calculate the present value of dividends over the five years.
b. Suppose you now forecast an issue of $28 million, 10 percent p.a. coupon debt at face value at the end of Year 2 with maturity beyond Year 5, and no change in forecasted cash investments. Recalculate the present value of the forecasted dividends over five years. Does the value change make sense?
c. Repeat the calculation in (b) with the maturity date for the debt at the end of Year 5.

E4.3. Debt Financing and DCF Techniques (Medium)

a. From the data in Exercise E4.2 (before the debt issue), calculate the present value of free cash flows.
b. Apply the DCF technique with the anticipated issue of debt in part (b) of Exercise E4.2 but with the original dividend payout unchanged.
c. Repeat the analysis with the maturity of the debt at the end of Year 5.

E4.4. Levered and Unlevered Cash Flow: Intel (Easy)

Some numbers from the financial statements of Intel Corporation, the semiconductor manufacturer, are below:

	1992	1993	1994	1995	1996	1997	1998
Reported cash flow from operations	1,635	2,801	2,981	4,026	8,743	10,008	9,191
Reported cash investments	1,480	3,337	2,903	2,687	5,268	6,859	6,506
Net investments in interest-bearing securities	252	1,404	462	(863)	2,244	2,358	2,043
Interest income	133	188	273	415	406	799	792
Interest expense	54	50	57	29	25	27	34

Calculate the levered and unlevered cash flow from operations and the free cash flow for each year. The firm has a 37 percent tax rate.

Real World Connection
See Exercise E9.1 in Chapter 9, Exercise E10.10. in Chapter 10, and Exercise E11.4. in Chapter 11 for more on Intel Corporation.

E4.5. Reconciling Earnings to Cash Flow from Operations: PepsiCo (Easy)

PepsiCo, the beverage and food conglomerate, reported net income of $1,076 million for the first half of 1999 and $992 million in levered cash flow from operations. How much of the net income reported was accruals?

E4.6. Reconciling Earnings to Free Cash Flow: Coca-Cola (Easy)

The Coca-Cola Company reported a levered free cash flow of $285 million for the first half of 1998. In the cash flow statement it reported that cash flow from operations was $62 million higher than net income, and cash investments were $1,466 million. What was the net income for the period?

Real World Connection
See Minicase M4.2 in this chapter and Minicase 13.2 in Chapter 13 for more analysis of Coca-Cola.

E4.7. Accounting Relations (Medium)

a. A firm reported $405 million in revenue and an increase in net receivables of $32 million. What was the cash generated by the revenues?
b. A firm reported wages expense of $335 million and cash paid for wages of $290 million. What was the change in wages payable for the period?
c. A firm reported net property, plant, and equipment (PPE) of $873 million at the beginning of the year and $923 million at the end of the year. Depreciation on the PPE was $131 million for the year. There were no disposals of PPE. How much new investment in PPE was there during the year?

E4.8. An Examination of Revenues: Microsoft (Easy)

Microsoft Corp. reported $19.747 billion in revenues for fiscal year 1999. Accounts receivable, net of allowances, increased from $1.460 billion in 1998 to $2.245 billion.

Microsoft has been criticized for underreporting revenue. Revenue from software licensed to computer manufacturers is not recognized in the income statement until the manufacturer sells the computers. Other revenues are recognized over contract periods with customers. As a result, Microsoft reported a liability, unearned revenue, of $4.239 billion in 1999, up from $2.888 billion earlier.

What was the cash generated from revenues in 1999?

Why might Microsoft want to underreport revenues?

Real World Connection

See Exercises E1.3, E3.8, and E17.3, and Minicase 8.1 in Chapter 8 for related material on Microsoft.

E4.9. Dividend Discounting and Simple Valuations: New York State Electric and Gas Corp. (Hard)

Under regulation, utilities have historically had smooth earnings and predictable dividend payments. So dividends have been relatively easy to forecast and, in many cases, dividend discounting has worked to value utilities. With deregulation, payouts have changed and, with more uncertainty, earnings have become less predictable.

a. New York State Electric and Gas Corp. was valued in the text in 1987 using discounted cash flow analysis. Using the data in Exhibit 4.1. value the firm at the end of 1987 based on the subsequent dividends that it paid.

b. Using the data in Exhibit 4.1, value the firm at the end of 1987 on the basis of the subsequent dividends it paid and the price payoff of $21.63 in 1996. Would the purchase of the stock at $20.88 in 1987 have been a good buy? Use a discount rate of 12 percent for the calculations. Why should the rate be different from the 9 percent rate used in the DCF analysis?

c. New York State Electric and Gas Corp. paid a dividend of $2.64 in 1987. Develop a simple valuation based on this dividend. Compare this valuation to the market price of $20.88 at the time. How much confidence do you have in this valuation?

d. In 1999 the shares of the firm (with its new name, Energy East Corp.) traded at $29 per share and paid $0.84 dividends per share. (These numbers are after a 2-for-1 stock split in April 1999.) Develop a simple valuation based on this dividend. What future growth in dividends does the market see in pricing the shares at $29? Why might this growth rate be higher than that in 1987? How might you go about determining whether this growth rate is appropriate?

e. The firm had a dividend payout rate of 70 percent in 1987. In 1999 its payout rate had dropped to 45 percent. What does this tell you about using dividends to value firms?

Minicases

M4.1

Comparison of Free Cash Flows and Profitability: Analog Devices, Inc.

Analog Devices, Inc., designs, manufactures, and markets a broad line of high-performance, linear, mixed-signal, and digital integrated circuits (ICs) that address a wide range of signal processing applications. The company's two principal product groups are general-purpose, standard-function linear and mixed-signal ICs and system-level ICs. The latter group includes general-purpose digital signal processing (DSP) ICs and application-specific devices that typically incorporate analog and mixed-signal circuitry and a DSP core. Analog's third product group consists of devices manufactured using assembled product technology. Nearly all of Analog's products are components that are typically incorporated by original equipment manufacturers (OEMs) in a wide range of equipment and systems for use in communications, computer, industrial, instrumentation, military/aerospace, automotive, and high-performance consumer electronics applications.

Review the company's website page at http://www.analog.com. It is a good example of informative reporting.

Exhibit 4.7 is a portion of Analog Devices's cash flow statements for 1997 and 1998.

A. Calculate the free cash flow that Analog Devices generated from operations in 1997 and 1998. With the aid of the summary following the exhibit, give a history of the free cash flow generated from 1992 to 1998.

B. The firm earned its highest return on common equity (ROCE) in 1995 and 1996 when its free cash flow was lowest. And it earned a relatively low ROCE in 1998 when it generated a relatively high free cash flow. Can you explain this negative correlation between profitability and cash flow? Will it always be the case? Can you find examples of firms with high profitability and high free cash flow?

C. Analog Devices's 164 million shares traded at $29 each at the end of 1998 and the firm carried little net debt. Calculate cash flow ratios for the firm. What do they mean?

M4.2

Discounted Cash Flow Valuation: Coca-Cola Company and Home Depot Inc.

The Coca-Cola Company and Home Depot have been very profitable companies, typically trading at high multiples of earnings, book values, and sales. To appreciate the difficulties involved, this case requires you to value the two companies using discounted cash flow analysis.

Coca-Cola, established in the nineteenth century, is a manufacturer and distributor of nonalcoholic beverages, syrups, and juices under recognized brand names. It operates in nearly 200 countries around the world. At the beginning of 1999, Coke traded at $67 per share, with a P/E of 47, a price-to-book ratio of 19.7, and a price-to-sales ratio of 8.8 on annual sales of $18.8 billion. With 2,465 million shares outstanding, the market capitalization of the equity was $165.2 billion, putting it among the top 20 U.S. firms in market capitalization.

EXHIBIT 4.7

ANALOG DEVICES, INC.
Partial Cash Flow Statement
(figures in thousands)

	Year End	
	October 31, 1998	November 1, 1997
Operations		
Cash flows from operations:		
Net income	$ 82,408	$ 178,219
Adjustments to reconcile net income to net cash provided by operations:		
Cumulative effect of change in accounting principal, net of $20 million of income taxes	37,080	0
Depreciation and amortization	127,560	103,554
Noncash portion of restructuring costs	10,000	0
Gain on sale of business	(13,100)	0
Equity in loss of WaferTech, net of dividends	10,907	211
Deferred income taxes	(12,372)	(6,134)
Change in operating assets and liabilities:		
Decrease (increase) in accounts receivable	51,061	(25,129)
Increase in inventories	(48,883)	(7,739)
Decrease (increase) in prepaid expenses and other current assets	240	(3,605)
Increase in investments—trading	(7,319)	(8,965)
Increase in accounts payable, deferred income, and accrued liabilities	(31,840)	4,828
Increase in income taxes payable	14,476	32,916
Increase in other liabilities	4,467	17,584
Total adjustments	142,277	107,521
Net cash provided by operations	224,685	285,740
Investments		
Cash flows from investments:		
Additions to property, plant, and equipment, net	(166,911)	(179,374)
Purchase of short-term investments available for sale	(143,449)	(153,269)
Maturities of short-term investments available for sale	152,880	192,073
Long-term investments	(56,110)	(51,599)
Proceeds from sale of business	27,000	0
Increase in other assets	(370)	(33,650)
Net cash used for investments	(186,960)	(225,819)

	1992	1993	1994	1995	1996	1997	1998
Reported cash flow from operations	33	89	183	210	144	286	225
Reported cash investments	66	67	163	239	306	226	187
Net investment in interest-bearing securities	0	0	73	9	62	12	47
Interest income	0	1	5	8	17	16	17
Interest expense	6	7	7	4	11	13	11
Return on common equity (ROCE)	4.1%	11.0%	15.6%	20.2%	22.7%	18.3%	7.4%

Home Depot is a more recent company, but it has expanded rapidly, building outlets for home improvement and gardening products throughout the United States, Canada, Mexico, and Argentina. By the end of its fiscal year ending January 1999, Home Depot operated nearly 900 stores as well as a number of design centers, adding stores at a rate of about 250 a year to become the second biggest retailer in the U.S. after Wal-Mart. It traded at $83 per share in January 1999, with a P/E ratio 53, a price-to-book ratio of 10.7, and a price-to-sales ratio of 4.1 on annual sales of $30.2 billion. With 1,475 million shares outstanding, the market capitalization of the equity was $122.4 billion, putting it also among the top 20 U.S. firms in market capitalization.

Listed below are partial statements of cash flow for Coca-Cola and Home Depot for three years, 1999–2001, along with some additional information (Home Depot's fiscal year, like most retailers, ends in January).

Suppose that you were observing these firms' stock prices at the beginning of 1999 and were trying to evaluate whether to buy the shares. Suppose, further, that you had the actual cash flow statements for the next three years (as given below), so you knew for sure what the cash flows were going to be.

A. Calculate free cash flows for the two companies for the three years using the information given in the statements below.

B. Attempt to value the shares of Coca-Cola and Home Depot at the beginning of 1999. Use a cost of capital of 9 percent for both firms.

As you have only three years of forecasts to deal with, your valuations will be only approximations. List the problems you run into and discuss the uncertainties you have about the valuations. For which firm do you feel most insecure in your valuation?

Real World Connection
See Minicase 13.2 in Chapter 13 on Coca-Cola and Minicase 14.1 in Chapter 14 on Home Depot.

THE COCA-COLA COMPANY AND SUBSIDIARIES
Consolidated Statements of Cash Flows
(in millions)

	Year Ended December 31,		
	2001	**2000**	**1999**
Operating Activities			
Net income	$3,969	$2,177	$2,431
Depreciation and amortization	803	773	792
Deferred income taxes	56	3	97
Equity income or loss, net of dividends	(54)	380	292
Foreign currency adjustments	(60)	196	(41)
Gains on issuances of stock by equity investees	(91)	—	—
Gains on sales of assets, including bottling interests	(85)	(127)	(49)
Other operating charges	—	916	799
Other items	34	119	119
Net change in operating assets and liabilities	(462)	(852)	(557)
Net cash provided by operating activities	4,110	3,585	3,883
Investing Activities			
Acquisitions and investments, principally trademarks and bottling companies	(651)	(397)	(1,876)
Purchases of investments and other assets	(456)	(508)	(518)
Proceeds from disposals of investments and other assets	455	290	176
Purchases of property, plant, and equipment	(769)	(733)	(1,069)
Proceeds from disposals of property, plant, and equipment	91	45	45
Other investing activities	142	138	(179)
Net cash used in investing activities	(1,188)	(1,165)	(3,421)

Other information:

Interest paid	304	458	199
Interest income	325	345	260
Borrowings at the end of 1998:	$4,990 million		
Investment in debt securities at the end of 1998:	$3,563 million		
Statutory tax rate:	36%		

HOME DEPOT INC.
Consolidated Statements of Cash Flows
(amounts in millions)

	Fiscal Year Ended		
	February 3, 2002	January 28, 2001	January 30, 2000
Cash Flows from Operations:			
Net earnings	$3,044	$2,581	$2,320
Reconciliation of net earnings to net cash provided by operations			
Depreciation and amortization	764	601	463
Increase in receivables, net	(119)	(46)	(85)
Increase in merchandise inventories	(166)	(1,075)	(1,142)
Increase in accounts payable and accrued liabilities	2,078	754	820
Increase in income taxes payable	272	151	93
Other	90	30	(23)
Net cash provided by operations	5,963	2,996	2,446
Cash Flows from Investing Activities:			
Capital expenditures, net of $5, $16, and $37 of noncash capital expenditures in fiscal 2002, 2001, and 2000, respectively	(3,393)	(3,558)	(2,581)
Payments for business acquired, net	(190)	(26)	(101)
Proceeds from sale of business, net	64	—	—
Proceeds from sales of property and equipment	126	95	87
Purchases of investments	(85)	(39)	(32)
Proceeds from sale of investments	25	30	30
Other	(13)	(32)	(25)
Net cash used in investing activities	(3,466)	(3,530)	(2,622)
Other information:			
Interest paid, net of interest capitalized	18	16	26
Interest income	53	47	37
Borrowings at the end of fiscal 1999:	$1,580 million		
Investment in debt securities at the end of fiscal 1999:	$81 million		
Statutory tax rate:	39%		

LINKS

Accrual Accounting and Valuation: Pricing Book Values

Link to previous chapters

Chapter 4 showed how accrual accounting modifies cash accounting to produce a balance sheet that reports shareholders' equity. However, Chapter 2 also explained that the book value in the balance sheet does not measure the value of shareholders' equity, so firms typically trade at price-to-book ratios different from 1.0.

This chapter

This chapter shows how to estimate the value omitted from the balance sheet and thus how to estimate intrinsic price-to-book ratios.

Link to next chapter

Chapter 6 complements this chapter. While Chapter 5 shows how to price the book value of equity, the "bottom line" of the balance sheet, Chapter 6 shows how to price earnings, the "bottom line" of the income statement.

Link to web page

Go to the web page for more applications of the techniques in this chapter.

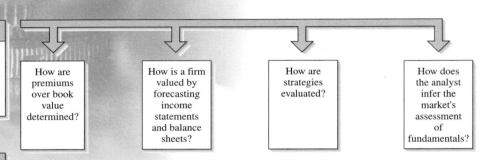

How are premiums over book value determined?

How is a firm valued by forecasting income statements and balance sheets?

How are strategies evaluated?

How does the analyst infer the market's assessment of fundamentals?

Firms typically trade at a price that differs from book value. Chapter 2 explained why: While some assets and liabilities are marked to market in the balance sheet, others are recorded at historical cost, and yet others are excluded from the balance sheet. Consequently, the analyst is left with the task of estimating the value that is omitted from the balance sheet. The analyst observes the book value of shareholders' equity and then asks how much value must be added to mark the book value to intrinsic value: What is the premium over book value at which a share should trade? Chapter 3 showed that asset-based valuation methods typically do not work. How, then, does the analyst proceed?

This chapter lays out a valuation model that guides the analyst in calculating the premium and intrinsic value. The model provides a framework for the five-step fundamental analysis that yields intrinsic values. It can also model strategy analysis. And the model provides directions to analyze firms to get at the sources of the value creation for strategy and valuation analysis.

The Analyst's Checklist

After reading this chapter you should understand:

- What "residual earnings" is.
- How forecasting residual earnings gives the premium over book value and the P/B ratio.
- What is meant by a normal price-to-book ratio.
- How residual earnings are driven by return on common equity (ROCE) and growth in book value.
- The difference between a Case 1, 2, and 3 valuation.
- How the residual earnings model applies to valuing bonds, projects, and strategies as well as equities.
- How the residual earnings model captures value added in a strategy.
- The advantages and disadvantages of using the residual earnings model and how it contrasts to dividend discounting and discounted cash flow analysis.
- How dividends, share issues, and share repurchases affect residual earnings.
- How residual earnings valuation protects the investor from paying too much for earnings.
- How residual earnings valuation protects the investor from paying for earnings that are created by accounting methods.
- How the residual earnings model is used in reverse engineering.

After reading this chapter you should be able to:

- Calculate residual earnings.
- Calculate the value of equities, bonds, projects, and strategies from forecasts of earnings and book value.
- Calculate an intrinsic price-to-book ratio.
- Calculate value added for a strategy.
- Calculate continuing values.
- Calculate an expected terminal value from a continuing value.
- Convert an analyst's earnings forecast into a valuation.
- Calculate an implied growth rate in residual earnings from the market price of a stock.

THE CONCEPT BEHIND THE PRICE-TO-BOOK RATIO

Book value represents shareholders' investment in the firm. Book value is also assets minus liabilities, that is, net assets. The value of the shareholders' investment—and the value of the net assets—is based on how much the investment (net assets) is expected to earn in the future. Therein lies the concept of the P/B ratio: Book value is worth more or less, depending upon the future earnings that the firm expects to generate. Book values do not measure value correctly, but the missing value is ultimately realized in the future earnings the book values produce.

This concept fits with our idea that shareholders buy earnings. Price, in the numerator of the P/B ratio, is based on the expected future earnings that investors are buying. So, the higher the expected earnings relative to book value, the higher the P/B ratio. The *rate of return on book value*—sometimes referred to as the *profitability*—is thus a measure that features strongly in the determination of P/B ratios.

This chapter supplies the formal valuation model to implement this concept of the P/B ratio, as well as the mechanics to apply the model faithfully. The formality is important, for formality forces one to be careful. In evaluating P/B ratios, one must proceed formally because one can pay too much for earnings if one is not careful.

Beware of Paying Too Much for Earnings

A basic precept of investing is that investments add value only if they earn above their required return. Firms may invest heavily—in an acquisition spree, for example—but that investment, while producing more earnings, adds value only if it delivers earnings above the required return on the investment. If a firm pays fair value for an acquisition or other investments, it may earn only the required return, and thus not add value. Indeed, a firm can increase earnings through investments even if those investments yield less than the required return (and thus lose value). This maxim leads to a modified P/B concept: The P/B ratio prices expected return on book value, but it does not price a return that is equal to the required return on book value.

The analysis in this chapter is designed to prevent you from making the mistake of paying too much for earnings. As you apply the model and methods in this chapter, you will see that P/B ratios increase only if earnings yield a return that is greater than the required return on book value. Indeed, with the tools in this chapter, you can assess whether the market is overpaying (or underpaying) for earnings and so detect cases where the P/B ratio is too high or too low.

PROTOTYPE VALUATIONS

Fundamental analysis anchors valuation in the financial statements. Book value provides an anchor. The investor anchors his valuation with the value that is recognized in the balance sheet—the book value—and then proceeds to assess value that is not recognized—the premium over book value:

$$\text{Value} = \text{Book value} + \text{Premium}$$

Two prototypes introduce you to the methods.

Valuing a Project

Suppose a firm invested $400 in a project that is expected to last for just one period and earn a return of 10 percent on investment, or $40 in that period. The required rate of return for the project is 10 percent. Following historical cost accounting, the asset would be recorded on the balance sheet at $400. How much value does this project add to the firm? The answer, of course, is zero because the asset is expected to earn a rate of return equal to its cost of capital.

A measure that captures the value added to book value is **residual earnings** or **residual income.** For the one period for this project (where the investment is at time 0,

$$\text{Residual earnings}_1 = \text{Earnings}_1 - (\text{Required return} \times \text{Investment}_0)$$

For earnings of $40, residual earnings is calculated as

$$\text{Residual earnings} = \$40 - (0.10 \times \$400) = \$0$$

If the project were to earn at a rate of 12 percent on the investment of $400 (that is, earn $48), residual earnings would be calculated as

$$\text{Residual earnings} = \$48 - (0.10 \times \$400) = \$8$$

The required dollar earnings for this project is $0.10 \times \$400 = \$40$. Residual earnings is the earnings in excess of these required dollar earnings. If the project earns $40, residual earnings is zero; if the project earns $48, residual earnings is $8. Residual earnings is sometimes referred to as **abnormal earnings** or **excess profit.**

A model that measures value added from forecasts of residual earnings is called the **residual earnings model:**

$$\text{Value} = \text{Book value of investment} + \text{Present value of expected residual earnings}$$

The one-period project is expected to earn a rate of return of 10 percent, that is, earn a residual earnings of zero, so the value of the project is

$$\text{Value} = \$400 + \frac{\$0}{1.10} = \$400$$

This project is worth its historical cost recorded on the balance sheet. If the project were expected to earn at a 12 percent rate, that is, earn residual earnings of $8,

$$\text{Value} = \$400 + \frac{\$8}{1.10} = \$407.27$$

In this case the project is worth more than its historical-cost book value because it is anticipated to generate positive residual earnings.

Valuing a Savings Account

The one-period project is a terminal investment, and we understand (from Chapter 3) that valuations that work with terminal investments may not work for going-concern investments. We introduced the accounting for a savings account in Box 2.2 of Chapter 2. The account there had a book balance of $100 that earned 5 percent per year. Suppose this investment were to continue indefinitely. How much would you pay for that account? Well, you would pay book value, $100. Why would you pay book value? Well, unless you have some reason to believe that the bank has made an error in calculating the book value, you know that $100 is the amount of cash that can be withdrawn from the account, its liquidation value. But $100 is also the going-concern value of the account.

Exhibit 5.1 lays out forecasts of book values, earnings, and dividends (withdrawals) for the $100 savings account for the first five years, 2001–2005. In the first scenario, earnings are paid out each year so that book value does not change. The required return for this savings account is 5 percent—that is the opportunity cost of the rate one could get at another bank across the street in an account with the same risk. So, forecasted residual earnings for each year is $5 - (0.05 \times \$100) = \$0$. As this asset is expected to yield no residual earnings, its value is equal to its book value, $100.

In the second scenario in Exhibit 5.1, no withdrawals are taken from the account. As a result, both earnings and book values grow as earnings are reinvested in the book values to earn within the account (numbers are rounded to two decimal places). But residual earnings is still zero for every year. For 2001, residual earnings is $5 - (0.05 \times \$100) = \$0$; for 2002, residual earnings is $5.25 - (0.05 \times \$105) = \$0$; for 2003, residual earnings is $5.51 - (0.05 \times \$110.25) = \$0$, and so on. As expected residual earnings are zero, the value of this asset in 2000 is its book value, $100.

EXHIBIT 5.1

Forecasts for a Savings Account with $100 Invested at the End of 2000, Earning 5% per Year.

	2000	Forecast Year				
		2001	2002	2003	2004	2005
Scenario 1: *Earnings withdrawn each year (full payout)*						
Earnings		$ 5	$ 5	$ 5	$ 5	$ 5
Dividends		5	5	5	5	5
Book value	$100	100	100	100	100	100
Residual earnings		0	0	0	0	0
Scenario 2: *No withdrawals (zero payout)*						
Earnings		$ 5	$ 5.25	$ 5.51	$ 5.79	$ 6.08
Dividends		0	0	0	0	0
Book value	$100	105	110.25	115.76	121.55	127.63
Residual earnings		0	0	0	0	0

These examples from the savings account bring out some important principles that we will carry through to the valuation of equities:

1. An asset is worth a premium or discount to its book value only if the book value is expected to earn nonzero residual earnings.

2. Residual earnings techniques recognize that earnings growth does not add value if that growth comes from investments earning the required return. In the second scenario, there is more earnings growth than in the first scenario, but that growth comes from reinvesting earnings in book values to earn at the required return of 5 percent. After charging earnings for the required return on the investment, there is no addition to residual earnings, even though there is growth in earnings. Accordingly, the value of the asset is the same for the case with no earnings growth.

3. Even though an asset does not pay dividends, it can be valued from its book value and earnings forecasts. Forecasting the zero cash flows (dividends) for the account in the second scenario will not work, but we have been able to value it from earnings and book values.

4. The valuation of the savings account does not depend on dividend payout. The two scenarios have different expected dividends but the same value: The valuation based on book values and earnings is insensitive to payout. This is desirable if, indeed, dividends are irrelevant to value, as discussed in Chapter 3.

The Normal Price-to-Book Ratio

The value of the savings account is equal to its book value. That is, the price-to-book ratio is equal to 1.0. A P/B ratio of 1.0 is an important benchmark case, for it is the case where the balance sheet provides the complete valuation. It is also the case where the forecasted return on book value is equal to the required rate of return, and forecasted residual earnings is zero—as with both the savings account and the project earning a 10 percent return.

The required return is sometimes referred to as the normal return for the level of risk in the investment. Accordingly, as an investment with a P/B of 1.0 earns a normal return, a P/B of 1.0 is sometimes referred to as a **normal P/B ratio.**

A MODEL FOR ANCHORING VALUE ON BOOK VALUE

The prototypes show us that one can value assets by anchoring the valuation on book value, and then adding extra value by forecasting future residual earnings. The prototypes lead us directly to a valuation model for equities that is anchored on book value. An equity investment is a going concern, and a going concern goes on indefinitely. So the value of its equity is

$$\text{Value of common equity } (V_0^E) = B_0 + \frac{\text{RE}_1}{\rho_E} + \frac{\text{RE}_2}{\rho_E^2} + \frac{\text{RE}_3}{\rho_E^3} + \cdots \qquad \textbf{(5.1)}$$

where RE is residual earnings for equity:

$$\text{Residual earnings} = \text{Comprehensive earnings} - (\text{Required return for equity} \\ \times \text{Beginning-of-period book value})$$

$$\text{RE}_t = \text{Earn}_t - (\rho_E - 1)B_{t-1}$$

B_0 is the current book value of equity on the balance sheet, and the residual earnings for each period in the future is the comprehensive earnings available to common equity for the period less a charge against the earnings for the book value of common equity at the beginning of the period, B_{t-1}, earning at the required return, $\rho_E - 1$.

We saw in Chapter 2 that Dell Computer reported $1,222 million of comprehensive income in 2002 on book value (assets minus liabilities) at the beginning of the year of $5,622 million. If Dell's shareholders require a 12 percent return, then its 2002 residual earnings was $1,222 - (0.12 \times 5,622) = $547.4 million. Dell added $547.4 million in earnings over a 12 percent return on the shareholders' investment in book value.

We calculate the value of equity by adding the present value of forecasted residual earnings to the current book value in the balance sheet. The forecasted residual earnings are discounted to present value at 1 plus the equity cost of capital, ρ_E. We calculate the intrinsic premium over book value, $V_0^E - B_0$, as the present value of forecasted residual income. This premium is the missing value in the balance sheet. The price-to-book (P/B) ratio is

$$\frac{V_0^E}{B_0} = 1 + \frac{\text{Present value of RE}}{B_0}$$

This makes sense: If we expect a firm to earn income for shareholders over that required on the book value of equity (a positive RE), its equity will be worth more than its book value and should sell at a premium. And the higher the earnings relative to book value, the higher will be the premium.

Table 5.1 shows that premiums (or P/B ratios) forecast subsequent residual earnings. This table groups all NYSE and AMEX firms into one of 20 groups based on their P/B ratio. The first group (Level 1) includes the firms with the highest 5 percent of P/B ratios, while the bottom group (Level 20) includes those with the lowest 5 percent. The median P/B for Level 1 is 6.68, while that for Level 20 is 0.42, as indicated in the P/B column of the table. The table gives the median RE for each level for the year that firms are grouped (Year 0) and for the subsequent five years. The RE is standardized by book value in Year 0. You can see that the RE entries in Years 1 to 5 are related to the P/B ratios in Year 0: High-P/B firms pay high RE, on average, while low-P/B firms pay low RE. Levels 14 and 15 have P/B close to 1.0 in Year 0 (a zero premium) and, correspondingly, their RE payoffs

TABLE 5.1
Price-to-Book Ratios and Subsequent Residual Earnings, 1965–1995.
High-P/B firms yield high residual earnings, on average, and low-P/B firms yield low residual earnings. Residual earnings for P/B ratios close to 1.0 (in Levels 14 and 15) are close to zero.

Source:
Company: Standard & Poor's
Data: Compustat® data.

P/B Level	P/B	Residual Earnings Each Year after P/B Groups Are Formed (Year 0)					
		0	**1**	**2**	**3**	**4**	**5**
1 (high)	6.68	0.181	0.230	0.223	0.221	0.226	0.236
2	3.98	0.134	0.155	0.144	0.154	0.154	0.139
3	3.10	0.109	0.113	0.106	0.101	0.120	0.096
4	2.59	0.090	0.089	0.077	0.093	0.100	0.099
5	2.26	0.076	0.077	0.069	0.068	0.079	0.071
6	2.01	0.066	0.067	0.059	0.057	0.076	0.073
7	1.81	0.057	0.048	0.043	0.052	0.052	0.057
8	1.65	0.042	0.039	0.029	0.039	0.050	0.044
9	1.51	0.043	0.034	0.031	0.038	0.046	0.031
10	1.39	0.031	0.031	0.028	0.036	0.047	0.028
11	1.30	0.024	0.026	0.023	0.035	0.036	0.030
12	1.21	0.026	0.028	0.023	0.036	0.039	0.038
13	1.12	0.016	0.021	0.012	0.031	0.039	0.026
14	1.05	0.009	0.008	0.009	0.026	0.034	0.032
15	0.97	0.006	0.005	0.011	0.018	0.031	0.017
16	0.89	−0.007	−0.011	−0.004	0.008	0.029	0.015
17	0.80	−0.017	−0.018	−0.004	0.006	0.023	0.008
18	0.70	−0.031	0.030	−0.030	−0.010	0.015	−0.001
19	0.58	−0.052	−0.054	−0.039	−0.015	−0.003	−0.008
20 (low)	0.42	−0.090	−0.075	−0.066	−0.037	−0.020	−0.039

are close to zero. Price-to-book ratios higher than 1.0 yield positive RE and low P/B ratios yield negative RE. In short, the data for actual firms behave just as the model says.[1] See also Box 5.1.

The forecasting to infinity that is required for the going-concern model (5.1) is a challenge. The criteria for a practical valuation technique presented in Chapter 3 require finite forecast horizons. If, as we forecasted further into the future, the present values of the RE were to become very small, we could stop forecasting RE at some point. But if not, a finite-horizon forecasting model would be needed for going concerns. Box 5.2 formally develops a model for forecasts over finite horizons and shows that it captures the returns to investing in stocks. For a forecast over a T-period horizon,

$$V_0^E = B_0 + \frac{\text{RE}_1}{\rho_E} + \frac{\text{RE}_2}{\rho_E^2} + \frac{\text{RE}_3}{\rho_E^3} + \cdots + \frac{\text{RE}_T}{\rho_E^T} + \frac{V_T^E - B_T}{\rho_E^T} \qquad \textbf{(5.2)}$$

where $V_T^E - B_T$ is the forecast of the intrinsic premium at the forecast horizon. So this model says that for forecasting 1, 2, 5, or 10 years ahead, we need three things (in addition to the equity cost of capital) to value the equity:

1. The current book value.

2. Forecasts of residual earnings to the horizon.

3. The forecasted premium at the horizon.

---

[1] The same required return for equity of 10 percent is used for all firms in the table. But using a CAPM cost of capital (and thus adjusting firms' required returns for their betas) gives similar patterns.

If a firm is trading at a discount to book value, it must be that the market expects negative residual earnings in the future.

Using a stock screener (accessed through the book's web page) you can identify stocks with P/B less than 1. A screen was made in 1999 for firms with P/B less than 1 and 1998 ROCE greater than 20 percent. With an ROCE of 20 percent or greater, a firm is reporting positive residual earnings for any reasonable estimate of the cost of capital. But a P/B less than 1 implies negative residual earnings in the future and future ROCE less than the cost of equity capital.

The screen produced the following firms (among others):

The forecasts of ROCE for 1999 and 2000 (derived from analysts' forecasts of earnings) indicate that ROCE were indeed expected to be lower than the cost of capital in the future. If this level of ROCE were expected to be a permanent condition, the firms should sell for less than book value, as they did.

Source of analysts' forecasts: Yahoo! Finance web page.

Firm	Business	Market Value	P/B	ROCE 1998	Beta	CAPM Equity Cost of Capital	ROCE Forecast	
							1999	2000
Advanta Corporation	Consumer financial services	$178.6 million	0.65	80.1%	1.13	12.2%	3.4%	3.9%
Allied Products Corporation	Machinery	$56.1 million	0.65	21.5	1.30	13.2	7.2	8.1
Bethlehem Steel Corporation	Steel	$1.10 billion	0.81	23.4	1.33	13.4	1.5	9.8
Natural Alternatives International, Inc.	Vitamins	$21.6 million	0.79	21.3	1.06	11.8	–9.4	–3.0

The equity cost of capital is given by a beta technology such as the capital asset pricing model (CAPM). Combining these three components of the value with the cost of capital according to the residual earnings formula accomplishes Step 4 of the fundamental analysis. Current book value is of course in the current balance sheet, leaving us with the task of forecasting residual earnings and the horizon premium. We also need to choose a forecast horizon. The **horizon premium**—the stock's expected value relative to book value T periods from now—appears to be a particular challenge. Indeed, the model appears circular: To determine the current premium we need to calculate a premium expected in the future. The calculation of this premium is the problem of a *continuing value* at the horizon. The section in this chapter titled Applying the Model to Equities deals with this problem.

The residual earnings model always yields the same value that we would get from forecasting dividends over an infinite forecasting horizon. This is important to appreciate, so that you can feel secure about the valuation, because share value is based on the dividends that the share is ultimately expected to pay. Box 5.2 derives the residual earnings model merely by substituting earnings and book values for dividends. That substitution means that we are really forecasting dividends; however, we get an appreciation of the ultimate dividends that a firm will pay using forecasts of earnings and book values over forecast horizons that are shorter than those typically required for dividend discounting methods.

We saw in Chapter 3 that values are determined by discounting payoffs to present value. Payoffs come over many periods but, to start simply, let's deal first with the one-period payoff to equity. The efficient equity price is the present value of the payoff that comes in the form of a dividend and a terminal price. So $P_0 = (d_1 + P_1)/\rho_E$, where P_0 is the current price, P_1 is the price one year ahead, d_1 is the dividend payoff one year ahead, and ρ_E is 1 plus the required rate of return on equity. The expected dividend component of the payoff is equal to forecasted comprehensive earnings minus the forecast change in book value: $d_1 = \text{Earn}_1 - (B_1 - B_0)$, by the stocks and flows accounting relation. So, substituting for dividends in the payoff,

$$P_0 = \frac{\text{Earn}_1 - (B_1 - B_0) + P_1}{\rho_E}$$

$$= \frac{B_0 + \text{Earn}_1}{\rho_E} + \frac{P_1 - B_1}{\rho_E}$$

$$= B_0 + \frac{\text{Earn}_1 - (\rho_E - 1)B_0}{\rho_E} + \frac{P_1 - B_1}{\rho_E}$$

The amount forecasted in the second term, $\text{Earn}_1 - (\rho_E - 1)B_0$, is the *residual earnings* for equity for the coming year.

The model says that we get the efficient price by forecasting next year's residual income and the premium at the end of the year, taking their present value, and adding the current book value in the balance sheet. We can extend the formula to longer forecast horizons by substituting comprehensive earnings and book values for dividends in each future period. For a forecast for T periods,

$$P_0 = B_0 + \frac{\text{RE}_1}{\rho_E} + \frac{\text{RE}_2}{\rho_E^2} + \frac{\text{RE}_3}{\rho_E^3} + \cdots + \frac{\text{RE}_T}{\rho_E^T} + \frac{P_T - B}{\rho_E^T}$$

Efficient prices are equal to intrinsic values, so we can express the model with intrinsic values rather than efficient prices. See model 5.2 in the text.

Residual Earnings Drivers and Value Creation

Residual earnings is the return on common equity, expressed as a dollar excess return rather than a ratio. For every earnings period t, we can restate residual earnings as

$$\text{Residual earnings} = (\text{ROCE} - \text{Required return on equity}) \quad \textbf{(5.3)}$$
$$\times \text{ Book value of common equity}$$

$$\underset{(1)}{\text{Earn}_t - (\rho_E - 1)B_{t-1}} = \underset{(2)}{[\text{ROCE}_t - (\rho_E - 1)]B_{t-1}}$$

where $\text{ROCE}_t = \text{Earn}_t/B_{t-1}$ is the **rate of return on common equity.** Box 5.3 takes you through the calculation of ROCE. Thus residual earnings compares ROCE to the required return, $\rho_E - 1$, and expresses the difference as a dollar amount by multiplying it by the beginning-of-period book value. Dell's (comprehensive) ROCE for 2002 was 21.74 percent (from Box 5.3). If its required return on equity were 12 percent, then its residual earnings was $(0.2174 - 0.12) \times \$5,622 = \$547.6$ million, which is the same number as we got before (adjusted for rounding error). If ROCE equals the required return, RE will be zero. If we forecast that the firm will earn an ROCE equal to its cost of capital indefinitely in the future, price will be equal to book value. If we forecast that ROCE will be greater than the cost of capital, the equity should sell at a premium. If we forecast that ROCE will be less than the cost of capital, the equity should sell at a discount. Look at Box 5.1 again.

You can see that RE is determined by two components, **(1)** and **(2)** in expression 5.3. The first is ROCE and the second is the amount of the book value of the equity investment (assets minus liabilities) that are put in place in each period. These two components are called **residual earnings drivers.** Firms increase their value over book value by

Return on common equity, ROCE, is comprehensive earnings to common earned during a period relative to the book value of net assets put in place at the beginning of the period. For period 1,

$$ROCE_1 = \frac{\text{Comprehensive earnings to common}_1}{\text{Book value}_0}$$

Comprehensive earnings to common are after preferred dividends and the book value is (of course) the book value of common shareholders' equity. Sometimes this measure is referred to as return on equity (ROE), but we will use ROCE to be clear that it is the return to common shareholders whose shares we are pricing. The ROCE is also referred to as a *book rate of return* or an *accounting rate of return* to distinguish it from the rate of return earned in the market from holding the shares.

Dell Computer's comprehensive income for 2002 was $1,222 million, and the book value of common shareholders' equity at the beginning of the year was $5,622 million (see Chapter 2). So Dell's ROCE for 2002 was $1,222/$5,622 = 21.74%.

Earnings are earned throughout the period and will change with changes in book values through share issues, stock repurchases, or dividends. But book value is measured at a point in time. For short periods, like a fiscal quarter, this does not matter much. But for longer periods, like a full fiscal year, it might. So ROCE for a year is often calculated as

$$ROCE_1 \equiv \frac{\text{Comprehensive earnings}_1}{\frac{1}{2}(B_1 + B_0)}$$

The denominator is the average of beginning and ending book value for the year. This calculation is approximate. More strictly, the denominator should be a weighted average of book values during the year. Significant errors will occur only if there are large share issues or stock repurchases near the beginning or end of a year. Based on average book value, Dell's 2002 ROCE was 23.69 percent.

The calculation can be done on a per-share basis:

$$ROCE_1 \equiv \frac{\text{eps}_1}{\text{bps}_0}$$

(with eps based on comprehensive income). The term bps is book value of common equity divided by shares outstanding (and shares outstanding is issued shares minus shares in treasury). The eps are weighted down for share issues and repurchases during the year by the weighted-average calculation. So this calculation keeps the numerator and denominator on the same per-share basis. Dell's 2002 ROCE on a per-share basis was 21.78 percent.

The three calculations typically give different answers but the difference is usually small. It is, however, dangerous to compare ROCE over time with calculations based on per-share amounts. To see this, suppose that proceeds from a share issue earn at the same rate as existing shareholders' equity. Then ROCE under the first calculation is unaffected by the share issue. The numerator in the second calculation, eps, may not be affected (as additional earnings generated by the share issue are deflated by additional shares outstanding) but bps usually will be affected. Share issues at market value change bps because dollar book value changes proportionally more than shares outstanding. If equity is $100 with 100 shares outstanding, bps = $1. If 50 new shares are issued at $2 per share, bps = $1.33 after the issue (whereas price per share does not change). Thus ROCE under the second calculation changes even though ROCE under the first does not. (The only exception is when price per share equals book value per share, the case of shares trading at a zero premium.)

The effect of share issues and share repurchases on ROCE (and on eps) is a little more complicated than this, as we will see, but the effect on bps is clear and instructs us not to compare ROCEs calculated on a per-share basis over time.

increasing their ROCE above the cost of capital. But they further increase their value by **growth in book values (net assets)** that will earn at this ROCE. For a given ROCE (over the cost of capital), a firm will add more value with more investments earning at that ROCE. Indeed these two drivers are sometimes referred to as *value drivers*. Determining the premium or discount at which a share should sell involves forecasting these two drivers. Figure 5.1 depicts how forecasts of the two drivers, along with the current book value, yield current value. Much of our analysis to uncover the value in a firm will involve uncovering the features of the business that determine these drivers. You also see how this model can be a strategy tool: Increase value by adopting strategies that increase ROCE above the required return and grow book values (net assets).

FIGURE 5.1 **The Drivers of Residual Earnings and the Calculation of the Value of Equity** Residual earnings is driven by return on common equity (ROCE) and the book value of investments put in place. Valuation involves forecasting future ROCE and the growth in the book values of net assets, discounting the residual income that they produce to present value, and adding the current book value.

$\text{ROCE}_t = \text{Earnings}_t / \text{Book value}_{t-1}$; Growth in book value$_t$ = Earnings$_t$ − Net dividends$_t$

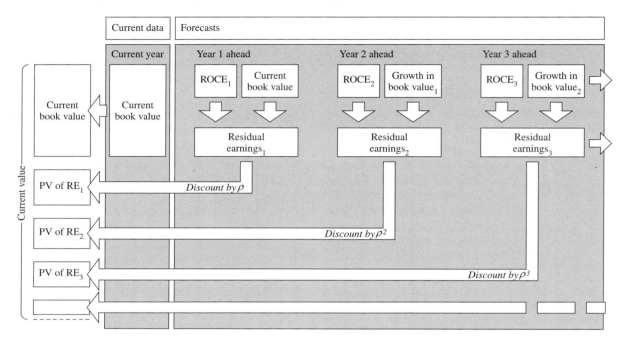

Table 5.2 gives percentiles of ROCE for NYSE and AMEX firms, along with percentiles of annual growth in the book value of common equity. Median ROCE (at the 50th percentile) is 12.2 percent, but there is variation, to 24.5 percent at the 90th percentile and –4.8 percent at the 10th percentile. Median growth in common shareholders' equity—which comes from retained earnings (after dividends) plus net share issues—is 9.0 percent per year, with variation from 33.2 percent at the 90th percentile to a decrease of 6.9 percent at the 10th percentile. It is useful to keep these historical benchmarks in mind when forecasting.

APPLYING THE MODEL TO EQUITIES

The case study on the next page applies Figure 5.1 to New York State Electric and Gas Corp., the New York State utility that we valued in Chapter 4 with discounted cash flow analysis. The first two lines give the firm's earnings per share (eps) and dividends per share (dps) for 1988 through 1993. Let's play the same game as in Chapter 4 and pretend that we are forecasting at the end of 1987 but know for sure what the subsequent earnings and dividends are going to be. From forecasts of eps and dps we can compute successive

TABLE 5.2
Percentiles of Annual ROCE and Annual Percentage Growth in Common Equity for NYSE and AMEX Firms, 1963–1997.
Note that the median ROCE is 12.2% and the median growth in common equity is 9.0%.

Source: D. Nissim and S. H. Penman, "Ratio Analysis and Equity Valuation: From Research to Practice," *Review of Accounting Studies,* March 2001, p. 129.

Percentile	ROCE	Growth in Common Equity %
95	31.0%	50.5%
90	24.5	33.2
75	17.6	17.3
50	12.2	9.0
25	6.3	2.7
10	–4.8	–6.9
5	–21.5	–18.0

CASE 1   New York State Electric and Gas Corporation

Required rate of return is 9 percent. In this case, residual earnings is expected to be zero after 1993.

	1987	Forecast Year					
		1988	**1989**	**1990**	**1991**	**1992**	**1993**
Eps		2.81	2.53	2.48	2.36	2.40	2.08
Dps		2.00	2.02	2.06	2.10	2.14	2.18
Bps	19.85	20.66	21.17	21.59	21.85	22.11	22.01
ROCE		14.2%	12.2%	11.7%	10.9%	11.0%	9.4%
RE (0.09 required return)		1.02	0.67	0.57	0.42	0.43	0.09
Discount factor (1.09^t)		1.090	1.188	1.295	1.412	1.539	1.677
PV of RE		0.94	0.56	0.44	0.30	0.28	0.05
Total PV of RE	2.57						
Value per share	22.42						

Forecasting residual earnings (1990):

Beginning bps (*a*)	21.17
Forecasted eps (*b*)	2.48
Forecasted dps	–2.06
Ending bps	21.59
Forecasted ROCE (*b/a*)	11.7%
Cost of equity capital	–9.0%
Excess ROCE (*c*)	2.7%
RE (*a* × *c*)	0.57
Discount factor	÷1.295
PV of RE	0.44
Alternatively,	
RE = 2.48 – (0.09 × 21.17)	0.57
Discount factor	÷1.295
PV of RE	0.44

book values per share (bps) by adding eps to beginning-of-period bps and subtracting dps. This just applies the stocks and flows accounting relation. So the forecast of bps for the end of 1990, for example, is 21.59, as shown below the valuation.[2]

With a forecast of eps and bps we can forecast RE. The CAPM cost of capital is 9 percent, so RE for 1990 is $2.48 - (0.09 \times 21.17) = 0.57$ or, calculating it from the forecasts of ROCE and book value, RE is $(0.117 - 0.09) \times 21.17 = 0.57$, as also shown below the valuation.

Now suppose we wished to value this firm at the end of 1987. We would take the present value of the RE forecasts (the discount factors are 1.09^t), sum them, and add the sum to the 1987 book value of $19.85 per share. This gives us a valuation of $22.42 per share, as shown. The calculated premium over book value is $22.42 - 19.85 = 2.57$. Is our valuation correct? Well, it would be if we forecasted RE after 1993 to be zero. You see the RE are declining over the years toward zero. Although the book value driver of RE is increasing, the ROCE driver is declining, and in 1993 it is 9.4 percent, close to the cost of capital. It looks as if RE after 1993 might be zero. If so, we have completed the valuation. We can write it as

$$V_0^E = B_0 + \frac{RE_1}{\rho_E} + \frac{RE_2}{\rho_E^2} + \frac{RE_3}{\rho_E^3} + \frac{RE_4}{\rho_E^4} + \frac{RE_5}{\rho_E^5} + \frac{RE_6}{\rho_E^6} \qquad \text{Case 1} \qquad (5.4)$$

where, in this case, Year 0 is 1987 and Year T (six years ahead) is 1993.

Compare this calculation with model 5.2. The continuing premium is missing here and this makes sense: If RE after the forecast horizon is forecasted to be zero, then the forecast of the premium at that point must be zero. We have forecasted $V_T^E - B_T = 0$. And so we expect the terminal value of the equity in 1993, V_T^E, to be equal to the expected book value of $22.01 per share at that point. In this example from historical numbers, we use per-share numbers. When forecasting, we will see that total dollar earnings, dividends, and book values are used, and per-share value is calculated by dividing the calculated value by shares outstanding.

The Forecast Horizon and the Continuing Value Calculation

We label this case of a forecast of a zero premium at the horizon as Case 1. How typical is it? Well, let's return to Wal-Mart, the firm we had difficulty valuing using discounted cash flow analysis in Chapter 4. Case 2 displays the same nine years as earlier, but now the eps, dps, and bps are given. Again pretending these actual numbers are numbers forecasted in 1987, forecasted RE and ROCE have been calculated. We charge Wal-Mart a 12 percent cost for using equity capital. The sum of the present values of the RE up to 1996 (2.05 per share), added to the 1987 book value of 75 cents per share, yield a valuation of 2.80 per share. But this is not correct because Wal-Mart is earning a positive RE in 1996 and is probably expected to earn more in years after. Wal-Mart has a declining ROCE driver, but its growth in book value more than offsets this to maintain its RE. The valuation of 2.80 per share is missing the continuing value, the continuing premium in model 5.2.

The continuing value is the value of residual earnings beyond the horizon. Look at the series of RE forecasts for Wal-Mart. You can see that although the RE entries are growing,

[2] In this and other examples we will use the approximate CAPM cost of capital, but other "asset pricing models" might also be used. We will also assume that the cost of capital is the same for all future periods. This may not be realistic for the equity cost of capital because it changes with leverage, as we will see. But we will also see (in Chapter 13) how valuations can be made ignoring leverage.

CASE 2 Wal-Mart Stores, Inc.

Required rate of return is 12 percent. In this case, residual earnings is expected to be constant, but non-zero, after 1996.

| | 1987 | **Forecast Year** | | | | | | | | |
		1988	1989	1990	1991	1992	1993	1994	1995	1996
Eps		0.28	0.37	0.48	0.57	0.70	0.87	1.02	1.17	1.19
Dps		0.03	0.04	0.06	0.07	0.09	0.11	0.13	0.17	0.20
Bps	0.75	1.00	1.33	1.75	2.25	2.86	3.62	4.51	5.51	6.50
ROCE		37.3%	37.0%	36.1%	32.6%	31.1%	30.4%	28.2%	25.9%	21.6%
RE (0.12)		0.19	0.25	0.32	0.36	0.43	0.53	0.59	0.63	0.53
Discount factor (1.12^t)		1.120	1.254	1.405	1.574	1.762	1.974	2.211	2.476	2.773
PV of RE		0.170	0.199	0.228	0.229	0.244	0.267	0.265	0.254	0.191
Total PV of RE	2.05									
Continuing value										4.42
PV of CV	1.59									
Value per share	4.39									

The continuing value:

$$CV = \frac{0.53}{0.12} = 4.42$$

$$PV \text{ of } CV = \frac{4.42}{2.773} = 1.59$$

the growth rate is slowing and the RE in 1996 is the same as in 1993. Suppose we forecast that RE beyond 1996 is going to be the same as the 0.53 in 1996 (and 1993): The subsequent RE will be a perpetuity. The value of the perpetuity is the capitalized amount of the perpetuity: $0.53/0.12 = 4.42$, as shown below the valuation. And as this is the value of expected REs after 1996, it is also the value of the expected premium at the end of 1996. So we can replace model 5.2 with

$$V_0^E = B_0 + \frac{RE_1}{\rho_E} + \frac{RE_2}{\rho_E^2} + \cdots + \frac{RE_T}{\rho_E^T} + \left(\frac{RE_{T+1}}{\rho_E - 1} \right) / \rho_E^T \qquad \textbf{Case 2} \qquad \textbf{(5.5)}$$

where, in Wal-Mart's case, T is nine years ahead. So the 1987 valuation for Wal-Mart is $4.39 = 0.75 + 2.05 + 4.42/2.773$. The calculated premium is $4.39 - 0.75 = 3.64$. The RE forecasts for 1997 and beyond supply the continuing value (CV) at the end of 1996 (Year 9) and this is the expected premium in 1996: $V_9^E - B_9 = 4.42$. And they supply the expected terminal value, V_9^E: As $B_9 = 6.50$, the expected terminal value is $6.50 + 4.42 = 10.92$.

We refer to the case of constant RE after the forecast horizon as Case 2. Cases 1 and 2 cover many of the cases you will run into in practice.[3] We might expect Case 1 to be typical: A firm might earn a positive RE for a while (ROCE greater than the cost of capital), but eventually competition will drive its profitability down so its ROCE will equal the cost of capital. High ROCE do decline, as illustrated by both New York State Electric and Gas and Wal-Mart, but it is quite common for ROCE and RE to level off at a positive amount. You can see this in Table 5.1. The RE there levels off to a constant amount for

---

[3] Forecasts of RE can be negative and so firms can sell at a discount. Negative RE also can be perpetual but, more likely, it recovers to zero or a positive amount.

CASE 3   General Electric Co.

Required rate of return is 12 percent. In this case, residual earnings is expected to grow at a 6% rate after 1992.

	1986	Forecast Year					
		1987	1988	1989	1990	1991	1992
Eps		3.20	3.75	4.36	4.85	3.03	5.51
Dps		1.33	1.46	1.70	1.92	2.08	2.32
Bps	16.57	18.44	20.73	23.39	26.32	27.27	30.46
Free cash flow ($ million)		(6,467)	(6,562)	(6,466)	(6,873)	(8,864)	(3,304)
ROCE		19.3%	20.3%	21.0%	20.7%	11.5%	20.2%
RE (0.12)		1.21	1.54	1.87	2.04	(0.13)	2.24
Discount factor (1.12^t)		1.120	1.254	1.405	1.574	1.762	1.974
PV of RE		1.08	1.23	1.33	1.30	(0.07)	1.13
Total PV of RE	6.00						
Continuing value							39.50
PV of CV	20.03						
Value per share	42.60						

The continuing value:

$$CV = \frac{2.37}{1.12 - 1.06} = 39.50$$

$$PV \text{ of } CV = \frac{39.50}{1.974} = 20.03$$

Note: Allow for rounding errors.

most levels of P/B, but for the top 15 P/B groups, the RE remains positive. This is a Case 2 pattern. Later in the book we will see that there are accounting reasons for RE to be positive and for ROCE to be greater than the cost of capital indefinitely: Firms keep book value low with conservative accounting like expensing R&D assets. RE is close to zero after a few years only for the lower P/B groups in Table 5.1. This is a Case 1 pattern. The table indicates that Case 1 or Case 2 applies over reasonable horizons. But while the RE patterns in the table are typical, they differ for many firms. The pattern for each firm is discovered by forecasting ROCE and growth in book value.

Case 3 is demonstrated with actual numbers for General Electric Company from 1986 to 1992. Like Wal-Mart, GE had negative free cash flows for these years. The RE are continually growing, except in 1991 when GE took a big charge to adopt new accounting for postemployment benefits. Its 1991 eps before extraordinary items and this charge was $5.10. This charge is relevant to the valuation because it represents a write-down for value owed to the employees. Thus the total present value of RE incorporates this unusual charge. However, the charge would not affect forecasts of earnings beyond 1992. The RE are growing because the firm is maintaining an ROCE of about 20 percent while increasing book value. It is probably unreasonable to expect RE to be constant or zero after 1992. If the growth is forecast to continue at a constant rate, the continuing value calculation can be modified:

$$V_0^E = B_0 + \frac{RE_1}{\rho_E} + \frac{RE_2}{\rho_E^2} + \frac{RE_3}{\rho_E^3} + \cdots + \frac{RE_T}{\rho_E^T} + \left(\frac{RE_{T+1}}{\rho_E - g}\right) / \rho_E^T \quad \text{Case 3} \quad \textbf{(5.6)}$$

where g is 1 plus the rate of growth.[4] GE's average RE growth rate from 1989 to 1992 is about 6 percent ($g = 1.06$). If this rate were expected to continue after 1992, the forecasted RE for 1993 would be $2.24 \times 1.06 = 2.37$. So the continuing value is 39.50, and its present value at the end of 1986 is 20.03, as indicated in the case study. The valuation at the end of 1986 (pretending these are forecasted numbers) is $V_0^E = 16.57 + 6.00 + 20.03 = 42.60$. And the expected value at the end of 1992 is $V_T^E = 30.46 + 39.50 = 69.96$. Note that we have been able to value GE even though the free cash flows (given in the case) are negative. Note also that Cases 1, 2, and 3 supply the terminal value that (as we saw in Chapter 4) is needed to apply the dividend discount model. See the appendix to this chapter, which emphasizes that the residual earnings model is just a rearrangement of the dividend discount model, such that we are able to work with shorter forecast horizons.

Case 3, along with Cases 1 and 2, completes the set of cases we are likely to meet in practice.[5] The long-term level of RE and its growth rate are sometimes referred to as the **steady-state condition** for the firm. The growth rate distinguishes Case 3 from Case 2 because Case 2 is just the case of no growth ($g = 1.0$). For the sake of our examples we have extrapolated growth rates. The forecast growth rate up to the horizon gives information about the long-term growth rate but it is unwise to extrapolate a rate in practice. It is even worse to assume a rate. Rather we should ask what the information tells us that the growth rate will be. The valuation can be quite sensitive to this growth rate. If, for example, we had specified a growth rate of 3 percent for Wal-Mart, the continuing value would have been $0.546/(1.12 - 1.03) = 6.07$, and the valuation would have been 4.99 rather than 4.39. The financial analysis of Parts Two and Three of the book is designed to uncover the growth rate.

On the web page for this chapter you will find a spreadsheet program to help you develop residual earnings valuation pro formas.

Converting an Analyst's Forecast to a Valuation

Analysts typically forecast earnings for one or two years ahead and then forecast "long-term" growth rates for subsequent years, usually three to five years. The forecasts for the immediate future are usually reliable (but buyer beware!); however, the long-term forecasts are often not much more than a guess. In any case, given the forecasts, the investor asks: How can the forecasts be converted to a valuation?

Table 5.3 gives an analyst's forecast for Hewlett-Packard made at the end of 1995. The analyst forecasted eps for three years, 1996–1998, and growth in eps of 17 percent per year for the five years after 1998. The bps at the end of fiscal 1995 was $23.22. This actual bps, along with the eps and dps forecasts, yields forecasts of bps. With the CAPM cost of equity capital of 12 percent, we can forecast RE, as in Table 5.3. Analysts typically do not forecast dps along with their eps forecasts, so the presumption in the pro forma is that the 1995 payout ratio will be maintained.[6] The 17 percent eps growth translates into a 16 percent RE growth, driven by a constant ROCE with growth in book value. It is doubtful that this can be maintained: You can see in the pro forma that the present

---

[4] The growth rate has to be less than the cost of capital or the terminal value calculation "blows up." It is unreasonable to expect a firm's RE to grow at a rate greater than the cost of capital indefinitely (and so have an infinite price).

[5] Growth could be negative at a horizon ($g < 1$). This is typically a case of a positive RE declining to zero: The forecast horizon can be extended to the point of zero RE, and Case I applies.

[6] Again, we will see that valuation with residual earnings methods is best done by forecasting the total dollar amounts rather than per-share amounts. But analysts forecast per-share amounts.

TABLE 5.3 **Analyst Forecast and Valuation: Hewlett-Packard Co.**
Required rate of return is 12 percent.

	1995A	1996E	1997E	1998E	1999E	2000E	2001E	2002E	2003E
Eps	4.63	5.45	6.35	7.32	8.56	10.01	11.72	13.71	16.04
Dps	0.70	0.94	1.10	1.25	1.46	1.70	1.99	2.33	2.73
Bps	23.22	27.73	32.98	39.05	46.15	54.46	64.19	75.57	88.88
ROCE		23.5%	22.9%	22.2%	21.9%	21.7%	21.5%	21.4%	21.2%
RE (0.12)		2.66	3.02	3.36	3.87	4.47	5.18	6.01	6.97
Discount factor		1.120	1.254	1.405	1.574	1.762	1.974	2.211	2.476
PV of RE		2.38	2.41	2.39	2.46	2.54	2.62	2.72	2.82
Total PV of RE	20.34								
Continuing value									58.08
PV of CV	23.46								
Value of equity	67.02								

TABLE 5.4
Analyst Forecast: Whirlpool Corp.

	Forecast Year			
	1994A	1995E	1996E	1997E
Eps	4.43	4.75	5.08	5.45
Dps	1.22	1.28	1.34	1.41
Bps	25.83	29.30	33.04	37.07
ROCE		18.4%	17.3%	16.5%
RE (0.10)		2.17	2.15	2.15

value of the RE is actually growing! Continued indefinitely, this would yield an infinite price. We don't know what earnings the analyst had in mind past 2003, so the calculation in the table assumes (with lack of any further analysis) that RE after 2003 will be constant. Thus the continuing value is 6.97/0.12 = 58.08. The valuation based on the analyst's forecast is $67.02 per share.

In converting the analyst's forecast to a valuation, we have run into some difficulties. So the valuation is tentative. Analysts often do not forecast dividends along with earnings forecasts, so, as we have done here, payout has to be assumed in order to forecast future book values. More importantly, analysts' forecasts are usually only for the immediate future. We have no idea of their forecasts for the long run, so we are left with the problem of supplying a continuing value at their forecast horizon.

In making these calculations we have determined the forecast horizon: It's the point where there is a pattern in forecasted RE such that Case 1, 2, or 3 applies. This horizon can be quite short. Look at the forecasts in Table 5.4 for Whirlpool Corporation, a household appliance manufacturer traded on the NYSE, made by a major brokerage house just before the end of 1994. For the RE calculation the cost of capital is 10 percent. Here the forecasts of RE are very similar from 1995 on, so the horizon is immediate. The Case 2 valuation is

$$V_{1994}^E = B_{1994} + \frac{RE_{1995}}{(\rho_E - 1)} = \$25.83 + \frac{2.17}{0.10} = 47.53$$

In 1999 a number of large insurance companies, including John Hancock Mutual Life Insurance, Metropolitan Life Insurance, and Prudential Insurance Company of America, announced that they intended to convert from mutual companies owned by policyholders to companies owned by shareholders. The process of "demutualization" involves issuing shares to policyholders and new investors in an initial public offering.

Analysts conjectured that these firms would be priced at book value. They were earning 9 percent–12 percent return on equity and analysts did not expect this rate of return to improve. Why might they trade at book value? Well, if the return that investors require to buy the initial share issue is also 9 percent–12 percent, the firms would be expected to generate zero residual earnings from their book values, and so should be priced at book value.

John Hancock's initial public offering was on January 27, 2000, when it became John Hancock Financial Services Inc. The firm's ROCE was 12 percent. It issued 331.7 million shares, 229.7 million to policyholders. These shares traded at $17¼ per share, a little above book value of $15 per share.

TABLE 5.5 Bond Valuation: Residual Earnings Approach
Required return on the bond: 8%

| | 0 | Forecast Year, *t* | | | | |
		1	2	3	4	5
Cash flow		$ 100.00	$ 100.00	$ 100.00	$ 100.00	$1,100.00
Interest income (8%)		86.39	85.30	84.12	82.85	81.48
Amortization of bond premium		13.61	14.70	15.88	17.16	18.52
Book value of bond	$1,079.85	1,066.24	1,051.54	1,035.66	1,018.50	0.00
Rate of return		8.0%	8.0%	8.0%	8.0%	8.0%
Residual interest income		0.00	0.00	0.00	0.00	0.00
PV of residual interest income	0.00					
Value of bond	1,079.85	Value added = $0.0				

At the time Whirlpool traded at about $47. This is a firm with very regular operations and very regular profitability, so expected RE settles down to a permanent level quickly. See also Box 5.4.

APPLYING THE MODEL TO DEBT

The model presented thus far applies to valuing equity. But it also applies to valuing debt. Consider again the valuation for the bond in Figure 3.6. The bond had a required return of 8 percent. Table 5.5 lays out the forecasts of the cash flows on the bond, as before, and also the interest income and book values that an accountant would record using the effective interest method. (Review this method if necessary: The interest recorded is the effective interest rate, 8 percent in this case, applied to the beginning-of-period book value of the bond. The difference between the cash coupon and the effective interest is the amount by which the bond premium over face value [$79.85] is amortized each year to yield the end-of-period book value. The first four rows of the table are the amortization table for the bond.) The interest income would be interest expense if we were accounting for the issuer rather than the purchaser of the bond.

The book value of the bond, when purchased, is its market price of $1,079.85. Subsequent book values follow the stocks and flows equation similar to that for equity:

$$\text{Book value}_t = \text{Book value}_{t-1} + \text{Income}_t - \text{Cash flow}_t$$

Thus the book value at the end of Year 1 is $1,079.85 + 86.39 - 100.00 = \$1,066.24$, and so for subsequent years.

From the forecasts of income and book values, we can value the bond using the RE formula:

$$V_0^D = \text{Book value}_0 + \text{PV of expected residual interest income}$$

But the residual incomes are forecast to be zero; for Year 3, for example, $84.12 - (0.08 \times 1,051.54) = 0$. Thus the value of the bond is its book value, which is also its market price.

This example demonstrates that bond valuation can be done using RE methods (as well as DCF methods), provided the income is accrual income, not the cash flow from the coupon. But it also shows how residual earnings calculations measure value added. We saw in Chapter 3 that a bond purchased at fair (market) value is a zero-NPV investment. But we can equivalently say it is a zero-RE investment: The forecasted rate of return here is 8 percent, equal to the required return for this bond. Buying this bond at market price does not generate RE and so it does not generate value.

With the valuation of equity and the valuation of bonds (debt) using RE methods, we can value the firm: $V_0^F = V_0^E + V_0^D$.

APPLYING THE MODEL TO PROJECTS AND STRATEGIES

The RE method also can be used to value projects within the firm. Project evaluation is typically done using NPV analysis (of cash flows), as we did for the project in Figure 3.6 that required an investment of $1,200. Table 5.6 accounts for that project using accrual accounting. The revenue is from the cash inflow but depreciation has been deducted to get the net income from the project. The depreciation is calculated using the straight-line method, that is, by spreading cost less estimated salvage value (the depreciation base) over the five years. The book value of the project each year is its original cost minus accumulated depreciation. And this book value follows the stocks and flows equation, similar to equities:

$$\text{Book value}_t = \text{Book value}_{t-1} + \text{Income}_t - \text{Cash flow}_t$$

So the book value in Year 1 is $1,200 + 214 - 430 = \$984$, and so for subsequent years. At the end of Year 5, the book value is zero as the assets in the project are sold for estimated salvage value. This is standard accrual accounting.

The value of the project is its book value plus the present value of expected residual income calculated from the forecasts of net income and book values. This value of $1,530 is the same as the discounted cash flow valuation in Chapter 3. The forecasts of RE have captured the value added over the cost of the investment: The present value of the forecasts of RE of $330 equals the NPV we calculated in Chapter 3.

Strategy involves a series of ongoing investments. Table 5.7 evaluates a strategy which (to keep it simple) requires investing $1,200 in the same project as before but in each year indefinitely. The revenues are those from all overlapping projects in existence in a given year: The revenue in Year 1 is $430 from the project begun in Year 0, the revenue in Year 2 of $890 is the second year's revenue ($460) from the project begun in Year 0 plus the first year's revenue from the project begun in Year 1 ($430), and so on.

TABLE 5.6 **Project Evaluation: Residual Earnings Approach**
Hurdle rate: 12%.

		Forecast Year, t				
	0	1	2	3	4	5
Revenues		$430	$460	$460	$380	$250
Depreciation		216	216	216	216	216
Project income		214	244	244	164	34
Book value	$1,200	984	768	552	336	0
Book rate of return		17.8%	24.8%	31.8%	29.7%	10.1%
Residual project income (0.12)		70	126	152	98	(6)
Discount rate (1.12^t)		1.120	1.254	1.405	1.574	1.762
PV of RE		62.5	100.5	108.2	62.3	(3.4)
Total PV of RE	330					
Value of project	$1,530			Value added = $330		

TABLE 5.7 **Strategy Evaluation**
Hurdle rate: 12%.

		Forecast Year, t					
	0	1	2	3	4	5	6 . . .
Residual Earnings Approach							
Revenues		$430	$890	$1,350	$1,730	$1,980	$1,980 . . .
Depreciation		216	432	648	864	1,080	1,080
Strategy income		214	458	702	866	900	900 . . .
Book value	$1,200	2,184	2,956	3,504	3,840	3,840	3,840 . . .
Book rate of return		17.8%	21.0%	23.8%	24.7%	23.4%	23.4%
Residual strategy income (0.12)		70	195.9	347.8	445.5	439.2	439.2 . . .
PV of RE		62.5	156.2	247.5	283.0	249.3	
Total PV of RE	999						
Continuing value[1]						3,660	
PV of CV	2,077						
Value of strategy	$4,276		Value added: $3,076				
Discounted Cash Flow Approach							
Cash inflow		$430	$890	$1,350	$1,730	$2,100	$2,100 . . .
Investment	$(1,200)	(1,200)	(1,200)	(1,200)	(1,200)	(1,200)	(1,200) . .
Free cash flow	(1,200)	(770)	(310)	150	530	900	900 . . .
PV of FCF		(687.5)	(247.2)	106.8	336.7	510.7	
Total PV of FCF	20						
Continuing value[2]						7,500	
PV of CV	4,256						
Value of strategy	$4,276		Net present value: $3,076				

[1]CV = 439.2/0.12 = $3,660.
[2]CV = 900/0.12 = $7,500.

Depreciation is the same as before ($216 per year for a project), so total depreciation is $216 times the number of projects operating at a time. By the fifth year into the strategy there are five projects operating each year with a steady stream of $1,980 in revenues and $1,080 in depreciation. Book value at all points is accumulated net investment less accumulated depreciation.

You see from the calculations that the strategy adds $3,076 of value to the initial investment of $1,200 if the required return is 12 percent, and this value added is the present value of expected residual income from the project. You also see from the second panel that this value added equals the NPV of the strategy calculated using discounted cash flow analysis.

Many of the strategic planning products marketed by consulting firms—with such names as economic profit models, economic value-added models, value driver models, and shareholder value-added models—are variations on the residual earnings model. To guide strategy analysis they focus on the two drivers of residual income and of value added: return on investment and growth in investment. They direct management to maximize return on investment and to grow investments that can earn a rate of return greater than the required return. These value-added measures are used, in turn, to evaluate and reward management on the success of their strategies.

FEATURES OF THE RESIDUAL EARNINGS MODEL

Box 5.5 lists the advantages and disadvantages of the residual earnings approach. Compare it to summaries for the dividend discount and discounted cash flow (DCF) models in Chapters 3 and 4. Some of the features listed will be discussed in more detail later in the book (as indicated). Some are discussed here.

Book Value Captures Value and Residual Earnings Captures Value Added to Book Value

The residual earnings approach employs the properties of accrual accounting that (typically) bring value recognition forward in time. More value is recognized earlier within a forecasting period, and less value is recognized in a continuing value about which we usually have greater uncertainty.

Residual earnings valuation recognizes the value that accountants have calculated in the current book value in the balance sheet, for a start; in addition, value is usually recognized in RE forecasts earlier than for free cash flow forecasts. You can see this by comparing the value captured in forecasts for one and two years ahead with the two methods in the strategy example we just went through: Free cash flows forecasts are negative for Years 1 and 2 but RE forecasts are positive. And you can see the earlier recognition of value by comparing the RE valuation for New York State Electric and Gas in this chapter with the DCF valuation in Chapter 4: More of the value is in the continuing value in the DCF valuation. In the strategy example in Table 5.7, the forecast horizon is the same five years using RE and DCF analysis (because free cash flows align with profitability and growth at the horizon). But for the DCF calculation, 99.5 percent of the value is in the continuing value, compared to 48.6 percent for the RE calculation. And if free cash flows are negative, DCF analysis can require longer forecast horizons, as we saw with Wal-Mart and General Electric.

Nevertheless, forecast horizons for DCF analysis and RE analysis are often the same. You see this in Table 5.7 where both methods forecast steady state (for the continuing value calculation) at Year 5. We detail the circumstances where this is so on the web page for Chapter 16.

ADVANTAGES

Focus on value drivers:	Focuses on profitability of investment and growth in investment, which drive value; directs strategic thinking to these drivers.
Incorporates the financial statements:	Incorporates the value already recognized in the balance sheet (the book value); forecasts the income statement and balance sheet rather than the cash flow statement.
Uses accrual accounting:	Uses the properties of accrual accounting that recognize value added ahead of cash flows, match value added to value given up, and treat investment as an asset rather than a loss of value.
Versatility:	Can be used with a wide variety of accounting principles (Chapter 16).
Aligned with what people forecast:	Analysts forecast earnings (from which forecasts of residual earnings can be calculated).
Validation:	Forecasts of residual earnings can be validated in subsequent audited financial statements.

DISADVANTAGES

Accounting complexity:	Requires an understanding of how accrual accounting works.
Suspect accounting:	Relies on accounting numbers, which can be suspect (Chapter 17).
Forecast horizon:	Forecast horizons can be shorter than for DCF analysis and more value is typically recognized in the immediate future. Forecasts up to the horizon give an indication of profitability and growth for a continuing value calculation; however, the forecast horizon does depend on the quality of the accrual accounting (Chapter 16).

Protection from Paying Too Much for Earnings Created by the Accounting

The prototype one-year project at the beginning of this chapter was recorded at its historical cost of $400. Suppose, instead, that the accountant decided to write down the asset to $360 before using it in operations. His manager wishes to give the asset a "conservative" valuation on the balance sheet. The asset must be fully depreciated by the end of the project (one year later), so the effect of the accounting will be to have lower depreciation expense in calculating earnings from the project, by the amount of $40. Accordingly, expected earnings for the project will be $40 higher, or $80. And the ROCE will be 22.2 percent rather than 10 percent.

By applying the required return to the written-down book value at the beginning of the earnings year, expected residual earnings will be $80 - (0.10 \times $360) = $44. Using the residual earnings valuation model,

$$\text{Value} = \$360 + \frac{\$44}{1.10} = \$400$$

This value is the same value as before. Although the forecast of earnings is higher, the value is unaffected (as it should be). The valuation model has dealt with the changed accounting: Even though we forecasted higher earnings from the project—because of the accounting—the model still confirms that the project adds no value.

The accounting here is a further example of the mismatching of revenues and expenses that we discussed in Chapter 2. The $40 expensed when the asset was purchased may be advertising costs that GAAP requires to be expensed. Or the manager may have written down the asset to report higher earnings later because his bonus was tied to the earnings. In either case, note that writing down assets always creates higher earnings later. Observant analysts would forecast $80 in earnings rather than $40. But this increase in earnings is just an accounting effect, it has no effect on the value of the project. Forecasted residual earnings would be higher, but when the forecast of residual earnings is combined with the lower book values in the calculation, the value is unaffected.

The same mechanism works with going concerns. Accounting rules might expense expenditures on assets like R&D and so report lower book values in the balance sheet. Because of the lower book values, this accounting gives the firm a higher premium. But the accounting also yields higher subsequent earnings because the asset does not have to be amortized against revenues. And the accounting yields higher residual earnings because, in addition, the net assets to be charged with the required return are lower. Or a manager may choose to record excessive estimated restructuring charges as liabilities—a common practice in the 1990s—and so report higher earnings in the future as the overestimates are reversed into income. But these accounting effects do not affect the underlying value of the firm, and the residual earnings valuation recognizes this.

At the beginning of this chapter we warned against paying too much for profitability, for investments must cover their required return to add value. The residual earnings model protects us by charging book values for the required return. We now see that future earnings and ROCE also can be created by accounting methods. This is not profitability that we want to pay for. However, the residual earnings model protects us from this danger also. Chapter 16 elaborates.

Residual Earnings Are Not Affected by Dividends, Share Issues, or Share Repurchases

In Chapter 3 we saw that share issues, share repurchases, and dividends typically do not create value if stock markets are efficient. But if residual earnings is based on book values (and earnings) and these transactions with shareholders affect book values, won't forecasts of residual earnings (and thus the valuation) be affected by expected dividends, share issues, and share repurchases? The answer is no. See Box 5.6.

What the Residual Earnings Model Misses

The residual earnings model captures the anticipated value to be generated within the business by applying shareholders' investment to earn profits from selling products and services to customers. We have recognized, however, that shareholders can also make money if shares are issued at a price greater than their fair value. This can happen if the market price is inefficient or if management (who acts on shareholders' behalf) has more information about the value of the firm than the buyers of the share issue. Gains also can be made (by some of the shareholders) from stock repurchases: If shares are repurchased at a price that is less than fair value, the shareholders who participate in the repurchase lose value to those who chose not to participate. In short, owners make money from selling or buying the firm at a price that is different from fair value. (They also can lose value if the management buys or sells shares at an unfavorable price relative to fair value.)

In the example with a share issue in Box 5.6, the residual earnings model calculates (appropriately) that there is no value added from an anticipated share issue at fair value unless the proceeds are invested in the firm to earn a return greater than the required return. The share issue itself does not create value. However, this is not so if the share issue is anticipated at a price that is greater than market value: The gain to the existing shareholders is not captured by the model.

We saw in Chapter 3 that share issues, share repurchases, and dividends typically do not create value if stock markets are efficient. So anticipated net share issues at fair value and dividends should not change a residual earnings valuation of a firm. Yet residual earnings is forecasted by forecasting book values, and book values are affected by share issues (and repurchases) and dividends. How, then, can the valuation be unaffected by these transactions with shareholders?

The example below values the equity of a firm with a book value of $1,000 and no expected dividends or share issues. The firm is expected to have positive residual earnings for two years and zero residual earnings thereafter.

Valuation of Equity with No Share Issues or Dividends
Cost of equity capital: 10%.

	0	1	2	3
Earnings		$150	$140	$129
Dividends		0	0	0
Share issues		0	0	0
Book value	$1,000	1,150	1,290	1,419
ROCE		15%	12.2%	10%
RE (0.10)		50	25	0
Total PV of RE	66			
Value of equity	$1,066			
Shares outstanding	100			
Value per share	$10.66			

This firm now anticipates a share issue of $100 in Year 1 and a dividend of $25 in Year 2.

Valuation of Equity with an Anticipated Share Issue and Dividend
Cost of equity capital: 10%.

	0	1	2	3
Earnings		$150	$150	$137.5
Dividends		0	25	0
Share issues		100	0	0
Book value	$1,000	1,250	1,375	1,512.5
ROCE		15%	12%	10%
RE (0.10)		50	25	0
Total PV of RE	66			
Value of equity	$1,066			
Shares outstanding	100			
Value per share	$10.66			

The two valuations are the same: Anticipated dividends and share issues are indeed irrelevant to the valuation. The share issue of 100 in the first year earns at the required return of 10 percent to add an extra 10 percent to earnings in Year 2. But it does not affect RE because the additional book value is charged at 10 percent also.[1] Of course, if proceeds of the issue were invested in a project earning greater than 10 percent, RE would be higher and added value would be recognized, appropriately, in the valuation. But the share issue itself does not add value. Similarly, the dividend in Year 3 reduces book value but not RE, so it does not affect the value. Again, if the management liquidated value-creating investments (earning greater than a 10 percent return) to make the dividend, value would be lost. But that dividend would not be value-irrelevant, and the RE valuation would reveal this.

These examples illustrate a more general principle: Only those investments that yield returns over the required return add to RE (and to the valuation). Share issues (investments in firms) and share repurchases and dividends (disinvestments) affect RE and value only if they affect investments within the firm that earn at a rate different from the required return.

We saw in Chapter 3 that share issues, repurchases, and dividends may "signal" about the value of the investments a firm makes. If so, that information revises RE forecasts and the value signaled is captured by an RE calculation.

[1] There may be leverage effects that are not incorporated. We deal with leverage effects in Chapter 13 and show that they do not affect the conclusion here. Treat the firm here as one with no leverage.

REVERSE ENGINEERING THE MODEL FOR ACTIVE INVESTING

We saw in Chapter 3 that one of the fundamental screens takes positions in stocks based on the P/B ratio. The P/B ratio is supposed to identify mispricing in the market: Buy low-P/B stocks, sell high-P/B stocks. We suggested that this simple screen could get you into trouble: A high P/B, for example, might be justified because considerable value is omitted in the balance sheet (and high RE are forecast for the future). It might even be that this omitted value is underpriced. The residual income valuation calculates the intrinsic P/B ratio and so indicates whether a high or low P/B is really due to mispricing.

There is another way of using the model in active trading strategies. On March 16, 1999, the Dow broke the 10000 mark for the first time. The S&P 500 Index stood at 1308, which priced the stocks in the index at about 4.6 times book value. A book-value multiple implies a certain RE forecast, so we can use the RE model to ask: What future RE is the market implicitly forecasting to price the S&P at 4.6 times book value? The S&P 500 firms earned an ROCE of about 16 percent in 1998, a good year. This group of firms is representative of the market as a whole and so has a beta of 1.0. Thus with a risk-free rate of 5.4 percent at the time and an equity risk premium of 6.0 percent, the CAPM required return is 11.4 percent. The RE model justifies a 4.6 multiple of each dollar of book value for an expected growth in RE, *g,* as follows:

$$4.6 = 1.0 + \frac{(0.16 - 0.114) \times g}{1.114 - g}$$

The solution for *g* is 1.0999, or a 9.99 percent rate. The amount, $0.16 - 0.114 = 0.046$ is the 1998 residual earnings for each dollar of book value. The growth rate of 9.99 percent is the **implied residual earnings growth rate,** that is, the rate at which the market implicitly expects this RE to grow in the future, perpetually. We could test the sensitivity of this calculation to different cost of capital estimates. But we can also ask: Is it reasonable to expect that the S&P 500 stocks are going to generate RE of such magnitude in the future? The growth in RE must come from higher ROCE and growth in book value. A glance at the historical ROCE in Table 5.2 might cast doubt on whether the current ROCE of 16 percent can be maintained: 16 percent looks high against the historical median of 12.2 percent, although note that Table 5.2 applies to a larger set of firms than the S&P 500. And historical median growth rates in RE since 1960 have been on the order of 4 percent per year. However, it might be that these firms are going to be much more profitable in the future. The market certainly expects so.

The *reverse engineering* that calculates implied forecasts from a market price is called *inverting the model* to read the market. This is similar to measuring implied forecast volatility of a stock price from an option price. Rather than calculating an intrinsic price from forecasts, we ask what are the **implied earnings forecast** in the market price. We then use this as a benchmark for our research: Can I justify the RE scenario that the market sees, or do I come to the conclusion that the market is mispriced? This is a different way of thinking about a trading strategy.

In a similar way we can invert the model to test a continuing value against the market's expectation. When valuing Hewlett-Packard at the end of 1995 in Table 5.3, we used an analyst's forecast of earnings to the year 2003, then (for lack of further analysis) assumed a zero growth rate in the continuing value. The intrinsic price was $67 but the market price was $84.5. Maybe the market forecasted a different growth rate at the horizon. We can impute the market's implied growth rate from the current market price using Case 3:

$$\$84.5 = 23.22 + \frac{2.66}{1.12} + \frac{3.02}{1.12^2} + \frac{3.36}{1.12^3} + \frac{3.87}{1.12^4} + \frac{4.47}{1.12^5} + \frac{5.18}{1.12^6}$$

$$+ \frac{6.01}{1.12^7} + \frac{6.97}{1.12^8} + \left(\frac{6.97 \times g}{1.12 - g}\right) / 1.12^8$$

We can solve for g; it is 1.048. If the market concurs with the analyst's forecasts of RE for 1996 to 2003, it implicitly sees perpetual growth in RE after 2003 of 4.8 percent per year. Is this rate realistic? Clearly this is a means of testing the market's forecast against the analyst's forecast but it is also a way of testing the analyst's forecast (or our own forecast) against the market: Does the market see something I don't see—some earnings that the firm can generate that I've not anticipated—or is the market missing something I see? We will have to go into deeper analysis—in Parts Two and Three of the book—to gain an appreciation of whether a 4.8 percent growth rate is appropriate.

Implied Earnings Forecasts

The implied residual earnings growth can be further engineered to convert it to an earnings forecast. Based on the implied RE growth rate, Hewlett-Packard's residual earnings in 2004 are the 2003 residual earnings of $6.97 growing at 4.8 percent, or $7.30. As book value at the end of 2003 is forecasted to be 88.88 (see Table 5.3), and residual earnings for 2004 are after a charge against that book value at the required return of 12 percent, earnings forecasted for 2004 are $(88.88 \times 0.12) + 7.30 = 17.97$. The formula to convert a residual earnings forecast to an earnings forecast is:

$$\text{Earnings forecast}_t = (\text{Book value}_{t-1} \times \text{Required return}) + \text{Residual earnings}_t$$

This formula reverse-engineers the residual earnings calculation.

Summary

This chapter has outlined an accrual accounting valuation model that can be applied to equities, bonds, projects, and strategies. The model utilizes information in the balance sheet and calculates the difference between balance sheet value and intrinsic value from forecasts of earnings and book values that will be reported in future forecasted income statements and balance sheets.

Residual earnings is the central concept in the model. Residual earnings measures the earnings in excess of those required if the book value were to earn at the required rate of return. Several properties of residual earnings have been identified in this chapter. Residual earnings treats investment as part of book value, so that an investment that is forecast to earn at the required rate of return generates zero residual earnings and has no effect on a value calculated. Residual earnings is not affected by dividends, share issues, and share repurchases, so using the residual income model yields valuations that are not sensitive to these (value-irrelevant) transactions with shareholders. Residual earnings uses accrual accounting, which captures added value over cash flows. And residual earnings valuation accommodates different ways of doing accrual accounting.

The Web Connection

Find the following on the web page for this chapter:

- Further applications of residual earnings valuation.

- A spreadsheet program to help you develop residual earnings pro formas.

- Further examples of how the residual earnings model protects the investor from paying for profitability that has been created by accounting methods.

- Directions to finding analysts' forecasts on the Web.

- Further examples of reverse engineering.

Above all, the residual earnings model provides a way of thinking about a business and about the value generation in the business. To value a business, it directs us to forecast profitability of investment and growth in investment, for these two factors drive residual earnings. And it directs management to add value to a business by increasing residual earnings, which, in turn, requires increasing ROCE and growing investment.

The residual earnings valuation approach has had a long history. Excess-profit approaches to valuation have been used as far back as the nineteenth century and have been permissible in tax court for a long time. But it is fair to say that, up to recently, cash flow approaches have dominated practice. Residual income techniques have been employed in management performance evaluation, led by General Electric in the 1950s.[7] In the 1990s, the techniques were applied in consulting, performance measurement, investment advising, and valuation practices, and most of these firms now have their variation of the model.

---

[7] Read a classic, D. Solomons, *Divisional Performance: Measurement and Control* (Burr Ridge, Ill.: Richard D. Irwin, 1965).

Key Concepts

implied earnings forecast is a forecast of earnings that is implicit in the market price. *164*

implied residual earnings growth rate is the perpetual growth in residual earnings that is implied by the market price. *164*

normal price-to-book ratio applies when price is equal to book value, that is the P/B ratio is 1.00 *144*

residual earnings is comprehensive earnings less a charge against book value for required earnings. Also referred to as **residual income, abnormal earnings,** or **excess profit.** *142*

residual earnings driver is a measure that determines residual earnings; the two primary drivers are **rate of return on common equity (ROCE)** and **growth in book value.** *148*

residual earnings model is a model that measures value added to book value from forecasts of residual earnings. *143*

steady-state condition is a permanent condition in forecast amounts that determines a continuing value. *155*

terminal premium or **horizon premium** is the premium at a forecast horizon (and is equal to the **continuing value** for the residual earnings valuation). *147*

The Analyst's Toolkit

Concept Questions

C5.1. Information indicates that a firm will earn a return on common equity above its cost of equity capital in all years in the future, but its shares trade below book value. Those shares must be mispriced. True or false?

C5.2. Jetform Corporation traded at a price-to-book ratio of 1.01 in May 1999. Its most recently reported ROCE was 10.1 percent and it is deemed to have a required equity return of 10 percent. What is your best guess as to the ROCE expected for the next fiscal year?

C5.3. Telesoft Corp. traded at a price-to-book ratio of 0.98 in May 1999 after reporting an ROCE of 52.2 percent. Does the market regard this ROCE as normal, unusually high, or unusually low?

C5.4. A share trades at a price-to-book ratio of 0.7. An analyst who forecasts an ROCE of 12 percent each year in the future, and sets the required equity return at 10 percent, recommends a hold position. Does his recommendation agree with his forecast?

C5.5. A firm cannot maintain an ROCE less than the required return and stay in business indefinitely. True or false?

C5.6. Look at the Case 3 valuation of General Electric in the chapter. Why are residual earnings increasing (except for 1991), although return on common equity (ROCE) is fairly constant?

C5.7. Look at Box 5.6 on residual earnings valuation and share issues and dividends.
   a. Why are the earnings different in the two scenarios (with and without a share issue and dividend)?
   b. Why is ROCE higher in Year 2 in the first scenario (with no share issue or dividends), although residual earnings are the same in both scenarios?

C5.8. Refer to the strategy evaluation that uses the residual earnings approach in Table 5.7. If the firm were to invest $1,400 per year (instead of $1,200 per year) at the same book rate of return, would it add value?

C5.9. When an analyst forecasts earnings, it must be comprehensive earnings. Why?

Exercises E5.1. **A Residual Earnings Valuation (Easy)**

An analyst presents you with the following pro forma (in millions of dollars) that gives her forecast of earnings and dividends for 2004–2008. She asks you to value the 1,380 million shares outstanding at the end of 2003, when common shareholders' equity stood at $4,310 million. Use a required return for equity of 10 percent in your calculations.

	2004E	2005E	2006E	2007E	2008E
Earnings	388.0	570.0	599.0	629.0	660.4
Dividends	115.0	160.0	349.0	367.0	385.4

a. Forecast book value, return on common equity (ROCE), and residual earnings for each of the years, 2004–2008.
b. Forecast growth rates for book value and growth in residual earnings for each of the years, 2005–2008.
c. Calculate the per-share value of the equity from this pro forma. Would you call this a Case 1, 2, or 3 valuation?
d. What is the premium over book value given by your calculation? What is the P/B ratio?

E5.2. **Residual Earnings and Value (Easy)**

The following forecasts of earnings per share (eps) and dividend per share (dps) were made at the end of 1999 for a firm with a book value per share of $22.00:

	2000E	2001E	2002E	2003E	2004E
Eps	3.90	3.70	3.31	3.59	3.90
Dps	1.00	1.00	1.00	1.00	1.00

The firm has an equity cost of capital of 12 percent per annum.

a. Calculate the residual earnings that are forecast for each year, 2000 to 2004.
b. What is the per-share value of the equity at the end of 1999 based on the residual income valuation model?
c. What is the forecasted per-share value of the equity at the end of the year 2004?
d. What is the expected premium in 2004?
e. Apply the dividend discount model to value this firm.

E5.3. **Residual Earnings Valuation and Return on Common Equity (Medium)**

A firm with a book value of $15.60 per share and 100 percent dividend payout is expected to have a return on common equity of 15 percent per year indefinitely in the future. Its cost of equity capital is 10 percent.

a. Calculate the intrinsic price-to-book ratio.
b. Suppose this firm announced that it was reducing its payout to 50 percent of earnings in the future. How would this affect your calculation of the price-to-book ratio?

E5.4. **Using Accounting-Based Techniques to Measure Value Added for a Project (Medium)**

A firm announces that it will invest $150 million in a project that is expected to generate a 15 percent rate of return on its beginning-of-period book value each year for the next five years. The required return for this type of project is 12 percent; the firm depreciates the cost of assets straight-line over the life of the investment.

    a. What is the value added to the firm from this investment?

    b. Forecast free cash flow for each year of the project. What is the net present value of cash flows for the project?

E5.5. Using Accounting-Based Techniques to Measure Value Added for a Going Concern (Medium)

A new firm announces that it will invest $150 million in projects each year forever. All projects are expected to generate a 15 percent rate of return on its beginning-of-period book value each year for five years. The required return for this type of project is 12 percent; the firm depreciates the cost of assets straight-line over the life of the investment.

    a. What is the value of the firm under this investment strategy? Would you refer to this valuation as a Case 1, 2, or 3 valuation?

    b. What is the value added to the initial investment of $150 million?

    c. Why is the value added greater than 15 percent of the initial $150 million investment?

E5.6. Residual Earnings Techniques: Bond Valuation (Easy)

Refer to the bond valuation problem in Exercise E3.10. Rather than valuing the bond using discounted cash flow techniques, value the bond at issue date using residual earnings techniques. (Table 5.5 will help you.)

E5.7. Analysts' Forecasts and Valuation: Hewlett-Packard (Medium)

In November 1999, Hewlett-Packard's shares traded at $83 each. Analysts were expecting the firm to announce earnings of $3.33 per share for the just-ended October 31 fiscal year and a book value per share of $19.36. The annual dividend per share for fiscal 1999 was 0.64.

    Analysts were also forecasting earnings for fiscal 2000 at $3.75 per share, $4.32 for 2001, and a growth rate in eps of 12 percent per year thereafter.

    a. The majority of analysts had a buy or strong buy on HP at the time. Are these recommendations consistent with the forecasts? Use a cost of equity capital of 12 percent.

    b. What was the market's implied long-term growth rate for residual earnings?

    c. List the difficulties you have answering these questions using the analysts' forecasts.

E5.8. Forecasting Target Prices Using Residual Earnings Techniques (Easy)

    a. In 2003 an analyst forecasted that the book value of the common equity of a firm would be $6,120 million at the end of 2005. He also forecasted that the firm would earn on this common equity a rate equal to the required return on equity, 11 percent. What is your forecast of the value of the equity at the end of 2005?

    b. How would your answer change if the analyst had forecasted that the firm would earn constant residual earnings of $25 million each year after 2005?

    c. How would your answer change if the analyst had forecasted $25 million of residual earnings for 2006, growing at a rate of 3 percent per year after that?

E5.9. Residual Earnings Valuation and Accounting Methods (Medium)

Refer back to the valuation in Exercise 5.1. In that pro forma, an analyst forecast $388 million for 2004 on a book value at the end of 2003 of $4,310 million, that is, a return on common equity of 9 percent. The forecasts were made at the end of 2003 based on preliminary reports from the firm.

    When the final report was published, however, the analyst discovered that the firm had decided to write-down its inventory at the end of 2003 by $114 million (following the lower-of-cost-or-market rule). As this was inventory that the analyst forecasted would be sold in 2004 (and thus the impairment affects cost of goods sold for that year), the analyst revised her earnings forecast for 2004. For questions (a) and (b), ignore any effect of taxes.

    a. What is the revised earnings forecast for 2004 as a result of the inventory impairment? What is the revised forecast of return on common equity (ROCE) for 2004?

    b. Show that the revision in the forecast of 2004 earnings does not change the valuation of the equity.

    c. Recognize, now, that the firm's income tax rate is 35 percent. Do your answers to questions (a) and (b) change?

E5.10.   Comparison Valuations: Hewlett-Packard, Dell Computer, and Compaq Computer (Hard)

In February 1996 an analyst from a major brokerage house provided the following eps forecasts for HP, Dell, and Compaq:

	1995A	1996E	1997E	Subsequent 3-Year Growth Rate
HP	4.63	5.60	6.60	16%
Dell	2.67	3.20	4.15	15
Compaq	2.88	4.50	5.75	13

At the time, HP traded at 95⅛, Dell at 36¾, and Compaq at 47⅞. Neither Dell nor Compaq paid dividends. Hewlett-Packard paid a dividend of $0.70 per share in 1995. Assume that the three firms have the same cost of capital of 12 percent. The book values per share for the three firms at the end of 1995 were:

HP	23.22
Dell	10.35
Compaq	17.27

    a. Given that the analyst's forecasts are representative of the market, what are the residual earnings growth rates that the market forecasts for each firm subsequent to 1997?

    b. The analyst recommended a hold for both HP and Dell and a buy for Compaq. The analyst also forecasted the following P/E ratios for the three firms at the end of 1997:

HP	14.0
Dell	12.0
Compaq	8.4

Do you see any inconsistency between these forecasts and the analyst's recommendations?

E5.11.   Did You Pay Too Much for Book Value? (Easy)

Consider the following per-share numbers from accounting reports for a firm:

	2000	2001	2002	2003
Book value, end of year	200	207	230	238
Dividends paid at end of year		15	0	15

Your opportunity cost of capital is 10 percent.

If you paid $220 per share for the firm at the beginning of 2000, do you think (with the advantage of hindsight) that you overpaid or underpaid?

E5.12. Did You Pay Too Much for Book Value?: Boeing, Lockheed, and McDonnell-Douglas (Medium)

At the end of 1988, you bought a share of each of three aerospace companies:

Company	Price	Bps
Boeing Co. (BA)	60⅝	35.267
Lockheed Corp. (LK)	41¼	41.728
McDonnell-Douglas Corp. (MD)	72¼	83.425

The following table shows their subsequent performance:

Year	Boeing		Lockheed		McDonnell-Douglas	
	Eps	Dps	Eps	Dps	Eps	Dps
1989	4.23	1.17	0.03	1.75	5.72	2.82
1990	4.01	0.95	5.30	1.80	7.99	2.82
1991	4.56	1.00	4.86	1.95	11.03	1.40
1992	1.62	1.00	−4.58	2.09	−20.10	1.40
1993	3.66	1.00	6.70	2.12	10.10	1.40

Boeing had a 1.5-for-1 split in 1989 and also in 1990. The eps and dps numbers reflect those splits.

Was the higher premium you paid for Boeing justified by these results? Which was the best buy? Your opportunity cost of capital for equity in this risk class is 12 percent.

E5.13. Implied Growth in Residual Earnings: Coca-Cola Company (Easy)

The Coca-Cola Company reports "economic profit" in the financial summary of its 10-K annual report. Economic profit is calculated in a similar way to residual earnings; the accountants use a required return of 9 percent in the calculation.

The economic profit for 1998 was $2.480 billion, reported along with earnings of $3.533 billion and a book value of common equity of $8.403 billion. Coke's 2.465 billion shares traded at 66½ at the end of 1998.

What growth in economic profit was the market imputing for Coca-Cola?

Real World Connection

See Minicase M13.2 in Chapter 13 on Coca Cola.

E5.14. Residual Earnings Growth and Growth in Earnings: Hewlett-Packard Company (Medium)

In October 1999 analysts were forecasting an eps of $3.75 for Hewlett-Packard's year ending October 31, 2000, on a book value per share of $19.36 at the end of October 1999. For the fiscal year ending October 31, 2001, the analysts were forecasting an eps of $4.32. The firm paid a dividend of $0.64 per share in 1999 and is expected to maintain a 19 percent payout ratio. It is assigned a cost of equity capital of 12 percent.

a. What growth in earnings must HP maintain after 2001 to give it constant residual earnings?

b. What change in premium do you forecast for each year after 2001 if the residual earnings are expected to be constant?

E5.15.   Forecast Revision and Change in Value: Weyerhaeuser Company (Medium)

On March 31, 1996, an analyst published the following eps forecast for Weyerhaeuser Co.:

	1995A	1996E	1997E	Five-Year Growth
Eps	3.93	3.40	4.10	10%

Weyerhaeuser paid dividends of $1.50 per share in 1995 and is expected to pay $1.60 per share in 1996 and 1997. The firm's book value per share was $22.57 at the end of 1995. Subsequently the analyst revised the forecast down to reflect a drop in paper prices:

	1995A	1996E	1997E
Eps	3.93	2.20	3.25

How would you revise the valuation as a result of this forecast revision? Use a cost of capital of 12 percent in your calculations.

Real World Connection

See Minicase M3.4 in Chapter 3 and Minicase M5.2 in this chapter on Weyerhaeuser.

E5.16.   Equivalent Valuation Methods (Hard: Uses the analysis in the appendix)

Refer to Box 5.6 in this chapter. A value of $10.66 per share was calculated under two scenarios (with and without a share issue or dividends). Show that the same value can be calculated by forecasting dividends and book value in Year 3 for both scenarios.

E5.17.   Impairment of Goodwill (Medium)

A firm made an acquisition at the end of 2001 and recorded the acquisition cost of $428 million on its balance sheet as tangible assets of $349 million and goodwill of $79 million. The firm used a required return of 10 percent as a hurdle rate when evaluating the acquisition and determined that it was paying fair value.

a. What is the projected residual income from the acquisition for 2002?

b. By the end of 2002, the tangible assets from the acquisition had been depreciated to a book value of $301 million. Management ascertained that the acquisition would subsequently earn an annual return of only 9 percent on book value at the end of 2002. What is the amount by which goodwill should be impaired under the FASB requirements for impairment?

Minicases	**M5.1**

The Goldman Sachs IPO

After considerable deliberation, the partners of Goldman Sachs, the global investment banking firm, converted the partnership to a corporation in 1999 and floated an initial public offering. Goldman was the last of the "bulge-bracket" investment banks to go public.

Commentators saw a big incentive for the 190 partners to make this move. At retirement, partners received book value for their stakes. But in the 1990s bull market, other investment banking firms such as Merrill Lynch and Morgan Stanley Dean Witter were trading at three to four times book value.

Some commentators saw the current partners as following the "greed creed" to the detriment of the long run. They argued that the partnership structure was a key to Goldman's value—the ability to attract talent to a tightly knit culture enhanced its human capital—and were concerned that the corporate environment could lead to its erosion.

Jon Corzine and Henry Paulson, the firm's co-chairmen when the IPO was proposed, claimed strategic reasons for the IPO: Going public would give the firm a currency—its own shares—with which to make acquisitions. There were fears that Goldman might be left behind in the recent consolidation in the industry, with the Travelers–Citicorp merger (which included Salomon Smith Barney), the Morgan Stanley and Dean Witter combination, and the Deutsche Bank and Bankers Trust union.

Goldman floated 15 percent of its shares in the IPO in May 1999 at $70 per share with the ticker GS. With 441.3 million shares outstanding, this gave it a market capitalization of $30.891 billion on its last-reported book value of $7.85 billion.

Analysts forecast an eps for Goldman of $4.69 for the fiscal year ending November 1999 (before special charges relating to the IPO) and $4.26 for 2000, and most gave it a hold recommendation. Goldman indicated it would pay a $0.48 per share dividend.

A. With these forecasts (and any other considerations you might raise), discuss whether the price-to-book ratio for the IPO price was justified. Use a required return of 10 percent.

B. Analyze the arguments for taking Goldman public. Have you considered those arguments in your answer to (a)?

C. Goldman's issue price was at approximately the same multiples of book value and earnings as those for Merrill Lynch and Morgan Stanley Dean Witter, two other bulge-bracket banks. Does this comparison justify the price for Goldman Sachs?

M5.2

Strategy and Valuation: Weyerhaeuser Company

Steven Rogel, formerly of Willamette Industries, a forest products producer, was appointed in 1998 as CEO of Weyerhaeuser, the forest products firm whose value was considered in minicase M3.4. He was given the mandate to lift Weyerhaeuser's return on equity from its historical level of 12 percent to 17 percent. Refer to the 1998 financial statements in the earlier minicase for an indication of the firm's profitability at the time.

Weyerhaeuser's revenues come from timber products, pulp, paper, and packaging products, and the development of residential real estate. Rogel planned to meet the target by increasing the timber harvest by 35 percent for the years 1999–2003 and by restructuring and cost cutting in the pulp, paper, and packaging segment. Reasonable estimates add $0.85 to 1999 per-share earnings over 1998 from the increase in the timber harvest and $0.72 from efficiencies gained in the pulp, paper, and packaging segment.

Weyerhaeuser's profitability in 1996–1998 had been depressed by the low commodity prices that prevailed at the time. The business is cyclical, partly due to commodity prices. At the peak of the last cycle in 1995, Weyerhaeuser reported $3.93 in per-share earnings, in contrast to $1.48 in 1998, and its return on common equity in 1995 was 18.2 percent. Analysts anticipate an increase in commodity prices, adding a further 40 cents to per-share earnings.

Excess production capacity has been a problem in the global paper industry. The industry has tended to reinvest cash flows at the peak of the demand cycle to build new plants that remain idle in the down cycle. The years 1996–1998 were such a down cycle. Anticipated increase in global demand in 1999 should use some of this excess capacity, adding 20 cents to eps.

Weyerhaeuser's shares traded at $55 each after its 1998 financial report was released and the new CEO's plans were known.

A. Will Rogel's plans achieve the objective of increasing return on equity to 17 percent?

B. What is the value of Weyerhaeuser's shares based on the plans? Would you buy the shares based on the CEO's initiatives? Use a 12 percent cost of capital in your calculations.

C. Why does utilization of capacity increase earnings?

D. What reservations do you have about incorporating the forecasts of higher return on equity in your valuation?

E. What difficulties did you have in getting answers to questions (a) and (b)? What further information would you seek?

Real World Connection
See Minicase M3.4. in Chapter 3 for related material on Weyerhaeuser Company.

M5.3
Chrysler Corporation: The Kerkorian Bid

In 1998, the German automobile manufacturer Daimler-Benz bid successfully for Chrysler Corporation, America's third largest automobile company. But there had been an earlier bid for Chrysler, by the colorful Kirk Kerkorian.

Kirk Kerkorian announced on April 11, 1995, that he and former Chrysler Chairman Lee A. Iacocca were planning to lead a hostile takeover of Chrysler Corporation, Detroit's No. 3 automaker. They offered $55 per share for 90 percent of 369 million shares outstanding. At the time Chrysler was trading at $39¾, but its share price jumped the next day to $49 on the news.

Kerkorian was a Las Vegas gambling mogul who owned about 10 percent of Chrysler through his Tracinda Corporation. He claimed that Chrysler was mismanaged under chairman and CEO Robert Eaton. A particular grievance was $7.5 billion in cash that Chrysler held. Kerkorian maintained that Chrysler had no use for this cash and that a payout to shareholders would increase the share price. Chrysler's management maintained that the $7.5 billion in cash was necessary to cover cash shortfalls during market downturns.

Others suspected Kerkorian's motives. He had spent $676 million in acquiring his stake in Chrysler. On April 15, after the bid, his stake was valued in the press at $1.4 billion. The charge against him was greenmail:

> What do takeover warriors of the 1980s such as Carl Icahn, Henry Kravis, Ron Perelman, the Bass Brothers, and Mike Milken think of the hostile Kerkorian–Iacocca attack on Chrysler (C)? They won't talk for attribution, and *Business Week* wasn't able to interview all of them. But the ones who spoke don't think a takeover will materialize. One of these pros privately described the Kerkorian caper this way: "The evidence clearly points to one thing— Kerkorian wants greenmail money, not Chrysler." So what's their advice? Short the stock. Icahn, for one, has taken big short positions in Chrysler.
>
> "Believe me," says one veteran of several leveraged-buyout deals, "There won't be a takeover." In the end, both sides will agree to a buyback, he says—probably at a price below 55. "I've been there. I know when somebody seriously wants to acquire a company. This case tells me in so many ways that Kerkorian wants out," says another central character of many '80s takeover battles. "What Kerkorian is telling [Chrysler chairman] Bob Eaton is that he [Kerkorian] will be a pain in the butt unless he's paid off. He has nothing to lose, and it's a smart move—for Kerkorian."[1]

Kerkorian had also been accused of being an "asset stripper" who destroyed viable businesses. Critics claimed that he viewed businesses as commodities to be broken up and sold in pieces. He had previously been involved in a number of controversial takeovers and dispositions.

In 1969 he bought 40 percent of MGM for $82 million in a hostile takeover. After buying United Artists for $380 million in 1982, he sold off assets from the two studios and combined them. This, it was said, weakened the two studios. He sold the package to Ted Turner for $1.5 billion five years later. Then in just five months he repurchased most of MGM/UA for $80 million when Turner ran into financial difficulties. Turner kept the film library for his cable television channels. Kerkorian again sold the studio in 1990 to Giancarlo Parretti's Pathé Communications Corp., this time for $1.3 billion. Both the Turner and Parretti transactions led to court cases with significant amounts paid in settlement by Kerkorian.

Kerkorian's supporters saw him as a value enhancer who, in running MGM as an operating studio for 20 years, increased its value considerably. They observed that he had made his fortune from running airlines and resort hotels, not through transactions for short-term gain.

Kerkorian's bid for Chrysler failed when he was unable to pin down financing. But he had been vigorous in making his case to Chrysler shareholders. Chrysler settled with Kerkorian in early February 1996 in order to head off a threatened proxy fight.

Chrysler's board agreed to give one seat to a Kerkorian nominee, agreed to change its poison pill grievance provision, and agreed to pay out large sums of cash. Kerkorian signed a five-year "standstill" agreement to keep his ownership below 13.7 percent. During 1996 Chrysler increased its dividend four times, repurchased $2.0 billion of its shares, and announced another $2.0 billion of repurchases for 1997.

---

[1] Source: K. Holland, D. Woodruff, and P. L. Zeig, "The Chrysler Bid: Are Any Backers Out There?" *Business Week,* May 1, 1995, p. 38.

Some information on Chrysler, assembled in early 1996, about the time when the Kerkorian affair was resolved, follows. It includes analysis of Chrysler and a summary of earnings forecasts that were being made by analysts at the time. The 1995 financial statements also are provided. More detail is available from the firm's SEC filings at http://www.sec.gov.

A. What possible motives, other than greenmail, might Kerkorian have in acquiring Chrysler at a premium over the current price of 39¾?

B. Is the $55 per share offer a fair price or a greenmail price? Try to get a valuation at the end of 1995, at the time when the Kerkorian affair was expected to be resolved. With the information at hand here you will not be able to do a thorough analysis to answer the question. But see what rough valuations you can come up with. Sometimes rough valuations—which don't require much work—are justified by more detailed analysis. As you attempt to get a valuation, make a list of the additional information you feel you need to give you more confidence in your analysis.

C. What do you think of Kerkorian's and management's claims regarding the $7.5 billion held in cash?

A REPORT ON CHRYSLER CORPORATION, FEBRUARY 1996

COMPANY OVERVIEW

Chrysler Corporation is the third largest automobile and truck manufacturer in the U.S. It produces Plymouth, Dodge, Eagle, Jeep, and Chrysler cars and utility vehicles, and Dodge trucks. It also produces automobile parts and accessories, and imports and sells Mitsubishi Motor's cars in the United States. During 1995 it began a program of selling off its defense businesses. Along with its automotive business, Chrysler also has a financing arm that provides financing with the sale of motor vehicles.

FIVE-YEAR SUMMARY

Sales, net income, eps, and dps for the five years up to 1995 are as follows (in millions, except per-share amounts):

Year	Revenue	Net Income	Eps	Dps
1995	53,195	2,004	5.30	2.00
1994	52,235	3,633	10.11	1.10
1993	43,600	−2,631	−7.62	0.65
1992	36,897	723	2.21	0.60
1991	29,370	−795	−3.28	0.60

After a big slump in 1990 and 1991, Chrysler has improved its performance steadily. (The loss in 1993 was after a charge for a change in accounting principle; earnings before this charge were $2,415 million, or $6.77 per share.) As well as increasing sales, Chrysler has made good progress in holding down marketing and development costs.

Chrysler's cheery outlook is in marked contrast to the darker moods at Ford and General Motors. Chrysler's record 207,000 unit sales in February bode well for 1996. Chrysler's truck line is its big edge. Trucks accounted for 70 percent of 1996 first-quarter production. With a lower cost base than its rivals, Chrysler is enjoying higher margins; the company is forecasted to earn $892 million on revenues of $13.9 billion in the first quarter of 1996, about $2.50 per share.

INDUSTRY ANALYSIS

The auto industry is cyclical. Industry sales in 1996 are forecasted to increase by 3–4 percent from 1995. However, a slowdown is expected after 1997. Many automakers, including foreign competitors, are planning to launch new or redesigned models. New plants are being built and it is expected that by 1998, there will be significant overinvestment in plant capacity worldwide.

FORECASTS

The analysis of industry conditions and Chrysler's market share lead to the following forecasts:

	1995A	1996E	1997E	1998E	1999E	2000E
Revenue	+1.9%	+4%	+3%	+ −0%	+2%	+2%
Gross margin	22.5%	22.5%	22.5%	21.0%	22.0%	22.0%
Capital spending	$3bn	$3bn	$3bn	$4bn	$3bn	$3bn

Based on Chrysler's strong performance in the first quarter in 1996, total revenue is expected to increase 3–4 percent in 1996 and 1997. But, with the market slump expected, growth in 1998 is expected to be 0 percent. In the long run, sales are expected to increase about 2 percent per year.

Chrysler has enjoyed high profitability due particularly to minivans and jeeps. However, prospective future competition both in the U.S. market and in the international market suggests lower profitability in the future. Gross margin in 1996 and 1997 is likely to be the same as 1995. However, estimates for 1998 and after 1999 are 21 percent and 22 percent, respectively.

CONSENSUS ANALYSTS' FORECASTS

In April 1995, the Institutional Brokers Estimate System (IBES) reported that analysts were forecasting eps for 1996 in a range of $4.14 to $6.23, with an average of $5.10. Their forecasts for 1997 ranged from $3.21 to $5.55, with an average of $4.38. The typical growth rate in eps forecasted for the three years after 1997 was 9 percent.

THE FINANCIAL STATEMENTS, YEAR ENDED DECEMBER 31, 1995
The Income Statement

	Year Ended December 31		
	1995	**1994**	**1993**
	(in millions of dollars)		
Sales of manufactured products	$49,601	$49,363	$40,831
Finance and insurance revenues	1,589	1,384	1,429
Other revenues	2,005	1,488	1,340
Total revenues	53,195	52,235	43,600
Costs, other than items below	41,304	38,032	32,382
Depreciation of property and equipment	1,100	994	969
Amortization of special tools	1,120	961	671
Selling and administrative expenses	4,064	3,933	3,377
Pension expense	405	714	756
Nonpension postretirement benefit expense	758	834	768
Interest expense	995	937	1,104
Gains on sales of automotive assets and investments	—	—	(265)
Total Expenses	49,746	46,405	39,762
Earnings before Income Taxes and Cumulative Effect of Changes in Accounting Principles	3,449	5,830	3,838
Provision for income taxes	1,328	2,117	1,423
Earnings before Cumulative Effect of Changes in Accounting Principles	2,121	3,713	2,415
Cumulative effect of changes in accounting principles	(96)	—	(4,966)
Net earnings (loss)	$2,025	$3,713	$(2,551)
Preferred stock dividends	21	80	80
Net earnings (loss) on common stock	$2,004	$3,633	$(2,631)
Primary Earnings (Loss) per Common Share	(in dollars or millions of shares)		
Earnings before cumulative effect of changes in accounting principles	$5.55	$10.11	$6.77
Cumulative effect of changes in accounting principles	(0.25)	—	(14.39)
Net earnings (loss) per common share	$5.30	$10.11	$(7.62)
Average common and dilutive equivalent shares outstanding	378.1	359.2	345.1
Fully Diluted Earnings per Common Share:			
Earnings before cumulative effect of changes in accounting principles	$5.35	$9.10	—
Cumulative effect of changes in accounting principles	(0.24)	—	—
Net earnings per common share	$5.11	$9.10	—
Average common and dilutive equivalent shares outstanding	396.1	407.8	—
Dividends Declared per Common Share	$2.00	$1.10	$0.65

The Balance Sheet

	December 31	
	1995	**1994**
	(in millions of dollars)	
Assets		
Cash and cash equivalents	$ 5,543	$ 5,145
Marketable securities	2,582	3,226
Accounts receivable—trade and other (less allowance for doubtful accounts: $58 million in 1995 and 1994)	2,003	1,695
Inventories	4,448	3,356
Prepaid taxes, pension, and other expenses	985	1,330
Finance receivables and retained interests in sold receivables	13,623	12,433
Property and equipment	12,595	11,073
Special tools	3,566	3,643
Intangible assets	2,082	2,162
Deferred tax assets	490	395
Other assets	5,839	5,081
Total assets	$53,756	$49,539
Liabilities		
Accounts payable	$8,290	$7,826
Short-term debt	2,674	4,645
Payments due within one year on long-term debt	1,661	811
Accrued liabilities and expenses	7,032	5,582
Long-term debt	9,858	7,650
Accrued noncurrent employee benefits	9,217	8,595
Other noncurrent liabilities	4,065	3,736
Total liabilities	42,797	38,845
Shareholders' Equity (shares in millions)		
Preferred stock—$1 per share par value; authorized 20.0 shares; Series A Convertible Preferred Stock; issued and outstanding: 1995 and 1994—0.1 and 1.7 shares, respectively (aggregate liquidation preference $68 million and $863 million, respectively)	*	2
Common stock—$1 per share par value; authorized 1,000.0 shares; issued: 1995 and 1994—408.2 and 364.1 shares, respectively	408	364
Additional paid-in capital	5,506	5,536
Retained earnings	6,280	5,006
Treasury stock—at cost: 1995—29.9 shares; 1994—9.0 shares	(1,235)	(214)
Total shareholders' equity	10,959	10,694
Total liabilities and shareholders' equity	$53,756	$49,539

The Cash Flow Statement

	Year Ended December 31		
	1995	**1994**	**1993**
	(in millions of dollars)		
Cash Flows from Operating Activities			
Net earnings (loss)	$2,025	$3,713	$(2,551)
Adjustments to reconcile to net cash provided by operating activities			
Depreciation and amortization	2,220	1,955	1,640
Provision for credit losses	372	203	209
Deferred income taxes	186	1,065	803
Cumulative effect of changes in accounting principles	96	—	4,966
Gains on sales of automotive assets and investments	—	—	(265)
Change in receivables	848	(1,158)	(2)
Change in inventories	(435)	129	(557)
Change in prepaid expenses and other assets	(702)	(1,898)	(1,472)
Change in accounts payable and accrued and other liabilities	2,089	2,613	(5)
Other	243	161	47
Net cash provided by operating activities	6,942	6,783	2,813
Cash Flows from Investing Activities			
Purchases of marketable securities	(5,410)	(5,425)	(4,700)
Sales and maturities of marketable securities	6,122	3,519	4,937
Finance receivables acquired	(24,437)	(20,149)	(16,809)
Finance receivables collected	5,040	5,236	9,616
Proceeds from sales of finance receivables	16,310	13,482	7,846
Proceeds from sales of nonautomotive assets	—	—	2,375
Proceeds from sales of automotive assets and investments	—	62	461
Expenditures for property and equipment	(3,060)	(2,847)	(1,761)
Expenditures for special tools	(1,049)	(1,177)	(1,234)
Other	585	351	446
Net cash (used in) provided by investing activities	(5,899)	(6,948)	1,177
Cash Flows from Financing Activities			
Change in short-term debt (less than 90-day maturities)	(1,971)	1,348	2,518
Proceeds under long-term borrowings and revolving lines of credit	4,731	1,305	6,995
Payments on long-term borrowings and revolving lines of credit	(1,687)	(1,011)	(13,592)
Proceeds from issuance of common stock, net of expenses	—	—	1,952
Repurchases of common stock	(1,047)	—	—
Dividends paid	(710)	(399)	(281)
Other	39	27	101
Net cash (used in) provided by financing activities	(645)	1,270	(2,307)
Change in cash and cash equivalents	398	1,105	1,683
Cash and cash equivalents at beginning of year	5,145	4,040	2,357
Cash and cash equivalents at end of year	$5,543	$5,145	$4,040

Appendix

Equivalent Valuation Methods: The Residual Earnings Model Supplies the Terminal Value for the Dividend Discount Model

In applying the RE model to value equity, we found that we could calculate not only the current value, V_0^E but also the expected terminal value: V_T^E = Expected book value at T + Expected premium (continuing value) at T. So for Wal-Mart, for example, the expected value at T was $6.50 + $4.42 = $10.92. Remember that in trying to apply the dividend discount model in Chapter 3, we abandoned the task because we did not know how to get the terminal payoff. Now we do so: with V_T^E in hand, we can value the equity with the dividend discount model as

$$V_0^E = \frac{d_1}{\rho_E^1} + \frac{d_2}{\rho_E^2} + \frac{d_3}{\rho_E^3} + \cdots + \frac{d_T}{\rho_E^T} + \frac{V_T^E}{\rho_E^T}$$

Indeed we can state the models for Cases 1, 2, and 3 in terms of discounted dividends plus the present value of an expected terminal value. In Case 1 we expect the terminal payoff to be equal to the forecast of book value, so the Case 1 valuation can be restated as

$$V_0^E = \frac{d_1}{\rho_E^1} + \frac{d_2}{\rho_E^2} + \frac{d_3}{\rho_E^3} + \cdots + \frac{d_T}{\rho_E^T} + \left[\frac{B_T}{\rho_E^T} \right] \quad \textbf{Case 1} \qquad \textbf{(5A.1)}$$

Go back to New York State Electric and Gas and discount the forecasts of dividends and 1993 book value of $22.01 to present value; you will get the same valuation as before.

The Case 2 valuation can be restated as

$$V_0^E = \frac{d_1}{\rho_E^1} + \frac{d_2}{\rho_E^2} + \frac{d_3}{\rho_E^3} + \cdots + \frac{d_T}{\rho_E^T} + \left[\frac{\text{Earn}_{T+1}}{\rho_E - 1} \right] / \rho_E^T \quad \textbf{Case 2} \qquad \textbf{(5A.2)}$$

The terminal value here is just the capitalized net income that is forecast for year $T + 1$. This is proofed for Wal-Mart in Table 5A.1. The expected earnings of $1.31 for 1997 are those that yield RE of 0.53 for that year: $0.53 = \text{Earn}_{1997} - (0.12 \times 6.50)$, so $\text{Earn}_{1997} = 1.31$. The terminal payoff is this earnings forecast, capitalized, and this is the same 10.92 that we calculated earlier. The 1987 equity value is the present value of this payoff plus the present value of the stream of dividends, or $4.39 per share, as before. You can make the same calculation for HP and find that the value is also as that in Table 5.3.

The corresponding calculation for Case 3 is a little more complicated. It is

$$V_0^E = \frac{d_1}{\rho_E^1} + \frac{d_2}{\rho_E^2} + \frac{d_3}{\rho_E^3} + \cdots + \frac{d_T}{\rho_E^T} + \left[\frac{\text{Earn}_{T+1} - (g - 1)B_T}{\rho_E - g} \right] / \rho_E^T \quad \textbf{Case 3} \qquad \textbf{(5A.3)}$$

You can proof this with the General Electric example. This formula is a good one to keep in mind because it captures all cases. If $g = 1$, then we have the Case 2 valuation in expression 5A.2. If $\text{Earn}_{T+1} = (\rho_E - 1)B_T$—that is, $\text{RE}_{T+1} = 0$—then we have the Case 1 valuation in expression 5A.1.

TABLE 5A.1 Case 2 (Dividend Discounting): Wal-Mart

		1987	1988	1989	1990	1991	1992	1993	1994	1995	1996	1997
						Forecast Year, t						
Dps			0.03	0.04	0.06	0.07	0.09	0.11	0.13	0.17	0.20	
Eps			0.28	0.37	0.48	0.57	0.70	0.87	1.02	1.17	1.19	1.31
Discount factor			1.12	1.254	1.405	1.574	1.762	1.974	2.211	2.476	2.773	
PV of dps			0.027	0.032	0.043	0.044	0.051	0.056	0.059	0.069	0.072	
Total PV of dps	0.46											
Terminal value (= 1.31/0.12)											10.92	
PV of TV	3.93											
V_0^E	4.39											

As these calculations are equivalent to the earlier RE valuations, you can make the calculation either way. With the dividend discount approach here, we forecast the earnings and book value at the horizon, combine them with the forecast of the growth rate (if any) according to equation 5A.3, and then add the present value of the dividend payoff up to the horizon. You recognize that this calculation corresponds exactly to the form of investment payoffs that we laid out in Chapter 3; payoffs are made up of dividends and a terminal payoff. So you can see directly that RE techniques (and the equivalent valuations here) forecast stock returns. And it is returns that investors, after all, are interested in.

In the strategy example in this chapter we saw that the RE valuation and the DCF valuation are equivalent for a five-year horizon. In the web page for Chapter 16 we will present the conditions where this is so. And we will see how the RE model supplies the continuing value for the DCF valuation as well as for the dividend discount valuation.

This appendix reinforces the point that the residual earnings model is really a restatement of the dividend discount model, but one that typically allows us to capture value over a shorter forecast horizon (with the terminal values above).

Chapter Six

Accrual Accounting and Valuation: Pricing Earnings

LINKS

Link to previous chapter

Chapter 5 showed how to price book values in the balance sheet and calculate intrinsic price-to-book ratios.

This chapter

This chapter shows how to price earnings in the income statement and calculate intrinsic price-earnings ratio.

Link to next chapter

Chapter 7 begins the financial statement analysis that is necessary to carry out the price-to-book and price-earnings valuations discussed in Chapters 5 and 6.

Link to web page

The web page has more applications of the techniques in this chapter.

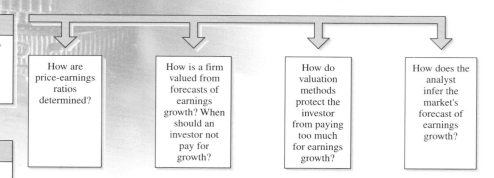

| How are price-earnings ratios determined? | How is a firm valued from forecasts of earnings growth? When should an investor not pay for growth? | How do valuation methods protect the investor from paying too much for earnings growth? | How does the analyst infer the market's forecast of earnings growth? |

The last chapter showed how to anchor valuations on the book value, the bottom line of the balance sheet. This chapter shows how to anchor valuations on earnings, the bottom line of the income statement. By anchoring on book value, the analyst develops the price-to-book ratio (P/B). By anchoring on earnings, the analyst develops the price-earnings ratio (P/E). So, while the last chapter asked how much one should pay per dollar of book value, this chapter asks how much one should pay per dollar of earnings.

The Analyst's Checklist

After reading this chapter you should understand:

- What "abnormal earnings growth" is.

- How forecasting abnormal earnings growth yields the intrinsic P/E ratio.

- What is meant by a normal P/E ratio.

- The difference between ex-dividend earnings growth and cum-dividend earnings growth.

- The difference between a Case 1 and Case 2 abnormal earnings growth valuation.

- The advantages and disadvantages of using an abnormal earnings growth valuation and how the valuation compares with residual earnings valuation.

- How dividends, share issues, and share repurchases affect abnormal earnings growth.

- That abnormal earnings growth is equal to the change in residual earnings.

- How abnormal earnings growth valuation protects the investor from paying too much for earnings growth.

- How abnormal earnings growth valuation protects the investor from paying for earnings that are created by accounting methods.

- How to use the abnormal earnings growth model in reverse engineering.

- What a PEG ratio is.

After reading this chapter you should be able to:

- Calculate cum-dividend earnings.

- Calculate abnormal earnings growth.

- Calculate the value of equities from forecasts of earnings and dividends.

- Calculate intrinsic forward P/E and trailing P/E ratios.

- Calculate continuing values for the abnormal earnings growth model.

- Convert an analyst's eps forecast to a valuation.

- Calculate implied earnings growth rates from the market price of a stock.

- Evaluate a PEG ratio.

THE CONCEPT BEHIND THE PRICE-EARNINGS RATIO

P/B ratios differ from 1.0 because accountants do not measure the full value of the equity in the balance sheet. However, the missing value is ultimately realized in the future earnings that assets produce, and these earnings can be forecasted: A price-to-book ratio is determined by expected earnings that have not yet been booked to book value, and the higher the future earnings relative to book value, the higher the P/B ratio.

A parallel idea lies behind the P/E ratio. Whereas book value is a measure of the stock of value, earnings is a measure of the change in value. In Chapter 2 we appreciated that, just as book value is an imperfect measure of the stock of value, earnings is also an imperfect measure of the value added for shareholders. Current earnings measure value added from current sales, whereas share prices change in anticipation of value to be added in earnings from future sales as well. So the P/E ratio compares the value of expected future earnings (in the numerator) to current earnings (in the denominator). Therein lies the concept of the P/E ratio. Just as the P/B ratio is based on expected earnings that have not yet been booked to book value, the P/E ratio is based on expected earnings that have not yet been recognized in current earnings. So P/E ratios are high when one forecasts considerably higher future earnings than current earnings, and P/E ratios are low when future earnings are forecasted to be lower than current earnings. In short, the P/E ratio prices earnings growth.

This chapter supplies the formal valuation model to implement this concept of the P/E ratio rigorously, as well as the mechanics to apply the model faithfully. The formality is warranted, for one can pay too much for earnings growth if one is not careful.

Beware of Paying Too Much for Earnings Growth

The stock market is often excited by earnings growth, and it rewards earnings growth with a higher P/E multiple. Analysts tend to advocate growth firms. Momentum investors push up stock prices of growth firms, anticipating yet more growth. However, growth in earnings does not necessarily imply higher value. Firms can grow earnings simply by investing more. If those investments fail to earn a return above the required return, they will grow earnings but they will not grow value. So, growth comes with a caveat: An investor should not pay for earnings growth that does not add value. This maxim leads to a modified P/E concept: The P/E prices earnings growth, but it does not price growth that does not add value.

A case in point is a firm that grows earnings dramatically through acquisitions. The market often sees acquisitive firms as growth firms and gives them high P/E multiples. But, if an acquirer pays fair value for an acquisition, it may not add value to the investment: Even though the acquisition adds a lot of earnings, the investment just earns the required return. Or worse, should an acquirer overpay for the acquisition—as is often the case with empire builders—he may actually destroy value while adding earnings growth.

During the 1990s, a number of firms went on an acquisition spree. Some acquisitions were for strategic reasons, while others appeared to be growth for growth's sake. Tyco International, a firm with $8,471 million in assets in 1996, grew to become a conglomerate with $111,287 million in assets by 2001. Its businesses included electronic components, undersea cables, medical supplies, fire suppression equipment, security systems, and flow control products, and it also ran a financing arm. It became a darling of the market, with its stock price increasing from $10 per share in 1996 to $60 in 2001. In 2002, much of its market value evaporated, with the price falling to $8, as the value of the acquisitions—and the accounting employed in reporting earnings from the acquisitions—came into question. WorldCom grew from a small Mississippi firm to the number two telecommunications firm in the U.S., acquiring (among others) MCI. Its stock price rose to over $60, but by 2002, due to an accounting scandal, it was trading at 25 cents per share and ultimately went bankrupt. Both Tyco and WorldCom were led by aggressive empire builders (who subsequently resigned under doubtful circumstances), both borrowed heavily to make acquisitions, and both ultimately ran into difficulties in servicing that debt.

The investor requires a model of the P/E ratio that discounts growth that does not add value. Indeed, the manager contemplating an acquisition requires such a model to ensure that he does not overpay for the earnings he is acquiring. The analysis in this chapter is designed to prevent you from making the mistake of pricing earnings growth that does not add value. Indeed, with the tools in this chapter, you can ascertain when the market is overpaying (or underpaying) for growth, and so detect cases where the P/E ratio is too high or too low.

PROTOTYPE VALUATION

In anchoring a valuation on earnings rather than book values, you need to appreciate that earnings is a measure of change in value—a flow rather than a stock. To convert flows to stocks, we simply capitalize the flow. The stock of value implied by earnings is:

$$\text{Stock of value} = \frac{\text{Earnings}}{\text{Required return}}$$

This was explained in Box 3.5 in Chapter 3. The way to think about anchoring value on earnings is as follows:

Value = Capitalized earnings + Extra value for forecasted earnings growth

To value earnings we always start with the anchor of capitalized earnings, and then ask what extra value must be added for anticipated earnings growth.

A savings account is easy to value, so we will begin with this simple asset as a prototype for valuing equities. Exhibit 6.1 presents the same savings account as in Exhibit 5.1 in Chapter 5 (and Box 2.2 in Chapter 2). The account involves $100 invested in 2000 to earn a 5 percent rate each year, from 2001 and thereafter. Two dividend payout scenarios are presented, full payout and no payout.

In both cases, expected residual earnings are zero, so the asset is valued at its book value of $100 in 2000 using the residual earnings model. However, the asset also can be valued by capitalizing forward 2001 earnings of $5:

$$\text{Value of savings account} = \frac{\text{Forward Earnings}}{\text{Required return}} = \frac{\$5}{0.05} = \$100$$

EXHIBIT 6.1

Forecasts for a Savings Account with $100 Invested at the End of 2000, Earning 5% per Year

		Forecast Year				
	2000	**2001**	**2002**	**2003**	**2004**	**2005**
Earnings withdrawn each year (full payout)						
Earnings		5	5	5	5	5
Dividends		5	5	5	5	5
Book value	100	100	100	100	100	100
Residual earnings		0	0	0	0	0
Earnings growth rate		0	0	0	0	0
Cum-dividend earnings		5	5.25	5.51	5.79	6.08
Cum-dividend earnings growth rate			5%	5%	5%	5%
No withdrawals (zero payout)						
Earnings		5	5.25	5.51	5.79	6.08
Dividends		0	0	0	0	0
Book value	100	105	110.25	115.76	121.55	127.63
Residual earnings		0	0	0	0	0
Earnings growth rate			5%	5%	5%	5%
Cum-dividend earnings		5	5.25	5.51	5.79	6.08
Cum-dividend earnings growth rate			5%	5%	5%	5%

Thus the savings account can be valued not only from its book value, but also by capitalizing forward earnings.

For the savings account, there is no extra value for anticipated earnings growth. However, you will notice that, while the earnings growth rate in the full-payout scenario is zero, it is 5 percent per year in the no-payout scenario. Yet the value of the account is the same in both cases. According to our calculations, we will not pay for the 5 percent growth. The growth of 5 percent comes from reinvesting earnings, but the reinvested earnings earn only the required return. The equivalent valuations demonstrate the principle that one does not pay for growth that comes from an investment that earns only the required return, for such an investment does not add value.

A little more formalism captures this idea and protects us from paying too much for growth. The earnings growth rates in the two scenarios look different, but in fact they are not. The earnings from the full-payout account are actually understated, for the dividends from the account can be reinvested in an identical account to earn 5 percent. So, for example, the $5 withdrawn in 2001 can be reinvested to earn 5 percent, or $0.25 in 2002, so that the total expected earnings for 2002 are $5.25, the same as the zero-payout account. Earnings from an asset arise from two sources, earnings earned by the asset and earnings earned from reinvesting dividends in another asset. So, by reinvesting dividends for all years, the earnings in the two payout scenarios here are the same; in the no-payout case, earnings are reinvested in the same account—that is, earnings are retained—and in the full-payout case, earnings can be reinvested in a different account, in both cases earning 5 percent.

The total earnings from an investment are referred to as **cum-dividend earnings**, that is, earnings with the dividend. Earnings without the reinvestment of dividends are called **ex-dividend earnings**. Value is always based on expected cum-dividend earnings and the P/E ratio is always based on cum-dividend earnings growth, for we must keep track of all sources of earnings from the investment. For any period, t

$$\text{Cum-dividend earnings}_t = \text{Earnings}_t + (\rho - 1)\text{dividend}_{t-1}$$

where ρ is (as before) 1 plus the required return. So, for the full-payout savings account, cum-dividend earnings for 2002 are $\text{Earnings}_{2002} + (0.05 \times \text{Dividend}_{2001}) = \$5 + (0.05 \times \$5) = \$5.25$.

On a cum-dividend basis, earnings growth in the two scenarios is the same, 5 percent per year, as you can see from Exhibit 6.1. However, in both cases, the earnings growth is not growth that we will pay for. We only pay for earnings growth that is greater than the required return. Earnings that are due to growth at the required return are called **normal earnings**. For any period, t

$$\text{Normal earnings}_t = \rho\text{Earnings}_{t-1}$$

So, for the savings account, normal earnings in $2002 = 1.05 \times \$5 = \$5.25$, that is, the prior year's earnings growing at 5 percent. The part of cum-dividend earnings for which we will pay is the cum-dividend earnings growth over these normal earnings, that is, the **abnormal earnings growth:**

$$\text{Abnormal earnings growth}_t = \text{Cum-dividend earnings}_t - \text{Normal earnings}_t$$

$$= [\text{Earnings}_t + (\rho - 1)\text{dividend}_{t-1}] - \rho\text{Earnings}_{t-1}$$

As cum-dividend earnings for the savings account in 2002 are $5.25, and as normal earnings also are $5.25, abnormal earnings growth is zero. And so for years 2003 and beyond. We will not pay for growth because, while we forecast growth, we do not forecast abnormal growth.

**P/E RATIOS AND EARNINGS GROWTH
FOR THE S&P 500**

The historical average forward P/E ratio for the S&P 500 is about 12 (and the average trailing P/E ratio is about 14). The historical average earnings per share growth rate is about 8.5 percent per year. If the required return for stocks in general is 10 percent, the normal forward P/E ratio is 10. These numbers present a riddle: If the growth rate is 8.5 percent, less than the required return of 10 percent, the forward P/E should be below the normal of 10, not above it at 12.

The riddle is solved as follows. Firms in the S&P 500 pay dividends; indeed, the historical dividend payout ratio has been about 45 percent of earnings (though it has been declining over the last 15 years). The 8.5 percent growth rate is an ex-dividend growth rate. The cum-dividend growth rate with 45 percent payout is about 13 percent. So, historically, earnings have really grown 13 percent per year, cum-dividend, above the assumed required return of 10 percent.

That puts the forward P/E ratio above the normal of 10, which indeed it has been.

GROWTH RATES FOR THE ECONOMY

Gross national product (GNP) is equal to national income. GNP and national income in the U.S. have grown historically at a rate of 3–4 percent per year. An investor would have grown income in a savings account at a higher rate than this, and a (government guaranteed) savings account is risk free. Earnings from corporations (in the S&P 500) have grown at 13 percent per year, cum-dividend. Why does national income grow at only 3–4 percent?

The riddle is solved as follows. The growth rate in national income is an ex-dividend growth rate. We consume out of national income, rather than reinvest in the economy: Income = Consumption + Savings; and Savings = Investment. Consumption is taking a dividend. The higher consumption, the lower the ex-dividend growth rate (all else being constant).

With these basic concepts in place, we now can move from the simple prototype to the valuation of equities. Here is a summary of the concepts we carry with us:

1. An asset is worth more than its capitalized earnings only if it can grow cum-dividend earnings at a rate greater than the required return. This recognizes that one pays only for growth that adds value.

2. When forecasting earnings growth, one must focus on cum-dividend growth. Ex-dividend growth ignores the value that comes from reinvesting dividends.

3. Dividend payout is irrelevant to valuation, for cum-dividend earnings growth is the same irrespective of dividends.

Box 6.1 solves two riddles about earnings growth.

The Normal Forward P/E Ratio

You will remember from Chapter 3 that the *forward* or *leading P/E* is price relative to the forecast of next year's earnings. For the savings account, the forward P/E ratio in 2000 is $100/$5 = 20. This is a particularly special P/E, referred to as the **normal forward P/E:**

$$\text{Normal forward P/E} = \frac{1}{\text{Required return}}$$

That is, the normal forward P/E is just $1 capitalized at the required return. For the savings account, the forward P/E is $1/$0.05 = 20.

The normal P/E embeds a principle that applies to all assets, including equities. If one forecasts no abnormal earnings growth (as with the savings account), the forward P/E ratio must be 1/required return. That is, a normal P/E implies that normal earnings growth is expected. For a required return of 10 percent, the normal forward P/E is 1/0.10, or 10. For a required return of 12 percent, the normal forward P/E is 1/0.12 = 8.33. If one forecasts cum-dividend earnings to grow at a rate greater than the required return, the P/E must be above normal: One pays extra for growth. If one forecasts cum-dividend earnings to grow at a rate lower than the required return, the P/E ratio must be lower than normal: One discounts for low growth.

The Normal Trailing P/E Ratio

Chapter 3 distinguished the *trailing P/E*—the multiple of current earnings—from the *forward or leading P/E*—the multiple of earnings forecasted one year ahead. Having calculated the value of the savings account from forecasts of forward earnings and earnings growth, it is, of course, straightforward to calculate the trailing P/E: Just divide the calculated value by the earnings reported in the income statement. But there is an adjustment to make.

For the savings account in Exhibit 6.1, suppose that $100 were invested in the account at the beginning of 2000 to earn 5 percent. Earnings for 2000 would be $5 and, if these earnings were paid out as dividends, the value of the account at the end of 2000 would still be $100. So it would appear that the trailing P/E is $100/$5 = 20, the same as the forward P/E. However, this is incorrect. How could the value of one more year of earnings be the same? Suppose the $5 earnings of 2000 were not paid out, so that the value in the account was $105. The P/E ratio then becomes $105/$5 = 21. The latter is the correct trailing P/E.

The amount that $1 of earnings is worth—the P/E multiple—should not depend on dividends. The $5 of earnings for a savings account produces $105 in value for the owner of the account—the $100 at the beginning of the period that produced the earnings, plus the $5 of earnings. If she leaves the earnings in the account, the owner has $105; if she withdraws the earnings, she still has $105, with $100 in the account and $5 in her wallet. The trailing P/E is 21. Thus the trailing P/E must always be based on cum-dividend prices:

$$\text{Trailing P/E} = \frac{\text{Price} + \text{Dividend}}{\text{Earnings}}$$

This measure is the dividend-adjusted P/E introduced in Chapter 3. The adjustment is necessary because dividends reduce the price (in the numerator) but do not affect earnings (in the denominator). The adjustment is not necessary for the forward P/E because both prices and forward earnings are reduced by the current dividend. P/E ratios published in the financial press do not make this adjustment. If the dividend is small, it matters little, but for high-payout firms, published P/E ratios depend on dividends as well as the ability of the firm to grow earnings.

Whereas the normal forward P/E is 1/Required return, the **normal trailing P/E** is:

$$\text{Normal trailing P/E} = \frac{(1 + \text{Required return})}{\text{Required return}}$$

For the savings account, the normal trailing P/E is $1.05/$0.05 = 21 (compared with 20 for the forward P/E). For a required return of 10 percent, the normal trailing P/E is $1.10/$0.10 = 11 (compared with 10 for the forward P/E), and for a required return of 12 percent, it is $1.12/$0.12 = 9.33 (compared with 8.33 for the forward P/E). The normal forward P/E and the normal trailing P/E always differ by 1.0, representing one current dollar earning at the required return for an extra year.

Just as a normal forward P/E implies that forward earnings are expected to grow, cum-dividend, at the required rate of return after the forward year, so a normal trailing P/E implies that current earnings are expected to grow, cum-dividend, at the required rate of return after the current year. So the trailing P/E for the savings account is 21 because the expected earnings growth rate is the required rate of 5 percent.

A Poor P/E Model

The following model for valuing equities from forward earnings is quite common:

$$\text{Value of Equity} = \frac{\text{Earn}_1}{\rho_E - g}$$

where g is (1 plus) the forecasted earnings growth rate. (You perhaps have seen this model with the letter r used to indicate the required return rather than ρ.) The model looks as if it should value earnings growth. The formula modifies the capitalized earnings formula (which worked for a savings account) for growth; indeed, the model is simply the formula for a perpetuity with growth that was introduced in Chapter 3. With this model, the forward P/E ratio is $1/(\rho - g)$.

This model is simple, but it is wrong. First, it is applied with forecasts of ex-dividend growth rates rather than cum-dividend growth rates. Ex-dividend growth rates ignore value from reinvesting dividends. Therefore, the higher the dividend payout, the higher the omitted value calculated by the formula; the lower the ex-dividend growth rate, the lower the value calculated by the formula. Second, the formula clearly does not work when the earnings growth rate is greater than the required return, for then the denominator is negative. You could apply the formula with cum-dividend growth rates rather than ex-dividend growth rates, but then you would be likely to have a negative denominator. For the savings account, the required return is 5 percent, but the expected cum-dividend growth rate is also 5 percent, so the denominator of this formula is zero (and the value of a savings account is infinite!). For equities, the cum-dividend growth rate is likely to be higher than the required return, resulting in a negative denominator: This is the case for the S&P 500 in Box 6.1, for example. A growth rate slightly lower than the required return would have you paying a very high price—and overpaying for growth.

This is a poor model; it leads you into errors. The denominator problem is a mathematical problem, but behind this mathematical problem lurks a conceptual problem. We need a valuation model that protects us from paying too much for growth.

A MODEL FOR ANCHORING VALUE ON EARNINGS

The model for valuing earnings growth anchors the valuation on capitalized earnings and then adds value from anticipated growth:

Value of equity = Capitalized forward earnings + Extra value for abnormal cum-dividend earnings growth

$$V_0^E = \frac{\text{Earn}_1}{\rho_E - 1} + \frac{1}{\rho_E - 1}\left[\frac{\text{AEG}_2}{\rho_E} + \frac{\text{AEG}_3}{\rho_E^2} + \frac{\text{AEG}_4}{\rho_E^3} + \cdots\right]$$

$$= \frac{1}{\rho_E - 1}\left[\text{Earn}_1 + \frac{\text{AEG}_2}{\rho_E} + \frac{\text{AEG}_3}{\rho_E^2} + \frac{\text{AEG}_4}{\rho_E^3} + \cdots\right] \qquad \textbf{(6.1)}$$

where AEG is abnormal (cum-dividend) earnings growth. (The ellipses indicate that forecasts continue on into the future, for equities are going concerns.) You see from the first version of the formula here that the discounted value of abnormal earnings growth supplies the extra value over that from forward earnings. The discounting calculates the

LIVERPOOL JOHN MOORES UNIVERSITY
Aldham Roberts L.R.C.
TEL 0151 231 3701/3634

value at the end of Year 1 of growth from Year 2 onward, and the value is then capitalized (to convert the value of flows to a stock of value). As both the value of growth and forward earnings are capitalized, the second version of the formula simplifies the calculation. So, to value a share, proceed through the following steps:

1. Forecast one-year-ahead earnings.

2. Add the present value (at the end of Year 1) of expected abnormal earnings growth for Year 2 ahead and onward.

3. Capitalize the total of forward earnings and the value of abnormal earnings growth.

Figure 6.1 directs you through these three steps. As with residual earnings valuation, earnings must be comprehensive earnings, otherwise value is lost in the calculation. Simply stated, the model says that value is based on future earnings, but with earnings from normal growth subtracted.

FIGURE 6.1 **Calculation of Equity Value Using the Abnormal Earnings Growth Model** Abnormal earnings growth is the difference between cum-dividend earnings and normal earnings. The present value of abnormal earnings growth for Year 2 and beyond is added to forward earnings for Year 1, and the total is then capitalized to calculate equity value.

$$\text{Abnormal earnings growth}_t = \text{Cum-dividend earnings}_t - \text{Normal earnings}_t$$
$$\text{Cum-dividend earnings}_t = \text{Earnings}_t + (\rho_E - 1)\,\text{dividend}_{t-1}$$
$$\text{Normal earnings}_t = \rho_E\,\text{Earnings}_{t-1}$$

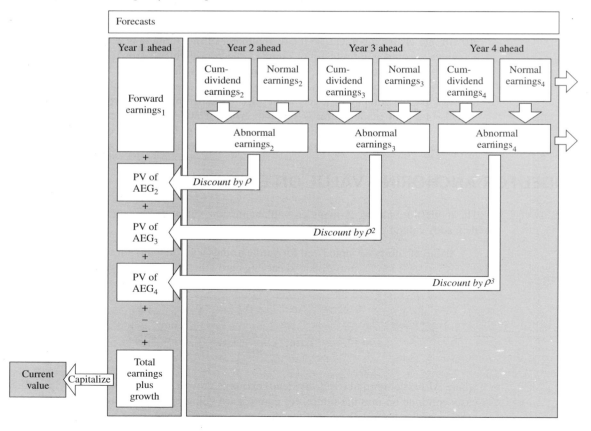

Under this model, the forward P/E is

$$\frac{V_0^E}{\text{Earn}_1} = \frac{1}{\rho_E - 1} + \frac{1}{\rho_E - 1}\left[\frac{\text{AEG}_2}{\rho_E} + \frac{\text{AEG}_3}{\rho_E^2} + \frac{\text{AEG}_4}{\rho_E^3} + \cdots\right] / \text{Earn}_1 \qquad \textbf{(6.2)}$$

So the forward P/E is calculated by capitalizing $1 plus the value of abnormal earnings growth relative to forward earnings. If no abnormal earnings growth is forecasted,

$$V_0^E = \frac{\text{Earn}_1}{\rho_E - 1}$$

and the P/E is normal:

$$\frac{V_0^E}{\text{Earn}_1} = \frac{1}{\rho_E - 1}$$

The P/E in model (6.2) is the normal P/E plus a premium for growth.

This model is referred to as the *abnormal earnings growth model*, or the *Ohlson-Juettner model* after its architects.[1]

Measuring Abnormal Earnings Growth

As for the savings account, abnormal earnings growth (AEG) is earnings (with dividends reinvested) in excess of earnings growing at the required return:

$$\text{Abnormal earnings growth}_t = \text{Cum-dividend earn}_t - \text{Normal earn}_t$$

$$= [\text{Earn}_t + (\rho_E - 1)\text{d}_{t-1}] - \rho_E\text{Earn}_{t-1} \qquad \textbf{(6.3)}$$

Calculations can be made on a per-share basis or on a total dollar basis. When working on a per-share basis, dividends are dividends per share; when working on a total dollar basis, dividends are net dividends (dividends plus share repurchases minus share issues). Here are calculations of abnormal earnings growth for 2002 for two firms, Dell Computer Corporation and Nike, Inc. A required return of 10 percent is used in both cases.

	Dell Computer	Nike, Inc.
Eps 2002	$0.48	$2.48
Dps 2001	$0.00	$0.48
Earnings on reinvested dividends (at 10%)	0.00	0.048
Cum-dividend earnings 2002	0.48	2.528
Normal earnings from 2001:		
Dell: 0.84 × 1.10; Nike: 2.18 × 1.10	0.924	2.398
Abnormal earnings growth (AEG) 2002	$–0.444	$0.130

Dell's eps for 2002 was $0.48, down from $0.84 for 2001. Dell paid no dividends, so its eps is cum-dividend eps. Assuming Dell had a required equity return of 10 percent, normal earnings for 2002 were 1.10 × $0.84 = $0.924, that is, 2001 earnings growing at 10 percent. So abnormal earnings growth for 2002 was $0.48 – $0.924 = –$0.444. Nike,

[1] See J. A. Ohlson and B. E. Juettner-Nauroth, "Expected EPS and EPS Growth as Determinants of Value," unpublished paper, New York University, 2000.

Inc., a firm that pays dividends, earned $2.48 per share for its fiscal 2002 year against $2.18 in 2001. It paid a dividend of $0.48 in 2001, so the cum-dividend earnings for a shareholder in 2002 (after reinvesting the 2001 dividend) were $2.48 + (0.10 \times $0.48) = $2.528, assuming a 10 percent shareholders' required return. So, with normal earnings of $1.10 \times $2.18 = $2.398, abnormal earnings growth was $2.528 - $2.398 = $0.13 per share.

Abnormal earnings growth can be expressed in terms of growth rates relative to required rates:

$$\text{Abnormal earnings growth}_t = [G_t - \rho_E] \times \text{Earnings}_{t-1} \qquad \textbf{(6.3a)}$$

where G_t is 1 plus the cum-dividend earnings growth rate for the period. That is, AEG is the dollar amount by which a prior year's earnings grow, cum-dividend, relative to the required rate. If G_t is equal to the required rate, there is no abnormal earnings growth. With eps of $0.48 for 2002 (and no dividends), Dell's cum-dividend earnings growth rate was $0.48/0.84 = -42.86 percent. So, with a required return of 10 percent, Dell's AEG for 2002 was $0.84 \times (0.5714 - 1.10) = -$0.444 per share, as before. With cum-dividend eps of $2.528 in 2002, a growth rate of 15.96 percent over 2001 eps of $2.18, Nike's AEG for 2002 was $2.18 \times (1.1596 - 1.10) = $0.13 per share, as before.

APPLYING THE MODEL TO EQUITIES

Exhibit 6.2 applies the abnormal earnings growth model in a simple example of a prototype firm with a required return of 10 percent whose earnings are expected to grow at 3 percent a year. A 3 percent growth rate looks low, but looks can be deceiving because the firm has a high payout ratio (76 percent of earnings).

Based on the earnings and dividend forecasts and the future book values they imply, residual earnings for the firm are forecasted to grow at a 3 percent rate, as indicated in the exhibit. So the firm can be valued in 2000 with a Case 3 residual earnings valuation by capitalizing 2001 residual earnings at this growth rate:

$$V_{2000}^E = 100 + \frac{2.36}{1.10 - 1.03} = 133.71$$

The P/B ratio is thus 1.34.

The exhibit also forecasts abnormal earnings growth (AEG), in order to apply the abnormal earnings growth model. Abnormal earnings growth each year is cum-dividend earnings less normal earnings. Calculations are described at the bottom of the exhibit using both the equation (6.3) and (6.3a) methods. You see that AEG is growing at 3 percent after 2001. So, the 2002 AEG can be capitalized with this growth rate:

$$V_{2000}^E = \frac{1}{0.10} \left[12.36 + \frac{0.071}{1.10 - 1.03} \right] = 133.74$$

The forward P/E ratio is 133.74/12.36 = 10.82, higher than the normal P/E of 10. You will notice at the bottom of the exhibit that the cum-dividend earnings growth rate is 10.57 percent, higher than the required return of 10 percent, and accordingly the P/E ratio is greater than the normal P/E. You also will notice that the cum-dividend earnings growth rate is considerably higher than the 3 percent rate forecasted for (ex-dividend) earnings.

The RE model and the AEG model give us the same valuation (the slight differences here are only due to rounding errors). This is always the case for the same forecasts of

EXHIBIT 6.2 **Forecasts for a Firm with Expected Earnings Growth of 3 Percent per Year (in Dollars)**

Required return is 10% per year.

		Forecast Year				
	2000	2001	2002	2003	2004	2005
Residual earnings forecasts:						
Earnings	12.00	12.36	12.73	13.11	13.51	13.91
Dividends	9.09	9.36	9.64	9.93	10.23	10.54
Book value	100.00	103.00	106.09	109.27	112.55	115.92
Residual earnings (RE)		2.360	2.431	2.504	2.579	2.656
RE growth rate			3%	3%	3%	3%
Abnormal earnings growth forecasts:						
Earnings	12.00	12.36	12.73	13.11	13.51	13.91
Dividends	9.09	9.36	9.64	9.93	10.23	10.53
Earnings on reinvested dividends		0.909	0.936	0.964	0.993	1.023
Cum-dividend earnings		13.269	13.667	14.077	14.499	14.934
Normal earnings		13.200	13.596	14.004	14.424	14.857
Abnormal earnings growth (AEG)		0.069	0.071	0.073	0.075	0.077
Abnormal earnings growth rate			3%	3%	3%	3%
Cum-dividend earnings growth rate		10.57%	10.57%	10.57%	10.57%	10.57%
Normal earnings growth rate		10.0%	10.0%	10.0%	10.0%	10.0%

The Calculations:

Earnings on reinvested dividends refers to the prior year's dividend earning at the required return. So, for 2002, earnings on reinvested dividends $0.10 \times 9.36 = 0.936$.

Cum-dividend earnings adds earnings on reinvested dividends to the ex-dividend earnings forecasted. So, cum-dividend earnings for 2002 are $12.73 + (0.10 \times 9.36) = 13.667$.

Normal earnings is the prior year's earnings growing at the required return. So, for 2002, normal earnings are $12.36 \times 1.10 = 13.596$.

Abnormal earnings growth is cum-dividend earnings – normal earnings. So, for 2002, AEG = $13.667 - 13.596 = 0.071$.

Abnormal earnings growth is also the prior year's earnings multiplied by the spread between the cum-dividend growth rate and the required rate. So, for 2002, AEG is $(1.1057 - 1.10) \times 12.36 = 0.071$.

Allow for rounding errors.

earnings, dividends, and book values. Further, the AEG model, like the RE model, gives the same valuation that one would get from forecasting dividends indefinitely into the future. That is, if we think of equity value as based on the dividends that a firm is ultimately expected to pay (in the very long run), both models give us this value. Indeed, the example has been constructed to demonstrate this point. Dividends are expected to grow at 3 percent per year in this example, so

$$V_{2000}^{E} = \frac{d_1}{\rho_E - g} = \frac{9.36}{1.10 - 1.03} = 133.71$$

This is a stylized case in which the dividend discount model works because the payout is tied directly to earnings with a fixed payout ratio, so growth in dividends is the same as growth in residual earnings and abnormal earnings growth. As we saw in Chapter 3, this is not usually the case; however, the accrual accounting models supply an answer.

Anchoring Valuation on Current Earnings

The valuation in this example prices forward earnings so, strictly speaking, it anchors on forecasted earnings rather than the current earnings in the financial statements. The value can be calculated by anchoring on current earnings: Capitalize current earnings, and then add the value of forecasted AEG from Year 1 onward. That is, shift the application of the model one period back in time. So, for the example in Exhibit 6.2,

$$V_{2000}^E + d_{2000} = 133.74 + 9.09 = \frac{1.10}{0.10}\left[12.00 + \frac{0.069}{1.10 - 1.03}\right] = 142.84$$

The value obtained is the cum-dividend value (price plus dividend) appropriate for valuing current earnings. The trailing P/E is \$142.84/\$12.00 = 11.90, higher than the normal trailing P/E of 11 (for a required return of 10 percent). The \$12.00 here is earnings for 2000 and the \$0.069 is forecasted AEG for Year 1, which is expected to grow at a 3 percent rate. The capitalization rate is 1.10/0.10, the normal trailing P/E, rather than 1/0.10, the normal forward P/E. The formal model for the calculation is:

$$V_0^E + d_0 = \frac{\rho_E}{\rho_E - 1}\left[\text{Earn}_0 + \frac{\text{AEG}_1}{\rho_E} + \frac{\text{AEG}_2}{\rho_E^2} + \frac{\text{AEG}_3}{\rho_E^3} + \cdots\right] \qquad \textbf{(6.4)}$$

Clearly, with no AEG after the current year, the trailing P/E is normal.

Anchoring valuation on current earnings anchors on actual earnings in the financial statements rather than a forecast of earnings. However, there is a good reason to apply the model to forward earnings rather than current earnings. As we will see when we come to analyze financial statements, current earnings often contain nonsustainable elements—unusual events and one-time charges, for example—that do not bear on the future. By focusing on forward earnings and using current earnings as a base for the forecast, we effectively focus on the sustainable portion of current earnings. Indeed, the financial statement analysis of Part Two of the book aims to identify sustainable earnings that are a sound anchor for forecasting forward earnings.

The web page for this chapter provides a spreadsheet to help you develop abnormal earnings growth pro formas.

The Forecast Horizon and the Continuing Value Calculation

The example in Exhibit 6.2 is similar to our prototype savings account example, except that this firm has some abnormal earnings growth whereas the savings account had none. The firm is somewhat special because AEG is forecasted to grow at a constant rate. It is a prototype for calculating continuing values for the AEG model. The model (6.1) requires infinite forecasting horizons, so we need continuing values to truncate the forecast horizon at a point where AEG is expected to evolve in a steady fashion. In the example, this occurs just one year ahead.

There are two types of continuing value calculations. Case 1 applies when one expects subsequent abnormal earnings growth to be zero. Case 2 applies when one expects subsequent abnormal earnings to grow at a constant rate.

Case 1 is illustrated using Wal-Mart as an example. Wal-Mart's CAPM equity cost of capital is 12 percent. The numbers in Case 1 are Wal-Mart's actual numbers but, as in Chapters 4 and 5, we treat them as forecasts at the end of 1987. Recall that we attempted to value Wal-Mart's shares using discounted cash flow valuation in Chapter 4 and ran into difficulties. However, we found we could value it with residual earnings methods in Chapter 5. The AEG valuation here produces the same \$4.39 per share value as the RE

CASE 1 Wal-Mart Stores, Inc.

In this case, abnormal earnings growth is expected to be zero after 1996.
Required rate of return is 12 percent.

					Forecast Year					
	1987	1988	1989	1990	1991	1992	1993	1994	1995	1996
Dps		0.03	0.04	0.06	0.07	0.09	0.11	0.13	0.17	0.20
Eps		0.28	0.37	0.48	0.57	0.70	0.87	1.02	1.17	1.19
Dps reinvested ($0.12 \times dps_{t-1}$)			0.004	0.005	0.007	0.008	0.011	0.013	0.016	0.020
Cum-dividend earnings (eps + dps reinvested)			0.374	0.485	0.577	0.708	0.881	1.033	1.186	1.210
Normal earnings ($1.12 \times Earn_{t-1}$)			0.314	0.414	0.538	0.638	0.784	0.974	1.142	1.310
Abnormal earnings growth (AEG)			0.060	0.071	0.039	0.070	0.097	0.059	0.044	−0.100
Discount rate (1.12^t)			1.120	1.254	1.405	1.574	1.762	1.974	2.211	2.476
PV of AEG			0.054	0.056	0.028	0.045	0.055	0.030	0.020	−0.040
Total PV of AEG to 1996		0.247								
Total		0.527								
Capitalization rate		0.12								
Value per share $\left(\dfrac{0.527}{0.12}\right)$	4.39 ←									

Allow for rounding errors.

valuation in Chapter 5. Wal-Mart's AEG continues growing up to 1993, but then it declines so that, by 1996, it is negative. The valuation is based on the forecast that AEG will be zero after 1996. That is, while Wal-Mart can grow cum-dividend earnings at a rate greater than the required return of 12 percent in the immediate future, earnings are expected to grow at a 12 percent rate after 1996. At the end of 1987, we forecast forward (1988) eps of $0.28, to which we add $0.247 for the present value of abnormal earnings growth up to 1996. The total of $0.527, capitalized at 12 percent, yields the value of $4.39.

A Case 2 valuation is demonstrated using General Electric, with a required rate of return of 12 percent. The numbers up to 1992 are the same as those in Chapter 5, where we valued the firm using residual earnings methods, with a continuing value based on a forecast that residual earnings would grow at a 6 percent rate after 1992. The numbers for 1993 and 1994 are those for this growth rate. The continuing value, calculated at the end of 1992, is now based on AEG growing at 6 percent (as the AEG for 1993 and 1994 confirms: 0.142/0.134 = 1.06, adjusted for rounding error). Accordingly, the continuing value is the 1993 AEG capitalized at this growth rate, that is, $2.238. The present value (in 1987) of this continuing value ($1.270) is added to the present value of AEG up to 1992 ($0.642) and 1987 forward earnings ($3.20), for a total of $5.112, yielding a value per share at the end of 1986, after capitalization, of $42.60. This value is the same as that obtained with residual earnings methods in Chapter 5.

Converting an Analyst's Forecast to a Valuation

Table 6.1 shows how to convert an analyst's forecast to a valuation. In June 2002, analysts' consensus forecast for Nike, Inc., was $2.83 per share for the fiscal year ending May 2003 and $3.22 for 2004. Analysts also forecasted an average growth rate for the three years thereafter (2005–2007) of just over 13 percent per year, and the forecasts for

CASE 2 General Electric Co.

In this case, abnormal earnings are expected to grow at a 6 percent rate after 1992.
Required rate of return is 12 percent.

	1986	1987	1988	1989	1990	1991	1992	1993	1994
					Forecast Year				
Dps		1.33	1.46	1.70	1.92	2.08	2.32	2.70	2.98
Eps		3.20	3.75	4.36	4.85	3.03	5.51	6.03	6.57
Dps reinvested at 12%			0.160	0.175	0.204	0.230	0.250	0.278	0.324
Cum-dividend earnings			3.910	4.535	5.054	3.260	5.760	6.305	6.894
Normal earnings			3.584	4.200	4.883	5.432	3.394	6.171	6.750
Abnormal earnings growth (AEG)			0.326	0.335	0.171	−2.172	2.366	0.134	0.142
Discount rate (1.12^t)			1.120	1.254	1.405	1.574	1.762		
PV of AEG			0.291	0.267	0.122	−1.380	1.343		
Total PV of AEG		0.642							
Continuing value (1992)							2.238		
PV of continuing value		1.270							
Total		5.112							
Capitalization rate		0.12							

Value per share $\left(\dfrac{5.112}{0.12}\right)$ 42.60

The continuing value calculation:

$$CV = \frac{0.134}{1.12 - 1.06} = 2.238$$

$$PV \text{ of } CV = \frac{2.238}{1.762} = 1.270$$

Allow for rounding errors.

TABLE 6.1 Analysts' Consensus Forecast and Valuation: Nike, Inc.

Required rate of return is 10 percent.

	2002	2003E	2004E	2005E	2006E	2007E
Dps		0.55	0.65	0.70	0.83	0.95
Eps		2.83	3.22	3.65	4.13	4.66
Dividend reinvested at 10%			0.055	0.065	0.070	0.083
Cum-dividend earnings			3.275	3.715	4.200	4.741
Normal earnings			3.113	3.542	4.015	4.543
Abnormal earnings growth (AEG)			0.162	0.173	0.185	0.198
Continuing value (2003)		5.40				
Total		8.23				
Capitalization rate		0.10				
Value per share	82.30					
Cum-dividend growth rate			15.72%	15.37%	15.07%	14.79%
Normal growth rate			10.0%	10.00%	10.00%	10.00%

The continuing value calculation:

$$CV = \frac{0.162}{1.10 - 1.07} = 5.40$$

Allow for rounding errors.

those years in the table reflect that growth rate. Dividends are forecasted at Nike's 2002 payout ratio of 20 percent. The table calculates abnormal earnings growth (AEG) implied by these forecasts, and you can see that, after 2003, AEG is expected to grow at a rate of 7 percent on forecasted cum-dividend growth rates of over 14 percent. Accordingly, assuming that the 7 percent growth rate will continue indefinitely, a continuing value can be calculated at the end of 2003 by capitalizing the expected 2004 abnormal earnings growth of $0.162, yielding a value per share in June 2002 as follows:

$$V_{2002}^{E} = \frac{1}{0.10}\left[2.83 + \frac{0.162}{1.10 - 1.07}\right] = \$82.30$$

As with residual earnings methods, the value implied by analysts' forecasts is incomplete. Unfortunately, many analysts do not give explicit dividend forecasts, so we are not sure what dividend their ex-dividend earnings forecasts are based on. Further, analysts do not forecast beyond a few years. Nike traded at $57 at the time of this forecast, so either the market views the forecasts for 2003–2007 as too optimistic or it sees less growth subsequent to 2007 than the 13 percent rate forecasted by analysts for 2005–2007.

FEATURES OF THE ABNORMAL EARNINGS GROWTH MODEL

Box 6.2 lists the advantages and disadvantages of the abnormal earnings growth model. Compare it to similar summaries for the dividend discount model (in Chapter 3), the discounted cash flow model (in Chapter 4), and the residual earnings model (in Chapter 5).

We have emphasized that AEG valuation, like the residual earnings valuation, protects us from paying too much for earnings growth. In this section we will discuss some other features of the model.

Buy Earnings

The abnormal earnings growth model adopts the perspective of "buying earnings." It embodies the idea that the value of a firm is based on what it can earn. As earnings represent value to be added from selling products and services in markets, the model anticipates the value to be added from trading with customers, after matching revenues from those customers with the values given up, in expenses, to generate the revenue.

The AEG model embraces the language of the analyst community. P/E ratios are more often referred to than P/B ratios. Analysts talk of earnings and earning growth, not residual earnings and residual earnings growth. So, converting an analyst's forecast to a valuation is more direct with this model than with the residual earnings model. (The language of the (Wall) street does not recognize how dividends affect growth, however; analysts talk of ex-dividend earnings growth rates, not cum-dividend rates.)

Abnormal Earnings Growth Valuation and Residual Earnings Valuation

On the other hand, the AEG model does not give as much insight into the value creation as the residual earnings model. Firms invest in assets and add value by employing these assets in operations. The residual earnings (RE) model explicitly recognizes the investment in assets, then recognizes that value is added only if that return is greater that the required return. The residual earnings model is a better lens on the business of generating value, the cycle of investment and return on investment. Accordingly, we have not proposed the AEG model as a model for strategy analysis (as we did with the RE model), for

ADVANTAGES

Easy to understand:	Investors think in terms of future earnings; investors buy earnings. Focuses directly on the most common multiple used, the P/E ratio.
Uses accrual accounting:	Embeds the properties of accrual accounting by which revenues are matched with expenses to measure value added from selling products.
Versatility:	Can be used under a variety of accounting principles (Chapter 16).
Aligned with what people forecast:	Analysts forecast earnings and earnings growth.

DISADVANTAGES

Accounting complexity:	Requires an understanding of how accrual accounting works.
Concept complexity:	Requires an appreciation of the concept of cum-dividend earnings; that is, value is based on earnings to be earned within the firm and from earnings from the reinvestment of dividends.
Sensitive to the required return estimate:	As the value derives completely from forecasts that are capitalized at the required return, the valuation is sensitive to the estimate used for the required return. Residual earnings valuations derive partly from book value that does not involve a required return.
Application to strategy:	Does not give an insight into the drivers of earnings growth, particularly balance sheet items; therefore, it is not suited to strategy analysis.
Suspect accounting:	Relies on earnings numbers that can be suspect (Chapter 17).
Forecast horizon:	Forecast horizons can be shorter than those for DCF analysis. and more value is typically recognized in the immediate future. But the forecast horizon does depend on the quality of the accrual accounting (Chapter 16).

strategy analysis involves investment. The central question in strategy analysis is whether the investment will add value.

The RE model and AEG model always yield the same valuation. Box 6.3 shows, indeed, that the concepts underlying the two models are not very different: Abnormal earnings growth is always equal to the change in residual earnings.

Abnormal Earnings Growth Is Not Affected by Dividends, Share Issues, or Share Repurchases

We saw in Chapter 5 that residual earnings valuation is not sensitive to expected dividend payout or share issues and share repurchases that do not add value. Such is also the case with the AEG model. Box 6.4 elaborates.

Accounting Methods and Valuation

The residual earnings model accommodates different accounting principles. As we saw in Chapter 5, this is because book values and earnings work together. Firms may create higher future earnings by the accounting they choose, but to do so they must write down book values. When the higher earnings are combined with the lower book values (in a residual earnings valuation), value is unaffected.

The AEG model and the RE model look different but are really quite similar. Both require forecasts of earnings and dividends, although the RE model adds the extra mechanical step of calculating book value forecasts from these forecasts. So the two models have the same forecasts as inputs.

Structurally, the two models are similar. The RE starts with book value as an anchor and then adds value by charging forecasted earnings by the required return applied to book value. The AEG model starts with capitalized earnings as an anchor and then adds value by charging forecasted (cum-dividend) earnings by the required return applied to prior earnings, rather than book value.

This structural difference is just a different arrangement of the inputs. A little algebra underscores the point. Abnormal earnings growth can be written in a different form:

$$AEG_t = [Earn_t + (\rho_E - 1)d_{t-1}] - \rho_E Earn_{t-1}$$

$$= Earn_t - Earn_{t-1} - (\rho_E - 1)(Earn_{t-1} - d_{t-1})$$

Using the stocks and flows equation for accounting for the book value of equity (Chapter 2), $B_{t-1} = B_{t-2} + Earn_{t-1} - d_{t-1}$, so $Earn_{t-1} - d_{t-1} = B_{t-1} - B_{t-2}$. Thus,

$$AEG_t = Earn_t - Earn_{t-1} - (\rho_E - 1)(B_{t-1} - B_{t-2})$$

$$= [Earn_t - (\rho_E - 1)B_{t-1}] - [Earn_{t-1} - (\rho_E - 1)B_{t-2}]$$

$$= RE_t - RE_{t-1}$$

So, abnormal earnings growth is always equal to the change in residual earnings. You can see this by comparing the changes in residual earnings with the AEG for the prototype firm in Exhibit 6.2:

	2001	2002	2003	2004	2005
Residual earnings	2.360	2.431	2.504	2.579	2.656
Change in residual earnings		0.071	0.073	0.075	0.077
Abnormal earnings growth		0.071	0.073	0.075	0.077

You can also test this relationship by comparing the abnormal earnings growth for Wal-Mart and General Electric in this chapter with the residual earnings for the two firms in Chapter 5. For example, Wal-Mart's residual earnings for 1989 are $0.25, an increase of $0.06 over the $0.19 for 1988, and that increase is equal to its abnormal earnings growth for 1989.

So, forecasting that there will be no abnormal earnings growth is the same as forecasting that residual earnings will not change. Or, as abnormal earnings growth of zero means that (cum-dividend) earnings are growing at the required rate of return, forecasting this normal growth rate is the same as forecasting that residual earnings will not change. Correspondingly, forecasting cum-dividend earnings growth above normal is the same as forecasting growth in residual earnings. Accordingly, one set of forecasts give us both measures.

The rearrangement of the inputs leads to the different anchors and different definitions of adding value to the anchors. Yet the underlying concepts are similar. AEG valuation enforces the point that a firm cannot add value from growing earnings unless it grows earnings at a rate greater than the required rate of return. Only then does it increase its P/E ratio. But that is the same as saying that the firm must grow residual earnings to increase its P/B ratio. That is, added value comes from investing to earn a return greater than the required return, and that added value has its manifestation in both growth in residual earnings and growth in cum-dividend earnings over a normal growth rate.

The AEG model, at first glance, looks as if it might not have this feature. A manager can create higher future earnings by writing down book values, and the AEG model values future earnings without carrying book values as a correcting mechanism. We do not want to pay for growth that does not add value, and accounting methods can create growth in earnings that we do not want to pay for. As it happens, the AEG model, like the residual earnings model, provides protection against paying for growth that is created by accounting. Box 6.5 explains.

Make sure you read the section titled "A Lesson for the Analyst" in Box 6.5. The trailing P/E indicates expected earnings from sales in the future relative to the earnings recognized from current sales. To measure the value added from sales, accounting methods match expenses with revenues. If that matching underestimates current expenses (by

Dividends involve the distribution of value, not the creation of value, so dividend payout should not affect a valuation. Further, share issues and repurchases at fair value should not affect a valuation.

DIVIDENDS

Consider the forecasts in Exhibit 6.2. Suppose the firm decided in 2000 that it would stop paying dividends. How would this affect the valuation?

For the prototype savings account in Exhibit 6.1, dividends did not affect the valuation. This is so for the equity investment in Exhibit 6.2 also. As no dividends will be paid in 2001, there will be no earnings from the reinvestment of dividends outside the firm in 2002. But, as the 2001 dividend of $9.36 is retained in the firm, it can earn at the required return of 10 percent. Accordingly, earnings forecasted within the firm for 2002 are $12.73 + (0.10 \times \$9.36) = \$13.667$, which is the amount of cum-dividend earnings if dividends were paid out. And so for all years, cum-dividend earnings are not affected by payout, as shown below. Accordingly, cum-dividend earnings growth and the present value of cum-dividend earnings growth are also unaffected.

Effect of Payout on Cum-Dividend Earnings Growth: Modifying Exhibit 6.2 for Zero Payout

	Forecast Year				
	2001	2002	2003	2004	2005
Earnings	12.36	13.667	16.077	14.499	14.934
Dividends	0.0	0.0	0.0	0.0	0.0
Cum-dividend earnings		13.667	14.077	14.499	14.934

If management liquidated value-adding investments to pay dividends, then value would of course be lost. In this case, dividends would no longer be value irrelevant. The AEG valuation then would (appropriately) recognize the loss of value in lower earnings forecasted because of the lower investment.

SHARE REPURCHASES AND SHARE ISSUES

Share repurchases are cash payouts, just like dividends. Accordingly, like dividends, repurchases at fair market value do not affect the total cum-dividend earnings inside and outside the firm. So, if the $9.36 of dividends in 2001 for the Exhibit 6.2 firm were paid out as a stock repurchase, cum-dividend earnings and the valuation would be the same as in Exhibit 6.2. Share issues (reverse share repurchases) similarly do not affect value. Value is added if the proceeds are invested in value-adding projects, but that is value added through investment, not as a matter of issuing shares.[1] The AEG valuation recognizes value added from investment with higher forecasted earnings, but it does not recognize value from share issues.

The point here underscores the principle that value is added by investment and operating activities, not fair-value financing activities, and a valid valuation model embeds this principle.

---

[1] There may be leverage effects on forecasted earnings, because leverage affects earnings and leverage can change with dividends, share repurchases, and share issues. Chapter 13 shows how leverage affects earnings growth, but it also shows that these leverage effects do not affect value. Treat the firm in Exhibit 6.2 as one with no leverage.

underestimating bad debts, for example), current earnings are higher. However, future earnings are lower—earnings are "borrowed from the future." Because more current earnings are recognized and less future earnings are expected (and value is not affected), the trailing P/E is lower. With lower future earnings, the forward P/E is higher. The converse is true if a firm recognizes more expenses in current earnings. In its third quarter of 2001, Cisco Systems, the manufacturer of routers for the Internet, wrote its inventory down by $2.25 billion; the firm found itself with excess inventory as the Internet bubble burst. This write-down created higher future profits with lower cost of goods sold and served to maintain Cisco's gross margins even though sales were declining. The discerning analyst might view subsequent margins with some skepticism and question whether they indeed add value or are just a result of the accounting methods used. Refer back to the Chapter 2 discussion on matching, and be prepared for a quality of earnings analysis that diagnoses this income shifting (in Chapter 17).

Exhibit 6.2 presented pro forma earnings and earnings growth for valuing the equity of a prototype firm. Suppose the manager of this firm has decided to create more earnings for 2001 by writing down inventory by $8 in 2000. This accounting adjustment changes the accounting numbers, but it should not affect the value. Here is the revised pro forma:

Creating Earnings with Accounting: Modifying Exhibit 6.2 for a Write-Down

	Forecast Year					
	2000	2001	2002	2003	2004	2005
Earnings	4.00	20.36	12.73	13.11	13.51	13.91
Dividends	9.09	9.36	9.64	9.93	10.23	10.54
Book value	92.00	103.00	106.09	109.27	112.55	115.92
Earnings on reinvested dividends			0.936	0.964	0.993	1.023
Cum-dividend earnings			13.667	14.077	14.499	14.934
Normal earnings			22.396	14.004	14.424	14.857
Abnormal earnings growth			(8.729)	0.073	0.075	0.077
Abnormal earnings growth rate					3%	3%

EFFECT ON VALUATION

As a result of the $8 write-down, the $12 reported for 2000 earnings is now $4 (and the book value is $92 instead of $100). Correspondingly, 2001 forward earnings increase by $8 to $20.36 because cost of goods sold is lower by $8. Cum-dividend earnings for 2002 are not affected but, because those earnings are now compared to normal earnings of $22.396, on the high base of $20.36 for 2001, abnormal earnings

growth for 2002 is (a decline of) –$8.729. Subsequent years are unaffected. The AEG valuation at the end of 2000 is

$$V_{2000}^E = \frac{1}{0.10}\left[20.36 - \frac{8.729}{1.10} + \frac{0.073}{1.10 - 1.03}\Big/1.10\right] = 133.74$$

This is the same as the value before the accounting change. While forward 2001 earnings have increased, the higher earnings of $20.36 mean higher normal earnings for 2002 and consequently lower earnings growth of –$8.729. The net effect is to leave the value unchanged.

EFFECT ON P/E RATIOS

While valuations are not affected by accounting methods, P/E ratios certainly are. The forward P/E for this firm is now $133.74/$20.36 = 6.57, down from 10.82. The trailing (dividend-adjusted) P/E is now ($133.74 + $9.09)/$4.00 = 35.71, up from 11.90. Shifting income from current earnings to forward earnings increases the trailing P/E; there is now more anticipated earnings growth next year and the P/E prices growth. However, shifting income to the future decreases the forward P/E—there is now less anticipated growth after the forward year, and the value of the earnings (in the numerator) does not change.

A LESSON FOR THE ANALYST

There is a lesson here. The diligent analyst discerns growth that comes from accounting from growth that comes from real business factors. If growth is induced by the accounting, he changes the P/E ratio, but he does not change the valuation. Applying the AEG model (or indeed the residual earnings model) protects him from making the mistake of pricing earnings that are due to accounting methods.

We opened this chapter with the caveat that we do not want to pay for growth that does not add value. We do not want to pay for earnings growth from added investment that earns only the required return. But we also do not want to pay for growth that is created by accounting methods. Using the residual earnings model or the abnormal earnings growth model protects us from both dangers.

REVERSE ENGINEERING THE MODEL FOR ACTIVE INVESTING

Like the residual earnings model, the AEG model can be reverse engineered. Consider the analysts' forecasts for Nike in Table 6.1 that we attempted to convert to a valuation earlier in the chapter. As analysts' forecasts are short-term, we were left with some uncertainty as to the valuation. Indeed, the value we calculated was $82.30, but the market was pricing Nike's shares at $57. Analysts were forecasting earnings growth of 13 percent for the near term. What is the market's implicit growth forecast?

Inverting the AEG model supplies the answer. In 2002, analysts were forecasting $2.83 for 2003 and $3.22 for 2004. With a forecast of $3.22 for 2004, we calculated AEG of $0.162 in Table 6.1. With these forecasts, a cost of capital of 10 percent, and a market price of $57,

$$\$57 = \frac{1}{0.10}\left[2.83 + \frac{0.162}{1.10 - g}\right]$$

Solving for g, the implied long-term growth rate for AEG is 4.4 percent: The market is pricing Nike's shares as if it expects abnormal earnings growth to grow indefinitely at 4.4 percent per year.

Implied Earnings Forecasts

The growth in AEG can be converted to eps forecasts. Analysts forecasted Nike's eps for 2003 and 2004. Using the implied growth rate of 4.4 percent, we can impute the market's eps forecasts for subsequent years. With $3.22 per-share earnings forecasted for 2004, normal earnings for 2005 are $1.10 \times \$3.22 = \$3.542$, as in Table 6.1. Adding the implied forecast of abnormal growth for 2005 of $0.169 (that is, 2004 AEG of $0.162 growing at 4.4 percent), and deducting the earnings of $0.065 from reinvesting the $0.65 dividend in 2004, forecasted eps for 2005 is $3.542 + 0.169 - 0.065 = \$3.65$. And so for subsequent years in the pro forma in Table 6.1. The formula for the conversion of an abnormal earnings growth forecast to an earnings forecast is:

Earnings forecast = Normal earnings forecast + AEG forecast
                    − Forecast of earnings from prior year's dividends

Applying this formula for forecasting Nike's 2006 eps using the implied growth rate of 4.4 percent, you should get a forecast of $4.12.

The fundamental analysts develops his own forecasts for Nike, then compares them with the market's **implied earnings forecasts**—forecasts that are implicit in the market price of the stock. Is the market forecasting earnings growth that is too high or too low? Are the $3.65 eps forecast for 2005 and the $4.12 forecast for 2006 reasonable? The answers to these questions dictate the analyst's buy, hold, or sell position in the stock. The analysis of profitability and growth—in Parts Two and Three of the book—is directed toward answering these questions. With daily revisions of implied forecasts as the market price changes, the investor maintains a watch on the stock and changes his position in the stock if the implied forecasts pass bounds he has established in his fundamental analysis.

Screening on Earnings Yield

Alan Greenspan, chairman of the Federal Reserve Bank during the 1990s, is known for his statements regarding the "irrational exuberance" of the stock market. According to *Barron's*, he uses an earnings yield screen. See Box 6.6.

The "Greenspan model" compares the expected *earnings yield* with the 10-year Treasury yield to assess whether stocks are overpriced. The expected earnings yield, measured as forward earnings/price, is just the inverse of the forward P/E ratio, so an earnings yield of 4.75 percent (at the time of the newspaper report) implies a forward P/E of 21.05. A Treasury yield of 5.60 percent implies a forward P/E of 17.86. The Greenspan model says that stocks are likely to be overpriced when the forward P/E for stocks rises above the P/E for Treasury notes. Is this a good screen?

The Greenspan model is not well calibrated. First, one expects the forward P/E for stocks to be different than that for bonds because stocks and bonds have different risk and

From an article in *Barron's* in 1998.

Fed Chairman Alan Greenspan hasn't said much about the stock market this year, but his favorite valuation model is just about screaming a sell signal. The so-called Greenspan model was brought to our attention last summer by Edward Yardeni, economist at Deutsche Morgan Grenfell, who found it buried in the back pages of a Fed report. The model's very presence in such a report was noteworthy because the Fed officials normally don't tip their hand about their views on the stock market. The model surfaced at a particularly interesting time: Stocks were near a high point, and the Greenspan model indicated that the market was about 20 percent higher than it should have been.

That turned out to be a pretty good call. By October 1998, stocks had fallen as much as 15 percent from their summer high point. By year-end, of course, the Dow had recovered to around 7900, but it still remained about 5 percent below its peak for the year.

Now that the Dow has climbed above 8600, Greenspan's model is again flashing a warning signal. To be exact, the Greenspan model now indicates that stocks are 18 percent overvalued.

The Fed's model arrives at its conclusions by comparing the yield on the 10-year Treasury note to the price-to-earnings ratio of the S&P 500 based on expected operating earnings in the coming 12 months. To put stocks and bonds on the same footing, the model uses the *earnings yield* on stocks, which is the inverse of the (forward) P/E ratio. So while the yield on the 10-year Treasury is now 5.60 percent, the earnings yield on the S&P 500, based on a (forward) P/E ratio of 21, is 4.75 percent.

In essence, the Fed's model asks, Why would anyone buy stocks with a 4.75 percent earnings return, when they could get a bond with a 5.60 percent yield?

The Fed's model suggests the S&P should be trading around 900, well under its current level of 1070.

Source: "Is Alan Addled? 'Greenspan Model' Indicates Stocks Today Are Overvalued by About 18%," *Barron's*, March 16, 1998, p. 21.

thus different required returns. The forward P/E of 17.86 for a bond is the normal P/E for a required return of 5.60 percent. Stocks are more risky; if the required return is 10 percent, the normal P/E is 10, considerably less than the P/E for a riskless government bond. Second, the Greenspan model does not explicitly build in growth after the forward year. A bond has no abnormal earnings growth (it is similar to a savings account), so the normal P/E is the appropriate P/E. But stocks with a normal P/E of 10 could be worth a P/E of 21 if abnormal earnings growth is anticipated after the forward year. Without forecasts of subsequent earnings, the P/E of 21 cannot be challenged effectively. The Greenspan model asks: Why would anyone buy stocks with a 4.75 percent earnings return, when they could get a bond with a 5.60 percent yield? Well, they would do so if they saw growth that they were willing to pay for. An earnings yield screen is too simplistic.

The two errors in applying the Greenspan model—ignoring differences in risk and expected growth—work in the opposite direction. Stocks should have a lower P/E because they are more risky, but they should have a higher P/E if they can deliver growth. By demanding that stocks have an earnings yield no less than the yield on Treasury notes, the model is saying that growth can never be high enough to compensate for the error of treating stocks as riskless securities like Treasury notes. Is that a good screen?

The comparison of earnings yields to Treasury rates does remind us that earnings yields and P/E ratios should change as interest rates change. See Box 6.7.

Screening on PEG Ratios

In recent years, the PEG ratio has come into prominence. The PEG (P/E-to-earnings-growth) ratio compares the P/E ratio to a forecast of percentage earnings growth rate in the following year:

$$\text{PEG ratio} = \frac{\text{P/E}}{\text{1-yr ahead percentage earnings growth}}$$

As P/E ratios involve the capitalization of earnings by the required return, and as the required return varies as interest rates change, P/E ratios should be lower in periods of high interest rates and higher in times of low interest rates. Correspondingly, earnings yields should be higher in times of high interest rates and lower in times of low interest rates. The figure below indicates that P/E ratios and interest rates have moved in the opposite directions in recent history.

When interest rates on government obligations were high in the late 1970s and early 1980s, P/Es were low; when interest rates were relatively low in the 1990s, P/Es were relatively high. But the relationship between P/E and interest rates is not strong. This is because expectations of future earnings growth are more important in determining the P/E than changes in interest rates.

Of course we must be cautious in our interpretations because the market may have been inefficient at times in pricing earnings. Were P/E ratios too low in the 1970s? Too high in the 1990s? Was the market underestimating future earnings growth in the 1970s and overestimating it in the 1990s?

Median P/E Ratios and Interest Rates (in Percentages) on One-Year Treasury Bills

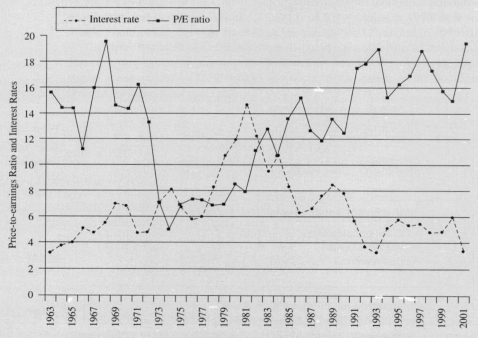

Source: P/E ratios were calculated from Standard & Poor's COMPUSTAT data. Company: Standard & Poor's. Data: Compustat® data. Interest rates are from the Federal Reserve Statistics Release (www.federalreserve.gov).

The P/E in the numerator is usually the forward P/E, but sometimes the trailing P/E is used. If the forward P/E is used, the appropriate measure of growth in the denominator of the PEG ratio is the forecasted one-year growth after the forward year, that is, growth for two years ahead. The ratio compares the traded P/E, the market's assessment of earnings growth after the forward year, with actual growth forecasts. Analysts' growth forecasts are typically used. If the ratio is less than 1.0, the screener concludes that the market is underestimating earnings growth. If it is greater than 1.0, the screener concludes that the market is too optimistic about growth.

The benchmark PEG ratio of 1.0 is consistent with the analysis in this chapter. If the required return for a stock is 10 percent (and thus the forward P/E is 10), the market is pricing the stock correctly if earnings are expected to grow (cum-dividend) at the required rate of 10 percent. If an analyst indeed forecasts a growth rate of 10 percent after the forward year, the PEG ratio is 10/10 = 1.0. (Note that the growth rate is in percentage terms). If, however, an analyst forecasts a growth rate of 15 percent, the PEG ratio is 10/15 = 0.67 and the analyst concludes that, at a P/E of 10, the market is underpricing expected growth.

Caution is called for in screening on PEG ratios. First, standard calculations (incorrectly) use the forecasted growth rate in ex-dividend earnings rather than the cum-dividend rate. Second, screening on just one year of anticipated growth ignores information about subsequent growth. For this reason, some calculations of the PEG ratio use annualized five-year growth rates in the denominator. In October 2002, Ford Motor Company's shares traded at $7.20 each on analysts' consensus forecast of eps for its December 2002 fiscal year of $0.43, giving a P/E of 16.7. Analysts were forecasting $0.65 in per-share earnings for 2003. As the firm indicated 40 cents per-share dividends in 2002, the cum-dividend forecast for 2003 was $0.69, assuming a required return of 10 percent. Thus the anticipated cum-dividend growth rate for 2003 was 60.5 percent and Ford's PEG ratio was 16.7/60.5 = 0.28. The PEG ratio indicates that Ford was underpriced. But the 2003 growth rate is probably due to the fact that the base year, 2002, was a particularly bad year for Ford. Ford would not be able to maintain a 60 percent growth rate into the future; the 2003 growth rate is not indicative of the long term. Indeed, analysts at the time were forecasting only an average 5 percent annual growth rate over the next five years. Using this growth rate in the denominator of the PEG ratio yields a ratio of 3.3.

Summary

The valuation methods in this chapter complement those in Chapter 5. They yield a direct calculation of intrinsic P/E ratios rather than P/B ratios. Rather than anchoring valuation on book value, the methods here anchor valuation on earnings. However, the form of the valuation is similar. With P/B valuation, one adds value to book value for earnings in excess of normal earnings (at the required return) on book value; with P/E valuation, one adds value to capitalized earnings for earnings in excess of normal earnings (at the required return) on prior earnings.

Abnormal earnings growth—earnings growth in excess of normal earnings growth—is the central concept for the valuation. This concept, in turn, requires an appreciation that, when the analyst focuses on earnings growth, she must focus on cum-dividend earnings growth because future earnings involve not only earnings earned in the firm but also earnings from reinvesting any dividends to be received.

As with residual earnings valuation, the application of the methods in this chapter protects the investor from paying too much for earnings. These methods also protect the investor from paying for earnings created by accounting methods. And, as with residual earnings, the abnormal earnings growth model facilitates reverse engineering: The analyst can deduce the earnings forecasts implicit in market stock prices.

The Web Connection

Find the following on the web page for this chapter:

- Further applications of abnormal earnings growth valuation.

- A spreadsheet program to help you develop abnormal earnings growth pro formas.

- Further examples of protection against paying for earnings created by accounting methods.

- Further examples of reverse engineering.

Key Concepts

abnormal earnings growth is earnings growth in excess of growth at a rate equal to the required return. Compare with **normal earnings growth**   188

ex-dividend earnings are earnings without consideration to the earnings that can be earned on dividends. Compare with **cum-dividend earnings**.   *188*

cum-dividend earnings are earnings that include earnings on prior dividends paid. Compare with **ex-dividend earnings**.   *188*

implied earnings forecast is a forecast that is implicit in the market price of a stock.   *204*

normal earnings growth is earnings growth at a rate equal to the required return.   *188*

normal forward P/E is a price-earnings ratio that is appropriate when earnings are expected to grow (cum-dividend) after the forward year at a rate equal to the required return; that is, normal earnings growth is expected.   *189*

normal trailing P/E is a price-earnings ratio that is appropriate when earnings are expected to grow (cum-dividend) after the current year at a rate equal to the required return   *190*

The Analyst's Toolkit

Analysis Tools	Page	Key Measures	Page	Acronymns to Remember
Abnormal earnings growth		Abnormal earnings growth	193	AEG abnormal earnings growth
model (6.1)	191	Continuing value		PEG price-to-earnings growth
Case 1	197	Case 1	197	RE residual earnings
Case 2	198	Case 2	198	
Forward P/E calculation (6.2)	193	Cum-dividend earnings	188	
Abnormal earnings		Earnings yield	204	
growth (6.3), (6.3a)	193	Ex-dividend earnings	188	
Trailing P/E model (6.4)	196	Forward P/E ratio	193	
Converting an analyst's		Implied abnormal earnings		
forecast to a valuation	197	growth rate	204	
Reverse engineering the		Normal earnings	188	
abnormal earnings		Normal Forward P/E ratio	189	
valuation model	203	Normal Trailing P/E ratio	190	
PEG ratio	205	PEG ratio	205	

**Concept
Questions**

C6.1. Explain why analysts' forecasts of earnings-per-share growth typically understimate the growth that an investor values when a firm pays dividends.

C6.2. The historical earnings growth rate for the S&P 500 companies has been about 8.5 percent. Yet the required growth rate for equity investors is considered to be about 12 percent. Can you explain the inconsistency?

C6.3. The following formula is often used to value shares, where Earn$_1$ is forward earnings, r is the cost of capital, and g is the expected earnings growth rate.

$$\text{Value of equity} = \frac{\text{Earn}_1}{r - g}$$

Explain why this formula can lead to errors.

C6.4. A firm's earnings are expected to grow at a rate equal to the required rate of return for its equity, 12 percent. What is the trailing P/E ratio? What is the forward P/E ratio?

C6.5. The normal forward P/E and the normal trailing P/E always differ by 1.0. Explain the difference.

C6.6. Explain why, for purposes of equity valuation, earnings growth forecasts must be for cum-dividend earnings growth, yet neither cum-dividend growth rates nor valuation are affected by expected dividends.

C6.7. Abnormal earnings growth is always equal to growth of (change in) residual earnings. Correct?

C6.8. A P/E ratio for a bond is always less than that for a stock. Correct?

C6.9. In an equity research report, an analyst calculates a forward earnings yield of 12 percent. Noting that this yield is considerably higher than the 7 percent yield on a 10-year Treasury, she heads her report with a buy recommendation. Could she be making a mistake?

C6.10. How do you interpret a PEG ratio?

C6.11. Look at Figure 2.3 in Chapter 2, which tracks median P/E ratios from 1963 to 2001. Explain why P/E ratios were low in the 1970s and high in the 1960s and 1990s.

C6.12. The earnings-to-price ratio for the S&P 500 stocks declined significantly from the late 1970s to the late 1990s. As this ratio is a "return" per dollar of price, some claimed that the decline indicated that the required return for equity investing had declined, and they attributed the increase in stock prices over the period to the decline in the required return. Why is this reasoning suspect?

C6.13. If the average cost of equity capital for firms in the economy is 10 percent, corporate earnings should grow at 10 percent per year, cum-dividend, before adjusting for any nonnormal growth. But gross domestic product typically grows at less than 4 percent per year. How can firms generate earnings growth at 10 percent per year while the economy grows less than 4 percent?

C6.14. Why might an analyst refer to a leading (forward) P/E ratio rather than a trailing P/E ratio?

C6.15. Can a firm increase its earnings growth yet not affect the value of its equity?

Exercises   **E6.1.**   **Valuation From Forecasting Abnormal Earnings Growth (Easy)**

An analyst presents you with the following pro forma (in millions of dollars). The pro forma gives her forecasts of earnings and dividends for 2004–2008. She asks you to value the 1,380 million shares outstanding at the end of 2003. Use a required return for equity of 10 percent in your calculations. (This is the same pro forma that was used for a residual earnings valuation in Exercise E5.1.)

	2004E	2005E	2006E	2007E	2008E
Earnings	388.0	570.0	599.0	629.0	660.45
Dividends	115.0	160.0	349.0	367.0	385.40

   a. Forecast growth rates for earnings and cum-dividend earnings for each year, 2005–2008.
   b. Forecast abnormal earnings growth for each of the years, 2005–2008.
   c. Calculate the per-share value of the equity at the end of 2003 from this pro forma. Would you call this a Case 1 or Case 2 abnormal earnings growth valuation?
   d. What is the forward P/E ratio for this firm? What is the normal forward P/E?

E6.2.   Abnormal Earnings Growth and Value (Easy)

The following forecasts of earnings per share (eps) and dividend per share (dps) were made at the end of 1999:

	2000E	2001E	2002E	2003E	2004E
Eps	3.90	3.70	3.31	3.59	3.90
Dps	1.00	1.00	1.00	1.00	1.00

The firm has an equity cost of capital of 12 percent per annum. (This is the same pro form a used in the residual earnings valuation in Exercise E5.2.)
   a. Calculate the abnormal earnings growth that is forecast for each year, 2001 to 2004.
   b. What is the expected per-share value of the equity at the end of 1999 based on the abnormal earnings growth valuation model?.
   c. What is the expected trailing P/E for 2004?
   d. What is the forecasted per-share value of the equity at the end of the year 2004?

E6.3.   Calculating Cum-Dividend Earnings Growth: Nike (Easy)

In early 2003, analysts were forecasting $2.77 for Nike's earnings per share for the fiscal year ending May 2003, and $3.13 for 2004, with a dividend per share of 56 cents expected for 2003. Compare the cum-dividend earnings growth forecasted for 2004 with ex-dividend earnings growth, using a required rate of return of 10 percent.

E6.4.   Calculating Cum-Dividend Earnings: General Motors (Easy)

General Motors reported earnings and paid dividends from 1994 to 1998 as follows:

	1994	1995	1996	1997	1998
Basic eps	5.22	7.28	6.06	8.70	4.26
Dps	0.80	1.10	1.60	2.00	2.00

Calculate cum-dividend earnings for General Motors for each years, 1995–1998. Assume a reinvestment rate for dividends of 10 percent.

E6.5.   Dividend Displacement and Value (Medium)

Two firms, A and B, which have very similar operations, have the same book value of 100 at the end of 2000 and their cost of capital is 11 percent. Both are forecast to have earnings of $16.60 in 2001. Firm A, which has 60 percent dividend payout, is forecast to have earnings of $17.80 in 2002. Firm B has zero payout.

    a. What is your best estimate of firm B's earnings for 2002?

    b. Would you pay more, less, or the same for firm B relative to firm A in 2000?

E6.6. Using Analysts' Forecasts to Calculate PEG Ratios and Evaluate Stock Prices: General Motors (Medium)

In early 2003, analysts were forecasting earnings for General Motors Corporation (GM) of $4.62 per share for 2003 and $6.77 for 2004. GM was expected to pay a dividend of $2 per share in 2003. Use a required return for the equity of 12 percent in the calculations below.

    a. Calculate cum-dividend earnings and the cum-dividend earnings growth rate forecasted for 2004.

    b. Calculate forecasted abnormal earnings growth for 2004.

    c. GM was trading at $39 in early 2003. Calculate the forward P/E that the market was giving this stock. Also calculate a PEG ratio that evaluates this forward P/E. What does this PEG ratio suggest to you?

    d. Would you conclude that the market price of $39 per share implies that abnormal earnings growth in 2004 will subsequently increase, decrease, or remain about the same?

E6.7. Forward P/E Ratios and Implied Earnings Growth: Hewlett-Packard (Medium)

Hewlett-Packard Corporation, the computer services and printer manufacturer, traded at $12 per share in September 2002, down considerably from $67 per share in 2000. Commentators were concerned about the effects of the acquisition of the then-unprofitable Compaq Computer, the personal computer and computer services firm. However, analysts were indicating that the Compaq operation would return to profitability in 2003 and were forecasting per-share earnings of $1.19 for Hewlett-Packard for the fiscal year ending October 2003.

    a. Calculate the forward P/E ratio at which the market was pricing the firm in October 2002.

    b. What growth rate is this forward P/E ratio implicitly forecasting for cum-dividend earnings for years after 2003? Use an equity cost of capital of 10 percent in your calculations.

    c. What abnormal earnings growth is this P/E ratio forecasting?

    d. Hewlett-Packard was forecasted to pay a dividend of 32 cents per share in 2003. What growth rate in ex-dividend earnings is the P/E in October 2002 forecasting?

Real World Connection

See Exercises E5.7 and E5.10 in Chapter 5 for more coverage of Hewlett-Packard.

E6.8. Using Earnings Growth Forecasts to Challenge a Stock Price: Toro Company (Medium)

Toro Company, a lawn products maker based in Minnesota, traded at $55 per share in October 2002. The firm had maintained a 20 percent annual eps growth rate over the previous five years, and analysts were forecasting $5.30 per share earnings for the fiscal year ending October 2003, with a 12 percent growth rate for the five years thereafter. Use a required return of 10 percent in answering the following questions.

    a. How much is a share of Toro worth based on the forward earnings of $5.30 only (ignoring any subsequent earnings growth)?

    b. Toro maintains a dividend payout of 10 percent of earnings. Based on the forecasted eps growth rate of 12 percent, forecast cum-dividend earnings for the five years, 2004–2008.

c. Forecast abnormal earnings growth for the years, 2004–2008.

d. Do your calculations indicate whether or not Toro is appropriately priced?

E6.9. **Abnormal Earnings Growth Valuation and Accounting Methods (Medium)**

Refer back to the valuation in Exercise 6.1. In the pro forma there, an analyst forecasted earnings of $388 million for 2004. The forecast was made at the end of 2003 based on preliminary reports from the firm.

When the final report was published, however, the analyst discovered that the firm had decided to write down its inventory at the end of 2003 by $114 million (following the lower-of-cost-or-market rule). As this was inventory that the analyst had forecasted would be sold in 2004 (and thus the impairment affects cost of goods sold for that year), the analyst revised her earnings forecast for 2004. For questions (a) and (b), ignore any effect of taxes.

a. What is the revised earnings forecast for 2004 as a result of the inventory impairment?

b. Show that the revision in the forecast of 2004 earnings does not change the valuation of the equity.

c. Now assume that the firm's income tax rate is 35 percent. Do your answers to questions (a) and (b) change?

E6.10. **Normal Trailing and Forward P/E Ratios: Whirlpool Corporation (Medium)**

Table 5.4 in Chapter 5 applies an analyst's forecast to a residual earnings valuation of Whirlpool Corporation, an appliance manufacturer, whose shares traded at $47 per share at the time. Whirlpool's required equity return is 10 percent.

a. Show that the analyst's forecast implies that Whirlpool should trade at a normal P/E multiple of the forward earnings of $4.75 per share.

b. Show that the analyst's forecast implies that Whirlpool should trade at a normal P/E multiple of the trading earnings of $4.43.

E6.11. **Is a Normal Forward P/E Ratio Appropriate? Maytag Corporation (Easy)**

A share of Maytag Corp., another appliance manufacturer, traded at $28.80 in January 2003. Analysts were forecasting earnings per share of $2.94 for 2003 and $3.03 for 2004, with dividends per share of 72 cents indicated for 2003. Analysts' 3–5 year growth rate for earnings per share after 2004 was 3.1 percent.

a. Calculate the normal forward P/E ratio for Maytag if its equity cost of capital is 10 percent. Compare the normal P/E to the actual traded P/E at the time.

b. Do the forecasts of earnings after 2003 indicate that the traded P/E is the appropriate pricing for the firm's shares?

E6.12. **Residual Earnings and Abnormal Earnings Growth (Medium)**

Consider the following pro forma for International Business Machines (IBM) based on analysts' forecasts in early 2003.

	2003E	2004E	Next Three Years
Earnings per share	4.32	5.03	Growth at 11%
Dividends per share	0.60	0.67	Growth at 11%

The book value of IBM's common equity at the end of 2002 was $23.4 billion, or $13.85 per share. Use a required return for equity of 12 percent in calculations.

a. Forecast residual earnings for each of the years, 2003–2007.

b. Forecast abnormal earnings growth for each of the years, 2004–2007.

c. Show that abnormal earnings growth is equal to the growth in residual earnings for every year.

E6.13. **Normal P/E Ratios (Easy)**

Prepare a schedule that gives the normal trailing and forward P/E ratios for the following levels of the cost of equity capital: 8, 9, 10, 11, 12, 13, 14, 15, and 16 percent.

E6.14. **Calculating an Intrinsic P/E Ratio: Maytag Corporation (Medium)**

The table below gives an analyst's forecast of earnings per share for Maytag Corporation. The forecast was made in early 1995 for earnings in 1995, 1996, and beyond.

MAYTAG CORP.
Analyst Forecast January 1995
(amounts in dollars per share)

	1993A	1994A	1995E	1996E	1997 and Beyond
Eps	0.48	1.40	1.55	1.65	Growth at 5%–9% p.a.
Dps	0.50	0.50	0.56	0.56	
Bps	5.50	6.82			

a. At what P/E ratio should Maytag trade based on this forecast? Use a required return for equity of 10 percent in your calculations.
b. Would you refer to this P/E ratio as a normal P/E ratio or a nonnormal P/E ratio?
c. What is the forecasted growth in cum-dividend earnings?

Minicases

M6.1

Borders Group: Reverse Engineering with Earnings Forecasts

Borders Group, Inc. (BGP), is a U.S. bookseller with subsidiaries in the United Kingdom and Australia and additional stores in Singapore and New Zealand. Borders operates "superstores" in competition with Barnes and Noble in the U.S. as well as smaller mall-based stores, most under the name of Waldenbooks. In 2001 it had 380 superstores, 821 mall stores, and 35 bookstores under the name of Books etc. in the United Kingdom.

After launching its superstore strategy in 1995, Borders came under increasing competition from Internet booksellers, notably Amazon.com. It was slow to adapt, but eventually launched its own e-commerce site in May 1998 under the Borders Online banner. The market greeted the change in strategy favorably, with its stock price increasing to $40 per share from $30 just six months earlier. The online operation was unsuccessful, however, and by April 2001, the price was down to $17. For its fiscal year ended January 2001, Borders reported earnings per share of 56 cents (down from $1.21 a year earlier) and 92 cents before a loss from discontinued operations. Borders pays no dividends.

In April 2001, analysts saw that Borders was taking steps to deal with its problems, including a thorough review of its strategic options. The consensus estimate of eps for the fiscal year ending January 2002 was $1.28, and $1.44 for fiscal 2003.

With the little information you have here, show how you would develop an analysis that addresses the question of whether the market price on $17 per share in April 2001 was a reasonable one. Use a cost of capital of 10 percent for Borders's equity.

Real World Connection

See Minicase M15.3 in Chapter 15 on Borders Group.

M6.2

Dell Computer Corporation: Pricing Earnings Forecasts with Sensitivity Analysis

Dell Computer traded at $22 per share in March 2001, down considerably from $43 a year earlier. Dell was a darling of the market throughout much of the 1990s, but during 2000 it revised projections for sales growth and profit margins downward. The firm reported earnings per share of $0.84 for the fiscal year ending February 2, 2001. Analysts' consensus eps forecasts were $0.63 for 2002 and $0.74 for 2003.

Carry out an analysis that challenges Dell's stock price. Use the analysts' forecasts and work with different growth rates and different rates for the required return to assess whether the $22 price in March 2001 was a reasonable one.

Real World Connection

See Minicases M10.1 (Chapter 10), M12.1 (Chapter 12), and M15.1 (Chapter 15) on Dell Computer.

M6.3

Should Cendant Corporation Buy Back Its Own Shares?

Cendant Corporation has wide-ranging businesses in travel and real estate services. Its hotel brands include Ramada Inn, Days Inn, Travelodge, Super 8 Motel, and Howard Johnson. It operates and franchises Avis, the car rental company, and in 2002 it bought the Budget car rental group out of bankruptcy. Cendant's real estate operations include Century 21, Coldwell Banker, and ERA. The firm also operates the travel-reservation platform, Galileo Services. Cendant acquired many of these businesses through a series of acquisitions during the 1990s.

In October 2002, Cendant was trading at $10 per share, a multiple of 7.9 times analysts' consensus earnings-per-share forecast of $1.27 for 2002, and a multiple of 6.3 times the $1.59 forecasted for 2003. With a book value per share of $8.61 at the beginning of 2002, the shares traded at a price-to-book ratio of 1.16. Cendant paid no dividends.

Cendant reported $0.42 earnings per share for 2001. An accounting scandal had enveloped Cendant in 1998, requiring payments totaling $2.9 billion over the subsequent years to fund the settlement of shareholder litigation arising from the scandal. In 2002, Cendant's share price, beaten down by the accounting scandal, was seen as cheap by some commentators. Most analysts had buy recommendations on the stock. Some institutional investors were calling on Cendant to repurchase its own stock. Rather than making more acquisitions—buying the stock of other firms—Cendant should, they argued, use its considerable cash flow from existing businesses to buy its own stock.

A. Why would commentators be calling for a stock repurchase? Do stock repurchases add value for shareholders?

B. Use the information here to evaluate whether Cendant's price of $10 per share was indeed cheap.

C. Calculate a PEG ratio for Cendant. Does this ratio indicate that Cendant's share price is cheap or expensive?

M6.4

Evaluation of Equity Research Report on Kmart Corporation

Equity research reports conclude with a stock recommendation. The investor reads the body of the report to be persuaded that the analysis in the report justifies the recommendation. She asks herself: Is the report credible? Is it internally consistent? Is there an imperative for the recommendation? Does the report give me a feeling of security in following the recommendation?

Reports all too often fail to give reassuring answers to these questions. And sometimes they exhibit inconsistencies and fallacies that reveal a lack of craftsmanship in how analysis is done.

Below are excerpts from an equity research report on Kmart Corporation, the discount retailer that is a close competitor of Wal-Mart. You might review the firm's web page at www.kmart.com before beginning the case.

Kmart Corp. March 1999   **(NYSE: KM)**
Current price per share: $17   **Recommendation: BUY**

Kmart Corp. is the second largest discount retailer in the United States and the world's third largest general merchandise retailer. It operates department stores in all 50 states in the United States and in Puerto Rico, the U.S. Virgin Islands, and Guam.

Some pertinent data for the 1999 fiscal year ending January 31 are below.

Earnings	$ 518 million
Dividends	0
Common equity	$5,979 million
Debt	$2,706 million
Cash flow from operations	$1,427 million
Cash investments	$ 795 million

Forecast: We forecast the following earnings and book values per share for fiscal years ending January 31, 2000 and 2001, along with forecasts of P/B ratios and P/E ratios.

	1999A	2000E	2001E
Eps	1.05	1.23	1.41
Bps	12.12	14.02	15.43
Shares outstanding ($ millions)	493.4	493.4	493.4
Price-to-book ratio	1.40	1.36	1.38
Price-earnings ratio	16.2	17.1	20.0

We forecast eps to increase at 6 percent per year after 2001. We also forecast free cash flow to grow at 6 percent per year from 1999 onwards.

Risk: We give Kmart a beta of 1.15 and a required return of 12 percent per year.

Recommendation: Our recommendation is based on the ability of the firm to grow its earnings and grow its P/E ratio. By 2001, we expect earnings to be fully flowing from its recent development of superstores in major metropolitan areas and see no reason why Kmart's shares should not be trading at a P/E of 20, the current average earnings multiplier for U.S. discount retailers.

What is wrong with this report?

The Analysis of Financial Statements

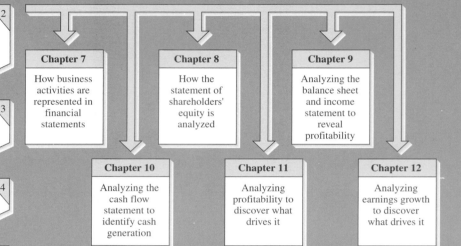

Knowing the business 1
- The products
- The knowledge base
- The competition
- The regulatory constraints

Strategy

Analyzing information 2
- In financial statements
- Outside of financial statements

Forecasting payoffs 3
- Specifying payoffs
- Forecasting payoffs

Converting forecasts 4
to a valuation

Trading on the 5
valuation

Outside investor:
Compare value with price to *buy*, *sell*, or *hold*

Inside investor:
Compare value with cost to *accept* or *reject* strategy

Chapter 7

How business activities are represented in financial statements

Chapter 8

How the statement of shareholders' equity is analyzed

Chapter 9

Analyzing the balance sheet and income statement to reveal profitability

Chapter 10

Analyzing the cash flow statement to identify cash generation

Chapter 11

Analyzing profitability to discover what drives it

Chapter 12

Analyzing earnings growth to discover what drives it

Part One of the book was concerned with concepts and with developing good thinking about valuation. Parts Two and Three apply good thinking to develop practical analysis.

The five steps in valuation analysis that were laid out in Chapter 3 are displayed here. Forecasting, in Step 3, is at the heart of the process and Part Three of the book focuses on forecasting. But to forecast, the forecaster must first analyze information in Step 2 of the process. This part of the book develops the financial statement analysis for Step 2 as a platform for forecasting in Step 3.

The valuation models outlined in Chapters 5 and 6 guide the forecasting. To add value to book value (and determine the price-to-book ratio), we must forecast future residual earnings, and to add value to capitalized earnings (and determine the price-earnings ratio), we must forecast abnormal earnings growth. Both residual earnings and abnormal earnings growth are driven by growth in investment and the profitability of investment.

Accordingly, the culmination of this part of the book is the analysis of ROCE and the analysis of growth. In analyzing financial statements, we discover the factors that drive current ROCE and growth and use them as a starting point for forecasting future ROCE and growth. Forecasting then becomes a question of how future ROCE and growth will be different from current ROCE and growth.

Step 1 of the valuation process requires that the analyst "know the business" before proceeding to Step 2. To begin financial statement analysis, the analyst must know how financial statements reflect the business that she has come to understand. Chapter 7 shows how business activities that drive value are represented in financial statements and shows how published financial statements are modified to highlight those activities. The modifications put the statements in a form that readies them for analysis.

Chapters 8, 9, and 10 analyze the financial statements. Chapter 8 deals with the statement of shareholders' equity, with a focus on uncovering comprehensive income and comprehensive ROCE, for correct analysis can proceed only if earnings are comprehensive. Chapter 9 analyzes the income statement and balance sheet. Here the focus is on distinguishing the firm's operating and financing activities and establishing the profitability of the two activities. Chapter 10 analyzes the statement of cash flows to identify the free cash flow from operations and the cash flows involved with financing.

Chapters 11 and 12 are the high point of this part of the book. They dissect the statements to discover the drivers of ROCE and growth in equity and so establish the platform for forecasting.

The financial statement analysis is done with a purpose: To discover what aspects of the financial statements tell us about the features of the business that determine a firm's value. You may have done some "ratio analysis" before—calculating ratios such as the current ratio or the inventory turnover—but after doing the calculations, you may have been left wondering: What now do I do with these ratios? In particular, what do the ratios tell me about the value of the firm? This part of the book outlines how you go about financial statement analysis in a systematic way to get an answer.

Business Activities
and Financial Statements

LINKS

Link to previous chapters

Chapter 1 introduced
the firm's operating,
investing, and financing
activities. Chapter 2
introduced the financial
statements. Chapters 5
and 6 outlined valuation
models that anchor on
those financial statements.

This chapter

This chapter shows how the
three business activities are
depicted in the financial
statements. It also shows
how the statements are
redesigned to highlight
these activities and to
prepare the statements for
applying the valuation
models in Chapters 5 and 6.

Link to next three chapters

Chapters 8, 9, and 10
reformulate the statements
according to the design
developed in this chapter.

Link to web page

Build your own financial
analysis spreadsheet based
on the chapter; for
assistance visit the BYOAP
feature on the text's website
at www.mhhe.com/
penman2e.

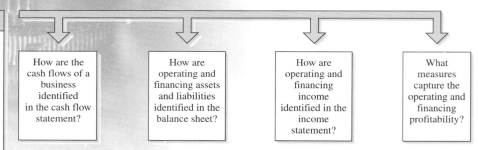

| How are the cash flows of a business identified in the cash flow statement? | How are operating and financing assets and liabilities identified in the balance sheet? | How are operating and financing income identified in the income statement? | What measures capture the operating and financing profitability? |

Every stock purchase is in fact the purchase of a business. And anyone who buys a business should know that business. This maxim, which was recognized in Chapter 1, requires the analyst to investigate "what makes the business tick." This might be done through factory visits and interviews with management. But we also observe the business through financial statements. Financial statements are the lens on the business, so we need to get a feel for not only how the business operates but also how its operations are represented in financial statements. Then we will understand the story behind the numbers.

This chapter builds on the introduction to businesses in Chapter 1 and the introduction to financial statements in Chapter 2. Chapter 2 showed how financial statements depict "stocks" and "flows" and how these articulating stocks and flows tell a story. This chapter shows how the three business activities introduced in Chapter 1—financing, investing, and operating activities—are depicted through stocks and flows in the statements. And it shows how this depiction is the basis for the analysis of the value generation in a business.

The Analyst's Checklist

After reading this chapter you should understand:

- How businesses are set up to generate value.

- Why reformatting financial statements is necessary for analysis.

- How operating and financing activities are depicted in reformatted financial statements.

- The four types of cash flows in a business.

- How the four types of cash flows relate to each other.

- How reformulated statements tie together as a set of stocks and flows.

- What operating activities involve.

- What financing activities involve.

- What determines dividends.

- What determines free cash flow.

- How free cash flow is disposed of.

- How free cash flow is a dividend from operating activities to the financing activities.

- How the financial statements are organized to measure value added for shareholders.

- Why free cash flow does not affect the accounting for value added.

After reading this chapter you should be able to:

- Apply the treasurer's rule.

- Lay out the form of reformulated cash flow statements, balance sheets, and income statements.

- Explain how net operating assets change over time.

- Explain how net financial obligations change over time.

- Explain how free cash flow is generated.

- Explain how free cash flow is disposed of.

- Add new accounting relations to your set of analyst's tools.

- Calculate return on net operating assets and net borrowing cost from reformulated statements.

Chapter 2 introduced the financial statements in the form in which they are presented under GAAP accounting and the disclosure rules issued by the Securities and Exchange Commission (SEC). That form does not quite give the picture we want to draw for valuation purposes. To improve our focus, we reformulate the statements in this chapter in a way that aligns the stocks and flows reported in the statements with the business activities that generate value. This reformulation readies the statements for the analysis in subsequent chapters which uncovers the factors that determine residual earnings and abnormal earnings growth, the primary valuation attributes in Chapters 5 and 6.

The emphasis in the chapter is on design. The chapter presents a template for reformulating financial statements and articulating the statements. See it as an engineering exercise. There are no examples; there are no numbers. These come in subsequent chapters where the template is applied to real companies and the analysis comes to life.

As you read the chapter, think of how you might build a spreadsheet program that inputs the financial statements in a way that readies them for analysis. In Chapter 2 the form of the financial statements was given by a set of accounting relations. Here, too, the form of the reformulated financial statements is given by a set of accounting relations. These accounting relations tell you how to structure a spreadsheet program that can, with further embellishments in subsequent chapters, be used to analyze financial statements and value firms. At the end of the chapter you will be introduced to a spreadsheet feature on the book's website that leads you in this direction.

BUSINESS ACTIVITIES: THE CASH FLOWS

In Chapter 1 we depicted the transactions between the firm and its shareholders and debtholders. The firm, however, was left as a black box and our aim in this and subsequent chapters is to fill out that box. Figure 7.1 begins to build the picture, to be completed in Figures 7.2 and 7.3. Figure 7.1 is similar to Figure 1.1 in Chapter 1, where cash flows to and from debtholders and shareholders are depicted. The cash flows to and from the debtholders and the firm have been reduced to a net flow, the *net debt financing flow,* labeled F in the figure. This is the net cash flow to bondholders, banks, and other creditors, that is, cash paid to debtholders in interest and principal repayments less cash paid into the firm from borrowing more from these creditors. Similarly, the *net dividend to shareholders* (*d* in the figure) is cash paid in dividends and stock repurchases less cash contributions to the firm from shareholders. The transactions between the two claimants and the firm are the firm's *financing activities*—debt and equity financing—and these take place in capital markets where the firm and these claimants trade.

A firm always begins with cash contributions from shareholders. Cash is a nonproductive asset so, until it is invested in operations, firms invest this cash in bonds or other interest-bearing paper, referred to as **financial assets** or sometimes as *marketable securities*. These financial assets are purchased in the capital market from debt issuers—governments (T-bills and bonds), banks (interest-bearing deposits), or other

FIGURE 7.1

Cash Flows between the Firm and Claimants in the Capital Market

Cash received from debtholders and shareholders is (temporarily) invested in financial assets. Cash payments to debtholders and shareholders are made by liquidating financial assets (that is, selling debt). Net financing assets are debt purchased from issuers, net of debt issued to debtholders. Net financing assets can be negative (that is, if debt sold to debtholders is greater than debt purchased).

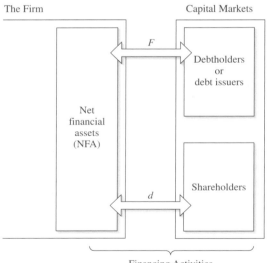

Key: F = Net cash flow to debtholders and issuers
        d = Net cash flow to shareholders
      NFA = Net financial assets = Financial assets – Financial liabilities

firms (corporate bonds or commercial paper). Like the issue of debt, the purchase of debt is also a financing activity. It is lending rather than borrowing, but both amount to buying and selling bonds or other financial claims. A firm can be a buyer of debt (of a debt issuer) if it has excess cash or can be an issuer of debt (to a debtholder) if it needs cash. In the first case it holds financial assets and interest and principal repayments flow into the firm. In the second case it has **financial obligations** or **financial liabilities,** and interest and principal repayments are paid out of the firm. In the first case, the net financing flow, *F,* is cash paid to buy bonds or paper less cash received in interest and from the sale of the bonds. In the second case, the net financing flow, *F,* is cash paid in interest and to redeem bonds less cash received in issuing (selling the firm's own) bonds.

Firms often issue debt and hold debt at the same time. Thus they hold both financial assets and financial obligations. The net debtholding is *net financial assets,* financial assets minus financial obligations, as depicted in Figure 7.1, or, if financial obligations are greater than financial assets, *net financial obligations.* Correspondingly, the net financing flow is the net cash outflow with respect to both borrowing and lending.

Figure 7.2 completes the cash flow picture. Firms typically are not primarily in the business of buying bonds but hold bonds only temporarily to invest idle cash. They invest in *operating assets*—land, factories, inventories, and so on—that produce products for sale. This is the firm's *investing activities* and the cash flows involved are *cash investment* or *cash flow in investment activities,* labeled *I* in the figure. To invest in operating assets, firms sell financial assets and buy operating assets with the proceeds. The arrows go both ways in the diagram because firms can also liquidate operating assets (in discontinued operations, for example) and buy financial assets with the proceeds. The operating

FIGURE 7.2

Cash Flows to Claimants and Cash Flows within the Firm
Cash generated from operations is invested in net financial assets (that is, it is used to buy financial assets or to reduce financial liabilities). Cash investment in operations is made by reducing net financial assets (that is, by liquidating financial assets or issuing financial obligations). Cash from operations and cash investment may be negative (such that, for example, cash can be generated by liquidating an operating asset and investing the proceeds in a financial asset).

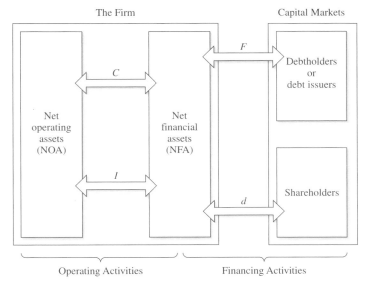

Key:
  F = Net cash flow to debtholders and issuers
  d = Net cash flow to shareholders
  C = Cash flow from operations
  I = Cash investment
  NFA = Net financial assets
  NOA = Net operating assets = Operating assets – Operating liabilities

assets, set to work, produce net cash flows (cash inflows from selling products less cash outflows from paying wages, rent, invoices, and so on) and this cash flow is referred to as *cash flow from operations*. This cash is invested in financial assets by buying bonds. The circle perpetuates. Cash from operations is never "left lying around" but is invested in financial assets to earn interest until needed. When needed, financial assets are liquidated to make cash investment in operations. Note that the term "investing activities" means investment in operating assets, not financial assets; indeed, investment in operating assets involves a liquidation of net financial assets.

Cash flow from operations and cash flow for investing activities were introduced in Chapter 4. We can now state a very important accounting identity known as the *cash conservation equation* or the *sources and uses of cash equation*. The four cash flows in Figure 7.2 always obey the relationship

$$\text{Free cash flow} = \text{Net dividends to shareholders}$$
$$+ \text{Net payments to debtholders and issuers} \qquad \textbf{(7.1)}$$
$$C - I = d + F$$

That is, cash flow from operations less cash investment in operations always equals the net cash flows paid to debtholders (or issuers) and shareholders. The left-hand side, $C - I$, is the *free cash flow*. If operations generate more cash than is used in investment, free cash flow is positive. If operations produce less cash than is needed for new investment, free cash flow is negative. A positive free cash flow is used either to buy bonds (F) or pay dividends (d). A negative free cash flow requires that a firm either issue bonds (negative F) or issue shares (negative d) to satisfy the cash shortfall. The cash conservation equation is called an identity because it's always true. Cash generated must be disposed of; the sources of cash must be equal to its uses.

You see now how a firm may have financial obligations rather than financial assets (and this is often so). Financial obligations are just negative financial assets. If free cash flow is negative, a firm can sell off financial assets to get cash; if these assets are all sold and if the firm chooses not to reduce its net dividend, however, the firm will have to issue debt to get the cash. Thus the firm becomes a net debtor rather than a creditor, a holder of net financial obligations rather than net financial assets. In either case it just trades in the debt market. If free cash flow is positive, the firm buys others' bonds with the cash or buys its own bonds (redeems them), holding net dividends constant. If free cash flow is negative, it sells bonds—either its own bonds or others' bonds which it holds. This is debt financing activity, and although sometimes it's done with banks (where the firm might have a loan or an interest-bearing deposit), you can think of it as trading in bonds. In doing so, the firm will have to cover any net dividend it wants to pay and, of course, net cash interest also generates or uses cash. The *treasurer's rule* summarizes this:

$$\text{If } C - I - i > d, \text{ then lend or buy down own debt.}$$

$$\text{If } C - I - i < d, \text{ then borrow or reduce lending.}$$

Here i is the net interest cash outflow (interest paid minus interest received).

The Reformulated Cash Flow Statement

The accountant keeps track of the cash flows in a statement of cash flows. A statement of cash flows that summarizes the four cash flows in Figure 7.2 is as follows (items in parentheses are negative amounts):

Reformulated Statement of Cash Flows		
Cash flows from operations		C
Cash investment		(I)
Free cash flow		$C - I$
Equity financing flows:		
Dividends and share repurchases	XX	
Share issues	(XX)	d
Debt financing flows:		
Net purchase of financial assets	XX	
Interest on financial assets	(XX)	
Net issue of debt	(XX)	
Interest on debt	XX	F
Total financing flows		$d + F$

This dummy statement is a little different from the GAAP statement of cash flows introduced earlier. It corresponds to the thought process of the treasurer or chief financial officer who is considering financing needs, and we want financial statements that reflect management activities. One of our tasks when we analyze the cash flow statement in Chapter 10 will be to reformulate the statement to identify the four cash flows clearly.

The Reformulated Balance Sheet

The cash flows in Figure 7.2 are flows into and out of stocks of net assets depicted by boxes. So a cash investment, for example, is a flow that reduces the stock of net financial assets and increases the stock of operating assets. The balance sheet keeps track of the stock of financial assets and obligations, and so reports the net indebtedness. The balance sheet keeps track of the stock of operating assets as well. Published balance sheets list assets and liabilities, usually classified into current and long-term categories. This division is useful for credit analysis (as we will see in Chapter 19). But for equity analysis, the published statements are better reformulated into operating and financial assets and operating and financial liabilities. Thus a dummy balance sheet that corresponds to Figure 7.2 looks like this:

Balance Sheet			
Assets		**Liabilities and Equity**	
Operating assets	OA	Operating liabilities	OL
Financial assets	FA	Financial obligations	FO
		Common stockholders' equity	CSE
Total assets	OA + FA	Total claims	OL + FO + CSE

Financing items can be assets or obligations (liabilities), as we have discussed. But operating items also can be positive or negative. If they are positive, they are called **operating assets** (OA). If they are negative, they are called **operating liabilities** (OL). Accounts receivable is an operating asset because it arises from selling products in operations. Accounts payable is an operating liability because it arises from buying goods and services in operations. So are wages payable, pension liabilities, and other accrued expenses. We will deal with these classifications in more detail when we analyze actual balance sheets in Chapter 9 and reformulate them along the lines of this dummy statement. For now note that operating liabilities arise as part of operations whereas financial liabilities arise as part of the financing activities to get cash to run the operations.

To distinguish operating and financing activities it helps to regroup these items in the balance sheet:

Reformulated Balance Sheet			
Operating Assets		**Financial Obligations and Owners' Equity**	
Operating assets	OA	Financial obligations	FO
Operating liabilities	(OL)	Financial assets	(FA)
		Net financial obligations	NFO
		Common shareholders' equity	CSE
Net operating assets	NOA		NFO + CSE

Note the following relations:

$$\text{Net operating assets (NOA)} = \text{OA} - \text{OL}$$

$$\text{Net financial assets (NFA)} = \text{FA} - \text{FO}$$

$$\text{Common shareholders' equity (CSE)} = \text{NOA} + \text{NFA}$$

Usually NFA is negative, in which case it is net financial obligations (NFO):

$$\text{CSE} = \text{NOA} - \text{NFO}$$

The difference between operating assets and operating liabilities is the *net operating assets* (NOA). The difference between financial assets and financial obligations is the *net financial assets* (NFA). If NFA is negative, we have *net financial obligations* (NFO), as in this dummy statement. If NFA is positive, it is placed on the left-hand side. The book value of common stockholders' equity, CSE, was previously indicated as *B*. The last two identities under the statement restate the standard balance sheet equation (Assets – Liabilities = Owners' equity) in terms of the two net stocks for operating and financial activities. The owners' equity is seen as an investment in net operating assets and net financial assets, and the investment in net financial assets can be negative.

BUSINESS ACTIVITIES: ALL STOCKS AND FLOWS

The picture in Figure 7.2 is not complete: How does the income statement fit in? Well, firms raise cash from capital markets to invest in financing assets which are then turned into operating assets. But they then use the operating assets in operations. This involves buying inputs from suppliers (of labor, materials, and so on) and applying them with the net operating assets (such as factories, plant, and equipment) to produce goods or services that are sold to customers. Financing activities involve trading in capital markets. *Operating activities* involve trading with these customers and suppliers in *product and input markets*. Figure 7.3 completes the picture.

Trading with suppliers involves giving up resources, and this loss of value is called **operating expense** (OE in the figure). The goods and services purchased have value in that they can be combined with the operating assets to yield products or services. These products or services are sold to customers to obtain **operating revenue**, or value gained (OR in the figure). The difference between operating revenue and operating expense is called **operating income**: OI = OR – OE. If all goes well, operating income is positive: The firm adds value. If not, operating income is negative: The firm loses value.

FIGURE 7.3

All Stocks and Flows for a Firm

Net operating assets employed in operations generate operating revenue (by selling goods and services to customers) and incur operating expenses (by buying inputs from suppliers). Δ indicates changes.

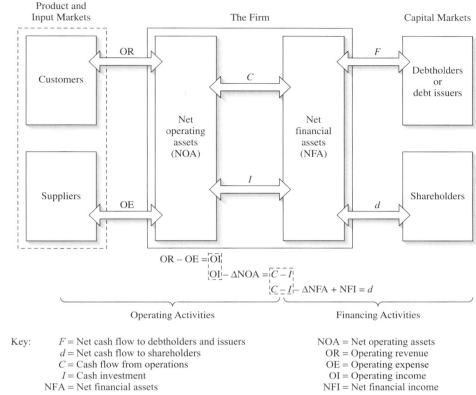

$$OR - OE = OI$$
$$OI - \Delta NOA = C - I$$
$$C - I - \Delta NFA + NFI = d$$

Operating Activities   Financing Activities

Key:
F = Net cash flow to debtholders and issuers   NOA = Net operating assets
d = Net cash flow to shareholders   OR = Operating revenue
C = Cash flow from operations   OE = Operating expense
I = Cash investment   OI = Operating income
NFA = Net financial assets   NFI = Net financial income

Figure 7.3 depicts the stocks and flows involved in the three business activities—financing, investing, and operating activities. It is common, however, to refer to the operating and investment activities together as operating activities (as in the figure), because investment is a matter of buying assets for operations. So analysts distinguish operating activities (which include investing activities) from financing activities (as in the figure).

The Reformulated Income Statement

The income statement summarizes the operating activities and reports the operating income or operating loss. The operating income is combined with the income or expense from financing activities to give the total value added to the shareholder, comprehensive income, or earnings:

Reformulated Income Statement		
Operating revenue		OR
Operating expense		(OE)
Operating income		OI
Financial expense	XX	
Financial revenue	(XX)	
Net financial expense		(NFE)
		Earnings

Operating revenues and operating expenses are not cash flows. They are measures of value in and value out as determined by the accountant. To capture that value, the accountant adds accruals to the cash flows, as we saw in Chapter 4. Similarly, interest income and interest expense (and other financing income and expenses) are not necessarily cash flows. As with operating income, the accountant determines what interest income and expense should be using an accrual: As cash interest on a discount bond (for example) does not represent the effective borrowing cost, the accountant adjusts the cash amount, as we saw with the valuation of a bond under the effective interest method in Chapter 5. The net amount of effective interest revenue (on financial assets) and effective interest expense (on financial obligations) is called **net financial income** (NFI) or, if interest expense is greater than interest revenue, **net financial expense** (NFE).

ACCOUNTING RELATIONS THAT GOVERN REFORMULATED STATEMENTS

We now have three reformulated statements. Just as published statements are governed by the accounting relations laid out in Chapter 2, so the reformulated statements are also governed by accounting relations. The cash flow and income statements are statements of flows over a period—operating flows and financing flows—and the balance sheet is a statement of the stocks—operating and financing stocks—at the end of a period. The flows during a period flow into and out of the stocks, as in the diagram, so the changes in the stocks are explained by the flows.

The flows and the changes in stocks are linked at the bottom of Figure 7.3. These links between stocks and flows are accounting relations. Accounting relations not only govern the form of the statements—how different components relate to each other—but they also describe what drives, or determines, each component. Financial analysis is a question of what drives financial statements, what drives earnings and book values. So the accounting relations we are about to lay out, though stated in technical terms here, will become analysis tools in subsequent chapters.

The Sources of Free Cash Flow and the Disposition of Free Cash Flow

Moving from left to right in Figure 7.3, we see how free cash flow is generated:

$$\text{Free cash flow} = \text{Operating income} - \text{Change in net operating assets} \qquad \textbf{(7.2)}$$

$$C - I = \text{OI} - \Delta\text{NOA}$$

where the Greek delta, Δ, indicates changes. Operations generate operating income, and free cash flow is the part of this income remaining after reinvesting some of it in net operating assets. In a sense, free cash flow is a dividend from the operations, the cash from operating profits after retaining some of the profits as assets. If the investment in NOA is greater than operating income, free cash flow is negative, and an infusion of cash (a negative dividend) into the operations is needed.

The right-hand side of the figure explains the disposition of free cash flow:

$$\text{Free cash flow} = \text{Change in net financial assets} \qquad \textbf{(7.3a)}$$
$$- \text{Net financial income} + \text{Net dividends}$$

$$C - I = \Delta\text{NFA} - \text{NFI} + d$$

That is, free cash flow and net financial income increase net financial assets and are also used to pay net dividends. If the firm has net financial obligations,

Free cash flow = Net financial expenses   **(7.3b)**
            − Change in net financial obligations + Net dividends

$$C - I = \text{NFE} - \Delta\text{NFO} + d$$

That is, free cash flow is applied to pay for net financial expenses, reduce net borrowing, and pay net dividends.

These two expressions for free cash flow will be important to cash flow analysis (in Chapter 10).

The Drivers of Dividends

Running all the way from left to right in Figure 7.3, you see how the value created in product and input markets and recorded in the accounting system flows through to the final dividend to shareholders: Operations yield value (operating income) that is invested in net operating assets; excess (or "free") cash from operations is invested in net financial assets, which yield net interest income; then these financial assets are liquidated to pay dividends. If operations need cash (negative free cash flow), financial assets are liquidated or financial obligations are created through borrowing. Alternatively, cash is raised from shareholders (a negative dividend) and temporarily invested in financial assets until needed to satisfy the negative free cash flow. And so the world turns.

The last point of this dividend generation is stated by the accounting relation to the right in Figure 7.3:

Net dividends = Free cash flow + Net financial income   **(7.4a)**
             − Change in net financial assets

$$d = C - I + \text{NFI} - \Delta\text{NFA}$$

which is a reordering of the free cash flow relation (7.3a). That is, dividends are paid out of free cash flow and interest earned on financial assets and by selling financial assets. If free cash flow is insufficient to pay dividends, financial assets are sold (or financial obligations incurred) to pay the dividend.

If the firm is a net debtor,

Net dividends = Free cash flow − Net financial expenses   **(7.4b)**
             + Change in net financial obligations

$$d = C - I - \text{NFE} + \Delta\text{NFO}$$

which is a reordering of the free cash flow relation (7.3b). That is, dividends are generated from free cash flow after servicing interest, but also by increasing borrowing. You see why dividends might not be a good indicator of the value generation in a business (at least in the short run): A firm can borrow to generate dividends (at least in the short run).

Dividends in these relations are net dividends, so cash is paid in by shareholders if free cash flow after net interest is less than net borrowing.

The Drivers of Net Operating Assets and Net Indebtedness

By reordering these accounting relations we explain changes in the balance sheet. From equation 7.2,

Net operating assets (end) = Net operating assets (beginning)   **(7.5)**
             + Operating income − Free cash flow

$$\text{NOA}_t = \text{NOA}_{t-1} + \text{OI}_t - (C_t - I_t)$$

or

$$\text{Change in net operating assets} = \text{Operating income} - \text{Free cash flow}$$

$$\Delta\text{NOA}_t = \text{OI}_t - (C_t - I_t)$$

Operating income is value added from operations, and that value increases the net operating assets. So, for example, a sale on credit increases both operating revenue and operating assets through a receivable; and purchase of materials on credit or a deferral of compensation increases both operating expense and operating liabilities through an accounts payable or wages payable. (This is just the debits and credits of accounting at work.) Free cash flow reduces net operating assets as cash is taken from operations and invested in net financial assets. Or, expressing the change in NOA as $\Delta\text{NOA} = \text{OI} - C + I$, you see that operating income and cash investment increase NOA, and NOA is reduced by the cash flows from operations that are invested in net financial assets.

Correspondingly, the change in net financial assets is determined by the income from net financial assets and free cash flows, along with dividends:

$$\text{Net financial assets (end)} = \text{Net financial assets (begin)} \qquad \textbf{(7.6a)}$$
$$+ \text{Net financial income}$$
$$+ \text{Free cash flow} - \text{Net dividends}$$

$$\text{NFA}_t = \text{NFA}_{t-1} + \text{NFI}_t + (C_t - I_t) - d_t$$

or

$$\text{Change in net financial assets} = \text{Net financial income} + \text{Free cash flow} - \text{Net dividends}$$

$$\Delta\text{NFA}_t = \text{NFI}_t + (C_t - I_t) - d_t$$

The net financial income earned on net financial assets adds to the assets, free cash flow increases the assets (as the cash from operations is invested in financial assets), and the assets are liquidated to pay net dividends. If the firm holds net financial obligations rather than net financial assets,

$$\text{Net financial obligations (end)} = \text{Net financial obligation (begin)} \qquad \textbf{(7.6b)}$$
$$+ \text{Net financial expense}$$
$$- \text{Free cash flow} + \text{Net dividends}$$

$$\text{NFO}_t = \text{NFO}_{t-1} + \text{NFE}_t - (C_t - I_t) + d_t$$

or

$$\text{Change in net financial obligations} = \text{Net financial expense} - \text{Free cash flow} + \text{Net dividends}$$

$$\Delta\text{NFO}_t = \text{NFE}_t - (C_t - I_t) + d_t$$

That is, interest obligations increase net indebtedness, free cash flow reduces indebtedness, and the firm has to borrow to finance the net dividend.

These accounting relations, remember, tell us what drives the various aspects of the (reformulated) statements. Net operating assets are driven by operating income and reduced by free cash flow, as in equation 7.5. Or, stated differently, NOA is increased by operating revenue, reduced by operating expenses, increased by cash investment, and reduced by cash from operations (which is not "left lying around" but invested in financial assets). The relations for net financial assets and obligations, equations 7.6a and 7.6b, explain what determines the borrowing or lending requirement and so restate the treasurer's rule: The amount of new debt to be purchased (and put on the balance sheet) is determined by the free cash flow after interest and the net dividend.

TYING IT TOGETHER FOR SHAREHOLDERS: WHAT GENERATES VALUE?

Figure 7.4 shows how reformulated financial statements articulate. The comparative balance sheet, at the center, reports the change in net operating assets, net financial obligations, and common shareholders' equity for a period. These changes are explained by the income statement and cash flow statement. Operating income increases net operating assets (and also increases shareholders' equity), and net financial expense increases net financial obligations (and decreases shareholders' equity). Free cash flow decreases net operating assets and also decreases the net indebtedness. Dividends are paid out of the net financial obligations—by liquidating financial assets (to get the cash) or by issuing debt. In short, the financial statements track the operating and financing flows of a business and show how they update the stocks of net operating assets, net financial obligations, and (as $\Delta CSE = \Delta NOA - \Delta NFO$) the change in shareholders' equity. The stocks and flows relations for NOA and NFO (or NFA) are similar in form to the stocks and flows equation for common stockholders' equity introduced in Chapter 2:

$$CSE_t = CSE_{t-1} + \text{Earnings}_t - \text{Net dividends}_t$$

That is, common equity is driven by comprehensive earnings and is reduced by net dividends. The expressions for NOA and NFO (equations 7.5 and 7.6b) also have a driver and a dividend. NOA is driven by operating income and reduced by a "dividend," free cash flow that is paid to the financing activities. And the net financial obligations are driven by the free cash flow received from the operating activities along with the financial expense they themselves incur, and they pay a dividend to the shareholders.

FIGURE 7.4

The Articulation of Reformulated Financial Statements. This figure shows how reformulated income statements, balance sheets, and the cash flow statements report the operating and financing activities of a business, and how the stocks and flows in Figure 7.3 are uncovered in the financial statements. Operating income increases net operating assets and net financial expense increases net financial obligations. Free cash flow is a "dividend" from the operating activities to the financing activities: Free cash flow reduces net operating assets and also reduces net financial obligations. Net dividends to shareholders are paid out of net financial obligations.

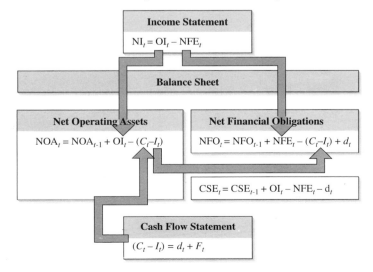

Income Statement
$NI_t = OI_t - NFE_t$

Balance Sheet

Net Operating Assets
$NOA_t = NOA_{t-1} + OI_t - (C_t - I_t)$

Net Financial Obligations
$NFO_t = NFO_{t-1} + NFE_t - (C_t - I_t) + d_t$

$CSE_t = CSE_{t-1} + OI_t - NFE_t - d_t$

Cash Flow Statement
$(C_t - I_t) = d_t + F_t$

The aim of the accounting system is to track value created for shareholders. The stocks and flows equation for shareholders indeed says this: Owners' equity is driven by a value-added measure, comprehensive income, and reduced by net distributions to owners. But common equity is also the net total of stocks in the balance sheet, the difference between net operating assets and net financial obligations:

$$CSE_t = NOA_t - NFO_t$$

So changes in common equity are driven by the drivers that change NOA and NFO. Figure 7.5 depicts how common shareholders' equity is generated by NOA and NFO. Line 1 explains the change in net operating assets from the beginning of a period and line 2 explains the change in net financial obligations. Line 3 explains the change in common equity (for the case of net financial obligations). The difference between the flows for NOA and NFO (line 1 minus line 2) explains the flow for common equity. The change in the common equity is explained by comprehensive earnings minus net dividends, but it is also explained by the flows that explain the net operating assets and net financial obligations.

You'll notice in this explanation of the change in shareholders' equity that although the free cash flow affects NOA and NFO, free cash flow drops out in the difference between the two when explaining the change in shareholders' equity: Take line 2 from line 1 to get line 3 and free cash flow drops out. The accounting says that free cash flow does not add value to shareholders. Free cash flow is a driver of the net financial position, not the operating activities, and the amount of free cash flow is irrelevant in determining the value of owners' equity. Rather, the profits from operating activities (OI) and financing activities (NFE), which together give earnings, increase or decrease shareholder wealth. Free cash flow is just a dividend of excess cash from the operating activities to the financing activities, not a measure of the value added from selling products. And free cash flows, just like dividends to shareholders, have little to do with value generated in the short run.

The explanations for the changes in NOA, NFO, and CSE work only if earnings refer to comprehensive income. Accordingly, the accounting for operating income and net financial expense must also be comprehensive: We must include all relevant flows in operating income and net financial expense. And the accounting must be clean: We must not mix financing flows with operating flows or financing assets and liabilities with operating assets and liabilities.

FIGURE 7.5

Change in common stockholders' equity is explained by changes (flows) in net operating assets (NOA) and net financial obligations (NFO). Take line 2 from line 1 and you see that free cash flow $(C - I)$ does not affect the change in common stockholders' equity.

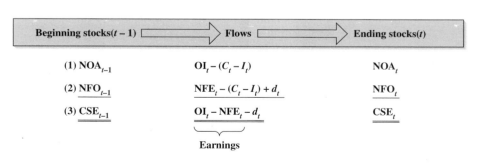

STOCKS AND FLOWS RATIOS: BUSINESS PROFITABILITY

The separation of operating and financing activities in the income statement identifies profit flows from the two activities. The corresponding stocks in the balance sheet identify the net assets or obligations put in place to generate the profit flows for the two activities. The comparison of the flows to the stocks yields ratios that measure profitability as a rate of return:

$$\text{Return on net operating assets (RNOA}_t) = \frac{OI_t}{\frac{1}{2}(NOA_t + NOA_{t-1})}$$

$$\text{Return on net financial assets (RNFA}_t) = \frac{NFI_t}{\frac{1}{2}(NFA_t + NFA_{t-1})}$$

RNOA is sometimes called return on invested capital (ROIC) or, confusingly with respect to our use of ROCE, return on capital employed (a different ROCE). Denominators are calculated as the average of beginning and ending dollar amounts. If a firm has net interest expense (and net financial obligations rather than net financial assets), the rate of return on financing activities is called the *net borrowing cost* (NBC):

$$\text{Net Borrowing cost (NBC}_t) = \frac{NFE_t}{\frac{1}{2}(NFO_t + NFO_{t-1})}$$

These ratios are primary ratios in the financial statement analysis we are about to develop, for they summarize the profitability of the two aspects of business, the operating activities and the financing activities, that have to be analyzed.

Summary

This chapter has laid out the bare bones of how a business works and how business activities are highlighted in reformulated financial statements. A series of accounting relations describe the drivers of reformulated statements and connect the statements together. These relations are summarized in the Analyst's Toolkit below, and you should try to commit them to memory. More importantly, you should appreciate what they are saying. Taken as a whole, these relations outline how value is passed from shareholders to the firm in share issues and, optimistically viewed, with value added passed back to shareholders. Figures 7.3 and 7.4 summarize this well. Put them firmly in your mind as you continue.

The chapter, indeed, is bare bones, and there is much flesh to be added in the following chapters. You have been given the form of the reformulated statements that distinguish the operating and financing activities of the firm, but the form has to be filled out. The distinction between the two types of activities is important for, as we observed in Chapter 3, it is the operating activities that are typically the source of the value generation, so it is these operating activities—and the return on net operating assets (RNOA)—that we will be particularly focused on as we analyze firms. Indeed, as we proceed with financial statement analysis, we will work with reformulated statements, not the published GAAP statements.

The accounting relations that govern the reformulated statements are also tools for the analyst. They explain how to pull the statements apart to get at the drivers. And they explain how to manipulate the statements to express one component in terms of others. The relations are stated in stark, technical terms here, but they, too, will come to life as the analysis develops. As a set, they give the form of a spreadsheet program that can be used to analyze reformulated statements and value firms. You will find yourself referring back to them and, as you do, you will appreciate how the summary of the financial statements in terms of the 6 relations (7.1–7.6) provides a succinct expression of the "story behind the numbers." It is now time to visit the Build Your Own Analysis Product (BYOAP) on the book's website. Refer to the Web Connection box that follows.

The Web Connection

BUILD YOUR OWN ANALYSIS PRODUCT (BYOAP)

The structure laid out in this chapter is a template for developing spreadsheets for analyzing the operating and financing activities of a firm and valuing the firm. The various accounting relations dictate the form that the spreadsheet must take to have integrity, and you will need to refer to these relations if you choose to develop your own analysis and valuation spreadsheet product.

You will find that developing such a product will be rewarding. Not only will you have a product that you can take into your professional life (and, indeed, use for your personal investing), but also the concepts will come alive as you go "hands-on." It is important that you develop a quality product. You do not want to lose any feature that is important to the valuation. Applying the framework in this chapter ensures that nothing is lost in your calculations.

You are not ready to develop the product yet. As the book proceeds, you will be able to build it using the architecture provided in this chapter, adding more bells and whistles as you go along. The feature **Build Your Own Analysis Product (BYOAP)** on the book's website will guide you in the practicalities. Rather than a final, off-the-shelf product that you can appropriate, BYOAP is a guide to building your own analysis product, so you learn as you go and gain an understanding of the engineering involved. With this understanding, you will be able to challenge the features of off-the-shelf products and reach the conclusion that yours is, indeed, a product with an edge.

For the moment, go to the BYOAP feature on the website, and familiarize yourself with the layout. We will refer to BYOAP as we proceed to develop the analysis in subsequent chapters.

Key Concepts

financial asset is an asset held to store cash temporarily and which is liquidated to invest in operations or pay dividends. Also called *marketable securities*. *222*

financial expense is an expense incurred on **financial obligations**. *228*

financial income is earnings on **financial assets**. The difference between financial expense and financial income is **net financial expense**. *228*

financial obligation or **financial liability** is an obligation incurred to raise cash for operations or to pay dividends. *223*

operating asset is an asset used in operations (to generate value from selling products and services). *225*

operating expense is the accounting measure of a loss of value from selling products (in operations). *226*

operating income is the accounting measure of net value added from operations. *226*

operating liability is an obligation incurred as part of operations (to generate value from selling products and services). *225*

operating revenue is the accounting measure of value gained from selling products (in operations). *226*

The Analyst's Toolkit

Analysis Tools	Page	Key Measures	Page	Acronymns to Remember
The treasurer's rule	224	Common stockholders' equity		BYOAP Build Your Own Analysis
If $C - I - i > d$, then lend		(CSE)	225	Product
or buy down debt		Financial assets (FA)	223	CSE common shareholders'
If $C - I - i < d$, then borrow		Financial obligations (FO)	223	equity
or reduce lending		Free cash flow	224	FA financial asset
Accounting relations		Net borrowing cost (NBC)	233	FO financial obligation
Cash conservation equation		Net financial assets (NFA)	223	NBC net borrowing cost
$C - I = d + F$ (7.1)	224	Net financial obligations (NFO)	223	NFA net financial assets
Free cash flow sources		Net financial expense (NFE)	228	NFE net financial expense
equation		Net financial income (NFI)	228	NFI net financial income
$C - I = OI - \Delta NOA$ (7.2)	228	Net operating assets (NOA)	226	NFO net financial obligations
Free cash flow disposition		Operating asset (OA)	225	NOA net operating assets
equations		Operating expense (OE)	226	OA operating assets
$C - I = \Delta NFA - NFI + d$		Operating income (OI)	226	OE operating expense
(7.3a)	228	Operating liabilities (OL)	225	OI operating income
$C - I = NFE - \Delta NFO + d$		Operating revenue (OR)	226	OL operating liabilities
(7.3b)	229	Return on net financial assets		OR operating revenue
Dividend driver equations		(RNFA)	233	RNFA return on net financial
$d = C - I + NFI - \Delta NFA$		Return on net operating assets		assets
(7.4a)	229	(RNOA)	233	RNOA return on net operating
$d = C - I - NFE + \Delta NFO$				assets
(7.4b)	229			
Net operating asset driver				
equation				
$\Delta NOA = OI - (C - I)$ (7.5)	229			
Net financial asset (or				
obligation) driver equations				
$\Delta NFA = NFI + (C - I) - d$				
(7.6a)	230			
$\Delta NFO = NFE - (C - I) + d$				
(7.6b)	230			

Concept Questions

C7.1. Why can free cash flow be regarded as a dividend, that is, as a distribution of value rather than the value created?

C7.2. A firm has positive free cash flow and a net dividend to shareholders that is less than free cash flow. What must it do with the excess of the free cash flow over the dividend?

C7.3. How can a firm pay a dividend with zero free cash flow?

C7.4. Distinguish an operating asset from a financial asset.

C7.5. Distinguish an operating liability from a financial liability.

C7.6. If an analyst has reformulated balance sheets and income statements, she does not need a cash flow statement to calculate free cash flow. True or false?

C7.7. What drives free cash flow?

C7.8. What drives dividends?

C7.9. What drives net operating assets?

C7.10. What drives net financial obligations?

C7.11. Free cash flow does not affect common shareholders' equity. True or false?

Exercises

E7.1. Free Cash Flow, Dividends, Debt Financing, and Growth in Net Operating Assets (Easy)

a: A firm that generated $143 million in free cash flow paid a dividend of $49 million to shareholders. How much was paid to debtholders?

b. The same firm reported operating income of $281 million. What was the growth in net operating assets during the period?

c. The same firm reported unlevered cash flow from operations of $239 million. What was the total of the accruals in operating income?

E7.2. Using Accounting Relations (Medium)

Below are a balance sheet and an income statement that have been reformulated according to the templates laid out in this chapter.

Balance Sheet

Assets			Liabilities and Equity		
	1999	1998		1999	1998
Operating assets	205.3	189.9	Operating liabilities	40.6	34.2
Financial assets	45.7	42.0	Financial liabilities	120.4	120.4
			Shareholders' equity	90.0	77.3
	251.0	231.9		251.0	231.9

Income Statement, 1999

Operating revenues	134.5
Operating expenses	(112.8)
Operating income	21.7
Interest revenues	2.5
Interest expenses	(9.6)
Comprehensive income	14.6

a. How much was paid out in net dividends during 1999?

b. What is free cash flow for 1999?

c. What was the return on net operating assets in 1999?

d. What was the firm's net borrowing cost?

E7.3. Using Accounting Relations (Medium)

Below are financial statements that have been reformulated using the templates in this chapter. Some items are missing; they are indicated by capital letters.

Income Statement, Six Months to June 30, 1999

Revenues		A
Operating expenses		
Cost of sales	2,453	
Research and development expenses	507	
Selling, administrative, and general expenses	2,423	
Other operating expenses, including taxes	2,929	B
Operating income after tax		850
Net financial expenses after tax		
Interest expense	153	
Interest income	C	59
Comprehensive income		791

Balance Sheet, June 30, 2000

	June 2000	December 1999		June 2000	December 1999
Operating assets	28,631	30,024	Operating liabilities	G	8,747
Financial assets	D	4,238	Financial liabilities	7,424	6,971
			Common equity	18,470	H
	33,088	E		33,088	F

Cash Flow Statement Six Months Ending June 30, 2000

Cash flow from operations	584
Cash investment	I
Free cash flow	J
Net dividends (dividends and share repurchases – share issues)	K
Payment to net debtholders	L
Total financing flows	M

a. Supply the missing numbers using the accounting relations laid out in this chapter.
b. What were the total new operating accruals in the first half of 1999?
c. How much new net debt was issued during this period?
d. What generated the net dividend in the period?

E7.4. Inferences Using Accounting Relations (Hard)

A firm with no financial assets or financial obligations generated free cash flow of $8.4 million in 1996. At the end of 1995 it had a market value of $224 million, or 1.6 times book value. At the end of 1996 it had a market value of $238 million, twice book value.

a. What was the rate of return from investing in the stock of this firm for 1996?
b. What were the earnings for this firm for 1996?

E7.5. Developing Spreadsheets (Hard)

The set of accounting relations in this chapter gives the template for a spreadsheet program that can be used to analyze past financial statements and forecast future residual earnings, free cash flows, and dividends. Carry through the minicase on Nike that follows to see how the forecasting works. Then develop a spreadsheet program that categorizes the financial statements as they are reformulated. Forecast future reformulated financial statements and then use the accounting relations to calculate forecasts of residual earnings, free cash flows, and dividends.

You may find this task to be too difficult at this stage. You might want to do this as you proceed through Chapters 8–12, where you will see how the reformulated financial statements work to highlight aspects of the business that drive residual earnings, free cash flows, and dividends. The BYOAP feature on the book's website will also help you. The aim of the spreadsheet exercise is to develop your own analysis, forecasting, and valuation product that can be applied in practice.

Minicase	**M7.1**

Accounting Relations, Forecasting, and Valuation: Nike, Inc.

The templates and accounting relations that are laid out in this chapter are very useful when it comes to forecasting and valuation. They organize the forecasting in a way that leads to an easy conversion of forecasts of profitability to a valuation. You will see this as you proceed through the book. The case here introduces you to forecasting with reformulated financial statements.

Nike is the sports and footwear manufacturer whose products became a household name during the 1990s. It is a firm that will be examined in some depth later in the text. Nike's top-selling footwear are basketball, cross-training, running, and children's shoes, but it also sells tennis, soccer, golf, baseball, football, bicycling, and other footwear, as well as some accessories such as athletic bags. It sells its products through approximately 18,000 retail outlets in the United States and around the world and through independent distributors and licensees. About 56 percent of Nike's sales in 1996 were in the United States. Foot Locker, the U.S. retail chain, accounted for 12 percent of 1996 sales.

The firm maintains an active research and development effort to improve its products. The company has manufacturing facilities in the United States, Asia, and South America. It had approximately 17,200 employees in 1996, but much of the manufacturing was through its independent contractors.

The market for footwear is highly competitive, with Reebok and Adidas being major competitors. Nike maintains a strongly recognized brand name through association with high-profile sporting events, sponsorship of sports teams, and intensive television and print advertising.

Nike's reformulated balance sheet for fiscal year 1995 is summarized as follows (in millions of dollars):

Reformulated Balance Sheet, May 31, 1995			
Operating assets	2,947	Operating liabilities	739
Financial assets	196	Financial liabilities	440
		Common equity	1,964
	3,143		3,143

In 1995, an analyst was forecasting a return on net operating assets (RNOA) for 1996 to 1999 as indicated in the pro forma below. The RNOA forecasts are for operating income relative to net operating assets at the beginning of the period, also given in the forecasted balance sheet in the pro forma. Nike's borrowing cost is 6.0 percent and it expects to earn the same return on the debt it holds in financial assets.

	1995A	1996E	1997E	1998E	1999E
RNOA		26.00%	24.80%	23.90%	21.00%
Operating assets	2,947	3,191	3,722	4,360	5,128
Operating liabilities	739	629	757	909	1,091
Financial assets	196	358	574	836	1,160
Financial liabilities	440	501	599	716	858

Using the pro forma, develop forecasts of earnings, dividends, free cash flows, residual earnings, and abnormal earnings growth. Attempt to value the equity from these forecasts. Use a cost of capital of 11 percent. Nike's 142,890 shares traded at $39 each at the end of its 1995 fiscal year.

Summarize the features of the forecasts you develop. What insights do they give as to how this firm is likely to evolve?

Real World Connection

See Exercise E1.5 in Chapter 1, Minicase M2.1 in Chapter 2, Exercise E6.3 in Chapter 6, Exercise E8.10 in Chapter 8, Exercise E9.5 in Chapter 9, Exercise E13.7 in Chapter 13, and the material on Nike, Inc., in Chapters 8–15.

The Analysis
of the Statement
# of Shareholders' Equity

LINKS

Link to previous chapter

Chapter 7 laid out a design for financial statements that prepares them for analysis.

This chapter

This chapter reformulates the statement of owners' equity according to the design in Chapter 7. The reformulation highlights comprehensive income.

Link to next chapter

Chapter 9 continues the reformulation with the balance sheet and the income statement.

Link to web page

For more applications of Chapter 8 content, visit the text's website at www.mhhe.com/ penman2e.

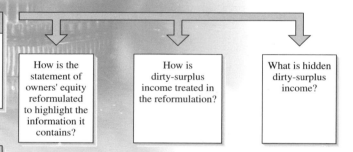

How is the statement of owners' equity reformulated to highlight the information it contains?

How is dirty-surplus income treated in the reformulation?

What is hidden dirty-surplus income?

The statement of shareholders' equity is usually not considered the most important part of the financial statements and is often ignored in analysis. In the United States it is not even required, although if it is not presented, a reconciliation of opening and closing balances of shareholders' equity must be displayed in footnotes. However, it is the first statement that the analyst should examine before going on to the other statements. It is a summary statement, tying together all transactions that affect shareholders' equity. By analyzing the statement, the analyst ensures that all aspects of the business that affect shareholders' equity are included in his analysis to value the equity.

We saw in Part One of the book that when accounting income is used in valuation, it must be comprehensive income. Otherwise value is lost in the calculation. The accounting relations in the last chapter hold only if income is comprehensive. We will use these relations as analysis tools in later chapters, but the tools will work only if income is on a comprehensive basis. Unfortunately, net income reported in most income statements in most countries is not comprehensive. The analysis of the statement of shareholders' equity

The Analyst's Checklist

After reading this chapter you should understand:

- How GAAP statements of shareholders' equity are typically laid out.

- Why reformulation of the statement is necessary.

- What is reported in "other comprehensive income" and where it is reported.

- What "dirty-surplus" items appear in the statement of shareholders' equity.

- How stock options work to compensate employees.

- How stock options and other contingent equity claims result in a hidden expense.

- How management can create value for shareholders with share transactions.

After reading this chapter you should be able to:

- Reformulate a statement of shareholders' equity.

- Distinguish the creation of value from the distribution of value in the equity statement.

- Calculate the net payout to shareholders.

- Calculate comprehensive income and comprehensive ROCE from the equity statement.

- Calculate payout and retention ratios.

- Calculate a growth rate for common shareholders' equity and analyze its components.

- Calculate the expense from exercise of stock options.

- Calculate gains and losses from put options.

- Calculate losses from the conversion of securities into common stock.

makes the correction. And it yields comprehensive income and comprehensive return on common equity (ROCE), which, as Chapters 5 and 6 showed are a particular focus in valuation analysis.

Another tenet of valuation theory is that value is generated for equity holders through operations, not by equity financing activities. We saw in Chapter 3 that share issues and repurchases at market value do not create value in efficient capital markets. But share issues are sometimes made in exchange for goods and services in operations, mostly for employee compensation. Unfortunately, GAAP accounting sometimes confuses the financing and operating aspects of these transactions, that is, it confuses the moneys raised for financing with the expenses incurred in operations. The analysis of the statement of shareholders' equity sorts out this accounting. Share issues to employees aside, share issues and repurchases can affect shareholder value if they are made at inefficient market prices. The chapter also discusses this issue.

REFORMULATING THE STATEMENT OF OWNERS' EQUITY

The ideal statement of owners' equity simply provides the reconciliation of beginning and ending owners' equity according to the stocks and flows equation introduced in Chapter 2: The change in owners' equity is explained by comprehensive income for the period plus capital contributions from share issues, less dividends paid in cash and stock repurchases. The GAAP statement is often—and unnecessarily—more complicated than this, however, so part of the analysis involves simplifying it. The ideal statement for a fiscal period has the following form:

Reformulated Statement of Common Shareholders' Equity

Beginning book value of common equity
\+ Net effect of transactions with common shareholders
   + Capital contributions (share issues)
   − Share repurchases
   <u>− Dividends</u>
   = Net cash contribution (negative net dividends)
\+ Effect of operations and nonequity financing
   + Net income (from income statement)
   + Other comprehensive income
   <u>− Preferred dividends</u>
   = Comprehensive income available to common
Closing book value of common equity

Notice three things about this statement:

1. With a view to valuing the common shareholders' equity, the reformulated statement excludes preferred equity. From the common shareholders' point of view, the preferred equity is an obligation to pay other claimants before themselves, and it is reclassified as a financial obligation in a reformulated balance sheet.

2. The net addition to common equity from transactions with shareholders—the negative net dividend—is separated from the addition to shareholders' equity that arises from business activities.

3. The total effect of operations and nonequity financing on the common shareholders is isolated in comprehensive income. This has three components: net income reported in the income statement, other comprehensive income reported outside the income statement, and preferred dividends. As preferred stock is effectively debt from the common shareholders' viewpoint, preferred dividends are an "expense" in calculating comprehensive income, just like interest expense.

Introducing Nike and Reebok

The analysis of financial statements in this and subsequent chapters will be demonstrated with the 1996 statements of Nike, Inc., and Reebok International Ltd., the sport and leisure footware companies. You will find it helpful to see a complete analysis of these firms carried out. The Build Your Own Analysis Product (BYOAP) feature on the book's website, introduced at the end of the last chapter, carries on the Nike analysis from 1996 to 2002. Accordingly, after covering the material in the book and in that web module, you will have a complete analysis history for Nike for a five-year period, 1996–2002. Take the Nike analysis in the book and the continued examples in BYOAP as a model for the analysis of any firm, and use the roadmap in BYOAP to develop spreadsheets that deliver a concrete analysis and valuation product.

We emphasized in both Chapters 1 and 3 that the first step in analysis and valuation is "knowing the business." Nike and Reebok are no doubt familiar to you: Their logos are visible on the clothes and shoes that many of us wear, from the greatest sports stars to the smallest of kid pretenders. The firms are fierce competitors. Boxes 8.1 and 8.2 give some further background on the two companies; however, in practice a much deeper understanding of a firm is required to carry out a capable analysis. The facts stated in the two boxes are as of 1996.

Incorporated in 1968, Nike (www.nike.com), like Reebok, is a leading manufacturer and marketer of sport and fashion footwear. The firm is headquartered in Beaverton, Oregon.

Strategy

Nike aims to dominate the market for athletic footwear and athletic footwear used for casual and leisure dress worldwide. It attempts to accomplish this through extensive promotion, often using high-profile sports figures and endorsements of sporting events.

Operations

Nike's top-selling footwear are basketball, cross-training, running, and children's shoes, but it also sells tennis, soccer, golf, baseball, football, bicycling, and other footwear, as well as some accessories such as athletic bags. It sells its products through approximately 18,000 retail outlets in the United States and around the world and through independent distributors and licensees. About 56 percent of Nike's sales in 1996 were in the United States. Foot Locker, the U.S. retail chain, accounted for 12 percent of 1996 sales.

The firm maintains an active research and development effort to improve its products. The company has manufacturing facilities in the United States, Asia, and South America. It has approximately 17,200 employees, but much of the manufacturing is through independent contractors.

The market for footwear is highly competitive, with Reebok and Adidas being major competitors. Changes in consumer preferences, changes in technology, and competition are seen as the main risk factors.

Debt Financing

With considerable free cash flow, Nike has little debt beyond short-term notes payable.

Equity Financing

Two classes of common shares have equal shares in profits. A total of 143,629 thousand shares were outstanding at the end of 1996. Nike has a continuing stock repurchase program and pays dividends. It aims for a dividend payout ratio in the range of 15 percent to 25 percent of earnings. A small number of redeemable preferred shares are held by an Asian supplier.

The company has an active stock compensation plan for employees. In 1996 options on 742 thousand shares were granted and options on 756 thousand shares were exercised at exercise prices ranging from $4.75 to $43.25 per share.

Summary Data

	1996	1995	1994
Basic earnings per share	$ 3.77	$ 2.72	$ 1.98
Diluted earnings per share	3.77	2.72	1.98
Dividends per share	0.55	0.45	0.40
Book value per share	16.93	13.75	11.89
Price per share, end of year	100.38	39.50	29.50
Price—high	104.25	40.94	37.38
Price—low	39.06	28.13	21.56
Trailing P/E ratio, end of year	26.6	14.5	14.9
P/B ratio, end of year	5.9	2.9	2.5

Reformulation Procedures

Exhibits 8.1 and 8.2 present the GAAP statements of shareholders' equity for Nike and Reebok, along with reformulated statements in the form of the template above. The GAAP statements are in thousands of dollars, but the reformulated statements are in millions of dollars to make the presentation even less detailed. Flags to the right of the GAAP statements indicate which items are transactions with shareholders (T) and which are components of comprehensive income (CI).

The reformulation follows three steps.

1. Restate beginning and ending balances for the period for items that are not part of common shareholders' equity:
   a. *Preferred Stock:* Preferred stock is included in shareholders' equity in the GAAP statement, but it is a liability for the common shareholders. So reduce the balances by the amount of preferred stock in those balances (and ignore any preferred stock transactions during the period in the reformulation). An exception is **mandatory redeemable preferred stock** which, under GAAP, is not part of equity but rather is reported on the balance sheet in a "mezzanine" between liabilities and equity. Nike's preferred stock is redeemable (as the footnote to the GAAP equity statement indicates), so no adjustment is required.

Organized in 1979 and incorporated in Massachusetts, Reebok (www.reebok.com), like Nike, is a leader in the design, manufacturing, and marketing of sport and leisure footwear.

Strategy

Reebok's strategy is very similar to Nike's. The firm was primarily focused on the fitness market until 1994, when it launched a "major strategic effort" to increase its on-field presence and establish its name as a sports brand. To do this it entered into promotion arrangements with leading athletes and endorsed high-profile sporting events. In addition, Reebok expanded its business beyond footwear to sports-related products such as sports and fitness videos, equipment, and fashion clothing. Like Nike, Reebok aims to be on the edge of footwear technology.

Operations

Reebok manufactures and markets a similar product line to Nike through its Reebok Division. This division also markets its Greg Norman apparel. It engages in heavy advertising and promotion and in continuing research and development to enhance products. In the United States, Reebok generally uses employee sales representatives who emphasize high-end retailers and avoid lower-margin mass merchandisers. The Reebok Division also licenses the Reebok name for such products as athletic gloves, videos, sunglasses, sport watches, uniforms, school supplies, and infant apparel.

Reebok's Rockport Division manufactures the Rockport brand of comfort footwear. Rockport also develops and markets the Ralph Lauren brand of footwear.

Virtually all of the company's products are manufactured through independent manufacturers, almost all of which are outside the United States. The company had 6,900 employees at the end of 1996.

Debt Financing

The firm carries more debt than Nike. Its debt increased substantially in 1996 as a result of a stock repurchase that was financed by borrowings. Agreements made to raise this debt bind the company to maintain a minimum interest coverage and restrict its asset acquisitions and capital expenditure.

Equity Financing

Reebok had 55,840 thousand common shares outstanding at the end of 1996. It has a stock option plan, and in 1996 options on 4,437 thousand shares were granted and options on 272 thousand shares were exercised at exercise prices ranging from $8.75 to $37.02 per share.

Concurrent with the stock repurchase, the company's board decided to suspend quarterly dividends.

Summary Data

	1996	1995	1994
Basic earnings per share	$ 2.00	$ 2.07	$ 3.02
Diluted earnings per share	2.00	2.07	3.02
Dividends per share	0.225	0.300	0.300
Book value per share	6.82	12.58	12.34
Price per share, end of year	$42.00	$28.25	$39.50
Price—high	45.25	39.63	40.25
Price—low	25.38	24.13	28.38
Trailing P/E ratio, end of year	21.0	13.65	13.08
P/B ratio, end of year	6.16	2.25	3.20

b. *Dividends Payable.* GAAP requires dividends payable to common shareholders to be reported as a liability. But shareholders cannot owe dividends to themselves. And dividends payable do not provide debt financing. Common dividends payable are part of the equity that the common shareholders have in the firm. So instead of reporting them as liabilities, reclassify them to the balances of shareholders' equity, as with Reebok.

c. *Unearned compensation* (or *deferred compensation*). When a firm issues shares at less than market value, current shareholders incur a loss. Firms grant shares to employees, often at 85 percent of market value, and in doing so they transfer value from shareholders to employees as compensation. The amount of the compensation is the difference between the market value of the shares issued and the price paid by employees. Reebok issued shares worth $1,505 thousand during 1996 (listed as "issuance of shares to certain employees") but the employees paid only

EXHIBIT 8.1 **GAAP statement and reformulated statement of common shareholders' equity for Nike, Inc.,**
May 31, 1996 The reformulated statement separates transactions with shareholders from comprehensive income. The flags on
the right of the GAAP statement indicate transactions with shareholders (T) and comprehensive income (CI).

NIKE, INC.
GAAP Statement of Equity
(dollar amounts in thousands)

	Common Stock				Capital in Excess of Stated Value	Foreign Currency Translation Adjustments	Retained Earnings	Total
	Class A		Class B					
	Shares	Amount	Shares	Amount				
Balance May 31, 1995	25,895	$ 155	45,550	$2,698	$122,436	$1,585	$1,837,815	$1,964,689
Stock options exercised			756	3	32,848			32,851 (T)
Conversion to Class B common stock	(655)	(2)	655	2				
Repurchase of Class B common stock			(200)	(1)	(451)		(18,304)	(18,756) (T)
Two-for-one stock split October 30, 1995	25,880		45,748					
Translation of statements of international operations						(18,086)		(18,086) (CI)
Net income							553,190	553,190 (CI)
Dividends on redeemable preferred stock							(30)	(30) (CI)
Dividends on common stock							(82,458)	(82,458) (T)
Balance May 31, 1996	51,120	$153	92,509	$2,702	$154,833	$(16,501)	$2,290,213	$2,431,400

Note: Nike's redeemable preferred shares are listed on its balance sheet below liabilities but above shareholders' equity at $300 thousand, in both 1996 and 1995.

Reformulated Statement of Common Equity (in millions)

Balance May 31, 1995		$1,965	
Transactions with shareholders			
Stock issues	$33		
Stock repurchases	(19)		
Common dividends	(82)	(68)	
Comprehensive income			
Net income reported	553		
Currency translations	(18)		
Preferred dividends	0	535	
Balance May 31, 1996		$2,431	

Notes: 1. As preferred shares are listed on the balance sheet apart from shareholders' equity, they are not deducted from balances in the reformulated statement.
  2. Preferred dividends of $300 thousand are rounded to $0 million in the reformulated statement.

$1,450 thousand. The difference, $55 thousand, is compensation that the equity
statement recognizes (appropriately) as deferred compensation. The compensation
is deferred as it is deemed to apply to future periods over which the employees
work, so it is amortized to the income statement over a service period; you see the
$292 thousand for the amortization in the current period in the statement. This ac-
counting is appropriate. However, the classification of the unearned compensation

EXHIBIT 8.2 **GAAP statement and reformulated statement of common shareholders' equity for Reebok International Ltd., December 31, 1996** The flags to the right of the GAAP statement indicate transactions with shareholders (T) and comprehensive income (CI).

REEBOK INTERNATIONAL LTD.
GAAP Statement of Equity (dollar amounts in thousands)

	Common Stock		Additional Paid-In Capital	Retained Earnings	Treasury Stock	Unearned Compensation	Foreign Currency Translation Adjustment	Total
	Shares	Par Value						
Balance December 31, 1995	111,015,133	$1,096	$0	$1,487,006	$(603,241)	$(1,208)	$11,636	$895,289
Net income				138,950				138,950 (CI)
Adjustment for foreign currency translation							(5,988)	(5,988) (CI)
Treasury shares repurchased					(14,379)			(14,379) (T)
Issuance of shares to certain employees	43,278			1,505		(55)		1,450 (T)
Amortization of unearned compensation						292		292 (Ignore)
Shares repurchased and retired	(18,931,403)	(190)		(672,900)		688		(672,402) (T)
Shares issued under employee stock purchase plans	157,134	2		4,042				4,044 (T)
Shares issued upon exercise of stock options	272,153	3		6,930				6,933 (T)
Put option contracts expired		15		39,825				39,840 (CI)
Income tax reductions relating to exercise of stock options				2,385				2,385 (?)
Dividends declared				(15,180)				(15,180) (T)
Balance December 31, 1996	92,556,295	$926	$0	$992,563	$(617,620)	$(283)	$5,648	$381,234

Notes: 1. Reebok lists dividends payable of $5,742 thousand on its balance sheet at the end of 1995. Reebok ceased to pay a dividend after its stock repurchase in 1996 so there were no dividends payable at the end of 1996. The cash flow statement lists cash paid for dividends of $20,922 thousand.
2. The stock repurchase occurred in August 1996.
3. Reebok listed a liability of $39,123 thousand at the end of 1995 for unexpired put options contracts on its stock. These options expired in 1996.

Reformulated Statement of Common Equity (in millions)

Balance December 31, 1995		$902
Transactions with shareholders		
Stock issues (1.4 + 4.0 + 6.9 + 2.4)	$15	
Stock repurchases (14.4 + 672.4)	(687)	
Common dividends (15.2 + 5.7)	(21)	(693)
Comprehensive income		
Net income reported	139	
Currency translations	(6)	
Put options expired	40	173
Balance December 31, 1996		$382

Notes: 1. The beginning balance in the reformulated statement is calculated as follows (in thousands):

Reported balance	$895,289
Dividends payable	5,742
Unearned compensation balance	1,208
	$902,239
The ending balance is calculated as follows:	
Reported balance	$381,234
Unearned compensation balance	283
	$381,517

2. The tax reduction from the exercise of stock options of $2,385 thousand is treated as proceeds from the issues of shares. Firms commonly net this tax benefit into the issuance amount under a heading, "Share issues for exercise of employee stock options, net of tax benefits."

as a contra to equity is not. It is an asset, like any other deferred charge or, indeed, prepaid wages, and should be classified as such. Increase beginning and ending balances of common equity by the amount of unearned compensation and ignore any transactions in the account during the period in the reformulated statement.

Nike's 1996 statement requires none of these adjustments. However, Reebok's statement does. The adjustments are summarized at the bottom of Exhibit 8.2.

2. Calculate *net transactions with shareholders* (the *net dividend*). This calculation nets dividends and stock repurchases against cash from share issues, as in the exhibits. Dividends must be cash dividends (calculated as follows), and not dividends declared as dividends payable:

Cash dividends = Dividends reported + Change in dividends payable

For Reebok (with no dividends payable at the end of the year), dividends paid are $15,180 + 5,742 = $20,922 thousand, which is the number for cash dividends in the cash flow statement (as intimated in the note to the GAAP statement).

3. Calculate *comprehensive income*. Comprehensive income combines net income and other income reported in the equity statement. Besides net income, the following items are garnered from the Nike and Reebok statements:

- Both firms have *currency translation losses* in the equity statement that must be included in comprehensive income.
- Nike has *preferred dividends.* Preferred dividends are an expense for the common shareholder.
- Reebok has a *gain from the lapse of put options* written on its own stock. These options give the holder of the options the right to sell Reebok's shares back to the firm at a fixed price, so they require Reebok to repurchase the shares at that price. Reebok recorded the amount of the premium paid for the options in 1995 as a liability (as note 3 to the GAAP statement in Exhibit 8.2 indicates). If the stock price rises above this strike price, the options lapse, as here, and the shareholders gain. The liability is written off to equity, but GAAP classifies it as an increase in paid-in capital and retained earnings, not income. But it is indeed a gain from trading in options, and it must be recognized as such: The shareholders are better off pocketing the $39,840 thousand because the options lapsed.

In reformulating Reebok's statement, we have added the tax reductions from the exercise of employee stock options to cash from share issues. Firms often treat the tax deduction they get when options are exercised as proceeds from share issues and report share issues net of the tax benefit. However, this treatment is to be questioned—as indicated by the (?) flag in the equity statement. Deeper issues lurk in the background. We defer these to the discussion of hidden dirty-surplus expenses below.

You will notice in this reformulation that we have not made any use of the distinction between stated value (or par value) of shares and additional (or excess) paid-in capital. This is of no import for equity analysis; better to know the company's telephone number than the par value of its stock. Retained earnings is a mixture of accumulated earnings, dividends, share repurchases, and stock dividends, and it does not bear on the analysis. Conversions of one class of common to another with zero effect do not change the book value of equity (as with Nike). Nor do stock splits (in Nike's statement) change the book value of equity; splits change the number of shares but do not change a given shareholder's claim.

The BYOAP feature on the book's website continues the reformulation for Nike over the years 1997–2000.

DIRTY-SURPLUS ACCOUNTING

Reporting income items as part of equity rather than in an income statement is known as *dirty-surplus accounting*. An equity statement that has no income other than net income from the income statement is a **clean-surplus accounting** statement. The terms are pejorative, and appropriately so. Under dirty-surplus accounting the income in the income statement is not "clean," it is not complete. "Net" income, as used in GAAP, is really a misnomer.

Table 8.1 lists the **dirty-surplus items** you are likely to see in the United States. Income items are designated as part of operating income or financial income (expense) to categorize them in a reformulated income statement. Some of the items you will rarely see. The three most common are unrealized gains and losses on securities, foreign currency translation gains and losses, and unrealized gains and losses on derivatives.

1. *Unrealized gains and losses on securities available for sale.* FASB Statement No. 115 distinguishes three types of securities:
   - Trading securities
   - Securities available for sale
   - Securities held to maturity

TABLE 8.1
Dirty-Surplus Accounting: U.S. GAAP
All dirty-surplus income items are reported net of tax.

Operating Income Items

Some income-increasing accounting changes (APB Opinion No. 20):
  Change from LIFO valuation of inventory
  Change in long-term contract accounting
  Change to or from full cost accounting in extractive industries
  Change triggered by a red line in an accounting standard (e.g., change from cost to
    equity method for long-term equities)
  Change made for the first time in conjunction with an IPO or business combination
Changes in accounting for contingencies (FASB Statement No. 11)
Additional minimum pension liability (FASB Statement No. 87)
Tax benefits of loss carryforwards acquired (FASB Statement No. 109)
Tax benefits of dividends paid to ESOPs (FASB Statement No. 109)
Unrealized gains and losses on equity securities available for sale (FASB Statement No. 115)

Financing Income (or Expense) Items

Preferred dividends
Unrealized gains and losses on debt securities available for sale (FASB Statement No. 115)
Losses on redemption of preferred stock
Gains on lapse of put options

Operating or Financing Income Items

Foreign currency translation gains and losses (FASB Statement No. 52)
Gains and losses on derivative instruments designated as cash-flow hedges
  (FASB Statement No. 133)

Balance Sheet Items to Be Reclassified

Deferred compensation relating to grant of employee stock options and stock
  (APB Opinion No. 25 and FASB Statement No. 123)
Dividends payable

Note: APB is the Accounting Principles Board, the predecessor body to the Financial Accounting Standards Board (FASB).

Accounting Clinic III

ACCOUNTING FOR MARKETABLE SECURITIES

Further detail on the accounting for securities is covered in Accounting Clinic III on the book's website. The clinic covers debt securities held by firms and equity securities representing less than 20 percent interest in other corporations. The accounting for equity investments of more than 20 percent is covered in Accounting Clinic V.

Trading securities are those held in a portfolio that is actively traded. These securities are marked to market value in the balance sheet and the unrealized gains and losses from changes in market value are reported in the income statement. Securities that are not actively traded but which might be sold before maturity are available for sale. These also are marked to "fair" market value but the unrealized gains and losses are reported as part of other comprehensive income. Securities that management intends to hold to maturity are recorded at cost on the balance sheet, so no unrealized gains and losses are reported. Realized gains and losses on all types of securities are reported in the income statement as part of net income. The rules apply to both debt securities and equity securities involving less than 20 percent ownership interest. Go to Accounting Clinic III.

2. *Foreign currency translation gains and losses.* The assets and liabilities of majority-owned foreign subsidiaries, measured in the foreign currency, must be consolidated into the statements of a U.S. parent in U.S. dollars. If the exchange rate changes over the reporting period, the value of the assets and liabilities changes in U.S. dollars. The resulting gain or loss is a translation gain or loss, to be distinguished from gains and losses on foreign currency transactions. Most transaction gains and losses are reported as part of net income. Translation gains and losses are part of other comprehensive income. Translation gains and losses can apply to both the operating and financing assets and liabilities of subsidiaries, so their income can affect operating or financing income as indicated in Table 8.1.

3. *Gains and losses on derivative instruments.* FASB Statement No. 133 requires most derivatives to be marked to fair value on the balance sheet, either as assets or liabilities. If the instrument hedges an existing asset or liability or a firm commitment by the company—a so-called *fair value hedge*—the gain or loss from marking the instrument to fair value is recorded as part of net income. (Under certain conditions, the gain or loss is offset in the income statement by the gain or loss on the hedged item.) If the instrument hedges the cash flow from an anticipated future transaction—a so-called *cash flow hedge*—the gain or loss is recorded to the equity statement, and then removed from the equity statement to net income when the hedged transaction affects earnings.[1]

Comprehensive Income Reporting

For years after 1998, FASB Statement No. 130 requires comprehensive income to be identified in the financial statements. It distinguishes net income from *other comprehensive*

---

[1] See M. A. Trombley, *Accounting for Derivatives and Hedging* (New York: McGraw-Hill/Irwin, 2003) for a primer on the accounting for derivatives.

income and permits the sum of the two, *comprehensive income,* to be reported in one of three ways:

1. Report comprehensive income in the statement of shareholders' equity by adding net income to other comprehensive income items reported in the equity statement.

2. Add other comprehensive income to net income in the income statement and close the total comprehensive income to shareholders' equity.

3. Present a separate statement of other comprehensive income apart from the income statement and close it to equity along with net income from the income statement.

Most firms follow the first approach.[2] So you now observe dirty-surplus income items added together into a number called "other comprehensive income" and other comprehensive income and net income added to "total comprehensive income"—all within the equity statement. This presentation facilitates the task of identifying comprehensive income. However, it is not, in fact, comprehensive; neither gains from the lapse of put options nor certain hidden dirty-surplus items (which we will identify toward the end of this chapter) are included.

The amount of dirty-surplus accounting in the United States is relatively small. In the United Kingdom, most items outside the income statement (the profit and loss account) are reported in a separate statement of recognized gains and losses, and so they are easily identified. But on the European continent and in Asia, the practice of reserving in the equity section is common. Unraveling these reserves to discover comprehensive income is quite a task. But unless this is done, the complete profitability cannot be discovered.

RATIO ANALYSIS

What does the reformatted statement of changes in owners' equity reveal? It gives the growth in equity over a period. And it distinguishes clearly between the growth in equity from new investment or disinvestment by the owners and additions to equity from running the business. Accordingly, the reformulated statement distinguishes the creation of value from the distribution of value. Indeed both ROCE and growth in equity—the two drivers of residual earnings—can be identified in the statement. A set of ratios analyzes the statement to refine this information.

Payout and Retention Ratios

The disinvestment by shareholders is described by payout ratio and retention ratios. The standard *dividend payout ratio* is the proportion of income paid out in cash dividends:

$$\text{Dividend payout} = \frac{\text{Dividends}}{\text{Comprehensive income}}$$

A calculation that you commonly see compares dividends to net income rather than comprehensive income. The dividend payout ratio involves payout in the form of dividends; total **payout** is dividends plus share repurchases. Some firms pay no dividends but have regular stock repurchases. Shareholders who are taxed on dividends will prefer

---

[2] For an example of the third approach, see the 1998 10-K filing for Pentair, Inc., on the SEC's EDGAR website. For an example of the second approach, see Chubb Corporation in Exercise E9.8 in Chapter 9.

stock repurchases to dividends if capital gains are taxed at a lower rate than dividends. The *total payout ratio* is

$$\text{Total payout ratio} = \frac{\text{Dividends} + \text{Stock repurchases}}{\text{Comprehensive income}}$$

calculated with total dollar amounts rather than per-share amounts. The difference between this ratio and the dividend payout ratio gives the percentage of earnings paid out as stock repurchases.

Note that stock dividends and stock splits are not involved. These simply change the share units, with no effect on the claim of each shareholder. Some splits and stock dividends involve a reclassification from retained earnings to additional paid-in capital, but again this has no effect on the value of claims.

Although the dividend payout ratio suggests that dividends are not paid out of earnings, they are really paid out of book value, out of assets. So a firm can pay a dividend even if it reports a loss. Payout, as a proportion of book value, is the rate of disinvestment by shareholders:

$$\text{Dividends-to-book value} = \frac{\text{Dividends}}{\text{Book value of CSE} + \text{Dividends}}$$

$$\text{Total payout-to-book value} = \frac{\text{Dividends} + \text{Stock repurchases}}{\text{Book value of CSE} + \text{Dividends} + \text{Stock repurchases}}$$

Usually ending book value of common shareholders' equity (CSE) is used in the denominator in these calculations (although, with dividends paid out over the year, average CSE is also appropriate).

Retention ratios focus on earnings retained rather than earnings paid out. The *standard retention ratio* involves only cash dividends (but can be modified to incorporate stock repurchases):

$$\text{Retention ratio} = \frac{\text{Comprehensive income} - \text{Dividends}}{\text{Comprehensive income}}$$

$$= 1 - \text{Dividend payout ratio}$$

Shareholder Profitability

The reformulated statement yields the comprehensive rate of return on common equity, ROCE, the profitability of the owners' investment for the period. In addition, ROCE is growth in equity from business activities. For Nike, the 1996 ROCE (using average equity for the year) is

$$\text{ROCE}_t = \frac{\text{Comprehensive earnings}}{\frac{1}{2}(\text{CSE}_t + \text{CSE}_{t-1})}$$

$$= \frac{535}{\frac{1}{2}(1,965 + 2,431)} = 24.3\%$$

The ROCE calculated on beginning common equity is 27.2 percent.

Had we calculated the ROCE based on net income, the number would have been 25.2 percent. Note that the income statement and balance sheet are not needed to calculate ROCE; rather, they provide the detail to analyze ROCE.

Growth Ratios

The growth in shareholders' equity is simply the change from beginning to ending balances. *Growth ratios* explain this growth as a rate of growth.

The part of the growth rate resulting from transactions with shareholders is the net investment rate:

$$\text{Net investment rate} = \frac{\text{Net transations with shareholders}}{\text{Beginning book value of CSE}}$$

Nike's net investment rate was a negative 3.5 percent because net cash was paid out; shareholders disinvested. The part of the growth rate that comes from business activities is given by the ROCE on beginning equity, 27.2 percent for Nike. The rate of growth of owners' equity from both sources—new shareholder financing and business activities—is the growth rate in common stockholders' equity:

$$\text{Growth rate of CSE} = \frac{\text{Change in CSE}}{\text{Beginning CSE}}$$

$$= \frac{\text{Comprehensive income} + \text{Net transactions with shareholders}}{\text{Beginning CSE}}$$

Nike's 1995 growth rate was 23.7 percent.

If ROCE is calculated with beginning CSE in the denominator, then

$$\text{Growth rate of CSE} = \text{ROCE} + \text{Net investment rate}$$

For Nike, the growth rate in common equity is 27.2 percent − 3.5 percent = 23.7 percent.

Return on common equity is the focus for the analysis of profitability. Growth in CSE is the focus for the analysis of growth. Together, the two drive residual earnings and earnings growth. As a first insight, we see that the growth rate is driven by ROCE and the rate of new investment.

HIDDEN DIRTY SURPLUS

The distinction between comprehensive income and transactions with shareholders in the reformulated statement of owners' equity separates the creation of value from the raising of funds and the distribution of value to shareholders. The premise is that transactions with shareholders do not create value. This is so when share transactions are at market value, but when shares are issued at less than market value, shareholders lose. And the losses do not appear in GAAP financial statements.

Issue of Shares in Operations

We have seen that when firms grant shares to employees at less than market price, the difference between market price and grant price is treated as (deferred) compensation to employees and ultimately amortized as an expense to the income statement. More frequently, though, shares are not granted to employees. Rather, *stock options* are granted and shares are issued later when the options are exercised. However, unlike the stock grant, compensation expense is not recorded.

Four events are involved in a stock option award: the grant of the option, the vesting of the option, the exercise of the option, and the lapse of the option. At the grant date employees are awarded the right to exercise at an exercise price; the vesting date is the first date at which they can exercise the option; the exercise date is the date on which they actually do exercise at the exercise price; and the lapse date is the date on which the option lapses should the employee choose not to exercise. Clearly the employee exercises if the stock is "in the money" at exercise date, that is, if the market price is greater than the exercise price.

If an option is granted in the money at grant date (with the exercise price set at less than the market price at grant date), GAAP accounting treats the difference between the market price and exercise price as compensation. Deferred compensation is recorded and then amortized to the income statement over the vesting period, as in the case of a stock grant. But most options are granted "at the money," with exercise price equal to the market price at grant date. So no compensation expense is recognized. And as time elapses and the market price of the stock moves "into the money," no compensation expense is recorded. Further, when options are indeed exercised, no compensation expense is recorded. You see in Reebok's statement of equity that the amount received on exercise is recorded as issued shares, but, unlike the stock grants, the expense—the difference between the market price and the issue price—is not recorded.

The appropriate accounting is to record the issue of shares at market price and recognize the difference between the market price and issue price as compensation expense. In the absence of this accounting there is a **hidden dirty-surplus expense**. The expense is not merely recorded in equity rather than the income statement; it is not recorded at all. But there has been a distribution of wealth to employees and that distribution has come at the expense of the shareholders: The value of their shares must drop to reflect the **dilution** of their equity. GAAP accounting treats this transaction, which is both a financing transaction—raising cash—and an operational transaction—paying employees—as if it is just a financing transaction. This hidden dirty-surplus accounting creates a hidden expense. Box 8.3 calculates Reebok's loss from the exercise of stock options during 1996.

Some commentators argue that, because options are granted at the money, there is no expense. Employees—and particularly management, who benefit most—say this adamantly. But there is no expense only if the options fail to move into the money. Paying employees with stock options that move into the money and are exercised substitutes for paying them with cash, and recording the expense is recording the cash-equivalent compensation: The firm is effectively issuing stock to employees at market price and giving them a cash amount equivalent to the difference between market and exercise prices to help pay for the stock. Recognizing this expense is at the heart of accrual accounting, for accrual accounting looks past cash flows to value flows; it sees a transfer of valuable stock for wages as no different from cash wages. If you are hesitant in viewing stock compensation as an expense, think of the case where a firm pays for all its operations—its materials, its advertising, its equipment—with stock options. (Indeed some sports stars have asked to be paid with stock options for promotions!) If the hidden expenses were not recognized, the income statement would have only revenues on it and no expenses. Stock options produce revenues and profits for shareholders if they present an incentive for employees and management. But GAAP accounting does not match the cost of the options against these revenues and profits. Value added must be matched with value lost.

With the large growth in stock compensation in the 1990s, the hidden expense has become quite significant, particularly in the high-tech sector. The Financial Accounting Standards Board addressed the issue but in Statement No. 123 came to an unsatisfactory conclusion. This statement requires an "expense" to be reported at grant date equal to the value of the option, priced using option-pricing formulas. This expense may be recognized in the income statement, but this is not required. The amount must be reported in footnotes along with an "as-if" net income that includes the option value as an expense. But granting options yields an expense only in recognition that exercise is possible. If the option lapses (because the stock does not go into the money), no expense is realized. An

Stock option loss is the difference between the exercise price and the market price of the shares at the date of exercise. This is the amount that shareholders lose by not issuing the shares at market price. The amount can be calculated in two ways.

METHOD 1

If options are **nonqualifying options,** the firm receives a tax deduction for the difference between market price and exercise price (and the employee is taxed on that difference). If the firm reports the tax benefit from the exercise of options, the amount of the tax deduction—the stock option expense—can be imputed using the firm's tax rate. Reebok's tax rate, gleaned from the tax footnote to the financial statements, is 35.4 percent. So, from the tax benefit of $2,385 thousand reported in the equity statement, the expense is $2,385/0.354 = $6,737 thousand. As the expense is a tax deduction, the after-tax option expense is calculated as follows (in thousands):

Stock option expense	$2,385/0.354	$6,737
Tax benefit at 35.4%		(2,385)
Stock option expense, after tax		$4,352

Note that the tax benefit from stock options is also reported as part of cash flow from operations in the cash flow statement. The cash flow statement recognizes the tax benefit without the associated expense, so firms increase reported cash from operations while incurring a loss for shareholders!

METHOD 2

If the options are **incentive options,** the firm does not receive a tax benefit, nor is the employee taxed on the difference between market and exercise price. (The employee is taxed when the shares are subsequently sold, however.) With no reported tax benefit to work from, the calculation must estimate the market price at exercise date. The midpoint of Reebok's high and low stock price during 1996 (in Box 8.2) is $35.31. With 272.153 thousand options exercised, the calculation is as follows:

Estimate market value of shares issued	272.153 × $35.31	$9,610
Exercise (issue) price, from equity statement		6,933
Stock option expense, before tax		2,677
Tax benefit at 35.4%		948
Stock option expense, after tax		$1,729

This calculation is tentative. If employees exercised above the $35.31 price (which is likely), the expense would be higher. Indeed, the Method 2 number is considerably less than the Method 1 number.

expense is realized only as the stock goes into the money and is exercised. And the difference between market and exercise price when the option is exercised is the amount of the expense.

Significantly, the Internal Revenue Service recognizes that compensation expense is incurred when options are exercised and gives the firm a tax deduction for it (if certain conditions are met). The firm books this **tax benefit** to equity: You see the entry in Reebok's equity statement (Exhibit 8.2), where $2,385 thousand in tax benefits are recorded. So, the accounting recognizes the tax benefit of the expense, increasing equity, but not the associated expense!

Exhibit 8.3 displays the 1996 stock option footnote for Reebok, as required by FASB Statement No. 123. The firm used a Black-Scholes valuation of options granted to calculated stock compensation expense. This expense is amortized against income over the option's vesting period, as described. The resultant expense reduced "pro forma" basic earnings per share from the $2 reported in the income statement to $1.96, that is, by $0.04 per share. After the corporate scandals of 2001–2002, when stock option accounting (appropriately) began to be criticized, many firms, in a move to "accounting quality," began to recognize the grant-date expense in their income statements, rather than just in footnotes. So you will now see stock compensation expense in the income statement (for some firms). At the time of this writing, the International Accounting Standards Board (IASB) has issued a proposal that would require the grant-date expense to be recognized in the income statement, and the FASB is considering the issue.

EXHIBIT 8.3

Extract from stock option footnote for Reebok International Ltd., 1996 Note pro forma earnings and earnings per share after including stock compensation expense calculated at grant date. The 1996 pro forma basic earnings per share of $1.96 compares to the $2 number reported in the income statement (without compensation expense).

Note 10: Stock Plans

Pro forma information regarding net income and earnings per share is required by Statement No. 123, which also requires that the information be determined as if the Company had accounted for its employee stock options granted subsequent to December 31, 1994, under the fair value method of that statement. The fair value for these options was estimated at the date of grant using a Black-Scholes option pricing model with the following weighted-average assumptions for 1995 and 1996, respectively: risk-free interest rates ranging from 5.19% to 7.65%; dividend yields of 0.89% and 0.68%; volatility factor of the expected market price of the Company's common stock of 0.27 in both years; and a weighted-average expected life of 4.2 years.

For purposes of pro forma disclosures, the estimated fair value of the options is amortized to expense over the options' vesting period.

The Company's pro forma information is as follows:

December 31,	1996	1995
Pro forma net income (in thousands)	$134,017	$163,404
Pro forma earnings per share	$1.96	$2.06
Weighted-average exercise price of options granted	$31.32	$34.90
Weighted-average fair value of options outstanding at the end of the period	$10.76	$11.63

Exercise prices for options outstanding ranged from $8.75–$41.63. Within that range, 2,933,609 options were outstanding between $8.75 and $20.46, and 6,982,097 options were outstanding between $20.47 and $41.63. The weighted-average contractual life of the options is seven years.

The following schedule summarizes the changes in stock options during the three years ended December 31, 1996:

Number of Shares Under Option		
	Nonqualified Stock Options	Option Price Per Share
Outstanding at December 31, 1993	6,406,968	8.75–41.74
Granted	212,797	28.88–38.88
Exercised	(352,255)	8.75–33.25
Canceled	(387,935)	11.38–41.74
Outstanding at December 31, 1994	5,879,575	8.75–39.77
Granted	1,361,502	28.75–36.75
Exercised	(361,400)	8.75–33.25
Canceled	(722,760)	11.38–39.77
Outstanding at December 31, 1995	6,156,917	8.75–38.88
Granted	4,436,947	26.75–41.63
Exercised	(272,153)	8.75–37.02
Canceled	(406,005)	11.38–37.02
Outstanding at December 31, 1996	9,915,706	8.75–41.63

However, GAAP *grant-date accounting* for stock option expense differs from the *exercise-date accounting* in Box 8.3. Reebok's expense from granting 4,436,947 options in 1996 was $0.04 per share. The exercise-date expense of $4,352 thousand for the 272,153 options exercised (under Method 1 in Box 8.3) is $0.08 per share on 55,568 thousand shares outstanding before the exercise.

This loss from the exercise of options results from options exercised in the current period. However, it does not capture the expected losses to shareholders from stock options in the future, and it is the expected costs of options with which we are concerned in valuation. In Exhibit 8.3 Reebok had 9,915,706 options outstanding at the end of 1996 at exercise prices ranging from $8.75 to $41.63 per share. Most of these options are in the money and are likely to be exercised. In valuing a Reebok share, the investor must consider the expected loss in value when these options are exercised; if one ignores this loss, one will overvalue the firm and pay too much for a share.

We return to the question of how anticipated losses from stock options are incorporated in valuation in Chapter 13. For the moment, however, note that Reebok reports a number in the footnote that is helpful to us. In Exhibit 8.3, the weighted average fair value of options outstanding (unexercised) at the end of 1996 (using a Black-Scholes option valuation) is $10.76, or $106,693 thousand on the 9,915,706 options outstanding. This is the **option overhang**, a contingent liability to issue shares at less than market value. Our valuations will build in this contingent liability.

Understanding some of the details of GAAP accounting and exercise-date accounting for options will help you in valuation. Go to Accounting Clinic IV.

Accounting Clinic IV

ACCOUNTING FOR STOCK COMPENSATION

GAAP accounting for stock options in the United States employs *grant-date accounting,* with firms given a choice between "pro forma" footnote disclosure or income statement recognition. The International Accounting Standards Board (IASB) also requires grant-date accounting but (at the time of this writing) is proposing that the compensation expense be booked to the income statement. Accounting Clinic IV leads you through grant-date accounting.

Accounting Clinic IV also lays out *exercise-date accounting* and takes you through the complete accounting that measures the effects of stock options on shareholders. Compensation costs are recorded at grant date, and then recognized as expense in the income statement over the period when employee services are given. Accordingly, the compensation cost is matched against the revenues that the employees produce. Subsequent to grant date, further losses are recognized as options go into the money. Here are the steps to effect sound accrual accounting for stock options:

1. Recognize the option value at grant date as a contingent liability, along with a deferred (unearned) compensation asset. This is the amount recognized with grant-date accounting under FASB Statement No. 123. The grant-date value given to employees is compensation, but it is contingent upon the options going into the money. The deferred compensation asset is similar to that which arises from stock issues to employees at less than market value.

2. Amortize the deferred compensation over an employee service period, usually the vesting period.

3. Mark the contingent liability to market as options go into the money to capture the value of the option overhang, and recognize a corresponding unrealized loss from stock options.

4. Extinguish the liability against the share issue (at market value) at exercise date. If options are not exercised, extinguish the liability and recognize a gain from stock options.

Exercise of stock options increases shares outstanding, so comparing *basic eps* with *diluted eps* (that anticipates the share issues) gives some idea of the extent of the problem. But the loss from stock options falls on the current shareholders, not the future shareholders from the exercise of options, and diluted eps does not make the distinction. Accounting Clinic IV outlines the calculation of diluted eps.

In Dell's statement of shareholders' equity for the fiscal year ending February 1, 2002, the following line item appeared (in millions):

	Shares	Amount
Repurchase of common shares	68	$3,000

This line suggests a routine stock repurchase. But further investigation reveals otherwise. Dividing the $3 billion paid out by the 68 million shares purchased, the average per-share purchase price is $44.12. But Dell's shares did not trade above $30 during the year, and the average price was $24. Footnotes reveal that Dell was forced to repurchase shares at the strike price of $44 on put options written to investors. In previous years, Dell had, like Reebok, gained from these options as the stock price continued to rise during the bubble. But with the share price falling (from a high of $60 in February 2000) as the stock market bubble burst, Dell was caught as these options went under water. Using the average price of $24 for 2002 as the market price when the shares were repurchased, the loss from the exercise of put options is as follows:

Market price for shares		
repurchase	$24 × 68 million	$1,632 million
Amount paid for shares repurchased		3,000
Loss on exercise of put options		$1,368 million

(The loss is not tax deductible.) On the 2,670 million shares outstanding before the repurchase, the loss is $0.51 per share, a significant amount compared to Dell's reported eps of $0.48. Dell effectively runs two types of businesses, a computer business earning $0.48 per share in 2002 and a business of betting on its own stock, earning a loss of $0.51 per share. GAAP does not report the latter.

The omission of this loss is a concern to the investor, and the investor must be vigilant. Shareholders lose when share prices fall, of course, but when the firm has written put options, the shareholder suffers twice; the loss from the price decline is levered. In 2002, Electronic Data Systems Corporation (EDS) announced that the firm had some accounting problems and that contract revenue would not be as previously expected. The stock price dropped 70 percent on the bad news. Later, the firm indicated that the drop in price would trigger the exercise of put options. The price dropped further.

Firms make similar commitments to buy back stock through **forward share purchase agreements**. They disclose the existence of put options and share purchase agreements in footnotes. In buying a stock of Dell in 2002, one must be aware of the put option overhang, for it might require further repurchases that lose value for shareholders. At the end of fiscal 2002, Dell has a further put option overhang for 51 million shares to be repurchased at $45 per share. In September 2002, when the shares were trading at $25, the options were in the money by $20 per share, a total of $1.020 billion, projecting a loss of $0.39 per outstanding share. Analysts were forecasting $0.80 eps for fiscal 2003, but that is GAAP earnings. Expected comprehensive earnings was $0.39 less, or $0.41 per share.

Issue of Shares in Financing Activities

Hidden losses occur not only with employee stock options but with the exercise of all **contingent equity claims**. Call and put options on the firm's own stock, warrants, rights, convertible bonds, and convertible preferred shares are all contingent equity claims that, if exercised, require the issue (or repurchase) of shares at a price that is different from market value.

To illustrate, consider the put options that arose in Reebok's equity statement. The options (to have shares repurchased by Reebok at a set price) lapsed in that case, yielding a gain to shareholders that was recognized in comprehensive income. Suppose the options were exercised, however, so that the firm was required to repurchase shares at a price higher than market value. How does GAAP deal with the issue? Well, not at all well. Look at Box 8.4.

Box 8.5 covers the accounting for convertible bonds and convertible preferred stock and shows how GAAP accounting does not recognize the full cost of financing with these instruments. GAAP accounting is not comprehensive, even though a nominal number, comprehensive income, is reported.

Convertible securities are securities, such as bonds and preferred stock, that can be converted into common shares if conditions are met. Textbooks propose two methods to record the conversion of a convertible bond or a convertible preferred stock into common shares:

The *book value method* records the share issue at the book value of the bond or preferred stock. Common equity is increased and debt or preferred stock is reduced by the same amount, so no gain or loss is recorded.

The *market value method* records the share issue at the market value of the shares issued in the conversion. The difference between this market value and the book value of the security converted is recorded as a loss on conversion.

The book value method is almost exclusively used in practice. It involves a hidden dirty-surplus loss. The market value method reports the loss. It accords the treatment of convertible securities the same treatment as nonconvertible securities. On redemption of nonconvertible securities before maturity, a loss (or gain) is recognized. The only difference with convertible securities is that shares rather than cash are used to retire them. In both cases there is a loss to the existing shareholders.

Convertible bonds carry a lower interest rate than nonconvertible bonds because of the conversion option. GAAP accounting records only this interest expense as the financing cost, so it looks as if the financing is cheaper. But the full financing cost includes any loss on conversion of the bonds into common shares—and this loss is not recorded.

In the 1990s, financing with convertible preferred stock became common. Only the dividends on the preferred stock were recorded as the financing cost, not the loss on conversion. Suppose a convertible preferred stock issue had no dividend rights but, to compensate, set a favorable conversion price to the buyer of the issue. Under GAAP accounting it would appear that this financing had no cost.

Share Transactions in Inefficient Markets

The maxim that share issues and repurchases at market value do not create value recognizes that in efficient stock markets, value received equals value surrendered; both sides of the transaction get what they paid for. In a share repurchase, for example, the firm gives up, and the seller receives, cash equal to the value of the stock.

But we recognized in Chapter 3 that if stock markets are inefficient, a firm can buy back shares at less than they are worth and issue shares at more than they are worth. The other side of the transaction—the shareholder who sells the shares or the new shareholder who buys—loses value. But the existing shareholders who do not participate in the transaction gain. These gains (or losses if shareholders lose in the transaction) are not revealed in the accounts.

Even if stock markets are efficient with respect to publicly available information, a firm's management might have private information about the value of their firm's shares and issue or repurchase shares at prices that are different from those that will prevail when the information is subsequently made public. Such transactions also generate value for existing shareholders. (In the United States there are legal constraints on this practice, however.)

The active investor who conjectures that the market may be inefficient at times is wary of share transactions with firms. As with all his trading in the stock market, he tests the market price against an estimate of intrinsic value. But he is particularly careful in this case because the firm's management may have a better feel for intrinsic value than he.

The active investor who understands the intrinsic value of a stock understands when it might be overvalued or undervalued. And he understands that management might use the mispricing to advantage. The management might, for example, use overvalued shares to make acquisitions, to acquire other firms cheaply. Indeed this is a reason why an investor might buy overvalued shares: He sees that value can be generated by using the shares as

Dell Computer explains its put option transactions (examined in Box 8.4) as "part of a share-repurchase program to manage the dilution resulting from shares issued under employee stock plans." It is common for firms to explain share repurchases in this way. The exercise of stock options increases shares outstanding and, as we have seen, dilutes existing shareholders' value. Buying back shares reduces shares outstanding. But does it reverse the dilution?

The answer is no. If shares are purchased at fair value, there is no change in the per-share value of the equity; the shareholder does not get extra value to compensate for the loss of value from stock options. Maintaining constant shares outstanding with share repurchases only gives the appearance of reversing the dilution.

During the stock market bubble, employees exercised options against the shareholders as prices soared. Firms then repurchased shares "to manage dilution." But purchasing shares at bubble prices (above intrinsic value) destroys value for shareholders. Shareholders lost twice, once with the employee options, and again with the repurchases. As some firms borrowed to finance the share repurchases, they were left with large debts that led to significant credit problems as the bubble burst.

currency in an acquisition. But this is a tricky business: If investors force up the prices of shares that are already overpriced, a price bubble can result. The fundamental investor bases his actions on a good understanding of the firm's acquisition possibilities and its acquisition strategy.

As for the management, they can take advantage of share mispricings to create value for shareholders with share transactions. They can choose to finance new operations with debt rather than equity if they feel the stock price is "too low." But they also can choose to exercise their stock options when the price is high—a double whammy for shareholders. They might also have misguided ideas about stock issues and repurchases. See Box 8.6.

THE EYE OF THE SHAREHOLDER

We have characterized the financial statements as a lens on the business. For equity analysis, the lens must be focused to the eye of the shareholder. GAAP accounting is inadequate for equity analysis because it does not have its eye on the shareholder. It does not account faithfully for the welfare of the shareholder, and nowhere else is this more apparent than with the accounting in the statement of shareholders' equity.

GAAP fails to see a sale of shares by current shareholders at less than market value as a loss. If the shareholders were forced to do so on their own account, they surely would make a loss. When the firm forces it on them, they also make a loss. GAAP fails to understand the distinction between cash transactions with shareholders (to raise cash and to pass out unneeded cash as a matter of financing) and value added (or lost) from operations that can be embedded in a share issue. It also fails to see that transactions between claimants—convertible bondholders and common shareholders, for example—can involve losses for the common shareholders.

In short, GAAP accounting does not honor the property rights of the common shareholder. This is so despite the fact that financial reports are prepared nominally for the shareholder, company directors (including the audit committee) have a fiduciary duty to the shareholders, and management and auditors formally present the financial reports to shareholders at the annual meeting. GAAP does not honor the shareholders as the owners of the firm. Consequently, the equity analyst must repair the accounting, as we have done in this chapter.

The Web Connection

Find the following on the web page for this chapter:

- Further demonstrations of reformulated statements of shareholders' equity.

- Further discussion of hidden expenses.

- More coverage of footnotes that pertain to the equity statement.

Summary

Misclassifications in the financial statements can lead to erroneous analysis of the financial statements and to erroneous valuations. Reformatting the statements classifies items correctly. The GAAP statement of equity sometimes comingles the results of operations with the financing of the operations. This chapter reformulates the statement to distinguish the creation of value in a firm from the distribution of value to shareholders in net dividends. The reformulation identifies dirty-surplus items in the statement and yields comprehensive income and comprehensive ROCE.

Omission in the financial statements is more pernicious than misclassification, and the chapter sensitizes the analyst to expenses that can arise from exercise of contingent claims but which are hidden by GAAP accounting. Failure to recognize these expenses in forecasting can lead to overvaluation of firms.

As always, a sense of perspective must be maintained in analyzing the statement of equity. For some firms with few dirty-surplus items and no stock compensation, there is little to be discovered. For many firms there are just two items—translation gains and losses and unrealized gains and losses on securities—that appear. And for many firms, the amounts of these items are small. In the United States, one can sometimes glance at the statement and dismiss the contents as immaterial. In other countries, the practice of dirty-surplus accounting is quite extensive. And in the United States, the use of stock options in compensation is widespread.

Key Concepts

clean-surplus accounting produces a statement of shareholders' equity that contains only net income (closed from the income statement) and transactions with shareholders.   *248*

contingent equity claim is a claim that may be converted into common equity if conditions are met. Examples are stock options, warrants, and **convertible securities**.   *257*

convertible securities are securities (such as bonds and preferred stock) that can be converted into common shares if conditions are met, but which have additional claims also.   *258*

dilution (to existing shareholders) occurs when shares are issued to new shareholders at less than market value.   *253*

dirty-surplus item is an accounting item in shareholders' equity other than transactions with shareholders or income closed from the income statement.   *248*

forward share purchase agreement is an agreement to buy back shares at a specified price in the future.   *257*

hidden dirty-surplus expense is an expense that arises from the issue of shares but is not recognized in the financial statements.   *253*

incentive options are employee stock options that are not taxed to the employee on exercise and are not tax deductible for the issuing firm. *254*

nonqualifying options are employee stock options that are taxable to the employee on exercise and tax deductible to the issuing corporation. *254*

option overhang is the value of stock options unexercised. *256*

payout is amounts paid to shareholders. The term is sometimes used to refer only to dividends, sometimes to dividends and stock repurchases. Compare with **retention**. *250*

redeemable securities are securities (such as bonds and preferred stocks) that can be redeemed by the issuer under specified conditions. *243*

retention is paying out less than 100 percent of earnings. Compare with **payout**. *251*

tax benefit is a tax deduction or credit given for specified transactions. *254*

The Analyst's Toolkit

Concept Questions

C8.1. Why is income in the equity portion of the balance sheet called "dirty-surplus" income?

C8.2. Why can "value be lost" if an analyst works with reported net income rather than comprehensive income?

C8.3. Are currency translation gains and losses real gains and losses to shareholders? Aren't they just an accounting effect that is necessary to consolidate financial statements prepared in different currencies?

C8.4. Why is it said that amortizations of deferred compensation are treated like an equity contribution under GAAP (generally accepted accounting principles)?

C8.5. Reebok's balance sheet for 1996 states that there were 55,840 thousand common shares outstanding at the end of 1996. Yet the equity statement in Exhibit 8.2 lists 92,556 thousand shares. Explain the difference. Which number should be used to calculate per-share numbers?

C8.6. In accounting for the conversion of convertible bonds to common stock, most firms record the issue of shares at the amount of the book value of the bonds. The issue of the shares could be recorded at their market value, with the difference between the market value of the shares and the book value of the bonds recorded as a loss on the conversion. Which treatment best reflects the effect of the transaction on the wealth of the existing shareholders?

C8.7. The compensation vice president of General Mills was quoted in *The Wall Street Journal* on January 14, 1997, as saying that option programs are "very attractive for shareholders" because they cut fixed costs and boost profits. So, for General Mills's 1996 year, selling, general, and administrative expenses, which include compensation, dropped by $222 million, or 9 percent, while pretax earnings from continuing operations rose by $194 million, or 34 percent. At the same time, the firm was distributing about 3 percent of its stock to employees annually.

What's wrong with this picture?

C8.8. In 1998, Chrysler Corporation, the American car and truck manufacturer, merged with Daimler-Benz, the German industrial group, to form DaimlerChrysler. In Germany, company officers could not be given stock options, so the executives of Chrysler who held options on their firm's shares were given shares in the new DaimlerChrysler instead of options. The executives, who held options on 30 million shares at an average exercise price of $27, converted the options into shares worth $60 each. What was the compensation paid to the Chrysler executives in the merger?

C8.9. Before it found the practice to be too expensive, Microsoft (and a number of other firms) was in the habit of repurchasing some of the shares that it issued each year as employees exercised stock options. The rationale, according to commentators, was to avoid the dilution from shares issued to employees.

a. Do share issues from the exercise of employee stock options cause dilution?
b. Do share repurchases reverse dilution?
c. Why would Microsoft feel that repurchasing shares is "too expensive"?

C8.10. Cisco Systems, the networking equipment firm, reported a tax benefit from the exercise of stock options of $837 million in its fiscal 1999 shareholders' equity statement. Over the previous years, the tax benefits had cut more than 25 percent off the firm's tax bills and in 1999 the tax benefit accounted for 19 percent of its reported cash flow from operations. Commentators saw this tax relief as a major source of value for the shareholders. Is this correct?

C8.11. In February 1999, Boots, the leading retail chemist in the United Kingdom, announced plans to reform its employee option compensation scheme. In the future, it said, the firm will purchase its own shares to provide shares to issue when options are exercised, and it will charge the difference between the market price and the issue price for the options against profits. The charge for the first year was expected to be £63 million ($103 million). What do you think of this scheme?

C8.12. In September 1999, Microsoft agreed to buy Visio Corporation for stock valued at $1.26 billion. Visio sells a popular line of technical drawing software. At the time, Microsoft had $14 billion of cash on its balance sheet. Why might Microsoft pay for the acquisition with its own stock rather than in cash?

Exercises

E8.1. Calculating ROCE from the Statement of Shareholders' Equity (Easy)

From the following information, calculate the return on common equity for the year 2000. (Amounts in millions of dollars.)

Common stockholders' equity, January 1, 2000	174.8
Dividends paid to common stockholders	8.3
Share issue on December 31, 2000	34.4
Common stockholders' equity, December 31, 2000	226.2

E8.2. Reformulation of a Statement of Owners' Equity: VF Corporation, 1993 (Easy)

Reformulate the 1993 statement of stockholders' equity for VF Corporation:

(in thousands)	Common Stock	Additional Paid-In Capital	Foreign Currency Translation	Retained Earnings
Balance January 2, 1993	$ 59,519	$ 301,336	$ 4,244	$ 788,872
Net income				246,415
Cash dividends:				
Common stock				(78,540)
Series B preferred stock				(4,291)
Tax benefit from preferred				
stock dividends				1,180
Redemption of preferred stock				(264)
Sale of common stock	4,600	227,468		
Exercise of stock options,				
net of shares surrendered	370	14,361		(761)
Foreign currency translation				
adjustments, less deferred				
income taxes of $6,927			(17,109)	
Balance January 1, 1994	$64,489	$543,165	($12,865)	$952,611

Real World Connection

See Minicase M11.2 in Chapter 11 for more material on VF Corporation.

E8.3. Deferred Compensation: Dell Computer (Medium)

The following statement of shareholders' equity for Dell Computer Corporation is from its annual report. Deferred compensation first arose during fiscal year ending January 1995. What is the balance of the deferred compensation asset at the end of January 1996?

	Preferred Stock and Capital in Excess of Par Value	Common Stock and Capital in Excess of Par Value	Retained Earnings	Other	Total
			Stockholders' Equity		
Balances at January 30, 1994	$120	$200	$171	$ (20)	$471
Net income			149		149
Issuance of 3,501,214 shares of common stock under employee plans, including tax benefits		42		(4)	38
Preferred stock dividends paid			(9)		(9)
Unrealized loss on marketable securities				(6)	(6)
Foreign currency translation adjustment				9	9
Balances at January 29, 1995	120	242	311	(21)	652
Net income			272		272
Issuance of 4,066,363 shares of common stock under employee plans, including tax benefits		74		(17)	57
Issuance of 10,020,968 shares of common stock due to preferred stock conversion	(114)	114			
Amortization of unearned compensation				2	2
Preferred stock dividends paid			(13)		(13)
Unrealized gain on marketable securities				3	3
Balances at January 28, 1996	$ 6	$430	$570	($33)	$973

Real World Connection

See the material on Dell Computer in Chapter 2, Exercise E1.1 in Chapter 1, Exercise E4.1 in Chapter 4, Exercise E5.10 in Chapter 5, Minicase M6.2 in Chapter 6, Exercise E8.8 in this chapter, Minicase 10.1 in Chapter 10, Minicase 12.1 in Chapter 12, and Minicase 15.1 in Chapter 15.

E8.4. Statement of Shareholders' Equity: Boise Cascade (Hard)

In the accompanying 1995 statement of shareholders' equity for Boise Cascade Corporation, the firm reported a liability of $213,934 thousand for "Guarantee of ESOP debt." The market price of a common share was $33 when the Series E preferred stock were converted.

a. Calculate comprehensive income to common shareholders for 1995 as best as you can with the information available.

b. What is the deferred ESOP benefit?

c. Calculate common shareholders' equity at December 31, 1995.

BOISE CASCADE CORPORATION
(in thousands)

Common Shares Outstanding		Shareholders' Equity	Preferred Stock	Deferred ESOP Benefit	Common Stock	Additional Paid-In Capital	Retained Earnings
38,284,186	Balance at						
	December 31, 1994	$1,364,858	$762,183	$(230,956)	$ 95,170		$ 737,921
	Net income	351,860					351,860
	Cash dividends declared						
	Common stock	(28,549)					(28,549)
	Preferred stock	(44,872)					(44,872)
8,625,000	Conversion of Series E						
	preferred stock		(191,466)		21,563	$169,903	
1,264,503	Stock options exercised	38,018			3,161	34,857	
(448,396)	Treasury stock						
	cancellations	(23,972)	(7,970)		(1,121)	(2,036)	(12,845)
34,653	Other	37,095		17,022	87	2,383	17,603
47,759,946	Balance at						
	December 31, 1995	$1,694,438	$562,747	$(213,934)	$119,400	$205,107	$1,021,118

E8.5.   Missing Shareholders' Equity Statement: J.C. Penney (Medium)

J.C. Penney, the retailer, did not include a statement of shareholders' equity in its 1995 10-K filing. However, the notes gave details of the changes in shareholders' equity. From the accompanying partial balance sheet and financial statement footnotes:

a. Reconstruct the statement as it might have been prepared under GAAP accounting.

b. Prepare a reformulated statement on a clean-surplus basis for the common shareholders.

c. Why are the preferred dividends net of taxes?

	1995	1994
Shareholders' equity (in millions)		
Preferred stock, without par value:		
Authorized, 25 million shares; issued, 1 million shares		
of Series B LESOP convertible preferred	603	630
Guaranteed LESOP obligation	(228)	(307)
Common stock, par value 50¢:		
Authorized, 1,250 million shares; issued, 224, and 227 million shares	1,112	1,030
Reinvested earnings	4,397	4,262
Total stockholders' equity	5,884	5,615

From the notes:

Consolidated Statements of Reinvested Earnings

(in millions)	1995	1994
Reinvested earnings at beginning of year	$4,262	$4,093
Net income	838	1,057
Net unrealized change in debt and equity securities and currency translation adjustments	72	(21)
Retirement of common stock	(301)	(435)
Common stock dividends declared	(434)	(392)
Preferred stock dividends declared, net of taxes	(40)	(40)
Reinvested earnings at end of year	$4,397	$4,262

Long-Term Debt

(in millions)	1995	1994
Original issue discount		
6% debentures, due 2006, $200 at maturity, effective rate 13.2%	$ 108	$ 104
Debentures and notes		
5.375% to 7.375%, due 1998 to 2023	2,500	1,500
8.25% to 8.375%, due 1996 to 2022	250	250
9% to 10%, due 1997 to 2021	835	1,000
Guaranteed LESOP notes		
8.17%, due 1998	228	307
Present value of commitments under capital leases	91	104
Other	68	70
Long-term debt	$4,080	$3,335
Average long-term debt outstanding	$3,241	$2,754
Average interest rates	7.9%	8.2%

Common Stock

Changes in Outstanding Common Stock	Shares (in thousands)		Paid-In Capital (in millions)	
	1995	1994	1995	1994
Balance at beginning of year	227,441	236,086	$1,030	$1,003
Common stock issued	3,858	1,455	113	70
Common stock purchased and retired	(7,374)	(10,100)	(31)	(43)
Balance at end of year	223,925	227,441	$1,112	$1,030

Preferred Stock

In 1988, a leveraged employee stock ownership plan (LESOP) was adopted. The LESOP purchased approximately 1.2 million shares of a new issue of Series B convertible preferred stock from the Company. These shares are convertible into shares of the Company's common stock at a conversion rate equivalent to 20 shares of common stock for each share of preferred stock. The conversion price is $30 per common share. The convertible preferred stock may be redeemed at the option of the Company or the LESOP, under certain limited circumstances. The redemption price may be satisfied in cash or common stock or a combination of both at the Company's sole discretion. The dividends are cumulative, are payable semiannually on January 1 and July 1, and yield 7.9 percent. The convertible preferred stock issued to the LESOP has been recorded in the stockholders' equity section of the consolidated section of the consolidated balance sheets, and the "Guaranteed LESOP obligation," representing borrowings by the LESOP, has been recorded as a reduction of stockholders' equity. As of January 27, 1996, approximately 827 thousand shares had been allocated to participants' accounts since 1988, and approximately 350 thousand shares were committed to be released in the next three years.

Real World Connection

See Exercise E2.4 in Chapter 2 and Exercise E3.12 in Chapter 3 for more material on J.C. Penney.

E8.6. **Analysis of the Statement of Shareholders' Equity: Sears, Roebuck and Company (Hard)**

Reformulate the 1995 statement of owners' equity for Sears, Roebuck that follows and identify comprehensive income. The following footnotes from the annual report will help you:

Discontinued Operations

On Nov. 10, 1994, the Company announced its intention to distribute in a tax-free dividend to the Company's common shareholders its 80% ownership interest in The Allstate Corporation. The distribution was approved by shareholders at a special meeting on March 31, 1995. On June 20, 1995, the Company's Board of Directors approved the distribution to Sears shareholders in a tax-free dividend. Sears shareholders of record on June 30, 1995, received, effective June 30, 1995, 0.93 shares of The Allstate Corporation for each Sears common share owned. This transaction resulted in a noncash dividend to Sears shareholders totaling $8.98 billion.

Preferred Shares

The Series A Mandatorily Exchangeable Preferred Shares [PERCS] were issued in the form of 28.75 million depository shares having an annual, cumulative dividend of $3.75 per depository share. The Company exchanged the PERCS for common shares on Mar. 20, 1995. Holders of depository shares received 1.24 common shares for each depository share. The total number of common shares delivered upon exchange was 35.7 million.

Profit Sharing Fund

Most domestic employees are eligible to become members of The Savings and Profits Sharing Fund of Sears Employees ("the Fund"). The Company contribution is based on 6% of consolidated income, as defined, for the participating companies. Company contributions are limited to 70% of eligible employee contributions.

The Fund includes an Employee Stock Ownership Plan ("the ESOP") to prefund a portion of the Company's anticipated contribution through 2004. The Company loaned the ESOP $800 million, which it used to purchase 25.9 million of Sears common shares. The loan is repaid with dividends on ESOP shares and Company contributions.

SEARS, ROEBUCK AND COMPANY

Consolidated Statements of Shareholders' Equity

	1995 (dollars in millions)	1995 (shares in thousands)
8.88% Preferred Shares, First Series		
Balance, beginning of year	$ 325	3,250
Issued during year		
Balance, end of year	$ 325	3,250
Series A Mandatorily Exchangeable Preferred Shares (PERCS)		
Balance, beginning of year	$1,236	7,188
Issued during year		
Exchanged to common shares during year	(1,236)	(7,188)
Balance, end of year		
Common Shares		
Balance, beginning of year	$ 294	392,310
Conversion of PERCS	27	35,673
Stock options exercised and other changes	1	1,700
Balance, end of year	$ 322	429,683
Capital in Excess of Par Value		
Balance, beginning of year	$2,385	
Stock options exercised and other changes	40	
Conversion of PERCS	1,209	
Balance, end of year	$3,634	

(continued)

	1995 (dollars in millions)	1995 (shares in thousands)
Retained Income		
Balance, beginning of year	$ 8,918	
Net income	1,801	
Preferred share dividends	(53)	
Common share dividends	(475)	
Distribution of The Allstate Corporation shares	(7,747)	
Balance, end of year	$ 2,444	
Treasury Stock-at-Cost		
Balance, beginning of year	$ (1,690)	(40,570)
Reissued under compensation plans	56	1,375
Balance, end of year	$ (1,634)	(39,195)
Minimum Pension Liability		
Balance, beginning of year		
Minimum liability adjustment during year	(285)	
Balance, end of year	$ (285)	
Deferred ESOP Expense		
Balance, beginning of year	$ (558)	
Reductions	305	
Balance, end of year	$ (253)	
Unrealized Net Capital Gains		
Balance, beginning of year	$ 32	
Net increase	1,176	
Distribution of The Allstate Corporation shares	(1,208)	
Balance, end of year		
Cumulative Translation Adjustments		
Balance, beginning of year	$ (141)	
Net unrealized loss during year	(7)	
Distribution of The Allstate Corporation shares	(20)	
Balance, end of year	$ (168)	
Total Common Shareholders' Equity and Shares Outstanding	$ 4,060	390,488
Total Shareholders' Equity	$ 4,385	

E8.7. Analysis of Shareholders' Equity for a U.K. Company: Cadbury Schweppes (Medium)

In the United Kingdom, firms are required to report a profit and loss statement (similar to the U.S. income statement) and a statement of movements in shareholders' funds (similar to the U.S. equity statement) and, between these two statements, a statement of total recognized gains and losses. The latter statement has gains and losses not reported in the profit and loss statement.

Cadbury Schweppes, the beverage and candy manufacturer, reported a profit after preferred dividends of £355 million in its profit and loss statement for 1998. Below are its statement of total recognized gains and losses and its reconciliation of movements in shareholder funds.

Calculate comprehensive income (profit) to the ordinary (common) shareholders for the year.

Statement of Total Recognized Gains and Losses

(Pounds in millions)	1998	1997	1996
Cadbury Schweppes plc.	£ (8)	£ 455	£ 130
Subsidiary undertakings	341	226	199
Associated undertakings	22	10	11
Profit for the Financial Year	355	691	340
Currency translation differences	(15)	(56)	(124)
Revaluation of fixed assets	(3)		
Total Recognized Gains and Losses for the Year	£ 337	£ 635	£ 216

Reconciliation of Movements in Shareholders' Funds

(Pounds in millions)	1998	1997	1996
Total recognized gains and losses for the year	£ 337	£ 635	£ 216
Dividends to ordinary shareholders	(194)	(182)	(171)
New share capital subscribed	31	39	33
Goodwill adjustments		(3)	(104)
Redemption of preference shares		(107)	
Other			(3)
Net Increase/(Decrease) in Shareholders' Funds	£ 174	£ 382	£ (29)
Shareholders' Funds at Beginning of Year	1,669	1,287	1,316
Shareholders' Funds at End of Year	£ 1,843	£ 1,669	£ 1,287

Real World Connection

See Exercise E10.11 in Chapter 10 for more material on Cadbury Schweppes.

E8.8.   **Exercise of Stock Options: Dell Computer (Medium)**

Dell Computer Corporation reported the following summary of stock option activity in a benefit plans footnote to its 1999 financial statements:

	Number of Shares (in millions)	Weighted-Average Exercise Price
Outstanding at beginning of year	439	$ 2.25
Granted	60	19.94
Canceled	(26)	2.63
Exercised	(110)	1.29
Outstanding at end of year	363	5.40
Exercisable at year-end	103	2.27

Dell's share price increased from $26 at the beginning of its 1999 fiscal year to $101 at the end of the year, and these prices were, respectively, close to the low and the high for the year.

a. Calculate, to the best of your ability given this information, the value lost to shareholders through the exercise of stock options during Dell's fiscal 1999 year. Dell's marginal tax rate is 35 percent.

b. Comment on the potential future value loss from options outstanding at the end of the year. If this loss were to be recognized in the accounts, how would it be treated?

Real World Connection

See Exercise E8.3 in this chapter. Also see Exercise E1.1 in Chapter 1, Exercise E4.1 in Chapter 4, Exercise E5.10 in Chapter 5, and Minicase M6.2 in Chapter 6.

E8.9.   Exercise of Stock Options and the Statement of Shareholders' Equity: Genentech (Medium)

Genetech's statement of shareholders' equity for fiscal 1999 below reports income tax benefits from employee stock option plans of $17,332 thousand. Genentech has a tax rate of 37 percent.

  a. What is your best estimate of the value loss to shareholders from the exercise of employee stock options during 1999?
  b. What do you think of the accounting treatment of adding the tax benefit to additional paid-in capital?

GENENTECH, INC.
Consolidated Statements of Stockholders' Equity (in thousands)

	Shares				Additional Paid-In Capital	Retained Earnings	Accumulated Other Comprehensive Income	Total
	Special Common Stock	Common Stock	Special Common Stock	Common Stock				
Balance December 31, 1997	47,607	76,621	$952	$1,532	$1,463,768	$511,141	$53,832	$2,031,225
Comprehensive income								
Net income						181,909		181,909
Net unrealized gain on securities available for sale							5,431	5,431
Comprehensive income								187,340
Issuance of stock upon exercise of options and warrants	2,460		49		86,835			86,884
Issuance of stock under employee stock plan	427		9		21,055			21,064
Income tax benefits realized from employee stock option exercises					17,332			17,332
Balance December 31, 1998	50,494	76,621	$1,010	$1,532	$1,588,990	$693,050	$59,263	$2,343,845

Real World Connection

See Exercise E2.5 in Chapter 2.

E8.10.   Ratio Analysis for the Equity Statement: Nike and Reebok (Easy)

Using the statements of shareholders' equity in Exhibits 8.1 and 8.2, carry out a ratio analysis that highlights the information about Nike and Reebok in those statements.

Minicases

M8.1

Analysis of the Equity Statement, Hidden Losses, and Off-Balance-Sheet Liabilities: Microsoft Corporation

Microsoft has undoubtedly been the most successful software firm ever. Between 1994 and 2000, the firm's revenues increased from $2.8 billion to $23.0 billion, and its earnings from $708 million to $9.4 billion. Over the two years, 1998 to early 2000, its stock price increased from $36 per share to almost $120, giving it a P/E ratio of 66 and a market capitalization at the height of the stock market bubble of over half a trillion dollars. By early 2003, Microsoft was trading at $50 per share with a market capitalization of $275 billion and a P/E ratio of 31.

Microsoft's success has been due to a strong product, market positioning, and innovative research and marketing. In terms of the buzzwords of the time, Microsoft has significant "knowledge capital" combined with dominant market positioning and network externalities. These intangible assets are not on its balance sheet, and accordingly the price-to-book ratio was over 12 in 2000. Yet, to develop and maintain the knowledge base, Microsoft had to attract leading technical experts with attractive stock option packages, with consequent costs to shareholders. Unfortunately, GAAP accounting did not report this cost of acquiring knowledge, nor did it report significant off-balance-sheet liabilities to pay for the knowledge. Knowledge liabilities, as well as knowledge assets, were missing from the balance sheet.

This case asks you to uncover the knowledge costs and the associated liabilities and to deal with other imperfections in the statement of shareholders' equity.

Microsoft's income statement for the first nine months of its June 30, 2000, fiscal year follows, along with its statement of shareholders' equity at the end of the nine months and the shareholders' equity footnote. At the time, Microsoft's shares were trading at $90 each. Reformulate the equity statement and then answer the questions that follow.

MICROSOFT CORPORATION
Income Statements
(in millions, except earnings per share)
(Unaudited)

	Nine Months Ended March 31, 2000
Revenue	$17,152
Operating expenses	
Cost of revenue	2,220
Research and development	2,735
Sales and marketing	2,972
General and administrative	825
Other expenses (income)	(13)
Total operating expenses	8,739
Operating income	8,413
Investment income	2,055
Gains on sales	156
Income before income taxes	10,624
Provision for income taxes	3,612
Net income	$ 7,012
Earnings per share:	
Basic	$ 1.35
Diluted	$ 1.27

Stockholders' Equity Statement (in millions) (Unaudited)

	Nine Months Ended March 31, 2000
Common stock and paid-in capital	
Balance, beginning of period	$13,844
Common stock issued	2,843
Common stock repurchased	(186)
Proceeds from sale of put warrants	472
Stock option income tax benefits	4,002
Balance, end of period	20,975
Retained earnings	
Balance, beginning of period	13,614
Net income	7,012
Net unrealized investment gains	2,724
Translation adjustments and other	166
Comprehensive income	9,902
Preferred stock dividends	(13)
Common stock repurchased	(4,686)
Balance, end of period	18,817
Total stockholders' equity	$39,792

Extract from the footnotes to the financial statements:

Stockholders' Equity

During the first three quarters of fiscal 2000, the Company repurchased 54.7 million shares of Microsoft common stock in the open market. In January 2000, the Company announced the termination of its stock buyback program.

To enhance its stock repurchase program, Microsoft sold put warrants to independent third parties. These put warrants entitle the holders to sell shares of Microsoft common stock to the Company on certain dates at specified prices. On March 31, 2000, 163 million warrants were outstanding with strike prices ranging from $69 to $78 per share. The put warrants expire between June 2000 and December 2002. The outstanding put warrants permit a net-share settlement at the Company's option and do not result in a put warrant liability on the balance sheet.

During 1996, Microsoft issued 12.5 million shares of 2.75% convertible exchangeable principal-protected preferred stock. Net proceeds of $980 million were used to repurchase common shares. The Company's convertible preferred stock matured on December 15, 1999. Each preferred share was converted into 1.1273 common shares.

A. What was the net cash paid out to shareholders during the nine months?

B. What was Microsoft's comprehensive income for the nine months?

C. Discuss your treatment of the $472 million from "proceeds from sale of put warrants." Why would Microsoft sell put warrants? How does GAAP account for put warrants, put options, and future share purchase agreements?

D. If the put warrants had been exercised rather than allowed to lapse, how would GAAP accounting report the transactions? How would you report the effect on shareholder value?

E. The equity statement shows that Microsoft repurchased $4.872 billion in common shares during the nine months. The firm had a policy of repurchasing the amount of shares that were issued in exercise of employee stock options, to "reverse the dilution," as it said. Microsoft discontinued the policy in 2000, as indicated in the shareholders' equity footnote. Does a repurchase reverse the dilution of shareholders' equity? Are repurchases at the share prices that prevailed in 2000 advisable from a shareholder's point of view?

F. Calculate the loss to shareholders from employees exercising stock options during the nine months. Microsoft's combined federal and state statutory tax rate is 37.5 percent.

G. The following is the financing section of Microsoft's cash flow statement for the nine months (in millions):

Financing	Nine month ending March 1999	Nine month ending March 2000
Common stock issued	$1,102	$1,750
Common stock repurchased	(1,527)	(4,872)
Put warrant proceeds	757	472
Preferred stock dividends	(21)	(13)
Stock option income tax benefits	2,238	4,002
Net cash from financing	$2,549	$1,339

Notice that the tax benefits from the exercise of stock options are included as financing cash flows. Later in 2000, the Emerging Issues Task Force of the Financial Accounting Standards Board required these tax benefits to be reported in the cash from operations section of the statement of cash flows. Which is the correct treatment?

H. The income statement reports income taxes of $3,612 million on $10,624 million of income. Yet press reports claimed that Microsoft paid no taxes at the time. Can you see why? What does the act of paying no taxes on a large income tell you about the quality of Microsoft's reported income?

I. Review the shareholders' equity footnote. What issues arise in the footnote that should be considered in valuing Microsoft's shares?

J. Microsoft's annual report for the year ending May 31, 2000, reported the following in the stock option footnote:

Stock Option Plans
For various price ranges, weighted-average characteristics of outstanding stock options at June 30, 2000, were as follows:

Range of Exercise Prices	Outstanding Options		
	Shares	Remaining Life (Years)	Weighted-Average Price
$ 0.56–$5.97	133	2.1	$ 4.57
5.98–13.62	104	3.0	10.89
13.63–29.80	135	3.7	14.99
29.81–43.62	96	4.5	32.08
43.63–83.28	198	7.3	63.19
83.29–119.13	166	8.6	89.91

The weighted average Black-Scholes value of options granted under the stock option plans during 1998, 1999, and 2000 was $11.81, $20.90, and $36.67, respectively. Value was estimated using a weighted-average expected life of 5.3 years in 1998, 5.0 years in 1999, and 6.2 years in 2000, no dividends, volatility of .32 in 1998 and 1999 and .33 in 2000, and risk-free interest rates of 5.7%, 4.9%, and 6.2% in 1998, 1999, and 2000, respectively.

What information does this footnote give you about the off-balance-sheet knowledge liability for the option overhang? Can you estimate the amount of the liability?

M8.2

Losses from Put Options: Household International

Household International is one of the largest U.S. lenders to consumers with poor credit histories, carrying receivables for auto loans, Mastercard and Visa credit card debt, and a significant amount of private noncredit card debt. In September 2002 Household issued 18.7 million shares, raising about $400 million. The issue, combined with a decision to sell $7.5 billion of receivables and deposits, was cheered by analysts concerned about the subprime lender's liquidity and credit rating. However, closer inspection revealed that Household International might have to use the cash raised for purposes other than bolstering its reserves.

A footnote in Household's 10-Q report for the third quarter ending September 30, 2002, reported the following:

Forward Purchase Agreements

At September 30, 2002, we had agreements to purchase, on a forward basis, approximately 4.9 million shares of our common stock with a weighted-average forward price of $52.99 per share. The agreements expire at various dates through August 2003. These agreements may be settled physically or on a net basis either in shares of our common stock or in cash, depending on the terms of the various agreements, at our option and consequently are accounted for as permanent equity. Under the terms of the various agreements, expiration dates accelerate if our stock price reaches certain triggers. Currently, these triggers vary between the agreements and range between $12 and $16 per share. During the current quarter, we received approximately 2.1 million shares at an average cost of $55.68 per share as a result of settlements under these forward contracts.

Under a net share settlement, if the price of our common stock falls below the forward price, we would be required to deliver common shares to the counterparty based upon the difference between the forward price and the then current stock price. Conversely, if the price of our common stock rises above the forward price, the counterparty would be required to deliver to us shares of our common stock based on the price difference. Based upon the closing price of our common stock of $28.31 at September 30, 2002, we would have been required to deliver approximately 4.2 million shares of our common stock to net share settle these contracts at September 30, 2002. If our common stock price had been $1 lower at September 30, 2002, we would have been required to deliver an additional 332,500 common shares to net share settle these contracts. If our common stock price had been higher by $1 at September 30, 2002, we would have been required to deliver a total of 3.9 million shares of our common stock to net share settle the contracts. These agreements, however, contain limits on the number of shares to be delivered under a net share settlement, regardless of the price of our common stock. At September 30, 2002, the maximum number of common shares we would be required to deliver to net share settle the 4.9 million shares currently outstanding was 29.8 million shares.

Since the beginning of 2001, Household had been both issuing and repurchasing shares. The maximum per-share amount received for share issues was $21.72, while the maximum amount per-share for repurchases was $53.88, contributing to its liquidity problems.

Discuss the information contained in the footnote. How does GAAP account for these transactions? What alternative accounting would better reflect the affect on shareholder value? Does it make a difference to your answers if the settlement is in cash or shares?

LIVERPOOL JOHN MOORES UNIVERSITY
Aldham Robarts L.R.C.
TEL 0151 231 3701/3634

The Analysis of the Balance Sheet and Income Statement

LINKS

Link to previous chapter

Chapter 8 reformulated and analyzed the statement of owners' equity.

This chapter

This chapter continues the reformulation and analysis with the balance sheet and income statement. The reformulation follows the design in Chapter 7.

Link to next chapter

Chapter 10 analyzes the cash flow statement.

Link to web page

More applications and analysis are on the text website at www.mhhe.com/ penman2e.

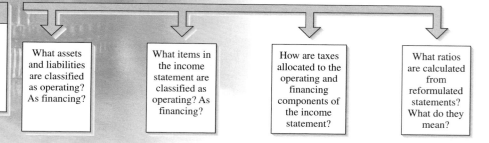

What assets and liabilities are classified as operating? As financing?

What items in the income statement are classified as operating? As financing?

How are taxes allocated to the operating and financing components of the income statement?

What ratios are calculated from reformulated statements? What do they mean?

The reformulated statement of shareholders' equity of the last chapter yields the overall profitability measure, the comprehensive return on common shareholders' equity, which, along with growth, drives residual earnings and value. The balance sheet and income statement give the detail to discover the sources of profitability and growth. This chapter takes you through the analysis of the two statements in preparation for the analysis of profitability and growth in Chapters 11 and 12.

Profitability that generates value comes from a firm's operations. Thus the analysis begins with a reformulation of the statements, following the templates of Chapter 7, which distinguishes operating activities from financing activities. This reformulation enforces the rule that one cannot value a firm without knowing the business, for distinguishing operating activities identifies the business the firm is in. And distinguishing operating items from financing items in financial statements requires understanding the role of each item in the business and how it contributes to the profitability of the firm. Reformulation of the financial statements—the lens on the business—brings the business activities into sharper focus. We understand the business better through the lens of reformulated financial statements. Reformulation is also a device for bringing considerably more detail into the statements, from the financial statements' footnotes and elsewhere, leading to a richer description of the firm than is presented in the published statements.

The Analyst's Checklist

After reading this chapter you should understand:

- Why reformulated income statements and balance sheets are desirable.

- How knowledge of the business is incorporated in reformulated statements.

- How operating and financing components of the two statements are identified.

- What assets and liabilities typically fall into operating and financing categories.

- Why income taxes are allocated to different parts of the income statement.

- What balance sheet and income statement ratios reveal.

After reading this chapter you should be able to:

- Reformulate income statements and balance sheets.

- Add footnote information to reformulated statements.

- Prepare a reformulated income statement on a comprehensive income basis.

- Allocate income taxes between operating income and financing income (or expense).

- Calculate effective tax rates for operations.

- Prepare and interpret a common-size, comparative analysis.

- Prepare and interpret a trend analysis.

- Calculate income statement ratios—including ratios that reveal the profitability of sales.

- Calculate balance sheet ratios—including financial leverage ratios and operating liability leverage ratios.

- Calculate summary profitability ratios.

- Calculate growth ratios.

The main aim of reformulating the balance sheet and income statements, however, is to discover the drivers of ROCE (return on common equity) and growth in preparation for forecasting and valuation. This discovery is made through ratio analysis, combined as always with a good knowledge of the business. This chapter introduces ratios calculated from these statements; these ratios become part of the comprehensive analysis of profitability and growth in Chapters 11 and 12.

REFORMULATION OF THE BALANCE SHEET

The typical balance sheet usually divides assets and liabilities into current and noncurrent (long-term) categories. For assets, this division is based on liquidity, and for liabilities, it is based on maturity, with the aim of giving an indication of the firm's ability to meet creditors' claims on cash. The analysis of credit risk in Chapter 19 will employ this division, but in Chapter 7 we overrode this classification with one that identifies the different sources of profitability, the operations and the financing activities. To discover a firm's ability to generate profits, we need to reformulate the balance sheet into operating and financing assets and liabilities.

Exhibit 9.1 lays out a typical balance sheet. It lists the standard line items you see in published statements. Balance sheets for specific firms do not include all these items, of course, and some items are often aggregated or grouped into "other assets" or "other liabilities" categories. In some industries you will see special line items that are not listed here.

EXHIBIT 9.1
The Typical GAAP Balance Sheet

Assets	Liabilities and Stockholders' Equity
Current assets:	Current liabilities:
Cash	Accounts payable
Cash equivalents	Accrued expenses
Short-term investments (marketable securities)	Deferred (unearned) revenues
Deposits and advances	Advances from customers
Accounts receivable (less allowances)	Warranty liabilities
Short-term notes receivable	Short-term notes payable
Other receivables	Short-term borrowings
Inventories	Deferred taxes (current portion)
Prepaid expenses	Current maturities of long-term debt
Deferred income taxes (current portion)	
Long-term assets:	Long-term liabilities:
Noncurrent receivables	Bank loans
Long-term debt investments	Bonds payable
Long-term equity investments—	Long-term notes payable
less than 20% ownership	Lease obligations
Long-term equity investments—	Commitments and contingencies
equity method	Deferred taxes
Property, plant, and equipment	Pension liabilities
(less accumulated depreciation)	Postemployment liabilities
Land	Minority interest
Buildings	
Equipment	
Leased assets	
Leasehold improvements	
Construction in progress	
Intangible assets	
Patents	
Licenses, franchises, and business rights	
Copyrights and trademarks	
Goodwill	
Software development costs	
Deferred taxes (noncurrent portion)	Preferred equity
Deferred charges	Common equity

    From Chapter 7 you'll remember that operating assets and liabilities are those involved in selling goods and services. Financing assets and liabilities are those that are involved in raising cash for operations and absorbing excess cash from operations. Before reformulating the statement, be sure to have an answer to the question: What business is the firm in? For it is the answer to this question that defines the operating assets and liabilities. Also keep in mind the parallel classification in the income statement (discussed later): Operating assets and liabilities generate operating income and financial assets and liabilities are those that produce financial income or incur financial expenses. See Box 9.1.

    The GAAP balance sheet is reformulated into operating and financial items as in Exhibit 9.2. This layout follows the template in Chapter 7.

Reformulating balance sheets involves distinguishing assets and liabilities that are used in operations—where the firm makes its money—from assets and liabilities that are used in financing—to raise cash for operations and temporarily store excess cash from operations. A firm "makes its money" by selling goods and services to customers, so identifying operating assets requires knowledge of goods and services the firm is delivering to customers.

Assets and liabilities with similar names on balance sheets may be financing items for one firm but operating items for another. Consider the following.

BANKS

Banks hold mainly (what look like) financial assets and financial liabilities in the form of customer deposits, bonds, and loans. But they make money from the spread between the interest they pay on their financial liabilities and the interest they earn on their financial assets. These apparent financial assets and liabilities are operating assets and liabilities.

CAPTIVE FINANCE SUBSIDIARIES

Automobile manufacturers like General Motors and Daimler-Chrysler consolidate finance subsidiaries into their financial statements. These finance subsidiaries hold (what look like) financial assets and liabilities. But they are used to support customers' purchases of automobiles, and often generous credit terms are used in promotions as effective price reductions. The finance subsidiaries are an integral part of operations and their assets and liabilities should be classified as such. The interest earned from the financing is operating income.

RETAILERS WITH CREDIT FACILITIES

Retailers make money from selling goods but often also make money from providing credit to customers. Accordingly, their interest income from the credit cards they issue and other credit facilities is operating income, and the financing receivables that generate the income are operating assets.

EXHIBIT 9.2

The Classification of Operating and Financing Items in the Balance Sheet

The Reformulated Balance Sheet

Assets	Liabilities and Stockholders' Equity
Financial assets:	Financial liabilities:
Cash equivalents	Short-term borrowings
Short-term investments	Current maturities of long-term debt
Short-term notes receivable (?)	Short-term notes payable (?)
Long-term debt investments	Long-term borrowing (bank loans, bonds payable, notes payable)
	Lease obligations
	Preferred stock
Operating assets:	Operating liabilities:
All else	All else
	Minority interest
	Common equity

Issues in Reformulating Balance Sheets

The layout of Exhibit 9.2 gives the classification of typical items found in balance sheets. Some issues arise:

- *Cash.* Working cash, or **operating cash,** which is needed as a buffer to pay bills as they fall due, is an operating asset. This is non–interest bearing, in the form of cash on hand or in a checking account. Just as the firm needs to invest in plant and equipment to carry out operations, it also has to invest in working cash. However, interest-bearing cash equivalents (investments with less than three months maturity) or cash invested in short-term securities are financial assets—they are investments of excess cash over that required to meet liquidity demands. Typically firms lump cash and cash equivalents together, so identifying the working cash is difficult. If the analyst knows the type of business well, she might impute the required working cash (as a percentage of sales, say) but, as many firms have cash swept daily into interest-bearing accounts, she would be safe in classifying all cash as a financial asset.

- *Short-term notes receivable.* Notes can be written by customers for goods received in trade, with or without interest, and, with interest, by borrowers. If the notes are temporary investments, treat them as financial assets. If they are trade notes, treat them as operating assets. Trade notes can be treated as financial assets if they bear the market rate of interest: The trade receivable has been converted to a financial claim. But if the firm is using credit to attract customers, treat the notes as operating assets: The firm is effectively offering a lower interest rate instead of a lower price for goods shipped. Correspondingly, the interest income should be classified as operating income, part of the income from selling goods with favorable credit terms. Finance receivables (for financing product sales) fall in the same category. See Box 9.1 again.

- *Debt investments.* For nonfinancial firms, investments in bonds and other interest-bearing investments are financial assets. Under FASB Statement No. 115, both current and noncurrent investments are marked to market (carried at market value on the balance sheet) if they are part of a trading portfolio or are available for sale, as we saw in the last chapter. They are recorded at cost if the firm intends to hold them to maturity. (The accounting for securities is covered in Accounting Clinic III in Chapter 8.) The footnotes give a schedule of all securities showing their historical costs and current fair values, along with the associated unrealized gains and losses which are income or expense in comprehensive income. If bonds are part of a trading portfolio, the firm is probably in the business of making money from bonds, so classify them as operating assets. Banks make money on the spread between borrowing and lending rates, so in their case, debt investments and liabilities are operating items.

- *Long-term equity investments.* Long-term equity investments (in the shares of other firms) are investments in the operations of other companies, and so they are classified as operating assets. If the holding is less than 20 percent of the shares of the other corporation, they are recorded on the balance sheet at market value if "available for sale" or at cost if "held to maturity." If the holding is greater than 20 percent and less than 50 percent, they are recorded as equity investments under the *equity method.* The equity method carries these investments at cost plus accumulated share of income of the subsidiary, less dividends paid by the subsidiary and any write-offs of the goodwill on purchase. If the holding is greater than 50 percent, **consolidation accounting** combines the financial statements of the related firms into one set of financial statements, so equity investments do not appear on the consolidated statement. Go to Accounting Clinic V.

  Equity investments in subsidiaries include the parent's share of net financial assets of subsidiaries. Thus they are investments in financial assets and obligations of these subsidiaries as well as their operating assets. Ideally we would like to go back into the subsidiaries' financial statements to sort out the operating and financial activities and divide the equity investments accordingly. This is often difficult to do if the subsidiary is not a public corporation, so as an expediency, treat the entire investment as an investment in an operating subsidiary.

- *Short-term equity investments.* Short-term marketable equity investments can be an exception to classifying equities as operating assets. If they are part of a trading

Accounting Clinic V

ACCOUNTING FOR EQUITY INVESTMENTS AND ACCOUNTING FOR BUSINESS COMBINATIONS

Accounting Clinic III covers the accounting for debt securities and equity securities that represent less than 20 percent ownership of another corporation. Accounting Clinic V deals with equity investments of 20 percent–50 percent ownership, where the *equity method* applies, and the

case of majority control (over 50 percent ownership), where *consolidation accounting* applies.

Firms acquire shares of other firms in mergers and acquisitions. Accounting Clinic V also covers the accounting for these *business combinations*, along with issues related to recognition, amortization, and the impairment of the goodwill acquired in business combinations.

portfolio, they are operating assets. If they are used to temporarily mop up excess cash, they are financial assets. These investments are marked to market.

- *Short-term notes payable.* Short-term notes can be written to generate cash, in which case they are financial obligations. However, notes also can be written to satisfy trade obligations, for the purchase of inventory, for example. If these are non–interest bearing, or carry an interest rate less than the market rate for this type of credit, classify them as operating liabilities; if they are interest-bearing at market rates, treat them as financial liabilities. A note written to satisfy a trade obligation results from operating activities but if it is interest-bearing at market rate, the operating liability (the accounts payable) has effectively been converted into a financial liability (the note payable). In the United States, GAAP requires the effective market rate of interest to be imputed on long-term notes payable (and receivable) so those items should be classified as financial obligations.

- *Accrued expenses.* These include liabilities to pay for the whole variety of operating expenses, including rent, insurance, wages, and taxes. Treat them as operating liabilities. But interest payable on financial obligations is a financing item.

- *Deferred revenues (Unearned revenues).* These include receipts from customers that are not yet recognized as revenue (because the firm has not performed on the sale) and obligations to complete performance such as warranties and guarantees. Treat them as operating liabilities.

- *Leases.* Leases that are capitalized are placed on the asset side of the balance sheet as a lease asset at the present value of the expected payouts under the lease agreement. The lease asset is an operating asset. The lease obligation is reported under liabilities and classified as a financial obligation in reformulated statements. Interest expense on the lease obligation is reported with other interest expenses in the income statement. Leases that are capitalized and placed on the balance sheet are called **capital leases.** Capital leases are essentially in-substance purchases granting the firm a right to use the asset for most of its useful life. Accordingly, if an asset satisfies criteria that indicate an in-substance purchase, the lease asset is treated similarly to any other property, plant, or equipment. And the obligation to service the lease is treated as if the firm had purchased the asset and borrowed to finance the purchase: The lease obligation is an effective loan to finance the purchase of the asset. Leases that are deemed not to be effective purchases are called **operating leases.** They do not appear on the balance sheet but the rent payments are included as rent expense in the income statement.

- *Deferred tax assets and liabilities* Deferred taxes arise almost always from accounting differences in calculating the operating income component of taxable income and reported book income. So they are operating assets or liabilities.

- *Dividends payable.* These are classified as shareholders' equity, not a liability, as explained in the last chapter.

- *Preferred stock.* From a common shareholders' focus, preferred stock are considered financial obligations.

- *"Other" items.* Balance sheets typically have a line for "other assets" and "other liabilities." The detail can be discovered from footnotes and sometimes from the management discussion and analysis (MD&A). If these sources prove fruitless, usually these items are considered operating. If any of the other liabilities are material amounts, firms are required to disclose them.

- *Minority interest.* It might be tempting to view minority interest in a consolidated subsidiary as a financial obligation from the common shareholders' point of view, an interest that has to be satisfied. But the **minority interest** is not an obligation, like debt, that is satisfied with cash generated from free cash flow. Rather it is an equity sharing in the results of the consolidated operations. In the reformulated statements treat it as a separate line item that shares with the common equity in the operating and financing assets and liabilities. The reformulated statement with minority interest has the following form: NOA – NFO = CSE + Minority interest.

Some people have trouble thinking of operating liabilities as part of operations and not part of the financial indebtedness. Indeed, you may have seen these included in debt and debt ratios in other books. As obligations to creditors, they are debt, and if we were making calculations to evaluate credit risk—or the ability to pay off debt—we would include these in relevant ratios (as in Chapter 19). However, our purpose here is to get a sense of operating profitability relative to the net assets put in place. And to the extent that a firm has operating liabilities, it reduces its net investment in operations, its net operating assets. Return on net operating assets (RNOA) compares operating income to the investment in net operating assets; to the extent that a firm can induce suppliers to give credit, this reduces the investment and increases the return on net operating assets. Just as firms lever up return on equity through financial liabilities, so they lever up return on operating assets with operating liabilities. The following examples illustrate:

- Dell Corporation is renowned in the computer business for its made-to-order system that keeps its investment in inventories low. Dell's fiscal 2002 balance sheet (in Chapter 2) reports $278 million in inventory, only 0.9 percent of sales.

  However, it also reports $5,075 million in accounts payable. Dell has managed to get material suppliers to give credit to "finance" the inventory (and more), so, in effect, Dell has negative investment in inventory. This generates value for shareholders as the shareholders do not need to use their funds to purchase inventories; indeed, creditors have supplied funds to finance other operating assets besides inventory. And shareholders need not service interest on financing debt.

- Oracle Corporation, the large software and information management firm, lists customer advances and unearned revenue of $1,276 million as a liability in its 2002 balance sheet.

This is cash that has been given to Oracle by customers in advance of receiving services from the firm. This cash generates shareholder value because it can be used to purchase operating assets for which shareholders would otherwise have to provide funds.

- General Motors, the automobile manufacturer, has a program to pay health benefits to employees after they retire. An amount of $34.5 billion was reported as a liability on its 2001 balance sheet for obligations under this benefit plan. The plan pays benefits later rather than using cash currently for wages that would be higher without the health benefits. The liability, like wages payable, arises from operations.

- Maytag Corporation, the appliance manufacturer, included sales warranties of $91.8 million in its accrued liabilities for 2001. These obligations to service sales effectively net against receivables and cash from the sales.

Exhibit 9.3 reproduces the published comparative balance sheets for Nike, Inc., for 1994–1996, along with reformulated balance sheets. Exhibit 9.4 reformulates Reebok's balance sheet. We introduced both of these firms in the last chapter. Notice several things about the reformulated statements (numbers below correspond to the numbers flagging items in the reformulated statements):

1. The reformulation maintains the balance sheet equation: CSE = NOA – NFO.

2. Net operating assets (NOA) is the difference between operating assets and operating liabilities.

3. Net financial obligations (NFO) is the difference between financial obligations and financial assets.

4. Cash and cash equivalents have been divided up between operating and financial assets.

5. Redeemable preferred stock is a financial obligation.

6. Minority interest in subsidiaries is not classified as either an operating or financing item on Reebok's balance sheet. Rather, as minorities share in both operating and financing assets and liabilities in subsidiaries, it is deducted from the net total for those activities in determining Reebok shareholders' share in the consolidated business. If the analyst has access to subsidiary financial statements, the allocation can be made or, if it is determined that the subsidiaries are likely to carry little net debt, minority interest can be classified as an operating item, thereby reducing the common shareholders' claim on net operating assets.

7. More information has been brought into the statements from the footnotes.

Reformulated balance sheets draw the following picture. Common shareholders' equity is represented as an investment in operations (net operating assets) less net debtholders' claim on those assets (net financial obligations). Net operating assets are net of the credit that suppliers and customers supply (operating liabilities), for this credit reduces the shareholders' investment in operations. Net financial obligations are net of financial assets, for financial assets are available to pay debt in satisfaction of the debtholders' claims. With this representation, the balance sheet is ready for an analysis of the profitability of operating and financing activities.

EXHIBIT 9.3   **GAAP Consolidated Balance Sheets and Reformulated Balance Sheets for Nike, Inc., 1994–1996.** The reformulated balance sheets reformat the GAAP statements into net operating assets (operating assets minus operating liabilities), net financial obligations (financial obligations minus financial assets), and common shareholders' equity (net operating assets minus net financial obligations).

NIKE, INC.
GAAP Balance Sheets
(in thousands)

	1996	May 31, 1995	1994
ASSETS			
Current assets:			
Cash and equivalents	$ 262,117	$ 216,071	$ 518,816
Accounts receivable, less allowance for doubtful accounts of $43,372, $32,663, and $28,291	1,346,125	1,053,237	703,682
Inventories (Note 2)	931,151	629,742	470,023
Deferred income taxes (Note 6)	93,120	72,657	37,603
Prepaid expenses	94,427	74,221	40,307
Total current assets	2,726,940	2,045,928	1,770,431
Property, plant, and equipment, net (Notes 3 and 5)	643,459	554,879	405,845
Identifiable intangible assets and goodwill (Note 1)	474,812	495,907	163,036
Deferred income taxes and other assets	106,417	46,031	34,503
Total assets	$3,951,628	$3,142,745	$2,373,815
LIABILITIES AND SHAREHOLDERS' EQUITY			
Current liabilities:			
Current portion of long-term debt (Note 5)	$ 7,301	$ 31,943	$ 3,857
Notes payable (Note 4)	445,064	397,100	127,378
Accounts payable (Note 4)	455,034	297,656	210,576
Accrued liabilities	480,407	345,224	181,889
Income taxes payable	79,253	35,612	38,287
Total current liabilities	1,467,059	1,107,535	561,987
Long-term debt (Notes 5 and 13)	9,584	10,565	12,364
Deferred income taxes (Note 6)	1,883	17,789	18,228
Other liabilities (Note 1)	41,402	41,867	39,987
Commitments and contingencies (Notes 11 and 14)	—	—	—
Redeemable preferred stock (Note 7)	300	300	300
Shareholders' equity (Note 8):			
Common Stock at stated value:			
Class A convertible: 51,120, and 51,790 shares outstanding	153	155	159
Class B: 92,509 and 91,100 shares outstanding	2,702	2,698	2,704
Capital in excess of stated value	154,833	122,436	108,284
Foreign currency translation adjustment	(16,501)	1,585	(15,123)
Retained earnings	2,290,213	1,837,815	1,644,925
Total shareholders' equity	2,431,400	1,964,689	1,740,949
Total liabilities and shareholders' equity	$3,951,628	$3,142,745	$2,373,815

Notes refer to notes to the published financial statements. Refer to the 1996 10-K.

(continued)

EXHIBIT 9.3   *(concluded)*

**Reformulated Balance Sheets
(in millions)**

	1996		1995		1994	
Net Operating Assets						
Operating assets						
Cash[1]		$ 27		$ 20		$ 15	**(4)**
Accounts receivable (less doubtful accounts of $43, $33, and $28)		1,346		1,053		704	
Inventories		931		630		470	
Prepaid expenses		94		74		40	
Property, plant, and equipment (net)		643		555		406	
Goodwill	$328		$330		$ 182		**(7)**
Trademarks and other intangibles	210		209		12		**(7)**
Accumulated amortization	(63)	475	(43)	496	(31)	163	**(7)**
Deferred income taxes and other assets		200		119		72	
		3,716		2,947		1,870	
Operating liabilities						
Accounts payable[2]	455		298		211		
Accrued liabilities	480		345		182		
Income taxes payable	79		36		38		
Deferred income taxes	2		18		18		
Other liabilities[3]	41	1,057	42	739	40	489	
		2,659		2,208		1,381	**(2)**
Net Financial Obligations						
Cash equivalents[1]	(235)		(196)		(503)		**(4)**
Current portion of long-term debt	7		32		4		
Notes payable[4]	446		397		127		
Long-term debt	10		11		12		
Redeemable preferred stock[5]	0	228	0	244	0	(360)	**(3)(5)**
Common Stockholders' Equity		2,431		1,964		1,741	**(1)**

[1]Cash and cash equivalents are split between operating cash and cash investments.
[2]Some accounts payable are interest bearing but this cannot be discovered.
[3]Other liabilities are primarily long-term deferred endorsement payments for promotions.
[4]Notes payable are interest bearing.
[5]Preferred stock is less than $0.5 million.

Some firms have financial assets in excess of financial obligations. Microsoft Corporation in Exhibit 9.5 is a case in point. In 2002, Microsoft has no financial debt but has considerable financial assets in the form of cash equivalents and short-term and long-term debt assets. The 2002 shareholders' equity of $52.180 billion is invested in $11.574 billion of net operating assets and $40.606 billion of net financial assets. Microsoft has generated considerable free cash flow from operations, which it has invested in Treasury bills and other interest-bearing investments. As in the case of a firm with net financial

EXHIBIT 9.4 **GAAP Balance Sheets and Reformulated Balance Sheets for Reebok International Ltd., 1994–1996**

REEBOK INTERNATIONAL LTD.
GAAP Balance Sheets
(in thousands)

	1996	December 31, 1995	1994
ASSETS			
Current assets:			
Cash and cash equivalents	$ 232,365	$ 80,393	$ 83,936
Accounts receivable, net of allowance for doubtful accounts ($43,527 and $46,401)	590,504	506,563	532,475
Inventory	544,522	635,012	624,625
Deferred income taxes	69,422	65,484	66,456
Prepaid expenses and other current assets	26,275	45,418	29,952
Total current assets	1,463,088	1,332,870	1,337,444
Property and equipment, net	185,292	192,033	164,848
Noncurrent assets:			
Intangibles, net of amortization	69,700	64,436	96,196
Deferred income taxes	7,850	5,455	2,910
Other	60,254	56,825	48,063
	137,804	126,716	147,169
Total assets	$1,786,184	$1,651,619	$1,649,461
LIABILITIES AND STOCKHOLDERS' EQUITY			
Current liabilities:			
Notes payable to banks	$ 32,977	$ 66,682	$ 63,837
Current portion of long-term debt	52,684	946	5,190
Accounts payable	196,368	166,037	170,622
Accrued expenses	169,344	144,585	157,479
Income taxes payable	65,588	47,956	102,392
Dividends payable		5,742	6,068
Total current liabilities	516,961	431,948	505,588
Long-term debt, net of current portion	854,099	254,178	131,799
Minority interest	33,890	31,081	21,569
Commitments and contingencies	—	—	—
Outstanding redemption value of equity put options	—	39,123	—
Stockholders' equity:			
Common stock, per value $.01; authorized 250,000,000 shares; issued 92,556,295 and 111,015,133 shares	926	1,096	169,125
Retained earnings	992,563	1,487,006	1,428,058
Less 36,716,227 and 36,210,902 shares in treasury at cost	(617,620)	(603,241)	(603,241)
Unearned compensation	(283)	(1,208)	(2,598)
Foreign currency translation adjustment	5,648	11,636	(839)
Total stockholders' equity	381,234	895,289	990,505
Total liabilities and stockholders' equity	$1,786,184	$1,651,619	$1,649,461

(continued)

EXHIBIT 9.4 *(concluded)*

Reformulated Balance Sheets
(in millions)

	1996		1995		1994		
Net Operating Assets							
Operating assets							
Cash[1]		$ 12		$ 8		$ 8	**(4)**
Accounts receivable (less doubtful accounts of $44, $46, and $45)		591		507		532	
Inventory		545		635		625	
Deferred taxes		77		71		69	
Prepaid expenses		26		45		30	
Property, plant, and equipment		185		192		165	
Goodwill	$ 34		$ 152				**(7)**
Trademarks and other intangibles	116		116				**(7)**
Accumulated amortization	(80)	70	(204)	64		96	**(7)**
Other assets[2]		60		57		50	
Operating assets		1,566		1,579		1,575	
Operating liabilities							
Accounts payable	196		166		171		
Accrued expenses	169		145		157		
Income taxes payable	66	431	48	359	102	430	
		1,135		1,220		1,145	**(2)**
Net Financial Obligations[3]							
Cash equivalents[1]	(220)		(72)		(76)		**(4)**
Notes payable	33		67		64		
Current portion of long-term debt	53		1		5		
Long-term debt	854		252		131		
Put option liability		720	39	287		124	**(3)**
CSE and Minority Interest		415		933		1,021	
Minority interest		34		31		22	**(6)**
Common Stockholders' Equity[2]		382		902		999	**(1)**

[1]Cash and cash equivalents divided between operating cash and cash investments.
[2]Common stockholders' equity includes dividends payable and excludes unearned compensation (which is added to other operating assets). See reformulated equity statement in Chapter 8.
[3]Excludes dividends payable, which is included in stockholders' equity.

obligations, the reformulated statement separates the assets and liabilities that are associated with operating activities from those that are associated with financial activities—in this case, assets that are storing excess cash. Note that equity investments are classified as operating items, and debt investments are classified as financing items, with the exception of convertible preferred debt in AT&T in connection with an (operating) investment in broadband.

EXHIBIT 9.5
Reformulated
Balance Sheet for
Microsoft
Corporation, 2002

MICROSOFT CORPORATION
Reformulated Comparative Balance Sheet, 2002
(in millions of dollars)

		Year ending June 30		
		2002		**2001**
Net Operating Assets				
Operating assets				
Working cash[1]		$ 50		$ 50
Accounts receivable, net		5,129		3,671
Inventories		673		83
Deferred income taxes		2,112		1,522
Property and equipment, net		2,268		2,309
Equity investments[2]		9,151		8,780
Convertible preferred debt[3]		3,036		3,925
Goodwill		1,426		1,511
Intangible assets, net		243		401
Other assets		2,952		3,372
		27,040		25,624
Operating liabilities				
Accounts payable	1,208		$1,188	
Accrued compensation	1,145		742	
Income taxes payable	2,022		1,468	
Unearned revenue	7,743		5,614	
Preferred income taxes	398		409	
Other liabilities	2,950	15,466	2,120	11,541
		11,574		14,083
Net financial assets				
Cash equivalents	2,966		3,872	
Short-term investments	35,636		27,678	
Long-term debt investments	2,004	40,606	1,656	33,206
Common Stockholders' Equity		52,180		47,289

[1]Cash and cash equivalents split between working cash and financial assets.
[2]Equity and other investments on GAAP statement split between equity and debt investments (financial assets), based on footnote information.
[3]Convertible debt of AT&T Corp., in connection with investment in broadband.

REFORMULATION OF THE INCOME STATEMENT

The income statement reports the profits and losses that the net operating assets and net financial assets have produced. The presentation of the GAAP statement varies but the typical line items found in the income statement are given in Exhibit 9.6.

The reformulated statement groups these items into operating and financing categories. However, it also includes dirty-surplus items removed from common equity to produce a statement of comprehensive operating income and comprehensive financial income, as in Exhibit 9.7. You see that the operating income typically reported is incomplete, hence the adjustments. Similarly, net interest expense usually reported does not capture all of the financing costs, and the adjustments are indicated. This statement describes financing flows as net expenses, but they are, of course, net financial income if financial assets are greater than financial obligations.

EXHIBIT 9.6
The Typical GAAP
Income Statement

Net sales (sales minus allowances)
+ Other revenue (royalties, rentals, license fees)
– Cost of sales
= Gross margin

– Marketing and advertising expenses
– General expenses
– Administrative expenses
– Pension expense
± Special items and nonrecurring items
    Restructuring charges
    Merger expenses
    Gains and losses on asset sales
    Asset impairments
    Litigation settlements
    Environmental remediation
– Research and development expense
= Operating income

+ Interest revenue
– Interest (expense)
± Realized gains and losses on securities
± Unrealized gains and losses on trading securities
+ Equity share in subsidiary income

= Income before tax
– Income taxes

= Income before extraordinary items and discontinued operations
± Discontinued operations
± Extraordinary items
    Gains and losses on debt retirement
    Abnormal gains and losses in operations
± Cumulative effect of an accounting change
– Minority interest
= (Net) income

Tax Allocation

The two components of income, operating and financing, both have tax consequences. Only one income tax number is reported in income statements, so this number must be allocated to the two components to put both on an after-tax basis. Referred to as **tax allocation,** this is done by first calculating the tax benefit of deducting interest expense on debt for tax purposes and allocating it to operating income. The tax benefit—sometimes referred to as the **tax shield** from debt—is calculated as

$$\text{Tax benefit} = \text{Net interest expense} \times \text{Tax rate}$$

and the after-tax net interest expense is

$$\text{After-tax net interest expense} = \text{Net interest expense} \times (1 - \text{Tax rate})$$

Firms are taxed on a schedule of tax rates, depending on the size of their income. The tax rate used in the calculation is the **marginal tax rate,** the highest rate at which income is taxed, for interest expense reduces taxes at this rate. This marginal rate is not to be confused with the **effective tax rate,** which is tax expense divided by income before tax in the income statement (and incorporates any tax benefits the firm generates). The effective

EXHIBIT 9.7
The Classification of Operating and Financing Items in the Income Statement

Reformulated Income Statement

Operating revenue as reported, minus any interest income included
− Operating expenses as reported
+ Share of subsidiary income
± Realized and unrealized gains and losses on equity securities
± Discontinued operations
± Cumulative effects of an accounting change
± Abnormal gains and losses in operations
± <u>Dirty-surplus operating items in Table 8.1</u>
= Operating income before tax

− Tax on operating income:
  + Tax as reported
  <u>+ Tax benefit from net interest expenses</u>
= Operating income after tax

− Net financial expenses after tax
  + Interest expense
  <u>− Interest revenue</u>
  ± Realized gains and losses on financial assets
  = Net interest expense before tax
  <u>− Tax benefit from net interest expenses</u>
  = Net interest expenses after tax
  ± Gains and losses on debt retirement
  ± Dirty-surplus financial items in Table 8.1 (including preferred dividends)
− Minority interest
= <u>Comprehensive income</u>

tax rate is reported in footnotes, but it is not to be used for the tax allocation. The marginal tax rate usually can be calculated from the notes to the statements. With little gradation in tax rates in the United States, the marginal rate is usually the maximum statutory rate for federal and state taxes combined. Foreign statutory tax rates are used if a multinational firm issues debt in another country and receives a tax deduction for interest paid on the debt in that country.

Without the tax benefit of debt, taxes on operating income would be higher, so the amount of the benefit that reduces the net interest expense is allocated to operating income. Thus the tax on operating income is

Tax on operating income = Tax expense as reported + (Net interest expense × Tax rate)

If there is net interest income (more financial assets than financial obligations), then the financial activities attract tax rather than reduce it, and this tax reduces the tax on operating activities. In both cases, the idea is to calculate after-tax operating income that is insensitive to the financing activities: What would after-tax operating income be if there were no financing activities? This provides a measure of the profitability from operations that takes into account the tax consequences of conducting operations.

The one circumstance where this tax calculation is not done is when the firm cannot get the benefit of tax deduction for interest expense because it has losses for tax purposes. In this case the marginal tax rate is zero. But this is not common in the United States. A net operating loss (or NOL) for tax purposes can be carried back and deducted from taxable income in the previous two years or carried forward to income for 20 future years. So a firm loses the tax benefit only if the loss cannot be absorbed into taxable income over the carryback and carryforward periods.

Accounting Clinic VI

ACCOUNTING FOR INCOME TAXES

Income taxes are recorded by matching taxes with the income that draws the tax, so the analyst understands the after-tax consequences of earnings income (or losses). As the income may not be taxed (on the firm's tax return) at the same time as it is reported (in the income statement), this matching leads to deferred tax liabilities and deferred tax assets.

Accounting Clinic VI takes you through the details of deferred tax accounting and covers other tax issues such as operating loss carryforwards and valuation allowances against deferred tax assets. It also shows how taxes are allocated over various components of income in reported financial statements.

Preferred dividends typically are not deductible in calculating taxes, so no benefit arises. An exception is preferred dividends paid to an ESOP for which the tax benefit is recognized as a dirty-surplus item and brought into the income statement. In a recent innovation, firms issue preferred stock through a wholly owned trust from which firms borrow the proceeds of the issue. In the consolidation of the trust into the firm's accounts, the firm gets the tax benefits of interest paid to the trust and recognizes the preferred dividends paid by the trust. This effectively gives the firm a tax benefit for the preferred dividends paid.

GAAP statements report other dirty-surplus items and extraordinary items net of tax (and reduce reported tax expense by the amount allocated to these items). These items thus already incorporate the tax they attract.

The tax allocation produces a revised effective tax rate that applies to the operations:

$$\text{Effective tax rate for operations} = \frac{\text{Tax on operating income}}{\substack{\text{Operating income before tax, equity income,} \\ \text{and extraordinary and dirty-surplus items}}}$$

The benefits of tax planning (from using investment and depreciation tax allowances and tax credits and utilizing loss carryforwards, for example) arise from operations, and this measure gives a sharper measure of those benefits. As income from equity in subsidiaries, extraordinary items, and dirty-surplus items is reported after tax, the denominator excludes these income items. Accounting Clinic VI deals with the accounting for income taxes.

Issues in Reformulating Income Statements

Apart from the tax allocation, the reformulating of the income statement, as with the balance sheet, is a mechanical reclassification exercise. But, as with the balance sheet, the analyst must know the business. Interest income is usually earned on financial assets, but interest income on a finance receivable from financing customer purchases is operating income. The following issues arise in the reformulation:

- Lack of disclosure is often a problem:
  The share of income of a subsidiary may include both financing income and operating income, but the two components are often not identifiable. As the investment in the subsidiary in the balance sheet is identified as an operating item, so should this corresponding income statement item.

Dividing currency translation gains and losses into financing and operating components is often difficult.

Detailing some expenses is often frustrating. In particular, selling, administrative, and general expenses are usually a large number with little explanation provided in the footnotes.

Interest income is often lumped together with "other income" from operations.

- Abnormal gains and losses in extraordinary items are, along with income from discontinued operations, operating items, but gains and losses from debt retirement, also in extraordinary items, are financing items.

- Under GAAP, interest that finances construction is capitalized into the cost of assets on the balance sheet. It is treated as a construction cost just like the labor and materials that go into the asset. This accounting practice confuses operating and financing activities; labor and material costs are investments in assets, and interest costs are costs of financing assets. The result may be that little interest expense appears in the income statement for debt on the balance sheet. But it is difficult to unscramble this capitalized interest: It is depreciated, along with other construction costs, through to the income statement and so is hard to trace. As the depreciation expense that includes interest is an operating expense, the practice also distorts the operating profitability.

- Reformulated statements can be prepared for segments of the firm—from the detail provided in the footnotes—to reveal more of the operations.

Exhibit 9.8 gives the GAAP comparative income statement for Nike, Inc., for 1996, along with the reformulated statement. Exhibit 9.9 reformulates Reebok's income statement. Note the following in the reformulated statement (numbers flag items in the exhibit):

1. Dirty-surplus items have been brought into the statement so the "bottom line" is the comprehensive income that was calculated in the last chapter.

2. The reformulation distinguishes operating income that comes from sales from operating income that does not come from sales, with taxes allocated to both components. (The nonrecurring charges from restructurings draw tax benefits, but currency translations are already reported after tax.) This distinction gives a clean measure of the profit margin from sales and also a clean measure of the effective tax rate on operating income.

3. Taxes have been allocated using federal and state statutory rates, 35 percent for the federal rate plus the state rate: The rates are ascertained from the tax footnote. Nike's effective tax rate on operating income for 1996 is 38.5 percent ($355/922 = 38.5\%$) while Reebok's is 35.1% ($93/265 = 35.1\%$).

4. Detail on expenses has been discovered in the footnotes. However, more detail on the large administrative and general expenses is not available. You will often be frustrated by such a lack of disclosure.

5. Minority interest in income (in Reebok's income statement) has not been divided over operating and financing income. The allocation should be made if one has access to the financial statements of the subsidiaries in which the minority has an interest, in order to determine the type of income in which the minority has interest. If the subsidiary is deemed to have little financing activities, minority interest income can be deducted from operating income.

EXHIBIT 9.8 **GAAP Consolidated Statements of Income and Reformulated Income Statements for Nike, Inc., 1994–1996** The reformulated statement reformats the GAAP statement into operating income (operating revenue minus operating expense) and net financial expense (financial expense minus financial income) and adds dirty-surplus income items.

NIKE, INC.
GAAP Income Statements (in thousands, except per-share data)

	Year Ended May		
	1996	1995	1994
Revenues	$6,470,625	$4,760,834	$3,789,668
Costs and expenses:			
Costs of sales	3,906,746	2,865,280	2,301,423
Selling and administrative	1,588,612	1,209,760	974,099
Interest expense (Notes 4 and 5)	39,498	24,208	15,282
Other income/expense, net (Notes 1, 9 and 10)	36,679	11,722	8,270
	5,571,535	4,110,970	3,299,074
Income before income taxes	899,090	649,864	490,594
Income taxes (Note 6)	345,900	250,200	191,800
Net income	$ 553,190	$ 399,664	$ 298,794
Net income per common share (Note 1)	$ 3.77	$ 2.72	$ 1.98

Notes refer to notes in the published statements. Refer to 1996 10-K.

Reformulated Income Statements
(in millions)

	1996		1995		1994		
Operating Income							
Revenues		$6,471		$4,761		$3,790	
Cost of sales		3,907		2,865		2,301	
Gross margin		2,564		1,896		1,489	
Operating expenses							
Administrative expenses	$977		$730		$614		
Advertising[1]	643		495		373		**(4)**
Amortization of intangibles[2]	22	1,642	13	1,238	8	995	**(4)**
Operating income from sales (before tax)		922		658		494	
Taxes							
Tax as reported	346		250		192		
Tax on other operating income			4		3		
Tax on financial items[3]	9	355	(1)	253	(2)	193	**(3)**
Operating income from sales		567		405		301	**(2)**
Other operating income (expense)							
Nonrecurring charge[2]			(11)		(7)		
Tax on other items			4		3		
			(7)		(4)		
Currency translations	(18)	(18)	16	9	(7)	(11)	**(1)(2)**
Operating income		549		414		290	

(continued)

EXHIBIT 9.8 *(concluded)*

	1996		1995		1994		
Financing Expense (Income)							
Interest expense	39		24		15		
Interest income[2]	(16)	23	(27)	(3)	(19)	(4)	
Tax effect[3]	(9)		1		2		
Net interest expense	14		(2)		(2)	**(3)**	
Preferred dividends	(0)		(0)		(0)	**(1)**	
	14		(2)		(2)		
Comprehensive Income to Common	535		416		292	**(1)**	

[1]Broken out from selling and administrative expenses in published income statement (from footnote information).
[2]Included in "other expense" in income statement. The nonrecurring charges in 1995 and 1994 relate to shutdown of certain facilities.
[3]Statutory tax rate was 38.5%, 38.5%, and 39.1% in 1996, 1995, and 1994, respectively, including both federal and state taxes.

EXHIBIT 9.9 GAAP Statements of Income and Reformulated Income Statements for Reebok International Ltd., 1994–1996

REEBOK INTERNATIONAL LTD.
GAAP Income Statements (in thousands except per-share data)

	Year Ended December		
	1996	**1995**	**1994**
Net sales	$3,478,604	$3,481,450	$3,280,418
Other income	4,325	3,126	7,165
	3,482,929	3,484,576	3,287,583
Costs and expenses:			
Cost of sales	2,144,422	2,114,084	1,966,138
Selling, general, and administrative	1,065,792	999,731	889,590
Special charges	—	72,098	—
Amortization of intangibles	3,410	4,067	4,345
Interest expense	42,246	25,725	16,515
Interest income	(10,609)	(7,103)	(6,373)
	3,245,261	3,208,602	2,870,215
Income before taxes and minority interest	237,668	275,974	417,368
Income taxes	84,083	99,753	153,994
Income before minority interest	153,585	176,221	263,374
Minority interest	14,635	11,423	8,896
Net income	$ 138,950	$ 164,798	$ 254,478
Net income per common share	$ 2.00	$ 2.07	$ 3.02

(continued)

EXHIBIT 9.9   *(concluded)*

Reformulated Income Statements

	1996		1995		1994		
Operating Income							
Sales		$3,479		$3,481		$3,280	
Cost of sales		2,144		2,114		1,966	
Gross margin		1,335		1,367		1,314	
Operating expenses							
Administrative expenses	$864		$842		$727		
Advertising[1]	202		158		163		**(4)**
Amortization of intangibles	4	1,070	4	1,004	3	893	**(4)**
Operating income from sales (before tax)		265		363		421	
Taxes							
Tax as reported	84		99		154		
Tax on other operating income	(2)		25		(3)		
Tax on financial items[3]	11	93	7	131	4	155	**(3)**
Operating income from sales		172		232		266	**(2)**
Other operating income (expense)							
Other income	4		3		7		
Nonrecurring charge[2]	___		(72)				
	4		(69)		7		
Tax on other items	(2)		25		(3)		
	2		(44)		4		
Currency translations	(6)	(4)	12	(32)	12	16	**(1)(2)**
Operating income		168		200		282	
Financing Expense (Income)							
Interest expense	42		26		17		
Interest income	(11)	31	(7)	19	(6)	11	
Tax effect[3]		(11)		(7)		(4)	**(3)**
Net interest expense		20		12		7	
Gain from expired put options		(40)		3		___	**(1)**
		(20)		9		7	
Minority interest		15		11		9	
Comprehensive Income to Common		173		180		266	**(1)**

[1]Broken out from selling and administrative expenses in published income statement.
[2]The charge in 1995 is due to consolidation and streamlining of facilities and to the sale of the Avia subsidiary.
[3]Marginal tax rate was 35.4%, 36.2%, and 36.9% for 1996, 1995, and 1994, respectively, including both federal and state taxes.

The reformulation of Nike's financial statements is continued on the BYOAP feature on the book's website. See Box 9.2.

Exhibit 9.10 presents reformulated income statements for Microsoft that correspond to the reformulated balance sheets in Exhibit 9.5. The GAAP income statement is given at the top of the exhibit. A line for "operating income" is identified in the GAAP statement, followed by losses on equity investments under the equity method and "investment income." Microsoft, as we observed in the balance sheet, holds considerable financial assets, and the interest on these assets is included in investment income. However, investment income also mixes in gains and losses on its (operating) equity investments. The reformulated statement, with the help of footnote information, sorts out the income into operating and financing components; further, it distinguishes operating income that

The reformulation of Nike's 1996 financial statements in this chapter begins an analysis of the firm that continues on the **Build Your Own Analysis Product (BYOAP)** on the book's website. By going to this feature, you can trace Nike over an extended period, so prepare yourself to carry out a valuation in 2002 with a considerable history behind you. Below are some summary numbers from the reformulated statements on BYOAP (in millions of dollars).

	2002	2001	2000	1999	1998	1997	1996
Sales	9,893	9,489	8,995	8,777	9,553	9,187	6,471
Operating income (after tax)	644	577	557	449	410	797	549
Comprehensive income	623	549	537	430	384	777	535
Net operating assets	4,400	4,517	4,402	3,993	4,042	3,674	2,659
Net financial obligations	561	1,022	1,254	658	780	518	228
Common shareholders' equity	3,839	3,495	3,148	3,335	3,262	3,156	2,431

EXHIBIT 9.10

GAAP Income Statements and Reformulated Statements for Microsoft Corporation, 2001–2002

MICROSOFT CORPORATION
GAAP Income Statements
(in millions)

	Year Ended June 30	
	2002	2001
Revenue	$28,365	. $25,296
Operating expenses:		
Cost of revenue	5,191	3,455
Research and development	4,307	4,379
Sales and marketing	5,407	4,885
General and administrative	1,550	857
Total operating expenses	16,455	13,576
Operating income	11,910	11,720
Losses on equity investments and other	(92)	(159)
Investment income (loss)	(305)	(36)
Income before income taxes	11,513	11,525
Provision for income taxes	3,684	3,804
Income before accounting change	7,829	7,721
Cumulative effect of accounting change (net of tax)		(375)
Net income	$ 7,829	$ 7,346

(continued)

EXHIBIT 9.10   *(concluded)*

Reformulated Income Statements
(in millions)

		Year ended June 30		
		2002		**2001**
Revenue		$28,365		$25,296
Operating expenses:				
Cost of revenue		5,191		3,455
Research and development		4,307		4,379
Sales and marketing		5,407		4,885
General and administrative		1,550		857
		16,455		13,576
Operating income from sales, before tax		11,910		11,720
Tax as reported	$3,684		$3,804	
Tax on other operating income	872		756	
Tax on financing income	(758)	3,798	(743)	3,817
Operating income from sales, after tax		8,112		7,903
Investment income in income statement:[1]				
Dividends	357		377	
Realized gains on sales of investments	2,121		3,003	
Permanent impairment of investments	(4,323)		(4,804)	
Unrealized losses on derivatives	(480)	(2,325)	(592)	(2,016)
Tax on investment income (at 37.5%)[2]		872		756
		(1,453)		(1,260)
Investment income in equity statement (after tax):				
Unrealized loss on convertible debt		—		(829)
Gains (losses) on derivatives		(91)		634
Unrealized losses on equity investments		(281)		(707)
Total investment income		(1,825)		(2,162)
Losses in equity subsidiaries		(92)		(159)
Currency translation and other		82		(39)
Cumulative effect of accounting change		—		(450)
Total other income		(1,835)		(2,810)
Total operating income		6,277		5,093
Net financing income				
Interest income[3]		1,762		1,808
Realized gains on short-term investments[1]		258		172
		2,020		1,980
Tax at 37.5%[4]		758		743
		1,262		1,237
Financing income in equity statement (after tax):				
Unrealized gain on financial assets		286		76
Total financing income		1,548		1,313
Comprehensive income		$ 7,825		$ 6,406

[1]Included in investment income is the GAAP statement; details from footnotes.
[2]Losses on investments draw a tax deduction.
[3]Interest income is included in investment income in the GAAP statement.
[4]With net financing income, financing activities draw further taxes rather than a tax benefit.

comes from sales from operating income that comes from Microsoft's portfolio of equity investments. The reformulated statement is, of course, on a comprehensive income basis so that both operating income and financing income in the equity statement have been brought into the reformulated income statement.

As Microsoft has net financing income (rather than expense), the financing activities attract tax (rather than reduce it), so the tax allocation to operating income reduces the tax on operating income. The net investment loss draws a tax benefit, and the allocation of this benefit back to operating income from sales recognizes that taxes would have been higher but for the investment losses. (Items from the equity statement are net of tax in that statement.)

The reformulated statement in Exhibit 9.10 draws the following picture. Microsoft is involved in software sales, runs an equity investment portfolio (with less than 20 percent ownership in other firms), and invests in subsidiaries with greater than 20 percent owner-ship where they are deemed to have substantial influence on the operations. The after-tax income for the three operating activities is identified, and considerably more information on the performance of the investments is added. Not only are the realized gains and losses in the GAAP income statement recognized, but so are the unrealized gains and losses from the equity statement. Therefore, one can understand the overall performance of the portfolio, irrespective of whether the firm sold investments or not. (The investor is not deceived, therefore, by a firm that engages in "cherry picking"—selling off investments that have appreciated so as to increase net income, but leaving unrealized losses in the eq-uity statement.) In addition to these operations, Microsoft invests excess cash in financial assets, and the income from these assets is identified (and not commingled with the re-sults of operations).

COMPARATIVE ANALYSIS OF THE BALANCE SHEET AND INCOME STATEMENT

To make judgments about a firm's performance the analyst needs benchmarks. Bench-marks are established by reference to other firms (usually in the same industry) or to the same firm's past history. Comparison to other firms is called *cross-sectional analysis*. Comparison to a firm's own history is called *time-series analysis*. Financial statements are prepared for cross-sectional comparisons using the techniques of *common-size analy-sis*. The statements are compared over time using *trend analysis*.

Common-Size Analysis

Common-size analysis is simply a standardization of line items to eliminate the effect of size. Line items are expressed per dollar of an attribute that reflects the scale of opera-tions. However, if that attribute is chosen carefully, and if reformulated statements are used, the scaling will reveal pertinent features of a firm's operations. And when com-pared across firms, or across time, common-size statements will identify unusual features that require further investigation.

Common-Size Income Statements

Exhibit 9.11 places Nike's reformulated 1996 income statement on a common-size basis and compares the statement to that of Reebok. Revenues and expenses, along with net comprehensive income, are expressed as a percentage of the revenue.

EXHIBIT 9.11
Comparative
Common-size Income
Statements for Nike,
Inc., and Reebok
International Ltd. for
1996. Dollar amounts
in millions.
Percentages are per
dollar of sales.
Common-size income
statements reveal the
profitability of sales
and the effect of each
expense item on the
profitability of sales.

	Nike		Reebok	
	$	%	$	%
Revenue	6,471	100.0	3,479	100.0
Cost of sales	3,907	60.4	2,144	61.6
Gross margin	2,564	39.6	1,335	38.4
Operating expenses				
Administrative	977	15.1	864	24.8
Advertising	643	9.9	202	5.8
Amortization	22	0.3	4	0.1
Operating income from sales				
(before tax)	922	14.2	265	7.6
Tax on operating income from sales	355	5.5	93	2.7
Other operating income from sales				
(after tax)	567	8.8	172	4.9
Other operating income	(18)	(0.3)	(4)	(0.1)
Operating income	549	8.5	168	4.8
Net financing expense (income)	14	0.2	(20)	(0.6)
Minority interest			15	0.4
Comprehensive income	535	8.3	173	5.0

The comparative common-size statements reveal two things:

• How firms do business differently and the different structure of revenues and expenses that result. These two firms have similar sources of revenue and expense, as valid comparables should. Looking at operating expenses, the firms have similar cost structures, but Nike has the lowest cost of sales per dollar of revenue (60.4 percent). Nike also maintains the lowest administrative costs at 15.1 percent of sales, but it has higher advertising costs (9.9 percent).

• Operating profitability per dollar of sales. As each operating item is divided through by sales revenue, the common-size number indicates the proportion of each dollar of sales the item represents. Thus the number for an operating expense is the percentage of sales that is absorbed by the expense, and the number for operating income is the percentage of sales that ends up in profit. The latter is particularly important:

Operating profit margin from sales = Operating income from sales (after tax)/Sales

This ratio is usually referred to simply as the *profit margin,* or more simply as the *margin.* Nike's profit margin is 8.8 percent, compared with a 4.9 percent margin for Reebok. Ratios also can be calculated for operating income before tax and for total operating income, as in the exhibit. Reviewing the expense ratios, we see that Reebok had a lower profit margin than Nike primarily because of cost of sales and administrative expenses. These differences highlight features of the business that need to be investigated. They direct the analyst to find information that will explain the differences and so explain why these firms might be valued differently.

The final comprehensive income number, expressed as a percentage of sales, is the (comprehensive) *net profit margin.* The comparison of this number to the operating profit

EXHIBIT 9.12
Comparative
Common-size
Balance Sheets for
Nike, Inc., and
Reebok International
Ltd. for 1996. Dollar
amounts in millions.
Common-size balance
sheets reveal the
percentage makeup of
operating assets,
operating liabilities,
financial assets, and
financial liabilities.

	Nike		Reebok	
	$	%	$	%
Operating assets				
Cash	27	0.7	12	0.8
Accounts renewable	1,346	36.2	591	37.7
Inventories	931	25.1	545	34.8
Prepaid expenses	94	2.5	26	1.7
Property, plant, and equipment	643	17.3	185	11.8
Goodwill	328	8.8	34	2.2
Trademarks and other intangibles	210	5.7	116	7.4
Accumulated amortization	(63)	(1.7)	(80)	(5.1)
Deferred taxes and other assets	200	5.4	137	8.7
	3,716	100.0	1,566	100.0
Operating liabilities				
Accounts payable	455	43.0	196	45.5
Accrued liabilities	480	45.4	169	39.2
Income taxes payable	79	7.5	66	15.3
Deferred taxes and other	43	4.0	—	—
	1,057	100.0	431	100.0
Net financial obligations				
Cash equivalents	(235)	(103.1)	(220)	(30.6)
Notes payable	7	3.1	33	4.6
Current portion of long-term debt	446	195.6	53	7.4
Long-term debt	10	4.4	854	118.6
Redeemable preferred stock	0	0.0	—	—
	228	100.0	720	100.0
Minority interest			34	
Common stockholders' equity	2,431		381	

margin reveals how much the firms increased or decreased their profits through financing activities. Nike earned a net 8.3 cents for every dollar of sales, compared to 5.0 cents for Reebok.

Common-Size Balance Sheets

Common-size balance sheets often standardize on total assets, but a more informative approach, using reformulated statements, standardizes operating assets and liabilities on their totals and financial assets and liabilities on their totals. The comparative common-size balance sheets for the two firms are shown in Exhibit 9.12. The percentages describe the relative composition of the net assets in the operating and financing activities. You can easily spot the differences when the balance sheets are in this form; try comparing the relative amounts of investments in accounts receivable, inventory, property, plant and equipment, and so on, for the two companies.

Trend Analysis *Horizontal*

Exhibit 9.13 presents trends for Nike, Inc., from 1996 to 2000. The numbers on which the analysis is based are in the BYOAP tool on the text's website. See Box 9.2. **Trend analysis** expresses financial statement items as an index relative to a base year. In Nike's case, the index is 100 for the base year of 1995.

EXHIBIT 9.13   **Trend Analysis of Selected Financial Statement Items for Nike, Inc., 1996–2000. Base = 100 for 1995**
Trend analysis reveals the growth or decline in financial statement items over time.

	2000	1999	1998	1997	1996	Base in 1995 ($ millions)
Sales	188.9	184.3	200.7	193.0	135.9	4,761
Cost of sales	188.6	191.7	211.7	192.1	136.4	2,865
Gross margin	189.4	173.2	183.9	194.3	135.2	1,896
Operating expenses	213.5	198.8	215.0	190.3	132.6	1,238
Operating income from sales (before tax)	144.1	125.0	125.6	201.7	140.2	658
Taxes	138.7	128.4	126.8	202.3	140.3	253
Operating income from sales (after tax)	147.5	122.8	124.9	201.4	140.1	405
Operating income	134.5	108.3	99.1	192.4	132.7	414
Comprehensive income	129.1	103.3	92.2	186.8	128.6	416
Balance Sheet						
Accounts receivable	148.8	146.3	159.0	166.6	127.8	1,053
Inventories	229.5	185.5	221.7	212.5	147.9	630
Property, plant, and equipment	285.3	228.1	207.8	166.2	115.9	555
Intangible assets	82.8	86.0	87.9	93.6	95.6	496
Deferred taxes and other assets	317.4	345.4	363.6	234.8	167.6	119
Operating assets	192.7	173.0	180.4	170.6	127.4	2,947
Accounts payable	182.5	158.9	198.6	230.6	152.7	298
Accrued liabilities	180.3	160.3	176.4	165.4	139.1	345
Other liabilities	114.9	83.1	84.6	100.0	127.7	96
Operating liabilities	172.7	149.7	172.4	183.2	143.2	739
Net operating assets	199.4	180.8	183.0	166.4	120.4	2,208
Net financial obligations	514.0	269.6	319.7	212.2	93.4	244
Common shareholders' equity	160.3	169.8	166.1	160.7	123.8	1,964

Trend analysis gives a picture of how financial statement items have changed over time. The index for net operating assets indicates whether the firm is growing investments in operations, and at what rate, or is liquidating. The index for common stockholders' equity tracks the growth or decline in the owners' investment. And the index for net financial obligations tracks the net indebtedness. Similarly, the indexes for the income statement track the income and the factors that affect it. Of particular interest are sales, operating income, and comprehensive income.

The picture drawn for Nike is one of fast-growing sales of 88.9 percent over the five years, resulting in growth in operating income from sales, after tax, of 47.5 percent and growth in comprehensive income of 29.1 percent. The indexes for specific line items indicate where the growth has come from, and year-to-year changes indicate the periods that have contributed most to growth. For Nike, growth in operating expenses exceeded growth in sales and gross margin over the period, leading to a lower growth rate in operating income and comprehensive income than in sales. Further, growth rates are considerably higher during the earlier years and slow significantly over the 1998–2000 period. From the balance sheet trends, we observe that net operating assets have grown a little faster than sales but that inventories and property, plant, and equipment have grown at a considerably faster rate, indicating that, as time has evolved, fewer sales have been earned for each dollar invested in these assets.

Year-to-year changes in the index represent year-to-year growth rates. For example, Nike's 1997 sales growth rate was (193.0 − 135.9)/135.9, or 42.0 percent, compared with the 2000 growth rate of (188.9 − 184.3)/184.3, or 2.5 percent. Comparisons of growth rates raise questions for the analyst. In 2000, sales grew by 2.5 percent, but inventories grew by a much larger amount: (229.5 − 185.5)/185.5 = 23.7%. Why? Was the inventory buildup due to Nike having trouble moving inventory, indicating lower demand and sales revenue in the future? Or was Nike building up inventory in anticipation of higher demand in the future? Why did operating expenses grow faster than sales revenue? Such questions provoke the analyst to further investigation.

Common-size and trend analysis can be combined by preparing trend statements on a common-size basis. This facilitates the comparison of one firm's trends with those of comparable firms.

RATIO ANALYSIS

From the reformulated statements we can calculate the two ratios that were introduced in Chapter 7 to summarize the profitability of the operating activities and the financing activities: return on net operating assets (RNOA), which is operating income after tax relative to net operating assets, and net borrowing cost (NBC), which is net financial expenses after tax relative to net financial obligations.

For Nike, Inc., the return on net operating assets for 1996 was

$$\text{RNOA} = \frac{549}{\frac{1}{2}(2{,}659 + 2{,}208)} = 22.6\%$$

Nike's net borrowing cost was

$$\text{NBC} = \frac{14}{\frac{1}{2}(228 + 244)} = 5.9\%$$

For Microsoft, the 2002 RNOA was

$$\text{RNOA} = \frac{6{,}277}{\frac{1}{2}(11{,}574 + 14{,}083)} = 48.9\%$$

and, as net financial expenses were negative, the return on net financial assets was

$$\text{RNFA} = \frac{1{,}548}{\frac{1}{2}(40{,}606 + 33{,}206)} = 4.2\%$$

These returns are, of course, after tax (and after the tax benefit of debt). The calculations use the average of beginning and ending balances in the denominator; they can be inaccurate if there are large changes in balance sheet items other than halfway through the year. Net borrowing cost is particularly sensitive to the timing of large changes in debt. Always compare the NBC against the cost of debt reported in the debt footnotes, as a check.

PROFIT MARGIN RATIOS

Profit margins are the percentage of sales that yield profits:

$$\text{Operating profit margin (PM)} = \frac{\text{OI (after tax)}}{\text{Sales}}$$

This profit margin is based on the total operating income on the last line of operating income before financial items. It can be divided into profit margin from income generated by sales and profit margin from income that does not come from sales:

$$\text{Sales PM} = \frac{\text{OI (after tax) from sales}}{\text{Sales}}$$

$$\text{Other items PM} = \frac{\text{OI (after tax) from other items}}{\text{Sales}}$$

These two margins sum to the operating profit margin. The most common other item in the income statement is the share of income (or loss) of subsidiaries. This income is from sales reported in the subsidiary, not from the reported sales in the parent's income statement. Including it in the analysis of the profitability of the sales in the parent's income statement results in an incorrect assessment of the profit margin on sales. Nike's sales PM is 8.8 percent in Exhibit 9.11, its other items PM is –0.3 percent, and its total operating profit margin is 8.5 percent.

$$\frac{\text{Financial income}}{\text{contribution ratio}} = \frac{\text{Net financial income}}{\text{Sales}}$$

This is the added contribution of financial activities to the profitability of each dollar of sales. It is –0.2 percent for Nike (as Nike has net expenses, not income). This ratio and the operating profit margin add to

$$\frac{\text{Net (comprehensive)}}{\text{income profit margin}} = \frac{\text{Comprehensive income}}{\text{Sales}}$$

EXPENSE RATIOS

Expense ratios calculate the percentage of sales revenue that is absorbed by expenses. They have the form

$$\text{Expense ratio} = \frac{\text{Expense}}{\text{Sales}}$$

This ratio is calculated for each expense item in operating income from sales so

$$1 - \text{Sales PM} = \text{Sum of expense ratios}$$

Expense ratios are given in Exhibit 9.11. For Reebok, cost of sales absorb 61.6 percent of sales. The firm's total expense ratios sum to 92.3 percent before tax and 95.1 percent after tax, with the remaining 4.9 percent of sales providing operating income after tax.

These profitability ratios will be analyzed in detail in Chapter 11. The commonsize analysis of the statements yield a number of ratios that will be used in that analysis. These ratios are summarized in Boxes 9.3 and 9.4.

Both profitability and growth are relevant for forecasting residual earnings. Trend analysis that documents past growth yields a number of growth ratios that will be used in the analysis of growth in Chapter 12. See Box 9.5.

COMPOSITION RATIOS

The percentages in common-size balance sheets (as in Exhibit 9.12) are composition ratios:

$$\text{Operating asset composition ratio} = \frac{\text{Operating asset}}{\text{Total operating assets}}$$

$$\frac{\text{Operating liability}}{\text{composition ratio}} = \frac{\text{Operating liability}}{\text{Total operating liabilities}}$$

$$\text{Financial asset composition ratio} = \frac{\text{Financial asset}}{\text{Total financial assets}}$$

$$\text{Financial liability composition ratio} = \frac{\text{Financial liability}}{\text{Total financial liabilities}}$$

The ratios for individual items sum to 100 percent within their category.

OPERATING LIABILITY LEVERAGE

The composition of net operating assets can be highlighted by comparing operating liabilities to net operating assets:

$$\text{Operating liability leverage (OLLEV)} = \frac{\text{Operating liabilities}}{\text{Net operating assets}}$$

The **operating liability leverage** ratio gives an indication of how the investment in net operating assets has been reduced by operating liabilities. It is called a leverage ratio because it can lever up the return on net operating assets (RNOA) with a lower denominator. For Nike the operating liability leverage ratio is 39.8 percent compared to 37.8 percent for Reebok. The operating liability composition ratios reveal which liabilities have contributed to the operating liability leverage.

FINANCIAL LEVERAGE

A second leverage ratio gives the relative size of net financial assets or obligations. Nike and Reebok have net debt while Microsoft holds net financial assets. The differences are captured by ratios that compare totals for net operating and net financing assets to owners' equity. These ratios are

$$\text{Capitalization ratio} = \text{NOA/CSE}$$

and

$$\text{Financial leverage ratio (FLEV)} = \text{NFO/CSE}$$

which is negative if the firm has positive net financial assets. **Financial leverage** is the degree to which net operating assets are financed by common equity. It is always the case that

$$\text{Capitalization ratio} - \text{Financial leverage ratio} = 1.0$$

Thus either measure can be used as an indication of the degree to which net financial assets are financed by common equity or net financial debt, but it is usual to refer to the financial leverage ratio. It is called a leverage ratio because, as we will see in Chapter 11, borrowing levers the ROCE up or down.

Nike has a capitalization ratio of 109.4 percent and a financial leverage ratio of 9.4 percent but Microsoft is a net creditor: Microsoft's financial leverage ratio is −77.8 percent and its capitalization ratio is 22.2 percent.

Trend analysis reveals growth. Four particular year-to-year growth rates are important to the growth component of valuation:

$$\text{Growth rate in sales} = \frac{\text{Change in sales}}{\text{Prior period's sales}}$$

$$\text{Growth rate in operating income} = \frac{\text{Change in operating income (after tax)}}{\text{Prior period's OI}}$$

$$\text{Growth in NOA} = \frac{\text{Change in net operating assets}}{\text{Beginning NOA}}$$

$$\text{Growth in CSE} = \frac{\text{Change in CSE}}{\text{Beginning CSE}}$$

Summary

We can put what we have done in this chapter in perspective by listing eight steps for financial statement analysis:

1. Reformulate the statement of stockholders' equity on a comprehensive income basis.

2. Calculate the comprehensive rate of return on common equity, ROCE, and the growth in equity from the reformulated statement of common stockholders' equity.

3. Reformulate the balance sheet to distinguish operating and financial assets and obligations.

4. Reformulate the income statement on a comprehensive income basis to distinguish operating and financing income.

5. Compare reformulated balance sheets and income statements with reformulated statements of comparison firms through a comparative common-size analysis and trend analysis.

6. Reformulate the cash flow statement.

7. Carry out the analysis of ROCE.

8. Carry out an analysis of growth.

Chapter 8 performed the first two steps. This chapter covers Steps 3–5, the next chapter covers Step 6, and the analysis of ROCE and growth in Steps 7 and 8 is done in Chapters 11 and 12.

Reformulation of the income statement and balance sheet is necessary to calculate ratios that correctly measure the results of the firm's activities. If financing items are classified as operating items, we get an incorrect measure of both operating profitability (RNOA) and financing profitability (NBC or RNFA). This chapter has led you through the reformulations. Reformulation looks like a mechanical exercise. But it requires a good knowledge of the business, an understanding of how the firm makes money. Indeed reformulation prompts the analyst to understand the business better. It requires her to dig into the footnotes and the management discussion and analysis to understand the GAAP statements and to incorporate more detail in the reformulated statements. With a rich set

The Web Connection

Find the following on the web page for this chapter:

- Further examples of reformulated balance sheets and income statements.

- Further discussion on distinguishing between operating and financing items.

- A discussion of financial disclosure (and lack thereof) and how poor transparency in the financial reports frustrates the analyst.

of reformulated statements accompanied by comparative common-size and trend statements, the analyst is prepared to proceed to the analysis of profitability and growth in Chapters 11 and 12.

You will sometimes find that lack of disclosure makes it difficult to classify items into operating and financing categories. The problem can be serious if a significant portion of earnings is in shares of subsidiaries' earnings under the equity method (where the firm holds less than 50 percent of the equity of a subsidiary). Reconstructing consolidated statements, or preparing statements on a segmented basis, helps rectify this problem. But to the extent that disclosure is insufficient, profitability measures will be less precise. At the other extreme, if disclosures—on the profitability of segments, for example—are plentiful, the analysis is improved.

Key Concepts

capital lease is a lease of an asset for substantially all of the asset's useful life and for which a lease asset and a lease obligation are placed on the balance sheet. *281*

consolidation accounting is the accounting process by which financial statements for one or more related firms are combined into one set of financial statements. *280*

effective tax rate is the average tax rate on income. *289*

financial leverage is the degree to which net operating assets are financed by net financial obligations. *304*

marginal tax rate is the rate at which the last dollar of income is taxed. *289*

minority interest is the share of shareholders in subsidiaries other than the common shareholders of the parent company. *282*

operating cash is cash used in operations (compared to cash invested in financial assets). *279*

operating lease is a lease which does not entitle the lessee to use the lease asset for substantially all of the asset's useful life and for which no asset or obligation is recognized on the balance sheet. *281*

operating liability leverage is the degree to which investment in net operating assets is made by operating creditors. *304*

tax allocation involves attributing income taxes to the appropriate component of income that attracts the taxes. *289*

tax shield is the effect that interest on debt has of reducing corporate taxes. *289*

trend analysis expresses financial statement items as an index relative to a base year. *300*

The Analyst's Toolkit

Analysis Tools	Page	Key Measures	Page	Acronymns to Remember
Reformulated balance sheets	277	Effective tax rate for		CSE common shareholders' equity
Reformulated income		operations	291	FLEV financial leverage
statements	288	Net financial income		NBC net borrowing cost
Tax allocation	289	(or expense) after tax	290	NFE net financial expense
Common-size analysis	298	Operating income		NOL net operating loss
Trend analysis	300	after tax (OI)	290	NOA net operating assets
Ratio analysis of the income		Ratios		OI operating income
statement and balance		Income statement ratios	303	OLLEV operating liability leverage
sheet	302	Operating profit margin		PM profit margin
		(PM)		RNFA return on net financial
		Sales PM		assets
		Other items PM		RNOA return on net operating
		Financial income contribution		assets
		ratio		ROCE return on common equity
		Net (comprehensive) income		
		profit margin		
		Expense ratio		
		Balance sheet ratios	304	
		Operating asset		
		composition ratio		
		Operating liability		
		composition ratio		
		Financial asset composition		
		ratio		
		Financial liability composition		
		ratio		
		Operating liability leverage		
		(OLLEV)		
		Financial leverage (FLEV)		
		Capitalization ratio		
		Growth ratios	305	
		Growth rate in sales		
		Growth rate in operating		
		income		
		Growth in NOA		
		Growth in CSE		

Concept Questions

C9.1. Why are reformulated statements necessary to discover operating profitability?

C9.2. Classify each of the following as a financial asset or an operating asset:

    a. Cash in a checking account used to pay bills.

    b. Accounts receivable.

    c. Finance receivables for an automobile firm.

    d. Cash in 90-day interest-bearing deposits.

    e. Debt investments held to maturity.

      f. Short-term equity investments.

      g. Long-term equity investments held to maturity.

      h. Goodwill.

      i. Lease assets.

      j. Deferred compensation.

C9.3. Classify each of the following as a financial liability, an operating liability, or neither:

      a. Accrued compensation.

      b. Deferred revenues.

      c. Preferred stock.

      d. Deferred tax liability.

      e. Lease obligations.

      f. Interest-bearing note payable.

C9.4. From the point of view of the common shareholders, minority interest is a financial obligation. Correct?

C9.5. What is meant by saying that debt provides a tax shield?

C9.6. When can a firm lose the tax benefit of debt?

C9.7. What does an operating profit margin reveal?

C9.8. What is operating liability leverage? What does it lever?

Exercises   E9.1.   A Reformulation: Intel Corporation (Easy)

Intel Corporation's 1998 income statement and balance sheet are below. The shareholders' equity statement reports unrealized gains on available-for-sale investments of $545 million for the year. The tax footnote reports an effective tax rate of 33.6 percent; the statutory rate for state and federal taxes is 38 percent.

    Reformulate the two statements in a way that highlights operating and financing activities of the business.

    a. What percentage of Intel's common stockholders' equity is in net financial assets?

    b. What percentage of Intel's income is in return on its net financial assets?

INTEL CORPORATION
Income Statement

	1998
Net revenues	$26,273
Cost of sales	12,144
Research and development	2,509
Marketing, general, and administrative	3,076
Purchased in-process research and development	165
Operating costs and expenses	17,894
Operating income	8,379
Interest expense	(34)
Interest income and other, net	792
Income before taxes	9,137
Provision for taxes	3,069
Net income	$ 6,068
Basic earnings per common share	$1.82
Diluted earnings per common share	$1.73

Balance Sheet

	1998	1997
Assets		
Current assets		
Cash and cash equivalents	$ 2,038	$ 4,102
Short-term investments	5,272	5,630
Trading assets	316	195
Accounts receivable, net of allowance for doubtful accounts of $62 ($65 in 1997)	3,527	3,438
Inventories	1,582	1,697
Deferred tax assets	618	676
Other current assets	122	129
Total current assets	13,475	15,867
Property, plant, and equipment		
Land and buildings	6,297	5,113
Machinery and equipment	13,149	10,577
Construction in progress	1,622	2,437
	21,068	18,127
Less accumulated depreciation	9,459	7,461
Property, plant, and equipment, net	11,609	10,666
Long-term investments	5,365	1,839
Other assets	1,022	508
Total assets	31,471	28,880
Liabilities and Stockholders' Equity		
Current liabilities		
Short-term debt	159	212
Long-term debt redeemable within one year		110
Accounts payable	1,244	1,407
Accrued compensation and benefits	1,285	1,268
Deferred income on shipments to distributors	606	516
Accrued advertising	458	500
Other accrued liabilities	1,094	842
Income taxes payable	958	1,165
Total current liabilities	5,804	6,020
Long-term debt	702	448
Deferred tax liabilities	1,387	1,076
Put warranties	201	2,041
Commitments and contingencies		
Stockholders' equity		
Preferred stock, $0.001 par value, 50 shares authorized; none issued		
Common stock, $0.001 par value, 4,500 shares authorized; 3,315 issued and outstanding (3,256 in 1997) and capital in excess of par value	4,822	3,311
Retained earnings	17,952	15,926
Accumulated other comprehensive income	603	58
Total stockholders' equity	23,377	19,295
Total liabilities and stockholders' equity	$31,471	$28,880

Real World Connection

See Exercise E4.4 in Chapter 4, Exercise E10.10 in Chapter 10, and Exercise E11.4 in Chapter 11 for more material on Intel Corporation.

E9.2. Testing Relationships in Reformulated Income Statements (Easy)

Fill in the missing numbers, indicated by capital letters, in the following reformulated income statement. Amounts are in millions of dollars. The firm's marginal tax rate is 35 percent.

Operating revenues		5,523
Cost of sales	3,121	
Other operating expenses	1,429	
Operating income before tax		A
Tax as reported	B	
Tax benefit of interest expense	C	
Operating income after tax		D
Interest expense before tax	E	
Tax benefit	(F)	
Interest expense after tax		42
Comprehensive income		610

What is the firm's effective tax rate on operating income?

E9.3. Where Did the Profits Come from? Hewlett-Packard (Medium)

In the mid-1990s, Hewlett-Packard reported earnings that were consistently growing on the order of 20 percent per year. The growth rate slowed down in the late 1990s. Earnings for the third quarter of 1998 were reported as "flat" when compared with the same period of the previous year. The income statement for HP's 1998 third quarter follows:

	Three Months Ended July 31	
	1998	**1997**
Net revenue		
Products	$ 9,213	$ 8,900
Services	1,766	1,571
	10,979	10,471
Cost and expenses		
Cost of products sold and services	7,505	7,053
Research and development	815	777
Selling, general, and administrative	1,885	1,816
	10,205	9,646
Earnings from operations	774	825
Interest income and other, net	154	109
Interest expense	54	53
Earnings before taxes	874	881
Provision for taxes	253	264
Net earnings	$ 621	$ 617
Net earnings per share		
Basic	$ 0.60	$ 0.60
Diluted	$ 0.58	$ 0.58

a. What is wrong with the interpretation that earnings were "flat" in 1998?
b. What is your best guess as to the change in free cash flow from the July 1997 quarter to the July 1998 quarter?

Real World Connection

See material on Hewlett-Packard in Chapter 5. Also see Exercise E1.2 in Chapter 1, Exercises E5.10 and E5.14 in Chapter 5, and Exercise E6.7 in Chapter 6.

E9.4. Cash Position: Chrysler Corporation (Easy)

In his bid for Chrysler in 1995, Kirk Kerkorian complained that Chrysler was holding too much of its capital in "cash." From the 1995 balance sheet and income statement given in Minicase M5.3 of Chapter 5, calculate the amount of "cash" (financial assets) and the firm's net financial asset position.

Real World Connection

See Minicase 5.3 in Chapter 5.

E9.5. Operating or Financial Liabilities? Nike, Inc. (Medium)

Nike, the sport and fashion shoe manufacturer, reported the following current liabilities in its 1999 balance sheet:

Current liabilities:	
Current portion of long-term debt (Note 5)	$ 1.0
Notes payable (Note 4)	419.1
Accounts payable (Note 4)	373.2
Accrued liabilities	653.6
Total current liabilities	$1,446.9

Note 4, referred to in the balance sheet, follows:

Note 4—Short-Term Borrowings and Credit Lines

Notes payable to banks and interest-bearing payable to Nissho Iwai American Corporation (NIAC) are summarized below:

	May 31, 1999	
	Borrowings (in millions)	**Interest Rate (%)**
Banks		
Non-U.S. operations	$239.8	3.87
U.S. operations	179.3	4.85
	419.1	
NIAC	$ 98.0	5.30

The company purchases through NIAC substantially all of the athletic footwear and apparel it acquires from non-U.S. suppliers. Accounts payable to NIAC are generally due up to 120 days after shipment of goods from the foreign port. Interest on such accounts payable accrues at the 90-day London Interbank Offered Rate (LIBOR) as of the beginning of the month of the invoice date, plus 0.30%.

Using the footnote information, classify each of the current liabilities into operating and financial categories.

Real World Connection

See the material on Nike, Inc., in Chapters 11–15. Also see Exercise E1.5 in Chapter 1, Minicase M2.1 in Chapter 2, Exercise E6.3 in Chapter 6, Minicase M7.1 in Chapter 7, and Exercise E8.10 in Chapter 8, and Exercise E13.7 in Chapter 13.

E9.6. Can Net Operating Assets Be Negative? Chubb Corporation (Hard)

Chubb, the property and casualty insurer, reported the balance sheet below for its June 30, 1999, quarter. Amounts are in millions.

	June 30, 1999
Assets	
Invested assets	
Short-term investments	$ 586.1
Fixed maturities	
Held-to-maturity—tax exempt (market $1,991.6)	1,900.8
Available-for-sale	
Tax exempt (cost $7,008.0)	7,176.0
Taxable (cost $4,364.5)	4,373.8
Equity securities (cost $629.9)	649.7
Total invested assets	14,686.4
Cash	25.4
Accrued investment income	225.9
Premiums receivable	1,253.6
Reinsurance recoverable on unpaid claims	1,239.2
Prepaid reinsurance premiums	126.3
Funds held for asbestos-related settlement	607.2
Deferred policy acquisition costs	746.3
Real estate assets	720.1
Deferred income tax	476.1
Other assets	958.9
Total assets	$21,065.4
Liabilities	
Unpaid claims	$10,584.7
Unearned premiums	2,989.8
Long-term debt	602.0
Dividend payable to shareholders	51.8
Accrued expenses and other liabilities	1,244.1
Total liabilities	15,472.4
Common stock, $1 par value; 175,977,128 and 175,989,202 shares	176.0
Paid-in surplus	520.7
Retained earnings	5,880.3
Accumulated other comprehensive income	
Unrealized appreciation of investments, net of tax	128.1
Foreign currency translation losses, net of tax	(44.4)
Receivable from employee stock ownership plan	(80.7)
Treasury stock, at cost, 14,075,468 and 13,722,376 shares	(987.0)
Total shareholders' equity	5,593.0
Total liabilities and shareholders' equity	$21,065.4

Calculate net operating assets employed in Chubb's insurance underwriting operations June 30, 1999. How can a company have negative net operating assets?

Real World Connection
See Exercise E9.8 in this chapter and Minicase M13.1 in Chapter 13 for more material on Chubb Corporation.

E9.7.   Effective Tax Rates: Home Depot, Inc. (Medium)
Home Depot is the largest home improvement retailer in the United States and, with 761 retail outlets, was one of the top 10 retailers in 1999.

Below is Home Depot's income statement for fiscal 1999, along with the tax footnote. Calculate the effective tax rate on operating income.

THE HOME DEPOT, INC. AND SUBSIDIARIES
Consolidated Statement of Earnings
(amounts in millions, except per-share data)

	Fiscal Year Ended January 31, 1999
Net sales	$30,219
Cost of merchandise sold	21,614
Gross profit	8,605
Operating expenses	
Selling and store operating	5,341
Pre-opening	88
General and administrative	515
Total operating expenses	5,944
Operating income	2,661
Interest income (expense)	
Interest and investment income	30
Interest expense	(37)
Interest, net	(7)
Earnings before income taxes	2,654
Income taxes (note 3)	1,040
Net earnings	$ 1,614
Basic earnings per share	1.10
Weighted-average number of common shares outstanding	1,471
Diluted earnings per share	$1,06
Weighted-average number of common shares outstanding assuming dilution	1,547

Note 3: Income Taxes

The provision for income taxes consisted of the following (in millions):

	Fiscal Year Ended		
	January 31, 1999	February 1, 1998	February 2, 1997
Current			
U.S.	$ 823	$653	$486
State	150	98	72
Foreign	20	15	10
	993	766	568
Deferred			
U.S.	46	(31)	23
State	(1)	1	6
Foreign	2	2	—
	47	(28)	29
Total	$1,040	$738	$597

The company's combined federal, state, and foreign effective tax rates for fiscal years 1998, 1997, and 1996, net of offsets generated by federal, state, and foreign tax incentive credits, were approximately 39.2%, 38.9%, and 38.9%, respectively. A reconciliation of income tax expense at the federal statutory rate of 35% to actual tax expense for the applicable fiscal years follows (in millions):

(continued)

	January 31, 1999	February 1, 1998	February 2, 1997
Income taxes at U.S. statutory rate	$ 929	$664	$537
State income taxes, net of federal income tax benefit	96	65	51
Foreign rate differences	—	2	2
Other, net	15	7	7
Total	$1,040	$738	$597

Real World Connection
See Minicase M14.1 in Chapter 14 for more material on Home Depot, Inc.

E9.8. ### Separating Sources of Income: Chubb Corporation (Medium)
Chubb's income statement and statement of comprehensive income for its second quarter, 1999, are below. Chubb is primarily involved in property and casualty insurance, but it also has commercial real estate operations in New Jersey and a residential real estate business in central Florida.

CHUBB CORP.
Income Statement, Quarter Ending June 30, 1999
(in millions)

Revenues	
Premiums earned	$1,377.5
Investment income	215.9
Real estate	47.3
Realized investment gains	45.9
Total revenues	1,686.6
Claims and expenses	
Insurance claims	924.3
Amortization of deferred policy acquisition costs	373.7
Other insurance operating costs and expenses	90.1
Real estate cost of sales and expenses	48.1
Investment expenses	3.0
Corporate expenses	11.5
Total claims and expenses	1,450.7
Income before federal and foreign income tax	235.9
Federal and foreign income tax	42.6
Net income	$ 193.3
Average common shares outstanding	161.3
Average common and potentially dilutive shares outstanding	163.9
Net income per share	
Basic	$ 1.19
Diluted	$ 1.18

Statement of Comprehensive Income, Quarter Ending June 30, 1999

Net income	$ 193.3
Other comprehensive income (loss)	
Change in unrealized appreciation of investments, net of tax	(206.1)
Foreign currency translation losses, net of tax	(13.3)
	(219.4)
Comprehensive income (loss)	(26.1)

Reformulate the accompanying statements into one statement that identifies the sources of Chubb's income. Use a marginal tax rate of 36 percent. Chubb's balance sheet (in Exercise E9.6) indicates that 67 percent of its fixed income investments are in tax-exempt securities. These securities provide about $110 million in tax-exempt investment revenue.

What does the reformulated statement reveal?

Real World Connection
See Exercise E9.6 in this chapter and Minicase M13.1 in Chapter 13 for more material on Chubb Corporation.

E9.9. Operating Profitability: Southwest Airlines (Medium)

A summary of income statements and balance sheets for Southwest Airlines from 1990 to 1994 follows. Southwest reported no income outside the income statement for these years. Use a marginal tax rate of 35 percent in the calculations below.

a. Calculate the free cash flow that Southwest Airlines generated in each year, 1991–1994.
b. Document changes in operating profitability over these five years.
c. Calculate percentage-borrowing costs for each year.
d. What observation can you make about Southwest's profitability and free cash flow?

SOUTHWEST AIRLINES
Income Statement, 1990–1994

	1990	1991	1992	1993	1994
Revenues					
Passenger	$1,144.4	$1,267.9	$1,623.8	$2,216.3	$2,533.8
Other	42.5	45.8	61.5	80.2	94.0
	1,186.9	1,313.7	1,685.3	2,296.5	2,627.8
Operating Expenses					
Salaries and benefits	357.4	408.0	501.9	641.7	762.8
Fuel and oil	242.0	225.5	243.5	304.4	319.9
Maintenance	82.9	97.6	120.6	163.4	192.4
Commissions	72.1	81.2	106.4	144.9	154.2
Aircraft rental	26.1	49.2	64.2	107.9	127.0
Landing and other	61.2	83.2	102.7	129.2	150.9
Depreciation	79.4	86.2	101.2	119.3	138.8
Other operating expenses	183.9	219.9	262.1	382.9	433.0
	1,105.0	1,250.8	1,502.6	1,993.7	2,279.0
Operating Income	81.9	62.9	182.7	302.8	348.8
Interest expense	20.0	28.6	43.6	40.7	28.3
Investment income	9.3	10.6	10.3	11.1	6.9
Other items	3.5	(1.0)	(2.5)	(13.5)	0.1
	7.2	19.0	35.8	43.1	21.3
Pretax Income	74.7	43.9	146.9	259.7	327.5
Taxes	27.7	16.9	55.8	105.4	129.7
Net Income	$ 47.1	$ 27.0	$ 91.1	$ 154.3	$ 197.8

Balance Sheets, 1990–1994

Assets	1990	1991	1992	1993	1994
Current Assets					
Cash and cash equivalents	$ 87,507	$ 260,856	$ 437,989	$ 295,571	$ 174,538
Accounts receivable	43,887	47,507	57,355	70,484	75,692
Inventories of parts and supplies at cost	15,460	23,036	30,758	31,707	37,565
Deferred income taxes				10,475	9,822
Prepaid expense and other current assets	10,973	8,602	15,792	23,787	17,281
Total current assets	157,827	340,001	541,894	432,024	314,898
Property and Equipment, at Cost					
Flight equipment	1,369,324	1,551,519	1,874,085	2,257,809	2,564,551
Ground property and equipment	194,118	218,522	294,458	329,605	384,501
Deposits on flight equipment purchase contracts	153,201	182,932	214,584	242,230	393,749
Less allowance for depreciation	406,106	458,779	559,034	688,280	837,838
Property and equipment, net	1,310,537	1,494,194	1,824,093	2,141,364	2,504,963
Other assets	2,774	3,096	2,869	2,649	3,210
Total Assets	$1,471,138	$1,837,291	$2,368,856	$2,576,037	$2,923,071

Liabilities and Stockholders' Equity	1990	1991	1992	1993	1994
Current Liabilities					
Accounts payable	51,172	54,970	82,023	94,040	117,599
Accrued liabilities	112,296	155,895	208,357	265,333	288,979
Air traffic liability	38,562	42,069	65,934	96,146	106,139
Income taxes payable	9,716	377	6,744	7,025	
Current maturities of long-term debt	13,612	6,583	16,234	16,068	9,553
Total Current Liabilities	225,358	259,894	379,292	478,612	522,270
Long-term debt less current maturities	326,956	617,016	735,754	639,136	583,071
Deferred income taxes	109,273	105,757	136,462	183,616	232,850
Deferred gains from sale and leaseback of aircraft	202,002	222,818	224,645	199,362	217,677
Other deferred liabilities	2,698	3,285	13,167	21,292	28,497
Stockholders' Equity					
Common stock, $1.00 par value	42,412	42,438	96,047	142,756	143,256
Capital in excess of par value	81,447	81,987	177,647	141,168	151,746
Retained earnings	484,559	507,259	605,928	770,095	943,704
Less treasury stock, at cost	3,567	3,163	86		
Total Stockholders' Equity	604,851	628,521	879,536	1,054,019	1,238,706
Total Liabilities and Stockholders' Equity	$1,471,138	$1,837,291	$2,368,856	$2,576,037	$2,823,071

Minicase

M9.1

Asset Leasing, Indebtedness, Profitability, and Leverage: UAL Corp.

UAL Corp. is the parent company for United Airlines, the U.S. domestic and international airline. In 1998, the airline flew 125 billion revenue passenger miles to make it the largest airline in the world on this measure. United is a founding member of Star Alliance, an integrated worldwide network of airlines that includes Lufthansa, Air Canada, SAS, Thai Airways, Varig, Singapore Airlines, Mexicana, and Spanair.

At the end of 1998, United Airlines leased 309 aircraft, 68 of them under capital leases and the remainder under operating leases. It also leased terminal space, aircraft hangers, and maintenance facilities, almost all under operating leases. The accounting treatment of the capital leases is outlined in a section in a footnote to the financial statements that summarizes UAL's accounting policies:

> Operating property and equipment—Owned operating property and equipment is stated at cost. Property under capital leases, and the related obligation for future lease payments, are initially recorded at an amount equal to the present value of those lease payments.
>
> Depreciation and amortization of owned depreciable assets is based on the straight-line method over their estimated service lives. Leasehold improvements are amortized over the remaining period of the lease or the estimated service life of the related asset, whichever is less. Aircraft are depreciated to estimated salvage values, generally over lives of 10 to 30 years; buildings are depreciated over a period of 25 to 45 years; and other property and equipment are depreciated over lives of 3 to 15 years.
>
> Properties under capital leases are amortized on the straight-line method over the life of the lease, or in the case of certain aircraft, over their estimated service lives. Lease terms are 10 to 30 years for aircraft and flight simulators and 25 years for buildings. Amortization of capital leases is included in depreciation and amortization expense.

(At this stage of the case, you should review the accounting for leases and be sure that you understand the difference between a capital lease and an operating lease.)

UAL's 1998 balance sheet and income statement are given at the end of this case. You see that capital lease assets are included as part of long-term assets and lease obligations are listed as liabilities. The lease footnote 10 gives more explanation about the leases:

> **10. Lease Obligations**
> The Company leases aircraft, airport passenger terminal space, aircraft hangers and related maintenance facilities, cargo terminals, other airport facilities, real estate, office computer equipment, and vehicles.
>
> Future minimum lease payments as of December 31, 1998, under capital lease (substantially all of which are for aircraft) and operating leases having initial or remaining noncancelable lease terms of more than one year are as follows:

	Operating Leases (in millions)		
	Aircraft	**Non-Aircraft**	**Capital Leases**
Payable during:			
1999	$ 869	$ 451	$ 317
2000	882	447	308
2001	865	439	399
2002	854	420	341
2003	892	413	242
After 2003	10,729	6,537	1,759
Total minimum lease payments	$15,091	$8,707	$3,366
Imputed interest (at rates of 5.3% to 12.2%)			(1,077)
Present value of minimum lease payments			2,289
Current portion			(176)
Long-term obligations under capital leases			$2,113

As of December 31, 1998, United leased 309 aircraft, 68 of which were under capital leases. These leases have terms of 10 to 26 years, and expiration dates range from 1999 through 2020.

In connection with the financing of certain aircraft accounted for as capital leases, United had on deposit at December 31, 1998, an aggregate 38 billion yen ($330 million), 324 million German marks ($193 million), 60 million French frances ($11 million), and $11 million in certain banks and had pledged an irrevocable security interest in such deposits to certain of the aircraft lessors. These deposits will be used to pay off an equivalent amount of capital lease obligations.

Amounts charged to rent expense, net of minor amounts of sublease rentals, were $1.385 billion in 1998, $1.416 billion in 1997, and $1.424 billion in 1996. Included in 1998 rental expense was $15 million in contingent rentals, resulting from changes in interest rates for operating leases under which rent payments are based on variable interest rates.

UAL also reported "Principal payments under capital leases" of $322 million as part of cash flow from financing activities in its 1998 cash flow statement.

A. On the basis of the financial statements and supplementary information, develop measures of operating profitability for UAL Corp. for 1998. Also develop a measure of its financial leverage and calculate the firm's 1998 net borrowing cost from the financial statements. Use a tax rate of 38 percent in your calculations.

Compare your measures of operating profitability with the standard measure, return on assets. Also compare your leverage measure with the standard debt-to-equity ratio. Discuss the differences between the measures.

B. There is often a fine line between designating a lease as an operating lease or a capital lease. Suppose that UAL treated all leases as operating leases. To the extent possible with the information before you, reconstruct the statements with this accounting and recalculate the measures of operating profitability and financial leverage.

Discuss how the accounting for leases comes into play in determining the alternative measures. Do you think the accounting for capital leases improves the reporting of leverage?

UAL CORPORATION
Statements of Consolidated Financial Position
(in millions)

	December 31 1998	December 31 1997
Assets		
Current assets		
Cash and cash equivalents	$ 390	$ 295
Short-term investments	425	550
Receivables, less allowance for doubtful accounts (1998, $22; 1997, $15)	1,138	1,051
Aircraft fuel, spare parts, and supplies less obsolescence allowance (1998, $39; 1997, $29)	384	355
Deferred income taxes	256	244
Prepaid expenses and other	315	453
	2,908	2,948
Operating property and equipment		
Owned		
Flight equipment	12,006	10,382
Advances on flight equipment	985	972
Other property and equipment	3,134	2,842
	16,125	14,196
Less accumulated depreciation and amortization	5,174	5,116
	10,951	9,080
Capital leases		
Flight equipment	2,605	2,221
Other property and equipment	97	98
	2,702	2,319
Less accumulated amortization	599	625
	2,103	1,694
	13,054	10,774
Other assets		
Investments in affiliates	304	223
Intangibles, less accumulated amortization (1998, $389; 1997, $374)	676	703
Aircraft lease deposits	545	318
Prepaid rent	631	60
Other	441	438
	2,597	1,742
	$18,559	$15,464
Liabilities and Stockholders' Equity		
Current liabilities		
Notes payable	$ 184	
Long-term debt maturing within one year	98	235
Current obligations under capital leases	176	171
Advance ticket sales	1,429	1,267
Accounts payable	1,151	1,030
Accrued salaries, wages, and benefits	952	869
Accrued aircraft rent	793	830
Other accrued liabilities	885	846
	5,668	5,248

(continued)

Long-term debt	2,858	2,092
Long-term obligations under capital leases	2,113	1,679
Other liabilities and deferred credits		
Deferred pension liability	89	25
Postretirement benefit liability	1,424	1,361
Deferred gains	1,180	1,210
Accrued aircraft rent	371	368
Deferred income taxes	398	79
Other	354	450
	3,816	3,493
Company-obligated mandatorily redeemable preferred securities of a subsidiary trust	100	101
Equity put options	32	—
Preferred stock committed to supplemental ESOP	691	514
Stockholders' equity	3,281	2,337
	$18,559	$15,464

UAL CORPORATION
Statements of Consolidated Operations
(in millions, except per share)

	Year Ended December 31	
	1998	**1997**
Operating revenues		
Passenger	$15,520	$15,342
Cargo	913	892
Other operating revenues	1,128	1,144
	17,561	17,378
Operating expenses		
Salaries and related costs	5,341	5,018
ESOP compensation expense	829	987
Aircraft fuel	1,788	2,061
Commissions	1,325	1,508
Purchased services	1,505	1,285
Aircraft rent	893	942
Landing fees and other rent	881	863
Depreciation and amortization	793	724
Aircraft maintenance	624	603
Other operating expenses	2,104	2,128
	16,083	16,119
Earnings from operations	1,478	1,259
Other income (expense)		
Interest expense	(355)	(286)
Interest capitalized	105	104
Interest income	59	52
Equity in earnings of affiliates	72	66
Gain on sale of partnership interest		275
Gain on sale of affiliate's stock		103
Miscellaneous, net	(103)	(49)
	(222)	265
Earnings before income taxes, distributions on preferred securities, and extraordinary item	1,256	1,524
Provision for income taxes	429	561
Earnings before distribution on preferred securities and extraordinary item	827	963
Distributions on preferred securities, net	(6)	(5)
Extraordinary loss on early extinguishment of debt, net	—	(9)
Net earnings	$ 821	$ 949
Per share, basic		
Earnings before extraordinary item	$ 12.71	$ 14.98
Extraordinary loss on early extinguishment of debt, net		(0.15)
Net earnings	$ 12.71	$ 14.83
Per share, diluted		
Earnings before extraordinary item	$ 6.83	$ 9.04
Extraordinary loss on early extinguishment of debt, net		(0.09)
Net earnings	$ 6.83	$ 8.95

The Analysis of the Cash Flow Statement

LINKS

Link to previous chapter

Chapter 9 reformulated the balance sheet and income statement to capture the operating and financing activities.

This chapter

This chapter reformulates the cash flow statement to capture the operating and financing activities.

Link to next chapter

Chapter 11 lays out the analysis of the reformulated financial statements.

Link to web page

Review the statement of cash flows for more real-world companies—visit the book's website at www.mhhe.com/penman2e.

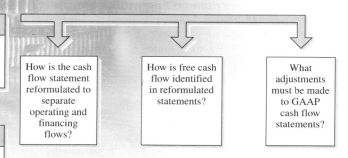

How is the cash flow statement reformulated to separate operating and financing flows?

How is free cash flow identified in reformulated statements?

What adjustments must be made to GAAP cash flow statements?

This chapter completes the preparation of the financial statements for analysis by reformulating the cash flow statement. The cash flow statement describes the cash generation in a business, and reformulation highlights the cash flows that are important to analysis.

If the equity analyst is using accounting-based valuation, he is concerned with profitability rather than cash flow, so his primary focus is on the balance sheet and income statement from which the profitability is calculated. But he cannot ignore the cash flow statement. Residual earnings valuation methods in Chapter 5 and abnormal earning growth methods in Chapter 6 rely on accrual accounting numbers and accrual accounting numbers can be distorted. A difference between accrual accounting earnings and operating cash flow is a "red flag" that could indicate manipulation, so the analyst must scrutinize the cash flows as well as accrual accounting earnings. Indeed earnings will be compared to cash flows in the analysis of the quality of earnings in Chapter 17.

If the valuation analyst chooses to apply discounted cash flow (DCF) analysis, (as in Chapter 4), the cash flow statement becomes the primary focus. This analyst has the primary task of forecasting free cash flows; to do so, he must have a good appreciation of the cash flow statement.

The Analyst's Checklist

After reading this chapter you should understand:	After reading this chapter you should be able to:
• How free cash flow can be calculated from reformulated income statements and balance sheets without a cash flow statement.	• Calculate free cash flow from reformulated income statements and balance sheets.
• How the cash conservation equation ties the cash flow statement together to equate free cash flow and financing cash flow.	• Calculate free cash flow from adjusted GAAP statements.
• The difference between the direct and indirect calculations of cash from operations.	• Reformulate GAAP statements of cash flow to identify operating, investing, and financing cash flows distinctly.
• Problems that arise in analyzing cash flows from GAAP statements of cash flow.	• Reconcile (approximately) the free cash flow from GAAP statements to that calculated from reformulated income statements and balance sheets.
• What reformulated cash flow statements tell you.	
• How free cash flow changes over a product's life cycle.	

Valuation issues aside, the analysis of the cash flow statement is necessary for *liquidity analysis* and *financial planning,* which will be covered in Part Five of the book. **Liquidity analysis** is involved in assessing the risk of debt, for liquidity (cash) is required to settle debt. So liquidity analysis is very much the tool of the credit analyst. **Financial planning** is the tool of the treasurer. She must ensure that financing is in place to meet the needs for cash—to make investments and cover dividends, as well as servicing debt. To understand the needs for cash, she must analyze the ability of the firm to generate cash. Like, valuation analysis, liquidity analysis and financial planning are prospective: The credit analyst and the treasurer are concerned about the ability of the firm to generate cash in the future, and they use current financial statements to forecast future cash flow statements. The analysis here, like that of the other statements, prepares you for forecasting.

Unfortunately, GAAP statements of cash flow are not in the form that identifies the cash flows used in these analyses, and indeed they misclassify some cash flows. Operating cash flows are confused with financing flows. This chapter reformulates the statement to distinguish the cash flows appropriately. The reformulation is important for preparing pro forma future cash flow statements for DCF analysis, liquidity analysis, and financial planning. If the analyst forecasts GAAP cash flows, a DCF valuation will be incorrect and a misleading picture of liquidity and financing needs will be drawn.

An important lesson emerges from this chapter. Forecasting free cash flow is best done by forecasting reformulated income statements and balance sheets. We can think of forecasting cash flow statements, but this is difficult without first forecasting the profitability of operations, which is understood from reformulated income statements and balance sheets. Further, once those statements are forecasted, free cash flow forecasts can be calculated immediately, as the first section of the chapter shows. And GAAP cash flow statements are messy, as the second section of the chapter shows, so forecasting them requires considerable adjustment.

Method 1:	$C - I = OI - \Delta NOA$			
	Operating income	1996		$549
	Net operating assets	1996	$2,659	
	Net operating assets	1995	2,208	(451)
	Free cash flow	1996		$ 98
Method 2:	$C - I = NFE - \Delta NFO + d$			
	Net financial expenses	1996		$14
	Net financial obligations	1996	$ 228	
	Net financial obligations	1995	244	16
	Net dividend	1996		68
	Free cash flow	1996		$ 98

THE CALCULATION OF FREE CASH FLOW

Free cash flow—the difference between cash flow from operations and cash investment in operations—is the main focus in DCF analysis, liquidity analysis, and financial planning. Free cash flow is the net cash generated by operations, which determines the ability of the firm to pay off its debt and equity claims.

If the analyst has gone through the analysis of the balance sheet and income statement in Chapter 9, he does not need a cash flow statement to get the free cash flow. If those statements are appropriately formatted, then the free cash flow is given by a quick calculation. In Chapter 7 we saw that

$$\text{Free cash flow} = \text{Operating income} - \text{Change in net operating assets} \quad \textbf{(10.1)}$$

$$C - I = OI - \Delta NOA$$

That is, free cash flow is operating income (in a reformulated income statement) less the change in net operating assets in the balance sheet.

For this quick calculation to work, the operating income must, of course, be comprehensive. Just as comprehensive income and changes in the book value of equity explain dividends to shareholders, so comprehensive operating income and the change in the book value of the net operating assets explain the "dividend" from the operating activities to the financing activities, the free cash flow.

The numbers for operating income and net operating assets for Nike, Inc., from Exhibits 9.3 and 9.8 in Chapter 9 are provided in Box 10.1. Free cash flow is calculated from these numbers under Method 1 in the display. Nike generated income from operations of $549 million, but its additional investment in net operating assets of $451 million produced a free cash flow of $98 million.

There is a second way to calculate free cash flow from reformulated statements. In Chapter 7 we also saw that free cash flow is applied as follows:

$$\text{Free cash flow} = \text{Net financial expense} \quad \textbf{(10.2)}$$
$$- \text{Change in net financial obligations}$$
$$+ \text{Net dividends}$$

$$C - I = NFE - \Delta NFO + d$$

Method 1:	$C - I = OI - \Delta NOA$			
	Operating income	1996		$168
	Net operating assets	1996	$1,135	
	Net operating assets	1995	1,220	85
	Free cash flow	1996		253
Method 2:	$C - I = NFE - \Delta NFO + d + MI$ in			
	income $- \Delta MI$ in balance sheet			
	Net financial expenses	1996		$ (20)
	Net financial obligations	1996	$ 720	
	Net financial obligations	1995	287	(433)
	Net dividend	1996		693
	Minority interest in income	1996		15
	Change in minority interest in balance sheet	1996		(3)
	Free cash flow (allow for refunding error)	1996		$253

that is, free cash flow is used to pay for net financial expense, reduce debt, and pay dividends. If minority interests are involved, the calculation is

$$C - I = NFE - \Delta NFO + d + \text{Minority interest in income} \quad \textbf{(10.2a)}$$
$$- \Delta\text{Minority interest in the balance sheet}$$

Again, the net financial expense must be comprehensive (of unrealized gains and losses on financial assets, for example, and of the tax benefit from interest expense). This second calculation is given for Nike, Inc., under Method 2 in Box 10.1. The net dividend is from the reformulated statement of common shareholders' equity in Exhibit 8.1 in Chapter 8.

The two calculations must agree if the reformulation of the equity statement is done on a comprehensive basis. The calculations in Box 10.2 are based on the reformulated statements for Reebok in Exhibits 9.4 and 9.9 in Chapter 9 and, for the net dividend, the reformulated equity statement in Exhibit 8.2 in Chapter 8. Note that Reebok has minority interest.

If the balance sheet and income statement have been reformulated, these calculations are straightforward. You'll agree that these methods are much simpler than the seven-step approach in Chapter 4. But, you may ask, Can't I simply read the cash flows on the statement of cash flows? This is not as easy as you would think.

GAAP STATEMENT OF CASH FLOWS AND REFORMULATED CASH FLOW STATEMENTS

For cash flow forecasting we need to distinguish clearly the cash generated by operations (the free cash flow) from the flows that involve paying that cash flow out to the firm's claimants. If operations use cash (and thus have negative free cash flow), we need to distinguish that negative free cash flow from the cash flows that involve claimants paying into the firm to cover the free cash flow deficit. An analyst forecasting free cash flow for discounted cash flow analysis must not confuse the free cash flow with the financing flows. And a treasurer forecasting the cash needs of the business must forecast the cash surplus or deficit as distinct from the financing flows that will dispose of the surplus or will be needed to meet the deficit.

As with the income statement and balance sheet, the template in Chapter 7 guides the reformulation of the cash flow statement to identify cash flows appropriately. Review that chapter before beginning this one; focus on Figure 7.3. Four types of cash flow are identified there. Two are cash flows generated by the operating activities within the firm: *cash from operations (C)* and *cash investments in those operations (I)*. Two involve financing activities between the firm and its claimants outside the firm: *net dividends to shareholders (d)* and *net payments to debtholders and issuers (F)*. The reformulated cash flow statement gives the details of these four flows.

The four cash flows are tied together according to the cash conservation equation that was introduced in Chapter 7:

Free cash flow = Net payments to shareholders + Net payments to debtholders and issuers

$$C - I = d + F$$

Free cash flow from operations (on the left) is applied (on the right) to financing payments to shareholders (as net dividends, d) and debtholders and issuers (as interest and principal payments, F). Free cash flow can be negative, in which case the financing flows to claimants must be negative, in the form of cash from share issues, debt issues, or the sale of financial assets.

The GAAP statement of cash flows has the appearance of giving us the free cash flow and the flows for financing activities, but it somewhat confuses the two. The form of the statement appears below, along with the form of the reformulated statement that follows the cash conservation equation. The GAAP statement can come in two forms,

---

GAAP Statement of Cash Flows

   Cash flow from operations
− Cash used in investing activities
+ <u>Cash from financing activities</u>
= <u>Change in cash and cash equivalents</u>

Reformulated Statement of Cash Flows

   Cash flow from operations
− <u>Cash investments</u>
= <u>Free cash flow from operating activities</u>
   Cash paid to shareholders
+ <u>Cash paid to debtholders and issuers</u>
= <u>Cash paid for financing activities</u>

---

one using the direct method and one using the indirect method. Box 10.3 explains the direct and indirect presentations.

Reclassifying Cash Transactions

Exhibit 10.1 gives Nike's 1996 comparative statement of cash flows. This statement uses the indirect method of presentation. Nike reports cash from operations of $330,021 thousand in 1996 and cash investment of $229,985 thousand so we might conclude that free cash flow equals the difference, $100 million. This number disagrees with our earlier calculation (in Box 10.1) of $98 million. Which is correct? In Nike's case, the difference is small. But this is not always the case.

The GAAP statement of cash flows is governed by FASB Statement No. 95. The statement suffers from a number of deficiencies, including transparent misclassifications of cash flow. Here are the main problems we encounter in trying to discover free cash flow

The direct and indirect cash flow statements differ in their presentation of cash flow from operations.

DIRECT METHOD

The direct method lists the separate sources of cash inflow and cash outflow in operations in the following form:

Cash inflows

  Cash from sales

  Cash from rents

  Cash from royalties

  Cash interest

Cash outflows

  Cash paid to suppliers

  Cash paid to employees

  Cash paid for other operating activities

  Cash paid for interest

  Cash paid for income taxes

The difference between cash inflows and cash outflows is cash from operations.

The cash from operations section of the 2001 comparative cash flow statement for Northrop Grumman Corp., the defense contractor, uses the direct method:

	Year Ended December 31, $ in millions	
	2001	2002
Operating Activities		
Sources of cash		
Cash received from customers		
Progress payments	3,102	1,438
Other collections	11,148	7,003
Interest received	17	17
Income tax refunds received	23	15
Other cash receipts	244	10
Cash provided by operating activities	14,534	8,483
Uses of cash		
Cash paid to suppliers and employees	13,251	7,250
Interest paid	333	165
Income taxes paid	126	57
Other cash payments	7	1
Cash used in operating activities	13,717	7,473
Net cash provided by operating activities	817	1,010

INDIRECT METHOD

The indirect method calculates cash from operations by adding back accrual (noncash) components of net income:

$$\begin{aligned} &\text{Net income} \\ +\ &\underline{\text{Accruals}} \\ =\ &\underline{\text{Cash from operations}} \end{aligned}$$

See Exhibit 10.1 for an example.

The indirect method has the feature of identifying the accruals made in calculating net income, and so it reconciles net income to cash flow. But the direct method has the advantage of listing the individual cash flows that generate the net cash, so it is more informative about the sources of cash flows. (If the direct method is used, a reconciliation of cash flow from operations to net income must be supplied.) Most firms use the indirect method.

from the GAAP statement.[1] Some have already been encountered in the discussion in Chapter 4.

1. **Change in cash and cash equivalents**. The GAAP statement is set up to explain the change in cash and cash equivalents (flagged 1 in Nike's statement). But cash generated has to be disposed of somewhere. Any change in cash needed for operations is an

[1] For a more detailed review, see H. Numberg, "Inconsistencies and Ambiguities in Cash Flow Statements under FASB Statement No. 95," *Accounting Horizons,* June 1993, pp. 60–75.

EXHIBIT 10.1
GAAP Consolidated Statement of Cash Flows for Nike, Inc., 1996 Numbers on the right-hand side flag the adjustments numbered in the text.

NIKE, INC.
GAAP Statement of Cash Flows
(in thousands)

	Year ended May 31			
	1996	**1995**	**1994**	
Cash provided (used) by operations:				
Net income	$553,190	$399,664	$298,794	**(3)(4)**
Income charges (credits) not affecting cash:				
Depreciation	97,179	71,113	64,531	
Deferred income taxes and purchased tax benefits	(73,279)	(24,668)	(23,876)	
Other liabilities	(465)	(1,359)	(3,588)	
Amortization and other	35,199	19,125	8,067	
Changes in certain working capital components:				
(Increase) decrease in inventory	(301,409)	(69,676)	160,823	
(Increase) decrease in accounts receivable	(292,888)	(301,648)	23,979	
(Increase) decrease in other current assets	(20,054)	(10,276)	6,888	
Increase (decrease) in accounts payable, accrued liabilities and income taxes payable	332,548	172,638	40,845	
Cash provided by operations	330,021	254,913	576,463	
Cash provided (used) by investing activities:				
Additions to property, plant, and equipment	(216,384)	(154,125)	(95,266)	
Disposals of property, plant, and equipment	12,775	9,011	12,650	
Additions to other assets	(26,376)	(6,260)	(5,450)	
Acquisition of subsidiaries:				
Identifiable intangible assets and goodwill	—	(345,901)	(2,185)	
Net assets acquired	—	(84,119)	(1,367)	
Cash used by investing activities	(229,985)	(581,394)	(91,618)	
Cash provided (used) by financing activities:				
Additions to long-term debt	5,044	2,971	6,044	
Reductions in long-term debt	(30,352)	(39,804)	(56,986)	
Increase (decrease) in notes payable	47,964	263,874	(2,939)	
Proceeds from exercise of options	21,150	6,154	4,288	
Repurchase of stock	(18,756)	(142,919)	(140,104)	
Dividends common and preferred	(78,834)	(65,418)	(60,282)	
Cash provided (used) by financing activities	(53,784)	24,858	(249,979)	
Effect of exchange rate changes on cash	(206)	(1,122)	(7,334)	
Net (decrease) increase in cash and equivalents	46,046	(302,745)	227,532	**(1)**
Cash and equivalents, beginning of year	216,071	518,816	291,284	
Cash and equivalents, end of year	$262,117	$216,071	$518,816	
Supplemental disclosure of cash flow information:				
Cash paid during the year for:				
Interest (net of amount capitalized)	$ 32,800	$ 20,200	$ 11,300	

investment in an operating asset that should be included in the cash investment section. The change in cash equivalents that earn interest is an investment of excess cash (over that needed for operations) in financial assets that should be in the debt financing section.

1. Change in Cash: Nike, Inc.

Nike's cash and cash equivalents increased by 46 million in 1996. In the reformulated balance sheet we attributed this to investment in cash equivalents (financial assets) of $39 million and an increase in operating cash of $7 million. So reclassify $7 million as cash investment in operations and $39 million as a debt financing flow.

2. **Transactions in financial assets**. Investments in financial assets such as short-term marketable securities and long-term debt securities are included in the investments section rather than in the financing section in the GAAP statement, but these investments are a disposition of free cash flow, not a reduction of free cash flow. If a firm invests its (surplus) free cash flow from operations in financial assets, the GAAP classification gives the appearance that the firm is reducing its free cash flow further. Similarly, sales of financial assets to provide cash for operations (or dividends) are classified in GAAP statements as investment flows rather than financing flows. These sales satisfy a free cash flow shortfall, they do not create it. There are no transactions in financial assets in Nike's statement, but see the box in this section that focuses on Lucent Technologies.

2. Transactions on Financial Assets: Lucent Technologies

Lucent Technologies is the telecommunications network supplier that was spun off from AT&T in 1996. The firm includes the research capabilities of the former Bell Laboratories. With the heavy network investment during the telecom boom of the late 1990s, Lucent became a "hot stock," with its share price rising to $60 by late 1999, yielding a P/E of 52. The firm was a darling of technology analysts, but some were concerned about the firm's declining cash flow from operations. Net income and cash from operations are given below for the years 1997–1999, along with the investment section of the firm's cash flow statement (in millions of dollars).

	Fiscal Year Ending September 30		
	1999	**1998**	**1997**
Net income	$ 4,766	$ 1,035	$ 449
Cash from operating activities	(276)	1,860	2,129
Cash in investing activities:			
Capital expenditures	(2,215)	(1,791)	(1,744)
Proceeds from the sale or disposal of property, plant, and equipment	97	57	108
Purchases of equity investments	(307)	(212)	(149)

(continued)

2. Transactions on Financial Assets: Lucent Technologies
(continued)

	Fiscal Year Ending September 30		
	1999	**1998**	**1997**
Sales of equity investments	156	71	12
Purchases of investment securities	(450)	(1,082)	(483)
Sales or maturity of investment securities	1,132	686	356
Dispositions of businesses	72	329	181
Acquisitions of businesses—net of cash acquired	(264)	(1,078)	(1,584)
Cash from mergers	61	—	—
Other investing activities—net	(69)	(80)	(68)
Net cash used in investing activities	(1,787)	(3,100)	(3,371)

Despite increasing profits, free cash flow (the difference between cash from operating activities and cash used in investing activities) appears to be negative in each of the three years. This is not unusual if a firm is increasing its investment to generate profits (as with Wal-Mart in Exhibit 4.2). However, Lucent reported a shortfall of cash from operations, before investment, of $276 million in 1999 (the shortfall after adding back after-tax net interest payments is $191 million). Cash investment also declined in 1999, but the $1,787 million number is misleading. This is the amount after selling interest-bearing investments for $1,132 million, as you see in the investing section of the statement. The net proceeds from these investments, after purchases of $450 million, is $682 million. So the actual investment in operations was $1,787 + $682 = $2,269 million, not $1,787 million.

Free cash flow calculated from GAAP numbers can be quite misleading. A firm like Lucent, faced with a cash shortfall, can sell securities in which it is storing excess cash to satisfy the shortfall. Under GAAP reporting, it looks as if it is increasing free cash flow by doing so, making it look less serious than it is. GAAP reporting mixes the cash flow deficit with the means employed to deal with the deficit.

Postscript: Lucent's negative cash flow in 1999 was an indicator of things to follow. With the bursting of the telecom bubble, Lucent's share price declined to below $2 per share by 2003. The firm's accounting came into question. See Minicase M17.2 in Chapter 17 where these same cash flow statements are investigated to raise accounting issues.

3. **Net cash interest**. Cash interest payments and receipts for financing activities are included in cash flow from operations rather than classified as a financing flow. In Nike's statement they are in cash flow from operations because they are in net income from which the accruals are subtracted. See the accompanying box for some more extreme examples.

An exception to including net interest in operations is interest capitalized during construction. This is classified, inappropriately, as cash investment because it is accounted for as an investment in constructed assets (see the note on interest payments in Nike's cash flow statement in Exhibit 10.1). But interest to finance construction projects is not part of the cost of construction and should be classified as a financing cash flow. Unfortunately, disclosure is usually not sufficient to sort this out.

3. Interest Payments: Westinghouse and Turner Broadcasting System

An extreme case of interest payments distorting cash flow from operations appears in the 1991 cash flow statement for Westinghouse. The reported cash flow was $703 million but that was after $1.006 billion of interest payments. If these interest payments had been classified as financing outflows, the cash flow from operations figure, before tax, would have been $1.709 billion, or 243 percent higher.

The peculiarity of treating interest as an operating flow can be seen in the case of zero coupon or deep discount debt. The repayment of the principal at face value is a financing flow, but GAAP requires the difference between face value and the issue amount (the issue discount) to be treated as an operating cash flow at maturity rather than part of the repayment of principal. So repayment of debt reduces operating cash flow. Accordingly, in 1990 Turner Broadcasting System deducted $206.1 million of issue discounts on zero coupon senior notes repaid in calculating an operating cash flow of $25.8 million. This is correct accounting according to GAAP, but the reported operating cash flow is an 89 percent distortion of the actual $231.9 million number.

4. **Tax on net interest.** Just as cash from interest income and expense is confused with operating cash flows, so are taxes paid on financing and operating income. All tax cash flows are included in cash from operations, even though some apply to financial income or are reduced by financial expenses. We seek to separate after-tax operating cash flows from after-tax financing cash flows, but the GAAP statement blurs this distinction. The accompanying box calculates Nike's after-tax net interest to adjust GAAP cash flow from operations.

4. Taxes on Net Interest Payments: Nike, Inc.

Nike's 1996 net interest payments after tax are calculated as follows (in thousands of dollars):

Interest payments	$32,800
Interest income	(16,000)
Net interest payments before tax	16,800
Tax benefit (38.5%)	6,468
Net interest payments after tax	10,332

The after-tax net interest of $10,332 thousand is added back to cash from operations in the reformulated statement and classified instead as a financing payment to debtholders.

Cash interest payments must be disclosed by firms in footnotes: Nike's disclosure of its interest payments is found at the bottom of the cash flow statement in Exhibit 10.1. Convert these interest payments to an after-tax basis at the marginal tax rate. Cash interest receipts are usually not reported. The accrual number in the income statement has to be used for interest receipts; this number will equal the cash number only if the opening and closing interest accruals are the same.

5. Noncash transactions. Nike had no noncash transactions in 1996, but it did report noncash transactions in 2000. See the accompanying box. In a **noncash transaction,** an asset is acquired or an expense is incurred by the firm by assuming a liability (by writing a note, for example) or by issuing stock. An acquisition of another firm for stock is a noncash transaction. Capitalized leases are recorded as assets and liabilities, but there is no cash flow for the purchase. A noncash transaction can involve an asset exchange (one asset for another) or a liability exchange, or a conversion of debt to equity or vice versa. With the exception of asset and liability exchanges within operating and financing categories, these noncash transactions affect the Method 1 and Method 2 calculations of free cash flow because they affect NOA or NFO. Implicitly we interpret these as if there were a sale of something for cash and an immediate purchase of something else with that cash. The GAAP statement recognizes these transactions as not involving cash flows. This of course is strictly correct but it obscures the investing and financing activities, and the "as-if" cash flow accounting uncovers them. Consider the following examples:

- Debt that is converted to equity is not indicated as a payment of a loan (in the financing section) in a GAAP statement even though the proceeds from the loan were recorded there in an earlier year when the debt was issued.

- If a firm acquires an asset by writing a note, the payment of the note is recorded in subsequent years but the original principal that is being paid off is not.

- For leases, nothing is recorded at the inception of the lease, but subsequent lease payments are divided between interest and principal repayments and recorded in the operating and financing sections, respectively, in the GAAP statement. The firm appears to be paying off a phantom loan.

- For an installment purchase of plant assets, only the initial installment is classified as investment. Subsequent payments are classified as financing flows. However, when a firm sells an asset, all installments are investing inflows from the liquidation. Obtaining details is difficult.

The upshot of all this is that we don't get a complete picture of firms' investment and financing activities. In all cases of noncash transactions, the "as-if" cash must be reported in supplemental disclosures so that implicit cash flows can be reconstructed.

5. Noncash Transactions: Nike, Inc., 2000

At the foot of its 2000 statement of cash flows, Nike reported the following (numbers in thousands):

Assumption of long-term debt to acquire property, plant, and equipment $108.9

This transaction was not incorporated in the GAAP cash flow statement. To adjust the statement, add $108.9 thousand to cash investments and $108.9 thousand to issue of debt in financing activities.

Tying It Together

Box 10.4 summarizes the adjustments that must be made to the GAAP statement of cash flows and makes the adjustment to Nike's statement. The numbers accompanying selected items flag them as one of the five adjustments above.

REFORMULATING GAAP CASH FLOW STATEMENTS

GAAP free cash flow
− Increase in operating cash	1
+ Purchase of financial assets	2
− Sale of financial assets	2
+ Net cash interest outflow (after tax)	3,4
− Noncash investments	5
− Investment in operating assets on installment basis	5
= Free cash flow	

GAAP financing flow
+ Increase in cash equivalents	1
+ Purchase of financial assets	2
− Sale of financial assets	2
+ Net cash interest outflow (after tax)	3,4
− Noncash financing	5
= Financing cash flow	

Nike, Inc.: Reformulated Cash Flow Statement, 1996 (in millions of dollars)

Free Cash Flow:			
Reported cash from operations			$330
3,4 Net interest paid after tax			10
			340
Cash investments reported		$230	
1 Investment in operating cash		7	237
Free cash flow			$103
Financing Flow to Claimants			
Debt financing:			
Additions to long-term debt		(5)	
Reductions to long-term debt		30	
Increase in notes payable		(48)	
3,4 Interest paid, after taxes		10	
1 Investments in cash equivalents		39	26
Equity financing:			
Share issues (from exercise of options)		(21)	
Repurchase of share		19	
Dividends		79	77
Total financing flows			$103

The free cash flow of $103 million in Nike's reformulated statement differs from the $98 million calculated under Method 1 and Method 2 (see Box 10.1). This often happens because of incomplete disclosures. In accounting terms, it is usually not possible to reconcile the cash flow statement to the income statement and balance sheet precisely. The likely reasons for the differences in the calculation are

- "Other assets" and "other liabilities" can't be classified into operating and financing items appropriately. In particular, interest receivable and payable (financing items) cannot be distinguished from operating items in these "other" categories.

- Cash dividends (in the cash flow statement) differ from dividends in the statement of equity, implying a dividend payable that cannot be discovered, as with Nike in 1996 (because it is probably lumped into "other liabilities").

- Cash received in share issues (in the cash flow statement) differs from the amount for those share transactions in the statement of equity, as with Nike. The difference implies a receivable (for shares issued but not paid) that has not been discovered.

- The details for adjustments 3, 4, and 5 above are not available.

- When foreign subsidiaries are involved, balance sheet items are translated into dollar amounts at beginning and end-of-year exchange rates while cash flow items are translated at average exchange rates.

If the difference between the two free cash flow calculations is small, it can of course be ignored. But if material, the analyst has to dig further, ask questions of the company, or guess.

The reconciliation of the two numbers is not only relevant to getting a sound free cash flow number. Any misclassification of operating and financing assets and liabilities that produces the difference also affects the calculation of operating profitability (RNOA) and net borrowing costs (NBC). So the exercise in calculating free cash flow using the different methods serves as a validity check on the analysis of the income statement and balance sheet. An error in reformatting the income statement or balance sheet produces a difference in the two free cash flow calculations. And an error in reformulating the income statement and balance sheet results in ratios (to be used in valuation) that are in error. So the analysis here is a prerequisite to sound ratio analysis in Chapters 11 and 12.

But let's not miss the forest for the trees. Calculations aside, what is the picture drawn here? Following the reformulated statement, Nike had a free cash flow from operations of $103 million because cash investments were less than cash from operations. The firm used this cash to pay out $26 million to debtholders and issuers and a net $77 million to shareholders.

CASH FLOW FROM OPERATIONS

Our calculations following Methods 1 and 2 yield a number for free cash flow but do not distinguish the two components, cash flow from operations and cash investments, in the free cash flow number. For that we need the cash flow statement. But, again, we run into problems with the reporting. The reason is that some of the cash flows that we might view as investment flows are included in cash from operations in the GAAP statement. Investment in research and development is part of cash from operations rather than part of the investment section. And investments in short-term assets are classified as cash from operations. Consider inventories. Investments in inventory are necessary to carry out operations just like plant and equipment. But the cash spent on building up inventory reduces GAAP cash from operations just like cash spent in inventory that is shipped to customers.

Potentially we could make further adjustments to cash flow from operations for these investments. But that should be done only if there is a clear purpose. For many analysis tasks, it is free cash flow that is needed, and a misclassification of an investment as an operating rather than investment flow does not affect this number. Because expenditures on R&D activities, a long-run investment, are classified as a decrease in cash from operations in financial statements, the R&D expenditures are added back to calculate the appropriate cash from operations. But the misclassification does not affect the calculation of free cash flow from the statement. The treatment of investment in brand name through advertising, which also reduces GAAP cash flow from operations, is similar.

Obviously, the analyst must handle the "cash flow from operations" number carefully. See Box 10.5.

CASH FLOW AND PRODUCT LIFE CYCLES

We observed in Chapter 4 that free cash flow is not a good measure of value added in a business. Firms that are very profitable can have negative free cash flow and firms that are marginally profitable can have considerable free cash flow. Free cash flow incorporates cash investment, which reduces net cash from operations. Profitable firms invest more, and when firms invest intensively for the future, free cash flow is low and even negative. When cash ultimately flows in from those investments, or when investments level off or decline, free cash flows are higher.

Commentators sometimes point to "cash from operations" as a pristine number on which to judge the operating performance of a firm. But the fundamental analyst is cynical.

CASH FLOW AND NONCASH CHARGES

Cash flow from operations is often promoted as a better number than earnings on which to rely because it dismisses noncash charges like depreciation. Analysts often view those charges as coming from "bookkeeping rules" that do not affect the cash generation. However, one ignores depreciation to one's peril. Depreciation is not a cash flow in the period when it is charged, but it certainly comes from cash outflows, made earlier, for investments. And those investments are necessary to generate cash from operations. If one refers to cash flows rather than earnings, one should refer to net cash flow—cash flow from operations less the cash invested to deliver cash from operations—which, of course, is free cash flow.

In 2001, Electronic Data Systems Corporation (EDS), the computer systems vendor, reported cash flow from operations of $1,722 million. This was more than the $1,363 million reported in earnings. However, this number was the result of adding back $1,482 million from earnings for depreciation of plant and amortization of software costs. Looking at the investment section of the cash flow statement, the analyst would find that the current expenditure in plant and software was $1,579 million (and free cash flow was –$1,902 million, a deficit). These expenditures were necessary to maintain cash from operations in the future. Touting cash from operations without considering the cash expenditures (or depreciation) needed to maintain the cash from operations gives a false impression of the ability of the firm to generate cash from operations.

Tax Benefits from Exercise of Stock Options

Tax benefits from the exercise of stock options—which we saw in Chapter 8 are recognized in the equity statement (incorrectly) as equity financing—are not recognized as equity financing in the GAAP cash flow statement. Rather they are recognized as cash from operations. This treatment is indeed appropriate (as the tax benefits arise from an operating activity, compensating employees), but the associated stock compensation expense which gives rise to the tax benefit is not recognized. Accordingly, cash flow from operations is overstated. In 2000, Intel reported $887 million from these tax benefits, Cisco Systems reported $2.5 billion, and Microsoft reported $5.5 billion, all part of cash from operations.

Delaying Payments

Firms can increase cash flow simply by delaying payments on accounts payable and other operating obligations. The delay does not affect earnings. Home Depot, the warehouse retailer, reported cash from operations of $5,942 million for fiscal year 2002, up from $2,977 million from the year earlier. But $1,643 million of the amount reported in 2002 came from an increase in accounts payable and taxes payable.

Advertising and R&D Expenditures

Because advertising and research and development expenditures are treated as cash from operations rather than cash investment under GAAP, cash from operations can be increased by reducing these expenditures (with adverse consequences for the future).

Advancing Payments of Receivables

Firms can increase cash flow by selling or securitizing receivables. This does not, however, represent an ability to generate cash from sales of products.

Noncash Transactions

Firms can increase cash from operations by paying for services with debt or share issues. Deferring the payment of wages with a payable or pension promise increases cash flow, as does compensation "paid" with stock options rather than cash (and the latter further increases cash flow through the tax benefit, as explained above).

The cash from operations number is useful for challenging the quality of earnings, so we return to cash flow in Chapter 17—but with the caveats above in mind.

So it is that free cash flow typically varies over a **product life cycle** or the life cycle of the firm, as depicted in Figure 10.1. In early stages of the life of a product or a firm, cash flow from operations is typically low as products take time to be accepted by the market. At the same time, the firm may be investing heavily to provide capacity to meet future demand and to generate brand recognition. So free cash flow is even lower. This stage of the life cycle is referred to as the *growth stage*. If demand for the product materializes, cash flows in. And if capacity from earlier investment is sufficient and brand presence is established, investment levels off, further generating free cash flow. This is the *maturity stage*. If demand should subsequently fall off, the product enters a *decline stage*, where

FIGURE 10.1

Cash Flow from Operations, Cash Investment, and Free Cash Flow over a Product or Firm Life Cycle In the growth stage, a firm invests heavily so that cash investment is higher than cash from operations, yielding negative free cash flow. In the mature stage, investments level off and cash flow from operations is greater than cash spent on investment. In the decline stage, cash inflows decline, but investments also decline.

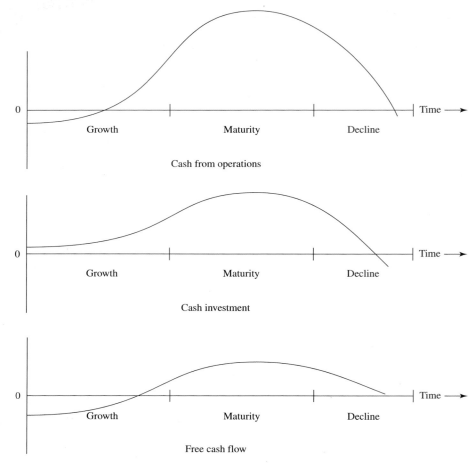

cash inflows from operations decline, but free cash flow is generated by reducing investments, at least for a period.

The Internet stocks were in the growth stage at the end of the 1990s, as were computer technology stocks in the 1980s and biotechnology stocks in the early 1990s. Firms like General Electric and Coca-Cola are now in the mature stage, as are the computer technology stocks like Microsoft, Intel, and Dell. In Chapter 4 we saw that Wal-Mart Stores was in a long growth stage until 1996, generating negative free cash flows, as indicated again in Table 10.1. But by 1997 Wal-Mart had entered a mature stage with increases in free cash flow from prior investment and a slowing down of the growth in investment.

As free cash flow always equals financing flows, the three stages are also stages in the financing of a firm. In the growth stage, firms need to raise cash from share issues and borrowing. In the mature and decline stages, cash generated pays down debt or is paid out to shareholders. If the cash generated is in excess of debt servicing and the net dividend, the firm invests in financial assets. Note, however, that the ability to pay a dividend is not necessarily related to the free cash flow: A firm can borrow to pay a dividend if free cash flow is insufficient.

The division of life cycles into three stages is a way to organize one's thinking for forecasting cash flows for the typical firm. But not all firms follow the pattern. Some

TABLE 10.1 **Wal-Mart Stores Inc.: Cash Flows**
Fiscal years ending January 31. Amounts in millions of dollars.

	1991	1992	1993	1994	1995	1996	1997	1998	1999	2000	2001	2002
Cash from operations	1,422	1,553	1,540	2,573	3,410	2,993	6,483	7,660	8,103	8,737	10,448	11,110
Cash investments	1,526	2,150	3,506	4,486	3,792	3,332	2,068	4,421	4,418	16,846	8,714	7,146
Free cash flow	(104)	(597)	(1,966)	(1,913)	(382)	(339)	4,415	3,239	3,685	(8,109)	1,734	3,964

successful firms, like Wal-Mart, are in growth mode for a long time and some, like Microsoft, are almost instantly mature. Some firms (like many Internet stocks) fail to progress out of the initial stage. The growth analysis of Chapter 12 is pertinent to the former, the default analysis of Chapter 19 is pertinent to the latter. Many firms adapt to threats of decline and are able to stay in a mature stage indefinitely. The adaption analysis of Chapter 18 is pertinent.

Summary

The analyst looks to the cash flow statement to assess the ability of the firm to generate cash. Free cash flow is a particular focus, for free cash flow is necessary to anticipate liquidity and financing requirements in the future. And free cash flow forecasts are required if the analyst employs discounted cash flow methods for valuation. Subsequent chapters that involve forecasting cash will rely on the analysis of this chapter.

Unfortunately, the GAAP statement of cash flows is a little messy. But, having reformulated income statements and balance sheets appropriately, free cash flow can be calculated simply by Methods 1 and 2 laid out in this chapter. So we will see in the forecasting part of the book that once forecasted (reformulated) income statements and balance sheets are prepared, forecasting free cash flow involves one simple calculation from these statements. It is hard to think of forecasting free cash flow without thinking of future sales, profitability, and investments that will be reported in the income statement and balance sheet, so forecasting these statements is needed to forecast free cash flow. And if those statements are in reformulated form, the forecasted free cash flow drops out of them immediately. This is a very efficient way of proceeding.

If we wish to read the free cash flow from the GAAP statement of cash flows, this chapter has presented the adjustments to the GAAP statement that are necessary. These adjustments reformulate the statement to categorize cash flows correctly, so that free cash flow is isolated and shown to be equal to the financing flows.

The Web Connection

Find the following on the web page for this chapter:

- Further examples of reformulated statements.

- Further discussion of problems raised by the GAAP presentation of the cash flow statement.

- Presentation of the cash flow statement under international accounting standards and U.K. GAAP.

- Further discussion of how firms can manipulate the cash from operations number.

Key Concepts

financial planning is planning to arrange financing to meet the future cash flow needs of the business. *323*

liquidity analysis is the analysis of current and future cash relative to the claims on cash. *323*

noncash transaction involves the acquisition of an asset or the incurring of an expense by assuming a liability or by issuing stock, without any cash involved. *332*

product life cycle of growth, maturity, and decline depicts stages of a product's life over which free cash flow is likely to vary. *335*

The Analyst's Toolkit

Analysis Tools	Page	Key Measures	Page
Method 1 for calculating free cash flow (equation 10.1)	324	Cash flow from operations	326
		Cash flow in financing activities	326
Method 2 for calculating free cash flow (equation 10.2)	324	Cash flow in investing activities	326
		Free cash flow	326
Direct method for cash flow from operations	327	Net cash interest	330
Indirect method for cash flow from operations	327	Tax on net interest	331
Reformulated cash flow statements	326		

Concept Questions

C10.1. Why might cash flow analysis be important for valuing firms?

C10.2. For what purposes might forecasting cash flows be an analysis tool?

C10.3. For a pure equity firm (with no net debt), how is free cash flow disposed of?

C10.4. By investing in short-term securities to absorb excess cash, a firm reduces its cash flow after investing activities in its published cash flow statement. What is wrong with this picture?

C10.5. Do you consider the direct method to be more informative than the indirect method of presenting cash flow from operations?

C10.6. GAAP cash flow statements treat interest capitalized during construction as investment in plant. Do you agree with this practice?

C10.7. Why is free cash flow sometimes referred to as a liquidation concept?

C10.8. Is a firm in a strong growth stage more likely to have positive or negative free cash flow?

C10.9. Why might an analyst not put much weight on a firm's current free cash flow as an indication of future free cash flow?

C10.10. What factors produce growth in free cash flow?

Exercises   E10.1.   Analyzing Cash Flows (Medium)

Consider the following comparative balance sheets for the Liquidity Company:

	December 31	
	2003	**2002**
Cash	$ 435,000	$ 50,000
Accounts receivable	40,000	-0-
Inventories	100,000	-0-
Land (unamortized cost)	400,000	800,000
Plant assets	200,000	200,000
Less: accumulated depreciation	(100,000)	-0-
	1,075,000	1,050,000
Accounts payable	25,000	-0-
Capital stock	1,050,000	1,050,000
	$1,075,000	$1,050,000

The company paid a dividend of $150,000 during 2003 and there were no equity contributions.

a. Calculate free cash flow generated during 2003.
b. Where did the increase in cash come from?
c. How would your calculation in part (a) change if the cash were invested in a financial asset at December 31, 2003?

E10.2.   Free Cash Flow for a Pure Equity Firm (Easy)

The following information is from the financial report of a pure equity company (one with no net debt). In millions of dollars.

Common shareholders' equity, December 31, 2002	174.8
Common dividends, paid December 2003	8.3
Issue of common shares on December 31, 2003	34.4
Common shareholders' equity, December 31, 2003	226.2

The firm had no share repurchases during 2003.
Calculate the firm's free cash flow for 2003.

E10.3.   Free Cash Flow for a Net Debtor (Easy)

The following information is for a firm that has net debt on its balance sheet. In millions of dollars.

Common shareholders' equity, December 31, 2002	174.8
Common dividends, paid December 2003	8.3
Issue of common shares, December 2003	34.4
Common shareholders' equity, December 31, 2003	226.2
Net debt, December 31, 2002	54.3
Net debt, December 31, 2003	37.4

There were no share repurchases during 2003. The firm reported net interest after tax of $4 million on its income statement for 2003, and this interest was paid in cash.
Calculate the firm's free cash flow for 2003.

E10.4. **Applying Cash Flow Relations (Easy)**

A firm reported free cash flow of $430 million and operating income of $390 million.

a. By how much did its net operating assets change during the period?

b. The firm invested $29 million cash in new operating assets during the period. What were its operating accruals?

c. The firm incurred net financial expenses of $43 million, paid a dividend of $20 million, and raised $33 million from share issues. What was the change in its net debt position during the period?

E10.5. **Applying Cash Flow Relations (Medium)**

An analyst prepared reformulated balance sheets for the years 2002 and 2003 as follows (in millions of dollars):

	2003	2002
Operating assets	$640	$590
Financial assets	250	110
	890	700
Financial debt	170	130
Operating liabilities	20	30
Common equity	700	540
	$890	$700

The firm reported $100 million in comprehensive income for 2003 and no net financial income or expense.

a. Calculate the free cash flow for 2003.

b. How was the free cash flow disposed of?

c. How can a firm with financial assets and financial liabilities have zero net financial income on expense?

E10.6. **Calculating Free Cash Flow: Ben & Jerry's (Medium)**

The 1996 comparative balance sheet and income statement for Ben & Jerry's Homemade, Inc., the manufacturer of premium ice cream and frozen yogurt, are summarized below. Ben & Jerry's statement of cash flows for 1996 is also given. All numbers, except per-share items, are in millions of dollars. The firm's marginal tax rate is 38 percent. From the three financial statements, calculate free cash flow in three different ways.

BEN & JERRY'S HOMEMADE, INC.
Balance Sheets

	1996	1995
Short-term investments	36.6	35.4
Trade receivables	8.7	11.7
Other receivables	0.3	0.9
Inventories	15.4	12.6
Other current operating assets	7.1	7.5
Current assets	68.1	68.1
Plant, net	65.1	59.6
Equity investments at market value	1.0	1.0
Other long-term operating assets	2.5	2.4
	136.7	131.1

Trade payables and accrued expenses	17.4	16.5
Current portion of long-term debt	0.6	0.5
	18.0	17.0
Long-term debt and lease obligations	31.1	32.0
Deferred tax liability	4.8	3.5
	53.9	52.5
Common stock	47.5	47.2
Retained earnings	35.2	31.3
Cumulative currency translation adjustment	0.1	0.1
	136.7	131.1

Income Statements

	1996	1995
Net sales	167.1	155.3
Cost of sales	115.2	109.1
Gross profit	51.9	46.2
Selling, general, and administrative expenses	45.5	36.4
	6.4	9.8
Other income (expense)		
Interest income	1.7	1.7
Interest expense	(2.0)	(1.5)
Other	0.2	(0.6)
Income before income taxes	6.3	9.4
Income taxes	2.4	3.5
Net income	3.9	5.9
Net income per common share	0.54	0.83

Statement of Cash Flows

	1996
Cash Flows from Operating Activities	
Net income (loss)	$ 3.9
Adjustments to reconcile net income (loss) to net cash provided by operating activities:	
Depreciation and amortization	7.1
Deferred income taxes	0.8
Provision for doubtful accounts	0.4
Changes in assets and liabilities	
Accounts receivable	3.1
Inventories	(2.7)
Prepaid expenses	0.9
Accounts payable and accrued expenses	0.8
Net cash provided by operating activities	14.3
Cash Flows from Investing Activities	
Additions to property, plant, and equipment	(12.3)
Proceeds from sale of property, plant, and equipment	0.1
Increase (decrease) in investments	(0.4)
Changes in other assets	(0.3)
Net cash used for investing activities	(12.9)

(continued)

Cash Flows from Financing Activities	
Net proceeds from long-term debt	
Repayments of long-term debt and capital leases	(0.6)
Net proceeds from issuance of common stock	0.2
Net cash (used for) provided by financing activities	(0.4)
Effect of exchange rate changes on cash	(0.2)
Increase in cash and cash equivalents	0.8
Cash and cash equivalents at beginning of year	35.4
Cash and Cash Equivalents at End of Year	36.2

Real World Connection

See E11.8 in Chapter 11, Exercise E13.8 in Chapter 13, and Exercise E14.2 in Chapter 14 for more material on Ben & Jerry's.

E10.7. **Unlevering Free Cash Flows: Waste Management, Inc. (Hard)**

Waste Management, Inc., the waste disposal firm, reported cash flow from operations for 1998 of $1,502,035 thousand. Its cash flows from investing activities in its cash flow statement was presented as follows (in thousands of dollars):

Cash flows from investing activities	
Short-term investments	$ 57,509
Acquisitions of businesses, net of cash acquired	(1,946,197)
Capital expenditures	(1,651,489)
Proceeds from sale of assets	545,143
Other investments	76,244
Acquisition of minority interests	(1,673,168)
Other	36,821
Net cash used in investing activities	$(4,555,137)

Footnotes to the financial statements indicate that total interest costs for 1998 were $722,958 thousand, and $26,829 thousand was recognized as interest income. But footnotes also revealed that $41,501 thousand in interest was capitalized in the construction of landfill projects and waste-to-energy facilities.

Calculate (unlevered) free cash flow from operations. Use a 38 percent tax rate.

E10.8. **Analyzing a Change in Free Cash Flow: Wal-Mart Stores (Medium)**

The excerpts from Wal-Mart's cash flow statements below show that reported free cash flow increased from a deficit of $949 million in 1996 to a surplus of $3,862 million in 1997. Yet net income increased by only $316 million.

	Fiscal Years Ended January 31	
(Amounts in millions)	1997	1996
Cash Flows from Operating Activities		
Net income	$3,056	$2,740
Adjustments to reconcile net income to net cash provided by operating activities		
Depreciation and amortization	1,463	1,304
Increase in accounts receivable	(58)	(61)
Increase/decrease in inventories	99	(1,850)
Increase in accounts payable	1,208	448
Increase in accrued liabilities	430	29
Deferred income taxes	(180)	76
Other	(88)	(303)

Net cash provided by operating activities	5,930	2,383
Cash Flows from Investing Activities		
Payments for property, plant, and equipment	(2,643)	(3,566)
Proceeds from sale of photo finishing plants	464	
Other investing activities	111	234
Net cash used in investing activities	(2,068)	(3,332)

a. Explain the change in reported free cash flow from 1996 to 1997.
b. The text (in Table 10.1) gives numbers for Wal-Mart's free cash flow that differ from the reported numbers here. Speculate as to what the differences might be.

E10.9.   **Analysis of Profitability and Cash Flows: Quantum (Medium)**

Quantum Corporation is a leading supplier of hard disk drives for personal computers, notebook computers, and workstations and a manufacturer of tape storage devices.

Below are balance sheets and income statements for Quantum Corporation that have been reformulated to place them on a comprehensive income basis and to distinguish operating and financing activities. Amounts are in millions of dollars.

a. Compare the operating and financing profitability from 1994 to 1996.
b. Calculate free cash flow for 1994, 1995, and 1996. Explain the changes in free cash flow.
c. Explain how the firm went from a net creditor position to a net debtor position from 1994 to 1996.

QUANTUM CORPORATION
Balance Sheets

	1993	1994	1995	1996
Net Operating Assets				
Accounts receivable, net of doubtful accounts	$266,992	$324,376	$497,887	$711,107
Inventories	223,107	194,083	324,650	459,538
Deferred taxes	37,479	32,821	44,054	109,625
Other current assets	13,094	14,365	35,580	81,472
Net property, plant, and equipment	74,698	85,874	280,099	364,111
Purchased intangibles	—	1,295	95,818	66,313
Other assets	19,034	14,585	15,187	18,437
Accounts payable	(215,909)	(267,189)	(355,117)	(498,829)
Accrued warranty expense	(42,410)	(55,617)	(57,001)	(62,289)
Accrued compensation	(17,189)	(15,315)	(54,917)	—
Income taxes payable	(19,020)	—	(17,566)	(11,232)
Accrued exit and restructuring costs	—	—	(32,213)	(103,165)
Other accrued liabilities	(21,825)	(35,545)	(77,227)	(152,734)
Net operating assets	318,051	293,733	699,234	982,354
Net Financial Obligations				
Cash and cash equivalents	(121,898)	(217,531)	(187,753)	(164,752)
Marketable securities	(170,751)	(112,508)	—	—
Short-term debt	—	—	50,000	4,125
Subordinated debentures	212,500	212,500	212,500	374,283
Long-term debt	—	—	115,000	223,875
Net financial obligations	(80,149)	(117,539)	189,747	437,531
Common Shareholders' Equity	$398,200	$411,272	$509,487	$544,823

Income Statements

	1993	1994	1995	1996
Core Operating Income				
Sales	$ 1,697,240	$ 2,131,054	$ 3,367,984	$ 4,422,726
Cost of sales	(1,374,422)	(1,892,211)	(2,804,271)	(3,880,309)
Operating expenses				
Research and development	(63,019)	(89,837)	(169,282)	(239,116)
Sales and marketing	(77,085)	(74,015)	(108,290)	(142,413)
General and administrative	(33,849)	(41,910)	(52,134)	(65,145)
Operating costs and expenses	(173,953)	(205,762)	(329,706)	(446,674)
Operating income	148,865	33,081	234,007	95,743
Tax on noncore income	(53,408)	(9,226)	(88,551)	(15,501)
Core operating income, after tax	95,457	23,855	145,456	80,242
Unusual Operating Income	—	(16,382)	(52,520)	(150,568)
Operating income	95,457	7,473	92,936	(70,326)
Net Financial Expenses	(1,646)	(4,799)	(11,345)	(20,130)
Net income available in common	$ 93,811	$ 2,674	$ 81,591	$ (90,456)

Real World Connection
See Exercise E12.3 in Chapter 12.

E10.10.   **What Is That in the Cash Flow Statement? Intel (Easy)**

Below are portions of the 1998 cash flow statement for Intel Corporation, the semiconductor manufacturer. The firm's 1998 income statement and balance sheet are given in exercise E9.1 of Chapter 9.

Calculate Intel's free cash flow for 1998. Use a 38 percent tax rate if necessary. Do you notice a particular feature in cash flow from operations that might raise an analyst's eyebrow?

INTEL CORPORATION
Statement of Cash Flow
(in millions of dollars)

	1998
Cash Flows Provided by (Used for) Operating Activities	
Net income	$6,068
Adjustments to reconcile net income to net cash provided by (used for) operating activities:	
Depreciation	2,807
Net loss on retirements of property, plant, and equipment	282
Deferred taxes	77
Purchased in-process research and development	165
Changes in assets and liabilities	
Accounts receivable	(38)
Inventories	167
Accounts payable	(180)
Accrued compensation and benefits	17
Income taxes payable	(211)
Tax benefit from employee stock plans	415
Other assets and liabilities	(378)
Total adjustments	3,123
Net cash provided by operating activities	$ 9,191

Cash Flows Provided by (Used for) Investing Activities

Additions to property, plant, and equipment	$(3,557)
Purchase of Chips and Technologies, Inc., net of cash acquired	(321)
Purchase of Digital Equipment Corporation semiconductor operations	(585)
Purchases of available-for-sale investments	(10,925)
Sales of available-for-sale investments	201
Maturities and other changes in available-for-sale investments	8,681
Net cash (used for) investing activities	$(6,506)

Real World Connection

See Exercise E4.4 in Chapter 4, Exercise E9.1 in Chapter 9, and Exercise E11.4 in Chapter 11.

E10.11. **Analysis of a Cash Flow Statement for a U.K. Company: Cadbury Schweppes, plc.**

The cash flow statement in the United Kingdom is laid out differently from the statement in the United States. The 1998 statement for Cadbury Schweppes, the confectionary and beverage manufacturer, is laid out under nine headings, as you see below.

a. From this statement, identify free cash flow and cash flow from financing activities. Use a 31 percent tax rate.

b. Compare this form of the cash flow statement with that for the U.S. statement. Which do you think is more transparent?

c. Discuss the "free cash flow" calculation at the bottom of the statement. Is it the same as the free cash flow you calculated?

CADBURY SCHWEPPES, PLC.
Group Cash Flow Statement
for the 52 weeks ended 2 January 1999

(Amounts in millions of pounds)	1998
Cash flow from operating activities	£ 686
Dividends received from associates	12
Returns on investments and servicing of finance	
Interest paid	(123)
Interest received	63
Dividends paid to minority interests	(30)
	(90)
Taxation	(122)
Capital expenditure and financial investments	
Purchases of tangible fixed assets	(157)
Disposals of tangible fixed assets	14
	(143)
Acquisitions and disposals	
Acquisitions of businesses	(96)
Expenditure on postacquisition restructuring	(4)
Proceeds from sale of investments, associates, and subsidiary undertakings	21
	(79)
Dividends paid to ordinary shareholders	(186)
Cash inflow/(outflow) before use of liquid resources and financing	78
Management of liquid resources	
Net change in commercial paper investments	24

Redemption of loan notes	278
Net change in bank deposits	(45)
Net change in bond investments	11
Net change in equity investments	(4)
	264

Financing

Issues of ordinary shares	31
Proceeds of new borrowings	129
Borrowings repaid	(484)
Proceeds of finance leases	6
Capital element of finance leases repaid	(6)
Net cash (outflow)/inflow from financing	(324)
Increase in cash	18

Free cash flow

Cash inflow/(outflow) before use of liquid resources and financing	78
Add back:	
Cash flows from acquisitions and disposals	79
	£ 157

Real World Connection

See Exercise E8.7 in Chapter 8.

Minicase

M10.1

Analysis of Cash Flows: Dell Computer

Dell Computer has been a very successful company, generating considerable cash flow from operations. The company can be analyzed thoroughly by working Minicase 12.1.

Dell's fiscal 2002 financial statements are given in Exhibit 2.1 of Chapter 2.

A. Reformulate the income statement and balance sheets to highlight the operating and financing activities, and calculate free cash flow from these statements. Compare this calculation to free cash flow calculated directly from the cash flow statement. Note, for your calculation, that Dell's marketable securities are substantially all debt securities and Dell's marginal tax rate is 35 percent. Can you speculate as to the reason for any discrepancies between the two calculations?

B. In 1999 Dell Computer Corporation began to report the cash benefit of taxes saved from employee stock option plans as part of cash flow from operations. Previously these tax benefits had been reported as part of financing cash flows.

What do you consider to be the appropriate classification of tax benefits from employee stock plans?

How does Dell's classification affect the reconciliation of the two cash flow numbers in question (A)?

C. Dell reports cash proceeds from the issue of common stock of $295 million in its 2002 cash flow statement. Yet it reports $853 million from the issue of stocks in its 2002 statement of shareholders' equity. Can you reconcile the two numbers?

D. What does your investigation of the cash flows tell you about the quality of Dell's financial statements?

Real World Connection

See material on Dell Computer in Chapter 2. Also see Exercise E1.1 in Chapter 1, Exercise E4.1 in Chapter 4, Exercise E5.10 in Chapter 5, Minicase M6.2 in Chapter 6, Exercises E8.3 and E8.8 in Chapter 8, Minicase M12.1 in Chapter 12, and Minicase M15.1 in Chapter 15.

Chapter **Eleven**

The Analysis of Profitability

LINKS

Link to previous chapters

Chapters 8, 9, and 10 reformulated the financial statements to prepare them for analysis.

This chapter

This chapter lays out the analysis of profitability that is necessary for forecasting future profitability and valuation.

Link to next chapter

Chapter 12 lays out the analysis of growth, to complete the analysis of the financial statements.

Link to web page

The website applies the analysis in this chapter to a wider range of firms (www.mhhe.com/ penman2e).

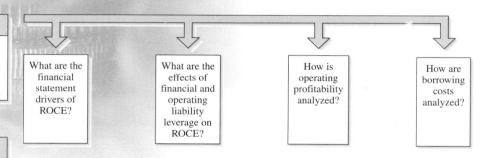

| What are the financial statement drivers of ROCE? | What are the effects of financial and operating liability leverage on ROCE? | How is operating profitability analyzed? | How are borrowing costs analyzed? |

The price-to-book valuation model of Chapter 5 directs us to forecast future residual earnings to value equities. The price-earnings valuation model of Chapter 6 directs us to forecast abnormal earnings growth. Residual earnings are determined by the profitability of shareholders' investment, ROCE, and the growth in equity investment. Earnings growth is also determined by growth in investment and the profitability of that investment. So forecasting involves forecasting profitability and growth. To forecast, we need to understand what drives ROCE and growth. The analysis of the drivers of ROCE is called **profitability analysis** and the analysis of growth is called **growth analysis**. This chapter covers profitability analysis. The next chapter covers growth analysis.

The reformulation of financial statements in the preceding chapters readies the statements for profitability and growth analysis. This and the next chapter complete the financial statement analysis.

Profitability analysis establishes where the firm is now. It discovers what drives current ROCE. Then, with this understanding of the present, the analyst begins to forecast

The Analyst's Checklist

After reading this chapter you should understand:

- How ratios aggregate to explain return on common equity (ROCE).
- How economic factors determine ratios.
- How financial leverage affects ROCE.
- How operating liability leverage affects ROCE.
- The difference between return on net operating assets (RNOA) and return on assets (ROA).
- How profit margins, asset turnovers, and their composite ratios drive RNOA.
- How borrowing costs are analyzed.
- How profitability analysis can be used to ask penetrating questions regarding the firm's activities.

After reading this chapter you should be able to:

- Calculate ratios that drive ROCE.
- Demonstrate how ratios combine to yield the ROCE.
- Perform a complete profitability analysis on reformulated financial statements.
- Prepare a spreadsheet program based on the design in this chapter. See the BYOAP feature on the text's website.
- Answer "what-if" questions about a firm using the analysis in this chapter.

(as we will see in Part Three of the book) by asking how future ROCE will be different from current ROCE. She aims to forecast ROCE, and to do so she forecasts the drivers that we lay out in this chapter. The forecasts, in turn, determine the value, so much so that the profitability drivers of this chapter are sometimes referred to as *value drivers*.

Value is generated by economic factors, of course. Accounting measures capture the economics. In understanding the profitability drivers, it is important to understand the aspects of the business that determine them. This, again, is part of "knowing the business." As you analyze the drivers, you learn more about the business. Profitability analysis has a mechanical aspect, and the analysis here can be transcribed to a spreadsheet program where the reformulated statements are fed in and numerous ratios are spat out. But that hardly gets at the economics of the value generation. So as you go through the mechanics, continually think of the activities of the firm that produce the ratios. The ratios focus the lens on the business.

With this thinking, profitability analysis becomes a tool for management planning, strategy analysis, and decision making, as well as valuation. The manager recognizes that generating higher profitability generates value. He then asks: What drives profitability? How will profitability change as a result of a particular decision and how does the change translate into value created for shareholders? If a retailer decides to reduce advertising and adopt a "frequent buyer" program instead, how does this affect ROCE and the value of the equity? What will be the effect of an expansion of retail floor space? Of an acquisition of another firm?

The purpose of analysis is to get answers to questions like these. So you will find a number of "what-if" questions in this chapter. And you will see how analysis provides the answers to these questions.

FIGURE 11.1 **The Analysis of Profitability** Return on common equity is broken down into its drivers over three levels of analysis. The first level identifies the effect of financing and operating liability leverage; the second level identifies the effect of profit margins and asset turnovers on operating profitability; and the third level identifies the drivers of profit margins, asset turnovers, and the net borrowing cost.

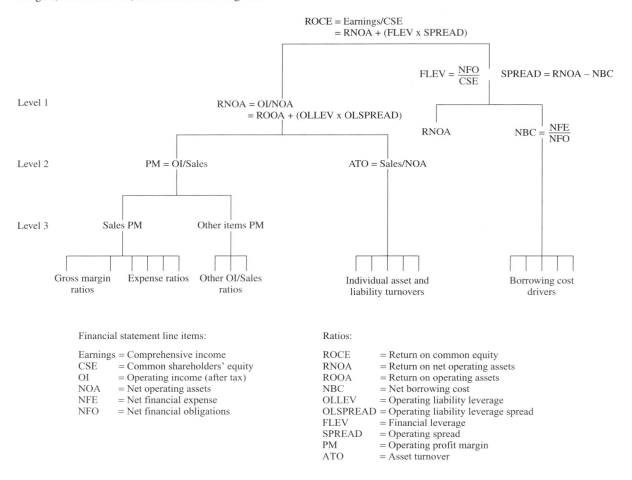

Financial statement line items:

Earnings	= Comprehensive income
CSE	= Common shareholders' equity
OI	= Operating income (after tax)
NOA	= Net operating assets
NFE	= Net financial expense
NFO	= Net financial obligations

Ratios:

ROCE	= Return on common equity
RNOA	= Return on net operating assets
ROOA	= Return on operating assets
NBC	= Net borrowing cost
OLLEV	= Operating liability leverage
OLSPREAD	= Operating liability leverage spread
FLEV	= Financial leverage
SPREAD	= Operating spread
PM	= Operating profit margin
ATO	= Asset turnover

CUTTING TO THE CORE OF THE OPERATIONS: THE ANALYSIS OF PROFITABILITY

As we have seen, the return on common stockholders' equity (CSE) is calculated as

$$\text{Return on common equity (ROCE)} = \frac{\text{Comprehensive income}}{\text{Average CSE}}$$

The ROCE is broken down into its drivers over three levels of analysis. These three levels are depicted in Figure 11.1, so follow this figure as we go through the analysis. The abbreviations and acronyms used are defined in the figure key.

$$ROCE = \frac{\text{Comprehensive earnings}}{\text{Average CSE}}$$

Comprehensive earnings in the numerator of ROCE is composed of operating income and net financial expense, as depicted in a reformulated income statement. Common shareholders' equity (CSE) in the denominator is net operating assets minus net financial obligations. Thus

$$ROCE = \frac{OI - NFE}{NOA - NFO}$$

(Balance sheet amounts are often averages over the period.) The operating income (OI) is generated by the net operating assets (NOA), and the operating profitability measure, RNOA, gives the percentage return on the net operating assets. The net financial expense (NFE) is generated by the net financial obligations (NFO), and the rate at which the NFE is incurred

is the net borrowing cost (NBC). So the ROCE can be expressed as

$$ROCE = \left(\frac{NOA}{CSE} \times RNOA\right) - \left(\frac{NFO}{CSE} \times NBC\right)$$

where, to remind you, RNOA = OI/NOA and NBC = Net financial expense/NFO. This expression for ROCE is a weighted average of the return from operations and the (negative) return from financing activities.

We get more insights by rearranging this expression:

$$ROCE = RNOA + \left[\frac{NFO}{CSE} \times (RNOA - NBC)\right]$$

$$= RNOA + (\text{Financial leverage} \times \text{Operating spread})$$

$$= RNOA + (FLEV \times SPREAD)$$

FIRST-LEVEL BREAKDOWN: DISTINGUISHING FINANCING AND OPERATING ACTIVITIES AND THE EFFECT OF LEVERAGE

We have seen that both operating activities (which produce operating income) and financing activities (which produce financial income or expense) affect the return to common shareholders. The first breakdown of ROCE distinguishes the profitability of these two activities. It also distinguishes the effect of leverage, which "levers" the ROCE up or down through liabilities. Leverage is also sometimes referred to as "gearing."

Financial Leverage

Financial leverage is the degree to which net operating assets are financed by net financial obligations (NFO) or by common equity. The measure FLEV = NFO/CSE, introduced in Chapter 9, captures financial leverage. To the extent that net operating assets are financed by net financial obligations rather than equity, the return on the equity is affected. The typical FLEV is about 0.4.

Financial leverage affects ROCE as follows (see Box 11.1):

Return on common equity = Return on net operating assets **(11.1)**
+ (Financial leverage × Operating spread)

$$ROCE = RNOA + [FLEV \times (RNOA - NBC)]$$

This expression for ROCE says that the ROCE can be broken down into three drivers:

1. Return on net operating assets (RNOA = OI/NOA).

2. Financial leverage (FLEV = NFO/CSE).

3. Operating spread between the return on net operating assets and the net borrowing cost (SPREAD = RNOA − NBC).

351

FIGURE 11.2

How Financial Leverage Affects the Difference Between ROCE and RNOA for Different Amounts of Operating Spread

FLEV is financial leverage and the SPREAD is the difference between RNOA and the net borrowing cost.

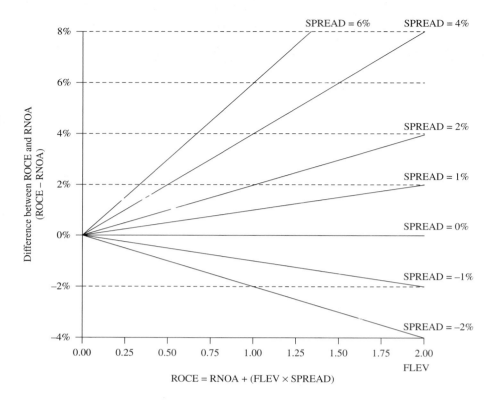

$$ROCE = RNOA + (FLEV \times SPREAD)$$

Both operating income and net financial expense must be after tax and comprehensive of all components, as in the reformulated income statements of Chapter 9, otherwise this breakdown will not work.

This formula says that the ROCE is levered up over the return from operations if the firm has financial leverage and the return from operations is greater than the borrowing cost. The firm earns more on its equity if the net operating assets are financed by net debt, provided those assets earn more than the cost of debt.

Figure 11.2 depicts how the difference between ROCE and RNOA changes with financial leverage according to the formula. If a firm has zero financial leverage, equation (11.1) says that ROCE equals RNOA. If the firm has financial leverage, then the difference between ROCE and RNOA is determined by the amount of the leverage and the **operating spread** between RNOA and the net borrowing cost. We will simply refer to the operating spread as the SPREAD. If a firm earns an RNOA greater than its after-tax net borrowing cost, it is said to have **favorable leverage** or **favorable gearing:** The RNOA is "levered up" or "geared up" to yield a higher ROCE. If the SPREAD is negative, the leverage effect is unfavorable, as shown for General Mills in Box 11.2. This highlights the "good news/bad news" nature of financial leverage: Financial leverage generates a higher return for shareholders if the firm earns more on its operating assets than its borrowing cost, but financial leverage hurts shareholder return if it doesn't. Accordingly, leverage is a component of the risk of equity as well as its profitability, as we will see in Chapter 13. We will also ask the following question in that chapter: Can a firm increase its equity value by increasing its ROCE through financial leverage, or will it reduce its equity value because of an increase in risk?

General Mills, a large manufacturer of packaged foods, has had considerable stock repurchases over the years. At the end of fiscal 1998 its common shareholders' equity was only $190.2 million on net operating assets of $2.251 billion. Its financial leverage was a huge 5.745, based on average balance sheet amounts.

The firm's ROCE for 1998 was 121.6 percent. Further analysis reveals that this very high number was driven by the high leverage:

$$ROCE = RNOA + [FLEV \times (RNOA - NBC)]$$

$$121.6\% = 21.6\% + [5.745 \times (21.6\% - 4.2\%)]$$

ROCE can exaggerate underlying operational profitability: RNOA is 21.6 percent but the high financial leverage, com-bined with a SPREAD over a borrowing cost of 4.2 percent, yields a much higher ROCE. Beware of firms boasting high ROCE: Is it driven by financial leverage?

A What-If Question

What if the RNOA at General Mills fell to 3 percent? What would be the effect on ROCE?

The answer is that the ROCE would fall to –3.9 percent:

$$-3.9\% = 3.0\% + [5.745 \times (3.0\% - 4.2\%)]$$

The unfavorable leverage would produce a negative ROCE on a positive RNOA.

How does the analysis change when a firm like Microsoft (see Box 11.3) has net financial assets (NFA) rather than net financial obligations (NFO)? In this case financial income will be greater than financial expense and the firm will have a positive return on financing activities (RNFA) rather than net borrowing costs. Return on common equity is related to RNOA as follows:

$$ROCE = RNOA - \left[\frac{NFA}{CSE} \times (RNOA - RNFA) \right] \qquad \textbf{(11.2)}$$

where (as in Chapter 9) RNFA = Net financial income/NFA, the return on net financial assets. Here a positive spread reduces the ROCE: Some of shareholders' equity is invested in financial assets and if financial assets earn less than operating assets, ROCE is lower than RNOA.

Operating Liability Leverage

Just as financial liabilities can lever up the ROCE, so can operating liabilities lever up the return on net operating assets. Operating liabilities are obligations incurred in the course of operations and are distinct from financial obligations incurred to finance the operations. Chapter 9 gave a measure of the extent to which the net operating assets (NOA) are comprised of operating liabilities (OL), the operating liability leverage:

$$\text{Operating liability leverage (OLLEV)} = \frac{OL}{NOA}$$

The typical OLLEV is about 0.4. Operating liabilities reduce the net operating assets that are employed and so lever the return on net operating assets. To the extent that a firm can get credit in its operations with no explicit interest, it reduces its investment in net operating assets and levers its RNOA. But credit comes with a price. Suppliers who provide credit without interest also charge higher prices for the goods and services they supply than would be the case if the firm paid cash. And so operating liability leverage, like financial leverage, can be unfavorable as well as favorable.

Microsoft has been very profitable. Look at the firm's reformulated statements for fiscal year 2002 in Exhibits 9.5 and 9.10 in Chapter 9. For fiscal 2002 the firm reported an ROCE of 15.7 percent on average common equity of $49.735 billion. But Microsoft had no financing debt. Instead Microsoft had considerable (average) financial assets of $36.906 billion from cash generated from its operations, giving it an average financial leverage that was negative: −0.742. The firm's return on average net financial assets was 4.2 percent.

The ROCE masks the profitability of operations of 48.9 percent:

$$ROCE = RNOA - [NFA/CSE \times (RNOA - RNFA)]$$

$$15.7\% = 48.9\% - [0.742 \times (48.9\% - 4.2\%)]$$

The RNOA of 48.9 percent is weighted down by the lower return on financing activities in the overall ROCE.

A What-If Question

Microsoft has regular stock repurchases. In 2002 the company used $6.069 billion of its financial assets to repurchase stock. What would the ROCE have been had it not undertaken the stock repurchase?

The answer is that with $3,035 billion more in average financial assets and common equity, the average financial leverage would have been −0.757 rather than −0.742, and the ROCE would have been

$$15.1\% = 48.9\% - [0.757 \times (48.9\% - 4.2\%)]$$

Stock repurchases (and dividends) increase ROCE.

To compute the leverage effect, first estimate the implicit interest that a supplier would charge for credit, using the firm's short-term borrowing rate for financial debt:

$$\text{Implicit interest on operating liabilities} = \text{Short-term borrowing rate (after tax)} \\ \times \text{Operating liabilities}$$

Then calculate a return on operating assets, ROOA, as if there were no operating liabilities:

$$\text{Return on operating assets (ROOA)} = \frac{OI + \text{Implicit interest (after tax)}}{\text{Operating assets}}$$

Then RNOA is driven by operating liability leverage as follows:

$$\text{Return on net operating assets} = \text{Return on operating assets} \qquad \textbf{(11.3)} \\ + (\text{Operating liability leverage} \\ \times \text{Operating liability leverage spread})$$

$$RNOA = ROOA + (OLLEV \times OLSPREAD)$$

where OLSPREAD is the **operating liability leverage spread**, that is, the spread of the return on operating assets over the after-tax short-term borrowing rate:

$$OLSPREAD = ROOA - \text{Short-term borrowing rate (after tax)}$$

This leverage expression for RNOA is similar in form to the financial leverage expression (11.1) for ROCE: RNOA is driven by the rate of return on operating assets as if there were no operating liability leverage, ROOA, plus a leverage premium that is determined by the amount of operating liability leverage, OLLEV, and the operating liability leverage spread, OLSPREAD. The effect of leverage can be favorable—if ROOA is greater than the short-term borrowing rate—or unfavorable—if ROOA is less than the short-term borrowing rate.

In calculating operating liability leverage and the implicit interest, ignore any operating liabilities, like pensions, where the accounting includes implicit interest in operating expenses, and ignore liabilities for which there is no implicit interest. Deferred tax liabilities are in the latter class because the government does not charge interest on the liabilities. See Box 11.4.

General Mills had average net operating assets of $2.310 billion during fiscal year 1998 of which $1.159 billion was in operating liabilities other than deferred taxes and pension liabilities. Thus its operating liability leverage ratio was 0.50. Its borrowing rate on its short-term notes payable was 5.4 percent, or 3.4 percent after tax. It reported operating income of $499.6 million, but applying the after-tax short-term borrowing rate to operating liabilities other than deferred tax and pension liabilities, this operating income includes implicit after-tax interest charges of $39.4 million. So

$$\text{ROOA} = \frac{499.6 + 39.4}{3,469.0} = 15.5\%$$

The effect of operating liability leverage is favorable:

$$\text{RNOA} = 21.6\% = 15.5\% + [0.50 \times (15.5\% - 3.4\%)]$$

A What-If Question

What if suppliers were to charge the short-term borrowing rate of 5.4 percent explicitly for the credit in accounts payable? What would be the effect on ROCE?

The answer is probably none. The interest would be an additional expense. But to stay competitive, the supplier would have to reduce prices of goods sold to the firm by a corresponding amount so that the total price charged (in implicit plus explicit interest) remains the same. But supplier markets may not work as efficiently as this supposes, so firms can exploit operating liability leverage.

Operating liability leverage can add value for shareholders, so it is important to identify if the analyst is to discover the source of the value generation. A firm that carries $400 million in inventory but has $400 million in accounts payable to the suppliers of the inventory effectively has zero net investment in inventory. The suppliers are carrying the investment in inventory which represents investment in the operations that the shareholders do not have to make (and can, rather, invest elsewhere to generate returns). See Box 11.5.

Summing Financial Leverage and Operating Liability Leverage Effects on Shareholder Profitability

Shareholder profitability, ROCE, is affected by both financial leverage and operating liability leverage. Without either type of leverage, ROCE would be equal to ROOA, the rate of return on operating assets. Operating liability leverage levers RNOA over ROOA and financial leverage levers ROCE over RNOA:

$$\text{ROCE} = \text{ROOA} + (\text{RNOA} - \text{ROOA}) + (\text{ROCE} - \text{RNOA})$$

So, for the General Mills examples in Boxes 11.2 and 11.4, the ROCE of 121.6 percent is determined by:

$$121.6\% = 15.5\% + (21.6\% - 15.5\%) + (121.6\% - 21.6\%)$$

Return on Net Operating Assets and Return on Assets

A common measure of the profitability of operations is the *return on assets* (ROA):

$$\text{ROA} = \frac{\text{Net income} + \text{Interest expense (after tax)}}{\text{Average total assets}}$$

(Minority interest in income, if any, is added to the numerator.) The net income in the numerator is usually reported net income rather than comprehensive income. But, this aside, the ROA calculation mixes up financing and operating activities. Interest income, part of

Dell Computer Corporation is recognized as an innovator in the process of producing and selling computers. Its direct-to-customer sales cut out the retail distribution layer and the higher markup that retailing requires. Its just-in-time inventory system means it carries little inventory, so not only does Dell have less investment in inventory but it also runs less risk of holding inventory as computer prices fall and technology changes, making inventory obsolete. As production is outsourced, Dell has a relatively low investment in plant, as well. It exerts pressure on its suppliers to carry inventory and delays payments to suppliers. Accordingly it carries high accounts payable relative to its investment in inventories and plant.

A reformulation of Dell's 2002 balance sheet (in Exhibit 2.1 in Chapter 2) gives the following composition of net operating assets (in millions of dollars):

Operating Assets		
Operating cash		$ 25
Accounts receivable		2,269
Inventories		278
Property, plant, and equipment		826
Other assets		1,875
		5,273
Operating Liabilities		
Accounts payable	5,075	
Accrued liabilities	2,444	
Other liabilities	802	8,321
Net Operating Assets		(3,048)
Net Financial Assets		7,742
Shareholders' Equity		$4,694

Dell has $7.742 billion invested in financial assets. But (remarkably for a manufacturer), shareholders have a negative investment in operations: Net operating assets are –$3.048 billion. On $31.168 billion in sales, Dell carries only $278 million in inventories and has only $826 million in property, plant, and equipment. With $5.075 billion in accounts payable and another $2.444 billion in accrued liabilities for services, operating liabilities exceed operating assets: The operating creditors are providing the investment in operations rather than the shareholders. Dell has extreme operating liability leverage.

Does this structure of the operations add value? Certainly, yes. Dell earned $1.284 billion from operations in 2002. Residual income from operations, on a (negative) investment in operations of –$3.048 billion (with a 9 percent required return), is

Residual income = $1.284 – (0.09 × –3.048) = $1.558 billion

The charge, at the required return, against a negative investment yields residual income greater than income. Effectively, shareholders add value in two ways. First they get value from the $1.284 billion in operating income and, second, they get value from investing the $3.048 billion they would otherwise have had to put into the business had the suppliers not supplied the investment. The suppliers are essentially providing a "float" that shareholders can invest elsewhere.

Note: You will notice that, because Dell has negative net operating assets, an RNOA cannot be calculated. This happens rarely. But, from a valuation point of view, this does not matter: Residual income from the operations can be calculated, as above, and valuation involves forecasting residual income.

financing activities, is in the numerator. Total assets are operating assets plus financial assets, so financial assets are in the base. Thus the measure mixes the return on operations with the (usually lower) return from investing excess cash in financial assets. Operating liabilities are excluded from the base. Thus the measure includes the cost of operating liabilities in the numerator (in the form of higher input prices as the price of credit) but excludes the benefit of operating liability leverage in the base. The RNOA calculation appropriately distinguishes operating and financial items. Since interest-bearing financial assets are treated as negative financial obligations, they do not affect the return on operations. Operating liabilities reduce the needed investment in operating assets, providing operating liability leverage, so they are subtracted in the base.

Thus ROA typically measures a lower rate of return than RNOA. The median ROA for all U.S. nonfinancial firms from 1963 to 2001 was 6.8 percent. This is below what we would expect the cost of capital to be: It looks more like a bond rate. The median RNOA

TABLE 11.1

Return on Net Operating Assets (RNOA) and Return on Assets (ROA) for Selected Firms for 1996 Fiscal Year
ROA typically understates operating profitability because it fails to incorporate operating liability leverage and includes the profitability of financial assets.

Industry and Firm	RNOA, %	ROA, %	Operating Liability Leverage (OLLEV)	Financial Assets/ Total Assets, %
Biotech				
Genentech, Inc.	11.2%	5.7%	0.37	52.8%
Amgen, Inc.	63.5	26.2	0.51	41.0
Chiron Corp.	6.2	3.8	0.31	10.3
High-tech				
Microsoft Corp.	197.0	25.4	1.69	64.7
Oracle Corp.	68.4	21.0	1.52	26.5
Cisco Systems, Inc.	121.8	32.5	0.87	48.5
Retailers				
Wal-Mart Stores, Inc.	12.7	9.3	0.35	1.0
Kmart Corp.	0.5	0.4	0.35	4.1
The Gap, Inc.	39.7	30.1	0.56	24.1
Oil producers and refiners				
Exxon Corp.	14.8	8.3	0.73	1.9
Chevron Corp.	13.9	8.2	0.64	4.4
Footwear and apparel manufacturers				
Nike, Inc.	22.6	16.3	0.37	6.1
Reebok Intl., Ltd.	14.1	9.8	0.32	7.2

was 10.1 percent, more in line with what we expect as a typical return from running businesses. ROA is a poor measure of operating profitability.

Table 11.1 compares ROA and RNOA for selected firms for 1996. That year was a very good profit year for many corporations and the high fliers included the high-tech firms you see in the table. In good profit years we expect the differences between RNOA and ROA to be higher because of favorable operating liability leverage, as it is for all firms in the table. Indeed you can see that ROA understates operating profitability. As a case in point, look at Exxon and Chevron. The ROAs for these firms look lackluster, to say the least. They are below what we would expect their cost of capital to be. The RNOAs, on the other hand, look respectable. And the RNOA measures identify Microsoft, Oracle, and Cisco Systems as the exceptional companies they indeed are.

Operating liability leverage (OLLEV) and the amount of financial assets relative to total assets explain the difference between RNOA and ROA, and you can see in the table that firms with the largest differences have high numbers for these ratios. Microsoft had an RNOA of 197.0 percent in 1996, but inclusion of financial assets (64.7 percent of total assets) in the ROA measure and the omission of the operating liability leverage of 1.69 reduces the profitability measure to 25.4 percent.

These observations reinforce two points. To analyze profitability effectively, two procedures must be followed:

1. Income must be calculated on a comprehensive (clean-surplus) basis.

2. There must be a clean distinction between operating and financing items in the income statement and balance sheet.

You will get "clean" measures only if these two elements are in place. So you can see the payoff to your work in this and the preceding chapters.

Financial Leverage and Debt-to-Equity Ratios

A common measure of financial leverage is the *debt-to-equity ratio,* calculated as total debt divided by equity. This measure is useful in credit analysis (see Chapter 19) but, for the analysis of profitability, it confuses operating liabilities (which create operating liability leverage) with financial liabilities (which create financial leverage). And, as usually defined, it does not net out financial liabilities against financial assets.

The difference can be sizable: The median debt-to-equity ratio for U.S. firms from 1963 to 2001 was 1.21 while the median FLEV was 0.42. Microsoft had 60.0 percent of its assets in financial assets at the end 2002 and, with an operating liability leverage of 0.428, had no financial obligations. Its debt-to-equity ratio was 0.22, but all the debt in the debt-to-equity ratio was operating debt. So using the firm's debt-to-equity ratio as an indication of financial leverage would be quite misleading: Microsoft's FLEV (which includes the financial assets as negative debt) was −0.742.

Table 11.2 analyzes the effect of leverage on shareholder profitability for the two firms, Nike and Reebok, for which we prepared reformulated statements in Chapter 9. The analysis, of course, uses the reformulated statements (the balance sheets are in Exhibits 9.3 and 9.4 and the income statements are in Exhibits 9.8 and 9.9). Table 11.2 compares the profitability of the two firms for 1995 and 1996 and lays out the profitability

TABLE 11.2
First Level
Breakdown: Nike
and Reebok

	1996		1995	
	Nike	**Reebok[1]**	**Nike**	**Reebok**
ROCE	24.3%	17.6%	22.5%	18.6%
ROCE before minority interest		18.8%		19.2%
RNOA	22.6%	14.1%	23.1%	16.9%
Financial leverage drivers				
NBC[2]	5.9%	4.9%	−3.4%	4.8%
SPREAD	16.7%	9.2%	19.7%	12.1%
FLEV	0.107	0.515	−0.031	0.187
Operating liability leverage drivers				
ROOA	17.3%	11.5%	18.0%	13.5%
Short-term borrowing rate (after tax)[2]	3.2%	3.2%	3.2%	3.2%
OLSPREAD	14.1%	8.3%	14.8%	10.3%
OLLEV	0.369	0.321	0.342	0.333

How the drivers combine for 1996:

$$ROCE = RNOA + (FLEV \times SPREAD)$$

Nike: $24.3\% = 22.6\% + (0.107 \times 16.7\%)$

Reebok: $18.8\% = 14.1\% + (0.515 \times 9.2\%)$

$$RNOA = ROOA + (OLLEV \times OLSPREAD)$$

Nike: $22.6\% = 17.3\% + (0.369 \times 14.1\%)$

Reebok: $14.1\% = 11.5\% + (0.321 \times 8.3\%)$

Summing leverage effects in 1996:

$$ROCE = ROOA + (RNOA - ROOA) + (ROCE - RNDA)$$

Nike: $24.3\% = 17.3\% + (22.6\% - 17.3\%) + (24.3\% - 22.6\%)$

Reebok: $18.8\% = 11.5\% + (14.1\% - 11.5\%) + (18.8\% - 14.1\%)$

[1]Reebok's 1996 ratios are calculated using weights of 2/3 and 1/3 applied to beginning and ending balance sheet amounts, respectively, to reflect timing of the large stock repurchase in August of 1996. The analysis for Reebok also excludes the gain from put options in order to evaluate the results from operating and financing the manufacture of products.
[2]The short-term borrowing rate is based on a before-tax rate of 5%. The after-tax rate is $5\% \times (1 - 0.37) = 3.2\%$.

nce of minority interest calls for a slight revision in lations of the effect of financial leverage. Minority unlike debtholder interests, does not affect the overall profitability of equity, the leverage, or the SPREAD. It just affects the division of rewards between different equity claimants. The minority, like the majority common, shares the costs and benefits of leverage. So the additional step with minority interest (MI) is to distinguish ROCE for all common claimants from that for the (majority) common owners of the parent corporation in the consolidation:

$$\text{ROCE} = \text{ROCE before MI} \times \text{MI sharing ratio}$$

where ROCE is the return on common equity to the shareholders of the parent company (the majority) and

$$\text{ROCE before MI} = \frac{\text{Comprehensive income before MI}}{\text{CSE} + \text{MI}}$$

$$\text{Minority interest sharing ratio} = \frac{\text{Comprehensive income/}}{\text{Comprehensive income before MI}} \Big/ \frac{\text{CSE/(CSE} + \text{MI})}{}$$

The first ratio here gives the return to total common equity, minority and majority. The second ratio gives the sharing of the return.

This calculation is cumbersome. However, it can be avoided if the minority interests' shares of operating and financing assets, liabilities, and income in subsidiaries can be identified and then subtracted from the relevant categories in the reformulated balance sheet. See Chapter 9. Minority interests are typically small in the U.S., and one can (as an approximation) often treat minority interest as a reduction in consolidated operating income and net operating assets.

drivers that we have been talking about. The calculations at the bottom of the table carry out the reconciliations in equations (11.1) and (11.3). (Allow for rounding errors.) Equation (11.2) applies to Nike in 1995 because in that year it had net financial assets.

You can see that Nike earned higher ROCE than Reebok in both years. This superior profitability came from higher RNOA, not financial leverage: Reebok had a better "kicker" from financial leverage but, because of its lower RNOA, it still produced lower ROCE. While Nike had a higher SPREAD in 1996, Reebok had higher financial leverage that levered up its ROCE more. In 1995 Nike was in fact a net creditor (with negative leverage). Nike's superior operating performance came in part from slightly higher operating liability leverage, which levered up its return on operating assets.

The calculations for Reebok differ from Nike's in two respects. First, as indicated in the notes in the exhibits, Reebok's large 1996 stock repurchase for $687 million was made in August and was financed by the issue of long-term debt (which you can see increased in the balance sheet). So average balance sheet amounts in the calculations are made by multiplying the beginning balances by 2/3 (eight months, relative to the beginning of the year) and the ending balances by 1/3 (four months, relative to the end of the year). Second, Reebok shares income, assets, and liabilities with minority interests in its subsidiaries. See Box 11.6.

SECOND-LEVEL BREAKDOWN: DRIVERS OF OPERATING PROFITABILITY

In the first-level breakdown, RNOA is isolated as an important driver of the ROCE. RNOA can be broken down further into its drivers so that

$$\text{ROCE} = \text{RNOA} + [\text{FLEV} \times (\text{RNOA} - \text{NBC})] \qquad \textbf{(11.4)}$$

$$= (\text{PM} \times \text{ATO}) + [\text{FLEV} \times (\text{RNOA} - \text{NBC})]$$

The two drivers of RNOA are

1. Operating profit margin (PM). This we calculated as a common-size ratio in Chapter 9:

$$PM = OI \text{ (after tax)}/Sales$$

The profit margin reveals the profitability of each dollar of sales.

2. Asset turnover (ATO):

$$ATO = Sales/NOA$$

The asset turnover reveals the sales revenue per dollar of net operating assets put in place. It measures the ability of the NOA to generate sales. It is sometimes referred to as its inverse, $1/ATO = NOA/Sales$, which indicates the amount of NOA used to generate a dollar of sales: If the ATO is 2.0, the firm is using 50 cents of net operating assets to generate a dollar of sales.

This decomposition of operating profitability is known as the *Du Pont model*. It says that profitability in operations comes from two sources. First, RNOA is higher the more of each dollar of sales ends up in operating income; second, RNOA is higher the more sales are generated from the net operating assets. The first is a profitability measure; the second is an efficiency measure. A firm generates profitability by increasing margins and can lever the margins up by using operating assets and operating liabilities more efficiently to generate sales.

The average profit margin is about 5.3 percent and the average asset turnover is about 2.0. But it is clear that a firm can produce a given level of RNOA with a relatively high profit margin but low turnover, or with a relatively high turnover but a low margin. Figure 11.3 plots median PM and ATO for 238 industries from 1963 to 1966. You see from the figure that industries with low asset turnovers tend to have high profit margins, and industries with high asset turnovers tend to have low profit margins. One could draw a curve—sloping down to the right—that connects dots with the same RNOA but different PMs and ATOs. An industry with a 10 percent margin and an ATO of 1.0 has the same 10 percent RNOA as a firm with a 3.33 percent margin and an ATO of 3.0.

FIGURE 11.3
Profit Margin and Asset Turnover Combinations for 238 Industries, 1963–1996 Industries with high profit margins tend to have low asset turnovers, and industries with low profit margins tend to have high asset turnovers.

Source: D. Nissim and S. H. Penman, "Ratio Analysis and Equity Valuation: From Research to Practice," *Review of Accounting Studies,* March 2001, p. 137.

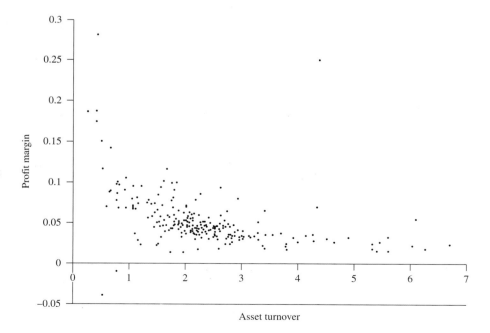

Table 11.3 gives median RNOAs, PMs, and ATOs for a number of industries. It ranks industries on their median ROCE and also gives their median financial leverage (FLEV) and operating liability leverage (OLLEV). This table will give you a sense of the typical amounts for these measures. The median ROCE over all industries is 12.2 percent, and the median RNOA is 10.3 percent. The difference is due to financial leverage and a positive SPREAD. The median FLEV over all industries is 0.403, but there is considerable variation, particularly in financial leverage. You can see that some industries—pipelines, utilities, and hotels—have produced ROCE through highly favorable financial leverage. Others—business services, printing and publishing, and chemicals—use little financial leverage to yield a high ROCE. Some—such as business services—have used operating liability leverage rather than financial leverage to lever ROCE. Others—such as trucking and airlines—have used both forms of leverage.

The PM and ATO tradeoff is apparent from the table. Some industries—printing and publishing and chemicals—produce a higher than average RNOA with both high profit margins and high asset turnovers. But industries with high margins typically have lower turnovers, and vice versa. Compare pipelines with food stores: Similar RNOAs are generated with quite dissimilar margins and turnovers. Capital-intensive industries such as pipelines, shipping, utilities, and communications have low turnovers but high margins. Firms in competitive businesses—food stores, wholesalers, apparel, and general retail—often have low profit margins but generate RNOA through higher turnover.

TABLE 11.3
Median Return on Common Equity (ROCE), Financial Leverage (FLEV), Operating Liability Leverage (OLLEV), Return on Net Operating Assets (RNOA), Profit Margins (PM), and Asset Turnovers (ATO) for Selected Industries, 1963–1996

Source:
Company: Standard & Poor's
Data: Compustat® data.

Industry	ROCE, %	FLEV	OLLEV	RNOA, %	PM, %	ATO
Pipelines	17.1%	1.093	0.154	12.0%	27.8%	0.40
Tobacco	15.8	0.307	0.272	14.0	9.3	1.70
Restaurants	15.6	0.313	0.306	14.2	5.0	2.83
Printing and publishing	14.6	0.154	0.374	13.6	6.5	2.20
Business services	14.6	0.056	0.488	13.5	5.2	2.95
Chemicals	14.3	0.198	0.352	13.4	7.1	1.91
Food stores	13.8	0.364	0.559	12.0	1.7	7.39
Trucking	13.8	0.641	0.419	10.1	3.8	2.88
Food products	13.7	0.414	0.350	12.1	4.4	2.74
Communications	13.4	0.743	0.284	9.1	12.5	0.76
General stores	13.2	0.389	0.457	11.3	3.5	3.55
Petroleum refining	12.6	0.359	0.487	11.2	6.0	1.96
Transportation equipment	12.5	0.369	0.422	11.2	4.5	2.47
Airlines	12.4	0.841	0.516	9.0	4.3	1.99
Utilities	12.4	1.434	0.272	8.2	14.5	0.59
Wholesalers, nondurable goods	12.2	0.584	0.461	10.2	2.3	3.72
Paper products	11.8	0.436	0.296	10.2	5.9	1.74
Lumber	11.7	0.312	0.384	10.4	4.0	2.60
Apparel	11.6	0.408	0.317	10.1	4.0	2.55
Hotels	11.5	1.054	0.201	8.5	8.2	1.04
Shipping	11.4	0.793	0.205	9.1	12.6	0.61
Amusements and recreation	11.4	0.598	0.203	10.1	9.5	1.10
Building and construction	11.4	0.439	0.409	10.6	4.5	2.06
Wholesalers, durable goods	11.2	0.448	0.354	9.9	3.4	2.84
Textiles	10.4	0.423	0.266	9.3	4.3	2.09
Primary metals	9.9	0.424	0.338	9.4	5.0	1.80
Oil and gas extraction	9.1	0.395	0.263	8.3	13.0	0.57
Railroads	7.3	0.556	0.362	7.1	9.7	0.78

Margins and turnovers reflect the technology for delivering products. Businesses with large capital investments—like telecommunications—typically have low turnovers and high margins. Firms that generate customers with advertising—like apparel makers—typically have lower margins (after advertising expense) but, as a result of the advertising, high turnovers. Margins and turnovers also reflect competition. An industry where high turnover can be achieved—food stores that can generate a lot of sales per square foot of retail space—will attract competition. That competition erodes margins, if there is little barrier to entry, as sales prices fall to maintain turnover (as with food stores).

THIRD-LEVEL BREAKDOWN

Profit Margin Drivers

The common-size analysis of the income statement in Chapter 9 broke the profit margin into two components:

$$PM = \text{Sales PM} + \text{Other items PM} \qquad (11.5)$$

Other items in the income statement include shares of subsidiary income, special items, and gains and losses. These sources of income are not a result of sales revenue at the top of the income statement. So calculating a PM that includes these items distorts the profitability of sales. The sales PM, based on operating income before other items, includes only expenses incurred to generate sales, thus isolating the profitability of sales.

The two components of the profit margin have further components:

$$\text{Sales PM} = \text{Gross margin ratio} - \text{Expense ratios} \qquad (11.6)$$

$$= \frac{\text{Gross margin}}{\text{Sales}} - \frac{\text{Administrative expense}}{\text{Sales}} - \frac{\text{Selling expense}}{\text{Sales}}$$

$$- \frac{\text{R\&D}}{\text{Sales}} - \frac{\text{Operating taxes}}{\text{Sales}}$$

$$\text{Other operating items PM} = \frac{\text{Subsidiary income}}{\text{Sales}} + \frac{\text{Other equity income}}{\text{Sales}} \qquad (11.7)$$

$$+ \frac{\text{Special items}}{\text{Sales}} + \frac{\text{Other gains and losses}}{\text{Sales}}$$

These component ratios are known as *profit margin drivers*. A good part of managerial accounting and cost accounting texts is devoted to an analysis of these drivers. The drivers should be analyzed further by segment if segment disclosures are available. Clearly, profit margins are increased by adding to gross margins (reducing cost of sales), by adding other items income, and by reducing expenses per dollar of sales.

Turnover Drivers

The net operating assets are made up of many operating assets and liabilities and so the overall ATO can be broken down into ratios for the individual assets and liabilities:

$$\frac{1}{\text{ATO}} = \frac{\text{Cash}}{\text{Sales}} + \frac{\text{Accounts receivable}}{\text{Sales}} + \frac{\text{Inventory}}{\text{Sales}} + \cdots + \frac{\text{PPE}}{\text{Sales}} \qquad (11.8)$$

$$+ \cdots - \frac{\text{Accounts payable}}{\text{Sales}} - \frac{\text{Pension obligations}}{\text{Sales}} - \cdots$$

Again, the balance sheet amounts are averages over the year. The turnover is expressed here as a reciprocal of the ATO, which is the amount of net operating assets to support a dollar of sales, as are the individual turnovers. Thus the individual turnovers aggregate conveniently (in a spreadsheet, for example) to the overall turnover. However, conventionally, individual turnover ratios are expressed as sales per dollar of investment in the asset. For example,

$$\text{Accounts receivable turnover} = \frac{\text{Sales}}{\text{Accounts receivable (net)}}$$

and

$$\text{PPE turnover} = \frac{\text{Sales}}{\text{Property, plant, and equipment (net)}}$$

(This is sometimes called the *fixed asset turnover.*)

A firm increases its turnover (and thus RNOA) by maintaining operating assets at a minimum while increasing sales. But the ATO is also affected by operating liability turnovers, and this of course reflects operating liability leverage: Operating liability leverage increases ATO and, if operating liability leverage is favorable, RNOA.

Turnover ratios are sometimes referred to as *activity ratios* or *asset utilization ratios.* Some activity ratios are calculated in different ways but with the same concept in mind. So, for example,

$$\text{Days in accounts receivable} = \frac{365}{\text{Accounts receivable turnover}}$$

(sometimes called days sales outstanding). This gives the typical number of days it takes to collect cash from sales. It highlights that efficiency is increased by turning sales into cash quickly and is often used as a metric to evaluate collection departments. The inventory turnover ratio is sometimes measured as

$$\text{Inventory turnover} = \frac{\text{Cost of goods sold}}{\text{Inventory}}$$

This differs from the sales/inventory calculation by not being affected by changes in profit margins. Using this definition, the efficiency of inventory management is sometimes expressed in terms of the average number of days that inventory is held, its shelf life:

$$\text{Days in inventory} = \frac{365}{\text{Inventory turnover}}$$

This ratio is best applied in wholesaling or retailing concerns where there is just one type of inventory, finished goods inventory. In a manufacturing concern, inventories include materials and work in progress, which take different times to complete into finished goods. Footnotes sometimes break down inventory into finished goods and other inventories, in which case ratios for finished goods inventory can be calculated.

A metric that assesses the ability to get operating liability leverage by extending credit from suppliers is

$$\text{Days in accounts payable} = \frac{365 \times \text{Accounts payable}}{\text{Purchases}}$$

where

$$\text{Purchases} = \text{Cost of goods sold} + \text{Change in inventory}$$

The turnover drivers can be reduced to two summary drivers, the *operating working capital driver* and the *long-term net operating asset driver:*

$$\frac{1}{\text{ATO}} = \frac{\text{Operating working capital}}{\text{Sales}} + \frac{\text{Long-term NOA}}{\text{Sales}}$$

Working capital is often defined as current assets minus current liabilities, but these may include financial items not involved in generating sales. So Operating working capital = Current assets − Current liabilities − Current financial assets + Current financial liabilities. The long-term NOA of course also exclude financial items and are usually made up of property, plant, and equipment, intangibles, and investments in subsidiaries.

The profit margins and turnovers for Nike and Reebok are given in Table 11.4, along with their drivers. The profit margin drivers sum to the overall PM, and the inverse of the turnover drivers sum to the inverse of the overall ATO, as laid out in equations (11.5), (11.6), and (11.8). You should prove that the breakdown in equation (11.4) also works.

TABLE 11.4   **Second- and Third-Level Breakdown: Nike and Reebok**

		1996			1995		
		Nike	Reebok		Nike	Reebok	
Second Level							
RNOA		22.6%	14.1%		23.1%	16.9%	
Profit margin		8.5%	4.8%		8.7%	5.7%	
Asset turnover		2.66	2.92		2.65	2.94	
Third Level[1]							
Profit margin drivers (%)							
Gross margin ratio	39.6		38.4		39.8		39.3
Administrative expense ratio	(15.1)		(24.8)		(15.3)		(24.2)
Advertising expense ratio	(9.9)		(5.8)		(10.4)		(4.5)
Amortization expense ratio	(0.3)		(0.1)		(0.3)		(0.1)
Sales PM before tax	14.2		7.6		13.8		10.4
Tax expense ratio	(5.5)		(2.7)		(5.3)		(3.8)
Sales PM	8.8		4.9		8.5		6.7
Other items PM	(0.3)	8.5	(0.1)	4.8	0.2	8.7	(0.9) 5.7
Asset turnover drivers (inverse)							
Cash turnover	0.004		0.003		0.004		0.002
Accounts receivable turnover	0.185		0.154		0.185		0.149
Inventory turnover	0.121		0.174		0.116		0.181
Prepayments turnover	0.013		0.011		0.012		0.011
PPE turnover	0.093		0.055		0.101		0.051
Intangibles turnover	0.075		0.019		0.069		0.023
Other assets turnover[2]	0.025		0.038		0.020		0.035
Operating asset turnover	0.515		0.453		0.506		0.453
Accounts payable turnover	(0.058)		(0.051)		(0.053)		(0.048)
Accrued expenses turnover	(0.064)		(0.044)		(0.055)		(0.043)
Taxes payable turnover	(0.009)		(0.016)		(0.008)		(0.021)
Other liabilities turnover	(0.008)	0.376		0.343	(0.012)	0.377	0.340

[1]Columns may not add precisely due to rounding error.
[2]Includes deferred tax assets.

Then look at the sources of the differences in RNOA for the two firms. Nike's higher RNOA is due to higher profit margins, which are due to higher gross margins and lower administrative expenses. Nike has higher profit margins in spite of the fact that it spends more of each dollar of sales on advertising (the advertising expense ratio). Nike levers up its higher profitability with advertising and promotion: It spends more per dollar of sales on advertising and promotion but this results in higher profit margins after advertising costs because of higher gross margins and lower expenses in production and administration. Nike also shows a higher RNOA despite its lower ATO, and this lower turnover occurs despite its higher operating liability leverage. In 1996 its accounts receivable turnover was 5.4 compared to 6.5 for Reebok (these numbers are the inverse of the numbers in the table). In days outstanding, these turnovers are 67 days and 56 days, respectively. Similarly, Nike's PPE turnover was 10.8 in 1996 compared with 18.2 for Reebok. Nike is also generating fewer sales from its purchased trademarks and goodwill than Reebok. However, Nike did carry lower inventory per dollar of sales: Its 1996 inventory turnover was 8.3 as against Reebok's 5.7. Measuring the inventory turnovers as cost of sales/inventory, the numbers are 5.0 and 3.5, respectively, and in days in inventory, the numbers are 73 and 104.

Bear in mind two caveats in interpreting these calculations. The first has to do with the averaging of beginning and ending balance sheet amounts in the turnover calculations. For Reebok this involved weighting the opening 1996 balance by 1/3 and the closing balance by 2/3 to accommodate the large reduction in CSE in August of that year. If the same weighting applied to CSE, NOA, and NFO, all calculations would aggregate pleasingly to the overall ROCE according to the formulas. But individual net operating assets may not have changed in the same pattern as CSE, so you should test the sensitivity of calculations to this averaging. Indeed, the August decrease in CSE was accompanied by an increase in NFO to finance the share repurchase, with no effect on operating assets. As it happens here, Reebok's beginning and ending balances of total operating assets and net operating assets are similar, so the weighting has little effect on calculations involving these totals. In principle, however, when there are significant changes, the assumption implied in the averaging should be investigated. Indeed the equal weighting of beginning and ending balances for Nike (and Reebok in 1995) should be examined against any information that would indicate that large changes in the balance sheet occurred other than at the midpoint of the year. The quarterly statements give balances at the end of each quarter.

The second caveat concerns the accounting. The turnover calculations are affected by the accounting for the net assets. So, for example, our calculations indicate that Nike's inventory turnover is lower than Reebok's, but inspection of the footnotes reveals that its U.S. inventories are carried at last-in-first-out (LIFO) cost whereas Reebok's are carried at first-in-first-out (FIFO). As LIFO inventory cost is typically lower than FIFO cost, the higher turnover may reflect this accounting difference. Nike's RNOA will also reflect the lower accounting values for inventory. So is it the case that Nike's higher RNOA is "manufactured" in part by the choice of accounting methods? This and other features of the accounting—and their implications for profitability analysis and valuation analysis—are investigated in Part Four of the book.

Analysis does not end with the calculation of ratios. Indeed the calculations are the tools of analysis. The analyst takes these tools and asks what-if questions—and gets answers. See Box 11.7.

Borrowing Cost Drivers

The final component of ROCE is the operating spread, RNOA – NBC. As the RNOA component of this spread has been analyzed, this leaves the analysis of the net borrowing cost or, in the case of net financial assets, the return from net financial assets.

What if Nike increased its accounts receivable turnover from 5.4 to Reebok's 6.5 in 1996? How would RNOA change?

Answer: The increase would result in a reduction of average accounts receivable by $204 million to $996 million. If this reduction had no effect on sales (and it might!), overall ATO would increase from 2.66 to 2.90 and RNOA from 22.6 percent to 24.6 percent.

What if Nike's gross margin ratio had declined to Reebok's 38.4 percent in 1996? How would RNOA change?

Answer: A reduction in gross margin of 1.2 percent is a reduction of 0.738 percent after tax at a rate of 38.5 percent. This results in a drop of operating PM after tax from 8.48 percent to 7.75 percent and a drop in RNOA to 20.6 percent.

What if Reebok increased its annual advertising expenditures by $50 million from the 1996 level, resulting in $300 million of additional sales at the same gross margin percentage?

Answer: The increased advertising would result in an additional $115.2 million in gross margin and, after the increase in advertising expenses, an additional $42.1 million in after-tax operating income, yielding a profit margin of 5.56 percent. The advertising expense ratio would increase from 5.8 percent to 6.7 percent of sales, but this increase produces an increased profit margin. If no further investment is needed to generate the sales, ATO also increases and the RNOA would increase from 14.1 percent to 17.6 percent. But if inventories and receivables and assets increase proportionally to support the sales, so that ATO remains unchanged, RNOA would increase to only 16.2 percent.

The net borrowing cost is a weighted average of the costs for the different sources of net financing. It can be calculated as

$$
\text{NBC} = \left[\frac{\text{FO}}{\text{NFO}} \times \frac{\text{After-tax interest on financial obligations (FO)}}{\text{FO}} \right]
$$

$$
- \left[\frac{\text{FA}}{\text{NFO}} \times \frac{\text{After-tax interest on financial assets (FA)}}{\text{FA}} \right]
$$

$$
- \left(\frac{\text{FA}}{\text{NFO}} \times \frac{\text{Unrealized gains on FA}}{\text{FA}} \right) + \left(\frac{\text{Preferred stock}}{\text{NFO}} \times \frac{\text{Preferred dividend}}{\text{Preferred stock}} \right) + \cdots
$$

Nike's 1996 borrowing cost is made up from the interest expense and interest income components as follows (refer, again, to the reformulated statements in Exhibits 9.3 and 9.8):

$$
\text{NBC} = \left[\frac{452}{236} \times \frac{39 \times (1 - 0.385)}{452} \right] - \left[\frac{216}{236} \times \frac{16 \times (1 - 0.385)}{216} \right]
$$

$$
= \left(\frac{452}{236} \times 5.31\% \right) - \left(\frac{216}{236} \times 4.56\% \right)
$$

$$
= 5.9\%
$$

The weights are calculated from average NFO ($236 million), average financial obligations ($452 million), and average financial assets ($216 million). (The preferred stock is ignored because it is a very small component.) This calculation separates the after-tax borrowing cost for the obligations (5.31 percent) from the return on financial assets (4.56 percent).

A lower rate of return on financial assets than the borrowing rate on obligations increases the composite net borrowing cost over that for the obligations (5.9 percent versus

The profitability analysis for Nike is continued on the **Build Your Own Analysis Product (BYOAP)** feature on the book's website, which provides a full analysis of the firm from 1996–2002. Here are some of the salient numbers:

	1996	1997	1998	1999	2000	2001	2002
Sales revenue ($ billions)	6.5	9.2	9.6	8.8	9.0	9.5	9.9
Profitability:							
Return on common equity (%)	24.3	27.8	12.0	13.0	16.6	16.5	17.0
Return on net operating assets (%)	22.6	25.0	10.6	11.2	13.3	12.9	14.4
Profit margin (%)	8.5	8.7	4.3	5.1	6.2	6.1	6.5
Asset turnover	2.7	2.9	2.5	2.2	2.1	2.1	2.2
Net borrowing cost (%)	5.9	5.1	4.1	2.6	2.1	2.5	2.7
Leverage:							
Financial leverage	0.107	0.140	0.202	0.218	0.295	0.342	0.216
Operating liability leverage	0.369	0.369	0.315	0.277	0.290	0.258	0.283

You see that Nike's return on common equity (ROCE) declined subsequent to 1996, even though financial leverage increased and net borrowing cost declined (as interest rates generally declined). The reason, of course, was a decline in operating profitability (RNOA), due to a decline in profit margins, assets turnovers, and operating liability leverage.

The next chapter analyzes the growth or decline in profitability in more depth. Chapter 12 also shows how changes in profitability combine with growth in investment to determine growth in earnings and residual earnings.

5.31 percent here). The difference in the rates for the two components is called the **spread between lending and borrowing rates** (–0.75 percent here). Banks make money with higher lending than borrowing rates and thus (if they are successful) their overall net rate, their RNFA, is higher than the borrowing rate. Nike has a negative lending and borrowing rate spread (typical of nonfinancial firms) and the overall contribution of financing activities to ROCE could be improved by selling off the financial assets and using the proceeds to reduce the financial obligations. Alternatively, Nike may wish to buy operating assets by selling off its financial assets and improve the ROCE through the RNOA driver.

The profitability analysis for Nike is continued on the BYOAP feature on the book's website. See Box 11.8.

As with all calculations, these numbers should be checked for their reasonableness. Footnotes give rates for some borrowings as a benchmark. If your calculated borrowing costs seem "out of line," it may be that you have misclassified operating and financing items (and this means that your RNOA is also incorrect). It may be that disclosures are not sufficient to make a clear distinction. In the case of Nike, the notes indicate that some accounts payable are interest bearing but the amount is not given. To the extent this is material, it will affect not only the net borrowing but also financial and operating leverage calculations. The inability to unravel capitalized interest will introduce errors. And errors will be made if the averaging of balance sheet amounts does not reflect the timing of changes in those amounts during the period.

The Web Connection

Find the following on the web page for this chapter:

- Further exploration of the effects of financial leverage, with consideration of both risk and profitability effects.

- Further exploration of operating liability leverage and how it is particularly pertinent for an insurance company.

- Profitability analysis for more firms.

Summary

This chapter has laid out the analysis of profitability. The analysis is summarized in Figure 11.1. The methods are orderly, with lower levels of analysis nested in higher levels. And the analysis aggregates up from the bottom to ROCE at the top, so it is amenable to simple programming. Once the reformulated income statement and balance sheet are entered into a spreadsheet program and the template in Figure 11.1 overlaid, the analysis proceeds at the press of a button.

The analysis uncovers the financial statement drivers of the return on common equity, but each of these drivers refers to an aspect of business activity. The analysis here is a way of penetrating the financial statements. But it is also a way of organizing your knowledge of the business and understanding the effects of business activities on value. Understanding how the business affects the financial statement drivers means that the analyst understands how the business affects ROCE and, in turn, how the business affects residual earnings and the value of the business. So, for example, the analyst understands how a change in the profit margin or asset turnover affects residual earnings. And the analyst—or the manager of the business—can ask "what-if" questions of how ROCE and the value might change with a planned or unplanned change in margins or turnovers.

The chapter has provided numbers for typical levels of ROCE, RNOA, financial leverage (FLEV), operating liability leverage (OLLEV), profit margins, asset turnovers, and more. Keep these numbers in mind, for they will provide useful benchmarks for what to expect when forecasting.

Key Concepts

favorable financial leverage (or favorable gearing) is an increase in ROCE over RNOA induced by borrowing. Compare with **unfavorable leverage**. *352*

favorable operating liability leverage is an increase in return on net operating assets over return on operating assets induced by operating liabilities. *354*

growth analysis is the analysis of the determinants of growth in residual earnings. *348*

operating liability leverage spread is the difference between the return on operating assets and the implicit borrowing rate for operating liabilities. *354*

operating spread is the difference between operating profitability and the net borrowing cost. *352*

profitability analysis is the analysis of the determinants of return on common equity (ROCE). *348*

spread is a difference between two rates of return. Examples are the **operating spread**, the **operating liability leverage spread**, and the **spread between borrowing and lending rates**. *352*

spread between borrowing and lending rates is the difference between the return on financial obligations and the return on financial assets. *367*

The Analyst's Toolkit

Concept Questions

C11.1. Under what conditions would a firm's return on common equity (ROCE) be equal to its return on net operating assets (RNOA)?

C11.2. Under what conditions would a firm's return on net operating assets (RNOA) be equal to its return on operating assets (ROOA)?

C11.3. State whether the following measures drive return on common equity (ROCE) positively, negatively, or depending on the circumstances:
a. Gross margin.
b. Advertising expense ratio.
c. Net borrowing cost.
d. Operating liability leverage.
e. Operating liability leverage spread.

        f. Financial leverage.

        g. Inventory turnover.

C11.4. Why might borrowing lever up the return on common equity?

C11.5. Why might operating liabilities lever up the return on net operating assets?

C11.6. A firm should always purchase inventory and supplies on interest-free credit rather than paying cash. Correct?

C11.7. A reduction in the advertising expense ratio increases return on common equity and share value. Correct?

C11.8. VF Corporation, the apparel manufacturer, states that one of its goals is to earn a return on common equity of 17–20 percent. What is wrong with setting a goal in terms of return on common equity?

C11.9. Why might operating losses increase after-tax borrowing cost?

C11.10. Some retail analysts use a measure called "inventory yield," calculated as gross profit-to-inventory. What does this measure tell you?

C11.11. Return on total assets (ROA) is a common measure of profitability. The historical average is about 6.8 percent. The historical yield on corporate bonds is about 6 percent. Why is the ROA so low? Would not investors expect more than a 0.8 percent higher return on risky operations?

Exercises E11.1. Leveraging Equations (Easy)

The following information is from reformulated financial statements (in millions of dollars):

	2002	2003
Operating assets	$2,000	$2,700
Marketable debt securities	400	100
Operating liabilities	(100)	(300)
Bonds payable	(1,400)	(1,300)
Book value (net)	$ 900	1,200
Sales		2,100
Operating expenses		(1,677)
Interest revenue		27
Interest expense		(137)
Tax expense (rate = 34%)		(106)
Earnings (net)		$ 207

a. (1) Calculate the dividends, net of capital contributions, for 2003.

    (2) Calculate ROCE for 2003; use average net book value in the denominator.

    (3) Calculate RNOA for 2003; use the average net operating assets in the denominator.

    (4) Supply the numbers for the formula

$$\text{ROCE} = \text{PM} \times \text{ATO} + [\text{Financial leverage} \times (\text{RNOA} - \text{Borrowing cost})]$$

b. The firm's short-term borrowing rate is 4.5 percent after tax. Supply the numbers for the formula

$$\text{RNOA} = \text{ROOA} + (\text{OLLEV} \times \text{OLSPREAD})$$

c. Repeat the exercise in part (a) using the following information:

	2002	2003
Operating assets	$2,000	$2,700
Marketable debt securities	800	1,000
Operating liabilities	(100)	(300)
Book value (net)	$2,700	3,400
Sales		2,100
Operating expenses		(1,677)
Interest revenue		90
Tax expense (rate = 34%)		(174)
Earnings		$ 339

E11.2. First-Level Analysis of Financial Statements (Easy)

A firm whose shares traded at three times their book value on December 31, 2002, had the accompanying financial statements. Amounts are in millions of dollars. The firm's marginal tax rate is 33 percent. There are no dirty-surplus income items in the balance sheet.

a. The firm paid no dividends and issued no shares during 2002, but it repurchased some stock. Calculate the amount of stock repurchase.

b. Calculate the following measures:

   Return on common equity (ROCE)
   Return on net operating assets (RNOA)
   Financial leverage (FLEV)
   The operating spread (SPREAD)
   Free cash flow

c. Does it make sense that this firm's shares should trade at three times book value?

Balance Sheet, December 31, 2002

Assets	2002	2001	Liabilities and Shareholders' Equity	2002	2001
Operating cash	$ 50	$ 20	Accounts payable	$ 215	$ 205
Short-term investments	150	150	Long-term debt	450	450
Accounts receivable	300	250			
Inventories	420	470	Common equity	1,095	1,025
Property and plant (net)	840	790			
	$1,760	$1,680		$1,760	$1,680

Income Statement, Year Ended December 31, 2002

Sales		$3,295
Interest income		9
Operating expenses	$3,048	
Interest expense	36	
Tax expense	61	(3,145)
Net income		$ 159

E11.3. Relationship between Rates of Return and Leverage (Medium)

a. A firm has a return on common equity of 13.4 percent, a net after-tax borrowing cost of 4.5 percent, and a return of 11.2 percent on net operating assets of $405 million. What is the firm's financial leverage?

b. The same firm has a short-term borrowing rate of 4.0 percent after tax and a return on operating assets of 8.5 percent. What is the firm's operating liability leverage?

c. The firm reported total assets of $715 million. Construct a balance sheet for this firm that distinguishes operating and financial assets and liabilities.

E11.4. Measures of Profitability and Leverage: Intel Corporation (Easy)

Refer to the income statement and balance sheet for Intel in Exercise E9.1 of Chapter 9.

a. Calculate the traditional return on assets (ROA) and compare it to Intel's return on net operating assets. Use a statutory tax rate of 38 percent.

b. Calculate the standard debt-to-equity ratio and compare it to the financial leverage measure that distinguishes operating from financing activities.

When might an analyst rely on the standard debt-to-equity ratio, and when might he or she rely on the measure that distinguishes operating activities from financing activities?

Real World Connection

See Exercise E4.4 in Chapter 4, Exercise E9.1 in Chapter 9, and Exercise E10.10 in Chapter 10 for more material on Intel Corporation.

E11.5. Profit Margins, Asset Turnovers, and Return on Net Operating Assets: A What-If Question (Medium)

A firm earns a profit margin of 3.8 percent on sales of $435 million and employs net operating assets of $150 million to do so. It considers adding another product line that will earn a 4.8 percent profit margin with an asset turnover of 2.3.

What would be the effect on the firm's return on net operating assets of adding the new product line?

E11.6. Analyzing Borrowing Costs: Reebok (Easy)

From the reformulated financial statements in the chapter, analyze Reebok's net borrowing cost for 1996.

E11.7. A What-If Question: Grocery Retailers (Medium)

In the late 1990s many grocery supermarkets shifted from regular storewide sales to issuing membership in discount and points programs, much like frequent flyer programs run by the airlines.

A supermarket chain with $120 million in annual sales and an asset turnover of 6.0 ponders whether to institute a customer membership program. It currently earns a profit margin of 1.6 percent on sales. Its marketing research indicates that a customer membership program would increase sales by $25 million and would require an additional investment in inventories of $2 million but no additional retail floor space. Costs to run the membership program, including the discounts offered to members, would reduce profit margins to 1.5 percent.

What would be the effect on the firm's return on net operating assets of adopting the customer membership program?

E11.8. Financial Statement Analysis: Ben & Jerry's (Medium)

Summaries of balance sheets and income statements for Ben & Jerry's Homemade, Inc., a manufacturer of premium ice cream, frozen yogurt, and novelty products, follow. Ben & Jerry's had 7.195 million shares outstanding on December 31, 1996. The firm's marginal tax rate is 38 percent.

Balance Sheets (amounts in millions)

	1996	1995
Short-term investments	$ 36.6	$ 35.4
Trade receivables	8.7	11.7
Other receivables	0.3	0.9
Inventories	15.4	12.6
Other current operating assets	7.1	7.5
Current assets	68.1	68.1
Plant, net	65.1	59.6
Equity investments at market value	1.0	1.0
Other long-term operating assets	2.5	2.4
	136.7	131.1
Trade payables and accrued expenses	17.4	16.5
Current portion of long-term debt	0.6	0.5
	18.0	17.0
Long-term debt and lease obligations	31.1	32.0
Deferred tax liability	4.8	3.5
	53.9	52.5
Common stock	47.5	47.2
Retained earnings	35.2	31.3
Cumulative currency translation adjustment	0.1	0.1
	$136.7	$131.1

Income Statements (amounts in millions)

	1996	1995
Net sales	$167.1	$155.3
Cost of sales	115.2	109.1
Gross profit	51.9	46.2
Selling, general, and administrative expenses	45.5	36.4
	6.4	9.8
Other income (expense)		
Interest income	1.7	1.7
Interest expense	(2.0)	(1.5)
Other	0.2	(0.6)
Income before income taxes	6.3	9.4
Income taxes	2.4	3.5
Net income	$ 3.9	$ 5.9
Net income per common share	0.54	0.83

a. Calculate financial leverage and operating liability leverage on December 31, 1996.
b. Calculate the appropriate measure of operating profitability for 1996.
c. Analyze what factors determined the operating profitability for 1996.

Real World Connection

See Exercise E10.6 in Chapter 10, Exercise E13.8 in Chapter 13, and Exercise E14.2 in Chapter 14.

Minicases

M11.1

Analysis with Equity Accounting and the Use of Proportional Consolidation: AirTouch Communications

Prior to being acquired, AirTouch Communications, Inc., was one of the largest wireless communications services companies in the world in 1999, serving 40 million cellular, PCS, and paging customers in the United States, Europe, Asia, and Africa. The firm's population area (referred to as POP in the business) was 724 million people in 13 countries, with 97 million of those POPs in the United States. AirTouch's aim is to be the premier provider of wireless telecommunications services worldwide and, in doing so, to develop scale advantages by spreading infrastructure costs over a large subscriber base.

AirTouch's ownership of international operations typically involves majority ownership at the time of the award of a license, but the share of ownership changes over time as a result of political, legal, and economic factors. In cases where the firm does not have majority control it attempts to maintain operating influence through board representation, the right to appoint key management, consent rights for significant corporate transactions, and rights of first refusal on sales of interests by partners and issuances of shares.

Some interests that involve greater than 50 percent ownership are accounted for by consolidating subsidiary accounts, some by the equity method (where AirTouch's interest is less than 50 percent but greater than 20 percent), and, in a very few cases (of less than 20 percent ownership), investments in subsidiaries are carried at cost. The firm's income statement for its June 30, 1999, quarter is below.

Income Statement for Three Months Ending June 30, 1999
(dollars in millions, except per-share information)

Operating revenues	$1,484
Operating expenses	
Cost of revenues	323
Selling and customer operations expenses	464
General, administrative, and other expenses	162
Depreciation and amortization expenses	285
Total operating expenses	1,234
Operating income	250
Equity in net income (loss) of unconsolidated wireless systems	
U.S.	9
International	193
Minority interests in net (income) loss of consolidated wireless systems	(46)
Interest	
Expense	(36)
Income	4
Merger-related costs	(116)
Miscellaneous income (expense)	21
Income before income taxes and preferred dividends	279
Income taxes	98
Income before preferred dividends	181
Preferred dividends	34
Net income applicable to common stockholders	$ 147

Notice that a considerable amount of the firm's earnings is reported as equity in the income of its subsidiaries. This reporting can frustrate analysis because, unlike the case where subsidiary accounts are consolidated, details of the revenues and expenses that generate the earnings are not given in the income statement. AirTouch reported the following Note F and Note D to its financial statements:

F. Investments in Unconsolidated Wireless Systems

The company's investments in unconsolidated wireless systems consist of the following:

(Dollars in millions)	June 30, 1999	December 31, 1998
Investments at equity	$3,714	$3,344
Investments at cost	188	147
	$3,902	$3,491

The company's equity in net income of its significant equity investee on December 31, 1998, Mannesmann Mobilfunk GmbH ("Mannesmann") was $101 million and $67 million for the three months ended June 30, 1999, and 1998, respectively. The company's equity in net income of Mannesmann differs from its proportionate share of Mannesmann's reported net income in the table below primarily due to amortization of intangibles and other adjustments. Condensed operating results for Mannesmann are as follows:

(Dollars in millions)	Three Months Ended June 30	
	1999	1998
Mannesmann Mobilfunk GmbH		
Operating revenues	$1,273	$958
Operating income	522	400
Net income	226	173

Firms are required to report profits by business segments. The schedule below, given in the segment information footnote, does this, but you will agree that the detail is minimal. In particular, it does not give much indication about the $202 million in equity of income in subsidiaries.

D. Segment Information

The following table presents the company's business segment information for the three and six months ended June 30, 1999, and 1998. There has not been a change in the basis of segmentation or the basis of measurement of the segment profit or loss for each of these segments from the Company's 1998 Annual Report on Form 10-K.

(Dollars in millions)	Three Months Ended June 30, 1999				
	U.S. Cellular Operations	International Operations	U.S. Paging Operations	Corporate and Other	Total Company
Operating revenues	$1,084	$287	$112	$ 1	$1,484
Net income applicable to common stockholders	91	215	5	(164)	147

To remedy the required GAAP reporting, AirTouch reports "proportionate data" outside its formal financial statements:

Selected Proportionate Financial Data (UNAUDITED)
Non-GAAP Supplemental Proportionate Data

The following tables are presented on a proportionate basis. Proportionate presentation is not permitted by generally accepted accounting principles ("GAAP") and is not intended to replace the consolidated operating results prepared and presented in accordance with GAAP. However, since significant wireless systems in which the Company has an interest are not consolidated, proportionate information is provided as supplemental data to facilitate a more detailed understanding and assessment of consolidated operating results prepared and presented in accordance with GAAP.

GAAP requires consolidation of wireless systems controlled by the company and the equity method of accounting for wireless systems in which the Company has significant influence but not a controlling interest. Proportionate presentation is a pro rata consolidation, which reflects the Company's share of revenues and expenses in both its consolidated and unconsolidated wireless systems. Proportionate results are calculated by multiplying the Company's ownership interest in each wireless system by each of the system's total operating results, and accordingly should not be compared with GAAP consolidated results of any company.

Net income under either GAAP or proportionate presentation is the same.

Proportionately reported amounts include results from the Company's equity investees, which the Company does not control. The Company does not have control over the revenues, expense, or cash flows of its equity investees that are reported in proportionate results and is only entitled to cash from dividends received from these entities. The Company does not own the underlying assets of its equity investees.

Total Company	
Service and other revenues	$2,297
Operating expenses before depreciation and amortization expenses (1)	1,400
Operating cash flow (2)	897
Depreciation and amortization expenses	395
Operating income	502
Interest and other income (expenses)	(133)
Income taxes	(188)
Income before preferred dividends	181
Preferred dividends	34
Net income applicable to common stockholders	$ 142
Operating cash flow margin (3)	39.1%
U.S. Cellular and PCS Operations	
Service and other revenues	$1,116
Operating expenses before depreciation and amortization expenses (1)	673
Operating cash flow (2)	443
Depreciation and amortization expenses	261
Operating income	182
Operating cash flow margin (3)	39.7%
International Operations	
Service and other revenues	$1,079
Operating expenses before depreciation and amortization expenses	629
Operating cash flow (2)	450
Depreciation and amortization expenses	112
Operating income	$ 338
Operating cash flow margin (3)	41.7%
U.S. Paging Operations	
Service and other revenues	$ 102
Operating expenses before depreciation and amortization expenses	72
Operating cash flow (2)	30
Depreciation and amortization expenses	20
Operating income	$ 10
Operating cash flow margin (3)	29.4%

Footnotes:
(1) Includes net loss on handsets sold.
(2) "Operating cash flow" is defined as "Operating income" plus "Depreciation and amortization expenses" and is not the same as "Cash flows from operating activities" in the Company's Consolidated Statements of Cash Flows. Proportionate "Operating cash flow" represents the Company's ownership interests in the respective entities' operating cash flows. As such, proportionate "operating cash flow" does not represent cash available to the Company.
(3) "Operating cash flow margin" is calculated by dividing "Operating cash flow" by "Service and other revenues."

Analyze the income of AirTouch in two steps:

A. Use only the income statement and the footnote information provided in the formal GAAP statements. Use a tax rate of 38 percent. Voice your frustrations with this limited information.

B. Use the full set of information, including the supplemental proportionate data.

Segment information rarely gives full details of segment or affiliate balance sheets. Voice the frustration and concerns you have about lack of balance sheet detail.

[Note: On June 30, 1999, AirTouch Communications, Inc., merged with the U.K. wireless operator Vodofone to form Vodofone AirTouch Plc. Vodafone then acquired Mannesmann to become the largest mobile phone operator in the world.]

M11.2

Analysis of Return on Common Equity and Some "What-If" Questions: VF Corporation

This case asks you to analyze the 1998 financial statements of VF Corporation and to conduct a sensitivity analysis of key ratios based on a series of what-if questions. As always, one must know the business before beginning because one understands analysis only in the context of the business's operations.

Founded in 1899, VF Corporation is the world's largest apparel manufacturer.

STRATEGY

VF Corporation aims to create and maintain stable clothing brands that have broad appeal to consumers and to maintain state-of-the-art distribution systems to retailers who look to deal with fewer, efficient suppliers.

The firm's "consumerism" philosophy focuses on reliability—fit, comfort, value for money—rather than fashion and glamour. It involves developing and maintaining strong brands, distinguishing up-market products from high-volume basic apparel, feeding the appropriate brands through each distribution channel, and being a leader in timely service.

The strategy is exercised through "coalition management" by which management groups are formed to focus on the consumer. The management relies on its Market Response System, an information technology that transmits point-of-sale data daily from retailers to generate next-day shipments and to manage inventory. This is supplemented with a Consumer Response System that tracks the needs of specific consumers and helps pinpoint the marketing of its brands.

OPERATIONS

VF Corporation's main product line is jeanswear, with brand names including Lee, Wrangler, Riders, Brittania, Rustler, and (in cotton casuals) Timber Creek by Wrangler. The jeans are sold through department stores, specialty stores, and discount stores throughout the world. In addition, the firm manufactures and sells work clothes, children's playwear, fleece wear, T-shirts, and intimate apparel. The firm is organized into six "coalitions"—Jeanswear, Workwear, Intimate Apparel, Knitwear, Playwear, and International.

The business is highly competitive, with major competitors being Levi's and the private labels. Wal-Mart is the biggest customer, accounting for 12.3 percent of sales in 1998. Sales to its 10 largest customers accounted for 41 percent of sales, and 16 percent of sales were international. Advertising is extensive, amounting to 5.2 percent of sales in 1998.

VF Corporation has 70,000 employees. It sponsors a noncontributory defined benefit pension plan covering substantially all full-time domestic employees. It also sponsors an employee stock ownership plan (ESOP).

DEBT FINANCING

The management has a target debt-to-equity ratio of 40 percent. About a third of its financing debt in 1998 was in short-term borrowings, with the remainder in long-term debt.

EQUITY FINANCING

The firm had 119,466 thousand common shares outstanding at January 2, 1999, net of 17,134 thousand shares in treasury and 233 thousand shares held in trust for deferred compensation plans. There is a "poison pill" provision in the event of a takeover bid. The firm has paid dividends annually since 1941 and has a target payout ratio of 30 percent.

The firm also has Series A preferred stock, of which none is issued, and 6.75 percent Series B preferred stock purchased by the ESOP. The Series B stock can be redeemed at $30.88 per share plus cumulative accrued dividends either by the company or, under certain circumstances, at the instigation of the ESOP trustee. They can also be converted to 1.6 shares of common for each preferred share. The ESOP's purchase of the preferred shares was funded by a loan of $65 million at an interest rate of 9.8 percent, payable in installments through 2002. Principal and interest obligations are satisfied through company contributions to the ESOP and preferred dividends.

The firm grants nonqualified stock options to officers, directors, and key employees at prices not less than fair market value of the common stock at grant date. The firm also grants restricted stock to selected employees, and 47,832 shares that vest in 2005 had been granted as of the end of 1998.

Summary Data

	1998	1997	1996
Basic earnings per share	$ 3.17	$ 2.76	$ 2.32
Diluted earnings per share	3.10	2.70	2.28
Dividends per share	0.81	0.77	0.73
Book value per share, end of year	17.30	15.40	15.44
Price per share, end of year	47	46	34
Price, high	54½	48¼	35
Price, low	33½	32¼	24
P/E ratio, end of year	14.8	16.7	14.7
P/B ratio, end of year	2.7	3.0	3.3

Note: See www.vfc.com for more information.

VF Corporation's reformulated financial statements for 1998 are below. Review those financial statements, and then answer the questions following.

Reformulated 1998 financial statements for VF Corporation

VF CORPORATION
Reformulated Statement of Common Equity
(in thousands of dollars)

Balance January 3, 1998		$1,866,769
Transactions with Shareholders		
Stock issues	$ 59,013	
Stock repurchases	(154,359)	
Common dividends	(97,943)	(193,289)
Comprehensive Income		
Net income	388,306	
Tax benefit of preferred dividends	568	
Loss on redemption of preferred stock	(2,763)	
Foreign currency translation gain	10,471	
Preferred dividends	(3,717)	392,865
Net Addition to Deferred Compensation		(37)
Balance January 2, 1999		$2,066,308

Reformulated Balance Sheet

	1998		1997	
Operating Assets				
Cash		$ 15,000		$ 12,000
Accounts receivable	$ 757,745		$ 627,510	
Less allowances for doubtful accounts	(52,011)	705,734	(39,576)	587,934
Inventories—Finished goods	552,729		434,000	
Work in process	185,929		166,947	
Materials	215,349	954,007	173,808	774,755
Other current assets		25,595		19,933
Property, plant, and equipment—Land	45,296		44,786	
Buildings	443,619		437,903	
Machinery	1,222,216		1,086,263	
	1,711,131		1,568,952	
Less accumulated depreciation	(935,040)	776,091	(862,962)	705,990
Goodwill	1,195,062		1,022,632	
Less accumulated amortization	(243,500)	951,562	(208,300)	814,332
Deferred income tax asset	235,044		212,975	
Less valuation allowance	(34,249)	200,795	(32,506)	180,469
Pension asset		35,164		27,713
Other assets		124,510		87,562
Deferred ESOP contributions		20,399		26,275
Operating assets		3,808,857		3,236,963

(continued)

Operating Liabilities

Accounts payable	341,126		301,103	
Accrued liabilities—Taxes payable	70,112		86,244	
Compensation payable	103,769		84,425	
Insurance payable	18,605		62,153	
Other	253,515		207,342	
Other liabilities—Deferred compensation	151,436		113,727	
Deferred income taxes	11,512		—	
Other	18,802	968,877	30,086	885,080
Net Operating Assets (NOA)		2,839,980		2,351,883
Net Financial Obligations (NFO)				
Short-term borrowings	244,910		24,191	
Current portion of long-term debt	969		450	
Long-term debt	521,657		516,226	
Preferred stock	54,344		56,341	
Financial obligations	821,880		597,208	
Cash equivalents	(48,208)	773,672	(112,094)	485,114
Common Shareholders' Equity (CSE)		$2,066,308		$1,866,769

Reformulated Income Statement

	1998		**1997**	
Net Sales		$ 5,478,807		$ 5,222,246
Cost of products sold		(3,586,686)		(3,440,611)
Gross margin		1,892,121		1,781,635
Miscellaneous income		3,300		6,684
		1,895,421		1,788,319
Advertising expense	$287,500		$309,300	
Administrative and general expense	911,354		866,298	
Other expense	9,098	(1,207,952)	964	(1,176,562)
		687,469		611,757
Tax benefit on preferred dividends to ESOP		568		700
Foreign currency translation gain		10,471		(42,538)
Operating income before tax		698,508		569,919
Tax reported	243,292		234,938	
Tax benefit of debt	21,231	(264,523)	9,833	(244,771)
Operating Income after Tax		433,985		325,148
Net Financial Expense				
Interest expense	62,282		49,695	
Interest income	(6,411)		(23,818)	
Net interest before tax	55,871		25,877	
Tax benefit of debt (38%)	(21,231)		(9,833)	
Net interest after tax	34,640		16,044	
Preferred dividends	3,717		3,804	
Loss on redemption of preferred stock	2,763	(41,120)	1,855	(21,703)
Comprehensive Income (Available to Common)		$ 392,865		$ 303,445

A. Analyze the firm's financial statements to discover the source of the profitability of the common shareholders' equity in 1998. Perform the necessary calculations but also express in words what you see as the drivers of the profitability.

B. Use your analysis of the financials to answer the following "what-if" questions:

(1) At what point would VF Corporation's financial leverage turn unfavorable?

(2) What would have been the return on net operating assets (RNOA) if VF had applied the $48 million in cash equivalents at the end of the period to buying down its debt? Consider the transaction to have taken place at the beginning of the period.

(3) What would have been the effect on return on common equity (ROCE) of the transaction in (2)?

(4) What would have been the effect on ROCE if the $48 million in cash had been applied to a stock repurchase at the beginning of the period?

(5) What would be the effect on the profitability of operations if VF could not get credit for its purchases, that is, if accounts payable were zero?

(6) What would be the effect on the return on common equity under the conditions in (5)?

(7) What would be the after-tax effect on VF's return on net operating assets if it could increase its gross profit margin by 1 percent by reducing materials cost?

(8) What would be the effect of the change in profit margin in (7) on ROCE? Using the residual earnings valuation model, estimate what the effect might be on VF Corporation's market value.

(9) VF's advertising expense dropped from 1997 to 1998. What would its return on net operating assets have been if advertising expenses had been maintained at their 1997 level with the same sales? What does this say about the quality of the 1998 RNOA?

C. Develop further questions that can be introduced into the analysis. How might these questions give answers to strategy issues confronting management?

Chapter Twelve

The Analysis of Growth and Sustainable Earnings

LINKS

Link to previous chapter

Chapter 11 laid out the analysis of profitability.

This chapter

This chapter lays out the analysis of growth that is necessary to complete the evaluation of P/B and P/E ratios.

Link to next chapter

Part Three of the book applies the analysis of profitability and growth to forecasting and valuation.

Link to web page

Explore the text website for more applications of Chapter 12 content (www.mhhe.com/penman2e).

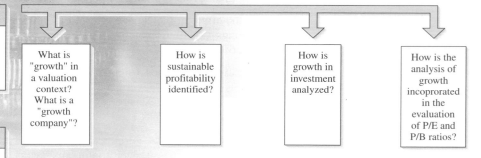

What is "growth" in a valuation context? What is a "growth company"?

How is sustainable profitability identified?

How is growth in investment analyzed?

How is the analysis of growth incorprorated in the evaluation of P/E and P/B ratios?

The price-to-book (P/B) valuation model of Chapter 5 showed that firms increase their price-to-book ratios if they can grow residual earnings. The price-earnings (P/E) valuation model of Chapter 6 showed that firms increase their price-earning ratios if they can grow abnormal earnings. Clearly, then, an assessment of a firm's ability to deliver growth is critical to valuation. This chapter lays out the analysis of growth.

Analysts often talk of growth in terms of a firm's ability to grow earnings. The chapter begins by reminding you that earnings growth is not a valid growth concept for valuation because, as shown in Chapters 5 and 6, firms can grow earnings without adding value. Rather, residual earnings growth and abnormal earnings growth are the relevant measures. Residual earnings growth is the focus when evaluating P/B ratios, and abnormal earnings growth is the focus when evaluating P/E ratios.

Growth in residual earnings is driven by increases in return on common equity (ROCE) and growth in equity investment. So the analysis of growth for the evaluation of P/B ratios amounts to an analysis of how ROCE and investment change over time. As earnings are just investment multiplied by the rate of return on investment, abnormal earnings growth is driven by the same factors that determine residual earnings growth. The analysis of growth uncovers these factors.

The Analyst's Checklist

After reading this chapter you should understand:	After reading this chapter you should be able to:
• Why the analysis of growth is important for valuation.	• Complete an analysis of a change in return on net operating assets (RNOA).
• Why growth analysis focuses on residual earnings growth and abnormal earnings growth, rather than earnings growth.	• Complete an analysis of a change in ROCE.
• Why abnormal earnings growth is equal to growth in residual earnings.	• Complete an analysis of growth in investment.
• What a growth firm is.	• Complete an analysis of growth in residual earnings.
• What constitutes sustainable earnings.	• Identify core or sustainable earnings in income statements.
• What transitory earnings are.	• Identify transitory or unusual items in income statements.
• What "quality of earnings" means.	• Analyze the effect of changes in financial leverage on ROCE.
• How operating leverage affects earnings as sales change.	• Analyze the effects of operating leverage on operating income and RNOA.
• How changes in ROCE can be created by borrowing.	• Identify core net borrowing cost.
• What the drivers of growth of the common shareholders' investment are.	

The question of whether future earnings will grow over current earnings can be couched in a different way: Are current earnings a good indicator of future earnings, or are there aspects of current earnings that are not likely to be repeated in the future? Earnings temporarily depressed by a strike are not indicative of future earnings. Earnings that reflect a one-time special contract may be abnormally high. Earnings reduced by restructuring charges may not be a good forecast of the future earnings that will likely benefit from the restructurings. Earnings that are indicative of a firm's long-run earning ability are called *sustainable earnings, persistent earnings,* or *core earnings.* Earnings based on temporary factors are called *unusual earnings* or *transitory earnings.* The sustainability of earnings affects forecasts of growth, so this chapter outlines an analysis that distinguishes sustainable earnings from transitory earnings.

The common-size analysis of Chapter 9 is a prerequisite for the profitability analysis of the last chapter. Correspondingly, the trend analysis of Chapter 9 is a prerequisite for the analysis of growth in this chapter, for trend analysis documents the historical growth in "bottom-line" numbers such as common equity, net operating assets, and operating income, and it explains their growth by growth in their component parts.

The analysis of growth bears on the determination of intrinsic P/B and P/E ratios. So the chapter begins by introducing the topic from that perspective, and the chapter ends by tying the analysis back to those ratios, in preparation for the forecasting and valuation that follows in Part Three of the book.

WHAT IS GROWTH?

The term "growth" is often used vaguely, or with a variety of meanings. People talk of "growth firms"—and of paying more for a growth firm—but their meaning is not always clear. Sometimes the term is used to mean growth in sales, sometimes growth in earnings, and sometimes growth in assets. Generally growth is seen as a positive attribute, an ability to generate value. But what is growth? What is a **growth firm?**

The valuation models of Chapters 5 and 6 provide the answer to this question.

Chapter 5 showed that one pays a premium over book value based on the ability of a firm to grow residual earnings (RE), where residual earnings is the difference between earnings and the required return on book value. For any year t,

$$\text{Residual earnings}_t\ (RE_t) = \text{Earnings}_t - [(\rho_E - 1) \times \text{Common shareholders' equity}_{t-1}]$$

where $\rho_E - 1$ is the required return for equity. Shareholders invest in firms, and the book value of their equity—the firm's net assets—measures this investment. Firms apply the net assets in operations to add value for shareholders. Residual earnings measure the value added to book value over that required to cover the cost of capital. So a sensible way of viewing growth that ties into value creation is in terms of growth in residual earnings: A growth firm is one that can grow residual earnings.

Chapter 6 showed that one pays more than a normal P/E based on the ability of a firm to generate abnormal earnings growth (AEG), where abnormal earnings growth is the difference between cum-dividend earnings and a charge for the prior year's earnings growing at the required rate. For any year t,

$$\text{Abnormal earnings growth}_t\ (AEG_t) = [\text{Earnings}_t + (\rho_E - 1)d_{t-1}] - \rho_E \text{Earnings}_{t-1}$$

where d_{t-1} is the net dividend paid in the prior year. Firms do not add to their P/E ratio if they can only grow earnings at the required rate of growth. They add value only if they can grow earnings at a rate greater that the required rate, that is, if they can deliver abnormal earnings growth. So another way of viewing growth that ties into the value creation is in terms of the ability of a firm to deliver abnormal earnings growth.

In both Chapters 5 and 6, we warned against paying too much for earnings growth. We emphasized that earnings growth alone is not a good measure of growth because earnings growth can be created by investment (that does not add value) and by accounting methods (that also do not add value). We showed how residual earnings and abnormal earnings growth measures isolate that part of earnings growth that is to be valued from that part which is not. Charging earnings for required earnings—required earnings on book value in the case of residual earnings and required earnings on prior earnings in the case of abnormal earnings growth—protects the investor from paying too much for earnings growth created by investment and accounting methods. In short, residual earnings growth and abnormal earnings growth are the growth measures we must focus on if we have valuation in mind.

Residual earnings is the relevant growth measure when evaluating the price-to-book (P/B) ratio. Abnormal earnings growth is the relevant growth measure when evaluating the price-earnings (P/E) ratio. However, we showed in Chapter 6 (in Box 6.3) that the two measures are just different ways of looking at the same thing: *Abnormal earnings growth is equal to the change in residual earnings.* If a firm has no growth in residual earnings, its abnormal earnings growth must be zero: The firm is a "no growth" firm. If a firm has residual earnings growth it must also have abnormal earnings growth: The firm is a "growth company." For most of this chapter, we will analyze growth in residual earnings with the understanding that the factors that grow residual earnings also produce abnormal earnings growth. Residual earnings growth involves both balance sheet and income statement features, so we gain a better appreciation of the determinants of growth from the analysis of growth in residual earnings.

Box 12.1 introduces you to some growth and no-growth firms. In each case, observe that abnormal earnings growth is equal to the change in residual earnings.

A GROWTH FIRM: GENERAL ELECTRIC

(Dollar amounts in millions)	1998	1997	1996	1995	1994	1993
Sales	100,469	90,840	79,179	70,028	60,109	55,701
Sales growth rate	10.6%	14.7%	13.1%	16.5%	7.9%	5.0%
Common equity	38,880	34,438	31,125	29,609	25,387	25,824
Common equity growth rate	12.9%	10.6%	5.1%	16.7%	−1.7%	10.1%
ROCE	26.2%	27.2%	22.5%	23.9%	18.5%	17.5%
Residual earnings (12%)	5,221	4,994	3,190	3,273	1,653	1,358
Abnormal earnings growth (12%)	227	1,804	(83)	1,620	295	—

General Electric has maintained a high growth rate in sales, which translates into both increasing ROCE and increasing investment. Accordingly, with the exception of 1996, residual earnings (based on a required return of 12 percent) was on a growth path and abnormal earnings growth was (mainly) positive.

A GROWTH FIRM? NIKE

(Dollar amounts in millions)	2002	2001	2000	1999	1998	1997	1996	1995
Sales	9,893	9,489	8,995	8,777	9,553	9,187	6,471	4,761
Sales growth rate	4.3%	5.5%	2.5%	−8.1%	4.0%	42.0%	35.9%	25.6%
Common equity	3,839	3,495	3,136	3,335	3,262	3,156	2,431	1,964
Common equity growth rate	9.8%	11.4%	−6.0%	2.2%	3.4%	29.8%	23.8%	12.8%
ROCE	19.1%	18.8%	17.4%	13.0%	12.0%	24.6%	24.3%	22.5%
Residual earnings (11.1%)	280	241	210	64	28	426	291	210
Abnormal earnings growth (11.1%)	39	31	146	36	(398)	135	81	106

Up to 1998, Nike grew sales at a high rate, along with high ROCE, increasing investment, increasing residual earnings, and delivering positive abnormal earnings growth. With a declining sales growth rate in 1998 and 1999, ROCE and residual earnings declined as ROCE and growth in investment declined. In the early 2000s, Nike once again delivered growth. Can Nike generate growth in the future?

A NO-GROWTH FIRM: REEBOK

(Dollar amounts in millions)	2001	2000	1999	1998	1997	1996	1995	1994
Sales	2,993	2,865	2,900	3,225	3,644	3,479	3,481	3,280
Sales growth rate	4.5%	−1.2%	−10.1%	−11.5%	4.7%	−0.1%	6.1%	13.3%
Common equity	720	608	529	524	507	381	941	999
Common equity growth rate	18.4%	14.9%	1.0%	3.4%	33.1%	−59.5%	−5.8%	16.7%
ROCE	16.9%	15.3%	2.1%	5.8%	24.3%	17.6%	18.6%	28.7%
Residual earnings (12%)	30	17	(52)	(32)	55	43	64	155
Abnormal earnings growth (12%)	13	69	(20)	(87)	12	(21)	(91)	39

Reebok generated increasing residual earnings and abnormal earnings growth in the early 1990s but, with declining sales growth rates and lower ROCE, was not able to maintain the growth. From 1995 to 2000, Reebok reported little growth in residual earnings, with both lower ROCE and investment growth. Correspondingly, abnormal earnings growth was negative in most years.

(continued)

A MODERATE-GROWTH COMPANY: ABBOTT LABORATORIES

(Dollar amounts in millions)	1998	1997	1996	1995	1994	1993
Sales	12,478	11,883	11,013	10,012	9,156	8,407
Sales growth rate	5.0%	7.9%	10.0%	9.3%	8.9%	7.1%
Common equity	5,713	4,999	4,820	4,397	4,049	3,734
Common equity growth rate	14.3%	3.7%	9.6%	8.6%	8.4%	9.5%
ROCE	43.6%	38.9%	40.5%	40.4%	40.3%	36.8%
Residual earnings (12%)	1,693	1,323	1,315	1,198	1,100	890
Abnormal earnings growth (12%)	370	8	117	98	210	—

Abbott Laboratories, the pharmaceutical and health care products company, has high ROCE, but from 1994 to 1997, the high ROCE translated into only moderate growth in residual earnings (using a 12 percent required return) because the firm could find only a moderate amount of additional investments to earn at the high ROCE. However, residual earnings grew considerably in 1998 with a higher ROCE and a 14.3 percent growth in investment. Accordingly, abnormal earnings growth was high in 1998. Is this growth sustainable?

A CYCLICAL FIRM: AMERICAN AIRLINES

(Dollar amounts in millions)	1998	1997	1996	1995	1994	1993
Sales	16,299	15,856	15,136	15,610	14,837	14,731
Sales growth rate	2.8%	4.8%	−3.0%	5.2%	0.7%	8.5%
Common equity	6,428	5,354	4,528	3,646	3,233	3,168
Common equity growth rate	20.1%	18.2%	24.2%	12.8%	2.1%	1.4%
ROCE	18.0%	16.2%	16.7%	6.0%	8.4%	0.7%
Residual earnings (14%)	238	107	112	(274)	(180)	(397)
Abnormal earnings growth (14%)	131	(5)	386	(94)	217	—

American Airlines, the air carrier, grew residual earnings from 1995 to 1998. (Residual earnings is calculated using a 14 percent required return, as befits a risky airline.) But airlines are cyclical, as the residual earnings and abnormal earnings growth for the earlier years show. Sales growth has been modest and variable, and the increase in ROCE from 1996 to 1998 has also been modest, with growth coming from growth in investment. Can American Airlines generate more growth in the future or is a cyclical pattern likely to be repeated?

In analyzing growth, the analyst has her eye on the future: Can the firm grow residual earnings in the future? Past growth is only an indicator of future growth. So, in asking whether American Airlines, Reebok, Nike, General Electric, and Abbott Laboratories are growth companies, the question is whether past growth can be sustained in the future.

INTRODUCTION TO GROWTH ANALYSIS

Residual earnings are driven by return on common equity (ROCE), the amount of common shareholder investment (CSE), and the cost of capital:

$$\text{Residual earnings}_t = (\text{ROCE}_t - \text{Cost of equity capital}_t) \times \text{CSE}_{t-1}$$

So, changes in residual earnings are driven by changes in ROCE, changes in the cost of equity capital, and changes in common shareholders' equity. We defer cost-of-capital

A simple formula calculates the change in residual earnings (RE) from its three drivers, the change in ROCE, the change in the cost of capital, and the change in the common shareholders' investment (CSE). For the change in residual earnings from Year 0 to Year 1,

Change in residual earnings = Change due to change in ROCE over the cost of capital + Change due to change in common equity

$$\Delta RE_1 = [\Delta(ROCE - Cost\ of\ capital)_1 \times CSE_0]$$
$$+ [\Delta CSE_1 \times (ROCE - Cost\ of\ capital)_1]$$

where Δ indicates changes. As abnormal earnings growth is the change in residual earnings, this calculation also explains abnormal earnings growth.

NIKE, INC.

Nike, Inc., was introduced in the last chapter. Some of the numbers from that chapter that are pertinent to an analysis of its growth are summarized here (dollar amounts in millions). All balance sheet numbers are averages for the year.

	1996	1995
Net operating assets	$2,434	$1,795
Net financial obligations	236	(58)
Common shareholders' equity	$2,198	$1,853
Sales	$6,471	$4,761
Operating income	$ 549	$ 414
Return on common equity (ROCE)	24.35%	22.45%
Return on net operating assets (RNOA)	22.56%	23.06%
Net borrowing cost (NBC)	5.9 %	–3.4%
Profit margin (PM)	8.48%	8.70%
Asset turnover (ATO)	2.66	2.65
Financial leverage (FLEV)	0.107	–0.031

In 1996, Nike had residual earnings of $291.2 million from a ROCE of 24.35 percent as follows:

Residual earnings$_{1996}$ = (24.35% – 11.1%) × $2,198 million
            = $291.2 million

(using average CSE, as in the ROCE calculation). And for 1995, Nike's residual earnings were

Residual earnings$_{1995}$ = (22.45% – 11.1%) × $1,853 million
            = $210.3 million

The change in residual earnings of $80.9 million is also the abnormal earnings growth for 1996. We have used a CAPM cost of capital of 11.1 percent for both years here. Nike's residual earnings in 1996 grew at a rate of 38.5 percent. With no change in the cost of capital, the growth was driven by an increase in ROCE of 1.9 percent, from 22.45 percent to 24.35 percent, and growth in CSE of $345 million to earn at this higher ROCE. Applying the simple formula,

$$\Delta RE_{1996} = (1.9\% \times \$1,853\ million)$$
$$+ [\$345\ million \times (24.35\% - 11.1\%)]$$

$$= \$35.2\ million + \$45.7\ million$$

$$= \$80.9\ million$$

The calculation shows that Nike's growth in residual earnings—and its abnormal earnings growth—came from two components. First, $35.2 million of the $80.9 million growth came from the 1995 equity earning at a 1.9 percent higher rate; second, $45.7 million of the growth came from the additions to equity in 1996 of $345 million that earned at the 1996 rate of 24.35 percent.

(continued)

issues until the next chapter and Part Five of the book, focusing our analysis of growth here on the analysis of changes in ROCE and the analysis of changes in CSE.

Box 12.2 shows how growth in residual earnings is formally broken down into its three components. The box continues the analysis of Nike and Reebok that was begun in the last chapter. Some of the numbers from the last chapter that will be used in this one are summarized in Box 12.2. Nike's residual earnings grew by 38.5 percent in 1996, while Reebok's residual earnings declined by 33.2 percent. As a benchmark, the median annual growth in residual earnings for NYSE and AMEX firms from 1963 to 2000 was 4.2 percent.

REEBOK INTERNATIONAL LTD.

Reebok's financial statement numbers are summarized below:

	1996	1995
Net operating assets	$ 1,191	$ 1,182
Net financial obligations	405	186
Minority interest	32	26
Common shareholders' equity	$ 754	$ 970
Sales	$ 3,479	$ 3,481
Operating income	$ 168	$ 200
Return on common equity (ROCE)	17.64%	18.56%
Return on common equity (before minority interest)	18.83%	19.18%
Return on net operating assets (RNOA)	14.11%	16.92%
Net borrowing cost (NBC)	4.9 %	4.8 %
Profit margin (PM)	4.83%	5.75%
Asset turnover (ATO)	2.92	2.94
Financial leverage (FLEV)	0.515	0.187

Reebok's 1996 growth in residual earnings was less impressive than that of Nike:

$$\text{Residual earnings}_{1996} = (17.64\% - 12.0\%) \times \$754 \text{ million}$$
$$= 42.5 \text{ million}$$

(again using average CSE for the year). And for 1995,

$$\text{Residual earnings}_{1995} = (18.56\% - 12.0\%) \times \$970 \text{ million}$$
$$= \$63.6 \text{ million}$$

Again, the cost of capital of 12.0 percent is estimated using the CAPM. Ignoring any changes in the cost of capital, Reebok's residual earnings declined by $21.1 million, or 33.2 percent. It also had negative abnormal earnings growth of $21.1 million. This decline was due to both a drop in the ROCE of 0.92 percent, from 18.56 percent to 17.64 percent, and a reduction of equity investment of $216 million, due partly to the large stock repurchase:

$$\Delta RE_{1996} = (-0.92\% \times \$970 \text{ million})$$
$$+ [-\$216 \text{ million} \times (17.64\% - 12.0\%)]$$
$$= -\$8.9 \text{ million} - \$12.2 \text{ million}$$
$$= -\$21.1 \text{ million}$$

These calculations ignore any changes in the cost of capital. The change in the cost of capital is likely to be important for Reebok because of the large change in leverage with the stock repurchase. We will see in the next chapter how this is accommodated.

We turn now to analyze the changes in ROCE and growth in common equity that drive the growth in residual earnings.

THE ANALYSIS OF CHANGES IN PROFITABILITY AND SUSTAINABLE EARNINGS

Return on common equity (ROCE) is driven by operations and by the financing of the operations. So the change in ROCE is explained by changes in the profitability of operations and by changes in financing.

Figure 12.1 guides the analysis of the changes in these two components. This figure corresponds to Figure 11.1 but directs the analyst to analyze changes in ROCE rather than the level of ROCE. Both changes in operating profitability (ΔRNOA) and changes in financing are analyzed through three levels of investigation. Remember that, as with the analysis of the level of ROCE in the last chapter, the financial statement drivers of changes in profitability are themselves driven by the business, so the analyst identifies the aspects of the business that produce the changes in the financial statement drivers.

FIGURE 12.1   **The Analysis of Changes in Return on Common Equity (ROCE), Where Δ Indicates Changes**
Changes in ROCE are analyzed by analyzing changes in the operating profitability component (ΔRNOA) and changes in the financing component of ROCE. Each of these two components is investigated through three levels of analysis.

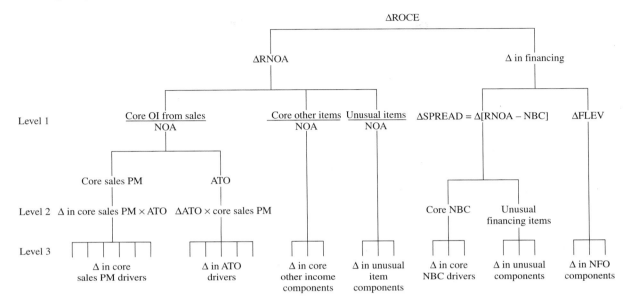

Analysis of Changes in Operations

To analyze changes in RNOA, proceed through the three levels in Figure 12.1.

Level 1. Distinguish Core and Unusual Components of RNOA

Changes in profitability can be partially explained by components of operating income that apply to a particular period, and so are nonrecurring. Nonrepeating components are referred to as **unusual items (UI)** or **transitory items**. Components that are generated by repetitive business are called **core income, persistent earnings, sustainable earnings**, or **underlying earnings**.[1] Thus

Return on net operating assets = Core RNOA + Unusual items to net operating assets

$$\text{RNOA} = \frac{\text{Core OI}}{\text{NOA}} + \frac{\text{UI}}{\text{NOA}}$$

The first component is the core RNOA. Separating income from sales from other operating income within the core RNOA,

$$\text{RNOA} = \frac{\text{Core OI from sales}}{\text{NOA}} + \frac{\text{Core other OI}}{\text{NOA}} + \frac{\text{UI}}{\text{NOA}}$$

---

[1] In the United Kingdom firms are required to report underlying earnings per share. But the analyst should check whether the firm's underlying earnings do exclude all transitory items.

To the extent that RNOA is driven by unusual, transitory items, it is said to be of "low quality." It is not sustainable. Identifying core earnings is sometimes referred to as **normalizing earnings** because it establishes "normal" ongoing earnings unaffected by one-time components.

Exhibit 12.1 lays out a template that adds to the reformulation of income statements in Chapter 9 to distinguish core (sustainable) and unusual operating income. Typical unusual items are listed there but the list is not exhaustive. The standard income statement identifies some items as "extraordinary" and these are of course unusual. But unusual items often appear above the extraordinary items section of the income statement also. Indeed you might identify aspects of the gross margin that are unusual because they are due to a special order or the effect of a strike that won't be repeated. Read the footnotes and

EXHIBIT 12.1
Reformulation of the Operating Income Section of the Income Statement to Identify Core and Unusual Items

Reformulated Operating Income

Core operating income
  Core sales revenue
  − <u>Core cost of sales</u>
  = Core gross margin
  − <u>Core operating expenses</u>
  = Core operating income from sales before tax
  − Tax on core operating income from sales
    + Tax as reported
    + Tax benefit from net financial expenses
    − Tax allocated to core other operating income
    − <u>Tax allocated to unusual items</u>
  = Core operating income from sales
  + Core other operating income
    + Equity income in subsidiaries
    + Earnings on pension assets
    + Other income not from sales
    − <u>Tax on core other operating income</u>
  = Core operating income
± **Unusual items**
  − Special charges
  − Special liability accruals
  ± Nonrecurring items
  − Asset write-downs
  ± Changes in estimates
  − Start-up costs expensed
  ± Profits and losses from asset sales
  − Restructuring charges
  ± Profits and losses from discontinued operations
  ± Extraordinary operating items
  ± Accounting changes
  ± Unrealized gains and losses on equity investments
  + Gains from share issues in subsidiaries
  ± Currency gains and losses
  ± Derivative gains and losses (operations)
  − <u>Tax allocated to unusual items</u>
= **Comprehensive operating income**

The Management Discussion and Analysis (MD&A) is management's report on the business and its prospects. It can sometimes be too optimistic, brushing over problems. But it often identifies elements of the business that are unusual. Indeed the SEC requires the MD&A to "describe any unusual or infrequent events or transactions or any significant economic changes that materially affected the amount of income from continuing operations and, in each case, indicate the extent to which income was so affected."

As well as discussing unusual items, the MD&A often reveals management's plans for the future that can indicate how the business might change and, accordingly, features of the current business that might not persist.

Focus on the results of operations section. It compares results over the recent three years, or more, with accompanying discussion of the changes. Be particularly sensitive to the discussion of changes in gross margins, because small percentage changes in those margins can have a large effect on the bottom line.

Management Discussion and Analysis for clues. See Box 12.3. The better you know the business, the better you will be in identifying these items. See Box 12.4.

With forecasting in mind we are interested in components that don't have any bearing in the future. Thus the unusual items category should include not only items that won't be repeated in the future but also items that appear each period but can't be forecast. Currency gains and losses and gains and losses from derivatives trading for an industrial firm are good examples. We might expect these as a normal feature of operations each period but presumably we cannot predict them: There will be either gains or losses in the future but we can't predict which, so their expected value is zero. A currency gain or loss is transitory; we don't expect it to persist. And so with all income items that are a result of marking balance sheet items to market value, because changes in market values are typically not predictable. Separate these gains and losses from current core income; otherwise core income will be affected by an item that is not representative of the future. Accordingly, we establish core operating income, which is a basis for predicting future operating income. Of course, if the firm is in the business of currency trading or securities trading, these gains and losses are part of core income: The firm attempts to exploit inefficiencies in the market or makes money from its lower transaction costs.

Issues in Identifying Sustainable Earnings

Here are the main issues in identifying sustainable operating income:

1. *Restructuring charges.* These are mostly unusual, but note this comment from management in the 1996 annual report of Cadbury Schweppes, which reports in the United Kingdom where firms are required to identify underlying earnings:

   Major restructuring costs are now widely recognised as a recurring item in major food manufacturers, estimated by some analysts at 0.5% of sales over the long term. We broadly subscribe to this view and accordingly accept that in normal circumstances it is no longer appropriate to exclude such costs from the underlying earnings.

2. *Unrealized gains and losses on equity investments.* These arise from equity holdings of less than 20 percent. They are due to marking the holdings to market value in the balance sheet. The market value of the holdings indicates their value, but changes in market value do not. Market values follow a "random walk," so changes in market value do not predict future changes in market value. Treat these unrealized gains and losses as transitory.

As with all analysis, knowing the firm's business is essential to identifying its core income. A firm's core business is defined by its business strategy, so the analyst must know the firm's business model before classifying items in the income statement.

Start-up costs for beginning new businesses are expensed in the income statement and would appear to be one-time charges. But for a retail chain like The Gap, the clothes retailer, or Starbucks, the coffee vendor, which are continually opening new stores as a matter of business strategy, these costs are ongoing.

Research and development expenditures on a special project might be considered a one-time expense, but R&D expenditures as part of a continuing R&D program—as is the case for a drug company like Abbott Laboratories—are persistent.

ABBOTT LABORATORIES (AND THE ANALYSIS OF R&D)

(in millions of dollars)	1998	1997	1996
Net sales	12,478	11,883	11,013
Cost of products sold	5,394	5,045	4,732
Research and development	1,222	1,302	1,205
Selling, general, and administrative	2,744	2,685	2,459
Total operating expenses	9,360	9,032	8,396
Operating earnings (before tax)	3,118	2,851	2,617
Sales growth rate	5.0%	7.9%	10.0%
R&D/sales	9.8%	11.0%	10.9%

Abbott Laboratories's sales growth rates are declining. Expenditures for R&D are persistent and reasonably flat, but they are declining as a percentage of sales. The analyst views R&D expenses as core expenses but sees the decline in R&D as a percentage of sales as a red flag. Will R&D decline further as a percentage of sales? Is research becoming less suc-

cessful in producing new products? Is the decline in the sales growth rate due to a failure to increase expenditure on R&D? Did the firm reduce R&D in 1999 to increase earnings that otherwise would be lower because of the slower sales growth? If the answer to the last question is yes, the reduction in R&D may be transitory, but the analyst has to ask whether the decrease in R&D will damage future sales.

COCA-COLA CO. (AND THE ANALYSIS OF ADVERTISING COSTS)

Marketing is an essential part of most firms' core strategy. A firm like Coca-Cola spends heavily on advertising to maintain its brand name. A one-time marketing campaign might be a transitory item but repetitive advertising, like Coke's, is persistent.

(In millions of dollars)	1998	1997	1996
Net operating revenues	18,813	18,868	18,673
Cost of goods sold	5,562	6,015	6,738
Gross profit	13,251	12,853	11,935
Selling, administrative, and general	8,284	7,852	8,020
Operating income (before tax)	4,967	5,001	3,915
Advertising expenses	1,597	1,576	1,441
Advertising expenses/sales	8.5%	8.4%	7.7%

Coke's income statement is very aggregated, with only two operating expense items. Advertising expenses are included in selling, administrative, and general expenses but are detailed in footnotes. Advertising expenses are a reasonably constant percentage of sales, so the analyst might use an advertising-to-sales ratio of 8.5 percent to forecast future advertising. As with R&D, the analyst must be sensitive to any drop or increase in the advertising-to-sales ratio. Is the change transitory? Is the firm temporarily reducing advertising to increase profits in the short run at the expense of the long run?

3. *Research and development.* A drop in R&D expenditure increases current earnings but may damage future earnings. Investigate whether changes in R&D are temporary. See Box 12.4.

4. *Advertising.* A drop in advertising expenditures increases current earnings but may damage future earnings. Investigate whether changes in advertising are temporary. See Box 12.4.

5. *Pension expense.* Firms report the cost of providing defined benefit pension plans as part of the cost of operating expenses. Pension expense, however, is a composite number, and the analyst must be aware of its makeup. The following summarizes the pension expense footnote for IBM for 2002.

INTERNATIONAL BUSINESS MACHINES (IBM)
Components of Pension Expense, 1999–2001
(in millions of dollars)

	2001	2000	1999
Service cost	1,042	1,008	1,041
Interest cost	3,838	3,787	3,686
Expected return on plan assets	(6,264)	(5,944)	(5,400)
Amortization of transition asset	(150)	(151)	(151)
Amortization of prior service cost	108	55	4
Actuarial losses (gains)	(24)	19	21
Net pension expense	(1,450)	(1,226)	(799)

Pension expense has six components, and you see all six components in IBM's summary.

• *Service cost:* The present value of the actuarial cost of providing future pensions for services of employees in the current year. This cost is, in effect, wages for employees to be paid in pension benefits when employees retire.

• *Interest cost:* The interest cost on the obligation to pay benefits, the effect of the time value of money as the date to pay pensions comes closer and the net present value of the obligation increases.

• *Expected return on plan assets:* The expected earnings on the assets of the pension fund, which reduce the cost of the plan to the employer. The expected earnings on plan assets is the market value of the assets multiplied by an expected rate of return. To make the pension expense less volatile in the financial statements, the actuary's expected return on plan assets is deducted in the calculation of pension expense, not actual gains and losses. If the difference between accumulated actual and expected gains and losses exceeds a limit, the difference is amortized into pension expense (none appears in IBM's pension expense).

• *Amortization of prior service cost:* The amortization of the cost of pension entitlements for service periods prior to the adoption or amendment of a plan. The amortization is over the estimated remaining service years for employees at the time of the change in the plan.

• *Amortization of transition asset or liability:* The amortization of the initial pension asset or liability established when pension accounting was first mandated (in 1985) for operations prior to 1985. (The amortization period was scheduled to expire by the year 2002.)

• *Actuarial gains and losses:* Changes in the pension liability due to changes in actuaries' estimates of employees' longevity and changes in discount rates to record the present value of the liability.

Service cost is a part of the core cost of paying employees. Interest cost is also a core cost; it is the cost, effectively paid to employees, to compensate them for the time value

Beware of Returns on Pension Assets

The expected return on plan assets component of pension expense must be handled with care. Below are three warnings.

1. RETURNS ON PENSION FUND ASSETS CAN BE A SIGNIFICANT PORTION OF EARNINGS

Pension expense is reduced by expected earnings on assets of the pension fund, and expected earnings on a fund's assets are of course based on the amount of the fund's assets. Pension plans invest in equities and, during the 1990s bull market, the prices of equities increased significantly, increasing the assets in these plans and the expected earnings on the plans. Such was the increase that for some firms, the expected earnings on fund assets, reported as a reduction in pension expense, was a significant part of the firm's earnings.

General Electric

General Electric sponsors a number of pension plans for its employees. Its 2001 pension footnote reported a service cost of $884 million, but $4,327 million in expected returns on plan assets was also reported, along with $2,065 million in interest on the pension liability. The net pension expense (with all components) was actually a gain of $2,095 million. This pension gain was netted against other expenses in the income statement. The $4,327 million in expected returns on plan assets was 22.0 percent of earnings before tax.

IBM Corporation

IBM reported a pension service cost of $931 million for 1998. But it also reported $4,862 million in expected returns on plan assets, along with $3,474 million in interest on the pension liability. The expected returns on plan assets were 53.1 percent of operating income before tax. IBM's expected return on plan assets for 1999–2001 (in the text) were 45.9 percent, 51.5 percent, and 57.2 percent of pretax income, respectively.

Earnings on pension plan assets are earnings from the operation of running a pension fund, not earnings from products and services. In all cases, list the expected return on plan assets as a separate component of core income so profit margins can be identified without this component, as in Exhibit 12.1.

2. RETURNS ON PENSION ASSETS CAN PERPETUATE A CHAIN LETTER

Consider the following scenario. In an overheated stock market, the assets of pension funds are inflated above their intrinsic values. Accordingly, the earnings of the firms sponsoring the pension funds for their employees are inflated through the reduction of pension expense for earnings of the pension funds. Analysts then justify a higher stock price for these firms based on the inflated earnings. So inflated stock prices feed on themselves. A chain letter is created.

As an extreme, consider the case of a company during the stock market bubble whose pension fund invested solely in the shares of the company (so employees could share in the success of the company). The earnings of the company would be exaggerated by the returns on the pension fund from the run-up of the firm's share price. Analysts look to earnings to assess the worth of firms' shares relative to their market price, but if the earnings reflect the market price of the shares, the analysis—if not done carefully—is circular. Good analysis penetrates the sources of firms' earnings and understands that stock prices are based on firms' ability to generate earnings from their core business, not the appreciation in stock prices.

Pension funds in the U.S. are permitted to hold only 10 percent of their assets in the sponsoring firm's shares, but they may well hold shares whose returns are highly correlated with the firm's own shares, inducing a similar effect.

3. BEWARE OF EXPECTED RATES OF RETURN ON PLAN ASSETS

Expected earnings of plan assets are calculated as an expected rate of return multiplied by the market value of the plan assets. The expected rate of return is an estimate that can be biased. Indeed, in the late 1990s, firms were using an expected rate of return of 10 percent and higher, considerably more than the 7 percent rate used in the early 1980s. This ambitious rate—perhaps influenced by the high bubble returns during the 1990s—led to higher pension gains in earnings when applied to high pension asset values.

The subsequent bursting of the bubble led to much lower returns—indeed, large negative returns—and firms revised their expected rates of return downward. The consequence was much lower pension gains in earnings in 2002, due in part from the drop in asset prices and in part from the lower expected rates of return. Indeed, many firms with defined benefit plans found that their pension obligations were underfunded and, in retrospect, their past earnings that incorporated the pension gains were overstated. An analyst with an understanding of pension accounting would have anticipated this scenario during the bubble.

Should firms lower their expected returns on plan assets in overheated stock markets—to anticipate the expected lower returns as prices drop in the future? If firms do not, the analyst should consider doing so.

Accounting Clinic VII

ACCOUNTING FOR PENSIONS

Accounting Clinic VII on the book's website gives a more thorough coverage of the accounting for pensions. The clinic explains how pension plans work and how defined benefit plans differ from defined contribution plans. The clinic also explains how the pension liability in the balance sheet is calculated as well as providing more detail on the pension expense in the income statement.

of money from receiving wages later, as a pension, rather than in the current year. Like service cost, interest cost is repetitive. Amortizations of prior service costs and transition assets and liabilities smooth out these items so, while they may eventually disappear, the smoothing is done over such a long period that they should be treated as repetitive rather than unusual. Similarly, actuarial gains and losses are smoothed.

Expected returns on plan assets, however, must be handled with care. You will notice that, in 1999–2001, IBM's net pension expenses were negative (that is, gains), primarily because of this item. These earnings on pension plan assets reduce IBM's obligation to support employees in retirement, so they are legitimately part of income. However, they are not earnings from the core business (of selling computers and technology in the case of IBM). The analyst must be careful to disentangle these earnings and attribute them to the profitability of the pension fund rather than the profitability of the business. Other dangers lurk in the pension expense number. See Box 12.5.

Accounting Clinic VII takes you through the accounting for pensions.

6. *Changes in estimates.* Some expenses like bad debts, warranty expenses, depreciation, and accrued expenses are estimates. When estimates for previous years turn out to be incorrect, the correction is made in the current year. Bad debts are usually estimated as a percentage of accounts receivable that is likely to go bad. If it is discovered that the estimate for last year (say) was too high—fewer creditors went bad than expected—the correction is made to the current year's bad debt expense. Thus the reported expense does not reflect the credit costs of the current period's sales. Firms also change estimates of residual values of lease receivables. The effect of these changes in estimates should be classified as unusual, leaving the core expense to reflect current operations. Unfortunately, published reports often do not give the necessary detail. A particularly pernicious change in estimate can follow restructuring changes. See Box 12.6.

7. *Gains and losses.* Many gains and losses (on asset sales, for example) are not detailed in the income statement. But they can be found in the cash flow statement in the reconciliation of cash flow from operations and net income. See Box 12.7.

8. *Income taxes.* Unusual aspects of income tax expense such as one-time or expiring credits and loss carryforwards can be found in the tax footnote.

9. *Other income.* Review the details of "other income" in footnotes, if provided. Often interest income is included with operating income in "other income."

Unusual items are identified in both operating income from sales and other operating income. For Nike and Reebok, all the unusual items are identified with other operating income in the reformulated statements in Exhibits 9.8 and 9.9 in Chapter 9. So, for these two firms, core operating income corresponds to operating income from sales, and the

When firms decide to restructure, they often write off the expected costs of restructuring against income before the actual restructuring begins, and recognize an associated liability, or "restructuring reserve" that is reduced later as restructuring costs are incurred. If later the firm finds that it has overestimated the charge, it must increase income for the correction. This is known as "bleeding back" the charge to income.

In moving its business away from computer hardware to a focus on information technology in the early 1990s, IBM wrote off considerable income with restructuring charges—$3.7 billion, $11.6 billion, and $8.9 billion, respectively, for 1991–1993. Examination of the firm's cash flow statement for subsequent years reveals the following item as an adjustment to net income to calculate cash from operations:

	1994	1995	1996	1997	1998
Effect of restructuring charges (in millions)	(2,772)	(2,119)	(1,491)	(445)	(355)

These amounts are negative; that is, they are deductions from net income to get cash from operations. Accordingly they were income, not expense, in the income statement.

IBM was bleeding back the earlier restructuring charges to increase operating income. This income, like the original restructuring charges themselves, must be identified as unusual income so that income from current activities is not dirtied by it.

When new management arrives at a firm, they are tempted to take restructuring charges to show they are innovating. The market often greets the restructuring as good news. If the new managers overestimate the restructuring charge, they get an added benefit: They can bleed it back to future income and report earnings improvement on their watch. This is a scheme to grow earnings.

In another scheme, firms take estimated merger charges when they make acquisitions. These charges reduce current income but increase future income if the charges are overestimated and subsequently bled back to income after the merger. Accordingly earnings from the merger make the merger look like a success.

The diligent analyst is attuned to these schemes.

Note: At the time of this writing, the FASB was proposing reform of the accounting for restructuring charges with a standard that would require firms to recognize the charges only as they occur, therefore eliminating the restructuring reserves from which firms can bleed back income.

---

other operating income is unusual. Thus the reformulated statements for the analysis of changes are made by a simple relabeling of those in the exhibits. Nike had a core RNOA in 1996 of 23.3 percent (compared with an overall RNOA of 22.6 percent) and Reebok had a core RNOA of 14.4 percent (compared with an overall RNOA of 14.1 percent). In 1995 there is a significant difference between Reebok's RNOA and its sustainable core RNOA, due to unusual items of 2.7 percent of average net operating assets.

To assess the profitability of the component parts of the income statement effectively, income taxes must be allocated to the component income that attracts the taxes, as in Exhibit 12.1. Taxes thus must be allocated not only over operating and financing components, but within the operating component also. You see in both the Nike and Reebok reformulated income statements (in Exhibits 9.8 and 9.9 in Chapter 9) that taxes have been deducted from other (unusual) operating income, and the taxes so deducted have reduced the tax calculated for core operating income. In making this allocation, keep in mind that extraordinary items and dirty-surplus income items are reported after tax in the United States, so do not allocate taxes to these items.

Level 2. Analyze Changes in Core Profit Margins and Turnovers

Having identified core RNOA, break it down into its profit margin and turnover components:

$$\text{RNOA} = (\text{Core sales PM} \times \text{ATO}) + \frac{\text{Core other OI}}{\text{NOA}} + \frac{\text{UI}}{\text{NOA}}$$

In the rising stock market of the 1990s, firms' holdings of equity securities appreciated. The sale of the shares sometimes provided a significant portion of profits.

INTEL

In its third quarter report for 1999, Intel reported net income of $1,458 million, with no indication of unusual items. Its cash flow statement, however, reported $556 million in gains on sales of investments, along with a $161 million loss on retirements of plant, as add backs to net income to calculate cash from operations.

DELTA AIR LINES

Delta reported operating income (before tax) of $350 million for its September quarter in 1999. However, notes to the report indicated that these earnings included pretax gains of $252 million from selling its interest in Singapore Airlines and Priceline.com.

IBM

IBM reported before-tax operating income of $4,085 million for its quarter ending June 1999. However, footnotes revealed that this income included a $3,430 million gain from the sale of IBM's Global Network to AT&T. This gain reduced selling, general, and administrative expenses in the income statement!

You see that the disclosure of these gains is often not transparent. The analyst must be careful to look for these gains—in the cash flow statement or in the footnotes—and separate them from core income from core operations. These gains or losses would be core income only if the firm is a portfolio management company. And watch firms with big equity portfolios: Microsoft had $9 billion in equity investments in 2002 and can realize gains into income should operating profitability from other operations decline.

As with gains from pension plan assets, gains from share appreciation can lead to mispricing and even create share price bubbles. Firms may sell shares when they feel that the shares are overvalued in the market. If an analyst mistakenly attributes profits that include these gains to persistent operating profits, he will overprice the firm. But he will overprice it more if the gains themselves are generated by mispricing. So the mispricing feeds on itself.

where

$$\text{Core sales PM} = \frac{\text{Core OI from sales}}{\text{Sales}}$$

This core sales PM uncovers a profit margin that is unaffected by unusual items, so it really "gets to the core" of the firm's ability to generate profits from sales.

With these distinctions, we are now ready to explain changes in RNOA. Look at Box 12.8, where Nike and Reebok's change in operating profitability is analyzed. The formula at the top gives the calculation that explains the change in RNOA. The first component of the change in RNOA is the effect due to change in the core PM in Year 1. To isolate the profit margin effect from the ATO effect, this is assessed holding ATO at the Year 0 level. The second component is the effect due to changes in ATO given the Year 1 core sales PM. The third and fourth components are the effects due to changes in other core operating income and unusual items. These changes can be analyzed by business segment.

Level 3. Analyze Drivers of Changes in PM, ATO, Other Income, and Unusual Items

The changes in core profitability are further explained by changes in the drivers of the core PM and ATO. The 1995 and 1996 drivers for Nike and Reebok are compared in the analysis of the second-level breakdown in Chapter 11. Reebok's decline in core profitability is due both to a decline in gross margins and an increase in expenses. Nike's gross margin decreased slightly but its expense ratios also decreased slightly. Overall turnovers for both firms remained about the same. Nike's inventory turnover decreased

Change in RNOA = Change in core sales profit margin at previous asset turnover level + Change due to change in asset turnover

+ Change due to change in other core income + Change due to change in unusual items

$$\Delta RNOA_{1996} = (\Delta \text{core sales PM}_{1996} \times ATO_{1995})$$

$$+ (\Delta ATO_{1996} \times \text{Core sales PM}_{1996})$$

$$+ \Delta\left(\frac{\text{Core other OI}}{\text{NOA}}\right) + \Delta\left(\frac{\text{UI}}{\text{NOA}}\right)$$

NIKE

Nike's decline in RNOA from 23.06 percent in 1995 to 22.56 percent in 1996 is explained as follows:

$$\Delta RNOA_{1996} = -2.8\%$$

$$= (-1.72\% \times 2.94) + (-0.026 \times 4.9\%$$

$$+ 0 + \left(-\frac{4}{1,191} + \frac{32}{1,182}\right)$$

(allow for rounding error). You see that while RNOA declined in 1996 (and overall profit margins declined), core profit margins actually increased, by 0.26 percent, producing a 0.69 percent boost to RNOA. Turnover also increased, producing a 0.06 percent increase. Accordingly, core profitability increased and the 1/2 percent reduction in RNOA was in fact due to items classified as unusual. In forecasting the future, we would conclude that the decrease in RNOA is not permanent but transitory, and we would base our forecast on the core RNOA of 23.3 percent rather than the RNOA of 22.6 percent.

REEBOK

Reebok's 1996 drop in RNOA from 16.92 percent to 14.11 percent is explained as

$$\Delta RNOA_{1996} = -2.8\%$$

$$= (-1.72\% \times 2.94) + (-0.026 \times 4.9\%)$$

$$+ 0 + \left(-\frac{4}{1,191} + \frac{32}{1,182}\right)$$

Here the decline in RNOA is attributable to a significant decline in the profitability of the core business, particularly the drop in core profit margin of 1.72 percent that reduced RNOA by 5.06 percent. Indeed unusual items served to increase the RNOA by 2.37 percent, due mainly to the large charge in 1995 from restructuring of operations, which was not repeated in 1996. With this analysis, the 1996 RNOA for Nike looks even better than that for Reebok. Nike maintained its ability to generate profits in its core business.

while Reebok's increased, and Reebok's accounts receivable turnover decreased. The property, plant, and equipment (PPE) turnover increased more for Nike than for Reebok.

The changes in other income and unusual items are apparent from the comparative reformulated statements.

Operating Leverage

Changes in core sales PM are determined by how costs change as sales change. Some costs are **fixed costs**: They don't change as sales change. Other costs are **variable costs**: They change as sales change. Depreciation, amortization, and many administrative expenses are fixed costs, while most labor and material costs in cost of sales are variable costs. The difference between sales and variable costs is called the *contribution margin* because it is this amount that contributes to covering fixed costs and providing profits. Thus

$$\text{Sales PM} = \frac{\text{Sales} - \text{Variable costs} - \text{Fixed costs}}{\text{Sales}}$$

$$= \frac{\text{Contribution margin}}{\text{Sales}} - \frac{\text{Fixed costs}}{\text{Sales}}$$

The first component here is called the *contribution margin ratio*. This is sometimes calculated as

$$\text{Contribution margin ratio} = 1 - \frac{\text{Variable costs}}{\text{Sales}} = \frac{\text{Contribution margin}}{\text{Sales}}$$

This ratio measures the change in income from a change in one dollar of sales. For a firm with variable costs that are 75 percent of sales, the contribution margin ratio is 25 percent: The firm adds 25 cents to income for each dollar increase in sales (and the fixed costs don't explain changes in profit margins).

The sensitivity of income to changes in sales is called the *operating leverage* (not to be confused with operating liability leverage). Operating leverage is sometimes measured by the ratio of fixed to variable expenses. But it is also measured by

$$\text{OLEV} = \frac{\text{Contribution margin}}{\text{Operating income}} = \frac{\text{Contribution margin ratio}}{\text{Profit margin}}$$

(Again, don't confuse OLEV with OLLEV!) If you are dealing with core income, then this calculation should include only core items. If there are fixed costs, OLEV will be greater than 1. The measure is not an absolute for the firm but changes as sales change. However, at any particular level of sales, it is useful to indicate the effect of a change in sales on operating income. Applying it to core operations,

$$\% \text{ Change in core OI} = \text{OLEV} \times \% \text{ Change in core sales}$$

An analyst inside the firm will have a relatively easy task of distinguishing fixed and variable costs. But the reader of annual financial reports will find it difficult. The depreciation and amortization component of fixed costs must be reported in the 10-K report, and it can be found in the cash flow statement. But other fixed costs—fixed salaries, rent expense, administrative expenses—are aggregated with variable costs in different line items on the income statement.

Analysis of Changes in Financing

Changes in RNOA partially explain changes in ROCE. The explanation is completed by an examination of financing. The steps appear on the right-hand side of Figure 12.1.

Level 1. Calculate Changes in Financial Leverage and the Operating Spread

The difference between ROCE and RNOA is explained by financial leverage (FLEV) and the operating spread (SPREAD). You'll remember from the last chapter that FLEV = NFO/CSE and the operating spread is the difference between the RNOA and the net borrowing cost (NBC): SPREAD = RNOA − NBC. Box 12.9 completes the analysis of the change in ROCE for Nike and Reebok. The calculation at the top incorporates the two additional components that, with the change in RNOA, explain the change in ROCE.

Level 2. Explain Change in Net Borrowing Cost

As the change in RNOA has been explained, the remaining change in spread is explained by the change in net borrowing cost. Like operating profitability, distinguish core financial expense and unusual financial expenses:

$$\text{Net borrowing cost} = \text{Core net borrowing cost} + \text{Unusual borrowing costs}$$

$$\text{NBC} = \frac{\text{Core net financial expenses}}{\text{NFO}} + \frac{\text{Unusual financial expenses}}{\text{NFO}}$$

Change in ROCE = Change in RNOA + Change due to change in spread at previous level of financial leverage

+ Change due to change in financial leverage

$$\Delta ROCE_{1996} = \Delta RNOA_{1996} + (\Delta SPREAD_{1996} \times FLEV_{1995})$$
$$+ (\Delta FLEV_{1996} \times SPREAD_{1996})$$

NIKE

For Nike, the explanation for the 1996 change in ROCE is

$$\Delta ROCE_{1996} = 1.9\%$$

$$= -0.5\% + (-3.1\% \times -0.031) + (0.138 \times 16.6\%)$$

$$= -0.5\% + 0.10\% + 2.29\%$$

While RNOA declined by ½ percent and the spread declined, ROCE increased, and this increase was due primarily to a 2.29 percent effect from the increase in leverage.

REEBOK

For Reebok, the 1996 change in ROCE (before minority interest) is

$$\Delta ROCE_{1996} = -0.3\%$$

$$= -2.8\% + (-2.9\% \times 0.187) + (0.328 \times 9.2\%)$$

$$= -2.8\% - 0.54\% + 3.02\%$$

The ROCE dropped less than the RNOA primarily because of a large change in leverage from the debt issue that financed the stock repurchase. The change in leverage increased ROCE by 3.02 percent. The change in spread also contributed to the reduction in ROCE (by 0.54 percent), but this was due mostly to the change in RNOA: The 1996 net borrowing cost was 4.9 percent relative to 4.8 percent for 1995.

and so for the case of a net financial asset position. The first term is the core net borrowing cost. As before, unusual financial items are those that are not likely to be repeated in the future or are unpredictable. They include realized and unrealized gains and losses on financial items and unusual interest income or expenses. Core income and expense is the rate at which the firm borrows or lends. So changes in core borrowing cost will reflect changes in these rates and, as the rates are after tax, this includes changes due to changes in tax rates.

Level 3. Explain Change in Financial Leverage

This step calculates the change in NFO/CSE and attributes it to different types of financing (long-term debt, short-term debt, and preferred stock changes).

As financial leverage typically does not change much, the change in spread is usually the more important aspect of the leverage effect. Typically the change in borrowing costs is also small, so the change in RNOA is usually the main driver of the leverage effect. If $\Delta FLEV$ and ΔNBC are small, then a useful approximation is

$$\Delta ROCE_1 = \Delta RNOA_1 \times [1 + \text{Average FLEV}_1]$$

If $\Delta FLEV$ and ΔNBC are not small, this will not work. If the change in leverage is not small, beware: Firms can create ROCE by borrowing, without any change in the profitability of their operations. See Box 12.10.

THE ANALYSIS OF GROWTH IN SHAREHOLDERS' EQUITY

The analysis of the statement of common equity in Chapter 8 indicated two drivers of the growth in common equity investment: ROCE and the equity net investment rate. But we can dig further, as Figure 12.2 depicts. The investment requirement is driven by the need

For most firms, issuing debt does not create value: They buy and sell debt at its fair value. The value generation is in the operations. Yet financial leverage can lever the ROCE above RNOA. Accordingly, firms can create ROCE by issuing debt. Beware of increases in ROCE. Analyze the change in profitability to see if it is driven by core operations or by changes in leverage.

Nike is a case in point. Its ROCE increased in 1996, despite a drop in RNOA, because financial leverage increased. But Reebok is an even more extreme example. Its financial leverage increased from 0.187 to 0.515 as a result of its borrowing to finance the large stock repurchase. Had Reebok not changed its debt-to-equity mix, its 1996 ROCE on a 1996 RNOA of 14.1 percent (with the 1995 financial leverage of 0.187) would have been 15.8 percent:

$$\text{ROCE} = \text{RNOA} + (\text{FLEV} \times \text{SPREAD})$$

$$\text{ROCE}_{1996} = 14.1 + [0.187 \times (14.1 - 4.9)]$$

$$= 15.8\%$$

Instead it reported a ROCE of 17.6 percent. The reported ROCE was less than the 18.6 percent in 1995, but the extent of the decline in operational profitability was masked by the increase in leverage. The change in ROCE is of "low quality."

Firms often state that their objective is to increase return on common equity. The management of VF Corporation, for example, states these "long-term financial goals":

1. Sales and income growth of 8 percent to 10 percent annually.

2. Return on equity of 17 percent to 20 percent.

3. Debt-to-capital ratio below 40 percent.

4. Dividend payout of 30 percent.

The number 2 aim, maximizing ROCE, is not entirely satisfactory. Maximizing RNOA is, and to the extent that increases in ROCE come from operations, increasing ROCE is a desirable goal, provided the cost of capital is covered. Tying management bonuses to ROCE would be a mistake: Management could increase managerial compensation by issuing debt.

Growing residual earnings generates value, as noted. But residual earnings are driven by ROCE, and ROCE can be generated by borrowing (which does not create value). There seems to be a contradiction. The riddle is solved in the next chapter.

FIGURE 12.2 The Analysis of Changes in Common Shareholders' Equity
Changes in common shareholders' equity are driven by changes in investment in net operating assets (ΔNOA) and changes in the amount of net debt (ΔNFO) to finance the investment in NOA. Changes in NOA are driven by sales growth (ΔSales) and changes in the amount of NOA that support each dollar of sales [Δ(1/ATO)].

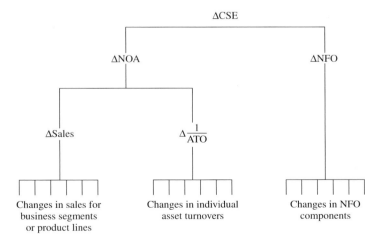

to invest in net operating assets. But to the extent that debt is used to finance net operating assets, the shareholders' investment is reduced:

$$\Delta CSE = \Delta NOA - \Delta NFO$$

Since ATO = Sales/NOA,

$$NOA = Sales \times \frac{1}{ATO}$$

So

$$\Delta CSE = \Delta\left(Sales \times \frac{1}{ATO}\right) - \Delta NFO$$

Sales require investment in net operating assets and the inverse of the asset turnover, 1/ATO, is the amount of net operating assets in place to generate $1 of sales. Nike's 1996 ATO was 2.66, so 1/2.66, or 37.6 cents of net operating assets, were in place to generate $1 of sales. The change in CSE can thus be explained by three components:

1. Growth in sales.

2. Change in net operating assets that support each dollar of sales.

3. Change in the amount of net debt that is used to finance the change in net operating assets rather than equity.

Sales growth is the primary driver. But sales growth requires more investment in net operating assets, which is financed by either net debt or equity.

Box 12.11 analyzes Nike and Reebok's growth in common equity. The calculation at the top incorporates the three components of the growth. Nike's common equity grew by 18.6 percent in 1996 and Reebok's declined by 22.3 percent. As a benchmark, note that the median annual growth in common equity for NYSE and AMEX firms from 1963 to 2000 was 9.0 percent.

Sales are the engine of growth; to create growth in order to create value, a manager grows sales. Sales require investment. And investments earn through ROCE and the factors that drive ROCE. Together, investment and ROCE drive residual earnings and abnormal earnings growth. The manager recognizes that there is a tension to growing CSE. Equity investment can easily be increased by issuing new shares or reducing dividends. But the new equity might not be used wisely. It could be invested in projects with low RNOA or financial assets with low returns, reducing ROCE, residual earnings, and value. That is why residual earnings is the focus, not ROCE or investment, but rather both used together. The manager aims to increase investment but also aims to have a low investment per dollar of sales—a high ATO—and a low investment per dollar of operating income— a high RNOA. The manager's aim is to maximize residual earnings and this involves two elements, increasing ROCE (through the RNOA) and increasing investment. To do this, she grows sales but minimizes the investment per dollar of sales (1/ATO) and maximizes the operating income per dollar of sales (PM).

GROWTH, SUSTAINABLE EARNINGS, AND THE EVALUATION OF P/B RATIOS AND P/E RATIOS

The analysis of current and past growth is a prelude to forecasting future growth in order to evaluate P/E and P/B ratios; the next part of the book proceeds with forecasting. We have three ratios on which we can base our pricing: the P/B ratio, the trailing P/E ratio,

Change in
common = Change due to change in sales at previous level of asset turnover
equity

+ Change due to change in asset turnover − change in financial leverage

$$\Delta CSE_{1996} = \left(\Delta Sales_{1996} \times \frac{1}{ATO_{1995}} \right)$$

$$+ \left(\Delta \frac{1}{ATO_{1996}} \times Sales_{1996} \right) - \Delta NFO_{1996}$$

NIKE

Nike's average common shareholders' equity increased by $345 million in 1996. This growth is attributed to a growth in sales of $1,710 million, a small increase in asset turnover from 2.65 to 2.66, and an increase in average net financial obligations of $294 million:

$$\Delta CSE_{1996} = (\$1,710 \text{ million} \times 0.377)$$
$$+ (-0.0014 \times \$6,471 \text{ million}) - \$294 \text{ million}$$

$$= \$645 \text{ million} - \$9 \text{ million} - \$294 \text{ million}$$

$$= \$345 \text{ million}$$

(allow for rounding error). As the asset turnover changed little, the change in CSE is explained mainly by sales growth and a change in net debt. Similar calculations can be made to explain the change in end-of-year equity rather than average equity over the year.

REEBOK

Reebok's average common equity declined by $216 million in 1996. As sales were almost the same as in 1996 (they declined by only $2 million) and the asset turnover changed little (from 2.94 to 2.92), the change in equity is attributable almost entirely to a change in financing and minority interest:

$$\Delta CSE_{1996} = (-\$2 \text{ million} \times 0.340)$$
$$+ (0.0023 \times \$3,479 \text{ million}) - \$225 \text{ million}$$

$$= -\$0.7 \text{ million} + \$8.0 \text{ million} - \$225.0 \text{ million}$$

$$= -\$216 \text{ million}$$

(again allow for rounding error). As the change in net operating assets in the consolidated balance sheet is financed by minority equity as well as net debt and common equity, the change in the minority interest is included with the change in net financial obligations here.

and the forward P/E ratio. Before proceeding to forecasting and valuation you should understand how these three ratios are related to each other. In this section we look at the relationship between P/B ratios and trailing P/E ratios and draw some lessons from the comparison.

Remember that zero abnormal earnings growth (AEG) implies no growth in residual earnings (RE), and positive AEG means there is positive growth in residual earnings. To reinforce this idea, Box 12.12 returns to Whirlpool Corporation, the firm for which a residual earnings valuation was developed in Chapter 5. The valuation yields a normal forward P/E and a normal trailing P/E ratio, and this valuation can be developed either by forecasting zero AEG or by forecasting no growth in residual earnings.

How Price-to-Book Ratios and Trailing P/E Ratios Articulate

The Whirlpool example is a case of normal P/E ratios but a non-normal P/B ratio. To focus on the question of how P/E and P/B ratios are related, ask the following question: Must a firm with a high P/B ratio also have a high (trailing) P/E ratio? Can a firm with a high P/B ratio have a low P/E ratio?

In order to appreciate the empirical relationship between the two ratios, Table 12.1 splits U.S. firms at their median (trailing) P/E and P/B each year from 1963 to 2001 and counts the number of times firms had a high P/B (above the median) and a high P/E (above the median), a low P/B (below the median) and a low P/E (below the median), and so on. You see that the relationship between P/B and P/E is positive: Firms with high P/B tend to have high P/E, and firms with low P/B tend to have low P/E also. Indeed

The table below gives an analyst's forecast of Whirlpool's earnings for 1995, 1996, and 1997 and the forecasted residual earnings calculated from the forecasted earnings. The forecast was made at the end of 1994. (Also displayed in Chapter 5.)

WHIRLPOOL CORP.
Analyst Forecast, December 1994
(amounts in dollars per share)
Required return to 10%

	1993A	1994A	1995E	1996E	1997E
Eps		4.43	4.75	5.08	5.45
Dps		1.22	1.28	1.34	1.41
Bps	22.85	25.83	29.30	33.04	37.07
RE		2.15	2.17	2.15	2.15
Cum-dividend earnings			4.87	5.21	5.58
Normal earnings			4.87	5.23	5.58
AEG			0.00	(0.02)	(0.00)

RESIDUAL EARNINGS VALUATION ON FORWARD RESIDUAL EARNINGS

Because the 1995 RE forecast looked similar to subsequent forecasted RE, Whirlpool was valued at $47.53 per share in Chapter 5 by capitalizing the 1995 RE forecast as a perpetuity at the cost of capital of 10 percent:

$$V_{1994}^E = CSE_{1994} + \frac{RE_{1995}}{\rho_E - 1} = \$25.83 + \frac{\$2.17}{0.10} = \$47.53$$

This value is close to Whirlpool's market price at the time of $47.25.

FORWARD EARNINGS VALUATION

The pro forma forecasts no growth in residual earnings from the forward year, 1995 onward. But no growth in residual earnings means abnormal earnings are zero, as shown (approximately) in the pro forma. With this expectation, the shares can be valued by capitalizing forward earnings, and the forward P/E must be 10, the normal forward P/E for a required return of 10 percent.

$$V_{1994}^E = \frac{\$4.75}{0.10}$$

$$= \$47.50, \text{or } 10 \text{ times forward earnings of } \$4.75.$$

RESIDUAL EARNINGS VALUATION ON CURRENT (TRAILING) RESIDUAL EARNINGS

The actual 1994 RE is $4.43 - (0.10 \times \$22.85) = \$2.15$. This is similar to the RE forecasted for the future. So, as no growth in RE is forecasted, we could have valued the firm by capitalizing the current 1994 RE:

$$V_{1994}^E = \$25.83 + \frac{\$2.15}{0.10} = \$47.33$$

TRAILING EARNINGS VALUATION

With no growth in residual earnings from the current year onward, and thus zero abnormal earnings growth, the shares can be valued by capitalizing trailing earnings, and the (cum-dividend) trailing P/E must be 11, the normal P/E for a required return of 10 percent:

$$V_{1994}^E + d_{1994} = 11 \times \$4.43 = \$48.73$$

So, as the dividend is $1.22, the ex-dividend value is $47.51 (allowing for approximation error).

This is a case of a firm with both a normal trailing P/E and a normal forward P/E, but a non-normal P/B.

TABLE 12.1
Frequency of High and Low P/B and P/E Ratios, 1963–2001

P/E Ratio	P/B Ratio	
	High	Low
High	23,146	10,848
	34.1%	16.1%
Low	10,849	23,147
	16.0%	34.1%

TABLE 12.2
Cell Analysis of the
P/B–P/E Relationship

P/E Ratio	P/B Ratio		
	High	**Normal**	**Low**
High	A	B	C
Normal	D	E	F
Low	G	H	I

TABLE 12.3
Cell Analysis of the
P/B–P/E
Relationship: Filling
in the Cells

P/E Ratio	P/B Ratio		
	High $(\overline{RE} > 0)$	**Normal** $(\overline{RE} = 0)$	**Low** $(\overline{RE} < 0)$
High	A $\overline{RE} > RE_0$	B $\overline{RE} > RE_0$ $RE_0 < 0$	C $\overline{RE} > RE_0$ $RE_0 < 0$
Normal	D $\overline{RE} = RE_0$ $RE_0 > 0$	E $\overline{RE} = RE_0$ $RE_0 = 0$	F $\overline{RE} = RE_0$ $RE_0 < 0$
Low	G $\overline{RE} < RE_0$ $RE_0 > 0$	H $\overline{RE} < RE_0$ $RE_0 > 0$	I $\overline{RE} < RE_0$

Key: $\overline{RE}$ = Expected future residual earnings.
   RE_0 = Current residual earnings.

two-thirds of cases fall on this diagonal. But one-third falls on the other diagonal: Firms can trade at a high P/B and a low P/E or a high P/B and a low P/E. What explains which of these cells a firm will fall into?

To answer this question, let's consider high, low, and normal P/Bs and P/Es in Table 12.2. Remember a normal P/B is equal to 1.0 and a normal trailing P/E in equal to $\rho_E/(\rho_E-1)$. There are nine cells, labeled **A** to **I**, and we want to enter the conditions under which firms fall into a particular cell. As with tic-tac-toe, start with the central cell, **E**. We know that expected future residual earnings must be zero here because P/B is normal. We also know that expected future RE must be the same as current RE for the P/E to be normal. Expected AEG must be zero. If we indicate the stream of expected future RE by $\overline{RE}$ (for short) and current RE by RE_0, it must be that $\overline{RE} = RE_0 = 0$ for firms in this central cell. That is, for both P/B and P/E to be normal, a firm must have zero expected future RE and current RE that is also zero (and thus current and future ROCE equal the cost of capital). This condition is entered in cell **E** in the solution to the problem in Table 12.3.

Now look at the other cells for a normal P/B, cells **B** and **H**. Here forecasted future RE must be zero. But, for high P/E in cell **B**, future RE must be forecasted as being higher than current RE (and forecasted AEG is positive). Thus RE_0 must be less than zero (and current ROCE must be less than the cost of capital). Correspondingly, firms should trade at a normal P/B and a low P/E in cell **H** when current RE is greater than zero (and current ROCE is greater than the cost of capital). In the other cells for a normal P/E (cells **D** and **F**), expected future RE must be at the same level as current RE but, as these are cases of nonnormal P/B, it must be that both current and future RE are greater than zero (cell **D**) or less than zero (cell **F**). Whirlpool falls into cell **D**.

The conditions for the four corner cells follow the same logic. To attribute both a high P/E and a high P/B to a firm (cell **A**), we must forecast future RE to be greater than zero and this RE must be greater than current RE. A firm can also have a high P/B and a low P/E. This is the cell **G** case where we expect residual earnings to be positive in the future but current residual earnings are even higher. And a firm can have a high P/E but a low P/B. This is the cell **C** case where we expect low (and negative) RE in the future but current RE is even lower. Finally cell **I** contains firms that have both forecasts of low and negative RE in the future but currently have a higher RE than the long-run level.

We can summarize all this in one statement: P/B is determined by the future RE a firm is expected to deliver but P/E is determined by the difference between current RE and the forecast of future RE, that is, growth in RE from current levels.

Look at Box 12.13 for examples of firms that fall in to the various cells. It looks as if the market is giving these firms the appropriate cell classification. But we could use the analysis to screen for firms that might be mispriced. Certain combinations of P/E, P/B, and current RE and forecasted RE are ruled out, so if these occur, mispricing is indicated. If a firm were reporting a high ROCE and RE, and reliable analysts' forecasts indicated positive RE in the future, we would expect the stock to trade at a P/B above 1.0. And if analysts' forecasts indicated that the current RE was particularly high and would be lower in the future, we would expect the P/E to be below normal and would classify the firm as a cell **G** firm. If the market were giving the firm a high P/B and a high P/E (as a cell **A** firm), it might be mispriced. (Of course, the market could be valuing earnings beyond the analysts' forecast horizon.)

You can summarize equity analysis and take positions based on the analysis in this way: Put a firm in the appropriate cell based on pro forma analysis of RE and then compare your classification with that of the market. In the late 1990s, the market placed many firms in cell **A**. Some claimed that earnings at that time were exceptionally high and could not be sustained. That claim puts firms in cell **G**. Who was correct?

Trailing Price-Earnings Ratios and Growth

A high-P/E stock is commonly referred to as a growth stock. But is this good thinking? We have seen that a high P/E implies high growth in earnings in the future. But the analysis we have just gone through gives us some reservation about calling every high-P/E firm a growth stock. A firm's P/E can be high but it may fall into cell **C**. That firm (like Rocky Shoes & Boots in Box 12.13) is expected to have low RE in the future (ROCE less than the cost of capital), and it has a high P/E only because current RE is even lower than that expected in the future. Rocky Shoes & Boots, in cell **C**, is hardly Nike, in cell **A**. This is not a firm that is able to pump out a lot of profits on book value. It is expected to have growth in earnings, yes, but low profitability. In contrast, a firm in cell **G** (like US Airways) is predicted to produce relatively high RE in the future, but it happens that current RE is even higher, and this produces a low P/E.

Which is the growth firm, the cell **C** firm or the cell **G** firm? It's a matter of definition, of course, but we might reserve the term **growth firm** for a firm that is capable of delivering residual earnings, growth and abnormal earnings growth in the future.

A. High P/B–High P/E

Nike, Inc. The market gave Nike a P/B of 6.1 and a P/E of 28 in 1996, both high relative to normal ratios. Current residual earnings were $291 million and analysts were forecasting earnings that indicated higher residual earnings (and positive abnormal earnings growth) in the future. This is a cell **A** firm.

B. Normal P/B–High P/E

Westcorp. Westcorp, a financial services holding company, reported earnings for 1998 of $0.65 per share and a ROCE of 5.4 percent. Analysts in 1999 forecasted earnings of $1.72 for 1999 and $2.00 for 2000, which translate into a ROCE of 13.6 percent and 14.1 percent, respectively. With a forecasted ROCE at about the (presumed) cost of capital but increasing from the current level, this is a cell **B** firm. The market gave the firm a P/B of 1.10 and a P/E of 24.

C. Low P/B–High P/E

Rocky Shoes & Boots, Inc. Like Nike, a footwear manufacturer, Rocky Shoes reported a ROCE of 1.8 percent for 1998 with earnings of $0.21 per share. Analysts forecast a ROCE of 6.2 percent for 1999 and 7.8 percent for 2000, on earnings of $0.72 and $0.95, respectively. The market gave the firm a P/B of 0.6 and a P/E of 33, appropriate for a firm with forecasted ROCE less than the (presumed) cost of capital but with increasing ROCE.

D. High P/B–Normal P/E

Whirlpool Corp. Whirlpool, with a positive but constant RE, was a cell **D** firm in 1994. Whirlpool was priced at 11 times earnings (cum-dividend), as we saw, and at 1.8 times book value.

E. Normal P/B–Normal P/E

Horizon Financial Corp. Horizon Financial Corp., a bank holding company, reported a ROCE of 10.3 percent for fiscal 1999. Analysts forecasted that ROCE would be 10.6 percent for 2000 and after, roughly at the same level. If the equity cost of capital is 10 percent, this firm should have a normal P/B and a normal P/E. The stock traded at 11 times earnings and 1.0 times book value.

F. Low P/B–Normal P/E

Rainforest Cafe Inc. In 1999, analysts covering Rainforest Cafe, a theme restaurant ("a wild place to eat"), forecasted earnings of $0.62 per share for 1999 and $0.71 for 2000, or a ROCE of 6.8 percent and 7.2 percent. The stock traded at a P/B of 0.6, reflecting the low anticipated ROCE. The ROCE for 1998 was 6.5 percent. With 1998 profitability similar to forecasted profitability, the stock should sell at a normal P/E ratio. And indeed it did: The P/E at the time of the forecasts was 11.

G. High P/B–Low P/E

US Airways Group. US Airways reported a ROCE of 81 percent in 1998. Analysts deemed 1998 to be a particularly good year and forecast ROCE for 1999 and 2000 down to 29 percent and 33 percent. The stock traded at 12.6 times book value, consistent with high ROCE in the future, but at a P/E of only 4.

H. Normal P/B–Low P/E.

America West Holdings. America West Holdings, the holding company for America West Airlines, had a ROCE of 15.0 percent in 1998. Analysts forecasted in 1999 that the ROCE would decline to 11.7 percent by 2000. The market gave the stock a P/B of 1.0 in 1999, in line with the forecasted ROCE equaling the cost of capital. But the P/E was 7, consistent with the expected drop in the ROCE.

I. Low P/B–Low P/E

UAL Corporation. United Airlines's holding company traded at a P/B of 0.7 in mid-1999 and a P/E of 6. It reported a ROCE of 29.2 percent for 1998, but its ROCE was expected by analysts to drop to 10.6 percent (before a special gain) in 1999 and to 9.1 percent in 2000.

Trailing Price-Earnings Ratios and Transitory Earnings

Because the trailing P/E is an indicator of the difference between current and future profitability, it is affected by current profitability. If a firm with strong ROCE forecasts has an exceptionally good year, it will have a low P/E and fall into cell **G**, like US Airways in 1998. A firm with poor prospects can fall into cell **C** with a high P/E because its current

TABLE 12.4
Subsequent Earnings Growth and Subsequent Residual Earnings for Different Levels of P/E, 1968–1985

Source: S. H. Penman, "The Articulation of Price-Earnings Ratios and Market-to-Book Ratios and the Evaluation of Growth," *Journal of Accounting Research,* Autumn 1996, pp. 235–259.

High-P/E firms in the current year (Year 0) have higher cum-dividend earnings growth in subsequent years than low-P/E firms. Residual earnings are higher in subsequent years than in the current year (Year 0) for high-P/E firms but lower for low-P/E firms. However, the relationship between P/E and growth is negative in the current year.

P/E Level	P/E	Year after Current Year (Year 0)				
		0	1	2	3	4
Cum-Dividend Eps Growth by P/E Level						
High	25.6	3.9%	52.2%	17.5%	17.8%	15.0%
Medium	10.6	14.5%	14.4%	13.3%	12.6%	13.1%
Low	5.2	20.9%	0.5%	7.0%	13.3%	14.4%
Residual Earnings by P/E Level						
High	25.6	0.009	0.034	0.038	0.054	0.061
Medium	10.6	0.040	0.043	0.043	0.044	0.051
Low	5.2	0.058	0.041	0.035	0.036	0.041

Earnings growth is the year-to-year change in eps divided by (the absolute value of) prior year's eps. Eps is adjusted for payout in the prior period and so is cum-dividend. Residual earnings are standardized by book value at the beginning of Year 0.

year's earnings are temporarily depressed, like Rocky Shoes. Earnings that are abnormally high or temporarily depressed are affected by transitory earnings or unusual earnings.

The effect of transitory earnings on the P/E has historically been referred to as the **Molodovsky effect**, after the analyst Nicholas Molodovsky, who highlighted the phenomenon in the 1950s. Table 12.4 shows the Molodovsky effect at work. The table shows the relationship between trailing P/E, residual earnings, and earnings growth for three P/E groups of NYSE and AMEX firms between 1968 to 1985. The "high"-P/E group had an average P/E of 25.6, the "medium" group an average P/E of 10.6, and the "low" group an average P/E of 5.2. The table gives median year-to-year cum-dividend eps growth rates for each P/E group, for the year when firms were assigned to the P/E group (Year 0) and for four subsequent years. Look at the medium P/E level. These firms have P/E ratios of 10.6 (on average) that are "normal" for what we would think of as a typical cost of capital for equity, 10 percent to 12 percent. (As normal P/E = $\rho_E/[\rho_{E-1}]$, a cost of capital of 10.4 percent implies P/E of 10.6.) These firms had subsequent earnings in the four years following Year 0 that grew on average at rates that also look like the typical cost of capital, or perhaps a tad higher, at 12 percent to 14 percent per year. Now look at the high-and low-P/E levels. High-P/E firms had relatively high earnings growth in the years following Year 0, whereas low-P/E firms had relatively low earnings growth. Thus the data confirm that P/E indicates future growth in earnings.

The table also gives residual earnings for the same P/E levels. These data also confirm that high-P/E firms have subsequent residual earnings above levels in Year 0, and low-P/E firms have subsequent residual earnings below that of Year 0. The residual earnings for the medium, "normal" P/E level are very similar in Years 1 to 4 to the level in Year 0, just like the Whirlpool case.

Now look at the growth rates in Year 0, the current year. Whereas P/E is positively related to future earnings growth, it is negatively related to current earnings growth. High-P/E firms are typically those whose earnings are down now but will rebound in the future. The low-P/E firms in the table have large increases in current earnings but these are not sustained subsequently. In short, the P/E is affected by temporary aspects of current earnings.

P/E Ratios and the Analysis of Sustainable Earnings

The analysis of sustainable earnings in this chapter identifies the transitory aspects of current earnings and so helps to ascertain the Molodovsky effect on the trailing P/E ratio. If earnings are temporarily high (and cannot be sustained), one should pay less per dollar of earnings—the P/E should be low. If, on the other hand, earnings can be sustained—or can grow because they are temporarily depressed—one should pay a higher multiple. Sustainable earnings analysis focuses on the future—for it is future earnings that the investor is buying—and helps the investor discount earnings for that part which is not sustainable.

As investors buy future earnings, it makes sense that a P/E valuation should focus on the forward P/E and thus the pricing of next year's earnings and growth after that year. Forward earnings are considerably less affected by the transitory items that do not contribute to permanent growth. For evaluation of the forward P/E, sustainable earnings analysis very much comes into play for, to forecast forward earnings after observing current earnings, we wish to identify the core earnings that can be sustained in the forward year.

Until recently, analysts talked most often in terms of the trailing P/E. But talk has shifted to the forward P/E. In light of our discussion here, that makes sense. For the most part, the valuation analysis in Part Three of the book focuses on the forward P/E.

Summary

Firms change over time and their financial statements change accordingly. This chapter has laid out the analysis of the changes in financial statements that are particularly relevant for valuation. The focus has been on changes in residual earnings and on changes in ROCE and growth in investment, which drive residual earnings and value. Change in residual earnings is the same as abnormal earnings growth.

Figures 12.1 and 12.2 summarize most of the growth analysis. A change in ROCE is analyzed by distinguishing changes that are due to operating profitability (changes in RNOA) and changes in the financing of operations. In both cases, core or sustainable components that are likely to drive profitability in the future are distinguished from transitory or unusual components that are nonrecurring. So the analyst "cuts to the core" of what will drive profitability in the future. Growth in equity investment, which combines with ROCE to produce growth in residual earnings, is determined primarily by sales growth but also by changes in the net operating asset investment needed to support sales growth and by changes in financing of this investment.

The analysis here has given an answer to the question raised at the beginning of the chapter: What is a growth firm? A growth firm is one that can earn a ROCE greater than the cost of capital and increase its residual earnings, either by increasing ROCE from core operations or by growing investment. And the chapter has given the tools required to analyze a growth firm by describing the drivers of changes in ROCE and growth in investment. A growth firm will have the following features:

1. Sustainable, growing sales (and with it, growing investment).

2. High or increasing profitability that is generated by core operations.

The analysis can be applied to understanding current and past changes in residual earnings, and to understanding abnormal earnings growth. But see it also as a tool for forecasting. How will the future be different from the present? The analysis of the chapter lays out the features that will drive changes in the future and so is a tool for forecasting, strategy analysis, and valuation in the next part of the book. And, as the last part of the chapter explained, the analysis comes to bear on the determination of P/B ratios and trailing and forward P/E ratios.

The Web Connection

Find the following on the web page for this chapter:

- Additional examples of the analysis of sustainable earnings.

- Further discussion of growth analysis.

- Further discussion of pension issues.

Key Concepts

fixed costs are costs that do not change with sales. Compare with **variable costs**. *398*

growth firm is a firm that grows residual earnings and has abnormal earnings growth. *384*

Molodovsky effect is the effect of transitory earnings on the P/E ratio. *408*

normalizing earnings is the process of purging earnings of transitory, abnormal components. *390*

sustainable earnings (also called **persistent earnings, core earnings**, or **underlying earnings**) are current earnings that are likely to be maintained in the future. Compare with **transitory items**. *389*

transitory items (or **unusual items**) are current earnings that are not likely to be repeated in the future. Compare with **sustainable earnings**. *389*

variable costs are costs that vary with sales. Compare with **fixed costs**. *398*

The Analyst's Toolkit

Concept Questions

C12.1. What is a growth firm?

C12.2. In analyzing growth, should the analyst focus on residual earnings, abnormal earnings growth, or both?

C12.3. What measure tells you that a firm is a no-growth firm?

C12.4. What features in financial statements would you look for to identify a firm as a growth company?

C12.5. Why would an analyst wish to distinguish the part of earnings that is sustainable?

C12.6. What are transitory earnings? Give some examples.

C12.7. Are unrealized gains and losses on financial assets persistent or transitory income?

C12.8. Distinguish operating leverage from operating liability leverage.

C12.9. The higher a firm's contribution margin ratio, the more leverage it gets from increasing sales. Correct?

C12.10. Would you see a high profit margin of, say, 6 percent for a grocery retailer as sustainable?

C12.11. What determines growth in equity investment in a firm?

C12.12. In 1996, Reebok's common equity declined from $941 million to $381 million. Refer to the analysis of Reebok in Chapter 11. How much of this change was attributable to operations and how much to financing changes?

C12.13. A firm can have a high trailing P/E ratio, yet have an expected cum-dividend earnings growth rate after the forward year that is less than the required rate. Is this so?

C12.14. For a firm with a normal trailing P/E ratio, expected future residual earnings must be the same as current residual earnings. Correct?

C12.15. Can a firm have a high P/E ratio yet a low P/B ratio? How would you characterize the growth expectations for this firm?

C12.16. Firms with high unsustainable earnings should have low (trailing) P/E ratios. Is this correct?

Exercises

E12.1. Calculating Core Profit Margin (Easy)

A firm reports operating income before tax in its income statement of $73.4 million on sales of $667.3 million. After net interest expense of $20.5 million and taxes of $18.3 million, its net income is $34.6 million. The following items are included as part of operating income:

Start-up costs for new venture	$ 4.3 million
Merger-related charge	$13.4 million
Gains on the disposal of plant	$ 3.9 million

The firm also reports a currency translation gain of $8.9 million as part of other comprehensive income.

Calculate the firm's core operating income (after tax) and core percentage profit margin. The firm's marginal tax rate is 39 percent.

E12.2. Explaining a Change in Profitability (Medium)

Consider the following financial information:

Summary Balance Sheets at December 31

	1998	1999	2000
Cash	$ 100	$ 100	$ 120
Short-term investments	300	300	330
Accounts receivable	900	1,000	1,250
Inventory	2,000	1,900	1,850
Property, plant, and equipment (net of accumulated depreciation)	8,200	9,000	10,500
Total assets	11,500	12,300	14,050
Accrued liabilities	600	500	550
Accounts payable	900	1,000	1,100
Bank loan	0	0	3,210
Bonds payable	4,300	4,300	1,000
Deferred taxes	490	500	600
Total liabilities	6,290	6,300	6,460
Preferred stock (8%)	1,000	1,000	1,000
Common stock	1,400	2,000	2,000
Retained earnings	2,810	3,000	4,590
Owners' equity	$ 5,210	$ 6,000	$ 7,590

Summary Income Statements

	1999	2000
Sales	$ 22,000	$ 24,000
Cost of goods sold	(13,000)	(13,100)
Selling and administration	(8,000)	(8,250)
Restructuring charges	(190)	0
Interest income	24	25
Interest expense	(430)	(430)
Earnings before taxes and extraordinary items	404	2,245
Tax expense	(134)	(675)
Earnings before extraordinary items	270	1,570
Gain due to retirement of bonds, net of taxes	0	100
Net income	$ 270	$ 1,670

Prepare a succinct analysis that explains the change in ROCE from 1999 to 2000. Assume that the marginal tax rate is 34 percent, and that the dividends paid on preferred stock cannot be deducted for tax purposes.

E12.3. **Explaining a Change in Operating Profitability: Quantum Corporation (Easy)**
Comparative reformulated financial statements for Quantum Corporation are given in Exercise E10.9 of Chapter 10. Analyze the change in the profitability of Quantum's operations from 1994 to 1996.

Real World Connection
See Exercise E10.9 in Chapter 10 for more material on Quantum Corporation.

E12.4. **Raising Questions Regarding a Change in Income:**
Boeing Company (Medium)
Below are the 1996, 1997, and 1998 income statements for Boeing Co., when the aerospace firm was headquartered in Seattle, Washington. The statements are as they were reported in the firm's 10-K report.

BOEING CO.
Income Statements
(dollars in millions except per share data)

Year Ended December 31	1998	1997	1996
Sales and other operating revenues	$56,154	$45,800	$35,453
Operating costs and expenses	50,546	40,644	29,383
General and administrative expense	1,993	2,187	1,819
Research and development expense	1,895	1,924	1,633
Share-based plans	153	(99)	133
Special charges		1,400	
Earnings (loss) from operations	1,567	(256)	2,485
Other income, principally interest	283	428	388
Interest and debt expense	(453)	(513)	(393)
Earnings (loss) before income taxes	1,397	(341)	2,480
Income taxes (benefit)	277	(163)	662
Net earnings (loss)	$ 1,120	$ (178)	$ 1,818
Earnings (loss) per share			
Basic	$ 1.16	$ (0.18)	$ 1.88
Diluted	$ 1.15	$ (0.18)	$ 1.85
Cash dividends per share	$ 0.56	$ 0.56	$ 0.55

Revenues increased in 1998 by 22.6 percent over 1997, and the firm reported income against a loss in 1997. However, the 1998 net income was less than that in 1996. What questions would you raise in trying to find out whether 1998 income is indicative of long-run profits? What questions can you answer from the limited information in the statements?

Real World Connection

See Exercise E5.12 in Chapter 5 and Exercise E12.6 in this chapter for more material on Boeing Company.

E12.5. Explaining Changes in Income: US Airways (Medium)

US Airways Group, the holding company for US Airways, reported the following income statements for 1997 and 1998 (in millions of dollars):

	1998	1997
Operating revenues		
Passenger transportation	$7,826	$7,712
Cargo and freight	168	181
Other	694	621
Total operating revenues	8,688	8,514
Operating expenses		
Personnel costs	3,101	3,179
Aviation fuel	623	805
Commissions	519	595
Aircraft rent	440	475
Other rent and landing fees	417	420
Aircraft maintenance	448	451
Other selling expenses	342	346
Depreciation and amortization	318	401
Other	1,466	1,258
Total operating expense	7,674	7,930
Operating income	1,014	584

(continued)

Other income (expense)		
Interest income	111	108
Interest expense	(223)	(256)
Interest capitalized	3	13
Equity in earnings of affiliates	1	30
Gains on sales of interests in affiliates		180
Other, net	(4)	13
Other income (expense), net	(112)	88
Income before taxes	902	672
Provision (credit) for income taxes	364	(353)
Net income	538	1,025
Preferred dividend requirement	(6)	(64)
Earnings applicable to common stockholders	$ 532	$ 961
Earnings per common share	$ 5.75	$ 12.32
Basic	$ 5.60	$ 9.87

a. Reported operating income before interest and taxes increased by 73.6 percent in 1998 over 1997 while revenues increased by only 2.0 percent. Why?

b. Despite the increase in operating income, net income available to common dropped by 44.6 percent. Why?

c. What might explain the negative tax expense in 1997? The following from the tax footnote might help you:

	1997	1996
Deferred tax assets (in thousands)		
Leasing transactions	$ 170,966	$ 154,732
Tax benefits purchased/sold	31,352	43,441
Gain on sale and leaseback transactions	125,169	135,308
Employee benefits	683,416	608,948
Net operating loss carryforwards	193,575	540,495
Alternative minimum tax credit carryforwards	158,441	33,459
Investment tax credit carryforwards	17,841	49,802
Other deferred tax assets	94,640	82,744
Total gross deferred tax assets	1,475,400	1,648,929
Less valuation allowance	(1,377)	(643,546)
Net deferred tax assets	1,474,023	1,005,383
Deferred tax liabilities		
Equipment depreciation and amortization	940,784	966,874
Other deferred tax liabilities	62,791	45,415
Total deferred tax liabilities	1,003,575	1,012,289
Net deferred tax liabilities (assets)	$ (470,448)	$ 6,906

d. If you were to forecast net income for 1999, would you rely on the 1998 or 1997 net income as an indication of "sustainable" income?

Real World Connection

See Exercise E12.8 in this chapter for more material on US Airways.

E12.6. **Analysis of Pension Expense: Boeing Co. (Medium)**

During the 1990s, the pension funds of many firms increased significantly as stock prices soared. It was claimed that the earnings on these funds were flowing through into income statements in the form of lower pension expense so that what looked like operating profitability was partially gains in investment assets in pension funds.

Boeing's pension expense is included in operating costs and general and administrative expense in its income statements. The income statements for 1996–1998 are given in Exercise E12.4. Boeing reported a pension asset of $3.273 billion in 1998, indicating an overfunded pension plan capable of generating considerable returns on its assets. The pension footnote gave the following detail (in millions):

	1998	1997
Benefit obligation		
Beginning balance	$25,845	$24,212
Service cost	573	506
Interest cost	1,793	1,727
Plan participants' contributions	1	1
Amendments	489	4
Actuarial loss	1,862	815
Benefits paid	(1,676)	(1,420)
Ending balance	$28,887	$25,845
Plan assets—fair value		
Beginning balance	$33,119	$28,259
Actual return on plan assets	1,146	5,932
Company contributions	18	345
Plan participants' contributions	1	1
Benefits paid	(1,659)	(1,409)
Exchange rate adjustment	(16)	(9)
Ending balance	$32,609	$33,119
Reconciliation of funded status to net amount recognized		
Funded status—plan assets in excess of (less than) benefit obligation	$ 3,722	$ 7,274
Unrecognized net actuarial gain	(1,699)	(4,938)
Unrecognized prior service costs	1,491	1,066
Unrecognized net transition asset	(241)	(331)
Net amount recognized	$ 3,273	$ 3,071
Amount recognized in statement of financial position		
Prepaid benefit cost	$ 3,513	$ 3,271
Intangible asset	105	
Accumulated other comprehensive income	37	
Accrued benefit liability	(382)	(200)
Net amount recognized	$ 3,273	$ 3,071

Components of net periodic benefit costs were as follows:

Year Ended December 31	1998	1997
Components of net periodic benefit cost—pensions		
Service cost	$ 573	$ 506
Interest cost	1,793	1,727
Expected return on plan assets	(2,507)	(2,163)
Amortization of transition asset	(86)	(86)
Amortization of prior service cost	101	101
Recognized net actuarial loss (gain)	5	(20)
Net periodic benefit cost (income)	$ (121)	$ 65

Demonstrate how this information indicates that Boeing's reported operating income may not be a good indication of its profitability in aerospace operations.

Real World Connection
See Exercise E5.12 in Chapter 5 and Exercise E12.4 in this chapter for more material on Boeing Company.

E12.7. **Transitory Taxes: Kimberly-Clark Corporation (Hard)**

Kimberly-Clark produces consumer and industrial products from natural and synthetic fibers. Kleenex, Scott paper towels, Huggies, and Kotex are among the household names in its brand portfolio.

In 1995, Kimberly-Clark reported a tax expense of $153.5 million on income before tax of $104.4 million. The income statement is below.

KIMBERLY-CLARK CORP.
Consolidated Statement of Income
Year Ended December 31, 1995
(in millions)

Net sales	$13,788.6
Cost of products sold	8,828.1
Gross profit	4,960.5
Advertising, promotion, and selling expenses	2,496.5
Research expense	207.2
General expense	603.8
Restructuring and other unusual charges	1,440.0
Operating profit	213.0
Interest expense	(245.5)
Other income (expense), net	136.9
Income before income taxes	104.4
Provision for income taxes	153.5
Income (loss) before equity interests	(49.1)
Share of net income of equity companies	113.3
Minority owners' share of subsidiaries' net income	(31.0)
Net income	$ 33.2

a. How can tax expense be greater than income before tax? The following excerpt from the tax footnote may help you answer this question.

A reconciliation of income tax computed at the U.S. federal statutory tax rate to the provision for income taxes applicable to continuing operations is as follows:

Millions of dollars

Income before income taxes:	
As reported	$ 104.4
Add back restructuring and other unusual charges	1,440.0
Income before income taxes excluding restructuring and other unusual charges	$1,544.4
Tax at U.S. statutory rate	$ 540.5
State income taxes, net of federal tax benefit	34.2
Operating losses for which no tax benefit was recognized	10.9
Net operating losses realized	(70.6)
Other—net	(1.5)
	513.5
Tax benefit of restructuring and other unusual charges	(360.0)
Provision for income taxes	$ 153.5

b. Recognizing that an effective tax rate of over 100 percent is transitory, reformulate the income statement to identify after-tax sustainable operating income from sales.
c. Calculate an effective tax rate on core operating income.
d. What aspect of the reporting here frustrates you in analyzing sustainable income?

E12.8. **Analysis of Effects of Operating Leverage: US Airways (Medium)**

Refer to the 1998 income statement for US Airways Group in Exercise E12.5 above. Of the total $7,674 million in operating expenses, suppose the following are fixed costs (in millions):

Personnel	$2,040
Aircraft rent	440
Other rent	350
Depreciation and amortization	318
Other	890
Total	$4,038

a. Calculate the firm's operating leverage.
b. What would be the percentage change in core operating income from sales before tax if there were a 1 percent increase in sales?
c. At what level of sales would the airline incur operating losses?

Real World Connection

See Exercise E12.5 in this chapter for more material on US Airways.

E12.9. **Analysis of Growth in Common Equity for a Firm with Constant Asset Turnover (Easy)**

An analyst summarizes the following information for a firm (dollar amounts in millions):

	2003	2002	2001
Common shareholders' equity	4,725	4,394	4,124
Net financial obligations	2,193	2,193	2,193
Net operating assets	2,532	2,201	1,931
Sales	7,100	6,198	5,939

Analyze the growth of average common shareholders' equity in 2003.

E12.10. **Analysis of Growth in Residual Earnings: Kmart Corporation (Medium)**

An analyst has reformatted the 1990 and 1991 income statements of Kmart, the discount retailer, as follows (in millions of dollars):

		1991		1990
Core Operating Income				
Revenue (less interest income)		32,452		29,898
Operating expenses		(30,907)		(28,387)
Operating income		1,545		1,511
Dirty surplus		(5)		(32)
Operating income, before tax		1,540		1,479
Tax, as reported	390		192	
Tax shield	144		128	
Tax on noncore income	0	(534)	230	(550)
Core operating income, after tax		1,006		929

(continued)

Unusual Operating Income

Restructuring charges			(640)
Tax benefit			230
Operating income		1,006	519
Net Financial Expenses (NFE)			
Interest expense	409		380
Interest income	(10)		(24)
	399		356
Tax effect (36%)	(144)	255	(128)	228
Comprehensive Income		751		291

The analyst also prepared a summary of average balance sheet amounts for 1991 and 1990 as follows:

	1991	1990
Net operating assets	8,972	8,578
Net financial obligations	3,794	3,606
Common shareholders' equity	5,178	4,972

Analyze the growth in Kmart's residual earnings on average common equity from 1990 to 1991. Use a cost of equity capital of 10 percent for calculating residual earnings.

Real World Connection

See Minicase M6.4 in Chapter 6 for more material on Kmart Corp.

E12.11. **P/E, P/B, and Return on Common Equity: Hilton Hotels (Hard)**

Hilton Hotels Corporation traded at the following P/E and P/B multiples from 1994 to 1996:

	1994	1995	1996
P/E	27.0	17.3	33.2
P/B	2.9	2.4	2.1
ROCE	10.8%	13.8%	4.8%

a. Explain why the P/E ratio was the lowest of the three years in 1995, yet the return on common equity (ROCE) in 1995 was the highest of the three years.
b. Explain why the P/E was the highest in 1996, yet ROCE declined to 4.8 percent.
c. In what cell in the cell analysis (in Table 12.3) would you place Hilton in each of the three years?
d. From 1997 to early 2000, Hilton's stock price declined from $30 a share to $8 a share. Would anything in the numbers above have forecasted this decline?

Minicases

M12.1

A Study in Value Creation: Dell Computer Corporation

The Wall Street Journal publishes an annual "Shareholder Scorecard" ranking the best and worst U.S. traded firms by market value generated for shareholders. Value generated is percentage increase in market price per share plus the value of dividends, that is, the stock rate of return.

In the 1998 scorecard, published on February 25, 1999, Dell Computer Corp., the Round Rock, Texas, personal computer manufacturer, ranked first in total return during the past 3, 5, and 10 years, a spectacular performance, and ranked tenth in return for 1998. A $1,000 investment in the company at the end of 1988 had a market value of $351,356 at the end of 1998, an average compound annual return of 79.7 percent. Returns for other periods are:

Annualized five-year return, 1994–1998	159.2%
Annualized three-year return, 1996–98	223.4%
1998 return	248.5%

In 1993 Dell Computer was the second largest personal computer vendor in the world (after Compaq) and the largest mail-order vendor. Michael Dell, the firm's founder, chairman, and CEO, started the business from his dorm room at the University of Texas in 1984. In the mid-1980s, Dell traded memory chips and assembled PC clones which were sold directly to the end user, thus avoiding the customary reseller distribution channel and its markup. This structure enabled Dell to sell PCs for 40 percent less than IBM. The company grew considerably through the 1980s and went public in 1988 with a $32 million stock offering.

After several years of record-setting earnings growth, Dell stumbled in 1990 as profits dropped 64 percent. The setback was due at least in part to rising inventory levels, high R&D expenditures, and an expensive and unsuccessful endeavor to develop a PC that used entirely proprietary technology.

The company rebounded the next year with the introduction of eight new products, new domestic distribution agreements with CompUSA and Staples, and a new production facility in Limerick, Ireland. In 1992 the company aggressively pursued international markets, opening subsidiaries in Japan and Austria, and signed several international distribution agreements, preferring direct sales to end users. In 1993 Dell experienced a margin squeeze from rising component costs and falling end-product prices. In 1994 Dell stopped selling computers domestically under retail store agreements and signed several more distribution agreements with international resellers, most notably in Asia.

Dell's product portfolio consists of desktop and notebook computers, workstations, network servers, its own branded software and accessories, and computer services and support. Its manufacturing is done in Austin, Texas, Limerick, Ireland, and Penang, Malaysia, with plans to build facilities in Brazil.

By 1998 Dell Computer was a darling of Wall Street analysts. It certainly had become an innovative manufacturer and marketer. Its strategy is centered around its "direct business model," which tries to deliver customized computers and services directly to the buyer. This approach aims to eliminate a large network of wholesalers and retailers with its higher markups, inventories, and competition for shelf space. The direct marketing approach is combined with an inventory system whereby computers, customized to consumers' needs, are manufactured to order. This system, along with online, prompt servicing and "comprehensive customer relationships" to understand customers' needs, is designed to promote customer satisfaction. But it also reduces the need to carry much inventory, an important consideration for computers, which can become obsolete through rapid technological change, and which, in 1998, experienced falling component prices.

Dell's direct sales and inventory systems are combined with organizational principles that continually divide operations into smaller areas focusing on customers. Managers, it is said, are rewarded for shrinking operations to create stronger focus rather than for amassing more functions under their control. And they are rewarded for innovations that create new focus areas.

DELL COMPUTER CORP.
Balance Sheets Fiscal Years Ending February 1
(in millions of dollars)

	1999	1998	1997	1996	1995	1994	1993
Current Assets							
Cash	$ 520	$ 320	$ 115	$ 55	$ 43	$ 3	$ 15
Marketable securities	2,661	1,524	1,237	591	484	334	81
Accounts receivable, gross	2,124	1,514	934	755	564	437	393
Allowance for bad debts	(30)	(28)	(31)	(29)	(26)	(26)	(19)
Accounts receivable, net	2,094	1,486	903	726	538	411	374
Inventories	273	233	251	429	293	220	303
Deferred tax assets	137	106	133	67	78	64	62
Other	654	243	108	89	34	16	18
Total current assets	6,339	3,912	2,747	1,957	1,470	1,048	853
Property, plant, and equipment, gross	775	509	374	292	208	152	113
Accumulated depreciation	(252)	(167)	(139)	(113)	(91)	(65)	43
Property, plant, and equipment, net	523	342	235	179	117	87	70
Other assets	15	14	11	12	7	5	4
Total assets	$6,877	$4,268	$2,993	$2,148	$1,594	$1,140	$927
Current Liabilities							
Accounts payable	2,397	$1,643	$1,040	$ 466	$ 403	$ 283	$295
Accrued and other	1,298	1,054	618	473	349	255	199
Total current liabilities	3,695	2,697	1,658	939	752	538	494
Long-term debt	512	17	18	113	113	100	48
Deferred revenue on warranty contracts	237	225	219	116	68		
Other	112	36	13	7	9	31	16
Commitments and contingent liabilities	—	—	—	—	—	—	—
Total liabilities	4,556	2,975	1,908	1,175	942	669	558
Put options			279				
Stockholders' equity							
Preferred stock and capital in excess of $0.01 par value				6	120	120	
Common stock and capital in excess of $0.01 par value	1,781	747	195	430	242	200	178
Retained earnings	606	607	647	570	311	171	209
Other	(66)	(61)	(36)	(33)	(21)	(20)	(18)
Total Stockholders' Equity	2,321	1,293	806	973	652	471	369
	$6,877	$4,268	$2,993	$2,148	$1,594	$1,140	$927

Shares outstanding on February 1, 1999, were 2,543 million. Dell's marketable securities are debt and preferred securities.

With its direct-to-customer policy, Dell was well placed to use the Internet, both to enhance customer relationships and to make more direct sales. Internet sales were a growing part of its business in 1998, accounting for 20 percent of its revenue.

Dell traded at 38 on March 25, 1999, some 66 times fiscal 1999 earnings and about 56 times book value. At http://www.bigcharts.com you can view a price chart for recent years. Analysts were forecasting eps of 0.74 for 2000 and 0.99 for 2001. Buy recommendations outpaced hold recommendations by 2 to 1 (with very few sell recommendations).

Dell's financial statements from 1993 to 1999 follow. These statements have been enhanced over the published statements to incorporate some footnote information. Dell has a 35 percent marginal tax rate. Dell's statements for 2001 and 2002 are in Exhibit 2.1 in Chapter 2.

Discover from these financial statements why Dell has been so successful in generating value for shareholders. Also identify the cash that Dell has generated for its shareholders.

Using the SEC EDGAR files, you can also compare Dell's drivers with those of Compaq Computer Corp. and Gateway 2000, two of Dell's strongest competitors.

Dell's website is at www.dell.com/us/en/gen/corporate/investor/investor.htm. It contains recent financial statements, including quarterly statements, earnings forecasts, and further investor information on the firm.

Income Statements
Fiscal Years Ending February 1
(in millions of dollars, except per-share items)

	1999	1998	1997	1996	1995	1994	1993
Net revenue	$18,243	$12,327	$7,759	$5,296	$3,475	$2,873	$2,014
Cost of revenue	14,137	9,605	6,093	4,229	2,737	2,440	1,565
Gross revenue	4,106	2,722	1,666	1,067	738	433	449
Operating expenses							
Selling, general, and administrative	1,589	1,065	739	512	361	346	208
Advertising expenses	199	137	87	83	63	77	60
Research, development, and engineering	272	204	126	95	65	49	42
Total operating expenses	2,060	1,406	952	690	489	472	310
Operating income	2,046	1,316	714	377	249	(39)	139
Financing and other	38	52	33	6	(36)	0	4
Income before taxes and extraordinary loss	2,084	1,368	747	383	213	(39)	143
Provision for income taxes	624	424	216	111	64	(3)	41
Income before extraordinary loss	1,460	944	531	272	149	(36)	102
Extraordinary loss, net of taxes			(13)				
Net income	1,460	944	518	272	149	(36)	102
Preferred stock dividends				(13)	(9)	(2)	
Net income available to common stockholders	$ 1,460	$ 944	$ 518	$ 259	$ 140	$ (38)	$ 102
Basic earnings per share	0.58	0.36	0.18	0.09	0.06	(0.02)	0.04
Diluted earnings per share	0.53	0.32	0.17	0.08	0.05	(0.04)	0.04

Per-share data have been adjusted for stock splits.

Statements of Shareholders' Equity
Fiscal Years Ending February 1
(dollar amounts in millions)

	Preferred Stock and Capital in Excess of Par Value	Common Stock and Capital in Excess of Par Value	Retained Earnings	Other	Total
Balances at February 2, 1992		166	107	1	274
Net income			102		102
Issuance of 1,056,328 shares of common under employee plans		12			12
Foreign currency translation adjustment				(19)	(19)
Balances at January 31, 1993		178	209	(18)	369
Net loss			(36)		(36)
Issuance of 1,250,000 shares of preferred stock	120				120
Issuance of 2,142,166 shares of common stock under employee plans, including tax benefits		22			22
Preferred stock dividends paid			(2)		(2)
Unrealized gain on marketable securities				3	3
Foreign currency translation adjustment				(5)	(5)
Balances at January 30, 1994	120	200	171	(20)	471
Net income			149		149
Issuance of 3,501,214 shares of common stock under employee plans, including tax benefits		42		(4)	38
Preferred stock dividends paid			(9)		(9)
Unrealized loss on marketable securities				(6)	(6)
Foreign currency translation adjustment				9	9
Balances at January 29, 1995	120	242	311	(21)	652
Net income			272		272
Issuance of 4,066,363 shares of common stock under employee plans, including tax benefits		74		(17)	57
Issuance of 10,020,968 shares of common stock due to preferred stock conversion	(114)	114			
Amortization of unearned compensation				2	2
Preferred stock dividends paid			(13)		(13)
Unrealized gain on marketable securities				3	3
Balances at January 28, 1996	6	430	570	(33)	973
Net income			518		518
Stock issuance under employee plans, including tax benefits		65		(18)	47
Purchase and retirement of 62 million shares		(22)	(388)		(410)
Purchase and reissuance of 19 million shares for employee plans and preferred stock conversion	(6)		(55)		(61)
Reclassification of put options		(279)			(279)
Other		1	2	15	18
Balances at February 2, 1997	0	195	647	(36)	806
Net income			944		944
Stock issuance under employee plans, including tax benefits		274		(11)	263
Purchases and retirement of 69 million shares		(39)	(984)		(1,023)
Reclassification of put options		279			279
Other		38		(14)	24
Balances at February 1, 1998	0	747	607	(61)	1,293
Net income			1,460		1,460
Stock issuance under employee plans, including tax benefits		1,092		(7)	1,085
Purchases and retirement of 149 million shares		(60)	(1,458)		(1,518)
Other		2	(3)	2	1
Balances at January 29, 1999	0	1,781	606	(66)	2,321

Statements of Cash Flow Fiscal Years
Ending February 1
(amounts in millions)

	1999	1998	1997	1996	1995	1994	1993
Cash flows from operating activities							
Net income	$ 1,460	$ 944	$ 518	$ 272	$ 149	$ (36)	$ 102
Adjustments to reconcile net income to net cash provided by operating activities							
Depreciation and amortization	103	67	47	38	33	31	20
Tax benefits of employee stock plans	444						
Other	11	24	29	22	25	4	
Changes in							
Operating working capital	367	529	659	(195)	(3)	97	(163)
Noncurrent assets and liabilities	51	28	109	38	39	17	2
Net cash provided by operating activities	2,436	1,592	1,362	175	243	113	(39)
Cash flows from investing							
Marketable securities							
Purchases	(16,459)	(12,305)	(9,538)	(4,545)	(4,644)	(2,588)	(1,808)
Maturities and sales	15,341	12,017	8,891	4,442	4,464	2,335	1,827
Capital expenditures	(296)	(187)	(114)	(101)	(64)	(48)	(47)
Net cash used in investing activities	(1,414)	(475)	(761)	(204)	(244)	(301)	(28)
Cash flows from financing activities							
Purchase of common stock	(1,518)	(1,023)	(495)				
Repayments of borrowings			(95)		(1)	(59)	
Issuance of common stock under employee plans	212	88	57	48	35	22	12
Cash received from sale of equity options		38					
Preferred stock dividends and other		(1)		(14)	(9)	(2)	
Proceeds from borrowing	494				14	97	15
Proceeds from issue of preferred stock						120	
Net cash (used in) provided by financing activities	(812)	(898)	(533)	34	39	178	27
Effect of exchange rate changes on cash	(10)	(14)	(8)	7	2	(2)	(1)
Net increase in cash	200	205	60	12	40	(12)	(41)
Cash at beginning of period	320	115	55	43	3	15	55
Cash at end of period	$ 520	$ 320	$ 115	$ 55	$ 43	$ 3	$ 14

Real World Connection

See material on Dell Computer Corp. in Chapter 2. Also see Exercise E1.1 in Chapter 1, Exercise E4.1 in Chapter 4, Exercise E5.10 in Chapter 5, Minicase M6.2 in Chapter 6, Exercises E8.3 and E8.8 in Chapter 8, Minicase M10.1 in Chapter 10, and Minicase 15.1 in Chapter 15.

M12.2

Analysis of Growth in Core Operating Income During the 1990s: International Business Machines

International Business Machines Corporation (IBM) was once the dominant mainframe computer manufacturer in the world and, from 1960–1980, the leading growth company. Indeed, in those years IBM became the very personification of a growth company. However, with the advent of decentralized computing and the personal computer in the 1980s, IBM's growth began to slow. Under the leadership of Louis Gerstner, Jr., the firm transformed itself in the early 1990s from a mainframe manufacturer to an information technology company, providing technology, system software, services, and financing products to customers. Mr. Gerstner's book, *Who Says Elephants Can't Dance? Inside IBM's Historic Turnaround,* published in 2002, gives the play-by-play. From revenues of $64.8 billion in 1991, IBM grew to a firm with $88.4 billion in revenues in 2000.

In turning around the business, IBM took large restructuring charges against its income in the early 1990s, resulting in net losses of $2.861 billion, $4.965 billion, and $8.101 billion for 1991–1993, respectively. Subsequently the firm delivered the earnings growth of yesteryear. You can see at the bottom of the income statements in Exhibit 12.2 that earnings per share grew from $2.56 in 1996 to $4.58 in 2000.

At a number of points, this chapter has analyzed the components of IBM's earnings in order to understand their sustainability. From the information extracted from IBM's financial statement footnotes below, restate the income statements from 1996–2000 in Exhibit 12.2 to identify core operating income that arises from selling products to customers. The footnotes are from the firm's 1999 10-K filing; you may also wish to look at the corresponding footnotes for other years. The extracts from the firm's cash flow statement in Exhibit 12.2 will also help you in your task.

Do you get a different picture of IBM's income growth during the last half of the 1990s than is suggested by growth in earnings per share?

EXHIBIT 12.2

INTERNATIONAL BUSINESS MACHINES CORPORATION AND SUBSIDIARY COMPANIES
Consolidated Statements of Earnings
(dollars in millions except per share amounts)

| | For the Year Ended December 31 | | | | |
	2000	1999	1998	1997	1996
Revenue	$88,396	$87,548	$81,667	$78,508	$75,947
Cost of revenue	55,972	55,619	50,795	47,899	45,408
Gross profit	32,424	31,929	30,872	30,609	30,539
Operating expenses					
Selling, general, and administrative	15,639	14,729	16,662	16,634	16,854
Research, development, and engineering	5,151	5,273	5,046	4,877	5,089
Total operating expenses	20,790	20,002	21,708	21,511	21,943
Operating income	11,634	11,927	9,164	9,098	8,596
Other income, principally interest	617	557	589	657	707

EXHIBIT 12.2
(continued)

Interest expense	717	727	713	728	716
Income before income taxes	11,534	11,757	9,040	9,027	8,587
Provision for income taxes	3,441	4,045	2,712	2,934	3,158
Net income	8,093	7,712	6,328	6,093	5,429
Preferred stock dividends	20	20	20	20	20
Net income applicable to common stockholders	$ 8,073	$ 7,692	$ 6,308	$ 6,073	$ 5,409
Earnings per share of common stock					
Assuming dilution	$ 4.44	$ 4.12	$ 3.29	$ 3.00	$ 2.51
Basic	$ 4.58	$ 4.25	$ 3.38	$ 3.09	$ 2.56

Statements of Cash Flows (partial) (dollars in millions)

	At December 31				
	2000	**1999**	**1998**	**1997**	**1996**
Cash flow from operating activities					
Net income	$ 8,093	$ 7,712	$ 6,328	$ 6,093	$ 5,429
Adjustments to reconcile net income to cash provided from operating activities					
Depreciation	4,513	6,159	4,475	4,018	3,676
Amortization of software	482	426	517	983	1,336
Effect of restructuring charges			(355)	(445)	(1,491)
Deferred income taxes	29	(713)	(606)	358	11
Gain on disposition of fixed and other assets	(792)	(4,791)	(261)	(273)	(300)
Other changes that (used) provided cash					
Receivables	(4,720)	(1,677)	(2,736)	(3,727)	(650)
Inventories	(55)	301	73	432	196
Other assets	(643)	(130)	219	(1,087)	(545)
Accounts payable	2,245	(3)	362	699	319
Other liabilities	122	2,817	1,257	1,814	2,294
Net cash provided from operating activities	9,274	10,111	9,273	8,865	10,275
Cash flow from investing activities					
Payments for plant, rental machines, and other property	(5,616)	(5,959)	(6,520)	(6,793)	(6,599)
Proceeds from disposition of plant, rental machines, and other property	1,619	1,207	905	1,130	1,314
Investment in software	(565)	(464)	(250)	(314)	(295)
Purchases of marketable securities and other investments	(1,079)	(3,949)	(4,211)	(1,617)	(1,613)
Proceeds from marketable securities and other investments	1,393	2,616	3,945	1,439	1,470
Proceeds from sale of the Global Network		4,880			
Net cash used in investing activities	$(4,248)	$(1,669)	$(6,131)	$(6,155)	$(5,723)

EXTRACTS FROM FOOTNOTES (FOR 1999)

D. Acquisitions/Divestitures

In December 1998, the company announced that it would sell its Global Network business to AT&T. During 1999, the company completed the sale to AT&T for $4,991 million. More than 5,300 IBM employees joined AT&T as a result of these sales of operations in 71 countries. The company recognized a pretax gain of $4,057 million ($2,495 million after tax, or $1.33 per diluted common share). The net gain reflects dispositions of plant, rental machines, and other property of $410 million, other assets of $182 million, and contractual obligations of $342 million.

M. Other Liabilities

Other liabilities (of $11,928 million in 1999) principally comprises accruals for nonpension postretirement benefits for U.S. employees ($6,392 million) and nonpension postretirement benefits, indemnity, and retirement plan reserves for non-U.S. employees ($1,028 million).

Also included in other liabilities are noncurrent liabilities associated with infrastructure reduction and restructuring actions taken through 1993. Other liabilities includes $659 million for postemployment preretirement accruals and $503 million (net of sublease receipts) for accruals for leased space that the company vacated.

P. Taxes

The significant components of activities that gave rise to deferred tax assets and liabilities that are recorded on the balance sheet were as follows:

Deferred Tax Assets (dollars in millions)

At December 31:	1999	1998	1997
Employee benefits	$ 3,737	$ 3,909	$ 3,707
Alternative minimum tax credits	1,244	1,169	1,092
Bad debt, inventory, and warranty reserves	1,093	1,249	1,027
Infrastructure reduction charges	918	863	1,163
Capitalized research and development	880	913	1,196
Deferred income	870	686	893
General business credits	605	555	492
Foreign tax loss carryforwards	406	304	202
Equity alliances	377	387	378
Depreciation	326	201	132
State and local tax loss carryforwards	227	212	203
Intracompany sales and services	153	182	235
Other	2,763	2,614	2,507
Gross deferred tax assets	13,599	13,244	13,227
Less: Valuation allowance	647	488	2,163
Net deferred tax assets	$12,952	$12,756	$11,064

Deferred Tax Liabilities (dollars in millions)

At December 31:	1999	1998	1997
Retirement benefits	$3,092	$2,775	$2,147
Sales-type leases	2,914	3,433	3,147
Depreciation	1,237	1,505	1,556
Software cost deferred	250	287	420
Other	2,058	1,841	1,413
Gross deferred tax liabilities	$9,551	$9,841	$8,683

The valuation allowance at December 31, 1999, principally applies to certain state and local and foreign tax loss carryforwards that, in the opinion of management, are more likely than not to expire before the company can use them.

As part of implementing its global strategies involving the relocation of certain of its manufacturing operations, the company transferred certain intellectual property rights to several non-U.S. subsidiaries in December 1998. Since these strategies, including this transfer, result in the anticipated utilization of U.S. federal tax credit carryforwards, the company reduced the valuation allowance from that previously required. The valuation allowance at December 31, 1998, principally applies to certain state and local and foreign tax loss carryforwards that, in the opinion of management, are more likely than not to expire before the company can utilize them.

A reconciliation of the company's effective tax rate to the statutory U.S. federal tax rate is as follows:

At December 31:	1999	1998	1997
Statutory rate	35%	35%	35%
Foreign tax differential	(2)	(6)	(3)
State and local	1	1	1
Valuation allowance related items		(1)	
Other		1	
Effective rate	34%	30%	33%

For tax return purposes, the company has available tax credit carryforwards of approximately $1,919 million, of which $1,244 million have an indefinite carryforward period, $199 million expire in 2004 and the remainder thereafter. The company also has state and local and foreign tax loss carryforwards, the tax effect of which is $633 million. Most of these carryforwards are available for 10 years or have an indefinite carryforward period.

Q. Selling and Advertising
Selling and advertising expense is charged against income as incurred. Advertising expense, which includes media, agency, and promotional expenses, was $1,758 million, $1,681 million, and $1,708 million in 1999, 1998, and 1997, respectively.

S. Research, Development, and Engineering
Research, development, and engineering expense was $5,273 million in 1999, $5,046 million in 1998, and $4,877 million in 1997. Expenses for product-related engineering included in these amounts were $698 million, $580 million, and $570 million in 1999, 1998, and 1997, respectively.

The company had expenses of $4,575 million in 1999, $4,466 million in 1998, and $4,307 million in 1997 for basic scientific research and the application of scientific advances to the development of new and improved products and their uses. Of these amounts, software-related expenses were $2,036 million, $2,086 million, and $2,016 million in 1999, 1998, and 1997, respectively. Included in the expense each year are charges for acquired in-process research and development.

W. Retirement Plans

Cost of the Defined Benefit Plans (dollars in millions)

	2000	1999	1998	1997	1996
Service cost	$ 1,008	$1,041	$ 931	$ 763	$ 796
Interest cost	3,787	3,686	3,474	3,397	3,427
Expected return on plan assets	(5,944)	(5,400)	(4,862)	(4,364)	(4,186)
Net amortization of unrecognized net actuarial gains, net transition asset, and prior service costs	(117)	(126)	(93)	(173)	(196)
Net periodic pension (benefit) cost	$(1,266)	$ (799)	$ (550)	(377)	$ (159)
Expected return on plan assets	10.0%	9.5%	9.5%	9.5%	9.25%
Discount rate for liability	7.25%	7.75%	6.5%	7.0%	7.75%

Real World Connection
See how leverage also contributed to IBM's earnings-per-share growth in Chapter 13.

Part **Three**

Forecasting and Valuation Analysis

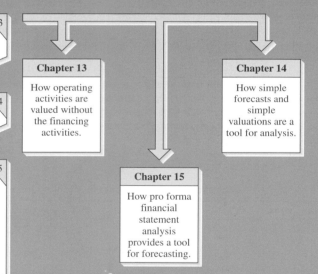

Knowing the business 1
• The products
• The knowledge base
• The competition
• The regulatory constraints

⬇ Strategy

Analyzing information 2
• In financial statements
• Outside of financial statements

Forecasting payoffs 3
• Specifying payoffs
• Forecasting payoffs

Converting forecasts to a valuation 4

Trading on the valuation 5

Outside investor:
    Compare value with price to *buy*, *sell*, or *hold*

Inside investor:
    Compare value with cost to *accept* or *reject* strategy

Chapter 13

How operating activities are valued without the financing activities.

Chapter 14

How simple forecasts and simple valuations are a tool for analysis.

Chapter 15

How pro forma financial statement analysis provides a tool for forecasting.

Part Two of the book analyzed financial statements in preparation for forecasting. This part of the book does the forecasting that leads to a valuation of the firm, its equity, and its strategies. It covers Step 3 of fundamental analysis.

The forecasting is developed gradually to enable you to see the building blocks clearly. And it is done with an eye to discovering simple forecasting schemes that make the task easier. Chapter 13 begins by showing that forecasting can be simplified by ignoring the financing activities if net financial obligations are measured on the balance sheet at market value. This has considerable practical advantages besides simplifying the forecasting: If financial leverage can be ignored, the analyst does not have to be concerned with continual changes in the equity cost of capital caused by changes in leverage. He need only focus on the operations and the risk of operations. And that focus leads him to evaluate price-to-book ratios and price-earnings ratios for the operations rather than for the equity.

The analyst looks for good, quick approximations before doing a lot of work. Chapter 14 lays out a scheme for making simple forecasts based only on the analysis of the operating activities in the current financial statements. These simple forecasts lead to simple valuations that usually are only approximate, although, with little effort, they are often a good first cut at the valuation. These simple forecasts and simple valuations are also useful analytical devices for asking "what-if" questions, employing reverse engineering, and prompting the analyst to find the broader information that leads to a better forecast and a sound valuation.

Chapter 15 develops a comprehensive scheme for forecasting, valuation, and strategy analysis utilizing the analyst's complete knowledge of the business. The building blocks of a forecast are laid out in the form of a template that can be incorporated in a standard spreadsheet analysis.

The financial statement analysis in Part Two of the book establishes where the firm is currently. Forecasting involves preparing pro forma financial statements to indicate where the firm will be in the future. The forecasting question is: How will the drivers of residual earnings and earnings growth differ in the future from their current levels?

The Value of Operations and the Evaluation of Enterprise Price-to-Book Ratios and Price-Earnings Ratios

LINKS

Link to previous chapter

Part Two of the book showed how to analyze the operating and financing activities of a firm and the profitability and growth they generate.

This chapter

This chapter develops valuations based only on operating profitability and growth and shows how to calculate intrinsic price-to-book ratios and price-earnings ratios for operations.

Link to next chapter

Chapter 14 will develop simple forecasting and valuation methods based on the valuation models for operations in this chapter.

Link to web page

Apply the methods of this chapter to valuing the operations of firms—visit the text website at www.mhhe.com/penman2e.

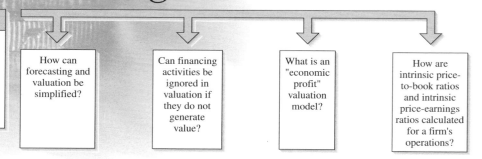

| How can forecasting and valuation be simplified? | Can financing activities be ignored in valuation if they do not generate value? | What is an "economic profit" valuation model? | How are intrinsic price-to-book ratios and intrinsic price-earnings ratios calculated for a firm's operations? |

The residual earnings model of Chapter 5 and the abnormal earnings growth model of Chapter 6 give us two ways to value equities from the financial statements: Price book values or price earnings. The analysis of financial statements in Part Two of the book provides an understanding of what drives residual earnings and earnings growth. We are now in a position to apply the analysis tools of Part Two to develop valuations using residual earnings and abnormal earnings growth methods.

With valuation in mind we want to forecast the aspects of the business that generate value. In Part Two of the book we took pains to distinguish operating activities from financing activities with the understanding that it is operations that generate value. This chapter shows how this distinction is incorporated in developing forecasts for valuation. It shows that if net financial obligations are measured in the balance sheet at market value, financing activities can be ignored in forecasting. You will see that this makes forecasting easier. In particular, complications that arise from the effect of leverage on residual earnings, abnormal earnings growth, and the cost of capital can be ignored. The simplification leads to a focus on income from operations rather than earnings that in-

The Analyst's Checklist

After reading this chapter you should understand:

- How, for an asset at market value on the balance sheet, expected residual income in the future must be zero.

- How a valuation based on forecasting residual income from operations differs from a residual earnings (RE) valuation based on forecasting full comprehensive income.

- Why forecasted residual income (or expense) on financial assets and liabilities is typically zero.

- How return on net operating assets and growth in net operating assets are the two drivers of residual operating income.

- How a valuation based on forecasting abnormal operating income growth differs from an abnormal earning growth (AEG) valuation.

- How the required return for operations and the required return for equity are related.

- How the required return for equity can be broken down into an operating risk premium and a financing risk premium.

- How financial leverage affects ROCE, earnings growth, and the required return for equity.

- How financial leverage affects a valuation.

- Why earnings growth that is created by leverage should not be valued.

- The difference between enterprise (unlevered) price multiples and levered multiples.

After reading this chapter you should be able to:

- Calculate residual operating income.

- Calculate abnormal operating income growth.

- Value a firm using the residual operating income model and the abnormal operating income growth model.

- Identify the drivers of residual operating income.

- Use reformulated balance sheets to value the financing activities of a business.

- Analyze the effect of a change in financial leverage on the value of a firm.

- Analyze the effect of financial leverage on ROCE, earnings growth, equity cost of capital, and P/B and P/E ratios.

- Calculate a weighted-average cost of capital using market values for debt and equity.

- Calculate the cost of capital for equity from the cost of capital for operations and the cost of debt.

- Explain the difference between a levered and unlevered price-to-book ratio.

- Explain the difference between a levered an unlevered price-earnings ratio.

- Calculate an unlevered P/E ratio using the abnormal operating income growth model.

- Reconcile levered and unlevered multiples.

- Calculate an unlevered price-to-book ratio using the residual operating income model.

cludes financing income and expense, and to a focus on net operating assets rather than common equity in the balance sheet.

The focus on operations brings a focus to *enterprise* or *unlevered* price-to-book ratios and price-earnings ratios rather than the more conventional *levered* ratios. If the financial assets and liabilities are measured at market value on the balance sheet, they do not contribute to the premium over book value. Rather it is the net operating assets that determine the premium. So an (enterprise) price-to-book ratio that reflects the pricing of the net operating assets gives a better measure of the omitted value in the balance sheet and of the value that, once calculated and added to book value, gives the value of the firm. Similarly, as value generating growth comes from the operating activities, an (enterprise) price-earnings ratio that prices operating income gives a better indication of the ability of a firm to add value through earnings growth.

A MODIFICATION TO RESIDUAL EARNINGS FORECASTING: RESIDUAL OPERATING INCOME

Let's remind ourselves of the residual earnings model for valuing equity:

$$V_0^E = \text{CSE}_0 + \text{Present value of forecasted residual earnings} \qquad \textbf{(13.1)}$$

$$= \text{CSE}_0 + \frac{\text{RE}_1}{\rho_E} + \frac{\text{RE}_2}{\rho_E^2} + \frac{\text{RE}_3}{\rho_E^3} + \cdots$$

where

Residual earnings (RE) = Earnings − Required earnings on book value of equity

$$\text{RE}_t = \text{Earn}_t - (\rho_E - 1)\,\text{CSE}_{t-1}$$

This RE model instructs us to anchor the valuation of equity on the book value of equity, then add value for earnings forecasted in excess of the required earnings on book value, where the required rate of return is the cost of capital for equity, $\rho_E - 1$.

We understand from this model that, if an asset is forecasted to earn at its required rate of return, forecasted residual earnings will be zero and the asset will be worth its book value. Correspondingly, if the book value of an asset is equal to its intrinsic value, then the residual earnings that it is expected to yield will be zero. We can make use of these properties in valuing equities even though the book value of equity is not equal to its value. If some assets are measured in the balance sheet at market value and if market value equals intrinsic value, then we know we don't have to forecast the residual earnings that they will produce; their forecasted residual earnings are zero. We only have to forecast residual earnings from assets not at market value. Accordingly, we can calculate the value of equity as

$$V_0^E = \text{CSE}_0 + \text{Present value of forecasted residual earnings from net assets not at}$$
market value

To carry out this valuation we have to be able to distinguish the earnings from assets or liabilities at market value from those that are not. The income from operating assets is usually earned by using assets jointly, which makes it difficult to identify the income from the separate assets. However, we have seen that we can usually separate operating income (generated by the net operating assets) from net financial expense (generated by the net financial obligations). And, net financial obligations are typically measured on the balance sheet at market value.

The two components of earnings identified by the reformulation of financial statements in Part Two of the book are listed in Table 13.1 along with the balance sheet component that generates them. Beside each component is the corresponding residual earnings measure. To get the residual earnings measure, each income component is matched with the corresponding balance sheet component and charged with the required earnings rate (the cost of capital) for the component. We will discuss the cost of capital in the next section but for now recognize that the required return for the different sources of income depends on the riskiness of that activity. Note that ρ_D is 1 plus the cost of capital for net debt (or, as it may be, the required return on net financial assets), and ρ_F is 1 plus the cost of capital for operating activities. In all cases the residual earnings is earnings in excess of the earnings (or expense) required for the asset (or liability) in the balance sheet to be earning at the relevant cost of capital.

TABLE 13.1
Components of Earnings and Book Value, and Corresponding Residual Earnings Measures

Earnings Component	Book Value Component	Residual Earnings Measure
Operating income (OI)	Net operating assets (NOA)	Residual operating income: $OI_t - (\rho_F - 1)\,NOA_{t-1}$
Net financial expense (NFE)	Net financial obligations (NFO)	Residual net financial expense: $NFE_t - (\rho_D - 1)\,NFO_{t-1}$
Earnings	Common stockholders' equity (CSE)	Residual earnings: $Earn_1 - (\rho_E - 1)\,CSE_{t-1}$

Residual earnings from net operating assets is *residual operating income,* and we will refer to it as ReOI:

$$\text{Residual operating income} = \text{Operating income (after tax)}$$
$$- \text{Required income on net operating assets}$$

$$ReOI_t = OI_t - (\rho_F - 1)NOA_{t-1}$$

Residual operating income charges the operating income with a charge for using the net operating assets. Residual operating income is also referred to as "economic profit" or "economic value added," and some consulting firms have taken these terms as trademarks for their valuation products. Residual earnings from the net financial obligations is *residual net financial expense,* $ReNFE = NFE_t - (\rho_D - 1)NFO_{t-1}$, or, if the firm has net financial assets, *residual net financial income.* Thus residual net financial expense is net financial expense less the required expense for the net debt. Box 13.1 gives forecasts of 1997 ReOI and ReNFE for Nike and Reebok, whose 1996 statements we analyzed in the last chapter. Analysts were forecasting $4.50 and $2.56 per-share earnings, respectively, for the two firms just after the end of their 1996 fiscal years. The box summarizes the 1996 balance sheets, breaks the 1997 forecasts down into operating and financial components, and calculates the 1997 forecasted residual earnings corresponding to each component by charging the forecast with a required amount based on the relevant 1996 balance sheet amount.

With forecasts of ReOI and ReNFE, we can value the NOA and NFO. The *value of the net financial obligations,* V_0^{NFO}, that mature at some time T in the future is

Value of NFO = NFO + Present value of expected residual net financial expense

$$V_0^{NFO} = NFO + \frac{ReNFE_1}{\rho_D} + \frac{ReNFE_2}{\rho_D^2} + \frac{ReNFE_3}{\rho_D^3} + \cdots + \frac{ReNFE_T}{\rho_D^T} \qquad \textbf{(13.2)}$$

We saw this valuation of debt in Chapter 5. If the NFO are measured at market value, it must be that forecasted ReNFE is zero (as for Nike and Reebok in Box 13.1, but so for all years in the future). Then $V_0^{NFO} = NFO$. The book value of the net financial obligations is their value. The *value of the net operating assets,* V_0^{NOA}, for a going concern is

Value of operations = Net operating assets + Present value of expected residual operating income

$$V_0^{NOA} = NOA_0 + \frac{ReOI_1}{\rho_F} + \frac{ReOI_2}{\rho_F^2} + \frac{ReOI_3}{\rho_F^3} + \cdots + \qquad \textbf{(13.3)}$$
$$\frac{ReOI_T}{\rho_F^T} + \frac{CV_T}{\rho_F^T}$$

Amounts in millions except per-share numbers	Nike	Reebok
Base data for 1996		
Net operating assets (NOA)	2,659	1,135
Net financial obligations (NFO)	228	720
Total equity	2,431	415
Minority interest		34
Common stockholders' equity (CSE)	2,431	381
Forecasts by analysts for 1997		
Analysts' consensus eps forecast	4.50	2.56
Shares outstanding	144	56
Analysts' earnings forecast	648	143
Analysts' implicit operating income (OI) forecast	656	187
Net financial expense (NFE) forecast:	(8)	(29)
NFO × Core net borrowing cost (NBC)		
Minority interest in earnings		(15)
Earnings forecast	648	143
Calculation of residual earnings measures		
Residual operating income (ReOI) forecast		
Nike: 656 − (0.110 × 2,659)	364	
Reebok: 187 − (0.101 × 1,135)		72
Residual net financial expense (ReNFE) forecast		
Nike: 8 − (0.035 × 228)	0	
Reebok: 29 − (0.040 × 720)		0

All forecasts are after tax. The cost of capital for operations is assumed to be 11.0 percent for Nike and 10.1 percent for Reebok (see later). Core net borrowing cost (after tax), core NBC, established from footnotes, is 3.5 percent for Nike and 4.0 percent for Reebok. The NFE forecast assumes that the book value of the NFO is at market value. This is reasonable. Financial assets are at fair (market) value under FASB Statement No. 115. Much of Reebok's debt is new debt (issued at market rates) and, with respect to the older debt, interest rates did not change much. Indeed fair-value disclosures in footnotes indicate that the book value of debt is close to fair value for both companies. Minority interest share of Reebok's income is forecasted to be the same as in 1996. (Allow for rounding error in proofing some of the calculations here.)

Analysts' implicit operating income forecast is their earnings forecast plus the NFE forecast and forecast of minority interest share of operating income. The zero residual net financial expense forecast follows from NFO being at market value on the balance sheet.

That is, the value is the book value of the NOA, plus the present value of expected residual operating income from these assets to a forecast horizon, plus a continuing value that is the value of expected residual operating income after the horizon. This model is the same form as the residual income model but applies to the net operating assets instead of the common shareholders' equity. Box 13.2 shows how the expected residual operating income beyond the forecast horizon can be captured in a continuing value.

The value of the operations is also called the *value of the firm.* It is also sometimes referred to as **enterprise value**. The value of the equity is $V_0^E = V_0^{NOA} - V_0^{NFO}$. So if the NFO are measured at market value on the balance sheet—that is, expected residual net financial expenses (ReNFE) are zero—then (recognizing that NOA − NFO = CSE) the value of the equity is

Continuing values summarize the analyst's expectation of a firm's performance beyond a forecast horizon. Continuing values can be calculated at a point where the analyst forecasts that performance will follow a regular pattern.

Corresponding to the three cases for the residual earnings model in Chapter 5 the continuing value for the residual operating income model can take three forms:

In Case 1 we expect residual operating income (ReOI) to be zero after the forecast horizon because we expect the net operating assets to earn at the cost of capital. In Case 2 we expect ReOI to be at a constant, permanent level, and in Case 3 we expect ReOI to grow perpetually at the rate g. The analyst's task, then, is to forecast the level and growth of residual operating income at the forecast horizon.

Case 1: $\quad CV_T = 0$

Case 2: $\quad CV_T = \dfrac{ReOI_{T+1}}{\rho_F - 1}$

Case 3: $\quad CV_T = \dfrac{ReOI_{T+1}}{\rho_F - g}$

$$\text{Value of common equity} = \text{Book value of common equity} \qquad \textbf{(13.4)}$$
$$+ \text{ Present value of expected residual}$$
$$\text{operating income}$$

$$V_0^E = CSE_0 + \frac{ReOI_1}{\rho_F} + \frac{ReOI_2}{\rho_F^2} + \frac{ReOI_3}{\rho_F^3} + \cdots + \frac{ReOI_T}{\rho_F^T} + \frac{CV_T}{\rho_F^T}$$

This model is the *residual operating income model.* Table 13.2 values Reebok using the model.

We saw in Box 13.1 that analysts' 1997 earnings forecasts for Reebok implied an operating income forecast of $187 million. This is an RNOA of 16.48 percent on 1996 net operating assets. The forecast of subsequent operating income applies this RNOA to net operating assets that are forecasted to grow at 7 percent per year. Accordingly, residual operating income is expected to grow at 7 percent per year. The continuing value calculation is based on a 7 percent growth rate also, giving a value per share of $45.52. Reebok traded in the range of $42 to $46 per share just after the end of 1996, so we have effectively modeled the forecast scenario for operations that is implicit in the market price (and might ask whether this scenario is reasonable): The market sees Reebok earning an RNOA of approximately 16.5 percent in the future, with ReOI growing 7 percent per year.

The residual operating income model makes sense. If debt and financial assets are zero residual earnings producers, then they add no value to their recorded value. We are going to get the valuation by forecasting the profitability of the operations that do add value. The model makes the forecasting task easier, too. It requires us to forecast operating income and net operating assets but we can forget about forecasting net financial expenses and net financial obligations. Of course if financial items are not measured at market value, the RE model in equation (13.1) must be used. But if the market value of these items is available, we can substitute the market value for the book value and proceed with ReOI valuation. In the United States, fair values of financial items can be

LIVERPOOL JOHN MOORES UNIVERSITY
Aldham Roberts L.R.C.
TEL 0151 231 3701/3634

TABLE 13.2 Residual Operating Income Valuation for Reebok International Ltd.
Required return for operations is 10.1%.

(Amounts in millions of dollars except per-share numbers)					
	1996A	**1997E**	**1998E**	**1999E**	**2000E**
Operating income (OI)		187.00	200.09	214.10	229.08
Net operating assets (NOA)	1,135	1,214.45	1,299.46	1,390.42	1,487.75
RNOA (%)		16.48	16.48	16.48	16.48
Residual operating income (ReOI)		72.37	77.48	82.90	88.71
Discount rate (1.101^t)		1.101	1.212	1.335	1.469
PV of ReOI		65.73	63.91	62.12	60.37
Total PV of ReOI	253				
Continuing value (CV)					3,061.93
PV of CV	2,084				
Value of NOA	3,472				
Book value of NFO	720				
Value of equity	2,752				
Value of minority interest	210				
Value of common equity	2,542				
Value per share (on 55.840 million shares)	$45.52				

The continuing value calculation:

$$CV = \frac{88.71 \times 1.07}{1.101 - 1.07} = 3,061.93$$

$$PV \text{ of } CV = \frac{3,061.93}{1.469} = 2,084.36$$

Value of minority interest is estimated as 14 times minority interest earnings.
Residual operating income (ReOI) is $OI_t - (\rho_F - 1)NOA_{t-1}$. So, for 1997,
ReOI = $187.00 - (0.101 \times 1,135) = 72.37$.

Allow for rounding errors.

found in statement footnotes. If the financial reporting is such that operating and financing activities cannot be separated, the RE model must be used.

Remember that for financial institutions, apparent interest-bearing financial assets and liabilities are really operating assets and liabilities. These firms make profits from financial assets and liabilities. The market value of these assets and liabilities might reflect the value of their operating assets, but they might not reflect the value in use to a particular firm. The analyst must explore how the firm makes money from financial items and forecast the residual operating income from them.

A final caveat: The market value of assets and liabilities on the balance sheet can be taken as their fair value only if the market value is an efficient one. See Box 13.3.

The Drivers of Residual Operating Income

We saw in Chapter 5 that residual earnings can be broken down into two components:

$$\text{Residual earnings} = (\text{ROCE} - \text{Required return for equity}) \times \text{Common equity}$$

$$RE_t = [ROCE_t - (\rho_E - 1)] \, CSE_{t-1}$$

$$\text{(1)} \qquad\qquad \text{(2)}$$

Equity investments that involve less than 20 percent ownership and are "available for sale" are carried on the balance sheet at market value. Market values are also given in the footnotes for "held-to-maturity" equity investments that are carried at cost on the balance sheet.

Microsoft Corporation held the following equity investments on its 1999 balance sheet:

Equity Securities (in millions of dollars)	Cost	Gains Recognized	Market Value
At market value on the balance sheet			
Comcast Corporation—			
common stock	$ 500	$1,394	$ 1,894
MCI Worldcom, Inc.—			
common stock	14	1,088	1,102
Other	849	1,102	1,951
Unrealized hedge loss		(785)	(785)
At cost on the balance			
sheet	3,845	—	6,100
	$5,208		$10,262

The analyst might accept the market values of these equity investments as their values. This considerably eases the valuation.

But what if these securities were mispriced in the market? The price of Microsoft's investments had risen significantly over cost. They were investments in "hot" technology and telecommunications stocks during a bubble. If shares of Microsoft—a technology company—were overpriced, might not the shares of other technology companies also be overpriced? So basing Microsoft's intrinsic value on the market price of these stocks might give the wrong impression. Indeed, we observed subsequent losses on these investments in Microsoft's reformulated income statements for 2001 and 2002 (in Exhibit 9.10 in Chapter 9).

These considerations require the analyst to investigate the value behind the market values of equities. Just as the analyst queries the market price of Microsoft through fundamental analysis, he also queries the price of Microsoft's equity investments through fundamental analysis of those investments.

We referred to the two components, ROCE and book values, as residual earnings drivers: RE is driven by the amount of shareholders' investment and the rate of return on this investment relative to the cost of equity capital. Residual operating income can similarly be broken down into two components:

$$\text{Residual operating income} = (\text{RNOA} - \text{Required return for operations}) \times \text{Net operating assets}$$

$$\text{ReOI}_t = [\text{RNOA}_t - (\rho_F - 1)]\,\text{NOA}_{t-1}$$

$$\text{(1)} \qquad\qquad \text{(2)}$$

The two components of ReOI are RNOA and net operating assets and we refer to these as *residual operating income drivers:* ReOI is driven by the amount of net operating assets put in place and the profitability of those assets relative to the cost of capital. The implied analysts' forecast of $364 million for Nike's 1997 residual operating income in Box 13.1 is a forecast of 1997 RNOA of 24.7 percent applied, after subtracting the cost of capital of 11.0 percent, to $2,659 million of net operating assets in place at the end of 1996: $(24.7\% - 11.0\%) \times 2,659 = 364$. The valuation of Reebok in Table 13.2 involved a forecast of a constant RNOA of 16.48 percent and future NOA growing at 7 percent per year. So, because RNOA was forecasted to be constant, forecasted ReOI growth is driven solely by growth in net operating assets.

Residual net financial expense (or income) also can be broken down into two drivers:

$$\text{Residual net financial expense} = (\text{Net borrowing cost} - \text{Cost of net debt}) \times \text{Net debt}$$

$$\text{ReNFE}_t = [\text{NBC}_t - (\rho_D - 1)]\,\text{NFO}_{t-1}$$

So ReNFE is driven by the amount of net financial debt and the net borrowing cost relative to the cost of debt. For a firm that issues debt for financing, expected borrowing costs are equal to the cost of the debt. So no matter how much debt is put in place, no value is added through the two drivers, and expected ReNFE is zero.

Rather, value is added to book value through the operations, and our breakdown tells us that this is done by earning an RNOA that is greater than the cost of capital for operations and by putting investments in place to earn at this rate. Accordingly, forecasting involves forecasting the two drivers, future RNOA and future NOA. We will see how these forecasts are developed in the next two chapters.

A MODIFICATION TO ABNORMAL EARNINGS GROWTH FORECASTING: ABNORMAL GROWTH IN OPERATING INCOME

Let us remind ourselves of the abnormal earnings growth model for valuing equity:

$$V_0^E = \text{Capitalized [Forward earnings + Present value of abnormal earnings growth]}$$

$$= \frac{1}{\rho_E - 1}\left[\text{Earn}_1 + \frac{\text{AEG}_2}{\rho_E} + \frac{\text{AEG}_3}{\rho_E^2} + \frac{\text{AEG}_4}{\rho_E^3} + \cdots\right] \qquad \textbf{(13.5)}$$

where

$$\text{Abnormal earnings growth}_t \ (\text{AEG}) = \text{Cum-dividend earnings}_t - \text{Normal earnings}_t$$

$$= [\text{Earnings}_t + (\rho_E - 1)d_{t-1}] - \rho_E\text{Earnings}_{t-1}$$

$$= [G_t - \rho_E] \times \text{Earnings}_{t-1}$$

where G_t is the cum-dividend earnings growth rate for the period. The AEG model instructs us to forecast forward (one-year ahead) earnings, then add value for subsequent cum-dividend earnings forecasted in excess of earnings growing at the required rate of return for equity. Forecasted earnings include earnings from reinvesting dividends, for a firm delivers two sources of earnings, one from earnings within the firm and the other from earnings that can be earned from reinvesting dividends paid by the firm. We understand from this model that earnings growth in itself does not add value, only abnormal growth over the required growth. If abnormal earnings growth is expected to be zero, the equity will be worth just the capitalized value of its forward earnings.

Consider now where abnormal growth comes from. Growth does not come from financing activities. To see this, refer back to the prototype savings account in Chapter 6 where abnormal earnings growth is always zero. Debt investments and debt obligations work just like a savings account: Debt is always expected to earn (or incur expenses) at the required return on the debt so, adjusting for any cash paid on the debt (the "dividend" from debt), net financial expense can grow only at a rate equal to the required return. To see it another way, we have just recognized that, if the net financial obligations are at market value on the balance sheet, residual income from the financing activities (ReNFE) is expected to be zero. So the change in residual income, period-to-period, is also expected to be zero, and abnormal earnings growth is always equal to the change in residual income.

Abnormal earnings growth is generated by operations. This makes sense for, once again, it is the operations that add value. As the financing activities do not contribute to growth over the required return, we focus on abnormal growth in operating income.

Abnormal Growth in Operating Income and the "Dividend" from Operating Activities

When introducing earnings growth in Chapter 6, we recognized that growth in (ex-dividend) earnings—the growth that analysts typically forecast—is not the growth that we should focus on. Earnings growth rates will be lower the more dividends are paid, but dividends can be reinvested to earn more, adding to growth. So any analysis of growth must focus on cum-dividend earnings growth. In focusing on growth in the operating income component of earnings, we also must not make the mistake of focusing on growth in operating income if cash that otherwise could be reinvested in operations is paid out of the operations. Dividends are net cash payments to shareholders out of earnings (that they can reinvest). What is the cash paid out of operations (that can be reinvested elsewhere)? What are the "dividends" from the operating activities?

Our depiction of business activities in Chapter 7 supplies the answer to this question. Look at Figure 7.3, which summarizes business activities, and Figure 7.4, which summarizes how those activities are represented in reformulated financial statements. Net dividends, d, are the dividends from the financing activities to the shareholders. Net payments to bondholders and debt issuers, F, are the "dividends" from the financing activities to these claimants. But the "dividend" from the operating activities to the financing activities is the free cash flow. Business works as follows: Operations pay a dividend to the financing activities—in the form of free cash flow—and the financing activities apply this cash to pay dividends to the outside claimants. Indeed, the reformulated cash flow statement is a statement that reports the cash dividend from the operating activities (free cash flow) and how that dividend is divided among cash to debtholders and cash to shareholders in the financing activities: $C - I = d + F$.

Accordingly, *abnormal operating income growth* is calculated as:

Abnormal operating income growth$_t$ (AOIG)

$$= \text{Cum-dividend operating income}_t - \text{Normal operating income}_t$$

$$= [\text{Operating income}_t + (\rho_F - 1)\text{FCF}_{t-1}] - \rho_F \text{ Operating income}_{t-1}$$

where free cash flow (FCF) is, of course, cash from operations minus cash investment $(C - I)$. Compare this measure to abnormal earnings growth (AEG) above. Operating income is substituted for earnings and free cash flow is substituted for dividends. And, as the income is from operations, the required return that defines normal growth is the required return for operations. A firm delivers abnormal operating income growth if growth in operating income—cum-dividend, after reinvesting free cash flow—is greater than the normal growth rate required for operations.

Just as AEG can be expressed in terms of cum-dividend growth rates relative to the required rate, so can abnormal operating income growth:

$$\text{Abnormal operating income growth}_t \text{ (AIOG)} = [G_t - \rho_F] \times \text{Operating income}_{t-1}$$

where G_t is now the cum-dividend operating income growth rate rather than earnings.

Table 13.3 lays out the abnormal earnings growth measures that correspond to the operating and financing components of earnings, in a similar way to the residual earnings breakdown in Table 13.1. A calculation for abnormal growth in net financial expense is included there, for completeness, but (like residual net financing expense) it is not a measure we will make use of because it is expected to be zero. (Note, for completeness, that the "dividend" for debt financing is the cash payment to debtholders, F.)

TABLE 13.3
Earnings
Components and
Corresponding
Abnormal Earnings
Growth Measures

Earnings Component	Abnormal Earnings Growth Measure
Operating income (OI)	Abnormal operating income growth: $[OI_t + (\rho_F - 1)FCF_{t-1}] - \rho_F OI_{t-1}$ $[G_t - \rho_F] \times OI_{t-1}$
Net financing expense (NFE)	Abnormal net financial expense growth: $[NFE_t + (\rho_D - 1)F_{t-1}] - \rho_D NFE_{t-1}$
Earnings	Abnormal earnings growth: $[Earn_t + (\rho_E - 1)d_{t-1}] - \rho_E Earn_{t-1}$ $[G_t^F - \rho_E] \times Earn_{t-1}$

With an understanding of abnormal growth in operating income, we can lay out an *abnormal operating income growth model* to value the equity. Forecasting abnormal operating income growth yields the value of the operations, just as forecasting residual operating income yields the value of the operations. Subtracting the value of the net financial obligations yields the value of the equity and, if net financial obligations are measured at market value on the balance sheet, the book value suffices for their value. So,

Value of common equity = Capitalized [Forward operating income
+ Present value of abnormal operating
income growth] − Net financial obligations

$$V_0^E = \frac{1}{\rho_F - 1}\left[OI_1 + \frac{AOIG_2}{\rho_F} + \frac{AOIG_3}{\rho_F^2} + \frac{AOIG_4}{\rho_F^3} + \cdots \right]$$
$$- NFO_0$$

(13.6)

You see that this is the same form as the AEG model (equation 13.5) except that operating income is substituted for earnings, and the cost of capital for the operations is substituted for the equity cost of capital. Like the ReOI model, this AOIG model simplifies the valuation task, for we need only forecast operating income and can ignore the financing aspects of future earnings. As the model values the enterprise or the firm before deducting the net financial obligations, the model (like the ReOI model) is referred to as an *enterprise valuation model* or a *valuation model for the firm*.

Table 13.4 applies the model to valuing Reebok, as in Table 13.2. The layout is the same as that for the abnormal earnings growth valuations in Chapter 6. As with the ReOI model, operating income and net operating assets are forecasted, but the net operating asset forecasts are then applied to forecast free cash flows: $C - I = OI - \Delta NOA$, as in the Method 1 calculation in Chapter 10. Free cash flow does not have to be forecasted in addition to the other forecasts—it is calculated directly from those forecasts. Expected abnormal operating income growth is calculated from forecasts of operating income and free cash flow, as described at the bottom of the table, and those forecasts are converted to a valuation as prescribed by the model. Note that abnormal operating income growth is forecasted to grow at a 7 percent rate, as was ReOI in Table 13.2. Note also that, just as AEG is always equal to the change in residual earnings (RE), AOIG is equal to the change in ReOI in each period (in Table 13.2). The valuation is, of course, the same as that obtained using ReOI methods.

TABLE 13.4   **Abnormal Operating Income Growth Valuation for Reebok International Ltd.**

Required return for operations is 10.1%.

(Amounts in millions of dollars except per-share numbers)					
	1996A	**1997E**	**1998E**	**1999E**	**2000E**
Operating income (OI)		187.00	200.09	214.10	229.08
Net operating assets (NOA)	1,135	1,214.45	1,299.46	1,390.42	1,487.75
Free cash flow (C–I = OI – ΔNOA)		107.55	115.08	123.31	131.76
Income from reinvested free cash flow					
(at 10.1%)			10.86	11.62	12.45
Cum-dividend OI			210.95	225.72	241.53
Normal OI			205.89	220.30	235.72
Abnormal OI Growth (AOIG)			5.06	5.42	5.81
Discount rate			1.101	1.212	1.335
PV of AOIG			4.60	4.46	4.35
Total PV of AOIG		13.41			
Continuing value					200.88
PV of continuing value		150.22			
Forward OI for 1997		187.00			
		350.63			
Capitalization rate		0.101			
Value of operations	3,472	↵			
Book value of NFO	720				
Value of equity	2,752				
Value of minority interest	210				
Value of common equity	2,542				
Value per share (on 55.840 million shares)	45.52				
Cum-dividend growth rate in OI			12.81%	12.81%	12.81%

The continuing value calculation:

$$CV = \frac{5.81 \times 1.07}{1.101 - 1.07} = 200.54$$

$$PV \text{ of } CV = \frac{200.54}{1.335} = 150.22$$

Value of minority interest is estimated as 14 times minority interest earnings.

Income from reinvested free cash flow is the prior year's free cash flow earning at the required rate of return of 10.1 percent. So, for 1998, income from reinvested free cash flow is $0.101 \times 107.55 = 10.86$.

Cum-dividend OI is operating income plus income from reinvesting free cash flow. So, for 1998, cum-dividend OI is $200.09 + 10.86 = 210.95$.

Normal OI is the prior year's operating income growing at the required rate of return. So, for 1998, normal OI is $187.00 \times 1.101 = 205.89$.

Abnormal OI growth (AOIG) is cum-dividend OI minus normal OI. So, for 1998, AOIG is $210.95 - 205.89 = 5.06$. AOIG is also given by $OI_{t-1} \times (G_t - \rho_F)$. So, for 1998, AOIG is $(1.1281 - 1.101) \times 187.00 = 5.06$.

Allow for rounding errors.

THE COST OF CAPITAL AND VALUATION

Step 4 of fundamental analysis combines forecasts from Step 3 with the cost of capital to get a valuation. The preceding models have shown how this is done, but now we have encountered three costs of capital: the cost of capital for equity, ρ_E; the cost of capital for debt, ρ_D; and the cost of capital for operations, ρ_F. These need a little explanation. We will not calculate them here but note that this is done using the beta technologies discussed in the appendix to Chapter 3, which are covered in corporate finance texts. (We will discuss how fundamental risk affects the cost of capital in Chapter 18.) Here you should be sure you have a good appreciation of the concepts, because with this understanding, forecasting and valuation can be simplified. We will see that just as residual income can be broken down into operating and financing components, so can the equity cost of capital. And we will see how the financing element of the cost of equity capital can be ignored in valuation.

The Cost of Capital for Operations

Residual earnings is earnings for the equity holders and so is calculated and discounted using the cost of capital for equity, ρ_E. Residual operating income is earnings for the operations and so is calculated and discounted using a cost of capital for the operations, ρ_F. Payoffs must be discounted at a rate that reflects their risk and the risk for the operations may be different from the risk for equity. The risk in the operations is referred to as *operational risk* or *firm risk*. Operational risk arises from factors that may hurt operating profitability. The sensitivity of sales and operating expenses to recessions and other shocks determines the operating risk. Airlines have relatively high operating risk because people fly less during recessions and fuel costs are subject to shocks in oil prices. The required return that compensates for this risk is called the *cost of capital for operations* or the *cost of capital for the firm*. This is what we have labeled ρ_F (where F is for "firm").

If you have taken a corporate finance class, you are familiar with this concept. The cost of capital for operations is sometimes referred to as the *weighted-average cost of capital,* or *WACC,* because of the following relationship:

$$\text{Cost of capital for operations} = \text{Weighted-average of cost of equity} \qquad \textbf{(13.7)}$$
$$\text{and cost of net debt}$$

$$= \left(\frac{\text{Value of equity}}{\text{Value of operations}} \times \text{Equity cost of capital} \right)$$

$$+ \left(\frac{\text{Value of debt}}{\text{Value of operations}} \times \text{Debt cost of capital} \right)$$

$$\rho_F = \frac{V_0^E}{V_0^{\text{NOA}}} \cdot \rho_E + \frac{V_0^D}{V_0^{\text{NOA}}} \cdot \rho_D$$

That is, the required return to invest in operations is a weighted average of the required return of the shareholders and the cost of net financial debt, and the weights are given by the relative values of the equity and debt in the value of the firm. See Box 13.4 for the calculations for Nike and Reebok.

The Cost of Capital for Debt

The cost of capital for debt is a weighted average of all components of net financial obligations, including preferred stock and financial assets. It is typically referred to as the

Beta services were reporting a capital asset pricing model (CAPM) stock beta of 0.95 for Nike and 1.10 for Reebok in 1996. The risk-free T-bill rate was 5.4 percent. Using a market risk premium of 6 percent, these betas imply a CAPM cost of equity capital of 11.1 percent for Nike and 12.0 percent for Reebok. The following are market values for the two firms at the end of their 1996 fiscal years (in millions of dollars):

	Nike	Reebok
Market value of equity	14,950	2,352
Net financial obligations	228	720
Market value of net operating assets	15,178	3,072

The book values of the NFO are deemed to be market value. The cost of capital for operations (the weighted-average cost of capital, WACC) is

Nike: $\left(\dfrac{14,950}{15,178} \times 11.1\% \right) + \left(\dfrac{228}{15,178} \times 3.5\% \right) = 11.0\%$

Reebok: $\left(\dfrac{2,352}{3,072} \times 12.0\% \right) + \left(\dfrac{720}{3,072} \times 4.0\% \right) = 10.1\%$

The after-tax cost of debt was calculated from footnote information, as before. These costs of capital for operations were those used in Box 13.1 and, in the case of Reebok's valuation, Tables 13.2 and 13.4.

cost of capital for debt but is better thought of as the cost of capital for all net financial obligations.

In Chapter 9 we allocated income taxes to operating and financing components of the income statement to restate net financial expenses on an after-tax basis. So too must the cost of net debt be calculated on an after-tax basis. The calculation is

$$\text{After-tax cost of net debt } (\rho_D) = \text{Nominal cost of net debt} \times (1 - t)$$

where t is the marginal income tax rate we used in Chapter 9. Reebok indicates in its financial statement footnotes that its borrowing rate for the new debt issued in 1996 was about 6.75 percent per year. With a tax rate of 36 percent, this is an after-tax rate of 4.32 percent. The after-tax cost of debt is sometimes referred to as the **effective cost of debt**, just like NFE is the effective financial expense, because what the firm effectively pays in interest is not the nominal amount but that amount less the taxes saved. So when we use ρ_D to indicate the cost of debt, always remember that this is the effective cost of capital for net financial obligations.

As both NFE and the cost of debt are on an after-tax basis, so is residual net financial expense. If the NFO are carried at market value, then forecasted ReNFE will be zero.

Operating Risk, Financing Risk, and the Cost of Equity Capital

The calculation of the WACC in equation (13.7) is a bit misleading because it looks as if the cost of capital for operations is determined by the costs of debt and equity. Although the operations have their inherent risk, this depends on the riskiness of the business and not on how the business is financed. Thus a standard notion in finance—another Modigliani and Miller concept—states that the cost of capital for the firm is unaffected by the amount of debt or equity in the financing of the operational assets. Rather than the required return for operations being determined by the cost of capital for equity and debt, the return that equity and debt investors require is determined by the riskiness of the operations. The operations have their interest risk, and this is imposed on the equity holders and the debtholders. The way to think about it is to see the cost of equity determined by the following formula. This is just a rearrangement of the WACC calculation (equation 13.7), putting the equity cost of capital on the left-hand side rather than the cost of capital for operations:

Required return for equity = Required return for operations $\quad\quad$ **(13.8)**
$\quad\quad\quad\quad\quad\quad\quad\quad\quad$ + (Market leverage × Required return spread)

$$\rho_E = \rho_F + \frac{V_0^D}{V_0^E}(\rho_F - \rho_D)$$

$$\text{(1)} \quad\quad\quad \text{(2)}$$

For Reebok, the cost of equity capital is 10.1% + [720/2,352 × (10.1% − 4.0%)] = 12% (allow for rounding error); the calculation for Nike is similar. Just as the payoff to shareholders has two components, operating and financing, the required return to investing for those payoffs has two components, **operating risk** and **financing risk** components. Component **1** is the risk the operations impose on the shareholder, and the return this requires is the cost of capital for the operations. If the firm has no net debt, the cost of equity capital is equal to the cost of capital for the operations, that is, $\rho_E = \rho_F$. If Reebok had no net debt, the shareholders would require a return of 10.1 percent, according to the CAPM calculations. This is sometimes referred to as the case of the **pure equity firm**. But if there are financing activities, component **2** comes into play; this is the additional required return for equity due to financing risk. As you can see, this premium for financing risk depends on the amount of debt relative to equity (the financial leverage) and the spread between the cost of capital for operations and that for debt. This makes sense. Financing risk arises because of leverage and the possibility of that leverage turning unfavorable. Leverage is unfavorable when the return from operations is less than the cost of debt, so the equity is more risky the more debt there is and the riskier the operations are relative to the cost of debt. The CAPM required return for operations is lower for Reebok than for Nike. But the equity investors require a higher return for Reebok than for Nike because of Reebok's higher leverage. So the financing risk premium is 1.9 percent for Reebok (12% − 10.1%) and only 0.1 percent for Nike (11.1% − 11%).

The leverage here is measured with the values of the debt and equity; it is referred to as **market leverage** to distinguish it from the **book leverage** (FLEV) discussed in Chapter 11.

If the firm has net financial assets rather than net debt,

Cost of equity captial = Weighted-average of cost of capital for operations $\quad$ **(13.9)**
$\quad\quad\quad\quad\quad\quad\quad\quad$ and required return on net financial assets

$$\rho_E = \frac{V_0^{NOA}}{V_0^E} \cdot \rho_F + \frac{V_0^{NFA}}{V_0^E} \cdot \rho_{NFA}$$

where ρ_{NFA} is the required return (yield to maturity) on the net financial assets. As financial assets are typically less risky than operations, the cost of equity capital is typically less than the cost of capital for the operations in this case. As an exercise, express this in the form of equation 13.8.

Box 13.5 provides a warning about using cost of capital estimates in fundamental analysis.

A basic tenant of fundamental analysis (discussed in Chapter 2) dictates that the analyst should always be careful to distinguish what she knows from speculation about what she doesn't know. Fundamental analysis is done to challenge speculative stock prices, so it must avoid incorporating speculation in any calculation. Unfortunately, standard cost-of-capital measures are speculative, so they must be handled with care. The appendix to Chapter 3 explained that, despite the elegant asset pricing models at hand, we really do not have a sound method to estimate the cost of capital.

SPECULATION ABOUT THE EQUITY RISK PREMIUM

Cost of capital measures that use the capital asset pricing model—like those for Nike and Reebok in Box 13.4—require an estimate of the market risk premium. We used 6 percent for Nike and Reebok, but estimates range, in texts and academic research, from 3.0 percent to 9.2 percent. With such a range, Reebok's equity cost of capital (with a beta of 1.10) would range from 8.7 percent to 15.5 percent. For a firm with a higher beta, the range would be even larger.

The truth is that the equity risk premium is a guess; it is a speculative number. Add to this the uncertainty as to what the actual beta is, and we have a highly speculative number for the cost of capital. Building this speculative number into a valuation results in a speculative valuation.

USING SPECULATIVE PRICES IN WEIGHTED-AVERAGE COST OF CAPITAL CALCULATIONS

We have warned against incorporating (possibly speculative) stock prices in a valuation. Thus, we warned of speculative pension fund gains in earnings in Chapter 12 and, in this chapter in Box 13.3, we warned about relying on (possibly speculative) equity prices on the balance sheet.

The WACC calculation in equation (13.7) weights equity and debt costs of capital by their respective (intrinsic) values. The standard practice is to use market values instead of intrinsic values in the weighting, as in the Nike and Reebok calculations in Box 13.4. This is done under the assumption that market prices are efficient. But we carry out fundamental valuations to question whether market prices are indeed efficient. It we build in possibly inefficient prices into our calculation, we compromise our ability to challenge those prices.

Indeed, you can see that the WACC calculation in equation (13.7) is circular: We wish to estimate the cost of capital in order to estimate equity value, but the estimate requires that we know the equity value! We need methods to break this circularity—without reference to speculative market prices. We turn to this problem in Chapter 18.

As with all instances where we have uncertainty, we get a feel for how that uncertainty affects valuations with sensitivity analysis. Sensitivity analysis is a feature of the cost of capital analysis of Chapter 18, and also of the pro forma analysis that leads to valuation in Chapter 15.

FINANCING RISK AND RETURN AND THE VALUATION OF EQUITY

Leverage and Residual Earnings Valuation

You will have noticed that the expression for the required return for equity in equation (13.8) has a similar form to the expression for the drivers of ROCE in Chapter 11. Both formulas are below, so you can compare them:

$$\text{Return on common equity} = \text{Return on net operating assets} + (\text{Book leverage} \times \text{Operating spread})$$

$$\text{ROCE} = \text{RNOA} + \left[\frac{\text{NFO}}{\text{CSE}} \times (\text{RNOA} - \text{NBC}) \right]$$

$$\text{Required return for equity} = \text{Required return for operations} + (\text{Market leverage} \times \text{Required return spread})$$

$$\rho_E = \rho_F + \frac{V_0^D}{V_0^F}(\rho_F - \rho_D)$$

The equity return in both cases is driven by the return on operating activities plus a premium for financing activities, where the latter is given by the financial leverage and the spread. The only difference is that the second equation refers to required returns rather than accounting returns and the leverage is market leverage rather than book leverage.

The comparison is insightful. Leverage increases the ROCE (and thus residual earnings) if the spread is positive, as we saw in Chapter 11. This is the "good news" aspect of leverage. But at the same time leverage increases the required return to equity because of the increased risk of getting a lower ROCE if the spread turns negative. This is the "bad news" aspect of leverage. "More risk, more return" is an old adage that you can see at work here. And you can see it at work in the RE valuation model: Equity value is based on forecasted RE and the rate at which RE is discounted to present value. The ROCE drives residual earnings. Given a positive spread between RNOA and the net borrowing cost, leverage will yield a higher ROCE and thus a higher RE. This is the good news effect on the present value. But at the same time the discount rate will increase to reflect the increased financing risk. This is the bad news effect on the present value. What is the net effect on the calculated value?

A standard notion in finance is that the two leverage effects are exactly offsetting, so leverage has no effect on the value of the equity. This is demonstrated in Table 13.5. The first valuation (A) values the equity from an operating income forecast of $135 million for all years in the future on a constant level of net operating assets. The perpetual forecasted ReOI of $18 million is capitalized at the cost of capital for operations of 9 percent to get a valuation (on 600 million shares) of $2.00 per share. The table then gives the valuation (B) for the equity using the RE model. The RE is calculated and capitalized using the equity cost of capital of 10 percent rather than the cost of capital for operations of 9 percent, but the valuation remains the same. Free cash flow after interest payments is paid out in dividends so, to keep it simple, there is no change in leverage forecasted from using free cash flow to buy down debt. But the final valuation (C) does have a leverage change. It is an RE valuation for the same firm recapitalized with a debt-for-equity swap. Two hundred shares were tendered in the swap at their value of $2.00 per share, reducing equity by $400 million and increasing debt by $400 million (leaving the net operating assets unchanged). The resulting leverage change increases the required return that shareholders demand from 10 percent to 12.5 percent, as indicated, to compensate them for the additional financing risk. It also increases ROCE from 12 percent to 16.7 percent, and residual earnings from $20 million to $25 million. But it does not change the per-share valuation of the equity.

In Chapter 12 we saw that Reebok's change in residual earnings and ROCE in 1996 was driven largely by a large change in financial leverage. Now look at Box 13.6. It analyzes the effect of Reebok's large stock repurchase on the value of the firm and its equity. You'll notice the large increase in ROCE that resulted from the big change in leverage in this transaction. Firms can increase ROCE with leverage. But the increased ROCE has no effect on the value of the firm.

These examples indicate that we can use either RE or ReOI forecasting to value equity. But the RE valuation is more complicated. The examples were constructed with just one leverage change. In reality, forecasted leverage will change every period as earnings, dividends, debt issues, and maturities change the equity and debt. So we have to adjust the discount rate every period. This tedious process requires more work, but there will be no effect on the value calculated. If, however, we apply residual operating income valuation, we remove all need to deal with financing activities. The operating income approach is a more efficient way of doing the calculation. It not only recognizes that expected residual earnings from net financing assets are zero but also recognizes that changes in

TABLE 13.5
Leverage Effects on the Value of Equity: Residual Earnings Valuation

	0	1	2	3
A. ReOI Valuation of a Firm with 9% Cost of Capital for Operations and 5% After-Tax Cost of Debt				
Net operating assets	1,300	1,300	1,300	1,300→
Net financial obligations	300	300	300	300→
Common shareholders' equity	1,000	1,000	1,000	1,000→
Operating income		135	135	135→
Net financial expense (300 × 0.05)		15	15	15→
Earnings		120	120	120 →
Residual operating income, ReOI [135 − (0.09 × 1,300)]		18	18	18→
PV of ReOI (18/0.09)	200			
Value of common equity	1,200			
Value per share (on 600 shares)	2.00			

$$P/B = \frac{1,200}{1,000} = 1.2$$

	0	1	2	3
B. RE Valuation of the Same Firm **Cost of equity capital** **= 9.0% + [300/1,200 × (9.0% − 5.0%)]** **= 10.0%**				
Net operating assets	1,300	1,300	1,300	1,300→
Net financial obligations	300	300	300	300
Common shareholders' equity	1,000	1,000	1,000	1,000
Earnings		120	120	120 →
ROCE		12%	12%	12%→
Residual earnings, RE [120 − (0.10 × 1,000)]		20	20	20 →
PV of RE (20/0.10)	200			
Value of common equity	1,200			
Value per share (on 600 shares)	2.00			

$$P/B = \frac{1,200}{1,000} = 1.2$$

	0	1	2	3
C. RE Valuation for the Same Firm after **Debt-for-Equity Swap** **Cost of equity capital** **= 9% + [700/800 × (9% − 5%)] = 12.5%**				
Net operating assets	1,300	1,300	1,300	1,300→
Net financial obligations	700	700	700	700→
Common shareholders' equity	600	600	600	600→
Operating income		135	135	135→
Net financial expense (700 × 0.05)		35	35	35 →
Earnings		100	100	100 →
ROCE		16.7%	16.7%	16.7%→
Residual earnings, RE [100 − (0.125 × 600)]		25	25	25→
PV of RE (25/0.125)	200			
Value of common equity	800			
Value per share (on 400 shares)	2.00			

$$P/B = \frac{800}{600} = 1.33$$

Note 2 to Reebok's 1996 financial statements reads:

2. Dutch Auction Self-Tender Stock Repurchase

On July 28, 1996, the Board of Directors authorized the purchase by the Company of up to 24.0 million shares of the Company's common stock pursuant to a Dutch Auction self-tender offer. The tender offer price range was from $30.00 to $36.00 net per share in cash. The self-tender offer, commenced on July 30, 1996, and expired on August 27, 1996. As a result of the self-tender offer, the Company repurchased approximately 17.0 million common shares at a price of $36.00 per share. Prior to the tender offer, the Company had 72.5 million common shares outstanding. As a result of the tender offer share repurchase, the Company had 55.8 million common shares outstanding at December 31, 1996. In conjunction with this repurchase and as described in Notes 6 and 8, the company entered into a new credit agreement underwritten by a syndicate of major banks.

At a purchase price of $36.00 per share, $601.2 million was paid to repurchase the 16.7 million shares. The company borrowed this amount at current market borrowing rates and so, with a reduction in equity and an increase in debt, leverage increased substantially. Here is the 1996 balance sheet and financial leverage compared with balance sheet and leverage as they would have been if the repurchase and simultaneous borrowing had not taken place (in millions of dollars):

	Actual 1996 Balance Sheet with Stock Repurchase	"As-If" 1996 Balance Sheet without Stock Repurchase
Net operating assets	1,135	1,135
Net financial obligations	720	119
Total equity	415	1,016
Minority interest	34	34
Common stockholders' equity	381	982
Financial leverage (FLEV)	1.73	0.12

The following is the forecasted 1997 income statement based on analysts' consensus eps forecast of $2.56 made in early 1997. It is compared with an "as-if" statement showing how that forecasted statement would have looked without the financing transaction:

	Pro Forma 1997 Income Statement with Stock Repurchase	"As-If" Pro Forma 1997 Income Statement without Stock Repurchase
Operating income	187	187
Net financial expense (4% of NFO)	(29)	(5)
Minority interest in earnings	(15)	(15)
Earnings forecast	143	167
Shares outstanding (millions)	55.840	72.540
Forecasted eps	2.56	2.30
Forecasts for 1997		
RNOA	16.5%	16.5%
SPREAD	12.5%	12.5%
ROCE	37.5%	17.0%

The forecast of operating income is unchanged by the change in leverage, since no NOA have been affected. Forecasted RNOA and the SPREAD also remain unchanged. But the change in leverage produces a big change in forecasted ROCE.

You see that a firm can earn a higher ROCE simply by increasing leverage (provided the spread is positive). But this has nothing to do with the underlying profitability of the operations. The financing adds no value. Here Reebok's valuation in Table 13.2 is compared with an "as-if" valuation of the 72.54 million shares had the leverage not changed:

	Valuation with Stock Repurchase	"As-If" Valuation without Stock Repurchase
Value of NOA	3,472	3,472
Book value of NFO	720	119
Value of equity	2,752	3,353
Value of minority interest	210	210
Value of common equity	2,542	3,143
Value per share	45.52	43.33

The operations were not affected by the financing, so their value is unaffected. It seems, however, that value per share increased. But the $45.52 per-share valuation is based on analysts' forecasts at the end of 1996 and is approximately the market price at that date. The stock was repurchased in August 1996, however, at $36 per share. If the 16.7 million shares had been repurchased at the $43.33 price that reflects the value in the later analysts' forecasts, the valuations before and after the transaction would be as follows:

	Valuation with Repurchase at $43.33 per Share	Valuation without Repurchase
Value of NOA	3,472	3,472
Book value of NFO	843	119
Value of equity	2,629	3,353
Value of minority interest	210	210
Value of common equity	2,419	3,143
Value per share	43.33	43.33

The valuation without the repurchase is the valuation at the end of 1996 as if there had not been a share repurchase, as before. The valuation with the repurchase just reflects a reduction of equity by the amount of the repurchase of $43.33 × 16.7 million shares = $724 million, and an increase in debt by the same amount. We saw in Chapter 3 that issuing or repurchasing shares at market value does not affect per-share price, and we see it here again. But we further see that issue of debt at market value also does not affect per-share value of $43.33. And we see that a change in leverage does not affect per-share value.

Of course, ex post (after the fact) the shareholders who did not participate in the stock repurchase did benefit from it. The $36.00 may have been a fair price, but the value went up subsequently: Our calculated value is $45.52 per share and that is close to the market value in early 1997. Without the repurchase, the per-share value would have gone from $36.00 to $43.33 based on analysts' forecast revisions. But the per-share value went to $45.52. The difference of $2.19 is the per-share gain to shareholders who did not participate in the repurchase from repurchasing the stock at $36.00 in August rather than at the later higher price. It is the loss to those who did repurchase (from selling at $36.00 rather than $43.33) spread over the remaining shares.

We stressed in Chapter 5 that residual earnings valuation techniques—as well as discounted cash flow techniques—value the business but miss out on value created from issuing and repurchasing shares at a market price that is not at fair value. Could Reebok have made the large stock repurchase because its analysis told it that the shares were underpriced? Reebok's share price rose from $36, the repurchase price in August 1996, to $43 in early 1997, so after the fact, shareholders who tendered their shares in the repurchase lost and those who did not gained. Did Reebok's management choose to make the stock repurchase when they thought the price was low? (Reebok's share prices subsequently dropped considerably.) Again, be careful which side of a share repurchase you choose to be on!

RE and the equity cost of capital that are due to leverage are not a consideration in valuation. Accordingly, the non-value generating financing activities are ignored and we can concentrate on the source of value creation, the operating activities.

Leverage and Abnormal Earnings Growth Valuation

You will notice that, as financial leverage increased with Reebok's stock repurchase in Box 13.6, forecasted earnings per share also increased—from $2.30 without the repurchase to $2.56 after the repurchase. Just as financial leverage increases ROCE (provided the spread is positive), financial leverage also increases earnings per share. An increase in leverage along with a stock repurchase increases earnings per share even more. With abnormal earnings growth valuation, we have said that we should pay more for earnings growth. But should we pay for eps growth that comes from leverage? Table 13.6 shows that the answer is no.

This table applies abnormal earnings growth methods to the same firm as in Table 13.5. The first valuation (A) applies the AOIG model of this chapter. As net operating assets do not change, free cash flow is the same as operating income, and cum-dividend operating income (after reinvesting free cash flow) is forecasted to equal normal operating income.

TABLE 13.6

Leverage Effects on the Value of Equity: Abnormal Earnings Growth Valuation

	0	1	2	3
A. AOIG Valuation of a Firm with 9% Cost of Capital for Operations and 5% After-Tax Cost of Debt				
Operating income		135	135	135→
Net financial expense (300 × 0.05)		15	15	15→
Earnings		120	120	120→
Eps (on 600 million shares)		0.20	0.20	0.20→
Free cash flow (C − I = OI − ΔNOA)		135	135	135→
Reinvested free cash flow (at 9%)			12	12→
Cum-dividend operating income			147	147→
Normal operating income (at 9%)			147	147→
Abnormal operating income growth (AOIG)			0	0→
Value of operations (135/0.09)	1,500			
Net financial obligations	300			
Value of equity	1,200			
Value per share (on 600 million shares)	2.00			
Forward P/E = 2.00/0.20 =10				
B. AEG Valuation of the Same Firm Cost of equity capital = 9.0% + [300/1,200 × (9% − 5%)] = 10.0%				
Operating income		135	135	135→
Net financial expense (300 x 0.05)		15	15	15→
Earnings		120	120	120→
Eps (on 600 million shares)		0.20	0.20	0.20→
Dividend (*d* = Earn − ΔCSE)		120	120	120→
Reinvested dividends (at 10%)			12	12→
Cum-dividend earnings			132	132→
Normal earnings (at 10%)			132	132→
Abnormal earning growth (AEG)			0	0→
Value of equity (120/0.10)	1,200			
Value per share (on 600 million shares)	2.00			
Forward P/E = 2.00/0.20 =10				
C. AEG Valuation for the Same Firm after Debt-for-Equity Swap Cost of equity capital = 9% + [700/800 × (9% − 5%)] = 12.5%				
Operating income		135	135	135→
Net financial expense (700 × 0.05)		35	35	35→
Earnings		100	100	100→
Eps (on 400 million shares)		0.25	0.25	0.25→
Dividends (*d* = Earn − ΔCSE)		100	100	100→
Reinvested dividends (at 12.5%)			12.5	12.5→
Cum-dividend earnings			112.5	112.5→
Normal earnings			112.5	112.5→
Abnormal earnings growth (AEG)			0	0→
Value of equity (100/0.125)	800			
Value per share (on 400 million shares)	2.00			
Forward P/E = 2.00/0.25 = 8				

Thus abnormal operating income growth from year 2 onward is forecasted to be zero and, accordingly, the value of the operations is equal to forward operating income ($135 million) capitalized at the required return for operations of 9 percent, or $1,500 million. The value of the equity, after subtracting net financial obligations, is $1,200, or $2.00 per share, the same valuation (of course) as that using ReOI methods.

Valuation (B) applies an AEG valuation rather than an AOIG valuation. Thus earnings and reinvested dividends are the focus rather than operating income and free cash flows. There is full payout, so dividends are the same as earnings. Now, however, the cost of equity capital is 10.0 percent, so abnormal earnings growth after the first year is forecasted to be zero. Therefore, the value of the equity is forward earnings of $120 million capitalized at 10 percent, or $1,200 as before. Value per share is $2.00, which is forward eps of $0.20 capitalized at 10 percent.

Valuation (C) is after the same debt-for-equity swap as in Table 13.5. The change in leverage decreases earnings (as there is now more interest expense with the same operating income) but increases eps to $0.25. The valuation shows that this increase in eps does not change the per-share value of the equity, for the cost of equity capital increases to 12.5 percent as a result of the increase in leverage to offset the increase in eps. The equity value—forward eps of $0.25 capitalized at a cost of equity capital of 12.5 percent—is $2.00, unchanged.

This example confirms that we can use either AEG or AOIG valuation methods to price earnings growth. But it also suggests that we are better off using AOIG methods that focus on the growth from operations. In practice, leverage changes each period so, if we were to use AEG valuation, we would have to change the equity cost of capital each period. It is easier to ignore the leverage and focus on the operations. Indeed, financing activities do not generate abnormal earnings growth, so why complicate the valuation (with a changing cost of capital from changing leverage) when leverage does not produce abnormal earnings growth?

Ignoring financing activities makes sense if you understand that a firm can't make money by issuing bonds at fair market value: These transactions are zero-NPV (and zero-ReNFE). It you forecast that a firm will issue bonds in the future and thus change its leverage—and the bond issue will be zero-NPV—current value cannot be affected. Similarly, an increase in debt to finance a stock repurchase cannot affect value if the stock repurchase is also at fair market value.

Leverage Creates Earnings Growth

The example in Table 13.6 provides a warning: Beware of earnings growth that is created by leverage. Leverage produces earnings growth, but not abnormal earnings growth. So the growth created by leverage is not to be valued. See Box 13.7 for a full explanation.

During the 1990s, many firms made considerable stock repurchases while increasing borrowings. The effect was to increase earnings per share. Below are some numbers for IBM.

INTERNATIONAL BUSINESS MACHINES (IBM) Share repurchases and financial leverage, 1995–2000						
	2000	**1999**	**1998**	**1997**	**1996**	**1995**
Share repurchases, net ($ billions)	6.1	6.6	6.3	6.3	5.0	4.7
Change in net debt ($ billions)	2.4	1.2	4.4	4.6	0.8	2.3
Financial leverage (FLEV)	1.21	1.10	1.22	0.98	0.68	0.62
Earnings per share	4.58	4.25	3.38	3.09	2.56	1.81

In introducing the P/B and P/E valuation models, Chapters 5 and 6 warned about paying too much for earnings and earnings growth. Beware of paying for earnings created by investment, for investment may grow earnings but not grow value. Do not pay for earnings created by accounting methods, for accounting methods do not add value. We now have another warning: Do not pay for earnings growth created by financing leverage. Here is the complete caveat:

- Beware of earnings growth created by investment.

- Beware of earnings growth created by accounting methods.

- Beware of earnings growth created by financial leverage.

Just as valuation models protect the investor from paying too much for earnings growth from the first two sources, so the models, faithfully applied, protect the investor from paying too much for earnings growth created by leverage.

The example in Table 13.6 looked at the effect of a one-time change in leverage. However, leverage changes each period, and if leverage increases each period (and the leverage is favorable), earnings and eps will continue to grow. But the growth is not growth to be paid for. The following pro formas compare the earnings growth and value of two firms with the same operations, one levered and the other not. The levered firm has higher expected earnings growth, but the same per-share equity value as the unlevered firm.

EARNINGS GROWTH WITH NO LEVERAGE

The pro forma below gives a forecast of earnings and eps growth for a pure equity firm (no financial leverage) with 10 million shares outstanding. The forecast is at the end of Year 0. The firm pays no dividends and its required return on operations is 10 percent (and so, with no leverage, the required return for the equity is also 10 percent). Dollar amounts are in millions, except per-share amounts.

	0	1	2	3	4
Net operating assets	100.00	110.00	121.00	133.10	146.41
Common equity	100.00	110.00	121.00	133.10	146.41
Operating income (equals comprehensive income)		10.00	11.00	12.10	13.31
Eps (on 10 million shares)		1.00	1.10	1.21	1.33
Growth in eps			10.0%	10.0%	10%
RNOA		10%	10%	10%	10%
ROCE		10%	10%	10%	10%
Residual operating income		0	0	0	0
Free cash flow		0	0	0	0
Cum-dividend OI			11.00	12.10	13.31
Normal OI			11.00	12.10	13.31
Abnormal OI growth			0	0	0
Value of equity[1]	100.00				
Per-share value of equity (10 million shares)	10.00				
Forward P/E ratio	10.0				
P/B ratio	1.0				

[1] As AOIG is zero after Year 1, value of equity $= \dfrac{10}{0.10} = 100$. The value of equity is also equal to book value of 100.

The forecast of RNOA of 10 percent yields residual operating income of zero. As forecasted residual income is zero, the equity is worth its book value of $100 million in Year 0, and the per-share value is $10. The P/B ratio is 1.0, a normal P/B.

The forecasts of operating income and free cash flow yield a forecast of zero abnormal operating income growth. So the firm (and the equity) is worth forward operating income capitalized at the required return of 10 percent, or $100 million, and $10 per share. The forward P/E ratio is 10.0, a normal P/E for a cost of capital of 10 percent.

The earnings and eps growth rates are both forecasted to be 10 percent (and accordingly, as 10 percent is also the required rate of return, abnormal earnings growth is forecasted to be zero).

EARNINGS GROWTH WITH LEVERAGE

The pro forma below is for a firm with the same operations, but with the operating assets in Year 0 financed by $50 million in debt and $50 million in equity (now with 5 million shares outstanding). The after tax cost of the debt is 5 percent.

	0	1	2	3	4
Net operating assets	100.00	110.00	121.00	133.10	146.41
Net financial obligations	50.00	52.50	55.12	57.88	60.77
Common equity	50.00	57.50	65.88	75.22	85.64
Operating income		10.00	11.00	12.10	13.31
Net financial expense		2.50	2.63	2.76	2.89
Comprehensive income		7.50	8.37	9.34	10.42
Eps (on 5 million shares)		1.50	1.68	1.87	2.08
Growth in eps			11.67%	11.57%	11.48%
RNOA		10%	10%	10%	10%
ROCE		15.0%	14.6%	14.2%	13.9%
Residual operating income		0	0	0	0
Free cash flow		0	0	0	0
Cum-dividend OI			11.00	12.10	13.31
Normal OI			11.00	12.10	13.31
Abnormal OI growth			0	0	0
Value of equity[1]	50.00				
Per-share value of equity (5 million shares)	10.00				
Forward P/E ratio	6.67				
P/B ratio	1.00				

[1] Value of equity is equal to the value of operations, 100, minus the net financial obligations, 50. The value of equity is also equal to book value of 50.

You will notice that, while earnings are lower than in the no-leverage case, eps is higher and both earnings growth and eps growth are higher. An analyst forecasting the higher growth rate of over 11 percent might be tempted to give this firm a higher valuation than the pure equity firm where the growth rate is just 10 percent. But that would be a mistake. Both ReOI and AOIG valuations yield the same $10 per-share value as is the case with no leverage. Just as the higher ROCE here is discounted by the appropriate valuation, so is the higher earnings growth.

While the valuation does not change with leverage, the P/E does. The forward P/E ratio is now 6.67 rather than 10.0, even though abnormal earnings growth is expected to be zero. You will understand the reason in the next section, but here is a hint: P/E ratios are determined not only by growth but also by the cost of capital, and the equity cost of capital increases with financing leverage. Exercise 13.9 explores this example further.

FIGURE 13.1

Median Financial Leverage for U.S. Firms, 1963–2001

Financial leverage is net financial obligations to common equity (FLEV).

Source:
Company: Standard & Poor's
Data: Compustat® data

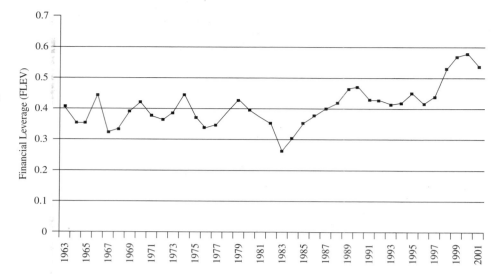

IBM delivered considerable per-share earnings growth during the 1990s. We saw in Chapter 12 that a significant portion of that growth came from pension fund gains, asset sales, and bleeding back of restructuring charges. The significant stock repurchases in this case, and the increase in financial leverage, further call into question the quality of IBM's earnings-per-share growth.

The increase in corporate debt during the 1990s contributed to strong earnings growth that the market rewarded with high earnings multiples. Figure 13.1 tracks financial leverage (FLEV) and earnings-per-share for U.S. firms from 1963–2001. For IBM, the outcome was favorable—it was able to maintain a favorable leverage position. But debt has a downside, and this downside risk increases the required return: If leverage becomes unfavorable, earnings will decline, perhaps precipitously. For some firms, the downside of debt became apparent in the early 2000s as they struggled to cover debt service, with large losses of shareholder value. Vivendi, Quest (and the many telecoms), United Airlines (and the many air carriers) are just a few examples. In many cases, the debt was issued to make acquisitions that also produced earnings growth. Analysts must be aware of earnings growth from acquisitions, but especially when the growth is financed with debt.

Debt and Taxes

Some people argue that, because interest is tax-deductible if paid by a corporation but is not deductible if paid by shareholders, there are tax savings to corporate borrowing. Shareholders can borrow on personal accounts to lever their equity, but they can also lever their equity by borrowing within the firm. If they borrow within the firm, they add value because they get a tax deduction for the interest cost incurred.

The claim is controversial. First, interest can (in the U.S.) be deducted on shareholders' own tax returns to the extent that it is matched by investment income. Second, the interest that is deductible by corporations is taxable in the hands of debtholders who receive the interest, and they will require a higher interest rate to compensate them for the taxes, mitigating the tax advantage to the corporate debt. The spread between interest rates on tax-free debt (like municipal debt) and corporate debt suggests this is so. Third, free cash flow must either be used to reduce corporate net debt or to make distributions

Typically it is argued that firms cannot create value by issuing debt: If the debt is issued at fair market value, the transaction is a zero-net present value transaction—or, equivalently, a zero-residual net financial expense transaction. Banks and other financial institutions make money from the spread between lending rates and borrowing rates and so create value from transacting in debt. And bond traders who discover mispricing of bonds also create value from transacting in debt. But for the firm that uses debt for financing, debt transactions are deemed not to create value.

There is an exception, however. Consider the following scenario. A firm with a particular risk profile that is given an AAB bond rating issues debt with a yield to maturity of 8 percent. Subsequently it engages in more risky business

and the bonds accordingly are downgraded to a BBB rating. The price of the bonds drops to yield an 11 percent return commensurate with the firm's new risk level. The firm then redeems the bonds and books a gain.

Firms can transfer value from bondholders to shareholders in this way. There is a message for bondholders: Beware and write bond agreements that give protection from this scenario. There is also a message for shareholders: Bondholders can be exploited in this way. There is also a message for the valuation analyst: Firms can create value for shareholders in this scenario. Applying residual earnings techniques will incorporate this value. If the scenario is anticipated, the analyst forecasts a realized gain from the redemption of bonds and, accordingly, a negative residual net financial expense (that is, residual income from bonds).

to shareholders: $C - I = d + F$. Both uses have tax effects. If cash flow is applied to reduce debt, shareholders lose the tax advantage of debt; if the firm wishes to maintain the debt, it must distribute cash flow to shareholders who are then taxed on the distributions. Either way, free cash flow is taxed, and shareholders cannot get the tax advantage of debt without incurring taxes at the personal level.

You can delve into these issues in a corporate finance text. Armed with the shareholders' personal tax rates and the corporate tax rate, you can revise the value calculations here by incorporating the present value of tax benefits if you are convinced that debt adds value. (But do not fall into the trap of thinking only about the tax benefit of debt without considering taxes on distributions to shareholders.)

Box 13.8 considers another way that firms might generate value for shareholders from debt if debtholders are not vigilant.

MARK-TO-MARKET ACCOUNTING: A TOOL FOR INCORPORATING THE COST OF STOCK OPTIONS IN VALUATION

The distinction between operating activities and financing activities shows us that there are two ways to proceed in valuation. We can forecast future earnings from an asset or liability, or we can mark the asset or liability to market. Marking to market is attractive because it relieves us of the forecasting task. But marking to market can only be done if market values are reliable measures of fair value. Market values of financial assets and liabilities measure up to this criterion, so we do not have to forecast the income and expenses arising from financing activities.

Chapter 8 explained that shareholders incur losses when employees exercise the stock options they have received as compensation. Yet GAAP accounting does not recognize this loss. Because of the omission, a valuation based on forecasting GAAP operating income will overestimate the value of the firm, leaving the investor with the risk of paying too much for a stock. The analyst must make adjustments. One might think that solution would involve reducing forecasts of GAAP earnings by forecasts of future losses from the exercise of options. Indeed, this is a solution. But forecasting those losses is not an easy task: As the loss is the difference between the market price and the exercise price at the exercise date, one would have to anticipate not only exercise dates but the market price of the stock at those dates.

Mark-to-market accounting—the alternative to forecasting—provides a solution. Fair values of options can be estimated, with reasonable precision, using option pricing methods. In Chapter 8, where the issue of stock options was introduced, we left open the treatment of Reebok's stock option costs. Refer back to the Reebok case there, and refresh yourself on the issue. Reebok's stock option footnote for 1996, in Exhibit 8.3, gives a pro forma eps number for the compensation expense incurred at grant date, as required by FASB Statement No. 123:

	December 31,	
	1996	**1995**
Pro forma net income (thousands)	$134,017	$163,404
Pro forma earnings per share	1.96	2.06
Weighted average exercise price of options granted	31.32	34.90
Weighted average fair value of options outstanding at the end of the period	10.76	11.63

By comparing the 1996 pro forma eps of $1.96 with the eps of $2.00 reported in the income statement, we understand that the compensation expense incurred from granting stock options was $0.04 per share. However, we also understand that this expense does not measure the full effect of stock options: Shareholders will also lose as options go into the money and are exercised. We have to consider the likely effect on share values of options that are outstanding but not exercised, a total of 9.916 thousand (in Exhibit 8.3). These outstanding options—the option overhang—amount to a contingent liability that affects shareholder value, just as a contingent liability under a product liability or environmental damage lawsuit is a contingent liability.

Reebok's footnote gives the weighted average of the fair value of options outstanding and explains (in Exhibit 8.3) how the fair values were arrived at using Black-Scholes methods. The weighted average option value is $10.76 (as shown above). Applying this value to the 9.916 thousand options outstanding, we arrive at an adjusted valuation for Reebok (in millions):

Value of equity before option overhang (from Tables 13.2 and 13.4)		$2,542
Liability for option overhang:		
Black-Scholes value of outstanding options: 9.916 × $10.76	$ 107	
Tax benefit (at 35.4%)	38	
Option liability, after tax		69
Value of equity		$2,473
Value per share on 55.640 million shares		$44.29

As the exercise of employee stock options draws a tax benefit, the liability is after tax.

Most firms are not as generous as Reebok in disclosing the fair value of outstanding options, so the analyst must produce his own valuations. Black-Scholes valuations provide an approximation. However, because employee options have different features than standard traded options, modifications are often made. One particular issue is the possibility that the options will not vest. Accordingly, the calculation above may be modified to price the number of options that are expected to be exercised, not the total outstanding options. The history of cancelled options (in Reebok's footnote in Exhibit 8.3) gives some indication of likely exercise. A floor valuation for the option overhang—that omits the value from stock price volatility—is given by the difference between current market price and exercise price. You will see this floor valuation being referred to (somewhat inappropriately) as the "intrinsic value" of the options.

Mark-to-market accounting for outstanding options does not quite avoid the need for forecasting. To the extent that future option grants are predictable, the option value to be given to employees as compensation at grant date and amortized to income must be anticipated. This is a tricky matter. But, if a firm voluntarily recognizes grant-date expense, or if the FASB adopts the IASB's proposal to require grant-date accounting for options, the expense will be included in GAAP income, leaving the analyst only with the task of marking the option overhang to market.

Mark-to-market methods essentially restate the book value on the balance sheet for an omitted liability. Mark-to-market accounting can be applied to other contingent liabilities. Apply the procedure above to incorporate outstanding put options on the firm's stock, warrants, and other convertible securities into a valuation. For contingent liabilities from lawsuits, deduct the present value of expected losses to be incurred. The contingent liability footnote provides (sparse) information about these liabilities.

ENTERPRISE MULTIPLES

In the example of leverage effects in Table 13.5 you will have noticed that the P/B ratio increased with the increase in leverage, from 1.2 to 1.33. You also will have noticed that the P/E ratio decreased with the increase in leverage in Table 13.6, from 10 to 8. Yet, in both cases, the value of the equity did not change. This suggests that we might be better served to think of P/B and P/E ratios without the effect of leverage.

Enterprise Price-to-Book Ratios

The value of equity is the value of the operations minus the value of the net financial obligations. So the intrinsic price-to-book (P/B) ratio can be expressed as

$$\frac{V_0^E}{\text{CSE}_0} = \frac{V_0^{\text{NOA}} - V_0^{\text{NFO}}}{\text{NOA} - \text{NFO}}$$

If the net financial obligations are measured at market value, they do not contribute to the premium over book value; the difference between price and book value is due to net operating assets not being measured at market value. Yet the expression here tells us that the P/B ratio will vary as the amount of net financial obligations changes relative to the operating assets. That is, the ratio is sensitive to leverage. So differences in firms' P/B ratios can derive from their financing even though price equals book value for financial items.

To avoid this confusion we should focus on the value of the operations relative to their book value. The ratio of the value of the net operating assets to their book value is the **enterprise P/B ratio** or the **unlevered P/B ratio**:

$$\text{Enterprise P/B ratio} = \frac{\text{Value of net operating assets}}{\text{Net operating assets}}$$

$$= \frac{V_0^{\text{NOA}}}{\text{NOA}_0}$$

The value of the net operating assets is, of course, the value of the equity plus the net financial obligations. So, to calculate a market (traded) enterprise P/B, just add the net financial obligations to the market value of the equity.

The standard price-to-book ratio for the equity is referred to as the **levered P/B ratio**. The two P/B ratios reconcile as follows:

Levered P/B ratio = Enterprise P/B ratio   **(13.10)**
$\qquad$ + [Financial leverage × (Enterprise P/B ratio − 1)]

$$\frac{V_0^E}{CSE_0} = \frac{V_0^{NOA}}{NOA_0} + FLEV\left(\frac{V_0^{NOA}}{NOA_0} - 1\right)$$

where FLEV is book financial leverage (NFO/CSE), as before. The difference between the two P/B ratios increases with leverage and the distance that the unlevered P/B is from the normal of 1.0. For an unlevered P/B of 1.0, the levered P/B is also 1.0 regardless of leverage. Figure 13.2a shows how the levered P/B ratio changes with leverage for six different levels of the unlevered P/B ratio. The conversion chart in Figure 13.2b charts unlevered P/B ratios corresponding to levered P/B ratios for different leverage levels.

The levered P/B ratio is the one that is commonly referred to. But it is the enterprise P/B on which we should focus. Reebok's levered P/B before its large stock repurchase

FIGURE 13.2A
Levered P/B Ratios and Leverage The figure shows how the levered P/B ratio (V^E/CSE) changes with financial leverage for different levels of unlevered P/B (V^{NOA}/NOA).

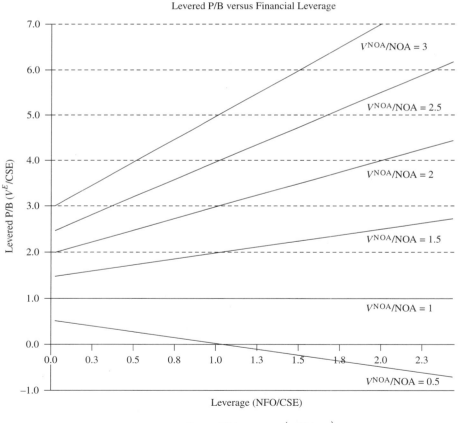

$$\frac{V^E}{CSE} = \frac{V^{NOA}}{NOA} + FLEV\left(\frac{V^{NOA}}{NOA} - 1\right)$$

and change in leverage in August 1996 was 2.70, but immediately after it was 6.0. This change does not reflect a change in the expected profitability of operations or a change in the premium one would have paid for the operations. It's a leverage-induced change: Reebok's enterprise P/B remained the same at 2.40. And the stock price was unchanged at about $36 from May to September; this repurchase and financing transaction had no effect on shareholders' per-share value, and this is also indicated by no change in the enterprise P/B ratio. Nike's levered P/B, with no change in leverage, remained at about 6.20 over the period (with an enterprise P/B of 5.70). If we compared the (similar) levered P/B ratios after Reebok's recapitalization, we might conclude that the two firms had similar profitability. But our analysis for 1996 in Chapter 11 revealed that Nike had higher RNOA that demanded a higher enterprise P/B ratio.

Figure 13.3 plots the median levered and unlevered price-to-book ratios for U.S. firms from 1963 to 2001. When unlevered P/B ratios were around 1.0 in the mid-1970s, so were the levered ratios. But when unlevered P/B ratios were above 1.0, the levered P/B ratios were higher than the unlevered ratios, the more so the higher the unlevered P/B.

FIGURE 13.2B

Levered P/B and Unlevered P/B Ratios
The figure shows how the levered P/B ratio (V^E/CSE) and the unlevered P/B ratio (V^{NOA}/NOA) relate for different levels of financial leverage (FLEV).

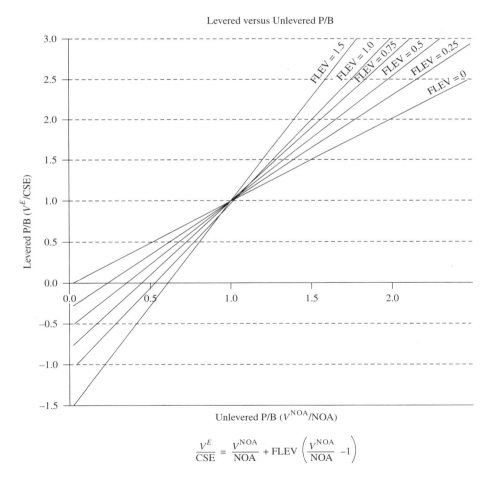

$$\frac{V^E}{\text{CSE}} = \frac{V^{\text{NOA}}}{\text{NOA}} + \text{FLEV}\left(\frac{V^{\text{NOA}}}{\text{NOA}} - 1\right)$$

FIGURE 13.3
Median Levered and Unlevered Price-to-Book Ratios for U.S. Firms, 1963–2001

Source:
Company: Standard & Poors'
Data: Compustat® data

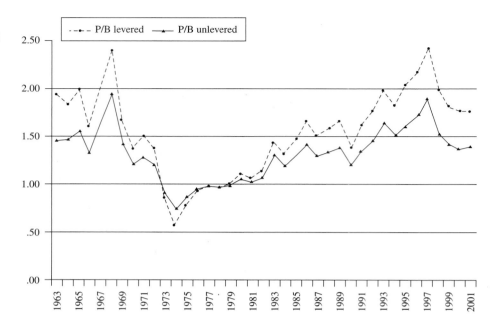

Enterprise Price-Earnings Ratios

The P/E ratio commonly referred to prices earnings after net interest expense, so it is a **levered P/E**. A levered P/E ratio anticipates earnings growth. However, earnings growth is affected by leverage, and anticipated growth from leverage is not growth to be valued. So it makes sense to think of a P/E ratio in terms of growth in earnings from operations. The **enterprise P/E ratio** or **unlevered P/E ratio** prices the operating income on the basis of expected growth in operating income.

The *forward enterprise P/E* is the value of the operations relative to forecasted one-year-ahead operating income:

$$\text{Forward} = \frac{\text{Value of operations}}{\text{Forward operating income}} = \frac{V_0^{NOA}}{OI_1}$$

The value of the operations is the value of the equity plus the net financial obligations. In Table 13.6, the enterprise P/E is the value of the operations, $1,500 million relative to Year 1 operating income of $135 million, or 11.11. This P/E does not change with an increase in leverage, whereas the levered P/E drops from 10 to 8 despite no change in operating income growth. The drop in the levered P/E reflects an increase in the required return due to leverage, but not a change in the price we would pay for growth.

The enterprise P/E in the Table 13.6 example is a normal P/E, for abnormal operating income growth after the forward year is forecasted to be zero. Indeed, the normal forward P/E for a 9 percent required return is 1/0.09 = 11.11. One would pay higher than 11.11 times forward earnings only if abnormal growth in operating income were forecasted. Reebok's forward enterprise P/E (from Table 13.4) is 3,472/187 = 18.6, which is higher than the normal P/E for a required return of 10.1 percent for operations (that is, 9.9) because abnormal operating income growth is forecasted. The change in leverage with the stock repurchase increased forward earnings from 2.30 to 2.56 (in Box 13.6) and reduced the forward levered P/E from 18.8 to 16.9, but with no effect on the value per share. The enterprise P/E did not change.

The *trailing enterprise P/E* compares the value of the operations to current operating income. There is an adjustment, however. Just as the levered trailing P/E must be cum-dividend (with dividends added to the numerator), so must the unlevered P/E. The dividend from operations is the free cash flow, so

$$\text{Trailing enterprise P/E} = \frac{\text{Value of operations} + \text{Free cash flow}}{\text{Current operating income}} = \frac{V_0^{\text{NOA}} + \text{FCF}_0}{\text{OI}_0}$$

The value of the operations is reduced by free cash flow (paid out to the financing activities) so, as the value of the operating income is independent of the cash paid out, free cash flow must be added to the numerator.

Nike, with little leverage, had a trailing enterprise P/E of 27.6 in 1996, only slightly higher than its levered P/E of 27.5. Reebok, with more leverage, had a trailing enterprise P/E of 22.2, compared with a levered P/E of 21.1.

The forward levered and unlevered P/E ratios reconcile as follows:

Levered forward P/E = Levered P/E + [Earnings leverage   **(13.11)**
$$\times \, (\text{Levered P/E} - 1/\text{Net borrowing cost})]$$

$$\frac{V_0^E}{\text{Earn}_1} = \frac{V_0^{\text{NOA}}}{\text{OI}_1} + \text{ELEV}_1 \left(\frac{V_0^{\text{NOA}}}{\text{OI}_1} - \frac{1}{\text{NBC}_1} \right)$$

Earnings leverage is the extent to which net financial expenses affect earnings: ELEV = NFE/Earnings, and NBC is the net borrowing cost. Think of the terms in parentheses as their reciprocals, operating income yield and the net borrowing cost. If the operating income yield, $\text{OI}_1/V_0^{\text{NOA}}$, is higher than the borrowing cost, leverage is favorable on earnings and the levered P/E is lower than the unlevered P/E, with the amount of the difference depending on the amount of earnings leverage, ELEV. The two ratios are the same when the operating earnings yield is equal to the net borrowing cost.

The two trailing P/E ratios reconcile in a similar way:

$$\frac{V_0^E + d_0}{\text{Earn}_0} = \frac{V_0^{\text{NOA}} + \text{FCF}_0}{\text{OI}_0} + \text{ELEV}_0 \left(\frac{V_0^{\text{NOA}} + \text{FCF}_0}{\text{OI}_0} - \frac{1}{\text{NBC}_0} - 1 \right) \quad \textbf{(13.12)}$$

For a given borrowing cost, you can set up conversion charts like those for enterprise and levered P/B ratios in Figures 13.2A and 13.2B.

Figure 13.4 plots median levered and unlevered trailing P/E ratios from 1963–2001. Typically, levered P/E ratios are less than unlevered ratios. In the earlier and later years in Figure 13.4, when unlevered P/E ratios were high, levered ratios were lower than unlevered ratios: Operating income yields were higher than borrowing costs. In the early 1980s, and early 1990s, when interest rates (and thus borrowing costs) were higher and/or yields were low, the relationship flipped.

The form of the relationship between levered and unlevered P/B ratios and P/E ratios is familiar: The levered amount is the unlevered amount plus a premium that depends on the leverage and a spread. We saw this in the relationship between levered and unlevered accounting returns and required returns. Table 13.7 summarizes the leverage effects we have discussed in this chapter.

FIGURE 13.4

Median Levered and Unlevered Trailing Price-to-Earnings Ratios for U.S. Firms, 1963–2001

Source:
Company: Standard & Poor's
Data: Compustat® data

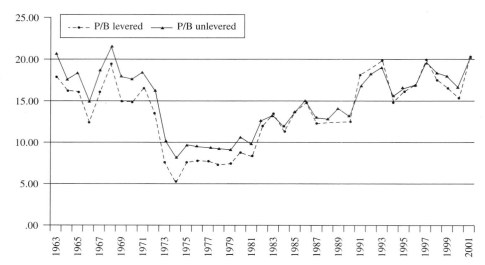

TABLE 13.7   **Relationships between Levered and Unlevered Measures**

Concept	Levered Measure	Unlevered Measure	Relationship
Profitability	ROCE	RNOA	$\text{ROCE} = \text{RNOA} + \text{FLEV}(\text{RNOA} - \text{NBC})$
Cost of capital	ρ_E	ρ_F	$\rho_E = \rho_F + \dfrac{V_0^D}{V_0^E}(\rho_F - \rho_D)$
P/B ratio	V_0^E/CSE_0	V_0^{NOA}/NOA_0	$\dfrac{V_0^E}{\text{CSE}_0} = \dfrac{V_0^{NOA}}{\text{NOA}_0} + \dfrac{\text{NFO}_0}{\text{CSE}_0}\left(\dfrac{V_0^{NOA}}{\text{NOA}_0} - 1\right)$
Forward P/E ratio	V_0^E/Earn_1	V_0^{NOA}/OI_1	$\dfrac{V_0^E}{\text{Earn}_1} = \dfrac{V_0^{NOA}}{\text{OI}_1} + \text{ELEV}_1\left(\dfrac{V_0^{NOA}}{\text{OI}_1} - \dfrac{1}{\text{NBC}_1}\right)$
Trailing P/E ratio	$\dfrac{V_0^E + d_0}{\text{Earn}_0}$	$\dfrac{V_0^{NOA} + \text{FCF}_0}{\text{OI}_0}$	$\dfrac{V_0^E + d_0}{\text{Earn}_0} = \dfrac{V_0^{NOA} + \text{FCF}_0}{\text{OI}_0} + \text{ELEV}_0\left(\dfrac{V_0^{NOA} + \text{FCF}_0}{\text{OI}_0} - \dfrac{1}{\text{NBC}_0} - 1\right)$

Summary

To the extent that accountants get the balance sheet correct, the analyst does not have to make a valuation. If, in the extreme, the balance sheet were perfect—giving the value of the equity—the analyst would have nothing to do; the accountant would have done the valuation. Balance sheets are typically not perfect, so the analyst has to forecast to get the missing value. But to the extent that the balance sheet gives the value, the analyst can avoid forecasting.

   This chapter has introduced valuation approaches that recognize the balance sheet values of net financial items as approximating their market values, but recognize that balance sheet amounts for net operating assets are typically not their values. Accordingly, valuation is based on forecasting residual income or abnormal earnings growth from operations. The valuation gives the value of the operations, and the value of the equity is then the value of the operations less the balance sheet value of the net debt (or the fair value of the net debt in the fair-value footnote).

The Web Connection

Find the following on the web page for this chapter:

- Further examples of residual operating income methods.
- Further examples of abnormal operating income growth methods.

- Demonstrations of how leverage affects ROCE, earnings growth, and valuations.
- More discussion of the tax effects of debt.

If the net debt on the balance sheet is close to its fair value, the appropriate way of thinking of a value multiple of book value is in terms of the unlevered or enterprise price-to-book ratio, that is, the pricing of the net operating assets rather than the equity. The chapter has laid out the calculation of the enterprise price-to-book ratio and has shown how it relates, through leverage, to the levered price-to-book ratio.

This chapter also focused on enterprise price-earnings ratios. It recognized that standard P/E ratios—levered P/E ratios—are based on prospective earnings growth that incorporates growth that is created by leverage. Yet, growth from leverage is not valued. Levered P/E ratios change with leverage, even if leverage has no effect on equity value. The analyst therefore prices growth from operations with an enterprise or unlevered P/E ratio.

We always want to carry out valuations efficiently. The residual operating income valuation approach and the abnormal operating income growth approach both reduce the forecasting task on which we will embark in the next two chapters. Only the operating components of comprehensive income and the net operating asset component on the balance sheet need to be forecasted. Further, in converting forecasts to a valuation using a required return, one can ignore changes in required returns that are due to changes in financial leverage.

Key Concepts

effective cost of debt is the after-tax cost of borrowing. *443*

enterprise value is the value of the operations. *434*

financing risk is the risk shareholders have of losing value in borrowing and lending activities. *444*

levered price-to-book ratio is the price multiple of common equity. Compare with **unlevered price-to-book ratio**. *458*

levered price-earnings ratio is the price multiple that prices (net) earnings. Compare with **unlevered price-earnings ratio**. *460*

market leverage is financial leverage measured by the ratio of the value of net

financial obligations to the value of common equity. *444*

operating risk is the risk shareholders and bondholders have of losing value in operations. *444*

pure equity firm is a firm with no net debt. *444*

unlevered price-to-book ratio or **enterprise price-to-book ratio** is the price multiple of net operating assets. Compare with **levered price-to-book ratio**. *457*

unlevered price-earnings ratio or **enterprise price-earnings ratio** is the price multiple that prices operating income. Compare with **levered price-earnings ratio**. *460*

The Analyst's Toolkit

Concept Questions

C13.1. Given the book value of an asset and its required return (and no other information), what is your prediction of the earnings from the asset? When will this forecast be a good forecast?

C13.2. If assets are at fair market value in the balance sheet, the income reported from those assets in the income statement does not give any information about the value of the assets. Is this correct?

C13.3. If assets are measured at their fair (intrinsic) value, the analyst must forecast that residual earnings from those assets will be zero. Is this correct?

C13.4. Why might the market value of the assets of a pure investment fund that holds only equity securities not be an indication of the fund's intrinsic value?

C13.5. What drives growth in residual operating income?

C13.6. Can residual operating income increase while, for the same period, residual earnings decrease?

C13.7. Explain what is meant by a financing risk premium in the equity cost of capital. When will a financing risk premium be negative?

C13.8. A firm with positive net financial assets will typically have a required return for equity that is greater than the required return for its operations. Is this correct?

C13.9. What is wrong with tying management bonuses to earnings per share? What measure would you propose as a management performance metric?

C13.10. The management of a firm that ties employee bonuses to return on common equity repurchases some of the firm's outstanding shares. What is the effect of this transaction on shareholders' wealth?

C13.11. An increase in financial leverage increases return on common equity (if the operating spread is positive), and thus increases residual earnings. The value of equity is based on forecasted residual earnings, yet it is claimed that the value of equity is not affected by a change in financial leverage. How is this seeming paradox explained?

C13.12. Levered price-to-book ratios are always higher than unlevered price-to-book ratios. Is this correct?

C13.13. During the 1990s, many firms repurchased stock and borrowed to do so. What is the typical effect of stock repurchases on earnings-per-share growth and return on common equity? Predict how a firm that excessively engaged in these practices would have fared in the downturn of the early 2000s.

C13.14. If an investor wants to buy a stock with high earnings growth but with low risk, she must pay a high multiple of earnings for it. Correct?

C13.15. Does an increase in financial leverage increase or decrease the (levered) P/E ratio?

C13.16. Established firms, like General Electric, have low beta risk, low earnings volatility, but consistently high earnings growth rates. These firms should have particularly high P/E ratios. Correct?

Exercises

E13.1. Using Market Values in the Balance Sheet: Pennzoil (Easy)

Pennzoil (now PennzEnergy Corporation), the oil company, has a substantial holding of Chevron Corporation, another oil company. But the holding (of 7.1 million shares at the end of 1998) is less than 20 percent of Chevron. The Chevron shares are classified as available for sale, so are carried at fair value on the balance sheet, with income recognized as dividends received plus unrealized gains or losses on the investments. PennzEnergy reported the following for 1998 (in thousands):

Dividend income	$34,026
Unrealized gains on securities	36,373

In its fair-value footnote the company gave the following information (in thousands):

	Cost	Estimated Fair Value	Accumulated Unrealized Gains
Investment in Chevron Corporation	$238,847	$588,228	$349,381

Outline how you would incorporate these numbers in a valuation of PennzEnergy.

E13.2. The Quality of Carrying Values for Equity Investments: SunTrust Bank (Easy)

In 1993, SunTrust Bank of Atlanta reported investment securities on its balance sheet of $10,644 million, an increase over the $8,715 million reported for 1992. Footnotes revealed that most of the securities were interest-bearing debt securities. But $1,077 million of the 1993 securities were shares held in the Coca-Cola Company, carried at market value. In 1992, the bank had carried these securities on the balance sheet at their historical cost of $110 million.

Which carrying value for the Coca-Cola shares do you see as the better quality number, the market value or the historical cost?

E13.3. Levered and Unlevered Price-to-Book Ratios: General Mills (Easy)

General Mills, the producer of packaged food products, reported the following balance sheet for its quarter ending August 29, 1999 (in millions):

	August 29, 1999
Assets	
Current assets	
Cash and cash equivalents	$ 46.0
Receivables	522.0
Inventories	
Valued primarily at FIFO	228.0
Valued at LIFO (FIFO value exceeds LIFO by $34.0)	282.1
Prepaid expenses and other current assets	77.4
Deferred income taxes	98.3
Total current assets	1,253.8
Land, buildings, and equipment, at cost	2,810.1
Less accumulated depreciation	(1,459.2)
Net land, buildings, and equipment	1,350.9
Intangibles	838.6
Other assets	1,061.0
Total assets	$4,504.3
Liabilities and Equity	
Current liabilities	
Accounts payable	$ 678.1
Current portion of long-term debt	129.6
Notes payable	751.1
Accrued taxes	184.7
Other current liabilities	274.8
Total current liabilities	2,018.3
Long-term debt	1,687.3
Deferred income taxes	293.6
Deferred income taxes—tax leases	111.5
Other liabilities	177.3
Total liabilities	4,288.0
Stockholders' equity	
Cumulative preference stock, none issued	—
Common stock, 408.3 shares issued	666.2
Retained earnings	1,902.7
Less common stock in treasury, at cost, shares of 104.1	(2,222.1)
Unearned compensation	(69.1)
Accumulated other comprehensive income	(61.4)
Total stockholders' equity	216.3
Total liabilities and equity	$4,504.3

The notes payable are interest-bearing. Cash and cash equivalents are regarded as financial assets.

a. General Mills's shares traded at $42 in August 1999. Calculate the firm's levered and unlevered price-to-book ratios. Which do you think is more important?

b. Give quantitative explanations of the factors that explain the differences between the two ratios.

E13.4. Levered and Unlevered P/E Ratios (Medium)

The following pro forma was prepared for a firm at the end of 2000 (in millions of dollars):

	2000	2001	2002	2003
Net operating assets	1,300	1,300	1,300	1,300
Net financial obligations	300	300	300	300
Common shareholders' equity	1,000	1,000	1,000	1,000
Operating income		135	135	135
Net financial expense		15	15	15
Earnings		120	120	120

The firm has a required return for its operations of 9 percent and a 5 percent after-tax cost of debt. Pro forma financial statements after 2003 are forecasted to be similar to those in 2003.

a. Forecast the value of the operations and the value of the equity at the end of years 2001 to 2003.
b. Forecast the levered and unlevered P/E ratios at the end of years 2001 to 2003.
c. Can you infer the required return for equity from the levered P/E ratios?

Real World Connection
This exercise builds on the example in Table 13.5.

E13.5. Calculating Residual Operating Income: Dell Computer (Easy)

Dell Computer reported after-tax operating income of $1,435 million for fiscal year 1999, along with average operating assets over the year of $3,080 million and average operating liabilities of $3,501 million.

Using a cost of capital for operations of 16 percent, calculate Dell's residual operating income for the year. Describe, in words, how Dell generated value during the year.

E13.6. Forecasting Residual Operating Income and Abnormal Operating Income Growth (Medium)

The following pro forma was developed at the end of 2003 for a firm which has a cost of capital for its operations of 10 percent (amounts in millions of dollars):

	2004	2005	2006
Cash flow from operations	30	70	40
Cash investment expenditures	45	55	90
Net financial obligations	150	150	240
Book value of common equity	140	170	190

The book value of equity at the end of 2003 was 130 and the net financial obligations at the same date were 120. Forecast residual operating income for 2004, 2005, and 2006 and abnormal operating income growth for 2005 and 2006.

E13.7. Valuation of Operations: Nike, Inc. (Medium)

The following summary numbers (in millions of dollars) were calculated from Nike's 1996 balance sheet:

Net operating assets	2,659
Net financial obligations	228
Common equity (144 million shares outstanding)	2,431

Analysts were forecasting $4.50 in earnings per share for 1997. Nike's after-tax core borrowing cost is 3.5 percent and its required return for operations is 11 percent.

a. What return on net operating assets (RNOA) are analysts implicitly forecasting for 1997?
b. Value a share of Nike on the assumption that the forecasted 1997 RNOA will continue indefinitely and residual operating income (ReOI) and net operating assets will grow at 7 percent per year.
c. Repeat the valuation from forecasts of abnormal operating income.
d. What is the value of Nike's operations with these forecasting assumptions?
e. If forecasted RNOA is expected to be constant in the future, how can residual operating income grow?

Real World Connection

See material on Nike in Chapters 8–15. Also see Exercise E1.5 in Chapter 1, Minicase M2.1 in Chapter 2, Exercise E6.3 in Chapter 6, Minicase M7.1. in Chapter 7, Exercise E8.10. in Chapter 8, and Exercise E9.5 in Chapter 9.

E13.8. Analyzing Value Generated from Operations: Ben & Jerry's (Medium)

The comparative income statement and balance sheet for Ben & Jerry's Homemade, Inc., for 1996 are given in Exercise E11.8 in Chapter 11. Commercial beta services were giving Ben & Jerry's an equity beta of 0.9 at the time and the risk-free borrowing rate was 5.0 percent. The firm's 7.2 million shares traded at $15 each.

a. Calculate the CAPM equity cost of capital for Ben & Jerry's. Use a market risk premium of 6 percent. Then calculate the cost of capital for operations that is implied by the firm's market capitalization at the time. What reservations do you have about these calculations?
b. Calculate residual operating income for 1996. Would you say that Ben & Jerry's was adding value?

Real World Connection

See Exercise E10.6 in Chapter 10, Exercise E11.8 in Chapter 11, and Exercise E14.2 in Chapter 14.

E13.9. Growth, the Cost of Capital, and the Normal P/E Ratio (Hard)

Box 13.7 in this chapter demonstrated how stock repurchases and leverage changes can increase earnings-per-share growth. Answer the following questions regarding the effect of the stock repurchase.

a. Why does the stock repurchase have no effect on the per-share value of the equity?
b. Why does forecasted earnings for Year 1 decrease from $10.00 million to $7.50 million?
c. Why does forecasted eps for Year 1 increase while forecasted earnings decrease?
d. The required return prior to the stock repurchase was 10 percent. What is the required return for the equity after the stock repurchase?
e. What is the expected residual earnings (on equity) for Year 1 after the repurchase?
f. Forecast the value of the equity at the end of Year 1 for both the case with no leverage and the case with leverage.
g. Forecast the P/E at the end of Year 1 for both the case with no leverage and the case with leverage. Why are they different?

E13.10.   Levered and Unlevered P/B and P/E Ratios (Easy)

A firm has the following summary balance sheet and income statement (in millions):

Net operating assets	$469
Net financial obligations	236
Common equity	$233
Operating income	$ 70
Net financial expense	14
Earnings	$ 56

The firm held the same amount of net financial obligations during the whole year for which the earnings were reported. The equity of this firm trades at a P/B ratio of 2.9. The firm pays no dividends.

a. Calculate the levered P/E ratio for this firm.

b. Calculate the enterprise P/B and P/E ratios.

Minicases

M13.1

Valuing the Operations and the Investments of a Property and Casualty Insurer: Chubb Corporation

Chubb Corporation is a property and casualty insurance holding company providing insurance through its subsidiaries in the United States, Canada, Europe, and parts of Australia, Latin America, and the Far East.

A frequently used measure of property and casualty insurance underwriting results is the combined loss and expense ratio. This ratio is the sum of the ratio of incurred losses and related loss adjustment expenses to premiums earned (the loss ratio) plus the ratio of underwriting expenses to premiums written (the expense ratio), after reducing both premium amounts by dividends to policyholders. When the combined ratio is under 100 percent, underwriting results are generally considered profitable; when the combined ratio is over 100 percent, underwriting results are generally considered unprofitable.

The net premiums and the loss, expense, and combined loss and expense ratios of the Chubb group of companies for the five years up to 1998 are shown below:

Year	Net Premiums (in millions) Written	Earned	Loss Ratios	Expense Ratios	Combined Loss and Expense Ratios
1994	$ 3,951.2	$ 3,776.3	67.0%	32.5%	99.5%
1995	4,306.0	4,147.2	64.7	32.1	96.8
1996	4,773.8	4,569.3	66.2	32.1	98.3
1997	5,448.0	5,157.4	64.5	32.4	96.9
1998	5,503.5	5,303.8	66.3	33.5	99.8
Total for five years ended December 31, 1998	$23,982.5	$22,954.0	65.7%	32.6%	98.3%

Chubb's combined loss and expense ratios are not at all impressive. But as well as underwriting, Chubb is involved in some commercial real estate operations—mainly in New Jersey and Florida—and earns investment income from its holdings of reserves. Exhibit 13.1 presents its income statement for the nine months ending September 30, 1999, along with its balance sheet of December 30, 1998. A statement of other comprehensive income is also given under net income. You will notice that, despite the high loss and expense ratios, Chubb reported net income for the nine months of $457.5 million on shareholders' equity at the beginning of the period of $5,644.1 million.

EXHIBIT 13.1

CHUBB CORPORATION
Income Statement for Nine Months Ending September 30, 1999
(in millions)

	Nine Months	
	1999	**1998**
Revenues		
Premiums earned	$ 4,209.4	$ 3,966.9
Investment income	654.8	613.8
Real estate	78.5	70.7
Realized investment gains	82.8	126.7
Total revenues	5,025.50	4,778.10
Claims and expenses		
Insurance claims	2,957.50	2,589.40
Amortization of deferred policy acquisition costs	1,136.10	1,096.30
Other insurance operation costs and expense	281.2	277.2
Real estate costs of sales and expenses	81.1	73.4
Investment expenses	11.2	10.2
Corporate expenses	39.9	22.7
Restructuring charge	—	40.0
Total claims and expenses	4,507.0	4,109.20
Income before federal and foreign income tax	518.5	668.9
Federal and foreign income tax	61.0	119.5
Net income	$ 457.50	$ 549.40
Other comprehensive income (loss)		
Change in unrealized appreciation of investments, net of tax	(400.3)	(24.0)
Foreign currency translation losses, net of tax	(9.4)	(12.1)
	(409.7)	(36.1)
Comprehensive income (loss)	$ 47.8	$ 513.3

Balance Sheet, December 31, 1998 (in millions)

	December 31, 1998
Assets	
Invested assets	
Short-term investments	$ 344.2
Fixed maturities	
Held-to-maturity—tax exempt (market $2,140.2)	2,002.2
Available-for-sale	
Tax exempt (cost $6,509.3)	6,935.1
Taxable (cost $4,259.0)	4,381.6
Equity securities (cost $1,002.6)	1,092.2
Total invested assets	14,755.3
Cash	8.3
Accrued investment income	221.0
Premiums receivable	1,199.3
Reinsurance recoverable on unpaid claims	1,306.6
Prepaid reinsurance premiums	134.6
Funds held for asbestos-related settlement	607.4

(continued)

LIVERPOOL JOHN MOORES UNIVERSITY
LEARNING & INFORMATION SERVICES

Deferred policy acquisition costs	728.7
Real estate assets	746.0
Deferred income tax	320.8
Other assets	718.0
Total assets	$20,746.0

Liabilities

Unpaid claims	10,356.5
Unearned premiums	2,915.7
Long-term debt	607.5
Dividend payable to shareholders	50.3
Accrued expense and other liabilities	1,171.9
Total liabilities	15,101.9

Commitments and Contingent Liabilities

Shareholders' equity

Preferred stock—authorized 4,000,000 shares; $1 par value, issued—none	—
Common stock—authorized 600,000,000 shares; $1 par value; issued 175,989,202 shares	176.0
Paid-in surplus	546.7
Retained earnings	5,604.0
Accumulated other comprehensive income	
Unrealized appreciation of investments, net of tax	414.7
Foreign currency translation losses, net of tax	(36.0)
Receivable from employee stock ownership plan	(86.3)
Treasury stock, at cost—13,722,376 shares	(975.0)
Total shareholders' equity	5,644.1
Total liabilities and shareholders' equity	$20,746.0

Chubb's 162.3 million shares traded at $50 each in October 1999. The firm's marginal tax rate on taxable income is 36 percent, but tax-exempt securities provided a significant portion of investment income for the nine months, yielding an effective tax rate on investment income of 15.4 percent in both 1999 and 1998.

A. Calculate Chubb's nine-month income from each of its activities: underwriting, real estate, and investments.

B. Based on the information before you, attempt to value a share of Chubb Corporation as of September 30, 1999. Use a cost of capital for operations of 10.5 percent.

C. Explain how each of the following featured in your valuations:
(1) Investment income.
(2) Realized investment gains.
(3) Change in unrealized appreciation of investments.
(4) Foreign currency translation losses.
(5) Net operating assets.
(6) Real estate assets.

D. Would you say that Chubb Corporation was particularly profitable? Would you say that it was creating value for its shareholders?

E. Calculate residual income on Chubb's "invested assets." How useful is this number for your valuation?

F. What features of Chubb Corporation's accounting—and of the accounting for insurers in general—might give you pause in basing a valuation on those financial statements?

G. If Chubb's current profitability were to continue, what would be your recommendation to management?

Real World Connection
See Exercises E9.6 and E9.8 in Chapter 9.

M13.2

Economic Profit and Value Generation: The Coca-Cola Company

The name Coca-Cola is known in households throughout the world. Of the approximately 48 billion beverage servings of all types drunk in the world each day, one billion bear the company's trade names: Coca-Cola, Diet Coke, Cherry Coke, Fanta, Sprite, TAB, Fresca, Minute Maid, and Hi-C, among many.

The Coca-Cola Company is a name that has also been a champion among investors, known for creating value for shareholders. From 1990 to 1997 Coke's sales grew from $10.3 billion to $18.9 billion and its share price increased from $12 per share to $67 per share. It traded at 40 times earnings at the end of 1997, and 23 times book value.

In its discussion and analysis in its annual report, Coca-Cola's management discussed performance measures that they feel indicate the value added in operations. One of those is a measure they refer to as "economic profit." Another is a measure they refer to as "economic value added":

> Economic profit and economic value added provide a framework by which we measure the value of our actions. We define economic profit as income from continuing operations after taxes, excluding interest, in excess of a computed capital charge for average operating capital employed. Economic value added represents the growth in economic profit from year to year. To ensure that our management team stays clearly focused on the key drivers of our business, economic value added and economic profit are used in determining annual incentive awards and long-term incentive awards for most eligible employees.

The company's review of selected financial data in its 1997 annual 10-K report includes a reference to economic profit, as seen in Exhibit 13.2. The company attaches a glossary to explain the terms in this schedule:

Glossary

Dividend Payout Ratio: Calculated by dividing cash dividends on common stock by net income available to common shareowners.

Economic Profit: Income from continuing operations, after taxes, excluding interest, in excess of a computed capital charge for average operating capital employed.

Free Cash Flow: Cash provided by operations less cash used in investing activities. The Company uses free cash flow along with borrowings to pay dividends and make share repurchases.

Net Debt and Net Capital: Debt and capital in excess of cash, cash equivalents and marketable securities not required for operations and certain temporary bottling investments.

Return on Capital: Calculated by dividing income from continuing operations—before changes in accounting principles, adjusted for interest expense—by average total capital.

Return on Common Equity: Calculated by dividing income from continuing operations—before changes in accounting principles, less preferred stock dividends—by average common shareowners' equity.

Total Capital: Equals shareowners' equity plus interest-bearing debt.

A. Show how Coke's economic profit measure is calculated. Use a tax rate of 37 percent.

B. What is the cost of capital (required return) that Coke uses for its operations?

C. Interpret what Coke's "economic profit" means.

D. How does Coke's measure of economic profit differ from the residual operating income measure in this chapter of the text? Calculate Coke's residual operating income for 1997. Also calculate the return on net operating assets (RNOA).

E. Coke has had considerable growth in economic profit, or as the firm calls this growth, economic value added. Calculate Coke's levered market price-to-book ratio. Do you think that the growth in economic profit justifies the multiple?

EXHIBIT 13.2

THE COCA-COLA COMPANY AND SUBSIDIARIES
Selected Financial Data
(in millions except per-share data, ratios, and growth rates)

	Year Ended December 31					
	1997	1996	1995	1994	1993	1992
Summary of Operations						
Net operating revenues	$18,868	$18,673	$18,127	$16,264	$14,030	$13,119
Cost of goods sold	6,015	6,738	6,940	6,168	5,160	5,055
Gross profit	12,853	11,935	11,187	10,096	8,870	8,064
Selling, administrative, and general expenses	7,852	8,020	7,161	6,459	5,771	5,317
Operating income	5,001	3,915	4,026	3,637	3,099	2,747
Interest income	211	238	245	181	144	164
Interest expense	258	286	272	199	168	171
Equity income	155	211	169	134	91	65
Other income (deductions)—net	583	87	86	(25)	7	(59)
Gains on issuances of stock by equity investees	363	431	74	—	12	—
Income from continuing operations before income taxes and changes in accounting principles	6,055	4,596	4,328	3,728	3,185	2,746
Income taxes	1,926	1,104	1,342	1,174	997	863
Income from continuing operations before changes in accounting principles	$ 4,129	$ 3,492	$ 2,986	$ 2,554	$ 2,188	$ 1,883
Net income	$ 4,129	$ 3,492	$ 2,986	$ 2,554	$ 2,176	$ 1,664
Preferred stock dividends	—	—	—	—	—	—
Net income available to common shareowners	$ 4,129	$ 3,492	$ 2,986	$ 2,554	$ 2,176	$ 1,664
Balance Sheet Data						
Cash, cash equivalents, and current marketable securities	$ 1,843	$ 1,658	$ 1,315	$ 1,531	$ 1,078	$ 1,063
Property, plant, and equipment—net	3,743	3,550	4,336	4,080	3,729	3,526
Depreciation	384	442	421	382	333	310
Capital expenditures	1,093	990	937	878	800	1,083
Total assets	16,940	16,161	15,041	13,873	12,021	11,052

Long-term debt	801	1,116	1,141	1,426	1,428	1,120
Total debt	3,875	4,513	4,064	3,509	3,100	3,207
Shareowners' equity	7,311	6,156	5,392	5,235	4,584	3,888
Total capital	11,186	10,669	9,456	8,744	7,684	7,095
Other Key Financial Measures						
Total debt-to-total capital	34.6%	42.3%	43.0%	40.1%	40.3%	45.2%
Net debt-to-net capital	21.9%	31.4%	32.2%	25.5%	29.0%	33.1%
Return on common equity	61.3%	60.5%	56.2%	52.0%	51.7%	46.4%
Return on capital	39.4%	36.7%	34.9%	32.7%	31.2%	29.4%
Dividend payout ratio	33.6%	35.7%	37.2%	39.4%	40.6%	44.3%
Free cash flow	$ 3,533	$ 2,413	$ 2,102	$ 2,146	$ 1,623	$ 873
Economic profit	$ 3,325	$ 2,718	$ 2,291	$ 1,896	$ 1,549	$ 1,300

Real World Connection

See Exercise E4.6 and Minicase M4.2 in Chapter 4, Exercise E5.13 in Chapter 5, Exercise E14.6 in Chapter 14, and Exercise E15.4 in Chapter 15.

M13.3

A Firm with Implied Value of Operations of Zero: Comverse Technology, Inc.

Comverse Technology Inc. designs and manufactures computer and telecommunications systems for multimedia communications. The company's subsidiaries are Comverse Inc., Verint Systems Inc., and Ulticom, Inc. The company's products are used in a broad range of applications by wireless and wireline telecommunications network operators and service providers, call centers, and other public and commercial organizations worldwide.

When the telecom sector collapsed in 2001 and 2002, the firm's sales and profits declined considerably. For its second quarter ended July 31, 2002, Comverse reported earnings of only 2 cents per share, down from 15 cents from the same quarter of the previous year. The balance sheet for the quarter is below.

COMVERSE TECHNOLOGY INC. AND SUBSIDIARIES
Condensed Consolidated Balance Sheets (in thousands, except share data)

	January 31, 2002	July 31, 2002
Assets		
Current Assets:		
Cash and cash equivalents	$1,361,862	$1,391,705
Bank time deposits and short-term investments	530,622	415,294
Accounts receivable, net	371,928	291,169
Inventories	56,024	51,055
Prepaid expenses and other current assets	76,667	69,344
Total current assets	2,397,103	2,218,567
Property and equipment, net	181,761	175,667
Other assets	125,299	139,581
Total assets	$2,704,163	$2,533,815
Liabilities and Stockholders' Equity:		
Current Liabilities:		
Accounts payable and accrued expenses	$ 322,402	$ 255,998
Advance payments from customers	39,576	44,563
Other current liabilities	4,875	47,051
Total current liabilities	366,853	347,612
Convertible debentures	600,000	434,000
Liability for severance pay	9,772	9,421
Other liabilities	49,827	9,997
Total liabilities	1,026,452	801,030
Minority interest	61,303	80,139
Stockholders' Equity:		
Common stock, $0.10 per value—authorized, 600,000,000 shares; issued and outstanding, 186,248,350 and 186,981,198	18,625	18,698
Additional paid-in capital	1,018,232	1,073,681
Retained earnings	574,763	555,110
Accumulated other comprehensive income	4,788	5,157
Total stockholders' equity	1,616,408	1,652,646
Total liabilities and stockholders' equity	$2,704,163	$2,533,815

After the second quarter report was published, shares of the firm traded at $7 each. Based on the July 2002 balance sheet, calculate the following:

A. Book value per share.

B. Net financial assets per share.

C. The unlevered price-to-book ratio.

D. The ratio of equity price to net financial assets.

What value is the market placing on the operations?

You will observe that the shares are trading at less than the amount of cash that the firm is holding. Analysts often consider this situation as a certain case of underpricing. What other information would you like to have before you purchase this stock?

Simple Forecasting and Simple Valuation

LINKS

Link to previous chapter

Chapter 13 developed a simplified valuation model based on forecasting operating profitability and growth in investment in operations.

This chapter

This chapter develops simple valuation models based on forecasts of operating profitability and growth, from information in the current financial statements.

Link to next chapter

Chapter 15 develops complete valuations based on information both within and outside the financial statements.

Link to web page

Learn more about simple forecasting and valuation—check out the text website at www.mhhe.com/penman2e.

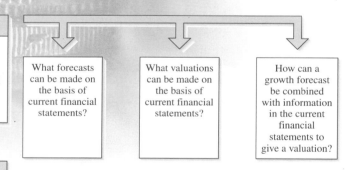

What forecasts can be made on the basis of current financial statements?

What valuations can be made on the basis of current financial statements?

How can a growth forecast be combined with information in the current financial statements to give a valuation?

In valuation analysts aim for simplicity. They strip away any features of the business that are not involved in value generation. And if some features are relatively important and others are of minor importance, analysts concentrate their efforts on those that are important. And they look for useful approximations that give a quick benchmark valuation before proceeding to a more complete, but more complex, valuation.

In this spirit, the last chapter stripped away the forecasting of financing activities to simplify the valuation. If the balance sheet measures the value of the net financial obligations, this is appropriate. The efficiencies are clear: Not only is the forecasting task reduced, but the analyst does not have to deal with changes in the discount rate arising from changes in leverage.

Simplicity comes not only from fewer factors to forecast, but also from using less information to make forecasts. A potentially large amount of information—from strategic planning, marketing research, the analysis of production costs, and an assessment of the viability of R&D, to name a few—is involved in forecasting. If we can limit ourselves to

The Analyst's Checklist

After reading this chapter you should understand:

- How simple forecasts reduce the valuation task.
- How simple forecasts give simple valuations.
- What forecasts can be obtained from the current financial statements.
- How components of income statements combine with components of balance sheets to give a simple forecast.
- How sales forecasts combine with financial statements to give simple forecasts.
- When simple forecasts and simple valuations work as reasonable approximations.
- How simple forecasting works as an analysis tool in sensitivity analysis.
- How simple valuation models work in reverse engineering.

After reading this chapter you should be able to:

- Make the three simple forecasts—SF1, SF2, and SF3—that are indicated by current financial statements.
- Integrate sales forecasts into a simple forecast.
- Calculate simple valuations from simple forecasts.
- Calculate enterprise price-to-book ratios price-earning ratios from simple forecasts.
- Value firms from short-term and long-term growth forecasts.
- Use simple forecasting in sensitivity analysis.
- Use simple valuation models in reverse engineering to challenge market speculation.

a small set of information that captures much of the broader information, yet still obtain reasonable value approximations, we are parsimonious in our endeavor. Simple schemes are justified if the benefit from reduced information analysis outweighs the cost of having only approximate valuations.

This chapter develops simple valuations based on limited information as a prelude to the next chapter, which utilizes the full set of information for forecasting. The focus is on the (limited) information that is available in the financial statements. In many cases—particularly for relatively mature firms—the financial statements aggregate considerable information and can be a reasonable indicator of the future. If, for example, profit margins or asset turnovers in current statements are good indicators of future margins and turnovers, the current financial statements are quite informative. The chapter asks the question: What forecasts and valuations can be made solely from information in the financial statements? In this chapter you will understand that historical financial statements are not "backward looking" but very much forward looking. You will also get a sense of the limits of the information provided by financial statements. With this in mind, the financial statement analysis of Part Two of the book—with its emphasis on core operating income as a basis for forecasting—is set up to elicit the information in the financial statements that is required for forecasting. It is now that you will strike pay dirt from the thorough reformulation and analysis of financial statements.

The focus of financial statement information has particular importance in fundamental analysis. The fundamental analyst, you'll remember, follows the rule of not mixing what he knows with speculation. Forecasting involves considerable speculation—particularly when forecasting the "long term" (for a continuing value calculation, for example). Financial statement information is what we know about the present (subject, of course, to the quality of the accounting). By isolating this more reliable information, we ensure we do not contaminate it with more speculative, softer information. Speculation can be added to the forecasting later (in the next chapter), but let's be sure of the relatively "hard" and "soft" inputs to our forecasting and give the former more weight. For Internet firms during the bubble, the weight given to speculative forecasts of rosy future profits, rather than current losses, turned out to be a mistake.

Simple valuations are only approximate—and sometimes are not only simple, but simple-minded. Yet even a simple valuation can serve as an analysis tool. The chapter will show that, by reverse engineering simple models, the analyst can compare the market's implicit forecast of profitability and growth with the forecasts provided in the financial statements. The market's forecast presumably uses wider information, but it is a speculation to be checked against "what we know" from the financial statements.

SIMPLE FORECASTS AND SIMPLE VALUATIONS FROM FINANCIAL STATEMENTS

The analysis of current financial statements reveals current profitability and growth. **Simple forecasts**—and the simple valuations derived from them—assume that current profitability and/or growth will continue in the future. We lay out three simple forecasts from the financial statements in the three sections that follow.

Forecasting from Book Values: SF1 Forecasts

A balance sheet has an implied forecast that is obtained by applying a required return to the balance sheet amount. The required return is the expected earnings rate, indicating future earnings that are expected if the book values (the net assets) earn at this rate. Table 14.1 gives one-year-ahead forecasts of earnings components that can be made from balance sheet components. We refer to this type of simple forecast as an SF1 forecast. Operating income is forecasted by expecting the net operating assets to earn at the required return for operations. Net financial expense is forecasted by expecting the net financial obligations to incur the expense at the cost of net debt. Full comprehensive earnings is forecasted by expecting the common shareholders' equity to earn at the required return for equity. These forecasts also can be restated as residual earnings forecasts, which are also given in the table. SF1 forecasts always forecast that residual earnings for the relevant component will be zero.

We know from the discussion in the last chapter that these SF1 forecasts are good forecasts if the relevant balance sheet amount is at fair value. So an SF1 forecast is a typically good forecast for the financing activities, but a poor forecast for the operating activities.

TABLE 14.1
Simple Forecasts from Book Values (SF1)

Earnings Component	Forecast of Earnings Component (forecast earnings and its components by forecasting that the relevant balance sheet component will earn at the required return)	Forecast of Residual Earnings (forecast that residual earnings and its components will be zero)
Operating	$OI_1 = (\rho_F - 1)NOA_0$	$OI_1 - (\rho_F - 1)NOA_0 = 0$
Financing	$NFE_1 = (\rho_D - 1)NFO_0$	$NFE_1 - (\rho_D - 1)NFO_0 = 0$
Earnings	$Earn_1 = (\rho_E - 1)CSE_0$	$Earn_1 - (\rho_E - 1)CSE_0 = 0$

To see how these SF1 forecasts tie together, consider the pro forma forecasted income statement for Year 1 for MS Inc. an equity investment fund that carries its net operating assets (equity investments) at market value on its balance sheet. The pro forma income statement using SF1 forecasts follows, along with the Year 0 balance sheet:

MS INC.
Balance Sheet, Year 0

Assets		Liabilities and Equity	
Marketable equity securities (at market)	23.4	Long-term (10%) debt (NFO)	7.7
		Common shareholders' equity (CSE)	15.7
Net operating assets (NOA)	23.4		23.4

Pro Forma Income Statement, Year 1

Operating income	2.654
Net financial expense: 0.10 × 7.7	(0.770)
Earnings: 0.12 × 15.7	1.884

If the equity investments and debt are at fair market value, we know that the equity of this firm is worth its book value, 15.7. The value of the operations is 23.4. This is a fair value balance sheet.

The required return for equity is 12 percent which, when applied to the book value of the equity, yields a Year 1 earnings forecast of $1.884 million. Forecasted net financial expense is the cost of debt (10 percent) applied to the book value of the debt. The forecasted operating income is $2.654 million, and you may have wondered how we got this. A plug, you say, because net financial expense was forecasted as $0.77 million, so operating income must be $1.884 million + $0.77 million. But it's more than a plug. The forecast of operating income is 11.34 percent of the $23.4 million invested in equity securities at the beginning of Year 1. And 11.34 percent is the required return for operations for MS Inc. using the weighted-average cost of capital calculation.[1] Knowing this cost of capital, we would have forecasted operating income for Year 1 as 0.1134 × 23.4 = 2.654. The pro forma Year 1 income statement would have been developed as follows:

MS INC.
SF1 Pro Forma Income Statement, Year 1

Earnings Component	Required Return × Balance Sheet Component	
Operating income	0.1134 × 23.4	2.654
Net financial expense	0.10 × 7.7	(0.770)
Earnings	0.12 × 15.7	1.884

So you see that each component of earnings is forecasted by applying the relevant required return to the beginning balance sheet amount, and these forecasts total to the earnings forecast that applies the required return for equity to the beginning common stockholders' equity.

---

[1] The required return for operations weights the equity cost of capital (12 percent) and the cost of debt (10 percent) by their respective values, given in the fair value balance sheet:

$$\text{Required return for operations} = \left[\frac{15.7}{23.4} \times 12.0\%\right] + \left[\frac{7.7}{23.4} \times 10.0\%\right] = 11.34\%$$

The SF1 residual earnings forecasts are zero for all future years. Thus the valuation of the common equity implied by the forecasts is

$$\text{Value of common equity} = \text{Book value of common equity} \qquad \textbf{(14.1)}$$

$$V_0^E = \text{CSE}_0$$

and this is appropriate for MS Inc.'s balance sheet. Also, the value of the operations is the book value of the net operating assets.

An SF1 forecast is usually a good forecast for the financing activities. But, if operating items on the balance sheet are not at market value, they will not yield sound SF1 forecasts. This is usually the case, of course. Even for an investment fund like MS Inc., where investments are marked to market, the market values on the balance sheet may not be a good indicator of future earnings (nor of value) if the market prices at which they are recorded are not efficient prices. Indeed, for an active fund that attempts to buy underpriced investments, we expect the market value to be lower than fair value and the fund to be worth a premium over book value.

Forecasting from Earnings and Book Values: SF2 Forecasts

With the balance sheet an imperfect predictor, we can turn to the income statement and use current earnings as a predictor. If we were to conclude that current (core) earnings are a good indicator of future earnings, we might forecast next year's earnings as equal to current (core) earnings. But that would be too simple, too naive. In making this extrapolation we'd want to take into account any new investments that would increase the earnings. Recognizing this, simple forecasts of earnings components based on current income statement and balance sheet numbers are given in Table 14.2, along with corresponding forecasts of residual earnings and abnormal earnings growth. We refer to these forecasts as SF2 forecasts. Because forecasts for financing activities are adequately provided by an SF1 forecast, we apply SF2 forecasts only to the operating income and total earnings.

The SF2 operating income forecast predicts that operating income will be the same as in the current year, but there will be an increase in operating income if there has been an increase in net operating assets in the current year; it further predicts that the addition to investment will earn at the required return. The comprehensive earnings forecast predicts an increase in earnings if there has been an increase in common shareholders' equity in the current year, with the increase earning at the required return for equity.

We illustrate the SF2 forecast using the financial statements for PPE Inc., a manufacturer with just one asset: property, plant, and equipment (PPE). The cash flow statement is derived from the income statement and balance sheet. Make sure you can prepare this.[2]

In Chapter 2 we discussed the reasons why accountants do not produce perfect balance sheets, the reasons why PPE Inc. is more typical than MS Inc. PPE Inc. looks simple but it is representative. The typical firm has many more net operating assets and net financial obligations, but they all fall into these two categories. And, typically, net financial obligations are measured at or close to market value, but most net operating assets are not. Many operating assets are measured at depreciated historical cost, as is the property,

---

[2] Free cash flow = OI − ΔNOA = 9.8 − 4.5 = 5.3. Net dividends paid can also be deduced from the change in shareholders' equity using the clean-surplus equation: d = Earnings − ΔCSE = 5.3. The investment in property, plant, and equipment (PPE) is the change in PPE in the balance sheet (4.5 million) plus the reduction of PPE of 21.4 million through depreciation.

TABLE 14.2 Simple Forecasts from Earnings and Book Values (SF2)

Earnings Component	Forecast of Operating Income and Earnings (forecast that earnings will be the same as in the current year, adjusted for changes in the balance sheet earning at the required return)	Forecast of Residual Earnings (forecast that residual earnings will be the same as in the current year)	Forecast of Abnormal Earnings Growth (forecast that abnormal earnings growth will be zero)
Operating Earnings	$OI_1 = OI_0 + (\rho_F - 1)\Delta NOA_0$ $Earn_1 = Earn_0 + (\rho_E - 1)\Delta CSE_0$	$ReOI_1 = ReOI_0$ $RE_1 = RE_0$	$AOIG = 0$ $AEG = 0$

plant, and equipment here; some operating assets are measured at zero, as in the case of omitted knowledge assets and other intangibles. This leaves us with the challenge of forecasting future residual earnings on abnormal earnings growth to determine the amount at which the equity should trade.

PPE INC.
Balance Sheet, December 31, Year 0

Assets	Year 0	Prior Year	Liabilities and Equity	Year 0	Prior Year
Property, plant, and equipment (at cost less accumulated depreciation)	74.4	69.9	Long-term debt (NFO)	7.7	7.0
			Common shareholders' equity (CSE)	66.7	62.9
Net operating assets (NOA)	74.4	69.9		74.4	69.9

Income Statement, Year 0

Operating income	
Sales of products	124.9
Cost of goods sold (including depreciation of 21.4)	(114.6)
	10.3
Other operating expenses	(0.5)
	9.8
Net financial expense: 0.10×7.0	(0.7)
Earnings	9.1

Statement of Cash Flows, Year 0

Cash flow from operations		
Operating income	9.8	
Depreciation	21.4	31.2
Cash flow in investing activities		
Investment in PPE (21.4 + 4.5)		(25.9)
Free cash flow		5.3
Cash flow in financing activities		
Net dividends paid		5.3

To develop a forecast of PPE Inc.'s Year 1 income statement with SF2 forecasts, suppose that the cost of capital for the firm's operations is the same as that for MS Inc., 11.34 percent:

PPE INC.

SF2 Pro Forma Income Statement, Year 1

Earnings Component	SF2 Forecasts of Operating Income and Earnings Current Earnings + (Required Return × Change in Balance Sheet Component)	
Operating income	$9.8 + (0.1134 \times 4.5)$	10.310
Net financial expense (SF1)	0.10×7.7	(0.770)
Earnings	$9.1 + (? \times 3.8)$	9.540

The changes in the balance sheet components here are the changes in Year 0 over the prior year. The earnings forecast nets the forecasts of operating income and interest expense. The earnings forecast cannot be obtained by forecasting from the current earnings and the change in equity for the current year until we know the cost of equity capital (thus the question mark in the pro forma statement). And we can't calculate that (using market leverage in equation (13.8) in the previous chapter) until we know the value of the equity.

These SF2 forecasts are the same thing as forecasting that the relevant residual income will be the same next year as it is currently, as indicated in the right-hand column of Table 14.2.[3] For PPE Inc., the forecast of operating income of 10.310 for Year 1 means forecasted ReOI for Year 1 is $10.310 - (0.1134 \times 74.4) = 1.873$, which is the same as its ReOI in Year 0, that is, $9.8 - (0.1134 \times 69.9) = 1.873$.

Extrapolating to future years, the SF2 forecast says that residual earnings is expected to be the same as it is now perpetually into the future. Using the residual operating income model, the valuation of the equity with a perpetuity in ReOI at the current level is

$$\text{Value of common equity} = \text{Book value of common equity} + \text{Capitalized current ReOI} \qquad \textbf{(14.2)}$$

$$7$$

For PPE Inc. the equity valuation is $66.7 + 1.873/0.1134 = 83.22$ and the levered price-to-book ratio is $83.22/66.7 = 1.25$. Just as the benchmark SF1 forecast gives us a benchmark valuation (of $V_0^E = CSE_0$), the benchmark SF2 forecast also gives us a benchmark valuation. The value of the operations is $V_0^{NOA} = 83.22 + 7.7 = 90.92$, and the enterprise P/B is $90.92/74.4 = 1.22$. This value for the operations can also be calculated as

$$V_0^{NOA} = NOA_0 + \frac{OI_1 - (\rho_F - 1)NOA_0}{\rho_F - 1}$$

---

[3] To see this algebraically,

$$OI_1 = OI_0 + (\rho_F - 1)\Delta NOA_{-1}$$

is the same as

$$OI_1 = OI_0 + (\rho_F - 1)NOA_0 - (\rho_F - 1)NOA_{-1}$$

Thus

$$OI_1 - (\rho_F - 1)NOA_0 = OI_0 - (\rho_F - 1)NOA_{-1}$$

and so on for the other components.

but, dividing through by $\rho_F - 1$, you can see that it can be calculated in an easier way:

Value of operations = Capitalized operating income forecasted for next year

$$V_0^{\text{NOA}} = \frac{\text{OI}_1}{\rho_F - 1} \qquad \textbf{(14.2a)}$$

that is, by just capitalizing the SF2 forecast of operating income for next year. For PPE Inc., this calculation is $10.310/0.1134 = 90.92$, as before.

The valuation in equation (14.2a) looks familiar: If value can be calculated by capitalizing forward operating income, it must be that abnormal operating income growth (AOIG) is expected to be zero. Indeed, Table 14.2 shows that an SF2 forecast is also a forecast that abnormal income growth is zero. This must of course, be the case, for abnormal earnings growth is always equal to the change in residual income, and an SF2 forecast is a forecast of no growth in residual income. For PPE Inc., expected abnormal operating income growth (AOIG) for Year 1 (from operating income of 9.8 and free cash flow of 5.3 in Year 0) is also $[10.31 + (0.1134 \times 5.3)] - (1.1134 \times 9.8) = 0$.

Accordingly, an SF2 forecast has a particular significance. Whereas an SF1 forecast implies a normal P/B ratio, an SF2 forecast implies a normal P/E ratio. To suggest that the P/E should be different from normal, one must make a forecast that differs from an SF2 forecast.

With the equity value now determined, we can calculate the equity cost of capital following equation (13.8) in the last chapter:

$$\text{Equity cost of capital} = 0.1134 + \left[\frac{7.7}{83.22} \times (0.1134 - 0.10) \right]$$

$$= 0.1146$$

And now we can complete the SF2 pro forma income statement for Year 1 by forecasting earnings directly using this cost of capital: Forecasted Year 1 earnings is $9.1 + (0.1146 \times 3.8) = 9.54$. Note, however, that we do not need this equity cost of capital to calculate the value of the equity. Valuing the operations suffices.

Box 14.1 gives SF2 valuations for Nike and Reebok. There is just one modification. Forecasts of future operating income, ReOI, and AOIG are based on current core operating income, that is, operating income purged of unusual items. If unusual items will not be repeated in the future, we should exclude them in forecasting. This is what the analysis of core income is designed to achieve—to give us a better forecast of future operating income. Always work with core income in forecasting.

Forecasting from Accounting Rates of Return: SF3 Forecasts

An SF2 forecast predicts that current income from assets in place at the beginning of the current period earning at the current rate of return will persist, but any addition to assets over the period will earn at the required rate of return. An alternative forecast predicts that all assets, both those in place at the beginning of the current period and those added over the period, will earn at the current rate of return. That is, an SF3 forecast predicts that a firm will maintain its current rate of return in the future. Table 14.3 summarizes SF3 forecasts.

The SF3 operating income forecast is made by predicting that the net operating assets in place at the beginning of Year 1 (those at the end of Year 0, NOA_0) will earn, in Year 1, at the RNOA in the current year, RNOA_0. If there are unusual items in the current year, the core RNOA_0 should be used. Similarly, the full earnings forecast is the current ROCE_0 applied to the common equity at the beginning of Year 1 (CSE_0).

NIKE, INC.

Required return for operations		11.0%
Core operating income	1996	$ 567 million
Net operating assets	1995	$2,208 million
	1996	$2,659 million
Core residual operating income	1996: 567 − (0.11 × 2,208)	$324.1 million
SF2 forecast of operating income	1997: 567 + (0.11 × 451)	$616.6 million
SF2 forecast of ReOI	1997	$324.1 million
SF2 forecast of AOIG (change in ReOI)	1998	0

Value of common equity:

$$V_{1996}^{E} = CSE_{1996} + \frac{ReOI_{1996}}{0.11} = 2,431 + \frac{324.1}{0.11}$$

$5,377 million

Value per share on 143.629 million shares

$37.44

$$V_{1996}^{NOA} = V_{1996}^{E} + NFO_{1996} = 5,377 + 228$$

$5,605 million

ReOI valuation of operations:

$$V_{1996}^{NOA} = NOA_{1996} + \frac{ReOI_{1996}}{0.11} = 2,659 + \frac{324.1}{0.11}$$

$5,605 million

AOIG valuation of operations:

$$V_{1996}^{NOA} = \frac{OI_{1997}}{0.11} = \frac{616.6}{0.11}$$

$5,605 million

Nike traded at $104 per share at the end of fiscal year 1996.

REEBOK INTERNATIONAL LTD.

Required return for operations		10.1%
Core operating income	1996	$ 174 million
Net operating assets	1995	$1,220 million
	1996	$1,135 million
Core residual operating income	1996: 174 − (0.101 × 1,220)	$ 50.8 million
SF2 forecast of operating income	1997: 174 − (0.101 × 85)	$165.4 million
SF2 forecast of ReOI	1997	$ 50.8 million
SF2 forecast of AOIG (change in ReOI)	1998	0

Value of common equity:

$$V_{1996}^{E} \text{ before minority interest (MI)} = CSE_{1996} + MI_{1996} + \frac{ReOI_{1996}}{0.101}$$

$$= 415 + \frac{50.8}{0.101}$$

$918 million

Value of minority interest (at 14 times 1996 MI earnings)	$210 million
Value of common equity	$708 million
Value per share on 55.840 million shares	$12.68

$$V_{1996}^{NOA} = V_{1996}^{E} \text{ before MI} + NFO_{1996} = 918 + 720 \qquad \text{\$1,638 million}$$

ReOI valuation of operations:

$$V_{1996}^{NOA} = NOA_{1996} + \frac{ReOI_{1996}}{0.101} = 1,135 + \frac{50.8}{0.101} \qquad \text{\$1,638 million}$$

AOIG valuation of operations:

$$V_{1996}^{NOA} = \frac{OI_{1997}}{0.101} = \frac{165.4}{0.101} \qquad \text{\$1,638 million}$$

Reebok traded at \$43 per share at the end of fiscal year 1996.

TABLE 14.3 **Simple Forecasts from Current Accounting Rates of Return (SF3)**

Earnings Component	Forecast of Operating Income and Earnings (forecast that the relevant balance sheet component will earn at the current profitability)	Forecast of Residual Earnings (forecast that residual earnings will change, not because of changes in profitability, but because of changes in the relevant balance sheet amounts earning at the current profitability)
Operating Earnings	$OI_1 = RNOA_0 \times NOA_0$ $Earn_1 = ROCE_0 \times CSE_0$	$[RNOA_1 - (\rho_F - 1)] NOA_0 = [RNOA_0 - (\rho_F - 1)] NOA_0$ $[ROCE_1 - (\rho_E - 1)] CSE_0 = [ROCE_0 - (\rho_E - 1)] CSE_0$

For PPE Inc. the current (Year 0) core RNOA, NBC, and ROCE (with beginning-of-year balance sheet amounts in the denominator) are 14.02 percent, 10.00 percent, and 14.47 percent, respectively.[4] The SF3 forecast of the income statement is as follows:

PPE INC.

SF3 Pro Forma Income Statement, Year 1

Earnings Component	SF3 Forecasts of Operating Income and Earnings Current Rate of Return × Balance Sheet Component	
Operating income	0.1402×74.4	10.431
Net financial expense (SF1)	0.10×7.7	0.770
Earnings	$(? \times 66.7)$	9.661

The forecasted OI minus interest expense nets to 9.661, but this earnings amount differs from the current ROCE applied to CSE. PPE's ROCE for Year 0 is 14.47 percent, so you might forecast Year 1 earnings as $0.1447 \times 66.7 = 9.651$, not 9.661 (so the

[4] These rates of return are 13.58 percent, 9.52 percent, and 14.04 percent if averages are used in the denominator. Averages were used in the denominator in Chapter 11 and, as these measure the earning rates better, they should be applied to assets put in place. We use beginning-of-year amounts in the denominator here to keep the calculations clear. When it comes to forecasting it is easier to think of assets and liabilities to be put in place at the beginning of a future period rather than average assets for the period. And it usually makes little difference because the timing of future investments within a year is usually not predictable.

appropriate ROCE is left as a question mark in the pro forma statement). What's wrong? ROCE is affected by financial leverage. The ROCE of 14.47 percent for Year 0 is based on CSE at the beginning of the year and is reconciled to the RNOA of 14.02 percent by financial leverage at the beginning of the year. But the leverage has changed from the beginning of Year 0 to the beginning of Year 1 (which is the end of Year 0). So we would expect the ROCE to change even though RNOA is not expected to change. We can remedy this by forecasting that the ROCE in Year 1 will be the same as that in Year 0 but with an adjustment for financial leverage:

$$\text{Leverage-adjusted ROCE}_0 = \text{RNOA}_0 + \frac{\text{NFO}_0 \text{ (end)}}{\text{CSE}_0 \text{ (end)}}(\text{RNOA}_0 - \text{NBC}_0)$$

where the financial leverage, $\text{NFO}_0/\text{CSE}_0$, is at the beginning of Year 1. When this ROCE is used to forecast, the RNOA will be the same as in Year 0 but ROCE will be different because of the change in leverage. For PPE Inc.,

$$\text{Leverage-adjusted ROCE}_0 = 0.1402 + \left[\frac{7.7}{66.7} \times (0.1402 - 0.10) \right] = 0.1448$$

Accordingly, the forecast of earnings for Year 1 is $0.1448 \times 66.7 = 9.661$ (corrected for rounding error). This is indeed the net amount of the OI and NFE forecasts in the pro forma income statement. The adjustment doesn't make much difference here and, given uncertainty about the cost of capital anyway, can usually be ignored. But it cannot be ignored if there has been a big change in leverage, as with Reebok in 1996. Note again, however, that we do not need the equity cost of capital for valuation. Valuing the operations suffices.

Just as an SF2 forecast implies a particular residual income and abnormal earnings growth forecast, so does an SF3 forecast. Residual operating income is driven by RNOA and investment in net operating assets. So residual operating income one-year-ahead, ReOI_1, is $\text{ReOI}_1 = [\text{RNOA}_1 - (\rho_F - 1)]\text{NOA}_0$. But, if we forecast that future RNOA will be the same as current core RNOA, so that $\text{RNOA}_1 = \text{Core RNOA}_0$, then

$$\text{SF3 forecast of ReOI}_1 = [\text{Core RNOA}_0 - (\rho_F - 1)]\text{NOA}_0$$

The forecast for residual earnings (RE) is similar, as Table 14.3 indicates. For PPE Inc., the ReOI forecast for Year 1 is $10.431 - (0.1134 \times 74.4) = 1.994$, which is also equal to the Year 0 RNOA of 14.02 percent applied to Year 0 net operating assets of 74.4: $(0.1402 - 0.1134) \times 74.4 = 1.994$. As this is greater than residual operating income of 1.873, this SF3 forecast predicts growth. Indeed, abnormal operating income growth (AOIG) is the increase in ReOI: Whereas forecasted AOIG for an SF2 forecast was zero, it is 0.121 for an SF3 forecast.

With an SF3 forecast, growth is forecasted by the current growth in net operating assets. One plus the growth rate in ReOI from Year 0 to Year 1 is:

$$\text{Growth rate in ReOI}_1 = \frac{[\text{RNOA}_1 - (\rho_F - 1)]\text{NOA}_0}{[\text{RNOA}_0 - (\rho_F - 1)]\text{NOA}_{-1}}$$

However, if we forecast $\text{RNOA}_1 = \text{RNOA}_0$, as we do with an SF3 forecast, the growth rate becomes

$$\text{Growth rate in ReOI}_1 = \frac{\text{NOA}_0}{\text{NOA}_{-1}}$$

That is, the forecasted growth in ReOI for the next year is given by the current growth of NOA. The growth forecast is given by information in the balance sheet.

Now suppose we use the SF3 forecasts for all future periods. That is, we predict that RNOA will be the same as current core RNOA indefinitely but NOA investments will continue to grow at the current rate. In this case ReOI will also grow indefinitely at this rate. Capitalizing the SF3 forecast of ReOI for Year 1 as a perpetuity with growth:

$$V_0^E = \text{CSE}_0 + \frac{[\text{Core RNOA}_0 - (\rho_F - 1)]\text{NOA}_0}{\rho_F - g} \qquad \textbf{(14.3)}$$

The growth rate is the forecasted growth in ReOI from Year 1 on, but in this case it is the forecasted growth in NOA at the current rate, $\text{NOA}_0/\text{NOA}_{-1}$. For PPE Inc., we forecasted ReOI_1 to be 1.994 and the current NOA grew at $74.4/69.9 = 1.0644$ from the previous year. So, using SF3 forecasts, the value of the equity is $66.7 + 1.994/(1.1134 - 1.0644) = 107.39$ and the levered P/B ratio is 1.61. The value of the operations is $107.39 + 7.7 = 115.09$, and the enterprise P/B is 1.55. The value of the operations can also be calculated as

$$V_0^{\text{NOA}} = \text{NOA}_0 + \frac{[\text{Core RNOA}_0 - (\rho_F - 1)]\text{NOA}_0}{\rho_F - g}$$

With a little rearrangement,

$$V_0^{\text{NOA}} = \text{NOA}_0 \times \frac{\text{Core RNOA}_0 - (g - 1)}{\rho_F - g} \qquad \textbf{(14.3a)}$$

(proof this for PPE Inc.) The multiplier here is the *enterprise price-to-book ratio*. The multiplier compares RNOA relative to the growth rate (in the numerator) to the required return relative to the growth rate (in the denominator). You can see the two ReOI drivers, RNOA and NOA, working together here. Remember that g is 1 plus the growth rate, so $g - 1$ is the growth rate. If the RNOA is greater than the required return for operations, then more value is added to book value the higher the RNOA is relative to the growth rate. But growth also contributes: For a given RNOA, (higher than the required return), more value is added if growth is higher. If RNOA equals the growth rate, the enterprise P/B is normal.

Correspondingly, an abnormal operating income growth valuation applies a multiplier that incorporates the growth rate to the SF3 forecast of forward operating income:

$$V_0^{\text{NOA}} = \text{OI}_1 \times \frac{1}{\rho_F - 1}\left[1 + \frac{\text{AOIG}_2 / \text{OI}_1}{\rho_F - g}\right] \qquad \textbf{(14.4)}$$

The multiplier is a *forward enterprise P/E ratio*. This multiplier also can be expressed as follows:

$$V_0^{\text{NOA}} = \text{OI}_1 \times \frac{1}{\rho_F - 1}\left[1 + \frac{G_2 - \rho_F}{\rho_F - g}\right] \qquad \textbf{(14.4a)}$$

where G_2 is 1 + the cum-dividend growth rate in operating income for Year 2 ahead (with free cash flow dividend from Year 1 reinvested), and g is still the growth rate in forecasted net operating assets. This multiplier has a similar form to the net operating assets multiplier: The numerator compares cum-dividend growth in operating income to the required return, and the denominator compares the required return to the growth rate.

TABLE 14.4 Simple Forecasts and Simple Valuation Models

Simple Forecast	Simple Valuation of the Equity	Simple Valuation of the Operations
SF1	$V_0^E = CSE_0$	$V_0^{NOA} = NOA_0$
SF2	$V_0^E = CSE_0 + \dfrac{Re\,OI_0}{\rho_F - 1}$	$V_0^{NOA} = NOA_0 + \dfrac{Re\,OI_0}{\rho_F - 1}$
		$= \dfrac{OI_1}{\rho_F - 1}$
SF3	$V_0^E = CSE_0 + \dfrac{[Core\,RNOA_0 - (\rho_F - 1)]NOA_0}{\rho_F - g}$	$V_0^{NOA} = NOA_0 + \dfrac{[Core\,RNOA_0 - (\rho_F - 1)]NOA_0}{\rho_F - g}$
		$= NOA_0 \times \dfrac{Core\,RNOA_0 - (g - 1)}{\rho_F - g}$
		$V_0^{NOA} = OI_1 \times \dfrac{1}{\rho_F - 1}\left[1 + \dfrac{AOIG_2\big/OI_1}{\rho_F - g}\right]$
		$= OI_1 \times \dfrac{1}{\rho_F - 1}\left[1 + \dfrac{G_2 - \rho_F}{\rho_F - g}\right]$

The calculation in equation (14.4a) requires a pro forma for Year 2 in order to forecast G.[5] The calculation in equation (14.3a) follows directly from the ReOI forecast for Year 1. Abnormal operating income growth for Year 2 ($AOIG_2$) is the forecasted growth in ReOI for that year, that is, the forecast of ReOI for Year 1 growing at the forecasted rate: $AOIG_2 = 1.994 \times 0.0644 = 0.1284$. So, for PPE Inc., the forward income multiplier is

$$\frac{1}{0.1134}\left[1 + \frac{0.1284\big/10.431}{1.1134 - 1.0644}\right] = 11.03.$$ Applying this multiplier to the SF3 forecast of Year 1 operating income of 10.431, the value of the operations is $10.431 \times 11.03 = 115.09$, as before (allowing for rounding error).

The SF1, SF2, and SF3 forecasts are summarized in Table 14.4, along with the **simple valuations** they yield. These valuations use only information in the financial statements. They should be seen as approximations, as starting points for more comprehensive valuations. The SF2 and SF3 forecasts are of no use for a firm with losses. The SF3 valuation works only for firms with positive residual income.

---

[5] For PPE Inc., the pro forma is developed as follows:

Forecasted $NOA_1 = NOA_0 \times g = 74.4 \times 1.0644 = 79.191$
Forecasted $OI_2 = NOA_1 \times RNOA_0 = 79.191 \times 0.1402 = \qquad 11.103$
$FCF_1 = OI_1 - \Delta NOA_1 = 10.431 - 4.791 = 5.64$
Reinvested FCF $= 5.64 \times 0.1134 = \qquad\qquad\qquad\underline{0.640}$
Cum-dividend OI $\qquad\qquad\qquad\qquad\qquad\qquad\underline{11.743}$

G_2 (cum-dividend growth rate in OI in Year 2) $= 11.743/10.431 = 1.1257$. Using this forecast of G_2 for the multiplier in equation (14.4a), the value of the operations is 115.07, as before.

SIMPLE FORECASTING: ADDING SPECULATION TO FINANCIAL STATEMENT INFORMATION

The SF3 valuation is based solely on information in financial statements. This information is (presumably) reliable information, but it is limited information. To enhance the valuation, the analyst adds speculation about how the future will be different from the picture presented in current financial statements.

The ReOI and AOIG models in equations (14.3) and (14.4) forecast growth on the basis of past growth in net operating assets. For Nike, net operating assets grew by 20.4 percent in 1996; Reebok's net operating assets declined by 7.0 percent. Neither number can be used in an SF3 valuation; one is negative and the other is greater than the required return (and the long-run growth rate can never be greater than the required return). One might use an average growth rate from the past three to five years instead. Alternatively, one might move to speculate about the future growth rate. The SF3 models can be adapted to a calculation that specifies any growth rate: Set *g* to the forecasted growth rate. The formulas also can be adapted to speculation about future profitability: Replace current RNOA in the models with a forecast of future RNOA. In doing so, of course, one is relying less on the financial statement information and shifting to speculation about the future.

Box 14.2 carries out a modified SF3 valuation for Nike and Reebok under the scenario of growth at 7 percent per year. This growth rate is arbitrary. The resulting valuations are less than the per-share market prices at the time, $104 for Nike and $43 for Reebok. Either this growth rate is too low or the market was overpricing these hot stocks. We shall see shortly that this valuation is a starting point for sensitivity analysis.

A Simple Forecast of Growth: Growth in Sales

Forecasting growth requires a sense of where the business is going. We will develop the apparatus to make the forecasts in the next chapter. But there is a simple forecast of NOA growth that can be made. Net operating assets are driven by sales and the asset turnover: NOA = Sales × 1/ATO. Thus if ATO is expected to be constant in the future, forecasting growth in sales is the same as forecasting growth in NOA. If Nike and Reebok have constant asset turnovers in manufacturing and selling footwear (and indeed they did over 1995 and 1996), then our 7 percent growth assumption in their SF3 calculations is a forecast for a 7 percent annual increase in sales. A sales forecast, you'll agree, is much easier to think about than an NOA forecast.

Recognize also that RNOA = Profit margin × ATO. So if we forecast a constant ATO, we forecast the constant RNOA in the SF3 forecast if we also forecast constant margins.

You see, then, that the SF3 valuation is likely to work best for firms that have fairly constant profit margins and turnovers and steady sales growth. Many retailers have this feature: Their current RNOA along with a sales growth forecast often give a good approximation. Look also at the valuation for the Coca-Cola Company in Box 14.3. On the other hand, firms that are changing their type of business (and thus their sales growth rates, profit margins, and asset turnovers) are not good candidates for an SF3 valuation. More analysis (as in the next chapter) is required.

NIKE, INC.

Cost of capital for operations		11%
Core RNOA	1996 (on average NOA)	23.3%
Forecasted growth rate for net operating assets		7%
Net operating assets	1996	$2,659 million
SF3 forecast of operating income	1997: 2,659 × 23.3%	$619.5 million
SF3 forecast of ReOI	1997	$327.1 million
SF3 forecast of AOIG (ReOI$_{1997}$ growing at 7%)	1998: 327.1 × 0.07	22.90 million

Value of common equity:

$$V^E_{1996} = CSE_{1996} + \frac{\overline{ReOI_{1997}}}{1.11-1.07} = 2,431 + \frac{327.1}{0.04} \qquad \$10,607 \text{ million}$$

Value per share on 143.629 million shares $\qquad\qquad$ $73.85

$$V^{NOA}_{1996} = V^E_{1996} + NFO_{1996} = 10,607 + 228 \qquad \$10,835 \text{ million}$$

ReOI valuation of operations:

$$V^{NOA}_{1996} = NOA_{1996} + \frac{(RNOA_{1996} - 0.11) \times NOA_{1996}}{1.11 - 1.07}$$

$$= 2,659 + \frac{(0.233 - 0.11) \times 2,659}{0.04} \qquad \$10,835 \text{ million}$$

$$V^{NOA}_{1996} = NOA_{1996} \times \frac{RNOA_{1996} - (g - 1)}{1.11 - 1.07}$$

$$= 2,659 \times \frac{(0.233 - 0.07)}{0.04} \qquad \$10,835 \text{ million}$$

AOIG valuation of operations
$$V^{NOA}_{1996} = OI_{1997} \times \frac{1}{0.11}\left[1 + \frac{AOIG_{1998}/OI_{1997}}{1.11 - 1.07}\right]$$

$$= 619.5 \times \frac{1}{0.11}\left[1 + \frac{22.90/619.5}{0.04}\right]$$

$\qquad\qquad$ $10,835 million

REEBOK INTERNATIONAL LTD.

Required return for operations		10.1%
Core RNOA	1996 (on average NOA)	14.8%
Forecasted growth rate for net operating assets		7.0%
Net operating assets	1996	$1,135 million
SF3 forecast of operating income	1997: 1,135 × 14.8%	$168.0 million
SF3 forecast of ReOI	1997	$ 53.4 million
SF3 forecast of AOIG (ReOI$_{1997}$ growing at 7%)	1998: 53.4 × 0.07	3.74 million

Value of common equity:

V_{1996}^E before minority interests = (MI) $2,136 million

$$CSE_{1996} + MI_{1996} + \frac{\overline{ReOI}_{1997}}{1.101 - 1.07}$$

Value of minority interest (at 14 times 1996 MI earnings)   <u>210</u> million

<u>$1,926</u> million

Value per share on 55.840 million shares $34.49

$V_{1996}^{NOA} = V_{1996}^E$ before MI + NFO_{1996} = $2,136 + 720 $2,856 million

ReOI valuation of operations:

$$V_{1996}^{NOA} = 1,135 + \frac{(0.148 - 0.101) \times 1,135}{0.031}$$ $2,856 million

$$V_{1996}^{NOA} = 1,135 \times \frac{(0.148 - 0.07)}{0.031}$$ $2,856 million

AOIG valuation of operations:

$$V_{1996}^{NOA} = 168.0 \times \frac{1}{0.101}\left[1 + \frac{3.74/168.0}{0.031}\right]$$ $2,856 million

THE APPLICABILITY OF SIMPLE VALUATIONS

The SF1, SF2, and SF3 valuations have the advantage of requiring little analysis of the future. They assume the future will be much like the present. They are the valuations we can make from the current financial statements—sometimes combined with a sales growth estimate—without analyzing much information outside the financial statements. They are quick and, yes, dirty. But they are benchmarks, starting points, to conduct a more thorough analysis. The thorough analysis requires extra work, as we will see; you must always ask how much the extra work will improve the valuation over one that assumes future profitability and/or growth in book value at the current level. Ask yourself: Will the more thorough analysis give me a competitive edge? For which firms are the simple assumptions in the simple valuations inappropriate?

The current ROCE explains some of the difference in firms' levered P/B ratios by itself. Look at Table 14.5. For this table we grouped all U.S. firms into 20 groups based on their ROCE. The table gives the median ROCE for the groups and also the median P/B ratio at which firms traded at the time the ROCE were reported. There is almost a monotonic relationship between ROCE and P/B here. The typical rank correlation between the two for individual firms is 0.35. This suggests that if you had to make a stab at what the P/B ratio might be based just on the current ROCE, you would be wrong, but you would have a good first guess. And calculating ROCE certainly does not require much analysis. Note further that the P/B is normal where the ROCE is about 12 percent (group 12), and 12 percent is what we think of as the typical historical cost of capital for equity.

Coca-Cola's shares rose from $22 per share at the end of 1993 to $67 per share by the end of 1997. It also paid a dividend, increasing from 34 cents per share in 1993 to 56 cents in 1997. It was one of the "high-flying" stocks of the 1990s, trading at 23 times book value by the end of 1997. The company's 10-K report for 1997 reported the following:

	1997	1996	1995	1994	1993
Return on capital[1]	39.4%	36.7%	34.9%	32.7%	31.2%
Sales profit margin (after tax)	17.2%	13.6%	14.4%	14.5%	14.4%
Asset turnover	2.3	2.7	2.4	2.3	2.2

Five-year annual sales growth rate, 1993–97: 7.5%

Net capital[1]	$11,186 million
Interest-bearing debt	3,875
Shareowners' equity	$ 7,311 million

[1]Coke defines net capital as equity plus interest-bearing debt, which is similar to net operating assets except that financial assets are treated as operating items.

Coke's asset turnovers are fairly constant. If this is to be the case in the future, the valuation relies primarily on a forecast of sales growth (which, with a constant ATO, is the forecast of NOA growth). If we forecast sales growth at the same 7.5 percent rate as the 1993–1997 period, a return on capital at the 1997 level of 39.4 percent, and assume a cost of capital of 10 percent, then a valuation of Coke at the end of 1997 can be calculated as follows:

$$V_{1997}^{NOA} = 11,186 + \frac{(0.394 - 0.10) \times 11,186}{1.10 - 1.075}$$

	= $142,733 million
Debt	3,875
V_{1997}^{E}	$138,858 million
Value per share on 2,471 million shares	$56.20

This seems like a reasonable valuation. Indeed you might argue that it's a little high. The 1997 return on capital and profit margin are higher than those in the earlier years: Can the 1997 rate of return be sustained? The assumed cost of capital for operations is not high; the CAPM rate (with a beta of 1.10) is close to 12 percent. And the sales growth rate may be optimistic: Coke's sales growth slowed substantially over the 1993–1997 period to only 1.0 percent in 1997 and 3.0 percent in 1996. How many thirsty people are there?

With Coke's market price of $70 at the end of 1997 you might well question if it was overvalued. (You would not have been the only skeptic at the time.) You could conduct a sensitivity analysis and ask what growth in sales and/or return on capital the market sees for the future and then ask whether such a forecast is reasonable. What does the market see that this optimistic simple valuation misses? (Coke's share price had declined to $40 by early 2003.)

There is another lesson here. Coke has a big brand-name asset that is not in the balance sheet. Some claim that because accountants do not record brand assets, it is difficult to value such firms. Not so. Valuation involves both the balance sheet and the income statement, and we see here that a valuation with both is indeed plausible. The simple valuation might be too simple, but you can see that modifying it with a more intelligent forecast of future RNOA and growth in RNOA will give an intelligent valuation even with a deficient balance sheet.

Correspondingly, RNOA gives an indication of enterprise P/B ratios. As an illustration, Figure 14.1 plots the enterprise P/B ratios for 300 industries in 1993 against their RNOA. The pattern is similar in other years: Higher RNOA indicates higher unlevered P/B ratios on average. Core RNOA gives a better indication of the enterprise P/B ratio, as will any indicator that forecasts growth as well as RNOA.

Figure 14.2 gives some idea of how applicable the simple valuations are. The three panels show how ReOI, RNOA, and growth in NOA typically behaved for NYSE and AMEX firms over five-year periods between 1964 and 1999. For these figures firms were placed in one of 10 groups based on their current (Year 0) ReOI (for Figure 14.2*a*), their current RNOA (for Figure 14.2*b*), and their current growth rate in NOA (for Figure 14.2*c*), with the firms with the highest 10 percent of the relevant measure in the top group and firms

TABLE 14.5
Median Levered Price-to-Book (P/B) Ratios for Firms Grouped on Return on Common Equity (ROCE), 1968–1985
Firms with high current ROCE tend to have high P/B and firms with low ROCE tend to have low P/B. The rank correlation between ROCE and P/B (for individual firms) is 0.35.

Source:
Company: Standard & Poor's
Data: Compustat® data

ROCE Group	ROCE, %	P/B
1	43.3	3.43
2	28.7	2.57
3	23.8	2.20
4	21.0	1.89
5	19.1	1.65
6	17.7	1.45
7	16.5	1.36
8	15.4	1.25
9	14.4	1.16
10	13.5	1.10
11	12.6	1.06
12	11.7	1.00
13	10.6	0.97
14	9.5	0.91
15	8.3	0.84
16	6.8	0.80
17	4.9	0.78
18	2.2	0.75
19	−3.2	0.74
20	−22.5	1.01

Based on all traded U.S. firms. The grouping is done each year; the numbers reported are averages for all years.

FIGURE 14.1
Plots of Unlevered Price-to-Book Ratios Against Return on Net Operating Assets (RNOA) for 300 Industries in 1993
The line through the plots is the best fit of the relationship between enterprise P/B ratios and RNOA.

Source:
Company: Standard & Poor's
Data: Compustat® data.

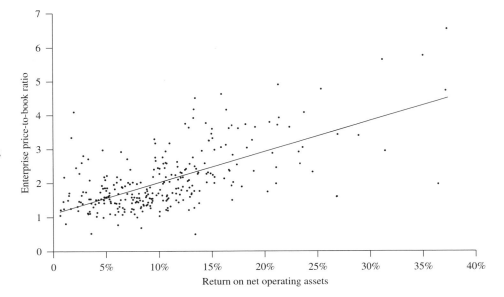

FIGURE 14.2
Patterns of Residual Operating Income (a), Return on Net Operating Assets (b), and Growth in Net Operating Assets (c) over Five-Year Periods for NYSE and AMEX Firms between 1964 and 1999

Source: D. Nissim and S. Penman, "Ratio Analysis and Equity Valuation: from Research to Practice," *Review of Accounting Studies*, March 2001, pp. 109–154.

(a) Residual operating income (ReOI). Firms with relatively high ReOI in the current year (Year 0) in the upper groups tend to maintain a high ReOI in the subsequent five years. Firms with relatively low ReOI in the current year in the lower groups tend to have low ReOI in the subsequent five years. Overall, ReOI tends to move toward zero for all groups. (ReOI is deflated by net operating assets at the beginning of Year 0.)

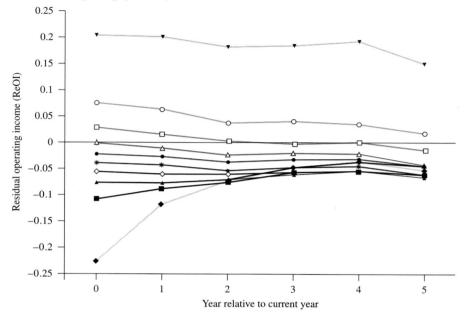

(b) Return on net operating assets (RNOA). RNOA also tends to move toward a common level for all firms, but firms with high RNOA in the current year, in the upper groups, tend to maintain high RNOA in the subsequent five years while firms with low RNOA in the current year, in the lower groups, tend to have low RNOA in the subsequent years.

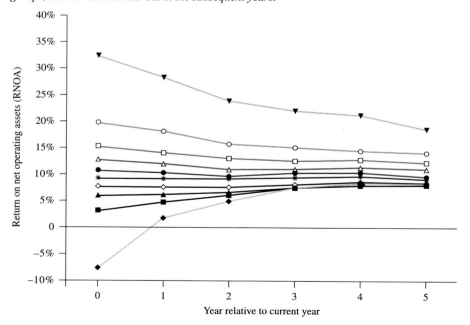

FIGURE 14.2
(Continued)

(c) Growth rate of net operating assets (growth in NOA). Growth in net operating assets also tends to move toward a common level. The growth rate for firms with high current growth in the upper groups tends to drop off, while growth for firms with low current growth in the lower groups tends to increase.

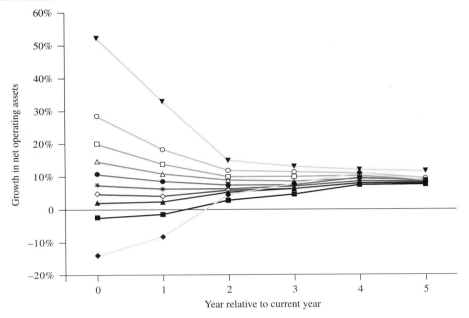

with the lowest 10 percent of the measure in the bottom group. The median measure for each group was then tracked over the subsequent five years, Years 1, 2, 3, 4, and 5 in the figures. The figures give the typical patterns for the three measures over time. Read the captions to the figures to be sure you understand what they are saying.

What you observe in these patterns is typical of many accounting measures: Extreme (high or low) measures tend to become more like the average measure as time goes on. In Figure 14.2*b*, which plots how RNOA behaves over time, there are large differences in current RNOA in Year 0, ranging from –7½ percent for the lowest group to 33 percent for the highest RNOA group. But after five years the differences are smaller, with the range reduced to 8 percent to 19 percent, and all groups except the top are in the range of 8 percent to 15 percent. This says that, based on past history, we typically expect RNOA to be in the range of 8 percent to 15 percent after five years. And similarly for growth in NOA in Figure 14.2*c* and, to a lesser extent, ReOI in Figure 14.2*a*.

This tendency for these measures to converge to typical, average levels is called **mean reversion**. High or low measures revert to the mean (the average) over time. Mean reversion means that high and low ReOI, RNOA, and growth in NOA are typically transitory as they are only temporarily high or low. Indeed, it was with these patterns in mind that financial statement analysis is designed to uncover transitory elements in RNOA.

You do well to keep these patterns in mind when forecasting because typical patterns are a good point of departure when forecasting for individual firms. The patterns are even sharper within industries. We will see (in the next chapter) how the economics of business causes mean reversion and (in Chapter 16) how the accounting also contributes. For now look at the patterns to judge how applicable the simple valuations are. The SF1 valuation usually does not work. The SF2 valuation, which forecasts constant ReOI, works best for firms with average ReOI and average RNOA (the central groups in Figures 14.2*a* and *b*). But the SF2 forecast will typically not work for firms with high or low RNOA or growth in NOA. It is these firms for which further analysis that forecasts future RNOA and growth in NOA is particularly necessary. The SF3 valuation, which forecasts growth in NOA at the current level but with constant RNOA, will work best for firms with average RNOA and average growth in NOA, that is, firms in central groups in Figures 14.2*b* and *c*. It is for these firms that both current RNOA and growth in NOA are indicative of future RNOA and growth in NOA. The SF3 valuation also works well for firms with reasonably constant profit margins and turnovers and steady sales growth rates (like Coke in Box 14.3).

Indeed, the term "steady-state" is the key to the effectiveness of simple valuations. If the firm has steady-state RNOA, growth in NOA, or growth in sales that are a good indication of the future, the current levels of these measures are a basis for valuation. If not, the simple valuations are approximate—or very wrong. They are just a starting point for full-information forecasting.

SIMPLE VALUATIONS WITH SHORT-TERM AND LONG-TERM GROWTH RATES

The simple forecasts above are based on one perpetual growth rate; they forecast that growth will continue at the specified rate into the long term. In many cases we expect firms to maintain relatively high growth rates in the short term and to fall off to a lower rate in the long term as competition challenges their business. In Nike's case, for example, the high sales growth rate of 35.9 percent in 1996 continued for a couple of years but dropped to 4 to 5 percent by the early 2000s.

Accommodating this pattern in a simple valuation is desirable not only because it fits with the facts, but because it also accommodates our dictum to separate more speculative aspects of a valuation from aspects about which we are more confident. Long-term growth rates are highly speculative, the most speculative part of any valuation. The discomfort you may have experienced in calculating continuing values (for the long term) is understandable. Analysts are more certain about their forecasts for the short run. They typically make point estimates of earnings for only one- and two-years ahead, then provide a growth rate for the following three to five years. Although these growth rates are referred to as "long-run" rates, they apply to only five years at most, and even for this period, they are usually considered to be so speculative that they are often dismissed. Long-term growth rates (beyond five years) are rarely made.

The simple valuation schemes can be modified to differentiate between short-term and long-term growth rates. A simple AOIG model accommodates the case where an analyst forecasts forward earnings, earnings for two years ahead, and a long-term growth rate:

$$V_0^{\text{NOA}} = \text{OI}_1 \times \frac{1}{\rho_F - 1} \left[\frac{G_2 - G_{\text{long}}}{\rho_F - G_{\text{long}}} \right] \qquad \textbf{(14.5)}$$

OI_1 is a forecast of forward operating income that is multiplied by a multiplier that incorporates two growth rates. G_2 is (1 plus) the growth rate forecasted for cum-dividend operating income two years ahead, and G_{long} is the same growth rate for the long term.[6] For

[6] The two-stage growth model was developed by Ohlson and Juettner-Nauroth. See, J. Ohlson and B. Juettner-Nauroth, "Expected EPS and EPS Growth as Determinants of Value," New York University, 2002.

In early 1997, analysts following Nike were forecasting eps of $4.50 for 1997 and $5.05 for 1998, up from $3.77 in 1996. Adjusting for expected net interest costs (as in Box 13.1 in the last chapter), these forecasts translated into operating income forecasts of $654 million and $732 million. With an expectation of net operating assets in the 1997 balance sheet of $2,932 million, a two-year pro forma is developed as follows:

	1996	1997	1998
Operating income		$ 654	$ 732
Net operating assets	$2,659	2,932	
Free cash flow (OI – ΔNOA)			381
Reinvested free cash flow (at 11%)			42
Cum-dividend operating income			774
Cum-dividend operating income growth rate: 774/654			18.35%

For the valuation: $G_2 = 1.1835$
$G_{long} = 1.04$
$\rho_F = 1.11$

The value of the operations is:

$$V_{1996}^{NOA} = 654 \times \frac{1}{0.11}\left[\frac{1.1835 - 1.04}{1.11 - 1.04}\right] = \$12,188 \text{ million}$$

$$V_{1996}^{E} = V_{1996}^{NOA} - \text{NFO} = 12,188 - 228 = \$11,960 \text{ million}$$

Value per share on 143.629 shares is $83.27.

The long-term growth rate specified here is 4 percent. Nike traded at $104 at the time. If one were reasonably confident in analysts' short-term forecasts, one would have to forecast that Nike's long-term growth rate in (cum-dividend) operating income would be considerably greater than 4 percent. Reverse engineering from a market price of $104 would establish the market's long-run growth forecast.

this model to work, the short-term growth rate must be higher than the long-term rate, which is very often the case. Box 14.4 applies this two-stage growth model to Nike, and Exercise E14.8 applies it to Cisco Systems.

SIMPLE VALUATION AS AN ANALYSIS TOOL

In the SF3 valuations of Nike and Reebok we substituted a forecasted NOA growth rate for the current growth rate. We chose 7 percent and this gave us a valuation. We could have chosen 5 percent or 9 percent and calculated a valuation with the same RNOA forecast. Or we could have substituted a forecasted RNOA that was different from the current core RNOA. Or we could have used a different cost of capital.

Setting different values for these features is called **sensitivity analysis**. This tests how a valuation changes as inputs to a model change, how the valuation is sensitive to alternative speculations about the future. The SF3 valuation model gives the form in which to conduct sensitivity analysis. The only drawback is that forecasts of RNOA and growth in NOA must be for constant amounts in the future. But, as an expediency, you might think of varying RNOA or NOA growth in terms of their average amounts. Remember, we are always looking for shortcuts that give reasonable approximations.

The SF3 model can be used in sensitivity analysis in the following ways.

Answering "As-If" Questions

This involves varying forecasts of RNOA and growth and observing the effect on the valuation. How does Nike's SF3 valuation in Box 14.2 change if we forecast that future RNOA will be 20.0 percent rather than 23.3 percent? Or if we forecast growth to be

5 percent rather than 7 percent? Indeed, we can construct a *valuation grid* that gives per-share values for different combined forecasts of the two drivers:

Valuation Grid for Nike, Inc., 1996 Required Return for Operations: 11%

Growth in NOA \ RNOA	15%	20%	23.3%	25%
0%	23.66	32.07	37.63	40.49
4%	27.50	40.73	49.46	53.95
7%	35.44	58.58	73.85	81.72
8.39%	45.30	80.76	104.00	116.23
9%	53.95	110.23	130.78	146.52

The valuation grid can be three-dimensional to incorporate different estimates of the required return. The two-dimensional grid here gives price per share, which we calculate for different combinations of RNOA and growth in NOA. If asset turnovers are forecasted to be constant, growth in NOA is replaced by sales growth. The grid expresses our uncertainty. We might be unsure about Nike's profitability in the future, so the grid displays the value of uncertain outcomes: What could the value drop to, or increase to, under reasonable scenarios? The grid also accommodates information we might have. We might have known that Nike was having trouble moving its inventory at the time and forecast a lower RNOA and growth rate; the grid gives us the valuation under this scenario. You might compare the speculations in this grid with the actual outcomes for Nike (in Chapters 9 and 11).

Imputing the Market's Forecast: Reverse Engineering

Nike traded at $104 at the end of its fiscal year 1996. What forecasts are implicit in this price? Well, the valuation grid indicates a price of $104 is justified by an RNOA forecast at the current level of 23.3 percent along with an 8.39 percent growth in NOA. Can Nike achieve this?

Market Forecast Pairs for Nike, Inc., 1996 Price = $104

RNOA	Growth in NOA
15%	10.15%
16	9.94
17	9.72
18	9.51
19	9.30
20	9.09
21	8.87
22	8.66
23	8.45
24	8.24
25	8.02
26	7.81
27	7.60
28	7.39
29	7.17
30	6.96

Many combinations of RNOA and NOA growth are possible for a given market price and these combinations are the *market forecast pairs*, as given in the table above. These pairs enable us to get a feel for whether the stock price is a reasonable one. Do reasonable scenarios justify any of the pairs for Nike? Or do we conclude that even if Nike could generate an RNOA of 30 percent indefinitely, it would be very difficult to maintain the perpetual growth in net operating assets of 6.96 percent that justifies a price of $104?

Discovering Value in an Analyst's Forecast

To claim to be adding value (as a forecaster) an analyst must discover information that improves upon a simple forecast. Our valuation of $45.52 per share for Reebok in Table 13.2 in the last chapter used analysts' consensus forecast of 1997 earnings that implied an RNOA of 16.5 percent and assumed 7 percent growth in NOA. Our SF3 valuation for Reebok, also with a 7 percent assumed growth rate, was $34.49. So the analysts' forecast causes a revision in the SF3 valuation by $11.16 per share.

Use the SF3 forecast to challenge analysts' forecasts. Is the analyst merely supplying a forecast that can be made from the (readily available) financial statements, or does the forecast reflect other information that he or she has incorporated?

Identifying a Focus for Analysis

The valuation grid displays values for possible uncertain outcomes. But it may also help point you in the right direction in resolving your uncertainty. You can see from Nike's valuation grid that at an 8.39 percent growth rate, there is not a large difference between Nike's value with a 23.3 percent and a 25.0 percent RNOA. But slight changes in the growth rate have significant effects. You might then concentrate on forecasting the growth rate if you feel that the RNOA in the future is likely to stay within this range.

Strategy and Planning

The valuation grid is a planning device within the firm. It translates actions into approximate valuations. A manager can ask: What will be the value effect of a cost-cutting program that increases RNOA by 1 percent? What if I increase NOA growth by 1 percent, but to do so have to invest in projects with lower RNOA than the current one?

Sensitivity analysis applies also to two-stage forecasting. If one is reasonably certain about short-term growth and profitability, the model in equation (14.5) provides the platform to examine sensitivities to alternative long-term growth rates. Or, if one assumes that long-term growth will be at the expected growth rate for GNP, one can simulate valuations with alternative short-term rates.

Summary

Simplicity is desirable. Simplicity, of course, also can yield poor approximations. Nevertheless, simple analysis serves as a starting point for more complicated analysis.

This chapter has presented three simple forecasts that can be developed from current and past financial statements without considering information outside the financial statements. These forecasts utilize the financial statement analysis of Part Two of the book to forecast the future. If core profitability is identified in that analysis, forecasts can be developed as if that core profitability is sustainable. Add to core profitability a measure of growth, and the analyst has a simple forecast (an SF3 forecast). If asset turnovers are constant, sustainable growth is given by a sales growth forecast.

The three simple forecasts yield simple valuations that give the analyst a first, quick-cut feel for the valuation and quick enterprise P/B and P/E ratios. Without much extra work, this is a considerable improvement over screening on multiples of current earnings, book values, and sales.

The Web Connection

Find the following on the web page for this chapter:

- More demonstrations of simple forecasts.
- A comparison of analysts' forecasts with simple forecasts.
- More applications of two-stage growth forecasting.
- More coverage of sensitivity analysis.

Simple forecasting follows the dictum of not contaminating what we know with what we do not know. To these simple forecasts, the analyst adds more speculative information. The chapter has shown how to incorporate more speculative forecasts into valuations in a way that maintains a simple form to the valuations and also incorporates the more reliable information in the financial statements.

The analyst who ignores information is at peril. The simple valuations will not work well when information outside the financial statements indicates that future profitability and growth will be different from current profitability and growth. The analyst calculates the simple valuations as starting points but then turns to full-information forecasting (discussed in the next chapter).

Notwithstanding, the simple valuations are an analysis tool to examine how valuations are sensitive to different scenarios for future profitability and growth—for asking "what-if" questions. And they lend themselves to reverse engineering to uncover the forecasts of profitability and growth that are implicit in the market price.

Key Concepts

mean reversion is the tendency of a measure to move over time toward the average or typical level for the measure. *497*

sensitivity analysis tests how value changes with different forecasts of the future or with different measures of the required return. *499*

simple forecasting involves forecasting from measures in the current financial statements. *480*

simple valuations are valuations calculated from simple forecasts. *490*

The Analyst's Tool Kit

Analysis Tools	Page	Key Measures	Page	Acronymns to Remember
SF1 forecasting	480	Abnormal operating income		AOIG abnormal growth in
SF2 forecasting	482	growth (AOIG)	485	operation income
SF3 forecasting	485	Change in balance sheet		CSE common shareholders'
SF1 valuation (equation 14.1)	482	components	484	equity
SF2 valuation (equation 14.2)	484	Core residual operating		G(1 plus) growth rate in cum-
SF3 valuation (equation 14.3)	489	income	484	dividend operating income
Enterprise P/B multiplier		Growth rate for cum-dividend		MI minority interest
(equation 14.3a)	489	operating income (G)	489	NFE net financial expense

The Analyst's Toolkit (continued)

Analysis Tools	Page	Key Measures	Page	Acronymns to Remember
Enterprise P/E multiplier (equations 14.4, 14.4a)	489	Growth rate in net operating assets	488	NFO net financial obligations
Combining sales forecasts with SF3 forecasts	491	Leverage-adjusted ROCE	488	NOA net operating assets
Two-stage growth forecasting (equation 14.5)	498	Market pairs	500	OI operating income
Valuation grid	500	Sales growth rate	491	ReOI residual operating income
Market-pairs analysis	500			ROCE return on common equity

Additional acronyms: RNOA return on net operating assets; SF1 simple forecast, type 1; SF2 simple forecast, type 2; SF3 simple forecast, type 3

Concept Questions

C14.1. Why is a simple forecast of operating income based on book value usually not a good forecast? When might such a forecast be a good forecast?

C14.2. A valuation that simply capitalizes a forecast of operating income for the next year implicitly assumes that residual operating income will continue as a perpetuity. Is this correct?

C14.3. What is the difference between an SF2 and an SF3 forecast?

C14.4. An analyst forecasts that next year's core operating income for a firm will be the same as the current year's core operating income. Under what conditions is this a good forecast?

C14.5. When is the forecasted growth rate in residual operating income the same as the forecasted growth rate in sales?

C14.6. Would you call a firm that is expected to have a high sales growth rate a growth firm?

C14.7. The higher the anticipated return on net operating assets (RNOA) relative to the anticipated growth in net operating assets, the higher will be the unlevered price-to-book ratio. Is this correct?

Exercises   E14.1.   Simple Forecasting and Valuation (Easy)

An analyst uses the following summary balance sheet to value a firm at the end of 2003 (in millions of dollars):

	2003	2002
Net operating assets	4,572	3,941
Net financial obligations	1,243	1,014
Common shareholders' equity	3,329	2,927

The analyst forecasts that the firm will earn a return on net operating assets (RNOA) of 12 percent in 2004 and a residual operating income of $91.4 million.

a. What is the implied rate of required return for operations that the analyst is using in his residual operating income forecast?

   b. The analyst forecasts that the residual operating income in 2004 will continue as a perpetuity. What value does this imply for the equity?

   c. Calculate the forecast of residual earnings (on common equity) that is implied by these forecasts. The firm's after-tax cost of debt is 6.0 percent.

E14.2. SF2 and SF3 Valuation: Ben & Jerry's (Easy)

The 1996 financial statements for Ben & Jerry's Homemade, Inc., the manufacturer of premium ice cream, frozen yogurt, and novelty products, are given in Exercise E11.8 in Chapter 11.

   a. Value Ben & Jerry's at the end of 1996 using just the information in the financial statements. Use a 10 percent cost of capital for operations. What further information would you seek to complete the valuation?

   b. Ben & Jerry's 7.195 million shares traded at 18-1/8. How might you explain the difference between your valuation and this price?

Real World Connection

For more analysis on Ben & Jerry's see Exercise E10.6 in Chapter 10, Exercise E11.8 in Chapter 11, and Exercise E13.8 in Chapter 13.

E14.3. Simple Forecasting and Sensitivity Analysis: Reebok International (Medium)

Reebok's 55.84 million shares traded at $43 each in early 1997, or 6.3 times their book value. The firm's year-end balance sheet for 1996 is summarized as follows (in millions of dollars):

Net operating assets	1,135
Net financial obligations	720
	415
Minority interest	34
Common stockholders' equity	381

During 1996, Reebok earned a core return on net operating assets (core RNOA) of 14.6 percent on an (after-tax) core profit margin of 4.94 percent and an asset turnover of 2.95. The required return on its operations is 10.1 percent.

   a. Calculate the unlevered price-to-book ratio at which Reebok traded in early 1997. Value the minority interest at 14 times minority interest earnings of $15 million.

   b. If Reebok were to maintain profit margins and asset turnovers at their 1996 level in the future, what sales growth rate would justify the unlevered price-to-book ratio?

   c. Calculate Reebok's unlevered price-to-book ratio if the sales growth rate you calculated in part (b) were to be maintained on an asset turnover of 2.95, but the profit margin were to fall to 3.5 percent of sales.

   d. If profit margins were to fall to 3.42 percent, how much would sales growth contribute to the value of the firm?

Real World Connection

See material on Reebok in Chapters 8–15. Also see Exercise E8.10 in Chapter 8 and Exercise E11.6 in Chapter 11.

E14.4. Idle Capacity and Value (Hard)

A firm with manufacturing facilities is currently running at 50 percent capacity. Its balance sheet is summarized as follows (in millions of dollars):

Accounts receivable	1.0
Inventory	4.3
Plant	10.7
	16.0
Financial liabilities	4.0
Common equity	12.0

The firm is generating sales of $32.0 million from its current production, earning an after-tax operating profit margin of 5.6 percent.

   a. Calculate the firm's return on net operating assets, its accounts receivable turnover, its inventory turnover, its turnover on plant, and its total asset turnover.

   b. The firm has a required return of 10 percent for its operations. Value the firm as if the current profitability will continue without any growth.

   c. Suppose the firm were to sell products at the full capacity of its plant with no change in selling prices or profit margins, and so earn revenues of $64.0 million. Receivables and inventories would increase to maintain the same accounts receivable and inventory turnovers as before. Calculate the value of the firm if it were to continue producing and selling at full capacity. Identify the aspects of the operations that have increased the value over that calculated in part (*b*).

E14.5. Value and Growth in Sales: Wal-Mart Stores (Medium)

For its year ending January 31, 1999, Wal-Mart Stores, the retailer, reported an after-tax profit margin of 3.65 percent and an asset turnover of 4.66 on net operating assets of $29.9 billion. The firm also reported net financial obligations of $8.0 billion.

In the previous few years Wal-Mart sales had been growing at 12 percent–16 percent per year, but analysts expect the rate to be 8 percent on average in the future. Analysts also expect profit margins and turnovers to continue at their 1999 level.

   a. Based on analysts' expectations, value the equity in 1999. Use a cost of capital for operations of 11 percent.

   b. Wal-Mart's shares traded at a total market capitalization of $200 billion at the end of fiscal 1999. If profit margins and turnovers were to continue at their 1999 level, what sales is the market forecasting for Wal-Mart in 2004 (five years in the future)?

Real World Connection

See material on Wal-Mart in Chapters 4 and 10. Also see Exercise E10.8 in Chapter 10.

E14.6. Preparing a Valuation Grid: Coca-Cola (Medium)

Refer to the valuation of the Coca-Cola Company in Box 14.3. Coke reported a "return on capital" of 39.4 percent (a measure similar to RNOA) on an after-tax profit margin of 17.2 percent and an asset turnover of 2.3. These measures were somewhat higher than in previous years.

Coke's operating capital at the end of 1997 was $11,186 million and its common equity was $7,311 million.

   a. Using a required return for operations of 10 percent, prepare a valuation grid giving the per-share value of Coke's 2,471 million outstanding shares under alternative scenarios for profit margins, turnovers, and growth in sales.

   b. Coke's shares traded at $70 at the end of 1997. What are the combinations of profitability (RNOA) and growth that would justify this price?

Real World Connection

See material on Coca-Cola in Exercise E4.6 and Minicase M4.2 in Chapter 4, Exercise E5.13 in Chapter 5, Minicase M13.2 in Chapter 13, and Exercise E15.4 in Chapter 15.

E14.7. A Simple Valuation Based on Abnormal Operating Income Growth: Coca-Cola (Medium)

Box 14.3 in this chapter developed a simple valuation of Coca-Cola using residual operating income methods. Using the same forecasted sales growth rate of 7.5 percent, carry out a simple valuation using abnormal operating income growth methods.

E14.8. A Simple Valuation with Short-Term and Long-Term Growth Rates: Cisco Systems (Easy)

In late 2002, analysts were forecasting fiscal 2003 and 2004 earnings per share for Cisco Systems of $0.54 and $0.61, respectively. Cisco's shares traded at $15 at the time. Assuming the long-term growth rate will be at 4 percent, the average rate of growth for gross national product, value Cisco using the model in equation (14.5) in this chapter. Apply the formula to earnings rather than operating income and use a required return for equity of 9 percent.

E14.9. Using Short-Term and Long-Term Growth Rates to Value Reebok (Medium)

In early 1997, analysts were forecasting earnings per share of $2.56 for Reebok's 1997 fiscal year. After adjusting for expected net interest costs, this forecast translates into a forecast of $187 million in operating income (see Box 13.1 in Chapter 13). Analysts were also forecasting earnings for 1998 that translated into $200 million of operating income. Reebok's net operating assets at the end of 1996 were $1,135 million and were expected to grow at a 7 percent rate for the next two years.

Using a required return for operations of 10.1 percent, prepare a valuation grid that values Reebok with alternative long-term growth rates using equation (14.5) in this chapter.

Minicase

M14.1

Simple Forecasting, Valuation, and Sensitivity Analysis: Home Depot

Home Depot, Inc., the home improvement retailer, had a market capitalization at the end of 1999 of $122.2 billion, sixteenth largest of all firms. Trading at $83 per share, its 12-month rolling P/E ratio was 53, its price-to-book ratio was 10.7, and its price-to-sales ratio was 4.1. Home Depot's stock price had appreciated 45 percent over the previous 12 months.

As of October 1999, Home Depot operated 878 do-it-yourself warehouse retail stores in 44 states in the U.S., Canada, and Latin America. These stores specialize in building materials, garden products, and interior design products, presented in a warehousing environment. The firm offers help and training to the "do-it-yourselfer," along with installation services. It has eight EXPO Design Center stores that offer high-end products for home interiors such as kitchen cabinetry, tiles, flooring, and lighting. Its Maintenance Warehouse subsidiary and its National Blind and Wallpaper subsidiary offer mail order services.

Home Depot is a concept retailer. Founded in 1978 by Bernard Marcus and Arthur Blank, its strategy is to target do-it-yourselfers, to give them the help and security needed to carry out home improvement tasks, to lever their labor with low competitive prices, and to supply high-quality, reliable merchandise to minimize their frustration and to promote satisfaction for a job well done. Most inventory is warehoused within the retail stores, giving customers a feeling that prices are low and promoting a back-to-basics mentality.

Warehouse stores offer significant discounts to customers. As discounting affects gross margins, the firm has to be careful in controlling merchandise, warehousing, and servicing costs. Home Depot has been particularly successful in offering low prices yet good service and quality. Accordingly, sales have grown from $7 million in 1979 to $750 million in 1986, $20 billion in 1996, and $30 billion in 1998. Its stock price rose from $2 per share in 1990 to $83 per share in late 1999.

Home Depot has been an outstanding retail success. But many in 1999 asked whether its future justified the high multiples at which it was trading. A sales-to-price ratio of 3.3 looked very expensive: At the firm's operating profit margin of about 5.0 percent, a sales multiple of 3.3 implies a lot of anticipated sales growth.

Home Depot's financial statements for 1996 to 1999 are given in Exhibit 14.1.

A. On the basis of the financial statements, develop forecasts for Home Depot that will enable you to value the equity. Analysts were forecasting earnings per share of 1.38 for fiscal 2000 at the time.

B. Value the equity on the basis of the forecasts you developed.

C. What issues did you encounter in developing the forecasts and the valuations? Do you think Home Depot lends itself to simple forecasting and valuation? What additional information would you look for to resolve these issues?

D. What were the implicit forecasts that the market was making at a price of $83 per share?

E. Prepare a valuation grid that helps you understand the possible scenarios for Home Depot's future.

In all your calculations, use a 10 percent required return for Home Depot's operations. Use a 39 percent marginal tax rate for income tax allocations.

EXHIBIT 14.1

HOME DEPOT, INC.
Income Statements

	Fiscal Year Ended		
(Amounts in millions, except per-share data)	January 31, 1999 (52 weeks)	February 1, 1998 (52 weeks)	February 2, 1997 (53 weeks)
Net sales	$30,219	$24,156	$19,535
Cost of merchandise sold	21,614	17,375	14,101
Gross profit	8,605	6,781	5,434
Operating expenses			
Selling and store operating	5,341	4,303	3,529
Preopening	88	65	55
General and administrative	515	413	324
Nonrecurring charge	—	104	—
Total operating expenses	5,944	4,885	3,908
Operating income	2,661	1,896	1,526
Interest income (expense):			
Interest and investment income	30	44	25
Interest expense	(37)	(42)	(16)
Interest, net	(7)	2	9
Earnings before income taxes	2,654	1,898	1,535
Income taxes	1,040	738	597
Net earnings	$ 1,614	$ 1,160	$ 938
Basic earnings per share	$1.10	$0.80	$0.65
Weighted-average number of common shares outstanding	1,471	1,459	1,438
Comprehensive Income			
Net income	1,614	1,160	938
Currency translation adjustments	(33)	(30)	8
Comprehensive income	$ 1,581	$ 1,130	$ 946

Balance Sheets

	January 31, 1999	February 1, 1998	February 2, 1997	January 28, 1996
Assets				
Current assets				
Cash and cash equivalents	$ 62	$ 172	$ 146	$ 53
Short-term investments	—	2	412	55
Receivables, net	469	556	388	325
Merchandise inventories	4,293	3,602	2,709	2,180
Other current assets	109	128	54	59
Total current assets	4,933	4,460	3,709	2,672

Property and equipment, at cost:				
Land	2,739	2,194	1,855	1,511
Buildings	3,757	3,041	2,470	1,886
Furniture, fixtures, and equipment	1,761	1,370	1,084	857
Leasehold improvements	419	383	339	315
Construction in progress	540	336	284	308
Capital leases	206	163	117	92
	9,422	7,487	6,149	4,969
Less accumulated depreciation and amortization	1,262	978	712	508
Net property and equipment	8,160	6,509	5,437	4,461
Long-term investments	15	15	8	25
Notes receivable	26	27	40	55
Cost in excess of the fair value of net assets acquired, net of accumulated amortization	268	140	87	87
Other	63	78	61	54
	$13,465	$11,229	$9,342	$7,354

Liabilities and Stockholders' Equity

Current liabilities				
Accounts payable	$ 1,586	$ 1,358	1,090	825
Accrued salaries and related expenses	395	312	249	198
Sales tax payable	176	143	129	113
Other accrued expenses	586	530	323	243
Income taxes payable	100	105	49	35
Current installments of long-term debt	14	8	2	2
Total current liabilities	2,857	2,456	1,842	1,416
Long-term debt, excluding current installments	1,566	1,303	1,247	720
Other long-term liabilities	208	178	134	116
Deferred income taxes	85	78	66	37
Minority interest	9	116	98	77

Stockholders' Equity

Common stock, par value $0.05. Authorized: 2,500,000,000 shares; issued and outstanding—1,475,452,000 shares at January 31, 1999	74	73	24	24
Paid-in capital	2,854	2,626	2,523	2,408
Retained earnings	5,876	4,430	3,406	2,579
Accumulated other comprehensive income	(61)	(28)	2	(6)
	8,743	7,101	5,955	5,005
Less: Shares purchased for compensation plans	3	3	0	(17)
Total stockholders' equity	8,740	7,098	5,955	4,988
	$13,465	$11,229	$9,342	$7,354

Real World Connection

See Exercise E9.7 in Chapter 9 on Home Depot.

Chapter **Fifteen**

Full-Information Forecasting, Valuation, and Business Strategy Analysis

LINKS

Link to previous chapter	Link to previous chapters
Chapter 14 developed simple forecasting schemes based on information in financial statements.	Chapters 11 and 12 laid out the analysis of financial statements that uncovers drivers of profitability and growth.

This chapter	
This chapter shows how information outside the financial statements is utilized to make forecasts that improve upon the simple forecasts in Chapter 14.	This chapter uses the financial statement analysis of Chapters 11 and 12 to develop a framework for full-information forecasting.

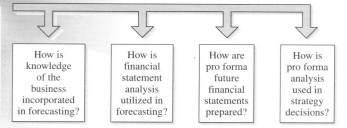

How is knowledge of the business incorporated in forecasting?	How is financial statement analysis utilized in forecasting?	How are pro forma future financial statements prepared?	How is pro forma analysis used in strategy decisions?

Link to next chapter
Chapter 16 begins an investigation of accounting issues that arise in forecasting and valuation.

Link to web page
Learn how to develop spreadsheet financial models to convert forecasts to valuations—visit the text website at www.mhhe.com/penman2e.

The simple forecasting schemes in the last chapter embedded all the concepts needed for valuation. But they did not exploit all of the information that is necessary to make the analyst feel secure about a valuation. The simple schemes focused on operating income and growth in net assets employed in operations, but they relied on current measures. Full-information forecasting digs deeper. It forecasts the full set of factors that drive operating income and net operating assets and, from these forecasts, builds up a forecast of residual earnings and abnormal earnings growth from which a valuation can be made.

Chapters 11 and 12 outlined the factors that drive profitability and growth enabling us to analyze current financial statements. But because those same factors drive future profitability and growth, the driver analysis of those chapters also gives us the framework for forecasting: The analyst forecasts the drivers—future core

The Analyst's Checklist

After reading this chapter you should understand:	After reading this chapter you should be able to:
• How forecasting is a matter of financial statement analysis for the future.	• Develop pro forma income statements and balance sheets for the future.
• How financial statement drivers translate economic factors into a valuation.	• Get forecasts of future residual operating income, abnormal operating income growth, and free cash flow from pro forma financial statements.
• What a driver pattern is and what economic forces affect them.	• Get valuations from pro forma financial statements.
• How to identify key drivers.	• Show how changes in forecasts for specific drivers change pro forma financial statements and valuations.
• How to conduct full-information pro forma analysis.	
• The 13 steps in pro forma analysis.	• Use pro forma analysis for sensitivity analysis.
• The seven steps involved in forecasting residual operating income and abnormal operating income growth.	• Calculate the effect of a proposed merger or acquisition on per-share value.
• How mergers and acquisitions are evaluated.	• Use pro forma analysis to evaluate strategy scenarios.
• How buyouts are evaluated.	
• The difference between dollar forecasting and per-share forecasting.	
• How pro forma analysis is used as a tool in strategy analysis.	

profit margins, turnovers, and so on—to develop forecasts. Financial statement analysis is an analysis of the present and past, to provide information for forecasts of the future. However, you will see in this chapter that forecasting is a matter of **financial statement analysis of the future**. Much of this chapter is the analysis of Chapters 11 and 12 rolled over to the future.

The drivers of profitability and growth are themselves driven by the "real" economic factors of the business. So knowing the business is an essential first step to discovering the information for full-information forecasting. You will see here how financial statement analysis provides the means of interpreting the many dimensions of business activity in a form that can be used for forecasting. Knowing the firm's strategy is also a prerequisite for forecasting, and you will also see how financial statement analysis interprets strategy. Moreover, you will see how the methods of forecasting are also the methods by which a manager evaluates alternative strategies.

The chapter develops a scheme for forecasting. The scheme ensures that all relevant aspects of the business are incorporated and irrelevant aspects are ignored. It is comprehensive and orderly so that no element is lost. By forcing the analyst to forecast in an orderly manner, the scheme disciplines speculative tendencies.

The simple forecasts of the last chapter are a starting point for full-information forecasting. They are based on current profitability and growth in net operating assets. Full-information forecasting asks how future profitability and growth will evolve from their current levels. If, through analysis of additional information, we forecast that indeed they will, then we will have improved on the simple forecasts and the simple valuations.

FINANCIAL STATEMENT ANALYSIS: FOCUSING THE LENS ON THE BUSINESS

We have repetitively said that one cannot value a business without a thorough understanding of the business; knowing the business is a prerequisite to valuation and strategy analysis—Step 1 of fundamental analysis. Before embarking on this chapter, look back to the section titled "The Analysis of Business" in Chapter 1, where the main factors that determine business success are discussed. The analyst must understand the business model and alternative, adaptive strategies available to the firm. She must understand the firm's product, its marketing and production methods, and its knowledge base. She must understand the competitive environment and have an appreciation of the firm's competitive advantage, if any, and its durability. She must understand the legal, regulatory, and political constraints on the firm.

Understanding these many economic factors is a prerequisite to forecasting. But we need a way of translating these factors into measures that lead to a valuation. We must recognize the firm's product, the competition in the industry, the firm's ability to develop product innovations, and so on, but we must also interpret this knowledge in a way that leads to a valuation. Economic factors are often expressed in qualitative terms that are suggestive but do not immediately translate into concrete dollar numbers. We might recognize that a firm has "market power," but what does this imply for its value? We might recognize that a firm is "under threat of competition," but what does this imply for its value? How are "growth opportunities" valued?

Accounting-based valuation models and the financial statement analysis of Chapters 11 and 12 provide the translation. Market power translates into higher margins; competition reduces them. The technology to produce sales is reflected in the asset turnover. And margins and turnovers are the drivers of profitability on which valuation is based. The structure of financial statement analysis is the means to interpret what we observe about business. It focuses the lens on the business. There is danger in relying on suggestive notions such as "market power," "competitive advantage," and "breakthrough technology" without a concrete analysis of what they mean. Investors can get carried away by enthusiasm for such ideas, leading to speculation in stock prices. Forecasting within a financial statement analysis framework disciplines investor exuberance and, indeed, investor pessimism. It brings both the bulls and the bears to a focus on the fundamentals.

There are four points of focus for translating business activities into a valuation.

1. Focus on Residual Operating Income and Its Drivers

The focus for the valuation of operations is on residual operating income (ReOI) for a P/B valuation or abnormal operating income growth (AOIG) for a P/E valuation. But AOIG is just the change in ReOI. So business activities are interpreted by their effect on ReOI. ReOI is driven by return on net operating assets (RNOA) and growth in net operating assets (NOA). RNOA is driven by four drivers:

$$\text{RNOA} = (\text{Core sales PM} \times \text{ATO}) + \frac{\text{Core other OI}}{\text{NOA}} + \frac{\text{Unusual items}}{\text{NOA}}$$

Combining these RNOA drivers with growth in NOA, we can capture the drivers of residual operating income in one expression that contains five drivers:

$$\text{ReOI} = \underbrace{\text{Sales}}_{\text{Product price} \,\times\, \text{Product quantity}} \times \left[\text{Core sales PM} - \frac{\text{Required return for operations}}{\text{ATO}} \right] \quad \textbf{(15.1)}$$

$$+ \text{ Core other OI} + \text{UI}$$

(It is often the case, however, that unusual items are expected to be zero.) The ATO is sales per dollar of net operating assets, so the ratio of the required return on operations to ATO here is a measure of operational efficiency in using net operating assets to generate sales relative to the required rate of return for those assets. We will refer to it as the *turnover efficiency ratio*, with a smaller ratio generating more ReOI. The RNOA drivers—core profit margin, asset turnover, core other income, and unusual items—are in this formula. And growth in NOA is embedded through its drivers: Since NOA is put in place to generate sales, NOA is driven by sales and 1/ATO, that is, by sales and the net operating assets required to generate a dollar of sales.

Forecasting residual operating income involves forecasting these drivers so, with valuation in mind, observations on the business are translated into forecasts of the five drivers:

- Sales
- Core sales profit margin
- Turnover efficiency
- Core other operating income
- Unusual items (UI)

Sales is the primary driver because, without customers and sales, no value can be added in operations. Much of our knowledge of the business—its products, its marketing, its R&D, its brand management, to name a few factors—is applied to forecasting sales. And as every basic economics course teaches, dollar sales is sales price multiplied by quantity sold. Both price and quantity involve analysis of consumer tastes, the price elasticity of consumer demand, substitute products, the technology path, competitiveness of the industry, and government regulations, to name a few. But equation (15.1) tells us that sales generate positive ReOI only if they are turned into positive margins. And sales generate positive ReOI only if these margins are greater than the turnover efficiency ratio.

As a first step in organizing your business knowledge, attach economic factors to ReOI drivers. What factors drive product prices and product quantities (and thus sales)? Among the answers will be competition, product substitutes, brand association, and patent protection. What factors drive margins? Among the answers will be the production technology, economies of scale and learning, and the competitiveness in labor and supplier markets.

2. Focus on Change

A firm's current drivers are discovered through financial statement analysis. Forecasting involves future drivers, so focus on business activities that may change ReOI drivers from their current levels. The analysis of changes in drivers is a question of earnings sustainability, or more strictly, *ReOI sustainability*. Analyze change in three steps.

Step A. Understand the Typical Driver Pattern for the Industry

Figure 14.2 in the last chapter displays historical patterns that are starting points for forecasting. The displays are of typical mean-reversion behavior of ReOI, RNOA, and growth in NOA to long-run average levels. They cover all NYSE and AMEX firms. Similar displays can be made for each industry or product sector from the historical data. And similar displays can be developed for core profit margins, asset turnovers, and the other drivers of ReOI.

These **driver patterns** are determined by two elements:

1. The current level of the driver relative to its typical (median) level for a comparison set of firms.

2. The rate of reversion to a long-run level.

Element 1 is established by the analysis of the current financial statements and element 2 is the subject of forecasting. The rate of reversion to a long-run level is sometimes referred to as the **fade rate** or **persistence rate**. Some analysts market their equity research as an analysis of fade rates. How long will a nontypical ReOI and nontypical ReOI drivers take to fade to the typical long-run level? How long will a nontypical level persist?

Economic factors affect firms in similar ways within industries, so driver pattern diagrams are best developed by industry. Industry is usually defined by the product brought to market. There are standard classifications, like the Standard Industrial Classification (SIC) system, which classifies firms by nested four-digit industry codes. Within an industry firms tend to become more like each other over time, or they go out of existence. Thus analysts talk of ReOI and its drivers fading to levels that are typical for the industry. Firms may have temporary advantages, new ideas, or innovations that distinguish them from others, but the **forces of competition** and the ability of existing and new firms to imitate them drive out the temporary advantage. Correspondingly, if these competitive forces are muted, we expect to see more sustained driver patterns than for a strongly competitive industry. As fade rates are driven by competition, some analysts refer to the period over which a driver fades to a typical level as the **competitive advantage period**.

Figure 15.1 gives historical patterns over five-year periods between 1964 and 1999 for the core RNOA driver for all NYSE and AMEX firms, along with patterns for core other income (relative to NOA) and items classified as unusual (also divided by NOA).[1] These figures, like those in the last chapter, track the drivers over five years from a base year (Year 0) for 10 groups of firms that differ in the amount of the drivers in the base year. The top group contains firms with the highest 10 percent of the driver in the base year and the bottom group contains firms with the lowest 10 percent. As you would expect, unusual items (in Figure 15.1c) fade out quickly—they are very transitory—but core RNOA (in Figure 15.1a) and other core income (in Figure 15.1b) also fade toward central values, with high profitability (in the upper groups) declining and low profitability (in the lower groups) increasing. The diagrams indicate that the forces of competition are at play to drive core RNOA to common levels. Firms in the top 10 percent of core RNOA in the current year have a median 29 percent RNOA that fades to 18 percent five years later. But there are long-run differences between core RNOA that have to be forecast: Firms with higher core RNOA currently tend to have higher core RNOA later, but differences in core RNOA decrease over time. We will see in Part Four that the accounting partly explains these permanent differences.

---

[1] As with Figure 14.2 in Chapter 14, the patterns in the figures here are averages of patterns from grouping firms on their drivers in 1964, 1969, 1974, 1979, 1984, 1989, and 1994, and tracking them.

FIGURE 15.1
Driver Patterns for Core RNOA, Core Other Income, and Unusual Operating Items, NYSE and AMEX Firms, 1964–1999
The patterns trace the median drivers over five years for 10 groups formed for different levels of the drivers in Year 0. Firms in the upper groups have high drivers in the current year (Year 0) and firms in the lower groups have low drivers in the current year.

Source: D. Nissim and S. Penman, "Ratio Analysis and Equity Valuation: from Research to Practice," *Review of Accounting Studies*, March 2001, pp. 109–154. Based on Standard & Poor's COMPUSTAT data.

(a) Core RNOA. Firms with high core RNOA currently (in the upper groups) tend to have declining profitability in the future; firms with low core RNOA (in the lower groups) tend to have increasing profitability in the future.

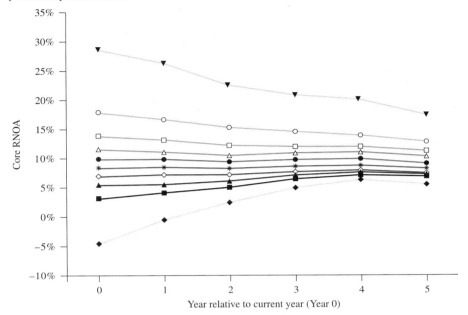

(b) Core other income/NOA. High core other income (for firms in the upper groups) tends to decline subsequently as a percentage of net operating assets; low core other operating income (for firms in the lower groups) tends to increase.

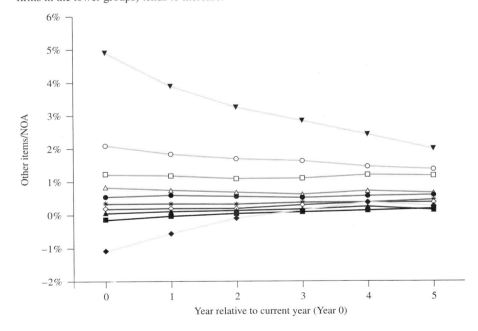

FIGURE 15.1
(Continued)

(c) Unusual operating items/NOA. Unusual items tend to disappear very quickly—as expected for a transitory item.

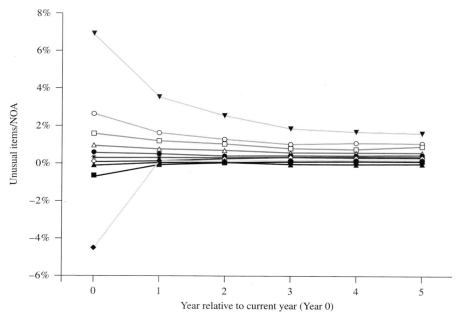

Driver patterns also can be established for change drivers that were analyzed in the analysis of growth in Chapter 12. Figure 15.2 gives historical patterns for sales growth rates, changes in core sales profit margins, and changes in asset turnovers. These patterns indicate the sustainability of increases or decreases in the drivers. Sales growth (in Figure 15.2*a*) is strongly mean reverting: Firms with large increases in sales tend to have lower increases in the future. And large increases or decreases in core sales profit margins (in Figure 15.2*b*) and asset turnovers (in Figure 15.2*c*) also tend to be temporary. Average changes in both drivers (represented by the fifth group from the top in Year 0) are close to zero, but all groups converge to this average over time.

The contrarian stock screening strategy (in Chapter 3) shorts stocks with high growth in sales and profits and buys stocks with low growth. The contrarians have these change patterns in mind but believe that the market does not. They believe that the market gets too excited with high sales and profit growth and thinks growth will continue rather than fade; and they believe the market does not understand that drops in sales and profits are often temporary.

Step B. Modify the Typical Driver Pattern for Forecasts for the Economy and the Industry

Historical industry patterns are a good starting point if the future is likely to be similar to the past. But indications may be to the contrary. Government or trade statistics may forecast a change in the direction for the (global) economy or for the specific industry. Forecasts of recession or a slowdown of GDP growth may signal a change from the past. Shifts in industrywide demand for the product may be indicated by changing demographics or changing consumer tastes. Knowing the business requires a knowledge of industry trends and a knowledge of the susceptibility of the industry to macroeconomic changes.

FIGURE 15.2
Driver Patterns for Sales Growth Rates, Changes in Core Sales Profit Margins, and Changes in Asset Turnovers, NYSE and AMEX Firms, 1964–1999

Source: D. Nissim and S. Penman, *Ratio Analysis and Equity Valuation*: from Research to Practice, *Review of Accounting Studies*, March 2001, pp. 109–154. Based on Standard & Poor's COMPUSTAT data.

(a) Sales growth rates. Sales growth tends to fade quickly: firms with high sales growth currently (in the upper groups) have lower sales growth subsequently; firms with low current sales growth (in the lower groups) have higher sales growth subsequently.

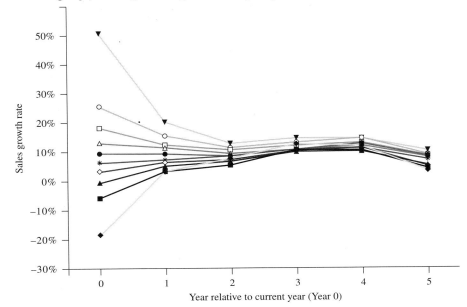

(b) Changes in core sales profit margins. Changes in core sales profit margins tend to fade quickly toward common levels close to zero.

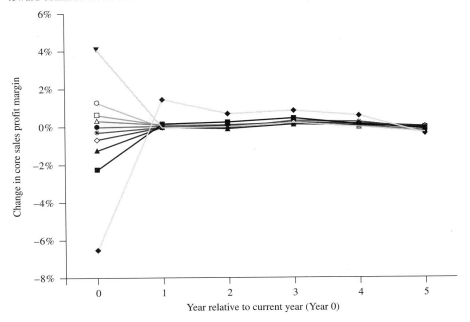

FIGURE 15.2
(Continued)

(c) Changes in asset turnovers. Changes in asset turnovers tend to revert toward common levels; large increases in asset turnovers (in the upper groups) are temporary, as are large decreases in asset turnovers (in the lower groups).

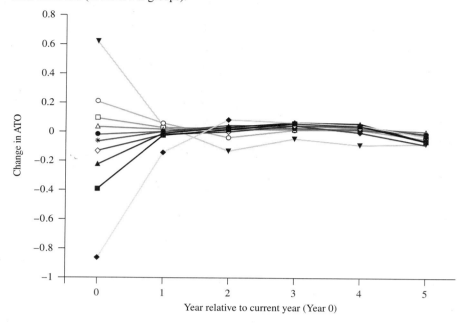

Historical driver patterns, adjusted if need be for macroeconomic and industry forecasts, modify the simple forecasts of the last chapter; forecasts based on current levels of the drivers are modified to incorporate typical fade rates. See Box 15.1.

Step C. Forecast How the Firm's Drivers Will Be Different from the Typical Pattern

Understanding typical drivers for an industry disciplines speculative tendencies. But firms have idiosyncratic features that yield drivers that are predictably different from industry patterns. So full-information forecasting is completed by asking how the firm's future drivers will be different from the typical pattern for the industry.

The main factor in determining fade rates is competition and firms' reactions to it. Competition causes abnormal RNOA to fade, and the ability of the firm to counter the forces of competition sustains RNOA higher than the industry average. Firms both create the forces of competition and counter those forces. Among the ways that they challenge other firms (with examples of specific firms or industries) are:

- Product price reductions (Wal-Mart, Home Depot, and other discount retailers).

- Product innovations (software developers, pharmaceutical companies).

- Product delivery innovations (Dell Computer, electronic commerce).

- Lower production costs (clothing manufacturers moving production to countries with low labor costs).

- Imitation of successful firms (PC cloners copying IBM; imitating Dell's inventory and distribution system).

- Entering industries where firms are earning abnormal profits (software, biotechnology).

Nike's ReOI drivers from 1994 to 1996 are as follows (dollar amounts in millions):

	1994	1995	1996
Sales	$3,790	$4,761	$6,471
Sales growth rate	–3.6%	25.6%	35.9%
Core sales PM	7.9%	8.5%	8.8%
Asset turnover	2.6	2.7	2.7
Required return for operations	11.0%	11.0%	11.0%
Turnover efficiency ratio	4.2%	4.1%	4.1%
Core other income	0	0	0
Core ReOI = Sales × (Core sales PM – Turnover efficiency ratio)	$ 140.2	$ 209.5	$ 304.1
Growth in core ReOI	—	49.4%	45.2%

Nike's sales growth has been phenomenal and has largely driven the growth in ReOI. But the historical data in athletic and fashion footwear sales indicates that such growth rates are unrealistic in the long run. Indeed an analyst forecasts long-run global demand to slow to an annual increase of 5 percent from 2000 on, with Nike's market share remaining constant. With these projections and a steady fade rate in sales growth to 5 percent by the year 2000, the analyst forecasts ReOI as follows if profit margins and operational efficiency ratios continue at the 1996 level. Note the fade in the sales growth and the growth in ReOI.

	1997E	1998E	1999E	2000E
Sales	$8,283	$9,939	$11,232	$11,793
Sales growth rate	28.0%	20.0%	13.0%	5.0%
Core sales PM	8.8%	8.8%	8.8%	8.8%
Turnover efficiency ratio	4.1%	4.1%	4.1%	4.1%
ReOI	$ 389.3	$ 467.1	$ 527.9	$ 554.3
Growth in ReOI	28.0%	20.0%	13.0%	5.0%

The valuation based on these forecasts is:

	1996A	1997E	1998E	1999E
PV of ReOI		$350.7	$379.1	$ 386.0
Total PV	$ 1,116			
Continuing value[1]				9,238.3
PV of CV	$ 6,755			
NOA$_{1996}$	2,659			
V_{1996}^{NOA}	$10,530			
NFO	228			
V_{1996}^{E}	$10,302			
Value per share on 143.629 million shares	$ 72			

[1]CV = 554.3/(1.11 – 1.05).

Compare this valuation to the simple Nike valuations in Chapter 14. The analyst might also apply fade rates to profit margins and turnovers: As demand for footwear falls, competition among suppliers could reduce prices, margins, and turnovers.

Postscript: Nike's actual 1997 sales were $9,187 million and 1998 sales were $9,553 million. Fiscal 1999 sales were down to $8,776.9 million, and 2000 sales were $8,995.1 million. The reversion in sales growth rates did happen. And sales profit margins were down to 4.3 percent in 1998, 5.1 percent in 1999, and 6.2 percent in 2000.

Among ways that firms counter competitive forces (with examples of specific firms or industries) are:

- Brand creation and maintenance; franchising (Coca-Cola, McDonald's).

- Creating proprietary knowledge that receives patent protection (pharmaceutical firms).

- Managing consumer expectations (beer and wine marketing).

- Forming alliances and agreements with competitors, suppliers, and firms with related technology (airline alliances, telecom alliances).

- Exploiting first-mover advantages (Wal-Mart, Amazon.com, Internet portal pioneers).

- Mergers (Netscape and AOL; AOL and Time-Warner).

- Creating superior production and marketing technologies (Dell Computer).

- Staying ahead on technological knowledge and production learning curve (Intel).

- Creating economies of scale that are difficult to replicate (telecom networks, banking networks).

- Creating a proprietary technological standard or a network that consumers and other firms must lock into (Microsoft).

- Government protection (agriculture).

Understanding the tension between the forces of competition and the counterforces is crucial to forecasting fade rates. Many actions of firms that challenge and counter competition create temporary advantages, but these advantages often disappear over time. Product innovation draws customers but ultimately is imitated if there is no patent protection. Success draws imitators unless there are natural or government-enforced barriers to entry. These factors yield decreasing returns (to use economists' language). Firms strive to maintain returns or generate increasing returns. A firm that can create a technological standard (like Microsoft with Windows) will enjoy sustained or even growing ReOI as customers are locked in. So will a pharmaceutical firm with patents for products in strong demand. So will a firm that has created consumer demand through a strong brand name.

Government policy attempts to balance the forces of competition against the forces to counter them. So government policy must be understood. Is the government disposed to free trade and competition? To protection? To political favoritism? What is the antitrust (monopolies) law? What are the trade laws and international trade treaties?

The driver pattern diagrams indicate not only that high profitability tends to decline but also that low profitability tends to increase. Firms on the latter trajectory include those that are entering an industry or establishing new products. These often have low initial profitability that gradually improves. The forecasting challenge is to assess the likely success of new products or innovations. Firms that fade up rather than down also include those whose core income is temporarily depressed because of product transition, competitive challenge, or a labor strike. The forecasting challenge is to assess the extent to which the low profitability is indeed temporary (so will recover) or is permanent. The diagrams here are based on actual data; the patterns therefore are for firms which survived to each future year. Forecasting survival and recovery is important for these low-profitability firms: The forces of competition drive out firms that cannot sustain ReOI in the long run. Chapter 19 deals with bankruptcy prediction.

The Coca-Cola Company manufactures concentrates and syrups and ships them to its bottlers for distribution in soft drinks. By keeping its cola formula secret, by careful quality control and by maintenance and promotion of its brand, Coke has consistently increased its sales and profits.

Coke's management says in its 10-K Discussion and Analysis that "our mission is to create share-owner value over time." In doing so they focus on improving what they call "economic profit," which is similar to residual operating income. Below are the economic profit figures that Coke has reported in its 10-Ks from 1990 to 1997, along with its drivers and stock prices.

	1990	1991	1992	1993	1994	1995	1996	1997
Net revenues ($ millions)	10,261	11,599	13,119	14,030	16,264	18,127	18,673	18,868
Return on capital[1] (%)	26.8	27.5	29.4	31.2	32.7	34.9	36.7	39.4
Sales profit margin (%)	13.1	13.5	14.4	15.2	15.4	15.3	15.9	18.0
Asset turnover	2.0	2.0	2.0	2.1	2.1	2.3	2.3	2.2
Economic profit ($ millions)	920	1,073	1,300	1,549	1,896	2,291	2,718	3,325
Growth in economic profit (%)		16.6	21.2	19.2	22.4	20.8	18.6	22.3
Stock price per share	12	20	21	22	26	37	53	67

[1]Coke defines return on capital in a similar way to RNOA. See Box 14.3 in Chapter 14.

Coke's stock price increased almost 5.6 times over the period, matched by increasing economic profit (ReOI). The economic profit has been driven by increasing sales and margins. This is a growth pattern, not a fade pattern. Can growth at this rate be maintained?

Fading (up or down) is a typical pattern, but many other driver patterns are possible. A not uncommon pattern is continuing high RNOA, without any fading, along with growth in ReOI because of growth in net operating assets. These are firms that counter competition successfully. Coca-Cola is a good example of a firm that has grown ReOI through brand management. See Box 15.2.

Drivers often interact. So declining RNOA may mean declining growth in NOA as the lower profitability encourages fewer investments. Lower sales growth rates are often accompanied by lower margins as competition affects both. And, to grow sales, firms may take on lower margin business. Dell Computer's stock price, driven by extraordinary sales growth and good margins to almost $60 in early 1999, fell to $47 over a week when it reported slower sales growth. In response, Dell indicated it was going into the hot market for small computers, selling for less than $1,000, but conceded that this would be lower margin business.

3. Focus on Key Drivers

For some firms, particular drivers are more important than others. A number of drivers might change slightly, but one or two drivers might change significantly. Drivers that require particular focus are **key drivers.** For Coca-Cola (in Box 15.2) sales and margins are key drivers. A simple forecast might suffice for a non–key driver, but key drivers require thorough investigation of the factors that drive them. In retailing, profit margins are often fairly constant, so forecasting focuses on sales and ATO where there is more uncertainty. Because sales and ATO are driven by sales per square foot, the retail analyst cuts through to this number first.

Box 15.3 identifies key economic factors for selected industries and the ReOI drivers associated with them. It also gives an analysis of key drivers for airlines and for Nike.

SELECTED INDUSTRIES

Industry	Key Economic Factors	Key ReOI Drivers
Automobiles	Model design and production efficiency	Sales and margins
Beverages	Brand management and product innovation	Sales
Cellular phones	Population covered (POP) and churn rates	Sales and ATO
Commercial real estate	Square footage and occupancy rates	Sales and ATO
Computers	Technology path and competition	Sales and margins
Fashion clothing	Brand management and design	Sales
Internet commerce	Hits per hour	Sales and ATO
Nonfashion clothing	Production efficiency	Margins
Pharmaceuticals	Research and development	Sales
Retail	Retail space and sales per square foot	Sales and ATO

AIRLINES

Airlines typically operate with a given fleet and a given gate allocation at airports, at least in the short run. Thus with a fixed number of flights their costs are mainly fixed costs, and profitability is driven largely by revenues. Below are statistics for the 10 largest carriers in the United States for 1994 to 1996.

U.S. Industry Statistics	1994	Change	1995	Change	1996	Change
Revenue miles seat (RMS) (thousands)	499,715	4.34%	512,612	2.58%	546,896	6.69%
Available seat miles (ASM) (thousands)	752,841	1.16%	762,550	1.29%	784,502	2.88%
Load factor	66.38%	3.14%	67.22%	1.27%	69.71%	3.70%
Yield (cent per RMS)	12.47	−1.88%	12.84	2.93%	13.08	1.90%
Revenues ($ millions)						
Passenger	62,332	2.38%	65,816	5.59%	71,553	8.72%
Cargo and other	7,572	−0.88%	7,653	1.07%	7,767	1.49%
Total	69,904	2.02%	73,469	5.10%	79,320	7.96%
Costs ($ millions)						
Labor	24,171	2.36%	24,093	−0.32%	25,507	5.87%
Fuel	8,099	−8.35%	8,193	1.16%	10,275	25.41%
Commissions	6,386	−0.05%	6,308	−1.22%	6,307	−0.02%
Rentals and landing fees	7,501	1.54%	7,824	4.31%	7,739	−1.09%
Maintenance	3,210	4.36%	2,989	−6.88%	3,485	16.59%
Depreciation and amortization	3,840	1.61%	3,791	−1.28%	3,825	0.09%
Other	14,741	3.92%	15,061	2.17%	15,767	4.69%
Total costs	67,948	1.01%	68,259	0.46%	72,905	6.81%
Commission rate	10.2%	−2.86%	9.6%	−5.88%	8.8%	−8.33%
Fuel price/gallon ($)	56.7	−8.55%	57.4	1.23%	70	21.95%
Average compensation ($ millions)	58,147	6.47%	59,849	2.93%	61,773	3.21%
Labor productivity[1]	1,811	5.22%	1,894	4.59%	1,900	0.30%
Unit labor cost/ASM	3.21	1.19%	3.16	−1.59%	3.25	2.91%

Note: Industry includes Alaska, America West, American, Continental, Delta, Northwest, Southwest, TWA, United, and US Airways.
[1]Thousands of available seat miles per employee.

The size of the fleet and gate allocation defines what the industry calls *available seat miles (ASM)*. A *load factor* determines *revenue miles seat (RMS)* and ticket prices determine the dollar yield per RMS. This yield, along with RMS, drives revenues so, for a given ASM, load factors and yields are the key drivers for airlines. The analyst cuts to these key factors but is also sensitive to any changes in available seat miles with new routes and new gate allocations. Other drivers such as labor productivity, labor costs, commission rates to travel agents, and fuel costs per mile (given in the table above) are also monitored.

NIKE, INC.

Nike's sales, profit margins, and asset turnovers for 1994 to 1996 (from the analysis in Chapters 11 and 12.) are given below. Gross margins are also given, along with the advertising-to-sales ratio.

	1994	1995	1996
Sales ($ millions)	$3,790	$4,761	$6,471
Core sales PM	7.9%	8.5%	8.8%
Asset turnover	2.6	2.7	2.7
Gross margin ratio	39.3%	39.8%	39.6%
Advertising and promotion/sales	9.8%	10.4%	9.9%

Gross margins and ATO are reasonably constant, so sales is a key driver: At these margins and turnovers, Nike must increase sales to increase ReOI. But sales are driven in part by Nike's extensive advertising and sports promotions. So a key driver is the amount of sales that advertising produces. The advertising-to-sales ratio, a measure of the productivity of advertising, has been reasonably constant at about 10 percent. Can Nike generate more sales by increasing advertising or will increased advertising be less productive so that advertising-to-sales ratios (and profit margins) fall? This is a key point of focus.

Analysts sometimes identify firms by **value types** according to their key drivers. So Coca-Cola is a *brand management firm* where value is driven by exploiting a brand. A firm where profit margins and asset turnovers quickly revert to typical levels is called a *company of averages*. A firm where value comes from growing sales and net operating assets is called a *growth firm*. A firm that has large fixed costs to be covered and where most of sales go to the bottom line after fixed costs are covered—like telecoms—is referred to as being *sales driven*. (This firm has declining ATO as sales increase.) A firm whose product is not yet clearly defined—like a start-up research biotech—is a *speculative* type. These names are helpful to bring focus but are often oversimplifications; be careful not to presume too much by typing a firm.

4. Focus on Choices versus Conditions

Economic factors and ReOI drivers can change in two ways. They are determined either by a change in the environment the firm is in or by choices made by management. Government regulations and tax rates are determined outside the firm (although the firm might try to influence regulations). Product price is often set by the market. The degree of competition in the industry is often outside management's control. These are **business conditions** under which the firm must operate. But other factors are the result of **strategic choices** made by management. Management chooses the product. Management chooses the location and form of the production process. They choose product quality. They decide on the R&D program. They make alliances with other firms. These choices, taken as a whole, amount to the firm's *strategy*.

Understanding both business conditions and the firm's strategy is a prerequisite for sound forecasting and valuation. When forecasting, the analyst asks how business conditions might change and how management's strategy might change—perhaps in reaction to changes in business conditions. But strategy, as a matter of choice, is itself the subject of valuation analysis.

FULL-INFORMATION FORECASTING AND PRO FORMA ANALYSIS

Full-information forecasting builds up pro forma future financial statements from forecasts of drivers. This is done in an orderly way to ensure that no element is overlooked.

The forecasting scheme follows a straightforward outline. Sales forecasting is the starting point. Then forecasted profit margins are applied to sales to yield forecasts of operating income. And forecasted ATO applied to sales yields the forecast of NOA to complete the ReOI calculation.

We will demonstrate the scheme with PPE Inc., the merchandising company for which we developed simple forecasts in the last chapter. Here are the relevant numbers in PPE's Year 0 statements (in millions of dollars):

Sales	124.90
Operating income	9.80
Net operating assets	74.42

These numbers indicate a sales PM of 7.85 percent and an ATO of 1.68. Suppose we forecast from a marketing analysis that sales for PPE Inc. will increase at a rate of 5 percent per year. Suppose also that we forecast that core profit margins will be the same in the future as they are currently (7.85 percent) and that there will be no other operating income or unusual items. To produce sales, an investment of net operating assets (more property, plant, and equipment) of 56¾ cents for each dollar of sales will have to be in place at the beginning of each year. This is just the inverse of the forecasted ATO, so the forecasted ATO is 1.762.

Based on these forecasts, we can develop the pro forma of Exhibit 15.1. Sales, as you see, are growing at the predicted 5 percent rate. Applying the forecasted PM to forecasted sales each year yields operating income: OI = Sales × PM. Applying the forecasted ATO to sales yields the forecast of net operating assets at the beginning of the year: NOA = Sales/ATO. So we produce the ingredients of residual operating income, OI and NOA. (Allow for some rounding errors when proofing these calculations.) The forecasted ReOI is given at the bottom of Exhibit 15.1. This is growing at a rate of 5 percent per year. So, with PPE's required return for operations of 11.34 percent, the value of the equity is

$$V_0^E = CSE_0 + \frac{\overline{ReOI_1}}{(\rho_F - g)}$$

$$= 66.72 + \frac{1.855}{1.1134 - 1.05}$$

$$= \$95.98 \text{ million}$$

and the intrinsic levered P/B ratio is 1.44. The value of the operations is $103.68 million and the unlevered P/B is 1.39. On 100 million shares outstanding, the per-share value is $0.96.

EXHIBIT 15.1

PPE INC.
Pro Forma Financial Statements, Operating Activities
(in millions of dollars)
(Required return for operations is 11.34%.)

	Year −1	Year 0	Year 1	Year 2	Year 3	Year 4	Year 5
Income Statement							
Sales		124.90	131.15	137.70	144.59	151.82	159.41
Core operating expenses		115.10	120.86	126.89	133.24	139.90	146.89
Core operating income		9.80	10.29	10.81	11.35	11.92	12.51
Financial income (expense)		(0.70)					
Earnings		9.10					
Balance Sheet							
Net operating assets	69.90	74.42	78.14	82.05	86.15	90.46	94.98
Net financial assets	(7.00)	(7.70)					
Common stockholders' equity							
(100 million shares outstanding)	62.90	66.72					
Cash Flow Statement							
OI		9.80	10.29	10.81	11.35	11.92	12.51
ΔNOA		4.52	3.72	3.91	4.10	4.31	4.52
Free cash flow (C − 1)		5.28	6.57	6.90	7.25	7.61	7.99
RNOA (%)		14.02	13.83	13.83	13.83	13.83	13.83
Profit margin (%)		7.85	7.85	7.85	7.85	7.85	7.85
Asset turnover		1.787	1.762	1.762	1.762	1.762	1.762
Growth in NOA (%)		6.5	5.0	5.0	5.0	5.0	5.0
Residual OI (0.1134)		1.87	1.855	1.948	2.046	2.148	2.256
Growth in ReOI (%)			5.0	5.0	5.0	5.0	5.0
Abnormal OI Growth (AOIG)				0.093	0.097	0.102	0.107
Growth in AOIG (%)				5.0	5.0	5.0	5.0

Allow for rounding errors.

The drivers of ReOI are given in the pro forma. The RNOA in all years is the same as that forecasted for Year 1 because its drivers, PM and ATO, are forecasted to stay the same: This is a firm with constant profitability but growing investment in NOA. But the forecast and the valuation implied differ from an SF3 forecast because ATO and growth in NOA are predicted to be different from current levels. Moreover, growth is not assumed but is forecasted by forecasting sales and the technology for producing sales that is captured by the ATO.

The pro forma in Exhibit 15.1 also forecasts abnormal operating income growth (AOIG). By recognizing that AOIG is the change in ReOI, the analysis avoids forecasting cum-dividend operating income and the free cash flow needed to calculate it. As AOIG is forecasted to grow at 5 percent per year, the AOIG equity valuation is

$$V_0^{CSE} = \frac{1}{0.1134}\left[10.295 + \frac{0.093}{1.1134 - 1.05}\right] - 7.70$$

$$= \$95.98 \text{ million}$$

or 0.96 per share (allow for rounding error.) That is, the equity value is the value of the operations less the value of the net financial obligations.

The forecasted OI and NOA are also the drivers of free cash flow ($C - I = $ OI $-$ ΔNOA), so the cash flow forecast in the pro forma falls out immediately.[2] These free cash flow forecasts can, in this case, be used to value the firm using discounted cash flow analysis. As the free cash flows are forecasted to grow at 5 percent per year after Year 1, the value of the equity is

$$V_0^E = \frac{\text{Free cash flow}_1}{\rho_E - g} - \text{NFO}_0$$

$$= \frac{6.574}{1.1134 - 1.05} - 7.70$$

$$= \$95.98 \text{ million}$$

or $0.96 per share (allow for rounding error).

This is a simple scenario, of course, but it highlights the ingredients in forecasting. The change in asset turnover and growth in net operating assets from current levels might be accompanied by changes in profit margins, but always the three forecasts—sales, PM, and ATO—along with any other operating income and unusual items, will determine the RNOA and growth in NOA, which produce residual operating income and abnormal operating income growth. You might put the PPE example into your spreadsheet program and see how the valuation changes with different predictions of the drivers.

The pro forma financial statements are not complete, but we can fill out the rest of the pro forma with just two further forecasts, one for net dividends and one for borrowing costs. The pro forma has free cash flow forecasts and so, if we forecast dividends and borrowing costs, we can forecast net financial obligations and expenses and fill out the income statement and balance sheet:

$$\text{NFO}_t = \text{NFO}_{t-1} - (C - I)_t + \text{NFE}_t + d_t \quad \text{and} \quad \text{NFE}_t = (\rho_D - 1)\text{NFO}_{t-1}$$

Suppose borrowing costs are 10 percent here. Let's set the future dividend at 40 percent of net income (a 40 percent payout ratio). The pro forma rolls out as in Exhibit 15.2.

Interest expense in the income statement is always 10 percent of net financial obligations in place at the beginning of the period and the change in net financial obligations is always determined by the treasurer's rule: Sell debt to cover the deficiency of free cash flow over interest and dividends. In this case there is a surplus, as indicated by the debt financing flows in the forecasted cash flow statement. This has been applied to buying bonds, first the firm's own bonds until Year 3 and then others' bonds after Year 3, to yield net financial assets rather than obligations. With both NOA and NFO forecasted, we have forecasted common stockholders' equity: CSE = NOA $-$ NFO.

---

[2] With these forecasts of free cash flow, one can forecast AOIG. The pro forma is developed as follows:

	Year 1	Year 2	Year 3	Year 4	Year 5
OI	10.295	10.810	11.351	11.918	12.514
Free cash flow	6.570	6.900	7.250	7.610	7.990
Reinvested FCF		0.745	0.782	0.822	0.863
Cum-dividend OI		11.555	12.133	12.740	13.377
Normal OI		11.462	12.036	12.638	13.270
AEG (for OI)		0.093	0.097	0.102	0.107

By forecasting AOIG as the change in ReOI, the forecasting is more efficient, for one avoids free cash flow forecasting.

EXHIBIT 15.2

PPE INC.
Pro Forma Financial Statements, All Activities
(in millions of dollars)

	Year −1	Year 0	Year 1	Year 2	Year 3	Year 4	Year 5
Income Statement							
Sales		124.90	131.15	137.70	144.59	151.82	159.41
Core operating expenses		115.10	120.86	126.89	133.24	139.90	146.89
Core operating income		9.80	10.29	10.81	11.35	11.92	12.51
Financial income (expense)		(0.70)	(0.77)	(0.57)	(0.35)	(0.10)	0.18
Earnings		9.10	9.52	10.24	11.00	11.82	12.69
Balance Sheet							
Net operating assets	69.90	74.42	78.14	82.05	86.15	90.46	94.98
Net financial assets	(7.00)	(7.70)	(5.71)	(3.47)	(0.97)	1.81	4.91
Common stockholders' equity							
(100 million shares outstanding)	62.90	66.72	72.44	78.58	85.19	92.27	99.89
Cash Flow Statement							
OI		9.80	10.29	10.81	11.35	11.92	12.51
ΔNOA		4.52	3.72	3.91	4.10	4.31	4.52
Free cash flow (C − I)		5.28	6.57	6.90	7.25	7.61	7.99
Dividends (payout: 40%)		5.28	3.81	4.10	4.40	4.73	5.08
Debt financing		0.00	2.76	2.80	2.85	2.88	2.91
Total financing flows		5.28	6.57	6.90	7.25	7.61	7.99

Allow for rounding errors.

The forecasting scheme can get into more detail, and that added detail will add further line items to the pro forma statements. Rather than forecasting profit margins, the detailed forecast predicts gross margins and expense ratios for each component of the margin and so builds up further line items for the forecasted income statement. And rather than forecasting the (total) asset turnover, the detailed forecast predicts individual asset and liability turnovers and so builds up the line items for the forecasted balance sheets. The forecaster decides what level of detail is necessary to improve a forecast, keeping in mind the cost of researching for more information. Box 15.4 builds up a detailed forecast for Nike.

A Forecasting Template

We can pull all this forecasting together as a series of steps that can be built into a spreadsheet program.

Step 1. Forecast Sales

The sales forecast is the starting point and usually involves the most investigation. Simple extrapolations with sales growth rates are a way to get going but a complete analysis involves a thorough understanding of the business. The following issues have to be considered:

1. The firm's strategy. What lines of business is it likely to be in? Are new products likely? What is the product quality strategy? At what point in the product life cycle is the firm? What is the firm's acquisition and takeover strategy?

2. The market for the products. How will consumer behavior change? What is the elasticity of demand for products? Are substitute products emerging?

A perceptive analyst forecasted in 1997 that Nike would not continue on its current trajectory. She felt that Nike's products would continue to be a hot fashion item through fiscal 1997 and 1998, spurred on by heavy promotion. But after 1998, Nike's luster would fade somewhat, particularly to the fashion-conscious teens. Indeed she forecasted increasing inventory buildup, anticipating that Nike would have trouble moving its inventory. And, with rising production costs and decreasing margins, she expected Nike would have to restructure some of its operations in 1998 and 1999 and take a charge against income.

She analyzed the effect of these trends on drivers as follows:

1. She forecasted that sales would increase by over 40 percent in 1997 to $9,200 million, remain at this level in 1998, and then drop to $8,500 million in 1999. Thereafter she forecasted sales to increase by 3 percent per year.

2. She forecasted gross margins of 39.8 percent for 1997, dropping to 36.5 percent in 1998 and thereafter as production costs increase.

Forecasts of other income statement ratios were as follows. The actual 1996 numbers are given for comparison.

	1996A	1997E	1998E	1999E and After
Advertising expense ratio (%)	9.9	10.6	12.3	12.3
Other expense ratio (%)	15.4	14.5	15.2	15.5
Tax rate (%)	38.5	38.0	38.0	38.0

The analyst forecasted profit margins to stabilize at 5.6 percent of sales after 1999, reflecting the benefits from restructuring. To achieve this margin the analyst forecasted that Nike would incur a restructuring charge of $130 million in 1998 and another of $50 million in 1999.

3. Turnover forecasts were as follows:

	1997E	1998E	1999E and After
Accounts receivable turnover	5.6	5.3	5.1
Inventory turnover	8.0	7.0	6.5
PPE turnover	9.9	8.0	4.5
Other NOA/sales	−6.77%	−6.95%	−11.34%

With these forecasts the analyst developed the following pro forma financial statements and valuation:

	1996A	1997E	1998E	1999E	2000E	2001E
Income Statement						
Sales	6,471	9,200	9,200	8,500	8,755	9,018
Cost of sales	3,907	5,538	5,842	5,397	5,559	5,726
Gross margin	2,564	3,662	3,358	3,103	3,196	3,292
SG&A expenses	1,642	2,309	2,530	2,363	2,434	2,507
Income from sales	922	1,353	828	740	762	785
Other operating income		32	20	28	29	30
Core operating income before tax	922	1,385	848	768	791	815
Taxes	355	526	322	292	301	310
Core operating income after tax	567	859	526	476	490	505
Restructuring charge			130	50		
Operating income	567	859	396	426	490	505

	1996A	1997E	1998E	1999E	2000E	2001E
Balance Sheet						
Accounts receivable	1,346	1,643	1,736	1,667	1,717	
Inventory	931	1,150	1,314	1,308	1,347	
Property, plant, and equipment	643	930	1,150	1,889	1,946	
Other NOA	(261)	(623)	(639)	(964)	(993)	
Net operating assets	2,659	3,100	3,561	3,900	4,017	
Operating income		859	396	426	490	
Change in NOA		441	461	339	117	
Free cash flow		418	(65)	87	373	
RNOA (on beginning NOA)		32.3%	12.8%	12.0%	12.6%	12.6%
ReOI (0.11)		566.5	55.0	34.3	61.0	62.9
Growth in ReOI			(90.3%)	(37.6%)	77.8%	3.0%
Total PV of ReOI to 2000	620					
Continuing value[1]					786	
PV of CV	518					
Value of operations	3,797					
NFO	228					
Value of common equity	3,569					
Value per share (on 143.629 million shares)	$24.85					

[1]CV = 62.9/(1.11 − 1.03).
(ReOI increasing at 3% after 2000.)

The analyst was most tentative about the long-run growth forecast. She saw Nike's product promotion as its key driver and forecasted that advertising would not be as productive (in generating sales) as Nike's products became less fashionable and competitors challenged Nike's market position. She expected sales at strong levels through the 1998 World Cup team sponsorship but was concerned about a Michael Jordan retirement and its effect on the Jordan Nike brand. So she forecasted a declining advertising-to-sales ratio but concluded that monitoring this driver was key to her ongoing valuation. You might put the forecasts here into a spreadsheet and carry out a sensitivity analysis of how Nike's value might change with changes in forecasted advertising-to-sales ratios.

This valuation of $24.85 per share is well below the market price of $104 in early 1997. As it turns out, the forecasts here for 1997–1999 are close to what Nike actually experienced in those years. Nike did have a downturn, but the market price declined from $104 to only about $80 in 1999 (before a 2-for-1 split), and $60 in 2000, well above the value implied by the actual results. At $60, the market must have seen significantly higher sales, growth rates, margins, or turnovers than forecasted here for 2000 and beyond. Look at subsequent results and see if the market's valuation of $60 ($30 after a split) in early 2000 was justified. Or did the market subsequently adjust to the picture here?

3. The firm's marketing plan. Are new markets opening? What is the pricing plan? What is the promotion and advertising plan? Does the firm have the ability to develop and maintain brand names?

Step 2. Forecast Asset Turnover and Calculate Net Operating Assets

The forecasted asset turnover, applied to sales, yields the NOA: NOA = Sales/ATO. Forecasting overall ATO involves forecasting its elements: receivables turnover, inventory turnover, PPE turnover, and so on. Accordingly the forecaster develops line items on forecasted balance sheets for receivables, inventories, PPE, and so on, that total to NOA.

The ATO forecast asks what assets need to be put in place to generate the forecasted sales. This of course requires a knowledge of the production technology: What plants need to be built and what level of inventories and receivables need to be carried to maintain the forecasted sales? It also requires a forecast of costs: How much will plants cost to build? In the Americas, in Asia, in Europe?

For PPE Inc. we forecasted that the amount of assets to be put in place will be proportional to sales. But this is probably unrealistic. Because plants do not always run at the same level of capacity, even without changes in technology the ATO will change if more sales can be generated with existing plants or if a forecasted drop in demand produces idle capacity. The ATO forecast captures the cost (in value lost) of idle capacity and the value gained by producing sales with existing capacity. If full capacity is reached, new plants will have to be built, but they may result in idle capacity to begin with.

Step 3. Revise Sales Forecasts

Capacity constraints limit sales. Forecasted ATO yields forecasted net operating assets, but if the assets cannot be put in place to produce the sales, the sales forecast must be revised.

Step 4. Forecast Core Sales Profit Margins

Core OI from sales = Sales × Core sales PM, so next forecast core sales PM. This involves forecasting all its components, gross margins, and expense ratios. This also requires a good knowledge of the business. What will be production costs? Is there a learning curve in production? Will technological innovations reduce costs? Will there be changes in labor costs or material prices? What will be the advertising budget? How much of each dollar of sales will be spent on R&D?

For firms with operating leverage, profit margins and expense ratios, like ATO, may not be proportional to sales. Variable costs might increase as a constant percentage of sales, but if some costs are fixed over a range of forecasted sales, margins will increase as sales increase over that range. Of course, as sales continue to increase all costs become variable as additional fixed costs are incurred to support the sales, but these fixed costs increase in lumps rather than continuously.

Step 5. Forecast Other Operating Income

The share of income in subsidiaries is the main item here and requires going to the subsidiaries and forecasting their earnings.

Step 6. Forecast Unusual Operating Items

These often can't be forecasted (they are forecasted to be zero). But if you can forecast a restructuring or a special charge, this is subtracted from core operating income to get total operating income.

Step 7. Calculate ReOI and AOIG

With the operating income and net operating asset forecasts and the operating cost of capital, calculate residual operating income: $OI_t = (\rho_F - 1)NOA_{t-1}$. Remember the shortcut:

$$ReOI = Sales \times \left(Core\ sales\ PM - \frac{Required\ return\ for\ operations}{ATO} \right) + Core\ other\ OI + UI$$

Abnormal operating growth is the change in ReOI over the previous period.

The valuation can now be done. In the PPE example we forecasted that the cost of capital was to remain constant, but we could use different rates in each period if the cost of capital were forecasted to change.

Step 8. Calculate Free Cash Flow

This is simply calculated from other forecasted amounts: $C - I = \text{OI} - \Delta\text{NOA}$.

Step 9. Forecast Net Dividend Payout

What will be the payout policy? Are stock repurchases anticipated? How much of new financing will come from share issues? Remember the net dividend is payout minus net share issues.

Step 10. Forecast Financial Expenses or Financial Income

With a forecast for NFO for the beginning of each year, the forecasted NFE for the next year applies a forecasted borrowing rate: $\text{NFE}_t = (\rho_D - 1)\text{NFO}_{t-1}$, and similarly for financial income with net financial assets. Remember that NFE is after tax and so too is the cost of capital for debt.

Step 11. Calculate Net Financial Obligations or Financial Assets

This, too, is by calculation: $\Delta\text{NFO}_t = (C - I)_t + \text{NFE}_t + d_t$. The net dividend is key here as it increases the borrowing requirement. Correspondingly, if funds are raised by share issues, the borrowing requirement is reduced. The amount of net financial obligations might be a matter of firm policy: The firm has a target leverage. If so, net dividend payout is determined by the leverage policy.

Step 12. Calculate Comprehensive Income

$$\text{Earnings} = \text{OI} - \text{NFE}.$$

Step 13. Calculate Common Stockholders' Equity

$$\text{CSE}_t = \text{NOA}_t - \text{NFO}_t = \text{CSE}_{t-1} + \text{Earnings}_t - d_t.$$

Step 14. Adjust the Valuation for any Stock Option Overhang

See Chapter 13.

Steps 1–6, and 9–10 require forecasting. All other steps are calculations from forecasted amounts using the accounting relations with which we are familiar from Chapter 7. (Step 7 could also involve a forecast of a change in the cost of capital for operations.) Only Steps 1–7 are necessary for valuation (before the adjustment for stock options). Yes, the seven steps. These seven steps are depicted diagrammatically in Figure 15.3.

The analyst can take some additional steps to test the pro forma statements:

1. Ensure that the two calculations of CSE in Step 13 agree. This validates that the pro forma articulates. We then know that we have been tidy and have not lost any element in the valuation. Note also that

$$\text{CSE} = \text{Sales} \times \frac{\text{NOA}}{\text{Sales}} \times \frac{\text{CSE}}{\text{NOA}} = \text{Sales} \times \frac{1}{\text{ATO}} \times \frac{1}{1 + \text{FLEV}}$$

2. Do a common-size analysis on the pro forma statements and test the numbers against industry norms to see if they are reasonable. Are they consistent with your prediction of how the firm's fade rates will differ from industry fade rates?

3. Watch for **financial asset buildup**. If operations are forecasted to generate positive free cash flow, financial obligations will be reduced and ultimately financial assets will be generated, as with PPE Inc. This can't go on indefinitely. You have to ask: What will they do with the financial assets? Will they pay them out as dividends or

FIGURE 15.3

Forecasting Residual Operating Income (ReOI) and Abnormal Operating Income Growth (AOIG)

The diagram summarizes the forecasting template; numbers indicate steps in the forecasting template. Beginning with a sales forecast, residual operating income forecasting is accomplished in the seven steps indicated. The abnormal operating income growth forecast is the change in forecasted residual operating income.

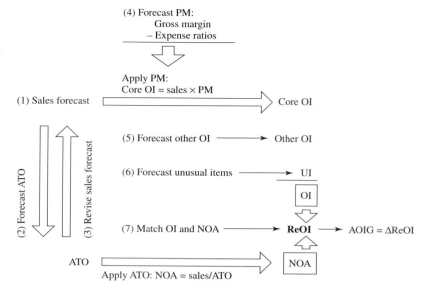

does management have a strategy that anticipates new investment that I have overlooked? These questions lead back to the issue that requires an answer before forecasting begins: What is the firm's strategy? Rethinking strategy as a result of forecasted financial asset buildup can induce you to revise the pro forma.

You now have all the tools required for building your own analysis and valuation product. See Box 15.5.

Features of Accounting-Based Valuation

The pro forma analysis highlights a number of desirable features of forecasting ReOI to value equity:

1. The method is efficient. It comes down to forecasting a few drivers: sales, PM, ATO, and their components.

2. The focus is on operations. The method focuses on the part of the business that adds value, the operations.

3. Dividends are irrelevant. The valuation is insensitive to dividend payout, and this is appropriate given our discussion of dividend irrelevance in Chapter 3. We valued PPE Inc. without a dividend forecast. The dividend forecast comes after Step 7 in the forecasting, and it is at Step 7 that a valuation is made. Indeed, you can change the payout in the example and you will see that the valuation is unaffected. Higher payout just means less cash to buy bonds under the treasurer's rule. Accordingly, only net financial assets are affected, not operating assets or operating income. To state it again, ReOI and AOIG are not affected by payout.

4. Financing is irrelevant. The valuation is not sensitive to financing. Buying and selling debt and the interest incurred on debt do not affect operating income or net operating assets. We could forecast stock issues in the PPE Inc. pro forma with the proceeds

With the financial statement analysis of Part Two of the book and the forecasting and valuation analysis of Part Three, you have all the equipment necessary to build a comprehensive analysis and valuation tool. The **BYOAP** feature on the book's website leads you through the construction of your own product. As an illustration, it values Nike in the year 2000.

You will find developing a product to be very satisfying. The concepts and tools in the book come to life as you apply them; you will understand them better and will appreciate how helpful they are. You will be gratified from working with a tool that has integrity, is consistent with the principles of sound fundamental analysis, and is disciplined by the accounting relations that must be obeyed if we are to avoid mistakes. Accordingly, you will have some added security in equity investing, by protecting yourself from the risk of paying too much for stocks. Take the product into your professional life and use it for your own personal investing. Add bells and whistles as you learn more.

used to reduce debt or purchase financial assets, but this has no affect on the valuation. This complements point 2 above. The focus is on value added and the valuation ignores the zero-NPV (zero-ReNFE) financing activities.[3]

5. Investments that add no value do not affect the valuation. To see this, suppose we modify the NOA forecast for PPE Inc. and predict that at the end of Year 2 PPE will invest another $50 million in operations, financed by an issue of debt at 10 percent. This investment is expected to earn at the same rate as the cost of capital of 11.34 percent and thus will increase the OI forecast by 5.67 percent in Year 3 and on. The ReOI will of course not be affected by the new debt or interest on the debt, but it will not be affected by the investment either. The expected addition to ReOI in Year 3 from the investment will be $5.67 - (0.1134 \times 50) = 0$. The effect on AOIG (the change in ReOI) will also be zero. And so for subsequent years of the investment's life. Accordingly, the firm's value based on the present value of ReOI is unaffected by the new investment. This would be called a zero-NPV investment in DCF analysis, a zero-ReOI investment here. Pro forma ReOI is affected only by investments that add (or decrease) value by earning at a rate different from the cost of capital.

6. Value-generating investments are uncovered and the source of the value generation is identified. By the same reasoning as in point 5, positive and negative ReOI investments that generate or decrease value are discovered by the pro forma analysis. In addition, the pro forma will reveal the reason for the value effect—in the PM or ATO. Suppose we forecast that in Year 1 management will make a new investment that will not produce any increase in sales. The forecasted ATO will decline, RNOA will decline, and so will ReOI. Accordingly, the effect on the valuation will be negative: We have uncovered a negative-value generator. This is an unlikely case, but it could be that frivolous corporate jet. It is sometimes said that management indulges in negative-value projects after free cash flow and financial asset buildup. This scenario is the so-called *free cash flow hypothesis* of management behavior: Management makes poor investments when they have a lot of free cash flow. This has to be monitored and pro forma analysis provides the means of anticipating financial asset buildup.

7. In applying the discount rate, we have to be concerned about only one discount rate, the cost of capital for operations. From the full pro forma statements in Exhibit 15.2, we could calculate RE and AEG from forecasted earnings and CSE and value PPE Inc.

[3] If you believe that there are tax advantages from corporate debt or tax disadvantages from paying dividends, the valuation can be adjusted by the present value of these tax effects.

from forecasts of RE and AEG rather than ReOI and AOIG. This would require the calculation of the cost of equity capital. But this varies with financing risk and must be recalculated for each period as financial leverage changes. The cost of capital for operations may also change as operations change but the task of forecasting the discount rate is reduced. Given the difficulty in estimating discount rates, changes in the discount rate for operations are likely to be not only small but also imprecise. So work with constant rates unless the nature of the business changes significantly.

8. The valuation avoids forecasting when mark-to-market accounting suffices, as with the valuation of financing activities and the cost of stock options.

VALUE GENERATED IN SHARE TRANSACTIONS

In introducing the residual earnings model in Chapter 5, we emphasized that the model does not capture value that may be generated or lost in share transactions. If there are no anticipated share issues or repurchases in the future or these transactions are expected to be for cash at fair value, then there is no problem. But if a firm can issue overpriced shares or repurchase underpriced shares, the resulting gain is not reflected in earnings or residual earnings. Nor is it captured by a discounted cash flow valuation. Two types of corporate transactions in particular can involve these gains: mergers and acquisitions and buyouts.

Mergers and Acquisitions

Mergers and acquisitions often involve the issue of shares. The acquiring firm issues shares to shareholders of the acquired firm (whose shares are retired), or sometimes shareholders of both firms receive shares in a new firm. The acquiring firm can add value in three ways:

1. Buying the acquiree's shares at less than fair value.

2. Using its own overvalued shares (as "overvalued currency") to buy the shares of the acquiree cheaply.

3. Generating value—synergies—by combining the operations of the two firms.

Residual earnings and DCF techniques anticipate the value of a business acquired and the synergies generated with pro forma analysis. But they don't capture the division of value between the shareholders of acquired and acquiring firms. Both have shares in the merged firm but their relative share of value depends on the terms of the share transactions. Points 1 and 2 determine those terms and those terms determine how the synergies in point 3 are divided. The acquirer buys the acquiree cheaply—for either reason 1 or 2— if it issues fewer of its shares for the shares of the acquiree, and so its shareholders get a larger share of any synergies from the merger.

The division of value in a merger is resolved in Box 15.6 from the point of view of the acquiring firms' shareholders. The same principles apply if the acquirees' shareholders wish to value an anticipated acquisition of their firm. The focus of the analysis is on the effect of the acquisition on the per-share value of an outstanding share.

A manager evaluates a potential acquisition by going through the same analysis: What is the effect of the transaction on the per-share value of the stock? Points 1, 2, and 3 above determine the answer. If the acquisition is made "cheaply," value is added to each share. If the acquiring firm overpays (either because it pays too much for the acquiree's shares or its own shares are undervalued), per-share value is lost. If there are synergies and, by the terms of the share transaction, the acquiring firms' shareholders share in those

PPE Inc. is expected to acquire another firm at the end of Year 2 by issuing 50 million shares to that firm's shareholders. The analyst follows the following steps:

1. Forecast the value of the new merged firm at the end of Year 2 from the forecasted balance sheet of the new merged firm at that date and the present value of subsequent residual earnings that the balance sheet is anticipated to generate.

2. Calculate the anticipated value per share at the acquisition date (at the end of Year 2) by dividing the merged firm's value by the total shares outstanding for the new firm.

3. Calculate the present value of this per-share value at Year 0.

4. Add the present value of expected per-share dividends from the premerged firm up to the merger date.

Suppose pro forma analysis calculates a value for the merged firm at the end of Year 2 of $180 million. With 150 million shares outstanding (100 million held by the original PPE shareholders and 50 million by the shareholders of the acquired firm), the per-share value is $1.20. The value of one of PPE's 100 million shares outstanding at Year 0 is calculated as follows:

Present value (at Year 0) of per-share Year 2 value:

$$\frac{1.20}{1.1134^2} \qquad \$0.97$$

Present value of Year 1 and Year 2 dividends per share:

$$\frac{0.038}{1.1134} + \frac{0.041}{1.1134^2} \qquad \underline{0.07}$$

Per-share value of PPE Inc. $\qquad \underline{\$1.04}$

As PPE was valued at $0.96 before the anticipated acquisition, this calculation indicates that the acquisition adds value to the current shareholders.

Real World Connection

See Exercise E15.7 for further calculations.

---

synergies, per-share value is added. The analysis in Box 15.6 shows that PPE's acquisition is expected to increase per-share value from the $0.96 calculated from the preacquisition pro formas earlier to $1.04. This value added is based on issuing 50 million shares in the merger. The acquisition analyst can ask: What would be the value added if the acquisition could be made by issuing only 40 million shares?

As a historical note, empirical studies have shown that much of the value generated in mergers and acquisitions typically goes to the shareholders of the acquiree. Prices of acquirees' shares tend to increase—often by significant amounts—while prices of acquirers' shares tend to be unaffected or even decline. These observations suggest that acquirees can extract most of the value in mergers. The acquirer's share price might decline because the market feels that it is overpaying for the acquisition. The price might also decline because the market interprets the bid as a signal that the acquirer's shares are overpriced.

Share Repurchases and Buyouts

If members of management feel that their firm's shares are undervalued in the market, they might generate value for shareholders—that is, increase per-share value—by buying back shares. It is for this reason that announcements of share repurchase programs are often seen as a signal of undervaluation, resulting in a share price increase. Research suggests that the market is slow to react, so that buying the shares on the announcement captures subsequent abnormal price appreciation as the market comes to realize that the shares are indeed undervalued.

But the investor must be careful. Share repurchases may just be the firm paying effective dividends. And they may involve distributions of cash not needed for investment—financial asset buildup—to shareholders. Indeed, the announcement of a repurchase may signal that the firm does not have investment opportunities.

The analyst must also be careful in interpreting repurchases in overheated markets: The firm may be paying too much for the shares, and the analyst tests this proposition with an analysis of intrinsic value. Many of the share repurchases in the bull market of the late 1990s did not result in price appreciations.

The *buyout* is a stock repurchase on a larger scale, often with borrowing (and is then a *leveraged buyout*, or *LBO*). If management is involved in gaining equity, the buyout is a *management buyout*. These transactions may add per-share value if managements who participate are more motivated to generate value in operations. But they also add value if shareholders interpret the buyout as a recognition that shares are undervalued.

For this reason, firms add the buyout to their set of tools for creating shareholder value. Buyouts were popular after the 1987 stock market crash. They also were proposed as a remedy for increasing the stock prices of "old-economy" firms in the late 1990s. At a time when investors were pricing technology stocks at very high multiples, old-economy firms traded at relatively low multiples. Their managements felt they were undervalued and proposed buyouts. Airlines were trading at multiples of earnings below 10. *The Wall Street Journal* (March 10, 2000, p. 1) reported the chief executive of Continental Airlines as saying, "If the market says this is all we're worth, then we ought to just buy the company."

Valuation Using Earnings-per-Share Forecasts

Residual earnings techniques calculate per-share value by calculating total dollar value— from forecasts of dollar residual earnings—and dividing the total dollar valuation by shares outstanding. You might ask: Do we reach the same value by forecasting per-share residual earnings and calculating a per-share value from these per-share forecasts? The answer is, no. Residual earnings valuation requires the stocks and flows accounting equation to hold for all future periods so that the comprehensive income forecasted is always equal to the change in book value plus dividends. This is always the case on a total dollar basis, but it is not the case on a per-share basis if there are changes in shares.

The requirement that the stocks and flows equation must hold does not apply to abnormal earnings growth methods: They do not involve forecasted book values, only forecasted earnings. So one can value a firm by forecasting future earnings per share and abnormal earnings per share growth.

Accordingly, the abnormal earnings growth model has a particular advantage when share issues or share repurchases are anticipated. If shares are repurchased cheaply (and so generate value), we expect earnings per share to be higher in the future, for we expect earnings on a lower number of shares than would have been issued for the same cash payment had the firm paid fair value. The abnormal earnings growth valuation is correspondingly higher. If a firm uses its overpriced shares as currency in an acquisition, it uses fewer shares to buy a given amount of earnings, so it increases expected earnings per share. Again, the abnormal earnings growth valuation is correspondingly higher.

The only complication is that, if we are to work with earnings-per-share forecasts, we must work with levered earnings. That implies an equity cost of capital. Accordingly, the cost of capital must be adjusted each future period ahead as changes in financial leverage are forecasted.

FINANCIAL STATEMENT INDICATORS AND RED FLAGS

Much of the information needed to determine how future operating income will be different from current operating income comes from outside the financial statements. But the financial statements themselves provide information that suggests that current income may not be indicative of the future. Box 15.7 lists features in financial statements that

Each of the following features of financial statements may indicate aspects of the current operational profitability that will not persist into the future. They are flags that cue the analyst to investigate causes and ask whether those causes indeed indicate that current operating income is not indicative of future income.

- Unusually high sales growth rates. High sales growth rates typically do not persist, as fade diagrams suggest.

- Unusually large changes in core RNOA. Large changes in core RNOA often don't persist, as fade diagrams suggest.

- Unusual changes in RNOA components.
  PM components:
    Gross margin ratio
    Advertising-to-sales ratio
    General and administrative expenses-to-sales ratio
    R&D-to-sales ratio
  ATO components:
    Inventories-to-sales ratio
    Accounts receivable-to-sales ratio
    Doubtful debts-to-sales ratio
    Other assets-to-sales ratio
    Operating liabilities-to-sales ratio

- RNOA is different from the industry average.
  Operating profitability typically reverts to the average for the industry.

- Components of RNOA are different from the industry average.

- Changes in RNOA components are different from the industry average.

- Changes in NOA are different from the industry average.

- Low effective tax rates. Low effective tax rates on operating income are usually due to tax concessions that are temporary: Firms' tax rates tend to revert to a common level close to the statutory rate over time.

Footnotes and the management discussion and analysis also provide indicators. Investigate the following:

- Order backlog.
  An accumulated order backlog indicates pending demand for the product. Computer and technology companies use the book-to-bill ratio—the ratio of sales orders outstanding to sales orders filled—as an indicator.

- Management earnings and sales forecasts.

- Changes in per-unit sales prices.

- Investment plans.

- Operational plans.

- Changes in labor force.

- Contingent liabilities and provisions.

- Expiration of loss carryforwards and loss of tax credits.

Some indicators are referred to as **red-flag indicators** because they indicate deterioration or even distress:

- Slower sales growth.

- Decline in order backlog.

- Increasing sales returns.
  This ratio may indicate growing customer dissatisfaction with the product.

- Increasing accounts receivable-to-sales ratio.
  This ratio may indicate customers are having credit problems or the firm is having difficulties making sales.

- Increasing inventory-to-sales ratio.
  This ratio may indicate inventory is building up due to difficulties in making sales. But it may also indicate a production buildup in anticipation of higher sales in the future.

- Deterioration in gross margin ratio.
  Analysts watch this ratio very closely. A small change in the gross margin ratio has a large effect on operating income.

- Increasing advertising-to-expense ratio.
  Increases in this ratio can indicate a decreasing effectiveness in advertising generating sales. But it can also indicate increased investment in advertising that will generate more future sales.

- Increasing selling and administrative expenses-to-sales ratio.
  This ratio will increase when sales decline if part of the expenses are fixed costs. Look at increases in the ratio due to variable costs; investigate an increasing ratio on increasing sales because, with fixed costs, the ratio is expected to decline with increases in sales.

raise questions. Each suggests that something might be unusual in core income or net operating assets. The analyst investigates to see whether the indicator points to transitory income or whether drivers have shifted to a new permanent level. Some indicators are red flags that warn about the future.

BUSINESS STRATEGY ANALYSIS AND PRO FORMA ANALYSIS

We have observed that pro forma analysis and valuation cannot begin without an appreciation of a firm's strategy. But pro forma analysis is also a means of evaluating strategies. Pro forma analysis uncovers the value generation. Thus it is also a means of investigating management strategies that generate value.

Pro forma analysis of residual operating income substitutes for discounted cash flow analysis. For a manager who wishes to maximize the value of the firm, the criterion of maximizing the present value of ReOI replaces the criterion of maximizing the net present value of cash flows. Forecasting ReOI cuts to the core of what drives value. It forecasts the drivers of the profitability of operations that connect management choices to value. Much of the framework we have developed in this book for the outside shareholder is, then, the framework for strategy analysis.

Strategy begins with ideas and good strategies begin with innovative ideas. Business strategy books lay out how to think about strategy in a way that leads to innovative ideas. Pro forma analysis converts those ideas into concrete numbers from which the ideas can be valued. But the forecasting framework is not just a method of analysis; it is a way of thinking about the business. And it simplifies that thinking. The manager knows that to generate value, he must focus on the drivers:

- Maximize RNOA relative to the required return.

- Grow net operating assets (if RNOA is greater than the required return).

To maximize RNOA, he maximizes (long-run) profit margins and asset turnovers. To grow net operating assets, he grows sales and maximizes asset turnovers. To maximize profit margins, he minimizes expense ratios, and so on down through the drivers of RNOA.

The manager understands the economic factors and how they affect ReOI drivers. She identifies which factors are business conditions and which involve her choices. Her focus is on change. She analyzes the effects of changes in business conditions and alternatives to deal with those changes (and create changes) with pro forma analysis. She knows key drivers where the business is most susceptible. And her strategy is always to sustain a high or growing ReOI. She understands the forces of competition that cause ReOI to fade and understands how she can counter the forces of competition to sustain a high ReOI.

Unarticulated Strategy

During the bubble, it was fashionable to reject financial analysis as the focus for strategic analysis. Some claimed that financial models constrain thinking and lead to mediocre organizations. The new strategists claimed that good thinking cannot be scripted. "Nonlinear thinking" must replace "linear thinking." The "intellectual capital model" must replace the financial model based on balance sheets and income statements, so that firms replace physical assets with knowledge assets as sources of value. Firms must be organized in ways that foster creativity and adaptability to change rather than focusing on the bottom line.

Such ideas are stimulating. They recognize the sources of value in modern economies, the value in human capital, adaptability, and invention. But there is considerable confusion in rejecting financial analysis to embrace these ideas. Ultimately firms must generate sales to add value, whether those sales are generated from investments in physical assets or investments in human capital and knowledge assets. Those sales must generate positive margins. And the RNOA must be high enough to recover investors' required return. We must have an idea of what future income statements and balance sheets will look like. The financial model must be used in conjunction with new ideas, to test those ideas and to discipline overenthusiasm for and speculation in ideas.

There is, however, a level of strategic analysis where financial analysis is difficult to apply. Strategic thinking can begin with general ideas that mature to specifics only as the thinking is executed. A firm might adopt a strategy of investing in basic R&D with the chance of discovering valuable products but, without an indication of what that product will be (let alone the sales and margins), financial analysis is very limited. To value a start-up biotech firm, study biochemistry. A firm might invest in reorganizing itself to be more dynamic, to foster creative thinking, and to develop its human capital and knowledge assets, but the form the payoffs will take is not clear.

Such strategies are **unarticulated strategies**. The less articulated the strategy, the less amenable it is to financial analysis. Investments in unarticulated strategies are highly speculative, approaching the form of a pure gamble. Financial information is of minimal use to reduce the uncertainty, although some technical information can be useful. It is for this reason that capital tends to flow to start-ups through venture capitalists (who specialize in technical information) rather than public stock markets where stocks are analyzed by financial analysis.

Nevertheless, the investor understands that ultimately a good strategy must "turn a profit." Strategic thinking, in its initial stages, does not submit to financial analysis well. But ultimately it must. Accordingly, the need for financial analysis of strategy enforces a discipline on strategic thinking, even at its most unarticulated level. The strategic thinker is pressed to develop her ideas further, to refine them to a level of specificity where they can be evaluated with financial analysis. By so doing, unarticulated strategies are articulated. The script is written. And, through the lens of financial analysis, the value generated by the idea becomes more transparent, the investment less speculative.

Scenario Analysis

The pro formas prepared for PPE Inc. in Exhibits 15.1 and 15.2 are for one particular scenario. The scenario is a particularly important one for it forecasts expected outcomes from which we wish to derive a valuation. Expected values are averages over a whole range of possible outcomes, however, and the pro forma analysis can be used to model all possible outcomes. What does the pro forma (and the valuation) look like if the sales growth rate is 4 percent rather than 5 percent? What is the effect if the forecasted profit margin drops to 6 percent? The pro forma under each condition is called a scenario, and an analysis that repeats the pro forma analysis under alternative scenarios for the future is called *scenario analysis*. Scenario analysis is the full-forecasting equivalent of the valuation grid applied to simple forecasting in the last chapter.

If you have built the pro forma forecasting framework into a spreadsheet (following the BYOAP road map) you can easily conduct scenario analysis. In doing so, you will understand the full range of possible outcomes and appreciate the upside and downside potential to the investment. Accordingly, scenario analysis is an important tool for assessing fundamental risk—as we will see when we take up the issue of risk and the required return in Chapter 18.

The Web Connection

Find the following on the web page for this chapter:

- More detailed and "real world" applications of pro forma analysis.

- A further introduction to the BYOAP feature.

- A discussion of "real option" approaches to valuation.

- A discussion of the valuation of intangible assets.

- A look at the connection between scenario planning and risk analysis.

Summary

This chapter has shown how to convert knowledge of a business into its valuation. Pro forma financial statement analysis is the tool. Pro forma analysis interprets the business in terms of its effect on value. And it provides a framework for developing forecasts and converting those forecasts to a valuation.

The forecasting template in the chapter develops the forecasting and valuation in a series of steps. Be sure you understand these steps and how the structure of the financial statements is used as a tool for forecasting.

As valuation involves forecasting future financial statements you can see that valuation and accounting are the same thing. Valuation is really a question of accounting for the future. Accounting is often thought of as a method to record the present, but really it is a system to think orderly about the future, a system to guide the development of forecasts of investment payoffs that can be converted to a valuation.

The formal structure of the accounting is of great benefit in valuation. We often have hazy concepts about firms' activities but getting a handle on their value implications is difficult. We can think a firm is "worth a lot," but measuring the worth is another thing. The accounting forces us to interpret imprecise notions in concrete terms such as margins and turnovers in a way that leads to a value inference. "Competitive advantage" translates into higher margins. "Strategic position" translates into higher margins and higher turnover. "Technological advantage" translates into lower expense ratios. Saying that an industry will become more competitive translates into lower profit margin forecasts and an explicit calculation of the loss in value. The "cost of idle capacity" is captured in the asset turnover and measured through the value calculation that forecasts this asset turnover. And we can go on. Accounting relations also play an important role, for these relations tie the pro forma together and make its components reconcile so no aspect of the value generation is lost.

But let's not get carried away. The analysis here relies on getting a good handle on long-term growth. That may be hard to do when our sense of a firm's value comes from the opinion that it is "strategically poised" to benefit from changes in technology or changes in consumer behavior. Measuring these potential benefits in a pro forma analysis might not be easy if the changes are not yet defined. We may feel that a firm has "superior management" that will generate value, but how the management might act to do this might not be clearly articulated. The firm might have R&D that may lead to new products, but what those products will be may be unclear, not to mention the profit margins and turnovers they will deliver. The firm may be positioned to make takeovers, but the firms involved and the timing might be unclear. Pro forma analysis serves to reduce our uncertainty. Pro forma analysis can be used to model our uncertainty (with scenario analysis). But pro forma analysis cannot eliminate our uncertainty.

Key Concepts

business condition is an economic factor that cannot be altered by management. Compare with **strategic choice**. *523*

competitive advantage period is the time that unusually high profitability takes to revert to a normal level. *514*

driver pattern is the behavior of a driver over time. *514*

fade rate is the rate at which a driver reverts to a typical level; also called **persistence rate**. *514*

financial asset buildup is increasing financial assets (from free cash flow net of dividends). *531*

financial statement analysis of the future is the structure of financial statement analysis applied in forecasting. *511*

forces of competition is the tendency of economic factors to force drivers to typical levels. *514*

full-information forecasting is forecasting with complete information about the economic factors affecting the business. Compare with **simple forecasting**. *524*

key driver is a driver that is particularly important to the value generation of a firm. *521*

red-flag indicator is information that indicates deterioration in a firm's profitability. *537*

strategic choice or **strategic plan** is a decision to determine an economic factor. Compare with **business condition**. *523*

unarticulated strategy is a strategy that is not specific enough to evaluate with pro forma analysis. *539*

value type classifies a firm by its **key driver**. *523*

The Analyst's Toolkit

Analysis Tools	Page	Key Measures	Page	Acronymns to Remember
Shortcut residual operating income calculation equation 15.1	513	Fade rates	514	AOIG abnormal operating income growth
Fade diagrams	514	Financial statement indicators	537	ATO asset turnover
Enhanced simple forecasting	519	Red-flag indicators	537	CSE common shareholders' equity
Forecasting template	527	Turnover efficiency ratio	513	CV continuing value
Seven steps to valuation	527			DCF discounted cash flow
Merger and acquisition valuation	534			FLEV financial leverage
Strategic planning analysis	538			LBO leveraged buyout
Scenario analysis	539			NFE net financial expense
				NFO net financial obligations
				NOA net operating value
				NPV net present value
				OI operating income
				PM profit margin
				R&D research and development
				ReOI residual operating income
				RNOA return on net operating assets
				UI unusual items

Concept Questions

C15.1. Why is it important to understand the "business concept" before valuing a firm?

C15.2. Explain why a fade diagram is helpful for forecasting.

C15.3. What factors determine the rate at which high operational profitability declines over time?

C15.4. What is meant by the "integrity" of a pro forma?

C15.5. Forecasted dividends affect forecasted shareholders' equity but do not affect the value calculated from forecasted financial statements. Why?

C15.6. What is a red-flag indicator?

C15.7. What is an unarticulated strategy?

C15.8. Why must the effect of a merger or acquisition on shareholder value be calculated on a per-share basis?

C15.9. When might management of a firm consider a leveraged buyout?

C15.10. Why might the shares of the acquiring firm in an acquisition decline on announcement of the acquisition?

Exercises

E15.1. Analysis of Value Added (Medium)

A firm has the following summary balance sheet (in millions of dollars):

Net operating assets	441
Net financial obligations	52
Common shareholders' equity	389

The firm is currently earning a return on net operating assets (RNOA) of 14 percent from sales of $857 million and after-tax operating income of $60 million. Its required return on operations is 10 percent. Forecasts indicate that RNOA is likely to continue at the same level in the future with growth in sales of 3 percent per year and growth in net operating assets to support the sales of 3 percent per year.

Management is considering a plan to introduce new products that are expected to increase the sales growth rate to 4 percent a year and maintain the current profit margin of 7 percent. But the plan will require additional investment in net operating assets that will reduce the firm's asset turnover to 1.67.

What effect will this plan have on the value of the firm?

E15.2. Forecasting Free Cash Flows and Residual Operating Income, and Valuing a Firm (Easy)

The following forecasts were prepared in 2003 for a firm with a cost of capital for its operations of 12 percent. Amounts are in millions of dollars.

Year	2004E	2005E	2006E	2007E	2008E
Dividends	70	75	75	75	75
Net debt	0	0	0	0	0
Investment expenditures	80	89	94	95	95
Common shareholders' equity	635	665	689	703	712

The common stockholders' equity at the beginning of 2004 is 596 and there is no net debt.

a. Forecast cash flow from operations and free cash flow for each of the five years.

b. Use residual operating income techniques to value this firm.

c. Attempt to value the firm using discounted cash flow analysis. Why do you get a different answer from part (*b*) of the exercise?

E15.3. Evaluating a Marketing Plan (Medium)

A firm with a current return on net operating assets of 15 percent anticipates growth in sales of 6 percent per year from its current net operating asset base of $498 million. It also anticipates that sales will deliver 7.5 percent after-tax profit margins and an RNOA of 15 percent on a consistent basis.

a. Value the operations of this firm for a required return on operations of 11 percent.
b. The marketing team believes that if it can structure extended delayed-payment terms with customers, it can increase the sales growth rate to 6.25 percent per year, with no change in profit margins. The effect of the increased receivables would be to reduce the asset turnover ratio to 1.9. Should the marketing plan be adopted?

E15.4. One-Step Residual Operating Income Calculation: Coca-Cola (Easy)

The Coca-Cola Company reported a profit margin of 22.1 percent on sales of $18.868 billion in 1997. Further analysis of the firm's financial statements revealed that the asset turnover was 2.2. Coke uses a 9 percent hurdle rate for its investment in operations. What was Coke's residual operating income for 1997?

Real World Connection

See Exercise E4.6 and Minicase M4.2 in Chapter 4, Exercise E5.13 in Chapter 5, Minicase M13.2 in Chapter 13, and Exercise E14.6 in Chapter 14 for more material on Coca-Cola.

E15.5. A Valuation from Operating Income Growth Forecasts: Nike, Inc. (Medium)

Box 15.1 in this chapter values Nike's shares based on a projected fading of growth rates. The valuation is done using residual operating income methods.

a. Modify the pro forma in Box 15.1 to forecast abnormal operating income growth, and value the shares from these forecasts.
b. Apply the simple forecast model (equation 14.5) in Chapter 14 that combines short-term and long-term growth rates.

E15.6. Integrity of Pro Formas (Hard)

An analyst developed the following set of pro forma financial statements as an input into a valuation:

(in millions of dollars)	2003A	2004E	2005E	2006E
Sales		454.0	481.2	510.1
Operating expenses		408.6	433.1	459.1
Operating income		45.4	48.1	51.0
Net financial expenses		6.4	10.5	12.9
Comprehensive income		39.0	37.6	38.1
Net operating assets	227.0	240.6	255.1	270.4
Net financial obligations	130.0	130.0	130.0	130.0
Common equity	97.0	110.6	125.1	140.4
Net dividends		25.0	25.0	25.0
Free cash flow		(19.0)	28.0	29.6

a. Spot the errors in the pro forma.
b. The analyst forecasts from these pro formas that residual operating income will grow at a rate of 8 percent per year. Do the pro formas justify this prediction?

E15.7.   Evaluating an Acquisition: PPE Inc. (Hard)

PPE Inc. is considering an acquisition. The acquisition, to be completed within one year, will bring the acquired firm onto PPE's balance sheet using the purchase method. Management has prepared the following pro forma, which anticipates this acquisition at the end of Year 1. This pro forma modifies the one in the text which yielded a valuation for PPE Inc. without the anticipated acquisition.

(in millions of dollars)	Year −1	Year 0	Year 1	Year 2	Year 3	Year 4	Year 5	Year 6
Income Statement								
Sales			124.90	131.15	189.00	200.34	212.36	225.10	238.61
Core operating expenses			115.10	120.86	168.87	179.00	189.74	201.13	213.19
Amortization of goodwill					11.00	11.00	11.00	0.00	0.00
Operating income			9.80	10.29	9.13	10.34	11.62	23.97	25.42
Balance Sheet								
Net operating assets other than goodwill	69.90	74.42	94.50	100.17	106.18	112.55	119.30	126.46
Goodwill			33.00	22.00	11.00	0.00	0.00	0.00
Net operating assets	69.90	74.42	127.50	122.17	117.18	112.55	119.30	126.46
Net financial obligations	7.00	7.70	5.71					
Common equity	62.90	66.72	121.79					

The pro forma balance sheet for the combined firm at the end of Year 1 includes the net operating assets of both firms and the goodwill on the purchase. This goodwill is amortized over the three subsequent years. Forecasted sales and operating expenses for the merged firm are given for years after Year 1. The merged firm is expected to have a required return for its operations of 11 percent.

Management anticipates that it will have to issue 120 shares to acquire the firm from its shareholders. PPE Inc. currently has 100 outstanding shares and, according to the pro forma in the text, is anticipated to pay a dividend of 3.81 cents per share at the end of Year 1.

a. Review the pro forma in Exhibit 15.1 without the acquisition and compare it to the one here. Will the proposed acquisition create value for PPE's shareholders?

b. Prior to FASB Statement No. 142, applicable from 2002 onward, firms amortized goodwill purchased in an acquisition, as in the pro forma here. Statement No. 142 does not require amortization. Rather, goodwill is carried on the balance sheet until it is deemed impaired; then it is written down. Reconstruct the pro forma without any amortization of goodwill.

c. Show that the equity value is the same with the revised pro forma.

Real World Connection
See Exercise E16.4 in Chapter 16.

E15.8.   Comprehensive Analysis and Valuation (Hard)

This exercise comes in two parts. Part I involves an analysis of a set of financial statements and Part II involves forecasting and valuation based on those financial statements.

Part I: Analysis

The following is a comparative balance sheet for a firm for fiscal year 2002 (in millions of dollars):

	2002	2001		2002	2001
Operating cash	$ 60	$ 50	Accounts payable	$1,200	$1,040
Short-term investments					
(at market)	550	500	Accrued liabilities	390	450
Accounts receivable	940	790	Long-term debt	1,840	1,970
Inventory	910	840			
Property and plant	2,840	2,710	Common equity	1,870	1,430
	$5,300	$4,890		$5,300	$4,890

The following is the statement of common shareholders' equity for 2002 (in millions of dollars):

Balance, end of fiscal year 2001	$1,430
Share issues from exercised employee stock options	810
Repurchase of 24 million shares	(720)
Cash dividend	(180)
Tax benefit from exercise of employee stock options	12
Unrealized gain on investments	50
Net income	468
Balance, end of fiscal year 2002	$1,870

The firm's income tax rate is 35 percent. The firm reported $15 million in interest income and $98 million in interest expense for 2002. Sales revenue was $3,726 million.

a. Calculate the loss to shareholders from the exercise of employee stock options during 2002.

b. The shares repurchased were in settlement of a forward purchase agreement. The market price of the shares at the time of the repurchase was $25 each. What was the effect of this transaction on the income for the shareholders?

c. Prepare a comprehensive income statement that distinguishes after-tax operating income from financing income and expense. Include gains or losses from the transactions in parts (a) and (b) above.

d. Prepare a reformulated comparative balance sheet that distinguishes assets and liabilities employed in operations from those employed in financing activities. Calculate the firm's financial leverage and operating liability leverage at the end of 2002.

e. Calculate free cash flow for 2002.

Part II: Forecasting and Valuation

Use a cost of capital for operations of 9 percent. Sales revenue is forecasted to grow at a 6 percent rate per year in the future, on a constant asset turnover of 1.25. Operating profit margins of 14 percent are expected to be earned each year.

a. Forecast return on net operating assets (RNOA) for 2003.

b. Forecast residual operating income for 2003.

c. Value the shareholders' equity at the end of the 2002 fiscal year using residual income methods.

d. Forecast abnormal growth in operating income for 2004.

e. Value the shareholders' equity at the end of 2002 using abnormal earnings growth methods.

f. After reading the stock compensation footnote for this firm, you note that there are employee stock options on 28 million shares outstanding at the end of 2002. These options vest in 2004 and after. A modified Black-Scholes valuation of these options is $15 each. How does this information change your valuation?

g. Forecast (net) comprehensive income for 2003.

Minicases

M15.1

Sensitivity Analysis, Valuation, and Strategy: Dell Computer

Dell Computer, the personal computer manufacturer, was investigated in some depth in Minicase M12.1 in Chapter 12. Its 2,543 million shares traded at $38 each in March 1999—at 66 times earnings. Most analysts gave Dell a buy recommendation or a strong buy.

1. From the information given in the earlier case, value Dell on the assumption that its residual operating income in 1999 will continue indefinitely (an SF2 valuation). Use a required return for operations of 16 percent.

2. What is the implied growth in residual operating income in the market price of $38 per share?

3. What questions would you ask in evaluating whether the price of $38 per share for Dell is a reasonable one? Consider, among other things, the fade diagrams in this chapter.

Real World Connection
See Exercise E1.1. in Chapter 1, Exercise E4.1 in Chapter 4, Exercise E5.10 in Chapter 5, Minicase M6.2 in Chapter 6, Exercises E8.3 and E8.8 in Chapter 8, Minicase M10.1 in Chapter 10, Minicase M12.1 in Chapter 12, and Exercise E13.5 in Chapter 13 for related material on Dell Computer Corp.

M15.2

Tracking Nike and Reebok

Nike, Inc., and Reebok International Ltd. have been referred to repeatedly in the text. Most examples covered the years 1994 to 1996, with valuations based on forecasts of years after 1996.

Exhibits 15.3 and 15.4 summarize both firms' financial statements, Nike from 1994 through fiscal 1999 (ending in May 1999) and Reebok from 1994 through fiscal 1998 (ending December 1998). The numbers in the exhibits give these firms' actual experience after 1996, which can be contrasted to the forecasts made in the book.

Nike traded at $52 per share just after its 1999 fiscal year end on 282.3 million outstanding shares. With an adjustment for an intervening 2-for-1 stock split, this price is the same as the per-share value of $104 in 1996.

Reebok traded at $15 per share in early 1999 on 56.6 million outstanding shares, down from $43 per share in early 1997.

A. Examine the financial history of the two firms in the exhibits. Track the changes in relevant drivers of residual operating income for each firm. How does the behavior of these drivers compare with the typical behavior in the fade diagrams in the text? Do the financial statements justify the changes in stock prices from 1996 to 1999?

EXHIBIT 15.3

NIKE, INC.
Financial Statement
(in millions of dollars)

	1999	1998	1997	1996	1995	1994
Sales	8,777	9,553	9,187	6,471	4,761	3,790
Cost of sales	5,494	6,066	5,503	3,907	2,865	2,301
Gross margin	3,283	3,487	3,684	2,564	1,896	1,489
Advertising expenses	979	1,130	978	643	495	373
General expenses	1,448	1,494	1,326	999	743	622
Core operating income, before tax	856	863	1,380	922	658	494
Tax on core operating income	338	335	532	355	253	193
Core operating income, after tax	518	528	848	567	405	301
Net operating assets	3,553	3,543	3,034	2,659	2,208	1,381
Net financial obligations	218	281	(122)	228	244	(360)
Common shareholders' equity	3,335	3,262	3,156	2,431	1,964	1,741

EXHIBIT 15.4

REEBOK INTERNATIONAL LTD.
Financial Statement
(in millions of dollars)

	1998	1997	1996	1995	1994
Sales	3,225	3,644	3,479	3,481	3,280
Cost of sales	2,037	2,294	2,144	2,114	1,966
Gross margin	1,188	1,350	1,335	1,367	1,314
Advertising expenses	144	165	202	158	163
General expenses	899	904	868	846	730
Core operating income, before tax	145	281	265	363	421
Tax on core operating income	50	56	93	131	155
Core operating income, after tax	95	225	172	232	266
Net operating assets	1,102	1,160	1,135	1,220	1,144
Net financial obligations	546	621	720	248	124
Minority interest	32	32	34	31	21
Common shareholders' equity	524	507	381	941	999

B. What forecasts would you make for Nike for 2000 and beyond based on the trends you see in your analysis? What forecasts would you make for Reebok for 1999 and beyond?

C. Value both firms based on your forecasts. (Value Reebok's minority interest at book value.) How do your valuations compare with the $52 per share price for Nike and the $15 price for Reebok? What might be missing from your analysis that could explain the discrepancies between your valuations and the market price? (Use a cost of capital for operations of 11 percent in your valuations for both firms.)

D. As time rolls on into 2000 and 2001, what features would you watch for in the firms' quarterly and annual reports that would be particularly important to you in revising your valuations?

Real World Connection

See material on Nike and Reebok in Chapters 8–15. Also see Exercise E1.5 in Chapter 1, Minicase M2.1 in Chapter 2, Exercise E6.3 in Chapter 6, Minicase 7.1 in Chapter 7, Exercise E8.10 in Chapter 8, Exercise E9.5 in Chapter 9, Exercise E11.6 in Chapter 11, Exercise E13.7 in Chapter 13, Exercises E14.3 and E14.9 in Chapter 14, and Exercise E15.5 in this chapter. Refer also to the BYOAP features on the website.

M15.3

Exploring Strategic Options: Borders Group

On March 6, 2000, *The Wall Street Journal* reported that Borders Group, the book and music retailer, was seeking advice from Merrill Lynch on options to enhance shareholder value. Under the headline "Borders Will Explore Strategic Options, Citing Frustration with Its Stock Price," the report indicated that Borders's management believed that the stock was significantly undervalued.

Borders went public in the summer of 1995 and its stock price rose to $40 per share by July 1998. But subsequently the price of its shares slowly eroded, to $11 by March 2000. At this price its P/E ratio was 8, its price-to-book ratio was 1.2, and its price-to-sales ratio was 0.3. There were 77.2 million shares outstanding in March 2000.

Borders came to the market in its 1995 IPO with a "superstore" concept that appealed to the market. These stores offer an extensive selection of books, videotapes, and recorded music, often emphasizing hard-to-find titles and recordings. The stores aim at providing a welcoming atmosphere, often featuring an espresso bar so customers can browse over coffee. Its Waldenbooks stores are smaller stores, often situated in shopping malls; they offer a more standard selection of best sellers, cooking, travel, and general-interest books.

Having established its superstores, Borders ran into significant competition from emerging Internet booksellers, particularly Amazon.com. It was slow to adapt to e-commerce retailing but eventually launched its own e-commerce site in May 1998 through Borders Online.

A. Borders's financial statements since its IPO are summarized in Exhibit 15.5. They are in reformulated form. Track how the financial statements have evolved. Do you see reasons for the declining stock price?

B. Based on the information in the financial statements—and any other considerations you might bring to the question—do you think Borders was undervalued in March 2000?

C. Discuss each of the following options which were being considered to increase the share price:
 (1) A merger.
 (2) A leveraged buyout.
 (3) Creating separate shares for the Internet business, following the lead of Wal-Mart, which had just floated Wal-Mart.com in a well-received offering.

EXHIBIT 15.5

BORDERS GROUP, INC.
Reformulated Income Statements, 1997–2000
(in millions of dollars, except per-share data)

	Fiscal Year Ending January						
	2000		**1999**		**1998**		**1997**
Sales	2,981.3		2,595.0		2,266.0		1,958.8
Cost of merchandise sold (includes occupancy)			1,859.4		1,634.3		1,437.8
Gross margin			735.6		631.7		521.0
Selling, general, and administrative expenses			557.6		484.9		409.6
Preopening expense			7.8		7.2		7.2
Goodwill amortization			2.9		1.6		1.1
Core operating income before tax	181.2		167.3		138.0		103.1
Tax, as reported		59.0		50.6		38.2	
Tax benefit of interest		6.0	65.0	2.7	53.3	2.6	40.8
Core operating income after tax	111.2		102.3		84.7		62.3
Foreign currency translations			0.0		(0.9)		0.0
Operating income			102.3		83.8		62.3
Net financial expense, after tax			10.2		4.5		4.4
Comprehensive income			92.1		79.3		57.9
Basic earnings per common share	1.38		1.20		1.06		0.77

Summary Reformulated Balance Sheets, 1996–1999
(in millions of dollars)

	Fiscal Year Ending January			
	1999	**1998**	**1997**	**1996**
Merchandise inventories	1,019.6	879.1	737.5	637.5
Accounts receivable, net	62.9	60.8	44.1	34.0
Property, plant, and equipment, net	493.8	373.7	289.2	243.5
Goodwill, net	106.0	109.5	38.5	39.6
Other assets	54.3	81.8	81.7	77.7
	1,736.6	1,504.9	1,191.0	1,032.3
Operating liabilities	854.7	754.1	604.0	482.4
Net operating assets	881.9	750.8	587.0	549.9
Net financial obligations	166.8	152.7	75.6	77.9
Common shareholders' equity	715.1	598.1	511.4	472.0

Financial reports for fiscal year 2000 had not been published by March 6, 2000. The limited income statement data is from the press release that gave preliminary numbers for 2000. Common equity at the end of fiscal year 2000 is estimated to be $704 million, based on the equity number in the third-quarter statement.

M15.4

Evaluating a P/E Ratio: Procter & Gamble

Procter & Gamble is a consumer products company that historically has been seen as a growth company able to generate value through product and packaging innovations and marketing.

Procter & Gamble produces and markets products in five categories: paper products, beauty care, food and beverages, laundry and cleaning products, and health care. Laundry and cleaning products accounted for 21 percent of its $38 billion in sales in 1999 and diaper sales were 14 percent of total sales. The firm's brand names include Pampers, Luvs, Tampax, Always, Bounty, and Charmin (in paper products); Dawn, Joy, Bounce, Downy, Comet, Tide, Ivory, Mr. Clean, Febreze, and Cascade (in laundry and cleaning products); Crisco, Folgers, Pringles, Sunny Delight, and Whirl (in food and beverages); Oil of Olay, Head and Shoulders, Secret, Old Spice, Vidal Sassoon, Clearasil, and Hugo Boss (in beauty care); and Vicks, Metamucil, Pepto-Bismol, Scope, and Crest (in health care products). These brands are protected by 25,000 patents.

The consumer products business is a highly competitive one. Procter & Gamble attempts to meet this competition with an extensive research and development program to develop new products and packaging ideas. Products, once launched, are supported with extensive advertising and a sales force that services the grocery stores and retail outlets through which products are primarily sold.

Procter & Gamble's product strategy has earned the support of financial markets. The following table is a record of the firm's (split-adjusted) share price from 1995 to 1999, along with its earnings per share and dividends per share during that period. Prices are at September 30 of each year. Earnings and dividends are for fiscal years ending June 30.

	1999	1998	1997	1996	1995
Share price	$98	$71	$65	$48	$35
Basic earnings per share	$2.75	$2.74	$2.43	$2.14	$1.85
Dividends per share	1.14	1.01	0.90	0.80	0.70

You see from this history that price-earnings (P/E) multiples have been increasing over the years, to over 35 in 1999. Yet earnings-per-share growth has been modest, particularly from 1997 to 1999. Concerns developed during 1999 about the ability of the firm to maintain its growth of earlier years. Competition was producing pricing pressure and the firm had lost some 10 percent of global market share over the prior five years. Sales were anticipated to grow at only 2 percent in 2000, at best. The firm was riding on old brands. The firm's R&D spending of over $1.7 billion ranked twenty-first of all U.S. corporations, but its last big innovation was the Always brand sanitary napkin in 1983. Despite these indicators, the trailing P/E reached 40 by the end of (calendar) 1999 and the price-to-sales ratio was 3.6. Clearly the market anticipated substantial earnings and sales growth.

Durk Jager, who took over as CEO in January 1999, recognized the problems. A reorganization—Organization 2005—was instituted to cut through a corporate culture that was slow to innovate and slow to move innovations to market. Operations were to be organized by brands rather than countries, innovation teams were to be established, new products were to be given to new managers rather than those managing old brands, and laboratory testing and new product marketing were to be streamlined.

Exhibit 15.6 is a summary of the financial statements from 1995 to 1999. A summary of analysts' consensus forecasts in late 1999 is also given. The firm's website is at www.pg.com.

EXHIBIT 15.6

Income Statement Summaries, 1995–1999
(in millions of dollars)

	1999	1998	1997	1996	1995
Net sales	$38,125	$37,154	$35,764	$35,284	$33,482
Cost of products sold	21,206	21,064	20,510	20,762	19,561
Marketing costs	3,538	3,704	3,466	3,254	3,284
Research and development	1,726	1,546	1,469	1,399	1,304
Other operating costs	5,402	4,785	4,831	5,054	5,089
Operating income before tax	6,253	6,055	5,488	4,815	4,244
Tax on operating income	2,233	2,056	1,922	1,677	1,445
Operating income after tax	4,020	3,999	3,566	3,138	2,799
Net income	$ 3,763	$ 3,780	$ 3,415	$ 3,046	$ 2,645
Basic earnings per share	$2.75	$2.74	$2.43	$2.14	$1.85
Diluted earnings per share	$2.59	$2.56	$2.28	$2.01	$1.74

Note: Opening income for 1999 includes an after-tax charge of $385 million, or $0.29 per share, for reorganizing the business. Other operating costs include goodwill amortizations; goodwill is amortized over 40 years.

Balance Sheet Summaries, 1994–1999
(in millions of dollars)

	1999	1998	1997	1996	1995	1994
Current operating assets	$ 8,558	$ 8,171	$ 7,676	$ 8,287	$ 8,664	$ 7,332
Property, plant, and equipment	12,626	12,180	11,376	11,118	11,026	10,024
Intangible assets	6,822	7,011	3,949	4,281	4,572	3,754
Other assets	1,307	1,198	1,433	1,524	1,685	1,769
	29,313	28,560	24,434	25,210	25,947	22,879
Operating liabilities	10,674	10,684	10,506	10,222	11,405	10,348
Net operating assets	18,639	17,876	13,928	14,988	14,542	12,531
Financial assets	(2,800)	(2,406)	(3,110)	(2,520)	(2,178)	(2,656)
Interest-bearing debt	9,381	8,046	4,992	5,786	6,131	6,355
Preferred equity	1,781	1,821	1,859	1,886	1,913	1,942
Common equity	$10,277	$10,415	$10,187	$ 9,836	$ 8,676	$ 6,890

Analysts' Forecasts for 2000, 2001, and Beyond

	2000	2001	After 2001
Earnings per share	3.22	3.66	Annual growth of 13%

Using this information, discuss Procter & Gamble's prospects for growth and evaluate the P/E ratio at the end of 1999. To guide the discussion, proceed through the following questions. Where necessary, use a required return for Procter & Gamble's operations of 9 percent and a required return for its equity of 11 percent.

A. Calculate the P/E ratio for each year from the price, earnings, and dividend history above.

B. Consider the analysts' forecasts of earnings per share. Attempt to calculate an intrinsic P/E from these forecasts by using the following formula:

$$\text{Intrinsic P/E} = \frac{g}{\rho_E - g}$$

where g is 1 plus the forecasted growth rate in earnings per share from its 1999 level of $2.75. This model calculates the value per dollar of current earnings from the forecasted growth rate for earnings per share. Is this a good model of the P/E ratio? What are the problems with it?

C. What is a "normal" P/E ratio for Procter & Gamble? What growth in earnings per share does it imply?

D. Consider alternative models of the P/E ratio to the one in part (C). Referring to your model, what do the financial statements from 1995 to 1999 indicate regarding the appropriate P/E for the firm? Do they suggest that a P/E of 40 is appropriate?

E. What other information might you seek to evaluate the P/E ratio? What features would you be most concerned with watching during 2000 to assess whether Procter & Gamble can deliver on a P/E of 40?

M15.5

Profitability and Growth Through Acquisitions, and Goodwill Amortization: Quaker Oats

Quaker Oats Company is a leading manufacturer and marketer of packaged foods. It sells cereals, pancake mixes, cornmeal, rice products, syrup, pasta products, frozen fruit juices, and other beverages. Among its brand products are Gatorade, Cap'n Crunch, Quaker Oatmeal, Rice-A-Roni, Golden Grain, Aunt Jemima, and Ardmore Farms.

The competition in the packaged food business is fierce. Companies have had difficulty gaining market share and growing sales. If you look at Quaker Oats's income statements in Exhibit 15.7 you will see that its sales declined over the 1990s. Firms in this industry attempt to increase sales by developing new brands internally, by targeting growing ethnic groups, and by expanding into markets overseas. But sales growth is constrained by the demographics. Firms thus resort to acquisitions of other companies with recognized brands. These acquisitions grow sales and earnings and give the manufacturers bargaining power in gaining access to supermarket shelves. Unilever, for example, acquired Ben & Jerry's in 2000 and also made an offer for Bestfoods.

EXHIBIT 15.7

QUAKER OATS CO.
Consolidated Statements of Income
(dollars in millions, except per-share data)

	1999	1998	1997	1996	1995	1994	1993
Net sales	4,725.2	4,842.5	5,015.7	5,199.0	5,954.0	6,211.1	5,730.6
Cost of goods sold	2,136.8	2,374.4	2,564.9	2,807.5	3,294.4	3,122.7	2,870.0
Gross profit	2,588.4	2,468.1	2,450.8	2,391.5	2,659.6	3,088.4	2,860.6
Selling, general, and administrative expenses	1,904.1	1,872.5	1,938.9	1,981.0	2,358.8	2,553.9	2,302.3
(Gains) losses on divestitures, restructuring charges, and asset impairments—net	(2.3)	128.5	1,486.3	(113.4)	(1,053.5)	108.6	20.5
Interest expense	61.9	69.6	85.8	106.8	131.6	101.5	65.6
Interest income	(11.7)	(10.7)	(6.7)	(7.4)	(6.2)	(4.0)	(10.5)
Foreign exchange loss—net	18.1	11.6	10.8	8.9	8.4	8.0	15.1
Income (loss) before income taxes	618.3	396.6	(1,064.3)	415.6	1,220.5	320.4	467.6
Provision (benefit) for income taxes	163.3	112.1	(133.4)	167.7	496.5	127.3	180.8
Net income (loss)	455.0	284.5	(930.9)	247.9	724.0	193.1	286.8
Preferred dividends—net of tax	4.4	4.5	3.5	3.7	4.0	4.0	4.2
Net income (loss) available for common	450.6	280.0	(934.4)	244.2	720.0	189.1	282.6
Per common share							
Net income (loss)	$3.36	$2.04	($6.80)	$1.80	$5.39	$1.41	$1.96
Analysis of divestiture gains and losses, restructuring charges, and asset impairments (from footnotes)							
(Gains) and losses from divestitures	(5.10)	0.70	1,420.4	(136.4)	(1,170.8)	(9.8)	(27.8)
Restructuring charges	12.7	89.7	65.9	23.0	117.3	118.4	48.3
Reversal of restructuring charges	(9.9)						
Asset impairment charges		38.1					
	(2.3)	128.5	1,486.3	113.4	1,053.5	108.6	20.5

Condensed Consolidated Balance Sheets

	1999	1998	1997	1996	1995	1994	1993	1992
Current assets, net of cash equivalents	746.7	815.0	1,073.0	789.7	1,000.1	1,133.6	1,027.6	1,176.2
Property, plant, and equipment, net	1,106.7	1,070.2	1,164.7	1,200.7	1,167.8	1,214.2	1,228.2	1,273.3
Intangible assets, net of amortization	236.9	245.7	350.5	2,237.2	2,309.2	493.4	431.3	427.4
Other assets	94.4	127.8	106.0	131.7	135.0	162.5	88.8	83.0
	2,184.7	2,258.7	2,694.2	4,359.3	4,612.1	3,003.7	2,775.9	2,959.9
Operating liabilities	1,306.9	1,406.0	1,431.5	1,583.9	1,759.6	1,566.4	1,443.9	1,382.3
Financial obligations	680.5	701.7	1,034.7	1,545.5	1,773.2	991.5	780.9	735.5
Shareholders' equity	197.3	151.0	228.0	1,229.9	1,079.3	445.8	551.1	842.1
	2,184.7	2,258.7	2,694.2	4,359.3	4,612.1	3,003.7	2,775.9	2,959.9

Quaker Oats has made a number of acquisitions and dispositions of businesses. Its income statements report gains and losses on dispositions of businesses every year, and its balance sheets contain considerable intangible assets that are largely goodwill from business acquisitions. Indeed, you see from these statements that gains and losses from selling businesses, along with restructuring charges on businesses, are a significant portion of earnings. Extensive footnotes in 10-K reports detail the transactions. Goodwill from acquisitions of businesses are a significant part of total assets.

In 1995, Quaker acquired Snapple, the drinks company, for $1.7 billion and at the same time sold off its pet food and candy businesses to generate cash for the purchase. You can see a large gain from the sales in the 1995 income statement and you can also see a large increase in goodwill (intangibles) in the 1995 balance sheet. The Snapple purchase was a disaster for Quaker Oats, and the firm sold Snapple for $300 million in 1997, taking a $1.4 billion loss that is recorded in the income statement for that year.

The following questions will help you focus on the creation of value from acquisitions by Quaker Oats.

A. What is the fallacy of "growing through acquisition"? Do acquisitions necessarily gain value? Does Quaker Oats's Snapple purchase make a point?

B. Calculate core return on net operating assets (core RNOA) for each year, 1993 to 1999. Does core RNOA capture all aspects of Quaker Oats's business that generate value?

C. Why does core RNOA decline significantly after the Snapple acquisition in 1995? Is there an accounting explanation? Why does the core RNOA increase after the sale of Snapple in 1997? Are there accounting explanations? In considering your answer, focus particularly on the goodwill in the balance sheet.

D. Quaker Oats amortizes goodwill over a period from 10 to 40 years. Almost all the purchase price of $1.7 billion for Snapple in 1995 went into goodwill. Do you think, in retrospect, that a 10–40 year amortization period was appropriate for the Snapple goodwill?

E. Discuss how goodwill accounting helps or hinders in valuation. What rules would you devise for amortizing goodwill? How would FASB statement No. 142—applicable from 2002 onward—change the accounting here?

F. Between 1996 and 1999, Quaker Oats's share price rose from $30 to almost $70. In May 2000 it traded at a P/E multiple of 24. Do you see anything in the numbers that justifies this price rise and this P/E ratio?

Part Four

Accounting Analysis and Valuation

Knowing the business *1*
- The products
- The knowledge base
- The competition
- The regulatory constraints

Strategy

Analyzing information *2*
- In financial statements
- Outside of financial statements

Forecasting payoffs *3*
- Specifying payoffs
- Forecasting payoffs

Converting forecasts to a valuation *4*

Trading on the valuation *5*

Outside investor:
Compare value with price to *buy*, *sell*, or *hold*

Inside investor:
Compare value with cost to *accept* or *reject* strategy

Chapter 16

How do accounting policies, applied on a consistent basis, affect measures of profitability and residual earnings? How does accounting policy affect valuations?

Chapter 17

How can firms use accounting methods to temporarily change their reported profitability? How can such manipulations be detected?

A valuation is as good as the forecasts on which it is based. The valuation analysis in this book is based on forecasting earnings and book values in future financial statements. But earnings and book values are determined in part by accounting methods. So an obvious question arises: If valuation is done on the basis of accounting numbers, won't the valuation be affected by how the accounting is done? Will the valuation depend on whether a firm uses accelerated depreciation methods versus straight-line methods or LIFO versus FIFO accounting for inventories? How does the analyst accommodate the expensing of research and development investments in income statements when these investments are assets that will produce future profits? Does she correct the accounting? This part of the book supplies answers to these questions, lays out the accounting issues that arise in valuation analysis, and shows how the accounting is accommodated.

Step 3 of the process of fundamental analysis, indicated here, has two aspects. First the analyst must specify what is to be forecasted and how it is measured in such a way as to capture a firm's value. Then, with this specification, he goes about the task of forecasting using the information he has analyzed in Step 2. Accordingly, accounting issues arise in valuation analysis in two ways. First is the issue of the accounting used to measure earnings forecasted for the future: Will forecasted residual earnings and abnormal earnings growth capture value added so that the analyst arrives at a sound valuation? If he forecasts earnings using GAAP, does he capture value? Should he adjust the GAAP accounting? Should he forecast cash flows instead? Second is the issue of the accounting in current financial statements that the analyst uses (in Step 2) to forecast future residual earnings. His financial statement analysis has uncovered core profitability as a basis for forecasting future profitability, but the measure of core profitability is based on accounting methods. Is that accounting transparent? Is it misleading? Does it help or hinder forecasting? The first issue is one of the quality of forecasted accounting. The second issue is one of the quality of the current accounting. Chapter 16 deals with the first issue; Chapter 17 examines the second.

In working through this part of the book you will be helped by a good knowledge of accounting. But detailed knowledge of accounting rules is not as important as appreciating how accounting works, particularly for valuation purposes. So the emphasis here will be on explaining the structure of accounting and how it aids—or hinders—valuation analysis. If you are hazy on the details of specific accounting methods, go to one of the many intermediate or advanced financial accounting texts that are available. The Accounting Clinics on the book's website will also help you.

Chapter **Sixteen**

Creating Accounting Value and Economic Value

LINKS

Link to previous chapters

Part Three of the book developed the analysis to calculate intrinsic price-to-book (P/B) ratios and price-earnings (P/E) ratios.

This chapter

This chapter shows how accounting policies, applied on a permanent basis, affect forecasts of profitability and growth and the P/B and P/E ratios calculated from these forecasts.

Link to next chapter

Chapter 17 reviews issues that arise when firms use accounting methods to shift income between the present and the future.

Link to web page

For more examples of how accounting methods are accommodated in valuation, visit the text website at www.mhhe.com/penman2e.

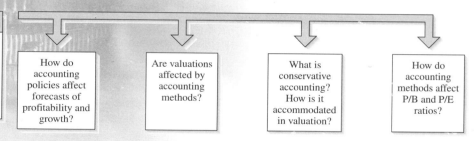

How do accounting policies affect forecasts of profitability and growth?

Are valuations affected by accounting methods?

What is conservative accounting? How is it accommodated in valuation?

How do accounting methods affect P/B and P/E ratios?

In this chapter we resolve a seeming paradox: Value is calculated by forecasting future earnings and earnings are measured using accounting methods, yet a firm's value cannot be affected by the accounting methods it uses.

Generally accepted accounting principles (GAAP) constrain the way that firms can account for their business. However, within GAAP firms have some latitude in choosing accounting methods, and these choices can affect the book values and earnings they report. Further, these choices can affect the future earnings and book values that must be forecasted for valuation purposes. In this chapter we ask how the choice of accounting method—as a matter of permanent accounting policy—affects the forecasts and the valuations made from them. If a firm uses LIFO rather than FIFO for inventory measurement, how will forecasts of residual earnings or abnormal earnings growth differ? Will valuation derived from these forecasts differ? How will price-to-book (P/B) ratios and price-earnings (P/E) ratios be affected? If a firm uses an accelerated depreciation method, capitalizes leases, or expenses costs of intangible assets, what will be the effect on residual earnings, earnings growth, valuations, and P/B and P/E ratios? Discounted cash flow valuations remove the effect of accounting methods (and focus rather on cash flows) under

The Analyst's Checklist

After reading this chapter you should understand:

- How accounting rates of return and residual earnings can be created by accounting methods.

- How growth in earnings, growth in residual earnings and abnormal earnings growth can be created by accounting methods.

- The difference between economic value added and accounting value added.

- How valuation techniques can produce valuations that are not affected by accounting methods.

- How accounting methods affect continuing value calculations.

- How price-to-book ratios are affected by accounting methods.

- How P/E ratios are affected by accounting methods.

- What "conservative accounting" means and what it implies for analysis of profitability, growth, and valuation.

- How firms create hidden reserves and how they can increase earnings by liquidating hidden reserves.

After reading this chapter you should be able to:

- Value firms in a way that incorporates their accounting methods.

- Forecast profitability and growth for firms with different accounting methods.

- Calculate intrinsic price-to-book ratios that reflect firms' accounting methods.

- Calculate intrinsic P/E ratios that reflect firms' accounting methods.

- Calculate continuing values that reflect firms' accounting methods.

- Identify when a firm is using conservative accounting.

the suspicion that valuations can be distorted by accounting methods. Do accounting methods indeed distort valuations? Does an analyst have to adjust firms' earnings for accounting methods before proceeding to a valuation?

We will see in this chapter how a firm can use accounting methods that will give it a high rate of return and thus high residual earnings: The firm can make itself look more profitable than it really is. We will also see that a firm's accounting methods can produce high earnings growth. But we will also see that residual earnings and earnings growth created by accounting methods do not affect the valuation of a firm. Residual earnings and earnings growth can be created by real factors and by accounting methods, but it is only the real factors that add economic value. Appropriate use of valuation methods distinguishes real value added from the accounting methods used to measure value added, and so yields valuations that reflect real factors only.

VALUE CREATION AND THE CREATION OF RESIDUAL EARNINGS

Consider a project that involves an investment of $400 at the end of the year 2000 and has a required return of 10 percent per year. The project has a two-year life and is expected to generate sales of $240 in 2001 and $220 in 2002. Depreciation is the only expense. Table 16.1 uses two different accounting treatments for this project. In Accounting Treatment 1 the initial cost is depreciated straight-line at $200 per year, so project income

TABLE 16.1
Accounting Treatments for a Project with a Required Return of 10% per Year and a Two-Year Life
Investment in the Project is $400.

	2000	2001	2002
Accounting Treatment 1			
Sales		240	220
Depreciation		200	200
Operating income		40	20
Net operating assets	400	200	0
Free cash flow		240	220
RNOA		10%	10%
ReOI (0.10)		0	0
PV of ReOI		0	0
Total PV of ReOI	0		
Value of project	400		
Accounting Treatment 2			
Sales		240	220
Start-up costs and depreciation	(40)	180	180
Operating income	(40)	60	40
Net operating assets	360	180	0
Free cash flow		240	220
RNOA		16.7%	22.2%
ReOI (0.10)		24	22
Present value of ReOI		21.82	18.18
Total PV of ReOI	40		
Value of project	400		

after depreciation is $40 and $20 for the two years. The book value of the project after depreciation (the net operating assets [NOA] for the project) declines to $200 at the end of 2001, yielding an expected return on net operating assets (RNOA) of 10 percent for each year, equal to the required return. Accordingly, residual operating income (ReOI) is forecasted to be zero for both years. This project does not add value over its investment cost so its value is its book value in 2000, that is, $400. By discounting the free cash flow numbers (given by operating income minus the change in net operating assets) at the 10 percent rate, you will also see that the project is a zero-NPV project.

The accountant who keeps the books with Accounting Treatment 2 is a conservative accountant. This does not refer to the accountant's clothes, hair style, or political beliefs. The conservative accountant likes to understate assets and overstate liabilities in the balance sheet. So he writes down the project to a book value of $360 in 2000. The reduced book value in 2000 results in reduced charges of $180 in straight-line depreciation in 2001 and 2002. He may classify the $40 write-down as a start-up cost (as in the table) or the part of the $400 investment that involves promotion to launch the project; GAAP requires both these costs to be expensed. The panel gives the ReOI forecasts with this accounting and the valuation from these forecasts.

There are two things to notice from comparing the two accounting treatments, summarized "accounting effects" and "valuation effects" in Box 16.1. The accounting effects demonstrate the intertemporal feature of accounting. Reducing book values lowers future expenses (in this case depreciation) and thus increases future earnings. Future RNOA is also higher because the higher operating income is divided by a lower book value for net operating assets. And future residual operating income is higher because higher income is compared to lower book values (charged with the cost of capital), to yield higher residual income.

ACCOUNTING EFFECTS

Residual earnings and RNOA can be created by the accounting. Treatment 1 yields forecasted RNOA of 10 percent for both 2001 and 2002 while Treatment 2 yields forecasted RNOA of 16.7 percent and 22.2 percent. Treatment 1 forecasts zero residual operating income for both years while Treatment 2 forecasts $24 and $22.

VALUATION EFFECTS

Residual earnings created by accounting methods does not affect the valuation: The value of the project is the same $400 under the two treatments and both treatments indicate no value added from the investment. Residual income valuation techniques accommodate different accounting methods so that any residual income that is created by the accounting has no effect on the value added that is measured.

In practice acquired assets are written off when R&D investments are expensed, when promotion and advertising that create brand-name assets are expensed, and when purchased goodwill is written off. Firms can also maintain low asset values for assets on the balance sheet by using accelerated depreciation for property, plant, and equipment, accelerated amortization of goodwill and other intangibles, and maintaining high bad debt estimates for receivables, for example. These practices create higher subsequent rates of return. Thus firms with large successful R&D programs typically generate high RNOA and ROCE in subsequent years when the R&D pays off, as earnings from the R&D are compared to low book values. Drug companies, which have large R&D programs, often report RNOA over 30 percent. Coca-Cola has brand-name assets that are not on the balance sheet and so has an RNOA in the order of 35 percent. Firms in the United Kingdom put brand-name assets in the balance sheet, so Cadbury-Schweppes typically has an RNOA of 25 percent, considerably less than Coke's. These rates of return may reflect real value added but certainly they are partly created by the accounting.

The practice of understating book values is called **conservative accounting.** But just as future RNOA and ROCE can be increased by writing down net assets, so can they be decreased by writing assets up. Writing up assets (or failing to write them down when they are impaired) is referred to as **liberal accounting.** Firms in the United Kingdom and Australia periodically revalue tangible assets upward, yielding lower RNOA and ROCE than comparable U.S. firms (which are not permitted to do so). Cadbury-Schweppes's lower RNOA (relative to Coca-Cola's) is due partly to asset revaluations.

Liberal accounting is a name sometimes given to less conservative accounting: A firm that capitalizes some software development costs but expenses other R&D (PeopleSoft, for example) is said to use more liberal accounting than a firm that expenses all R&D (Microsoft, for example). But both use conservative accounting overall. A benchmark that draws the line between conservative and liberal accounting is **neutral accounting.** This is accounting that yields an expected return on equity (equal to the cost of capital) and thus zero residual income for investments that do not add value. Accounting Treatment 1 is an example of neutral accounting. Conservative and liberal accounting, in contrast, yield profitability that is different from the required return when there in fact is no value added. Conservative accounting produces higher future profitability than the required return; liberal accounting lowers future profitability.

So you see that **economic value added** and **accounting value added** differ. High RNOA and residual earnings are not necessarily indicative of value added. So beware of those who point to accounting measures as indicators of economic value added. Examine products that consultants sell as measures of economic value added. All measures are accounting measures of some form and the form of the accounting must be considered in accepting the measures as economic value added.

The valuation effect of different accounting methods (described in Box 16.1) is referred to as the **value conservation principle:** Valuations using residual income techniques are not affected by the accounting for current book value. Value is calculated as current book value plus the present value of future residual income forecasted. An accounting method that changes current book value changes future residual income, but it does not change the value calculated because the change in the residual income is exactly offset, in present value terms, by the change in current book value. So expensing R&D creates higher future residual earnings but lower current book value, and the valuation is not affected. Value is affected only by residual income generated by real economic profitability, not accounting-induced profitability.

ACCOUNTING METHODS, PRICE-TO-BOOK RATIOS, PRICE-EARNINGS RATIOS, AND THE VALUATION OF GOING CONCERNS

The example in the last section involves a single project. Similar observations can be made about a going-concern firm which keeps its book values low (or high) continually. Here again the value does not depend on the accounting. But P/B and P/E ratios will. The effects depend on the amount of investment growth, so first we look at the case of no growth in investment and then at the case where a firm grows its investment.

Accounting Methods with a Constant Level of Investment

Going concerns have repetitive investment. Table 16.2, the first in a series of five tables illustrating accounting methods, gives the valuation for a firm that invests $400 in the same zero-value-added project in 2000 (as before) but is also forecasted to invest $400 in each subsequent year, again with zero value added. The table gives forecasted operating income and net operating assets for the firm, and it calculates forecasted RNOA, residual operating income (ReOI), and abnormal operating income growth (AOIG) from these forecasts, along with profit margin, asset turnover, and growth drivers. As before, the project generates $240 in sales in its first year and $220 in its second, and again its cost is depreciated straight-line over two years. The totals for operating income after 2001 are the sum of incomes from the projects put in place over the prior two years, and net operating assets is the sum of the investments just made ($400) and the (partially depreciated) book value of the continuing investment in place.

You see that operating income is $60 once the firm reaches its permanent level of net operating assets of $600. Accordingly, the RNOA is forecasted to be 10 percent in all years, equal to the cost of capital; the ReOI is forecasted to be zero; and the value of the firm is $400, its book value in 2000. The AOIG is also forecasted to be zero after the forward year (2001), so the value of $400 is also equal to capitalized forward operating income. This is neutral accounting: The firm does not add value to its investments (like the project before) and the accounting method confirms this since the rate of return equals the cost of capital, and abnormal income growth equals zero. And for a zero-value-added firm, neutral accounting yields a normal intrinsic P/B ratio of 1.0 and normal trailing and forward P/E ratios, as you see at the bottom of the table. For this reason neutral accounting can be referred to as *normal accounting*.

Look now at Table 16.3. Here the firm's investment and sales are the same as in Table 16.2 in all years, but now conservative accounting is used. The accountant writes off 10 percent (or $40) of investment immediately, charged against income. Consider

TABLE 16.2
**Neutral Accounting:
A Firm Investing
$400 Each Year with
No Value Added
(Required return is
10%)**

	2000	2001	2002	2003	2004
Sales					
From investments in 2000		240	220		
From investments in 2001			240	220	
From investments in 2002				240	220
From investments in 2003					240
		240	460	460	460
Operating expenses (depreciation)					
For investments in 2000		200	200		
For investments in 2001			200	200	
For investments in 2002				200	200
For investments in 2003					200
		200	400	400	400
Operating income		40	60	60	60
Net operating assets (NOA)					
For investments in 2000	400	200			
For investments in 2001		400	200		
For investments in 2002			400	200	
For investments in 2003				400	200
For investments in 2004					400
	400	600	600	600	600
Investment	400	400	400	400	400
Free cash flow	(400)	(160)	60	60	60
RNOA (%)		10.0	10.0	10.0	10.0
Profit margin (%)		16.7	13.0	13.0	13.0
Asset turnover		0.60	0.77	0.77	0.77
Growth in NOA (%)		50	0	0	0
ReOI (0.10)		0	0	0	0
AOIG (0.10)			0	0	0
Value of firm	400	600	600	600	600
Premium over book value	0	0	0	0	0
P/B	1.0	1.0	1.0	1.0	1.0
Trailing P/E		11.0	11.0	11.0	11.0
Forward P/E	10.0	10.0	10.0	10.0	10.0

ReOI value of firm = Book value = 400

AOIG value of firm = Capitalized forward income = $\dfrac{40}{0.10}$ = 400

Values in all years in Tables 16.2–16.5 and 16.7 are the value in 2000 growing at the 10 percent cost of capital, less free cash flows paid out. So the forecasted value at the end of 2001 is $(400 \times 1.10) + 160 = 600$ and that at the end of 2002 is $(600 \times 1.10) - 60 = 600$. The P/B ratios are unlevered P/B ratios (or levered P/B if there is no debt financing). As premiums are unaffected by financing they are both the premiums for the firm and premiums for the equity. P/E ratios are also unlevered P/E ratios. For each year they are calculated as (Value + Free cash flow)/OI, as in Chapter 13. The effects on levered P/E ratios are similar (and the P/E ratios here are indeed levered P/E ratios if the firm has no net debt).

this as the R&D component of the project or promotion costs that are expensed immediately according to GAAP. Comparing Table 16.3 with Table 16.2, you observe the accounting and valuation effects of conservative accounting relative to normal accounting. Liberal accounting would have the same effect, except in the opposite direction. Box 16.2 lists the accounting and valuation effects of conservative accounting for this firm that invests a constant amount each year.

TABLE 16.3
Conservative
Accounting: A Firm
Investing $400 Each
Year with No Value
Added; 10% of
Investment Expensed
Immediately
(Required return is
10%)

	2000	2001	2002	2003	2004
Sales					
From investments in 2000		240	220		
From investments in 2001			240	220	
From investments in 2002				240	220
From investments in 2003					240
		240	460	460	460
Operating expenses					
For investments in 2000	40	180	180		
For investments in 2001		40	180	180	
For investments in 2002			40	180	180
For investments in 2003				40	180
For investments in 2004					40
	40	220	400	400	400
Operating income	(40)	20	60	60	60
Net operating assets (NOA)					
For investments in 2000	360	180			
For investments in 2001		360	180		
For investments in 2002			360	180	
For investments in 2003				360	180
For investments in 2004					360
	360	540	540	540	540
Investment	400	400	400	400	400
Free cash flow	(400)	(160)	60	60	60
RNOA (%)		5.6	11.1	11.1	11.1
Profit margin (%)		8.3	13.0	13.0	13.0
Asset turnover (%)		0.67	0.85	0.85	0.85
Growth in NOA (%)		50	0	0	0
ReOI (0.10)		(16)	6	6	6
AOIG (0.10)			22	0	0
Value of firm	400	600	600	600	600
Premium over book value		60	60	60	60
P/B	1.11	1.11	1.11	1.11	1.11
Trailing P/E		22.0	11.0	11.0	11.0
Forward P/E	20	10.0	10.0	10.0	10.0

$$\text{ReOI value of firm} = 360 - \frac{16}{1.10} + \left(\frac{6}{0.10}\right) / 1.10 = 400 \text{ (A Case 2 valuation)}$$

$$\text{AOIG value of firm} = \frac{1}{0.10}\left[20 + \frac{22}{1.10}\right] = 400$$

The valuation of $400 in Table 16.3 is the same as that with neutral accounting; again the accounting does not affect the valuation. But note now that intrinsic price-to-book ratios are higher—and permanently so—because of the lower book value. Intrinsic trailing and forward P/E ratios are affected temporarily (because earnings are transitory) but they are unaffected once the permanent level of investment is reached: Earnings are unaffected by the accounting (as, of course, is value). The AOIG is expected to be zero, so the P/E ratio remains a normal P/E ratio. Research and development and brand-generating

ACCOUNTING EFFECTS

1. *Operating income* is not affected by conservative accounting once a permanent level of investment is reached. Income is lower with the conservative accounting while the level of investment is being built up (in 2001) but it is the same $60 after 2001. This is always a feature of accounting: Accounting methods don't affect income if there is no change in investment because total expenses and revenues are always the same, regardless of the accounting for expenses and revenues.

2. *Net operating assets*, although constant, are lower with conservative accounting and permanently so. As with the project, the accounting affects book value, but it does so permanently.

3. *RNOA* and *residual operating income* (and ROCE and residual earnings) are permanently higher with conservative accounting than with neutral accounting.

4. *Abnormal operating income growth* is not affected by conservative accounting once a permanent level of investment is reached.

VALUATION EFFECTS

1. *Value* is unaffected by the accounting. As with the single project, residual earnings created by the accounting have no effect on the value calculated.

2. *P/B ratios* are nonnormal (greater than 1). Conservative accounting reduces book values and thus induces a premium over book value. Not only is there an effect on current premiums, but there is also a permanent effect on subsequent premiums.

3. *P/E ratios* are not affected by the accounting once the permanent level of investment is reached: Earnings and value are both unaffected by the accounting.

firms typically have high RNOA and residual earnings, so they typically have high price-to-book ratios. But that does not mean that they necessarily have high P/E ratios.

The form of the valuation for the firm with conservative accounting differs from that for the firm with neutral accounting. As residual operating income is expected to be greater than zero permanently, the ReOI valuation is a Case 2 valuation (introduced in Chapter 5), as shown at the bottom of Table 16.3: ReOI is a perpetuity, so it is capitalized at the required return. It is sometimes said that continuing values should be calculated at a point in the future where the rate of return is expected to equal the cost of capital. Rates of return decline toward a normal return, it is said, as competition drives excess profits to zero. Excess economic profits may indeed be dissipated through competition, but that does not mean that the accounting measure of profitability, RNOA, will fall to the level of the required return: Conservative accounting will create a permanent level of RNOA above the required return even if there is no real value generated. So a Case 1 valuation (where ReOI is expected to be zero) will typically not apply to an R&D firm, for example.

Accounting Methods with a Changing Level of Investment

In Tables 16.2 and 16.3 the firm reaches a constant level of investment. But the picture changes when the level of investment is forecasted to change. Table 16.4 deals with the same firm as in Table 16.2, except that investment, which again is depreciated straight-line, is forecasted to grow at 5 percent per year. Each dollar of investment is expected to generate the same sales as before but, as investment is growing, so are sales revenue, operating income, and cum-dividend operating income. Because the firm is employing neutral accounting, even though operating income and net operating assets are forecasted to grow, forecasted RNOA is 10 percent and ReOI is zero. The value of the firm is still $400: The expanding investment with growing earnings does not add value.

TABLE 16.4
Neutral Accounting:
A Firm with
Investment Growing
at 5% per Year with
No Value Added
(Required return is
10%)

	2000	2001	2002	2003	2004
Sales					
From investments in 2000		240.0	220.0		
From investments in 2001			252.0	231.0	
From investments in 2002				264.6	242.6
From investments in 2003					277.8
		240.0	472.0	495.6	520.4
Operating expenses (depreciation)					
For investments in 2000		200.0	200.0		
For investments in 2001			210.0	210.0	
For investments in 2002				220.5	220.5
For investments in 2003					231.5
For investments in 2004					
		200.0	410.0	430.5	452.0
Operating income (OI)		40.0	62.0	65.1	68.4
Net operating assets (NOA)					
For investments in 2000	400.0	200.0			
For investments in 2001		420.0	210.0		
For investments in 2002			441.0	220.5	
For investments in 2003				463.1	231.5
For investments in 2004					486.2
	400.0	620.0	651.0	683.6	717.7
Investment	400	420	441	463.1	486.2
Free cash flow	(400)	(180)	31	32.5	34.4
RNOA (%)		10.0	10.0	10.0	10.0
Profit margin (%)		16.7	13.1	13.1	13.1
Asset turnover		0.60	0.76	0.76	0.76
Growth in NOA (%)		55	5	5	5
ReOI (0.10)		0	0	0	0
Growth in ReOI (%)		—	0	0	0
Growth in cum-dividend OI (%)		—	10	10	10
AOIG (0.10)			0	0	0
Value of firm	400	620.0	651.0	683.6	717.7
Premium over book value	0	0	0	0	0
P/B	1.0	1.0	1.0	1.0	1.0
Trailing P/E		11.0	11.0	11.0	11.0
Forward P/E	10.0	10.0	10.0	10.0	10.0

ReOI value of firm = 400

AOIG value of firm = $\dfrac{40}{0.10}$ = 400

Growth in cum-dividend OI is growth in operating income adjusted for reinvesting free cash flow at the required return of 10 percent. The free cash flow is the "dividend" from operations.

Look now at Table 16.5. Here the conservative accountant is at work writing off 10 percent of the investment as R&D and promotion expenditures each year. This results in positive residual earnings and a nonnormal P/B ratio, as before, but there are additional effects. Forecasted operating income is increasing through time but is lower in all years than in Table 16.4 because the write-off also increases at a 5 percent rate. But the cum-dividend operating income (after reinvesting the free cash flow "dividend" at the cost of capital) is

TABLE 16.5
Conservative Accounting: A Firm with Investment Growing at 5% per Year with No Value Added; 10% of Investment Expensed Immediately (Required return is 10%)

	2000	2001	2002	2003	2004
Sales					
From investments in 2000		240.0	220.0		
From investments in 2001			252.0	231.0	
From investments in 2002				264.6	242.6
From investments in 2003					277.8
		240.0	472.0	495.6	520.4
Operating expenses					
For investments in 2000	40.0	180.0	180.0		
For investments in 2001		42.0	189.0	189.0	
For investments in 2002			44.1	198.5	198.5
For investments in 2003				46.3	208.4
For investments in 2004					48.6
	40.0	222.0	413.1	433.8	455.5
Operating income	(40.0)	18.0	58.9	61.8	64.9
Net operating assets (NOA)					
For investments in 2000	360.0	180.0			
For investments in 2001		378.0	189.0		
For investments in 2002			396.9	198.5	
For investments in 2003				416.8	208.4
For investments in 2004					437.6
	360.0	558.0	585.9	615.2	646.0
Investment	400	420	441	463.1	486.2
Free cash flow	(400)	(180)	31	32.5	34.2
RNOA (%)		5.0	10.6	10.6	10.6
Profit margin (%)		7.5	12.5	12.5	12.5
Asset turnover (%)		0.67	0.85	0.85	0.85
Growth in NOA (%)		55	5	5	5
ReOI (0.10)		(18.0)	3.10	3.26	3.42
Growth in ReOI (%)		—	—	5	5
Growth in cum-dividend OI (%)		—	127	10.3	10.3
AOIG (0.10)			21.10	0.155	0.163
Growth in AOIG (%)			—	—	5
Value of firm	400.0	620.0	651.0	683.6	717.7
Premium over book value		62.0	65.1	68.4	71.8
P/B	1.11	1.11	1.11	1.11	1.11
Trailing P/E		24.4	11.6	11.6	11.6
Forward P/E	22.2	10.5	10.5	10.5	10.5

$$\text{ReOI value of firm} = 360 - \frac{18}{1.10} + \left(\frac{3.1}{1.10 - 1.05}\right) / 1.10 = 400 \text{ (A Case 3 valuation)}$$

$$\text{AOIG value of firm} = \frac{1}{1.10}\left[18 + \frac{21.10}{1.10} + \left(\frac{0.155}{1.10 - 1.05}\right) / 1.10\right] = 400$$

Some numbers don't add precisely due to rounding.

LIVERPOOL JOHN MOORES UNIVERSITY
Aldham Roberts L.R.C.
TEL 0151 231 3701/3634

ACCOUNTING EFFECTS

1. *Operating income* is lower with conservative accounting if assets are growing.

2. *RNOA* and *residual operating income* are higher with conservative accounting, as before. Although there is an effect on income (in the numerator of RNOA), the effect is proportionately larger on the denominator. But, due to the effect on income in the numerator, rates of return and residual earnings are not as large as with constant investment.

3. *Growth in income* is induced by conservative accounting if assets are growing.

4. *Growth in residual operating income* is induced by conservative accounting if assets are growing.

5. *Abnormal income growth* is induced by conservative accounting if assets are growing.

VALUATION EFFECTS

1. *Value* is unaffected by the accounting, as always.

2. *P/B ratios* are higher with conservative accounting, but no higher than in the no-growth case. But conservative accounting with growth results in increasing premiums over time, reflecting induced residual earnings growth. P/B ratios do not change from the no-growth case because the percentage increase in the numerator is the same as that in the denominator.

3. *P/E ratios* are higher than in the no-growth case: The accounting does not affect firm value but yields lower earnings. The higher P/E ratios reflect the higher forecasted growth in abnormal operating income induced by the accounting.

growing at a rate that is greater than the cost of capital rather than the 10 percent rate in Table 16.4.[1] Further, ReOI and AOIG are increasing at 5 percent, not constant as before. Nothing has changed here from Table 16.4 except the accounting. The conservative accounting has produced growth in operating income, growth in ReOI and abnormal income growth: An RNOA above the required return combined with growing net operating assets yields growing ReOI, and growing ReOI implies abnormal income growth.

As the growing ReOI is just an accounting effect, it does not change the $400 valuation. This is also a zero-value-added firm. But note that the ReOI value calculation (at the bottom of the table) is now a Case 3 valuation that accommodates the growing ReOI: ReOI is capitalized at the 5 percent growth rate. The AOIG valuation also is based on a 5 percent growth rate but the value of $400 is the same as the case with no growth.

The accounting and valuation effects of conservative accounting with growing investment for a firm with zero value added are summarized in Box 16.3. The accounting effects for liberal accounting are in the opposite direction.

Table 16.6 summarizes the effects of conservative and liberal accounting that we have observed for operating income, residual operating income, growth in residual operating income, abnormal operating income growth, the P/B ratio, and the P/E ratio. The effects are the same on earnings and residual earnings, but they are compounded by the effects of financial leverage that we examined in Chapter 13. The effects are for the firm that does not add value; the results of neutral accounting are given as a benchmark. The effects are given for declining investment as well as growing investment. Under all conditions (of constant, growing, or declining investment), P/B and P/E ratios are normal for normal accounting. Conservative and liberal accounting produce opposite effects, but the direction

[1] Reported income grows at a slower rate but this does not recognize the earnings from reinvesting dividends. The "dividends" from the operations are the free cash flow and the growth rates in operating income in corporate earnings from this free cash flow invested at 10 percent.

TABLE 16.6 **Accounting Effects for a Firm with Zero Value Added**

Accounting Method	Investment Pattern	RNOA	Residual OI		Abnormal OI Growth		P/B	P/E
			Level	Pattern	Level	Pattern		
Neutral	Constant	Normal	Zero	Constant	Zero	Constant	Normal	Normal
Conservative	Constant	Above normal	Positive	Constant	Zero	Constant	Above normal	Normal
Liberal	Constant	Below normal	Negative	Constant	Zero	Constant	Below normal	Normal
Neutral	Growing	Normal	Zero	Constant	Zero	Constant	Normal	Normal
Conservative	Growing	Above normal	Positive	Growing	Positive	Growing	Above normal	Above normal
Liberal	Growing	Below normal	Negative	Declining	Negative	Declining	Below normal	Below normal
Neutral	Declining	Normal	Zero	Constant	Zero	Constant	Normal	Normal
Conservative	Declining	Above normal	Positive	Declining	Negative	Declining	Above normal	Below normal
Liberal	Declining	Below normal	Negative	Growing	Positive	Growing	Below normal	Above normal

A normal RNOA is one that equals the required return for operations; a normal P/B is equal to 1.0; a normal trailing P/E is equal to (1 + Required Return)/Required return; a normal forward P/E is equal to 1/Required return.

of some of the effects depends on whether investment is growing or declining. (Note that declining investment cannot continue indefinitely.) Price-to-book ratios with conservative accounting and growth in investment are higher than normal, but they are unchanged from the no-growth case. But P/E ratios are higher than in the no-growth case (and higher than normal P/E ratios), because conservative accounting yields lower earnings (and value is unaffected). A higher P/E is, of course, appropriate: P/E is higher than normal if positive AOIG is expected, and conservative accounting creates AOIG.

We have observed in earlier chapters that P/E ratios and P/B ratios tend to be above normal. This makes sense in light of our analysis here. Conservative accounting is commonly practiced, so firms tend to have P/B above normal. But firms also have been growing assets, so the conservative accounting produces high P/E ratios as well.

The examples we have been through are for a firm that doesn't add value. The idea is to show you how the accounting can give the appearance of value added when there is none. Economic factors that add value will yield higher forecasted ReOI and AOIG than that generated by the accounting, and thus higher premiums over book value and higher P/E ratios. ReOI and AOIG are always a result of both real and accounting effects.

Because accounting methods don't affect the value, we don't have to worry about distinguishing real profitability from accounting profitability. But there is a proviso. The earnings we forecast must be comprehensive earnings. If any component of earnings is left out of the forecast, we will lose value in the calculation.

An Exception: LIFO Accounting

There is one exception to the principle that accounting does not create value. If firms are required to use the same accounting methods in their financial reports as they use for filing tax returns, the choice of accounting will affect their values. If, for example, firms choose methods that reduce or postpone taxes, they will have higher values. In some countries there is a link between tax and financial reporting rules. In the United States the link applies only to LIFO (last in, first out) accounting for inventories; if a firm uses LIFO for tax, it must also use it in its financial reports.

LIFO is a conservative accounting method when inventory quantities and costs are rising. Inventory on the balance sheet is measured at the low prices of older inventory purchases while cost of goods sold is measured at recent, higher purchase prices. The low book values yield higher inventory turnovers, asset turnovers, rates of return, and P/B ratios. It is sometimes said that LIFO results in lower earnings also. But this is not necessarily so. Cost of goods sold equals purchases minus change in inventory; thus if inventories on the balance sheet remain level, cost of goods sold (and earnings) are the same under LIFO and FIFO (first in, first out) accounting, equal to the cost of current purchases. This is another example of what we saw in Table 16.3: The accounting does not affect income when there is no change in net operating assets (in inventories here). But if inventories are growing (and inventory costs are rising), the effects observed in Table 16.5 surface: LIFO yields higher cost of goods sold along with lower gross margins, profit margins, and earnings, and it yields higher P/B and P/E ratios.

If inventories and their costs are expected to grow, the higher LIFO cost of goods sold will result in lower taxes. Firms therefore adopt LIFO for tax and book purposes and so generate value. What adjustments are required to incorporate this added value from using the LIFO method? None: The higher value is incorporated in forecasts of residual income. The lower forecasted taxes increase forecasted after-tax profit margins and RNOA. Accordingly, forecasted residual earnings are higher and so are their present values.

HIDDEN RESERVES AND THE CREATION OF EARNINGS

We have just seen that when investments are growing, conservative accounting depresses earnings and profit margins but raises residual earnings and abnormal income growth. But it is also the case that if the rate of investment subsequently slows, conservative accounting generates higher earnings and profit margins and even higher residual earnings and abnormal income growth.

Look at Table 16.7. This involves the same investment as Table 16.5 up to the year 2004. Then, in 2005, investment is forecasted to level off at the amount in 2004 instead of growing at 5 percent. Sales and expenses from 2006 on are thus forecasted for this level of investment, producing a permanent level of operating income of $72.9. But the ratio of depreciation to revenue declines, yielding higher profit margins. So RNOA increases from 10.6 percent to 11.1 percent by 2006, the same RNOA as that with no growth in investment in Table 16.3. Residual operating income also increases, driven by the higher RNOA, and, as in Table 16.3, is forecasted to be constant. The decline in the rate of growth has generated profit margins, turnovers, RNOA, residual operating income, and (temporarily) abnormal operating income growth.

This example illustrates the phenomenon of **hidden reserves** and their liquidation. Hidden reserves are profits that might have been booked with less conservative accounting. Conservative accounting, with growth, reduces earnings because of higher expenses. But the charging of higher expenses builds up hidden profit reserves that can be realized with a slowing of investment. They are "hidden" because they are book value that is missing from the balance sheet due to conservative accounting: Reporting lower earnings means that net assets (and equity) must be lower by exactly the same amount.[2] If the accounting were not conservative, the net operating assets would be carried at a higher amount. If the growth of investment slows or levels off, or if investment declines, more profits can be generated; this is referred to as **liquidating hidden reserves.** Yes, this is strange! Firms can generate profits by reducing investment. Table 16.5 shows the effect

---

[2]The term, hidden reserves, is sometimes used to refer to allowances and liabilities that have been overestimated; so excessive bad debt allowances and unearned revenue estimates create hidden reserves. These are just particular cases of conservative accounting. The understatement or omission of any asset, or overstatement of any liability, creates a hidden reserve.

TABLE 16.7   **Creation and Liquidation of Hidden Reserves with Conservative Accounting: A Firm with Investment Initially Growing at 5% and Then Leveling Off, with No Value Added; 10% of Investment Expensed Immediately (Required return is 10%)**

	2000	2001	2002	2003	2004	2005	2006	2007
Sales								
From investments in 2000		240.0	220.0					
From investments in 2001			252.0	231.0				
From investments in 2002				264.6	242.6			
From investments in 2003					277.8	254.7		
From investments in 2004						291.7	267.4	
From investments in 2005							291.7	267.4
From investments in 2006								291.7
		240.0	472.0	495.6	520.4	546.4	559.1	559.1
Operating expenses								
For investments in 2000	40.0	180.0	180.0					
For investments in 2001		42.0	189.0	189.0				
For investments in 2002			44.1	198.5	198.5			
For investments in 2003				46.3	208.4	208.4		
For investments in 2004					48.6	218.8	218.8	
For investments in 2005						48.6	218.8	218.8
For investments in 2006							48.6	218.8
For investments in 2007								48.6
	40.0	222.0	413.1	433.8	455.5	475.8	486.2	486.2
Operating income (OI)	(40.0)	18.0	58.9	61.8	64.9	70.6	72.9	72.9
Net operating assets (NOA)								
For investments in 2000	360.0	180.0						
For investments in 2001		378.0	189.0					
For investments in 2002			396.9	198.5				
For investments in 2003				416.8	208.4			
For investments in 2004					437.6	218.8		
For investments in 2005						437.6	218.8	
For investments in 2006							437.6	218.8
For investments in 2007								437.6
	360.0	558.0	585.9	615.2	646.0	656.4	656.4	656.4
Investment	400	420	441	463.1	486.2	486.2	486.2	486.2
Free cash flow	(400)	(180)	31	32.5	34.2	60.2	72.9	72.9
RNOA (%)		5.0	10.6	10.6	10.6	10.9	11.1	11.1
Profit margin (%)		7.5	12.5	12.5	12.5	12.9	13.0	13.0
Asset turnover		0.67	0.85	0.85	0.85	0.85	0.85	0.85
Growth in NOA (%)		55	5	5	5	1.6	0.0	0.0
ReOI (0.10)		(18.0)	3.10	3.26	3.42	6.02	7.29	7.29
Growth in ReOI (%)		—	—	5	5	76	21	0
Growth in cum-dividend OI (%)		—	127	10.3	10.3	14.0	11.8	10.0
AOIG (0.10)			21.10	0.155	0.163	2.602	1.270	0.0
Growth in AOIG (%)		—						
ReOI value of firm	400.0	620.0	651.0	683.6	717.7	729.3	729.3	729.3
Premium over book value		62.0	65.1	68.4	71.7	72.9	72.9	72.9
P/B	1.11	1.11	1.11	1.11	1.11	1.11	1.11	1.11
Trailing P/E		24.4	11.6	11.6	11.6	11.2	11.0	11.0
Forward P/E	22.2	10.5	10.5	10.5	10.2	10.0	10.0	10.0

$$\text{ReOI value of firm} = 360 - \frac{18}{1.10} + \frac{3.1}{1.21} + \frac{3.25}{1.331} + \frac{3.42}{1.464} + \frac{6.02}{1.611} + \frac{7.29}{0.10} \Big/ 1.611 = 400$$

Some numbers don't add exactly due to rounding.

of the creation of hidden reserves (reducing income); Table 16.7 shows the effects of their liquidation (increasing income).

The use of LIFO is a case in point. If physical inventories and inventory costs are increasing, LIFO produces higher cost of goods sold and lower earnings, creating hidden reserves. These hidden reserves are reflected in a lower balance sheet number for inventories over what it would have been under FIFO. In the United States GAAP requires the amount of the hidden reserve, referred to as the *LIFO reserve*, to be reported. It is typically given in footnotes. The LIFO reserve is the cumulative amount of additional earnings that would have been recognized in the past if the firm had used FIFO. It is always the case that

$$\text{LIFO inventory} = \text{FIFO inventory} - \text{LIFO reserve}$$

so you can always calculate what the inventory number would have been if the firm used FIFO. And it is always the case that, for any fiscal period,

$$\text{LIFO cost of goods sold} = \text{FIFO cost of goods sold} + \text{Change in LIFO reserve}$$

The difference in after-tax operating income under FIFO and LIFO is the change in the LIFO reserve multiplied by the tax rate. If you want to compare profit margins, turnovers, and RNOA of a LIFO and FIFO firm, you can put them on the same basis by using these relationships.

Table 16.8 gives the median LIFO reserve as a percentage of shareholders' equity for NYSE and AMEX firms using LIFO for the years 1976 to 1991, along with the 75th and 25th percentiles. You see that the median reserve ranged from 13.3 percent of shareholders'

TABLE 16.8   **LIFO Reserves and Changes in LIFO Reserves for NYSE and AMEX Firms, 1976–1991**

Year	Percentage Change in CPI	LIFO Reserves/Shareholders' Equity, %			Change in LIFO Reserves/ Revenue, %		
		75th Percentile	Median	25th Percentile	75th Percentile	Median	25th Percentile
1976	4.86	14.8	9.6	4.9	0.9	0.4	0.1
1977	6.70	15.4	9.8	4.8	0.9	0.5	0.1
1978	9.02	16.4	10.3	5.1	1.0	0.6	0.2
1979	13.29	20.7	12.4	6.4	1.8	1.0	0.5
1980	12.52	22.4	13.3	6.4	1.5	0.8	0.3
1981	8.92	21.2	12.7	6.1	1.1	0.5	0.1
1982	3.83	19.9	11.5	5.2	0.3	−0.0	−0.6
1983	3.79	18.1	10.3	4.6	0.2	−0.0	−0.4
1984	3.95	16.5	9.1	3.8	0.2	0.0	−0.3
1985	3.80	14.8	7.8	3.1	0.1	−0.1	−0.5
1986	1.10	13.1	6.3	2.4	0.1	−0.1	−0.5
1987	4.43	12.6	6.1	2.5	0.4	0.1	−0.1
1988	4.42	13.7	6.9	2.8	0.6	0.3	0.1
1989	4.65	13.0	6.4	2.6	0.4	0.1	−0.0
1990	6.11	13.3	6.4	2.4	0.3	0.1	−0.1
1991	3.06	12.4	5.9	2.0	0.1	0.0	−0.3

The table gives the amount of LIFO reserve (as a percentage of shareholders' equity) and the change in the LIFO reserve (as a percentage of revenue). The LIFO reserve is the difference between LIFO inventories and the FIFO carrying amount. The change in the LIFO reserve is the difference between LIFO and FIFO cost of goods sold.

Source: R. Jennings, P. Simko, and R. Thompson II, "Does LIFO Inventory Accounting Improve the Income Statement at the Expense of the Balance Sheet?" *Journal of Accounting Research*, Spring 1996, pp. 89–90.

equity in 1980 to 5.9 percent in 1991. So, at the median, firms would have had 13.3 percent higher equity in 1980 if they had used FIFO, and 5.9 percent more equity in 1991. LIFO reserves increase when inventory costs rise and the change in the Consumer Price Index (CPI) reported in the table indicates that 1980 was a high inflation year, while 1991 was a low one. The table also gives numbers for changes in the LIFO reserve as a percentage of revenue. Changes in LIFO reserves are the difference between LIFO and FIFO cost of goods sold, so, as the changes are divided by revenue in the table, the numbers are the LIFO effect on before-tax gross margins and profit margins relative to FIFO. They ranged from 1.0 percent in 1979 to –0.1 percent in 1985 and 1986 as a percentage of revenues.

Just as growing LIFO inventories reduce earnings and increase (hidden) LIFO reserves, declining LIFO inventories create earnings by liquidating LIFO reserves: Lower, older costs are brought into cost of goods sold, yielding higher earnings than under FIFO. The additional earnings are called *LIFO liquidation profits*. (Taxes, deferred by using LIFO when inventories were growing, will also be realized against the liquidation profits.) Table 16.8 indicates there were four years when median changes in LIFO reserves were negative, and in each year from 1982 to 1991, except 1988, LIFO reserves declined at the 25th percentile: Over 25 percent of LIFO firms reported higher profits than they would have under FIFO.

A decline in physical inventories reduces the LIFO reserve if inventory costs are rising. But the LIFO reserve will also decline if inventory costs fall, because LIFO costs of goods sold (based on recent, lower prices) are then lower than under FIFO (based on older, higher prices). Often quantities and prices both fall as a result of lower demand for the product. Some companies separate LIFO reserve declines due to inventory liquidation from those due to price declines in their footnotes.

Hidden reserves can arise from any application of conservative accounting. Reducing investment in plant and equipment that has been depreciated rapidly will generate profits. Constant or declining sales after a period of sales growth will yield profits if there has been a policy of overestimating warranty liabilities on bad debts provisions.

Some analysts take special care to recognize hidden reserves and add value to the firm for them. Some maintain that LIFO reserves, which must be reported under U.S. GAAP (usually in footnotes), are an asset whose value must be added to correct the book value. But we have to be careful. Hidden reserves are an accounting phenomenon, and accounting can't generate value. Look at the valuation at the bottom of Table 16.7. This is the same firm as in the previous tables; it does not generate value. And applying residual earnings techniques—now with the forecast horizon at the steady-state year beginning 2006—we get the same valuation as before, $400. (You might do the AOIG valuation also.) The presence of unrealized hidden reserves in Table 16.5 did not give us an incorrect valuation. Provided we forecast ReOI to a steady-state level that recognizes the investment path, hidden reserves are not a concern. Perpetual growth (in the Table 16.5 valuation) means we anticipate hidden reserves will never be realized. But expected realization of hidden reserves (in Table 16.7) does not change the valuation. A forecast of higher ReOI (in Table 16.7) is exactly offset by a forecast of a lower growth rate for ReOI.

By now you should be aware of a number of fallacies with respect to interpreting accounting data. These fallacies often lead to misstatements—in the press and even by analysts—so it is useful to flag them. Box 16.4 lists statements that are sometimes erroneously made about the relationship between accounting numbers and value. Each statement can be true if the accounting captures real phenomena, and often that is the case. But each attribute can also result from accounting methods. Most of the fallacies

These statements are not necessarily true:

- Firms with higher anticipated earnings growth are worth more.
  Rejoinder: Earnings growth can be created by accounting methods (and by financial leverage) rather than economic factors.

- Firms with high anticipated return on equity are worth more.
  Rejoinder: High return on equity means a higher premium over book value but not a higher value; ROCE can be created by the accounting (and by financial leverage).

- Increasing residual earnings indicate a firm that is adding more and more value.
  Rejoinder: Probably, but growth in residual earnings can be induced with conservative accounting.

- If a firm is earning an RNOA that is higher than the cost of capital, it will add value by investing more.
  Rejoinder: A firm can create a high RNOA through accounting methods but may not be able to add value through investment.

- If RNOA is higher than the cost of capital, a reduction in investment (or slowing of its growth rate) reduces residual earnings.
  Rejoinder: A reduction of investment can create residual earnings if conservative accounting has created hidden reserves.

- Low profit margins mean a firm cannot generate much value from sales.
  Rejoinder: Low profit margins may be induced by conservative accounting if net assets are growing.

- High asset turnovers mean a firm is efficient in generating sales.
  Rejoinder: High turnovers can be produced by keeping asset values low with conservative accounting.

- Conservative accounting reduces profits and results in higher P/E ratios.
  Rejoinder: Not always; only if investment is growing.

arise from naively focusing on earnings growth or rates of return. Earnings growth and rates of return can be affected by the accounting, so they must be interpreted by combining forecasted residual earnings with current book value in a residual earnings valuation, or by charging earnings growth for required earnings growth in an AOIG valuation. Don't be too quickly impressed with growing earnings, growing residual earnings, and high rates of return. Reserve judgment until you have tested to see if these attributes are real or induced.

With respect to earnings growth, you now have three warnings about interpreting earnings growth. In Chapters 5 and 6 we saw that investment can generate earnings growth but may not add value. In Chapter 13 we saw that financial leverage can generate earnings growth but does not add value. And here we see that conservative accounting can generate earnings growth but does not add value. In all cases, the use of appropriate valuation techniques determines whether growth adds value.

CONSERVATIVE AND LIBERAL ACCOUNTING IN PRACTICE

While the focus of some accounting methods is on measuring earnings, all methods have an effect on both earnings and book value. This is just the debits and credits of accounting: One can't affect earnings without also affecting the balance sheet. So all methods can be thought of in terms of their effect on book value and thus on accounting rates of return, residual income, and the P/B ratio. They can be thought of in terms of their effects on earnings, profit margins, and the P/E ratio, but only with changing investment. So think first in terms of the effect on book values. For example, "accelerated depreciation" results in lower book values for property, plant, and equipment; high bad debt estimates

CONSERVATIVE ACCOUNTING

Practices that decrease book values:

- Accelerated depreciation of tangible assets.

- Accelerated amortization of intangible assets such as patents, copyrights, and purchased goodwill.

- LIFO inventory methods.

- Underestimates of:
  Net accounts receivable (high bad debt estimates).
  Impairment values (high impairment write-offs).

- Pooling accounting (rather than purchase accounting) for mergers.

- Overestimates of:
  Pension and postemployment benefit liabilities.
  Warranty liabilities.
  Provisions for restructurings and other future events.
  Deferred revenue.

Practices that record no book values at all:

- Expensing R&D expenditures.

- Expensing advertising expenditures.

- Expensing investment in intellectual and human capital.

LIBERAL ACCOUNTING

Practices that increase book values:

- Revaluing tangible assets upward (U.K.).

- Booking brand-name assets (U.K.).

- Charging no depreciation (some firms in U.K.).

- Overstating deferred tax assets through low valuation allowances (U.S.).

Practices that record no book values at all:

- Omitting contingent liabilities for environmental damage, lawsuits, and stock compensation, for example.

result in lower net receivables; and LIFO measurement of cost of goods sold results in lower inventories (when inventory prices are rising). These conservative methods yield higher P/B ratios. They yield lower earnings and higher P/E ratios only with increasing property, plant, and equipment, receivables, and inventories.

The accounting profession in most countries typically takes a conservative approach. It is sometimes claimed that this conservative accounting leads to lower income and lower rates of return, giving a "conservative" picture of the firm. Don't be confused. Conservative accounting policies will yield lower profits if investments are growing. But they will always result in higher rates of return and thus higher apparent profitability. And if investments are growing, they will result in growing residual income and higher earnings growth. Conservative accounting—supposedly designed to yield a conservative balance sheet—actually produces higher profitability, which is not a conservative view.

Box 16.5 lists common accounting practices that affect book values and accounting rates of return. They are classified as conservative or liberal but many of the conservative methods can be liberal (and some liberal methods conservative) if applied in the opposite direction. For example, accelerated depreciation and amortization methods yield lower book values and higher rates of return and so are conservative. But methods that depreciate or amortize assets very slowly are liberal methods, just like asset revaluations.

The rest of this chapter illustrates the effects of accounting methods.

LIFO versus FIFO

We saw in Chapter 11 that in 1996 Nike had higher RNOA than Reebok, 22.6 percent compared to Reebok's 14.1 percent. But Nike uses LIFO for its U.S. inventories while Reebok uses FIFO. Table 16.9 lists some measures for 1996 and 1997 that reflect inventory accounting for the two firms.

Nike's inventory turnover ratios are higher than Reebok's, due in part to lower LIFO inventories. This contributes to a higher RNOA. Nike's large growth in inventory has the

TABLE 16.9
Nike versus Reebok

	1997		1996	
	Nike	**Reebok**	**Nike**	**Reebok**
RNOA (%)	25.7	16.0	22.6	14.1
Asset turnover	3.0	3.2	2.7	2.9
Inventory turnover	8.1	6.6	8.3	5.8
Gross margin (%)	40.1	37.0	36.9	38.4
Profit margin (%)	8.7	4.9	8.5	4.8
Inventory ($ thousand)	1,338,640	563,735	931,151	544,522
Growth in inventory (%)	43.8	3.5	47.8	−14.2
LIFO reserve ($ thousand)	20,716	—	16,023	—

effect of lower profit margins because of higher cost of goods sold, but the effect of lower margins on the RNOA is not as great as that of the asset turnover, so RNOA is larger than it would be under FIFO. With the amounts for the LIFO reserve (taken for Table 16.9 from the inventory footnote), we can calculate Nike's RNOA for 1997 as if it were using FIFO. Inventories would be higher by the amount of the LIFO reserve and so then would net operating assets in the denominator of RNOA. Operating income in the numerator would be higher by the amount of the change in the LIFO reserve from 1996 to 1997, that is, $4,693 thousand before tax and $2,886 thousand after tax at Nike's 38.5 percent tax rate. The adjusted RNOA (based on average net operating assets in the denominator) is 25.6 percent, immaterially different from the LIFO RNOA. We see that Nike had large increases in inventory but conclude that with the small increase in the LIFO reserve relative to its inventory, it does not have significant cost increase in manufacturing inventories.

These adjustments help in the comparison of firms' ratios. But for valuation purposes they are unnecessary: We can value both Nike and Reebok by forecasting their RNOA as measured, without adjustment for differences in the accounting. However, other considerations aside, Nike, with lower net operating assets under LIFO, has a (slightly) higher intrinsic P/B ratio than Reebok and, with its growth in inventories depressing earnings, a slightly higher intrinsic P/E.

Research and Development in the Pharmaceuticals Industry

Table 16.10 gives simulated ROCE, P/B, and E/P ratios (the reciprocal of the P/E ratios) generated by a simulation of a firm's R&D program. In the simulation a firm spends a set amount each year for basic R&D on a number of drugs with a set probability of success. If the research on a drug is successful, the firm moves to preclinical testing and clinical trials, again with a set probability of a successful outcome. Successful drugs are launched commercially with estimated revenues, production costs, and marketing costs. All estimates, including the probability of R&D success, are based on experience in the drug industry, lending them a certain realism.

The numbers in Table 16.10 are averages over many trials in the simulation. This representative firm starts an R&D program in Year 1 and in early years there are no revenues as drug development moves through to commercial launch. The development period is quite long, and Year 14 is the first year that revenues are generated. The table gives ROCE, P/B, and E/P for that year, as well as Years 20, 26, and 32. The firm is not leveraged, so the ROCE is equal to the RNOA. The three ratios are given for three different accounting methods. The expensing method expenses all drug development costs when incurred, as required under GAAP. The full costing method capitalizes development costs

TABLE 16.10 Ratios from a Simulated Research and Development Program Using Different Accounting Methods

Year from Beginning of R&D Program	ROCE, %			P/B Ratios			P/E Ratios		
	Expense Method	Full Costing	Successful Efforts	Expense Method	Full Costing	Successful Efforts	Expense Method	Full Costing	Successful Efforts
14	−92.3	−3.4	−15.2	17.9	2.7	4.5	−0.043	−0.012	−0.035
20	8.1	10.7	11.0	11.4	2.9	5.2	0.016	0.029	0.018
26	54.8	27.8	39.6	7.3	2.7	4.5	0.098	0.101	0.098
32	54.0	26.4	39.3	7.4	2.6	4.5	0.096	0.097	0.096

The table shows how ROCE, P/B ratios, and E/B ratios change as R&D programs mature, for three different accounting methods that differ in the degree of conservative accounting. Expensing R&D is the most conservative accounting, full costing the least conservative. The R&D program generates losses up to Year 14 (for all three methods) because R&D expenses exceed revenues. Positive profitability is reported after Year 14, but the profitability is higher the more conservative the accounting method.

Source: P. Healy, S. Myers, and C. Howe, "R&D Accounting and the Relevance–Objectivity Tradeoff: A Simulation Using Data from the Pharmaceutical Industry," Sloan School of Management, MIT, 1998. See also "R&D Accounting and the Tradeoff between Relevance and Objectivity," *Journal of Accounting Research*, June 2002, pp. 677–710, by the same authors.

and amortizes them straight-line over 10 years from commercial launch. The successful efforts costing method capitalizes all development costs, writes off unsuccessful projects when they fail to move to the next stage of development, and amortizes successful projects over 10 years from commercial launch. Prices in the E/P and P/B ratios are intrinsic prices calculated from forecasting cash flows in the stimulation.

Expensing R&D is the most conservative accounting, full costing the least. Steady state is reached in Year 26 and you can see that at that point expensing yields the highest ROCE, full costing the lowest. Accordingly, P/B ratios are highest under the expensing method, lowest under full costing. Because the firm commits a set amount of expenditure to R&D each year, once steady state is reached there is no growth in investment. Correspondingly, there is little change in earnings and ROCE (from Year 26 to Year 32), as in the Table 16.3 example earlier. There is also little change in E/P ratios and P/B ratios regardless of accounting method, again as in Table 16.3. And E/P ratios look normal: As there is no growth in ROCE or growth in expenditures (and no growth in earnings or book values), residual earnings are constant, so P/Es are normal.

The steady-state ratios are typical of a mature R&D firm with no growth in its R&D program. With growth, steady-state ROCE would be lower but P/E higher: The steady state would be a Table 16.5 rather than a Table 16.3 example. The ratios for the expensing method prior to steady state are typical of an R&D start-up. Expenditures for R&D are expensed but revenues are not yet forthcoming, so the firm reports very low profitability.

Purchase versus Pooling Accounting

Up to 2001 the United States permitted both purchase and pooling accounting in mergers and acquisitions. Under purchase accounting the full purchase price of an acquisition is recorded, with the difference between the purchase price and the fair value of the net assets acquired recorded as goodwill. This goodwill is amortized against future earnings over its expected life, up to 40 years. Under pooling, the net assets of the combining firms are combined in the balance sheet at their book values, and no goodwill is recorded.

As pooling results in no amortization of goodwill, subsequent earnings are higher than under purchase accounting, as are residual earnings, because book values are lower. But is current book value plus the present value of expected residual earnings—that is, value—higher? No: Purchase accounting results in lower earnings and lower residual

TABLE 16.11
Glaxo Wellcome PLC

Source: C. Higson, "Value
Metrics in Equity Analysis,"
Institute of Finance and
Accounting, London Business
School, 1998.

Return on Operations, %	1991	1992	1993	1994	1995	1996
As reported	50.6	54.2	51.5	55.5	75.5	96.4
With R&D capitalized	39.8	41.2	39.4	39.4	50.5	55.0

earnings but the same value of current book value plus the present value of expected residual earnings. Pooling is relatively conservative accounting, purchase accounting is relatively liberal accounting, but the accounting does not affect the valuation.

Some claim that the lower earnings under purchase accounting result in lower valuations, and that is why firms prefer pooling accounting. Pooling accounting generates earnings and firms can grow earnings with successive pooling mergers. But pooling accounting does not generate value. If, as is claimed, the market values earnings from poolings more highly, the market is in error, and an appropriate residual earnings analysis will uncover the mispricing.

Issues do arise with respect to impairment of goodwill under purchase accounting. These, too, should not affect the valuation, but an analyst has to be aware of them. If a firm writes down goodwill excessively, it is practicing conservative accounting that will induce higher future profitability and earnings growth.

Expensing Goodwill and Research and Development Expenditures

The first line of Table 16.11 gives the reported operating profitability for Glaxo Wellcome, the large U.K. pharmaceutical firm, from 1991 to 1996. Glaxo bought Wellcome in 1995, so earlier figures are preacquisition (the firm is now part of Glaxo Smithkline PLC). Glaxo Wellcome expenses R&D expenditures. The second line gives the profitability recalculated by capitalizing R&D and amortizing it at a rate of 25 percent of declining balance each year. The period was one of growing investment in R&D which, when expensed, reduces operating income in the numerator. But the overall impact of the conservative accounting is to increase the return on operating assets over that from capitalizing and amortizing.

Prior to 1998 firms in the United Kingdom expensed all goodwill in the year that it was purchased as a dirty-surplus charge to equity. (They now capitalize it and subject it to impairment rules.) This was very conservative accounting that effectively gives the same result as pooling. You can see that the write-off from the acquisition of Wellcome in 1995 produced a large reported rate of return of 96.4 percent in 1996. When goodwill is capitalized, the 1996 return falls to 38.6 percent; it falls to 31.5 percent when both R&D and goodwill are capitalized.

Liberal Accounting: Breweries and Hotels

Many breweries, hotels, and leisure companies in the United Kingdom regularly revalue assets upward and also charge little in depreciation. Their argument is that asset values increase rather than decline and regular maintenance slows economic depreciation. Such firms accordingly have low accounting rates of return and low P/B ratios. Table 16.12 compares numbers for Forte PLC, a U.K. hotel and restaurant chain (before it was taken over by Granada in 1996), and Hilton Hotels, the U.S. hotel chain. These firms have large investments in depreciable assets (hotels), yet Forte's depreciation-to-sales ratio is much lower than Hilton's. And a high percentage of Forte's book value comes from

TABLE 16.12
Forte versus Hilton

	1991	1992	1993	1994	1995
Forte PLC					
ROCE (%)	1.2	1.2	4.1	2.4	3.8
Depreciation/sales (%)	3.0	3.3	3.6	4.6	4.9
Revaluation reserve/equity (%)	69.8	71.0	67.5	73.9	70.9
P/B	0.58	0.61	0.58	1.03	0.94
Hilton Hotels Corp.					
ROCE (%)	9.0	10.6	10.3	11.1	14.5
Depreciation/sales (%)	9.1	8.9	8.5	8.9	8.6
P/B	2.01	2.06	2.75	2.90	2.37

TABLE 16.13
General Motors Corporation

	1988	1989	1990	1991	1992	1993	1994	1995	1996
Unlevered P/B	0.7	0.8	0.7	0.7	1.2	1.5	1.3	1.2	1.2
RNOA (%)	9.7	7.2	2.5	0.0	−20.8	6.3	11.1	11.0	7.5
Core PM (%)	6.7	6.9	4.1	1.5	1.8	4.2	5.0	5.5	3.8
ATO	1.5	1.0	1.0	1.0	1.3	1.9	2.2	1.9	1.7
NOA ($ billion)	118.3	125.1	124.1	118.4	81.8	63.3	76.7	96.2	95.3

revaluations (which are not permitted in the United States). Accordingly, its liberal accounting produced low ROCE and low P/B ratios. Forte's P/B ratios of less than 1.0 forecast negative residual earnings for the future. Hilton's P/B ratios forecast positive residual earnings.

Profitability in the 1990s

In the middle to late 1990s many firms reported strong profitability. In the early 1990s many of those same firms reported low profitability. The low profitability was due partly to recession but also to major restructurings and to the recognition of employee benefit liabilities. Some claim that the subsequent high profitability and earnings growth, though no doubt deriving from cost efficiencies introduced by the restructurings, was partly created by the lower book values from asset write-offs and the recognition of the new liabilities. Correspondingly, the high P/B ratios of the middle to late 1990s were due partly to the accounting having become more conservative.

In the late 1980s, General Motors Corporation traded below book value with correspondingly low book rates of return, as you can see in Table 16.13. After a period of very low profitability in the early 1990s, due significantly to restructuring and recognition of post-employment liabilities, profitability recovered to higher levels in 1994 and 1995, and the firm traded at a premium. Core profit margins recovered but the higher RNOA relative to 1988 and 1989 was driven by a higher ATO. The higher ATO probably reflects real efficiencies in using assets but also is a result of the accounting in 1990 to 1992. And the higher P/B ratios reflect the lower book values of net operating assets.

Economic-Value-Added Measures

Consultants in recent years have developed residual earnings measures that adjust GAAP accounting to measure "economic value added" or "economic profit." These products may be good as value-based management tools—as performance incentives to maximize shareholder value—but users should be careful about demanding the adjustments for valuation. These measures redo the accounting, but the accounting may not matter. The measures typically undo accounting conservatism—by capitalizing and amortizing R&D and advertising, for example—but we have seen that this is not necessary. Indeed capitalizing and amortizing introduces the problem of estimating amortization rates to measure the decline in economic value of intangibles. This is a nontrivial exercise.

ACCOUNTING METHODS AND THE FORECAST HORIZON

The analysis in this chapter has shown that, for valuation purposes, we do not have to distinguish real economic profitability from accounting profitability: Accounting methods do not affect the valuation. That is just as well, for—despite consultants' claims that their products measure "economic profit" and "economic value added"—we really cannot observe true economic profitability. While accountants and consultants strive to improve measurement, we are ultimately forced to work with imperfect measurements. There are, however, two provisos to our conclusion:

1. The earnings forecasted must be comprehensive earnings. If any component of earnings is left out of the forecast, value is lost in the calculation.

2. The valuation is insensitive to the accounting only if steady state is predicted. Different accounting methods result in different (Case 1, 2, or 3) steady-state profitability, but once this difference in permanent profitability is recognized, the valuations are the same. If we value firms with forecasts up to a point before steady state is reached, however, we will not get the same valuation.

The first point has been emphasized consistently throughout the book. The second point is clear from comparing the valuations in Tables 16.4 and 16.5. With neutral accounting (in Table 16.4), the forecast horizon is very short; steady state is reached one year ahead. With conservative accounting (Table 16.5), the forecast horizon is longer; steady state is reached two years ahead. In the case of the pharmaceuticals industry in Table 16.10, the accounting takes a considerable amount of time to uncover the profitability of bringing drugs to the market, the more so for (very conservative) GAAP accounting that expenses investment in R&D immediately.

These observations give you a sense of another feature of the accounting that bears upon the valuation. Valuations are uncertain, but more so the further into the future we have to forecast. All else being equal, we prefer to value a firm from forecasts over a short forecasting horizon. Accounting methods that recognize value added earlier are to be preferred to accounting methods that require us to forecast well into the future. Accordingly, we can think of "good accounting" as accounting that shortens the forecast horizon and "bad accounting" as accounting that forces us to forecast into the distant future. That is, accounting is judged by the practical criterion—established in Chapter 3—of establishing valuations from relatively short forecast horizons. Mark-to-market accounting for financial assets and liabilities is considered good accounting because it removes the need for forecasting. The simple valuations of Chapter 14 use very short forecast horizons. Indeed, the forecast horizon is immediate because those valuations rely only on the current financial statements. But those valuations only work if the accounting for the present is good enough to give us an indication of the long run.

The neutral accounting outlined in this chapter is ideal, for it uncovers economic profitability and results in short forecast horizons. This is the accounting that consultants strive for when they attempt to measure "economic profit." However, care is required in reconstructing GAAP accounting to this ideal. Accounting that purports to be closer to the ideal is only a good forecast of the long run if it is reliable. If, with the pretense of measuring real profitability, the accountant builds in a lot of speculation, we have lost our anchor; we have contaminated what we know with what we don't know. Consultants who measure "economic value added" typically capitalize R&D expenditures as assets on the balance sheet and then amortize this cost to earnings. If the outcome of the R&D program is highly speculative, the book value is also highly speculative. If, in addition, the amortization rates are highly uncertain, earnings also are contaminated by the speculation about the future, and we lose information about what we do know about the current profitability that might help us forecast future profitability. Conservative accounting (that expenses R&D immediately, for example) excludes such speculation and forces us to speculate over longer forecast horizons. Conservative accounting that is justified by uncertainty satisfies the fundamental analyst's desire to leave speculation to the forecasting and exclude it from the accounting.

The web page for this chapter lays out the accounting issues that determine the length of the forecast horizon.

The Quality of Cash Accounting and Discounted Cash Flow Analysis

This discussion brings us back to the point where we embraced accrual accounting valuation models (in Chapter 4). We did so because cash accounting—and discounted cash flow analysis—can lead to long forecasting horizons to uncover the underlying value, especially if free cash flows in the short term are negative. Using the language above, cash accounting is not good accounting for valuation.

Discounted cash flow analysis forecasts cash flows, and its seeming appeal is that it uses reliable numbers. Cash flows are said to be "real" and not affected by accrual accounting rules and estimates. "Cash is king" is the cry, so forecast cash. The implication is that cash flow forecasts are better quality than earnings forecasts for capturing value. But we saw earlier in the book that free cash flow is doubtful as a value-added measure. It is the "dividend" from the operations, not the value created by the operations.

To remind ourselves, Table 16.14 gives the free cash flows for Starbucks from 1994 to 1997. As $C - I = \text{OI} - \Delta\text{NOA}$, the first two lines give operating income and net operating assets. The free cash flows here are negative. Was Starbucks losing value over this period? If we were valuing the firm in 1993 and had been given these cash flows as short-term forecasts for 1994 to 1997, would we accept them as good quality indicators of profitability? As measures of cash flows they are of course "real." But they are not good quality for valuing the firm.

		1994	1995	1996	1997
Operating income		15,051	24,406	31,081	53,252
Net operating assets	93,589	191,416	342,648	412,958	578,237
Free cash flow ($C - I$)	—	(82,776)	(126,826)	(39,229)	(112,027)
Core profit margin (%)		5.3	5.2	4.5	5.6
Asset turnover		2.00	1.74	1.84	1.95
Core RNOA (%)		10.6	9.0	8.3	10.9
Growth in NOA (%)		104.5	80.5	20.6	40.0

TABLE 16.14
Starbucks
Corporation: Free
Cash Flows and
Accrual Accounting
Measures, 1994–1997
(in thousands of
dollars)

TABLE 16.15
Return on Common
Equity (ROCE),
Price-to-Book Ratios
(P/B), and Price-
Earnings Ratios (P/E)
for Varying Levels of
Levered Free Cash
Flow (FCF),
1973–1990

Source: Standard & Poor's
COMPUSTAT.

FCF Group	FCF/Price	ROCE	P/B	P/E
1	87.1%	4.7%	0.78	17.4
2	23.4	9.2	0.91	10.3
3	10.8	12.1	1.10	9.6
4	6.3	13.7	1.32	10.4
5	2.2	14.6	1.55	11.6
6	−1.4	13.2	1.58	13.0
7	−6.1	12.6	1.49	12.8
8	−13.4	11.6	1.36	12.5
9	−25.9	9.9	1.14	12.2
10	−78.8	4.2	0.94	22.7

Note: Firms are grouped into 10 groups according to their levered free cash flow, with the highest 10 percent in group 1 and the lowest 10 percent in group 10. The table gives median free cash flow (to stock price), ROCE, P/B, and P/E for each group. Based on all listed U.S. firms. The grouping is done each year, the numbers reported are averages from all years. Levered free cash flow is free cash flow minus after-tax interest and preferrred dividends.

In contrast, the accrual accounting numbers for Starbucks in Table 16.14—profit margins, asset turnover, RNOA, and growth in net operating assets—give some indication of profitability. They do not necessarily indicate long-run profitability, but they are a starting point to project how this firm can add value from profitability and growth. We begin by recognizing the current profitability and growth and then, with other information about the firm's business plan, product demand, and so on, we forecast into the future. The web page for this chapter discusses how one would combine the accrual accounting information for Starbucks with other information to reach a valuation. But staring at the free cash flows does not help. Starbucks's new investment each year is large relative to cash flow from operations, so forecasted free cash flows are negative. If investment continues apace as the firm expands into Europe and the Asia/Pacific region, forecasted free cash flows might be negative for a long time after 1997. The forecast horizon might have to be very long indeed to capture the value the firm can generate.

Table 16.15 shows how free cash flow (FCF) was related to return on common equity (ROCE) from 1973 to 1990. The 10 groups are from a ranking of all listed U.S. firms on their free cash flow (less interest on debt and preferred dividends) as a percentage of share price. Group 1 is firms with the top 10 percent of free cash flow and group 10 is firms with the lowest 10 percent. The second column gives the average free cash flow for the groups as a percentage of share price, and the third column gives the ROCE. The ROCE numbers tell you that free cash flow is not a good indication of firms' profitability: Lower ROCE numbers are associated with both low and high free cash flow and there's not much difference in ROCE over a wide range of positive and negative free cash flows. If ROCE is a value driver, then forecasting free cash flow is not likely to capture the value. The table shows further that current free cash flow is not a good indicator of the P/B ratio or the P/E ratio. Whereas ROCE varies with the level of P/B in the table, low P/B is associated with both high and low cash flows, and similarly so for P/E ratios. The amount of free cash flows that a firm generates is not a good indicator of the premium or the multiple of earnings at which the firm should trade.

In practice DCF analysts often adjust forecasted cash flows to get a better quality forecast. They recognize liabilities for pension costs and deferred taxes. They adjust investments for those investments they consider to be unnecessary for sustaining the cash flows. This effectively yields a normal depreciation charge. But any adjustment to a cash flow is an accrual that serves the role of producing higher quality measures of value added. The adjustments are effectively redoing the accounting with particular accrual methods. In the end, the quality of the forecast will depend on the quality of the added accruals, which raises the question of what is good accrual/accounting and what is poor accrual accounting.

The alternative approach is to start with GAAP earnings forecasts which already have many of the desired accruals. An analyst might be so distrustful of the estimates in accrual accounting as to back them out altogether. But he would have to then consider whether the resulting number—free cash flow—is really a higher quality number.

In a "fundamental" sense, the forecasting of accrual earnings is unavoidable. Even if we were satisfied with forecasted cash flows, it is difficult to imagine forecasting them without getting a feel for profitability. Try to forecast the cash flow statement without a forecasted income statement. How would you forecast investment without a sense of the profitability of investment? And how would you forecast the cash flow from operations without forecasting earnings and the profitability of investments? Indeed forecasting cash sales is more difficult than forecasting sales: One has to forecast customers' payment patterns as well as sales. Forecasting RNOA is particularly important. The RNOA, PM, and ATO give transparency; you see where the value is coming from. So prescriptions for DCF analysis require you to first forecast the earnings and then "back out the accruals" to get to the cash flows: $C - I = OI - \Delta NOA$. Thus much of the pro forma analysis we have been through is essential for DCF analysis. Having done the analysis, we must ask whether the accruals should be eliminated if the result is a lower quality number.

Discounted cash flow analysis always gives the same valuation as residual earnings techniques if the forecast horizon is long enough. If one forecasts free cash flow to steady state, one recovers the valuation. Again, the issue is a question of working with reasonable horizons. But there are also circumstances where the DCF valuation is the same as the residual earnings valuation with the same forecast horizon. The web page for this chapter lays out these circumstances and also contrasts other features of DCF and residual earnings valuation.

Summary

Residual earnings and abnormal earning growth are accounting measures. So are measures marketed by consultants as "economic profit," "economic value added," and the like. These measures are not necessarily measures of (real) value added. They are measures that are determined by real economic factors, but also by the accounting used in their calculation.

In a series of examples, this chapter has shown how accounting can create earnings, profitability, and residual earnings. And it has shown how accounting can create growth in earnings and growth in residual earnings, with the resultant effect on P/B ratios and P/E ratios. A benchmark case of a firm that adds no value with its investment was used to demonstrate the accounting effects. In general, profitability and growth result from both accounting effects and real economic factors that create value.

The chapter has shown that the way to view accounting methods is in terms of their effect on book value, for it is the accounting for book value that generates higher profitability and growth. So accounting methods were categorized as "conservative," "liberal," or "neutral" depending on their effect on book value. Indeed, while people often think of accounting methods in terms of their effect on earnings, the chapter has shown that the accounting does not affect earnings or P/E ratios if investment is constant. But the accounting does, in this case, affect profitability, residual earnings measures, and P/B ratios. Only if investment is increasing does the accounting affect earnings and P/E ratios, and in this case it creates growth in earnings and residual earnings even though no value is added by the growing investment.

The Web Connection

Find the following on the web page for this chapter:

- More examples of the effects of conservative accounting on profitability and earnings growth.

- A spreadsheet program for analyzing the effect of conservative accounting on profitability and growth.

- An examination of the accounting adjustments that consultants make to measure "economic value added."

- A look at cases in which discounted cash flow methods give the same valuation as accrual accounting methods with the same forecast horizon.

- An examination of the accounting issues involved in making valuations from short-term forecasts, with an application to Starbucks Corporation.

Despite the fact that book value and earnings are determined by both economic and accounting factors, the chapter comes with the assurance that if accrual accounting techniques are applied, firms can be valued and value added can be measured. The proviso is that steady state must be forecasted so that a continuing value can be calculated. The chapter also reconsidered the case where the analyst removes the accruals completely and uses discounted cash flow analysis, reiterating that this cash accounting is poor quality for value.

Key Concepts

accounting value added is (accounting) earnings in excess of that required for book value to earn at the required return. Compare with **economic value added**. *561*

conservative accounting is accounting that understates assets on the balance sheet or overstates liabilities. Compare with **liberal accounting**. *561*

economic value added is value generated from investment in excess of that to compensate for the required return on the investment. Compare with **accounting value added**. *561*

hidden reserve is income that has not been recognized in the past because conservative accounting has been practiced. Equivalently, hidden reserves are amounts of net assets that have not been recognized on the balance sheet because of conservative accounting. An example is the LIFO reserve. *570*

liberal accounting is accounting that overstates (or gives relatively higher) assets on the balance sheet or understates liabilities. Compare with **conservative accounting**. *561*

liquidation of hidden reserve is an increase in income that arises from slowing investments in assets that have been measured with conservative accounting. *570*

neutral accounting is accounting that yields an accounting rate of return equal to the required return for investments that add no (economic) value. *561*

value conservation principle is the principle by which value is insensitive to the accounting for book values: Accounting methods affect forecasts of residual earnings but, because of the offsetting effect on book value, do not affect value. *562*

The Analyst's Toolkit

Additional acronyms: NOA net operating assets; OI operating income; P/B price-to-book ratio; P/E price-earnings ratio; PM profit margin; PV present value; R&D research and development; RE residual earnings; ReOI residual operating income; RNOA return on net operating assets; ROCE return on common equity

Concept Questions

C16.1. Firms with a return on net operating assets (RNOA) that is higher than the required return on operations are adding value with their investments and so should trade at a premium over their book value. Is this statement correct?

C16.2. Why are LIFO accounting and the expensing of R&D expenditures referred to as conservative accounting policies?

C16.3. Explain how intrinsic price-to-book (P/B) ratios are affected by conservative accounting (such as expensing R&D expenditures).

C16.4. Does conservative accounting result in higher or lower accounting rates of return?

C16.5. Explain how intrinsic P/E ratios are affected by conservative accounting (such as expensing R&D expenditures).

C16.6. Consultants talk of "economic profit," or "economic value added." What is it? Can it be observed?

C16.7. How is it that accounting policies affect the measurement of residual income but the value calculated using residual income methods may not be affected by accounting policies?

C16.8. A firm that uses LIFO accounting for inventory in times of rising inventory costs will always report lower profit margins than if it used FIFO. Is this correct?

C16.9. A firm using LIFO accounting for inventory is likely to have a lower inventory turnover ratio than one using FIFO. Is this correct?

C16.10. Firms with anticipated earnings-per-share growth are worth more. Is this statement always correct?

C16.11. What is a "hidden reserve"? What does it mean to "release hidden reserves"?

C16.12. What is meant by "steady state"?

C16.13. In the United Kingdom, firms revalue tangible assets upward and recognize the value of brands on the balance sheet. In the United States, this accounting is not permitted. In which country would you expect the average return on common equity for firms to be higher?

C16.14. On January 29, 1999, *The Wall Street Journal* reported: "Sears, Roebuck & Co. is moving toward more conservative accounting methods used by competing credit-card issuers, which will boost its loan losses by about $200 million during the next 5 quarters." What effect will this new policy have on future return on net operating assets?

C16.15. Expensing research and development costs raises accounting quality issues similar to those raised in cash accounting. Explain.

Exercises

E16.1. **Inventory Accounting, P/B, and P/E Ratios: Ford Motor Company (Medium)**

Ford Motor Company uses the last in, first out (LIFO) method for most of its inventories in its Automotive Division. The amounts of the LIFO reserve reported in footnotes for 1999 were

	1999	1998
LIFO reserve	$1.1 billion	$1.2 billion

Ford reported total shareholders' equity of $27.537 billion at the end of 1999 and $23.409 billion at the end of 1998, and it reported earnings for 1999 of $7.237 billion. The firm's 1.21 billion outstanding shares traded at $53 at the end of 1999. Ford faces a statutory tax rate of 36 percent.

a. What would have been Ford's shareholders' equity at the end of 1999 and 1998 if it had used the first in, first out (FIFO) method to record its inventories?

b. What return on common equity would Ford have reported in 1999 if it had used FIFO?

c. Compare Ford's price-to-book ratios at the end of 1999 under LIFO and FIFO, and explain the difference.

d. Compare the firm's P/E ratio under LIFO and FIFO, and explain the difference.

E16.2. **The Accounting for Research and Development and Economic Profit Measures (Hard)**

Many consultants recognize that expensing R&D investments gives a poor indication of the performance of a firm or its managers because investing in R&D results in lower income. So they adjust GAAP accounting by capitalizing R&D expenditures and amortizing the capitalized amount over the estimated life of the revenues that flow from the expenditures.

a. Below is a series of R&D expenditures that are expected for the years 2000 to 2005 under a firm's R&D program (in millions of dollars). The R&D program began in 1999 with a $100 million investment. Expected net operating assets for the firm are also given for net assets other than those created by the R&D expenditures. Expenditures for R&D are expected to generate $1.60 of revenue over each of the subsequent five years for each dollar spent. Expenses other than R&D expenses are expected to be 80 percent of sales.

	1999A	2000E	2001E	2002E	2003E	2004E	2005E
R&D expenditure	100	100	100	100	100	100	100
Net operating assets	80	80	80	80	80	80	80

Calculate expected operating income, return on net operating assets (RNOA), and residual operating income for each year, 2000 to 2005, under GAAP accounting (where R&D expenditures are expensed against income). Use a required return for operations of 10 percent.

b. Now calculate the RNOA and residual operating income for each year under an accounting that capitalizes R&D expenditures and amortizes them over five years.

c. Compare the RNOA and residual operating income calculated under the two accounting treatments for each year. Why are they different?

d. Forecast RNOA and residual operating income for 2006 under the two accounting treatments. Why do these forecasts differ?

e. Value the firm at the end of 1999 using the two different accounting treatments. Do the valuations differ? Why?

f. If you tried to value this firm by forecasting only to 2002, what difficulties would you face under the two methods?

E16.3. Depreciation Methods, Profitability, and Valuation (Medium)

A start-up firm embarks on an investment program in 2000 to manufacture and market a new switching device to be used in communications. The program requires an initial investment of $600 million in plant and equipment, increasing by $100 million each year for four years up to 2004, and then continuing at $1,000 million per year thereafter.

The founders of the firm are keen to look profitable when they expect to take the firm public in an initial public offering (IPO) in early 2005. After awarding him stock options, they ask the newly hired chief financial officer (CFO) to prepare pro forma statements of earnings and return on investment. The marketing manager supplies the CFO with the following sales forecasts (in millions of dollars), and he and the production manager estimate that operational expenses before depreciation will be 70 percent of sales.

	2001E	2002E	2003E	2004E	2005E	2006E	2007E
Sales	250	1,530	3,540	4,295	4,305	4,410	4,500

Sales after 2007 are expected to be at the level of those in 2007.

The CFO understands that with the rapid technological change that is expected, estimated useful lives of assets are quite uncertain and thinks he can justify either a three-year estimated life or a five-year estimated life for the plant and equipment. So he prepares two sets of pro formas, one depreciating the investments in plant and equipment straight-line over three years, and one depreciating them straight-line over five years.

a. Prepare the operating section of the pro forma income statements and balance sheets under both depreciation methods. Ignore tax effects.

b. Which set of pro formas shows the firm to be more profitable in 2004, just prior to the anticipated public offering? Why?

c. The CFO wishes to show the management that the depreciation method does not affect the intrinsic value of the firm at the time of the IPO. Prepare the calculations to give this demonstration, using the hurdle rate of 10 percent that the founders have set for investments.

d. Despite your calculation, the founders insist that the market will give a higher value if higher earnings are reported at the time of the IPO. What would be your reply to them?

e. The CFO points out that his and the founders' stock options vest in 2009, not at the time of the IPO in 2005. He therefore suggests that the focus should be on profits expected to be reported in 2009. What arguments might be made to justify using one depreciation method over the other?

E16.4. Purchase and Pooling Accounting and Rates of Return: MS Inc. and PPE Inc. (Hard)

MS Inc. and PPE Inc. are two fictitious companies that have been used in examples in Chapters 14 and 15 and in Exercise E15.7 (in Chapter 15).

The balance sheets of the two firms at Year 0 are reproduced here. MS Inc.'s balance sheet (Exhibit 16.1) is measured at market value so that its equity value is equal to its book value of $15.7 million or, with $15.7 million shares outstanding, $1.00 per share. PPE Inc.'s balance sheet (Exhibit 16.2) is not measured at market value, so its pro forma (forecasted) income statement for Year 1 is given to help with a valuation. Analysts forecast that operating income and residual operating income after Year 1 will continue at the same level as in Year 1. So the value of PPE's equity, with a cost of capital for operations of 11.34 percent, is $83.22 million or, with 83.22 million shares outstanding, $1.00 per share.

The two firms announce at the end of Year 0 that MS Inc. will acquire PPE Inc. with an exchange of one share in PPE Inc. for one share of MS Inc. Analysts see the merger as one of a portfolio company with a manufacturing operation, yielding no value-added synergies from the merger. Accordingly, they forecast that future earnings from the combined firm will be the sum of those for the individual firms.

a. Construct the balance sheet for the new combined firm if pooling accounting is used in the merger. Compare this balance sheet to that which would be prepared if purchasing accounting were used in the merger.

b. Calculate the unlevered price-to-book ratios for the new firm under pooling and purchasing accounting.

c. Prepare operating income and net operating asset forecasts for the combined firm for the next five years using analysts' forecasts for PPE above. Assume that the marketable securities held by MS Inc. in Year 0 will continue to be held and will earn at a rate of 11.34 percent, with any dividends reinvested in the securities. Prepare the forecasts for both purchase and pooling accounting. For purchase accounting, amortize the goodwill on purchase over 20 years. For each of the five years, also forecast

   (1) Return on net operating assets.

   (2) Residual operating income (with a required return of 11.34 percent). Compare these two measures under purchase and pooling accounting. Why do they differ? Compare the way in which these two measures change over time. Can you explain the difference?

d. Calculate the value of the merged firm from the two sets of pro formas using purchase and pooling accounting. Do the two values differ?

e. Suppose that MS Inc. paid for PPE Inc. by issuing 1.5 of its shares for each PPE share. Was value created or lost in this transaction?

f. Prepare the balance sheets and the five-year pro formas under purchase and pooling accounting for the transaction on the terms in part (e). Which type of accounting do you think is more revealing of the value created by the merger?

Real World Connection

See Exercise E15.7 in Chapter 15.

EXHIBIT 16.1

MS INC.
Balance Sheet, December 31, Year 0

Assets	Year 0	Prior Year	Liabilities and Equity	Year 0	Prior Year
Marketable equity securities (at market)	23.4	20.3	Long-term debt	7.7	7.0
			Common shareholders' equity	15.7	13.3
Net operating assets	23.4	20.3		23.4	20.3

EXHIBIT 16.2

PPE INC.
Balance Sheet, December 31, Year 0

Assets	Year 0	Prior Year	Liabilities and Equity	Year 0	Prior Year
Property, plant, and equipment (at cost less accumulated depreciation)	74.4	69.9	Long-term debt	7.7	7.0
			Common shareholders' equity	66.7	62.9
Net operating assets	74.4	69.9		74.4	69.9

PPE INC.
Pro Forma Income Statement for Year 1

Operating income	10.31
Net financial expense	0.77
Earnings	9.54

E16.5. The Quality of Free Cash Flow and Residual Operating Income: Coca-Cola Company (Easy)

The Coca-Cola Company reports a number called "economic profit" that is very similar to residual operating income (see Minicase 13.2 in Chapter 13). It also reports free cash flow in its annual summary of selected financial data. The respective numbers for 1992–1999 are given below (in millions of dollars), along with what Coke calls total capital (similar to net operating assets) and return on total capital (similar to return on net operating assets):

	1992	1993	1994	1995	1996	1997	1998	1999
Economic profit	1,300	1,549	1,896	2,291	2,718	3,325	2,480	1,128
Free cash flow	873	1,623	2,146	2,102	2,413	3,533	1,876	2,332
Total capital	7,095	7,684	8,744	9,456	10,669	11,186	13,552	15,740
Return on capital	29.4%	31.2%	32.7%	34.9%	36.7%	39.4%	30.2%	18.2%

a. Economic profit and free cash flow are similar, in most years, and their growth patterns are similar. Why?

b. Based on this past history, would you be indifferent in valuing Coke using discounted cash flow methods or residual operating income methods?

Real World Connection

See Exercise E4.6 and Minicase M4.2 in Chapter 4, Exercise E5.13 in Chapter 5, Minicase M13.2 in Chapter 13, Exercise E14.6 in Chapter 14, and Exercise E15.4 in Chapter 15 for related material on the Coca-Cola Company.

E16.6. Research and Development Expenditures and Valuation (Medium)

A new pharmaceutical firm has patented a technology and has committed to spending $350 million annually for the next five years to develop further products from the technology. The program is currently spending $350 million on R&D, yielding $1,000 million in sales and a loss of $150 million after R&D, production and advertising costs, and taxes. However, revenues from the R&D are expected to grow by $500 million per year over the next five years, reaching $3,500 million. After that, revenues are expected to grow at 5 percent per year, with growth in R&D expenditures also of 5 percent per year to support the additional sales. Production and advertising costs are expected to be at the same percentage of sales as currently. The firm requires an investment in net operating assets such as to maintain an asset turnover of 1.4. Currently net operating assets stand at $714 million.

a. Value the firm using a hurdle rate for operations of 10 percent.

b. Comment on the quality of the earnings forecasts for the next three years as a basis for valuation.

c. Calculate the forecasted R&D-to-sales ratio for each of the next five years. Why is this ratio an indicator of the quality of the earnings forecasted?

E16.7. The Quality of Forecasted Residual Operating Income and Free Cash Flow (Medium)

A start-up begins operations in 2000 by investing $400 million in plant and equipment. It expects to increase investment by $40 million each year, indefinitely, depreciating it straight-line over two years. The investment program is expected to generate sales for the next four years, as follows (in millions of dollars):

	2000A	2001E	2002E	2003E	2004E	2005E
Sales		240	484	530	576	622
Investment	400	440	480	520	560	600

a. Prepare a schedule of pro forma operating income, return on net operating assets (RNOA), residual operating income, and net operating assets for the years 2001 to 2005. Depreciation of the investment is the only operating expense. The firm has a 10 percent hurdle rate for its operations. Calculate the value of this firm using residual operating income methods.

b. Forecast free cash flow for 2001 to 2005. Do you think that forecasted free cash flow is a good quality number on which to base a valuation? What features in the pro forma explain why the pattern of free cash flows is different from that for residual operating income?

E16.8. The Quality of Return on Net Operating Assets Forecasts (Medium)

A firm begins an investment program in 2000 with an investment of $400 million. The program involves increasing investments by 5 percent per year up to 2004, then continuing investments after 2004 at the same level as in 2004. The projected investments, along with the sales they are expected to generate (in millions of dollars) are:

	2000	2001	2002	2003	2004	2005	2006	2007
Investment	400	420	441	463	486	486	486	486
Sales		240	472	496	520	546	559	559

The firm charges 10 percent of the investment each year to income as start-up costs. Depreciation, the only other operating expense, is charged on a straight-line basis over two years.

a. Forecast return on net operating assets (RNOA) from this investment program for each year 2001 to 2007. Is the RNOA for years 2001 to 2004 a good indicator of subsequent RNOA? Why or why not? Table 16.7 will be of help to you in answering this question.

b. Value the firm from your forecasts using a 10 percent discount rate. How does the quality of RNOA forecasted for years 2001 to 2004 affect the valuation?

Minicases

M16.1

ACCOUNTING VALUE AND ECONOMIC VALUE: SARA LEE CORPORATION

Sara Lee Corporation is a consumer products company with operations in more than 140 countries. Its packaged meat, frozen foods, and bakery products are displayed on most supermarket shelves in the United States, and it markets leading coffee and tea brands, Kiwi brand shoe care products, body care products, insecticides, and air fresheners. It runs the fourth largest food service operation in the United States, supplying both institutions and restaurants. Sara Lee apparel lines include such brand names as Bali, Hanes, Wonderbra, Bleecker, and L'eggs, with licenses for other products under the DKNY brand.

By 1996 Sara Lee had become a far-flung but vertically integrated conglomerate. Management decided to restructure. The restructuring program was explained in the 1998 annual report in the following words:

> In fiscal 1998 Sara Lee embarked on a program designed to reshape the Corporation to enable the Corporation to produce higher returns on a smaller asset base. Sara Lee's decision to undertake the program was prompted by fundamental changes in the economic environment in which it operates. Historically, Sara Lee has manufactured the branded consumer products it markets. The Corporation's strategy was to vertically integrate the manufacturing processes into the business in order to assure a readily available product source that met quality standards. In recent years, alternative sources of competitively priced manufactured products have increased and excess manufacturing capacity has developed in the markets for certain of the Corporation's products. These competitive sources have allowed the Corporation to purchase needed commodities from a number of suppliers at prices which are less than, or equal to, prior manufacturing costs. These forces also create opportunities for Sara Lee to build stockholder value and Sara Lee intends to take advantage of these opportunities by focusing Sara Lee's energies on knowledge-based skills that will characterize successful companies of the future.
>
> Sara Lee announced its new strategic direction on September 15, 1997. The program is intended to more tightly focus Sara Lee's business activity and make Sara Lee more competitive. The goal of the program is to create an organization that is less vertically integrated (by divesting, to the extent practical and possible, operating assets), owns fewer fixed assets and uses knowledge-based skills to develop and market products. Sara Lee has coined the term "de-verticalization" to describe this process. Sara Lee has also committed to repurchase $3 billion of the Corporation's common stock by the end of fiscal year 2000. As of August 31, 1998, Sara Lee had completed the repurchase of approximately 29 million shares at a total cost of $1.6 billion. In connection with Sara Lee's adoption of a new strategic focus, Sara Lee also restructured its worldwide operations. The restructuring resulted in an after-tax charge of $1.625 billion in the second quarter of fiscal 1998. The planned restructuring activities include the disposition of 116 manufacturing and distribution facilities. The restructuring charge was related primarily to the sale and write-down of assets that Sara Lee has determined it does not need to own in order to fulfill its primary mission of building brands on a global basis. Of the total after-tax provision, 89%, or approximately $1.45 billion, is non-cash and 11%, or approximately $176 million, will require cash outflows.

Sara Lee was embracing the concept of "weightlessness" that appeared in management textbooks at the time. By selling off its many factories, outsourcing, and turning itself into a "knowledge-based" brand management company with a lower asset base, it hoped to add value.

The stock market liked the concept. The share price increased from $20 per share in September 1997 when the announcement was made to $30 by the following March. However, the stock price subsequently declined over the course of 1999 to a low of $15 in March 2000 as investors became disillusioned with the results of the reorganization.

Exhibit 16.3 is a summary of Sara Lee's annual financial statements from 1995 to 1999, and Exhibit 16.4 offers some more detail on the restructuring. You can see from the balance sheets how assets declined (on increasing sales), particularly property assets. Common equity declined from $4.280 billion in 1997 to 1.266 billion in 1999.

EXHIBIT 16.3

SARA LEE CORPORATION
Condensed Consolidated Balance Sheets
(dollars in millions except per-share data)

	July 3, 1999	June 27, 1998	June 28, 1997	June 29, 1996	July 1, 1995
Assets					
Cash and equivalents	$ 279	$ 273	$ 272	$ 243	$ 202
Trade accounts receivable (net)	1,744	1,800	1,841	1,728	1,653
Inventories					
Finished goods	1,710	1,809	1,803	1,802	1,782
Work in process	470	443	497	381	423
Materials and supplies	463	630	673	624	625
	2,643	2,882	2,973	2,807	2,830
Other current assets	321	265	305	303	243
Total current assets	4,987	5,220	5,391	5,081	4,928
Trademarks and other assets	533	501	536	636	615
Property					
Land	103	126	126	132	136
Buildings and improvements	1,762	1,895	2,008	1,924	1,879
Machinery and equipment	2,845	2,742	3,777	3,657	3,462
Construction in progress	261	184	293	263	206
	4,971	4,947	6,204	5,976	5,683
Accumulated depreciation	2,802	2,857	3,125	2,969	2,719
Property, net	2,169	2,090	3,079	3,007	2,964
Intangible assets, net	2,832	3,178	3,947	3,878	3,924
	$10,521	$10,989	$12,953	$12,602	$12,431
Operating liabilities	$ 4,982	$ 5,231	$ 4,972	$ 4,839	$ 4,745
Financial liabilities	3,660	3,382	3,178	2,920	3,228
Minority interest in subsidiaries	613	560	523	523	519
Common equity	1,266	1,816	4,280	4,320	3,939
	$10,521	$10,989	$12,953	$12,602	$12,431

Minority interest consists of preferred stock in subsidiary corporations.

(continued)

EXHIBIT 16.3
(Continued)

SARA LEE CORPORATION
Consolidated Statements of Income
(in millions except per-share data)

	Years Ended			
	July 3, 1999	June 27, 1998	June 28, 1997	June 29, 1996
Net sales	$20,012	$20,011	$19,734	$18,624
Cost of sales	12,208	12,331	12,267	11,470
Selling, general, and administrative expenses	6,053	5,907	5,824	5,603
Interest expense	237	224	202	228
Interest income	(96)	(48)	(43)	(55)
Unusual items				
Product recall	76	—	—	
Gain on sale of business	(137)	—	—	
Restructuring charge	—	2,040	—	
	18,341	20,454	18,250	17,246
Income (loss) before income taxes	1,671	(443)	1,484	1,378
Income taxes	480	80	475	462
Net income (loss)	1,191	(523)	1,009	916
Preferred dividends	(12)	(14)	(26)	(27)
Net income (loss) available for common stockholders	$ 1,179	$ (537)	$ 983	$ 889
Net income (loss) per common share—basic	$ 1.31	$ (0.57)	$ 1.02	$ 0.92

Condensed Consolidated Statements of Cash Flows
(dollars in millions)

	Years Ended			
	July 3, 1999	June 27, 1998	June 28, 1997	June 29, 1996
Net cash from operating activities	$ 1,603	$ 1,935	$1,552	$1,304
Investment Activities				
Purchases of property and equipment	(535)	(474)	(547)	(542)
Acquisitions of businesses	(234)	(393)	(674)	(216)
Dispositions of investments and businesses	412	451	114	12
Sales of property	158	140	59	49
Other	7	1	6	4
Net cash used in investment activities	(192)	(275)	(1,042)	(693)
Financing Activities				
Issuances of common stock	111	86	93	93
Purchases of common stock	(1,279)	(1,500)	(393)	(103)
Redemption of preferred stock	—	(200)	(100)	
Issuance of equity securities by subsidiary	50	—	—	—
Borrowings of long-term debt	20	594	495	354
Repayments of long-term debt	(284)	(296)	(252)	(369)
Short-term borrowings, net	451	113	119	(135)
Payments of dividends	(464)	(447)	(430)	(395)
Net cash used in financing activities	(1,395)	(1,650)	(468)	(555)
Effect of changes in foreign exchange rates on cash	(10)	(9)	(13)	(15)
Increase in cash and equivalents	6	1	29	41
Cash and equivalents at beginning of year	273	272	243	202
Cash and equivalents at end of year	$ 279	$ 273	$ 272	$ 243

EXHIBIT 16.4   **Excerpt from the Financial Statement Footnotes for 1999**

Restructuring Provision
(in millions)

	Original Restructuring Reserves	Write-Down of Long-Lived Assets to Net Realizable Value	Recognition of Curtailment Loss and Special Termination Benefits	Cash Payments	Foreign Exchange Impacts	Restructuring Reserves as of July 3, 1999
Anticipated losses associated with disposal of long-lived assets	$1,729	$(1,729)	$ —	$ —	$—	$ —
Pension and social costs	219	—	(39)	(107)	—	73
Anticipated expenditures to close and dispose of idled facilities—includes noncancelable lease obligations	47	—	—	(31)	—	16
Anticipated loss associated with the disposal of equity and cost method investments	45	(45)	—	—	—	—
	2,040	(1,774)	(39)	(138)	—	89
Foreign exchange impacts	—	—	—	—	(8)	(8)
Total restructuring reserves	$2,040	$(1,774)	$(39)	$(138)	$ (8)	$ 81

In the second quarter of 1998, the Corporation provided for the cost of restructuring its worldwide operations. The planned restructuring activities include the disposition of 116 manufacturing and distribution facilities—86 facilities are owned and 30 are leased. This restructuring provision reduced income before income taxes, net income, and net income per common share in 1998 by $2,040, $1,625, and $3.46 per share, respectively. The 1998 pretax income includes charges for restructuring as follows: Branded Apparel—$1,574; Sara Lee Foods—$208; Household and Body Care—$185; Coffee and Tea—$71; and Foodservice—$2.

A. From the financial statements, track Sara Lee's profitability over the years from 1996 to 1999. Track both return on net operating assets (RNOA) and return on common equity (ROCE). Also track residual operating income over a 9 percent hurdle rate. Analysts were forecasting earnings per share of $1.35 for the June 30, 2000, fiscal year on 884 million outstanding shares. Use this forecast to predict RNOA, ROCE, and residual operating income for fiscal 2000. Use a 37 percent tax rate if needed in calculations. You will see that the reorganization increased the firm's profitability significantly. Why, then, did the stock price decline?

B. The income statements show that Sara Lee had considerable growth in earnings per share (before unusual items) over the years. Why might stock prices decline while earnings per share increase?

C. In April 2000, when the stock was trading at $16 and a P/E ratio of 12 on 1999 earnings, analysts were forecasting earnings per share of $1.35 for the June 30, 2000, fiscal year, $1.50 for the June 2001 fiscal year, and 11.5 percent earnings-per-share growth for the five years thereafter. The firm was paying a 53 cents per share annual dividend at the time. What is the per-share value of the equity and the P/E ratio that is implied by these forecasts?

M16.2

ADVERTISING, LOW QUALITY ACCOUNTING, AND VALUATION: E*TRADE

New businesses take time to get established, and the new Internet firms of the late 1990s were no exception. Internet portal firms and e-commerce firms traded at high multiples of sales on the promise of large profits, but most of them were generating losses from their sales.

In statements to the press, these firms maintained that their "business model" required them to incur substantial losses in order to generate future profits. Investments were required in infrastructure. Considerable expenditure was required for advertising and promotion to establish a customer base and to create brand recognition. So these firms appealed to investors to ignore the bottom line and focus rather on their ability to generate revenues. Accordingly, the price-to-sales ratio became the typical multiplier that investors referred to. And analysts referred to other indicators like "hit rates" and "page views" (on websites) to assess the price-to-sales ratio.

In arguing that the losses they were reporting were not indicative of the value in their business model, Internet entrepreneurs argued that the GAAP accounting they were required to use was of low quality. But clearly investors were left with the question of whether these firms would actually become profitable in the end and whether the size of the profits would justify the high stock prices at which these firms traded. Rather than the crude indicators like hit rates, they looked for more substantial financial analysis.

ONLINE TRADING FIRMS

During 1999 there was a dramatic shift by investors to online stock trading on the Internet. E*Trade, TD Waterhouse, National Discount Brokers, and others battled with Charles Schwab, the traditional discount broker, and with each other for market share. Morgan Stanley Dean Witter, a more traditional broker, offered online trading through its Discovery brokerage. Merrill Lynch, after initially indicating that it might shun the online business, entered the fray in late 1999 with a $29.95 per-trade fee.

Figures as of September 1999 for some of the firms selling online trading services follow. Earnings and sales are rolling 12-month numbers to June 30, 1999 (M = millions; B = billions):

	Sales	Eps	Market Value	P/E Ratio	Price-to-Book Ratio	Price-to-Sales Ratio
E*Trade	$464M	−0.23	$ 5.75B	—	5.5	12.4
TD Waterhouse	896M	0.25	5.13B	47	2.6	5.7
National Discount Brokers	250M	1.28	458.6M	20	2.6	1.8
Ameritrade	274M	0.15	3.28B	119	9.2	12.0
Charles Schwab	3.361B	4.11	27.6B	56	14.4	8.2

In the fall of 1999, these firms began an advertising war. In the industry, market share is referred to as "share of voice." Customers are sticky, it is said: They tend to stay with the same brokerage, so attracting them—and building a brand name to attract them—is seen as the driver of ultimate success.

Schwab, with a large discount brokerage business prior to the advent of online trading, led with a 25 percent share of voice on the Internet. But in early 1999, E*Trade increased its share to 14 percent with what was judged a very successful advertising campaign on prime-time TV shows such as "Ally McBeal" and "E.R." and on the Super Bowl, the most expensive advertising time of all. Others imitated so that by the end of 1999 it was said that these firms had committed to a total of $1.5 billion in advertising over the subsequent 18 months.[1] To give a sense of perspective, this amount is roughly equal to the annual advertising budget of Coca-Cola.

Estimates varied, but industry analysts maintained that in a market saturated with competitors, it takes $400 to $500 in advertising and inducements to sign up each new customer, with repeat advertising of $100 per customer to retain them and maintain the brand.

E*TRADE

E*Trade was one of the first online trading firms to challenge Schwab and the traditional brokers. It spent $322 million on sales marketing for its fiscal year ended September 30, 1999, increasing the number of trading accounts by 1 million to 1.55 million and producing revenues of $657 million. Based on its marketing expenses for the first quarter of fiscal 2000, its annual advertising budget was running at $450 million.

Exhibit 16.5 presents summary financial statements for E Trade Group, the firm that runs E*Trade, for the September 1999 fiscal year.

A. Why are the earnings reported by start-up firms considered to be a "low quality" number?

B. Why should investors be wary of price-to-sales ratios? Why should they be skeptical about hit rates and page views on websites?

C. Develop an analysis that tests E*Trade's business model with the marketing information in the case.

D. E Trade Group traded at $25 per share at the end of September 1999, giving it a price-to-sales ratio of 10.5. Given your analysis in part (C), was the firm appropriately priced at the time?

E. What other strategies might E*Trade pursue to add value?

F. By early 2000, the number of online brokerage firms had exploded to about 140 and competition was fierce. The industry needed consolidation, it was said, to deal with the glut in capacity. Should E*Trade consider acquisitions to consolidate the dominant position it holds and compete more effectively with Charles Schwab? Stock market values for the larger online firms in the preceding table were such as to value each customer account at about $3,000 each.

Real World Connection
See Exercise E3.7 in Chapter 3 on Charles Schwab's valuation.

---

[1] As reported in Joseph Kahn's article, "The Media Business: Advertising: The On-Line Brokerage Battle," *The New York Times*, October 4, 1999, p. C1. Copyright © 1999 by The New York Times Co. Reprinted with permission. Text not being quoted, but is cited in publication.

EXHIBIT 16.5

E TRADE GROUP INC.
Consolidated Balance Sheets
(in thousands, except per-share amounts)

	September 30	
	1999	1998
Assets		
Cash and equivalents	$ 124,801	$ 71,317
Cash and investments required to be segregated under federal or other regulations	104,500	7,400
Brokerage receivables—net	2,912,581	1,365,247
Mortgage-backed securities	1,426,053	1,012,163
Loans receivable—net	2,154,509	904,854
Investments	830,329	812,093
Property and equipment—net	178,854	54,805
Goodwill and other intangibles	17,211	19,672
Other assets	159,386	101,372
Total assets	$7,908,224	$4,348,923
Liabilities and Shareowners' Equity		
Liabilities		
Brokerage payables	$2,824,212	$1,244,513
Banking deposits	2,162,682	1,209,470
Borrowings by bank subsidiary	1,267,474	876,935
Subordinated notes	0	29,855
Accounts payable, accrued and other liabilities	203,971	101,920
Total liabilities	6,458,339	3,462,693
Company-obligated mandatorily redeemable preferred securities	30,584	38,385
Shareowners' equity		
(275 million shares outstanding in 1999)	1,419,301	847,845
Total liabilities and shareowners' equity	$7,908,224	$4,348,923

Consolidated Statements of Operations
(in thousands, except per-share amounts)

	Years Ended September 30	
	1999	1998
Revenues		
Transaction revenues	$ 355,830	$162,097
Interest income	368,053	185,804
Global and institutional	110,959	95,829
Other	40,543	28,163
Gross revenues	875,385	471,893
Interest expense	(215,452)	(120,334)
Provision for loan losses	(2,783)	(905)
Net revenues	657,150	350,654
Cost of services	292,910	145,018
Operating Expenses		
Selling and marketing	321,620	124,408
Technology development	76,878	33,926
General and administrative	102,138	50,067
Merger-related expenses	7,174	1,167
Total operating expenses	507,810	209,568
Total cost of services and operating expenses	800,720	354,586
Operating income (loss)	$(143,570)	$ (3,932)

EXHIBIT 16.5
(Continued)

	Years Ended September 30	
	1999	**1998**
Nonoperating Income (Expense)		
Corporate interest income—net	$ 19,639	$ 11,036
Gain on sale of investments	54,093	0
Equity in income (losses) of investments	(8,838)	531
Other	(71)	(1,098)
Total nonoperating income	64,823	10,469
Pretax income (loss)	(78,747)	6,537
Income tax expenses (benefit)	(31,306)	1,873
Minority interest in subsidiary	2,197	1,362
Income (loss) before cumulative effect of accounting change and extraordinary loss	(49,638)	3,302
Cumulative effect of accounting change, net of tax	(469)	0
Extraordinary loss on early extinguishment of subordinated debt, net of tax	(1,985)	0
Net income (loss)	(52,092)	3,302
Preferred stock dividends	222	2,352
Income (loss) applicable to common stock	($52,314)	$ 950
Income (loss) per share before cumulative effect of accounting change and extraordinary loss		
Basic	($0.19)	$0.00
Diluted	($0.19)	$0.00
Income (loss) per share		
Basic	($0.20)	$0.00
Diluted	($0.20)	$0.00

M16.3

The Quality of Accounting Rates of Return: Starbucks

Analysts base their forecasts of future rates of return from operations on past rates of return. Difficulties arise when rates of return are distorted by the accounting. In particular, if a firm is growing, past rates of return may not be a good indicator of future rates of return if the firm expenses start-up costs, advertising and promotion costs, and research and development costs. Increasing expenditures on these items can depress rates of return, which may then recover once the growth stage is over.

Starbucks Corporation is the world's largest specialty coffee retailer, with sales of $1.68 billion in 1999 and a market capitalization in March 2000 of nearly $8 billion. Starbucks purchases and roasts coffees and sells them through its own retail coffee shops in high traffic, high-visibility locations, along with teas, pastries, coffeemaking equipment, and specialty items. About 70 percent of its products are beverages served in the coffee shops, 15 percent are food items, and 10 percent are whole coffee beans. By the end of 1999 the firm operated 2,135 stores in the United States, Canada, and the United Kingdom, with plans for expansion elsewhere. Eighty-four percent of revenues came from these stores, with the remainder from sales to wholesalers, sales through its website, and licensing fees. Visit the firm's website at www.starbucks.com.

Starbucks has enjoyed a following among investors who have seen it as a strong growth company. At the end of March 2000 it was trading at $42 per share, or 75 times earnings reported for the fiscal year ending September 1999. Its price-to-book ratio was 8.0.

At this price-to-book ratio the market expected the firm to generate a considerable rate of return on book value. Yet Starbucks's financial statements for the past several years revealed close to average rates of return. The rates of return from 1993 to 1997 were given in Table 16.14; it appears that that market viewed these rates of return as low quality as indicators of long-run profitability. The financial statements for 1997 to 1999 are given in Exhibit 16.6.

Review these financial statements and discuss whether the profitability they reveal is indeed low quality as an indicator of the profitability that Starbucks is ultimately likely to generate. Would you expect Starbucks to be a firm that can earn above-average rates of return? Attempt to value the firm's shares. Is the $42 price warranted in your view? Use a 9 percent required return for operation.

EXHIBIT 16.6

STARBUCKS CORPORATION
Income Statements (in thousands)

	Fiscal Year (Ending September)		
	1999	**1998**	**1997**
Net revenues	$1,680,145	$1,308,702	$975,389
Cost of sales and related occupancy costs	741,010	578,483	436,942
Gross margin	939,135	730,219	538,447
Store operating expenses	543,572	418,476	314,064
Other operating expenses	51,374	43,479	28,239
Depreciation and amortization	97,797	72,543	52,801
General and administrative expenses	89,681	77,575	57,144
Merger expenses		8,930	
Operating income	156,711	109,216	86,199
Interest and other income	8,678	8,515	12,393
Interest and other expense	(1,363)	(1,381)	(7,282)
Earnings before income taxes	164,026	116,350	91,310
Income taxes	62,333	47,978	36,099
Net earnings	$ 101,693	$ 68,372	$ 55,211
Net earnings per common share—basic	$ 0.56	$ 0.39	$ 0.35
Net earnings per common share—diluted	$ 0.54	$ 0.37	$ 0.33

EXHIBIT 16.6
(Continued)

Consolidated Balance Sheet
(in thousands)

	Fiscal Year (Ending September)		
	1999	**1998**	**1997**
Assets			
Current assets			
Cash and cash equivalents	$ 66,419	$101,663	$ 70,126
Short-term investments	51,367	21,874	83,504
Accounts receivable	47,646	50,972	31,231
Inventories	180,886	143,118	119,767
Prepaid expenses and other current assets	19,049	11,205	8,763
Deferred income taxes, net	21,133	8,448	4,164
Total current assets	386,500	337,280	31,755
Joint ventures and other investments	68,060	38,917	34,464
Property, plant, and equipment, net	760,289	600,794	488,791
Deposits and other assets	23,474	15,685	16,342
Goodwill, net	14,191	79	
Total assets	$1,252,514	$992,755	$857,152
Liabilities and Shareholders' Equity			
Current liabilities			
Accounts payable	$ 56,108	$ 49,861	$ 47,987
Checks drawn in excess of bank balances	64,211	33,634	28,582
Accrued compensation and related costs	43,872	35,941	25,894
Accrued occupancy costs	23,017	17,526	12,184
Accrued taxes	30,752	18,323	
Other accrued expenses	33,637	24,190	30,829
Total current liabilities	251,597	179,475	145,476
Deferred income taxes, net	32,886	18,983	12,946
Convertible subordinated debentures			165,020
Long-term debt	7,018		
Total liabilities	$ 291,501	$198,458	$323,442
Shareholders' equity			
Common stock—authorized, 300,000,000 shares; issued and outstanding, 183,282,095 in 1999, respectively (includes 848,550 common stock units in both years)	$ 651,020	$589,214	$391,284
Retained earnings	313,939	212,246	142,426
Accumulated other comprehensive loss	(3,946)	(7,163)	
Total shareholders' equity	$ 961,013	$794,297	$533,710
Total liabilities and shareholders' equity	$1,252,514	$992,755	$857,152

Chapter **Seventeen**

Analysis of the Quality of Financial Statements

LINKS

Link to previous chapter

Chapter 16 showed how accounting policies, consistently applied, affect profitability and earnings growth on a permanent basis.

This chapter

This chapter shows how accounting methods can affect earnings temporarily, making current earnings a poor indicator of future earnings. It also develops diagnostics to detect when reported earnings are of poor quality.

Link to next chapter

Part Five of the book analyzes the fundamental determinants of risk and the cost of capital.

Link to web page

Explore further examples of accounting quality analysis by visiting the text website at www.mhhe.com/penman2e.

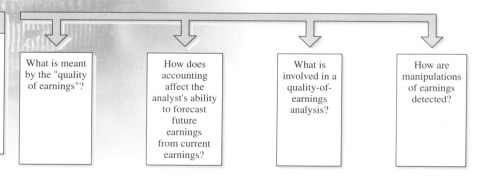

What is meant by the "quality of earnings"?

How does accounting affect the analyst's ability to forecast future earnings from current earnings?

What is involved in a quality-of-earnings analysis?

How are manipulations of earnings detected?

Some analysts specialize in examining the quality of the accounting in financial reports. Quality analysts advise clients—some of whom are other analysts—on the integrity of the accounting in representing the underlying operations of the firm. Accounting methods can be used to "package" the firm, to make it look better than it is. Quality analysts unwrap the packaging and if the accounting is being used to obscure, they issue warnings.

This chapter leads you through a quality analysis. The analysis can be used for examining accounting quality in any context but the focus is on using the accounting for valuation. Quality warnings hit the news headlines and often cause sudden drops in share prices. The equity analyst tries to avoid being caught by surprise; the analyst who first gets a sense that there is something wrong with the accounting is very much at an advantage.

With the bursting of the stock market bubble in 2001, accounting quality problems surfaced for many firms. The pressure to produce earnings was too much for some firms,

The Analyst's Checklist

After reading this chapter you should understand:

- How accounting methods and estimates determine, in part, the sustainability of earnings.

- What quality accounting is.

- What "quality of earnings" means.

- How accounting quality determines, in part, the quality of earnings.

- The accounting devices that management can use to manipulate earnings.

- How firms can time transactions to determine their earnings.

- What disclosure quality means.

- In what situations a quality analyst is more likely to detect accounting manipulation.

- How diagnostics are developed to detect manipulation in financial statements.

After reading this chapter you should be able to:

- Carry out a complete accounting quality analysis on a set of financial statements.

- Identify sensitive situations where manipulation of the financial statements is more likely.

- Apply a set of diagnostics that raises questions about the quality of the accounting in financial statements.

- Combine accounting quality analysis with the financial statement analysis and red-flag analysis discussed earlier in the book to assess the sustainability of earnings.

leading them to apply a variety of accounting methods to deliver earnings growth. But such methods can only maintain growth in the short run. As the bubble burst, firms like Xerox, Enron, Tyco, Lucent Technologies, WorldCom, Bristol-Myers Squibb, and Royal Ahold found their accounting called into question, in some cases with disastrous effects on their stock prices.

This chapter lays out an analysis of the quality of the accounting in financial statements. Valuation involves forecasting future financial statements, but current financial statements are analyzed to uncover the core profitability on which to base forecasts. Current financial statements are of poor quality if they mislead us in making forecasts. Accounting quality issues arise in forecasting because of the way that accounting reverses. If a firm charges too-low depreciation in order to increase current earnings, it must charge higher depreciation in the future (often in the form of a restructuring charge), and so report lower future earnings. If it overestimates restructuring charges to reduce current earnings, it must **bleed back** the overestimates to income statements in the future and so create future profits. These types of practices are low-quality accounting because they make current earnings a poor indicator of future earnings. If the practices are detected, forecasts can be adjusted to anticipate the reversals. If left undetected, however, low-quality accounting leads to low-quality forecasts and low-quality valuations.

The accounting issues in this chapter are not to be confused with those in the last. The last chapter dealt with accounting methods that are applied on a consistent, permanent basis—always expensing research and development (R&D) and advertising expenses, always maintaining accelerated depreciation methods, or always using LIFO for inventory, for instance. Those conservative accounting methods, consistently applied, consistently produce higher accounting rates of return and earnings growth. This chapter deals with the effects of accounting that are temporary, thus making current earnings a poor indicator of future earnings. If a firm always overestimates bad debts (so always to be "conservative"), it will consistently report a higher return on net operating assets. But if it temporarily increases or lowers its debt estimate to change current earnings, it will produce a return on net operating assets that is a poor indicator of future profitability.

Accounting quality analysis is a further dimension to the analysis of sustainable earnings. If current earnings are overstated by accounting methods but will reverse in the future, those earnings are not sustainable. The analysis of core earnings in Chapter 12 was designed to identify sustainable earnings. This chapter completes the analysis of sustainable earnings by investigating the accounting methods used to measure core earnings.

FIVE QUESTIONS ABOUT ACCOUNTING QUALITY

In analyzing the quality of the accounting, the analyst seeks answers to five questions:

1. **GAAP quality**: Are generally accepted accounting principles deficient? If forecasts are based on GAAP statements but GAAP does not capture all the value-relevant aspects of the firm, valuations will be deficient. We have seen (in Chapter 8) that GAAP fails to capture the expense of stock compensation. In Chapter 12 we saw that GAAP earnings can include stock market bubble gains. In some countries pension and employment liabilities and related expenses are not recorded. Expensing R&D can obscure the profitability of research and development activities.

2. **Audit quality**: Is the firm violating GAAP or committing outright fraud? GAAP accounting might be appropriate, but a firm might not be applying GAAP according to the rules. Is it booking receivables without having firm commitments from customers? Is it failing to recognize expenses or amortize costs as required? Is it using methods not approved by GAAP? To answer these questions the analyst usually has to be close to the business, so audit quality is the province of the auditor and enforcement agencies with subpoena powers (the Securities and Exchange Commission [SEC] in the United States). The analyst typically relies on the audit. But she needs to be sensitive to the possibility of audit failure or to situations where an auditor with a conflict of interest might be generous to management in drawing a line through a gray area.

3. **GAAP application quality**: Is the firm using GAAP accounting to manipulate reports? Generally accepted accounting principles restrict the accounting methods that a firm can use but permit some choice among methods. That choice can be taken as a license to manipulate the numbers to achieve a desired effect, and with approval of auditors. Managers manage firms but they can also manage earnings. The issue is particularly sensitive when estimates are involved—estimates of bad debts, useful lives of assets, warranty expenses, pension costs, and estimated restructuring charges, for example. Such manipulations change both current and future earnings and, if detected, can be accommodated with appropriate valuation methods as shown in Chapters 5 and 6. But detection is the key. Otherwise one might be misled to accept current profit margins (say) as a good indicator of future margins and so forecast earnings incorrectly.

4. **Transaction timing quality**: Is the firm manipulating its business to accommodate the accounting? A firm may employ GAAP faithfully but then arrange transactions around the accounting to achieve desired results. This is manipulation of the business, not the

accounting, but it relies on features of the accounting. It takes two forms, the manipulation of revenues and the manipulation of expenses:

    a. **Revenue timing**. Typically GAAP requires revenues be recognized when goods or services are shipped or delivered to customers. Firms might ship a lot of goods prior to the end of a period to increase profits for the period or delay shipping when they want to defer profits. This is referred to as **channel stuffing**.

    b. **Expenditure timing**. Firms may time expenditures that go straight to the income statement to manipulate income. Deferring R&D and advertising expenditures to the next period increases income, whereas advancing them to the current period decreases income.

5. **Disclosure quality**: Are disclosures adequate to analyze the business? Disclosures are made within the financial statements, in the footnotes, and in the management discussion and analysis. Management also gives additional commentary in meetings with analysts. Much of the financial analysis that we have been through relies on good disclosures, to understand the business and how it is represented in the financial statements. For valuation, four types of disclosures are particularly important:

    a. Disclosures that distinguish operating items from financial items in the statements.

    b. Disclosures that distinguish core operating profitability from unusual items.

    c. Disclosures that reveal the drivers of core profitability.

    d. Disclosures that explain the accounting used so the analyst can investigate the quality of the application of GAAP.

Without adequate disclosures it is difficult to forecast from a good measure of current core operating income, so low-quality disclosures lead to low-quality valuations.

All five of these questions require a thorough knowledge of accounting. But they also require a thorough knowledge of the business so that the analyst has an appreciation of what, for the particular business, a "high-quality" financial report would look like.

You might think of applying quality scores on the basis of answers to these five questions: Score a firm on each question and then total the scores for an overall accounting quality score for the firm. A qualified audit report would indicate low quality, but so would manipulation and limited disclosure. Indeed an equity research report might be prefaced with a review of the quality of the accounting that the analyst has had to work with, and assigning an overall score is a way to communicate that quality.

All five quality questions must be answered to discover the quality of the accounting. GAAP quality (question 1) has arisen at several points in this book, particularly in Chapters 2, 8, and 12. Audit quality (question 2) is a matter of auditing principles and is left to auditing books. In this chapter we deal with the problem of earnings manipulated by the accounting (question 3) or by transaction timing (question 4). But disclosure quality (question 5) arises at many points because we can't carry out any analysis with confidence if disclosures are poor.

ACCOUNTING QUALITY, EARNINGS QUALITY, AND FORECASTING

We have already gained some appreciation of when accounting quality matters for valuing firms. We have recognized that perfect balance sheets are not necessary. Indeed residual earnings methods are designed to solve the problem of "low-quality" balance sheets where the book value does not give fundamental value. So it is not necessary, for example, for the balance sheet to include the value of R&D. But with imperfect balance sheets the focus shifts to the income statement as an indicator of future residual earnings: We can't typically forecast from the balance sheet with an SF1 forecast, so we forecast from the income statement with an SF2 or SF3 forecast. This brings the focus to the quality of earnings.

Accounting quality analysis is a matter of establishing the integrity of the accounting to be used in forecasting. But quality analysts go further to establish the quality of the earnings. They understand that real factors also determine whether current earnings are a good indicator of future earnings. Having established the accounting quality in a report, they ask whether the report indicates there are aspects of the operations that raise concerns about the future. They may, for example, identify red flags raised in the report and evaluate the warnings they give. Current income may be up but there also may be a decrease in the inventory turnover (sales-to-inventory) ratio. Does this mean that the firm is having trouble moving its inventories or does it mean that it is building up inventory in anticipation of higher future sales? What explains a decrease in accounts receivable turnover? Does increased advertising expense (which lowers current earnings) actually mean higher future earnings (because the increased advertising will produce more sales)? These questions are about the quality of the operations, not just the accounting.

This broader type of inquiry is commonly referred to as a **quality-of-earnings** analysis. So the analysis of the quality of the accounting is just part of the analysis of the quality of the current earnings as an indicator of future earnings.

It should be clear that much of the apparatus that we have laid out in this book contributes to a quality-of-earnings analysis. The separation of operating from financing items in Chapter 9 identifies a component of net income—operating income—that is pertinent for forecasting what's important for value, future residual operating income and abnormal operating income growth. Operating income is a "higher quality" number than net income because it removes the component that comes from financial activities. The financial statement analysis in Chapter 12 drove harder to purge operating income of unusual, transitory items, to cut to core operating income and core profit margins, which are "higher quality" numbers to forecast the future. And the analysis in Chapter 15 hoisted some red flags.

One further element is needed to complete an earnings-quality analysis. Current operating income and its components may be affected by accounting methods. So we have to analyze the quality of the accounting for core operating income. We have to cut through the accounting to get to the core. This is the issue of accounting quality.

Quality-of-earnings analysis thus has three components, as depicted in Figure 17.1. The first, accounting quality analysis, is the prerequisite for further quality analysis. It involves the five quality questions above. Secure in the accounting, financial statement analysis cuts to the core of the operations to identify sustainable earnings. Then the analyst interprets red flags in the statements. The complete quality-of-earnings analysis is a preamble to forecasting. Doubts about quality at any point introduce doubts in forecasting. If disclosure quality makes core profit margins or unusual items harder to identify, forecasts are more tentative. If GAAP is being manipulated and the manipulation can be discovered, adjustments can be made. But if the analyst suspects manipulation but can't be sure (possibly because of poor disclosure), then forecasts are more tentative. If red flags are raised but the message can't be interpreted, forecasts are more tentative.

CUTTING THROUGH THE ACCOUNTING: DETECTING MANIPULATION

With forecasting in mind, a quality analysis focuses on the return on net operating assets (RNOA), which drives residual operating income. The central idea is that if there is manipulation, current RNOA cannot be maintained in the future. As current RNOA (for

FIGURE 17.1

Components of a Quality-of-Earnings Analysis The analyst analyzes the quality of the accounting used to report current profitability. He then analyzes the financial statements to uncover core operating profitability on which to base a forecast. Finally he scrutinizes the financial statements for red flags that may indicate that the firm cannot sustain the current core profitability.

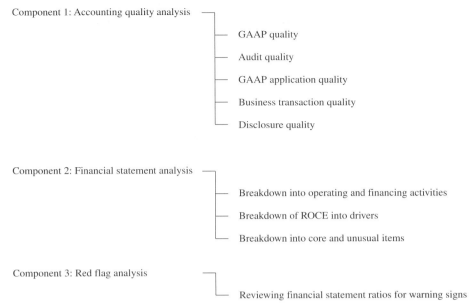

Component 1: Accounting quality analysis
— GAAP quality
— Audit quality
— GAAP application quality
— Business transaction quality
— Disclosure quality

Component 2: Financial statement analysis
— Breakdown into operating and financing activities
— Breakdown of ROCE into drivers
— Breakdown into core and unusual items

Component 3: Red flag analysis
— Reviewing financial statement ratios for warning signs

Year 0) is $RNOA_0 = OI_0/NOA_{-1}$, then manipulation in the current period involves altering operating income. But we have seen that

$$OI = \text{Free cash flow} + \Delta NOA$$

Thus, since cash flows are not affected by the accounting, a change in operating income (OI) must change net operating assets (NOA) by a corresponding amount. But those net operating assets are the base for next year's RNOA. Next year's RNOA is $RNOA_1 = OI_1/NOA_0$ so, unless the manipulation is perpetuated after Year 1, increasing current operating income by manipulation reduces next year's RNOA because of a higher NOA in the denominator. And a decrease in current operating income increases next year's RNOA through a lower denominator. But there is an additional effect. The higher NOA that results from the manipulation will have to be written off to higher expenses, reducing operating income in the future (and a lower NOA will increase operating income in the future). If cost of goods sold, depreciation expense, or pension expense is measured lower now (to yield a higher current RNOA), RNOA must be lower in the future. This is the *reversal property* of accounting. The implications for forecasting and valuation are clear: Unless we detect the manipulation, we will not forecast a change in the future RNOA, which drives residual operating income.

Manipulation that inflates current operating income is referred to as **borrowing income from the future.** It always involves either an increase in sales or a decrease in expenses. Both increase NOA: An increase in net sales increases accounts receivable or reduces bad debt or sales return allowances; a decrease in expenses increases the unamortized value of assets or decreases operating liabilities like accrued expense liabilities and pension liabilities. Manipulation that reduces current operating income is called **saving** or **banking income for the future.** It always involves either a decrease in sales or an increase in expenses, both of which decrease NOA. Overestimating restructuring charges, for example, increases expenses and estimated liabilities. The motivation for borrowing from the future is fairly clear: Management wants to make profitability look better than it really is. Saving income for the future might arise when managers' bonuses are tied to future earnings. An extreme version is called "taking a big bath": A new management writes off a lot of expenses, attributes the lower income (or loss) to the old management it has replaced, and generates more future income on which it will be rewarded.

This intertemporal shifting of income, which is the hallmark of manipulation, means that earnings quality is not only doubtful in the year of the manipulation but also in subsequent years when the borrowing or saving of income "comes home to roost." Some claim that the large amount of restructuring in the early 1990s produced excessive restructuring charges and liabilities, which created higher profits in the late 1990s. The market was very excited about earnings in the late 1990s, resulting in high multiples. But these earnings were partly created by the earlier restructuring charges.

Manipulation of the current accounting differs from accounting that reflects permanent accounting policy. A conservative depreciation policy, which always calculates high depreciation, will result in lower income (with growth in assets) and higher RNOA permanently, as in the examples in the tables in the last chapter. But a high depreciation charge for just one period will have a temporary effect of increasing RNOA, which will reverse in the future. Accordingly, conservative accounting or liberal accounting does not result in low-quality earnings, as is sometimes said. The term **aggressive accounting** (not liberal accounting) is best used to indicate manipulation that temporarily increases income. And the term **big-bath accounting** might be used to indicate manipulation that temporarily reduces income (not conservative accounting), although the term is typically used when income is reduced by large amounts. However, firms with permanent conservative accounting policies are less likely to be manipulative. Liberal accounting creates income that might not be permanent and net operating assets that might have to be written down later.

In the last chapter we listed conservative and liberal accounting practices that can be used to change operating income and net operating assets. They are referred to there as a part of permanent accounting policy, but many can be used on a one-time basis for manipulation. Used for manipulation, being temporarily more conservative in the current period (increasing bad debt allowances, increasing estimated liabilities) banks income for the future, while being temporarily more liberal or "aggressive" (extending useful lives of assets, reducing bad debt allowances) borrows income from the future.

Prelude to a Quality Analysis

Before beginning a quality investigation, the analyst should understand four things well:

- The business.
- The accounting policy.
- The business areas where accounting quality is most doubtful.
- Situations in which management is particularly tempted to manipulate.

On the first point, knowing the business is necessary to get a feel for what the appropriate accounting is for the type of business. What are normal bad debt rates for the business and does the firm's allowance for bad debts seem out of line? What is the standard useful life of depreciable assets in this line of business?

On the second point, the accounting policy for the firm establishes a benchmark for detecting deviations from the policy. A firm's accounting policy is determined from its accounting footnote (usually the first footnote). The policy may be conservative, liberal,

Industry	Flash Point
Banking	Credit losses: Quality of loan loss provisions
Computer hardware	Technological change: Quality of receivables and inventory
Computer software	Marketability of products: Quality of capitalized research and development
	Revenue recognition of servicing contracts: Quality of receivables
Retailing	Credit losses: Quality of net accounts receivable
	Inventory obsolescence: Quality of carrying values of inventory
	Rebate programs: Quantity of supplier rebates recognized
Manufacturing	Warranties: Quality of warranty liabilities
	Product liability: quality of estimated liabilities
Automobiles	Overcapacity: Quality of depreciation allowances
Telecommunications	Technological change: Quality of depreciation allowances
Equipment leasing	Lease values: Quality of carrying values for leases
Tobacco	Liabilities for health effects of smoking: Quality of estimated liabilities
Pharmaceuticals	R&D: Quality of R&D expenditures
	Product liability: Quality of estimated liabilities
Real estate	Property values: Quality of carrying values for real property
Aircraft and ship manufacturing	Revenue recognition: Quality of estimates under percentage of completion method and "program accounting"
Subscriber services	Development of customer base: Quality of capitalized promotion costs
	Subscriptions paid in advance: Quality of deferred revenue

or neutral. It determines the level of current and future RNOA. This permanent effect does not frustrate the valuation, as we saw in the last chapter. But deviations from the policy may be manipulations. Beware of firms whose accounting policy is different from the standard for the industry. Watch for firms whose accounting estimates have been incorrect in the past. If a firm regularly recognizes large gains from asset sales, its depreciation charges might be too high. If it regularly reports losses from asset sales, or restructuring charges, its depreciation might be too low.

On the third point, some businesses have particular flash points where manipulation is more likely. In equipment leasing it is the estimate of leases' residual values and allowances for defaults. For computer manufacturers it is sales returns. They sometimes book sales on shipment to retailers but allow returns. They sometimes guarantee distributors' inventories off balance sheet. Product obsolescence is a factor in this industry, so the quality of sales is also in doubt. Box 17.1 gives the typical flash points for a number of industries. The suspect balance sheet item (NOA) is given in most cases. For each there is a corresponding income statement item. As a test of your accounting, can you name the income statement item?

On the fourth point, a number of conditions coincide to make manipulation more attractive to managers. Box 17.2 lists them. The quality analyst needs to be aware of these flash points in order to direct her efforts to cases where manipulation is more likely.

Caveat emptor, and beware when buying shares. But be particularly careful when buying shares from the firm itself. It is well known that returns to buying stock in an initial public offering (IPO) are not particularly good; indeed, after an initial period when an IPO might be "hot," risk-adjusted stock returns subsequent to an IPO are negative on average. Look at the diagnostics in Table 17.1. They are medians from 1,682 IPOs between

Institutional conditions:

- The firm is in the process of raising capital or renegotiating borrowing. Watch public offerings.

- Debt covenants are likely to be violated.

- Management changes.

- Auditor changes.

- Management rewards (like bonuses) are tied to earnings.

- Management is repricing executive stock options.

- Governance structure is weak: Inside management dominates the board; there is a weak audit committee or none at all.

- Regulatory requirements (like capital ratios for banks and insurance companies) are likely to be violated.

- Transactions are conducted with related parties rather than at arm's length.

- Special events such as union negotiations and proxy fights.

- The firm is "in play" as a takeover target.

- Earnings meet analysts' expectations, but just barely.

- The firm engages in exotic arrangements like off-balance-sheet special purpose entities and stylized derivative contracts.

Accounting and financial statement conditions:

- A change in accounting principles or estimates.

- An earnings surprise.

- A drop in profitability after a period of good profitability.

- Constant sales or falling sales.

- Earnings growing faster than sales.

- Very low earnings (that might be a loss without manipulation).

- Small or zero increases in profit margins (that might be a decrease without manipulation).

- A firm meets analysts' earnings expectations, but just barely.

- Differences in expenses for tax reporting and financial reporting.

- Financial reports are used for other purposes, like tax reporting and union negotiations.

- Accounting adjustments in the last quarter of the year.

TABLE 17.1
Accounting Numbers Around Initial Public Offerings

Source: S. Teoh, T. Wong, and G. Rao, "Are Accruals During Initial Public Offerings Opportunistic?" *Review of Accounting Studies*, 1998, pp. 175–208.

Diagnostic, %	Year of IPO	Year after IPO					
		1	2	3	4	5	6
Net income/sales	4.6	2.8	2.1	1.6	1.3	1.3	1.8
Abnormal accruals/book value	5.5	1.6	−0.4	−0.8	−2.0	−1.4	−2.7
Allowance for uncollectibles/gross accounts receivable	2.91	3.32	3.46	3.62	3.81	3.77	3.85

1980 and 1990. The net income-to-sales ratio was high for these firms in the year they went public but declined thereafter. Was management manipulating the accounting to give a better profitability picture for the IPO? Well, look at the abnormal accounting accruals in the table. These are accruals in excess of those you would expect from the increase in sales and capital investments for the year (expressed relative to book value in the table). They were high in the IPO year, increasing income, but considerably lower later. Indeed they were negative later; they reversed. And allowances for bad debts were low in the IPO year, increasing later.

Does the apparent manipulation explain the poor returns from buying IPOs? The market might indeed have been deceived by the good earnings reported with the IPO, thus valuing the firms too high. And then, when prices dropped as lower earnings were reported, the market realized that the earlier earnings were "low quality." Indeed, there is evidence that the amount of implied manipulation predicts post-IPO returns.[1] If so, a quality analyst who diagnosed the accounting would have been able to earn superior returns.

We have referred to the indicators of manipulation as "diagnostics" here. We now develop **quality diagnostics** that help the forensic accountant to detect manipulation. Figure 17.2 guides you through the analysis. These diagnostics must be seen as red flags; they raise questions about accounting quality but do not resolve the question. Each diagnostic can arise for legitimate reasons, and it is up to the quality analyst to dig further to discover whether real operations or the application of accounting methods is the cause. It is to this point that disclosure quality is important, particularly disclosures about the accounting. If disclosures are inadequate, the quality analyst can only flag the possible problem but cannot sort it out. Provided the audit quality is good, red flags are explained by legitimate operational factors in most cases.

Many of the diagnostics are accounting ratios. Like all financial statement ratios, they should be evaluated relative to the past (in time series) and relative to those for comparison firms (in cross section). Look for differences from the past and differences from other firms, and compare changes from the past with changes from the past for comparison firms.

To develop diagnostics of the quality of operating income, focus on how operating income is measured:

$$\text{Operating income (OI)} = \text{Free cash flow} + \Delta\text{Net operating assets}$$

Free cash flow is a "hard" number that cannot be manipulated by accounting. The change in net operating assets (ΔNOA) can be "soft." It depends on real increases in investment in operations but also on accruals. And accruals can be manipulated. So diagnostics aim to uncover the quality of the change in net operating assets during a period.

Diagnostics to Detect Manipulated Sales

Sales are of good quality if they are unbiased estimates of the cash that the sales will generate. A sale might be booked but there is a chance that goods may be returned, a warranty claim may be made, or a receivable may not be paid. Focus, then, is on net sales after allowances for sales returns, warranties, and credit losses:

$$\text{Net sales} = \text{Cash from sales} + \Delta\text{Net accounts receivable} \\ - \Delta\text{Unearned revenue} - \Delta\text{Warranty liabilities}$$

Lack of disclosure might frustrate this calculation. If so, use net sales as reported by GAAP, that is, sales less estimated sales returns and allowances in the diagnostics that follow. Cash cannot be manipulated by the accounting, so any quality question arises from accruals that affect changes in net receivables (that are net of estimated sales returns and bad debts), unearned revenue, and warranty liabilities. Manipulation diagnostics look for changes in sales relative to cash generated by sales and changes in sales relative to changes in the net operating assets that relate to sales:

Diagnostic: Net sales/Cash from sales

Diagnostic: Net sales/Net accounts receivable

Diagnostic: Net sales/Unearned revenue

Diagnostic: Net sales/Warranty liabilities

[1] See S. Teoh, I. Welch, and T. Wong, "Earnings Management and the Long-Run Market Performance of Initial Public Offerings," *Journal of Finance*, December 1998, pp. 1935–1974.

FIGURE 17.2

Diagnostics to Detect Manipulation in Operating Income
First investigate the quality of sales revenues. Then investigate the quality of core expenses. Finally investigate unusual items.

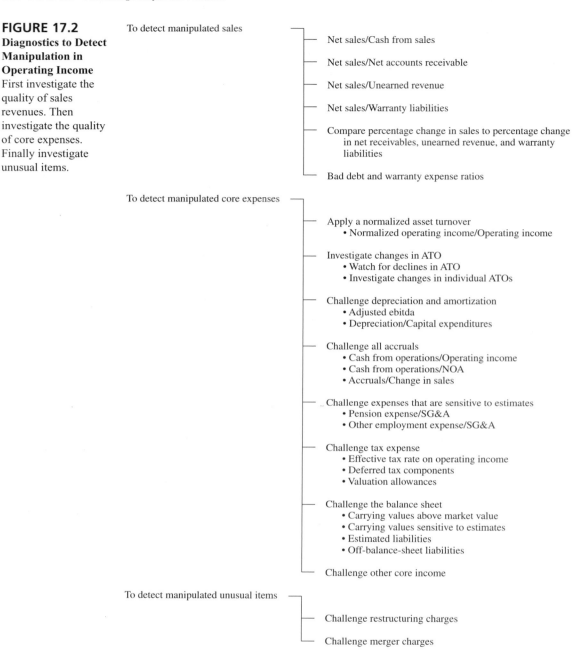

If firms are aggressively recognizing revenue or underestimating returns and credit losses (and thus have no legitimate receivables that are being paid off in cash), the first ratio will increase and the second will decrease. If net sales are increasing because of reduced estimates of unearned (deferred) revenue or warranty liabilities, the last two ratios will increase. Changes in these ratios should be investigated over time. Comparisons of

From *The Wall Street Journal*, November 4, 1996.

In a recent report, Sanford Bernstein analyst David Poneman argues that Sear's earnings growth this year of 24 percent or $134 million, has been aided by a 1993 balance-sheet maneuver that softens the impact of soaring levels of bad credit-card debt among its 50 million card holders.

Wall Street got a wake-up call in the second quarter, when Sears increased its provision for bad credit-card debt by $254 million, up 73 percent from the year earlier. Then in the third quarter, it made another $286 million provision, a 53 percent increase. Yet the retailer posted a 22 percent gain in third-quarter net. How so? "Sears is using its super-abundant balance sheet to smooth out its earnings," says Mr. Poneman. He says Sears has a "quality-of-earnings issue."

Mr. Poneman is referring to a $2 billion reserve for credit losses that Sears set up in 1993, half of it to cover potential credit-card losses, some resulting from the closing of its catalog division. As it turned out, the reserve was higher than it needed to be. Three years later, Sears still has a nearly $1 billion reserve on its balance sheet to cover credit-card losses. That's nearly twice the size of reserves at most credit-card companies as a percentage of receivables, for instance.

The credit-card reserve was part of a big bath that also included restructuring charges that Sears took in 1993, shortly after Arthur Martinez became chief executive officer. Such charges and reserves can be a big help for a new CEO who wants to generate a pattern of improving results in future years. Mr. Poneman says the big addition to reserves "moved income out of 1992 and 1993 and into 1995 and 1996."

Although Sears's earnings were reduced by credit-card charge-offs of $239 million in the second quarter and $272 million in the third quarter, Mr. Poneman says the retailer isn't replenishing the reserve to reflect the growing problem. Even though Sears's credit-card delinquencies are 70 percent higher than they were at the end of 1993, the size of the reserve remains the same as it was then.

Why is that bad? From the point of view of some investors and Mr. Poneman, the overly large reserve has allowed Sears to prop up its earnings at a time when losses in its huge credit-card business, which currently accounts for about 50 percent of its earnings, have been soaring. Credit-card delinquencies stood at a total of $1.2 billion at the end of the third quarter, or about 5 percent of its $25 billion portfolio. So far this year, Sears's delinquencies have risen by $420 million.

"Considering that increased delinquencies exceed year-to-date increased earnings, it could be argued that the increase in Sears's year-to-date earnings has depended entirely on its over-reserved condition entering 1996," Mr. Poneman wrote clients in a recent report.

Allen Lacey, Sears's chief financial officer, says in response to Mr. Poneman's assertions, "When you make an actuarial estimate for something like credit-card debt, it can be higher or lower than what you actually experience." But, he maintains, Sears has not used its credit-card reserves as a way of avoiding earnings hiccups.

Mr. Lacey says it's true that Sears's reserves as a percent of total receivables has dropped to about 4 percent from 5 percent since 1993. But he said the company had over-reserved in the mistaken expectation that closing the catalog would drive up catalog-customer credit-card defaults.

Bernstein's Mr. Poneman says Sears is operating well within the bounds of accepted accounting rules. "Our point is that the properly stated profits from an accounting perspective have little to do with the ongoing economics of the business," if reserves are being diluted relative to future bad debts.

---

percentage changes in net sales to percentage changes in net receivables, warranty expenses, and unearned revenue are also revealing. Watch increases in sales that are accompanied by decreases in warranty liabilities or unearned revenue.

Of course these ratios can change for legitimate reasons, like unusual credit sales growth and customers taking longer to pay receivables. The ratios can also be red flags about the business, to signal lower customer interest in products or price discounting to attract customers. These are issues pertaining to the overall quality of earnings but not accounting quality.

Box 17.3 is a report from the "Heard on the Street" column of *The Wall Street Journal*. A large provision for credit card losses at Sears, Roebuck in 1993 was allegedly "bled back" to create higher income and income growth from 1994 to 1996. Read the details and note the implied motivation for the accounting. This practice suggests three further diagnostics (if disclosures permit):

Diagnostic: Bad debt expense/Actual credit losses

Diagnostic: Bad debt reserves/Accounts receivable (gross)

Diagnostic: Bad debt expense/Sales

Similarly investigate warranty liability estimates (if disclosures permit):

Diagnostic: Warranty expense/Actual warranty claims

Diagnostic: Warranty expense/Sales

Also monitor estimated liabilities for rebate programs such as frequent-flier programs and incentives on retail credit cards.

Diagnostics to Detect Manipulation of Core Expenses

Manipulations are also perpetrated through the recording of expenses. Here is a way to investigate.[2]

1. Investigate Changes in Net Operating Assets with Normalized Asset Turnover

As we have shown, manipulation of operating income leaves a trail: Net operating assets must also change as operating income changes. We have seen that

$$\Delta NOA = \text{Cash investment} + \text{New operating accruals}$$

Cash investment is not affected by the accounting but accruals are, so the task is to distinguish justified accruals in net operating assets from manipulation. We have seen that net operating assets are driven by sales and the asset turnover: NOA = Sales/ATO. The amount of NOA that is required for a given level of sales is determined by the normal or usual ATO, and the ΔNOA that should be recorded for the current change in sales is determined by the normal or usual ATO. If the ΔNOA is higher than that expected from the change in sales, suspect manipulation of the expenses.

If you are satisfied with the integrity of sales (from the diagnostics above), calculate

$$\text{Normalized OI} = \text{Free cash flow} + \Delta\text{Normalized NOA}$$

$$= \text{Free cash flow} + \Delta\text{Sales/Normal ATO}$$

The normal ATO is calculated from average asset turnovers over past years or from comparison firms with similar operations and accounting policies. The following diagnostic flags the possible manipulation:

Diagnostic: (Normalized OI)/OI

If this ratio differs from 1.0, a flag is hoisted.

2. Investigate Changes in Asset Turnover

Manipulation of operating expenses always changes both profit margin (PM) and ATO, but in opposite directions: Lower expenses mean higher income to sales but, as net operating assets increase, lower expenses also mean lower sales to net operating assets. So a change in ATO may indicate manipulation. And if firms are using manipulation to

---

[2] This material incorporates teaching notes of Jim Ohlson at New York University.

TABLE 17.2   **Changes in Return on Net Operating Assets (RNOA) and Profit Margins (PM) for Different Changes in Asset Turnover (ATO)**

Group, Year 0:	1 (High)	2	3	4	5	6	7	8	9	10 (Low)
Core RNOA (%)	57.4	35.5	28.3	23.8	20.2	17.3	14.2	11.3	8.2	3.9
Change in RNOA Next Year, Year 1 (%)										
High ΔATO	−6.72	−0.77	−0.18	−0.61	0.12	0.35	0.74	0.69	0.97	1.49
Low ΔATO	−12.57	−4.90	−2.92	−2.54	−1.41	−0.13	−0.63	−0.45	0.12	0.59
Change in PM Next Year, Year 1 (%)										
High ΔATO	−1.14	−0.32	−0.04	−0.13	−0.15	−0.08	−0.31	0.06	0.32	0.88
Low ΔATO	−2.74	−1.68	−0.94	−1.07	−0.54	−0.51	−0.32	−0.14	0.04	0.29

Source: P. Fairfield and T. Yohn, "Using Asset Turnover and Profit Margin to Forecast Changes in Profitability," unpublished paper, School of Business Administration, Georgetown University, 1999. A published version of this paper (but without this table) is in *Review of Accounting Studies*, 2001, pp. 371–385.

increase or maintain profit margins, the corresponding decrease in ATO will signal a subsequent decrease in future profit margins as the accounting reverses.

Table 17.2 pertains to firms grouped on their core RNOA before taxes (Year 0) for the years 1978 to 1996. Group 1 has the highest RNOA, group 10 the lowest. The average core RNOA for each group is given under the group number in the column headings. The table then gives median changes in RNOA and profit margins for each group in the next year (Year 1). These are given for firms with the top third of changes in asset turnover in Year 0 in each group (high-ΔATO firms) and for firms with the lowest third of ΔATO (low-ΔATO firms). For all groups, next year's change in RNOA is lower if the current change in ATO is low, and for all except one group, next year's change in profit margin is lower if the current change in ATO is low. And the differences are higher for firms that have high current RNOA: A high current RNOA is likely to be followed by a decrease in RNOA, but the decrease is likely to be greater if the firm has a small change in ATO.

These relationships may not arise from accounting quality but certainly bear on the overall question of earnings quality. So analyze changes in ATO. Compare changes in sales to changes in ATO. Be sensitive to cases where profit margins increase or are constant but the asset turnover declines. This may be the case of a firm that is otherwise experiencing falling margins but wants to maintain profit margins and RNOA at previous levels. And watch for cases where there has been a large increase in NOA but a small or negative change in ATO.

Changes in individual turnovers should be investigated to isolate the possible manipulation. Pay attention to turnovers involving estimates: intangible asset turnover, PPE turnover, deferred asset turnover, pension liability turnover, and other estimated liability turnovers. Watch for declines in turnovers. Is there an explanation?

3. Investigate Line Items Directly

a. Challenge Depreciation and Amortization Expense.   Low depreciation or amortization usually means there will be future write-downs of assets, usually through restructuring charges or losses on disposals of assets. Too high depreciation or amortization results in later gains from asset disposals.

In 1988 General Motors reported $4.9 billion in profits. Analysts claimed that $790 million of this came from extending the useful lives of assets from 35 to 45 years, thereby reducing depreciation, and $270 million came from changing assumptions for estimated

LIVERPOOL JOHN MOORES UNIVERSITY
Aldham Roberts L.R.C.
TEL 0151 231 3701/3634

residual values on car leases. This accounting continued for a few years, but then came the large restructuring charges of the early 1990s. These charges, it was claimed, were partly corrections for underdepreciation in the past. Indeed, GM had so many restructurings in the 1990s that analysts claimed they could not at any time work out what profits GM was really making.

To investigate, adjust operating income before depreciation and amortization (ebitda) with a normal capital charge:

$$\text{Adjusted ebitda} = \text{OI (before tax)} + \text{Depreciation and amortization} \\ - \text{Normal capital expense}$$

The diagnostic compares this adjusted ebitda to operating income before tax (ebit), which is based on the reported depreciation and amortization:

Diagnostic: (Adjusted ebitda)/ebit

Normal capital expense is approximated by the average capital expenditure over past years or, to accommodate growth, normal depreciation and amortization for the level of sales, calculated from past (Depreciation + Amortization)-to-sales ratios. Also calculate, for the past few years,

Diagnostic: Depreciation/Capital expenditures

If this ratio is less than 1.0, future depreciation is likely to increase.

Some analysts employ models of required depreciation that are more forward looking. These models identify under- or overdepreciation by forecasting write-downs and disposal gains and losses, and they set the appropriate depreciation charge as that which will produce no write-downs, gains, or losses. For example, if there is overcapacity in an industry—as with automobile manufacturing and telecoms in the 1990s—these models forecast that firms will have to write off the excess plant unless current depreciation is adjusted to reflect the cost of the investment in overcapacity. Or if technological change will render current plant obsolete, depreciation is adjusted. These models may also attempt to calculate the depreciation that is necessary to sustain sales, usually approximated by annualizing capital expenditures necessary to replace facilities. This is desirable when there are anticipated increases in the cost of new plants that will replace current plants but will generate the same sales, or where technological change will require the updating of the production facilities to deliver sales. Current depreciation, so adjusted, becomes a better predictor of future depreciation, a higher quality number. Technological change has been rapid in telecommunications and so these methods are desirable there. See Box 17.4.

Some analysts, wary of depreciation and amortization charges, add back depreciation to operating income and work with ebitda as a measure of income from operations for profitability analysis. This is bad analysis. Depreciation is a cost of generating sales, just like wages. Plants rust, wear out, and become obsolete, so value is lost. Depreciation captures value loss; ebitda is a low-quality measure of value added. If the analyst has questions about the quality of depreciation and amortization, she can work with adjusted ebitda, which uses a normal capital charge.

b. Challenge Both Depreciation and Amortization and Working Capital Accruals. We have seen that cash flow from operations = OI − New operating accruals. Thus calculate

Diagnostic: CFO/OI

In June 1998 AT&T, the largest U.S. telecommunications group, made a bid of $45.5 billion to acquire Telecommunications Inc. (TCI), the country's biggest cable television company. AT&T's strategy was to build systems for delivery of voice, television, and Internet service to homes, circumventing the Baby Bells (the local telephone companies).

The press at the time claimed that the purchase price of 14 times 1997 earnings before interest, tax, depreciation, and amortization (ebitda) was "a bit stiff," and indeed AT&T's shares dropped 15 percent in the two weeks after the bid. High or not, quoting prices as multiples of ebitda is appropriate if, with rapid technological change, there is a question of whether reported depreciation is too low. Indeed the many restructuring charges in the industry at the time were in part adjustments for low depreciation charged in the past. It was also recognized that AT&T would have to spend heavily to upgrade TCI's network to maintain the business under competition.

Quoting a bid price as a multiple of earnings before depreciation and amortization allows the analyst to plug in a normalized depreciation calculated to accommodate technological change and to anticipate expenditures necessary to sustain the business.

As the accounting does not affect cash flow from operations (CFO), manipulation of operating income (OI) with unjustified accruals will affect this ratio. Also calculate

Diagnostic: CFO/Average NOA

Any increase in NOA due to manipulation will affect the average NOA in the denominator.

If these ratios are different from the past (or from comparison firms), inspect each accrual listed in the reconciliation of net income to CFO in the cash flow statement, such as changes in prepaid expenses, payables, and accrued expenses. For each accrual other than depreciation and amortization, look at

Diagnostic: Accrual/ΔSales

For example, a drop in the change in accrued expenses (an accrual in the cash flow statement) may indicate that too few expenses have been recognized. Be particularly aware of accruals that increase income, especially when the change in sales is close to zero, lower than in the past, or negative. (If the change in sales is zero or negative, the ratio form of the diagnostic will not work but accruals and change in sales can still be compared.)

c. Challenge Other Expense Components that Depend on Estimates.

Diagnostic: Pension expense/SG&A expense

Diagnostic: Other postemployment expenses/SG&A expense

Pensions and other employment expenses can be manipulated by changing actuarial estimates of projected payouts and discount rates for the liabilities, and by changing the expected return on plan assets. Go to the pension footnote and investigate the components of pension expense (as in Chapter 12). To the extent disclosure allows, investigate other components of SG&A expenses; this item tends to be a large one on the income statement.

d. Challenge Tax Expense.
Effective tax rates usually converge to the statutory rate over time. So investigate

Diagnostic: Operating tax expense/OI before taxes

If this rate is below the statutory rate, find out when tax credits are likely to expire. But also investigate the portion of the tax expense that is subject to estimates: deferred taxes.

The Cash Flow Statement Is a Source of Information on Accruals 17.5

The focus in an accounting quality analysis is on distinguishing "hard" numbers, which result from cash flows, and "soft" numbers in the accruals, which are subject to estimates. The cash flow statement separates cash flows (from operations and investment) from the accruals.

Accruals are reported between net income and cash from operations in an indirect method statement of cash flows. Use these accruals as follows:

- Compare changes in net accounts receivable with changes in sales for sales quality diagnostics.

- Compare changes in unearned revenue and warranty liabilities with changes in sales for sales quality diagnostics.

- Use the depreciation and amortization number for the adjusted ebitda and depreciation diagnostics.

- Compare changes in prepaid expenses with changes in sales.

- Compare changes in accrued expenses with changes in sales.

- Use the deferred tax number for deferred tax diagnostics.

- Track restructuring charges and their reversals.

Changes in balance sheet items should be taken from the cash flow statement rather than from consecutive balance sheets because the latter are affected by acquisitions. The cash flow statement records assets acquired in acquisitions as cash investments and reduces changes in assets in the cash from operations section accordingly.

Go to the tax footnote and investigate reasons for changes in deferred tax assets and liabilities. If these are changing at a rate different from sales, a flag is raised.

Deferred taxes are taxes on the difference between income reported in the financial statements (using GAAP) and income reported on the tax return (using tax rules for measuring income). If the firm is using estimates to generate higher GAAP income, it must recognize more deferred taxes. So investigate the extent to which tax expense is composed of deferred taxes. Investigate the components of deferred taxes (in the tax footnote). Watch, particularly, deferred taxes arising from depreciation: If the deferred tax from depreciation relative to depreciation expense is high (compared to similar firms) or increasing relative to investment growth, the firm may be reporting low GAAP depreciation expense by estimating long useful lives for assets. Investigate deferred taxes arising from bad debt estimates, unearned revenue, and warranty expenses. If a firm increases GAAP income by lowering its bad debt estimate, for example, it will also recognize more deferred taxes because bad debts are accounted for on a cash basis on tax returns. Watch deferred taxes arising from sales-type leases that require estimates of residual values for GAAP income measurement.

If a firm has deferred tax assets, one feature requires particular monitoring: the valuation allowance. Deferred tax assets arise from features that yield lower GAAP income to taxable income. If the income tax benefits in these assets are deemed "more likely than not" *not* to be realized in the future, deferred tax assets are reduced by the allowance. But, to say the least, the allowance is a subjective number. Now look at Box 17.5.

4. Investigate Balance Sheet Line Items Directly

If carrying values of operating assets are too high in the balance sheet, they will have to be written off in the future, reducing RNOA. Particular suspects are:

- Assets whose carrying values are above their market values: These are likely impairment candidates. (Market values may be difficult to ascertain, however.)

- Assets whose carrying values and amortization rates are subject to estimate. Watch intangible assets, deferred tax assets, and nontypical capitalization of expenses such as

Prior to 1996, America Online (AOL) capitalized marketing costs in developing a subscriber base on its balance sheet and amortized them over a two-year period. It had been a "hot stock," increasing its share price from $10 in early 1995 to over $35 in April 1996. But concerns about the quality of its capitalized marketing costs set in during 1996 and its price dropped back almost to $10 by September 1996. Analysts queried whether subscribers would renew. To meet the concerns, AOL wrote off the $385 million capitalization in its first fiscal 1997 quarter ending September 1996, producing a loss of $3.80 per share for the quarter. Earnings per share for 1997 were –$2.61 compared to 14 cents in 1996. One might say that 1996 earnings were low quality (they did not reflect appropriate marketing expenses) and that the low quality resulted in lower future earnings. In evaluating the quality of the asset one would have to consider the retention rate in holding on to new subscribers, and that was the point on which quality analysts were focusing.

start-up costs, advertising and promotion, product development, and software development costs. Look at trends in these assets relative to total operating assets.

- Assets recorded at fair value. If estimates of fair value are used, they may have to be revised in the future.

Similarly, the carrying value of operating liabilities should be investigated. Focus on:

- Estimated liabilities such as pension liabilities, other employment liabilities, warranties, and deferred revenue. Look at trends in these liabilities relative to total operating liabilities.

- Off-balance-sheet liabilities such as loan guarantees, recourse for assigned receivables or debt, purchase commitments, contingent liabilities for lawsuits and regulatory penalties, and contingent obligations from off-balance-sheet special purpose entities. These liabilities are usually mentioned in footnotes. The footnote should be studied thoroughly to avoid a surprise in the outcome of the contingency. Environmental liabilities (for cleanup of pollution) are a current issue.

While focusing on the balance sheet, this analysis is a quality-of-earnings analysis also: If distorted carrying values were recorded at an appropriate amount or the contingent liabilities were recognized on the balance sheet, income would be affected (through a charge), and omission of this charge yields low quality earnings. See Box 17.6 as a case in point.

Diagnostics to Detect Manipulation of Unusual Items

Unusual items are isolated to identify core income in order to improve earnings quality. From an earnings quality point of view they are low quality and thus are discarded for forecasting. But the analyst does have to be careful that unusual items identified indeed have no implications for the future.

A quality issue arises if unusual items involve estimates. A notorious example is estimated restructuring charges and impairments. Firms may decide to restructure in the future but will include an estimate of the cost in current income, along with an estimated liability in the balance sheet. And they may overestimate the liability, take a bath, and "bleed back" income to income statements in the future as actual expenses are less than anticipated.

Box 17.7 is a case in point. If aggressive accounting was in fact practiced, Borden attempted to bleed 1992 income to later periods through an estimated restructuring charge.

In 1992 Borden, the food and chemicals company, took a $642 million special restructuring charge against income and reported a loss of $439.6 million. In 1993, under pressure from the SEC, Borden reversed $119.3 million of the charge retrospectively, increasing 1992 income and reducing 1993 income. In addition, Borden was required to reclassify $145.5 million of the charges that were for "packaging modernization" and marketing as ordinary operating expense.

In the fourth quarter of 1993 Borden took another restructuring charge of $637.4 million for estimated losses on disposal of businesses, unrelated to the earlier charge. Its 1994 third quarter results included a $50 million credit from having overestimated these losses in 1993.

Indeed the restatement of the 1992 charge reduced 1993 income. The unrelated 1993 fourth quarter charge was, it turns out, also an overstimate which increased income in 1994. See also the coverage of IBM in Chapter 12.

The Borden case raises another point about estimated charges. Borden included (what the SEC concluded) was $145.5 million of 1992 core operating expense in the 1992 restructuring charge, thus inflating core income. Investigate the components of the charge to see whether this is going on.

Estimated merger costs also warrant investigation. Firms can overestimate these costs and then bleed back the overestimates to increase profits in the future. This makes the merger look more profitable than it is.

Special charges can of course be underestimated as well as overestimated. The analyst watches for charges that should be taken and are not. AT&T took four major charges between 1986 and 1993. The firm reported an average of nearly 10 percent annual profit growth over the period before the charges were subtracted, from $1.21 per share in 1996 to $3.13 per share in 1995. But the total of the restructuring charges of $14.2 billion exceeded the total reported net income of $10.3 billion over the period. AT&T maintained that the write-offs were caused by rapid technological change that hadn't been anticipated. But quality analysts raised a question: Were the profits before restructuring low quality, overstated profits that would have to be written off later? What was AT&T really making in profits during the period? Would an insightful analyst have adjusted the low quality earnings with "normalized depreciation"? Monitor normalized core operating income relative to reported core operating income. Watch particularly for cases where this ratio is low but other costs to sales are high; these conditions may signal a restructuring.

In view of the AT&T case, one must be skeptical about classifying restructuring charges as unusual. They may be repetitive, particularly during times of technological and organizational change. Citicorp took restructuring charges six years in a row, from 1988 to 1993, when changes shook the banking industry. Eastman Kodak did the same for five out of six years from 1989 to 1994. And Cadbury-Schweppes maintained in its 1996 report that "major restructuring costs are now widely recognized as a recurring item in major food manufacturers, estimated by some analysts as 0.5 percent of sales over the long term," and thus felt it no longer appropriate to exclude these costs from underlying (core) earnings.

The diagnostics here raise the alarm. They might be incorporated together in a model that yields a score of accounting quality. The scoring model would, at the heart of it, distinguish discretionary accruals from those that are justified by the business.[3] Such a

---

[3] Simple models of this type are developed in J. Jones, "Earnings Management during Import Relief Investigations," *Journal of Accounting Research* 29 (1991), pp. 193–223, and P. Dechow, R. Sloan, and A. Sweeney, "Detecting Earnings Management," *Accounting Review* 70 (1995), pp. 193–225.

model cannot substitute for knowing the business and pulling the financial statements apart but can, at a minimum, screen firms whose accounting quality is questionable and should be investigated.

DETECTING TRANSACTION MANIPULATION

Firms can choose accounting methods only as GAAP permits. Where GAAP is inflexible, they can sometimes arrange their business to accommodate GAAP to achieve a desired result.

Core Revenue Timing

Recognizing sales by shipping products in one fiscal year rather than another shifts income. Unfortunately this "channel stuffing" is hard to pick up unless one has details of monthly shipments. Watch for

- Unexpected shipments and sales increases or decreases in the final quarter.

- Structuring of lease transactions to qualify as sales-type leases in lessors' books.

Core Expense Timing

Firms can time expenditures, and these will affect income if they are expensed immediately. So look at R&D and advertising expenses. Investigate

> Diagnostic: R&D expense/Sales

> Diagnostic: Advertising expense/Sales

If these ratios are low, a firm might be deferring expenditures to the future to increase current income.

Advertising and R&D expenses may have more the quality of an asset because they may produce future profits. Increasing expenditures will reduce current income but may increase future income. Understand the technology and the markets for products to evaluate whether the expenditures will in fact produce future profits. Look at trends in the ratios over time. Look particularly for earnings that are generated by declining R&D or advertising. These may be low quality earnings because future earnings may suffer from the reduced expenditures.

Generally accepted accounting principles require most investments (other than R&D and advertising) to be capitalized as assets in the balance sheet so investment timing cannot affect income. But there is another thing to watch even if investments are capitalized. If the firm uses conservative accounting (as a matter of policy), we saw in the last chapter (in Table 16.7) that hidden reserves are created. If the growth in investment slows, hidden reserves are liquidated and profits increase. So a firm can slow investments temporarily to increase profits temporarily. This practice is sometimes referred to as *cookie-jar accounting*, dipping into the cookie jar (of hidden reserves) to generate profits. So watch firms you have identified as having conservative accounting policies and inspect their changes in inventory, plant, and intangibles.

A particular case is a firm using LIFO for inventories. If inventories are reduced, LIFO liquidation profits are realized as hidden reserves are released. We saw in Table 16.8 in Chapter 16 that over 25 percent of NYSE and AMEX firms on LIFO increased earnings with LIFO liquidations from 1982 to 1991. This is referred to as **LIFO dipping.** The footnotes are helpful here because the inventory note must give the amount of the LIFO reserve and the SEC requires that firms report the impact of LIFO dipping on income. Is it temporary? Firms can dip into LIFO inventories to boost profits temporarily, but a LIFO liquidation can also be the precursor to a long-run decline in the demand for the firm's products. And a drop in the LIFO reserve can follow a drop in prices, not inventory liquidation, and this is more likely to be permanent.

FIFO accounting is less open to manipulation. But because cost of goods sold is based on older costs (and inventory on more recent costs), FIFO cost of goods sold and FIFO earnings are sometimes said to be low quality if inventory costs are rising: Cost of goods sold does not indicate what firms are currently paying for inventory or will have to pay in the future. This is not of great concern, however, in the typical situation of rapid inventory turnover.

Other Core Income Timing

Look at the results reported by Coca-Cola Co. from 1995 to 1997 (in millions of dollars):

	1995	1996	1997
Operating income	4,026	3,915	5,001
Equity income in subsidiaries	169	211	155
Other income	86	87	583
Gain on issuances of stock by equity investees	74	431	363

Coke, as we have seen, has been very profitable. But increasingly a significant share of income from subsidiaries has come from gains that are recognized on a parent's equity investment when a subsidiary issues shares. Some issues were of one subsidiary's shares to another. Coke presumably has "significant influence" in issuing these shares and so might be able to arrange share issues to time the recognition of gains in its own accounts. Coke might maintain that this is a device to represent the real profitability of subsidiaries. But it can also be used for manipulation. And since the gains are from share issues, not operations, they are low quality.

Unusual Income Timing

Firms time asset sales to increase or decrease net income by recognizing gains or losses on the sales. Classifying these gains and losses as unusual deals with the quality issue, but beware of sales that are made of good quality business just to affect income. A firm may sell an asset with low book value relative to its market value to record a gain that increases current income, but future income is impaired by the loss of earnings from the asset.

Organizational Manipulation: Off-Balance-Sheet Operations

Firms can sometimes arrange their affairs to get some aspect of operations off the books. These off-balance-sheet operations are called **shells** and setting them up is called the *shell game*.

R&D Partnerships

Expenditures for R&D reduce income. Firms therefore sometimes set up a shell company—perhaps with other partners—to carry out the R&D. The original company may actually do the research but then charge the R&D partnership, creating revenue for itself to offset its R&D expenditure. If the R&D is unsuccessful, the investment in the shell has to be written off, and past revenues from the R&D would be fictitious.

Pension Funds

Pension funds can become overfunded, as happened in the 1990s with the long bull market in stocks (held by pension funds). This overfunding is technically the property of the employees, but firms find ways to use the overfunding to pay for operational expenses. They apply it to early retirement plans, retiree health benefits, and merger financing, the cost of which would otherwise be borne in the income statement.

Special Purpose Entities

These entities are designed to hold assets that might otherwise be on a firm's balance sheet, like leased assets and assets that have been securitized. Although the firm may not have control of these entities (and thus the entities are not consolidated), it may have some recourse liability for the obligations of the entity.

JUSTIFIABLE MANIPULATION?

It is claimed that Coca-Cola realizes gains from stock issues to report the underlying profitability in subsidiaries that investors might not otherwise see. General Electric is alleged to "smooth" earnings to give a picture of regular, predictable profit growth.

Managements smooth earnings by borrowing income from the future or by shifting income to the future. They borrow earnings in bad years and bank earnings in good years. All's well and good if they can be sure that a bad year will be followed by good years from which they borrow. Indeed, such practices will help with forecasting as the current year's earnings will be a better indicator of future earnings. One might argue the quality of earnings is better (for forecasting) if they are smoothed!

But what if bad years are followed by bad years? Then the quality of current earnings, increased to make them look better, is doubtful. Thus analyzing this practice is a tricky business and the analyst has to be very sure of a firm's long-run earnings prospects before accepting the manipulated earnings as high quality. Accept a high, manipulated RNOA only if the firm has the real profitability to maintain the RNOA in the future. In Coke's case, what if profitability declined but profits could no longer be propped up with the gains from shares in subsidiaries?

DISCLOSURE QUALITY

News Corporation (of which Rupert Murdoch is chairman) is engaged in publishing, entertainment, television, and sports franchises. Prior to 1998 it ran these businesses through hundreds of companies in scores of countries. Its consolidated statements were hard to sort out, to say the least, and analysts often requested greater transparency. They had difficulty discovering where profits were coming from. And, while a large proportion of revenues and profits came from film, television, and sports in the United States, News Corporation was priced more like a publishing concern than an entertainment company: It traded in 1998 at 8.5 times estimated 1998 earnings as compared to 16 and higher for competitors like Disney, Viacom, and Time Warner. In June 1998 Murdoch announced that the U.S. entertainment assets, including 20th Century Fox, the Fox television network, the Los Angeles Dodgers, and part interest in the New York Knicks and Rangers would be bundled into a separate company—Fox Group—and a public offering made of 20 percent of its stock. News Corporation's stock price rose 12 percent on the news of the spinoff. Was this the reward for disclosure? Other factors may have contributed but analysts hailed the added transparency that would result as a reason for valuing the earnings higher. "Tracking" or "letter" stocks for a division of a company—like the Hughes Electronics unit of General Motors—have the same effect (and also separate out an earnings stream, which some investors might want), but the shareholder usually doesn't have voting rights.

The News Corporation spinoff indicates that poor disclosure leads to lower valuations: Investors discount the price for the risk from not having information. The price effect of poor disclosure is sometimes couched in terms of the cost of capital: Low-quality disclosure raises the required return to compensate for additional risk.

Disclosure issues permeate all aspects of financial analysis and by now you will have accumulated a list of problems you have had with disclosures in getting to this point. The following (and many more!) should be on your list:

- Consolidation accounting often makes the source of profitability hard to discover.

- Line of business and geographical segment reporting is often not detailed enough.

- Earnings in unconsolidated subsidiaries are hard to analyze. (Think of a firm that has all its earnings in subsidiaries in which it has less than 50 percent ownership: Core profit margins are not transparent.)

- Disclosure is insufficient to reconcile free cash flow in the cash flow statement to free cash flow calculated (as $OI - \Delta NOA$) from the income statement and balance sheet. Some of the problems arise from uncertainty about items to be included in operating income and net operating assets.

- Disclosures to calculate stock compensation overhang are thin.

- Information is often not available to calculate losses on conversion of convertible claims into common equity.

- Details on selling, general, and administrative expenses are often scarce.

ABNORMAL RETURNS TO QUALITY ANALYSIS

Many analysts claim that the market is "fixated" on reported earnings. The market takes earnings at face value, so managers are tempted to manipulate earnings to affect stock prices. A person who believes in efficient markets would maintain that the market sees through any accounting tricks to the real profitability. But if history is any indication, a quality analyst who believed otherwise might find that piercing through the accounting will discover mispricing that leads to abnormal returns.

Figure 17.3 gives annual returns, from 1962 to 1991, that have been documented from taking long positions in stocks with low operating accruals and short positions in stocks with high operating accruals. The returns are the sum of those to the long and short positions which, together, involve zero investment: The proceeds from the short position are used to invest in the long position so the investor has no money invested except that to finance the short positions. The historical analysis is based on all nonfinancial NYSE and AMEX firms. Accruals are measured relative to total assets (with a revenue accrual being positive and an expense accrual negative), so they are the part of the return on total assets deriving from accruals. Manipulation can be accomplished with accruals, so the idea is that particularly high accruals are suggestive of earnings and return on assets that have been manipulated up (aggressive accounting) and particularly low accruals are suggestive of big-bath accounting.

FIGURE 17.3 **Returns by Calendar Year to a Hedge Portfolio That Takes a Long Position in the Stocks of Firms with the Lowest 10 Percent of the Amount of Accruals Reported and a Short Position in the Stocks of Firms with the Highest 10 Percent of Accruals.** Accruals are the change in noncash current assets, less the change in current liabilities (exclusive of short-term debt and taxes payable), less depreciation expense, all divided by average total assets. The combined return to the long and short positions—the hedge portfolio return—is positive in all but two years. The hedge position requires zero investment, so if stocks are priced efficiently, the position should earn zero returns.

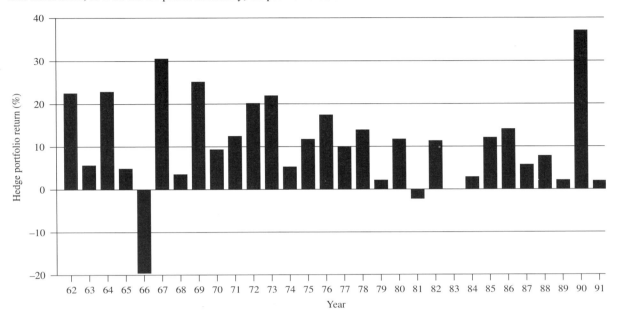

Source: R. Sloan, "Do Stock Prices Fully Reflect Information in Accruals and Cash Flows about Future Earnings?" *Accounting Review* 71 (1996), p. 312.

It's clear from the figure that this trading strategy would have been profitable in all except two years. Firms whose return on assets are measured with a lot of income-increasing accruals tend to be overvalued, and their stock prices subsequently decline. Firms whose return on assets are measured with a lot of income-decreasing accruals tend to be undervalued, and their stock prices subsequently increase. The findings suggest that the mispricing can be exploited to earn abnormal returns, that is, returns with no investment required. And this is so with a very simple quality analysis—distinguishing accruals from cash flow from operations as in the CFO/OI diagnostic.

Why might the strategy work? Figure 17.4 gives the pattern of earnings (relative to total assets) for the firms with the high and low accruals in the short and long portfolios in the trading strategy, for five years before and after Year 0, the year when accruals are identified as high or low. You see that for firms with high accruals, earnings increase up to Year 0 but decline subsequently, and for firms with low accruals, earnings decline up to Year 0 but increase subsequently. This is a pattern one would expect if accruals subsequently reverse. The earnings in Year 0 are low quality for both groups. It appears that the market did not appreciate that high and low accruals can be temporary. The market price "corrected" as subsequent earnings were reported. A quality analyst would have understood the accounting quality and the market's apparent misconception.

You can work out the approximate reward to quality analysis. If you adjust core operating profit margins by 1 percent and the asset turnover is 2.0, the adjustment translates to

FIGURE 17.4 **Patterns of Earnings for High- and Low-Accrual Firms** Year 0 is the year in which firms are assigned to high- and low-accrual portfolios. Earnings are measured as income from continuing operations scaled by average total assets for the year. For high-accrual firms, earnings increase up to Year 0 but subsequently decline. For low-accrual firms, earnings decline up to Year 0 but subsequently increase.

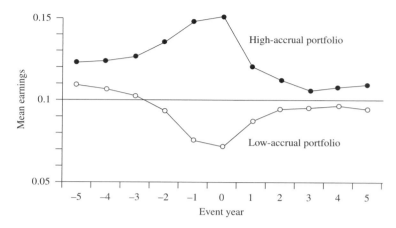

Source: R. Sloan, "Do Stock Prices Fully Reflect Information in Accruals and Cash Flows about Future Earnings?" *Accounting Review* 71 (1996), p. 301.

a change in the core RNOA of 2 percent. If you revise your forecast of long-run RNOA accordingly, then, capitalizing the 2 percent effect at a 10 percent cost of capital (say), the change in your valuation (and the premium) is 20 cents for every dollar of book value if no growth in book value is forecast. This calculation applies to the SF2 valuation. If net operating assets are forecasted to grow, the effect is larger.

Summary

When forecasting from the current financial statements, the analyst must be concerned with the quality of the accounting used in those statements. If accounting methods and estimates temporarily increase or decrease reported profitability, the analyst knows that the effect will reverse in the future.

This chapter has developed a set of diagnostics to use in an accounting quality analysis. These diagnostics are merely suggestive, flags to raise suspicions about the accounting numbers. They lead to further investigation and to questions to management, to resolve the suspicions that they raise. To reach an overall judgment of accounting quality, the analyst is aware of situations when manipulation is more likely and is aware of the sensitive issues in particular industries. The chapter has outlined situations where the analyst must have particular concerns about the quality of the accounting.

Accounting quality analysis is part of the wider analysis of sustainable earnings. So marry the material in this chapter with that on sustainable earnings in Chapter 12. And use the red-flag analysis of Chapter 15 to raise further questions about the ability of the firm to maintain current profitability in the future.

The Web Connection

Find the following on the web page for this chapter:

- Further examples of low quality accounting.

- A discussion of recent quality problems that have surfaced at companies.

- An introduction to methods that score firms on their accounting quality.

- Results from research that investigates earnings quality.

- More on the abnormal returns that have been reported from using quality-of-earnings diagnostics.

Key Concepts

aggressive accounting is accounting that recognizes more current income than alternative accounting methods. Compare with **big-bath accounting**. *608*

audit quality refers to the integrity of the audit in ensuring that generally accepted accounting principles have been adhered to. *604*

banking (or saving) income for the future refers to the practice of reducing current income and deferring it to the future. Compare with **borrowing income from the future**. *607*

big-bath accounting is accounting that reduces current income (usually by large amounts). Compare with **aggressive accounting**. *608*

bleeding back income is the practice of recognizing income that has previously been banked for the future. *603*

borrowing income from the future refers to the (aggressive accounting) practice of recognizing income currently that would otherwise be recognized in the future. Compare with **banking income for the future**. *607*

channel stuffing is the practice of advancing sales to the current period to recognize more revenue. *605*

disclosure quality is the degree to which financial statements and their footnotes give the detail necessary to analyze them. *605*

expenditure timing is the practice of timing expenditures to accounting periods. *605*

GAAP application quality is the degree to which a firm uses GAAP accounting to give a "true and fair" view of the firm's activities: A firm can use accounting methods available within GAAP to give a distorting view of the firm's activities. *604*

GAAP quality is the degree to which generally accepted accounting principles (GAAP) capture the transactions that are relevant to the valuation of a firm. *604*

LIFO dipping is the practice of reducing LIFO inventories to increase current income by the liquidation of LIFO reserves. *621*

quality diagnostic is a measure that raises questions as to the quality of accounting in financial statements. *611*

quality of earnings is the degree to which current earnings serve as an indicator of future earnings. *606*

revenue timing is the method of assigning revenue to accounting periods. *605*

shell is an operation that is part of a firm's business but is organized in such a way as to keep the operation off the firm's balance sheet. *622*

transaction timing refers to the practice of arranging a firm's business around the accounting rules so as to recognize transactions in particular accounting periods. *604*

The Analyst's Toolkit

Analysis Tools	Page	Key Measures	Page	Acronymns to Remember
Five questions about quality	604	Diagnostics		ATO asset turnover
Prelude to quality analysis	608	Net sales/Cash from sales	611	CFO cash flow from operations
Diagnostics to detect		Net sales/Net accounts		ebit earnings before interest and
manipulated accounting:		receivable	611	taxes
Sales	611	Net sales/Unearned revenue	611	ebitda earnings before interest,
Core expenses	614	Net sales/Warranty liabilities	611	taxes, depreciation, and
Unusual items	619	Bad-debt ratios	614	amortization
Diagnostics to detect		Warranty expense ratios	614	FIFO first in, first out
transaction timing:		Normalized OI/OI	614	IPO initial public offering
Core revenue timing	621	Change in asset turnover	614	LIFO last in, first out
Core expense timing	621	Adjusted ebitda/ebit	616	NOA net operating assets
Other core income timing	622	Depreciation/Capital		OI operating income
Unusual income timing	622	expenditures	616	PM profit margin
Organizational		Cash flow from		R&D research and development
manipulation	622	operations/OI	616	RNOA return on net operating
		Cash flow from		assets
		operations/Average NOA	617	SEC U.S. Securities and Exchange
		Expense accrual diagnostics	617	Commission
		Effective tax rate on		SG&A selling, general, and
		operations	617	administrative (expenses)
		R&D expense/Sales	621	
		Advertising expense/Sales	621	

Concept Questions

C17.1. A firm can create future income by temporarily increasing its bad debt allowance. Is this correct?

C17.2. Low depreciation charges forecast losses in future income statements. Is this correct?

C17.3. A decrease in warranty liabilities increases net sales. Is this correct?

C17.4. Increasing profit margins by underestimating expenses creates net operating assets. Is this correct?

C17.5. Why is a change in the asset turnover an indicator of future profitability?

C17.6. Why do analysts compare cash flow from operations with earnings to assess the quality of the earnings?

C17.7. Why should an analyst view a large merger charge suspiciously?

C17.8. Why should an analyst view an increase in deferred taxes from bad debt allowances suspiciously?

C17.9. IBM reported a 3 percent increase in income for its first quarter of 2000, beating analysts' estimates. But it also reported a decline in revenue. Its stock price dropped in response to the report.

What explanations would you give for the drop in stock price on an earnings increase?

What is your prediction for the change in IBM's asset turnover over the quarter?

C17.10. Excite signed a pact with Netscape in 1999 under which it paid $86.1 million to share revenues from co-branded search-and-directory services. It wrote off two-thirds of the cost—or $56.8 million—against income immediately.

Analysts objected. Why should they?

C17.11. Shares of Pitney Bowes dropped 10 percent after it announced earnings per share from continuing operations of $0.70 for its September quarter of 1999, up from $0.49 in the same quarter in the year before. Revenues also increased 8 percent.

Analysts raised concerns about the quality of the earnings, citing a decrease in the firm's effective tax rate. Why might the effective tax rate be of concern to analysts?

C17.12. If you saw a deferred tax liability from depreciation increase significantly over a year, what might you conclude?

C17.13. A firm has a capital expenditure-to-depreciation ratio of 1.6 over three years. What might you infer from this ratio?

C17.14. Some firms suggest that investors focus on "pro forma" earnings rather than reported earnings. Their pro forma earnings usually exclude amortizations of goodwill and shares of losses in subsidiaries. Is this good advice?

C17.15. In July 1999, Federal Reserve Chairman Alan Greenspan stated that corporate profits in the United States were understated, particularly in the technology sector. To what do you think he was referring?

C17.16. The realization principle, which recognizes revenues at point of sale, is said to be an accounting principle that improves the quality of reporting. Companies cannot estimate their future revenues; rather they must have a firm customer before they can recognize revenue. Do you see the realization principle as a desirable accounting principle?

C17.17. Matching costs to revenue—the matching principle—is seen as producing "good quality" earnings numbers. Why?

Exercises

E17.1. **Quality of Earnings per Share: Reebok (Easy)**

Reebok International reported the following for 1996 and 1997 (amounts in thousands, except per-share data):

	Year Ended December 31	
	1997	**1996**
Net sales	$3,643,599	$3,478,604
Income before income taxes and minority interest	158,085	237,668
Net income	135,119	138,950
Basic earnings per share	2.41	2.06

Review the analysis of Reebok in Chapters 11, 12, and 13. Why did net income decline from 1996 to 1997 yet earnings per share increased?

E17.2. **Stock Market Reactions to Earnings Announcements: Eastman Kodak and Intel (Medium)**

For its September quarter of 1998, Eastman Kodak, the imaging products manufacturer, reported a net profit of $398 million, up 72 percent from one year earlier and in line with analysts' expectations. However, when it was also revealed that its sales had fallen 10 percent to $3.4 billion, its stock price dropped 13 percent.

EXHIBIT 17.1

EASTMAN KODAK
Partial Cash Flow Statements
(in millions of dollars)

	Three Quarters	
	1998	**1997**
Cash Flows from Operating Activities		
Net earnings	1,118	749
Adjustments to reconcile above earnings to net cash provided by operating activities, excluding the effect of initial consolidation of acquired companies		
Depreciation and amortization	619	600
Purchased research and development	—	186
Deferred taxes	(63)	(76)
(Gain) loss on sale or retirement of businesses, investments, and properties	(107)	1
Increase in receivables	(216)	(57)
Increase in inventories	(334)	(156)
Decrease in liabilities excluding borrowings	(553)	(285)
Other items, net	(26)	(97)
Total adjustments	(680)	116
Net cash provided by operating activities	438	865

For the same quarter, Intel, the world's biggest computer chip manufacturer, reported that its net income of $1.6 billion was much the same as a year earlier, but sales rose 9 percent to $6.7 billion. Its stock price increased by 8 percent after the announcement.

a. Calculate the changes in the net profit margins in the September 1999 quarter over the quarter for the year earlier for both firms. Why would the price reaction be so different to the two earnings announcements?

b. Exhibit 17.1 is the cash flow from operations section of Eastman Kodak's cash flow statements for the first three quarters of 1998 and 1997. Sales were $9.843 billion for the first three quarters of 1998 and $10.759 billion for the corresponding period for 1997. Do these statements provide any information about earnings quality?

E17.3. The SEC and Microsoft (Easy)

a. In 1999, Microsoft Corporation announced that the Securities and Exchange Commission (SEC) was investigating some of its accounting practices. Exhibit 17.2 presents the asset and liability sections of Microsoft's comparative balance sheet at the end of the first quarter of its 2000 fiscal year. Can you see a reason for the SEC's concern?

b. Exhibit 17.3 is the cash from operations section of Microsoft's cash flow statement for the same quarter. Microsoft reported revenues of $5.384 billion in the quarter to September 30, 1999, and $4.193 billion for the corresponding quarter for 1998.

Does it appear that the SEC's concerns were justified in the 1999 period?

Real World Connection

See Exercises E1.3 in Chapter 1, E3.8 in Chapter 3, E4.8 in Chapter 4, and Minicase M8.1 in Chapter 8 for related material on Microsoft.

EXHIBIT 17.2

MICROSOFT CORPORATION
Partial Balance Sheets
(in millions)

	Sept. 30, 1999	June 30, 1999
Assets		
Current assets		
Cash and short-term investments	$18,902	$17,236
Accounts receivable	2,207	2,245
Other	854	752
Total current assets	21,963	20,233
Property and equipment	1,657	1,611
Equity and other investments	14,910	14,372
Other assets	1,142	940
Total assets	$39,672	$37,156
Liabilities and Stockholders' Equity		
Current liabilities		
Accounts payable	$ 997	$ 874
Accrued compensation	313	396
Income taxes payable	1,136	1,607
Unearned revenue	4,129	4,239
Other	1,757	1,602
Total current liabilities	$ 8,332	$ 8,718

EXHIBIT 17.3

MICROSOFT CORPORATION
Partial Cash Flow Statements
(in millions)

	Three Months Ended September 30	
	1999	1998
Operations		
Net income	$2,191	$1,683
Depreciation	440	179
Gains in sales	(156)	(160)
Unearned revenue	1,253	1,010
Recognition of unearned revenue from prior periods	(1,363)	(765)
Other current liabilities	(345)	360
Accounts receivable	64	341
Other current assets	(94)	(64)
Net cash from operations	$1,990	$2,584

E17.4. **A Financial Statement Restatement: Sunbeam (Medium)**

By the mid-1990s, Sunbeam Corporation, the once celebrated household appliance manufacturer, was reporting lackluster sales and losses. New management, engaged in 1996 to turn the company around, implemented a major restructuring and trumpeted higher sales and profitability. The firm's stock price rose 50 percent over 1997 as results confirmed the predictions.

In 1998, the firm restated its annual reports for 1996 and 1997 with the following introduction:

> Subsequent to the issuance of the Company's Consolidated Financial Statements for the fiscal years ended December 28, 1997, and December 29, 1996, it was determined that the reported results generally inflated 1997 results at the expense of 1996 results.

The firm's stock price dropped from $50 to $10 after the announcement of the restatement.

Part of the restatement had to do with improperly recognized sales. Net sales for 1997 were restated from $1.168 billion down to $1.073 billion but those for 1996 were unchanged. Expenses in both years were affected, however. Exhibits 17.4 and 17.5 are the original and restated cash flow from operations. What were the aspects of the original reports that had to be restated?

EXHIBIT 17.4
From Original Cash Flow Statement (in Millions)

SUNBEAM CORPORATION		
	1997	**1996**
Operating Activities		
Net earnings (loss)	$109,415	($228,262)
Adjustments to reconcile net earnings (loss) to net cash provided by (used in) operating activities		
Depreciation and amortization	38,577	47,429
Restructuring, impairment, and other costs	—	154,869
Other noncash special charges	—	128,800
Loss on sale of discontinued operations, net of taxes	13,713	32,430
Deferred income taxes	57,783	(77,828)
Increase (decrease) in cash from changes in working capital		
Receivables, net	(84,576)	(13,829)
Inventories	(100,810)	(11,651)
Accounts payable	(1,585)	14,735
Restructuring accrual	(43,378)	—
Prepaid expenses and other current assets and liabilities	(9,004)	2,737
Income taxes payable	52,844	(21,942)
Payment of other long-term and nonoperating liabilities	(14,682)	(27,089)
Other, net	(26,546)	13,764
Net cash provided by (used in) operating activities	$ (8,249)	$ 14,163

EXHIBIT 17.5
From Restated Cash
Flow Statement
(in Millions)

SUNBEAM CORPORATION		
	Restated 1997	**Restated 1996**
Operating Activities		
Net earnings (loss)	$38,301	($208,481)
Adjustments to reconcile net earnings (loss) to net cash (used in) provided by operating activities		
Depreciation and amortization	39,757	47,429
Restructuring and asset impairment (benefits) charges	(14,582)	110,122
Other noncash special charges	—	70,847
Loss on sale of discontinued operations, net of taxes	14,017	39,140
Deferred income taxes	38,824	(69,206)
Increase (decrease) in cash from changes in operating assets and liabilities from continuing operations		
Receivables, net	(57,843)	(845)
Proceeds from accounts receivable securitization	58,887	—
Inventories	(140,555)	11,289
Accounts payable	4,261	11,029
Restructuring accrual	(31,957)	—
Prepaid expenses and other current assets and liabilities	(16,092)	39,657
Income taxes payable	52,052	(21,942)
Payment of other long-term and nonoperating liabilities	(1,401)	(27,089)
Other, net	10,288	12,213
Net cash (used in) provided by operating activities	$ (6,043)	$ 14,163

E17.5.   Analysis of Restructuring Charges: EDS (Easy)

Electronic Data Systems (EDS) reported net income of $420.9 million for 1999, $743.4 million for 1998, and $730.6 million for 1997. Sales for the corresponding periods were $18.6 billion, $16.9 billion, and $15.2 billion. It also reported the following in its footnotes for 1999:

The following table summarizes activity in the restructuring accruals for the years ended December 31, 1999, 1998, and 1997 (in millions):

	1997 Restructuring Charge	1998 Restructuring Charge	1999 Restructuring Charge
Balance at December 31, 1996	$97.5	$ —	$ —
1997 Restructuring charge	—	125.3	—
Cash payments	(51.2)	(55.1)	—
Balance at December 31, 1997	46.3	70.2	—
Cash payments	(7.4)	(53.1)	—
Reversal of residual accruals	(11.4)	(10.8)	—
Balance at December 31, 1998	27.5	6.3	—
1999 Restructuring charge	—	—	759.2
Cash payments	(6.4)	(0.5)	(293.9)
Reversal of residual accruals	(11.0)	(3.7)	(14.7)
Balance at December 31, 1999	$10.1	$ 2.1	$450.6

What does this footnote tell you about the quality of the firm's earnings?

E17.6. Analyzing Earnings Quality with the Deferred Tax Footnote: Tandem Computers (Hard)

Tandem Computers, Inc., accounted for its deferred tax assets and liabilities in the footnote to its 1996 annual report as follows (in thousands):

	1996	1995
Deferred tax assets		
Restructuring accruals	$ 26,916	$ 32,381
Inventory reserves	19,192	10,108
Deferred income	12,975	17,492
Intercompany profit eliminations	25,885	28,408
Federal tax credit carryovers (expire beginning 1997)	53,621	36,470
Federal net operating loss carryover (expires in 2010)	53,077	50,497
Foreign net operating loss carryovers (expire beginning 1997)	11,311	10,504
Foreign taxes on unremitted foreign earnings, net of the related U.S. tax liability	53,349	49,811
Expenses not currently deductible	37,272	28,051
Other	21,536	6,593
Total deferred tax assets	315,134	270,315
Valuation allowance for deferred tax assets	(200,043)	(163,384)
Net deferred tax assets	$115,091	$106,931
Deferred tax liabilities		
Capitalized software	$ (53,614)	$ (43,084)
Operating leases for income tax reporting	(32,763)	(41,208)
Accelerated depreciation	(10,635)	(11,900)
Total net deferred tax liabilities	$ (97,012)	$ (96,192)
Total net deferred tax assets	$ 18,079	$ 10,739

What issues does this footnote raise about the quality of Tandem's earnings?

E17.7. The Quality of Revenues: Bausch & Lomb (Easy)

Bausch and Lomb, Inc., the optical products company, reported the following sales and receivables from 1990 to 1993 (in millions of dollars):

	1990	1991	1992	1993
Net sales	1,368.6	1,520.1	1,709.1	1,872.2
Trade receivables, less allowances	203.0	205.3	277.3	385.0

Subsequently it was discovered that the firm had booked revenues incorrectly. Do the numbers here raise concerns about the quality of the reported revenues?

Minicases

M17.1

A QUALITY ANALYSIS: XEROX CORPORATION

Xerox Corporation is a long-established company whose very name has been lent to the process of copying documents. The firm develops copying technology through an extensive research program and manufactures and markets a large range of document processing products. Many of its sales are made with lease financing arrangements through its Xerox Credit Corporation in the United States and through other subsidiaries worldwide. The firm's traditional black and white lens copiers (which provided 40 percent of revenues in 1999) were under challenge in the late 1990s from new digital technology, and Xerox developed digital copiers, printers, and production publishers in response.

Xerox initiated a major restructuring of its operations in 1998, and the implementation of the restructuring caused some difficulties in the field. In 1999, total revenues of $19.2 billion were down 1 percent from $19.4 billion in 1998. An announcement that revenues would not meet expectations in October 1999 resulted in a 24 percent share price drop. During 1999 Xerox's share price dropped from $59 to $24. However, income from continuing operations for the full 1999 year, ending December 31, was $1.43 billion, up from $585 million in 1998.

Xerox's income statements for 1997, 1998, and 1999 are reproduced in Exhibit 17.6, along with sections of its cash flow statements. Also given are extracts from the 1999 footnotes.

EXHIBIT 17.6

XEROX CORP.
Income Statements
(in millions, except per-share data)

	Year Ended December 31		
	1999	1998	1997
Revenues			
Sales	$10,346	$10,696	$ 9,881
Service and rentals	7,856	7,678	7,257
Finance income	1,026	1,073	1,006
Total revenues	19,228	19,447	18,144
Costs and Expenses			
Cost of sales	5,744	5,662	5,330
Cost of service and rentals	4,481	4,205	3,778
Inventory charges	0	113	0
Equipment financing interest	547	570	520
Research and development expenses	979	1,040	1,065
Selling, administrative, and general expenses	5,144	5,321	5,212
Restructuring charge and asset impairments	0	1,531	0
Other, net	297	242	98
Total costs and expenses	17,192	18,684	16,003
Income before income taxes, equity income, and minority interests	2,036	763	2,141
Income taxes	631	207	728
Equity in net income of unconsolidated affiliates	68	74	127
Minority interests in earnings of subsidiaries	49	45	88
Income from continuing operations	1,424	585	1,452
Discontinued operations	0	(190)	0
Net income	$ 1,424	$ 395	$ 1,452

(continued)

EXHIBIT 17.6
(continued)

Partial Cash Flow Statements
(in millions)

	Year Ended December 31		
	1999	**1998**	**1997**
Cash Flows from Operating Activities			
Income from continuing operations	$1,424	$ 585	$1,452
Adjustments required to reconcile income to cash flows from operating activities			
Depreciation and amortization	935	821	739
Provision for doubtful accounts	359	301	265
Restructuring charge and other charges	0	1,644	0
Provision for postretirement medical benefits, net of payments	41	33	29
Cash charges against 1998 restructuring reserve	(437)	(332)	0
Minorities' interests in earnings of subsidiaries	49	45	88
Undistributed equity in income of affiliated companies	(68)	(27)	(84)
Decrease (increase) in inventories	68	(558)	(170)
Increase in on-lease equipment	(401)	(473)	(347)
Increase in finance receivables	(1,788)	(2,169)	(1,629)
Proceeds from securization of finance receivables	1,495	0	0
Increase in accounts receivable	(94)	(540)	(188)
(Decrease) increase in accounts payable and accrued compensation and benefit costs	(94)	127	250
Net change in other current and noncurrent liabilities	277	(192)	361
Change in current and deferred income taxes	(78)	67	83
Other, net	(464)	(497)	(377)
Total	1,224	(1,165)	472
Cash Flows from Investing Activities			
Cost of additions to land, buildings, and equipment	(594)	(566)	(520)
Proceeds from sales of land, buildings, and equipment	99	74	36
Acquisitions, net of cash acquired	(107)	(380)	(812)
Other, net	(25)	5	45
Total	$(627)	$(867)	$(1,251)

Peruse the statements and footnotes. What questions arise about the quality of the earnings reported in 1998 and 1999?

Extracts from Footnotes

The following footnote extracts refer to 1999. Dollar amounts are in millions.

2 Restructuring

In 1998, we announced a worldwide restructuring program intended to enhance our competitive position and lower our overall cost structure. In connection with this program, we recorded a pretax provision of $1,644. The program includes the elimination of approximately 9,000 jobs, net, worldwide, the closing and consolidation of facilities, and the write-down of certain assets. The charges associated with this restructuring program include

$113 of inventory charges recorded as cost of revenues and $316 of asset impairments. Included in the asset impairment charge is facility fixed asset write-downs of $156 and other asset write-downs of $160. Key initiatives of the restructuring include:

1. Consolidating 56 European customer support centers into one facility and implementing a shared services organization for back-office operations.
2. Streamlining manufacturing, logistics, distribution, and service operations. This will include centralizing U.S. parts depots and outsourcing storage and distribution.
3. Overhauling our internal processes and associated resources, including closing one of four geographically organized U.S. customer administrative centers.

The reductions are occurring primarily in administrative functions, but also impact service, research, and manufacturing.

The following table summarizes the status of the restructuring reserve (in millions):

	Total Reserve	Charges against Reserve	12/31/99 Balance
Severance and related costs	$1,017	$ 717	$300
Asset impairment	316	316	0
Lease cancellation and other costs	198	104	94
Inventory charges	113	113	0
Total	$1,644	$1,250	$394

5 Finance Receivables, Net

Finance receivables result from installment sales and sales-type leases arising from the marketing of our business equipment products. These receivables generally mature over two to five years and are typically collateralized by a security interest in the underlying assets. The components of finance receivables, net at December 31, 1999, 1998, and 1997 follow:

	1999	1998	1997
Gross receivables	$14,666	$16,139	$14,094
Unearned income	(1,677)	(2,084)	(1,909)
Unguaranteed residual values	752	699	557
Allowance for doubtful accounts	(423)	(441)	(389)
Finance receivables, net	13,318	14,313	12,353
Less current portion	5,115	5,220	4,599
Amounts due after one year, net	$ 8,203	$ 9,093	$ 7,754

6 Inventories

The components of inventories at December 31, 1999, 1998, and 1997 follow:

	1999	1998	1997
Finished goods	$1,800	$1,923	$1,549
Work in process	122	111	97
Raw materials	363	464	406
Equipment on operating leases, net	676	771	740
Inventories	$2,961	$3,269	$2,792

7 Investments in Affiliates, at Equity

Investments in corporate joint ventures and other companies in which we generally have a 20 to 50 percent ownership interest at December 31, 1999, 1998, and 1997 follow:

	1999	1998	1997
Fuji Xerox	$1,513	$1,354	$1,231
Other investments	102	102	101
Investments in affiliates, at equity	$1,615	$1,456	$1,332

Xerox Limited owns 50 percent of the outstanding stock of Fuji Xerox, a corporate joint venture with Fuji Photo Film Co. Ltd. (Fuji Photo). Fuji Xerox is headquartered in Tokyo and operates in Japan and other areas of the Pacific Rim, Australia, and New Zealand, except for China. Condensed financial data of Fuji Xerox for its last three fiscal years follow:

	1999	1998	1997
Summary of Operations			
Revenues	$7,751	$6,809	$7,415
Costs and expenses	7,440	6,506	6,882
Income before income taxes	311	303	533
Income taxes	201	195	295
Net income	$ 110	$ 108	$ 238
Balance Sheet Data			
Assets			
Current assets	$3,521	$2,760	$2,461
Noncurrent assets	3,521	3,519	2,942
Total assets	$7,042	$6,279	$5,403
Liabilities and Shareholders' Equity			
Current liabilities	$2,951	$2,628	$2,218
Long-term debt	169	101	286
Other noncurrent liabilities	1,079	1,028	679
Shareholders' equity	2,843	2,522	2,220
Total liabilities and shareholders' equity	$7,042	$6,279	$5,403

8 Segment Reporting

Our reportable segments are as follows: Core Business, Fuji Xerox, Paper and Media, and Other.

	Document Processing Segments			
	Core Business	Fuji Xerox	Paper and Media	Other
1999				
Information about profit or loss				
Revenues from external customers	$15,224	$0	$1,148	$1,830
Finance income	1,016	0	0	10
Intercompany revenues	(206)	0	0	206
Total segment revenues	16,034	0	1,148	2,046
Depreciation and amortization	930	0	0	5
Interest expense	803	0	0	0
Segment profit (loss)	2,014	0	62	(40)
Earnings of nonconsolidated affiliates	13	$55	0	0
Information about assets				
Investments in nonconsolidated affiliates	102	1,513	0	0
Total assets	25,319	1,513	86	1,896
Capital expenditures	580	0	0	14

M17.2

A QUALITY ANALYSIS: LUCENT TECHNOLOGIES

Lucent Technologies, Inc., was formed from AT&T's Bell Laboratories research organization after the breakup of AT&T into the Baby Bells. Lucent designs, develops, and manufactures communication systems, supplying these systems to most of the world's telecom operators for both wired and wireless services for voice, data, and video delivery. In 1999 Lucent reported $38.301 billion in revenues, against $31.806 billion in 1998 and $27.611 billion in 1997.

Analysts have complained about the quality of Lucent's reported earnings over the years.

A. What questions arise regarding the quality of Lucent's earnings for 1997, 1998, and 1999 from the partial cash flow statements in Exhibit 17.7?

EXHIBIT 17.7

Partial Consolidated Statements of Cash Flows
(dollars in millions)

	Year Ended September 30		
	1999	**1998**	**1997**
Operating Activities			
Net income	$4,766	$1,035	$ 449
Adjustments to reconcile net income to net cash (used in) provided by operating activities, net of effects from acquisitions of businesses			
Cumulative effect of accounting change	(1,308)	0	0
Business restructuring reversal	(141)	(100)	(201)
Asset impairment and other charges	236	0	81
Depreciation and amortization	1,806	1,411	1,499
Provision for uncollectibles	75	149	136
Tax benefit from stock options	367	271	88
Deferred income taxes	1,026	56	(21)
Purchased in-process research and development	15	1,683	1,255
Adjustment to conform Ascend and Kenan's fiscal years	169	0	0
Increase in receivables—net	(3,183)	(2,161)	(484)
Increase in inventories and contracts in process	(1,612)	(403)	(316)
Increase (decrease) in accounts payable	668	231	(18)
Changes in other operating assets and liabilities	(2,320)	155	(397)
Other adjustments for noncash items—net	(840)	(467)	58
Net cash (used in) provided by operating activities	$ (276)	$1,860	$2,129

B. How do deferred tax footnotes help in ascertaining the quality of the accounting? Does the note below (from the 1999 report) raise any quality questions?

The components of deferred tax assets and liabilities at September 30, 1999, and 1998 are as follows:

	September 30		
Deferred Income Tax Assets	**1999**	**1998**	**1997**
Employee pensions and other benefits—net	$ 442	$1,520	$1,777
Business restructuring	6	165	112
Reserves and allowances	1,009	1,137	887
Net operating loss/credit carryforwards	226	239	107
Valuation allowance	(179)	(261)	(234)
Other	344	526	664
Total deferred tax assets	$1,848	$3,326	$3,313
Deferred income tax liabilities			
Property, plant, and equipment	$ 628	$ 399	$ 478
Other	511	391	240
Total deferred tax liabilities	$1,139	$ 790	$ 718

C. Lucent reported effective tax rates of 33.9 percent in 1999, 35.3 percent in 1998, and 36.8 percent 1997. Do these rates raise quality questions?

D. Look at the footnote for the pension cost that follows. Does this note revise your assessment as to the quality of earnings reported from 1997 to 1999?

Components of Net Periodic Benefit Cost

	Year Ended September 30		
	1999	**1998**	**1997**
Pension Cost			
Service cost	$ 509	$ 331	$ 312
Interest cost on projected benefit obligation	1,671	1,631	1,604
Expected return on plan assets	(2,957)	(2,384)	(2,150)
Amortization of unrecognized prior service cost	461	164	149
Amortization of transition asset	(300)	(300)	(300)
Amortization of net loss	2	0	0
Charges for plan curtailments	0	0	56
Net pension credit	$ (614)	$ (558)	$ (329)
Postretirement Cost			
Service cost	$80	$63	
Interest cost on accumulated benefit obligation	537	540	
Expected return on plan assets	(308)	(263)	
Amortization of unrecognized prior service cost	53	53	
Amortization of net loss (gain)	6	3	
Charges for plan curtailments	0	0	
Net postretirement benefit cost	$ 368	$ 396	
Pension and Postretirement Benefits			
Weighted-average assumptions as of September 30			
Discount rate	7.25%	6.0%	
Expected return on plan assets	9.0%	9.0%	
Rate of compensation increase	4.5%	4.5%	

Effective October 1, 1998, Lucent changed its method for calculating the market-related value of plan assets used in determining the expected return-on-asset component of annual net pension and postretirement benefit cost. Under the previous accounting method, the calculation of the market-related value of plan assets included only interest and dividends immediately, while all other realized and unrealized gains and losses were amortized on a straight-line basis over a five-year period. The new method used to calculate market-related value includes immediately an amount based on Lucent's historical asset returns and amortizes the difference between that amount and the actual return on a straight-line basis over a five-year period. The new method is preferable under Statement of Financial Accounting Standards No. 87 because it results in calculated plan asset values that are closer to current fair value, thereby lessening the accumulation of unrecognized gains and losses while still mitigating the effects of annual market value fluctuations.

The cumulative effect of this accounting change related to periods prior to fiscal year 1999 of $2,150 ($1,308 after-tax, or $0.43 and $0.42 per basic and diluted share, respectively) is a one-time, noncash credit to fiscal 1999 earnings. This accounting change also resulted in a reduction in benefit costs in the year ended September 30, 1999, that increased income by $427 ($260 after-tax, or $0.09 and $0.08 per basic and diluted share, respectively) as compared with the previous accounting method. A comparison of pro forma amounts below shows the effects if the accounting change were applied retroactively:

	Year Ended September 30	
	1998	**1997**
Pro forma net income	$1,276.00	$657.00
Earnings per share—basic	$0.43	$0.23
Earnings per share—diluted	$0.42	$0.22

The Analysis of Risk

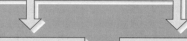

Knowing the business	1

- The products
- The knowledge base
- The competition
- The regulatory constraints

Strategy

Analyzing information	2

- In financial statements
- Outside of financial statements

Forecasting payoffs	3

- Specifying payoffs
- Forecasting payoffs

Converting forecasts to a valuation	4

Trading on the valuation	5

Outside investor:
Compare value with price to *buy*, *sell*, or *hold*

Inside investor:
Compare value with cost to *accept* or *reject* strategy

Chapter 18
How do the fundamentals of a business affect equity risk? How is fundamental risk analyzed?

Chapter 19
How does fundamental analysis aid in the evaluation of default risk on bonds and other business debt?

Investing involves both risk and return. For much of this book we have been concerned with forecasting payoffs to investing. But forecasts are expected amounts and expected amounts are averages of possible outcomes, so investors must consider the possibility of getting an outcome different from that expected. The chance of getting an outcome different from that expected is the risk of the investment. Of particular concern is getting a "bad outcome," an outcome worse than expected.

This part of the book analyzes business risk. The two chapters here give you an understanding of what determines risk. With that understanding, the investor sets his required return for investing. So these chapters also deal with the problems of measuring the required return. And, as the investor's required return is the firm's cost of capital, this part of the book deals with problems of measuring the cost of capital.

Chapter 18 analyzes the risk of equity investment. The risk in equity investing is the risk of not getting the stock return expected. Standard beta models, like the capital asset pricing model, measure this return risk: These models were outlined in the appendix to Chapter 3 and are covered in detail in corporate finance and investments texts. But the risk in returns is determined by the risk of the underlying business. So Chapter 18 focuses on the fundamental determinants of risk and on how fundamental analysis can help to gain insight into the risk of equity investing.

Chapter 19 analyzes the risk of investing in business debt, such as corporate bonds and bank loans. The risk involved is that which a debt ranking agency or a bank loan officer has to evaluate: the risk that a firm might default on its debt. Default risk determines the effective interest rate on the debt—the cost of debt to the firm—and the value of the debt. The emphasis in Chapter 19 is on applying fundamental analysis to determine default risk.

The required return is the final ingredient needed to calculate a value—as indicated in Step 4 of fundamental analysis here. The required return for equity converts forecasts of the payoffs from business activity to a valuation, typically by discounting or capitalizing those payoffs to present value. Similarly, the required return for debt is used to discount forecasted cash flows from debt to a present value. In both cases the discount rate is determined by risk, and fundamental analysis aids in assessing that risk.

The Analysis of Equity Risk and the Cost of Capital

LINKS

Link to previous chapters

Chapter 3 (and its appendix) reviewed standard beta technologies to measure the cost of capital. Chapter 13 distinguished operating risk and financing risk.

This chapter

This chapter analyzes the fundamental determinants of operating and financing risk in equity investing. It also introduces price risk and outlines ways to incorporate risk when valuing firms and trading in their shares.

Link to next chapter

Chapter 19 analyzes the risk of firms' debt.

Link to web page

Go to the text website at www.mhhe.com/penman2e for further discussion of risk.

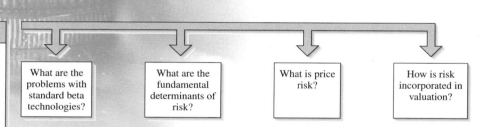

What are the problems with standard beta technologies?

What are the fundamental determinants of risk?

What is price risk?

How is risk incorporated in valuation?

Valuation involves both risk and expected return, so we have referred to risk at many points in this text. Risk determines an investor's required return, and expected payoffs must cover the required return before an investment can be said to add value. As the book has proceeded, we have seen that to value investments and to measure value added, expected payoffs must be discounted for the required return. Indeed, Step 4 of fundamental analysis requires expected payoffs to be discounted using the required return to arrive at a valuation.

But we also have seen that valuations can be quite sensitive to estimates of the required return. In most applications in the book we have estimated the required return using the one-factor capital asset pricing model (CAPM). But we have done so with considerable discomfort because of problems in measuring the inputs into the model. Alternative multifactor models have been proposed (as discussed in the appendix to Chapter 3), but these beta technologies only compound the measurement problems.

So-called asset pricing models seemingly do not refer to fundamentals. They are composed of betas and risk premium. Betas are defined as correlations between investment

The Analyst's Checklist

After reading this chapter you should understand:

- That precise measures of the cost of capital are difficult to calculate.

- What risk is.

- How business investment can yield extreme (high and low) returns.

- How diversification reduces risk.

- Problems with using the standard capital asset pricing model and other beta technologies.

- The difference between fundamental risk and price risk.

- The determinants of fundamental risk.

- The determinants of price risk.

- How fundamental analysis protects against price risk.

- How pro forma analysis can be adapted to prepare value-at-risk profiles.

- How fundamentals help to measure predicted betas.

After reading this chapter you should be able to:

- Plot a distribution of return outcomes, like those for the S&P 500.

- Analyze a firm's risk drivers.

- Generate a value-at-risk profile.

- Incorporate value-at-risk analysis in strategy formulation.

- Calculate a fundamental beta (at least in broad outline).

- Assign firms to a risk class.

- Conduct relative value investing.

- Invest with a margin of safety.

returns, and risk premiums are defined in terms of expected returns. Typically betas and risk premiums are measured from stock returns. However, risk, like return, is driven by the fundamentals of the firm, the type of business it is engaged in, and its leverage; in short, a firm's operating and financing activities determine its risk. This chapter analyzes the fundamentals that determine risk, so that you can understand why one firm would have a higher required return than another.

Market prices reflect fundamentals if the market is efficient. The perspective of this book is that of the active investor who considers that the market may not be efficient at all times. So this chapter also deals with the analysis of investment risk in inefficient markets. In inefficient markets the investor—both the outside investor and the investor inside the firm who sets hurdle rates for projects—cannot accept a required return that is estimated from market prices as indicative of fundamental risk. But there is another concern. The outside investor must also be aware of price risk—the possibility that she might be hurt by a deviation of prices from the intrinsic price at which she hopes to sell—as well as fundamental risk. This chapter considers both fundamental risk and price risk.

Despite an enormous amount of research on the issue, measures of the cost of capital remain elusive. You will not find a way to estimate the required return with assured precision in this chapter. You will find the material here to be more qualitative than quantitative. But the chapter will conclude with ways to finesse the difficulties of estimating the required return in equity investing.

THE NATURE OF RISK

Each year *The Wall Street Journal* reports a "Shareholder Scorecard," which ranks 1,000 major U.S. companies on their stock return performance. The year 1998 was a particularly good year for stocks, with the 1,000 firms earning an average return of 24.2 percent. But 377 of them had negative returns while 386 generated returns of more than 20 percent. Table 18.1 gives the top and bottom 2 1/2 percent of performers for 1998.

When investing we often talk of expected returns, and the historical average return to investing in U.S. equities has been about 13 percent per year. Table 18.1 gives you some idea of how actual returns vary from average returns. There is a chance of doing better than 13 percent—very much better as the best performers in the table indicate—and a chance of "losing one's shirt"—as the large negative returns in the table indicate. This variation in possible outcomes is the risk of investing.

The investor's perception of this variation determines the return she requires for an investment—how much she will charge in terms of expected return to invest—and the return required by investors is the firm's cost of capital. If no variation in returns is expected, the investment is said to be risk free. So the required return for a risky investment is determined as

$$\text{Required return} = \text{Risk-free return} + \text{Premium for risk}$$

United States government securities are seen as risk free, and the yields on these securities are readily available. The difficult part of determining a required return is calculating the premium for risk.

The Distribution of Returns

The set of possible outcomes and the probability of outcomes that an investor faces is referred to as the **distribution of returns.** Risk models typically characterize return distributions in terms of probability distributions that are familiar in statistical analysis. A probability distribution assigns to each possible outcome a probability, the chance of getting that outcome. The average of all outcomes, weighted by their probabilities, is the mean of the distribution, or the expected outcome. The investor is seen as having an expected return but also is aware of the probabilities of getting outcomes different from the expected return. And the risk premium she requires depends on her perception of the form of the distribution around the mean.

Figure 18.1*a* plots the familiar bell-shaped curve of the **normal distribution.** If returns were distributed according to the normal distribution, approximately 68 percent of outcomes would fall within 1 standard deviation of the expected return (the mean) and 95 percent within 2 standard deviations, as depicted. The typical *standard deviation* of annual returns among stocks is about 30 percent. So, with a mean of 13 percent, we expect returns to fall between –47 percent and +73 percent exactly 95 percent of the time if returns follow a normal distribution.

But look at Table 18.1. The stocks listed there are 5 percent of the Shareholder Scorecard's 1,000, that is, 2½ percent with the best performance and 2½ percent with the worst, so their returns are those outside 95 percent of outcomes. The top performers have returns considerably greater than 73 percent; the worst performers have returns less than –47 percent (and 1998 was a particularly good year for stocks, with none of the 1,000 firms failing with 100 percent of value lost).

These extreme returns are not uncommon. Figure 18.1*b* compares the actual distribution of annual stock returns to the normal distribution in Figure 18.1*a*. You notice two

TABLE 18.1   **Best and Worst 1998 Stock Return Performance for the 1,000 Firms in *The Wall Street Journal's* Shareholder Scorecard**

The Best Performers		The Worst Performers	
Company Name	Stock Return, %	Company Name	Stock Return, %
Amazon.com	+966.4%	Sunbeam	−83.7%
Network Solutions	+896.8	MedPartners	−76.5
Metromedia Fiber Network	+706.1	Parker Drilling	−73.8
CMGI	+604.1	AGCO	−73.0
America Online	+585.6	Harnischfeger Industries	−70.4
Yahoo!	+584.3	IKON Office Solutions	−69.2
MindSpring Enterprises	+444.8	Venator Group	−68.1
Infoseek	+359.3	ENSCO International	−67.9
Earthlink Network	+342.7	Rowan Companies	−67.6
Dell Computer	+248.5	Santa Fe International	−64.2
Best Buy	+232.9	Case	−63.7
Century Communications	+225.3	Global Marine	−63.4
Apple Computer	+211.9	Weatherford International	−62.6
EMC	+209.8	Union Pacific Resources Group	−62.1
Lagato Systems	+199.7	Thermo Electron	−61.5
At Home Corp. Internet Service	+195.5	Polaroid	−60.9
Level 3 Communications	+191.4	Baker Hughes	−59.0
EchoStar Communications	+188.8	Starwood Hotels & Resorts Worldwide	−58.8
International Network Services	+187.6	Security Capital Group	−58.3
Excite	+180.4	Sensormatic Electronics	−57.8
Lucent Technologies	+175.9	Noble Drilling	−57.8
Lycos	+168.6	Tidewater	−57.4
Ascend Communications	+168.4	Nabors Industries	−57.3
Allegiance Corp.	+165.2	Thermo Instrument Systems	−56.3
Lexmark International	+164.5	UCAR International	−55.4

Note: The best performers listed are 2 1/2 percent of the total, as are the worst performers. Stock return includes changes in share prices, reinvestment of dividends, rights and warrant offerings, and cash equivalents (such as stock received in spinoffs).

Source: *The Wall Street Journal*, February 25, 1999. Analysis performed by L.E.K. Consulting LLC.

things. First, stock returns can't be less than −100 percent, but there is significant potential for returns greater than +100 percent, as Table 18.1 indicates.[1] Second, the probability of getting very high or low returns is greater than if returns were normally distributed. In statistical terms, the first observation says that returns are **skewed** to the right. The second observation says that the distribution of return is **fat-tailed** relative to the normal; that is, there is more probability in the tails (the extremes) of the distribution, as the comparison of Figures 18.1*a* and *b* indicates.

This all says that in evaluating risk we should be apprehensive of models that rely on the normal distribution. There is a chance of being badly damaged in equity investing:

---

[1] With limited liability, returns cannot be less than −100 percent because losses are limited to the amount invested. That is, stock prices cannot drop below zero. But investing in ventures not protected by limited liability can yield returns less than −100 percent because creditors can make claims against assets outside the business.

FIGURE 18.1

(a) The Normal Distribution and (b) the Typical Distribution of Actual Stock Returns. (c) The Hypothetical Normal Distribution of S&P 500 Returns and (d) the Empirical Distribution of S&P 500 returns. The actual distribution of returns indicates that the chance of getting very low returns or very high returns is higher than indicated by the normal distribution. Even for a large portfolio, like the S&P 500, there are more extreme negative and positive returns than are likely under the normal distribution.

Source: © CRSP. *Center for Research in Security Prices*. The University of Chicago, Graduate School of Business. Used with permission. All rights reserved.

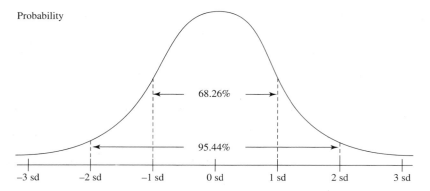

(*a*) The normal distribution. With a normal distribution, there is a 68.26% probability that a return will be within 1 standard deviation (sd) of the mean and a 95.44% probability that a return will be within 2 standard deviations of the mean.

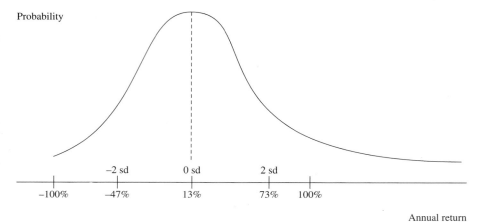

(*b*) The empirical distribution of annual stock returns.

(continued)

The probability of getting very bad returns (greater than 2 standard deviations from the mean, say) cannot be taken lightly. This is sometimes referred to as **downside risk**. Correspondingly, equity investing has the potential of yielding very large rewards—on the order of 1,000 percent and greater. This is sometimes referred to as **upside potential**. Indeed, we might view equity investing as buying a significant chance of losing a considerable amount but with the compensation of upside potential. Amazon, at the top of the list in Table 18.1 with a 966.4 percent return in 1998, experienced a large negative return of –80.2 percent in 2000. The firm's experience since 1998—the bubble and the bursting of the bubble—has reinforced this principle.

The mean and standard deviation do not capture this feature of investing entirely. In assessing risk premiums, the investor might require a higher premium for downside risk and a lower premium for upside potential. His required return for a start-up biotech firm that has a significant probability of losing 100 percent of value but also a significant probability of generating 500 percent returns may be different from his required return for a mature firm like General Motors, which has a very small chance of either.

FIGURE 18.1
(Continued)

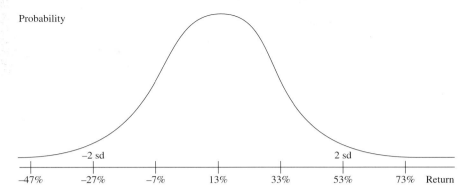

(*c*) The normal distribution of annual returns on the S&P 500 stock portfolio with a mean of 13% and a standard deviation of 20%.

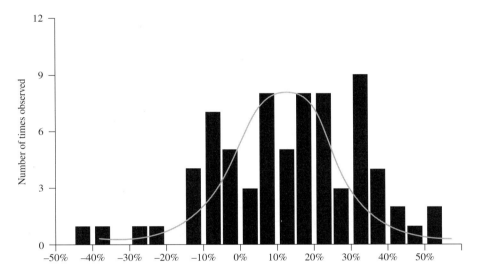

(*d*) The empirical distribution of annual returns on the S&P 500 stock portfolio 1926–1998.

Diversification and Risk

A major tenet of modern finance states that the investor reduces risk by holding stocks (or any other investment) in a portfolio with other stocks (or investments). Positive returns cancel negative returns in a portfolio, just like the positive returns in Table 18.1 compensate for the negative returns for anyone holding the 1,000 stocks covered by the Shareholder Scorecard. And if returns on the different investments in the portfolio are not perfectly correlated, the standard deviation of the portfolio return is less than the average standard deviation of return for stocks in the portfolio.

This reduction in the variation of returns in a portfolio is the reduction of risk through **diversification**. Figure 18.2 shows how the standard deviation of return on a portfolio declines as the number of securities in an investment portfolio increases. An investor holding one or two investment assets (stocks, for example) exposes himself to considerable

FIGURE 18.2

The Effect on the Standard Deviation of Return from Adding More Securities to a Portfolio The standard deviation declines as the number of securities in the portfolio increases, but the amount of the decline from adding yet more securities is less as the number of securities in the portfolio grows.

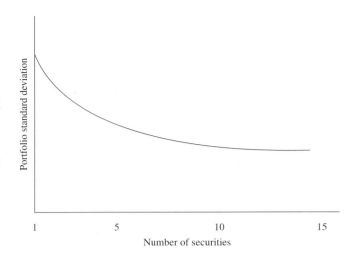

standard deviation of return, but by adding more assets he reduces this variation. At some point, however, adding more investments reduces the standard deviation of return only slightly; there is little further gain to diversification. If the investor holds all available investment assets, he is said to hold the market portfolio and the variation of return for this portfolio is variation that cannot be further reduced. The variation that remains after being fully diversified is **nondiversifiable risk**, or **systematic risk**; it is risk that affects all investments in common. Risk that can be diversified away is called **diversifiable risk** or **unsystematic risk**.

The S&P 500 stocks are typically seen as approximating the market portfolio. The historical standard deviation of returns for the S&P 500 has been about 20 percent per year, around a mean of 13 percent. Figure 18.1*c* depicts a normal distribution with a mean of 13 percent and a standard deviation of 20 percent. With a standard deviation of 20 percent, we expect returns to fall between –27 percent and 53 percent (within 2 standard deviations of the mean) 95 percent of the time if they are distributed normally, as Figure 18.1*c* shows. Compare this normal distribution with the distribution of individual stock returns in Figure 18.1*b*. The probability of returns falling between –27 percent and 53 percent in Figure 18.1*c* is greater than that in 18.1*b* because the standard deviation of return on a portfolio is less than that of the average standard deviation for individual stocks. This comparison illustrates the benefits of diversification.

Figure 18.1*d* gives the actual empirical distribution of annual returns for the S&P 500 from 1926 to 1998. You'll notice that the actual distribution of returns in the history does not follow the normal distribution in Figure 18.1*c* exactly. As in the case of individual stocks, there are more extreme returns than would be the case if returns were normally distributed. So portfolios, while giving the benefit of diversification, do not entirely eliminate the chance of getting extreme returns. And that chance is greater than would be predicted by the normal distribution. In 1930 the stock market dropped by 25 percent, followed by a 43 percent drop in 1931 and a 35 percent drop in 1937. In 1974 it dropped by 26 percent, and on "Black Monday" in October 1987 it dropped by 29 percent in one day. On the other hand, 1933 yielded a return of 54 percent, 1935 a return of 48 percent, 1954 a return of 53 percent, 1958 a return of 43 percent 1995 a return of 38 percent, and 1997 a return of 34 percent. Look at Box 1.1 in Chapter 1 for stock market behavior since 1998: the pattern perpetuates.

What do we learn from these observations? The investor can reduce risk through diversification, and if this can be done without much transaction cost, the market will not reward the investor for bearing diversifiable risk. The investor will be rewarded only for the risk that has to be borne in a well-diversified portfolio. So we must think of risk in terms of factors whose effect on returns cannot be diversified away. But we should also realize that diversification does not entirely eliminate the possibility of getting large (positive and negative) returns.

Asset Pricing Models

An asset pricing model translates the features of the return distribution into a risk premium, and so calculates a required return. Review the material on asset pricing models and beta technologies in the appendix to Chapter 3; for more detail, go to a corporate finance or investments text.[2]

The capital asset pricing model (CAPM), which is widely used, recognizes the diversification property. It says that the only nondiversifiable risk that has to be borne is the risk in the market as a whole. Accordingly, the risk premium for an investment is determined by a premium for the (systematic) risk of the market portfolio and by an investment's sensitivity to that risk, the investment's beta. But the CAPM assumes that returns follow a normal distribution,[3] like that in Figure 18.1a. That is, it assumes that if you think about the standard deviation of return, you will have captured all aspects of an investment's risk. But we have seen that the standard deviation underweights the probability of extreme returns.

Even if we accept the CAPM assumptions, we run into severe problems applying it. Warren Buffett, the renowned fundamental investor, claims that the CAPM is "seductively precise." It uses fancy machinery and looks as if it gives you a good estimate of the required return. But there are significant measurement problems:

- The CAPM requires estimates of firms' betas, but these estimates typically have errors. A beta estimated as 1.3 may, with significant probability, be somewhere between 1.0 and 1.6. With a market risk premium of 6.0 percent, an error in beta of 0.1 produces an error of 0.6 percent in the required return.

- The market risk premium is a big guess. Research papers and textbooks estimate it in the range of 3.0 percent to 9.2 percent. Pundits keen to rationalize the "high" stock market at the end of the 1990s were brave enough to state that it had declined to 2 percent. With a beta of 1.3, the difference between a required return for a market risk premium of 3.0 percent and one for a market risk premium of 9.2 percent is 8.06 percent.

Compound the error in beta and the error in the risk premium and you have a considerable problem. The CAPM, even if true, is quite imprecise when applied. No one knows what the market risk premium is. And adopting multifactor pricing models adds more risk premiums and betas to estimate. These models contain a strong element of smoke and mirrors.

---

[2] See, for example, R. A. Brealey and S. C. Myers, *Principles of Corporate Finance*, 7th ed. (New York: McGraw-Hill, 2000); S. A. Ross, R. W. Westerfield, and J. Jaffe, *Corporate Finance*, 5th ed. (New York: McGraw-Hill, 2002); and W. F. Sharpe, G. J. Alexander, and J. V. Bailey, *Investments*, 6th ed. (Upper Saddle River, N.J.: Prentice Hall, 1999).
[3] On a technical point, the CAPM is also valid if investors have quadratic utility for any form of the return distribution. But we don't know enough about people's utility functions to test if they are quadratic (and they probably are not), whereas we know something about the actual distribution of returns.

Warren Buffett made another observation on asset pricing models.[4] The CAPM says that if the price of a stock drops more than the market, it has a high beta: it's high risk. But if the price goes down because the market is mispricing the stock relative to other stocks, then the stock is not necessarily high risk: The chance of making an abnormal return has increased, and paying attention to fundamentals makes the investor more secure, not less secure. The more a stock has "deviated from fundamentals," the more likely is the "return to fundamentals" and the less risky is the investment in the stock.

Buffett's point is that risk cannot be appreciated without understanding fundamentals. Risk is generated by the firm, and in assessing risk, it might be more useful to refer to those fundamentals rather than estimating risk from (possibly inefficient) market prices. But the possibility of inefficient prices changes our view about investment risk. We may find a stock whose price has dropped considerably to be low risk. But we may also find a stock whose price may deviate from the intrinsic value path in the future to be high risk: In an inefficient market an investor can be caught by prices moving against him for reasons other than those relating to fundamentals. The next section of this chapter deals with the issue of fundamental risk; later in the chapter, we deal with the issue of price risk.

To see the difficulty in relying on market prices to estimate the required return, consider the weighted-average cost of capital (WACC) calculation for operations (or the cost of capital for the firm), ρ_F, that we outlined in Chapter 13:

$$\text{Cost of capital for operations} = \left(\frac{\text{Value of equity}}{\text{Value of operations}} \times \text{Equity cost of capital} \right) \quad \textbf{(18.1)}$$
$$+ \left(\frac{\text{Value of debt}}{\text{Value of operations}} \times \text{Cost of debt capital} \right)$$

$$\rho_F = \frac{V_0^E}{V_0^{\text{NOA}}} \bullet \rho_E + \frac{V_0^D}{V_0^{\text{NOA}}} \bullet \rho_D$$

This weighted-average cost of capital requires a measure of the equity cost of capital, ρ_E, as an input. This is often estimated from market prices using the CAPM without reference to fundamentals, producing the reservations that Buffett expresses. But, further, the cost of capital for equity and the after-tax cost of capital for debt, ρ_D, are usually weighted not with intrinsic values as in equation (18.1) but with the market prices of equity and debt. This is odd. We want to estimate the cost of capital for operations in order to get the value of the firm and the value of the equity. We do this to see if the market price is correct. But if we use the market price as an input to the calculation—and assume it is correct—we are defeating our purpose. In valuation we must always try to estimate fundamental value independently of prices to assess whether the market price is a reasonable one. To break the circularity in the WACC calculation, we must assess risk by reference to fundamentals, not market prices.

FUNDAMENTAL RISK

Fundamental risk is the risk that an investor bears as a result of the way a firm conducts its activities. The firm conducts its activities through financing, investment, and operations, as we have seen. The risk from investing and operating activities, combined, is

---

[4] Buffett's commentary on asset pricing models, along with other aspects of corporate finance, can be found in L. A. Cunningham, ed., *The Essays of Warren Buffett: Lessons for Corporate America* (New York: Cardozo Law Review, 1997).

called *operating risk* or *business risk*. If a firm invests and operates in countries with political uncertainty, it has high operating risk. It has high operating risk if it chooses to produce products for which demand drops considerably in recessions. Financing activities that determine financial leverage produce additional risk for shareholders, called *financial risk* or *leverage risk*.

We introduced these two risk components in Chapter 13. We saw that the required return for an equity investor is made up as follows:

Required return for equity = Required return for operations   **(18.2)**
                    + (Market leverage × Required return spread)

$$\rho_E = \rho_F + \frac{V_0^D}{V_0^E}(\rho_F - \rho_D)$$

$$\quad\quad\quad\quad\;\; \textbf{(1)} \quad\quad\quad \textbf{(2)}$$

The two components, operating risk **(1)** and financial risk **(2)**, are the basic *fundamental determinants* of equity risk. But just as payoffs are determined by drivers, so these risks are also driven by further fundamental determinants. Indeed, you see in the expression that financing risk is decomposed into two drivers, market financial leverage and the spread of the required return for operations over the after-tax cost of debt.

To understand the determinants of operating and financing risk, appreciate first what is at risk. Well, shareholder value is at risk, and shareholder value is driven by expectations of future residual earnings:

$$V_0^E = CSE_0 + \frac{RE_1}{\rho_E} + \frac{RE_2}{\rho_E^2} + \frac{RE_3}{\rho_E^3} + \ldots$$

This valuation is based on expected residual earnings (RE). But value is at risk because expected residual earnings are at risk: The firm might not earn the earnings relative to book value that are expected, so anticipated value might not be delivered. Indeed, instead of earnings adding to current book values, the book values might be used up with losses in operations. Accordingly, expected RE are "discounted" for this possibility with a required return, ρ_E, that incorporates the risk. As a consequence, the calculated value reflects risk as well as expected return.

The same drivers that yield RE also can drive RE away from its expected level. Thus the analysis of risk determinants closely follows the analysis of RE drivers in Chapters 11 and 12. Residual earnings are generated by return on common equity (ROCE) and growth in investment. So risk is determined by the chance that a firm will not earn the forecasted ROCE or will not grow investments to earn at the ROCE. We deal with these determinants in turn.[5]

Figure 18.3 depicts how the drivers of return on common equity and growth determine fundamental risk. Follow this diagram as we proceed. The risk determinants are expressed in terms of financial statement drivers, but just as economic factors drive residual income, so risk determinants are driven by economic risk factors. Analyzing risk amounts to identifying these economic factors and attaching them to observable features in the financial statements. And identifying economic risk factors amounts to "knowing the business."

---

[5] If value is calculated as discounted free cash flows, the same drivers of risk apply: Free cash flow is just an accounting transformation of residual earnings, as we have seen, so the factors that drive residual earnings also drive free cash flow over the long term. But one would not want to view the variation of free cash flow in the short term as indicative of risk: A negative free cash flow may be caused by large, low-risk investments rather than a bad outcome.

FIGURE 18.3

The Determinants of Fundamental Risk

Risk of not earning an expected ROCE is determined by the risk of not earning the expected return on operations (operating risk 1), compounded by the risk of financial leverage turning unfavorable (financing risk). The risk of not earning expected residual earnings is the ROCE risk compounded by growth risk (operating risk 2).

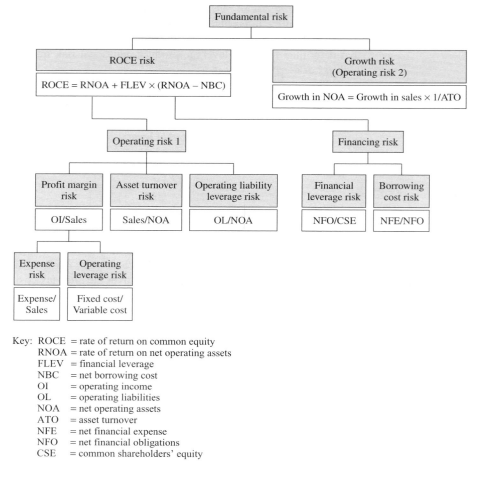

Key: ROCE = rate of return on common equity
RNOA = rate of return on net operating assets
FLEV = financial leverage
NBC = net borrowing cost
OI = operating income
OL = operating liabilities
NOA = net operating assets
ATO = asset turnover
NFE = net financial expense
NFO = net financial obligations
CSE = common shareholders' equity

Return on Common Equity Risk

We have seen that return on common equity is driven by return on operations and a premium for financing in the same way as the required return in Eq. 18.2:

Return on common equity = Return on net operating assets **(18.3)**
+ (Financial leverage × Operating spread)

$$\text{ROCE} = \text{RNOA} + \frac{\text{NFO}}{\text{CSE}}(\text{RNOA} - \text{NBC})$$

Just as the drivers here determine the expected ROCE, so they determine the risk that the expected ROCE will not be earned. We analyze each in turn.

Operating Risk

The potential variation in return on net operating assets (RNOA) generates operating risk. And variation in RNOA is driven by variation in profit margins and asset turnovers. We refer to the risks that profit margins and asset turnovers will not be at their expected levels as *profit margin (PM) risk* and *asset turnover (ATO) risk*. The RNOA is also determined by operating liability leverage, and we refer to possible variation in operating liability leverage as *operating liability leverage (OLLEV) risk*.

Asset turnover risk recognizes the chance that sales will fall, by a fall either in prices or in volumes, if demand from customers changes or competitors erode market share. If net operating assets are inflexible—they cannot be reduced immediately—ATO falls with a drop in sales, reducing RNOA. The decrease in ATO is, in turn, driven by lower inventory turnover (a buildup of inventory relative to sales and thus excess investment in inventory), lower property, plant, and equipment turnover (and thus value lost in idle capacity), and other individual net asset turnovers. Firms with fixed capital equipment in place, such as investments in large communications networks, are particularly susceptible to ATO risk. Firms with large inventories for which consumer demand can shift to substitute products, such as a new generation of computers or new models of cars, are susceptible to ATO risk.

Profit margin risk is the risk of profit margins changing for a given level of sales. It is driven by *expense risk:* the risk of labor and material costs increasing, per dollar of sales, selling expenses increasing, and so on. Profit margins will also be affected by the fixed and variable cost structure of expenses, which we referred to as *operating leverage (OLEV)* in Chapter 12. If sales fall, profit margins fall by a larger amount if costs are fixed rather than variable (and adaptable to the change in sales). So fixed salary commitments and a tradition that frowns on dismissing employees generate higher profit margin risk. Long-term rental agreements increase profit margin risk.

Operating liability leverage risk is the chance that operating liabilities will fall as a percentage of net operating assets. If the firm gets into difficulties that cause margins and turnovers to fall, suppliers may not grant credit, reducing payables and OLLEV. The ability to collect cash ahead of sales may fall, reducing deferred revenues and OLLEV. These scenarios reduce RNOA and ROCE.

Financing Risk

Financing risk is driven by the amount of financial leverage and the variation in the spread, that is, the RNOA relative to the net borrowing cost. The operating spread varies, of course, as RNOA varies, but the financing component of the spread is the net borrowing cost. So we talk of *financial leverage (FLEV) risk* and *net borrowing cost (NBC) risk* as the determinants of financing risk.

A fall in RNOA reduces the operating spread and the effect on ROCE is magnified, or levered, by the FLEV. As long as the operating spread is positive, financial leverage is favorable (for firms with positive leverage). Should the operating spread turn negative, however, the leverage turns unfavorable, reducing ROCE below RNOA.

Borrowing cost risk increases the chance that operating spreads will decline. Firms with variable-interest-rate debt have higher borrowing cost risk than firms with fixed-rate debt; if interest rates increase with variable-rate debt, ROCE declines, but if interest rates decrease, ROCE increases. Firms that hedge interest rates reduce borrowing cost risk. Net borrowing costs are after-tax, so if firms incur operating losses and cannot get the tax benefit from losses carried forward or back, their after-tax borrowing costs will increase.

Growth Risk

Residual earnings are driven by both ROCE and growth in investment, so ROCE risk is compounded by the risk that common equity will not increase as expected. For a given financial leverage, growth in common equity is driven by growth in net operating assets. So uncertainty about whether the firm can grow investment in net operating assets is an additional aspect of operating risk. That is, uncertainty about a firm's investment opportunities adds to risk.

Growth in net operating assets is driven by sales. For a given asset turnover, the amount of net operating assets to be put in place is determined by sales, so growth risk is driven by the risk of sales not growing as expected. Indeed sales risk is viewed as the foremost business risk, affecting both the growth in net operating assets and the RNOA. A reduction of sales may not reduce net operating assets because net operating assets are inflexible, but if so, it will reduce RNOA and residual earnings as asset turnovers decrease. If net operating assets are flexible, a sales decline will reduce residual earnings through the reduction in net operating assets. This growth risk is labeled operating risk 2 in Figure 18.3 to distinguish it from RNOA risk, which is labeled operating risk 1.

You see how risk components interact, compounding sales risk through the system depicted in Figure 18.3. A fall in sales reduces net operating assets growth and asset turnovers. The fall in asset turnover reduces RNOA, which reduces the operating spread. Operating creditors may reduce credit, reducing operating liability leverage, and borrowing costs may increase because of lower profitability. These effects compound to reduce residual earnings and the compounding effect can cause considerable distress, or even failure. These compounding effects increase the probability of extreme returns.

In valuing the operations by forecasting residual operating income (ReOI), only operating risk needs to be considered, both operating risk 1 and operating risk 2 in Figure 18.3.

VALUE-AT-RISK PROFILES

In Figure 18.1 risk was depicted as a distribution of possible return outcomes. Each possible return implies a valuation—how much the investor would be willing to pay for that return—so risk can also be depicted as a distribution of values. Plotting that distribution of values—depicting how value might differ from expected value—prepares a *value-at-risk profile*.

Cast back to the full-information, pro forma financial statement forecasting in Chapter 15. Following the template laid out there, we forecasted operating income and net operating assets for the simple firm PPE Inc. and, from the forecasts, calculated forecasted residual operating income. We then converted these forecasts to a valuation. The pro forma financial statements that we prepared were based on expected sales, profit margins, and turnovers. But expected values are averages of a whole range of possible outcomes and the distribution of outcomes determines the risk of the investment. Value-at-risk profiles are developed by preparing pro forma financial statements for each possible outcome and then calculating the values for each outcome.

To develop value-at-risk profiles, follow the five steps outlined next.

1. *Identify economic factors that will affect the risk drivers in Figure 18.3*. Like valuation more generally, identifying these factors requires "knowing the business." Consider airlines. What factors affect airlines' profits? General economic conditions affect asset turnover risk since airlines sell fewer tickets at lower prices on fixed capacity in recessions than in boom times. Airlines are subject to shocks in oil prices, affecting expense risk. Airlines are subject to changes in government regulation, affecting growth risk. Airlines are subject to price challenges from competitors and new entrants to the industry, affecting RNOA and growth risk.

2. *Identify risk protection mechanisms in place within the firm*. An airline may hedge oil prices to reduce the effects of oil price shocks. Currency risk may be hedged. Incorporation is a risk-protection device to limit liability. The investigation of risk exposures is part of knowing the business. Indeed, the aspects of business that are exposed to risk

really define the business. If a gold company hedges its gold reserves against changes in the price of gold, it creates a gold mining business (with risk in production costs) rather than a gold mining and trading business (with risk in production costs and sale prices). If a downstream oil company hedges oil prices, an investor should realize that she is buying a firm that is more like a marketing company than an oil company. A firm hedging currency risk has decided that it is not in the business of trading currencies. If a firm hedges all risks, the investor is buying an investment that is more like the risk-free asset than an equity.

Disclosure is important to the discovery of risk exposure. Look at the derivatives and financial instrument disclosures. Examine the management discussion and analysis. Just as poor disclosure frustrates the identification of operating assets (what business the firm really is in), so poor disclosure frustrates discovery of risk exposures. A manager seeking to maximize the market value of the firm indicates clearly what type of business the firm is in and so attracts investors who seek the risk and returns to that type of business. If she fails to disclose exposures, she imposes disclosure risk on the investor.[6]

3. *Identify the effect of economic factors on the fundamental risk elements in Figure 18.3.* If valuations are made by forecasting operations, only operating risk drivers need be considered. If valuations are made on the basis of full residual income, both operating and financing drivers need to be considered.

4. *Prepare pro forma financial statements under alternative scenarios for the future fundamental risk drivers.*

5. *Calculate projected residual operating income for each scenario and, from these projections, calculate the set of values that each scenario implies.* Use the risk-free rate (the rate on secure government obligations) to calculate residual incomes and to discount them. (The reason for this will become clear shortly.)

A value-at-risk profile is developed by considering all risk factors to which the firm and its shareholders are exposed. With the profile—and an understanding of the risk factors that generate it—the investor considers his strategy to deal with risk. He chooses his exposures. He avoids firms with particular risk features. He uses financial and commodity hedging instruments to protect himself against particular exposures. For example, if he wants exposure to oil price risk, he might buy an oil company, but because he does not want exposure to interest rate risk, he might hedge against interest rate effects on a highly leveraged oil company. Further, the investor understands that risk can be diversified by holding a large portfolio of stocks. Value-at-risk profiles for individual firms are then an input to determining the risk profile of a portfolio of stocks. And the investor understands that portfolios can be engineered to give exposure to one type of risk while minimizing exposure, through diversification, to other types of risk. Value-at-risk profiles help him in weighting his portfolio toward particular types of risk. In implementing his risk-exposure strategy, the investor appreciates the risk protection mechanisms in place within the firm (discussed in point 2 above) and mixes his own strategy with that of the firm to engineer his desired exposure to risk.

---

[6] Some argue that managers should not be concerned with protecting shareholders from risk. With the availability of risk protection instruments on the market and with the ability to diversify, shareholders can protect themselves if they wish, and so arrange their own risk exposures. But to the extent that firms do manage risk, the investor must be aware.

The identification of economic risk factors in Step 1—and the attachment to financial statement drivers in Step 3—follows closely the identification of the economic determinants of residual earnings in Chapter 15. The preparation of pro forma financial statements in Step 4 completes the full-information forecasting of Chapter 15 by considering not only information about expected residual income but information about the possible variation in residual income also.

The values calculated in Step 5 use the risk-free rate. So for each outcome scenario, using residual operating income valuation,

$$V_0^{NOA} = NOA_0 + \frac{OI_1 - (R-1)NOA_0}{R} + \frac{OI_2 - (R-1)NOA_1}{R^2} \qquad \textbf{(18.4)}$$
$$+ \frac{OI_3 - (R-1)NOA_2}{R^3} + \ldots$$

where R is $1 +$ risk-free rate. Forecasts are made up to a steady-state year.

Most spreadsheet programs have sensitivity analysis features that facilitate this analysis. The example in Table 18.2 keeps it simple by considering only one risk factor (albeit an important one), the variation in the performance of the economy as a whole as measured by the growth in gross domestic product (GDP). This factor is like the "market factor" in the capital asset pricing model. This factor affects only three drivers in the example: sales, profit margins, and asset turnovers. Table 18.2 gives sales for two firms, A and B, for seven growth rates in GDP indicated at the top of the table. Both firms, you notice, have the same sales for a given GDP growth scenario and so have the same sales risk from the GDP factor. But the two firms differ on PM risk and ATO risk. Profit margin risk is driven by operating leverage, the ratio of fixed costs to variable costs. Firm A has a higher fixed-cost component to expenses than B, $20 million compared to $4 million (as indicated at the bottom of the table) and accordingly, with variable costs of 72 percent of sales rather than 88 percent, Firm A has higher operating leverage risk and profit margin risk. Firm A also has less adaptable net operating assets, with $30.7 million invested in inflexible assets compared to $18.7 million for Firm B (as indicated at the bottom of the table). Accordingly, Firm A has higher ATO risk. View the inflexible portion of net operating assets as plant and the variable portion (36 percent of sales for A and 48 percent of sales for B) as inventory and receivables.

These differing sensitivities to the performance of the economy produce different ReOI under the seven scenarios. If GDP grows at 2 percent, both firms will deliver $100 million of sales, a PM of 8 percent, an ATO of 1.50, and an RNOA of 12 percent. And they will deliver $4 million in ReOI over that required with NOA earning at the risk-free rate (assumed to be 6 percent). But Firm A delivers lower RNOA and ReOI than B if GDP growth falls below 2 percent. On the other hand, Firm A delivers considerably more RNOA and ReOI if GDP growth is over 2 percent: Operating leverage and ATO flexibility determine downside risk, but they also work to reward downside risk with upside potential.

The value of each outcome is given at the bottom of Table 18.2. The valuation (again, to keep it simple) is based on each outcome being a perpetuity: $V_0^{NOA} = NOA_0 +$ Forecasted ReOI/0.06. For scenarios 1 and 2 for Firm A and scenario 1 for Firm B, the negative value is the amount of NOA put in place: A perpetual negative RNOA implies all value is lost and, with limited liability, the loss is limited to 100 percent of investment. So the set of possible values reflects not only sales risk, PM risk, and ATO risk but also protection from risk through limited liability. Value-at-risk profiles are completed by

TABLE 18.2 Value-at-Risk Profiles for Two Firms

Firm A

Scenario:	1	2	3	4	5	6	7
Factor: GDP growth	-1%	0%	1%	2%	3%	4%	5%
Probability of scenario	0.1	0.1	0.2	0.2	0.2	0.1	0.1
Fundamentals affected							
Sales ($ million)	25	50	75	100	125	150	175
Operating expenses ($ million)							
Fixed costs	20	20	20	20	20	20	20
Variable costs	18	36	54	72	90	108	126
Total expenses	38	56	74	92	110	128	146
Operating income ($ million)	-13	-6	1	8	15	22	29
Profit margin	-52%	-12%	1.3%	8.0%	12%	14.7%	16.6%
Asset turnover	0.63	1.03	1.30	1.50	1.65	1.77	1.87
RNOA	-32.7%	-12.3%	1.7%	12.0%	19.8%	26.0%	30.9%
Beginning NOA ($ million)	39.7	48.7	57.7	66.7	75.7	84.7	93.7
ReOI ($R = 1.06$)	-15.4	-8.9	-2.5	4.0	10.5	16.9	23.4
Value with limited liability	-40	-49	-16	133	251	366	484

PM risk driver: Operating expense = 20 + 72% of sales
ATO risk driver: Net operating assets = 30.7 + 36% of sales

Firm B

Scenario:	1	2	3	4	5	6	7
Factor: GDP growth	-1%	0%	1%	2%	3%	4%	5%
Probability of scenario	0.1	0.1	0.2	0.2	0.2	0.1	0.1
Fundamentals affected							
Sales ($ million)	25	50	75	100	125	150	175
Operating expenses ($ million)							
Fixed costs	4	4	4	4	4	4	4
Variable costs	22	44	66	88	110	132	154
Total expenses	26	48	70	92	114	136	158
Operating income ($ million)	-1	2	5	8	11	14	17
Profit margin	-4%	4%	6.7%	8.0%	8.8%	9.3%	9.7%
Asset turnover	0.81	1.17	1.37	1.50	1.59	1.65	1.70
RNOA	-3.3%	4.7%	9.1%	12.0%	14.0%	15.4%	16.6%
Beginning NOA ($ million)	30.7	42.7	54.7	66.7	78.7	90.7	102.7
ReOI ($R = 1.06$)	-2.8	-0.6	1.7	4.0	6.3	8.6	10.8
Value with limited liability	-31	33	83	133	184	234	283

PM risk driver: Operating expense = 4 + 88% of sales
ATO risk driver: Net operating assets = 18.7 + 48% of sales

FIGURE 18.4

Value-at-Risk Profiles for Firm A and Firm B The profiles are generated for seven scenarios for GDP growth in Table 18.2. Firm A has higher profit margin risk and higher asset turnover risk. These risk factors give Firm A a higher probability of low-value outcomes but also a higher probability of high-value outcomes.

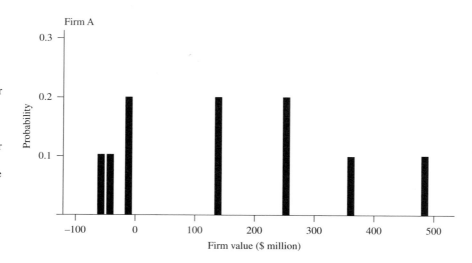

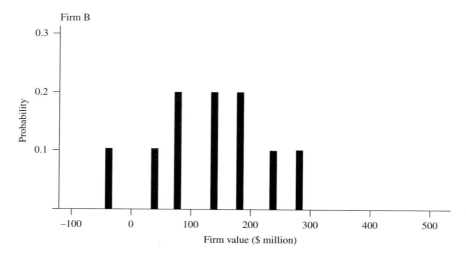

attaching the probability of outcomes to the value of outcomes. Profiles for firms A and B are depicted in Figure 18.4.

The comparison of the two profiles illustrates the tradeoff between upside potential and downside risk. The expected value of a set of outcomes is the sum of each outcome multiplied by the probability of the outcome. So for both firms expected sales are $100 million (which happens also to be the median sales in scenario 4). At this level of sales both firms generate $4 million in ReOI and, forecasting this ReOI as a perpetuity, both firms' values are $V_0^{NOA} = 66.7 + 4.0/0.06 = \$133$ million. But the distribution of values around this expected value differ, so the firms are not equivalent investments. Their risk profiles differ. Firm A has the chance of generating considerably higher value than B but takes on a higher chance of losing value on the downside.

The value-at-risk profile for Firm A is similar to the fat-tailed, right-skewed distribution of stock returns that is typically observed, as depicted in Figure 18.1*b*. But now we have uncovered the drivers of those distributions through fundamental analysis. We understand what drives firms' risk. Rather than assuming a return distribution, like the normal distribution, we have determined the form of the distribution through analysis. We understand return distributions—and corresponding value-at-risk profiles—may not be normally distributed. And we understand why the standard deviation of return may not capture all aspects of risk: Operating leverage and ATO risk can combine to give the chance of large returns but also the chance of very poor returns.

The examples here are very stylized. They ignore other aspects of operating risk such as expense risk and operating liability leverage risk. They ignore factors beside GDP growth that might affect sales. They are based on a distribution of sales for just one period. Growth risk is not incorporated, for growth risk takes on meaning only over a longer period of time. Nevertheless, the examples illustrate the form of the analysis. Other risk factors can be accommodated. Political risk from a change in government or a change in regulations might lead the analyst to specify sales outcomes for both GDP and political outcome scenarios. The analysis can be repeated for each forecast year ahead and for steady-state sales, PM, ATO, and growth at a forecast horizon. All that changes is the computational complexity, for which a computer is required. Many more possible outcomes and outcome paths over time are considered and many more values associated with these paths are calculated, along with associated probabilities. Accordingly, the value profile typically takes a form closer to the "smooth" distribution of values over every value in a range, like those in Figure 18.1.

Adaptation Options and Growth Options

The examples for firms A and B specify the response of net operating assets to sales in a simple way: The ATO risk driver has just two components, a fixed component and a component that is proportional to sales. This asset structure does not recognize the variety of ways that a firm can adapt to changes in sales. It is unlikely that a firm would stay in a scenario 1 situation. If it found that, for any reason, the demand for its products faced a scenario 1 outcome, it would adapt. It might liquidate, returning some value to claimants rather than losing all value as in the examples. Or it might adapt into other related or unrelated products.

The ability to liquidate or adapt and avoid worst-case outcomes is called the **adaptation option**. A firm's adaptation option depends on how it is structured, how easily its technology can be liquidated or adapted to alternative use. A farmer can adapt to falling demand for his crop by growing alternative crops or grazing animals. A maker of gasoline-powered automobiles presumably can adapt to solar-powered vehicles should demand shift to them. But a highly specialized producer—the manufacturer of a drug that is replaced by a superior drug—may have few options and may choose to adapt by liquidating. The adaptation option is the ability of firms to "reinvent themselves."

Analysts talk of valuing the adaptation option. The value is captured within the analysis here by specifying more sales outcomes (which will result if the adaptation option is taken) and more complicated ATO drivers for these outcomes, and assigning probabilities that the adaptation will occur. The value in liquidation can also be considered within the analysis.

Analysts also talk of **growth options** and the need to attach a value to them. Like adaptation options, a growth option is an option to adapt, but in particularly good scenarios rather than bad scenarios. The growth option amounts to being able to put assets in place—to expand net operating assets—to exploit new opportunities. Adaptation options limit downside risk; growth options generate upside potential. We characterized growth risk in Figure 18.3 as the risk that sales may not grow. But as with all risks, growth risk has an upside, and firms may have differential ability to capitalize on unexpected growth in sales.

A retailer who signs a lease with an option to rent additional floor space has created an explicit growth option. But most growth operations are not as explicit. Firms create growth options by building excess capacity—in factories, telephone networks, distribution systems, airline routes, and satellite networks. Growth options also come from a firm placing itself "in the right place at the right time." Its knowledge base may give it the ability to capitalize on technological change as it occurs. Its market position, brand name, and customer loyalty may give it the ability to capitalize on product innovations and adapt to changes in consumer tastes. Identifying these options adds to the upside potential in the value-at-risk profile. Indeed we saw Firm A had a built-in growth option (relative to Firm B) by having fixed-cost plant that could be utilized if sales materialized above their expected amount.

These growth options, and the profits and value they may generate, are captured by a value-at-risk analysis. As with Firm A, lay out the sales, profit margin, and asset turnover scenarios if growth options are exercised and assign a probability to these scenarios.

Strategy and Risk

Value-at-risk profiles are a tool for analyzing strategies. The business strategist must not only appreciate the expected value of a strategy but also understand the upside potential and downside risk it generates. And he needs to trade off upside potential for downside risk. So he prepares a value-at-risk profile for each proposed strategy.

Firm A and Firm B in the example above represent different strategies for structuring a business with the same sales outcomes, and these strategies generate different value-at-risk profiles. Strategies with different sales outcomes can be evaluated in the same way. More generally, each component of fundamental risk is explicitly considered in each strategy and its effect on the value-at-risk profile is documented. Should the firm build in growth options? Should it build in adaptation options? What is the cost of these options?

With an understanding of risk, the manager manages risk with *scenario planning*. He lays out the possible scenarios, but he also plans how to run the business in each possible scenario. He plans the adaptation to avoid bad outcomes should pessimistic scenarios be realized. He plans how to handle growth, should it come. This contingent planning, in turn, yields more detailed scenarios and more insights into generating value and reducing risk. Accordingly, value-at-risk analysis is an aid to formulating plans as well as analyzing them for the risk that they involve.

Discounting for Risk

For both firms A and B we calculated a value of $133 million based on expected sales. But this valuation assumed the investments were risk free: The discount rate used in the calculations was the risk-free rate. Given the risk profiles indicated possible variation around the value of $133 million, the risk-averse investor would pay something less than $133 million for the gambles.

The difference between the risk-free valuation and a risk-adjusted valuation is the discount for risk. Buying at the lower risk-adjusted price creates an expected return above the risk-free return; therefore, the discount for risk also can be viewed as an increase in the expected (required) return over the risk-free rate, or as a risk premium in the required return. The valuation question is how to measure this premium (or discount, if that's how you view it).

The standard deviation in the values for Firm A is $198.8 million, compared to $103.3 million for Firm B. One approach might be to determine the risk premium on the basis of this standard deviation. This approach requires a model of how the risk premium is related to standard deviation. But such an approach does not recognize that standard deviation can be reduced through diversification. Asset pricing models do, but they do not yield a reliable measure of the risk premium. Further, the standard deviation and asset pricing models do not capture the risk in extreme returns that is indicated by the analysis of fundamental risk and observed in stock returns.

The technology to measure the risk premium has not yet been developed in a satisfactory way. The CAPM is the model that is most frequently used. The analysis here does not give you an alternative. It does, however, describe how business fundamentals determine risk and how outcomes affect value. And it has developed a skepticism in taking asset pricing models at face value.

FUNDAMENTAL BETAS

Fundamentals can play a role in the beta technologies that emanate from asset pricing models. Beta is the sensitivity of a firm's returns to systematic marketwide factors such as GDP growth and, as we saw with the examples for firms A and B in the last section, these sensitivities depend on characteristics of the firm. A firm with high financial leverage or high operating leverage, for example, will have a high CAPM beta, all else being equal. Firm A will have a higher beta than Firm B. So information on these fundamental characteristics can be of help in estimating betas.

Betas estimated from stock returns (without any consideration of fundamentals) are called *historical betas*. The estimation of a historical beta for Firm i is done by running a regression for returns over past periods in the form

$$\text{Return}(i) = \alpha + \beta(i) \times \text{Return on the market} + e(i) \qquad \textbf{(18.5)}$$

The return on the market determines the systematic portion of the return; $\alpha + e(i)$, sometimes referred to as residual return is the portion of the firm's return that is not explained by movements in the market. Sometimes the regression is run with returns measured as the excess over the risk-free rate. The firm's beta, $\beta(i)$, is the sensitivity of its return to movements in the market.

Historical betas are calculated after the fact. That is, they measure the sensitivity of returns to the market return in the past. But the investor is concerned with the beta she will experience in the future while she holds the investment. Betas change because firms change. Firms change their type of business, their leverage, and their asset turnover risk. All of the risk determinants in Figure 18.3 can change over time. Indeed historical beta estimates are known to change over time. In particular, like a lot of financial measures we have investigated, they are mean reverting: High betas tend to decline over time and low betas tend to increase. For this reason, some beta services adjust historical betas as follows:

$$\text{Adjusted historical } \beta(i) = 0.35 + 0.65 \times \text{Historical } \beta(i)$$

This adjustment has the effect of pulling the historical beta toward 1.0, the average beta for all firms. So if the historical beta is 1.70, the adjusted beta for the future is 1.455. But the adjustment is ad hoc.

Another way to proceed is to predict future betas from fundamentals. If betas reflect firms' characteristics, then they can be predicted from those characteristics. Such betas are called *predicted betas* or, because they are predicted using fundamentals, *fundamental betas*. The firm BARRA, Inc., pioneered the marketing of fundamental betas based on academic research.

A predictive beta model is built in two steps. We illustrate it with just two fundamental predictors, financial leverage (FLEV) and operating leverage (OLEV). In the first step, a relationship between historical betas and past fundamentals is estimated from the cross section of firms:

$$\text{Historical } \beta(i) = b_0 + b_1 \text{ FLEV}(i) + b_2 \text{ OLEV}(i) + u(i)$$

In the second step, estimated coefficients from the first step, b_0, b_1, and b_2, are used to predict future betas for particular firms from their most recent fundamentals:

$$\text{Predicted } \beta(i) = b_0 + b_1 \text{FLEV}(i) + b_2 \text{ OLEV}(i)$$

Models also can be developed that incorporate both historical betas (estimated from returns) and fundamentals.[7]

Fundamental beta models typically include many more fundamental characteristics than the two used here, along with indicators for industry sector and lines of business. Some other fundamental measures that have been used are:

- Earnings variability
- Cash flow variability
- Size
- Growth in earnings or sales
- Growth in assets
- P/E ratio
- P/B ratio
- Dividend yield

These characteristics are usually selected on the basis of what works in the data, with not a lot of theoretical justification that they should capture risk. Look to Figure 18.3 for additional fundamental risk attributes that might be beta predictors.

PRICE RISK

Fundamental risk arises from the uncertainty of outcomes to business investment, and fundamental risk contributes to uncertainty about stock returns. But there is another aspect of risk with which the investor must be concerned. If prices deviate from fundamental value, the investor can be at risk—and be rewarded—by trading at prices that are not at fundamental value. This risk, which has nothing to do with fundamentals, is called **price risk**. Price risk comes in two forms, market inefficiency risk and liquidity risk.

---

[7] Because betas determine expected returns (according to the CAPM), a model of returns is sometimes estimated in the first step by including fundamental characteristics, in addition to the market factor, in the return model (equation 18.5). So fundamentals are added to the market return and the historical beta to explain returns in the past. Then, in the second step, estimates from this model are used to combine fundamental characteristics with historical betas to predict future stock returns rather than betas.

Market Inefficiency Risk

The passive investor who trusts that the market for shares is efficient recognizes that he is subject to fundamental risk: Efficient market prices will change in response to changes in fundamentals. The active investor maintains that prices can be inefficient. He tries to exploit the inefficiencies, but he also recognizes that the market can be inefficient in an uncertain way. Prices can move against him. **Market inefficiency risk** is the risk of prices moving in a way that is not justified by fundamentals.

Consider two scenarios for exploiting market inefficiency. You might predict that the price at which you will liquidate the investment at some future time, P_T, will be appropriately priced but recognize that the current price, P_0, is mispriced. That is, you predict that you will get a fair price when you sell at time T, and you make an abnormal return by buying the stock at the current price that you judge is incorrect. Alternatively, you might conclude that the stock is appropriately priced at present in P_0 but will be mispriced in the future in P_T. Using V to indicate an intrinsic value, the two scenarios are depicted in the two panels of Figure 18.5. Each panel gives current and expected future market prices for the investment, P_0 and P_T^C. P_T^C (the expected future price with a C attached to it) indicates that the expected price at time T is cum-dividend for dividends paid from 0 to T, for dividends are always part of the return. P_0 and P_T^C are compared to intrinsic values at time 0 and T, V_0 and V_T^C. The intrinsic value at time T is also cum-dividend.

In Scenario A, the fundamental analyst perceives the stock to be currently mispriced and invests to capture an abnormal return as the price returns to fundamental value. An investor who fails to detect overpricing might buy a stock that is overvalued and then lose value as the price falls in its return to fundamental value. An investor who fails to detect an underpricing (as in the figure) might sell (short) and lose the value as the price rises toward fundamental value. In either case, there is a risk of trading at the wrong price. The risk is referred to as *Scenario A risk*. Scenario A can bring rewards but it also involves risk.

In Scenario B the investor buys a stock at its fundamental value and sees the stock deviating from fundamental value in the future. So he invests to capture the abnormal return that he predicts. However, a fundamental investor who thinks he is buying at fundamental value but does not anticipate Scenario B may actually lose value should a Scenario B outcome materialize and the stock deviate down from fundamental value. We refer to this risk as *Scenario B risk*. Like all investing, Scenario B can be exploited for reward but can also bring risks.

The two scenarios differ in the expectation of how future prices will behave. Scenario A predicts that the market will ultimately recognize the mispricing and correct itself (as future earnings reports become available, for example). Scenario B predicts the market will be "carried away" from fundamental value. In a Scenario B one might, for example, forecast that acquirers, in the process of "empire building," will bid up the price of takeover targets above fundamental value. The investor might buy likely takeover targets in anticipation of this. Or one might forecast inflated prices of takeover targets during "merger booms" as acquirers compete for the acquisitions. One might anticipate supply and demand for stocks and forecast that strong demand for stocks (or lack of demand) will drive them away from their intrinsic values. A number of investors explained the perceived overvaluation of stocks in the 1990s as the effect of baby boomers getting too enthusiastic about stocks and investing their wealth indiscriminately, pushing the price up. These are so-called liquidity theories of stock prices. And one might forecast that stock prices will be carried away from fundamentals by fashions, fads, or a

FIGURE 18.5

In These Scenarios for Earning Abnormal Returns, P_0 Is Market Price at Time 0 and V_0 Is Intrinsic Value at Time 0. P_T^C Is Expected Cum-dividend Price at Time T and V_T^C Is Expected Cum-dividend Intrinsic Value at T In Scenario A the investor expects the cum-dividend price in the future to be at fundamental value but sees the current price as different from fundamental value. Thus she makes abnormal returns as prices move toward fundamental value. In Scenario B the investor sees the current price as equal to fundamental value but expects the price to move away from fundamental value in the future. Thus she makes abnormal returns as prices deviate from fundamental value.

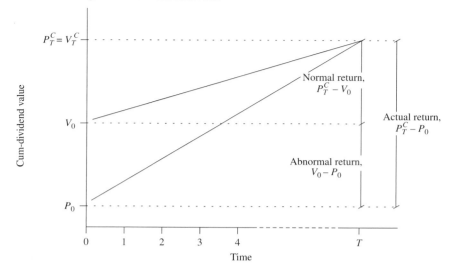

Scenario A: Price gravitates to fundamental value

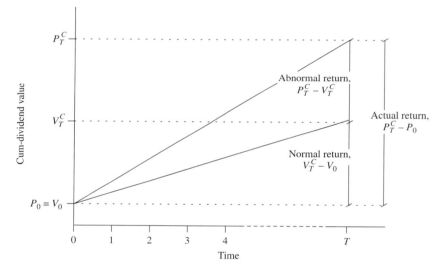

Scenario B: Price deviates from fundamental value

herd mentality that introduces misconceived popular beliefs of a stock's worth. These are so-called psychological theories of the stock market. These theories try to explain how investors can be seemingly irrational. The study of the forces that drive stocks away from their values is called **behavioral finance.**

Scenario A risk and Scenario B risk can be operating at the same time. An investor may think that a stock is undervalued and so buy in anticipation of a Scenario A return, but Scenario B forces can drive the price even lower. In the mid-1990s, many fundamental investors saw stocks as overvalued, so they moved out of stocks, only to find that over the late 1990s stocks became more overvalued (in their view)—and they missed out on a good deal of the bull market. And those who sold short in the mid-1990s had considerable losses. Assured of their insights into fundamentals (and fundamental risk), they were still exposed to price risk.

The risk in both scenarios arises from buying or selling at the wrong price, a price that is not consistent with information about fundamentals. Fundamental analysis is a protection against price risk. This was the appeal to fundamental analysis that we made in the very first chapter of this book: Analysis reduces the uncertainty in investing.

But fundamental analysis alone may not be enough to protect against Scenario B risk. Scenario B arises from factors that drive prices away from fundamentals and understanding those "irrational" market forces helps to predict Scenario B. Indeed, that understanding also helps predict Scenario A because if you think, based on fundamental analysis, that a stock is mispriced and, as well, you have an explanation of why the prices are not at fundamental value, you are doubly assured.

Fundamental analysis does not explain stock prices fully. Stock price theory, based on behavioral theories of price movements, completes the explanation. Understanding price formation protects against price risk. But just as fundamental analysis protects against price risk while it exploits (Scenario A) mispricing, so stock price theory helps in exploiting (Scenario B) mispricing. Unfortunately, the behavioral theory of stock prices is not well developed; it is rather at the level of (interesting) conjecture. Absent such a theory, the fundamental investor might well take the advice of the fundamental analysts of old: Invest for the long term with considerable patience (for prices to ultimately reflect fundamental value). This view asserts the mispricing is a temporary phenomenon that will (ultimately) correct itself.

The manager investing in projects within the firm is not concerned with price risk. The risk in projects and business strategies is fundamental risk. However, that manager must be careful in using hurdle rates for investment that are estimated from market prices, like those based on historical CAPM betas. Such hurdle rates might reflect price risk, not fundamental risk.

Liquidity Risk

Selling at a price less than fundamental value can harm returns. But an investor can get a poor price by simply not finding other investors to sell to. Desiring to sell, the investor may find she has to take a low price to attract a buyer.

The risk of having to trade at a price that is different from intrinsic value because of a scarcity of traders is called **liquidity risk**. Sellers face liquidity risk, but so do buyers who do their fundamental analysis but can't find sellers. Short sellers run considerable risk if they can't find buyers when they wish to buy the stock to cover positions. And the more leveraged the trading position, the worse is the effect of liquidity risk.

Liquidity risk can be a permanent feature of some markets. Shares in privately held firms that rarely trade have considerable liquidity risk. Shares in large publicly traded firms have low liquidity risk. But liquidity risk can change unpredictably also. Investors may lose interest in particular stocks. And if the firm fares poorly, the investor may find it difficult to dispose of shares, to find willing buyers. Entire markets face liquidity risk should investors flee the market in a "crash," and regulators and central bankers are concerned with this "systematic" liquidity risk.

The discount that a seller takes for illiquidity is the *liquidity discount*. Market mechanisms develop to reduce this discount. The stockbroker performs the function of finding buyers or sellers on the other side of a trade and so reduces liquidity risk (for which he charges a fee). The market maker matches buy and sell orders on stock exchanges and so reduces liquidity risk (for which traders pay an implicit fee in the bid–ask spread). Investment banks find buyers for large issues of securities, and specialized brokers arrange for sales of private firms (for which they charge fees). Indeed transactions costs in trading are the cost of minimizing liquidity risk. Expected returns to investing are reduced by liquidity risk and expected returns to investing are reduced by transactions costs (which reduce liquidity risk).

INFERRING RISK FROM MARKET PRICES

In Chapter 5, we saw that we can infer growth rates in residual income from market prices by reverse engineering if we know (or assume) the cost of capital. Defining P_0 as the market price,

$$P_0 = \text{CSE}_0 + \frac{\text{RE}_1}{\rho_E} + \frac{\text{RE}_2}{\rho_E^2} + \ldots \frac{\text{RE}_T}{\rho_E^T} + \left(\frac{\text{RE}_{T+1}}{\rho_E - g}\right) / \rho_E^T$$

Then, if we know the equity cost of capital, ρ_E, we can calculate the expected growth, g, implied by the market price, P_0, if we have forecasts of residual earnings. Thus if we have analysts' forecasts for the next three years, we can input the market's long-term growth rate in RE after those three years.

In the same vein, we can calculate an implied cost of capital from the market price if we are confident in our earnings forecasts and long-term growth forecasts. If the market price were efficient (and our forecasts of earnings and growth were good ones), we would have a reliable estimate of the market's required return. And that estimate would be forward looking. It would not be based on historical analysis but would rather provide an estimate of the risk the investor is to bear in the future and of the risk premium the market would be giving him for buying at the market price.

Recent research has estimated the equity cost of capital along these lines. Claus and Thomas[8] assume long-run RE growth at the current real risk-free rate to calculate an average risk premium for equities of about 3.5 percent from prices observed from 1985 to 1996. This estimate is considerably lower than the 6 percent–9 percent typically estimated from historical stock returns. Gebhardt, Lee, and Swaminathan[9] assume fade rates for growth, along the lines of the fade diagrams of Chapter 15, and measure an average equity risk premium of about 3 percent over the period 1979–1995. They also calculate implied required equity returns for different industries and show that these required returns vary according to attributes that we normally associate with risk. Easton, Shroff, Sougiannis, and Taylor[10] estimate average implied risk premiums for Dow Jones Industrial stocks of 6.0 percent from 1981 to 1998. Gode and Mohanram infer the cost of capital for firms by reverse engineering the abnormal earnings growth model.[11]

Some of these estimates seem low, although the cost of capital is elusive. More research along these lines could be promising. But beware; these methods of inferring the cost of capital work only if market prices are efficient. Indeed, an active investor might view an implied equity risk premium of 3 percent as too low and so conclude that the price that implies this premium is too high.

[8] J. Claus and J. Thomas, "Equity Premia as low as Three Percent? Evidence from Analysts' Earnings Forecasts for Domestic and International Stock Markets," *Journal of Finance* (October 2001), pp. 1629–1666.

[9] W. Gebhardt, C. Lee, and B. Swaminathan, "Towards an Ex Ante Cost-of-Capital," *Journal of Accounting Research* (June 2001), pp. 135–176.

[10] P. Easton, P. Shroff, T. Sougiannis, and G. Taylor, "Using Forecasts of Earnings to Simultaneously Estimate Growth and the Rate of Return on Equity Investment," *Journal of Accounting Research* (June 2002) pp. 657–676.

[11] D. Gode and P. Mohanram, "Inferring the Cost of Capital Using the Ohlson-Juettner Model," *Review of Accounting Studies*, December 2003.

ADAPTING TO THE RISK MEASUREMENT PROBLEM

Clearly, the present state of the technology cannot guarantee a reliably precise measure of the cost of capital. We have presented the determinants of risk here but have not found any persuasive way of converting risk characteristics into a risk premium.

The qualitative analysis of risk in this chapter is of some help, however. While qualitative analysis does not yield the precise measures that quantitative analysis promises, it can get us "in the ball park." Here are ways to incorporate the qualitative analysis of risk into investing.

Relative Value Analysis: Evaluating Firms within Risk Classes

The qualitative analysis gives us a sense of relative riskiness. By establishing value-at-risk profiles, we can distinguish more risky firms from less risky firms. Firm A is seen as more risky than Firm B in our example. Think of identifying firms into *risk classes* according to the shape of their profiles. Firms with high operating risk and high financing risk might be distinguished from firms with high operating risk but low financing risk. And firms with higher upside potential but higher downside risk (Firm A) might be placed in a separate risk class from those that are structured to minimize downside risk and lose upside potential (Firm B). Cruder risk classes might be based simply on industry and financial leverage differences.

Having established a risk class, we would conclude that, with the current state of the technology, we cannot see any significant difference in risk between firms within the class. We would not have a measured cost of capital for the class, but in selecting investments, we can proceed with *relative value investing*, which finesses the need to estimate the cost of capital.

To understand relative value investing, understand that the valuations we have been making with a (presumed) estimate of the cost of capital are a form of relative value. The calculation V_0^E is the amount of value in units of cash that we would have to give up to buy the investment; it's a value relative to the value of cash. Cash can be invested at the risk-free rate. The risk-adjusted discount rate in the value calculation gives a value that is an alternative to cash, or an alternative to investing cash at the risk-free rate. So, effectively, the use of a risk-adjusted discount rate places the investment in the same risk class, so to speak, as cash. In technical terms, cash is the *numéraire*, the unit of measurement.

Now, rather than calculating the value in units of cash, calculate the value per unit of value of another stock in the same risk class, that is, with a similar value-at-risk profile. Rather than thinking of the alternative as investing cash at the risk-free rate, think of the alternative as investing in another asset with the same value-at-risk profile. Calculate a *relative value ratio* for the investment being considered, investment 1, relative to the alternative investment in the same risk class, investment 2:

$$\text{Relative value ratio} = \frac{V_0^E(1)/P_0(1)}{V_0^E(2)/P_0(2)}$$

The value for both investments $V_0^E(1)$ and $V_0^E(2)$ is calculated by discounting expected residual earnings at the risk-free rate. $P_0(1)$ and $P_0(2)$ are the market prices for the two investments set by the market's assessment of risk.

If both investments are risky, the ratio of their values (calculated using the risk-free rate) to the current price, $V_0^E(1)/P_0(1)$ in the numerator and $V_0^E(2)/P_0(2)$ in the denominator of the relative value ratio, should be greater than 1.0. If not, the numerator or denominator would indicate sell. But a buy or sell also would be indicated if the overall relative value ratio were different from 1.0. If the ratio is greater than 1.0, buy investment 1 because its market price, $P_0(1)$, discounts the risk-free equivalent value for risk more than investment 2, for the same risk. And, to hedge against the risk that is common to both, sell investment 2 short. If the relative value ratio is less than 1.0, reverse these positions. You can also conduct the analysis with the alternative investment being a portfolio of all firms in the same risk class. This reduces possible error from having assigned investment 2 to the wrong risk class and averages out idiosyncratic risk in any one stock.

The most difficult part of the analysis is the assignment of firms to risk classes. Price risk must be considered along with fundamental risk. Focus on industries that have the same operating characteristics.

Analysts do concentrate on specific industries and their knowledge of the industry should enable them to generate value-at-risk profiles. Table 18.3 gives "perceived risk" measures from a survey of analysts published in 1985. Analysts were asked to rank the risk of stocks on a scale of 1 to 9, assuming that the stocks were to be added to a well-diversified portfolio. Thus the risk they were asked to assess is systematic risk. The

TABLE 18.3
Analysts' Perceived Risk and Fundamental Attributes for 25 Stocks in 1985

Source: G. E. Farrelly, K. R. Ferris, and W. R. Reichenstein, "Perceived Risk, Market Risk, and Accounting Determined Risk Measures," *Accounting Review*, April 1985, pp. 278–288.

Name of Stock	Perceived Risk Mean	Perceived Risk Variance	Asset Size	Financial Leverage	Variability in Earnings
AT&T	1.89	1.22	11.83	0.165	1.09
Procter & Gamble	2.36	1.74	8.85	0.318	2.79
IBM	2.39	1.52	10.30	0.338	1.95
General Electric	2.69	1.64	9.95	0.468	1.29
Exxon	2.70	1.97	11.33	0.277	2.25
Commonwealth Edison	3.20	2.40	9.32	0.620	1.76
Dow Jones & Co.	3.57	2.38	6.28	0.477	2.96
McDonald's	3.87	2.36	7.97	0.413	2.32
Sears, Roebuck	3.91	1.69	10.24	0.573	1.42
DuPont	4.11	1.91	10.08	0.508	1.64
Safeway	4.28	3.27	8.21	0.691	2.01
Citicorp	4.30	2.37	11.69		1.52
Dr. Pepper	4.32	2.03	5.11	0.215	2.26
General Motors	4.59	2.43	10.57	0.422	
Xerox	4.69	2.45	8.95	0.397	1.04
American Broadcasting Company	4.86	1.83	7.37	0.370	0.47
Holiday Inn Worldwide	5.13	1.86	7.43	0.536	1.34
Tandy	5.54	2.00	6.84	0.225	3.27
Litton Industries	5.66	1.78	8.21	0.552	2.52
RCA	5.67	2.02	8.97	0.855	
Georgia-Pacific	5.88	2.51	8.53	0.450	3.13
Emery Air Freight	5.92	2.58	5.62	0.697	2.28
E.F. Hutton	6.37	2.75	8.64		1.80
U.S. Homes	7.23	2.60	6.63		20.18
International Harvester	8.78	0.41	8.58	0.704	

Note: A blank indicates that data were not available. Perceived risk is a ranking of risk as perceived by analysts, on a scale from 1 to 9; asset size is the natural logarithm of total assets; financial leverage is senior debt divided by total assets; and variability in earnings is the past standard deviation of the price-earnings ratio.

average responses for each firm are given along with three fundamental attributes that are commonly accepted as indicators of risk. The average perceived risks are in ascending order and seem to be correlated with the fundamentals. Indeed the correlations between perceived risk and asset size, financial leverage, and earnings variability are –0.46, 0.52, and 0.48, respectively. This analysis is fairly primitive but gives promise that analysts can combine their knowledge of business with fundamental analysis to assign firms to risk classes.

Investing is highly personal and different investors may have different risk attributes with which they are concerned when benchmarking with a risk class. Investors have different tolerances for risk and like or dislike different features of variance-at-risk profiles. Accordingly, they desire different exposures to risk and different hedges against risk. It is probably for this reason that mutual funds provide menus of funds for investors to choose from. A set of risk classes is such a menu.

Conservative and Optimistic Forecasting and the Margin of Safety

The analyst can adjust for risk by being conservative in forecasting, that is, calculate values by forecasting a conservative scenario for residual earnings and discounting these forecasts by the risk-free rate. If the market price is greater than a value calculated with conservative forecasting, buy. Similarly, if selling is being entertained, forecast an optimistic scenario and calculate a value (by discounting at the risk-free rate) under this scenario. If the market price is greater than this value, sell.

The same ad hoc accommodation of risk can be made by using risk-adjusted discount rates but specifying rates that a value-at-risk profile would indicate are excessive in evaluating a buy. A high rate would tend to undervalue the firm. Similarly, use a low rate that tends to overvalue the firm for a sell evaluation.

Biasing forecasts or biasing discount rates builds in what traditional fundamental analysts call a *margin of safety*. Either form of bias produces a valuation which is deemed to be incorrect but which is wrong by an amount—the margin of safety—that is a protection against being wrong with estimates. The margin of safety is particularly important to the defensive investor. Investing is inherently uncertain and uncertainty about the risks requires caution.

Summary

This chapter has not given you a precise cost of capital. So we cannot list the cost of capital as one of the key measures at the end of the chapter. We must be realistic and not pretend that a precise measure can be calculated. Fake precision is of no help in practical investing. Rather, take an honest approach, admit that imprecision is inescapable, and think of ways of finessing the problem. Indeed the last section of the chapter offered some ways of doing this.

The centerpiece of this chapter is the material in the "Fundamental Risk" section on the determinants of fundamental risk. Understand the drivers of fundamental risk; they are summarized in Figure 18.3. And understand how value-at-risk profiles, like those in Figure 18.4, are developed from an analysis of these drivers. Understand also how the analysis is used for strategy and scenario planning.

An understanding of the fundamental determinants yields a qualitative assessment of risk. Wise and prudent investors understand risk even if they cannot measure it precisely. And they understand that price risk as well as fundamental risk is involved, and how fundamental analysis helps to reduce price risk.

The Web Connection

Find the following on the web page for this chapter:

- A further look at the distribution of stock returns.

- More discussion on extreme returns and how downside risk is rewarded with upside potential.

- Reverse engineering the cost of capital.

- More on Scenario A and Scenario B investing.

Key Concepts

adaptation option is the ability to alter the business after a bad outcome. *661*

behavioral finance is the study of why stock prices seemingly behave irrationally *666*

distribution of returns is the set of possible outcomes that an investor faces with probabilities assigned to those outcomes. *646*

diversification of risk involves reducing risk by holding many investments in a portfolio. *649*

downside risk is the probability of receiving extremely low returns. *648*

fat-tailed distribution of outcomes has a probability of extreme (high and low) outcomes that is higher than that for the **normal distribution**. *647*

fundamental risk is the risk that is generated by business activities. Compare with **price risk**. *652*

growth option is the ability to grow assets (and profits) if an opportunity arises. *661*

liquidity risk is the risk of not finding a buyer or seller at the intrinsic value. *667*

market inefficiency risk is the risk of prices changing in a way that is not justified by fundamentals. *665*

normal distribution is a set of outcomes characterized solely by its mean and standard deviation. *646*

price risk is the risk of trading at a price that is different from the fundamental value, either because of **market inefficiency risk** or **liquidity risk**. Compare with **fundamental risk**. *664*

skewed distribution of outcomes is one that has higher probability in one extreme than the other. *647*

systematic risk or **nondiversifiable risk** is risk that cannot be diversified away in a portfolio. Compare with **unsystematic risk**. *650*

upside potential is the probability of yielding extremely high returns. Compare with **downside risk**. *648*

unsystematic risk or **diversifiable risk** is the risk that can be diversified away in a portfolio. Compare with **systematic risk**. *650*

The Analyst's Toolkit

Analysis Tools	Page	Key Measures	Page	Acronymns to Remember
Value-at-risk analysis	656	Asset turnover risk	654	ATO asset turnover
Scenario planning	662	Borrowing cost risk	655	CAPM capital asset pricing model
Historical beta estimation	663	Expense risk	655	CSE common shareholders' equity
Fundamental (predicted) beta		Financial leverage risk	655	FLEV financial leverage
estimation	663	Fundamental beta	663	GDP gross domestic product
Implicit cost of capital		Growth risk	655	NBC net borrowing cost
estimation (from market		Operating leverage risk		NFE net financial expense
price)	668	Operating liability leverage		NFO net financial obligations
Relative value investing	669	risk	655	NOA net operating assets
Conservative forecasting	671	Profit margin risk	654	OI operating income
		Relative value ratio	669	OLEV operating leverage
		Risk class	669	OLLEV operating liability leverage
		Standard deviation of returns	646	PM profit margin
				RE residual earnings
				ReOI residual operating income
				ROCE return on common equity
				RNOA return on net operating assets
				WACC weighted-average cost of capital

Concept Questions

C18.1. Why might the normal distribution of returns not characterize the risk of investing in a business?

C18.2. Comment on the following statement. The challenge in measuring the required return for investing is to measure the size of the risk premium over the risk-free rate, but the capital asset pricing model largely leaves this measurement as a guessing game.

C18.3. Can you explain why diversification lowers risk?

C18.4. Why does operating liability leverage increase operating risk?

C18.5. Why are growth stocks often seen as high risk?

C18.6. Explain asset turnover risk.

C18.7. Airlines are said to have high operating risk. Why?

C18.8. Why might stock returns have greater risk than is justified by the fundamentals of the firm's business activities?

C18.9. Should firms manage risk on behalf of their shareholders?

C18.10. Suppose one calculated the intrinsic value of two firms using residual earnings techniques with the risk-free rate as a discount rate. The price-to-value (P/V) ratio of these two firms, so calculated, should be the same if they have the same risk characteristics. Is this so?

C18.11. Explain the difference between Scenario A and Scenario B investing and the risks involved in each.

Exercises **E18.1.** **Balance Sheets and Risk (Easy)**

Below are balance sheets for two firms with similar revenues. Amounts are in millions of dollars. Which firm looks more risky for shareholders? Why?

FIRM A			
Assets		**Liabilities and Equity**	
Cash	$ 17	Accounts payable	$ 14
Accounts receivable	43	Long-term debt	200
Inventory	102		
Property, plant, and equipment	194		
Long-term debt investments	104	Common equity	246
	$460		$460

FIRM B			
Assets		**Liabilities and Equity**	
Cash	$ 15	Accounts payable	$ 37
Accounts receivable	72	Long-term debt	200
Inventory	107		
Property, plant, and equipment	289	Common equity	246
	$483		$483

E18.2. **Income Statements and Risk (Medium)**

The statements below are for two firms in the same line of business (in millions of dollars).

FIRM A		
Sales		$1,073
Expenses		
Labor and materials	$536	
Administration	121	
Depreciation	214	
Selling expenses	84	955
		118
Interest expense		25
Income before taxes		93
Income taxes		34
Income after taxes		$ 59

FIRM B

Sales		$1,129
Expenses		
Labor and materials	$793	
Administration	42	
Depreciation	79	
Selling expenses	91	1,005
		124
Interest expense		4
Income before taxes		120
Income taxes		43
Income after taxes		$ 77

a. Analyze the risk drivers in these income statements. Which firm looks more risky for stockholders? Why?

b. On the basis of the relationships in these income statements, develop pro forma income statements under the following scenarios:

(1) Sales drop to $532 million for both firms.

(2) Sales increase to $2,140 million for both firms. What does this analysis tell you?

E18.3. Ranking Firms on Risk (Medium)

Below are income statements and balance sheets for three firms. Rank these firms on what you perceive to be the relative riskiness of their equity from these statements. What features in the statements determined your ranking? All numbers are in millions of dollars. All three firms face a statutory tax rate of 36 percent.

FIRM A
Income Statement

Sales		$542
Cost of sales		
Labor and materials	$345	
Depreciation	89	434
		108
Selling expenses	9	
Administrative expenses	26	
Research and development expenses	24	59
		49
Net interest expense		7
Income before taxes		42
Income taxes		15
Income after taxes		$ 27

FIRM A
Balance Sheet

Assets		Liabilities and Equity	
Cash	$ 7	Accounts payable	$ 42
Short-term investments	4	Long-term debt	104
Accounts receivable	27		
Inventory	64		
Property, plant, and equipment	215	Common equity	171
	$317		$317

FIRM B
Income Statement

Sales		$796
Cost of sales		
Labor and materials	$590	
Depreciation	47	637
		159
Selling expenses	53	
Administrative expenses	19	
Research and development expenses	15	87
		72
Net interest expense		4
Income before taxes		68
Income taxes		24
Income after taxes		$ 44

FIRM B
Balance Sheet

Assets		Liabilities and Equity	
Cash	$ 5	Accounts payable	$ 36
Short-term investments	47	Long-term debt	104
Accounts receivable	78		
Inventory	192		
Property, plant, and equipment	159	Common equity	341
	$481		$481

FIRM C
Income Statement

Sales		$649
Cost of sales		
Labor and materials	$454	
Depreciation	65	519
		130
Selling expenses	36	
Administrative expenses	28	
Research and development	8	72
		58
Net interest expense		14
Income before taxes		44
Income taxes		16
Income after taxes		$ 28

FIRM C
Balance Sheet

Assets		Liabilities and Equity	
Cash	$ 6	Accounts payable	$ 39
Short-term investments	10	Long-term debt	210
Accounts receivable	66		
Inventory	97		
Property, plant, and equipment	195	Common equity	125
	$374		$374

E18.4. Analyzing Risk (Hard)

Two firms, Firm A and Firm B, have $1,000 million invested in net operating assets in the same line of business. Firm A has $25 million in net financial obligations while Firm B has $600 million in net financial obligations. Both firms face a statutory tax rate of 36 percent.

Below are forecasted pro forma income statements for the two firms for the upcoming year (in millions of dollars).

FIRM A
Forecasted Income Statement

Sales		$2,140
Fixed costs	$ 643	
Variable costs	1,240	1,883
		257
Interest expense		2
Income before taxes		255
Income taxes		91
Income after taxes		$ 164

FIRM B
Forecasted Income Statement

Sales		$2,140
Fixed costs	$1,240	
Variable costs	643	1,883
		257
Interest expense		48
Income before taxes		209
Income taxes		75
Income after taxes		$ 134

a. Calculate the forecasted return on common equity for the two firms. Would you attribute the difference between the two measures to differences in risk? If so, why is the risk of the equity different for the two firms?

b. Calculate the value of the operations of these two firms, assuming that the residual operating income indicated by the pro forma income statements will continue indefinitely in the future. Use a risk-free rate of 5 percent in your calculations to derive a value that is not risk adjusted.

c. Would you pay more or less for the operations of Firm A than for Firm B? Why?

d. As an equity investor, would your required return be higher for Firm A than Firm B? Why?

e. What would residual operating income for the two firms be if sales fell to $1,500 million? Does this calculation justify your answer to part (c)?

The Analysis of Credit Risk

LINKS

Link to previous chapter

Chapter 18 showed how the analysis of fundamentals helps in the evaluation of equity risk. Value-at-risk profiles were developed to assess equity risk.

This chapter

This chapter shows how fundamental analysis helps in the evaluation of the risk of a firm defaulting on its debt. Value-at-risk profiles are developed to assess default risk.

Link to web page

To learn even more about risk, visit the text website at www.mhhe.com/penman2e.

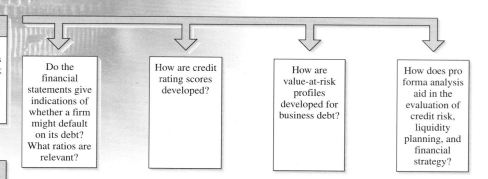

Do the financial statements give indications of whether a firm might default on its debt? What ratios are relevant?

How are credit rating scores developed?

How are value-at-risk profiles developed for business debt?

How does pro forma analysis aid in the evaluation of credit risk, liquidity planning, and financial strategy?

Most of the analysis in the book to this point has been concerned with the valuation of the firm and the valuation of the equity claim on the firm. This chapter deals with the other major claim on the firm, the debt. Thus far we have accepted the market value of debt as its value. But buyers and sellers of debt need to know how to establish the market value of debt.

In most debt contracts, the payoffs to debt are specified in the contract. So Step 3 of fundamental analysis—forecasting payoffs—is trivial. But forecasted payoffs have to be discounted (in Step 4) to get a valuation. Discounting requires a measure of the required return for debt, and this required return, like that for equity, depends on the riskiness of the debt: The required return for debt is the risk-free rate for the term of the debt plus a **default premium** that varies with default risk. **Default risk**, or **credit risk**, is the risk of

The Analyst's Checklist

After reading this chapter you should understand:

- Who the alternative suppliers of debt financing to the firm are and how they contract with the firm.

- How default risk determines the price of credit and the cost of debt capital for the firm.

- What determines default risk.

- How default risk is analyzed.

- What bond rating agencies do.

- How credit scoring models work.

- The difference between Type I and Type II errors in predicting default.

- How pro forma analysis identifies default scenarios.

- How value-at-risk analysis is incorporated into default analysis.

- How financial strategy works.

After reading this chapter you should be able to:

- Reformulate and annotate financial statements in preparation for credit analysis.

- Calculate liquidity, solvency, and operational ratios that are pertinent to credit analysis.

- Calculate credit scores using financial ratios.

- Calculate a probability of bankruptcy using financial ratios.

- Trade off Type I and Type II default forecasting errors.

- Prepare pro formas for default scenarios.

- Prepare value-at-risk profiles for debt.

- Forecast default points.

- Prepare a default strategy.

default; that is, the risk of not receiving timely interest and return of principal as specified in the debt agreement. This chapter brings fundamental analysis to the task of evaluating default risk.

Analysts talk of the required return for debt. But debt taken on by the firm is also credit supplied by those who purchase the debt. Accordingly, we can talk of the required return for debt as also being the **price of credit**. Whatever the terminology, the amount charged by suppliers of credit is the *cost of debt* for the firm.

THE SUPPLIERS OF CREDIT AND THE PRICE OF CREDIT

Suppliers of credit to the firm include the following:

- *Public debt market investors*, who include (long-term) bondholders and (short-term) commercial paper holders. Typically, publicly traded debt is unsecured, that is, not collateralized by specific assets. Bondholders are protected by bond covenants, which restrict the firm from specified actions that might increase default risk, and violation of a bond covenant is technically a default. To evaluate default risk, investors in this type of debt rely on those corporate disclosures about the overall health of the firm that are required by the Securities and Exchange Commission (SEC) for all publicly traded securities. They also rely on *bond ratings*, which are published by rating agencies to indicate default risk. Accordingly, it is the rating agencies that are particularly concerned with the analysis of risk, and they develop rating models that involve the analysis of fundamentals.

- *Commercial banks*, which make loans to firms. They are usually closer to a firm's business than a bondholder, so they have access to more information regarding default risk. The loan officer serves as the credit analyst, and loan officers, like bond rating agencies, have models that aid in *credit scoring*. Their credit scoring methods are tied into their bank's internal risk management, to protect the bank and to satisfy regulatory constraints on its exposure to risk. Banks originate loans on the basis of credit scores. They then use credit scoring to measure the quality of loans that they sell on to other institutions and to monitor the default risk of loans they retain.

- *Other financial institutions*, such as insurance companies, finance houses, and leasing firms, make loans, much like banks, but usually with specific assets serving as **collateral**. They also arrange specialty financing such as leases of long-term assets.

- *Suppliers* to the firm, who grant (usually short-term) credit upon delivery of goods and services. The credit can be granted with or without interest. The firm also is a supplier of credit—to its customers.

Each supplier of credit has a price for granting credit—the required return—and each needs to analyze the risk of default and charge accordingly. Bondholders charge a yield to maturity based on their risk assessment and set bond prices accordingly. Banks charge an interest rate over a base rate (the prime rate for their safest customers) that depends on default risk. And suppliers charge a higher price for goods and services if the default risk is high. If risk is deemed to be unacceptable, no price is acceptable to the lender, so credit is denied.

The explicit price is only one dimension of the price. Just as a supplier might charge no explicit interest for credit but charge a higher price for goods supplied to compensate, a bondholder will charge a lower yield if bond covenants have more protection, a finance firm will charge less with collateral, and a bank will charge less for loans with personal or parent company guarantees. Such restrictions increase the (implicit) cost of capital to the borrowing firm.

RATIO ANALYSIS FOR CREDIT EVALUATION

Equity analysis calls for a particular ratio analysis (of profitability and growth), which was laid out in Chapters 11 and 12. **Credit analysis** calls for a different analysis, and many of the ratios involved are different from those for equity analysis. As with equity analysis, the emphasis is on forecasting. Rather than identifying those ratios that forecast profitability and growth, credit analysis identifies ratios that indicate the likelihood of default. Therefore, it is also referred to as **default analysis**. As with equity analysis, the credit analyst identifies ratios from financial statements that have first been reformulated for the purpose.

Reformulated Financial Statements

For the equity analysis financial statements were reformulated to uncover what is most important to equity investors, core operating profitability. For credit analysis the statements must be in a form to uncover what is most important to creditors, the ability to repay the debt.

Reformulation, as before, involves reclassifying items in the financial statements and bringing more dollar detail into the financial statements from the footnotes. In addition, the discovery process leads to some annotation of the statements. *Annotation* involves summarizing features of the financing that cannot be expressed as dollar amounts on the balance sheet but which are pertinent to the risk of default.

Balance Sheet Reformulation and Annotation

The ability to repay depends on having cash at maturity. Maturities differ, but it is standard practice to distinguish debt as short-term (usually thought of as maturing within one year) and long-term (maturing in more than one year). Published balance sheets are usually prepared with a division into current and noncurrent (long-term) assets and liabilities, so the balance sheet needs little reformulation. Indeed, it is because balance sheets are structured with the creditor in mind that we had to reformulate them for equity analysis. For credit analysis, there is no need to distinguish operating debt from financing debt. Both are claims that have to be paid.

Some reformulation and annotation is called for, however. The reformulation may differ for short-term and long-term debt analysis as follows:

- Details on different classes of debt and their varying maturities are available in the debt footnotes; these details can be inserted in the body of reformulated statements.

- Debt of unconsolidated subsidiaries (where the parent owns less than 50 percent but has effective control) should be recognized. For example, oil companies sometimes raise cash through joint ventures in which they hold less than 50 percent interest, and they cover the debt of the joint venture if revenues in the venture are insufficient to service its debt. The Coca-Cola Company owns less than 50 percent of its bottling companies but effectively borrows through these subsidiaries. The debt of these subsidiaries or joint ventures should be included in a consolidated reformulated statement if the parent company is ultimately responsible for it. Use proportional consolidation methods, as described in Minicase M11.1 in Chapter 11.

- Long-term marketable securities are sometimes available for sale in the short term if a need for cash arises. For analyzing short-term liquidity, therefore, reclassify them as a short-term asset.

- Long-term debt can be presented on a net basis. If a firm has long-term debt assets of similar maturity to its long-term debt liabilities, its effective (net) debt is its long-term debt minus its long-term debt assets. Such netting is effective **defeasance**. (Current debt investments should not be netted against current liabilities because net amounts are calculated in ratios calculated from the statements, as in the next subsection.)

- Remove deferred tax liabilities that are unlikely to revert from liabilities to shareholders' equity. Such deferred taxes, created by a reduction of earnings and equity, are liabilities that are unlikely to be paid. So classify them back to equity.

- Add the LIFO reserve to inventory and to shareholders' equity to convert LIFO inventory to a FIFO basis. FIFO inventory is closer to current cost, so it is a better indicator of cash that can be generated from inventory.

- Off-balance-sheet debt can be recognized on the face of the statement. See Box 19.1.

- Contingent liabilities that can be estimated should be included in the reformulated statements. Contingent liabilities that cannot be estimated should be noted as part of the annotation. Contingent liabilities include liabilities under product, labor, and environmental litigation. In the United States, GAAP requires these liabilities to be put on the balance sheet if the liability is "probable" and the amount of the loss can be

Off-balance-sheet financing transactions are arrangements to finance assets and create obligations that do not appear on the balance sheet. Some types of off-balance-sheet financing are:

- Operating leases. Leases that are in substance purchases, called *capital leases*, appear on the balance sheet, with the leased asset as part of property, plant, and equipment and the lease obligation as part of liabilities. Leases that are not in substance a purchase, called *operating leases*, do not appear on the balance sheet; they are summarized in footnotes. However, lessees and lessors have been creative in writing lease agreements to get around the letter of the rules for capitalizing leases. Examine operating leases in the footnotes and assess whether these are effectively an obligation to use an asset for most of its useful life. If so, bring them onto the balance sheet as a capital lease. The lease amount is the present value of the payments under the lease.

- Agreements and commitments can create obligations that should be recognized:
  Third-party agreements: A third party purchases an asset for the firm and the firm agrees to service the third party's debt on the purchase.
  Throughput agreements: A firm agrees to pay for the use of the facilities of another firm.
  Take-or-pay agreements: A firm agrees to pay for goods in the future, regardless of whether it takes delivery.

Repurchase agreements: A firm sells inventory but agrees to repurchase the inventory at selling price or guarantees a resale price to the customer.

- Sales of receivables with recourse. A firm sells its receivables for cash, removing them from the balance sheet, but has an obligation to indemnify the holder of the receivables.

- Unfunded pension liabilities. In some countries (but not the United States) significant pension liabilities may not be on the balance sheet.

- Guarantees of third-party or related-party debt. Watch for guarantees of the debt of nonconsolidated subsidiaries by a parent company.

- **Special purpose entities**, *off-balance-sheet partnerships*, and *structured finance vehicles*. Firms can create entities, in which others have control (so they are not consolidated), to accomplished specific purposes—like the securitization of assets or acquiring assets with off-balance-sheet leases ("synthetic leases"). Although the firm does not have control, it might retain residual risk if these entities run into financial difficulties. The obligations may be in the form of recourse liabilities or put options on the firm's own stock. The Enron affair highlighted the danger of these special purpose entities.

"reasonably estimated." Footnote disclosure is otherwise required, unless the possibility of loss is "remote."

- The risk in derivatives and other financial instruments should be noted. Inspect the financial instruments footnote.

Reformulated Income Statements

The analyst reviews the income statement to assess the ability of the firm to generate operating income to cover net interest payments. Thus the reformulated income statement that distinguishes after-tax operating income from after-tax net financial expense serves debt analysis well. So does the distinction in reformulated statements between core and unusual items for, with a view to future default, the issue is whether future core income will cover future core financial expense.

Reformulated Cash Flow Statements

The reformulated cash flow statement prepared for equity analysis also serves debt analysis. In particular, the reformulation of GAAP cash flow from operations to exclude after-tax net interest identifies (unlevered) cash flow from operations that is available to pay after-tax interest. And the reclassification of investments in financial assets (which GAAP places in the investing section) as financing flows rather than investment flows captures net amounts of bond issuing activity.

With reformulated financial statements in hand, the ratio analysis can begin. With the two types of maturities in mind—short-term and long-term—ratio analysis groups ratios into two types, short-term *liquidity ratios* and long-term *solvency ratios*. Both sets of ratios are indicators of the ability to repay, but at different maturity dates. The ratio analysis is completed with some of the *operational ratios* that we have already covered.

All three sets of ratios are benchmarked with comparisons to similar firms and with trend analysis over time. The credit analyst looks for deteriorations in the ratios over time and relative to comparison firms.

Short-Term Liquidity Ratios

Short-term creditors—suppliers, short-term paper holders, and long-term lenders of debt that is shortly to mature, for example—are concerned with the firm's ability to have enough cash to repay in the near future. The long-term lender is also interested in short-term liquidity because if the firm cannot survive the short term, there is no long term.

Working capital is current assets minus current liabilities. As *current assets* are those expected to generate cash within one year and *current liabilities* are obligations due to mature within one year, working capital and its components are the focus of liquidity analysis.

The typical balance sheet has five types of current assets:

1. Cash and cash equivalents

2. Short-term investments

3. Receivables

4. Prepaid expenses

5. Inventories

Each item has an expected date for realization into cash. Inventories typically have the longest time to cash as they first have to be sold and converted into a receivable, and then the receivable has to be turned into cash. Short-term investments (to which readily marketable long-term securities can be added in the balance sheet reformulation) may be closer to cash than receivables or prepaid expenses, depending on the maturity of the investments. Under historical cost accounting, the carrying amount for inventories usually understates their cash value, although the lower-of-cost-or-market rule for inventories can give them a market valuation when the firm is in distress.

There are three types of current liabilities on the typical balance sheet:

1. Trade payables

2. Short-term debt

3. Accrued liabilities

All three are typically close to their cash value.

The balance sheet is a statement of stocks, so it gives the stocks (amounts) of net liquid assets at a point in time. Liquidity flows are in the cash flow statement. Liquidity ratios involve both the balance sheet stocks of cash and near-cash items and flows of cash in the cash flow statement.

Liquidity Stock Measures

$$\text{Current ratio} = \frac{\text{Current assets}}{\text{Current liabilities}}$$

$$\text{Quick (or acid test) ratio} = \frac{\text{Cash} + \text{Short-term investments} + \text{Receivables}}{\text{Current liabilities}}$$

$$\text{Cash ratio} = \frac{\text{Cash} + \text{Short-term investments}}{\text{Current liabilities}}$$

These measures indicate the ability of near-cash assets to pay off the current liabilities. The numerators of these ratios indicate different cash maturities. So, for example, the quick ratio includes only *quick assets* in the numerator by excluding inventories that may take some time to turn into cash (and whose carrying values are not usually their cash values). The cash ratio involves only assets with almost immediate liquidity.

Liquidity Flow Measures

$$\text{Cash flow ratio} = \frac{\text{Cash flow from operations}}{\text{Current liabilities}}$$

$$\text{Defensive interval} = \frac{\text{Cash} + \text{Short-term investments} + \text{Receivables}}{\text{Capital expenditures}} \times 365$$

$$\frac{\text{Cash flow to}}{\text{capital expenditures}} = \frac{\text{(Unlevered) cash flow from operations}}{\text{Capital expenditures}}$$

Levered cash flow, you'll remember, is cash flow after interest. Unlevered cash flow is levered cash flow plus after-tax net interest payments. The first measure indicates how well the cash flow from operations covers the cash needed to settle liabilities in the short term. It is conventional to use the reported (levered) cash flow from operations, and average current liabilities are sometimes used in the denominator. The second ratio measures the liquidity available to meet capital expenditures without further borrowing. Multiplying by 365 yields the number of days expenditures can be maintained out of near-cash resources. The third measure is free cash flow in ratio form and indicates to what extent capital expenditures can be financed out of cash from operations. Sometimes forecasted expenditures are used in the denominators of the second and third measures.

Long-Term Solvency Ratios

Long-term debtholders watch the firm's immediate liquidity, but they are primarily concerned with its ability to meet its obligations in the more distant future. Focus therefore moves to incorporate the noncurrent sections of the balance sheet in ratios.

Solvency Stock Measures

$$\text{Debt to total assets} = \frac{\text{Total debt (Current} + \text{Long-term)}}{\text{Total assets (Liabilities} + \text{Total equity)}}$$

$$\text{Debt to equity} = \frac{\text{Total debt}}{\text{Total equity}}$$

$$\text{Long-term debt ratio} = \frac{\text{Long-term debt}}{\text{Long-term debt} + \text{total equity}}$$

The first two ratios capture all debt, the third just long-term debt. The first two differ in the denominator but capture similar characteristics. Net debt can be used in the numerator when financial assets are available to pay off the debt (in this case the denominators of the first and third ratios are reduced by debt assets).

Solvency Flow Measures

$$\text{Interest coverage (times interest earned)} = \frac{\text{Operating income}}{\text{Net interest expense}}$$

$$\text{Interest coverage (cash basis)} = \frac{\text{Unlevered cash flow from operations}}{\text{Net cash interest}}$$

$$\text{Fixed-charge coverage} = \frac{\text{Operating income} + \text{Fixed charges}}{\text{Fixed charges}}$$

$$\text{Fixed-charge coverage (cash basis)} = \frac{\text{Unlevered cash flow from operations} + \text{Fixed charges}}{\text{Fixed charges}}$$

$$\text{CFO to debt} = \frac{\text{Unlevered cash flow from operations}}{\text{Total debt}}$$

It is conventional to measure the flows in these ratios before tax (although an after-tax calculation is also justified). The ratios are improved (as indicators of the future) by measuring operating income and net interest as core income and expense.

The two interest coverage ratios give the number of times operating earnings and cash flow from operations, respectively, cover the interest requirement. The numerators and denominators are from the reformulated income and cash flow statements. Some definitions consider only interest expense, in which case the numerator includes interest income and the denominator excludes it.

Fixed charges are interest and principal repayments (including those on leases) and preferred dividends, so fixed-charge coverage measures the number of times total debt service is covered. The last ratio measures cash flow relative to total debt repayments to be made, not just the current repayment.

These ratios give not only an indication of solvency but also an indication of a firm's **debt capacity**. Low coverage ratios suggest that a firm has capacity to assume more debt (all else being equal).

Operating Ratios

The ratios just listed pertain directly to liquidity and solvency. But liquidity and solvency are driven in large part by the outcome of operations, so operating ratios are also indicators of debt risk. It is sometimes the case that a firm can be quite profitable in operations and still have short-term liquidity difficulties, but it is far more likely that both short-term liquidity and long-term solvency problems are induced by poor operating profitability.

Interest coverage, for example, is just a restatement of the FLEV × SPREAD, and so is driven by financial leverage (FLEV) and the operating spread (SPREAD), that is, the return on net operating assets relative to net borrowing costs. And these measures, in turn, are driven by lower-order drivers. Thus to complete the ratio analysis, analyze profitability and changes in profitability along the lines of earlier parts of the book. And watch for the "red flag" indicators (in Chapter 15) that indicate deterioration. If receivables or inventory turnover increases, for example, liquidity problems could result.

FORECASTING AND CREDIT ANALYSIS

Liquidity, solvency, and operational ratios reveal the current state of the firm. But the credit analyst is concerned with default in the future. Do the ratios predict default? Some of them might be symptoms of financial distress rather than predictors. Discovering that interest coverage is low is important to the analyst. But anticipation of a low interest coverage ahead of time is also important. And so for all ratios. Indeed, once liquidity and coverages have deteriorated, it might be too late.

The analyst thus turns to forecasting. His aim is to produce a credit score that indicates the probability of default.

Prelude to Forecasting: The Interpretive Background

Before forecasting, the analyst must have a good understanding of the conditions under which credit is given to the firm. Such an understanding provides the information necessary for forecasting. It enables the analyst to bring her judgment to supplement quantitative techniques. And it provides perspective to interpret ratios and other financial data. A particular ratio—a current ratio of less than 1.0, for example—might be seen as inadequate for a firm with large inventories and receivables but quite adequate for a firm with no inventories or receivables.

The analyst needs to understand the following points and include salient ones in the annotations to the reformulated statements:

- Know the business. Just as the equity analyst must know the business before attempting to value the equity, so must the credit analyst. Understand the business strategy and understand the drivers of value in the strategy. And understand the risks that the strategy exposes the firm to.

- Appreciate the "moral hazard" problem of debt. The interest of debtholders is not the prime consideration for management. Members of management serve the shareholders (and themselves), not the debtholders. So they can take actions that benefit the shareholders at the expense of debtholders. They can borrow to pay a large dividend to shareholders. They can pursue highly risky strategies with high upside potential and use debt to leverage the upside payoff. If the strategy is successful, shareholders benefit enormously, but debtholders just get their fixed return. If they fail, debtholders (and shareholders) can lose all.

- Understand the financing strategy. What is the firm's target leverage ratio? What is the firm's target payout ratio? What sources of financing will the firm rely on? Does the firm hedge interest rate risk? If borrowing across borders, does it hedge currency risk?

- Understand the current financing arrangements. What are the firm's banking relationships? Does it have open lines of credit? When might they expire? What is the current composition of the firm's debt? What debt is secured? What debt has seniority? What are the maturity dates for the debt? What are the restrictions on the firm in its debt agreements?

- Understand the quality of the firm's accounting.

- Understand the auditor's opinion, particularly any qualifications to the opinion.

With this background, the analyst develops forecasts. We cover two forecasting tools here. The first develops credit scores based on predictions from financial ratios. The second brings the pro forma profitability analysis and value-at-risk analysis of earlier chapters to the task of credit analysis.

FIGURE 19.1
The Behavior of Selected Financial Statement Ratios over Five Years prior to Bankruptcy, for Firms that Failed and Comparable Firms that did not Fail.
Ratios for failed firms are of lower quality than those for nonfailed firms, and they deteriorate as bankruptcy approaches.

Source: W. H. Beaver, "Financial Ratios as Predictors of Failure," *Journal of Accounting Research*, Supplement, 1966, p. 82.

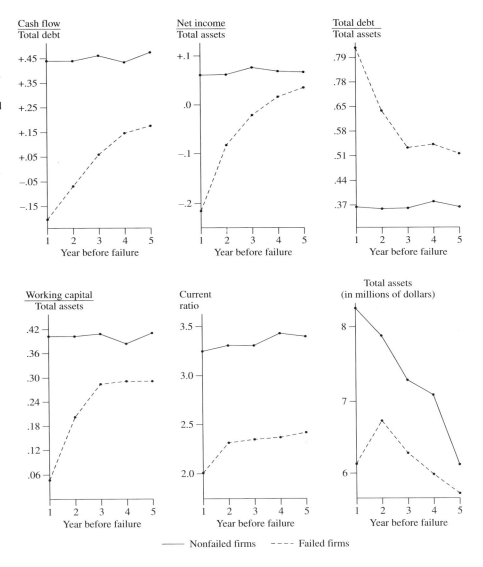

Ratio Analysis and Credit-Scoring

Figure 19.1 depicts the deterioration of a number of ratios over five years prior to bankruptcy (failure). The graphs are from one of the original studies on bankruptcy prediction by William Beaver in the 1960s. Average ratios for bankrupt firms are compared with those of comparable firms that did not go bankrupt. The ratios for firms going bankrupt are of lower quality than those for nonbankrupt firms, even five years before bankruptcy. And they become significantly worse as bankruptcy approaches. So, benchmarking ratios against those for comparable firms, combined with a trend analysis, does give an indication of future bankruptcy.

Two issues arise in getting default predictions from accounting ratios:

1. There are many ratios to be considered and the analyst needs to summarize the information they provide as a whole. A low interest coverage but a high current ratio may

have different implications than a low interest coverage and a low current ratio. A composite credit score needs to be developed.

A *bond rating* of the sort published by Standard & Poor's and Moody's is a composite score. Standard & Poor's ratings range from AAA (for firms with highest capacity to repay interest and principal) through AA, A, BBB, BB, B, CCC, CC, C to D (for firms actually in default). The ability to repay debt rated BB and below is deemed to have significant uncertainty. Moody's rankings are similar: Aaa, Aa, and A for high-grade debt, then Baa, Ba, B, Caa, Ca, C, and D. These debt ratings are published as an indicator of the required bond yield, and indeed the ratings are highly correlated with yields.

A bank typically summarizes information about the creditworthiness of a firm in a credit score. This score can be in the form of a number ranging from one to seven or one to nine, or qualitative categories such as "normal acceptable risk," "doubtful," and "nonperforming."

2. Errors in predicting default and the cost of prediction errors have to be considered. The financial ratios of failing and nonfailing firms are different on average but some failing firms can have ratios that are similar to those of healthy firms. A firm going bankrupt could have the same current ratio and interest coverage ratio as one that will survive. A bank loan officer might then classify both firms as low default risk, approve loans to both, and generate loan losses for the bank (from the bankrupt firm). Alternatively she might classify them both as having high default risk and deny credit, losing good business for the bank (from the nonbankrupt firm).

The first issue calls for a method of combining ratios into one composite score that indicates the overall creditworthiness of the firm. The second issue calls for a method of trading off the two types of errors that can be made. We deal with each in turn.

Credit Scoring Models

Credit scoring models combine a set of ratios that pertain to default into a credit score. A credit scoring model has the form

$$\text{Credit score} = (w_1 \times \text{Ratio}_1) + (w_2 \times \text{Ratio}_2) + (w_3 \times \text{Ratio}_3) + \cdots + (w_N \times \text{Ratio}_N)$$

That is, the model sums ratios that are weighted by weights w. A variety of statistical techniques can be used to determine the weights, but two common ones are multiple discriminant analysis and logit analysis.

Multiple Discriminant Analysis. Z-score analysis, pioneered by Edward Altman,[1] utilizes discriminant analysis techniques. The model has been refined over time but the original model, developed in the 1960s, took the form

$$Z\text{-score} = 1.2\left(\frac{\text{Working capital}}{\text{Total assets}}\right) + 1.4\left(\frac{\text{Retained earnings}}{\text{Total assets}}\right)$$

$$+ \; 3.3\left(\frac{\text{Earnings before interest and taxes}}{\text{Total assets}}\right)$$

$$+ \; 0.6\left(\frac{\text{Market value of equity}}{\text{Book value of liabilities}}\right) + 1.0\left(\frac{\text{Sales}}{\text{Total assets}}\right)$$

[1] E. Altman, "Financial Ratios, Discriminant Analysis, and the Prediction of Corporate Bankruptcy," *Journal of Finance*. September 1968, pp. 589–609.

To identify predictors in a model like this, select a sample of firms that went bankrupt in the past and a random sample of firms that did not. Calculate a full set of liquidity, solvency, and operational ratios for these firms. Discriminant analysis, applied to the historical data, then selects those ratios that jointly best discriminate between firms that subsequently went bankrupt and those that did not, and then calculates coefficients on the selected ratios that weight them into a Z-score. The weights are calculated to minimize the differences in Z-scores within bankrupt or nonbankrupt groups but to maximize the differences in scores between the two groups. The Z-score indicates the relative likelihood of a firm not going bankrupt, so a firm with a high score is less likely, a firm with a low score is more likely, and those with intermediate level scores are in a gray area.

The Z-score model is based on firms going bankrupt, but models also can be estimated with default on debt or other conditions of financial distress as the defining event. And the model can be adapted to situations having more than two outcomes. So a model of bond ratings (with several classes) also can be built. Other ratios, such as asset size, interest coverage, the current ratio, and the variability of earnings, have appeared in similar published models.

Logit Analysis.   Logit analysis is based on different statistical assumptions from discriminant analysis and delivers a score between zero and 1 that indicates the probability of default. An early application of logit analysis to bankruptcy prediction by James Ohlson[2] produced the following model:

$$y = -1.32 - 0.407(\text{size}) + 6.03\left(\frac{\text{Total liabilities}}{\text{Total assets}}\right)$$

$$-1.43\left(\frac{\text{Working capital}}{\text{Total assets}}\right) + 0.0757\left(\frac{\text{Current liabilities}}{\text{Current assets}}\right)$$

$$-2.37\left(\frac{\text{Net income}}{\text{Total assets}}\right) - 1.83\left(\frac{\text{Working capital flow from operations}}{\text{Total liabilities}}\right)$$

$$+0.285\left(\begin{array}{l}1 \text{ if net income was negative for the last two years} \\ 0 \text{ if net income was not negative for the last two years}\end{array}\right)$$

$$-1.72\left(\begin{array}{l}1 \text{ if total liabilities exceed total assets} \\ 0 \text{ if total liabilities do not exceed total assets}\end{array}\right)$$

$$-0.521\left(\frac{\text{Change in net income}}{\text{Sum of absolute values of current and prior years' net incomes}}\right)$$

Size is measured here as the natural logarithm of total assets divided by the GNP implicit price deflator (with a base of 100 in 1978). Working capital flow is cash flow from operations plus changes in other working capital items. The score from this model is transformed into a probability:

$$\text{Probability of bankruptcy} = \frac{1}{1 + e^{-y}}$$

where e is approximately 2.718282 and y is the score estimated from the ratios above.

[2] J. A. Ohlson, "Financial Ratios and the Probabilistic Prediction of Bankruptcy," *Journal of Accounting Research*, Spring 1980, pp. 109–131.

The models here serve to indicate the form of credit scoring. The estimates were made quite a while ago, so the analyst should reestimate the models from more recent data. Coefficients will be different and other ratios may be found to be relevant. Nonaccounting information might be included. The models here are unconditional models. Conditional models might be estimated for different conditions, such as industry, country, or macro conditions. Predictors and their coefficients may be different in recessions than in boom times, for example.

It is unrealistic to expect financial ratios to capture all the information that indicates the probability of default. The interpretive background and the annotations to reformulated statements yield other insights, as does the pro forma analysis of the next subsection. So credit analysts use the scores from these types of models to supplement their broader judgment (and as a check on their judgment). The credit scores that combine financial statement scores with other information are typically a ranking from one to seven or one to nine rather than the Z-scores and probabilities estimated here.

Prediction Error Analysis

A bank loan officer who assigns credit scores on a scale of one to nine (say) has to decide at what score he will reject a loan application. Is it three, or is it four or five? A bond rater has to decide what Z-score or probability score indicates significant probability of default in order to assign the firm to a BB or lower rating. Set the cutoff point too high and too many firms are deemed to be high credit risk. Set the cutoff too low and too many firms will be considered safe investments.

Classifying a firm as not likely to default when it actually does default is called a **Type I error**. Classifying a firm as likely to default when it does not default is called a **Type II error**. Both errors have costs. In a Type I error, the bank or bondholder loses in the default. In a Type II error, the bank or bond investor misses out on a good investment. For a bank the cost of a Type II error may be considerable: It may lose good loans and good customers and business might migrate to banks with better credit models and better error analysis.

Errors are reduced by developing better scoring models. But inevitably these will be gray areas. In his original study, Altman found that firms with Z-scores of less than 1.81 went bankrupt within one year while scores higher than 2.99 always indicated nonbankruptcy. Scores from 1.81 to 2.99 were the gray areas.

Error analysis aims to determine the optimal cutoff for classifying firms. One simple way is to choose a cutoff point that minimizes the total of Type I and Type II errors. This cutoff can be discovered from historical data analysis (preferably on a set of firms that were not used to estimate the credit scoring model), and this historical analysis can be updated through experience. Altman's original analysis found that a Z-score of 2.675 minimized the number of total errors. For Ohlson's logit analysis, a probability of 0.038 gave the optimal cutoff.

This simple method assumes that Type I and Type II errors are equally costly. If this is not so, the bank or the investor must analyze the cost of each type and weight the errors accordingly in setting a cutoff. Many consider a Type I error more costly than a Type II.

Full-Information Forecasting

Credit scoring from ratios uses the limited information in current financial statements. The full information about firms is captured by the pro forma analysis of Chapter 15. This analysis, along with the value-at-risk analysis of the last chapter, can readily be adapted to assess the likelihood of default.

Pro Forma Analysis and Default Prediction

Rather than using current liquidity, solvency, and operational ratios to forecast default, pro forma analysis uses the full information available to the analyst to forecast future liquidity, solvency, and operational ratios that result in default. And pro forma analysis explicitly forecasts the firm's ability to generate cash to meet debt payments.

Scenario 1 in Table 19.1 calculates ratios from the pro formas for PPE Inc., the firm used in the pro forma analysis of Chapter 15. More ratios could be calculated with more detailed financial statements. The forecasts underlying these pro formas were a sales growth of 5 percent per year, a profit margin (PM) of 7.85 percent, an asset turnover (ATO) of 1.762, and a dividend payout of 40 percent of net income. Under this scenario, the firm is projected to pay down debt from positive free cash flow after dividends by Year 4 and become a holder of net financial assets. Debt to total assets and the debt to equity ratio are thus decreasing and interest and fixed-charge coverages are increasing. The debt is expected to mature at the end of Year 4. But the debt is retired by that date without need of further financing. Default is not anticipated: Scenario 1 is a nondefault scenario. Indeed, the firm is projected to increase its debt capacity.

Scenario 2 gives a different picture. Here sales are expected to decline by 5 percent each year and the profit margins are expected to be only 1 percent. Net operating assets decline with sales but they are not perfectly flexible, so asset turnover decreases. The firm is expected to drop its dividend in Year 1 in anticipation of liquidity problems, but the poor cash flow still leaves a reduced capacity to service the debt. When the debt matures in Year 4, the firm is expected to default. Scenario 2 is a **default scenario**.

Default occurs when *cash available for debt service* is less than the *debt service requirement*:

$$\text{Cash available for debt service} = \text{Free cash flow} - \text{Net dividends}$$

$$= \text{OI} - \Delta\text{NOA} - \text{Net dividends}$$

$$\text{Debt service requirement} = \text{Required interest and preferred dividend payments}$$
$$+ \text{Required net principal payments} + \text{Lease payments}$$

In scenario 2, PPE Inc. is forecasted to have $1.42 million available for debt service in Year 4 when the debt matures. The debt service requirement is $4.25 million. Thus it is anticipated to default. Note that cash available for debt service is after net dividends, that is, dividends net of new equity financing. So default can be avoided if cash can be raised from equity issues. Similarly, the debt service requirement is for net principal repayments (debt repayments minus new debt issued). So default can be avoided if cash can be raised from issuing new debt (which debt restructuring effectively involves).

Pro forma analysis for equity valuation focuses on forecasting operating income and net operating assets for the residual income calculation. Pro forma analysis for credit evaluation focuses on forecasting cash available for debt service. Accordingly, the "bottom line" in the pro formas in Table 19.1 is the cash available for debt service line. In terms of the forecasting template in Chapter 15, the pro forma analysis for equities is completed at Step 6, where residual income can be calculated. The pro forma analysis for debt is completed at Step 9, where cash available for debt service can be calculated.

Value-at-Risk Analysis and the Probability of Default

Scenario 2 is a default scenario, but it is just one default scenario: It forecasts a particular sales growth, profit margin, and so on. It also forecasts that the dividend would be dropped (to increase cash available for debt service) and that no cash would be raised

TABLE 19.1 PPE Inc.: Pro Forma Financial Statements and Default Prediction under Two Scenarios

	Year 0	Year 1	Year 2	Year 3	Year 4	Year 5
Scenario 1						
Sales (growth = 5% per year)	124.90	131.15	137.70	144.59	151.82	159.41
Core operating income (PM = 7.85%)	9.80	10.29	10.81	11.35	11.92	12.51
Financial income (expense)	(0.70)	(0.77)	(0.57)	(0.35)	(0.10)	0.18
Net income	9.10	9.52	10.24	11.00	11.82	12.69
Net operating assets (ATO = 1.762)	74.42	78.15	82.05	86.16	90.46	94.99
Net financial assets	(7.70)	(5.71)	(3.47)	(0.97)	1.81	4.91
Common equity	66.72	72.44	78.58	85.19	92.27	99.90
Free cash flow	5.28	6.57	6.90	7.25	7.61	7.99
Dividend	5.28	3.81	4.10	4.40	4.73	5.08
Cash available for debt service	0.0	2.76	2.80	2.85	2.88	2.91
Debt to total assets (%)	10.3	7.3	4.3	1.1	-2.0	-5.2
Debt to equity (%)	11.5	7.9	4.4	1.1	-2.0	-4.9
Interest coverage*	14.0	13.4	19.0	32.4	19.2	—
Fixed-charge coverage†	—	4.7	4.9	5.0	5.1	—
RNOA (%)	14.0	13.8	13.8	13.8	13.8	13.8
ROCE (%)	14.5	14.3	14.1	14.0	13.9	13.8
Debt service requirement‡	0.0	0.0	0.0	0.0	0.0	0.0
Scenario 2						
Sales (decline = 5% per year)	124.90	118.66	112.72	107.09	101.73	96.65
Core operating income (PM = 1%)	9.80	1.19	1.13	1.07	1.02	0.97
Financial income (expense)	(0.70)	(0.77)	(0.69)	(0.60)	(0.52)	(0.42)
Net income	9.10	0.42	0.44	0.47	0.50	0.55
Net operating assets	74.42	74.00	73.60	73.20	72.80	72.40
Net financial assets	(7.70)	(6.86)	(6.02)	(5.15)	(4.25)	Default
Common equity	66.72	67.14	67.58	68.05	68.55	Default
Free cash flow	5.28	1.61	1.53	1.47	1.42	1.37
Dividend	5.28	0.0	0.0	0.0	0.0	0.0
Cash available for debt service	0.0	1.61	1.53	1.47	1.42	1.37
Debt to total assets (%)	10.3	9.3	8.2	7.0	5.8	
Debt to equity (%)	11.5	10.2	8.9	7.6	6.2	
Interest coverage*	14.0	1.5	1.6	1.8	2.0	
Fixed-charge coverage†	—	1.7	1.7	1.7	1.7	
RNOA (%)	14.0	1.6	1.5	1.5	1.4	1.3
ROCE (%)	14.5	0.6	0.7	0.9		
Debt service requirement‡	0.0	0.0	0.0	0.0	4.25	Default

*Interest coverage = Operating income/Financial expense.
†Fixed-charge coverage = (Operating income + Debt service)/Debt service.
‡The debt is zero-coupon, thus there are no interest payments.

from new debt to reduce the debt service requirement. Other operating and financing scenarios are possible and the analyst is interested in the full set of default scenarios.

The value-at-risk analysis of the last chapter is a method for examining the full set of likely scenarios. The analysis was applied to equities but is also applicable to debt: Under what set of scenarios is the value of debt at risk?

The equity analysis profiles the possible variation in residual income. The debt analysis profiles the possible variation in cash available for debt service. Follow these steps:

FIGURE 19.2

Value-at-Risk Profile for Debt and the Identification of Default Scenarios The profile plots cash available for debt service under alternative scenarios and the probability of each outcome. The default point—where cash available for debt service is less than the debt service requirement—distinguishes defaulting scenarios from nondefaulting scenarios. The probability of default is the total probability of defaulting scenarios.

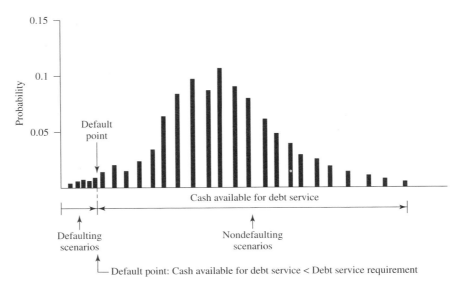

1. Generate profiles of cash available for debt service for a full set of scenarios from pro forma analysis.

2. Establish the debt service requirement.

3. Identify the *default point* where cash available for debt service is below the debt service requirement, and so identify the default scenarios.

4. Assess the probability of the set of default scenarios occurring.

As debt has to be serviced each year, a profile should be generated for each year ahead, with particular attention to years where large amounts of debt are to mature.

A profile of cash available for debt service from Step 1 is depicted in Figure 19.2. The default scenarios are to the left of the point where cash available for debt service is less than the required debt service. To the left of this default point, value is lost to the debtholder; to the right of the default point, debt value is preserved.

The probability of default is the sum of the probabilities of the defaulting scenarios (about 3.5 percent in the figure). Stated formally, the default probability is

Probability of default = Pr {Cash available for debt service < Debt service requirement}

where Pr is probability. This probability is the basis for setting the price of credit (and the cost of debt capital for the firm).

This metric is similar to the value-at-risk (VaR) metric that is commonly used to assess the market (price) risk of a portfolio of financial assets. The formal definition of VaR is given by

$$\text{Prespecified probability} = \text{Pr } \{\Delta P_t \leq \text{VaR}\}$$

Here ΔP_t is the change in market value of a financial asset over a period t. So VaR is an amount such that, for a prespecified probability, losses equal to or larger than the VaR occur. A hedge fund, for example, might assess that it will lose 50 percent of the value of its fund in one month with a probability of 0.02 percent. It might discover this from historical simulation of price changes for its portfolio.

Similarly, a bank might assess, for a stated probability, how much of its loan portfolio it will lose over a year. To do this it might refer to its historical experience in lending, just like the hedge fund does. Or it might produce the value-at-risk profiles for its current portfolio which employ fundamental analysis. And a banking syndicate that wishes to sell its loans to a pension fund might use the profiles to price the sale.

LIQUIDITY PLANNING AND FINANCIAL STRATEGY

Just as the pro forma analysis of operating profitability can be used to formulate business strategy, so can the pro forma analysis here be used to formulate financial strategy.

Financial planning is the task of the corporate treasurer. Her task is to ensure that the debt and equity financing is in place to support the firm's operational strategy. With targets for the debt-to-equity mix and dividends that are set by management, she plans the financing under the most likely scenario. And she plans, contingently, for scenarios that vary from the likely scenario. How will a surplus of cash under an optimistic operational scenario be applied? To a stock repurchase? To a purchase of bonds? And how will a cash deficiency be handled under a pessimistic scenario?

Planning for pessimistic scenarios sets a **default strategy**. Default planning is part of scenario planning that we introduced in the last chapter. Scenario 2 in the PPE Inc. example embeds a default strategy: Drop the dividend to generate more cash for debt service. Other strategies (that generate other scenarios to deal with default) are

- Modify operations to reduce operational risk that generates default risk.

- Issue equity.

- Issue or roll over debt.

- Establish an open line of credit.

- Sell off assets.

- Sell off the whole firm (in a takeover).

- Hedge risks.

Some strategies, such as issuing new debt or equity or rolling over a line of credit, might not be feasible in some scenarios.

Each strategy has a different set of default scenarios and a different value-at-risk profile. And each profile yields a different probability of default and thus a different borrowing cost. The benefit of lowering the cost of capital by reducing the probability of default is traded off against the cost of lowering the probability. Open lines of credit require fees. Hedging is costly. Do the benefits outweigh the costs?

Two principles guide this tradeoff:

1. Strategy indifference. In well-functioning capital markets the arrangements to avoid default might be priced to equal the benefits from avoidance. So the treasurer is indifferent. She might hedge default risk with a financial instrument, but the cost of that hedge will reflect the probability of default and the cost of the firm's debt.

2. Shareholder indifference. Shareholders might be able to hedge themselves against the consequences of default in financial markets and so are indifferent to the firm doing it for them.

The Web Connection

Find the following on the web page for this chapter:

- Examples of proportional consolidation to reflect debt in subsidiaries.

- Examples of reformulated balance sheets set up for credit evaluation

- A discussion of special purpose entities and the dangers they pose.

Summary

This chapter has shown how the analysis of financial statements and the development of pro forma financial statements aid in determining the creditworthiness of a firm.

The risk of default is the primary concern in the analysis of debt. To gain an appreciation of this risk, the credit analyst, like the equity analyst, is familiar with the business and its operations. Like the equity analyst, she understands the risk in the operations. She understands the contracts between the debtholders and the firm. And she understands how financial statements and pro forma analysis of financial statements can help her in evaluating credit risk.

This chapter has laid out an analysis of financial statements for credit evaluation. It has identified a number of liquidity and solvency ratios and has shown how these ratios can be combined to yield credit ratings and to indicate the probability of default.

The pro forma analysis for equities has been adapted in this chapter to credit analysis, this time with the objective of forecasting cash available for debt service. That analysis generates a value-at-risk profile for debt that depicts cash available for debt service under alternative scenarios and identifies default scenarios. The chapter also shows how these profiles are used in financial strategy analysis and default planning.

Key Concepts

collateral refers to assets that can be repossessed if a debtor defaults.   *682*

credit analysis or **default analysis** analyzes information to determine the likelihood of a borrower defaulting on debt.   *682*

debt capacity is a firm's ability to borrow.   *687*

default is a failure to make timely payments on debt or other violation of a debt agreement.   *681*

default premium is the price of debt in excess of the risk-free rate to compensate for **default risk**.   *680*

default risk or **credit risk** is the risk that a debtor will **default**.   *680*

default scenario is a forecast under which a firm defaults.   *693*

default strategy or **default planning** is a strategy to deal with default.   *696*

defeasance sets aside cash or securities to service debt and removes both the debt and the offsetting cash and securities from the balance sheet.   *683*

off-balance-sheet financing is financing that creates an obligation that is not shown on a balance sheet.   *684*

price of credit is the lending rate charged by a creditor, the creditor's required return (and the borrower's borrowing rate).   *681*

special purpose entity is an entity (often a partnership) setup off-balance-sheet to accomplish a specific task, but not controlled by the firm.   *684*

Type I default prediction error is classifying as not likely to default a firm which does default.   *692*

Type II default prediction error is classifying as likely to default a firm which does not default.   *692*

The Analyst's Toolkit

Concept Questions

C19.1. Explain what a default premium is.

C19.2. What is the objective in reformulating financial statements for credit analysis? How does the reformulation for credit analysis differ from that for equity analysis?

C19.3. Describe off-balance-sheet financing.

C19.4. What is the "moral-hazard" problem with business debt?

C19.5. Distinguish a Type I error in predicting default from a Type II error.

C19.6. What is a default point?

C19.7. How does pro forma analysis of financial statements help in credit analysis?

C19.8. Why might a deferred tax liability not be considered a liability for credit scoring?

C19.9. What is a default strategy?

C19.10. Explain the danger posed by special purpose entities.

Exercises   E19.1.   Pro Forma Analysis and Default Points (Medium)

A firm has the following balance sheet and income statement (in millions of dollars):

Balance Sheet

Operating cash	$ 4
Receivables	29
Inventories	138
Plant and equipment	942
	1,113
Operating liabilities	288
Long-term debt (8%)	695
	983
Stockholders' equity	130
	$1,113

Income Statement

Revenues	$908
Operating expenses	817
Operating income	91
Interest expense	55
Income before tax	36
Income taxes	13
Income after tax	$ 23

The long-term debt is 8 percent coupon debt maturing in five years. The statutory tax rate is 38 percent. Prepare pro forma financial statements for the next five years under the two following scenarios. Also forecast cash available for debt service and the debt service requirement under both scenarios. The firm pays no dividends.

a. Sales are expected to grow at 4 percent per year, with the current operating profit margin being maintained and with an asset turnover of 1.14.

b. Sales are expected to decline by 4 percent per year and operating profit margins are expected to decline to 2 percent. With some assets inflexible, asset turnovers are expected to decline to 0.98.

Do either of these two scenarios forecast default on the debt?

E19.2.   Z-Scoring (Medium)

Below are ratios for some of the firms that have appeared in this book, for their 1998 fiscal year.

Firm	Working Capital Total Assets	Retained Earnings Total Assets	Earnings before Interest and Taxes Total Assets	Market Value of Equity Book Value of Liabilities	Sales Total Assets
Coca-Cola	−0.12	1.05	0.29	15.4	0.98
Nike	0.34	0.58	0.15	9.0	1.67
Reebok	0.43	0.66	0.06	0.7	1.85
Hewlett-Packard	0.24	0.50	0.13	3.6	1.40
Dell Computer	0.38	0.09	0.31	27.9	2.65
Gateway Computer	0.27	0.34	0.19	5.2	2.59
Microsoft	0.45	0.34	0.32	46.7	0.65

a. Calculate Z-scores from these ratios.
b. Explain why Nike has a different Z-score from Reebok.
c. What reservations do you have about the Z-score as an indicator of creditworthiness?

E19.3.   Tracking Credit Risk Measures: Toys "R" Us (Hard)

Toys "R" Us, Inc., is the world's largest toy retailer, with sales of nearly $12 billion in 1999. It has been challenged in recent years, particularly in e-commerce, losing market share from 20.2 percent in 1993 to 16.8 percent in 1999. The firm's stock price was down to $11 in early 2000 from a high of $36 in 1998. Management had begun, however, to take strategic initiatives to return the firm to the leading position it once enjoyed.

The firm's balance sheets and income statements for fiscal years ending January of 1997 to 2000 are given in Exhibit 19.1, along with share price and shares outstanding information. Track the profitability of the firm over the years and also its creditworthiness, as indicated by relevent ratios and Z-scores.

EXHIBIT 19.1
Toys "R" Us, Inc.

Balance Sheets (in millions of dollars)				
	1997	**1998**	**1999**	**2000**
Assets				
Cash	$ 761	$ 214	$ 410	$ 584
Accounts and other receivables	142	175	204	182
Merchandise inventories	2,215	2,464	1,902	2,027
Prepaid expenses and other current assets	42	51	81	80
Total current assets	3,160	2,904	2,597	2,873
Net property, plant, and equipment	4,047	4,212	4,226	4,455
Goodwill	365	356	347	374
Deposits and other assets	451	491	729	651
Total assets	8,023	7,963	7,899	8,353
Liabilities				
Short-term borrowings	304	134	156	278
Accounts payable	1,346	1,280	1,415	1,617
Accrued expenses and other current liabilities	720	680	696	836
Income taxes payable	171	231	224	107
Total current liabilities	2,541	2,325	2,491	2,838
Deferred income taxes	222	219	333	362
Long-term debt	909	851	1,222	1,230
Other liabilities	160	140	229	243
Total liabilities	3,832	3,535	4,275	4,673
Shareholders' Equity				
Common stock	30	30	30	30
Additional paid-in capital	489	467	459	453
Retained earnings	4,120	4,610	4,478	4,757
Foreign currency translation adjustments	(60)	(122)	(100)	(137)
Treasury	(388)	(557)	(1,243)	(1,423)
Shareholders' equity	4,191	4,428	3,624	3,680
Total liabilities and equity	$ 8,023	$ 7,963	$ 7,899	$ 8,353
Share price	$22	$27	$17	$11
Shares outstanding (millions)	288	282	251	240

Income Statements
(in millions of dollars)

	1997	1998	1999	2000
Net sales	$9,932	$11,038	$11,170	$11,862
Cost of sales	6,892	7,710	8,191	8,321
Gross profit	3,040	3,328	2,979	3,541
Selling, advertising, general, and administrative expenses	2,020	2,231	2,443	2,743
Depreciation, amortization, and asset write-offs	206	253	255	278
Restructuring and other charges	60	0	294	0
Total operating expenses	2,286	2,484	2,992	3,021
Operating (loss) income	754	844	(13)	520
Interest expense	98	85	102	91
Interest and other income	(17)	(13)	(9)	(11)
Earnings before income taxes	673	772	(106)	440
Income taxes	246	282	26	161
Net earnings (loss)	$ 427	$ 490	$ (132)	$ 279

Minicase

M19.1

ANALYSIS OF DEFAULT RISK: FRUIT OF THE LOOM

Fruit of the Loom Ltd. fared poorly from 1997 to 1999. Between April 1997 and October 1999, its stock price dropped from $38 to $3, a 92 percent loss in market value.

Fruit of the Loom manufactures men's and boys' underwear. It had an estimated 32 percent share of the U.S. market in 1999, second only to the Sara Lee Corporation's Hanes brand, which holds a 37 percent share. The firm has had a checkered history. It was controlled by a financier, William Farley, who took the firm through a leveraged transaction in the mid-1980s and began considerable cost cutting. It was one of those "small-town America" companies where conflicts between management and labor arose with the cost cutting associated with leveraging and reorganization and with the shipping of production overseas to countries with cheaper labor. Remember the movie *Other People's Money?*

With the cost cutting and dispersion of production came quality control problems and difficulty managing inventories. Financial difficulties in other apparel holdings forced Farley to reduce his stake in Fruit of the Loom and, analysts claimed, distracted him from the business. In late summer 1999, Farley gave up control to Dennis Bookshester, an outside director and a veteran of the retail trade, who found the firm's computer and control systems were in a mess. Some numbers on the firm are shown in Table 19.2.

The problems, most analysts claimed, were fixable. Product market share had declined slightly but was still at a respectable 32 percent. The market was pricing these sales at a low multiple of 0.11. The infrastructure from the cost-cutting program was still in place. Many of the production and inventory coordination problems could be fixed with better computer systems, and computer consultants were working to do so.

In the fall of 1999, some analysts were forecasting that the firm would break even for the rest of 1999 and were forecasting an eps of $0.79 for the year ending December 31, 2000. Subject to qualifications about the firm's ability to get its systems under control, these analysts were also forecasting continuing profitability in the years after 2000. But other analysts warned that the firm might be heading for bankruptcy.

For the nine months ending October 2, 1999, the firm reported a loss of $253.2 million against a profit of $146.9 million for the same period of the previous year. Exhibit 19.2 presents the firm's financial statements covering the first nine months of 1999.

TABLE 19.2
Fruit of the Loom Ltd.

	1995	1996	1997	1998	1999
Revenues	2,403	2,447	2,140	2,170	2,045
EBIT	50.4	325.3	−283.1	234.9	102.3
Net income	−227.3	151.2	−487.6	135.9	28.1
Dividends	0	0	0	0	0
Eps	−300	1.98	−6.55	1.88	0.39
Net profit margin (%)	−9.5	6.2	−22.8	6.3	1.4
Book value per share	11.78	13.90	5.87	7.61	6.82
P/E ratio	—	19.1	—	73	7.7
P/B ratio	2.11	2.70	4.41	1.86	0.44
Price-to-sales ratio	0.77	1.19	0.86	0.46	0.11

1999 numbers are based on 12 months to June 30, 1999.
Shares outstanding: 66.923 million.

Figures in millions of dollars, except as per-share numbers and ratios.

EXHIBIT 19.2

FRUIT OF THE LOOM LTD.
Condensed Consolidated Balance Sheet
(in thousands of dollars)

	October 2, 1999	January 2, 1999
Assets		
Current assets		
Cash and cash equivalents (including restricted cash)	$ 37,000	$ 1,400
Notes and accounts receivable (less allowance for possible losses of $10,800 and $12,000 respectively)	80,200	109,700
Inventories		
Finished goods	645,200	500,700
Work in progress	135,800	183,100
Materials and supplies	52,500	58,200
Total inventories	833,500	742,000
Due from receivable financing subsidiary	26,800	—
Other	45,400	41,100
Total current assets	1,022,900	894,200
Property, plant, and equipment	1,157,200	1,192,100
Less accumulated depreciation	745,900	758,200
Net property, plant, and equipment	411,300	433,900
Other assets		
Goodwill (less accumulated amortization of $356,200 and $336,200 respectively)	666,300	686,300
Deferred income taxes	36,700	36,700
Other	146,500	238,700
Total other assets	849,500	961,700
	$ 2,283,700	$ 2,289,800
Liabilities and Stockholders' Equity		
Current liabilities		
Current maturities of long-term debt	$ 650,200	$ 270,500
Trade accounts payable	87,300	119,700
Other accounts payable and accrued expenses	299,200	226,700
Total current liabilities	1,036,700	616,900
Noncurrent liabilities		
Long-term debt	682,200	856,600
Notes and accounts payable—affiliates	438,600	—
Other	266,000	267,400
Total noncurrent liabilities	1,386,000	1,124,000
Preferred stock	71,70	—
Common stockholders' equity (deficiency)[1]	(211,500)	548,900
	$ 2,283,700	$ 2,289,800

[1]Common stockholders' equity at October 2, 1999, includes retained earnings of $20,700 thousand compared to retained earnings of $276,600 thousand at January 2, 1999.

(continued)

EXHIBIT 19.2
(Continued)

Condensed Consolidated Statement of Operations (Unaudited)
(in thousands of dollars)

	Nine Months Ended	
	Oct. 2, 1999	**Sept. 26, 1999**
Net sales		
Unrelated parties	$1,508,400	$1,678,900
Affiliates	275,000	—
	1,783,400	1,678,900
Cost of sales		
Unrelated parties	1,253,900	1,145,500
Affiliates	355,400	—
	1,609,300	1,145,500
Gross earnings (loss)	174,100	533,400
Selling, general, and administrative expenses	315,400	281,100
Goodwill amortization	19,900	19,900
Operating earnings (loss)	(161,200)	232,400
Interest expense	(72,700)	(74,600)
Other expense—net	(18,100)	(3,100)
Earnings (loss) before income tax provision	(252,000)	154,700
Income tax provision	1,200	7,800
Net earnings (loss)	$ (253,200)	$ 146,900

A. Stock screeners would say that this stock has all the features of a buy: low P/E, low P/B, and low price-to-sales ratio. How comfortable would you be with issuing a buy recommendation on this stock at a price of $3 per share? What other information would you like to see to make you more secure in your recommendation?

B. Carry out an analysis of financial statement ratios that indicate the likelihood of bankruptcy in October 1999.

C. Calculate a Z-score using the Z-score model in this chapter. Annualize ratios based on nine months for the calculation. How did the firm's Z-score change between January and October 1999?

Note: Fruit of the Loom filed for Chapter 11 bankruptcy protection in December 1999. Warren Buffett subsequently bought the firm out of bankruptcy.

EXHIBIT 19.2
(Continued)

Condensed Consolidated Statement of Cash Flows (Unaudited)
(in thousands of dollars)

	Nine Months Ended	
	Oct. 2, 1999	**Sept. 26,1999**
Cash flows from operating activities		
Net earnings (loss)	$ (253,200)	$ 146,900
Adjustments to reconcile to net cash provided by (used for) operating activities		
Depreciation and amortization	90,200	84,900
Deferred income tax provision	—	(4,900)
Increase in working capital	(117,000)	(189,100)
Other—net	(24,700)	(13,600)
Net cash provided by (used for) operating activities	(304,700)	24,200
Cash flows from investing activities		
Capital expenditures	(28,000)	(25,000)
Proceeds from asset sales	20,500	68,200
Payment on Acme Boot debt guarantee	—	(60,800)
Other—net	(19,600)	(4,100)
Net cash used for investing activities	(27,100)	(21,700)
Cash flows from financing activities		
Proceeds from issuance of long-term debt	240,200	—
Proceeds under line-of-credit agreements	676,800	754,300
Payments under line-of-credit agreements	(486,800)	(643,400)
Principal payments on long-term debt and capital leases	(236,400)	(122,200)
Increase in affiliate notes and accounts payable	174,700	—
Preferred stock dividends	(1,100)	—
Common stock issued	—	6,800
Common stock repurchased	—	(3,000)
Net cash provided by (used for) financing activities	367,400	(7,500)
Net increase (decrease) in cash and cash equivalents (including restricted cash)	35,600	(5,000)
Cash and cash equivalents (including restricted cash) at beginning of period	1,400	16,100
Cash and cash equivalents (including restricted cash) at end of period	$ 37,000	$ 11,100

Appendix

A Summary of Formulas

CHAPTER 3

$$\text{Unlevered price/sales} = \frac{\text{Market value of equity} + \text{Net debt}}{\text{Sales}}$$

Page 69

$$\text{Unlevered price/ebit} = \frac{\text{Market value of equity} + \text{Net debt}}{\text{ebit}}$$

Page 69

$$\text{Unlevered price/ebitda} = \frac{\text{Market value of equity} + \text{Net debt}}{\text{ebitda}}$$

Page 69

$$\text{Trailing P/E} = \frac{\text{Price per share}}{\text{Most recent eps}}$$

Page 69

$$\text{Rolling P/E} = \frac{\text{Price per share}}{\text{Sum of eps for most recent four quarters}}$$

Page 69

$$\text{Forward or leading P/E} = \frac{\text{Price per share}}{\text{Forecast of next year's eps}}$$

Page 69

$$\text{Dividend-adjusted P/E} = \frac{\text{Price per share} + \text{Annual dps}}{\text{eps}}$$

Page 69

Value of a bond = Present value of expected cash flows

$$V_0^D = \frac{CF_1}{\rho_D} + \frac{CF_2}{\rho_D^2} + \frac{CF_3}{\rho_D^3} + \frac{CF_4}{\rho_D^4} + \cdots + \frac{CF_T}{\rho_D^T}$$

Page 82

(ρ_D is 1 + Required return for the bond)

Value of a project = Present value of expected cash flows

$$V_0^P = \frac{CF_1}{\rho_P} + \frac{CF_2}{\rho_P^2} + \frac{CF_3}{\rho_P^3} + \frac{CF_4}{\rho_P^4} + \cdots + \frac{CF_T}{\rho_P^T}$$

Page 83

(ρ_P is 1 + Hurdle rate for the project)

Value of equity = Present value of expected dividends

$$V_0^E = \frac{d_1}{\rho_E} + \frac{d_2}{\rho_E^2} + \frac{d_3}{\rho_E^3} + \frac{d_4}{\rho_E^4} + \cdots$$

Page 89

(ρ_E is 1 + Required return for the equity)

Value of equity = Present value of expected dividends + Present value of expected terminal price

$$V_0^E = \frac{d_1}{\rho_E} + \frac{d_2}{\rho_E^2} + \frac{d_3}{\rho_E^3} + \cdots + \frac{d_T}{\rho_E^T} + \frac{P_T}{\rho_E^T}$$

Page 90

Perpetuity dividend model:

$$V_0^E = \frac{d_1}{\rho_E} + \frac{d_2}{\rho_E^2} + \frac{d_3}{\rho_E^3} + \cdots + \frac{d_T}{\rho_E^T} + \left(\frac{d_{T+1}}{\rho_E - 1}\right) / \rho_E^T$$

Page 90

Dividend growth model:

$$V_0^E = \frac{d_1}{\rho_E} + \frac{d_2}{\rho_E^2} + \frac{d_3}{\rho_E^3} + \cdots + \frac{d_T}{\rho_E^T} + \left(\frac{d_{T+1}}{\rho_E - g}\right) / \rho_E^T$$

Page 90

CHAPTER 4

Value of the firm = Present value of expected free cash flows

$$V_0^F = \frac{C_1 - I_1}{\rho_F} + \frac{C_2 - I_2}{\rho_F^2} + \frac{C_3 - I_3}{\rho_F^3} + \frac{C_4 - I_4}{\rho_F^4} + \frac{C_5 - I_5}{\rho_F^5} + \cdots \qquad \text{Page 112}$$

(ρ_F is 1 + Required return for the firm)

Value of the equity = Present value of expected free cash flows minus value of net debt

$$V_0^E = \frac{C_1 - I_1}{\rho_F} + \frac{C_2 - I_2}{\rho_F^2} + \frac{C_3 - I_3}{\rho_F^3} + \cdots + \frac{C_T - I_T}{\rho_F^T} + \frac{CV_T}{\rho_F^T} - V_0^D \qquad \text{Page 113}$$

If free cash flows after T are forecasted to be a (constant) perpetuity,

$$CV_T = \frac{C_{T+1} - I_{T+1}}{\rho_F - 1} \qquad \text{Page 113}$$

If free cash flows are forecasted to grow at a constant rate after the horizon,

$$CV_T = \left(\frac{C_{T+1} - I_{T+1}}{\rho_F - g} \right) \qquad \text{Page 114}$$

Cash flow from operations = reported cash flow from operations
+ After-tax net interest payments   Page 119

Cash investment in operations = Reported cash flow from investing
− Net investment in interest-bearing
instruments   Page 119

Revenue = Cash receipts from sales + New sales on credit
− Cash received for previous periods' sales
− Estimates of credit sales not collectible − Estimated sales returns
− Deferred revenue for cash received in advance of sale
+ Revenue previously deferred   Page 123

Expense = Cash paid for expenses + Amounts incurred in generating
revenues but not yet paid − Cash paid for generating revenues
in future periods + Amounts paid in the past for generating
revenues in the current period   Page 123

Earnings = Levered cash flow from operations + Accruals

$$\text{Earnings} = (C - i) + \text{Accruals} \qquad \text{Page 123}$$

Earnings = Free cash flow − Net cash interest + Investment + Accruals

$$\text{Earnings} = (C - I) - i + I + \text{Accruals} \qquad \text{Page 124}$$

CHAPTER 5

The value of common equity $(V_0^E) = B_0 + \dfrac{RE_1}{\rho_E} + \dfrac{RE_2}{\rho_E^2} + \dfrac{RE_3}{\rho_E^3} + \cdots$ \qquad Page 145

Residual earnings = Comprehensive earnings – (Required return for equity
× Beginning-of-period book value of equity)   Page 145

$$RE_t = Earn_t - (\rho_E - 1)B_{t-1}$$

The price-to-book (P/B) ratio:

$$\frac{V_0}{B_0} = 1 + \frac{\text{Present value of RE}}{B_0}$$ Page 145

Residual earnings = (ROCE – Required return on equity)
× Beginning-of-period book value of common equity

$$Earn_t - (\rho_E - 1)B_{t-1} = [ROCE_t - (\rho_E - 1)]B_{t-1}$$ Page 148

Case 1 valuation: RE forecasted to be zero after some point:

$$V_0^E = B_0 + \frac{RE_1}{\rho_E} + \frac{RE_2}{\rho_E^2} + \frac{RE_3}{\rho_E^3} + \ldots + \frac{RE_T}{\rho_E^T}$$ Page 152

Case 2 valuation: No growth:

$$V_0^E = B_0 + \frac{RE_1}{\rho_E} + \frac{RE_2}{\rho_E^2} + \cdots + \frac{RE_T}{\rho_E^T} + \left(\frac{RE_{T+1}}{\rho_E - 1}\right)\!\Big/\rho_E^T$$ Page 153

Case 3 valuation: Growth is forecasted to continue at a constant rate:

$$V_0^E = B_0 + \frac{RE_1}{\rho_E} + \frac{RE_2}{\rho_E^2} + \frac{RE_3}{\rho_E^3} + \cdots + \frac{RE_T}{\rho_E^T} + \left(\frac{RE_{T+1}}{\rho_E - g}\right)\!\Big/\rho_E^T$$ Page 154

CHAPTER 6

Normal forward P/E $= \dfrac{1}{\text{Required return}}$ Page 189

Normal trailing P/E $= \dfrac{(1 + \text{Required return})}{\text{Required return}}$ Page 190

Value of equity = Capitalized forward earnings
+ Extra value for abnormal cum-dividend earnings growth

$$V_0^E = \frac{Earn_1}{\rho_E - 1} + \frac{1}{\rho_E - 1}\left[\frac{AEG_2}{\rho_E} + \frac{AEG_3}{\rho_E^2} + \frac{AEG_4}{\rho_E^3} + \cdots\right]$$

$$= \frac{1}{\rho_E - 1}\left[Earn_1 + \frac{AEG_2}{\rho_E} + \frac{AEG_3}{\rho_E^2} + \frac{AEG_4}{\rho_E^3} + \cdots\right]$$ Page 191

Abnormal earnings growth$_t$ (AEG$_t$) = Cum-dividend earn$_t$ – Normal earn$_t$ Page 193

$$= [Earn_t + (\rho_E - 1)d_{t-1}] - \rho_E Earn_{t-1}$$

Abnormal earnings growth$_t$ (AEG$_t$) = [G$_t$ – ρ_E] × Earnings$_{t-1}$ Page 194

Value of equity (cum-dividend) = Capitalized current earnings
+ Extra value for abnormal cum-dividend abnormal
earnings growth

$$V_0^E + d_0 = \frac{\rho_E}{\rho_E - 1}\left[\text{Earn}_0 + \frac{\text{AEG}_1}{\rho_E} + \frac{\text{AEG}_2}{\rho_E^2} + \frac{\text{AEG}_3}{\rho_E^3} + \cdots\right]$$

Page 196

$$\text{PEG ratio} = \frac{\text{P/E}}{\text{1-year ahead percentage earnings growth}}$$

Page 205

CHAPTER 7

Free cash flow = Net dividends to shareholders + Net payments to debtholders and issuers

$$C - I = d + F$$

Page 224

Treasurer's rule:

If $C - I - i > d$: Lend or buy down own debt.
If $C - I - i < d$: Borrow or reduce lending

Page 224

Free cash flow = Operating income − Change in net operating assets

$$C - I = \text{OI} - \Delta\text{NOA}$$

Page 228

Free cash flow = Change in net financial assets − Net financial income
+ Net dividends

$$C - I = \Delta\text{NFA} - \text{NFI} + d$$

Page 228

Free cash flow = Net financial expenses − Change in net financial obligations
+ Net dividends

$$C - I = \text{NFE} - \Delta\text{NFO} + d$$

Page 229

Net dividends = Free cash flow + Net financial income
− Change in net financial assets

$$d = C - I + \text{NFI} - \Delta\text{NFA}$$

Page 229

Net dividends = Free cash flow − Net financial expenses
+ Change in net financial obligations

$$d = C - I - \text{NFE} + \Delta\text{NFO}$$

Page 229

Net operating assets (end) = Net operating assets (beginning)
+ Operating income − Free cash flow

$$\text{NOA}_t = \text{NOA}_{t-1} + \text{OI}_t - (C_t - I_t)$$

Page 229

Change in net operating assets = Operating income − Free cash flow

$$\Delta\text{NOA}_t = \text{OI}_t - (C_t - I_t)$$

Page 230

Net financial assets (end) = Net financial assets (begin)
                    + Net financial income + Free cash flow
                    − Net dividends

$$NFA_t = NFA_{t-1} + NFI_t + (C_t - I_t) - d_t$$ Page 230

Change in net financial assets = Net financial income + Free cash flow
                    − Net dividends

$$\Delta NFA_t = NFI_t + (C_t - I_t) - d_t$$ Page 230

Net financial obligations (end) = Net financial obligations (begin)
                    + Net financial expense − Free cash flow
                    + Net dividends

$$NFO_t = NFO_{t-1} + NFE_t - (C_t - I_t) + d_t$$ Page 230

Change in net financial obligations = Net financial expense − Free cash flow
                    + Net dividends

$$\Delta NFO_t = NFE_t - (C_t - I_t) + d_t$$ Page 230

Stocks and flows equation for common stockholders' equity:

$$CSE_t = CSE_{t-1} + Earnings_t - \text{Net dividends}_t$$ Page 231

$$CSE_t = NOA_t - NFO_t$$ Page 232

$$\text{Return on net operating assets } (RNOA_t) = \frac{OI_t}{\frac{1}{2}(NOA_t + NOA_{t-1})}$$ Page 233

$$\text{Return on net financial assets } (RNFA_t) = \frac{NFI_t}{\frac{1}{2}(NFA_t + NFA_{t-1})}$$ Page 233

$$\text{Net borrowing cost } (NBC_t) = \frac{NFE_t}{\frac{1}{2}(NFO_t + NFO_{t-1})}$$ Page 233

CHAPTER 8

$$\text{Dividend payout} = \frac{\text{Dividends}}{\text{Comprehensive income}}$$ Page 250

$$\text{Total payout ratio} = \frac{\text{Dividends + Stock repurchases}}{\text{Comprehensive income}}$$ Page 251

$$\text{Dividends-to-book value} = \frac{\text{Dividends}}{\text{Book value of CSE + Dividends}}$$ Page 251

$$\text{Total payout-to-book value} = \frac{\text{Dividends + Stock repurchases}}{\text{Book value of CSE + Dividends + Stock repurchases}}$$ Page 251

LIVERPOOL JOHN MOORES UNIVERSITY
Aldham Roberts L.R.C.
TEL 0151 231 0000

$$\text{Retention ratio} = \frac{\text{Comprehensive income} - \text{Dividends}}{\text{Comprehensive income}}$$

$$= 1 - \text{Dividend payout ratio} \qquad \text{Page 251}$$

$$\text{Net investment rate} = \frac{\text{Net transactions with shareholders}}{\text{Beginning book value of CSE}} \qquad \text{Page 252}$$

$$\text{Growth rate of CSE} = \frac{\text{Change in CSE}}{\text{Beginning CSE}} \qquad \text{Page 252}$$

$$= \frac{\text{Comprehensive income} + \text{Net transactions with shareholders}}{\text{Beginning CSE}}$$

$$\text{Growth rate of CSE} = \text{ROCE} + \text{Net investment rate} \qquad \text{Page 252}$$

CHAPTER 9

$$\text{Tax benefit of net debt} = \text{Net interest expense} \times \text{Marginal tax rate} \qquad \text{Page 289}$$

$$\text{After-tax net interest expense} = \text{Net interest expense} \times (1 - \text{Marginal tax rate}) \qquad \text{Page 289}$$

$$\text{Tax on operating income} = \text{Tax expense as reported}$$
$$+ (\text{Net interest expense} \times \text{Tax rate}) \qquad \text{Page 290}$$

$$\text{Effective tax rate for operations} = \qquad \text{Page 291}$$

$$\frac{\text{Tax on operating income}}{\text{Operating income before tax, equity income, and extraordinary and dirty-surplus items}}$$

$$\text{Operating profit margin (PM)} = \frac{\text{OI (after tax)}}{\text{Sales}} \qquad \text{Page 303}$$

$$\text{Sales PM} = \frac{\text{OI (after tax) from sales}}{\text{Sales}} \qquad \text{Page 303}$$

$$\text{Other items PM} = \frac{\text{OI (after tax) from other items}}{\text{Sales}} \qquad \text{Page 303}$$

$$\text{Net (comprehensive) income profit margin} = \frac{\text{Comprehensive income}}{\text{Sales}} \qquad \text{Page 303}$$

$$\text{Expense ratio} = \frac{\text{Expense}}{\text{Sales}} \qquad \text{Page 303}$$

$$1 - \text{Sales PM} = \text{Sum of expense ratios} \qquad \text{Page 303}$$

$$\text{Operating asset composition ratio} = \frac{\text{Operating asset}}{\text{Total operating assets}} \qquad \text{Page 304}$$

$$\text{Operating liability composition ratio} = \frac{\text{Operating liability}}{\text{Total operating liabilities}} \qquad \text{Page 304}$$

$$\text{Financial asset composition ratio} = \frac{\text{Financial asset}}{\text{Total financial asset}}$$

Page 304

$$\text{Financial liability composition ratio} = \frac{\text{Financial obligation}}{\text{Total financial obligations}}$$

Page 304

$$\text{Operating liability leverage (OLLEV)} = \frac{\text{Operating liabilities}}{\text{Net operating assets}}$$

Page 304

$$\text{Capitalization ratio} = \frac{\text{Net operating assets}}{\text{Common stockholders' equity}} = \text{NOA/CSE}$$

Page 304

$$\text{Financial leverage ratio (FLEV)} = \frac{\text{Net financial obligations}}{\text{Common stockholders' equity}} = \text{NFO/CSE}$$

Page 304

$$\text{Capitalization ratio} - \text{Financial leverage ratio} = 1.0$$

Page 304

$$\text{Growth rate in sales} = \frac{\text{Change in sales}}{\text{Prior period's sales}}$$

Page 305

$$\text{Growth rate in operating income} = \frac{\text{Change in operating income (after tax)}}{\text{Prior period's OI}}$$

Page 305

$$\text{Growth in NOA} = \frac{\text{Change in net operating assets}}{\text{Beginning NOA}}$$

Page 305

$$\text{Growth in CSE} = \frac{\text{Change in CSE}}{\text{Beginning CSE}}$$

Page 305

CHAPTER 10

$$\text{Free cash flow} = \text{Operating income} - \text{Change in net operating assets}$$

$$C - I = \text{OI} - \Delta\text{NOA}$$

Page 324

$$\text{Free cash flow} = \text{Net financial expense} - \text{Change in net financial obligations} + \text{Net dividends}$$

$$C - I = \text{NFE} - \Delta\text{NFO} + d$$

Page 324

CHAPTER 11

$$\text{ROCE} = \left(\frac{\text{NOA}}{\text{CSE}} \times \text{RNOA}\right) - \left(\frac{\text{NFO}}{\text{CSE}} \times \text{NBC}\right)$$

Page 351

$$\text{ROCE} = \text{RNOA} + \left[\frac{\text{NFO}}{\text{CSE}} \times \left(\text{RNOA} - \text{NBC}\right)\right]$$

$$= \text{RNOA} + \left(\text{Financial leverage} \times \text{Operating spread}\right)$$

$$= \text{RNOA} + \left(\text{FLEV} \times \text{SPREAD}\right)$$

Page 351

$$\text{ROCE} = \text{RNOA} - \left[\frac{\text{NFA}}{\text{CSE}} \times \left(\text{RNOA} - \text{RNFA}\right)\right]$$

Page 353

Implicit interest on operating liabilities = Short-term borrowing rate (after tax)
$$\times \text{Operating liabilities} \qquad \text{Page 354}$$

$$\text{Return on operating assets (ROOA)} = \frac{\text{OI} + \text{Implicit interest (after tax)}}{\text{Operating assets}} \qquad \text{Page 354}$$

Return on net operating assets = Return on operating assets + (Operating liability
leverage × Operating liability leverage spread)

$$\text{RNOA} = \text{ROOA} + (\text{OLLEV} \times \text{OLSPREAD}) \qquad \text{Page 354}$$

$$\text{OLSPREAD} = \text{ROOA} - \text{Short-term borrowing rate (after tax)} \qquad \text{Page 354}$$

$$\text{ROCE} = \text{ROCE before MI} \times \text{MI sharing ratio} \qquad \text{Page 354}$$

$$\text{ROCE before minority interest (MI)} = \frac{\text{Comprehensive income before MI}}{\text{CSE} + \text{MI}} \qquad \text{Page 359}$$

$$\frac{\text{Minority interest}}{\text{sharing ratio}} = \frac{\text{Comprehensive income/Comprehensive income before MI}}{\text{CSE/ (CSE} + \text{MI})} \qquad \text{Page 359}$$

$$\text{ROCE} = (\text{PM} \times \text{ATO}) + [\text{FLEV} \times (\text{RNOA} - \text{NBC})] \qquad \text{Page 359}$$

$$\text{PM} = \text{OI (after tax)/Sales} \qquad \text{Page 359}$$

$$\text{ATO} = \text{Sales/NOA} \qquad \text{Page 360}$$

$$\text{PM} = \text{Sales PM} + \text{Other items PM} \qquad \text{Page 362}$$

$$\text{Sales PM} = \text{Gross margin ratio} - \text{Expense ratios} \qquad \text{Page 362}$$

$$\frac{1}{\text{ATO}} = \frac{\text{Cash}}{\text{Sales}} + \frac{\text{Accounts receivable}}{\text{Sales}} + \frac{\text{Inventory}}{\text{Sales}} + \ldots + \frac{\text{PPE}}{\text{Sales}}$$
$$+ \ldots - \frac{\text{Accounts payable}}{\text{Sales}} - \frac{\text{Pension obligations}}{\text{Sales}} - \ldots \qquad \text{Page 362}$$

$$\text{Accounts receivable turnover} = \frac{\text{Sales}}{\text{Accounts receivable (net)}} \qquad \text{Page 363}$$

$$\text{PPE turnover} = \frac{\text{Sales}}{\text{Property, plant, and equipment (net)}} \qquad \text{Page 363}$$

$$\text{Days in accounts receivable} = \frac{365}{\text{Accounts receivable turnover}} \qquad \text{Page 363}$$

(sometimes called days sales outstanding)

The inventory turnover ratio is sometimes measured as:

$$\text{Inventory turnover} = \frac{\text{Cost of goods sold}}{\text{Inventory}} \qquad \text{Page 363}$$

$$\text{Days in inventory} = \frac{365}{\text{Inventory turnover}} \qquad \text{Page 363}$$

$$\text{Days in accounts payable} = \frac{365 \times \text{Accounts payable}}{\text{Purchases}} \qquad \text{Page 363}$$

The net borrowing cost is a weighted average of the costs for the different sources of net financing:

$$NBC = \left(\frac{FO}{NFO} \times \frac{\text{After-tax interest on financial obligations (FO)}}{FO} \right)$$

$$- \left(\frac{FA}{NFO} \times \frac{\text{After-tax interest on financial assets (FA)}}{FA} \right)$$

$$- \left(\frac{FA}{NFO} \times \frac{\text{Unrealized gains on FA}}{FA} \right)$$

$$+ \left(\frac{\text{Preferred stock}}{NFO} \times \frac{\text{Preferred dividends}}{\text{Preferred stock}} \right) + \cdots$$

Page 366

CHAPTER 12

Change in residual earnings = Change due to change in ROCE over the cost of capital + Change due to change in common equity

Page 387

$$\Delta RE_1 = [\Delta(ROCE - \text{Cost of capital})_1 \times CSE_0]$$
$$+ [\Delta CSE_1 \times (ROCE - \text{Cost of capital})_1]$$

Page 387

Return on net operating assets = Core RNOA
+ Unusual items to net operating assets

Page 389

$$RNOA = \frac{\text{Core OI}}{NOA} + \frac{UI}{NOA}$$

Page 389

$$RNOA = \frac{\text{Core OI from sales}}{NOA} + \frac{\text{Core other OI}}{NOA} + \frac{UI}{NOA}$$

Page 389

$$RNOA = \left(\text{Core sales PM} \times ATO \right) + \frac{\text{Core other OI}}{NOA} + \frac{UI}{NOA}$$

where   Core sales PM $= \dfrac{\text{Core OI from sales}}{\text{Sales}}$

Page 396

$$\text{Change in RNOA} = \begin{array}{c}\text{Change in core sales}\\\text{profit margin at}\\\text{previous asset}\\\text{turnover level}\end{array} + \begin{array}{c}\text{Change due to}\\\text{change in asset}\\\text{turnover}\end{array} + \begin{array}{c}\text{Change due to}\\\text{change in other}\\\text{core income}\end{array} + \begin{array}{c}\text{Change due to}\\\text{change in}\\\text{unusual items}\end{array}$$

Page 398

$$\Delta RNOA_1 = \left(\Delta \text{Core sales PM}_1 \times ATO_0 \right) + \left(\Delta ATO_1 \times \text{Core sales PM}_1 \right)$$

$$+ \Delta \left(\frac{\text{Core other OI}}{NOA} \right) + \Delta \left(\frac{UI}{NOA} \right)$$

Page 398

$$\text{Sales PM} = \frac{\text{Sales} - \text{Variable cost} - \text{Fixed costs}}{\text{Sales}}$$

$$= \frac{\text{Contribution margin}}{\text{Sales}} - \frac{\text{Fixed costs}}{\text{Sales}}$$

Page 398

$$\text{Contribution margin ratio} = 1 - \frac{\text{Variable costs}}{\text{Sales}} = \frac{\text{Contribution margin}}{\text{Sales}}$$

Page 399

$$\text{OLEV} = \frac{\text{Contribution margin}}{\text{Operating income}} = \frac{\text{Contribution margin ratio}}{\text{Profit margin}}$$

(Don't confuse OLEV with OLLEV!)   Page 399

% Change in core OI = OLEV × % Change in core sales   Page 399

Net borrowing cost = Core net borrowing cost + Unusual borrowing costs   Page 399

$$\text{NBC} = \frac{\text{Core net financial expenses}}{\text{NFO}} + \frac{\text{Unusual financial expenses}}{\text{NFO}}$$

Page 399

$$\text{Change in ROCE} = \text{Change in RNOA} + \underset{\substack{\text{Change due to change in} \\ \text{spread at previous level} \\ \text{of financial leverage}}}{} + \underset{\substack{\text{Change due to} \\ \text{change in financial} \\ \text{leverage}}}{}$$

Page 400

$$\Delta\text{ROCE}_1 = \Delta\text{RNOA}_1 + (\Delta\text{SPREAD}_1 \times \text{FLEV}_0) + (\Delta\text{FLEV}_1 \times \text{SPREAD}_1)$$

If ΔFLEV and ΔNBC are small, then a useful approximation is:

$$\Delta\text{ROCE}_1 = \Delta\text{RNOA}_1 \times (1 + \text{Average FLEV}_1)$$

Page 400

$$\text{NOA} = \text{Sales} \times \frac{1}{\text{ATO}}$$

Page 402

$$\Delta\text{CSE} = \Delta\left(\text{Sales} \times \frac{1}{\text{ATO}}\right) - \Delta\text{NFO}$$

Page 402

$$\text{Change in common equity} = \underset{\substack{\text{Change due to change} \\ \text{in sales at previous} \\ \text{level of asset turnover}}}{} + \underset{\substack{\text{Change due to change} \\ \text{in asset turnover}}}{} - \underset{\substack{\text{Change in} \\ \text{financial} \\ \text{leverage}}}{}$$

$$\Delta\text{CSE}_1 = \left(\Delta\text{Sales}_1 \times \frac{1}{\text{ATO}_0}\right) + \left(\Delta\frac{1}{\text{ATO}_1} \times \text{Sales}_1\right) - \Delta\text{NFO}_1$$

Page 403

CHAPTER 13

Residual operating income = Operating income − (Required return for operations
× Beginning net operating assets)

$$\text{ReOI}_t = \text{OI}_t - (\rho_F - 1)\text{NOA}_t - 1$$

Page 433

Residual operating income = (RNOA − Required return for operations)
× Net operating assets

$$\text{ReOI}_t = [\text{RNOA}_t - (\rho_F - 1)]\text{NOA}_t - 1$$

Page 437

Value of operations = Net operating assets
+ Present value of expected residual operating income

$$V_0^{\text{NOA}} = \text{NOA}_0 + \frac{\text{ReOI}_1}{\rho_F} + \frac{\text{ReOI}_2}{\rho_F^2} + \frac{\text{ReOI}_3}{\rho_F^3} + \dots + \frac{\text{ReOI}_T}{\rho_F^T} + \frac{\text{CV}_T}{\rho_F^T}$$

Page 433

Value of common equity = Book value of common equity
+ Present value of expected residual operating income

$$V_0^E = \text{CSE}_0 + \frac{\text{ReOI}_1}{\rho_F} + \frac{\text{ReOI}_2}{\rho_F^2} + \frac{\text{ReOI}_3}{\rho_F^3} + \ldots + \frac{\text{ReOI}_T}{\rho_F^T} + \frac{\text{CV}_T}{\rho_F^T}$$ Page 435

Abnormal operating income growth$_t$ (AOIG)

= Cum-dividend operating income$_t$ − Normal operating income$_t$

= [Operating income$_t$ + (ρ_F − 1)FCF$_{t-1}$] − $\rho_F$operating income$_{t-1}$

= [OI$_t$ + (ρ_F − 1)FCF$_{t-1}$] − ρ_FOI$_{t-1}$

= [G$_t$ − ρ_F] × OI$_{t-1}$ Page 438

Value of common equity = Capitalized (Forward operating income + Present
value of abnormal operating income growth)
− Net financial obligations

$$V_0^E = \frac{1}{\rho_F - 1}\left[\text{OI}_1 + \frac{\text{AOIG}_2}{\rho_F} + \frac{\text{AOIG}_3}{\rho_F^2} + \frac{\text{AOIG}_4}{\rho_F^3} + \cdots\right] - \text{NFO}_0$$ Page 440

Cost of capital for operations = Weighted-average cost of equity and cost of net debt

$$= \left(\frac{\text{Value of equity}}{\text{Value of operations}} \times \text{Equity cost of capital}\right)$$

$$+ \left(\frac{\text{Value of debt}}{\text{Value of operations}} \times \text{Cost of debt capital}\right)$$

$$\rho_F = \frac{V_0^E}{V_0^{\text{NOA}}} \cdot \rho_E + \frac{V_0^D}{V_0^{\text{NOA}}} \cdot \rho_D$$ Page 442

After-tax cost of net debt (ρ_D) = Nominal cost of net debt × (1 − Tax rate) Page 443

Required return on equity = Required return for operations
+ (Market leverage × Required return spread)

$$\rho_E = \rho_F + \frac{V_0^D}{V_0^E}\left(\rho_F - \rho_D\right)$$ Page 444

Unlevered P/B ratio $= \dfrac{\text{Value of net operating assets}}{\text{Net operating assets}}$

$$= \frac{V_0^{\text{NOA}}}{\text{NOA}_0}$$ Page 457

Levered P/B ratio = Unlevered P/B ratio + [Financial leverage
× (Unlevered P/B ratio − 1)]

$$\frac{V_0^E}{\text{CSE}_0} = \frac{V_0^{\text{NOA}}}{\text{NOA}_0} + \text{FLEV}\left(\frac{V_0^{\text{NOA}}}{\text{NOA}_0} - 1\right)$$ Page 458

Forward enterprise P/E ratio $= \dfrac{\text{Value of operations}}{\text{Forward operating income}} = \dfrac{V_0^{\text{NOA}}}{\text{OI}_1}$ Page 460

$$\text{Trailing enterprise P/E ratio} = \frac{\text{Value of operations} + \text{Free cash flow}}{\text{Current operating income}}$$

$$= \frac{V_0^{\text{NOA}} + \text{FCF}_0}{\text{OI}_0} \qquad \text{Page 461}$$

$$\text{Forward enterprise P/E ratio} = \frac{V_0^E}{\text{Earn}_1} = \frac{V_0^{\text{NOA}}}{\text{OI}_1} + \text{ELEV}_1\left(\frac{V_0^{\text{NOA}}}{\text{OI}_1} - \frac{1}{\text{NBC}_1}\right) \qquad \text{Page 461}$$

$$\text{Trailing enterprise P/E ratio} = \frac{V_0^E + d_0}{\text{Earn}_0} \qquad \text{Page 461}$$

$$= \frac{V_0^{\text{NOA}} + \text{FCF}_0}{\text{OI}_0} + \text{ELEV}_0\left(\frac{V_0^{\text{NOA}} + \text{FCF}_0}{\text{OI}_0} - \frac{1}{\text{NBC}_0} - 1\right)$$

CHAPTER 14

SF1 forecast: Page 480

Earnings Forecast	Residual Earnings Forecast
$\text{OI}_1 = (\rho_F - 1)\text{NOA}_0$	$\text{OI}_1 - (\rho_F - 1)\text{NOA}_0 = 0$
$\text{NFE}_1 = (\rho_D - 1)\text{NFO}_0$	$\text{NFE}_1 - (\rho_D - 1)\text{NFO}_0 = 0$
$\text{Earn}_1 = (\rho_E - 1)\text{CSE}_0$	$\text{Earn}_1 - (\rho_E - 1)\text{CSE}_0 = 0$

SF1 valuation:
Value of common equity = Book value of common equity

$$V_0^F = \text{CSE} \qquad \text{Page 482}$$

SF2 forecast: Page 483

Earnings Forecast	Residual Earnings Forecast	Abnormal Earnings Growth Forecast
$\text{OI}_1 = \text{OI}_0 + (\rho_F - 1)\Delta\text{NOA}_0$	$\text{ReOI}_1 = \text{ReOI}_0$	$\text{AOIG}_1 = 0$
$\text{Earn}_1 = \text{Earn}_0 + (\rho_E - 1)\Delta\text{CSE}_0$	$\text{RE}_1 = \text{RE}_0$	$\text{AOIG}_2 = 0$

SF2 valuation:
Value of common equity = Book value of common equity + Capitalized current ReOI

$$V_0^E = \text{CSE}_0 + \frac{\text{ReOI}_0}{\rho_F - 1} \qquad \text{Page 484}$$

Value of operations = Capitalized operating income forecasted for next year

$$V_0^{\text{NOA}} = \frac{\text{OI}_1}{\rho_F - 1} \qquad \text{Page 485}$$

SF3 forecast: Page 487

Earnings Forecast	Residual Earnings Forecast
$OI_1 = RNOA_0 \times NOA_0$	$[RNOA_1 - (\rho_F - 1)]NOA_0 = [RNOA_0 - (\rho_F - 1)]NOA_0$
$Earn_1 = ROCE_0 \times CSE_0$	$[ROCE_1 - (\rho_E - 1)]CSE_0 = [ROCE_0 - (\rho_E - 1)]CSE_0$

SF3 valuation:
  Value of common equity:

$$V_0^E = CSE_0 + \frac{\left[RNOA_0 - (\rho_F - 1)\right]NOA_0}{\rho_F - g}$$

Page 489

  Value of operations:

$$V_0^{NOA} = NOA_0 + \frac{\left[RNOA_0 - (\rho_F - 1)\right]NOA_0}{\rho_F - g}$$

$$= NOA_0 \times \frac{RNOA_0 - (g - 1)}{\rho_F - g}$$

Page 489

  Unlevered price-to-book ratio:

$$\frac{V^{NOA}}{NOA_0} = \frac{RNOA_0 - (g - 1)}{\rho_F - g}$$

Page 489

$$V_0^{NOA} = OI_1 \times \frac{1}{\rho_F - 1}\left[1 + \frac{AOIG_2 \big/ OI_1}{\rho_F - g}\right]$$

$$= OI_1 \times \frac{1}{\rho_F - 1}\left[1 + \frac{G_2 - \rho_F}{\rho_F - g}\right]$$

Page 489

A simple valuation with short-term and long-term growth rates:

$$V_0^{NOA} = OI_1 \times \frac{1}{\rho_F - 1}\left[\frac{G_2 - G_{long}}{\rho_F - G_{long}}\right]$$

Page 498

CHAPTER 15

$$ReOI = Sales \times \left(Core\ sales\ PM - \frac{Required\ return\ for\ operations}{ATO}\right)$$
$$+ \ Core\ other\ OI + Unusual\ items$$

Page 513

CHAPTER 17

Quality diagnostics:
    Net sales/Cash from sales
    Net sales/Net accounts receivable
    Net sales/Unearned revenue
    Net sales/Warranty liabilities   Page 611

    Bad debt expense/Actual credit losses
    Bad debt reserves/Accounts receivable (gross)
    Bad debt expense/Sales   Page 614

    Warranty expense/Actual warranty claims
    Warranty expense/Sales   Page 614

$$\frac{\text{Normalized OI}}{\text{OI}}$$

where

$$\text{Normalized OI} = \text{Free cash flow} + \Delta \text{Normalized NOA}$$
$$= \text{Free cash flow} + \Delta \text{Sales/Normal ATO} \qquad \text{Page 614}$$

$$\frac{\text{Adjusted ebitda}}{\text{ebit}} \qquad \text{Page 616}$$

$$\frac{\text{Depreciation}}{\text{Capital expenditures}} \qquad \text{Page 616}$$

$$\frac{\text{Cash flow from operations (CFO)}}{\text{Operating income}} \qquad \text{Page 616}$$

$$\frac{\text{CFO}}{\text{Average NOA}} \qquad \text{Page 617}$$

$$\frac{\text{Pension expense}}{\text{SG\&A expense}} \qquad \text{Page 617}$$

$$\frac{\text{Other postemployment expenses}}{\text{SG\&A expenses}} \qquad \text{Page 617}$$

$$\frac{\text{Operating tax expense}}{\text{OI before taxes}} \qquad \text{Page 617}$$

$$\frac{\text{R\&D expense}}{\text{Sales}} \qquad \text{Page 621}$$

$$\frac{\text{Advertising expense}}{\text{Sales}} \qquad \text{Page 621}$$

CHAPTER 18

$$\text{Relative value ratio} = \frac{V_0^E (1)/P_0(1)}{V_0^E (2)/P_0(2)} \qquad \text{(for two investments, 1 and 2)} \qquad \text{Page 669}$$

CHAPTER 19

$$\text{Current ratio} = \frac{\text{Current assets}}{\text{Current liabilities}}$$
Page 686

$$\text{Quick (or acid test) ratio} = \frac{\text{Cash + Short-term investments + Receivables}}{\text{Current liabilities}}$$
Page 686

$$\text{Cash ratio} = \frac{\text{Cash + Short-term investments}}{\text{Current liabilities}}$$
Page 686

$$\text{Defensive interval} = \frac{\text{Cash + Short-term investments + Receivables}}{\text{Capital expenditures}} \times 365$$
Page 686

$$\frac{\text{Cash flow to}}{\text{capital expenditures}} = \frac{\text{(Unlevered) cash flow from operations}}{\text{Capital expenditures}}$$
Page 686

$$\text{Debt to total assets} = \frac{\text{Total debt (current + long-term)}}{\text{Total assets (liabilities + total equity)}}$$
Page 686

$$\text{Debt to equity} = \frac{\text{Total debt}}{\text{Total equity}}$$
Page 686

$$\text{Long-term debt ratio} = \frac{\text{Long-term debt}}{\text{Long-term debt + Total equity}}$$
Page 686

$$\text{Interest coverage} = \frac{\text{Operating income}}{\text{Net interest expense}} \quad \text{(times interest earned)}$$
Page 687

$$\text{Interest coverage} = \frac{\text{Unlevered cash flow from operations}}{\text{Net cash interest}} \quad \text{(cash basis)}$$
Page 687

$$\text{CFO to debt} = \frac{\text{Unlevered cash flow from operations}}{\text{Total debt}}$$
Page 687

$$\text{Cash available for debt service} = \text{Free cash flow} - \text{Net dividends}$$
$$= \text{OI} - \Delta\text{NOA} - \text{Net dividends}$$
Page 693

$$\text{Debt service requirement} = \text{Required interest and preferred dividend payments}$$
$$+ \text{Required net principal payments}$$
$$+ \text{Lease payments}$$
Page 693

Index